Webster's
French-English
Dictionary

Webster's French-English Dictionary

Created in Cooperation with the Editors
of Merriam-Webster

FEDERAL
STREET
PRESS

A Division of Merriam-Webster, Incorporated
Springfield, Massachusetts

This edition published by Federal Street Press
a Division of Merriam-Webster Incorporated
P.O. Box 281
Springfield, MA 01102

Federal Street Press books are available for bulk purchase for sales promotion and premium use. For details write the manager of special sales,
Federal Street Press, P.O. Box 281, Springfield, MA 01102

ISBN 1-892859-79-3

Printed in the United States of America
05 06 07 08 09   5 4 3 2

Contents

Preface

This dictionary is a concise reference for the core vocabulary of French and English. Its 40,000 entries and over 50,000 translations provide up-to-date coverage of the basic vocabulary and idioms in both languages. In addition, the book includes vocabulary specific to the Canadian province of Quebec.

IPA (International Phonetic Alphabet) pronunciations are given for all words. Included as well are tables of irregular verbs in both languages and the most common French abbreviations.

This book shares many details of presentation with larger French-English Dictionaries, but for reasons of conciseness it also has a number of features uniquely its own. Users need to be familiar with the following major features of this dictionary.

Main entries follow one another in strict alphabetical order, without regard to intervening spaces or hyphens.

Homographs (words spelled the same but having different meanings or parts of speech) are run on at a single main entry if they are closely related. Run-on homograph entries are replaced in the text by a boldfaced swung dash (as **devoir**. . .*vt*. . . — ∼ *nm* . . .). Homographs of distinctly different origin (as **date**[1] and **date**[2]) are given separate entries.

Run-on entries for related words that are not homographs may also follow the main entry. Thus we have the main entry **calculer** *vt* followed by run-on entries for — **calcul** *nm,* — **calculateur, -trice** *adj,* and — **calculatrice** *nf.* However, if a related word falls later in the alphabet than a following unrelated main entry, it will be entered at its own place; **ear** and its run-on — **eardrum** precede the main entry **earl** which is followed by the main entry **earlobe.**

Variant spellings appear at the main entry separated by *or* (as **judgment** *or* **judgement; paralyze** *or Brit* **paralyse;** or **lis** *or* **lys**).

Inflected forms of English verbs, adjectives, adverbs, and nouns are shown when they are irregular (as **wage** . . . **waged; waging; ride** . . . **rode; ridden; good** . . . **better; best;** or **fly** . . . *n, pl* **flies**) or when there might be doubt about their spelling (as **ego** . . . *n, pl* **egos**). Inflected forms of French irregular verbs are shown in the section Conjugation of French Verbs on page 6a; numerical references to this table are included at the main entry (as **tenir** {92} *vt*). Irregular plurals of French nouns or adjectives are shown at the main entry (as **mondial, -diale** *adj, mpl* **-diaux**).

Cross-references are provided to lead the user to the appropriate main entry (as **mice** → **mouse** or **fausse** → **faux**[2]).

Pronunciation information is either given explicitly or implied for all English and French words. A full list of the pronunciation symbols used appears on page 20a.

The grammatical function of entry words is indicated by an italic **functional label** (as *vt, adj,* or *nm*). Italic **usage labels** may be added at the entry or sense as well (as **artilleur** . . . *nm Can* : pitcher (in baseball); **center** *or Brit* **centre** . . . *n* . . .; or **tuyau** . . . *nm* . . . **2** *fam* : tip, advice). These labels are also included in the translations (as **bet** . . . *n* : pari *m,* gageure *f Can*).

Usage notes are occasionally placed before a translation to clarify meaning or use (as **moins** . . . *prep* . . . **2** (*in expressions of time*) : to, of).

Synonyms may appear before the translation word(s) in order to provide context for the meaning of an entry word or sense (as **poursuivre** . . . *vt* . . . **2** CONTINUER : carry on with; or **meet** . . . *vt* . . . **2** SATISFY : satisfaire).

Bold notes are sometimes used before a translation to introduce a plural sense or a common phrase using the main entry word (as **meuble** . . . *nm* . . . **2** ∼**s** *nmpl* : furniture; or **call** . . . *vt* . . . **3** ∼ **off** : annuler). Note that when an entry word is repeated in a bold note, it is replaced by a swung dash

Conjugation of French Verbs

Simple Tenses

-ER **Verbs** (parler)		-IR **Verbs** (grandir)	
PRESENT INDICATIVE			
je parle	nous parlons	je grandis	nous grandissons
tu parles	vous parlez	tu grandis	vous grandissez
il parle	ils parlent	il grandit	ils grandissent
PRESENT SUBJUNCTIVE			
je parle	nous parlions	je grandisse	nous grandissions
tu parles	vous parliez	tu grandisses	vous grandissiez
il parle	ils parlent	il grandisse	ils grandissent
PRETERIT INDICATIVE			
je parlai	nous parlâmes	je grandis	nous grandîmes
tu parlas	vous parlâtes	tu grandis	vous grandîtes
il parla	ils parlèrent	il grandit	ils grandirent
IMPERFECT INDICATIVE			
je parlais	nous parlions	je grandissais	nous grandissions
tu parlais	vous parliez	tu grandissais	vous grandissiez
il parlait	ils parlaient	il grandissait	ils grandissaient
IMPERFECT SUBJUNCTIVE			
je parlasse	nous parlassions	je grandisse	nous grandissions
tu parlasses	vous parlassiez	tu grandisses	vous grandissiez
il parlât	ils parlassent	il grandît	ils grandissent
FUTURE INDICATIVE			
je parlerai	nous parlerons	je grandirai	nous grandirons
tu parleras	vous parlerez	tu grandiras	vous grandirez
il parlera	ils parleront	il grandira	ils grandiront
CONDITIONAL			
je parlerais	nous parlerions	je grandirais	nous grandirions
tu parlerais	vous parleriez	tu grandirais	vous grandiriez
il parlerait	ils parleraient	il grandirait	ils grandiraient
IMPERATIVE			
	parlons		grandissons
parle, parlez	parlez	grandis, grandissez	grandissez
PRESENT PARTICIPLE (GERUND)			
parlant		grandissant	
PAST PARTICIPLE			
parlé		grandi	

Perfect Tenses

The *perfect* tenses are formed with *avoir* and the past participle:

PRESENT PERFECT
j'ai parlé, nous avons parlé, etc. (*indicative*)
j'aie parlé, nous ayons parlé, etc. (*subjunctive*)

PAST PERFECT
j'avais parlé, nous avions parlé, etc. (*indicative*)
j'eusse parlé, nous eussions parlé, etc. (*subjunctive*)

PRETERIT PERFECT
j'eus parlé, nous eûmes parlé, etc.

FUTURE PERFECT
j'aurai parlé, nous aurons parlé, etc.

CONDITIONAL PERFECT
j'aurais parlé, nous aurions parlé, etc.
or
j'eusse parlé, nous eussions parlé, etc.

PAST IMPERATIVE
aie parlé, ayons parlé, ayez parlé

The perfect tenses of the following verbs are formed with *être*:
aller, arriver, décéder, devenir, échoir, éclore, entrer, mourir, naître, partir, repartir, rentrer, rester, retourner, sortir, tomber, venir, revenir, parvenir, survenir

For example, the present perfect of *arriver* would be as follows:
je suis arrivé, nous sommes arrivés, etc. (*indicative*)

Irregular Verbs

The *imperfect subjunctive*, the *conditional*, and the first and second person plural of the *imperative* are not included in the model conjugations list but can be derived from other verb forms:

The *imperfect subjunctive* is formed by using the second person singular of the preterit indicative, removing the final *s*, and adding the following suffixes: *-sse, -sses, -t* (and adding a circumflex accent on the preceding vowel), *-ssions, -ssiez, -ssent. Servir* is conjugated as follows:

PRETERIT INDICATIVE, SECOND PERSON SINGULAR	servis – *s* = servi
IMPERFECT SUBJUNCTIVE	je servisse, tu servisses, il servît, nous servissions, vous servissiez, ils servissent

The *conditional* is formed by using the stem of the future indicative and adding the following suffixes: *-ais, -ais, -ait, -ions, -iez,- aient. Prendre* is conjugated as follows:

FUTURE INDICATIVE	je prendrai – *ai* = prendr
CONDITIONAL	je prendrais, tu prendrais, il prendrait, nous prendrions, vous prendriez, ils prendraient

The first and second person plural of the *imperative* are the same as the corresponding forms of the present indicative.

Model Conjugations of Irregular Verbs

The model conjugations below include the following simple tenses: the *present indicative* (*IND*), the *present subjunctive* (*SUBJ*), the *preterit indicative* (*PRET*), the *imperfect indicative* (*IMPF*), the *future indicative* (*FUT*), the second person singular form of the *imperative* (*IMPER*), the *present participle* or *gerund* (*PRP*), and the *past participle* (*PP*). Each set of conjugations is preceded by the corresponding infinitive form of the verb, shown in bold type. Only tenses containing irregularities are listed, and the irregular verb forms within each tense are displayed in bold type.

Also note that some conjugated verbs are labeled *defective verb*. This refers to a verb lacking one or more of the usual forms of grammatical inflection (tense, mood, etc.), for example, in French, the verbs *bruire* and *ouïr*.

Each irregular verb entry in the French-English section of this dictionary is cross-referred by number to one of the following model conjugations. These cross-reference numbers are shown in curly braces { } immediately preceding the entry's functional label.

The three main categories of verbs are:

                   1) Verbs ending in -ER
                   2) Verbs ending in -IR

Present indicative endings for verbs in these categories are:

-is, -is, -it, -issons, -issez, -issent

For example, *j'arrondis, nous arrondissons*, etc. for infinitive *arrondir*

                   3) Verbs ending in -IR/-OIR/-RE

Present indicative endings for verbs in these categories are:

-e, -es, -e, -ons, -ez, -ent

For example, *j'accueille, nous accueillons*, etc. for infinitive *accueillir*

or

-s(x), -s(x), -t(d), -ons, -ez, -ent

For example, *je rends, nous rendons*, etc. for infinitive *rendre*

Note that in the third group there are two different sets of endings for both the present indicative and preterit indicative depending on the verb in question, as shown above for the present indicative. For clarity, these forms are included in the model conjugations in an attempt to prevent the reader from inadvertently choosing the wrong endings.

1   **absoudre** : *IND* **j'absous, tu absous, il absout, nous absolvons, vous absolvez, ils absolvent;** *SUBJ* **j'absolve, tu absolves, il absolve, nous absolvions, vous absolviez, ils absolvent;** *PRET* (*not used*); *IMPF* **j'absolvais, tu absolvais, il absolvait, nous absolvions, vous absolviez, ils absolvaient;** *IMPER* **absous;** *PRP* **absolvant;** *PP* **absous**

2   **accroire** (*defective verb*) *Used only in the infinitive*

3   **accueillir** : *IND* **j'accueille, tu accueilles, il accueille,** nous accueillons, vous accueillez, ils **accueillent;** *PRET* **j'accueillis, tu accueillis, il accueillit, nous accueillîmes, vous accueillîtes, ils accueillirent;** *FUT* **j'accueillerai, tu accueilleras, il accueillera, nous accueillerons, vous accueillerez, ils accueilleront;** *IMPER* **accueille**

4   **advenir** (*defective verb*) *Used only in the infinitive and in the following tenses* : *IND* **il advient;** *SUBJ* **il advienne;** *PRET* **il advint;** *IMPF* **il advenait;** *FUT* **il adviendra;** *PRP* **advenant;** *PP* **advenu**

5   **aller** : *IND* **je vais, tu vas, il va, nous allons, vous allez, ils vont;** *SUBJ* **j'aille, tu ailles, il aille, nous allions, vous alliez, ils aillent;** *FUT* **j'irai, tu iras, il ira, nous irons, vous irez, ils iront;** *IMPER* **va**

Conjugation of French Verbs

6   **annoncer :** *IND* j'annonce, tu annonces, il annonce, **nous annonçons,** vous annoncez, ils annoncent; *PRET* **j'annonçai, tu annonças, il annonça, nous annonçâmes, vous annonçâtes, ils annoncèrent;** *IMPF* **j'annonçais, tu annonçais, il annonçait, nous annoncions,** vous annonciez, ils annonçaient; *PRP* **annonçant**

7   **apparaître :** *IND* j'apparais, tu apparais, il **apparaît, nous apparaissons,** vous apparaissez, **ils apparaissent;** *SUBJ* **j'apparaisse, tu apparaisses, il apparaisse, nous apparaissions, vous apparaissiez, ils apparaissent;** *PRET* **j'apparus, tu apparus, il apparut, nous apparûmes, vous apparûtes, ils apparurent;** *IMPF* **j'apparaissais, tu apparaissais, il apparaissait, nous apparaissions, vous apparaissiez, ils apparaissaient;** *IMPER* **apparais;** *PRP* **apparaissant;** *PP* **apparu**

8   **appeler :** *IND* **j'appelle, tu appelles, il appelle,** nous appelons, vous appelez, **ils appellent;** *SUBJ* **j'appelle, tu appelles, il appelle,** nous appelions, vous appeliez, **ils appellent;** *FUT* **j'appellerai, tu appelleras, il appellera, nous appellerons, vous appellerez, ils appelleront;** *IMPER* **appelle**

9   **asseoir :** *IND* **J'assieds** *or* **j'assois, tu assieds** *or* **tu assois, il assied** *or* **il assoit, nous asseyons** *or* **nous assoyons, vous asseyez** *or* **vous assoyez, ils asseyent** *or* **ils assoient;** *SUBJ* **j'asseye** *or* **j'assoie, tu asseyes** *or* **tu assoies, il asseye** *or* **il assoie, nous asseyions** *or* **nous assoyions, vous asseyiez** *or* **vous assoyiez, ils asseyent** *or* **ils assoient;** *PRET* **j'assis, tu assis, il assit, nous assîmes, vous assîtes, ils assirent;** *IMPF* **j'asseyais** *or* **j'assoyais, tu asseyais** *or* **tu assoyais, il asseyait** *or* **il assoyait, nous asseyions** *or* **nous assoyions, vous asseyiez** *or* **vous assoyiez, ils asseyaient** *or* **ils assoyaient;** *FUT* (*not used*); *IMPER* **assieds** *or* **assois;** *PRP* **asseyant** *or* **assoyant;** *PP* **assis**

10   **avoir :** *IND* **j'ai, tu as, il a, nous avons, vous avez, ils ont;** *SUBJ* **j'aie, tu aies, il ait, nous ayons, vous ayez, ils aient;** *PRET* **j'eus, tu eus, il eut, nous eûmes, vous eûtes, ils eurent;** *IMPF* **j'avais, tu avais, il avait, nous avions, vous aviez, ils avaient;** *FUT* **j'aurai, tu auras, il aura, nous aurons, vous aurez, ils auront;** *IMPER* **aie, ayons, ayez;** *PRP* **ayant;** *PP* **eu**

11   **balayer :** *IND* **je balaie** *or* je balaye, **tu balaies** *or* tu balayes, **il balaie** *or* il balaye, nous balayons, vous balayez, **ils balaient** *or* ils balayent; *SUBJ* **je balaie** *or* je balaye, **tu balaies** *or* tu balayes, **il balaie** *or* il balaye, nous balayions, vous balayiez, **ils balaient** *or* ils balayent; *FUT* **je balaierai** *or* je balayerai, **tu balaieras** *or* tu balayeras, **il balaiera** *or* il balayera, **nous balaierons** *or* nous balayerons, **vous balaierez** *or* vous balayerez, **ils balaieront** *or* ils balayeront; *IMPER* **balaie** *or* balaye

12   **battre :** *IND* **je bats, tu bats, il bat,** nous battons, vous battez, ils battent; *PRET* **je battis, tu battis, il battit, nous battîmes, vous battîtes, ils battirent;** *IMPER* **bats;** *PP* **battu**

13   **boire :** *IND* je bois, tu bois, il boit, **nous buvons, vous buvez, ils boivent;** *SUBJ* **je boive, tu boives, il boive, nous buvions, vous buviez, ils boivent;** *PRET* **je bus, tu bus, il but, nous bûmes, vous bûtes, ils burent;** *IMPF* **je buvais, tu buvais, il buvait, nous buvions, vous buviez, ils buvaient;** *PRP* **buvant;** *PP* **bu**

14   **bouillir :** *IND* **je bous, tu bous, il bout,** nous bouillons, vous bouillez, ils bouillent; *PRET* **je bouillis, tu bouillis, il bouillit, nous bouillîmes, vous bouillîtes, ils bouillirent;** *IMPER* **bous**

15   **braire** (*defective verb*) *Used only in the infinitive and in the following tenses :* *IND* **il brait, ils braient;** *IMPF* **brayait, brayaient;** *FUT* **il braira, ils brairont**

16   **bruire** (*defective verb*) *Used only in the infinitive and in the following tenses :* *IND* **il bruit, ils bruissent;** *SUBJ* (*not used*); *PRET* (*not used*); *IMPF* **il bruissait, ils bruissaient;** *PRP* **bruissant;** *PP* **bruit**

17   **changer :** *IND* je change, tu changes, il change, **nous changeons,** vous changez, ils changent; *PRET* **je changeai, tu changeas, il changea, nous changeâmes, vous changeâtes, ils changèrent;** *IMPF* **je changeais, tu changeais, il changeait,** nous changions, vous changiez, **ils changeaient;** *PRP* **changeant**

18   **choir** (*defective verb*) *Used only in the following tenses :* *IND* **je chois, tu chois, il choit, ils**

choient; *SUBJ* (*not used*); *PRET* **il chut**; *IMPF* (*not used*); *FUT* il choira; *IMPER* (*not used*); *PRP* (*not used*); *PP* **chu**

19 **clore** (*defective verb*) *Used only in the following tenses* : *IND* je clos, tu clos, **il clôt, ils closent**; *SUBJ* **je close, tu closes, il close, nous closions, vous closiez, ils closent**; *PRET* (*not used*); *IMPF* (*not used*); *FUT* (*used but regularly formed*); *PRP* **closant**; *PP* **clos**

20 **congeler** : *IND* **je congèle, tu congèles, il congèle**, nous congelons, vous congelez, **ils congèlent**; *SUBJ* **je congèle, tu congèles, il congèle**, nous congelions, vous congeliez, **ils congèlent**; *FUT* **je congèlerai, tu congèleras, il congèlera, nous congèlerons, vous congèlerez, ils congèleront**; *IMPER* **congèle**

21 **conquérir** : *IND* **je conquiers, tu conquiers, il conquiert**, nous conquérons, vous conquérez, **ils conquièrent**; *SUBJ* **je conquière, tu conquières, il conquière**, nous conquérions, vous conquériez, **ils conquièrent**; *PRET* **je conquis, tu conquis, il conquit, nous conquîmes, vous conquîtes, ils conquirent**; *FUT* **je conquerrai, tu conquerras, il conquerra, nous conquerrons, vous conquerrez, ils conquerront**; *IMPER* **conquiers**; *PP* **conquis**

22 **coudre** : *IND* je couds, tu couds, il coud, **nous cousons, vous cousez, ils cousent**; *SUBJ* **je couse, tu couses, il couse, nous cousions, vous cousiez, ils cousent**; *PRET* **je cousis, tu cousis, il cousit, nous cousîmes, vous cousîtes, ils cousirent**; *IMPF* **je cousais, tu cousais, il cousait, nous cousions, vous cousiez, ils cousaient**; *PRP* **cousant**; *PP* **cousu**

23 **courir** : *IND* je cours, tu cours, il court, nous courons, vous courez, ils courent; *PRET* **je courus, tu courus, il courut, nous courûmes, vous courûtes, ils coururent**; *FUT* **je courrai, tu courras, il courra, nous courrons, vous courrez, ils courront**; *IMPER* **cours**; *PP* **couru**

24 **croire** : *IND* je crois, tu crois, il croit, **nous croyons, vous croyez**, ils croient; *SUBJ* je croie, tu croies, il croie, **nous croyions, vous croyiez**, ils croient; *PRET* **je crus, tu crus, il crut, nous crûmes, vous crûtes, il crurent**; *IMPF* **je croyais, tu croyais, il croyait, nous croyions, vous croyiez, ils croyaient**; *PRP* **croyant**; *PP* **cru**

25 **croître** : *IND* **je croîs, tu croîs, il croît, nous croissons, vous croissez, ils croissent**; *SUBJ* **je croisse, tu croisses, il croisse, nous croissions, vous croissiez, ils croissent**; *PRET* **je crûs, tu crûs, il crût, nous crûmes, vous crûtes, ils crûrent**; *IMPF* **je croissais, tu croissais, il croissait, nous croissions, vous croissiez, ils croissaient**; *IMPER* **croîs**; *PRP* **croissant**; *PP* **crû**

26 **décevoir** : *IND* **je déçois, tu déçois, il déçoit**, nous décevons, vous décevez, **ils déçoivent**; *SUBJ* **je déçoive, tu déçoives, il déçoive**, nous décevions, vous déceviez, **ils déçoivent**; *PRET* **je déçus, tu déçus, il déçut, nous déçûmes, vous déçûtes, ils déçurent**; *IMPER* **déçois**; *PP* **déçu**

27 **déchoir** (*defective verb*) *Used only in the following tenses* : *IND* je déchois, tu déchois, il déchoit *or* il déchet, **nous déchoyons, vous déchoyez, ils déchoient**; *SUBJ* je déchoie, tu déchoies, il déchoie, **nous déchoyions, vous déchoyiez, ils déchoient**; *PRET* **je déchus, tu déchus, il déchut, nous déchûmes, vous déchûtes, ils déchurent**; *IMPF* (*not used*); *FUT* (*used but regularly formed*); *IMPER* (*not used*); *PRP* (*not used*); *PP* **déchu**

28 **devoir** : *IND* **je dois, tu dois, il doit**, nous devons, vous devez, **ils doivent**; *SUBJ* **je doive, tu doives, il doive**, nous devions, vous deviez, **ils doivent**; *PRET* **je dus, tu dus, il dut, nous dûmes, vous dûtes, ils durent**; *IMPER* **dois**; *PRP* **dû**

29 **dire** : *IND* je dis, tu dis, il dit, **nous disons, vous dites, ils disent**; *SUBJ* **je dise, tu dises, il dise, nous disions, vous disiez, ils disent**; *PRET* **je dis, tu dis, il dit, nous dîmes, vous dîtes, ils dirent**; *IMPF* **je disais, tu disais, il disait, nous disions, vous disiez, ils disent**; *PRP* **disant**; *PP* **dit**

30 **dormir** : *IND* **je dors, tu dors, il dort**, nous dormons, vous dormez, ils dorment; *PRET* **je dormis, tu dormis, il dormit, nous dormîmes, vous dormîtes, ils dormirent**; *IMPER* **dors**

31 **échoir** (*defective verb*) *Used only in the following tenses* : *IND* **il échoit, ils échoient**; *SUBJ* **il échoie**; *PRET* **il échut, ils échurent**; *IMPF* (*not used*); *FUT* il échoira *or* **il écherra**; ils échoiront *or* **ils écherront**; *IMPER* (*not used*); *PRP* **échéant**; *PP* **échu**

32 **éclore** (*defective verb*) *Used only in the following tenses* : *IND* **il éclot**; *PP* **éclos**

33 **écrire** : *IND* j'écris, tu écris, il écrit, **nous écrivons, vous écrivez, ils écrivent**; *SUBJ* **j'écrive, tu écrives, il écrive, nous écrivions, vous écriviez, ils écrivent**; *PRET* j'écrivis, tu écrivis, il écrivit, nous écrivîmes, vous écrivîtes, ils écrivirent; *IMPF* j'écrivais, tu écrivais, il écrivait, nous écrivions, vous écriviez, ils écrivaient; *PRP* **écrivant**; *PP* **écrit**

34 **enclore** (*defective verb*) *Used only in the following tenses* : *IND* j'enclos, tu enclos, il enclot, **nous enclosons, vous enclosez, ils enclosent**; *SUBJ* **j'enclose, tu encloses, il enclose, nous enclosions, vous enclosiez, ils enclosent**; *PRET* (*not used*); *IMPF* (*not used*); *FUT* (*used but regularly formed*); *IMPER* enclos; *PRP* **enclosant**; *PP* **enclos**

35 **ensuivre (s')** (*defective verb*) *Used only in the following tenses* : *IND* il s'ensuit; *SUBJ* il s'ensuive; *PRET* il s'ensuivit; *IMPF* il s'ensuivait; *FUT* il s'ensuivra; *PP* s'ensuivi

36 **envoyer** : *IND* j'envoie, tu envoies, il envoie, nous envoyons, vous envoyez, **ils envoient**; *SUBJ* **j'envoie, tu envoies, il envoie,** nous envoyions, vous envoyiez, **ils envoient**; *FUT* **j'enverrai, tu enverras, il enverra, nous enverrons, vous enverrez, ils enverront**; *IMPER* **envoie**

37 **éteindre** : *IND* j'éteins, tu éteins, il éteint, nous éteignons, vous éteignez, ils éteignent; *SUBJ* **j'éteigne, tu éteignes, il éteigne, nous éteignions, vous éteigniez, ils éteignent**; *PRET* **j'éteignis, tu éteignis, il éteignit, nous éteignîmes, vous éteignîtes, ils éteignirent**; *IMPF* **j'éteignais, tu éteignais, il éteignait, nous éteignions, vous éteigniez, ils éteignaient**; *IMPER* **éteins**; *PRP* **éteignant**; *PP* **éteint**

38 **être** : *IND* **je suis, tu es, il est, nous sommes, vous êtes, ils sont**; *SUBJ* **je sois, tu sois, il soit, nous soyons, vous soyez, ils soient**; *PRET* **je fus, tu fus, il fut, nous fûmes, vous fûtes, ils furent**; *IMPF* **j'étais, tu étais, il était, nous étions, vous étiez, ils étaient**; *FUT* **je serai, tu seras, il sera, nous serons, vous serez, ils seront**; *IMPER* **sois**; *PRP* **étant**; *PP* **été**

39 **exclure** : *IND* **j'exclus, tu exclus, il exclut, nous excluons, vous excluez, ils excluent**; *PRET* **j'exclus, tu exclus, il exclut, nous exclûmes, vous exclûtes, ils exclurent**; *IMPER* **exclus**; *PP* **exclu**

40 **extraire** : *IND* j'extrais, tu extrais, il extrait, **nous extrayons, vous extrayez,** ils extraient; *SUBJ* j'extraie, tu extraies, il extraie, **nous extrayions, vous extrayiez,** ils extraient; *PRET* (*not used*); *IMPF* **j'extrayais, tu extrayais, il extrayait, nous extrayions, vous extrayiez, ils extrayaient**; *PRP* **extrayant**; *PP* **extrait**

41 **faillir** (*defective verb*) *Used only in the infinitive and as a PP* **failli**

42 **faire** : *IND* je fais, tu fais, il fait, **nous faisons, vous faites, ils font**; *SUBJ* **je fasse, tu fasses, il fasse, nous fassions, vous fassiez, ils fassent**; *PRET* **je fis, tu fis, il fit, nous fîmes, vous fîtes, ils firent**; *IMPF* **je faisais, tu faisais, il faisait, nous faisions, vous faisiez, ils faisaient**; *FUT* **je ferai, tu feras, il fera, nous ferons, vous ferez, ils feront**; *PRP* **faisant**; *PP* **fait**

43 **falloir** (*defective verb*) *Used only in the following tenses* : *IND* **il faut**; *SUBJ* **il faille**; *PRET* **il fallut**; *IMPF* **il fallait**; *FUT* **il faudra**; *IMPER* (*not used*); *PRP* (*not used*); *PP* **fallu**

44 **forfaire** (*defective verb*) *Used only in the infinitive and in the following tenses* : *IND* **il forfait**; *PP* **forfait**

45 **frire** (*defective verb*) *Used only in the following tenses* : *IND* **je fris, tu fris, il frit**; *FUT* je frirai, tu friras, il frira, nous frirons, vous frirez, ils friront; *IMPER* **fris**; *PP* **frit**

46 **fuir** : *IND* je fuis, tu fuis, il fuit, **nous fuyons, vous fuyez, ils fuient**; *SUBJ* je fuie, **nous fuyions, vous fuyiez, ils fuient**; *PRET* je fuis, tu fuis, il fuit, **nous fuîmes, vous fuîtes, ils fuirent**; *IMPF* **je fuyais, tu fuyais, il fuyait, nous fuyions, vous fuyiez, ils fuyaient**; *PRP* **fuyant**; *PP* **fui**

47 **gésir** (*defective verb*) *Used only in the following tenses* : *IND* **je gis, tu gis, il gît, nous gisons, vous gisez, ils gisent**; *IMPF* **je gisais, tu gisais, il gisait, nous gisions, vous gisiez, ils gisaient**; *PRP* **gisant**

48 **haïr** : *IND* je hais, tu hais, il hait, **nous haïssons, vous haïssez, ils haïssent**; *SUBJ* **je haïsse, tu haïsses, il haïsse, nous haïssions, vous haïssiez, ils haïssent**; *PRET* **je haïs, tu haïs, il haït**

nous haïmes, vous haïtes, ils haïrent; *IMPF* je haïssais, tu haïssais, il haïssait, nous haïssions, vous haïssiez, ils haïssaient; *IMPER* hais; *PRP* haïssant; *PP* haï

49 **instruire** : *IND* j'instruis, tu instruis, il instruit, **nous instruisons, vous instruisez**, ils instruisent; *SUBJ* j'instruise, tu instruises, il instruise, nous instruisions, vous instruisiez, ils instruisent; *PRET* j'instruisis, tu instruisis, il instruisit, nous instruisîmes, vous instruisîtes, ils instruisirent; *IMPF* j'instruisais, tu instruisais, il instruisait, nous instruisions, vous instruisiez, ils instruisaient; *PRP* instruisant; *PP* instruit

50 **joindre** : *IND* je joins, tu joins, il joint, nous joignons, vous joignez, ils joignent; *SUBJ* je joigne, tu joignes, il joigne, nous joignions, vous joigniez, ils joignent; *PRET* je joignis, tu joignis, il joignit, nous joignîmes, vous joignîtes, ils joignirent; *IMPF* je joignais, tu joignais, il joignait, nous joignions, vous joigniez, ils joignaient; *IMPER* joins; *PRP* joignant; *PP* joint

51 **lire** : *IND* je lis, tu lis, il lit, **nous lisons, vous lisez, ils lisent**; *SUBJ* je lise, tu lises, il lise, nous lisions, vous lisiez, ils lisent; *PRET* je lus, tu lus, il lut, nous lûmes, vous lûtes, ils lurent; *IMPF* je lisais, tu lisais, il lisait, nous lisions, vous lisiez, ils lisaient; *PRP* lisant; *PP* lu

52 **mener** : *IND* je mène, tu mènes, il mène, nous menons, vous menez, ils mènent; *SUBJ* je mène, tu mènes, il mène, nous menions, vous meniez, ils mènent; *FUT* je mènerai, tu mèneras, il mènera, nous mènerons, vous mènerez, ils mèneront; *IMPER* mène

53 **mettre** : *IND* je mets, tu mets, il met, nous mettons, vous mettez, ils mettent; *PRET* je mis, tu mis, il mit, nous mîmes, vous mîtes, ils mirent; *IMPER* mets; *PP* mis

54 **moudre** : *IND* je mouds, tu mouds, il moud, **nous moulons, vous moulez, ils moulent**; *SUBJ* je moule, tu moules, il moule, nous moulions, vous mouliez, ils moulent; *PRET* je moulus, tu moulus, il moulut, nous moulûmes, vous moulûtes, ils moulurent; *IMPF* je moulais, tu moulais, il moulait, nous moulions, vous mouliez, ils moulaient; *PRP* moulant; *PP* moulu

55 **mourir** : *IND* je meurs, tu meurs, il meurt, nous mourons, vous mourez, **ils meurent**; *SUBJ* je meure, tu meures, il meure, nous mourions, vous mouriez, **ils meurent**; *PRET* je mourus, tu mourus, il mourut, nous mourûmes, vous mourûtes, ils moururent; *FUT* je mourrai, tu mourras, il mourra, nous mourrons, vous mourrez, ils mourront; *IMPER* meurs; *PRP* mourant; *PP* mort

56 **mouvoir** : *IND* je meus, tu meus, il meut, nous mouvons, vous mouvez, **ils meuvent**; *SUBJ* je meuve, tu meuves, il meuve, nous mouvions, vous mouviez, **ils meuvent**; *PRET* je mus, tu mus, il mut, nous mûmes, vous mûtes, ils murent; *IMPER* meus; *PP* mû

57 **naître** : *IND* je nais, tu nais, il naît, nous naissons, vous naissez, ils naissent; *SUBJ* je naisse, tu naisses, il naisse, nous naissions, vous naissiez, ils naissent; *PRET* je naquis, tu naquis, il naquit, nous naquîmes, vous naquîtes, ils naquirent; *IMPF* je naissais, tu naissais, il naissait, nous naissions, vous naissiez, ils naissaient; *IMPER* nais; *PRP* naissant; *PP* né

58 **nettoyer** : *IND* je nettoie, tu nettoies, il nettoie, nous nettoyons, vous nettoyez, **ils nettoient**; *SUBJ* je nettoie, tu nettoies, il nettoie, nous nettoyions, vous nettoyiez, **ils nettoient**; *FUT* je nettoierai, tu nettoieras, il nettoiera, nous nettoierons, vous nettoierez, ils nettoieront; *IMPER* **nettoie**

59 **oindre** (*defective verb*) *Used only in the infinitive and as a PP* oint

60 **ouïr** (*defective verb*) *Used only in the infinitive and as a pp* ouï

61 **paître** (*defective verb*) *Used only in the following tenses* : *IND* **je pais, tu pais, il paît, nous paissons, vous paissez, ils paissent**; *SUBJ* je paisse, tu paisses, il paisse, nous paissions, vous paissiez, ils paissent; *PRET* (*not used*); *IMPF* **je paissais, tu paissais, il paissait, nous paissions, vous paissiez, ils paissaient**; *FUT* (*used but regular*); *IMPER* pais; *PRP* **paissant**; *PP* (*not used*)

62 **parfaire** (*defective verb*) *Used only in the infinitive and in the following tenses* IND **il parfait**; *PP* **parfait**

63 **perdre** : *IND* je perds, tu perds, **il perd**, nous perdons, vous perdez, ils perdent; *PRET* **je perdis, tu perdis, il perdit, nous perdîmes, vous perdîtes, ils perdirent**; *PP* perdu

Conjugation of French Verbs

64 **piéger** : *IND* je piège, tu pièges, il piège, nous piégeons, vous piégez, ils piègent; *SUBJ* je piège, tu pièges, il piège, nous piégions, vous piégiez, ils piègent; *PRET* je piégeai, tu piégeas, il piégea, nous piégeâmes, vous piégeâtes, ils piégèrent; *IMPF* je piégeais, tu piégeais, il piégeait, nous piégions, vous piégiez, ils piégeaient; *IMPER* piège; *PRP* piégeant; *PP* piégé

65 **plaindre** : *IND* je plains, tu plains, il plaint, **nous plaignons, vous plaignez, ils plaignent;** *SUBJ* je plaigne, tu plaignes, il plaigne, nous plaignions, vous plaigniez, ils plaignent; *PRET* je plaignis, tu plaignis, il plaignit, nous plaignîmes, vous plaignîtes, ils plaignirent; *IMPF* je plaignais, tu plaignais, il plaignait, nous plaignions, vous plaigniez, ils plaignaient; *PRP* plaignant; *PP* plaint

66 **plaire** : *IND* je plais, tu plais, **il plaît, nous plaisons, vous plaisez, ils plaisent;** *SUBJ* je plaise, tu plaises, il plaise, nous plaisions, vous plaisiez, ils plaisent; *PRET* je plus, tu plus, il plut, nous plûmes, vous plûtes, ils plurent; *IMPF* je plaisais, tu plaisais, il plaisait, nous plaisions, vous plaisiez, ils plaisaient; *PRP* plaisant; *PP* plu

67 **pleuvoir** (*defective verb*) *Used in the infinitive and in the following tenses* *IND* **il pleut, ils pleuvent** (*only in the figurative*); *SUBJ* **il pleuve, ils pleuvent** (*only in the figurative*); *PRET* **il plut;** *IMPF* **il pleuvait, ils pleuvaient** (*only in the figurative*); *FUT* **il pleuvra;** *IMPER* (*not used*); *PRP* **pleuvant;** *PP* **plu**

68 **pourvoir** : *IND* je pourvois, tu pourvois, il pourvoit, nous pourvoyons, vous pourvoyez, ils pourvoient; *SUBJ* je pourvoie, tu pourvoies, il pourvoie, nous pourvoyions, vous pourvoyiez, ils pourvoient; *PRET* je pourvus, tu pourvus, il pourvut, nous pourvûmes, vous pourvûtes, ils pourvurent; *IMPF* je pourvoyais, tu pourvoyais, il pourvoyait, nous pourvoyions, vous pourvoyiez, ils pourvoyaient; *FUT* je pourvoirai, tu pourvoiras, il pourvoira, nous pourvoirons, vous pourvoirez, ils pourvoiront; *IMPER* pourvois; *PRP* pourvoyant; *PP* pourvu

69 **pouvoir** : *IND* je peux *or* je puis, tu peux, il peut, nous pouvons, vous pouvez, ils peuvent; *SUBJ* je puisse, tu puisses, il puisse, nous puissions, vous puissiez, ils puissent; *PRET* je pus, tu pus, il put, nous pûmes, vous pûtes, ils purent; *FUT* je pourrai, tu pourras, il pourra, nous pourrons, vous pourrez, ils pourront; *IMPER* (*not used*); *PP* pu

70 **prendre** : *IND* je prends, tu prends, **il prend, nous prenons, vous prenez, ils prennent;** *SUBJ* je prenne, tu prennes, il prenne, nous prenions, vous preniez, ils prennent; *PRET* je pris, tu pris, il prit, nous prîmes, vous prîtes, ils prirent; *IMPF* je prenais, tu prenais, il prenait, nous prenions, vous preniez, ils prenaient; *PRP* prenant; *PP* pris

71 **prévaloir** : *IND* je prévaux, tu prévaux, il prévaut, nous prévalons, vous prévalez, ils prévalent; *PRET* je prévalus, tu prévalus, il prévalut, nous prévalûmes, vous prévalûtes, ils prévalurent; *FUT* je prévaudrai, tu prévaudras, il prévaudra, nous prévaudrons, vous prévaudrez, ils prévaudront; *IMPER* prévaux; *PP* prévalu

72 **rassir** (*defective verb*) *Used only in the infinitive and as a PP* **rassis**

73 **ravoir** (*defective verb*) *Used only in the infinitive*

74 **résoudre** : *INF* je résous, tu résous, il résout, nous résolvons, vous résolvez, ils résolvent; *SUBJ* je résolve, tu résolves, il résolve, nous résolvions, vous résolviez, ils résolvent; *PRET* je résolus, tu résolus, il résolut, nous résolûmes, vous résolûtes, ils résolurent; *IMPF* je résolvais, tu résolvais, il résolvait, nous résolvions, vous résolviez, ils résolvaient; *IMPER* résous; *PRP* résolvant; *PP* résolu

75 **résulter** (*defective verb*) *Used only in the infinitive and in the following tenses* : *IND* **il résulte;** *PRP* **résultant**

76 **rire** : *IND* je ris, tu ris, il rit, nous rions, vous riez, ils rient; *SUBJ* je rie, tu ries, il rie, **nous riions, vous riiez,** ils rient; *PRET* je ris, tu ris, il rit, nous rîmes, vous rîtes, ils rirent; *IMPER* ris; *PP* ri

77 **rompre** : *IND* je romps, tu romps, **il rompt,** nous rompons, vous rompez, ils rompent; *PRET* je rompis, tu rompis, il rompit, nous rompîmes, vous rompîtes, ils rompirent; *PP* rompu

78 **saillir** : *IND* **je saille, tu sailles, il saille,** nous saillons, vous saillez, ils saillent; *PRET* **je saillis, tu sallis, il saillit, nous saillîmes, vous saillîtes, ils saillirent;** *FUT* **je saillerai, tu sailleras, il saillera, nous saillerons, vous saillerez, ils sailleront;** *IMPER* **saille**

79 **savoir** : *IND* je sais, tu sais, il sait, nous savons, vous savez, ils savent; *SUBJ* **je sache, tu saches, il sache, nous sachions, vous sachiez, ils sachent;** *PRET* je sus, tu sus, il sut, nous sûmes, vous sûtes, ils surent; *FUT* je saurai, tu sauras, il saura, nous saurons, vous saurez, ils sauront; *IMPER* sache, sachons, sachez; *PRP* **sachant;** *PP* su

80 **seoir** (*defective verb*) *Used only in the following tenses* : *IND* **il sied, ils siéent;** *SUBJ* **il siée, ils siéent;** *PRET* (*not used*); *IMPF* **il seyait, ils seyaient;** *FUT* **il siéra, ils siéront;** *IMPER* (*not used*); *PRP* **séant** *or* **seyant;** *PP* (*not used*)

81 **servir** : *IND* je sers, tu sers, il sert, nous servons, vous servez, ils servent; *PRET* **je servis, tu servis, il servit, nous servîmes, vous servîtes, ils servirent;** *FUT* **je servirai, tu serviras, il servira, nous servirons, vous servirez, ils serviront;** *IMPER* sers; *PP* servi

82 **sortir** : *IND* je sors, tu sors, il sort, nous sortons, vous sortez, ils sortent; *PRET* **je sortis, tu sortis, il sortit, nous sortîmes, vous sortîtes, ils sortirent;** *FUT* **je sortirai, tu sortiras, il sortira, nous sortirons, vous sortirez, ils sortiront;** *IMPER* sors; *PRP* **sortant;** *PP* sorti

83 **souffrir** : *IND* **je souffre, tu souffres, il souffre,** nous souffrons, vous souffrez, ils souffrent; *PRET* **je souffris, tu souffris, il souffrit, nous souffrîmes, vous souffrîtes, ils souffrirent;** *FUT* **je souffrirai, tu souffriras, il souffrira, nous souffrirons, vous souffrirez, ils souffriront;** *IMPER* **souffre;** *PP* **souffert**

84 **sourdre** (*defective verb*) *Used only in the infinitive and in the following tenses* : *IND* **il sourd, ils sourdent;** *IMPF* **il sourdait, ils sourdaient**

85 **stupéfaire** (*defective verb*) *Used only in the following tense* *PP* **stupéfié**

86 **suffire** : *IND* je suffis, tu suffis, il suffit, **nous suffisons, vous suffisez, ils suffisent;** *SUBJ* **je suffise, tu suffises, il suffise, nous suffisions, vous suffisiez, ils suffisent;** *PRET* **je suffis, tu suffis, il suffit, nous suffîmes, vous suffîtes, ils suffirent;** *IMPF* **je suffisais, tu suffisais, il suffisait, nous suffisions, vous suffisiez, ils suffisaient;** *PRP* **suffisant;** *PP* suffi

87 **suggérer** : *IND* **je suggère, tu suggères, il suggère,** nous suggérons, vous suggérez, **ils suggèrent;** *SUBJ* **je suggère, tu suggères, il suggère,** nous suggérions, vous suggériez, **ils suggèrent;** *IMPER* **suggère**

88` **suivre** : *IND* **je suis, tu suis, il suit,** nous suivons, vous suivez, ils suivent; *PRET* **je suivis, tu suivis, il suivit, nous suivîmes, vous suivîtes, ils suivirent;** *IMPER* suis; *PP* suivi

89 **suppléer** : *IND* **je supplée, tu supplées, il supplée, nous suppléons, vous suppléez, ils suppléent;** *SUBJ* **je supplée, tu supplées, il supplée, nous suppléions, vous suppléiez, ils suppléent;** *PRET* **je suppléai, tu suppléas, il suppléa, nous suppléâmes, vous suppléâtes, ils suppléèrent;** *FUT* **je suppléerai, tu suppléeras, il suppléera, nous suppléerons, vous suppléerez, ils suppléeront;** *IMPER* **supplée;** *PP* **suppléé**

90 **surseoir** : *IND* **je sursois, tu sursois, il sursoit, nous sursoyons, vous sursoyez, ils sursoient;** *SUBJ* **je sursoie, tu sursoies, il sursoie, nous sursoyions, vous sursoyiez, ils sursoient;** *PRET* **je sursis, tu sursis, il sursit, nous sursîmes, vous sursîtes, ils sursirent;** *IMPF* **je sursoyais, tu sursoyais, il sursoyait, nous sursoyions, vous sursoyiez, ils sursoyaient;** *FUT* **je surseoirai, tu surseoiras, il surseoira, nous surseoirons, vous surseoirez, ils surseoiront;** *IMPER* **sursois;** *PRP* **sursoyant;** *PP* **sursis**

91 **taire** : *IND* je tais, tu tais, **il tait, nous taisons, vous taisez, ils taisent;** *SUBJ* **je taise, tu taises, il taise, nous taisions, vous taisiez, ils taisent;** *PRET* **je tus, tu tus, il tut, nous tûmes, vous tûtes, ils turent;** *IMPF* **je taisais, tu taisais, il taisait, nous taisions, vous taisiez, ils taisaient;** *PRP* **taisant;** *PP* tu

92 **tenir** : *IND* **je tiens, tu tiens, il tient,** nous tenons, vous tenez, **ils tiennent;** *SUBJ* **je tienne, tu tiennes, il tienne,** nous tenions, vous teniez, **ils tiennent;** *PRET* **je tins, tu tins, il tint, nous**

tînmes, vous tîntes, ils tinrent; *FUT* je tiendrai, tu tiendras, il tiendra, nous tiendrons, vous tiendrez, ils tiendront; *IMPER* tiens; *PP* tenu

93 **tressaillir** ; *IND* je tressaille, tu tressailles, il tressaille, nous tressaillons, vous tressaillez, ils tressaillent; *PRET* je tressaillis, tu tressaillis, il tressaillit, nous tressaillîmes, vous tressaillites, ils tressaillirent; *FUT* je tressaillirai, tu tressailliras, il tressaillira, nous tressaillirons, vous tressaillirez, ils tressailliront; *IMPF* tressaille; *PP* tressailli

94 **vaincre** : *IND* je vaincs, tu vaincs, il vainc, nous vainquons, vous vainquez, ils vainquent; *SUBJ* je vainque, tu vainques, il vainque, nous vainquions, vous vainquiez, ils vainquent; *PRET* je vainquis, tu vainquis, il vainquit, nous vainquîmes, vous vainquîtes, ils vainquirent; *IMPF* je vainquais, tu vainquais, il vainquait, nous vainquions, vous vainquiez, ils vainquaient; *IMPER* vaincs; *PRP* vainquant; *PP* vaincu

95 **valoir** : *IND* je vaux, tu vaux, il vaut, nous valons, vous valez, ils valent; *SUBJ* je vaille, tu vailles, il vaille, nous valions, vous valiez, ils vaillent; *PRET* je valus, tu valus, il valut, nous valûmes, vous valûtes, ils valurent; *FUT* je vaudrai, tu vaudras, il vaudra, nous vaudrons, vous vaudrez, ils vaudront; *IMPER* vaux; *PP* valu

96 **vérifier** : *SUBJ* je vérifie, tu vérifies, il vérifie, **nous vérifiions, vous vérifiiez,** ils vérifient; *IMPF* je vérifiais, tu vérifiais, il vérifiait, **nous vérifiions, vous vérifiiez,** ils vérifiaient

97 **vêtir** : *IND* je vêts, tu vêts, il vêt, nous vêtons, vous vêtez, ils vêtent; *PRET* **je vêtis, tu vêtis, il vêtit, nous vêtîmes, vous vêtîtes, ils vêtirent;** *FUT* je vêtirai, tu vêtiras, il vêtira, nous vêtirons, vous vêtirez, ils vêtiront; *IMPER* vêts; *PP* vêtu

98 **vivre** : *IND* je vis, tu vis, il vit, nous vivons, vous vivez, ils vivent; *PRET* **je vécus, tu vécus, il vécut, nous vécûmes, vous vécûtes, ils vécurent;** *IMPER* vis; *PP* vécu

99 **voir** : *IND* je vois, tu vois, il voit, **nous voyons, vous voyez,** ils voient; *SUBJ* je voie, tu voies, il voie, **nous voyions, vous voyiez,** ils voient; *PRET* **je vis, tu vis, il vit, nous vîmes, vous vîtes, ils virent;** *IMPF* je voyais, tu voyais, il voyait, nous voyions, vous voyiez, ils voyaient; *FUT* je verrai, tu verras, il verra, nous verrons, vous verrez, ils verront; *PRP* voyant; *PP* vu

100 **vouloir** : *IND* je veux, tu veux, il veut, nous voulons, vous voulez, **ils veulent;** *SUBJ* je veuille, tu veuilles, il veuille, nous voulions, vous vouliez; **ils veuillent;** *PRET* je voulus, tu voulus, il voulut, nous voulûmes, vous voulûtes, ils voulurent; *FUT* **je voudrai, tu voudras, il voudra, nous voudrons, vous voudrez, ils voudront;** *IMPER* veux *or* veuille; *PP* voulu

Irregular English Verbs

INFINITIVE	PAST	PAST PARTICIPLE
arise	arose	arisen
awake	awoke	awoken *or* awaked
be	was, were	been
bear	bore	borne
beat	beat	beaten *or* beat
become	became	become
befall	befell	befallen
begin	began	begun
behold	beheld	beheld
bend	bent	bent
beseech	beseeched *or* besought	beseeched *or* besought
beset	beset	beset
bet	bet	bet
bid	bade *or* bid	bidden *or* bid
bind	bound	bound
bite	bit	bitten
bleed	bled	bled
blow	blew	blown
break	broke	broken
breed	bred	bred
bring	brought	brought
build	built	built
burn	burned *or* burnt	burned *or* burnt
burst	burst	burst
buy	bought	bought
can	could	—
cast	cast	cast
catch	caught	caught
choose	chose	chosen
cling	clung	clung
come	came	come
cost	cost	cost
creep	crept	crept
cut	cut	cut
deal	dealt	dealt
dig	dug	dug
do	did	done
draw	drew	drawn
dream	dreamed *or* dreamt	dreamed *or* dreamt
drink	drank	drunk *or* drank
drive	drove	driven
dwell	dwelled *or* dwelt	dwelled *or* dwelt
eat	ate	eaten
fall	fell	fallen
feed	fed	fed
feel	felt	felt
fight	fought	fought
find	found	found
flee	fled	fled
fling	flung	flung
fly	flew	flown
forbid	forbade	forbidden
forecast	forecast	forecast

INFINITIVE	PAST	PAST PARTICIPLE
forego	forewent	foregone
foresee	foresaw	foreseen
foretell	foretold	foretold
forget	forgot	forgotten *or* forgot
forgive	forgave	forgiven
forsake	forsook	forsaken
freeze	froze	frozen
get	got	got *or* gotten
give	gave	given
go	went	gone
grind	ground	ground
grow	grew	grown
hang	hung	hung
have	had	had
hear	heard	heard
hide	hid	hidden *or* hid
hit	hit	hit
hold	held	held
hurt	hurt	hurt
keep	kept	kept
kneel	knelt *or* kneeled	knelt *or* kneeled
know	knew	known
lay	laid	laid
lead	led	led
leap	leaped *or* leapt	leaped *or* leapt
leave	left	left
lend	lent	lent
let	let	let
lie	lay	lain
light	lit *or* lighted	lit *or* lighted
lose	lost	lost
make	made	made
may	might	—
mean	meant	meant
meet	met	met
mow	mowed	mowed *or* mown
pay	paid	paid
put	put	put
quit	quit	quit
read	read	read
rend	rent	rent
rid	rid	rid
ride	rode	ridden
ring	rang	rung
rise	rose	risen
run	ran	run
saw	sawed	sawed *or* sawn
say	said	said
see	saw	seen
seek	sought	sought
sell	sold	sold
send	sent	sent
set	set	set
shake	shook	shaken
shall	should	—
shear	sheared	sheared *or* shorn
shed	shed	shed
shine	shone *or* shined	shone *or* shined

INFINITIVE	PAST	PAST PARTICIPLE
shoot	shot	shot
show	showed	shown *or* showed
shrink	shrank *or* shrunk	shrunk *or* shrunken
shut	shut	shut
sing	sang *or* sung	sung
sink	sank *or* sunk	sunk
sit	sat	sat
slay	slew	slain
sleep	slept	slept
slide	slid	slid
sling	slung	slung
smell	smelled *or* smelt	smelled *or* smelt
sow	sowed	sown *or* sowed
speak	spoke	spoken
speed	sped *or* speeded	sped *or* speeded
spell	spelled	spelled
spend	spent	spent
spill	spilled	spilled
spin	spun	spun
spit	spit *or* spat	spit *or* spat
split	split	split
spoil	spoiled	spoiled
spread	spread	spread
spring	sprang *or* sprung	sprung
stand	stood	stood
steal	stole	stolen
stick	stuck	stuck
sting	stung	stung
stink	stank *or* stunk	stunk
stride	strode	stridden
strike	struck	struck
swear	swore	sworn
sweep	swept	swept
swell	swelled	swelled *or* swollen
swim	swam	swum
swing	swung	swung
take	took	taken
teach	taught	taught
tear	tore	torn
tell	told	told
think	thought	thought
throw	threw	thrown
thrust	thrust	thrust
tread	trod	trodden *or* trod
wake	woke	woken *or* waked
waylay	waylaid	waylaid
wear	wore	worn
weave	wove *or* weaved	woven *or* weaved
wed	wedded	wedded
weep	wept	wept
will	would	—
win	won	won
wind	wound	wound
withdraw	withdrew	withdrawn
withhold	withheld	withheld
withstand	withstood	withstood
wring	wrung	wrung
write	wrote	written

French Numbers

Cardinal Numbers

1	un	24	vingt-quatre
2	deux	25	vingt-cinq
3	trois	26	vingt-six
4	quatre	27	vingt-sept
5	cinq	28	vingt-huit
6	six	29	vingt-neuf
7	sept	30	trente
8	huit	31	trente et un
9	neuf	40	quarante
10	dix	50	cinquante
11	onze	60	soixante
12	douze	70	soixante-dix
13	treize	80	quatre-vingts
14	quatorze	90	quatre-vingt-dix
15	quinze	100	cent
16	seize	101	cent un
17	dix-sept	200	deux cents
18	dix-huit	1 000	mille
19	dix-neuf	1 001	mille un
20	vingt	2 000	deux mille
21	vingt et un	100 000	cent mille
22	vingt-deux	1 000 000	un million
23	vingt-trois	1 000 000 000	un milliard

Ordinal Numbers

1st	premier, première	16th	seizième
2nd	deuxième *or* second	17th	dix-septième
3rd	troisième	18th	dix-huitième
4th	quatrième	19th	dix-neuvième
5th	cinquième	20th	vingtième
6th	sixième	21st	vingt et unième
7th	septième	22nd	vingt-deuxième
8th	huitième	30th	trentième
9th	neuvième	40th	quarantième
10th	dixième	50th	cinquantième
11th	onzième	60th	soixantième
12th	douzième	70th	soixante-dixième
13th	treizième	80th	quatre-vingtième
14th	quatorzième	90th	quatre-vingt-dixième
15th	quinzième	100th	centième

Abbreviations in this Work

adj	adjective
adv	adverb
adv phr	adverbial phrase
Bel	Belgium
Brit	Great Britain
Can	Canada
conj	conjunction
conj phr	conjunctive phrase
esp	especially
etc	et cetera
f	feminine
fam	familiar or colloquial
fpl	feminine plural
interj	interjection
m	masculine
mf	masculine or feminine
mpl	masculine plural
n	noun
nf	feminine noun
nfpl	feminine plural noun
nfs & pl	invariable singular or plural feminine noun
nm	masculine noun
nmf	masculine or feminine noun
nmfpl	plural noun invariable for gender
nmfs & pl	noun invariable for both gender and number
nmpl	masculine plural noun
nms & pl	invariable singular or plural masculine noun
npl	plural noun
ns & pl	noun invariable for plural
pl	plural
pp	past participle
prep	preposition
prep phr	prepositional phrase
pron	pronoun
qqch	quelque chose (something)
qqn	quelqu'un (someone)
s	singular
s.o.	someone
sth	something
Switz	Switzerland
usu	usually
v	verb (transitive and intransitive)
v aux	auxiliary verb
vi	intransitive verb
v impers	impersonal verb
vr	reflexive verb
vt	transitive verb

Pronunciation Symbols

VOWELS

æ — ask, bat, glad
ɑ — cot, bomb
ã — *French* chant, ennui
a — *New England* aunt, *British* ask, glass
e — *French* été, aider, chez
ɛ — egg, bet, fed
ɛ̃ — *French* lapin, main
ə — about, javelin, Alabama
ə — when italicized as in *ə*l, *ə*m, *ə*n, indicates a syllabic pronunciation of the consonant as in bottle, prism, button
i — very, any, thirty
i: — eat, bead, bee
ɪ — id, bid, pit
o — Ohio, yellower, potato
o: — oats, own, zone, blow
ɔ — awl, maul, caught, paw
ɔ̃ — ombre, mon
ʊ — sure, should, could
u — *French* ouvert, chou, rouler
u: — boot, two, coo
ʌ — under, putt, bud
eɪ — eight, wade, bay
aɪ — ice, bite, tie
aʊ — out, gown, plow
ɔɪ — oyster, coil, boy
ər — further, stir
ø — *French* deux, *German* Höhe
œ — *French* bœuf, *German* Gött
œ̃ — *French* lundi, parfum

CONSONANTS

b — baby, labor, cab
d — day, ready, kid
ʤ — just, badger, fudge
ð — then, either, bathe
f — foe, tough, buff
g — go, bigger, bag
h — hot, aha
j — yes, vineyard
k — cat, keep, lacquer, flock
l — law, hollow, boil
m — mat, hemp, hammer, rim
n — new, tent, tenor, run
ŋ — rung, hang, swinger
ɲ — *French* digne, agneau
p — pay, lapse, top
r — rope, burn, tar
s — sad, mist, kiss
ʃ — shoe, mission, slush
t — toe, button, mat
t̬ — indicates that some speakers of English pronounce this sound as a voiced alveolar flap, as in later, catty, battle
ʧ — choose, batch
θ — thin, ether, bath
v — vat, never, cave
w — wet, software
ɥ — *French* cuir, appui
x — *German* Bach, *Scottish* loch
z — zoo, easy, buzz
ʒ — azure, beige

h,k, when italicized indicate sounds which
p,t are present in the pronunciation of some speakers of English but absent in the pronunciation of others, so that *whence* [ˈʰwɛnt̬s] can be pronounced as [ˈʰwɛns], [ˈhwɛnts], [ˈwɛnts], or [ˈwɛns].

OTHER SYMBOLS

ˈ — high stress pen**man**ship
ˌ — low stress penman**ship**
ʼ — aspiration; when used before French words in *h*-, indicates absence of liaison, as in *le héros* [lə ʼero]
( ) — indicate sounds that are present in the pronunciation of some speakers of French but absent in that of others, as in *cenellier* [s(ə)nɛlje], *but* [by(t)]

French-English
Dictionary

A

a [a] *nm* : a, first letter of the alphabet

à [a] *prep* **1** : to **2** ~ **deux heures** : at two o'clock **3** ~ **la** : in the manner of, like **4** ~ **l'heure** : per hour **5** ~ **mon avis** : in my opinion **6** ~ **pied** : on foot **7** ~ **vendre** : for sale **8 la femme aux yeux verts** : the woman with green eyes **9 un ami** ~ **moi** : a friend of mine **10 voler aux riches** : steal from the rich

abaisser [abese] *vt* **1** : lower, reduce **2** HUMILIER : humble — **s'abaisser** *vr* **1** : lower oneself **2** ~ **à** : stoop to

abandonner [abɑ̆dɔne] *vt* : abandon — **s'abandonner** *vr* **1** : neglect oneself **2** ~ **à** : give oneself up to — **abandon** [abɑ̆dɔ̃] *nm* **1** : abandonment, neglect **2** DÉSINVOLTURE : abandon

abasourdir [abazurdir] *vt* : stun

abat–jour [abaʒur] *nms & pl* : lampshade

abats [aba] *nmpl* **1** : entrailes **2** ~ **de volaille** : giblets

abattant [abatɑ̆] *nm* : flap, leaf

abattis [abati] *nmpl* : giblets

abattoir [abatwar] *nm* : slaughterhouse

abattre [abatr] {12} *vt* **1** : knock down, cut down **2** ÉPUISER : wear out **3** DÉMORALISER : dishearten — **s'abattre** *vr* **1** : fall, crash **2** ~ **sur** : descend on — **abattement** [abatmɑ̆] *nm* **1** : reduction, allowance **2** : despondency — **abattu, -tue** [abaty] *adj* : downcast

abbaye [abei] *nf* : abbey — **abbé** [abe] *nm* **1** : abbot **2** PRÊTRE : priest

abcès [apsɛ] *nm* : abscess

abdiquer [abdike] *v* : abdicate — **abdication** [abdikasjɔ̃] *nf* : abdication

abdomen [abdɔmɛn] *nm* : abdomen — **abdominal, -nale** [abdɔminal] *adj, mpl* **-naux** [-no] : abdominal

abécédaire [abesedɛr] *nm* : primer, speller

abeille [abɛj] *nf* : bee

aberrant, -rante [aberɑ̆, -rɑ̆t] *adj* : absurd — **aberration** [aberasjɔ̃] *nf* : aberration

abêtir [abetir] *vt* : make stupid

abhorrer [abɔre] *vt* : abhor

abîme [abim] *nm* : abyss, depths — **abîmer** [abime] *vt* : spoil, damage — **s'abîmer** *vr* **1** : be spoiled **2** : sink, founder

abject, -jecte [abʒɛkt] *adj* : despicable, abject

abjurer [abʒyre] *vt* : renounce, abjure

abnégation [abnegasjɔ̃] *nf* : self-denial

aboiement [abwamɑ̆] *nm* : barking — **abois** [abwa] *nmpl* **aux** ~ : at bay

abolir [abɔlir] *vt* : abolish — **abolition** [abɔlisjɔ̃] *nf* : abolition

abominable [abɔminabl] *adj* : abominable

abonder [abɔ̃de] *vi* : abound — **abondamment** [abɔ̃damɑ̆] *adv* : abundantly — **abondance** [abɔ̃dɑ̃s] *nf* : abundance — **abondant, -dante** [abɔ̃dɑ̆, -dɑ̆t] *adj* : abundant

abonner [abɔne] *vt* : subscribe to — **abonné, -née** [abɔne] *n* : subscriber — **abonnement** [abɔnmɑ̆] *nm* : subscription

aborder [abɔrde] *vt* **1** : approach **2** : tackle, deal with — *vi* : (reach) land — **abord** [abɔr] *nm* **1** : approach **2 d'** ~ : at first **3** ~**s** *nmpl* : surroundings — **abordable** [abɔrdabl] *adj* **1** : approachable **2** : affordable — **abordage** [abɔrdaʒ] *nm* : boarding

aborigène [abɔriʒɛn] *nmf* : aborigine, native — ~ *adj* : aboriginal

abortif, -tive [abɔrtif, -tiv] *adj* : abortive

aboutir [abutir] *vi* **1** : succeed **2** ~ **à** : result in — **aboutissement** [abutismɑ̆] *nm* : result

aboyer [abwaje] {58} *vi* : bark

abraser [abraze] *vt* : abrade — **abrasif, -sive** [abrazif, -ziv] *adj* : abrasive

abréger [abreʒe] {64} *vt* : shorten, abridge — **abrégé** [abreʒe] *nm* : summary — **abrègement** [abrɛʒmɑ̆] *nm* : abridgment

abreuver [abrœve] *vt* **1** : water **2** ~ **de** : shower with — **s'abreuver** *vr* : drink — **abreuvoir** [abrœvwar] *nm* : watering place

abréviation [abrevjasjɔ̃] *nf* : abbreviation

abri [abri] *nm* **1** : shelter **2 à l'**~ : under cover — **abriter** [abrite] *vt* **1** : shelter **2** HÉBERGER : house

abricot [abriko] *nm* : apricot

abrier [abrije] {96} *vt Can* : cover

abroger [abrɔʒe] {17} *vt* : repeal

abrupt, -brupte [abrypt] *adj* **1** ESCARPÉ : steep **2** BRUSQUE : abrupt

abrutir [abrytir] *vt* : make stupid — **abruti, -tie** [abryti] *n fam* : fool, idiot

absenter [apsɑ̆te] *v* **s'absenter** *vr* : leave, go away — **absence** [apsɑ̃s] *nf* : absence — **absent, -sente** [apsɑ̆, -sɑ̆t] *adj* : absent — ~ *n* : absentee

absolu, -lue [apsɔly] *adj* : absolute — **absolu** *nm* : absolute — **absolument** [-lymɑ̆] *adv* : absolutely

absolution [apsɔlysjɔ̃] *nf* : absolution

absorber [apsɔrbe] *vt* **1** : absorb **2** : take (medicine) — **absorbant, -bante** [apsɔrbɑ̆, -bɑ̆t] *adj* **1** : absorbent **2** : engrossing — **absorption** [apsɔrpsjɔ̃] *nf* : absorption

absoudre [apsudr] {1} *vt* : absolve

abstenir [apstənir] {92} *v* **s'abstenir** *vr* **1**
: abstain **2** ~ **de** : refrain from — **absti-**
nence [apstinɑ̃s] *nf* : abstinence
abstraction [apstraksjɔ̃] *nf* **1** : abstraction **2**
faire de ~ ... : abstraire [apstrɛr]
{40} *v* : abstract — **abstrait, -traite** [apstrɛ,
-trɛt] *adj* : abstract — **abstrait** *nm* : abstract
absurde [apsyrd] *adj* : absurd — **absurdité**
[apsyrdite] *nf* : absurdity
abuser [abyze] *vt* : deceive — *vi* ~ **de 1**
: misuse **2** : exploit — **s'abuser** *vr* : be mistaken — **abusif, -sive** [abyzif, -ziv] *adj* **1**
EXAGÉRÉ : excessive **2** IMPROPRE : incorrect
académie [akademi] *nf* : academy —
académique [akademik] *adj* : academic
Acadien, -dienne [akadjɛ̃, -djɛn] *n* **1** : Acadian **2** : Cajun — **acadien, -dienne** *adj* **1**
: Acadian **2** : Cajun
acajou [akaʒu] *nm* : mahogany
acariâtre [akarjatr] *adj* : cantankerous
accabler [akable] *vt* **1** ÉCRASER : overwhelm **2** : condemn — **accablant, -blante**
[akablɑ̃, -blɑ̃t] *adj* : overwhelming — **ac-**
cablement [akabləmɑ̃] *nm* : despondency
accalmie [akalmi] *nf* : lull
accaparer [akapare] *vt* : monopolize
accéder [aksede] {87} *vi* **1** ~ **à** : reach, obtain **2** ~ **à** : accede to
accélérer [akselere] {87} *v* : accelerate —
accélérateur *nm* : accelerator — **accéléra-**
tion [akselerasjɔ̃] *nf* : acceleration
accent [aksɑ̃] *nm* **1** : accent **2** : stress, emphasis — **accentuer** [aksɑ̃tɥe] *vt* **1** : accent,
stress **2** : emphasize — **s'accentuer** *vr*
: become more pronounced
accepter [aksɛpte] *vt* : accept, agree to —
acceptable [aksɛptabl] *adj* : acceptable —
acceptation [aksɛptasjɔ̃] *nf* : acceptance
acception [aksɛpsjɔ̃] *nf* : sense, meaning
accès [aksɛ] *nm* **1** : access **2** : entry **3**
CRISE : fit, attack — **accessible** [aksɛsibl]
adj : accessible
accession [aksɛsjɔ̃] *nf* ~ **à** : accession to,
attainment of
accessoire [aksɛswar] *nm* **1** : accessory **2**
: prop — ~ *adj* : incidental, secondary
accident [aksidɑ̃] *nm* : accident — **acci-**
denté, -tée [aksidɑ̃te] *adj* **1** : damaged, injured **2** : rough, uneven — ~ *n* : accident
victim — **accidentel, -telle** [aksidɑ̃tɛl] *adj*
: accidental — **accidentellement** [-tɛlmɑ̃]
adv : accidentally
acclamer [aklame] *vt* : acclaim, cheer — **ac-**
clamation [aklamasjɔ̃] *nf* : cheering
acclimater [aklimate] *vt* : acclimatize —
s'acclimater *vr* : adapt
accolade [akɔlad] *nf* **1** ÉTREINTE : embrace
2 : brace sign, bracket
accommoder [akɔmɔde] *vt* : accommodate

— **s'accommoder** *vr* ~ **de** : put up with
— **accommodant, -dante** [akɔmɔdɑ̃,
-dɑ̃t] *adj* : obliging — **accommodement**
[akɔmɔdmɑ̃] *nm* : compromise
accompagner [akɔ̃paɲe] *vt* : accompany —
accompagnement [akɔ̃paɲmɑ̃] *nm* : ac-
companiment
accomplir [akɔ̃plir] *vt* : accomplish —
s'accomplir *vr* : take place — **accompli,**
-plie [akɔ̃pli] *adj* : finished — **accom-**
plissement [akɔ̃plismɑ̃] *nm* : accomplishment
accordéon [akɔrdeɔ̃] *nm* : accordion
accorder [akɔrde] *vt* **1** : reconcile **2** OC-
TROYER : grant, bestow — **s'accorder** *vr*
: be in agreement — **accord** [akɔr] *nm* **1**
: agreement **2** : approval, consent **3** : chord
(in music)
accoster [akɔste] *vt* : approach — *vi* : dock,
land
accotement [akɔtmɑ̃] *nm* : shoulder (of a
road)
accoucher [akuʃe] *vt* : deliver (a baby) — *vi*
1 : be in labor **2** ~ **de** : give birth to — **ac-**
couchement [akuʃmɑ̃] *nm* : childbirth
accouder [akude] *v* **s'accouder** *vr* ~ **à** *or*
~ **sur** : lean (one's elbows) on — **ac-**
coudoir [akudwar] *nm* : armrest
accoupler [akuple] *vt* : couple, link —
s'accoupler *vr* : mate — **accouplement**
[akupləmɑ̃] *nm* **1** : coupling **2** : mating
accourir [akurir] {23} *vi* : come running
accoutrement [akutrəmɑ̃] *nm* : outfit
accoutumer [akutyme] *vt* : accustom —
s'accoutumer *vr* ~ **à** : get accustomed to
— **accoutumé, -mée** [akutyme] *adj* : customary
accréditer [akredite] *vt* **1** : accredit **2** : sub-
stantiate (a rumor, etc.)
accroc [akro] *nm* **1** : rip, tear **2** OBSTACLE
: hitch, snag
accrocher [akrɔʃe] *vt* **1** SUSPENDRE : hang
up **2** : hook, hitch **3** HEURTER : bump into
4 ~ **l'œil** : catch the eye — *vi* : catch, snag
— **s'accrocher** *vr* : hang on, cling — **ac-**
crochage [akrɔʃaʒ] *nm* **1** : hanging, hook-
ing **2** : collision **3** QUERELLE : dispute —
accrocheur, -cheuse [akrɔʃœr, -ʃøz] *adj*
1 OPINIÂTRE : tenacious **2** ATTRAYANT
: eye-catching
accroire [akrwar] {2} *vt* **en faire** ~ **à** : take
in, dupe
accroître [akrwatr] {25} *vt* : increase —
s'accroître *vr* : grow — **accroissement**
[akrwasmɑ̃] *nm* : growth, increase
accroupir [akrupir] *v* **s'accroupir** *vr* : squat
accueillir [akœjir] {3} *vt* : greet — **accueil**
[akœj] *nm* : welcome, reception — **accueil-**
lant, -lante [akœjɑ̃, -jɑ̃t] *adj* : welcoming,
hospitable

acculer [akyle] *vt* : corner
accumuler [akymyle] *vt* : accumulate —
s'accumuler *vr* : pile up — **accumulation**
[akymylasjɔ̃] *nf* : accumulation
accuser [akyze] *vt* **1** : accuse **2 ~ réception de** : acknowledge receipt of — **accusateur, -trice** [akyzatœr, -tris] *adj* : incriminating — **accusation** [akyzasjɔ̃] *nf* : accusation — **accusé, -sée** *n* : defendant, accused
acerbe [asɛrb] *adj* : acerbic
acéré, -rée [asere] *adj* : sharp
acharner [aʃarne] *v* **s'acharner** *vr* **1** S'OBSTINER : persevere **2 ~ sur** : persecute, hound — **acharné, -née** [aʃarne] *adj* : relentless — **acharnement** [aʃarnəmɑ̃] *nm* : relentlessness
achat [aʃa] *nm* **1** : purchase **2 faire des ~s** : go shopping
acheminer [aʃmine] *vt* **1** : transport **2** : forward (mail) — **s'acheminer** *vr* **~ vers** : head for — **acheminement** [aʃminmɑ̃] *nm* : dispatch, routing
acheter [aʃte] {20} *vt* : buy, purchase — **acheteur, -teuse** [aʃtœr, -tøz] *n* : buyer
achever [aʃve] {52} *vt* : complete, finish — **s'achever** *vr* : draw to a close — **achèvement** [aʃɛvmɑ̃] *nm* : completion
acide [asid] *adj* & *nm* : acid — **acidité** [asidite] *nf* : sourness, acidity
acier [asje] *nm* : steel — **aciérie** [asjeri] *nf* : steelworks
acné [akne] *nf* : acne
acolyte [akɔlit] *nm* : accomplice
acompte [akɔ̃t] *nm* : deposit, installment
à-côté [akote] *nm, pl* **à-côtés** : extra, perk
à-coup [aku] *nm, pl* **à-coups** : jerk, jolt
acoustique [akustik] *adj* : acoustic — **~** *nf* : acoustics
acquérir [akerir] {21} *vt* **1** : acquire **2** : purchase — **acquéreur, -reuse** [akerœr, -røz] *n* : buyer
acquiescer [akjese] {6} *vi* : agree
acquis, -quise [aki, -kiz] *adj* **1** : acquired **2** : established — **acquis** *nms* & *pl* : knowledge — **acquisition** [akizisjɔ̃] *nf* : acquisition
acquitter [akite] *vt* **1** : acquit **2** PAYER : pay — **s'acquitter** *vr* **~ de 1** : carry out **2** : pay off — **acquit** [aki] *nm* : receipt — **acquittement** [akitmɑ̃] *nm* : payment (of a debt)
acre [akr] *nf* : acre *Can*
âcre [akr] *adj* : acrid — **âcreté** [akrəte] *nf* : bitterness
acrobate [akrɔbat] *nmf* : acrobat — **acrobatie** [akrɔbasi] *nf* : acrobatics — **acrobatique** [akrɔbatik] *adj* : acrobatic
acrylique [akrilik] *adj* & *nm* : acrylic
acte [akt] *nm* **1** : action, deed **2** : act (in theater) **3** : certificate, document **4 ~s** *nmpl* : proceedings
acteur, -trice [aktœr, -tris] *n* : actor, actress *f*
actif, -tive [aktif, -tiv] *adj* : active — **actif** *nm* **1** : assets *pl* **2** : active voice
action [aksjɔ̃] *nf* **1** : action, act EFFET : effect **3** : share (in finance) — **actionnaire** [aksjɔnɛr] *nmf* : shareholder — **actionner** [aksjɔne] *vt* **1** : engage, set in motion **2** : sue
activer [aktive] *vt* **1** : activate **2** HÂTER : speed up — **s'activer** *vr* : bustle about
activiste [aktivist] *adj* & *nmf* : activist — **activisme** [aktivism] *nm* : activism
activité [aktivite] *nf* : activity
actualité [aktɥalite] *nf* **1** : current events *pl* **2 ~s** *nfpl* : news — **actualiser** [aktɥalize] *vt* : update, modernize
actuel, -tuelle [aktɥɛl] *adj* : current, present — **actuellement** [-tɥɛlmɑ̃] *adv* : at present
acuité [akɥite] *nf* : acuteness
acupuncture [akypɔ̃ktyr] *nf* : acupuncture
adage [adaʒ] *nm* : adage
adapter [adapte] *vt* : adapt, fit — **s'adapter** *vr* : adapt — **adaptation** [adaptasjɔ̃] *nf* : adaptation — **adaptateur** [adaptatœr] *nm* : adapter
additif [aditif] *nm* : additive
addition [adisjɔ̃] *nf* **1** : addition **2** NOTE : bill, check — **additionnel, -nelle** [adisjɔnɛl] *adj* : additional — **additionner** [adisjɔne] *vt* : add (up)
adepte [adɛpt] *nmf* : follower
adéquat, -quate [adekwa, -kwat] *adj* **1** SUFFISANT : adequate **2** APPROPRIÉ : appropriate
adhérer [adere] {87} *vi* **1** : adhere **2 ~ à** : join — **adhérence** [aderɑ̃s] *nf* : adhesion, grip — **adhérent, -rente** [aderɑ̃, -rɑ̃t] *adj* : adhering, sticking — **~** *n* : member
adhésif, -sive [adezif, -ziv] *adj* : adhesive — **adhésif** *nm* : adhesive — **adhésion** [adezjɔ̃] *nf* **1** : adhesion **2** : adherence, support **3** AFFILIATION : membership
adieu [adjø] *nm, pl* **adieux** : farewell, goodbye
adjacent, -cente [adʒasɑ̃, -sɑ̃t] *adj* : adjacent
adjectif [adʒɛktif] *nm* : adjective
adjoindre [adʒwɛ̃dr] {50} *vt* **1** : appoint **2** : add, attach — **s'adjoindre** *vr* **~ qqn** : take s.o. on, hire s.o. — **adjoint, -jointe** [adʒwɛ̃, -ʒwɛ̃t] *adj* & *n* : assistant
adjonction [adʒɔ̃ksjɔ̃] *nf* : addition
admettre [admɛtr] {53} *vt* : admit
administrer [administre] *vt* : administer — **administrateur, -trice** [administratœr, -tris] *n* : director, administrator — **administratif, -tive** [administratif, -tiv] *adj* : admin-

istrative — **administration** [administrasjɔ̃] *nf* : administration

admirer [admire] *vt* : admire — **admirable** [admirabl] *adj* : admirable — **admirateur, -trice** [admiratœr, -tris] *n* : admirer — **admiratif, -tive** [admiratif, -tiv] *adj* : admiring — **admiration** [admirasjɔ̃] *nf* : admiration

admissible [admisibl] *adj* : acceptable, eligible — **admission** [admisjɔ̃] *nf* : admittance

admonester [admɔnɛste] *vt* : admonish

ADN [adeɛn] *nm* (*acide désoxyribonucléique*) : DNA

adolescence [adɔlesɑ̃s] *nf* : adolescence — **adolescent, -cente** [-lesɑ̃, -sɑ̃t] *adj* & *n* : adolescent

adopter [adɔpte] *vt* : adopt — **adoptif, -tive** [adɔptif, -tiv] *adj* : adoptive, adopted — **adoption** [adɔpsjɔ̃] *nf* : adoption

adorer [adɔre] *vt* : adore, worship — **adorable** [adɔrabl] *adj* : adorable

adosser [adose] *vt* : lean — **s'adosser** *vr* ~ **à** *or* ~ **contre** : lean back against

adoucir [adusir] *vt* 1 : soften 2 : alleviate, ease — **s'adoucir** *vr* : become milder, mellow — **adoucissement** [adusismɑ̃] *nm* 1 : softening 2 : alleviation

adresser [adrese] *vt* : address — **adresse** [adrɛs] *nf* 1 : address 2 HABILETÉ : skill — **s'adresser** *vr* ~ **à** : speak to

adroit, -droite [adrwa, -drwat] *adj* HABILE : skillful

adulte [adylt] *adj* & *nmf* : adult

adultère [adyltɛr] *nm* : adultery — ~ *adj* : adulterous

advenir [advənir] {4} *v impers* 1 : happen, occur 2 ~ **de** : become of

adverbe [advɛrb] *nm* : adverb

adversaire [advɛrsɛr] *nmf* : opponent — **adverse** [advɛrs] *adj* : opposing — **adversité** [advɛrsite] *nf* : adversity

aérer [aere] {87} *vt* : air out — **s'aérer** *vr* : get some fresh air

aérien, -rienne [aerjɛ̃, -rjɛn] *adj* : air, aerial

aérobic [aerɔbik] *nm* : aerobics

aérodynamique [aerɔdinamik] *adj* : aerodynamic

aérogare [aerɔgar] *nf* : air terminal

aéroglisseur [aerɔglisœr] *nm* : hovercraft

aéroport [aerɔpɔr] *nm* : airport

aérosol [aerɔsɔl] *nm* : aerosol

affable [afabl] *adj* : affable

affaiblir [afeblir] *vt* : weaken — **s'affaiblir** *vr* 1 : become weak 2 ATTÉNUER : fade

affaire [afɛr] *nf* 1 : affair 2 CAS : matter 3 ENTREPRISE : business 4 TRANSACTION : deal 5 ~**s** *nfpl* : belongings 6 ~**s** *nfpl* : business 7 **avoir** ~ **à** : deal with — **affairer** [afere] *v* **s'affairer** *vr* : be busy — **affairé, -rée** [afere] *adj* : busy

affaisser [afese] *v* **s'affaisser** *vr* : collapse, give way — **affaissement** [afɛsmɑ̃] *nm* : sagging, sinking

affaler [afale] *v* **s'affaler** *vr* : collapse

affamé, -mée [afame] *adj* : famished

affecter [afɛkte] *vt* 1 : affect 2 NOMMER : appoint 3 ASSIGNER : allocate 4 FEINDRE : feign — **affectation** [afɛktasjɔ̃] *nf* 1 : appointment 2 ~ **des fonds** : allocation of funds — **affecté, -tée** [afɛkte] *adj* : mannered, affected

affectif, -tive [afɛktif, -tiv] *adj* : emotional

affection [afɛksjɔ̃] *nf* 1 : affection 2 : ailment — **affectionner** [afɛksjɔne] *vt* : be fond of — **affectueux, -tueuse** [afɛktɥø, -tɥøz] *adj* : affectionate — **affectueusement** [-tɥøzmɑ̃] *adv* : fondly

afférent, -rente [aferɑ̃, -rɑ̃t] *adj* ~ **à** : pertaining to

affermir [afɛrmir] *vt* : strengthen

affiche [afiʃ] *nf* : poster, notice — **affichage** [afiʃaʒ] *nm* 1 : posting, publicizing 2 ~ **numérique** : digital display — **afficher** [afiʃe] *vt* 1 : post, put up 2 : show, display

affilée [afile] **d'~** *adv phr* : in a row

affiler [afile] {96} *vt* : sharpen

affilier [afilje] *vt* : affiliate — **s'affilier** *vr* ~ **à** : join

affiner [afine] *vt* : refine

affinité [afinite] *nf* : affinity

affirmatif, -tive [afirmatif, -tiv] *adj* : affirmative — **affirmative** *nf* : affirmative

affirmer [afirme] *vt* : affirm, assert — **s'affirmer** *vr* : assert oneself — **affirmation** [afirmasjɔ̃] *nf* : assertion

affliger [afliʒe] {17} *vt* : afflict, distress — **affliction** [afliksjɔ̃] *nf* : affliction — **affligeant, -geante** [afliʒɑ̃, -ʒɑ̃t] *adj* : distressing

affluer [aflye] *vi* 1 COULER : flow 2 ~ **vers** : flock to — **affluence** [aflyɑ̃s] *nf* 1 : crowd 2 **heure d'~** : rush hour — **affluent** [aflyɑ̃] *nm* : tributary

afflux [afly] *nm* : influx, rush

affoler [afɔle] *vt* EFFRAYER : terrify — **s'affoler** *vr* : panic — **affolé, -lée** [afɔle] *adj* : frightened — **affolement** [afɔlmɑ̃] *nm* : panic

affranchir [afrɑ̃ʃir] *vt* 1 LIBÉRER : liberate, free 2 : stamp (a letter) — **affranchissement** [afrɑ̃ʃismɑ̃] *nm* 1 : liberation 2 : stamping, postage

affréter [afrete] {87} *vt* : charter

affreux, -freuse [afrø, -frøz] *adj* : horrible — **affreusement** [afrøzmɑ̃] *adv* : horribly

affronter [afrɔ̃te] *vt* : confront — **s'affronter** *vr* : confront each other — **affront** [afrɔ̃] *nm* : affront — **affrontement** [afrɔ̃tmɑ̃] *nm* : confrontation

affûter [afyte] *vt* : sharpen — **affût** [afy] *nm* **être à l'~ de** : be on the lookout for

afin [afɛ̃] *adv* **1** ~ **de** : in order to **2** ~ **que** : so that

africain, -caine [afrikɛ̃, -kɛn] *adj* : African

agacer [agase] {6} *vt* : irritate — **agaçant, -çante** [agasɑ̃, -sɑ̃t] *adj* : annoying — **agacement** [agasmɑ̃] *nm* : annoyance

âge [aʒ] *nm* **1** : age (of a person) **2** : age, era — **âgé, -gée** [aʒe] *adj* **1** VIEUX : elderly **2** ~ **de 10 ans** : 10 years old

agence [aʒɑ̃s] *nf* : agency, office

agencer [aʒɑ̃se] {6} *vt* : arrange, lay out — **agencement** [aʒɑ̃smɑ̃] *nm* : layout

agenda [aʒɛ̃da] *nm* : appointment book

agenouiller [aʒnuje] *v* **s'agenouiller** *vr* : kneel

agent, -gente [aʒɑ̃, -ʒɑ̃t] *n* **1** : agent **2** ~ **de police** : police officer

agglomération [aglɔmerasjɔ̃] *nf* : urban area

agglutiner [aglytine] *vt* : stick together

aggraver [agrave] *vt* : aggravate, make worse — **s'aggraver** *vr* EMPIRER : worsen — **aggravation** [agravasjɔ̃] *nf* : worsening

agile [aʒil] *adj* : agile — **agilité** [aʒilite] *nf* : agility

agir [aʒir] *vi* **1** : act **2** SE COMPORTER : behave **3** : take effect (of medication) — **s'agir** *vr* **il s'agit de** : it is a question of — **agissements** [aʒismɑ̃] *nmpl* : schemes, dealings

agiter [aʒite] *vt* **1** SECOUER : shake **2** TROUBLER : disturb — **s'agiter** *vr* **1** : bustle about **2** : fidget — **agitation** [aʒitasjɔ̃] *nf* **1** : agitation **2** : (political) unrest — **agité, -tée** [aʒite] *adj* **1** : restless **2** : rough, choppy

agneau [aɲo] *nm, pl* **agneaux** : lamb

agonie [agɔni] *nf* : (death) throes *pl* — **agoniser** [agɔnize] *vi* : be dying

agrafe [agraf] *nf* **1** : hook, fastener **2** : staple — **agrafer** [agrafe] *vt* **1** : fasten **2** : staple — **agrafeuse** [agraføz] *nf* : stapler

agrandir [agrɑ̃dir] *vt* : enlarge — **s'agrandir** *vr* : expand, grow — **agrandissement** [agrɑ̃dismɑ̃] *nm* : enlargement, expansion

agréable [agreabl] *adj* : nice, pleasant — **agréablement** [-abləmɑ̃] *adv* : pleasantly

agréer [agree] *vt* **1** : accept **2 veuillez ~ l'expression de mes sentiments distingués** : sincerely yours — **agréé, agréée** [agree] *adj* : authorized

agrégé, -gée [agreʒe] *n France* : certified teacher or professor — **agrégation** [agregasjɔ̃] *nf France* : qualifying exam for teachers or professors

agrément [agremɑ̃] *nm* **1** : charm, appeal **2 voyage d'~** : pleasure trip — **agrémenter** [agremɑ̃te] *vt* : embellish

agrès [agrɛ] *nmpl* : (gymnastic) apparatus

agresser [agrese] *vt* : attack, assault — **agresseur** [agresœr] *nm* : attacker — **agressif, -sive** [agresif, -siv] *adj* : aggressive — **agression** [agresjɔ̃] *nf* **1** : attack **2** : aggression — **agressivité** [agresivite] *nf* : aggressiveness

agricole [agrikɔl] *adj* : agricultural — **agriculteur, -trice** [agrikyltœr, -tris] *n* : farmer — **agriculture** [agrikyltyr] *nf* : agriculture, farming

agripper [agripe] *vt* : clutch, grab — **s'agripper** *vr* ~ **à** : cling to, clutch

agrumes [agrym] *nmpl* : citrus fruits

aguets [agɛ] **aux** ~ *adv phr* : on the lookout

ah [a] *interj* : oh!, ah!

ahuri, -rie [ayri] *adj* : dumbfounded — **ahurissant, -sante** [ayrisɑ̃, -sɑ̃t] *adj* : astounding

aider [ede] *vt* : help — **aide** *nf* **1** : aid **2 à l'~ de** : with the help of — **aide** *nmf* : assistant

aïe [aj] *interj* : ouch!, ow!

aïeux [ajø] *nmpl* : ancestors

aigle [ɛgl] *nm* : eagle

aigre [ɛgr] *adj* : sour, tart — **aigredoux, -douce** [ɛgrədu, -dus] *adj* : bittersweet — **aigreur** [ɛgrœr] *nf* : sourness — **aigri** [egri] *adj* : embittered

aigu, -guë [egy] *adj* **1** : sharp, keen **2** VIF : acute **3** STRIDENT : shrill

aiguille [egɥij] *nf* **1** : needle **2** : hand (of a clock)

aiguillon [egɥijɔ̃] *nm* **1** : goad **2** : stinger (of an insect)

aiguiser [egize] *vt* **1** : sharpen **2** ~ **l'appétit** : whet the appetite

ail [aj] *nm* : garlic

aile [ɛl] *nf* **1** : wing **2** : fender (of an automobile) — **ailier** [elje] *nm* : wing, end (in sports)

ailleurs [ajœr] *adv* **1** : elsewhere **2 d'~** : besides, moreover **3 par** ~ : furthermore

aimable [emabl] *adj* : kind — **aimablement** [emabləmɑ̃] *adv* : kindly

aimant¹, -mante [emɑ̃, -mɑ̃t] *adj* : loving, caring

aimant² *nm* : magnet

aimer [eme] *vt* **1** : love, like **2** ~ **mieux** : prefer

aine [ɛn] *nf* : groin

aîné, -née [ene] *adj* **1** : older, oldest **2** : senior — ~ *n* **1** : elder child, eldest child **2 aînés** *nmpl* : elders **3 il est mon aîné** : he's older than me

ainsi [ɛ̃si] *adv* **1** : in this way, thus **2** ~ **que** : just as **3** ~ **que** : as well as **4 et** ~ **de suite** : and so on **5 pour** ~ **dire** : so to speak

air [ɛr] *nm* **1** : air **2** MÉLODIE : tune **3** EXPRESSION : air, look **4 avoir l'~** : look, seem

aire [ɛr] *nf* **1** : area **2** ~ **d'atterrissage** : landing strip

aisance [ezɑ̃s] *nf* **1** : ease **2** PROSPÉRITÉ : affluence — **aise** *nf* **1** : ease **2 être à l'**~ : be comfortable, **aisé,** **aisée** [ɛze] *adj* **1** : easy **2** RICHE : well-off — **aisément** [ezemɑ̃] *adv* : easily

aisselle [ɛsɛl] *nf* : armpit

ajourner [aʒurne] *vt* : adjourn — **ajournement** [aʒurnəmɑ̃] *nm* : adjournment

ajouter [aʒute] *vt* : add — **ajout** [aʒu] *nm* : addition

ajuster [aʒyste] *vt* : adjust — **ajustement** [aʒystəmɑ̃] *nm* : adjustment

alarmer [alarme] *vt* : alarm — **s'alarmer** *vr* : become alarmed — **alarmant, -mante** [alarmɑ̃, -mɑ̃t] *adj* : alarming — **alarme** [alarm] *nf* : alarm

album [albɔm] *nm* : album

alcool [alkɔl] *nm* : alcohol — **alcoolique** [alkɔlik] *adj & nmf* : alcoholic — **alcoolisé, -sée** [alkɔlize] *adj* : alcoholic — **alcoolisme** [-kɔlism] *nm* : alcoholism

alcôve [alkov] *nf* : alcove

aléa [alea] *nm* : risk — **aléatoire** [aleatwar] *adj* **1** : risky, uncertain **2** : random

alentour [alɑ̃tur] *adv* : around, surrounding — **alentours** [alɑ̃tur] *nmpl* **aux** ~ **de** : around, in the vicinity of

alerter [alɛrte] *vt* : alert, warn — **alerte** [alɛrt] *adj* : alert, lively — **alerte** *nf* : alert, warning

algèbre [alʒɛbr] *nf* : algebra

algérien, -rienne [alʒerjɛ̃, -rjɛn] *adj* : Algerian

algue [alg] *nf* : seaweed

alias [aljas] *adv* : alias

alibi [alibi] *nm* : alibi

aliéner [aljene] {87} *vt* : alienate — **aliénation** [aljenasjɔ̃] *nf* : alienation

aligner [aliɲe] *vt* : align — **s'aligner** *vr* : fall into line — **alignement** [aliɲmɑ̃] *nm* : alignment

alimenter [alimɑ̃te] *vt* **1** : feed **2** APPROVISIONNER : supply — **aliment** [alimɑ̃] *nm* : food — **alimentation** [alimɑ̃tasjɔ̃] *nf* **1** : diet, nourishment **2 magasin d'**~ : grocery store

alinéa [alinea] *nm* : paragraph

alité, -tée [alite] *adj* : bedridden

allaiter [alete] *vt* : nurse, breast-feed — **allaitement** [alɛtmɑ̃] *nm* : breast-feeding

allant [alɑ̃] *nm* : drive, spirit

allécher [aleʃe] {87} *vt* : allure, tempt — **alléchant, -chante** [aleʃɑ̃, -ʃɑ̃t] *adj* : tempting

allée [ale] *nf* **1** : path, lane, walk **2** : aisle **3** ~**s et venues** : comings and goings

allégation [alegasjɔ̃] *nf* : allegation

allégeance [aleʒɑ̃s] *nf* : allegiance

alléger [aleʒe] {64} *vt* **1** : lighten **2** SOULAGER : alleviate

allègre [alɛgr] *adj* : cheerful, lively — **allégresse** [alegrɛs] *nf* : elation

alléguer [alege] {87} *vt* : allege

allemand, -mande [almɑ̃, -mɑ̃d] *adj* : German — **allemand** *nm* : German (language)

aller [ale] {5} *vi* **1** : go **2** MARCHER : work **3** : proceed, get along **4** ~ **à** : fit, suit **5 allons-y** : let's go **6 comment allez-vous?** : how are you? **7 elle va bien** : she is fine — *v aux* : be going to, be about to — **s'en** ~ *vr* : go away — ~ *nm* **1** *or* ~ **simple** : one-way (ticket) **2 aller–retour** : round-trip (ticket)

allergie [alɛrʒi] *nf* : allergy — **allergique** [alɛrʒik] *adj* : allergic

alliage [aljaʒ] *nm* : alloy

allier [alje] *vt* : combine — **s'allier** *vr* ~ **à** : become allied with — **alliance** [aljɑ̃s] *nf* **1** : alliance **2** : wedding ring **3 par** ~ : by marriage — **allié, -liée** *n* : ally

alligator [aligatɔr] *nm* : alligator

allô [alo] *interj* : hello

allocation [alɔkasjɔ̃] *nf* **1** : allocation **2** ~ **de chômage** : unemployment benefit

allocution [alɔkysjɔ̃] *nf* : short speech, address

allonger [alɔ̃ʒe] {17} *vt* **1** : lengthen **2** ÉTIRER : stretch (out) — *vi* : get longer — **s'allonger** *vr* SE COUCHER : lie down

allouer [alwe] *vt* : allocate

allumer [alyme] *vt* **1** : light, ignite **2** : turn on, switch on — **s'allumer** *vr* : come on, light (up) — **allumage** *nm* **1** : lighting **2** : (automobile) ignition — **allumette** [alymɛt] *nf* : match

allure [alyr] *nf* **1** APPARENCE : appearance **2** : speed, pace **3 à toute** ~ : at full speed

allusion [alyzjɔ̃] *nf* : allusion

almanach [almana] *nm* : almanac

alors [alɔr] *adv* **1** : then **2** ~ **que** : while, when **3** ~ **que** : even though **4 et** ~? : so?, so what? **5 ou** ~ : or else

alouette [alwɛt] *nf* : lark

alourdir [alurdir] *vt* : weigh down — **s'alourdir** *vr* : become heavy

alphabet [alfabɛ] *nm* : alphabet — **alphabétique** [alfabetik] *adj* : alphabetical

alpin, -pine [alpɛ̃, -pin] *adj* : alpine — **alpinisme** [alpinism] *nm* : mountain climbing

altérer [altere] {87} *vt* **1** : distort **2** ABÎMER : spoil — **s'altérer** *vr* : deteriorate

alterner [altɛrne] *v* : alternate — **alternatif, -tive** [altɛrnatif, -tiv] *adj* : alternative — **alternative** [altɛrnativ] *nf* : alternative

altesse [altɛs] *nf* **son Altesse** : His (Her) Highness

altier, -tière [altje, -tjɛr] *adj* : haughty

altitude [altityd] *nf* : altitude

altruisme [altrɥism] *nm* : altruism

aluminium [alyminjɔm] *nm* ; aluminum

amabilité [amabilite] *nf* : kindness

amadouer [amadwe] *vt* : cajole

amaigrir [amegrir] *vt* : make thin — **amaigrissement** [amegrismɑ̃] *nm* : weight loss

amalgame [amalgam] *nm* : mixture

amande [amɑ̃d] *nf* 1 : almond 2 : kernel (of a fruit or nut)

amant, -mante [amɑ̃, -mɑ̃t] *n* : lover

amarrer [amare] *vt* : moor — **amarrage** [amaraʒ] *nm* : mooring

amas [ama] *nm* : pile, heap — **amasser** [amase] *vt* ACCUMULER : amass — **s'amasser** *vr* : pile up

amateur [amatœr] *nm* 1 : enthusiast 2 : amateur

ambages [ɑ̃baʒ] **sans ~** *adv phr* : plainly

ambassade [ɑ̃basad] *nf* : embassy — **ambassadeur, -drice** [ɑ̃basadœr, -dris] *n* : ambassador

ambiance [ɑ̃bjɑ̃s] *nf* : atmosphere — **ambiant, -biante** [ɑ̃bjɑ̃, -bjɑ̃t] *adj* : surrounding

ambigu, -guë [ɑ̃bigy] *adj* : ambiguous — **ambiguïté** [ɑ̃bigɥite] *nf* : ambiguity

ambitieux, -tieuse [ɑ̃bisjø, -sjøz] *adj* : ambitious — **ambition** [ɑ̃bisjɔ̃] *nf* : ambition

ambivalent, -lente [ɑ̃bivalɑ̃, -lɑ̃t] *adj* : ambivalent

ambre [ɑ̃br] *nm* : amber

ambulant, -lante [ɑ̃bylɑ̃, -lɑ̃t] *adj* : itinerant — **ambulance** [ɑ̃bylɑ̃s] *nf* : ambulance

ambulatoire [ɑ̃bylatwar] *adj* : ambulatory

âme [am] *nf* 1 : soul 2 **état d'~** : state of mind

améliorer [ameljɔre] *vt* : improve — **s'améliorer** *vr* : get better — **amélioration** [ameljɔrasjɔ̃] *nf* : improvement

aménager [amenaʒe] {17} *vt* : fit out — **aménagement** [amenaʒmɑ̃] *nm* 1 : fitting out 2 : development (of a region, etc.)

amender [amɑ̃de] *vt* : amend — **amende** [amɑ̃d] *nf* : fine — **amendement** [amɑ̃dmɑ̃] *nm* : amendment

amener [amne] {52} *vt* 1 : bring 2 OCCASIONNER : cause

amenuiser [amənɥize] *v* **s'amenuiser** *vr* : dwindle

amer, -mère [amɛr] *adj* : bitter — **amèrement** [amɛrmɑ̃] *adv* : bitterly

américain, -caine [amerikɛ̃, -kɛn] *adj* : American

amérindien, -dienne [amerɛ̃djɛ̃, -djɛn] *adj* : Native American

amertume [amɛrtym] *nf* : bitterness

ameublement [amœbləmɑ̃] *nm* 1 : furnishing 2 MEUBLES : furniture

ami, -mie [ami] *n* 1 : friend 2 *or* **petit ~** : boyfriend 3 *or* **petite ~e** : girlfriend

amiable [amjabl] *adj* **à l'~** : amicable

amiante [amjɑ̃t] *nm* : asbestos

amibe [amib] *nf* : amoeba

amical, -cale [amikal] *adj, mpl* **-caux** [-ko] : friendly

amidon [amidɔ̃] *nm* : starch — **amidonner** [amidɔne] *vt* : starch

amincir [amɛ̃sir] *vt* : make thinner — **s'amincir** *vr* : get thinner

amiral [amiral] *nm, pl* **-raux** [-ro] : admiral

amitié [amitje] *nf* 1 : friendship 2 **~s** *nfpl* : best regards

ammoniaque [amɔnjak] *nf* : ammonia

amnésie [amnezi] *nf* : amnesia

amnistie [amnisti] *nf* : amnesty

amoindrir [amwɛ̃drir] *vt* : lessen — **s'amoindrir** *vr* : diminish

amollir [amɔlir] *vt* : soften

amonceler [amɔ̃sle] {18} *vt* : accumulate — **s'amonceler** *vr* : pile up — **amoncellement** [amɔ̃sɛlmɑ̃] *nm* : pile, heap

amont [amɔ̃] *nm* **en ~** : upstream

amorce [amɔrs] *nf* 1 DÉBUT : beginning(s) 2 APPÂT : bait 3 : detonator, fuse — **amorcer** [amɔrse] {6} *vt* 1 COMMENCER : begin 2 APPÂTER : bait 3 : boot (a computer) — **s'amorcer** *vr* : begin

amorphe [amɔrf] *adj* : listless

amorti [amɔrti] *nm Can* : bunt (in baseball)

amortir [amɔrtir] *vt* : cushion, deaden — **amortisseur** [amɔrtisœr] *nm* : shock absorber

amour [amur] *nm* : love — **amoureusement** [amurøzmɑ̃] *adv* : lovingly — **amoureux, -reuse** [amurø, -røz] *adj* 1 : loving 2 **être ~** : be in love — **~** *n* : lover — **amour–propre** [amurprɔpr] *nm* : self-esteem

amovible [amɔvibl] *adj* : removable

amphibien [ɑ̃fibjɛ̃] *nm* : amphibian

amphithéâtre [ɑ̃fiteatr] *nm* 1 : amphitheater 2 : lecture hall

ample [ɑ̃pl] *adj* : ample — **ampleur** [ɑ̃plœr] *nf* : extent, range

amplifier [ɑ̃plifje] {96} *vt* 1 : amplify 2 : expand — **s'amplifier** *vr* : increase — **amplificateur** [ɑ̃plifikatœr] *nm* : amplifier

ampoule [ɑ̃pul] *nf* 1 : lightbulb 2 CLOQUE : blister 3 : vial (in medicine)

amputer [ɑ̃pyte] *vt* 1 : amputate 2 : cut drastically — **amputation** [ɑ̃pytasjɔ̃] *nf* 1 : amputation 2 : drastic cut

amuse–gueule [amyzgœl] *nms & pl* : appetizer

amuser [amyze] *vt* : amuse — **s'amuser** *vr* 1 : play 2 : enjoy oneself — **amusant, -sante** [amyzɑ̃, -zɑ̃t] *adj* : amusing — **amusement** [amyzmɑ̃] *nm* : amusement

amygdale   **10**

amygdale [amidal] *nf* : tonsil

an [ɑ̃] *nm* 1 : year 2 le Nouvel An : New Year's Day

analgésique [analʒezik] *adj & nm* : analgesic

analogie [analɔʒi] *nf* : analogy — analogue [analɔg] *adj* : similar

analphabète [analfabɛt] *adj* : illiterate — analphabétisme [analfabetism] *nm* : illiteracy

analyse [analiz] *nf* 1 : analysis 2 : (blood) test — analyser [analize] *vt* : analyze — analytique [analitik] *adj* : analytic, analytical

ananas [anana(s)] *nms & pl* : pineapple

anarchie [anarʃi] *nf* : anarchy

anatomie [anatɔmi] *nf* : anatomy — anatomique [anatɔmik] *adj* : anatomic(al)

ancêtre [ɑ̃sɛtr] *nmf* : ancestor

anchois [ɑ̃ʃwa] *nms & pl* : anchovy

ancien, -cienne [ɑ̃sjɛ̃, -sjɛn] *adj* 1 : former 2 VIEUX : ancient, old — anciennement [ɑ̃sjɛnmɑ̃] *adv* : formerly — ancienneté [ɑ̃sjɛnte] *nf* 1 : oldness 2 : seniority

ancre [ɑ̃kr] *nf* : anchor — ancrer [ɑ̃kre] *vt* : anchor

andouille [ɑ̃duj] *nf fam* 1 : andouille (sausage) 2 *fam* : fool, sap

âne [an] *nm* : ass, donkey

anéantir [aneɑ̃tir] *vt* 1 DÉTRUIRE : annihilate 2 ACCABLER : overwhelm — anéantissement [aneɑ̃tismɑ̃] *nm* : annihilation

anecdote [anɛkdɔt] *nf* : anecdote

anémie [anemi] *nf* : anemia — anémique [anemik] *adj* : anemic

ânerie [anri] *nf* : stupid mistake or remark

anesthésie [anɛstezi] *nf* : anesthesia — anesthésique [anɛstezik] *adj & nm* : anesthetic

aneth [anɛt] *nm* : dill

ange [ɑ̃ʒ] *nm* : angel — angélique [ɑ̃ʒelik] *adj* : angelic

anglais, -glaise [ɑ̃glɛ, -glɛz] *adj* : English — anglais *nm* : English (language)

angle [ɑ̃gl] *nm* 1 : angle 2 : corner

anglophone [ɑ̃glɔfɔn] *adj* : English-speaking

anglo–saxon, -saxonne [ɑ̃glɔsaksɔ̃, -saksɔn] *adj* : Anglo-Saxon

angoisser [ɑ̃gwase] *vt* : distress — angoissant, -sante [ɑ̃gwasɑ̃, -sɑ̃t] *adj* : agonizing — angoisse [ɑ̃gwas] *nf* : anguish

anguille [ɑ̃gij] *nf* : eel

anguleux, -leuse [ɑ̃gylø, -løz] *adj* : angular

animal [animal] *nm, pl* -maux [-mo] : animal

animateur, -trice [animatœr, -tris] *n* 1 : moderator 2 : (television show) host

animer [anime] *vt* : enliven — s'animer *vr* : come to life — animation [animasjɔ̃] *nf* : animation — animé, -mée [anime] *adj* : animated, lively

animosité [animɔzite] *nf* : animosity

anis [ani(s)] *nm* : anise

ankyloser [ɑ̃kiloze] *v* s'ankyloser *vr* : stiffen (up)

anneau [ano] *nm, pl* -neaux : ring

année [ane] *nf* 1 : year 2 ~ bissextile : leap year

annexe [anɛks] *adj* 1 : adjoining, attached 2 : related — ~ *nf* : annex — annexer [anɛkse] *vt* : annex

annihiler [aniile] *vt* : annihilate — annihilation [aniilasjɔ̃] *nf* : annihilation

anniversaire [anivɛrsɛr] *nm* 1 : anniversary 2 : birthday

annoncer [anɔ̃se] {6} *vt* 1 : announce 2 DÉNOTER : indicate — s'annoncer *vr* : appear (to be) — annonce [anɔ̃s] *nf* 1 : announcement 2 : advertisement — annonceur, -ceuse [anɔ̃sœr, -søz] *n* 1 : advertiser 2 *Can* : (radio) announcer

annoter [anɔte] *vt* : annotate — annotation [anɔtasjɔ̃] *nf* : annotation

annuaire [anɥɛr] *nm* 1 : yearbook 2 ~ téléphonique : telephone directory

annuel, -nuelle [anɥɛl] *adj* : annual — annuellement [anɥɛlmɑ̃] *adv* : annually

annulaire [anylɛr] *nm* : ring finger

annuler [anyle] *vt* 1 : cancel 2 RÉVOQUER : annul — annulation [anylasjɔ̃] *nf* 1 : cancellation 2 : annulment

anodin, -dine [anɔdɛ̃, -din] *adj* 1 : insignificant 2 : harmless

anomalie [anɔmali] *nf* : anomaly

anonyme [anɔnim] *adj* : anonymous — anonymat [anɔnima] *nm* : anonymity

anorexie [anɔrɛksi] *nf* : anorexia

anormal, -male [anɔrmal] *adj, mpl* -maux [-mo] : abnormal

anse [ɑ̃s] *nf* 1 : handle 2 : cove

antagonisme [ɑ̃tagɔnist] *adj* : antagonistic

antan [ɑ̃tɑ̃] d'~ *adj phr* : of yesteryear

antarctique [ɑ̃tarktik] *adj* : antarctic

antécédent, -dente [ɑ̃tesedɑ̃, -dɑ̃t] *adj* : previous — antécédents *nmpl* : (medical) history, (criminal) record

antenne [ɑ̃tɛn] *nf* : antenna

antérieur, -rieure [ɑ̃terjœr] *adj* 1 PRÉCÉDENT : previous 2 : front (of a part, etc.) — antérieurement [ɑ̃terjœrmɑ̃] *adv* : previously

anthologie [ɑ̃tɔlɔʒi] *nf* : anthology

anthropologie [ɑ̃trɔpɔlɔʒi] *nf* : anthropology

antibiotique [antibiɔtik] *adj & nm* : antibiotic

anticiper [ɑ̃tisipe] *vt* : anticipate — *vi* : think ahead — anticipation [ɑ̃tisipasjɔ̃] *nf* : anticipation

anticorps [ɑ̃tikɔr] *nms & pl* : antibody

antidote [ɑ̃tidɔt] *nm* : antidote

antigel [ɑ̃tiʒɛl] *nm* : antifreeze

antilope [ɑ̃tilɔp] *nf* : antelope

antipathie [ɑ̃tipati] *nf* : antipathy

antique [ɑ̃tik] *adj* : ancient, antique — **antiquité** [ɑ̃tikite] *nf* 1 : antiquity 2 : antique

antisémite [ɑ̃tisemit] *adj* : anti-Semitic

antiseptique [ɑ̃tisɛptik] *adj & nm* : antiseptic

antonyme [ɑ̃tɔnim] *nm* : antonym

antre [ɑ̃tr] *nm* : den, lair

anus [anys] *nms & pl* : anus

anxieux, anxieuse [ɑ̃ksjø, -sjøz] *adj* : anxious — **anxiété** [ɑ̃ksjete] *nf* : anxiety

août [u(t)] *nm* : August

apaiser [apeze] *vt* : appease — **s'apaiser** *vr* : quiet down — **apaisement** [apɛzmɑ̃] *nm* : calming (down)

apanage [apanaʒ] *nm* : prerogative

apathie [apati] *nf* : apathy — **apathique** [apatik] *adj* : apathetic

apercevoir [apɛrsəvwar] {26} *vt* : perceive, see — **s'apercevoir** *vr* 1 ~ **de** : notice 2 ~ **que** : realize that — **aperçu** [apɛrsy] *nm* : general idea, outline

apéritif [aperitif] *nm* : aperitif

à–peu–près [apøprɛ] *nms & pl* : approximation

apeuré, -rée [apœre] *adj* : frightened

apitoyer [apitwaje] {58} *v* **s'apitoyer** *vr* ~ **sur** : feel sorry for — **apitoiement** [apitwamɑ̃] *nm* : pity

aplanir [aplanir] *vt* 1 : level 2 : resolve (a problem) — **s'aplanir** *vr* : flatten out

aplatir [aplatir] *vt* : flatten

aplomb [aplɔ̃] *nm* 1 : aplomb, composure 2 **d'**~ : steady, balanced

apocalypse [apɔkalips] *nf* : apocalypse

apogée [apɔʒe] *nm* : peak

apostrophe [apɔstrɔf] *nf* : apostrophe — **apostropher** [apɔstrɔfe] *vt* : address rudely

apothéose [apɔteoz] *nf* : crowning moment

apôtre [apotr] *nm* : apostle

apparaître [aparɛtr] {73} *vi* : appear — *v impers* **il apparaît que** : it seems that

apparat [apara] *nm* 1 : pomp 2 **d'**~ : ceremonial

appareiller [apareje] *vi* : set sail — *vt* : match up — **appareil** [aparɛj] *nm* 1 : apparatus, appliance 2 : telephone 3 ~ **auditif** : hearing aid 4 ~ **digestif** : digestive system 5 ~ **photo** : camera

apparence [aparɑ̃s] *nf* 1 : appearance 2 **en** ~ : outwardly — **apparent, -rente** [aparɑ̃, -rɑ̃t] *adj* : apparent — **apparemment** [aparamɑ̃] *adv* : apparently

apparenté, -tée [aparɑ̃te] *adj* : related

apparition [aparisjɔ̃] *nf* 1 MANIFESTATION : appearance 2 SPECTRE : apparition

appartement [apartəmɑ̃] *nm* : apartment

appartenir [apartənir] {92} *vi* ~ **à** : belong to — *v impers* **il m'appartient de** : it's up to me to — **appartenance** [apartənɑ̃s] *nf* : membership, belonging

appâter [apate] *vt* 1 : bait 2 : lure, entice — **appât** [apɑ] *nm* : bait, lure

appauvrir [apovrir] *vt* : impoverish — **s'appauvrir** *vr* : become impoverished

appeler [aple] {8} *vt* 1 : call 2 NÉCESSITER : call for, require 3 **en** ~ **à** : appeal to — *vi* : call — **s'appeler** *vr* : be named, be called — **appel** [apɛl] *nm* 1 : call 2 : appeal

appendice [apɑ̃dis] *nm* : appendix — **appendicite** [apɑ̃disit] *nf* : appendicitis

appentis [apɑ̃ti] *nm* : shed

appesantir [apəzɑ̃tir] *vt* : weigh down — **s'appesantir** *vr* 1 : grow heavier 2 ~ **sur** : dwell on

appétit [apeti] *nm* 1 : appetite 2 **bon** ~! : enjoy your meal! — **appétissant, -sante** [apetisɑ̃, -sɑ̃t] *adj* : appetizing

applaudir [aplodir] *v* : applaud — **applaudissements** [aplodismɑ̃] *nmpl* : applause

appliquer [aplike] *vt* : apply — **s'appliquer** *vr* 1 : apply oneself 2 ~ **à** CONCERNER : apply to — **applicateur** [aplikatœr] *nm* : applicator — **application** [aplikasjɔ̃] *nf* : application — **appliqué, -quée** [aplike] *adj* : industrious, painstaking

appoint [apwɛ̃] *nm* 1 : contribution, support 2 **d'**~ : extra 3 **faire l'**~ : make exact change — **appointements** [apwɛ̃təmɑ̃] *nmpl* : salary

apporter [apɔrte] *vt* 1 AMENER : bring 2 FOURNIR : provide — **apport** [apɔr] *nm* : contribution

apposer [apoze] *vt* : put, affix

apprécier [apresje] {96} *vt* 1 : appreciate 2 : appraise — **appréciation** [apresjasjɔ̃] *nf* : assessment, appraisal

appréhender [apreɑ̃de] *vt* 1 ARRÊTER : apprehend, arrest 2 : dread — **appréhension** [apreɑ̃sjɔ̃] *nf* : apprehension

apprendre [aprɑ̃dr] {70} *vt* 1 : learn 2 ENSEIGNER : teach

apprenti, -tie [aprɑ̃ti] *n* : apprentice — **apprentissage** [aprɑ̃tisaʒ] *nm* 1 : apprenticeship 2 : learning

apprêter [aprɛte] *v* **s'apprêter** *vr* : get ready

apprivoiser [aprivwaze] *vt* : tame

approbateur, -trice [aprɔbatœr, -tris] *adj* : approving — **approbation** [aprɔbasjɔ̃] *nf* : approval

approcher [aprɔʃe] *vt* : approach — *vi* : draw near — **s'approcher** *vr* ~ **de** : come up to — **approchant, -chante** [aprɔʃɑ̃, -ʃɑ̃t] *adj* : similar — **approche** [aprɔʃ] *nf* : approach

approfondir [aprɔfɔ̃dir] *vt* 1 : deepen 2 PÉNÉTRER : delve into — **approfondi, -die** [aprɔfɔ̃di] *adj* : thorough

approprier [aprɔprije] {96} v **s'approprier** vr : appropriate — **approprié, -priée** [aprɔprije] adj : appropriate

approuver [apruve] vt : approve (of)

approvisionner [aprɔvizjɔnel vt : supply — **s'approvisionner** vr : stock up — **approvisionnement** [aprɔvizjɔnmɑ̃] nm : supply, provision

approximation [aprɔksimasjɔ̃] nf : approximation — **approximatif, -tive** [aprɔksimatif, -tiv] adj : approximate — **approximativement** [-tivmɑ̃] adv : approximately

appuyer [apɥije] {58} vt 1 : rest, lean 2 SOUTENIR : support — vi ~ sur : push, press — **s'appuyer** vr 1 ~ à or ~ contre : lean against 2 ~ sur : rely on — **appui** [apɥi] nm : support

âpre [apr] adj : bitter, harsh

après [aprɛ] adv : afterwards — ~ prep 1 : after 2 : beyond 3 ~ tout : after all 4 d'~ : according to — **après–demain** [aprɛdmɛ̃] adv : the day after tomorrow — **après–midi** [apremidi] nmfs & pl : afternoon

à–propos [aprɔpo] nm 1 : aptness 2 : presence of mind

apte [apt] adj : capable — **aptitude** [aptityd] nf : aptitude

aquarelle [akwarɛl] nf : watercolor

aquarium [akwarjɔm] nm : aquarium

aquatique [akwatik] adj : aquatic

aqueduc [akdyk] nm : aqueduct

arabe [arab] adj : Arab, Arabic — ~ nm : Arabic (language)

arachide [araʃid] nf : peanut

araignée [arɛɲe] nf : spider

arbitraire [arbitrɛr] adj : arbitrary

arbitre [arbitr] nm 1 : arbitrator 2 : referee 3 libre ~ : free will — **arbitrer** [arbitre] vt 1 : arbitrate 2 : referee

arborer [arbɔre] vt : bear, display

arbre [arbr] nm 1 : tree 2 : shaft

arbrisseau [arbriso] nm : shrub

arbuste [arbyst] nm : bush

arc [ark] nm 1 : arc, curve 2 : bow (in archery)

arcade [arkad] nf : arch, archway

arc–boutant [arkbutɑ̃] nm, pl **arcs–boutants** : flying buttress

arc–en–ciel [arkɑ̃sjɛl] nm, pl **arcs–en–ciel** : rainbow

archaïque [arkaik] adj : archaic

arche [arʃ] nf 1 : arch 2 : ark

archéologie [arkeɔlɔʒi] nf : archaeology

archet [arʃɛ] nm : bow (in music)

archevêque [arʃəvɛk] nm : archbishop

archipel [arʃipɛl] nm : archipelago

architecture [arʃitɛktyr] nf : architecture — **architecte** [arʃitɛkt] nmf : architect

archives [arʃiv] nfpl : archives

arctique [arktik] adj : arctic

ardent, -dente [ardɑ̃, -dɑ̃t] adj 1 : burning 2 PASSIONNÉ : ardent — **ardemment** [ardamɑ̃] adv : ardently — **ardeur** [ardœr] nf 1 CHALEUR : heat 2 : ardor

ardoise [ardwaz] nf : slate

ardu, -due [ardy] adj : arduous

arène [arɛn] nf 1 : arena 2 ~s : bullring, amphitheater — **aréna** [arena] nm Can : arena

arête [arɛt] nf 1 : fish bone 2 : ridge, bridge (of the nose)

argent [arʒɑ̃] nm 1 : money 2 : silver 3 ~ comptant : cash — **argenté, -tée** [arʒɑ̃te] adj 1 : silver-plated 2 : silvery — **argenterie** [arʒɑ̃tri] nf : silverware

argile [arʒil] nf : clay

argot [argo] nm : slang

argument [argymɑ̃] nm : argument — **argumentation** [argymɑ̃tasjɔ̃] nf : rationale — **argumenter** [argymɑ̃te] vi : argue

aride [arid] adj : arid

aristocrate [aristɔkrat] nmf : aristocrat — **aristocratique** [-kratik] adj : aristocratic — **aristocratie** [aristɔkrasi] nf : aristocracy

arithmétique [aritmetik] nf : arithmetic

armature [armatyr] nf : framework

armer [arme] vt 1 : arm 2 : cock (a gun) — **arme** [arm] nf 1 : weapon 2 ~s nfpl : coat of arms — **armée** [arme] nf : army — **armement** [armɔmɑ̃] nm : armament

armistice [armistis] nm : armistice

armoire [armwar] nf 1 : cupboard 2 : wardrobe, closet

armoiries [armwari] nfpl : coat of arms

armure [armyr] nf : armor

arnaquer [arnake] vt fam : swindle — **arnaque** [arnak] nf fam : swindle

aromate [arɔmat] nm : spice, herb

arôme [arom] nm 1 : aroma 2 : flavor — **aromatique** [arɔmatik] adj : aromatic — **aromatiser** [arɔmatize] vt : flavor

arpenter [arpɑ̃te] vt 1 : pace up and down 2 MESURER : survey

arqué, -quée [arke] adj : curved, arched

arrache–pied [araʃpje] d'~ adv phr : relentlessly

arracher [araʃe] vt 1 : pull up or out 2 DÉCHIRER : tear off 3 : snatch, grab

arranger [arɑ̃ʒe] {17} vt 1 : arrange 2 RÉPARER : fix 3 CONVENIR : suit, please 4 RÉGLER : settle — **s'arranger** vr 1 : come to an agreement 2 : get better — **arrangement** [arɑ̃ʒmɑ̃] nm : arrangement

arrestation [arɛstasjɔ̃] nf : arrest

arrêter [arete] vt 1 : stop 2 FIXER : fix 3 APPRÉHENDER : arrest 4 DÉTERMINER : decide on — **s'arrêter** vr 1 : stop, cease 2 ~ de faire : stop doing — **arrêt** [arɛ] nm 1 : stopping, halt **2** : decree **3** ~ **d'autobus** : bus stop

arrhes [ar] *nfpl France* : deposit

arrière [arjɛr] *adj* : back, rear — ~ *nm* **1** : back, rear **2 en ~** : backwards **3 en ~ de** : behind — **arriéré, -rée** [arjere] *adj* **1** : overdue **2** : backward — **arriéré** *nm* **1** : arrears *pl* **2** : backlog — **arrière–goût** [arjɛrgu] *nm, pl* **arrière–goûts** : aftertaste — **arrière–grand–mère** [arjɛrgrɑ̃mɛr] *nf, pl* **arrière–grands–mères** : great-grand-mother — **arrière–grand–père** [arjɛrgrɑ̃pɛr] *nm, pl* **arrière–grands–pères** : great-grandfather — **arrière–pays** [arjɛrpei] *nms & pl* : hinterland — **arrière–pensée** [arjɛrpɑ̃se] *nf, pl* **arrière–pensées** : ulterior motive — **arrière–plan** [arjɛrplɑ̃] *nm, pl* **arrière–plans** : background

arrimer [arime] *vt* **1** : stow **2** FIXER : secure, fix

arriver [arive] *vi* **1** : arrive, come **2** RÉUSSIR : succeed **3** SE PASSER : happen, occur **4** ~ **à** ATTEINDRE : reach — **arrivée** [arive] *nf* **1** : arrival **2 or ligne d'**~ : finish line — **arriviste** [arivist] *adj* : pushy — ~ *nmf* : upstart

arrogant, -gante [arɔgɑ̃, -gɑ̃t] *adj* : arrogant — **arrogance** [arɔgɑ̃s] *nf* : arrogance

arroger [arɔʒe] {17} *v* **s'arroger** *vr* : claim (without right)

arrondir [arɔ̃dir] *vt* **1** : make round **2** : round off (a number)

arrondissement [arɔ̃dismɑ̃] *nm* : district

arroser [aroze] *vt* **1** : water **2** : baste (in cooking) **3** CÉLÉBRER : drink to — **arrosoir** [arozwar] *nm* : watering can

arsenal [arsənal] *nm, pl* **-naux** [-no] **1** : shipyard **2** : arsenal

arsenic [arsənik] *nm* : arsenic

art [ar] *nm* : art

artère [artɛr] *nf* **1** : artery **2** : main road

arthrite [artrit] *nf* : arthritis

artichaut [artiʃo] *nm* : artichoke

article [artikl] *nm* **1** : article **2** ~**s de toilette** : toiletries

articuler [artikyle] *vt* : articulate — **articulation** [artikylasjɔ̃] *nf* **1** : articulation **2** : joint (in anatomy)

artifice [artifis] *nm* : trick, device

artificiel, -cielle [artifisjɛl] *adj* : artificial — **artificiellement** [-sjɛlmɑ̃] *adv* : artificially

artillerie [artijri] *nf* : artillery

artilleur [artijœr] *nm Can* : pitcher (in baseball)

artisan, -sane [artizɑ̃, -zan] *n* : artisan, craftsman — **artisanal, -nale** *adj, pl* **-naux** : made by craftsmen, homemade — **artisanat** [artizana] *nm* **1** : artisans *pl* **2** : arts and crafts *pl*

artiste [artist] *nmf* : artist — **artistique** [artistik] *adj* : artistic

as [ɑs] *nm* : ace

ascendant, -dante [asɑ̃dɑ̃, -dɑ̃t] *adj* : ascending — **ascendant** *nm* **1** : influence **2** ~**s** *nmpl* : ancestors — **ascendance** [asɑ̃dɑ̃s] *nf* : ancestry

ascenseur [asɑ̃sœr] *nm* : elevator

ascension [asɑ̃sjɔ̃] *nf* : ascent

ascète [asɛt] *nmf* : ascetic — **ascétique** [asetik] *adj* : ascetic

asiatique [azjatik] *adj* : Asian

asile [azil] *nm* **1** : (political) asylum **2** ABRI : refuge

aspect [aspɛ] *nm* **1** : aspect **2** ALLURE : appearance

asperge [aspɛrʒ] *nf* : asparagus

asperger [aspɛrʒe] {17} *vt* : sprinkle, spray

aspérité [asperite] *nf* : bump, protrusion

asphalte [asfalt] *nm* : asphalt

asphyxier [asfiksje] {96} *vt* : asphyxiate, suffocate — **s'asphyxier** *vr* : suffocate — **asphyxie** [asfiksi] *nf* : asphyxiation

aspirer [aspire] *vt* **1** : suck up (a liquid) **2** : inhale — *vi* ~ **à** : aspire to — **aspiration** [aspirasjɔ̃] *nf* **1** AMBITION : aspiration **2** : suction **3** : inhaling — **aspirateur** [aspiratœr] *nm* **1** : vacuum cleaner **2 passer l'**~ : vacuum

aspirine [aspirin] *nf* : aspirin

assagir [asaʒir] *vt* : calm, quiet — **s'assagir** *vr* : quiet down

assaillir [asajir] {93} *vt* : attack — **assaillant, -lante** [asajɑ̃, -jɑ̃t] *n* : attacker

assainir [asenir] *vt* : purify, clean up

assaisonner [asɛzɔne] *vt* : season — **assaisonnement** [asɛzɔnmɑ̃] *nm* : seasoning

assassiner [asasine] *vt* : murder, assassinate — **assassin** *nm* : murderer, assassin

assaut [aso] *nm* **1** : assault **2 prendre d'**~ : storm

assécher [aseʃe] {87} *vt* : drain

assembler [asɑ̃ble] *vt* : assemble — **s'assembler** *vr* : gather — **assemblée** [asɑ̃ble] *nf* **1** RÉUNION : meeting **2** : (political) assembly

asséner [asene] {87} *vt* : strike (a blow)

assentiment [asɑ̃timɑ̃] *nm* : assent, consent

asseoir [aswar] {9} *vt* : seat, sit — **s'asseoir** *vr* : sit down

assermenté, -tée [asɛrmɑ̃te] *adj* : sworn

assertion [asɛrsjɔ̃] *nf* : assertion

asservir [asɛrvir] *vt* : enslave

assez [ase] *adv* **1** SUFFISAMMENT : enough **2** : rather, quite

assidu, -due [asidy] *adj* : diligent — **assiduité** [asidɥite] *nf* : diligence

assiéger [asjeʒe] {64} *vt* : besiege

assiette [asjɛt] *nf* : plate, dish — **assiettée** [asjete] *nf* : plateful

assigner [asiɲe] *vt* : assign, allot — **assignation** [asiɲasjɔ̃] *nf* 1 : allocation 2 : summons, subpoena

assimiler [asimile] *vt* 1 : assimilate 2 ~ **à** : equate with, compare to — **assimilation** [asimilasjɔ̃] *nf* : assimilation

assis, -sise [asiz] *adj* : seated, sitting down

assise *nf* 1 : foundation, base 2 ~s *nfpl* : court

assister [asiste] *vt* : assist — *vi* ~ **à** : attend — **assistance** [asistɑ̃s] *nf* 1 : assistance 2 : audience — **assistant, -tante** [asistɑ̃, -tɑ̃t] *n* : assistant

associer [asɔsje] {96} *vt* 1 : associate 2 ~ **qqn à** : include s.o. in — **s'associer** *vr* : join together — **association** [asɔsjasjɔ̃] *nf* : association — **associé, -ciée** [asɔsje] *n* : associate

assoiffé, -fée [aswafe] *adj* : thirsty

assombrir [asɔ̃brir] *vt* : darken — **s'assombrir** *vr* : darken

assommer [asɔme] *vt* 1 : stun, knock out 2 *fam* : bore stiff — **assommant, -mante** [asɔmɑ̃, -mɑ̃t] *adj* : boring

assortir [asɔrtir] *vt* : match — **assorti, -tie** [asɔrti] *adj* 1 : matched 2 : assorted — **assortiment** [asɔrtimɑ̃] *nm* : assortment

assoupir [asupir] *v* **s'assoupir** *vr* : doze off

assouplir [asuplir] *vt* : make supple, soften — **s'assouplir** *vr* : loosen up

assourdir [asurdir] *vt* 1 : deafen 2 ÉTOUFFER : muffle

assouvir [asuvir] *vt* : appease

assujettir [asyʒetir] *vt* 1 : subjugate 2 ~ **à** : subject to

assumer [asyme] *vt* : assume, take on

assurer [asyre] *vt* 1 : assure 2 FOURNIR : provide 3 : insure (one's property, etc.) — **s'assurer** *vr* ~ **de** : make sure of — **assurance** [asyrɑ̃s] *nf* 1 : assurance 2 : insurance 3 ~-**vie** : life insurance — **assuré, -rée** [asyre] *adj* : confident, certain — **assurément** [asyremɑ̃] *adv* : certainly

astérisque [asterisk] *nm* : asterisk

asthme [asm] *nm* : asthma

asticot [astiko] *nm* : maggot

astiquer [astike] *vt* : polish

astre [astr] *nm* : star

astreindre [astrɛ̃dr] {37} *vt* : compel — **astreignant, -gnante** [astrɛɲɑ̃, -ɲɑ̃t] *adj* : demanding

astrologie [astrɔlɔʒi] *nf* : astrology

astronaute [astrɔnot] *nmf* : astronaut

astronomie [astrɔnɔmi] *nf* : astronomy

astuce [astys] *nf* 1 : cleverness 2 TRUC : trick 3 PLAISANTERIE : joke — **astucieux, -cieuse** [astysjø, -sjøz] *adj* : astute, clever — **astucieusement** [-sjøzmɑ̃] *adv* : cleverly

atelier [atəlje] *nm* 1 : studio 2 : workshop

athée [ate] *adj* : atheistic — ~ *nmf* : atheist

athlète [atlet] *nmf* : athlete — **athlétique** [atletik] *adj* : athletic — **athlétisme** [atletism] *nm* : athletics

atlantique [atlɑ̃tik] *adj* : Atlantic

atlas [atlas] *nm* : atlas

atmosphère [atmɔsfɛr] *nf* : atmosphere — **atmosphérique** [atmɔsferik] *adj* : atmospheric

atome [atom] *nm* : atom — **atomique** [atɔmik] *adj* : atomic

atomiseur [atɔmizœr] *nm* : atomizer

atout [atu] *nm* 1 : trump (card) 2 AVANTAGE : asset

âtre [atr] *nm* : hearth

atroce [atrɔs] *adj* : atrocious — **atrocité** [atrɔsite] *nf* : atrocity

atrophier [atrɔfje] {96} *v* **s'atrophier** *vr* : atrophy

attabler [atable] *v* **s'attabler** *vr* : sit down at the table

attacher [ataʃe] *vt* : tie (up), fasten — **s'attacher** *vr* 1 : fasten 2 ~ **à** : attach oneself to 3 ~ **à** : apply oneself to — **attachant, -chante** [ataʃɑ̃, -ʃɑ̃t] *adj* : appealing, likeable — **attache** [ataʃ] *nf* 1 : fastener 2 LIEN : tie, bond — **attaché, -chée** [ataʃe] *n* : attaché — **attachement** [ataʃmɑ̃] *nm* : attachment

attaquer [atake] *v* : attack — **s'attaquer** *vr* ~ **à** : attack — **attaque** [atak] *nf* : attack

attarder [atarde] *v* **s'attarder** *vr* : linger — **attardé** [atarde] *adj* 1 : late 2 : retarded 3 DÉMODÉ : old-fashioned

atteindre [atɛ̃dr] {37} *vt* 1 : reach, attain 2 FRAPPER : strike, hit 3 AFFECTER : affect — **atteinte** [atɛ̃t] *nf* 1 : attack 2 **hors d'**~ : out of reach 3 **porter** ~ **à** : undermine

atteler [atle] {8} *vt* : harness — **s'atteler** *vr* ~ **à** : apply oneself to — **attelage** [atlaʒ] *nm* : team (of animals)

attelle [atɛl] *nf* : splint

attenant, -nante [atnɑ̃, -nɑ̃t] *adj* : adjoining

attendre [atɑ̃dr] {63} *vt* 1 : wait for 2 ESPÉRER : expect — *vi* 1 : wait 2 **faire** ~ **qqn** : keep s.o. waiting 3 **en attendant** : in the meantime — **s'attendre** *vr* ~ **à** : expect

attendrir [atɑ̃drir] *vt* 1 ÉMOUVOIR : move 2 : tenderize (meat) — **s'attendrir** *vr* : be moved — **attendrissant, -sante** [atɑ̃drisɑ̃, -sɑ̃t] *adj* : moving, touching

attendu, -due [atɑ̃dy] *adj* 1 : expected 2 : long-awaited — **attendu** *prep* ~ **que** : since, considering that

attente [atɑ̃t] *nf* 1 : wait 2 ESPOIR : expectation

attenter [atɑ̃te] *vi* ~ **à** : make an attempt on — **attentat** [atɑ̃ta] *nm* : attack

attention [atɑ̃sjɔ̃] *nf* 1 : attention 2 ~!

: look out!, beware! **3 faire ~** : pay attention — **attentionné, -née** [atãsjɔne] *adj* : considerate — **attentif, -tive** [atãtif, -tiv] *adj* **1** : attentive **2** : careful **3 être ~ à** : pay attention to — **attentivement** [-tiv-mã] *adv* : attentively

atténuer [atenɥe] *vt* **1** : tone down **2** : ease, allay — **s'atténuer** *vr* : subside

atterrer [atere] *vt* : dismay, appall

atterrir [aterir] *vi* : land — **atterrissage** [aterisaʒ] *nm* : landing

attester [atɛste] *vt* : attest, testify to — **attestation** [atɛstasjɔ̃] *nf* **1** : affidavit **2** : certificate

attirail [atiraj] *nm fam* : gear, paraphernalia

attirer [atire] *vt* : attract, draw — **attirance** [atirãs] *nf* : attraction — **attirant, -rante** [atirã, -rãt] *adj* : attractive

attiser [atize] *vt* : stir up, kindle

attitré, -trée [atitre] *adj* **1** : authorized **2** HABITUEL : regular

attitude [atityd] *nf* : attitude

attouchement [atuʃmã] *nm* : touching, fondling

attraction [atraksjɔ̃] *nf* : attraction (in science)

attrait [atrɛ] *nm* : appeal, attraction

attraper [atrape] *vt* : catch

attrayant, -trayante [atrɛjã, -trɛjãt] *adj* ATTIRANT : attractive

attribuer [atribɥe] *vt* : attribute, assign — **s'attribuer** *vr* : claim for oneself — **attribut** [atriby] *nm* : attribute — **attribution** [atribysjɔ̃] *nf* : allocation, allotment

attrister [atriste] *vt* : sadden

attrouper [atrupe] *v* **s'attrouper** *vr* : gather — **attroupement** [atrupmã] *nm* : crowd

au [o] → **à, le**

aubaine [obɛn] *nf* : good fortune, godsend

aube [ob] *nf* : dawn, daybreak

aubépine [obepin] *nf* : hawthorn

auberge [obɛrʒ] *nf* **1** : inn **2 ~ de jeunesse** : youth hostel — **aubergiste** [obɛr-ʒist] *nmf* : innkeeper

aubergine [obɛrʒin] *nf* : eggplant

auburn [oboern] *adj* : auburn

aucun, -cune [okœ̃, -kyn] *adj* **1** : no, not any **2 plus qu'aucun autre** : more than any other — **~** *pron* **1** : none, not any **2** : any, anyone **3 d'aucuns** : some (people) — **aucunement** [okynmã] *adv* : not at all

audace [odas] *nf* **1** : audacity **2** COURAGE : boldness — **audacieux, -cieuse** [odasjø, -jøz] *adj* **1** : audacious **2** HARDI : daring

au–dedans [odədã] *adv* **1** : inside **2 ~ de** : within

au–dehors [odəɔr] *adv* **1** : outside **2 ~ de** : outside (of)

au–delà [odəla] *adv* **1** : beyond **2 ~ de** : beyond

au–dessous [odsu] *adv* **1** : below **2 ~ de** : below, under

au–dessus [odsy] *adv* **1** : above **2 ~ de** : above, over

au–devant [odvã] *adv* **1** : ahead **2 aller ~ de** : go to meet

audible [odibl] *adj* : audible

audience [odjãs] *nf* **1** : audience **2 ~s publiques** : public hearings

audio [odjo] *adj* : audio — **audiovisuel, -suelle** [odjovizɥɛl] *adj* : audiovisual

auditeur, -trice [oditœr, -tris] *n* : listener

audition [odisjɔ̃] *nf* **1** : hearing **2** : audition (in theater) — **auditionner** [odisjɔne] *v* : audition — **auditoire** [oditwar] *nm* : audience — **auditorium** [oditɔrjɔm] *nm* : auditorium

auge [oʒ] *nf* : trough

augmenter [ogmãte] *v* : increase — **augmentation** [ogmãtasjɔ̃] *nf* : increase, raise

augurer [ogyre] *vt* : augur — **augure** [ogyr] *nm* : omen

aujourd'hui [oʒurdɥi] *adv & nm* : today

aumône [omon] *nf* : alms *pl*

aumônier [omonje] *nm* : chaplain

auparavant [oparavã] *adv* : before(hand)

auprès [oprɛ] *adv* **~ de 1** : beside, near, next to **2** : compared with **3 ambassadeur ~ des Nations Unies** : ambassador to the United Nations

auquel, -quelle [okɛl] → **lequel**

auréole [oreɔl] *nf* **1** : halo **2** TACHE : ring

auriculaire [orikylɛr] *nm* : little finger

aurore [ɔrɔr] *nf* AUBE : dawn

ausculter [oskylte] *vt* : examine (with a stethoscope)

auspices [ospis] *nmpl* **sous les ~ de** : under the auspices of

aussi [osi] *adv* **1** : too, also, as well **2** TELLEMENT : so **3 ~ ... que** : as ... as

aussitôt [osito] *adv* **1** : immediately **2 ~ que** : as soon as

austère [ostɛr] *adj* : austere — **austérité** [osterite] *nf* : austerity

austral, -trale [ostral] *adj, mpl* -trals : southern

australien, -lienne [ostraljɛ̃, -jɛn] *adj* : Australian

autant [otã] *adv* **1** *or* **~ de** : as much, as many, so much, so many **2 ~ que** : as much as, as many as, as far as **3 d'~ plus** : all the more **4 pour ~** : for all that

autel [otɛl] *nm* : altar

auteur [otœr] *nm* **1** : author **2** : person responsible, perpetrator

authentique [otãtik] *adj* : authentic

auto [oto] *nf* : car, automobile

autobiographie [otobjɔgrafi] *nf* : autobiography

autobus [otɔbys] *nm* : bus

autocar [otɔkar] *nm* : bus, coach
autochtone [otɔktɔn] *adj & nmf* : native
autocollant, -lante [otɔkɔlã, -lãt] *adj* : self-adhesive — **autocollant** *nm* : sticker
autocuiseur [otɔkɥizœr] *nm* : pressure cooker
autodéfense [otɔdefãs] *nf* : self-defense
autodidacte [otɔdidakt] *adj* : self-taught
autodiscipline [otɔdisiplin] *nf* : self-discipline
autographe [otɔgraf] *nm* : autograph
automation [otɔmasjɔ̃] *nf* : automation — **automatique** [otɔmatik] *adj* : automatic — **automatiquement** [-tikmã] *adv* : automatically
automatiser [otɔmatize] *vt* : automate — **automatisation** [otɔmatizasjɔ̃] *nf* : automation
automne [otɔn] *nm* : autumn, fall
automobile [otɔmɔbil] *adj* : automotive — ~ *nf* : automobile, car — **automobiliste** [otɔmɔbilist] *nmf* : motorist, driver
autonome [otɔnɔm] *adj* : autonomous — **autonomie** [otɔnɔmi] *nf* : autonomy
autoportrait [otɔpɔrtrɛ] *nm* : self-portrait
autopsie [otɔpsi] *nf* : autopsy
autoriser [otɔrize] *vt* : authorize — **autorisation** [otɔrizasjɔ̃] *nf* 1 : authorization 2 PERMIS : permit
autorité [otɔrite] *nf* : authority — **autoritaire** [otɔritɛr] *adj* : authoritarian
autoroute [otɔrut] *nf* 1 : highway, freeway 2 ~ à péage : turnpike
auto–stop [otɔstɔp] *nm* **faire de l'**~ : hitchhike — **auto–stoppeur, -peuse** [otɔstɔpœr, -pøz] *n* : hitchhiker
autosuffisant, -sante [otɔsyfizã, -zãt] *adj* : self-sufficient
autour [otur] *adv* 1 ~ **de** : around, about 2 **tout** ~ : all around
autre [otr] *adj* 1 ~ : other, different 2 ~ **chose** : something else — ~ *pron* : other, another
autrefois [otrəfwa] *adv* : in the past, formerly
autrement [otrəmã] *adv* 1 : differently 2 SINON : otherwise 3 ~ **dit** : in other words
autruche [otryʃ] *nf* : ostrich
autrui [otrɥi] *pron* : others
auvent [ovã] *nm* : awning
auxiliaire [oksiljɛr] *adj & nmf* : auxiliary, assistant — ~ *nm* : auxiliary (verb)
auxquels, -quelles [okɛl] → **lequel**
avachi, -chie [avaʃi] *adj* : shapeless, limp
aval [aval] *nm* **en** ~ : downstream
avalanche [avalãʃ] *nf* : avalanche
avaler [avale] *vt* : swallow
avancer [avãse] {6} *vt* : move forward, put ahead — *vi* 1 : advance, go forward 2 : be fast (of a watch) — **s'avancer** *vr* 1 : move

forward 2 : progress — **avance** [avãs] *nf* 1 : advance 2 : lead 3 à l'~ or d'~ : in advance 4 **en** ~ : early — **avancé, -cée** [avãse] *adj* : advanced — **avancement** [avãsmã] *nm* : promotion
avant [avã] *adv* 1 : before 2 : first 3 ~ **de** : before 4 ~ **que** : before, until — ~ *adj* : front — ~ *nm* 1 : front 2 : forward (in sports) 3 **en** ~ : forward, ahead 4 **en** ~ **de** : ahead of — ~ *prep* 1 : before, by 2 ~ **tout** : above all
avantager [avãtaʒe] {17} *vt* 1 FAVORISER : favor 2 : flatter — **avantageux, -geuse** [avãtaʒø, -ʒøz] *adj* : profitable, worthwhile — **avantage** [avãtaʒ] *nm* 1 : advantage 2 ~**s sociaux** : fringe benefits
avant–bras [avãbra] *nms & pl* : forearm
avant–dernier, -nière [avãdɛrnje, -njɛr] *adj* : next to last
avant–garde [avãgard] *nf, pl* **avant–gardes** : avant-garde
avant–goût [avãgu] *nm, pl* **avant–goûts** : foretaste
avant–hier [avãtjɛr] *adv* : the day before yesterday
avant–midi [avãmidi] *nfs & pl Can, nms & pl Bel* : morning
avant–poste [avãpɔst] *nm, pl* **avant–postes** : outpost
avant–première [avãprəmjɛr] *nf, pl* **avant–premières** : preview
avant–propos [avãprɔpo] *nms & pl* : foreword
avant–toit [avãtwa] *nm* : eaves *pl*
avare [avar] *adj* : miserly — ~ *nmf* : miser
avarié [avarje] *adj* : spoiled, rotten
avec [avɛk] *prep* : with — ~ *adv fam* : with it, with them
avenant, -nante [avnã, -nãt] *adj* : pleasant
avènement [avɛnmã] *nm* 1 : accession (to a throne) 2 DÉBUT : advent
avenir [avnir] *nm* 1 : future 2 à l'~ : in the future
avent [avã] *nm* l'~ : Advent
aventure [avãtyr] *nf* 1 : adventure 2 : love affair — **aventurer** [avãtyre] *vt* : risk — **s'aventurer** *vr* : venture — **aventureux, -reuse** [avãtyrø, -røz] *adj* : adventurous
avenu [avny] *adj m* **nul et non** ~ : null and void
avenue [avny] *nf* : avenue
avérer [avere] {87} *v* **s'avérer** *vr* : turn out to be
averse [avɛrs] *nf* : shower, storm
aversion [avɛrsjɔ̃] *nf* : aversion, dislike
avertir [avɛrtir] *vt* 1 : warn 2 INFORMER : inform — **avertissement** [avɛrtismã] *nm* : warning — **avertisseur** [avɛrtisœr] *nm* 1 : (car) horn 2 : alarm

aveu [avø] *nm, pl* **-veux** : confession, admission

aveugle [avœgl] *adj* : blind — ~ *nmf* : blind person — **aveuglant, -glante** [avœglɑ̃, -glɑ̃t] *adj* : blinding — **aveuglement** [avœgləmɑ̃] *nm* : blindness — **aveuglément** [avœglemɑ̃] *adv* : blindly — **aveugler** [avœgle] *vt* : blind

aviateur, -trice [avjatœr, -tris] *n* : pilot — **aviation** [avjasjɔ̃] *nf* : aviation

avide [avid] *adj* **1** CUPIDE : greedy **2** ~ **de** : eager for — **avidité** [avidite] *nf* **1** CUPIDITÉ : greed **2** : eagerness

avilir [avilir] *vt* : debase

avion [avjɔ̃] *nm* : airplane

aviron [avirɔ̃] *nm* RAME : oar

avis [avi] *nm* **1** : opinion **2** ANNONCE : notice **3** CONSEIL : advice — **aviser** [avize] *vt* : inform, notify — **avisé, -sée** [avize] *adj* : sensible

aviver [avive] *vt* : revive

avocat[1], -cate [avɔka, -kat] *n* : lawyer, attorney

avocat[2] *nm* : avocado

avoine [avwan] *nf* : oats *pl*

avoir [avwar] {10} *vt* **1** POSSÉDER : have **2** OBTENIR : get **3** ~ **dix ans** : be ten years old **4** ~ **à** : have to **5** ~ **mal** : be hurt — *v impers* **1 il y a** : there is, there are **2 qu'est-ce qu'il y a?** : what's wrong? — *v aux* : have — ~ *nm* : assets *pl*

avoisiner [avwazine] *vt* : be near, border on — **avoisinant, -nante** [avwazinɑ̃] *adj* : neighboring

avorter [avɔrte] *vi* : abort — **avortement** [avɔrtəmɑ̃] *nm* : abortion

avouer [avwe] *vt* : admit, confess to — **s'avouer** *vr* : confess, own up

axe [aks] *nm* **1** : axis **2** ~ **routier** : major road — **axer** [akse] *vt* : center, focus

axiome [aksjom] *nm* : axiom

azote [azɔt] *nm* : nitrogen

azur [azyr] *nm* : sky blue

B

b [be] *nm* : b, second letter of the alphabet

babeurre [babœr] *nm* : buttermilk

babiller [babije] *vi* : babble, chatter — **babillage** [babijaʒ] *nm* : babbling — **babillard** [babijar] *nm Can* : bulletin board

babiole [babjɔl] *nf* : trinket

babouin [babwɛ̃] *nm* : baboon

baby-sitter [bebisitœr] *nmf, pl* **baby-sitters** *France* : baby-sitter — **baby-sitting** [bebisitiŋ] *nm* **faire du** ~ *France* : baby-sit

baccalauréat [bakalɔrea] *nm* **1** *France* : school-leaving certificate **2** *Can* : bachelor's degree

bâche [baʃ] *nf* : tarpaulin

bâcler [bakle] *vt* : rush through

bacon [bekɔn] *nm* : bacon

bactéries [bakteri] *nfpl* : bacteria

badaud, -daude [bado, -dod] *n* : (curious) onlooker

badge [badʒ] *nm* : badge

badiner [badine] *vi* **1** : joke, jest **2** ~ **avec** : toy with — **badinage** [badinaʒ] *nm* : banter, joking

bafouer [bafwe] *vt* : ridicule, scorn

bafouiller [bafuje] *v* : mumble, stammer — **bafouillage** [bafujaʒ] *nm* : mumbling, gibberish

bagage [bagaʒ] *nm* : baggage, luggage

bagarrer [bagare] *vi* : fight — **se bagarrer** *vr* : fight, brawl — **bagarre** [bagar] *nf* : fight, brawl

bagatelle [bagatɛl] *nf* : trifle, trinket

bagne [baɲ] *nm* : labor camp

bagnole [baɲɔl] *nf fam* : jalopy

bague [bag] *nf* : ring

baguette [bagɛt] *nf* **1** : stick, rod, baton **2** : baguette (loaf of French bread) **3** ~ **de tambour** : drumstick **4** ~**s** *nfpl* : chopsticks

baie [bɛ] *nf* **1** : bay **2** : berry

baigner [beɲe] *vt* : bathe, wash — *vi* : soak, steep — **se baigner** *vr* **1** : take a bath **2** : go swimming — **baignade** [beɲad] *nf* : swimming — **baigneur, -gneuse** [beɲœr, -ɲøz] *n* : swimmer, bather — **baignoire** [beɲwar] *nf* : bathtub

bail [baj] *nm, pl* **baux** [bo] : lease

bâiller [baje] *vi* **1** : yawn **2** : be ajar (of a door) — **bâillement** [bajmɑ̃] *nm* : yawn

bâillonner [bajɔne] *vt* : gag, muzzle — **bâillon** [bajɔ̃] *nm* : gag

bain [bɛ̃] *nm* : bath

bain-marie [bɛ̃mari] *nm, pl* **bains-marie** : double boiler

baïonnette [bajɔnɛt] *nf* : bayonet

baiser [beze] *vt* : kiss — ~ *nm* : kiss

baisser [bese] *vt* : lower, reduce (volume, light, etc.) — *vi* : drop, decline — **se**

baisser *vr* : bend down — **baisse** [bɛs] *nf* : fall, drop

bal [bal] *nm* : ball, dance

balader [balade] *v* **se balader** *vr* 1 : go for a walk 2 : go for a drive — **balade** [balad] *nf* 1 : stroll, walk 2 : drive, ride

balafre [balafr] *nf* : gash, slash

balai [balɛ] *nm* : broom, brush

balancer [balɑ̃se] {6} *vt* 1 : sway, swing (one's arms, etc.) 2 : balance (an account) 3 *fam* : chuck, junk — **se balancer** *vr* : rock, sway — **balance** [balɑ̃s] *nf* : scales *pl*, balance

balancier [balɑ̃sje] *nm* : pendulum

balançoire [balɑ̃swar] *nf* 1 : child's swing 2 BASCULE : seesaw

balayer [baleje] {11} *vt* 1 : sweep 2 : scan (in computer science) — **balayage** [balejaʒ] *nm* : sweeping — **balayeuse** [balejøz] *nf* 1 : street-cleaning truck 2 *Can* : vacuum cleaner

balbutier [balbysje] {96} *v* : stammer, stutter — **balbutiement** [balbysimɑ̃] *nm* 1 : stammering, stuttering 2 ~s *nmpl* : beginnings

balcon [balkɔ̃] *nm* : balcony

baldaquin [baldakɛ̃] *nm* : canopy

baleine [balɛn] *nf* : whale

balise [baliz] *nf* : buoy, beacon — **baliser** [balize] *vt* : mark with beacons

balistique [balistik] *adj* : ballistic

balivernes [balivɛrn] *nfpl* : nonsense

ballade [balad] *nf* : ballad

balle [bal] *nf* 1 : ball (in sports) 2 : bullet 3 *France fam* : franc

balle-molle [balmɔl] *nf Can* : softball

ballet [balɛ] *nm* : ballet — **ballerine** [balrin] *nf* : ballerina

ballon [balɔ̃] *nm* 1 : (foot)ball 2 : balloon — **ballon-panier** [balɔ̃panje] *nm Can* : basketball (game)

ballot [balo] *nm* BALUCHON : pack, bundle

ballotter [balɔte] *vt* SECOUER : shake, toss about — *vi* : toss, roll around

balloune [balun] *nf Can* : balloon

balnéaire [balneɛr] *adj* : seaside

balourd, -lourde [balur, -lurd] *adj* : awkward, clumsy

baluchon [balyʃɔ̃] *nm* : pack, bundle

balustrade [balystrad] *nf* : guardrail

bambin, -bine [bɑ̃bɛ̃, -bin] *n* : child, toddler

bambou [bɑ̃bu] *nm* : bamboo

ban [bɑ̃] *nm* 1 : round of applause 2 ~s *nmpl* : banns 3 **mettre au ~** : ostracize

banal, -nale [banal] *adj, mpl* -**nals** : commonplace, trite — **banalité** [banalite] *nf* : triviality

banane [banan] *nf* : banana

banc [bɑ̃] *nm* 1 : bench 2 : school (of fish) 3 ~ **de sable** : sandbank 4 ~ **de neige** *Can* : snowbank

bancaire [bɑ̃kɛr] *adj* : banking, bank

bancal, -cale [bɑ̃kal] *adj, mpl* -**cals** ; wobbly, rickety

bandage [bɑ̃daʒ] *nm* 1 : bandaging 2 PANSEMENT : bandage

bande [bɑ̃d] *nf* 1 : gang, group, pack (of animals) 2 : tape, (reel of) film 3 ~ **dessinée** : comic strip

bandeau [bɑ̃do] *nm, pl* -**deaux** 1 : blindfold 2 : headband

bander [bɑ̃de] *vt* 1 : bandage 2 ~ **les yeux à** : blindfold

banderole [bɑ̃drɔl] *nf* : banner, pennant

bandit [bɑ̃di] *nm* VOLEUR : bandit, robber

bandoulière [bɑ̃duljɛr] *nf* : shoulder strap

banlieue [bɑ̃ljø] *nf* : suburbs *pl*

bannière [banjɛr] *nf* : banner

bannir [banir] *vt* : banish, exile

banque [bɑ̃k] *nf* 1 : bank 2 **travailler dans la ~** : work in banking — **banqueroute** [bɑ̃krut] *nf* : bankruptcy

banquet [bɑ̃kɛ] *nm* : banquet, feast

banquette [bɑ̃kɛt] *nf* : bench, seat (in a booth or vehicle)

banquier, -quière [bɑ̃kje, -kjɛr] *n* : banker

baptême [batɛm] *nm* : baptism — **baptiser** [batize] *vt* : baptize, christen

bar [bar] *nm* 1 : sea bass 2 CAFÉ : bar

baragouin [baragwɛ̃] *nm* : gibberish — **baragouiner** [baragwine] *vi* : talk gibberish, jabber

baraque [barak] *nf* 1 : hut, shack 2 : stall, booth (at a fair, etc.)

barbare [barbar] *adj* : barbaric — ~ *nmf* : barbarian

barbe [barb] *nf* : beard

barbecue [barbəkju] *nm* : barbecue

barbelé, -lée [barbəle] *adj* **fil barbelé** : barbed wire

barbiche [barbiʃ] *nf* : goatee

barbier [barbje] *nm Can* : barber

barbouiller [barbuje] *vt* 1 : smear 2 GRIBOUILLER : scribble

bardeau [bardo] *nm, pl* -**deaux** : shingle

barème [barɛm] *nm* : scale, table, list

baril [baril] *nm* TONNELET : barrel, keg

bariolé, -lée [barjɔle] *adj* : multicolored

barman [barman] *nm, pl* -**mans** *or* -**men** : bartender

baromètre [barɔmɛtr] *nm* : barometer

baron, -ronne [barɔ̃, -rɔn] *n* : baron *m*, baroness *f*

barque [bark] *nf* : small boat

barrage [baraʒ] *nm* 1 : dam 2 ~ **routier** : roadblock

barre [bar] *nf* 1 : bar, rod 2 NIVEAU : mark, level 3 **prendre la ~** : take the helm — **barreau** [baro] *nm, pl* -**reaux** 1 : bar 2 : rung — **barrer** [bare] *vt* 1 : bar, block 2

: cross out (a word) **3** : steer (a boat) **4** *Can* : lock

barricader [barikade] *vt* : barricade — **barricade** [barikad] *nf* : barricade

barrière [barjɛr] *nf* : barrier

baryton [baritɔ̃] *nm* : baritone

bas *nms & pl* **1** : bottom, lower part **2** : stocking **3 à ~** : down with **4 en ~** : below **5 en ~ de** : at the bottom of — **~** *adv* **1** : low **2 parler tout ~** : whisper, speak softly — **bas, basse** [ba (baz *before a vowel or mute h*), bas] *adj* **1** : low **2** VIL : base, vile

basané, -née [bazane] *adj* : tanned, sunburned

bascule [baskyl] *nf* **1** BALANCE : balance, scales *pl* **2** BALANÇOIRE : seesaw — **basculer** [baskyle] *vi* : tip, topple

base [baz] *nf* **1** : base **2** FONDEMENT : basis **3 ~ de données** : database

baseball *or* **base–ball** [bezbol] *nm* : baseball — **baseballeur, -leuse** [bɛzbolœr, -løz] *n Can* : baseball player

baser [baze] *vt* FONDER : base, found

basilic [bazilik] *nm* : basil

basilique [bazilik] *nf* : basilica

basket [baskɛt] *or* **basket–ball** [baskɛtbol] *nm* : basketball — **basketteur, -teuse** [baskɛtœr, -tøz] *n* : basketball player

basque [bask] *adj & nm* : Basque

basse [bas] *nf* : bass (in music)

bassin [basɛ̃] *nm* **1** : basin (in geography) **2** : pond, pool **3** : pelvis — **bassine** [basin] *nf* : bowl

basson [basɔ̃] *nm* : bassoon

bataille [bataj] *nf* : battle, fight — **batailler** [bataje] *vi* : fight, struggle (hard) — **batailleur, -leuse** [batajœr, -jøz] *adj* : quarrelsome — **~** *n* : fighter

bâtard, -tarde [batar, -tard] *adj & n* : bastard

bateau *nm, pl* **-teaux 1** : boat, ship **2 ~ à voiles** : sailboat

batifoler [batifole] *vi* : frolic

bâtir [batir] *vt* **1** CONSTRUIRE : build, erect **2** FAUFILER : baste, tack — **bâtiment** [batimɑ̃] *nm* **1** : building, structure **2** NAVIRE : ship — **bâtisseur, -seuse** [batisœr, -søz] *n* : builder

bâton [batɔ̃] *nm* **1** : rod, stick, staff **2** *Can* : bat (in sports) **3 ~ de rouge** : lipstick

battre [batr] {12} *vt* **1** FRAPPER : hit, strike **2** VAINCRE : defeat **3** : shuffle (cards) — *vi* : beat (of the heart) — **se battre** *vr* : fight — **battant, -tante** [batɑ̃, -tɑ̃t] *adj* **1** : beating, pounding **2 pluie battante** : pouring rain — **batte** [bat] *nf* : bat (in sports) — **battement** [batmɑ̃] *nm* **1** : beating **2 ~ de cœur** : heartbeat — **batterie** [batri] *nf* **1** : battery (of a car) **2** ENSEMBLE : set, group **3** : drums, drum set — **batteur** [batœr,

-tøz] *nm* **1** : whisk, eggbeater **2** : drummer **3** : batter (in sports)

baume [bom] *nm* : balm

baux → bail

bavard, -varde [bavar, -vard] *adj* : talkative — **~** *n* : chatterbox — **bavarder** [bavarde] *vi* **1** : chatter **2** : gossip — **bavardage** [bavardaʒ] *nm* : idle talk, chatter

bave [bav] *nf* : dribble, spittle — **baver** [bave] *vi* **1** : dribble, drool **2** COULER : leak — **bavoir** [bavwar] *nm* : (baby's) bib

bavure [bavyr] *nf* **1** : smudge **2** GAFFE : blunder

bazar [bazar] *nm* **1** : bazaar **2** *fam* : clutter, mess

beau [bo] (**bel** [bɛl] *before vowel or mute h*), **belle** [bɛl] *adj, mpl* **beaux** [bo] **1** : beautiful, handsome **2** : good (of a performance, etc.) **3** : considerable (in quantity) **4 ~ temps** : nice weather — **~** *adv* **1 avoir ~** : do (something) in vain **2 il fait ~** : it's nice outside

beaucoup [boku] *adv* **1** : much, a lot **2 ~ de** : much, many, a lot of **3 de ~** : by far

beau–fils [bofis] *nm, pl* **beaux–fils 1** : son-in-law **2** : stepson — **beau–frère** [bofrɛr] *nm, pl* **beaux–frères 1** : brother-in-law **2** : stepbrother — **beau–père** [bopɛr] *nm, pl* **beaux–pères 1** : father-in-law **2** : stepfather

beauté [bote] *nf* : beauty

beaux–arts [bozar] *nmpl* : fine arts

beaux–parents [boparɑ̃] *nmpl* : in-laws

bébé [bebe] *nm* : baby, infant

bec [bɛk] *nm* **1** : beak, bill **2** *fam* : mouth **3** EMBOUCHURE : mouthpiece **4** : point (of a pen) **5** : spout, lip (of a jug, etc.) **6** *Can fam* : kiss

bêche [bɛʃ] *nf* : spade — **bêcher** [beʃe] *vt* : dig (up)

bedaine [bədɛn] *nf fam* : paunch

bée *adj* [be] → **bouche**

beffroi [befrwa] *nm* : belfry

bégayer [begeje] {11} *v* : stutter, stammer

béguin [begɛ̃] *nm fam* : crush, infatuation

beige [bɛʒ] *adj & nm* : beige

beignet [bɛɲɛ] *nm* **1** : doughnut **2** : fritter — **beigne** [bɛɲ] *nm Can* : doughnut

bel [bɛl] → **beau**

bêler [bele] *vi* : bleat — **bêlement** [bɛlmɑ̃] *nm* : bleat

belette [bəlɛt] *nf* : weasel

belge [bɛlʒ] *adj* : Belgian

bélier [belje] *nm* : ram

belle [bɛl] *adj* → **beau**

belle–famille [bɛlfamij] *nf, pl* **belles–familles** : in-laws *pl* — **belle–fille** [bɛlfij] *nf, pl* **belles–filles 1** : daughter-in-law **2** : stepdaughter — **belle–mère** [bɛlmɛr] *nf, pl* **belles–mères 1** : mother-in-law **2** : stepmother — **belle–sœur** [bɛlsœr] *nf, pl* **belles–sœurs** : sister-in-law

belligérant, -rante [beliʒerɑ̃, -rɑ̃t] *adj & n* : belligerent

belliqueux, -queuse [bɛlikø, -køz] *adj* GUERRIER : warlike

bémol [bemɔl] *adj & nm* : flat (in music)

bénédiction [benediksjɔ̃] *nf* : blessing, benediction

bénéfice [benefis] *nm* **1** AVANTAGE : benefit, advantage **2** GAIN : profit — **bénéficiaire** [benefisjɛr] *nmf* : beneficiary — **bénéficier** [benefisje] {96} *vi* ~ **de** : benefit from — **bénéfique** [benefik] *adj* : beneficial

bénévole [benevɔl] *adj* : voluntary — ~ *nmf* : volunteer

bénin, -nigne [benɛ̃, beniɲ] *adj* **1** : slight, minor **2** : benign (of a tumor)

bénir [benir] *vt* : bless — **bénit, -nite** [beni, -nit] *adj* : blessed

benjamin, -mine [bɛ̃ʒamɛ̃, -min] *n* CADET : youngest child

béquille [bekij] *nf* **1** : crutch **2** : kickstand

bercer [bɛrse] {6} *vt* **1** : rock (a baby) **2** APAISER : soothe, lull — **se bercer** *vr* : rock, swing — **berceau** [bɛrso] *nm, pl* **-ceaux** : cradle — **berceuse** [bɛrsøz] *nf* **1** : lullaby **2** : rocking chair

béret [berɛ] *nm* : beret

berge [bɛrʒ] *nf* RIVE : bank (of a river, etc.)

berger, -gère [bɛrʒe, -ʒɛr] *n* : shepherd, shepherdess *f* — **berger** *nm* : sheepdog

berline [bɛrlin] *nf* : sedan

berlingot [bɛrlɛ̃go] *nm* **1** : carton (for milk, etc.) **2** : hard candy

berner [bɛrne] *vt* : fool, deceive

besogne [bazɔɲ] *nf* : task, job

besoin [bazwɛ̃] *nm* **1** : need **2 avoir** ~ **de** : need **3 dans le** ~ : needy

bestiole [bɛstjɔl] *nf* : bug, tiny creature

bétail [betaj] *nm* : livestock, cattle *pl*

bête [bɛt] *nf* ANIMAL : animal, creature — ~ *adj* : stupid, silly — **bêtement** [bɛtmɑ̃] *adv* : foolishly — **bêtise** [betiz] *nf* **1** : stupidity **2** : stupid thing, nonsense

béton [betɔ̃] *nm* : concrete

bette [bɛt] *nf* : Swiss chard

betterave [bɛtrav] *nf* : beet

beugler [bøgle] *vi* **1** : moo, bellow **2** : blare (of a radio, etc.) — *vt* : bellow out

beurre [bœr] *nm* : butter — **beurrer** [bœre] *vt* : butter

bévue [bevy] *nf* : blunder

biais [bjɛ, bjɛz] *nm* **1** : means, way **2 de** ~ : diagonally — **biaiser** [bjeze] *vi* : hedge, dodge the issue

bibelot [biblo] *nm* : trinket, curio

biberon [bibrɔ̃] *nm* : baby bottle

Bible [bibl] *nf* **la** ~ : the Bible — **biblique** [biblik] *adj* : biblical, scriptural

bibliographie [biblijɔgrafi] *nf* : bibliography

bibliothèque [biblijɔtɛk] *nf* **1** : library **2** : bookcase — **bibliothécaire** [biblijɔtekɛr] *nmf* : librarian

bicarbonate [bikarbɔnat] *nm* ~ **de soude** : baking soda

biceps [bisɛps] *nms & pl* : biceps

biche [biʃ] *nf* : doe

bicoque [bikɔk] *nf* : shack, shanty

bicyclette [bisiklɛt] *nf* : bicycle

bidon [bidɔ̃] *nm* : can, flask

bien [bjɛ̃] *adv* **1** : well, satisfactorily **2** TRÈS : very, quite **3** RÉELLEMENT : definitely, really **4** VOLONTIERS : readily, happily **5** ~ **des fois** : many times **6** ~ **que** : although **7** ~ **sûr** : of course — ~ *adj* **1** : good, fine, satisfactory **2** : well, in good health **3** BEAU : good-looking **4** RESPECTABLE : nice **5** : comfortable (of shoes, etc.) — ~ *nm* **1** : good **2** ~**s** *nmpl* : possessions, property — ~ *interj* : OK, all right, very well — **bien–aimé, -aimée** [bjɛ̃neme] *adj & n* : beloved — **bien–être** [bjɛ̃nɛtr] *nm* **1** : well-being **2** : comfort

bienfaisance [bjɛ̃fazɑ̃s] *nf* : charity, kindness — **bienfaisant, -sante** [bjɛ̃fazɑ̃, -zɑ̃t] *adj* **1** : charitable **2** BÉNÉFIQUE : beneficial — **bienfait** [bjɛ̃fɛ] *nm* AVANTAGE : benefit — **bienfaiteur, -trice** [bjɛ̃fɛtœr, -tris] *n* : benefactor

bientôt [bjɛ̃to] *adv* : soon, shortly

bienveillance [bjɛ̃vejɑ̃s] *nf* : kindness, benevolence — **bienveillant, -lante** [bjɛ̃vejɑ̃, -jɑ̃t] *adj* : kind, benevolent

bienvenu, -nue [bjɛ̃vny] *adj* : welcome — ~ *n* **soyez le** ~ : you are welcome (here) — **bienvenue** *nf* : welcome

bière [bjɛr] *nf* : beer

biffer [bife] *vt* : cross out

bifteck [biftɛk] *nm* : steak

bifurquer [bifyrke] *vi* : to fork — **bifurcation** [bifyrkasjɔ̃] *nf* : fork (in a road)

bigot, -gote [bigo, -ɔt] *adj* : overly devout — ~ *n* : (religious) zealot

bigoudi [bigudi] *nm* : hair curler

bijou [biʒu] *nm, pl* **-joux 1** : jewel **2** MERVEILLE : gem — **bijouterie** [biʒutri] *nf* **1** BIJOUX : jewelry **2** : jewelry store — **bijoutier, -tière** [biʒutje, -tjɛr] *n* : jeweler

bilan [bilɑ̃] *nm* **1** : assessment **2** : balance sheet (in finance)

bilatéral, -rale [bilateral] *adj, mpl* **-raux** [-ro] : bilateral

bile [bil] *nf* **1** : bile **2 se faire de la** ~ : worry

bilingue [bilɛ̃g] *adj* : bilingual

billard [bijar] *nm* : billiards *pl*

bille [bij] *nf* **1** : (playing) marble **2** : billiard ball

billet [bijɛ] *nm* **1** : bill, banknote **2** TICKET : ticket **3** ~ **doux** : love letter — **billetterie** [bijɛtri] *nf* **1** GUICHET : ticket office **2** : automatic teller machine

billion [biljɔ̃] *nm* : trillion (US), billion (Brit)

bimensuel, -suelle [bimãsɥɛl] *adj* : semimonthly

binette [binɛt] *nf* : hoe

biochimie [bjoʃimi] *nf* : biochemistry

biographie [bjɔgrafi] *nf* : biography — **biographe** [bjɔgraf] *nmf* : biographer — **biographique** [bjɔgrafik] *adj* : biographical

biologie [bjɔlɔʒi] *nf* : biology — **biologique** [bjɔlɔʒik] *adj* : biological

bis [bis] *adv* **1** : twice (in music) **2** : A (in an address) — ~ *nm & interj* : encore

biscotte [biskɔt] *nf* : cracker

biscuit [biskɥi] *nm* **1** : cookie **2** : sponge cake

bise [biz] *nf* **1** : north wind **2** *fam* : kiss, smack

biseau [bizo] *nm* **1** : bevel **2 en** ~ : beveled

bisexuel, -sexuelle [bisɛksɥɛl] *adj* : bisexual

bison [bizɔ̃] *nm* : bison, buffalo

bissextile [bisɛkstil] *adj* **année** ~ : leap year

bistouri [bisturi] *nm* : lancet

bistro *or* **bistrot** [bistro] *nm* : café

bit [bit] *nm* : bit (unit of information)

bizarre [bizar] *adj* : bizarre, strange — **bizarrement** [-zarmã] *adv* : oddly, strangely

blafard, -farde [blafar, -fard] *adj* : pale, pallid

blague [blag] *nf* PLAISANTERIE : joke — **blaguer** [blage] *vi* PLAISANTER : joke, kid around — **blagueur, -gueuse** [blagœr, -gøz] *n* : joker

blaireau [blɛro] *nm, pl* **-raux** : badger

blâmer [blame] *vt* : blame, criticize — **blâme** [blam] *nm* DÉSAPPROBATION : blame, censure

blanc, blanche [blɑ̃, blɑ̃ʃ] *adj* **1** : white **2** PÂLE : pale **3** : pure, innocent **4 page blanche** : blank sheet — **blanc** *nm* **1** : white **2** INTERVALLE : gap, blank space

blanchir [blɑ̃ʃir] *vt* **1** : whiten, bleach **2** : launder (one's clothes) **3** : blanch (vegetables) — *vi* : turn white — **blanchissage** [blɑ̃ʃisaʒ] *nm* : laundering — **blanchisserie** [blɑ̃ʃisri] *nf* : laundry

blasé, -sée [blaze] *adj* : blasé, jaded

blason [blazɔ̃] *nm* : coat of arms

blasphème [blasfɛm] *nm* : blasphemy

blatte [blat] *nf* : cockroach

blazer [blazɛr] *nm* : blazer

blé [ble] *nm* : wheat

blême [blɛm] *adj* : pale, wan

blesser [blese] *vt* : injure, wound — **blessé,**

-sée [blese] *n* : casualty, injured person — **blessure** [blesyr] *nf* : injury, wound

bleu, bleue [blø] *adj* **1** : blue **2** : very rare (of steak, etc.) — **bleu** *nm* **1** : blue **2** : bruise

bleuet [bløɛ] *nm Can* : blueberry

blindé, -dée [blɛ̃de] *adj* : armored — **blindé** *nm* : armored vehicle

bloc [blɔk] *nm* **1** : block **2 en** ~ : as a whole

blocage [blɔkaʒ] *nm* **1** : obstruction **2** : freezing (of prices, etc.)

blocus [blɔkys] *nm* : blockade

blond, blonde [blɔ̃, blɔ̃d] *adj & n* : blond

blonde *nf Can fam* : girlfriend

bloquer [blɔke] *vt* **1** : block (an entrance) **2** : jam on (the brakes) **3** : freeze (a bank account, etc.), stop (a check) — **se bloquer** *vr* : jam, stick

blottir [blɔtir] *v* **se blottir** *vr* : cuddle, snuggle

blouse [bluz] *nf* **1** CHEMISIER : blouse **2** SARRAU : smock

blouson [bluzɔ̃] *nm* : jacket

blue-jean [bludʒin] *nm, pl* **blue-jeans** : jeans *pl*

bluffer [blœfe] *vi* : bluff — **bluff** [blœf] *nm* : bluff

bobine [bɔbin] *nf* : reel, spool

bocal [bɔkal] *nm, pl* **-caux** [bɔko] : jar

bœuf [bœf] *nm, pl* **bœufs** [bø] : beef

bohème [bɔɛm] *adj* : bohemian — **bohémien, -mienne** [bɔemjɛ̃, -mjɛn] *n* : gypsy

boire [bwar] {13} *vt* **1** : drink **2** ABSORBER : absorb — *vi* : drink

bois [bwa] *nms & pl* **1** : wood **2** FORÊT : woods *pl* **3** ~ **de chauffage** : firewood **4** ~ *nmpl* : antlers — **boisé, -sée** [bwaze] *adj* : wooded — **boisé** *nm Can* : woods *pl*

boisseau [bwaso] *nm* : bushel

boisson [bwasɔ̃] *nf* **1** : drink, beverage **2 en** ~ *Can* : drunk

boîte [bwat] *nf* **1** : (tin) can **2** : box **3** ~ **de nuit** : nightclub

boiter [bwate] *vi* : limp — **boiteux, -teuse** [bwatø, -tøz] *adj* **1** : lame **2** BRANLANT : wobbly, shaky — **boitiller** [bwatije] *vi* : limp slightly, hobble

boîtier [bwatje] *nm* : casing, housing

bol [bɔl] *nm* **1** : bowl **2** : bowlful

bombarder [bɔ̃barde] *vt* : bomb, bombard — **bombardement** [bɔ̃bardəmã] *nm* : bombing, bombardment — **bombardier** [bɔ̃bardje] *nm* : bomber (plane)

bombe [bɔ̃b] *nf* **1** : bomb **2** ATOMISEUR : aerosol spray

bomber [bɔ̃be] *vt* : puff out, swell

bon, bonne [bɔ̃ (**bon** *before a vowel or mute h*), bɔn] *adj* **1** : good **2** CORRECT

: correct, proper **3 ~ marché** : inexpensive **4 ~ sens** : common sense **5 pour de ~** : for good, for keeps — **bon** *adv* **faire ~** : be nice — **~** *nm* **1** : good thing **2** : voucher, bond

bonbon [bɔ̃bɔ̃] *nm* : candy

bond [bɔ̃] *nm* **1** SAUT : bound, leap **2** : bounce (of a ball)

bondé, -dée [bɔ̃de] *adj* : crammed, packed

bondir [bɔ̃dir] *vi* : jump, leap

bonheur [bɔnœr] *nm* **1** : happiness, pleasure **2 par ~** : luckily

bonhomme [bɔnɔm] *nm, pl* **bonshommes 1** *fam* : fellow, guy **2 ~ de neige** : snowman

bonjour [bɔ̃ʒur] *nm* **1** : hello, good morning, good afternoon **2** *Can* : good-bye

bonne [bɔn] *nf* DOMESTIQUE : maid

bonnement [bɔnmɑ̃] *adv* **tout ~** : quite simply

bonnet [bɔnɛ] *nm* : cap, hat

bonneterie [bɔnɛtri] *nf* : hosiery

bonsoir [bɔ̃swar] *nm* : good evening, good night

bonté [bɔ̃te] *nf* : goodness, kindness

bord [bɔr] *nm* **1** : edge, rim **2** : bank, shore **3 à ~** : on board, aboard **4 au ~ de** : on the verge of

bordeaux [bɔrdo] *nm* : Bordeaux, claret (wine)

bordée [bɔrde] *nf* **1** : volley **2 ~ de neige** *Can* : snowstorm

bordel [bɔrdɛl] *nm fam* **1** : brothel **2** PAGAILLE : mess, shambles

border [bɔrde] *vt* **1** : border, line **2** : tuck in

bordereau [bɔrdəro] *nm, pl* **-reaux** [-ro] **1** : note (in finance) **2 ~ de dépôt** : deposit slip

bordure [bɔrdyr] *nf* : border, edge

borne [bɔrn] *nf* **1** : milestone, landmark **2 ~s** *nfpl* : limits — **borné, -née** [bɔrne] *adj* : narrow-minded — **borner** [bɔrne] *vt* RESTREINDRE : limit, restrict — **se borner** *vr* : confine oneself

bosquet [bɔske] *nm* : grove, copse

bosse [bɔs] *nf* **1** : hump (of a person or animal) **2 se faire une ~** : get a bump — **bosseler** [bɔsle] {8} *vt* : dent (a bumper, etc.) — **bosser** [bɔse] *vi France fam* : work, slave away

botanique [bɔtanik] *nf* : botany — **~** *adj* : botanical

botte [bɔt] *nf* **1** : boot **2** : bunch (of radishes), sheaf (of hay) — **botter** [bɔte] *vt* : kick (in sports)

bottin [bɔtɛ̃] *nm* : (telephone) directory

bouche [buʃ] *nf* **1** : mouth **2** ENTRÉE : opening, entrance **3 ~ bée** : flabbergasted **4 ~ d'incendie** : fire hydrant — **bouchée** [buʃe] *nf* : mouthful

boucher[1] [buʃe] *vt* : stop up, block — **se boucher** *vr* : become blocked — **bouchon** [buʃɔ̃] *nm* **1** : cork, stopper **2** : float (in fishing) **3** EMBOUTEILLAGE : traffic jam

boucher[2], **-chère** [buʃe, -ʃɛr] *n* : butcher — **boucherie** [buʃri] *nf* : butcher's shop

boucler [bukle] *vt* **1** : buckle (a belt), fasten (a seat belt) **2** : complete (a task) — *vi* : curl — **boucle** [bukl] *nf* **1** : buckle **2** : curl **3 ~ d'oreille** : earring — **bouclé, -clée** [bukle] *adj* : curly

bouclier [buklije] *nm* : shield

bouddhiste [budist] *adj & nmf* : Buddhist — **bouddhisme** [budism] *nm* : Buddhism

bouder [bude] *vt* : avoid — *vi* : sulk, pout — **bouderie** [budri] *nf* : sulkiness — **boudeur, -deuse** [budœr, -døz] *adj* : sulky

boudin [budɛ̃] *nm* : blood sausage

boue [bu] *nf* : mud — **boueux, boueuse** [buø, buøz] *adj* : muddy

bouée [bwe] *nf* : buoy

bouffant, -fante [bufɑ̃, -fɑ̃t] *adj* : baggy (of pants) — **bouffi, -fie** [bufi] *adj* : puffy, swollen

bouffe [buf] *nf fam* : grub, chow — **bouffer** [bufe] *vt fam* : eat, gobble up

bouffée [bufe] *nf* **1** : puff, gust **2** : surge, fit (of rage, etc.)

bouffon, -fonne [bufɔ̃, bufɔn] *adj* : comical — **bouffon** *nm* : clown, buffoon

bougeoir [buʒwar] *nm* : candlestick

bouger [buʒe] {17} *vt* : move — *vi* : budge, stir

bougie [buʒi] *nf* **1** : candle **2** : spark plug (of a car)

bougonner [bugɔne] *vi* : grumble — **bougon, -gonne** [bugɔ̃, -gɔn] *adj* : grumpy

bouillabaisse [bujabɛs] *nf* : fish soup

bouillir [bujir] {14} *vi* **1** : boil **2** : seethe (with anger, etc.) — **bouillie** [buji] *nf* : baby cereal, gruel — **bouilloire** [bujwar] *nf* : kettle, teakettle — **bouillon** [bujɔ̃] *nm* : broth, stock — **bouillonner** [bujɔne] *vi* **1** : bubble, foam **2 → bouillir**

boulanger, -gère [bulɑ̃ʒe, -ʒɛr] *n* : baker — **boulangerie** [bulɑ̃ʒri] *nf* : bakery

boule [bul] *nf* **1** : ball **2 ~ de neige** : snowball

bouleau [bulo] *nm, pl* **-leaux** : birch

bouledogue [buldɔg] *nm* : bulldog

boulet [bulɛ] *nm* **1** : cannonball **2** : ball and chain

boulette [bulɛt] *nf* **1** : pellet **2** : meatball

boulevard [bulvar] *nm* : boulevard

bouleverser [bulvɛrse] *vt* **1** : upset, turn upside down **2** PERTURBER : overwhelm — **bouleversant, -sante** [bulvɛrsɑ̃, -sɑ̃t] *adj* : distressing, upsetting — **bouleversement** [bulvɛrsəmɑ̃] *nm* : upheaval, upset

boulon [bulɔ̃] *nm* : bolt

boulot [bulo] *nm fam* **1** : work, task **2** EMPLOI : job — **boulot, -lotte** [bulo, -lɔt] *adj* : plump, chubby

boum [bum] *nm* **1** : bang **2** : boom (of business, etc.)

bouquet [bukɛ] *nm* : bouquet, bunch (of flowers)

bouquin [bukɛ̃] *nm fam* : book — **bouquiniste** [bukinist] *nmf* : secondhand bookseller

bourbier [burbje] *nm* : swamp, quagmire

bourde [burd] *nf* : blunder

bourdon [burdɔ̃] *nm* : bumblebee — **bourdonnement** [burdɔnmɑ̃] *nm* : buzz, hum, droning — **bourdonner** [burdɔne] *vi* : buzz, hum

bourgeois, -geoise [burʒwa, -ʒwaz] *adj & n* : bourgeois — **bourgeoisie** [burʒwazi] *nf* : bourgeoisie

bourgeon [burʒɔ̃] *nm* : bud — **bourgeonner** [burʒɔne] *vi* : bud

bourgogne [burgɔɲ] *nm* : Burgundy (wine)

bourrage [buraʒ] *nm* : filling, stuffing

bourreau [buro] *nm, pl* **-reaux 1** : executioner **2** ~ **de travail** : workaholic

bourrer [bure] *vt* : fill, stuff, cram — *vi* : be filling — **se bourrer** *vr* : stuff oneself

bourru, -rue [bury] *adj* : gruff, surly

bourse [burs] *nf* **1** PORTE-MONNAIE : purse **2** : scholarship **3 la Bourse** : the stock market — **boursier, -sière** [bursje, -sjɛr] *adj* : stock, stock-market

boursoufler [bursufle] *vt* : puff up, cause to swell — **se boursoufler** *vr* : blister — **boursouflure** [bursuflyr] *nf* : blister (of paint, etc.)

bousculer [buskyle] *vt* **1** : jostle, shove **2** PRESSER : rush — **se bousculer** *vr* : jostle — **bousculade** [buskylad] *nf* : rush, scramble

bousiller [buzije] *vt fam* : bungle, botch

boussole [busɔl] *nf* : compass

bout [bu] *nm* **1** EXTRÉMITÉ : end, tip **2** MORCEAU : bit **3 au** ~ **de** : after **4 à** ~ **portant** : point-blank

bouteille [butɛj] *nf* : bottle

boutique [butik] *nf* : shop, boutique

bouton [butɔ̃] *nm* **1** : button **2** BOURGEON : bud **3** : pimple **4** *or* ~ **de porte** : doorknob — **boutonner** [butɔne] *vt* : button — **boutonnière** *nf* : buttonhole

bovins [bɔvɛ̃] *nmpl* : cattle

bowling [buliŋ] *nm* : bowling

box [bɔks] *nm, pl* **boxes** : stall (for a horse)

boxe [bɔks] *nf* : boxing — **boxer** [bɔkse] *vi* : box — **boxeur** [bɔksœr] *nm* : boxer, fighter

boyau [bwajo] *nm, pl* **boyaux 1** INTESTIN : intestine, gut **2** : inner tube (of a tire)

boycotter [bɔjkɔte] *vt* : boycott — **boycottage** [bɔjkɔtaʒ] *nm* : boycott

bracelet [braslɛ] *nm* : bracelet

braconner [brakɔne] *vi* : poach (of game)

braguette [bragɛt] *nf* : fly (of pants, etc.)

braille [braj] *nm* : braille

brailler [braje] *vi fam* : bawl, howl

braire [brɛr] {15} *vi* : bray

braise [brɛz] *nf* : embers *pl*

brancard [brɑ̃kar] *nm* CIVIÈRE : stretcher

branche [brɑ̃ʃ] *nf* **1** : branch **2** : sidepiece (of eyeglasses) — **branché, -chée** [brɑ̃ʃe] *adj fam* : trendy — **brancher** [brɑ̃ʃe] *vt* **1** : connect (a utility) **2** : plug in (a device)

branchie [brɑ̃ʃi] *nf* : gill (of a fish)

brandir [brɑ̃dir] *vt* : brandish, wave

branler [brɑ̃le] *vi* : wobble, be loose — **branlant, -lante** [brɑ̃lɑ̃, -lɑ̃t] *adj* : unsteady — **branle** [brɑ̃l] *nm* **mettre en** ~ : set in motion

braquer [brake] *vt* **1** DIRIGER : aim **2** : turn (a steering wheel) **3** *fam* : point a gun at **4** ~ **qqn contre qqch** : turn s.o. against sth

bras [bra] *nms & pl* : arm — **brasser** [brase] *vt* **1** : mix **2** : brew (beer) — **brasserie** [brasri] *nf* **1** : brewery **2** : restaurant — **brassière** [brasjɛr] *nf Can* : bra, brassiere

brave [brav] *adj* **1** GENTIL : good, nice **2** COURAGEUX : brave — **bravement** [bravmɑ̃] *adv* : bravely, boldly — **braver** [brave] *vt* : brave

break [brɛk] *nm France* : station wagon — ~ *nm Can* : break, rest

brebis [brəbi] *nf* : ewe

brèche [brɛʃ] *nf* : gap

bredouiller [brəduje] *v* : mumble, mutter

bref, brève [brɛf, brɛv] *adj* : brief, short — **bref** [brɛf] *adv or* **en** ~ : briefly, in short

brésilien, -lienne [breziljɛ̃, -ljɛn] *adj* : Brazilian

bretelle [brətɛl] *nf* **1** : strap **2** : (access) ramp **3** ~**s** *nfpl* : suspenders

breton, -tonne [brətɔ̃, brətɔn] *n* : Breton

breuvage [brœvaʒ] *nm* : beverage

brevet [brəvɛ] *nm* **1** : patent **2** : diploma, certificate — **breveter** [brəvte] {8} *vt* : patent

bribes [brib] *nfpl* : bits, pieces

bric-à-brac [brikabrak] *nms & pl* : odds and ends

bricoler [brikɔle] *vi* : do odd jobs, putter — *vt* : fix up — **bricolage** [brikɔlaʒ] *nm* : do-it-yourself work — **bricoleur, -leuse** [brikɔlœr, -løz] *n* : handyman

bride [brid] *nf* : bridle — **brider** [bride] *vt* **1** : bridle (a horse) **2** CONTENIR : keep in check

bridge [bridʒ] *nm* : bridge (card game)

brièveté [brijɛvte] *nf* : brevity — **brièvement** [brijɛvmɑ̃] *adv* : briefly

brigade [brigad] *nf* : brigade, squad

briller [brije] *vi* : shine — **brillant, -lante** [brijɑ̃, -jɑ̃t] *adj* **1** : bright, shiny **2** REMARQUABLE : brilliant, outstanding — **brillant** *nm* **1** gloss, shine

brimer [brime] *vt* : bully

brin [brɛ̃] *nm* **1** : blade (of grass), sprig **2** : little bit, iota **3** : strand (of thread, etc.)

brindille [brɛ̃dij] *nf* : twig

bringue [brɛ̃g] *nf fam* : binge

brio [brijo] *nm* **1** : brilliance, panache **2** avec ～ : brilliantly

brioche [brijɔʃ] *nf* **1** : brioche **2** *fam* : paunch

brique [brik] *nf* : brick

briquet [brikɛ] *nm* : (cigarette) lighter

brise [briz] *nf* : breeze

briser [brize] *vt* **1** : break, smash **2** DÉTRUIRE : ruin, wreck — **se briser** *vr* : shatter, break

britannique [britanik] *adj* : British

broche [brɔʃ] *nf* **1** : brooch **2** : spit, skewer (in cooking) — **brochette** [brɔʃɛt] *nf* : skewer

brochure [brɔʃyr] *nf* : brochure, pamphlet

brocoli [brɔkɔli] *nm* : broccoli

broder [brɔde] *vt* : embroider — **broderie** [brɔdri] *nf* : embroidery

bronchite [brɔ̃ʃit] *nf* : bronchitis

bronze [brɔ̃z] *nm* : bronze — **bronzage** [brɔ̃zaʒ] *nm* : suntan — **bronzé, -zée** [brɔ̃ze] *adj* : suntanned — **bronzer** [brɔ̃ze] *vi* : get a suntan

brosse [brɔs] *nf* : brush — **brosser** [brɔse] *vt* **1** : brush **2** : paint (a picture) — **se brosser** *vr* ～ **les cheveux** : brush one's hair

brouette [bruɛt] *nf* : wheelbarrow

brouiller [bruje] *vt* **1** : mix up, scramble **2** TROUBLER : blur, cloud — **se brouiller** *vr* **1** : quarrel **2** : cloud over (of the weather) — **brouillard** [brujar] *nm* : fog, mist — **brouillon, -lonne** [brujɔ̃, -jɔn] *adj* : disorganized, untidy — **brouillon** *nm* : rough draft

broussailles [brusaj] *nfpl* : undergrowth

brousse [brus] *nf* **la** ～ : bush, wilderness

brouter [brute] *vi* : graze

broyer [brwaje] {58} *vt* : grind, crush

bru [bry] *nf* : daughter-in-law

bruine [brɥin] *nf* : drizzle — **bruiner** [brɥine] *vi* : drizzle

bruire [brɥir] {16} *vi* : rustle, murmur, hum — **bruissement** [brɥismɑ̃] *nm* : rustling, murmuring — **bruit** [brɥi] *nm* **1** : noise **2** VACARME : commotion, fuss **3** RUMEUR : rumor

brûler [bryle] *vt* **1** : burn, scald **2** : run (a red light) — *vi* : burn (up) — **se brûler** *vr* : burn oneself — **brûlant, -lante** [brylɑ̃, -lɑ̃t] *adj* **1** : burning hot **2** : ardent — **brûleur**

[brylœr] *nm* : burner — **brûlure** [brylyr] *nf* **1** : burn **2** ～**s d'estomac** : heartburn

brume [brym] *nf* : mist, haze — **brumeux, -meuse** [brymø, -møz] *adj* : misty, foggy

brun, brune [brœ̃, bryn] *adj* : brown — **brun** *n* = **brunet** ～ *nm* : brown — **brunette** [brynɛt] *nf* : brunette

brusque [brysk] *adj* : brusque, abrupt — **brusquement** [bryskəmɑ̃] *adv* : abruptly, suddenly — **brusquer** [bryske] *vt* : rush, hurry

brut, brute [bryt] *adj* **1** : raw, crude **2** : dry (of wine) **3 poids** ～ : gross weight

brutal, -tale [brytal] *adj, mpl* **-taux** [bryto] : brutal — **brutalement** [-talmɑ̃] *adv* **1** : brutally **2** : suddenly — **brutaliser** [brytalize] *vt* : abuse, mistreat — **brutalité** [brytalite] *nf* : brutality — **brute** [bryt] *nf* : brute

bruyant, bruyante [brɥijɑ̃, -jɑ̃t] *adj* : noisy, loud — **bruyamment** [brɥijamɑ̃] *adv* : noisily, loudly

bruyère [brɥijɛr] *nf* : heather

buanderie [bɥɑ̃dri] *nf* **1** : laundry room **2** *Can* : self-service laundry

buccal, -cale [bykal] *adj, mpl* **-caux** [byko] : oral

bûche [byʃ] *nf* : log — **bûcher** [byʃe] *vi fam* : work, slave away — **bûcheron, -ronne** [byʃrɔ̃, -rɔn] *n* : logger, lumberjack

budget [bydʒɛ] *nm* : budget — **budgétaire** [bydʒetɛr] *adj* : budgetary — **budgétiser** [bydʒezite] *vt* : budget

buée [bɥe] *nf* : steam, mist

buffet [byfe] *nm* **1** : sideboard **2** : buffet

buffle [byfl] *nm* : buffalo

buisson [bɥisɔ̃] *nm* : bush, shrub

bulbe [bylb] *nm* : bulb (of a plant)

bulldozer [byldozɛr] *nm* : bulldozer

bulle [byl] *nf* : bubble

bulletin [byltɛ̃] *nm* **1** : report, bulletin **2** ～ **de vote** : ballot

bureau [byro] *nm, pl* **-reaux 1** : office, study **2** SECRÉTAIRE : desk **3** : department, bureau — **bureaucrate** [byrokrat] *nmf* : bureaucrat — **bureaucratie** [byrokrasi] *nf* : bureaucracy — **bureaucratique** [-kratik] *adj* : bureaucratic

bus [bys] *nm* AUTOBUS : bus

buste [byst] *nm* **1** : chest, bust **2** : bust (in sculpture)

but [by(t)] *nm* **1** : aim, goal **2** *Can* : base (in baseball)

buter [byte] *vi* ～ **contre** *or* ～ **sur** : stumble on, trip over — *vt* : antagonize — **se buter** *vr* : become obstinate — **buté, -tée** [byte] *adj* : obstinate

butin [bytɛ̃] *nm* : loot

butte [byt] *nf* **1** : small hill, mound **2 être en** ～ **à** : come up against

buveur, -veuse [byvœr, -vøz] *n* : drinker

C

c [se] *nm* : c, third letter of the alphabet

ça [sa] *pron* **1** : that, this **2** : it **3** ~ **va?** : how's it going? **4** ~ **y est** : there, that's it

cabane [kaban] *nf* : cabin, hut — **cabanon** [kaban5] *nm* : shed

cabaret [kabaʀɛ] *nm* : nightclub

cabine [kabin] *nf* **1** : cabin, cab (of a truck, etc.) **2** ~ **téléphonique** : telephone booth **3** ~ **de pilotage** : cockpit

cabinet [kabinɛ] *nm* **1** : office **2** : cabinet (in government) **3** ~ **de toilette** *France* : toilet

câble [kabl] *nm* **1** : cable **2** : cable television

cabosser [kabɔse] *vt* : dent

cabriole [kabrijɔl] *nf* : somersault

cacahouète [kakaɥɛt] *nf* : peanut

cacao [kakao] *nm* : cocoa

cache-cache [kaʃkaʃ] *nms & pl* : hide-and-seek

cachemire [kaʃmir] *nm* : cashmere

cacher [kaʃe] *vt* : hide, conceal — **se cacher** *vr* : hide

cachet [kaʃɛ] *nm* **1** COMPRIMÉ : tablet, pill **2** *or* ~ **de la poste** : postmark **3** : fee **4** : character, style — **cacheter** [kaʃte] {8} *vt* : seal

cachette [kaʃɛt] *nf* : hiding place

cachot [kaʃo] *nm* : dungeon

cachottier, -tière [kaʃotje, -tjɛr] *adj* : secretive — **cachotterie** [kaʃotri] *nf* : little secret

cacophonie [kakɔfɔni] *nf* : cacophony

cactus [kaktys] *nms & pl* : cactus

cadavre [kadavr] *nm* : corpse

cadeau [kado] *nm, pl* **-deaux** : gift, present

cadenas [kadna] *nm* : padlock — **cadenasser** [-nase] *vt* : padlock

cadence [kadɑ̃s] *nf* : cadence, rhythm

cadet, -dette [kadɛ, -dɛt] *adj* : younger, youngest — ~ *n* **1** : younger, youngest (son, daughter, child) **2** : junior

cadran [kadrɑ̃] *nm* **1** : dial, face **2** *Can fam* : alarm clock

cadre [kadr] *nm* **1** : frame **2** : setting, surroundings *pl* **3** STRUCTURE : framework **4** : executive

caduc, -duque [kadyk] *adj* **1** : obsolete **2** : deciduous

cafard [kafar] *nm* **1** : cockroach **2 avoir le** ~ : have the blues

café [kafe] *nm* **1** : coffee **2** : café, bar — **caféine** [kafein] *nf* : caffeine — **cafetière** [kaftjɛr] *nf* : coffeepot — **cafétéria** [kafeterja] *nf* : cafeteria

cage [kaʒ] *nf* **1** : cage **2** ~ **d'escalier** : stairwell

cageot [kaʒo] *nm* : crate

cagnotte [kaɲɔt] *nf* : pool, kitty

cagoule [kagul] *nf* : hood

cahier [kaje] *nm* : notebook, exercise book

cahoter [kaɔte] *vi* : bump along — **cahoteux, -teuse** [kaɔtø, -tøz] *adj* : bumpy

cailler [kaje] *vi* **1** : curdle **2** : clot (of blood) — **caillot** [kajo] *nm* : clot

caillou [kaju] *nm, pl* **-loux** : pebble, stone

caisse [kɛs] *nf* **1** BOÎTE : box, crate **2** *or* ~ **enregistreuse** : cash register **3** ~ **d'épargne** : savings bank **4** ~ **populaire** *Can* : cooperative bank — **caissier, -sière** [kesje, -sjɛr] *n* **1** : cashier **2** : (bank) teller

cajoler [kaʒɔle] *vt* **1** : fuss over, cuddle **2** ENJÔLER : cajole

cajun [kaʒœ̃] *adj* : Cajun

cake [kɛk] *nm* : fruitcake

calamité [kalamite] *nf* : calamity

calcaire [kalkɛr] *nm* : limestone — ~ *adj* : chalky

calciner [kalsine] *vt* : char

calcium [kalsjɔm] *nm* : calcium

calculer [kalkyle] *vt* : calculate — **calcul** [kalkyl] *nm* **1** : calculation, sum **2** : arithmetic **3** ~ **biliaire** : gallstone — **calculateur, -trice** [kalkylatœr, -tris] *adj* : calculating — **calculatrice** *nf* : calculator

cale [kal] *nf* **1** : wedge **2** : hold (of a ship)

calé, -lée [kale] *adj fam* : brainy

calèche [kalɛʃ] *nf* : (horse-drawn) carriage

caleçon [kalsɔ̃] *nm* **1** : boxer shorts *pl* **2** : leggings *pl* **3** *or* ~**s de bain** : swimming trunks

calembour [kalɑ̃bur] *nm* : pun

calendrier [kalɑ̃drije] *nm* : calendar

calepin [kalpɛ̃] *nm* : notebook

caler [kale] *vt* : wedge — *vi* : stall (of an engine)

calibre [kalibr] *nm* **1** : caliber **2** : grade, size — **calibrer** [kalibre] *vt* : calibrate, grade

califourchon [kalifurʃɔ̃] **à** ~**s** *adv phr* : astride

câliner [kaline] *vt* : cuddle — **se câliner** *vr* : cuddle (up)

calmant, -mante [kalmɑ̃, -mɑ̃t] *adj* : soothing — **calmant** *nm* : sedative

calmar [kalmar] *nm* : squid

calme [kalm] *nm* **1** : calm **2 du** ~**!** : quiet down! — ~ *adj* : calm — **calmer** [kalme] *vt* : calm, soothe — **se calmer** *vr* : calm down

calomnie [kalɔmni] *nf* : slander, libel — **calomnier** [kalɔmnje] {96} *vt* : slander, libel

calorie [kalɔri] *nf* : calorie

calorifère [kalɔrifɛr] *nm* : heater, stove

calquer [kalke] *vt* **1** : trace (a drawing) **2** : copy, imitate — **calque** [kalk] *nm* : (exact) copy

calvaire [kalvɛr] *nm* : ordeal, suffering

calvitie [kalvisi] *nf* : baldness

camarade [kamarad] *nmf* **1** : friend **2** ~ **de classe** : classmate — **camaraderie** [kamaradri] *nf* : friendship

cambrer [kãbre] *vt* : curve, arch

cambrioler [kãbrijɔle] *vt* : burglarize — **cambriolage** [kãbrijɔlaʒ] *nm* : burglary — **cambrioleur, -leuse** [kãbrijɔlœr, -løz] *n* : burglar

cambrure [kãbryr] *nf* : arch, curve

camelot [kamlo] *nm Can* : paperboy

camelote [kamlɔt] *nf fam* : trash, junk

caméra [kamera] *nf* : movie or television camera

camion [kamjɔ̃] *nm* : truck — **camionnette** [kamjɔnɛt] *nf* : van — **camionneur, -neuse** [kamjɔnœr, -nøz] *n* : truck driver

camoufler [kamufle] *vt* : camouflage — **camouflage** [kamuflaʒ] *nm* : camouflage

camp [kã] *nm* **1** : camp **2** PARTI : side, team

campagne [kãpaɲ] *nf* **1** : country, countryside **2** : campaign (in politics, etc.) — **campagnard, -gnarde** [kãpaɲar, -ɲard] *adj* : country, rustic

camper [kãpe] *vi* : camp — **campement** [kãpmã] *nm* : encampment — **campeur, -peuse** [kãpœr, -pøz] *n* : camper — **camping** [kãpiŋ] *nm* **1** : camping **2** : campground

campus [kãpys] *nm* : campus

canadien, -dienne [kanadjɛ̃, -djɛn] *adj* : Canadian — **canadien–français, canadienne–française** *adj, pl* **canadiens–français, canadiennes–françaises** : French-Canadian

canal [kanal] *nm, pl* **-naux** [kano] **1** : canal **2** : channel

canapé [kanape] *nm* : sofa, couch

canard [kanar] *nm* : duck

canari [kanari] *nm* : canary

cancer [kãsɛr] *nm* : cancer — **cancéreux, -reuse** [kãserø, -røz] *adj* : cancerous

candeur [kãdœr] *nf* : ingenuousness

candidat, -date [kãdida, -dat] *n* : candidate — **candidature** [kãdidatyr] *nf* : candidacy

candide [kãdid] *adj* : ingenuous, naïve

cane [kan] *nf* : (female) duck — **caneton** [kantɔ̃] *nm* : duckling

canette [kanɛt] *nf* **1** : (small) bottle **2** : can (for a beverage)

caniche [kaniʃ] *nm* : poodle

canicule [kanikyl] *nf* : heat wave

canif [kanif] *nm* : pocketknife

canine [ˈkeɪˌnaɪn] *nf* : canine (tooth)

caniveau [kanivo] *nm, pl* **-veaux** : gutter (in a street)

canne [kan] *nf* **1** : cane **2** ~ **à pêche** : fishing rod **3** ~ **à sucre** : sugar-cane

canneberge [kanbɛrʒ] *nf* : cranberry

cannelle [kanɛl] *nf* : cinnamon

cannibale [kanibal] *nmf* : cannibal

canoë [kanɔe] *nm* : canoe

canon [kanɔ̃] *nm* **1** : cannon **2** : barrel (of a gun) **3** : canon, rule

canot [kano] *nm* **1** *France* : boat **2** *Can* : canoe **3** ~ **de sauvetage** : lifeboat

cantaloup [kãtalu] *nm* : cantaloupe

cantine [kãtin] *nf* : canteen, cafeteria

cantique [kãtik] *nm* : hymn

canton [kãtɔ̃] *nm* **1** *France* : district, canton **2** *Can* : township

canular [kanylar] *nm* : hoax

canyon [kaɲɔ̃] *nm* : canyon

caoutchouc [kautʃu] *nm* **1** : rubber **2** ~**s** *nmpl* : galoshes — **caoutchouteux, -teuse** [kautʃutø, -tøz] *adj* : rubbery

cap [kap] *nm* **1** PROMONTOIRE : cape **2** ÉTAPE : milestone

capable [kapabl] *adj* : capable

capacité [kapasite] *nf* **1** : capacity **2** APTITUDE : ability

cape [kap] *nf* : cape, cloak

capitaine [kapitɛn] *nm* : captain

capital, -tale [kapital] *adj, mpl* **-taux** [-to] **1** : major, crucial **2** **peine capitale** : capital punishment — **capital** *nm, pl* **-taux** : capital, assets *pl* — **capitale** *nf* : capital (city)

capitalisme [kapitalism] *nm* : capitalism — **capitaliste** [kapitalist] *adj* : capitalist(ic)

capiteux, -teuse [kapitø, -tøz] *adj* : heady

caporal–chef [kapɔralʃef] *nm, pl* **caporaux–chefs** [-ro] : corporal

capot [kapo] *nm* : hood (of an automobile) — **capoter** [kapɔte] *vt* : overturn, capsize

caprice [kapris] *nm* : whim — **capricieux, -cieuse** [kaprisjø, -sjøz] *adj* : temperamental

capsule [kapsyl] *nf* **1** : capsule **2** : cap (of a bottle)

capter [kapte] *vt* **1** : pick up (radio signals) **2** ~ **l'attention de** : capture the attention of

captif, -tive [kaptif, -tiv] *adj & n* : captive — **captiver** [kaptive] *vt* : captivate — **captivité** [kaptivite] *nf* : captivity

capture [kaptyr] *nf* **1** : capture, seizure **2** ATTRAPE : catch — **capturer** [kaptyre] *vt* : capture, catch

capuche [kapyʃ] *nf* : hood — **capuchon** [kapyʃɔ̃] *nm* **1** : hood **2** : cap, top (of a pen, etc.)

caqueter [kakte] {8} *vi* : cackle

car[1] [kar] *nm* : bus, coach

car[2] *conj* : for, because

carabine [karabin] *nf* : rifle

caractère [karaktɛr] *nm* **1** : letter, character **2** TEMPÉRAMENT : character, nature — **caractériser** [karakterize] *vt* : characterize — **caractéristique** [karakteristik] *adj & nf* : characteristic

carafe [karaf] *nf* : carafe, decanter

caramel [karamɛl] *nm* **1** : caramel **2** ~ **mou** : fudge

carapace [karapas] *nf* : shell

carat [kara] *nm* : carat, karat

caravane [karavan] *nf* **1** : caravan **2** : trailer

carbone [karbɔn] *nm* : carbon — **carboniser** [karbɔnize] *vt* : burn, char

carburant [karbyrɑ̃] *nm* : fuel — **carburateur** [karbyratœr] *nm* : carburetor

carcasse [karkas] *nf* : carcass

cardiaque [kardjak] *adj* : cardiac

cardigan [kardigɑ̃] *nm* : cardigan

cardinal, -nale [kardinal] *adj, mpl* **-naux** [-no] : cardinal, chief — **cardinal** *nm, pl* **-naux 1** : cardinal (in religion) **2** : cardinal number

carence [karɑ̃s] *nf* : lack, deficiency

caresser [karese] *vt* **1** : caress **2** : cherish, dream of — **caresse** [karɛs] *nf* : caress

cargaison [kargɛzɔ̃] *nf* : cargo, freight — **cargo** [kargo] *nm* : freighter

caricature [karikatyr] *nf* : caricature

carie [kari] *nf* : tooth decay, cavity

carillon [karijɔ̃] *nm* : bell, chime — **carillonner** [karijɔne] *v* : chime

carnage [karnaʒ] *nm* : carnage, bloodshed

carnaval [karnaval] *nm, pl* **-vals** : carnival

carnet [karnɛ] *nm* **1** : notebook **2** : book (of stamps, tickets, etc.)

carotte [karɔt] *nf* : carrot

carré, -rée [kare] *adj* **1** : square **2** : straightforward — **carré** *nm* : square

carreau [karo] *nm, pl* **-reaux 1** : tile **2** VITRE : windowpane **3** : diamond (in playing cards) **4 à ~x** : checkered

carrefour [karfur] *nm* : intersection, crossroads

carreler [karle] {8} *vt* : tile — **carrelage** [karlaʒ] *nm* : tiled floor

carrément [karemɑ̃] *adv* **1** : bluntly, directly **2** : downright

carrière [karjɛr] *nf* **1** : career **2** : stone quarry

carrosse [karɔs] *nm* : (horse-drawn) coach

carrure [karyr] *nf* : build (of the body)

carte [kart] *nf* **1** : card **2** : (road) map **3** : menu (in a restaurant) **4** *or* ~ **à jouer** : playing card **5** ~ **de crédit** : credit card **6** ~ **des vins** : wine list **7** ~ **postale** : postcard

cartilage [kartilaʒ] *nm* : cartilage, gristle

carton [kartɔ̃] *nm* **1** : cardboard **2** : cardboard box

cartouche [kartuʃ] *nf* : cartridge

cas [ka] *nms & pl* **1** : case **2 en aucun ~** : on no account **3 en ~ de** : in case of

cascade [kaskad] *nf* **1** : cascade, torrent **2** : waterfall

case [kaz] *nf* **1** : box (on a form) **2** ~ **postale** *Can* : post office box

caserne [kazɛrn] *nf* **1** *France* : barracks *pl* **2** ~ **de pompiers** *France* : fire station

casier [kazje] *nm* **1** : pigeonhole **2** ~ **judiciaire** : police record

casino [kazino] *nm* : casino

casque [kask] *nm* **1** : helmet **2** : headphones *pl* — **casquette** [kaskɛt] *nf* : cap

casser [kase] *v* : break — **se casser** *vr* **1** : break (one's leg, etc.) **2 casse-toi!** *fam* : get out of here! — **cassable** [kasabl] *adj* : breakable — **casse-croûte** [kaskrut] *nms & pl* **1** : snack **2** *Can* : snack bar — **casse-noix** [kasnwa] *nms & pl* : nutcracker

casserole [kasrɔl] *nf* : saucepan

casse-tête [kastɛt] *nms & pl* **1** : puzzle **2** PROBLÈME : headache

cassette [kasɛt] *nf* : cassette

cassonade [kasɔnad] *nf* : brown sugar

cassure [kasyr] *nf* : break

castor [kastɔr] *nm* : beaver

catalogue [katalɔg] *nm* : catalog

cataracte [katarakt] *nf* : cataract

catastrophe [katastrɔf] *nf* : catastrophe — **catastrophique** [katastrɔfik] *adj* : catastrophic

catéchisme [kateʃism] *nm* : catechism

catégorie [kategɔri] *nf* : category — **catégorique** [kategɔrik] *adj* : categorical

cathédrale [katedral] *nf* : cathedral

catholique [katɔlik] *adj* : Catholic — **catholicisme** [katɔlisism] *nm* : Catholicism

catimini [katimini] **en ~** *adv phr* : on the sly

cauchemar [koʃmar] *nm* : nightmare

cause [koz] *nf* **1** : cause, reason **2** : (legal) case **3 à ~ de** : because of, on account of — **causer** [koze] *vt* PROVOQUER : cause — *vi* : chat — **causerie** [kozri] *nf* : talk, chat

caution [kosjɔ̃] *nf* **1** : surety, guarantee **2 libérer sous ~** : release on bail

cavalerie [kavalri] *nf* : cavalry — **cavalier, -lière** [kavalje, -ljɛr] *n* : rider, horseman *m*, horsewoman *f* — **cavalier** *nm* : knight (in chess)

cave [kav] *nf* : cellar

caverne [kavɛrn] *nf* GROTTE : cavern, cave

caviar [kavjar] *nm* : caviar

cavité [kavite] *nf* : cavity, hollow

CD [sede] *nm* (compact disc) : CD

ce [sə] (**cet** [sɛt] *before a vowel or mute h*), **cette** [sɛt] *adj, pl* **ces** [se] **1** : this, that, these, those **2 cette fois-ci** : this time **3 cette idée!** : what an idea! — **ce** (**c'** [s] *be-*

fore a vowel) *pron* **1** : it, that, these, those **2**
~ que, **~ qui**, **~ dont** : what, which **3**
c'est : it is **4 ce sont** : they are **5 c'est**
cela : that's right

ceci [səsil] *pron* : this

cécité [sesite] *nf* : blindness

céder [sede] {87} *vt* : give up, yield — *vi*
: give in

cédille [sedij] *nf* : cedilla

cèdre [sɛdr] *nm* : cedar

cégep [seʒɛp] *nm* (collège d'enseignement
général et professionnel) *Can* : junior college

ceinture [sɛ̃tyr] *nf* **1** : belt **2 ~ de sauvetage** : life belt **3 ~ de sécurité** : safety
belt

cela [səla] *pron* : that, it

célébrer [selebre] {87} *vt* : celebrate —
célébration [selebrasjɔ̃] *nf* : celebration —
célèbre [selɛbr] *adj* : famous — **célébrité**
[selebrite] *nf* **1** : fame, renown **2** : celebrity
(person)

céleri [sɛlri] *nm* : celery

céleste [selɛst] *adj* : heavenly

célibataire [selibater] *adj* : single, unmarried — **~** *nmf* : single person

celle, celles → celui

cellule [selyl] *nf* : cell

celui [səlɥi], **celle** [sɛl] *pron, pl* **ceux** [sø],
celles [sɛl] : the one(s), those — **celui-ci**
[səlɥisi], **celle-ci** [sɛlsi] *pron, pl* **ceux-ci**
[søsi], **celles-ci** [sɛlsi] **1** : this (one), these
2 : the latter — **celui-là** [səlɥila], **celle-là**
[sɛlla] *pron, pl* **ceux-là** [søla], **celles-là**
[sɛlla] **1** : that (one), those **2** : the former

cendre [sãdr] *nf* : ash — **cendrier** [sãdrije]
nm : ashtray

censé, -sée [sãse] *adj* **être ~ faire** : be sup-
posed to do

censurer [sãsyre] *vt* : censor, ban — **censure** [sãsyr] *nf* **1** : censorship **2** : censure

cent [sã] *adj* : a hundred, one hundred — **~**
nm **1** : hundred **2** : cent **3 pour ~** : percent — **centaine** [sãten] *nf* : about a hundred — **centenaire** [sãtner] *adj* : hundred-
year-old — **~** *nm* : centennial — **centième**
[sãtjem] *adj & nmf & nm* : hundredth

centigrade [sãtigrad] *adj* : centigrade

centime [sãtim] *nm* : centime

centimètre [sãtimɛtr] *nm* **1** : centimeter **2**
: tape measure

central, -trale [sãtral] *adj, mpl* **-traux** [sãtro]
: central — **central** *nm* **~ téléphonique**
: telephone exchange — **centrale** *nf* **1**
: power plant **2 ~ syndicale** : labor union
— **centraliser** [sãtralize] *vt* : centralize

centre [sãtr] *nm* **1** : center **2 ~ commercial** : shopping center — **centrer** [sãtre] *vt*
: center — **centre-ville** [sãtrəvil] *nm, pl*
centres-villes : downtown

cependant [səpãdã] *conj* : however, yet

céramique [seramik] *nf* : ceramics

cerceau [sɛrso] *nm, pl* **-ceaux** : hoop

cercle [sɛrkl] *nm* **1** : circle **2** : group (of
friends, etc.)

cercueil [sɛrkœil] *nm* : coffin

céréale [sereal] *nf* : cereal

cérémonie [seremɔni] *nf* **1** : ceremony **2**
sans ~ : informally

cerf [sɛr] *nm* : stag

cerf-volant [sɛrvolã] *nm, pl* **cerfs-volants**
: kite

cerise [səriz] *nf* : cherry — **cerisier** [sərizje]
nm : cherry tree

cerner [sɛrne] *vt* **1** : surround **2** DÉFINIR
: define, determine — **cerne** [sɛrn] *nm* **avoir
des ~s** : have rings under one's eyes

certain, -taine [sɛrtɛ̃, -tɛn] *adj* **1** : certain,
sure **2** : certain, some — **certainement**
[sɛrtɛnmã] *adv* : certainly — **certains, cer-
taines** [sɛrtɛ̃, -tɛn] *pron pl* : some (people),
certain (ones)

certes [sɛrt] *adv* : of course, indeed

certifier [sɛrtifje] {96} *vt* : certify — **certificat** [sɛrtifika] *nm* : certificate

certitude [sɛrtityd] *nf* : certainty

cerveau [sɛrvo] *nm, pl* **-veaux** : brain

ces → ce

cesser [sese] *v* : cease, stop — **cesse** [sɛs] *nf*
sans ~ : constantly — **cessez-le-feu**
[seselfø] *nms & pl* : cease-fire

c'est-à-dire [sɛtadir] *conj* : that is (to say)

cet, cette → ce — ceux → celui — ceux-ci
→ celui-ci — ceux-là → celui-là

chacun, chacune [ʃakœ̃, -kyn] *pron* **1**
: each (one) **2** : everybody, everyone

chagrin [ʃagrɛ̃] *nm* PEINE : grief, sorrow —
chagriner [ʃagrine] *vt* : grieve, distress

chahut [ʃay] *nm* : uproar, din

chaîne [ʃɛn] *nf* **1** : chain **2** : (television)
channel **3** : (stereo) system — **chaînon**
[ʃɛnɔ̃] *nm* : link

chair [ʃɛr] *nf* **1** : flesh **2** : meat **3 ~ de
poule** : goose bumps

chaire [ʃɛr] *nf* **1** : (university) chair **2** : pulpit

chaise [ʃɛz] *nf* **1** : chair, seat **2 ~ roulante**
: wheelchair

chaland [ʃalã] *nm* : barge

châle [ʃal] *nm* : shawl

chalet [ʃalɛ] *nm* **1** : chalet **2** *Can* : cottage

chaleur [ʃalœr] *nf* **1** : heat **2** : warmth —
chaleureux, -reuse [ʃalœrø, -røz] *adj*
: warm, friendly

chaloupe [ʃalup] *nf* : rowboat

chamailler [ʃamaje] *v* **se chamailler** *vr*
: bicker

chambarder [ʃãbarde] *vt fam* : mess up

chambre [ʃãbr] *nf* **1** : room, bedroom **2**
: (legislative) chamber, house

chameau [ʃamo] *nm, pl* **-meaux** : camel**

champ [ʃɑ̃] *nm* **1** : field **2** ~ **de bataille** : battlefield **3** ~ **de courses** : racetrack
champagne [ʃɑ̃paɲ] *nm* : champagne
champêtre [ʃɑ̃pɛtr] *adj* : rural
champignon [ʃɑ̃piɲɔ̃] *nm* : mushroom
champion, -pionne [ʃɑ̃pjɔ̃, -pjɔn] *n* : champion — **championnat** [ʃɑ̃pjɔna] *nm* : championship
chance [ʃɑ̃s] *nf* **1** : luck, fortune **2** POSSIBILITÉ : chance, possibility **3 par** ~ : fortunately
chanceler [ʃɑ̃sle] {8} *vi* : stagger — **chancelant, -lante** [ʃɑ̃slɑ̃, -lɑ̃t] *adj* : unsteady
chancelier [ʃɑ̃səlje] *nm* : chancellor
chanceux, -ceuse [ʃɑ̃sø, -søz] *adj* : lucky
chandail [ʃɑ̃daj] *nm* : sweater
chandelle [ʃɑ̃dɛl] *nf* : candle — **chandelier** [ʃɑ̃dəlje] *nm* : candlestick
changer [ʃɑ̃ʒe] {17} *vt* **1** REMPLACER : change **2** MODIFIER : alter — *vi* **1** ~ **de** : change **2** ~ **d'avis** : change one's mind — **se changer** *vr* : change one's clothes — **change** [ʃɑ̃ʒ] *nm* : exchange (in finance) — **changement** [ʃɑ̃ʒmɑ̃] *nm* : change
chanson [ʃɑ̃sɔ̃] *nf* : song — **chant** [ʃɑ̃] *nm* **1** : song, hymn **2** : singing
chantage [ʃɑ̃taʒ] *nm* : blackmail
chanter [ʃɑ̃te] *v* **1** : sing **2 faire** ~ : blackmail — **chanteur, -teuse** [ʃɑ̃tœr, -tøz] *n* : singer
chantier [ʃɑ̃tje] *nm* **1** : (construction) site **2** ~ **naval** : shipyard
chantonner [ʃɑ̃tɔne] *v* : hum
chanvre [ʃɑ̃vr] *nm* : hemp
chaos [kao] *nm* : chaos — **chaotique** [kaɔtik] *adj* : chaotic
chapeau [ʃapo] *nm, pl* **-peaux** : hat, cap
chapelet [ʃaplɛ] *nm* : rosary
chapelle [ʃapɛl] *nf* : chapel
chapelure [ʃaplyr] *nf* : bread crumbs *pl*
chaperon [ʃaprɔ̃] *nm* : chaperon
chapiteau [ʃapito] *nm, pl* **-teaux** : circus tent
chapitre [ʃapitr] *nm* **1** : chapter (of a book) **2** : subject matter
chaque [ʃak] *adj* : each, every
char [ʃar] *nm* **1** : chariot **2** : cart, wagon, float (in a parade) **3** ~ **d'assaut** : tank
charabia [ʃarabja] *nm fam* : gibberish
charbon [ʃarbɔ̃] *nm* **1** : coal **2** ~ **de bois** : charcoal
charcuterie [ʃarkytri] *nf* **1** : delicatessen **2** : cooked pork products
charger [ʃarʒe] {17} *vt* **1** : load **2** : charge (a battery) **3** ~ **de** : put in charge of — **se charger** *vr* ~ **de** : take care of — **charge** [ʃarʒ] *nf* **1** : load **2** RESPONSABILITÉ : responsibility **3** : (electrical) charge **4** FONCTION : office **5** ~**s** : costs **6 à la** ~ **de** : dependent on — **chargé, -gée** [ʃarʒe] *adj*

: busy — **chargement** [ʃarʒəmɑ̃] *nm* **1** : loading **2** : load, cargo
chariot [ʃarjo] *nm* : cart, wagon
charisme [karism] *nm* : charisma — **charismatique** [-rismatik] *adj* : charismatic
charité [ʃarite] *nf* : charity — **charitable** [ʃaritabl] *adj* : charitable
charlatan [ʃarlatɑ̃] *nm* : charlatan
charmer [ʃarme] *vt* : charm — **charmant, -mante** [ʃarmɑ̃, -mɑ̃t] *adj* : charming, delightful — **charme** [ʃarm] *nm* : charm, attraction — **charmeur, -meuse** [ʃarmœr, -møz] *adj* : charming — ~ *n* : charmer
charnière [ʃarnjɛr] *nf* : hinge
charnu, -nue [ʃarny] *adj* : fleshy
charpente [ʃarpɑ̃t] *nf* **1** : framework **2** : build (of the body) — **charpentier** [ʃarpɑ̃tje] *nm* : carpenter
charrette [ʃarɛt] *nf* : cart
charrue [ʃary] *nf* : plow
charte [ʃart] *nf* : charter — **charter** [ʃarte] *nm* : charter flight
chas [ʃa] *nm* : eye (of a needle)
chasser [ʃase] *vt* **1** : hunt **2** EXPULSER : chase away — **chasse** [ʃas] *nf* **1** : hunting **2** POURSUITE : chase **3** *or* ~ **d'eau** : flush (of a toilet) — **chasse-neige** [ʃasnɛʒ] *nms & pl* : snowplow — **chasseur, -seuse** [ʃasœr, -søz] *n* : hunter
châssis [ʃasi] *nm* : frame (of a window)
chaste [ʃast] *adj* : chaste — **chasteté** [ʃastəte] *nf* : chastity
chat, chatte [ʃa, ʃat] *n* : cat
châtaigne [ʃatɛɲ] *nf* : chestnut
château [ʃato] *nm, pl* **-teaux 1** : castle **2** ~ **fort** : stronghold
châtier [ʃatje] {96} *vt* : chastise — **châtiment** [ʃatimɑ̃] *nm* : punishment
chaton [ʃatɔ̃] *nm* : kitten
chatouiller [ʃatuje] *vt* : tickle — **chatouilleux, -leuse** [ʃatujø, -jøz] *adj* : ticklish
châtrer [ʃatre] *vt* : castrate
chatte → **chat**
chaud, chaude [ʃo, ʃod] *adj* : warm, hot — **chaud** [ʃo] *adv* **1 avoir** ~ : feel warm or hot **2 il fait** ~ : it's warm, it's hot — ~ *nm* : heat, warmth — **chaudière** [ʃodjɛr] *nf* : boiler — **chaudron** [ʃodrɔ̃] *nm* : cauldron
chauffage [ʃofaʒ] *nm* : heating
chauffard [ʃofar] *nm* : reckless driver
chauffer [ʃofe] *vt* : heat, warm — *vi* : warm up — **se chauffer** *vr* : warm (oneself) up
chauffeur [ʃofœr] *nm* : driver, chauffeur
chaussée [ʃose] *nf* : roadway
chausser [ʃose] *vt* **1** : put on (shoes) **2** ~ **du 7** : take size 7 (in shoes) — **chaussette** [ʃosɛt] *nf* : sock — **chausson** [ʃosɔ̃] *nm* **1** : slipper **2** ~ **aux pommes** : apple turnover — **chaussure** [ʃosyr] *nf* : shoe, footwear

chauve [ʃov] *adj* : bald — **chauve–souris** [ʃovsuri] *nf, pl* **chauves–souris** : bat (animal)

chauvin, -vine [ʃovɛ̃, -vin] *adj* : chauvinistic

chaux [ʃo] *nf* **1** : lime **2 lait de ~** ... à ... white wash

chavirer [ʃavire] *v* : capsize

chef [ʃɛf] *nm* **1** : leader, head, chief **2** *or* **~ cuisinier** : chef **3 ~ d'orchestre** : conductor **4 en ~** : (in) chief — **chef–d'œuvre** [ʃɛdœvr] *nm, pl* **chefs–d'œuvre** : masterpiece

chemin [ʃəmɛ̃] *nm* **1** : road, path **2 ~ de fer** : railroad

cheminée [ʃəmine] *nf* **1** : fireplace **2** : chimney

cheminer [ʃəmine] *vi* **1** : walk along **2** PROGRESSER : progress

chemise [ʃəmiz] *nf* **1** : shirt **2** DOSSIER : folder **3 ~ de nuit** : nightgown — **chemisier** [ʃəmizje] *nm* : blouse

chenal [ʃənal] *nm, pl* **-naux** [ʃəno] : channel

chêne [ʃɛn] *nm* : oak

chenille [ʃənij] *nf* : caterpillar

chèque [ʃɛk] *nm* : check

cher, chère [ʃɛr] *adj* **1** : dear, beloved **2** COÛTEUX : expensive — **~** *n* **mon cher, ma chère** : my dear — **cher** *adv* **coûter ~** : cost a lot

chercher [ʃɛrʃe] *vt* : look for, seek — **chercheur, -cheuse** [ʃɛrʃœr, -ʃøz] *n* : researcher

chérir [ʃerir] *vt* : cherish — **chéri, -rie** [ʃeri] *adj & n* : darling, dear

chétif, -tive [ʃetif, -tiv] *adj* : puny, weak

cheval [ʃəval] *nm, pl* **-vaux** [ʃəvo] **1** : horse **2** *or* **cheval–vapeur** : horsepower

chevalerie [ʃəvalri] *nf* : chivalry

chevalet [ʃəvalɛ] *nm* : easel

chevalier [ʃəvalje] *nm* : knight

chevaucher [ʃəvoʃe] *vt* **1** : straddle **2** : overlap — **se chevaucher** *vr* : overlap

chevelure [ʃəvlyr] *nf* : hair — **chevelu, -lue** [ʃəvly] *adj* : hairy

chevet [ʃəvɛ] *nm* : bedside

cheveu [ʃəvø] *nm, pl* **-veux 1** POIL : hair **2 ~x** *nmpl* : (head of) hair

cheville [ʃəvij] *nf* : ankle

chèvre [ʃɛvr] *nf* : goat — **chevreau** [ʃəvro] *nm, pl* **-vreaux** : kid (goat)

chevreuil [ʃəvrœj] *nm* : roe deer

chevron [ʃəvrɔ̃] *nm* : rafter

chez [ʃe] *prep* **1** : at (the house of) **2** PARMI : among, in **3 ~ soi** : at home

chez–soi [ʃeswa] *nms & pl* : home

chic [ʃik] *adj s & pl* **1** : stylish **2** SYMPATHIQUE : nice

chicane [ʃikan] *nf* : squabble

chicorée [ʃikɔre] *nf* **1** : endive **2** : chicory (for coffee)

chien, chienne [ʃjɛ̃, -ʃjɛn] *n* : dog, bitch *f*

chiffon [ʃifɔ̃] *nm* : rag — **chiffonner** [ʃifɔne] *vt* : crumple

chiffre [ʃifr] *nm* **1** : figure, numeral **2** : amount, sum (in finance) **3** CODE : code **4 ~ d'affaires** : turnover — **chiffrer** [ʃifre] *vt* : calculate, assess — **se chiffrer** *vr* **~ à** : amount to

chignon [ʃiɲɔ̃] *nm* : (hair) bun

chimie [ʃimi] *nf* : chemistry — **chimique** [ʃimik] *adj* : chemical — **chimiste** [ʃimist] *nmf* : chemist

chimpanzé [ʃɛ̃pɑ̃ze] *nm* : chimpanzee

chinois, -noise [ʃinwa, -nwaz] *adj* : Chinese — **chinois** *nm* : Chinese (language)

chiot [ʃjo] *nm* : puppy

chips [ʃips] *nfpl* : potato chips

chirurgie [ʃiryrʒi] *nf* : surgery — **chirurgical, -cale** [ʃiryrʒikal] *adj, mpl* **-caux** [-ko] : surgical — **chirurgien, -gienne** [ʃiryrʒjɛ̃, -ʒjɛn] *n* : surgeon

chlore [klɔr] *nm* : chlorine

choc [ʃɔk] *nm* **1** : shock **2** : impact, crash

chocolat [ʃɔkɔla] *nm* : chocolate

chœur [kœr] *nm* **1** : choir **2** : chorus

choir [ʃwar] {18} *vi* : drop, fall

choisir [ʃwazir] *vt* : choose — **choix** [ʃwa] *nm* **1** : choice **2 de ~** : choice, first-rate

cholestérol [kɔlɛsterɔl] *nm* : cholesterol

chômage [ʃomaʒ] *nm* : unemployment — **chômeur, -meuse** [ʃomœr, -møz] *n* : unemployed person

choquer [ʃɔke] *vt* : shock, offend — **choquant, -quante** [ʃɔkɑ̃, -kɑ̃t] *adj* : shocking

choral, -rale [kɔral] *adj, mpl* **-rals** *or* **-raux** [kɔro] : choral — **chorale** *nf* : choir

chose [ʃoz] *nf* **1** : thing **2** AFFAIRE : matter

chou [ʃu] *nm, pl* **choux** : cabbage — **chou-chou, -choute** [ʃuʃu, -ʃut] *n fam* : pet, favorite — **choucroute** [ʃukrut] *nf* : sauerkraut

chouette [ʃwɛt] *nf* : owl — **~** *adj fam* : terrific, neat

chou–fleur [ʃuflœr] *nm, pl* **choux–fleurs** : cauliflower

choyer [ʃwaje] {58} *vt* : pamper

chrétien, -tienne [kretjɛ̃, -tjɛn] *adj & n* : Christian — **christianisme** [kristjanism] *nm* : Christianity

chrome [krom] *nm* **1** : chromium **2 ~s** *nmpl* : chrome

chronique [krɔnik] *adj* : chronic — **~** *nf* : (newspaper) column, (televison) report — **chroniqueur, -queuse** [krɔnikœr, -køz] *n* : columnist

chronologie [krɔnɔlɔʒi] *nf* : chronology — **chronologique** [krɔnɔlɔʒik] *adj* : chronological

chronomètre [krɔnɔmɛtr] *nm* : stopwatch

— **chronométrer** [krɔnɔmetre] {87} *vt*
: time

chuchoter [ʃyʃɔte] *v* : whisper — **chuchotement** [ʃyʃɔtmɑ̃] *nm* : whisper

chum [tʃɔm] *nm Can fam* : boyfriend

chut [ʃyt] *interj* : sh!, hush!

chute [ʃyt] *nf* **1** : fall **2** *or* ~ **d'eau** : waterfall **3** ~ **de pluie** : rainfall

ci [si] *adv* **1 ce livre-ci** : this book **2 cette fois-ci** : this time **3 ceux-ci** : these ones **4 par-ci par-là** : here and there — ~ *pron* **1** ~ **et ça** : this and that **2** → **comme** — **ci–après** [siaprɛ] *adv* : hereafter — **ci–bas** [siba] *adv* : below

cible [sibl] *nf* : target

ciboule [sibul] *nf* : scallion — **ciboulette** [sibulɛt] *nf* : chive

cicatrice [sikatris] *nf* : scar — **cicatriser** [sikatrize] *v* **se cicatriser** *vr* : heal (up)

ci–contre [sikɔ̃tr] *adv* : opposite

ci–dessous [sidəsu] *adv* : below

ci–dessus [sidəsy] *adv* : above

cidre [sidr] *nm* : cider

ciel [sjɛl] *nm* **1** *pl* **ciels** : sky **2** *pl* **cieux** [sjø] : heaven

cierge [sjɛrʒ] *nm* : candle (in a church)

cigare [sigar] *nm* : cigar — **cigarette** [sigarɛt] *nf* : cigarette

cigogne [sigɔɲ] *nf* : stork

ci–inclus, -cluse [siɛ̃kly, -klyz] *adj* : enclosed — **ci–inclus** [siɛ̃kly] *adv* : enclosed

ci–joint, -jointe [siʒwɛ̃, -ʒwɛ̃t] *adj* : enclosed — **ci–joint** [siʒwɛ̃] *adv* : enclosed, herewith

cil [sil] *nm* : eyelash

cime [sim] *nf* : summit, peak

ciment [simɑ̃] *nm* : cement

cimetière [simtjɛr] *nm* : cemetery

cinéaste [sineast] *nmf* : film director

cinéma [sinema] *nm* **1** : movie theater **2 aller au** ~ : go to the movies

cinglant, -glante [sɛ̃glɑ̃, -glɑ̃t] *adj* : cutting, biting

cinq [sɛ̃k] *adj* **1** : five **2** : fifth (in dates) — ~ *nms & pl* : five

cinquante [sɛ̃kɑ̃t] *adj & nms & pl* : fifty — **cinquantaine** [sɛ̃kɑ̃tɛn] *nf* **une** ~ **de** : about fifty — **cinquantième** [sɛ̃kɑ̃tjɛm] *adj & nmf & nm* : fiftieth

cinquième [sɛ̃kjɛm] *adj & nmf & nm* : fifth

cintre [sɛ̃tr] *nm* : coat hanger

cirage [siraʒ] *nm* : shoe polish

circoncire [sirkɔ̃sir] {86} *vt* : circumcise — **circoncision** [sirkɔ̃sizjɔ̃] *nf* : circumcision

circonférence [sirkɔ̃ferɑ̃s] *nf* : circumference

circonflexe [sirkɔ̃flɛks] *adj* **accent** ~ : circumflex (accent)

circonscrire [sirkɔ̃skrir] {33} *vt* : limit, contain — **circonscription** [sirkɔ̃skripsjɔ̃] *nf* : district, ward

circonspect, -specte [sirkɔ̃spɛ, -spɛkt] *adj* : cautious, circumspect

circonstance [sirkɔ̃stɑ̃s] *nf* : circumstance, occasion

circuit [sirkɥi] *nm* **1** : circuit **2** *or* **coup de** ~ *Can* : home run (in baseball)

circulaire [sirkyler] *adj & nf* : circular

circuler [sirkyle] *vi* **1** : circulate **2** SE DÉPLACER : move (along) **3** : run (of buses, etc.) **4 faire** ~ **des bruits** : spread rumors — **circulation** [sirkylasjɔ̃] *nf* **1** : circulation **2** : traffic

cire [sir] *nf* : wax — **ciré** [sire] *nm* : oilskin — **cirer** [sire] *vt* : wax, polish

cirque [sirk] *nm* **1** : circus **2** *fam* : chaos

cisailles [sizaj] *nfpl* : shears

ciseau [sizo] *nm, pl* **-seaux 1** : chisel **2** ~**x** *nmpl* : scissors — **ciseler** [sizle] {20} *vt* : chisel

citadelle [sitadɛl] *nf* : citadel

citadin, -dine [sitadɛ̃, -din] *n* : city dweller

citation [sitasjɔ̃] *nf* **1** : quotation **2** : summons (in law)

cité [site] *nf* **1** : city **2** ~ **universitaire** *France* : college dormitories *pl* **3** ~ **universitaire** *Can* : college campus

citer [site] *vt* **1** : quote **2** MENTIONNER : name, cite

citerne [sitɛrn] *nf* : tank, reservoir

citoyen, citoyenne [sitwajɛ̃, -jɛn] *n* : citizen — **citoyenneté** [sitwajɛnte] *nf* : citizenship

citron [sitrɔ̃] *nm* : lemon — **citronnade** [sitrɔnad] *nf* : lemonade

citrouille [sitruj] *nf* : pumpkin

civière [sivjɛr] *nf* : stretcher

civil, -vile [sivil] *adj* **1** : civil **2** : secular — ~ *n* : civilian — **civilisation** [sivilizasjɔ̃] *nf* : civilization — **civiliser** [sivilize] *vt* : civilize — **civilité** [sivilite] *nf* : civility

civique [sivik] *adj* : civic

clair, claire [klɛr] *adj* **1** : clear **2** LUMINEUX : bright **3** PÂLE : light-colored — **clair** *adv* : clearly — **clair** [klɛr] *nm* **1** ~ **de lune** : moonlight **2 mettre au** ~ : make clear — **clairement** [klɛrmɑ̃] *adv* : clearly — **clairière** [klɛrjɛr] *nf* : clearing

clairon [klɛrɔ̃] *nm* : bugle

clairsemé, -mée [klɛrsəme] *adj* : scattered, sparse

clamer [klame] *vt* : proclaim — **clameur** [klamœr] *nf* : clamor

clan [klɑ̃] *nm* : clan, clique

clandestin, -tine [klɑ̃dɛstɛ̃, -tin] *adj* **1** : clandestine **2 passager** ~ : stowaway

clapier [klapje] *nm* : (rabbit) hutch

clapoter [klapɔte] *vi* : lap (of waves)

claque [klak] *nf* **1** : slap, smack **2** ~**s** *nfpl Can* : rubbers, galoshes — **claquement** [klakmɑ̃] *nm* : bang(ing), slam(ming) — **claquer** [klake] *vt* **1** GIFLER : slap **2** : slam (a door) — *vi* **1 faire ∼ ses doigts** : snap one's fingers **2 il claque des dents** : his teeth are chattering — **claquettes** [klakɛt] *nfpl* : tap dancing

clarifier [klarifje] {96} *vt* : clarify — **clarification** [-rifikasjɔ̃] *nf* : clarification

clarinette [klarinɛt] *nf* : clarinet

clarté [klarte] *nf* **1** : light, brightness **2** NETTETÉ : clarity

classe [klas] *nf* **1** : class, category **2** : classroom **3 aller en ∼** : go to school — **classement** [klasmɑ̃] *nm* **1** : classification **2** RANG : ranking, place — **classer** [klase] *vt* : class, classify — **se classer** *vr* : rank — **classeur** [klasœr] *nm* **1** : binder **2** : filing cabinet

classifier [klasifje] {96} *vt* : classify — **classification** [klasifikasjɔ̃] *nf* : classification

classique [klasik] *adj* : classic(al) — **∼** *nm* : classic (of a book, etc.)

clause [kloz] *nf* : clause

claustrophobie [klostrɔfɔbi] *nf* : claustrophobia

clavecin [klavsɛ̃] *nm* : harpsichord

clavicule [klavikyl] *nf* : collarbone

clavier [klavje] *nm* : keyboard

clé *or* **clef** [kle] *nf* **1** : key **2** : clef (in music) **3 ∼ anglaise** : monkey wrench — **∼** *adj* : key

clément, -mente [klemɑ̃, -mɑ̃t] *adj* **1** : lenient **2** DOUX : mild, clement — **clémence** [klemɑ̃s] *nf* : leniency

clémentine [klemɑ̃tin] *nf* : tangerine

clenche [klɑ̃ʃ] *nf* : latch

clergé [klɛrʒe] *nm* : clergy

clérical, -cale [klerikal] *adj, mpl* **-caux** [-ko] : clerical

cliché [kliʃe] *nm* : cliché

client, cliente [kliɑ̃, kliɑ̃t] *n* **1** : customer, client **2** : patient — **clientèle** [kliɑ̃tɛl] *nf* **1** : customers *pl* **2** : practice (of a doctor)

cligner [kliɲe] *vi* **1 ∼ de l'œil** : wink **2 ∼ des yeux** : blink — **clignotant** [kliɲɔtɑ̃] *nm* : blinker, directional signal — **clignoter** [kliɲɔte] *vi* **1** : flicker, flash **2 →** **cligner 2**

climat [klima] *nm* : climate — **climatisation** [klimatizasjɔ̃] *nf* : air-conditioning — **climatisé, -sée** [klimatize] *adj* : air-conditioned — **climatiseur** [klimatizœr] *nm* : air conditioner

clin [klɛ̃] *nm* **1 ∼ d'œil** : wink **2 en un ∼ d'œil** : in a flash

clinique [klinik] *nf* : clinic — **∼** *adj* : clinical

cliquer [klike] *vi* : click (on a computer)

cliqueter [klikte] {8} *vi* : clink, jingle, clack — **cliquetis** [klikti] *nm* : jingle, clatter

clochard, -charde [klɔʃar, -ʃard] *n* : tramp

cloche [klɔʃ] *nf* : bell — **clocher** [klɔʃe] *nm* : belfry, steeple

cloison [klwazɔ̃] *nf* : partition — **cloisonner** [klwazɔne] *vt* : partition (off)

cloître [klwatr] *nm* : cloister

cloque [klɔk] *nf* : blister

clore [klɔr] {19} *vt* : close, conclude — **clos, close** [klo, -kloz] *adj* : closed, shut — **clôture** [klotyr] *nf* **1** : fence **2** : end, closure — **clôturer** [klotyre] *vt* **1** : enclose **2** : bring to a close

clou [klu] *nm, pl* **∼s 1** : nail **2** : high point **3** FURONCLE : boil **4 ∼ de girofle** : clove — **clouer** [klue] *vt* **1** : nail **2** : pin down

clown [klun] *nm* : clown

club [klœb] *nm* : club

coaguler [kɔagyle] *v* : coagulate — **se coaguler** *vr* : coagulate, clot

coalition [kɔalisjɔ̃] *nf* : coalition

coasser [kɔase] *vi* : croak

cobaye [kɔbaj] *nm* : guinea pig

cocaïne [kɔkain] *nf* : cocaine

cocasse [kɔkas] *adj* : comical

coccinelle [kɔksinɛl] *nf* : ladybug

cocher [kɔʃe] *vt* : check (off)

cochon [kɔʃɔ̃] *nm* **1** : pig **2 ∼ d'Inde** : guinea pig — **cochonnerie** [kɔʃɔnri] *nf* : junk, trash

cocktail [kɔktɛl] *nm* : cocktail

coco [kɔkɔ] *nm or* **noix de ∼** : coconut — **cocotier** [kɔkɔtje] *nm* : coconut palm

cocon [kɔkɔ̃] *nm* : cocoon

cocotte [kɔkɔt] *nf* : casserole dish

code [kɔd] *nm* **1** : code **2 ∼ postal** : zip code — **coder** [kɔde] *vt* : code, encode

coéquipier, -pière [kɔekipje, -jɛr] *n* : teammate

cœur [kœr] *nm* **1** : heart **2** : center, core **3** : hearts *pl* (in playing cards) **4** COURAGE : courage **5 à ∼ joie** : to one's heart's content **6 avoir mal au ∼** : feel sick, feel nauseous **7 de bon ∼** : willingly

coffre [kɔfr] *nm* **1** : (toy) chest **2** COFFRE-FORT : safe **3** : trunk (of a car) — **coffre–fort** [kɔfrəfɔr] *nm, pl* **coffres–forts** : safe — **coffret** [kɔfrɛ] *nm* : small box, case

cognac [kɔɲak] *nm* : cognac

cogner [kɔɲe] *vt* : knock, bang — *vi* : knock — **se cogner** *vr* **1** : bump oneself **2 ∼ la tête** : hit one's head

cohabiter [kɔabite] *vi* : live together

cohérent, -rente [kɔerɑ̃, -rɑ̃t] *adj* : coherent — **cohérence** [-erɑ̃s] *nf* : coherence

cohue [kɔy] *nf* : crowd

coiffe [kwaf] *nf* : headdress — **coiffer** [kwafe] *v* **se coiffer** *vr* : do one's hair — **coiffeur, -feuse** [kwafœr, -føz] *n* : hairdresser — **coiffure** [kwafyr] *nf* **1** : hairdo **2** : hairdressing

coin [kwɛ̃] *nm* **1** : corner **2** ENDROIT : place, spot

coincer [kwɛ̃se] {6} vt 1 : wedge, jam 2 fam : corner, nab — vi : get stuck

coïncider [koɛ̃side] vi : coïncide — coïncidence [koɛ̃sidɑ̃s] nf : coïncidence

col [kɔl] nm 1 : collar 2 : neck (of a bottle)

colère [kɔlɛr] nf 1 : anger 2 se mettre en ~ : get angry — coléreux, -reuse [kɔlerø, -røz] adj : bad-tempered, irritable — colérique [kɔlerik] adj : bad-tempered

colimaçon [kɔlimasõ] nm 1 : snail 2 escalier en ~ : spiral staircase

colique [kɔlik] nf 1 : diarrhea 2 or ~s nfpl : colic

colis [kɔli] nms & pl : parcel, package

collaborer [kɔlabɔre] vi : collaborate — collaborateur, -trice [kɔlabɔratœr, -tris] n : colleague — collaboration [-bɔrasjõ] nf : collaboration

collant, -lante [kɔlɑ̃, -lɑ̃t] adj : sticky — collant nm 1 : panty hose pl 2 ~s mpl : tights

collation [kɔlasjõ] nf : snack

colle [kɔl] nf 1 : paste, glue 2 : trick question

collecte [kɔlɛkt] nf : collection — collecter [kɔlɛkte] vt : collect (funds) — collectif, -tive [kɔlɛktif, -tiv] adj : collective, joint — collection [kɔlɛksjõ] nf : collection — collectionner [kɔlɛksjɔne] vt : collect — collectionneur, -neuse [kɔlɛksjɔnœr, -nøz] n : collector

collège [kɔlɛʒ] nm 1 France : junior high school 2 Can : vocational college — collégial, -giale [kɔleʒjal] adj, mpl -giaux [-ʒjo] : collegiate — collégien, -gienne [kɔleʒjɛ̃, -ʒjɛn] n France : schoolboy m, schoolgirl f

collègue [kɔlɛg] nmf : colleague

coller [kɔle] vt : stick, glue — vi à : stick to, adhere to

collet [kɔlɛ] nm 1 : collar (of a shirt) 2 être ~ monté : be prim and proper

collier [kɔlje] nm 1 : necklace 2 : (animal) collar

colline [kɔlin] nf : hill

collision [kɔlizjõ] nf 1 : collision 2 entrer en ~ avec : collide with

colloque [kɔlɔk] nm : symposium

colombe [kɔlõb] nf : dove

colon [kɔlõ] nm : settler

côlon [kolõ] nm : colon (in anatomy)

colonel [kɔlɔnɛl] nm : colonel

colonie [kɔlɔni] nf 1 : colony 2 ~ de vacances : summer camp — colonial, -niale [kɔlɔnjal] adj, mpl -niaux [-njo] : colonial — coloniser [kɔlɔnize] vt : colonize, settle

colonne [kɔlɔn] nf 1 : column 2 ~ vertébrale : spine, backbone

colorer [kɔlɔre] vt : color, tint — colorant [kɔlɔrɑ̃] nm : dye, stain — coloré, -rée [kɔlɔre] adj 1 : colorful 2 : colored — colorier [kɔlɔrje] {96} vt : color (a drawing) — coloris [kɔlɔri] nm : shade, color

colporter [kɔlpɔrte] vt : hawk, peddle — colporteur, -teuse [kɔlpɔrtœr, -tøz] n : peddler

coma [kɔma] nm : coma

combattre [kɔbatr] {12} v : fight — combat [kɔba] nm 1 : fight(ing) 2 ~ de boxe : boxing match — combattant, -tante [kɔbatɑ̃, -tɑ̃t] n 1 : combatant, fighter 2 ancien combattant : veteran — combatif, -tive [kɔbatif, -tiv] adj : combative

combien [kɔbjɛ̃] adv 1 : how much, how many 2 ~ de : how much, how many 3 ~ de fois : how often 4 ~ de temps : how long

combiner [kɔbine] vt 1 : combine 2 PRÉPARER : work out, devise — combinaison [kɔbinezõ] nf 1 : combination 2 : coveralls pl, suit — combiné [kɔbine] nm : (telephone) receiver

combler [kɔble] vt 1 : fill (in) 2 : satisfy, fulfill — comble [kɔbl] adj : packed — ~ nm le ~ de : the height of

combustible [kɔbystibl] adj : combustible — ~ nm : fuel — combustion [kɔbystjõ] nf : combustion

comédie [kɔmedi] nf : comedy — comédien, -dienne [kɔmedjɛ̃, -djɛn] n : actor m, actress f

comestible [kɔmɛstibl] adj : edible

comète [kɔmɛt] nf : comet

comique [kɔmik] adj : comic, funny — ~ nmf : comedian, comic

comité [kɔmite] nm : committee

commander [kɔmɑ̃de] vt 1 : command 2 : order (a meal, etc.) — commandant [kɔmɑ̃dɑ̃] nm 1 : commander 2 : major (in the army) 3 ~ de bord : captain — commande [kɔmɑ̃d] nf 1 : order 2 ~ à distance : remote control — commandement [kɔmɑ̃dmɑ̃] nm 1 : command, authority 2 : commandment (in religion)

comme [kɔm] adv : how — ~ conj 1 : as, like 2 : since 3 : when, as 4 ~ ci, ~ ça : so-so 5 ~ il faut : properly — ~ prep : like, as

commémorer [kɔmemɔre] vt : commemorate — commémoration [kɔmemɔrasjõ] nf : commemoration

commencer [kɔmɑ̃se] {6} v : begin, start — commencement [kɔmɑ̃smɑ̃] nm : beginning, start

comment [kɔmɑ̃] adv 1 : how 2 : what 3 ~ ça va? : how is it going?

commenter [kɔmɑ̃te] vt : comment on — commentaire [kɔmɑ̃tɛr] nm 1 : comment 2 : commentary

commérages [kɔmeraʒ] nmpl fam : gossip

commerce [kɔmɛrs] nm : business, trade — commercer [kɔmɛrse] {6} vi : trade, deal — commerçant, -çante [kɔmɛrsɑ̃, -sɑ̃t] n

: merchant, storekeeper — **commercial**
[kɔmɛrsjal] *adj, mpl* -**ciaux** [-sjo] : commercial — **commercialiser** [kɔmɛrsjalize] *vt*
: market
commère [kɔmɛr] *nf* : gossip (person)
commettre [kɔmɛtr] {53} *vt* : commit
commis [kɔmi] *nm* **1** : clerk **2** ~
voyageur : traveling salesman
commissaire [kɔmisɛr] *nm* : superintendent,
commissioner — **commissariat** [kɔmis-
arja] *nm* ~ **de police** : police station
commission [kɔmisjɔ̃] *nf* **1** : committee **2**
~**s** *nfpl* : shopping
commode [kɔmɔd] *adj* **1** : handy **2 pas** ~
: awkward — ~ *nf* : chest of drawers —
commodité [kɔmɔdite] *nf* : convenience
commotion [kɔmɔsjɔ̃] *nf* ~ **cérébrale**
: concussion
commun, -mune [kɔmœ̃, -myn] *adj* **1**
: common, shared **2** : usual, ordinary —
commun *nm* **1 en** ~ : in common **2 hors
du** ~ : out of the ordinary
communauté [kɔmynote] *nf* **1** : community **2** : commune — **communautaire**
[kɔmynotɛr] *adj* : communal
communication [kɔmynikasjɔ̃] *nf* **1** : communication **2** ~ **téléphonique** : telephone
call
communion [kɔmynjɔ̃] *nf* : communion
communiquer [kɔmynike] *v* : communicate
— **communiqué** [kɔmynike] *nm* : press release
communisme [kɔmynism] *nm* : communism — **communiste** [kɔmynist] *adj & nmf*
: communist
commutateur [kɔmytatœr] *nm* : (electric)
switch
compact, -pacte [kɔ̃pakt] *adj* : compact,
dense — **compact** *nm* : compact disc
compagnie [kɔ̃paɲi] *nf* **1** : company **2 tenir**
~ **à qqn** : keep s.o. company — **com-
pagne** [kɔ̃paɲ] *nf* : (female) companion,
partner — **compagnon** [kɔ̃paɲɔ̃] *nm* : companion
comparer [kɔ̃pare] *vt* : compare — **comparaison** [kɔ̃parɛzɔ̃] *nf* : comparison
compartiment [kɔ̃partimɑ̃] *nm* : compartment
compas [kɔ̃pa] *nms & pl* : compass
compassion [kɔ̃pasjɔ̃] *nf* : compassion
compatible [kɔ̃patibl] *adj* : compatible —
compatibilité [kɔ̃patibilite] *nf* : compatibility
compatir [kɔ̃patir] *vi* : sympathize — **compatissant, -sante** [kɔ̃patisɑ̃, -sɑ̃t] *adj*
: compassionate
compatriote [kɔ̃patrijɔt] *nmf* : compatriot
compenser [kɔ̃pɑ̃se] *vt* : compensate for —
compensation [kɔ̃pɑ̃sasjɔ̃] *nf* : compensation

compétent, -tente [kɔ̃petɑ̃, -tɑ̃t] *adj* : competent — **compétence** [-petɑ̃s] *nf* : compe-
tence
compétiteur, -trice [kɔ̃petitœr, -tris] *n*
: competitor, rival — **compétitif, -tive**
[kɔ̃petitif, -tiv] *adj* : competitive — **compétition** [kɔ̃petisjɔ̃] *nf* : competition
complaisant, -sante [kɔ̃plɛzɑ̃, -zɑ̃t] *adj* **1**
AIMABLE : obliging, kind **2** INDULGENT
: indulgent
complément [kɔ̃plemɑ̃] *nm* : complement
— **complémentaire** [kɔ̃plemɑ̃tɛr] *adj*
: complementary
complet, -plète [kɔ̃plɛ, -plɛt] *adj* **1** : complete **2** PLEIN : full (of a hotel, etc.) — **complet** *nm* : suit — **complètement** [kɔ̃plɛtmɑ̃]
adv : completely — **compléter** [kɔ̃plete]
{87} *vt* : complete
complexe [kɔ̃plɛks] *adj & nm* : complex —
complexité [kɔ̃plɛksite] *nf* : complexity
complication [kɔ̃plikasjɔ̃] *nf* : complication
complice [kɔ̃plis] *adj* : knowing (of a look,
etc.) — ~ *nmf* : accomplice
compliment [kɔ̃plimɑ̃] *nm* : compliment —
complimenter [kɔ̃plimɑ̃te] *vt* : compliment
compliquer [kɔ̃plike] *vt* : complicate —
compliqué, -quée [kɔ̃plike] *adj* : complicated
complot [kɔ̃plo] *nm* : plot — **comploter**
[kɔ̃plote] *v* : plot, scheme
comporter [kɔ̃pɔrte] *vt* **1** CONTENIR : include **2** : entail (risks, etc.) — **se comporter** *vr* : behave — **comportement**
[kɔ̃pɔrtəmɑ̃] *nm* : behavior
composer [kɔ̃poze] *vt* **1** : compose (music)
2 : constitute, make up **3** : dial (a number)
— **se composer** *vr* ~ **de** : consist of —
composant [kɔ̃pozɑ̃] *nm* ÉLÉMENT : component — **composé, -sée** [kɔ̃poze] *adj*
: compound — **composé** *nm* : compound
— **compositeur, -trice** [kɔ̃pozitœr, -tris] *n*
: composer — **composition** [kɔ̃pozisjɔ̃] *nf*
: composition
compote [kɔ̃pɔt] *nf* ~ **de pommes** : apple
sauce
compréhensif, -sive [kɔ̃preɑ̃sif, -siv] *adj*
: understanding — **compréhension** [kɔ̃-
preɑ̃sjɔ̃] *nf* : understanding, comprehension
comprendre [kɔ̃prɑ̃dr] {70} *vt* **1** : consist
of, comprise **2** : understand **3 mal** ~
: misunderstand
compression [kɔ̃prɛsjɔ̃] *nf* : compression
comprimer [kɔ̃prime] *vt* : compress —
comprimé [kɔ̃prime] *nm* : tablet, pill
compris, -prise [kɔ̃pri, -priz] *adj* **1** INCLUS
: included **2 y compris** : including
compromettre [kɔ̃prɔmɛtr] {53} *vt* : compromise — **compromis** [kɔ̃prɔmi] *nm*
: compromise

comptable [kɔ̃tabl] *nmf* : accountant — **comptabilité** [kɔ̃tabilite] *nf* : accounting

comptant [kɔ̃tɑ̃] *adv* **payer** ~ : pay cash

compte [kɔ̃t, -tœ] *nm* **1** . (*banlr*) account **2** **au bout du** ~ : in the end **3** ~ **à rebours** : countdown **4** **se rendre** ~ **de** : realize — **compter** [kɔ̃te] *vt* **1** : count **2** ESPÉRER : expect **3** ~ **faire** : intend to do — *vi* **1** CALCULER : count **2** IMPORTER : matter **3** ~ **sur** : count on

compte–rendu [kɔ̃trɑ̃dy] *nm, pl* **comptes–rendus** : report

compteur [kɔ̃tœr] *nm* : meter

comptoir [kɔ̃twar] *nm* : counter, bar

comte, comtesse [kɔ̃t, -tɛs] *n* : count *m*, countess *f*

comté [kɔ̃te] *nm* : county

concave [kɔ̃kav] *adj* : concave

concéder [kɔ̃sede] {87} *vt* : grant, concede

concentrer [kɔ̃sɑ̃tre] *vt* : concentrate — **se concentrer** *vr* **1** : concentrate **2** ~ **sur** : center on — **concentration** [kɔ̃sɑ̃trasjɔ̃] *nf* : concentration

concept [kɔ̃sɛpt] *nm* : concept — **conception** [kɔ̃sɛpsjɔ̃] *nf* : conception

concerner [kɔ̃sɛrne] *vt* **1** : concern **2** **en ce qui me concerne** : as far as I'm concerned — **concernant** [kɔ̃sɛrnɑ̃] *prep* : concerning, regarding

concert [kɔ̃sɛr] *nm* **1** : concert **2** **de** ~ : together — **se concerter** [kɔ̃sɛrte] *vr* : consult, confer — **concerté, -tée** [kɔ̃sɛrte] *adj* : concerted

concession [kɔ̃sesjɔ̃] *nf* : concession — **concessionnaire** [kɔ̃sesjɔnɛr] *nmf* : dealer, agent

concevoir [kɔ̃səvwar] {26} *vt* **1** : conceive (a child) **2** IMAGINER : conceive of, design

concierge [kɔ̃sjɛrʒ] *nmf* : janitor

concilier [kɔ̃silje] {96} *vt* : reconcile — **conciliant, -liante** [kɔ̃siljɑ̃, -ljɑ̃t] *adj* : conciliatory

concis, -cise [kɔ̃si, -siz] *adj* : concise — **concision** [kɔ̃sizjɔ̃] *nf* **avec** ~ : concisely

conclure [kɔ̃klyr] {39} *vt* : conclude — **concluant, -cluante** [kɔ̃klyɑ̃, -klyɑ̃t] *adj* : conclusive — **conclusion** [kɔ̃klyzjɔ̃] *nf* : conclusion

concombre [kɔ̃kɔ̃br] *nm* : cucumber

concorder [kɔ̃kɔrde] *vi* : agree, match — **concordant, -dante** [kɔ̃kɔrdɑ̃, -dɑ̃t] *adj* : in agreement

concourir [kɔ̃kurir] {23} *vi* **1** : compete **2** ~ **à** : work toward — **concours** [kɔ̃kur] *nm* : competition, contest

concret, -crète [kɔ̃krɛ, -krɛt] *adj* : concrete — **concrétiser** [kɔ̃kretize] *vt* : give shape to — **se concrétiser** *vr* : materialize

concurrencer [kɔ̃kyrɑ̃se] {6} *vt* : rival, compete with — **concurrence** [kɔ̃kyrɑ̃s] *nf* : competition, rivalry — **concurrent, -rente** [kɔ̃kyrɑ̃, -rɑ̃t] *adj* : competing, rival — ~ *n* : competitor

condamner [kɔ̃dane] *vt* **1** : condemn **2** : sentence (in law) — **condamnation** [kɔ̃danasjɔ̃] *nf* **1** : condemnation **2** PEINE : sentence

condenser [kɔ̃dɑ̃se] *vt* : condense — **condensation** [kɔ̃dɑ̃sasjɔ̃] *nf* : condensation

condescendant, -dante [kɔ̃desɑ̃dɑ̃, -dɑ̃t] *adj* : condescending

condiment [kɔ̃dimɑ̃] *nm* : condiment

condition [kɔ̃disjɔ̃] *nf* **1** : condition **2** ~ **s** *nfpl* : conditions, circumstances **3** **sous** ~ **que** : provided that — **conditionnel, -nelle** [kɔ̃disjɔnɛl] *adj* : conditional

condoléances [kɔ̃dɔleɑ̃s] *nfpl* : condolences

conduire [kɔ̃dɥir] {49} *vt* **1** : drive **2** ~ **à** : lead to — **se conduire** *vr* : behave — **conducteur, -trice** [kɔ̃dyktœr, -tris] *n* : driver — **conducteur** *nm* : conductor (of electricity) — **conduite** [kɔ̃dɥit] *nf* **1** : behavior, conduct **2** TUYAU : pipe **3** ~ **à droite** : right-hand drive

cône [kon] *nm* : cone

confection [kɔ̃fɛksjɔ̃] *nf* **1** : making **2** **la** ~ : the clothing industry — **confectionner** [kɔ̃fɛksjɔne] *vt* : make (a meal, a garment, etc.)

confédération [kɔ̃federasjɔ̃] *nf* : confederation

conférence [kɔ̃ferɑ̃s] *nf* **1** : conference **2** COURS : lecture — **conférencier, -cière** [kɔ̃ferɑ̃sje, -sjɛr] *n* : lecturer

conférer [kɔ̃fere] {87} *v* : confer

confession [kɔ̃fesjɔ̃] *nf* **1** : confession **2** : denomination — **confesser** [kɔ̃fese] *vt* : confess

confettis [kɔ̃feti] *nmpl* : confetti

confiant, -fiante [kɔ̃fjɑ̃, -fjɑ̃t] *adj* **1** : confident, trusting **2** ASSURÉ : self-confident — **confiance** [kɔ̃fjɑ̃s] *nf* **1** : confidence, trust **2** ~ **en soi** : self-confidence

confidence [kɔ̃fidɑ̃s] *nf* **1** : confidence **2** **faire des** ~ **s à** : confide in — **confident, -dente** [kɔ̃fidɑ̃, -dɑ̃t] *n* : confidant, confidante *f* — **confidentiel, -tielle** [kɔ̃fidɑ̃sjɛl] *adj* : confidential

confier [kɔ̃fje] {96} *vt* **1** ~ **à qqn** : confide to s.o. **2** ~ **(qqch) à qqn** : entrust (sth) to s.o. — **se confier** *vr* ~ **à qqn** : confide in s.o.

confiner [kɔ̃fine] *vt* : confine — **confins** [kɔ̃fɛ̃] *nmpl* : limits, confines

confirmer [kɔ̃firme] *vt* : confirm — **confirmation** [kɔ̃firmasjɔ̃] *nf* : confirmation

confiserie [kɔ̃fizri] *nf* **1** : candy store **2** : candy

confisquer [kɔ̃fiske] *vt* : confiscate

confiture [kɔ̃fityr] *nf* : jam, preserves *pl*
conflit [kɔ̃fli] *nm* : conflict
confondre [kɔ̃fɔ̃dr] {63} *vt* **1** : confuse, mix up **2** ÉTONNER : baffle
conformer [kɔ̃fɔrme] *v* **se conformer** *vr* ~ **à** : conform to — **conforme** [kɔ̃fɔrm] *adj* **1** ~ **à** : in keeping with **2** ~ **à** : true to — **conformément** [kɔ̃fɔrmemɑ̃] *adv* ~ **à** : in accordance with — **conformité** [kɔ̃fɔrmite] *nf* : conformity
confort [kɔ̃fɔr] *nm* : comfort — **confortable** [kɔ̃fɔrtabl] *adj* : comfortable
confrère [kɔ̃frɛr] *nm* : colleague
confronter [kɔ̃frɔ̃te] *vt* **1** : confront **2** COMPARER : compare
confus [kɔ̃fy] *adj* **1** : confused **2** : embarrassed — **confusion** [kɔ̃fyzjɔ̃] *nf* **1** DÉSORDRE : confusion **2** GÊNE : embarrassment **3** ERREUR : mix-up
congé [kɔ̃ʒe] *nm* **1** VACANCES : vacation **2** : leave, time off — **congédier** [kɔ̃ʒedje] {96} *vt* : dismiss (an employee)
congeler [kɔ̃ʒle] {20} *vt* : freeze — **congélateur** [kɔ̃ʒelatœr] *nm* : freezer
congestion [kɔ̃ʒɛstjɔ̃] *nf* : congestion — **congestionner** [kɔ̃ʒɛstjɔne] *vt* : congest
congrès [kɔ̃grɛ] *nm* : congress, conference
conifère [kɔnifɛr] *nm* : conifer
conjecturer [kɔ̃ʒɛktyre] *v* : conjecture — **conjecture** [kɔ̃ʒɛktyr] *nf* : conjecture
conjoint, -jointe [kɔ̃ʒwɛ̃, -ʒwɛ̃t] *adj* : joint — ~ *n* ÉPOUX : spouse — **conjointement** [-ʒwɛ̃tmɑ̃] *adv* ~ **avec** : in conjunction with
conjonction [kɔ̃ʒɔ̃ksjɔ̃] *nf* : conjunction
conjoncture [kɔ̃ʒɔ̃ktyr] *nf* : circumstances *pl*, juncture
conjugaison [kɔ̃ʒygɛzɔ̃] *nf* : conjugation
conjugal, -gale [kɔ̃ʒygal] *adj, mpl* **-gaux** [-go] : marital
conjuguer [kɔ̃ʒyge] *vt* : conjugate (a verb)
connaître [kɔnɛtr] {7} *vt* **1** : know **2** ÉPROUVER : experience — **se connaître** *vr* **1** : know each other **2 s'y** ~ **en** : know about, be an expert in — **connaissance** [kɔnɛsɑ̃s] *nf* **1** : knowledge **2** : acquaintance **3** CONSCIENCE : consciousness **4 à ma** ~ : as far as I know **5 faire** ~ **avec qqn** : meet s.o. **6** ~**s** *nfpl* : knowledge, learning — **connaisseur, -seuse** [kɔnɛsœr, -søz] *n* : expert
connecter [kɔnɛkte] *vt* : connect
connexe [kɔnɛks] *adj* : related
connu, -nue [kɔny] *adj* : well-known
conquérir [kɔ̃kerir] {21} *vt* **1** : conquer **2** : win over — **conquérant, -rante** [kɔ̃kerɑ̃, -rɑ̃t] *n* : conqueror — **conquête** [kɔ̃kɛt] *nf* : conquest
consacrer [kɔ̃sakre] *vt* **1** : consecrate **2** ~ **à** : devote to — **se consacrer** *vr* ~ **à** : dedicate oneself to

conscience [kɔ̃sjɑ̃s] *nf* **1** : conscience **2** : consciousness — **consciemment** [kɔ̃sjamɑ̃] *adv* : consciously — **consciencieux, -cieuse** [kɔ̃sjɑ̃sjø, -sjøz] *adj* : conscientious — **conscient, -ciente** [kɔ̃sjɑ̃, -sjɑ̃t] *adj* : conscious, aware
consécutif, -tive [kɔ̃sekytif, -tiv] *adj* : consecutive — **consécutivement** [-tivmɑ̃] *adv* : consecutively
conseil [kɔ̃sɛj] *nm* **1** : (piece of) advice **2** : council **3** ~ **d'administration** : board of directors **2** — **conseiller** [kɔ̃seje] *vt* **1** : advise **2** RECOMMANDER : recommend — **conseiller, -lère** [kɔ̃seje, -jɛr] *n* **1** : counselor, advisor **2** : councillor
consentir [kɔ̃sɑ̃tir] {82} *vi* ~ **à** : consent to, agree to — **consentant, -tante** [kɔ̃sɑ̃tɑ̃, -tɑ̃t] *adj* : willing — **consentement** [kɔ̃sɑ̃tmɑ̃] *nm* : consent
conséquence [kɔ̃sekɑ̃s] *nf* **1** : consequence **2 en** ~ : consequently — **conséquent, -quente** [kɔ̃sekɑ̃, -kɑ̃t] *adj* : consistent, logical — **conséquent** *nm* **par** ~ : consequently
conservateur, -trice [kɔ̃sɛrvatœr, -tris] *adj* : conservative — ~ *n* **1** : conservative **2** : curator — **conservation** [kɔ̃sɛrvasjɔ̃] *nf* : conservation
conservatoire [kɔ̃sɛrvatwar] *nm* : academy, conservatory
conserver [kɔ̃sɛrve] *vt* GARDER : keep, retain — **se conserver** *vr* : keep, stay fresh — **conserve** [kɔ̃sɛrv] *nf* **1** : canned food **2 en** ~ : canned
considérable [kɔ̃siderabl] *adj* : considerable
considérer [kɔ̃sidere] {87} *vt* **1** : consider **2** ESTIMER : think highly of — **considération** [kɔ̃siderasjɔ̃] *nf* **1** : consideration **2** ESTIME : respect
consigner [kɔ̃siɲe] *vt* : check (luggage, etc.) — **consigne** [kɔ̃siɲ] *nf* **1** ORDRE : instructions *pl* **2** : checkroom
consister [kɔ̃siste] *vi* **1** ~ **en** : consist of **2** ~ **dans** : lie in **3** ~ **à faire** : consist in doing — **consistance** [kɔ̃sistɑ̃s] *nf* : consistency — **consistant, -tante** [kɔ̃sistɑ̃, -tɑ̃t] *adj* **1** ÉPAIS : thick **2** NOURRISSANT : substantial
consoler [kɔ̃sɔle] *vt* : console, comfort — **consolation** [kɔ̃sɔlasjɔ̃] *nf* : consolation
consolider [kɔ̃sɔlide] *vt* : consolidate
consommer [kɔ̃sɔme] *vt* : consume — *vi* : have a drink — **consommateur, -trice** [kɔ̃sɔmatœr, -tris] *n* : consumer — **consommation** [kɔ̃sɔmasjɔ̃] *nf* **1** : consumption **2** BOISSON : drink — **consommé** [kɔ̃sɔme] *nm* : clear soup
consonne [kɔ̃sɔn] *nf* : consonant
conspirer [kɔ̃spire] *vi* : conspire, plot — **conspiration** [kɔ̃spirasjɔ̃] *nf* : conspiracy

constant, -tante [kɔ̃stã, -tãt] *adj* : constant, continual — **constamment** [kɔ̃stamã] *adv* : constantly

constater [kɔ̃state] *vt* REMARQUER : notice — **constatation** [kɔ̃statasjɔ̃] *nf* : observation

constellation [kɔ̃stelasjɔ̃] *nf* : constellation

consternation [kɔ̃stɛrnasjɔ̃] *nf* : dismay — **consterner** [kɔ̃stɛrne] *vt* : dismay

constipation [kɔ̃stipasjɔ̃] *nf* : constipation — **constiper** [kɔ̃stipe] *vt* : constipate

constituer [kɔ̃stitɥe] *vt* 1 COMPOSER : constitute 2 ÉLABORER : set up, form — **constitution** [kɔ̃stitysjɔ̃] *nf* 1 : constitution 2 ÉTABLISSEMENT : setting up — **constitutionnel, -nelle** [kɔ̃stitysjɔnɛl] *adj* : constitutional

constructeur, -trice [kɔ̃stryktœr, -tris] *n* : builder — **constructif, -tive** [kɔ̃stryktif, -tiv] *adj* : constructive — **construction** [kɔ̃stryksjɔ̃] *nf* : building, construction — **construire** [kɔ̃strɥir] {49} *vt* : construct, build

consulat [kɔ̃syla] *nm* : consulate

consultant, -tante [kɔ̃syltã, -tãt] *n* : consultant — **consultation** [kɔ̃syltasjɔ̃] *nf* : consultation (with a doctor, etc.) — **consulter** [kɔ̃sylte] *vt* 1 : consult 2 : refer to — **se consulter** *vr* : confer

consumer [kɔ̃syme] *vt* : burn, destroy

contact [kɔ̃takt] *nm* 1 : contact, touch 2 **couper le ~** : switch off the ignition 3 **rester en ~** : keep in touch — **contacter** [kɔ̃takte] *vt* : get in touch with, contact

contagieux, -gieuse [kɔtaʒjœ, -ʒjøz] *adj* : contagious

contaminer [kɔ̃tamine] *vt* 1 : contaminate 2 INFECTER : infect — **contamination** [-minasjɔ̃] *nf* : contamination

conte [kɔ̃t] *nm* 1 : tale, story 2 **~ de fées** : fairy tale

contempler [kɔ̃tãple] *vt* : contemplate — **contemplation** [-tãplasjɔ̃] *nf* : contemplation

contemporain, -raine [kɔ̃tãpɔrɛ̃, -rɛn] *adj & n* : contemporary

contenir [kɔ̃tnir] {92} *vt* 1 : hold, contain 2 RETENIR : restrain — **se contenir** *vr* : control oneself — **contenance** [kɔ̃tnãs] *nf* ALLURE : bearing, attitude

content, -tente [kɔ̃tã, -tãt] *adj* : content, pleased — **contentement** [kɔ̃tãtmã] *nm* : satisfaction — **contenter** [kɔ̃tãte] *vt* : satisfy, please — **se contenter** *vr* **~ de** : be contented with

contentieux [kɔ̃tãsjø] *nm* 1 : dispute 2 : legal department

contenu [kɔ̃tny] *nm* : contents *pl*

conter [kɔ̃te] *vt* : tell (a story)

contester [kɔ̃tɛste] *vt* : contest, dispute — *vi*

: protest — **contestation** [kɔ̃tɛstasjɔ̃] *nf* 1 DISPUTE : dispute 2 : (political) protest

conteur, -teuse [kɔ̃tœr, -tøz] *n* : storyteller

contexte [kɔ̃tɛkst] *nm* : context

contigu, -guë [kɔ̃tigy] *adj* : adjacent

continent [kɔ̃tinã] *nm* : continent — **continental, -tale** [-nãtal] *adj, mpl* **-taux** [-to] : continental

continuer [kɔ̃tinɥe] *vt* 1 : continue 2 PROLONGER : extend — *vi* : continue, go on — **continu, -nue** [kɔ̃tiny] *adj* : continuous — **continuation** [kɔ̃tinɥasjɔ̃] *nf* : continuation — **continuel, -nuelle** [kɔ̃tinɥɛl] *adj* : continuous, continual — **continuellement** [kɔ̃tinɥɛlmã] *adv* : continually — **continuité** [kɔ̃tinɥite] *nf* : continuity

contorsion [kɔ̃tɔrsjɔ̃] *nf* : contortion — **contorsionner** [kɔ̃tɔrsjɔne] *v* **se contorsionner** *vr* : contort oneself

contour [kɔ̃tur] *nm* : outline, contour — **contourner** [kɔ̃turne] *vt* 1 : bypass 2 : get around (a difficulty, etc.)

contraceptif, -tive [kɔ̃trasɛptif, -tiv] *adj* : contraceptive — **contraceptif** *nm* : contraceptive — **contraception** [kɔ̃trasɛpsjɔ̃] *nf* : contraception

contracter [kɔ̃trakte] *vt* 1 : contract (a muscle) 2 : incur (a debt) 3 : catch (a cold, etc.) — **contraction** [kɔ̃traksjɔ̃] *nf* : contraction, tensing

contradiction [kɔ̃tradiksjɔ̃] *nf* : contradiction — **contradictoire** [kɔ̃tradiktwar] *adj* : contradictory

contraindre [kɔ̃trɛ̃dr] {65} *vt* **~ à** : compel to, force to — **contrainte** [kɔ̃trɛ̃, -trɛ̃t] *nf* : constraint, coertion

contraire [kɔ̃trɛr] *adj & nm* : contrary, opposite — **contrairement** [kɔ̃trɛrmã] *adv* **~ à** : contrary to

contrarier [kɔ̃trarje] {96} *vt* : annoy, vex — **contrariant, -riante** [kɔ̃trarjã, -rjãt] *adj* : annoying — **contrariété** [kɔ̃trarjete] *nf* : annoyance

contraste [kɔ̃trast] *nm* : contrast

contrat [kɔ̃tra] *nm* : contract

contravention [kɔ̃travãsjɔ̃] *nf* : (parking) ticket

contre [kɔ̃tr] *prep* 1 : against 2 : versus (in law) 3 : (in exchange) for 4 **trois ~ un** : three to one — **~** *nm* **le pour et le ~** : the pros and cons — **~** *adv* 1 **par ~** : on the other hand 2 **parler ~** : speak in opposition — **contre–attaque** [kɔ̃tratake] *nf, pl* **contre–attaques** : counterattack — **contrebande** [kɔ̃trəbãd] *nf* : smuggling — **contrebandier, -dière** [kɔ̃trəbãdje, -djɛr] *n* : smuggler — **contrebas** [kɔ̃trəba] **en ~** *adv phr* : (down) below — **contrebasse** [kɔ̃trəbas] *nf* : double bass — **contrecarrer** [kɔ̃trəkare] *vt* : thwart — **contrecœur** [kɔ̃-

trəkœr] **à ~** *adv phr* : unwillingly — **con-trecoup** [kɔ̃trəku] *nm* : consequence — **contredire** [kɔ̃trədir] {29} *vt* : contradict — **se contredire** *vr* : contradict oneself — **contrefaire** [kɔ̃trəfɛr] {42} *vt* : counterfeit, forge — **contrefaçon** [kɔ̃trəfasɔ̃] *nf* : counterfeiting, forgery — **contrefort** [kɔ̃trəfɔr] *nm* **1** : buttress **2 ~s** *nmpl* : foothills — **contremaître** [kɔ̃trəmɛtr] *n* : foreman — **contrepartie** [kɔ̃trəparti] *nf* **1** : compensation **2 en ~** : in return — **contrepoids** [kɔ̃trəpwa] *nm* : counterbalance — **contrer** [kɔ̃tre] *vt* : counter — **contresens** [kɔ̃trəsɑ̃s] **à ~** *adv phr* : the wrong way — **contretemps** [kɔ̃trətɑ̃] *nm* : hitch, setback — **contrevenir** [kɔ̃trəvnir] {92} *vi* **~ à** : contravene

contribuer [kɔ̃tribɥe] *vi* : contribute — **contribuable** [kɔ̃tribɥabl] *nmf* : taxpayer — **contribution** [kɔ̃tribysjɔ̃] *nf* : contribution

contrit, -trite [kɔ̃tri, -trit] *adj* : contrite

contrôle [kɔ̃trol] *nm* **1** : checking, inspection **2 ~ de soi-même** : self-control — **contrôler** [kɔ̃trole] *vt* **1** : check, inspect **2** MAÎTRISER : supervise, control — **contrôleur, -leuse** [kɔ̃trolœr, -løz] *n* : (ticket) inspector, (bus) conductor

controverse [kɔ̃trɔvɛrs] *nf* : controversy — **controversé, -sée** [kɔ̃trɔvɛrse] *adj* : controversial

contusionner [kɔ̃tyzjɔne] *vt* : bruise — **contusion** [kɔ̃tyzjɔ̃] *nf* : bruise

convaincre [kɔ̃vɛ̃kr] {94} *vt* : convince — **convaincant, -cante** [kɔ̃vɛ̃kɑ̃, -kɑ̃t] *adj* : convincing

convalescence [kɔ̃valesɑ̃s] *nf* : convalescence

convenir [kɔ̃vnir] {92} *vt* : agree, admit — *vi* **~ à** : suit, fit — *v impers* **il convient de** : it is advisable to — **convenable** [kɔ̃vnabl] *adj* **1** ACCEPTABLE : adequate **2** : proper, decent — **convenance** [kɔ̃vnɑ̃s] *nf* **1 à votre ~** : at your convenience **2 ~s** *nfpl* : conventions, proprieties

convention [kɔ̃vɑ̃sjɔ̃] *nf* **1** USAGE : custom **2** ACCORD : agreement **3** ASSEMBLÉE : convention, assembly — **conventionnel, -nelle** [kɔ̃vɑ̃sjɔnɛl] *adj* : conventional

convenu, -nue [kɔ̃vny] *adj* : agreed

converger [kɔ̃vɛrʒe] {17} *vi* : converge, meet

conversation [kɔ̃vɛrsasjɔ̃] *nf* : conversation — **converser** [kɔ̃vɛrse] *vi* : converse

convertir [kɔ̃vɛrtir] *vt* : convert — **conversion** [kɔ̃vɛrsjɔ̃] *nf* : conversion

conviction [kɔ̃viksjɔ̃] *nf* CERTITUDE : conviction

convier [kɔ̃vje] {96} *vt* : invite

convive [kɔ̃viv] *nmf* : guest (at a meal)

convoi [kɔ̃vwa] *nm* **1** : convoy **2** *or* **~ funèbre** : funeral procession

convoiter [kɔ̃vwate] *vt* : covet

convoquer [kɔ̃vɔke] *vt* **1** : convene **2** : summon

convulsion [kɔ̃vylsjɔ̃] *nf* : convulsion

coopérer [kɔɔpere] {87} *vi* : cooperate — **coopératif, -tive** [kɔɔperatif, -tiv] *adj* : cooperative — **coopération** [-perasjɔ̃] *nf* : cooperation — **coopérative** *nf* : cooperative

coordination [kɔɔrdinasjɔ̃] *nf* : coordination — **coordonner** [kɔɔrdɔne] *vt* : coordinate

copain, -pine [kɔpɛ̃, -pin] *n* **1** : friend, buddy **2** *or* **petit copain, petite copine** : boyfriend *m*, girlfriend *f*

copeau [kɔpo] *nm, pl* **-peaux** : chip (of wood, etc.)

copie [kɔpi] *nf* **1** : copy, duplicate **2** DEVOIR : paper, schoolwork — **copier** [kɔpje] {96} *vt* **1** : copy **2 ~ sur** : copy from, crib from

copieux, -pieuse [kɔpjø, -pjøz] *adj* : plentiful, copious

copilote [kɔpilɔt] *nmf* : copilot

copine → copain

copropriété [kɔprɔprijete] *nf* **1** : joint ownership **2 immeuble en ~** : condominium

coq [kɔk] *nm* : rooster

coque [kɔk] *nf* **1** : hull (of a boat) **2 œuf à la ~** : soft-boiled egg

coquelicot [kɔkliko] *nm* : poppy

coquet, -quette [kɔke, -kɛt] *adj* **1** ÉLÉGANT : stylish **2** : attractive **3** *fam* : tidy, considerable

coquille [kɔkij] *nf* **1** : shell **2** FAUTE : misprint **3 ~ Saint-Jacques** : scallop — **coquillage** [kɔkijaʒ] *nm* **1** : shellfish **2** COQUILLE : shell

coquin, -quine [kɔkɛ̃, -kin] *adj* : mischievous — **~** *n* : rascal, scamp

cor [kɔr] *nm* **1** : horn (in music) **2** : corn (on one's foot)

corail [kɔraj] *nm, pl* **-raux** [kɔro] : coral

Coran [kɔrɑ̃] *nm* : Koran

corbeau [kɔrbo] *nm, pl* **-beaux** : crow

corbeille [kɔrbɛj] *nf* **1** : basket **2 ~ à papier** : wastepaper basket

corbillard [kɔrbijar] *nm* : hearse

corde [kɔrd] *nf* **1** : rope **2** : string **3 ~s vocales** : vocal cords — **cordage** [kɔrdaʒ] *nm* **1** : rope **2 ~s** *nmpl* : rigging

cordial, -diale [kɔrdjal] *adj, mpl* **-diaux** [-djo] : cordial — **cordialement** [-djalmɑ̃] *adv* : cordially

cordon [kɔrdɔ̃] *nm* **1** : cord (in anatomy) **2 ~ de soulier** : shoelace — **cordonnerie** [kɔrdɔnri] *nf* : shoe repair shop — **cordonnier, -nière** [kɔrdɔnje, -njɛr] *n* : shoemaker, cobbler

coréen, -réenne [kɔreɛ̃, -rɛɛn] *adj* : Korean — **coréen** *nm* : Korean (language)

coriace [kɔrjas] *adj* : tough

corne [kɔrn] *nf* **1** : antler, horn **2** : horn (instrument) **3** ~ **de brume** : foghorn

cornée [kɔrne] *nf* : cornea

corneille [kɔrnɛj] *nf* : crow

cornemuse [kɔrnəmyz] *nf* : bagpipes *pl*

cornet [kɔrnɛ] *nm* **1** : cone **2** ~ **de crème glacée** : ice-cream cone

corniche [kɔrniʃ] *nf* : cliff road

cornichon [kɔrniʃɔ̃] *nm* : pickle

corporation [kɔrpɔrasjɔ̃] *nf* : corporation

corporel, -relle [kɔrpɔrɛl] *adj* : bodily

corps [kɔr] *nm* **1** : body **2** : corps (in the army, etc.) **3** : professional body **4 prendre** ~ : take shape

corpulent, -lente [kɔrpylɑ̃, -lɑ̃t] *adj* : stout

correct, -recte [kɔrɛkt] *adj* : correct — **correctement** [-rɛktəmɑ̃] *adv* : correctly — **correcteur, -trice** [kɔrɛktœr, -tris] *adj* : corrective — **correction** [kɔrɛksjɔ̃] *nf* **1** : correction **2** : grading, marking **3** PUNITION : beating

corrélation [kɔrelasjɔ̃] *nf* : correlation

correspondre [kɔrɛspɔ̃dr] {63} *vi* **1** : correspond, write **2** : communicate (by telephone, etc.) **3** ~ **à** : correspond to — **correspondance** [kɔrɛspɔ̃dɑ̃s] *nf* **1** : correspondence **2** : connection (of a plane, etc.) — **correspondant, -dante** [kɔrɛspɔ̃dɑ̃, -dɑ̃t] *n* **1** : correspondent **2** : person being called (on the telephone)

corrida [kɔrida] *nf* : bullfight

corridor [kɔridɔr] *nm* : corridor

corriger [kɔriʒe] {17} *vt* **1** : correct **2** : grade, mark

corroborer [kɔrɔbɔre] *vt* : corroborate

corroder [kɔrɔde] *vt* : corrode

corrompre [kɔrɔ̃pr] {77} *vt* **1** : corrupt **2** SOUDOYER : bribe — **corrompu, -pue** [kɔrɔ̃py] *adj* : corrupt

corrosif, -sive [kɔrɔzif, -ziv] *adj* : corrosive — **corrosion** [kɔrɔzjɔ̃] *nf* : corrosion

corruption [kɔrypsjɔ̃] *nf* **1** : corruption **2** : bribery

corsage [kɔrsaʒ] *nm* **1** : blouse **2** : bodice (of a dress)

corsé, -sée [kɔrse] *adj* : full-bodied (of wine), strong (of coffee, etc.)

corser [kɔrse] *v* **se corser** *vr* : get more complicated

cortège [kɔrtɛʒ] *nm* : procession

corvée [kɔrve] *nf* : chore

cosmétique [kɔsmetik] *nm* : cosmetic — ~ *adj* : cosmetic

cosmique [kɔsmik] *adj* : cosmic

cosmopolite [kɔsmɔpɔlit] *adj* : cosmopolitan

cosmos [kɔsmos] *nm* : universe, cosmos

cosse [kɔs] *nf* : pod, husk

costaud, -taude [kɔsto, -tod] *adj fam* : sturdy, burly

costume [kɔstym] *nm* **1** : costume **2** COMPLET : suit — **costumer** [kɔstyme] *v* **se costumer** *vr* ~ **en** : dress up as

cote [kɔt] *nf* **1** : (stock) quotation **2** CLASSEMENT : rating **3** : call number (of a library book) **4** NIVEAU : level

côte [kot] *nf* **1** : coast **2** : rib (in anatomy) **3** : chop, cutlet **4** PENTE : hill **5** ~ **à** ~ : side by side

côté [kote] *nm* **1** : side **2** : way, direction **3 à** ~ : nearby **4 à** ~ **de** : next to **5 de** ~ : sideways **6 de mon** ~ : for my part **7 mettre de** ~ : put aside

coteau [kɔto] *nm, pl* **-teaux** : hill, hillside

côtelé, -lée [kotle] *adj* **velours côtelé** : corduroy

côtelette [kotlɛt] *nf* : chop

coter [kɔte] *vt* : quote (in finance)

coterie [kɔtri] *nf* : clique

côteux, -teuse [kotø, -tøz] *adj Can* : hilly

côtier, -tière [kotje, -tjɛr] *adj* : coastal

cotiser [kɔtize] *vi* : subscribe, pay one's dues — **cotisation** [kɔtizasjɔ̃] *nf* : dues *pl*, fee

coton [kɔtɔ̃] *nm* : cotton

côtoyer [kotwaje] {58} *vt* **1** : skirt, run alongside of **2** FRÉQUENTER : mix with

cou [ku] *nm* : neck

coucher [kuʃe] *vt* **1** : put to bed **2** : lay down flat — *vi* : sleep, spend the night — **se coucher** *vr* **1** : lie down, go to bed **2** : set (of the sun) — ~ *nm* **1** : bedtime **2** ~ **du soleil** : sunset — **couche** [kuʃ] *nf* **1** : layer, stratum **2** : coat (of paint) **3** : (baby) diaper **4 fausse** ~ : miscarriage — **couchette** [kuʃɛt] *nf* : berth, bunk

coucou [kuku] *nm* : cuckoo

coude [kud] *nm* **1** : elbow **2** COURBE : bend, angle **3** ~ **à** ~ : shoulder to shoulder

cou–de–pied [kudpje] *nm, pl* **cous–de–pied** : instep

coudre [kudr] {22} *v* : sew

couler [kule] *vt* **1** : sink **2** : cast (metal) — *vi* **1** : flow, run **2** : leak (of a faucet) **3** : sink (of a boat)

couleur [kulœr] *nf* **1** : color **2** : suit (of cards)

coulisser [kulise] *vi* : slide (in a groove) — **coulisses** [kulis] *nfpl* : backstage, wings

couloir [kulwar] *nm* **1** : corridor **2** : lane (in transportation)

coup [ku] *nm* **1** : knock, blow **2** CHOC : shock **3** : stroke, shot (in sports) **4** : (political) coup **5** ~ **de feu** : gunshot **6** ~ **de foudre** : love at first sight **7** ~ **de pied** : kick **8** ~ **de poing** : punch **9** ~ **de soleil** : sunburn **10** ~ **de téléphone** : telephone call **11** ~ **d'œil** : glance **12 tout à** ~ : suddenly

coupable [kupabl] *adj* : guilty — **~** *nmf* : culprit

coupant, -pante [kupɑ̃, -pɑ̃t] *adj* 1 : sharp 2 CAUSTIQUE : cutting, curt

couper [kupe] *vt* 1 : cut, cut up 2 : cut off, block 3 CROISER : intersect 4 DILUER : dilute — *vi* : cut — **se couper** *vr* 1 : cut oneself 2 : intersect — **coupe** [kup] *nf* 1 : fruit dish 2 : cup (in sports) 3 *or* **~ de cheveux** : haircut 4 *or* **~ transversale** : cross section — **coupe-ongles** [kupɔ̃gl] *nms & pl* : nail clippers — **coupe-papier** [kuppapje] *nms & pl* : letter opener

couple [kupl] *nm* : couple — **coupler** [kuple] *vt* : pair (up)

coupon [kupɔ̃] *nm* : coupon

coupure [kupyr] *nf* 1 : cut 2 BILLET : banknote

cour [kur] *nf* 1 : court (of law) 2 : courtyard 3 : courtship 4 **~ de récréation** : playground

courage [kuraʒ] *nm* : courage — **courageux, -geuse** [kuraʒø, -ʒøz] *adj* : courageous

courant, -rante [kurɑ̃, -rɑ̃t] *adj* 1 : (electric) current 2 COMMUN : common, usual — **courant** *nm* 1 : (electric) current 2 : course (of the day, etc.) 3 **~ d'air** : draft 4 **être au ~ de** : know all about — **couramment** [kuramɑ̃] *adv* 1 : fluently 2 SOUVENT : commonly

courbature [kurbatyr] *nf* : stiffness, ache — **courbaturé, -rée** [kurbatyre] *adj* : aching

courber [kurbe] *vt* : bend, curve — **se courber** *vr* : bend, curve — **courbe** [kurb] *nf* : curve

coureur, -reuse [kurœr, -røz] *n* : runner

courge [kurʒ] *nf* : gourd — **courgette** [kurʒɛt] *nf* : zucchini

courir [kurir] {23} *vt* 1 : run in, compete in 2 FRÉQUENTER : frequent 3 PARCOURIR : roam through 4 : run (a risk, etc.) — *vi* 1 : run 2 SE PRESSER : rush

couronner [kurɔne] *vt* : crown — **couronne** [kurɔn] *nf* 1 : crown 2 : wreath — **couronnement** [kurɔnmɑ̃] *nm* 1 : coronation 2 : crowning achievement

courrier [kurje] *nm* 1 : mail, correspondence 2 **~ électronique** : electronic mail, e-mail — **courriel** [kurjɛl] *nm Can* : electronic mail

courroie [kurwa] *nf* : strap, belt

cours [kur] *nm* 1 : course, class 2 : flow, current 3 **au ~ de** : in the course of, during 4 **~ d'eau** : river, stream 5 **~ du soir** : night school 6 **en ~** : in progress

course [kurs] *nf* 1 : running 2 COMPÉTITION : race, competition 3 COMMISSION : errand 4 **faire des ~s** : go shopping

court, courte [kur, kurt] *adj* : short — **court**

[kur] *adv* 1 **à ~ de** : short of 2 **s'arrêter ~** : stop short 3 **tout ~** : simply — **court** *nm* : court (in sports) — **court-circuit** [kursirkɥi] *nm, pl* **courts-circuits** : short circuit

courtier, -tière [kurtje, -tjɛr] *n* 1 : broker, agent

courtiser [kurtize] *vt* : court, woo

courtois, -toise [kurtwa, -twaz] *adj* : courteous — **courtoisie** [kurtwazi] *nf* : courtesy

cousin, -sine [kuzɛ̃, -zin] *n* : cousin

coussin [kusɛ̃] *nm* : cushion

coût [ku] *nm* : cost — **coûtant** [kutɑ̃] **à prix ~** *adv phr* : at cost

couteau [kuto] *nm, pl* **-teaux** 1 : knife 2 **~ de poche** : pocketknife

coûter [kute] *vt* 1 : cost 2 **~ cher** : be expensive 3 **ça coûte combien?** : how much is it? — *vi* : cost — **coûteux, -teuse** [kutø, -tøz] *adj* : costly

coutume [kutym] *nf* : custom — **coutumier, -mière** [kutymje, -mjɛr] *adj* : customary

couture [kutyr] *nf* 1 : sewing 2 : dressmaking 3 : seam (of a garment) — **couturier** [kutyrje] *nm* : fashion designer — **couturière** [kutyrjɛr] *nf* : dressmaker

couvée [kuve] *nf* : brood

couvent [kuvɑ̃] *nm* : convent

couver [kuve] *vt* 1 : hatch 2 PROTÉGER : overprotect 3 : be coming down with (an illness) — *vi* 1 : smolder 2 : be brewing

couvercle [kuvɛrkl] *nm* 1 : lid, cover 2 : top (of a spray can, etc.)

couvert, -verte [kuvɛr, -vɛrt] *adj* 1 : covered 2 NUAGEUX : overcast — **couvert** *nm* 1 : place setting (at a table) 2 **~s** *nmpl* : flatware 3 **à ~** : under cover — **couverture** [kuvɛrtyr] *nf* 1 : cover (of a book, etc.) 2 : blanket 3 : roofing 4 : news coverage

couveuse [kuvøz] *nf* : incubator

couvrir [kuvrir] {83} *vt* : cover — **se couvrir** *vr* 1 : dress warmly 2 : become overcast 3 **~ de** : be covered with — **couvre-feu** [kuvrəfø] *nm, pl* **couvre-feux** : curfew — **couvre-lit** [kuvrəli] *nm, pl* **couvre-lits** : bedspread

cow-boy [kɔbɔj] *nm, pl* **cow-boys** : cowboy

coyote [kɔjɔt] *nm* : coyote

crabe [krab] *nm* : crab

cracher [kraʃe] *v* : spit

craie [krɛ] *nf* : chalk

craindre [krɛdr] {65} *vt* 1 REDOUTER : fear, be afraid of 2 **~ que** : regret that, fear that — **crainte** [krɛt] *nf* 1 : fear, dread 2 **de ~ que** : for fear that — **craintif, -tive** [krɛtif, -tiv] *adj* : fearful, timid

crampe [krɑ̃p] *nf* : cramp

crampon [krɑ̃pɔ̃] *nm* : clamp — **cramponner** [krɑ̃pɔne] *v* **se cramponner** *vr* **~ à** : cling to

cran [krɑ̃] *nm fam* : courage, guts

crâne [kran] *nm* : skull

crapaud [krapo] *nm* : toad

craquer [krake] *vi* 1 : crack, snap, creak 2 SE DÉCHIRER : tear, rip 3 *fam* : break down — **craquement** [krakmɑ̃] *nm* : crack, creak

crasse [kras] *nf* : filth — **crasseux, -seuse** [krasø, -søz] *adj* : filthy

cratère [krater] *nm* : crater

cravache [kravaʃ] *nf* : horsewhip

cravate [kravat] *nf* : necktie

crayon [krɛjɔ̃] *nm* 1 : pencil 2 ~ **à bille** : ballpoint pen

créancier, -cière [kreɑ̃sje, -sjɛr] *n* : creditor

créateur, -trice [kreatœr, -tris] *adj* : creative — ~ *n* : creator — **création** [kreasjɔ̃] *nf* : creation — **créativité** [kreativite] *nf* : creativity

créature [kreatyr] *nf* : creature

crèche [krɛʃ] *nf France* : nursery

crédible [kredibl] *adj* : credible — **crédibilité** [-dibilite] *nf* : credibility

crédit [kredi] *nm* 1 : credit 2 ~**s** *nmpl* : funds — **créditer** [kredite] *vt* : credit — **créditeur, -trice** [kreditœr, -tris] *n* : creditor

crédule [kredyl] *adj* : credulous — **crédulité** [-dylite] *nf* : credulity

créer [kree] {89} *vt* : create

crémaillère [kremajɛr] *nf* **pendre la** ~ : have a housewarming (party)

crème [krɛm] *nf* 1 : cream 2 ~ **glacée** *Can* : ice cream — **crémerie** [krɛmri] *nf France* : dairy shop — **crémeux, -meuse** [kremø, -møz] *adj* : creamy

créneau [kreno] *nm, pl* **-neaux** 1 : slot, gap 2 **faire un** ~ : back into a parking space

crêpe [krɛp] *nf* : pancake, crepe — ~ *nm* : crepe (fabric)

crépiter [krepite] *vi* : crackle — **crépitement** [krepitmɑ̃] *nm* 1 : crackling 2 : patter (of rain)

crépu, -pue [krepy] *adj* : frizzy

crépuscule [krepyskyl] *nm* : twilight, dusk

cresson [krɛsɔ̃] *nm* : watercress

crête [krɛt] *nf* 1 : crest, peak 2 : comb (of a rooster)

crétin, -tine [kretɛ̃, -tin] *n* : idiot

creuser [krøze] *vt* : dig, hollow out — **se creuser** *vr* ~ **la tête** *fam* : rack one's brains — **creux, creuse** [krø, krøz] *adj* 1 : hollow 2 : sunken (of eyes) — **creux** *nm* 1 CAVITÉ : hollow, cavity 2 : pit (of the stomach)

crevaison [krəvɛzɔ̃] *nf* : flat tire

crevasse [krəvas] *nf* : crevice, crack

crever [krəve] {52} *vt* 1 : burst, puncture 2 *fam* : wear out — *vi* 1 : burst 2 ~ **de faim** : be starving — **crevé, -vée** [krəve] *adj* 1 : punctured, flat (of a tire) 2 *fam* : dead tired

crevette [krəvɛt] *nf* : shrimp, prawn

cri [kri] *nm* 1 : cry, shout 2 **le dernier** ~ : the latest thing — **criant, criante** [krijɑ̃, krijɑ̃t] *adj* : glaring, obvious — **criard, criarde** [krijar, krijard] *adj* 1 : shrill 2 : gaudy

cribler [krible] *vt* 1 : sift, screen 2 ~ **de** : riddle with — **crible** [kribl] *nm* : sieve

cric [krik] *nm* : (car) jack

cricket [krikɛt] *nm* : cricket (sport)

crier [krije] {96} *vi* : shout, yell — *vt* : shout (out)

crime [krim] *nm* 1 : crime 2 MEURTRE : murder — **criminel, -nelle** [kriminɛl] *adj* : criminal — ~ *n* 1 : criminal 2 MEURTRIER : murderer

crinière [krinjɛr] *nf* : mane

criquet [krikɛ] *nm* : locust (insect)

crise [kriz] *nf* 1 : crisis 2 ACCÈS : fit, outburst 3 ~ **cardiaque** : heart attack

crispé, -pée [krispe] *adj* : tense, clenched

crisser [krise] *vi* : screech, squeal (of tires)

cristal [kristal] *nm, pl* **-taux** [kristo] : crystal

critère [kritɛr] *nm* : criterion

critique [kritik] *adj* : critical — ~ *nf* 1 : criticism 2 : critique, review — ~ *nmf* : critic, reviewer — **critiquer** [kritike] *vt* : criticize

croasser [krɔase] *vi* : caw, croak

croc [kro] *nm* : fang

crochet [krɔʃɛ] *nm* 1 : hook 2 : square bracket 3 **faire du** ~ : crochet 4 **faire un** ~ : make a detour — **crochu, -chue** [krɔʃy] *adj* : hooked

crocodile [krɔkɔdil] *nm* : crocodile

croire [krwar] {24} *vt* 1 : believe 2 PENSER : think, believe — *vi* ~ **à** *or* ~ **en** : believe in

croisade [krwazad] *nf* : crusade

croiser [krwaze] *vt* 1 : cross 2 : intersect 3 RENCONTRER : pass, meet 4 : crossbreed — *vi* : cruise (of a ship) — **se croiser** *vr* 1 : cross, cut across 2 : pass each other — **croisement** [krwazmɑ̃] *nm* 1 : junction 2 : crossbreeding — **croiseur** [krwazœr] *nm* : cruiser (ship) — **croisière** [krwazjɛr] *nf* : cruise

croître [krwatr] {25} *vi* : grow, increase — **croissant, -sante** [krwasɑ̃, -sɑ̃t] *adj* : growing, increasing — **croissant** *nm* : croissant — **croissance** [krwasɑ̃s] *nf* : growth, development

croix [krwa] *nf* : cross

croquer [krɔke] *vt* : crunch, munch — *vi* ~ **dans** : bite into (an apple, etc.) — **croquant, -quante** [krɔkɑ̃, -kɑ̃t] *adj* : crunchy — **croque–monsieur** [krɔkməsjø] *nms & pl* : grilled ham and cheese sandwich

croquis [krɔki] *nm* : sketch

crosse [krɔs] *nf* : butt (of a gun)

crotte [krɔt] *nf* : droppings *pl*, dung — **crottin** [krɔtɛ̃] *nm* : (horse) manure

crouler [krule] *vi* s'EFFONDRER : crumble, collapse

croupir [krupir] *vi* 1 stagner 0 ..... dans : wallow in

croustillant, -lante [krustijɑ̃, -jɑ̃t] *adj* : crisp, crispy

croûte [krut] *nf* 1 : (pie) crust 2 : scab — **croûton** [krutɔ̃] *nm* 1 : crust (of bread) 2 : crouton

croyance [krwajɑ̃s] *nf* : belief — **croyant, croyante** [krwajɑ̃, -jɑ̃t] *n* : believer

cru, crue [kry] *adj* 1 : raw, uncooked 2 OSÉ : crude 3 : harsh (of light, etc.) — **cru** *nm* 1 VIGNOBLE : vineyard 2 : vintage (of wine)

cruauté [kryote] *nf* : cruelty

cruche [kryʃ] *nf* : jug, pitcher

crucial, -ciale [krysjal] *adj, mpl* -ciaux [-sjo] : crucial

crucifier [krysifje] {96} *vt* : crucify — **crucifix** [krysifi] *nms & pl* : crucifix — **crucifixion** [krysifiksjɔ̃] *nf* : crucifixion

crudités [krydite] *nfpl* : raw vegetables

crue [kry] *nf* : rise in water level

cruel, cruelle [kryɛl] *adj* : cruel — **cruellement** [-ɛlmɑ̃] *adv* : cruelly

crustacés [krystase] *nmpl* : shellfish

crypte [kript] *nf* : crypt

cube [kyb] *adj* : cubic — ～ *nm* : cube — **cubique** [kybik] *adj* : cubic

cueillir [kœjir] {3} *vt* : pick, gather — **cueillette** [kœjɛt] *nf* : picking, gathering

cuillère *or* **cuiller** [kɥijɛr] *nf* 1 : spoon 2 : spoonful 3 ～ à thé *or* ～ à café : teaspoon — **cuillerée** [kɥijere] *nf* 1 : spoonful 2 ～ à café : teaspoonful

cuir [kɥir] *nm* 1 : leather 2 ～ chevelu : scalp

cuire [kɥir] {49} *vt* : cook, bake — *vi* : cook

cuisine [kɥizin] *nf* 1 : kitchen 2 : cooking, cuisine 3 faire la ～ : cook — **cuisiner** [kɥizine] *v* 1 : cook 2 *fam* : interrogate, grill — **cuisinier, -nière** [kɥizinje, -njɛr] *n* : chef, cook — **cuisinière** *nf* : stove

cuisse [kɥis] *nf* 1 : thigh 2 : leg (in cooking)

cuisson [kɥisɔ̃] *nf* : cooking, baking

cuit, cuite [kɥi, kɥit] *adj* 1 : cooked 2 bien ～ : well-done

cuivre [kɥivr] *nm* 1 : copper 2 *or* ～ jaune : brass 3 ～s *nmpl* : brass (musical instruments)

culbute [kylbyt] *nf* 1 : somersault 2 CHUTE : tumble, fall

cul-de-sac [kydsak] *nm, pl* **culs-de-sac** : dead end

culinaire [kylinɛr] *adj* : culinary

culminer [kylmine] *vi* : culminate, peak — **culminant, -nante** [kylminɑ̃, -nɑ̃t] *adj* **point culminant** : high point

culot [kylo] *nm* *fam* **avoir du ～** : have a lot of nerve

culotte [kylɔt] *nf* 1 PANTALON : pants *pl* 2 : panties *pl*

culpabilité [kylpabilite] *nf* : guilt

culte [kylt] *nm* 1 VÉNÉRATION : worship, cult 2 : religion

cultiver [kyltive] *vt* : cultivate, grow — **cultivateur, -trice** [kyltivatœr, -tris] *n* AGRICULTEUR : farmer — **cultivé, -vée** [kyltive] *adj* 1 : cultivated 2 : cultured, educated — **culture** [kyltyr] *nf* 1 CONNAISSANCES : culture 2 : cultivation, growing 3 : crop 4 ～ physique : physical education — **culturel, -relle** [kyltyrɛl] *adj* : cultural — **culturisme** [kyltyrism] *nm* : bodybuilding

cumuler [kymyle] *vt* 1 : accumulate 2 : hold concurrently — **cumulatif, -tive** [kymylatif, -tiv] *adj* : cumulative

cupide [kypid] *adj* : greedy — **cupidité** [kypidite] *nf* : greed

cure [kyr] *nf* : treatment, cure

curé [kyre] *nm* : pastor, parish priest

curer [kyre] *v* se **curer** *vr* : clean (one's nails, teeth, etc.) — **cure-dent** *or* **cure-dents** [kyrdɑ̃] *nm, pl* **cure-dents** : toothpick

curieux, -rieuse [kyrjø, -rjøz] *adj* 1 : curious 2 ÉTRANGE : strange, odd — ～ *n* : onlooker — **curieusement** [kyrjøzmɑ̃] *adv* : curiously, strangely — **curiosité** [kyrjozite] *nf* : curiosity

curry [kyri] *nm* : curry

curseur [kyrsœr] *nm* : cursor

cuver [kyve] *vi* : ferment — **cuve** [kyv] *nf* : vat, tank — **cuvée** [kyve] *nf* : vintage — **cuvette** [kyvɛt] *nf* : basin

cyanure [sjanyr] *nm* : cyanide

cycle [sikl] *nm* : cycle — **cyclique** [siklik] *adj* : cyclic, cyclical

cycliste [siklist] *nmf* : cyclist, bicyclist — **cyclisme** [siklism] *nm* : cycling, bicycling

cyclomoteur [siklomotœr] *nm* : moped

cyclone [siklon] *nm* : cyclone

cygne [siɲ] *nm* : swan

cylindre [silɛ̃dr] *nm* : cylinder — **cylindrique** [silɛ̃drik] *adj* : cylindrical

cymbale [sɛ̃bal] *nf* : cymbal

cynique [sinik] *adj* : cynical — ～ *nmf* : cynic — **cynisme** [sinism] *nm* : cynicism

cyprès [siprɛ] *nm* : cypress

D

d [de] *nm* : d, fourth letter of the alphabet
dactylographier [daktilɔgrafje] {96} *vt* : type — **dactylo** [daktilo] *or* **dactylographe** [daktilɔgraf] *nmf* : typist
daigner [deɲe] *vt* : deign
daim [dɛ̃] *nm* **1** : deer **2** : suede
dalle [dal] *nf* : slab, paving stone
daltonien, -nienne [daltɔnjɛ̃, -njɛn] *adj* : color-blind
dame [dam] *nf* **1** : lady **2** : queen (in games) **3** ~**s** *nfpl or* **jeu de** ~**s** : checkers — **damier** [damje] *nm* : checkerboard
dandiner [dɑ̃dine] *v* **se dandiner** *vr* : waddle
danger [dɑ̃ʒe] *nm* : danger — **dangereux, -reuse** [dɑ̃ʒrø, -røz] *adj* : dangerous
dans [dɑ̃] *prep* **1** : in **2** : into, inside **3** : from, out of **4** ~ **la journée** : during the day **5** ~ **les 20 ans** : in about 20 years **6** **monter** ~ **l'auto** : get into the car
danser [dɑ̃se] *v* : dance — **danse** [dɑ̃s] *nf* : dance, dancing — **danseur, -seuse** [dɑ̃sœr, -søz] *n* : dancer
dard [dar] *nm* **1** : stinger (of an insect) **2** *Can* : dart
date [dat] *nf* : date — **dater** [date] *vi* **1** : be dated, be old-fashioned **2** ~ **de** : date from
datte [dat] *nf* : date (fruit)
dauphin [dofɛ̃] *nm* : dolphin
davantage [davɑ̃taʒ] *adv* **1** PLUS : more **2** : (any) longer
de [də] (**d'** *before vowels and mute h*) *prep* **1** : of **2** (*before infinitive*) : to, of **3 de l', de la, du, des** : some, any **4** ~ **Molière** : by Molière **5** ~ **Montréal** : from Montreal **6** **moins** ~ **cinq** : less than five
dé [de] *nm* **1** : die, dice *pl* **2** ~ **à coudre** : thimble
déambuler [deɑ̃byle] *vi* : stroll, wander about
débâcle [debakl] *nf* : fiasco
déballer [debale] *vt* : unpack, unwrap
débandade [debɑ̃dad] *nf* : stampede
débarquer [debarke] *vt* : unload (goods) — *vi* : disembark (of passengers) — **débarquement** [debarkəmɑ̃] *nm* **1** : unloading **2** : landing
débarrasser [debarase] *vt* : clear, rid — **se débarrasser** *vr* ~ **de** : get rid of
débarrer [debare] *vt Can* : unlock
débattre [debatr] {12} *vt* : debate, discuss — **se débattre** *vr* : struggle — **débat** [deba] *nm* **1** : debate, discussion **2** ~**s** *nmpl* : proceedings
débaucher [deboʃe] *vt* **1** CORROMPRE : cor-

rupt **2** LICENCIER : lay off — **débauche** [deboʃ] *nf* : debauchery
débiliter [debilite] *vt* : debilitate — **débile** [debil] *adj fam* : stupid
débiter [debite] *vt* **1** : debit **2** VENDRE : sell, retail **3** FOURNIR : produce **4** : recite, reel off — **débit** [debi] *nm* **1** : debit **2** : turnover (of merchandise, etc.) **3** : (rate of) flow — **débiteur, -trice** [debitœr, -tris] *n* : debtor
déblayer [debleje] {11} *vt* : clear (away)
débloquer [deblɔke] *vt* : free, release
déboires [debwar] *nmpl* ENNUIS : difficulties
déboîter [debwate] *vt* : dislocate (a joint) — *vi* : pull out, change lanes
débonnaire [debɔnɛr] *adj* : easygoing, good-natured
déborder [debɔrde] *vi* : overflow — *vt* **1** : extend beyond **2** SUBMERGER : overwhelm — **débordé, -dée** [debɔrde] *adj* : overwhelmed
déboucher [debuʃe] *vt* : open, unblock — *vi* ~ **sur** : open onto, lead to — **débouché** [debuʃe] *nm* **1** : outlet, market **2** : opportunity, prospect
débourser [deburse] *vt* : pay out
debout [dəbu] *adv* **1** : standing up **2** : upright, on end **3** : up, out of bed
déboutonner [debutɔne] *vt* : unbutton, undo
débraillé, -lée [debraje] *adj* : disheveled
débrancher [debrɑ̃ʃe] *vt* : unplug, disconnect
débrayer [debreje] {11} *vi* **1** : disengage the clutch **2** : go on strike — **débrayage** [debrɛjaʒ] *nm* **1** : disengaging the clutch **2** : strike, walkout
débris [debri] *nms & pl* **1** : fragment **2** ~ *nmpl* : rubbish, scraps
débrouiller [debruje] *vt* DÉMÊLER : disentangle — **se débrouiller** *vr* : manage, cope — **débrouillard, -larde** [debrujar, -jard] *adj* : resourceful
débuter [debyte] *v* : begin — **début** [deby] *nm* **1** : beginning **2** ~**s** *nmpl* : debut, early stages — **débutant, -tante** [debytɑ̃, -tɑ̃t] *n* : beginner, novice
décacheter [dekaʃte] {8} *vt* : unseal, open
décadence [dekadɑ̃s] *nf* : decadence — **décadent, -dente** [dekadɑ̃, -dɑ̃t] *adj* : decadent
décaféiné, -née [dekafeine] *adj* : decaffeinated
décalage [dekalaʒ] *nm* **1** : gap, interval **2** ~ **horaire** : time difference
décamper [dekɑ̃pe] *vi* : clear out
décaper [dekape] *vt* **1** : clean, scour **2**

: strip (paint, etc.) — **décapant** [dekɑpɑ̃]
nm : paint stripper

décapotable [dekapɔtabl] *adj & nf* : convertible

décapsuleur [dekapsylœr] *nm* : bottle opener

décéder [desede] {87} *vi* : die — **décédé, -dée** [desede] *adj* : deceased

déceler [desle] {20} *vt* **1** DÉCOUVRIR : detect **2** RÉVÉLER : reveal

décembre [desɑ̃br] *nm* : December

décence [desɑ̃s] *nf* : decency

décennie [deseni] *nf* : decade

décent, -cente [desɑ̃, -sɑ̃t] *adj* : decent

déception [desɛpsjɔ̃] *nf* : disappointment

décerner [deserne] *vt* : award

décès [desɛ] *nm* : death

décevoir [desəvwar] {26} *vt* : disappoint — **décevant, -vante** [desəvɑ̃, -vɑ̃t] *adj* : disappointing

déchaîner [deʃene] *vt* : unleash — **se déchaîner** *vr* : erupt, burst out — **déchaîné, -née** [deʃene] *adj* : raging, unbridled — **déchaînement** [deʃɛnmɑ̃] *nm* : outburst

décharger [deʃarʒe] {17} *vt* **1** : unload **2** : discharge (a firearm, etc.) **3** SOULAGER : relieve, unburden — **décharge** [deʃarʒ] *nf* **1** : discharge **2** : garbage dump

décharné, -née [deʃarne] *adj* : gaunt

déchausser [deʃose] *v* **se déchausser** *vr* : take off one's shoes

déchéance [deʃeɑ̃s] *nf* : decay, decline

déchet [deʃɛ] *nm* **1** : scrap **2** ~**s** : waste, refuse

déchiffrer [deʃifre] *vt* : decipher

déchiqueter [deʃikte] {8} *vt* : tear into pieces

déchirer [deʃire] *vt* : tear up, tear apart — **déchirant, -rante** [deʃirɑ̃, -rɑ̃t] *adj* : heart-rending — **déchirure** [deʃiryr] *nf* : tear

déchoir [deʃwar] {27} *vi* : fall, decline (in prestige)

décider [deside] *vt* **1** : decide **2** CONVAINCRE : persuade **3** ~ **de** : decide on, determine — **se décider** *vr* : make up one's mind — **décidé, -dée** [deside] *adj* **1** : decided, settled **2** DÉTERMINÉ : determined — **décidément** [desidemɑ̃] *adv* : definitely, really

décimal, -male [desimal] *adj, mpl* -**maux** [-mo] : decimal — **décimale** *nf* : decimal

décision [desizjɔ̃] *nf* **1** : decision **2** : decisiveness — **décisif, -sive** [desizif, -ziv] *adj* : decisive

déclarer [deklare] *vt* **1** PROCLAMER : declare **2** : register, report — **se déclarer** *vr* : break out (of fire, etc.) — **déclaration** [deklarasjɔ̃] *nf* : declaration, statement

déclencher [deklɑ̃ʃe] *vt* **1** : set off, trigger **2** LANCER : launch — **déclenchement** [deklɑ̃ʃmɑ̃] *nm* : onset, outbreak

déclic [deklik] *nm* : click

décliner [dekline] *v* : decline — **déclin** [deklɛ̃] *nm* : decline

décoller [dekɔle] *vt* : unstick, remove — *vi* : take off (of an airplane, etc.) — **décollage** [dekɔlaʒ] *nm* : takeoff

décolleté, -tée [dekɔlte] *adj* : low-cut

décolorer [dekɔlɔre] *vt* : bleach — **se décolorer** *vr* : fade

décombres [dekɔ̃br] *nmpl* : rubble, debris

décommander [dekɔmɑ̃de] *vt* : cancel

décomposer [dekɔ̃poze] *vt* : decompose — **décomposition** [dekɔ̃pozisjɔ̃] *nf* : decomposition, rotting

décompter [dekɔ̃te] *vt* **1** : count, calculate **2** DÉDUIRE : deduct — **décompte** [dekɔ̃t] *nm* **1** : count, breakdown **2** DÉDUCTION : deduction

déconcerter [dekɔ̃serte] *vt* : disconcert

décongeler [dekɔ̃ʒle] {20} *v* : thaw, defrost

déconnecter [dekɔnɛkte] *vt* : disconnect

déconseiller [dekɔ̃seje] *vt* : dissuade, advise against — **déconseillé, -lée** [dekɔ̃seje] *adj* : inadvisable

décontracté, -tée [dekɔ̃trakte] *adj* : relaxed, casual

décorer [dekɔre] *vt* ORNER : decorate — **décor** [dekɔr] *nm* **1** : decor **2** : scenery (in theater, etc.) — **décoration** [dekɔrasjɔ̃] *nf* : decoration — **décorateur, -trice** [dekɔratœr, -tris] *n* : interior decorator — **décoratif, -tive** [dekɔratif, -tiv] *adj* : decorative

décortiquer [dekɔrtike] *vt* : shell, hull

découler [dekule] *vi* : result, follow

découper [dekupe] *vt* **1** : cut up, carve **2** : cut out (a picture)

décourager [dekuraʒe] {17} *vt* : discourage — **se décourager** *vr* : lose heart — **découragement** [dekuraʒmɑ̃] *nm* : discouragement

décousu, -sue [dekuzy] *adj* **1** : unstitched **2** : disjointed, disconnected

découvrir [dekuvrir] {83} *vt* **1** : discover **2** : uncover — **se découvrir** *vr* : clear up (of weather) — **découvert** [dekuver] *nm* : overdraft (in banking) — **découverte** [dekuvert] *nf* : discovery

décrépit, -pite [dekrepi, -pit] *adj* : decrepit

décret [dekre] *nm* : decree, edict — **décréter** [dekrete] {87} *vt* : decree

décrire [dekrir] {33} *vt* : describe

décrocher [dekrɔʃe] *vt* **1** : unhook, take down **2** *fam* : get, land (a job, etc.) — *vi fam* : drop out, give up

décroître [dekrwatr] {25} *vi* : decrease, decline

déçu, -çue [desy] *adj* : disappointed

dédaigner [dedeɲe] *vt* : disdain, scorn — **dédaigneux, -neuse** [dedɛɲø, -ɲøz] *adj*

: disdainful, scornful — **dédain** [dedɛ̃] *nm*
MÉPRIS : disdain, scorn

dédale [dedal] *nm* : maze, labyrinth

dedans [dədɑ̃] *adv* **1** : inside, in **2 en ~**
: on the inside, within — **~** *nm* : inside, interior

dédicace [dedikas] *nf* : dedication — **dédicacer** [dedikase] {6} *vt* : inscribe, dedicate

dédier [dedje] {96} *vt* : dedicate

dédommager [dedɔmaʒe] {17} *vt* : compensate — **dédommagement** [dedɔmaʒmɑ̃]
nm INDEMNITÉ : compensation

déduire [dedɥir] {49} *vt* **1** : deduct **2** CON-
CLURE : deduce, infer — **déduction**
[dedyksjɔ̃] *nf* : deduction

déesse [dees] *nf* : goddess

défaillir [defajir] {93} *vi* : weaken, fail —
défaillance [defajɑ̃s] *nf* : failing, weakness

défaire [defɛr] {42} *vt* **1** : undo **2** : unpack
— **se défaire** *vr* **1** : come undone **2 ~ de**
: part with — **défait, -faite** [defɛ, -fɛt] *adj*
1 : undone **2** : defeated — **défaite** *nf* : defeat

défaut [defo] *nm* **1** IMPERFECTION : flaw, defect **2** FAIBLESSE : shortcoming **3** MANQUE
: lack **4 faire ~** : be lacking

défavoriser [defavɔrize] *vt* : put at a disadvantage — **défavorable** [defavɔrabl] *adj*
: unfavorable

défectueux, -tueuse [defɛktɥø, -tɥøz] *adj*
: defective, faulty — **défectuosité** [defɛk-
tɥozite] *nf* **1** : defectiveness **2** DÉFAUT : defect, fault

défendre [defɑ̃dr] {63} *vt* **1** : defend **2** PRO-
TÉGER : protect, uphold **3** INTERDIRE : forbid — **se défendre** *vr* : defend oneself —
défendeur, -deresse [defɑ̃dœr, -drɛs] *n*
: defendant

défense [defɑ̃s] *nf* **1** : defense **2** INTERDIC-
TION : prohibition **3** : tusk (of an elephant,
etc.) — **défenseur** [defɑ̃sœr] *nm* : defender
— **défensif, -sive** [defɑ̃sif, -siv] *adj* : defensive — **défensive** *nf* : defensive

défi [defi] *nm* : challenge, dare

déficit [defisit] *nm* : deficit

défier [defje] {96} *vt* **1** : challenge, dare **2**
BRAVER : defy

défigurer [defigyre] *vt* **1** : disfigure **2 ~
les faits** : distort the facts

défiler [defile] *vi* **1** : march, parade **2**
: stream past **3** : scroll (on a computer) —
défilé [defile] *nm* **1** : parade, procession **2**
: stream (of visitors, etc.)

définir [definir] *vt* : define — **défini, -nie**
[defini] *adj* **1** : defined **2** : definite —
définitif, -tive [definitif, -tiv] *adj* : definitive, final — **définition** [definisjɔ̃] *nf* : definition — **définitivement** [definitivmɑ̃] *adv*
: definitively, for good

défoncer [defɔ̃se] {6} *vt* : smash, break down

déformer [defɔrme] *vt* : deform, distort —
déformation [defɔrmasjɔ̃] *nf* : distortion

défraîchi, -chie [defreʃi] *adj* : faded, worn

défrayer [defreje] {11} *vt* : pay (s.o.'s expenses)

défunt, -funte [defœ̃, -fœ̃t] *adj & n* : deceased

dégager [degaʒe] {17} *vt* **1** : free **2** DÉBAR-
RASSER : clear (the way, etc.) **3** EXTRAIRE
: bring out **4** ÉMETTRE : emit — **se dégager** *vr* **1** : clear (up) **2** : emanate **3 ~
de** : get free of — **dégagé, -gée** [degaʒe]
adj **1** : clear, open **2** : free and easy

dégâts [dega] *nmpl* : damage

dégeler [deʒle] {20} *v* : thaw — **dégel**
[deʒɛl] *nm* : thaw

dégénérer [deʒenere] {87} *vi* : degenerate

dégingandé, -dée [deʒɛ̃gɑ̃de] *adj* : lanky

dégivrer [deʒivre] *vt* : defrost

dégonfler [degɔ̃fle] *vt* : deflate — **se dégonfler** *vr* : deflate, go flat

dégoûter [degute] *vt* : disgust — **se dégoûter** *vr* **~ de** : get sick of — **dégoût**
[degu] *nm* : disgust — **dégoûtant, -tante**
[degutɑ̃, -tɑ̃t] *adj* : disgusting

dégoutter [degute] *vi* : drip

dégrader [degrade] *vt* : degrade

dégrafer [degrafe] *vt* : unhook

degré [dəgre] *nm* **1** : degree **2** : step (of a
staircase) **3 par ~s** : gradually

dégueulasse [degœlas] *adj fam* : disgusting

déguiser [degize] *vt* : disguise — **se
déguiser** *vr* **~ en** : dress up as —
déguisement [degizmɑ̃] *nm* : disguise

déguster [degyste] *vt* **1** : taste **2** SAVOURER
: savor, enjoy

dehors [dəɔr] *adv* **1** : outside **2 en ~** : (toward the) outside **3 en ~ de** : outside of,
apart from — **~** *nms & pl* : outside, exterior

déjà [deʒa] *adv* : already

déjeuner [deʒœne] *nm* **1** : lunch **2** *Can*
: breakfast — **~** *vi* **1** : have lunch **2** *Can*
: have breakfast

déjouer [deʒwe] *vt* : thwart

delà [dəla] *adv* → **au–delà, par–delà**

délabrer [delabre] *v* **se délabrer** *vr* : become dilapidated — **délabrement** [de-
labrəmɑ̃] *nm* : dilapidation, disrepair

délai [delɛ] *nm* **1** : time limit **2** : extension
(of time) **3** : waiting period

délaisser [delese] *vt* **1** ABANDONNER : abandon, desert **2** : neglect

délasser [delase] *vt* : relax — **se délasser**
vr : relax

délayer [deleje] {11} *vt* **1** DILUER : dilute **2**
: drag out (a speech, etc.)

déléguer [delege] {87} *vt* : delegate —
délégué, -guée [delege] *n* : delegate —
délégation [delegasjɔ̃] *nf* : delegation

délibérer [delibere] {87} *vi* : deliberate — **délibéré, -rée** [delibere] *adj* **1** : deliberate **2** DÉCIDÉ : determined

délicat, -cate [delika, -kat] *adj* **1** : delicate ▮ ▮ ▮ ▮ ▮ **0** ▮▮▮▮▮▮▮▮▮▮ ▮ ▮▮▮▮▮ **délicatement** [delikatmã] *adv* **1** : delicately **2** : finely, precisely — **délicatesse** [delikatɛs] *nf* **1** : delicacy **2** : tactfulness

délice [delis] *nm* : delight — **délicieux, -cieuse** [delisjø, -sjøz] *adj* : delicious, delightful

délier [delje] {96} *vt* **1** : untie **2** ~ **de** : release from

délimiter [delimite] *vt* : demarcate

délinquant, -quante [delɛ̃kã, -kãt] *adj & n* : delinquent

délire [delir] *nm* **1** : delirium **2 en ~** : delirious, frenzied — **délirant, -rante** [delirã, -rãt] *adj* **1** : delirious **2** : frenzied — **délirer** [delire] *vi* **1** : be delirious **2** : rave

délit [deli] *nm* : crime, offense

délivrer [delivre] *vt* **1** : set free **2** : issue, award **3** ~ **de** : relieve of — **délivrance** [delivrãs] *nf* **1** : freeing, release **2** : delivery, issue **3** SOULAGEMENT : relief

déloger [delɔʒe] {17} *vt* **1** : evict **2** : remove, dislodge

déloyal, -loyale [delwajal] *adj*, *mpl* **-loyaux** [-jo] **1** : disloyal **2** : unfair — **déloyauté** [delwajote] *nf* : disloyalty

delta [dɛlta] *nm* : delta

déluge [delyʒ] *nm* **1** : deluge, flood **2** AVERSE : downpour

demain [dəmɛ̃] *adv & nm* : tomorrow

demander [dəmãde] *vt* **1** : ask for, request **2** : ask (about) **3** NÉCESSITER : call for, require — **se demander** *vr* : wonder — **demande** [dəmãd] *nf* **1** : request **2** : application (form) **3 l'offre et la ~** : supply and demand

démanger [demãʒe] {17} *vi* : itch — **démangeaison** [demãʒɛzɔ̃] *nf* : itch, itching

démarche [demarʃ] *nf* **1** ALLURE : gait, walk **2** REQUÊTE : step, action

démarrer [demare] *v* : start (up) — **démarreur** [demarœr] *nm* : starter

démêler [demele] *vt* : disentangle — **démêlé** [demele] *nm* **1** : quarrel **2 ~s** *nmpl* : problems, trouble

déménager [demenaʒe] {17} *v* : move, relocate — **déménagement** [demenaʒmã] *nm* : moving, relocation

démence [demãs] *nf* : madness, insanity

démener [demne] {52} *v* **se démener** *vr* : struggle, thrash about

dément, -mente [demã, -mãt] *adj* : insane, demented

démentir [demãtir] {82} *vt* : refute, deny — **démenti** [demãti] *nm* : denial

démesuré, -rée [deməzyre] *adj* : excessive, immoderate

démettre [demɛtr] {53} *vt* : dismiss, fire — **se démettre** *vr* **1** : resign **2** : dislocate (one's shoulder, etc.)

demeurer [dəmœre] *vi* **1** (*with* **être**) : remain **2** (*with* **avoir**) : reside — **demeure** [dəmœr] *nf* : residence

demi, -mie *adj* **1** : half **2 et ~** : and a half, half past — ~ *n* : half — **demi** *nm France* : half-pint (of beer) — **à ~** *adv phr* : half, halfway

démission [demisjɔ̃] *nf* : resignation — **démissionner** [demisjɔne] *vi* : resign

démocratie [demɔkrasi] *nf* : democracy — **démocratique** [demɔkratik] *adj* : democratic

démodé, -dée [demɔde] *adj* : old-fashioned, out-of-date

demoiselle [demwazɛl] *nf* **1** : young lady **2** ~ **d'honneur** : bridesmaid

démolir [demɔlir] *vt* : demolish — **démolition** [demɔlisjɔ̃] *nf* : demolition

démon [demɔ̃] *nm* : demon

démonstration [demɔ̃strasjɔ̃] *nf* : demonstration — **démonstrateur, -trice** [demɔ̃stratœr, -tris] *n* : demonstrator — **démonstratif, -tive** [demɔ̃stratif, -tiv] *adj* : demonstrative

démonter [demɔ̃te] *vt* : dismantle, take down

démontrer [demɔ̃tre] *vt* : demonstrate, show

démoraliser [demɔralize] *vt* : demoralize

démunir [demynir] *vt* : deprive

dénégation [denegasjɔ̃] *nf* : denial

dénicher [deniʃe] *vt* : unearth

dénier [denje] {96} *vt* : deny

dénigrer [denigre] *vt* : disparage

dénombrer [denɔ̃bre] *vt* : count, enumerate

dénommer [denɔme] *vt* : name, call — **dénomination** [denɔminasjɔ] *nf* : name, designation

dénoncer [denɔ̃se] {6} *vt* : denounce, inform on — **dénonciation** [denɔ̃sjasjɔ̃] *nf* : denunciation

dénoter [denɔte] *vt* : denote

dénouement [denumã] *nm* : outcome

dénouer [denwe] *vt* : untie, undo

denrée [dãre] *nf* **1** : commodity **2 ~s alimentaires** : foods

dense [dãs] *adj* : dense — **densité** [dãsite] *nf* : density, denseness

dent [dã] *nf* **1** : tooth **2** : cog (of a wheel), prong (of a fork) — **dentaire** [dãtɛr] *adj* : dental

dentelé, -lée [dãtle] *adj* : jagged, serrated

dentelle [dãtɛl] *nf* : lace

dentiste [dãtist] *nmf* : dentist — **dentier** [dãtje] *nm* : dentures *pl* — **dentifrice** [dãtifris] *nm* : toothpaste — **dentition** [dãtisjɔ̃] *nf* : teeth *pl*

dérouler

dénuder [denyde] *vt* **1** : make bare **2** : strip (off)

dénué, -nuée [denɥe] *adj* ~ **de** : devoid of, lacking in

déodorant [deodorã] *adj & nm* : deodorant

dépanner [depane] *vt* **1** : fix, repair **2** : help out (s.o.) — **dépanneur** [depanœr] *nm Can* : convenience store

dépareillé, -lée [depareje] *adj* : odd, not matching

départ [depar] *nm* **1** : departure **2** : start (in sports)

département [departəmã] *nm* : department

départir [departir] {82} *v* **se départir** *vr* ~ **de** : abandon, depart from

dépassé, -sée [depase] *adj* : outdated, outmoded

dépasser [depase] *vt* **1** : pass, go past **2** EXCÉDER : exceed **3** SURPASSER : surpass **4** **cela me dépasse!** : that's beyond me! — *vi* : stick out — **dépassement** [depasmã] *nm* : passing

dépayser [depeize] *vt* **1** : disorient **2** : provide with a change of scenery

dépecer [depəse] {6} *and* {52} *vt* : cut up, tear apart

dépêcher [depeʃe] *vt* : dispatch — **se dépêcher** *vr* : hurry up — **dépêche** [depeʃ] *nf* : dispatch

dépeindre [depɛ̃dr] {37} *vt* : depict, describe

dépendre [depãdr] {63} *vi* ~ **de** : depend on — *vt* : take down — **dépendance** [depãdãs] *nf* : dependence — **dépendant, -dante** [depãdã, -dãt] *adj* : dependent

dépenser [depãse] *vt* **1** : spend (money) **2** : use up, expend (energy) — **se dépenser** *vr* : exert oneself — **dépens** [depã] *nmpl* **aux** ~ **de** : at the expense of — **dépense** [depãs] *nf* **1** : spending, expenditure **2** : expense — **dépensier, -sière** [depãsje, -sjɛr] *adj* : extravagant

dépérir [deperir] *vi* **1** : wither (of a plant) **2** : waste away (of a person)

dépister [depiste] *vt* **1** : detect, discover **2** : track down (a criminal)

dépit [depi] *nm* **1** : spite **2** **en** ~ **de** MALGRÉ : in spite of, despite

déplacer [deplase] {6} *vt* : move, shift — **se déplacer** *vr* : move about — **déplacé, -cée** [deplase] *adj* : out of place

déplaire [depler] {66} *vi* **1** : be disliked **2** ~ **à** : displease — **déplaisant, -sante** [deplɛzã, -zãt] *adj* : unpleasant

dépliant [deplijã] *nm* : brochure, pamphlet

déplier [deplije] {96} *vt* : unfold

déplorer [deplɔre] *vt* : deplore — **déplorable** [deplɔrabl] *adj* : deplorable

déployer [deplwaje] {58} *vt* **1** : deploy **2** DÉPLIER : unfold, spread out

déposer [depoze] *vt* **1** : put down **2** : deposit (a sum of money) **3** : drop off, leave **4** : register, file (a complaint) — *vi* : testify — **se déposer** *vr* : settle

dépôt [depo] *nm* **1** : deposit **2** ENTREPÔT : warehouse, store **3** : (train) station **4** ~ **d'ordures** : (garbage) dump — **dépotoir** [depotwar] *nm* : dump

dépouiller [depuje] *vt* ~ **qqn de** : deprive s.o. of

dépourvu, -vue [depurvy] *adj* ~ **de** : without, lacking in — **au dépourvu** *adv phr* : by surprise

déprécier [depresje] {96} *vt* **1** : devalue **2** : disparage — **se déprécier** *vr* : depreciate — **dépréciation** [depresjasjõ] *nf* : depreciation

dépression [depresjõ] *nf* : depression

déprimer [deprime] *vt* : depress — **déprimant, -mante** [deprimã, -mãt] *adj* : depressing — **déprimé, -mée** [deprime] *adj* : depressed, dejected

depuis [dəpɥi] *prep* **1** : since **2** : from **3** ~ **deux ans** : for two years — ~ *adv* : since (then) — **depuis que** *adv phr* : (ever) since

député, -tée [depyte] *n* : representative (in government)

déraciner [derasine] *vt* : uproot

dérailler [deraje] *vi* : derail — **déraillement** [derajmã] *nm* : derailment

déraisonnable [derɛzɔnabl] *adj* : unreasonable

déranger [derãʒe] {17} *vt* **1** : bother, disturb **2** DÉRÉGLER : disrupt, upset — **se déranger** *vr* : put oneself out — **dérangement** [derãʒmã] *nm* **1** : trouble, bother **2** : (stomach) upset

déraper [derape] *vi* **1** GLISSER : skid, slip **2** : get out of hand (of a situation)

dérégler [deregle] {87} *vt* **1** : put out of order **2** : upset, disturb — **se dérégler** *vr* : go wrong

dérision [derizjõ] *nf* : derision, mockery — **dérisoire** [derizwar] *adj* : ridiculous, pathetic

dériver [derive] *vt* **1** : divert **2** ~ **de** : derive from — *vi* : drift, be adrift — **dérivé** [derive] *nm* **1** : derivation (of a word) **2** : by-product

dernier, -nière [dɛrnje, -njɛr] *adj* **1** : last, previous **2** : latest (of a novel, etc.) **3** : final, last **4** : lowest (of a step, etc.) — ~ *n* **1** : last (one) **2 ce dernier, cette dernière** : the latter — **dernièrement** [dɛrnjɛrmã] *adv* : recently

dérobé, -bée [derɔbe] *adj* : hidden — **à la dérobée** *adv phr* : on the sly

dérouler [derule] *vt* : unwind, unroll — **se dérouler** *vr* : take place — **déroulement** [derulmã] *nm* : development, progress

dérouter [derute] *vt* : disconcert, confuse — **déroute** [derut] *nf* : rout

derrière [dɛrjɛr] *adv & prep* : behind — ~ *nm* **1** : back, rear **2** *fam* : buttocks *pl*, bottom

des → **de**

dès [dɛ] *prep* **1** : from **2** ~ **lors** : from then on **3** ~ **que** : as soon as

désaccord [dezakɔr] *nm* : disagreement

désagréable [dezagreabl] *adj* DÉPLAISANT : disagreeable, unpleasant

désagréger [dezagreʒe] {64} *vt* : break up — **se désagréger** *vr* : disintegrate

désagrément [dezagremã] *nm* : annoyance

désapprouver [dezapruve] *vt* : disapprove of — **désapprobation** [dezaprɔbasjɔ̃] *nf* : disapproval

désarmer [dezarme] *vt* : disarm — **désarmement** [dezarməmã] *nm* : disarmament

désarroi [dezarwa] *nm* : confusion, distress

désastre [dezastr] *nm* : disaster — **désastreux, -treuse** [dezastrø, -trøz] *adj* : disastrous

désavantage [dezavãtaʒ] *nm* : disadvantage — **désavantager** [dezavãtaʒe] {17} *vt* : put at a disadvantage — **désavantageux, -geuse** [dezavãtaʒø, -ʒøz] *adj* : disadvantageous

désaveu [dezavø] *nm*, *pl* **-veux** : repudiation, denial

désavouer [dezavwe] *vt* RENIER : deny, repudiate

descendre [dəsãdr] {63} *vt* **1** : go down (the stairs, etc.) **2** : take (sth) down — *vi* **1** : go down, come down **2** : get off (of a passenger) **3** ~ **de** : be descended from — **descendant, -dante** [desãdã, -dãt] *n* : descendant — **descente** [desãt] *nf* **1** : descent **2** : (police) raid **3** PENTE : slope

description [dɛskripsjɔ̃] *nf* : description — **descriptif, -tive** [dɛskriptif, -tiv] *adj* : descriptive

désemparé, -rée [dezãpare] *adj* **1** : distraught **2** : in distress

déséquilibrer [dezekilibre] *vt* : unbalance — **déséquilibre** [dezekilibr] *nm* : imbalance

désert, -serte [dezɛr, -zɛrt] *adj* : desert, deserted — **désert** *nm* : desert

déserter [dezɛrte] *v* : desert — **déserteur** [dezɛrtœr] *nm* : deserter

désespérer [dezɛspere] {87} *vi* : despair — *vt* : drive to despair — **désespéré, -rée** [dezɛspere] *adj* : desperate — **désespoir** [dezɛspwar] *nm* : desperation, despair

déshabiller [dezabije] *vt* : undress — **se déshabiller** *vr* : get undressed

déshonneur [dezɔnœr] *nm* : dishonor, disgrace — **déshonorant, -rante** [dezɔnɔrã, -rãt] *adj* : dishonorable — **déshonorer** [dezɔnɔre] *vt* : dishonor, disgrace

déshydrater [dezidrate] *vt* : dehydrate

désigner [deziɲe] *vt* **1** : designate, indicate ▯ ▯▯▯.▯▯.▯▯▯▯ ▯ ▯▯▯▯▯▯▯

désillusion [dezilyzjɔ̃] *nf* : disillusionment — **désillusionner** [dezilyzjɔne] *vt* : disillusion

désinfecter [dezɛ̃fɛkte] *vt* : disinfect — **désinfectant** [dezɛ̃fɛktã] *nm* : disinfectant

désintégrer [dezɛ̃tegre] {87} *v* **se désintégrer** *vr* : disintegrate

désintéressé, -sée [dezɛ̃terese] *adj* : impartial, disinterested

désinvolte [dezɛ̃vɔlt] *adj* : casual, offhand — **désinvolture** [dezɛ̃vɔltyr] *nf* : offhand manner

désirer [dezire] *vt* : want, desire — **désir** [dezir] *nm* : desire — **désireux, -reuse** [dezirø, -røz] *adj* : anxious, eager

désobéir [dezɔbeir] *vi* : disobey — **désobéissance** [dezɔbeisãs] *nf* : disobedience — **désobéissant, -sante** [dezɔbeisã, -sãt] *adj* : disobedient

désobligeant, -geante [dezɔbliʒã, -ʒãt] *adj* : disagreeable

désoler [dezɔle] *vt* : distress — **se désoler** *vr* : be upset — **désolé, -lée** [dezɔle] *adj* **1** : desolate **2** être ~ : be sorry

désopilant, -lante [dezɔpilã, -lãt] *adj* : hilarious

désordonné, -née [dezɔrdɔne] *adj* **1** : disorganized **2** : untidy — **désordre** [dezɔrdr] *nm* **1** : disorder **2** : untidiness

désorganiser [dezɔrganize] *vt* : disorganize

désorienté, -tee [dezɔrjãte] *adj* : disoriented, confused

désormais [dezɔrmɛ] *adv* : henceforth, from now on

désosser [dezɔse] *vt* : bone (a fish)

desquels, desquelles → **lequel**

dessécher [deseʃe] {87} *vt* : dry up, parch

desserrer [desere] *vt* : loosen

dessert [desɛr] *nm* : dessert

desservir [desɛrvir] {81} *vt* **1** : serve (by providing transportation) **2** : clear (the table) **3** : do a disservice to

dessin [desɛ̃] *nm* **1** : drawing **2** : design, pattern **3** CONTOUR : outline **4** ~ **animé** : (animated) cartoon — **dessinateur, -trice** [desinatœr, -tris] *n* **1** : artist **2** : designer — **dessiner** [desine] *vt* **1** : draw **2** : outline — *vi* : draw, sketch — **se dessiner** *vr* **1** : stand out **2** APPARAÎTRE : appear, take shape

dessous [dəsu] *adv* : underneath — ~ *nms & pl* **1** : underneath, underside **2** ~ *nmpl* : underwear, lingerie **3** en ~ : underneath, down below **4** en ~ de : below — **dessous-de-verre** [d(ə)ɛsudvɛr] *nms & pl* : coaster

dessus [dəsy] *adv* : on top, on (it) — ～ *nms & pl* **1** : top **2** : upper (of a shoe) **3** : upper floor, upstairs **4 en ～** : on top, above

destiner [dɛstine] *vt* **1** : destine **2 ～ qqch à qqn** : intend sth for s.o. — **destin** [dɛstɛ̃] *nm* : fate, destiny — **destinataire** [dɛstinatɛr] *nmf* : addressee — **destination** [dɛstinasjɔ̃] *nf* : destination — **destinée** [dɛstine] *nf* : fate, destiny

destruction [dɛstryksjɔ̃] *nf* : destruction — **destructeur, -trice** [dɛstryktœr, -tris] *adj* : destructive

désuet, -suète [dezɥɛ, -zɥɛt] *adj* : outdated, obsolete — **désuétude** [dezɥetyd] *nf* **tomber en ～** : fall into disuse

désunir [dezynir] *vt* : separate, divide

détacher [detaʃe] *vt* **1** : detach, tear off **2** : untie, unfasten — **se détacher** *vr* **1** : come undone **2 ～ de** : grow apart from — **détaché, -chée** [detaʃe] *adj* : detached

détailler [detaje] *vt* **1** : sell retail **2** ÉNUMÉRER : detail, itemize — **détail** [detaj] *nm* **1** : detail **2** : retail

détecter [detɛkte] *vt* : detect — **détecteur** [detɛktœr] *nm* : detector, sensor — **détection** [detɛksjɔ̃] *nf* : detection — **détective** [detɛktiv] *nm* : detective

détendre [detɑ̃dr] {63} *vt* **1** : slacken, loosen **2** : relax, ease — **se détendre** *vr* **1** : become slack **2** : relax, unwind — **détendu, -due** [detɑ̃dy] *adj* : relaxed

détenir [detnir] {92} *vt* **1** POSSÉDER : hold, possess **2** : detain (a suspect)

détente [detɑ̃t] *nf* **1** REPOS : relaxation **2** : trigger (of a firearm)

détenteur, -trice [detɑ̃tœr, -tris] *n* : holder

détention [detɑ̃sjɔ̃] *nf* **1** : possession **2** EMPRISONNEMENT : detention

détenu, -nue [detny] *n* : prisoner

détergent [detɛrʒɑ̃] *nm* : detergent

détériorer [deterjɔre] *vt* : damage — **se détériorer** *vr* : deteriorate — **détérioration** [deterjɔrasjɔ̃] *nf* : deterioration

déterminer [detɛrmine] *vt* : determine — **se déterminer** *vr* **～ à** : make up one's mind to — **détermination** [detɛrminasjɔ̃] *nf* : determination — **déterminé, -née** [detɛrmine] *adj* **1** : determined, resolute **2** : specified, definite

déterrer [detere] *vt* : dig up, unearth

détester [detɛste] *vt* : detest — **détestable** [detɛstabl] *adj* : hateful

détoner [detɔne] *vi* : explode — **détonation** [detɔnasjɔ̃] *nf* : explosion

détourner [deturne] *vt* **1** : divert, reroute **2** : hijack (an airplane) **3** : embezzle (funds) — **détour** [detur] *nm* : detour — **détourné, -née** [deturne] *adj* : indirect, roundabout — **détournement** [deturnəmɑ̃] *nm* **1** : diver-

sion, rerouting **2** : hijacking **3** : embezzlement

détraquer [detrake] *vt* **1** : put out of order, break **2** *fam* : upset (one's stomach) — **ne détraquer** *vr* : break down, go wrong

détresse [detrɛs] *nf* : distress

détriment [detrimɑ̃] *nm* **au ～ de** : at the cost of

détritus [detrity(s)] *nmpl* : waste, rubbish

détroit [detrwa] *nm* : strait

détruire [detrɥir] {49} *vt* : destroy

dette [dɛt] *nf* : debt

deuil [dœj] *nm* : bereavement, mourning

deux [dø] *adj* **1** : two **2** : second (in dates) **3 ～ fois** : twice — ～ *nm* **1** : two **2 tous les ～** : both (of them) — **deuxième** [døzjɛm] *adj & nmf* : second — **deuxièmement** [døzjɛmmɑ̃] *adv* : secondly, second

deux-points [døpwɛ̃] *nms & pl* : colon

dévaliser [devalize] *vt* : rob (a bank, etc.)

dévaloriser [devalɔrize] *vt* **1** : reduce the value of **2** : belittle (s.o.)

devancer [dəvɑ̃se] {6} *vt* **1** : be ahead of **2** ANTICIPER : anticipate

devant [dəvɑ̃] *adv* : in front, ahead, before — ～ *nm* : front — ～ *prep* **1** : in front of **2** : ahead of

devanture [dəvɑ̃tyr] *nf* **1** : storefront **2** : shopwindow

dévaster [devaste] *vt* : devastate

développer [devlɔpe] *vt* : develop — **se développer** *vr* : develop — **développement** [devlɔpmɑ̃] *nm* : development

devenir [dəvnir] {92} *vi* **1** : become **2 qu'est-ce que tu deviens?** : what are you up to?

déverser [devɛrse] *vt* : pour (out) — **se déverser** *vr* **～ dans** : flow into

déviation [devjasjɔ̃] *nf* **1** : deviation **2** DÉTOUR : detour — **dévier** [devje] {96} *vt* : deflect, divert (traffic) — *vi* **1** : veer, swerve **2 ～ de** : deviate from

deviner [dəvine] *vt* **1** : guess **2** APERCEVOIR : perceive **3** PRÉDIRE : foretell

devinette [dəvinɛt] *nf* : riddle

devis [dəvi] *nms & pl* : estimate

devise [dəviz] *nf* **1** : motto **2** : currency (money)

dévisser [devise] *vt* : unscrew

dévoiler [devwale] *vt* : unveil, reveal

devoir [dəvwar] {28} *vt* : owe — *v aux* **1** : have to, should **2** (*expressing obligation*) : must — ～ *nm* **1** : duty **2 ～s** *nmpl* : homework

dévorer [devɔre] *vt* : devour

dévot, -vote [devo, -vɔt] *adj* : devout, pious — **dévotion** [devosjɔ̃] *nf* : devotion, piety

dévouer [devwe] *vt* : devote — **se dévouer** *vr* : devote oneself — **dévoué, -vouée**

[devwe] *adj* : devoted — **dévouement** [devumɑ̃] *nm* : dedication, devotion
dextérité [dɛksterite] *nf* : dexterity, skill
diabète [djabɛt] *nm* : diabetes — **diabétique** [djabetik] *adj & nmf* : diabetic
diable [djabl] *nm* : devil — **diabolique** [djabɔlik] *adj* : diabolical
diagnostic [djagnɔstik] *nm* : diagnosis — **diagnostiquer** [djagnɔstike] *vt* : diagnose
diagonal, -nale [djagɔnal] *adj, mpl* **-naux** [-no] : diagonal — **diagonale** *nf* 1 : diagonal 2 **en ~** : diagonally
diagramme [djagram] *nm* : graph, chart
dialecte [djalɛkt] *nm* : dialect
dialogue [djalɔg] *nm* : dialogue
diamant [djamɑ̃] *nm* : diamond
diamètre [djamɛtr] *nm* : diameter
diaphragme [djafragm] *nm* : diaphragm
diapositive [djapɔzitiv] *nf* : slide, transparency
diarrhée [djare] *nf* : diarrhea
dictateur [diktatœr] *nm* : dictator
dicter [dikte] *vt* : dictate — **dictée** [dikte] *nf* : dictation
dictionnaire [diksjɔnɛr] *nm* : dictionary
dièse [djɛz] *nm* 1 : sharp (in music) 2 : pound sign
diesel [djezɛl] *adj & nm* : diesel
diète [djɛt] *nf* RÉGIME : diet
dieu [djø] *nm, pl* **dieux** 1 : god 2 **Dieu** : God
diffamer [difame] *vt* : slander, libel — **diffamation** [difamasjɔ̃] *nf* : slander, libel
différence [diferɑ̃s] *nf* 1 : difference 2 **à la ~ de** : unlike — **différencier** [diferɑ̃sje] {96} *vt* : differentiate — **différend** [diferɑ̃] *nm* : disagreement — **différent, -rente** [diferɑ̃, -rɑ̃t] *adj* : different — **différer** [difere] {87} *vt* : defer, postpone — *vi* : differ, vary
difficile [difisil] *adj* : difficult — **difficilement** [difisilmɑ̃] *adv* : with difficulty — **difficulté** [difikylte] *nf* : difficulty
difforme [difɔrm] *adj* : deformed, misshapen — **difformité** [difɔrmite] *nf* : deformity
diffuser [difyze] *vt* 1 : broadcast 2 PROPAGER : spread, distribute — **diffusion** [difyzjɔ̃] *nf* 1 : broadcasting 2 : distribution
digérer [diʒere] {87} *vt* 1 : digest 2 *fam* : put up with — **digestif, -tive** [diʒɛstif, -tiv] *adj* : digestive — **digestion** [diʒɛstjɔ̃] *nf* : digestion
digital, -tale [diʒital] *adj, mpl* **-taux** [-to] : digital
digne [diɲ] *adj* 1 : dignified 2 **~ de** : worthy of — **dignité** [diɲite] *nf* : dignity
digue [dig] *nf* : dike
dilapider [dilapide] *vt* : squander
dilater [dilate] *vt* : dilate — **se dilater** *vr* : dilate
dilemme [dilɛm] *nm* : dilemma

diluer [dilɥe] *vt* : dilute
dimanche [dimɑ̃ʃ] *nm* : Sunday
dimension [dimɑ̃sjɔ̃] *nf* : dimension
diminuer [diminɥe] *vt* RÉDUIRE : lower, reduce — *vi* : diminish, decrease — **diminution** [diminɥsjɔ̃] *nf* : reduction, decreasing
dinde [dɛ̃d] *nf* : (female) turkey — **dindon** [dɛ̃dɔ̃] *nm* : (male) turkey
dîner [dine] *vi* 1 : dine, have dinner 2 *Can* : have lunch — *~ nm* 1 : dinner 2 *Can* : lunch — **dîneur, -neuse** [dinœr, -nœz] *n* : diner (person)
dinosaure [dinozɔr] *nm* : dinosaur
diplomate [diplɔmat] *adj* : diplomatic, tactful — *~ nmf* : diplomat — **diplomatie** [diplɔmasi] *nf* : diplomacy — **diplomatique** [diplɔmatik] *adj* : diplomatic
diplôme [diplom] *nm* : diploma — **diplômé, -mée** [diplome] *adj* : qualified, certified — *~ n* : graduate
dire [dir] {29} *vt* 1 : say 2 : tell 3 **qu'en dis-tu?** : what do you think? 4 **vouloir ~** : mean — **se dire** *vr* 1 : tell oneself 2 **comment se dit ... en français?** : how do you say ... in French? — *~ nm* 1 : statement 2 **au ~ de** : according to
direct, -recte [dirɛkt] *adj* : direct — **direct** *nm* 1 : express train 2 **en ~** : live, in person — **directement** [-təmɑ̃] *adv* : directly, straight
directeur, -trice [dirɛktœr, -tris] *adj* : directing, guiding — *~ n* 1 : manager, director 2 **directeur général** : chief executive officer
direction [dirɛksjɔ̃] *nf* 1 : direction 2 GESTION : management 3 : steering (mechanism)
directive [dirɛktiv] *nf* : order
dirigeant, -geante [diriʒɑ̃, -ʒɑ̃t] *adj* : ruling — *~ n* : leader, director
diriger [diriʒe] {17} *vt* 1 : direct, manage 2 CONDUIRE : steer 3 MENER : conduct 4 **~ sur** : aim at — **se diriger** *vr* **~ vers** : head toward
discerner [disɛrne] *vt* : discern — **discernement** [disɛrnəmɑ̃] *nm* : discernment
disciple [disipl] *nm* : disciple
discipline [disiplin] *nf* : discipline — **discipliner** [disipline] *vt* : discipline
discorde [diskɔrd] *nf* : discord
discours [diskur] *nms & pl* : speech
discréditer [diskredite] *vt* : discredit
discret, -crète [diskrɛ, -krɛt] *adj* : discreet — **discrétion** [diskresjɔ̃] *nf* 1 : discretion 2 **à ~** : unlimited, as much as one wants
discrimination [diskriminasjɔ̃] *nf* : discrimination
disculper [diskylpe] *vt* : clear, exonerate
discussion [diskysjɔ̃] *nf* : discussion
discuter [diskyte] *vt* 1 : discuss, debate 2

CONTESTER : question — *vi* **1** : talk **2** PRO-TESTER : argue **3** ~ **de** : discuss

diseuse [dizøz] *nf* ~ **de bonne aventure** : fortune-teller

dingrâoe [disgras] *nf* : disgrace

disloquer [dislɔke] *vt* LUXER : dislocate

disparaître [disparɛtr] {7} *vi* **1** : disappear **2** MOURIR : die — **disparition** [disparisjɔ̃] *nf* **1** : disappearance **2** MORT : extinction, death

disparité [disparite] *nf* : disparity

disparu, -rue [dispary] *adj* : missing — ~ *n* **1** : missing person **2** : dead person

dispenser [dispɑ̃se] *vt* **1** : exempt, excuse **2** DISTRIBUER : dispense — **se dispenser** *vr* ~ **de** : avoid — **dispense** [dispɑ̃s] *nf* : exemption

disperser [dispɛrse] *vt* : disperse, scatter — **se disperser** *vr* : disperse

disponible [dispɔnibl] *adj* : available — **disponibilité** [dispɔnibilite] *nf* : availability

disposer [dispoze] *vt* **1** PLACER : arrange **2** INCITER : incline, dispose — *vi* ~ **de** : have at one's disposal — **disposé, -sée** [dispoze] *adj* **1** : arranged **2** ~ **à** : disposed to, willing to — **dispositif** [dispozitif] *nm* **1** : device, mechanism **2** PLAN : plan of action — **disposition** [dispozisjɔ̃] *nf* **1** : arrangement, layout **2** APTITUDE : aptitude **3** TENDANCE : tendency **4 à la** ~ **de** : at the disposal of **5** ~**s** *nfpl* : steps, measures

disproportionné, -née [disprɔpɔrsjɔne] *adj* : disproportionate

disputer [dispyte] *vt* **1** : compete in, play **2** *fam* : tell off **3** *Can* : scold — **se disputer** *vr* : quarrel, fight — **dispute** [dispyt] *nf* : argument, quarrel

disqualifier [diskalifje] {96} *vt* : disqualify

disque [disk] *nm* **1** : (phonograph) record **2** : disk — **disquette** [diskɛt] *nf* : floppy disk

disséminer [disemine] *vt* : scatter

dissentiment [disɑ̃timɑ̃] *nm* : dissent

dissertation [disɛrtasjɔ̃] *nf* : essay (in school)

dissimuler [disimyle] *vt* : conceal, hide — **se dissimuler** *vr* : hide oneself — **dissimulation** [disimylasjɔ̃] *nf* **1** : deceit **2** : concealment

dissiper [disipe] *vt* **1** : disperse **2** : squander (one's fortune) — **se dissiper** *vr* : clear (up), vanish

dissolu, -lue [disɔly] *adj* : dissolute — **dissolution** [disɔlysjɔ̃] *nf* **1** : dissolution, breakup **2** : dissolving — **dissolvant** [disɔlvɑ̃] *nm* **1** : solvent **2** : nail polish remover

dissoudre [disudr] {1} *vt* : dissolve — **se dissoudre** *vr* : dissolve

dissuader [disɥade] *vt* : dissuade, deter

distance [distɑ̃s] *nf* : distance — **distant, -tante** [distɑ̃, -tɑt] *adj* : distant

distiller [distile] *vt* : distill

distinct, -tincte [distɛ̃, -tɛ̃kt] *adj* : distinct — **distinctif, -tive** [distɛ̃ktif, -tiv] *adj* : distinctive — **distinction** [distɛ̃ksjɔ̃] *nf* : distinction

distinguer [distɛ̃ge] *v* : distinguish — **distingué, -guée** [distɛ̃ge] *adj* : distinguished

distraction [distraksjɔ̃] *nf* **1** : distraction **2** PASSE-TEMPS : recreation

distraire [distrɛr] {40} *vt* **1** : distract **2** DIVERTIR : amuse, entertain — **se distraire** *vr* : amuse oneself — **distrait, -traite** [distrɛ, -trɛt] *adj* : distracted, absentminded

distribuer [distribɥe] *vt* **1** : distribute **2** : deliver (mail) — **distributeur** [distribytœr] *nm* **1** : distributor **2** *or* ~ **automatique** : dispenser, vending machine — **distribution** [distribysjɔ̃] *nf* **1** : distribution **2** : casting, cast (of actors)

district [distrikt] *nm* : district

dit, dite [di, dit] *adj* **1** : agreed upon, stated **2** : called, known as

divaguer [divage] *vi* : rave

divan [divɑ̃] *nm* : couch

divergence [-vɛrʒɑ̃s] *nf* : difference — **diverger** [divɛrʒe] {17} *vi* : diverge

divers, -verse [divɛr, -vɛrs] *adj* **1** VARIÉ : diverse **2** PLUSIEURS : various — **diversifier** [divɛrsifje] {96} *vt* : diversify — **diversion** [divɛrsjɔ̃] *nf* : diversion — **diversité** [divɛrsite] *nf* : diversity, variety

divertir [divɛrtir] *vt* : amuse, entertain — **se divertir** *vr* : amuse oneself — **divertissement** [divɛrtismɑ̃] *nm* : entertainment, pastime

dividende [dividɑ̃d] *nm* : dividend

divine, -vine [divɛ̃, -vin] *adj* : divine — **divinité** [divinite] *nf* : divinity

diviser [divize] *vt* : divide — **se diviser** *vr* : divide — **division** [divizjɔ̃] *nf* : division

divorcer [divɔrse] {6} *vi* : get a divorce — **divorce** [divɔrs] *nm* : divorce

divulguer [divylge] *vt* : divulge, disclose

dix [dis, *before a consonant* di, *before a vowel or mute h* diz] *adj* **1** : ten **2** : tenth (in dates) — ~ *nms & pl* : ten

dix-huit [dizɥit] *adj* **1** : eighteen **2** : eighteenth (in dates) — ~ *nms & pl* : eighteen — **dix-huitième** [dizɥitjɛm] *adj & nmf & nm* : eighteenth

dixième [dizjɛm] *adj & nmf & nm* : tenth

dix-neuf [diznœf] *adj* **1** : nineteen **2** : nineteenth (in dates) — ~ *nms & pl* : nineteen — **dix-neuvième** [diznœvjɛm] *adj & nmf & nm* : nineteenth

dix-sept [disɛt] *adj* **1** : seventeen **2** : seventeenth (in dates) — ~ *nms & pl* : seventeen

— **dix–septième** [disɛtjɛm] *adj & nmf & nm* : seventeenth
dizaine [dizɛn] *nf* : ten, about ten
docile [dɔsil] *adj* : obedient
dock [dɔk] *nm* : dock
docteur [dɔktœr] *nm* : doctor
doctrine [dɔktrin] *nf* : doctrine
document [dɔkymã] *nm* : document — **documentation** [dɔkymãtasjɔ̃] *nf* : literature, leaflets *pl* — **documenter** [dɔkymãte] *v se documenter* *vr* ~ **sur** : research
dodu, -due [dɔdy] *adj* : plump, chubby
dogme [dɔgm] *nm* : dogma
doigt [dwa] *nm* 1 : finger 2 ~ **de pied** : toe — **doigté** [dwate] *nm* TACT : tact
dollar [dɔlar] *nm* : dollar
domaine [dɔmɛn] *nm* 1 : domain 2 PROPRIÉTÉ : estate
dôme [dom] *nm* : dome
domestique [dɔmɛstik] *adj* 1 : domestic 2 : domesticated — ~ *nmf* : servant — **domestiquer** [dɔmɛstike] *vt* APPRIVOISER : domesticate
domicile [dɔmisil] *nm* : residence, home
dominer [dɔmine] *v* : dominate — **dominant, -nante** [dɔminã, -nãt] *adj* : dominant
dommage [dɔmaʒ] *nm* 1 PRÉJUDICE : harm, injury 2 DÉGÂTS : damage 3 **c'est** ~ : that's too bad
dompter [dɔ̃te] *vt* : tame
don [dɔ̃] *nm* : gift — **donateur, -trice** [dɔnatœr, -tris] *n* : donor, giver — **donation** [dɔnasjɔ̃] *nf* : donation
donc [dɔ̃k] *conj* 1 : so, therefore, consequently 2 : so, then
donner [dɔne] *vt* 1 : give 2 : produce, yield 3 MONTRER : indicate, show 4 CAUSER : cause 5 : deal (cards) — *vi* 1 : produce a crop 2 ~ **dans** : fall into 3 ~ **sur** : overlook — **se donner** *vr* ~ **à** : devote oneself to — **donne** [dɔn] *nf* : deal (in card games) — **donné, -née** [dɔne] *adj* 1 : given 2 **c'est** ~ : it's a bargain — **donnée** *nf* 1 : fact 2 ~**s** *nfpl* : data — **donneur, -neuse** [dɔnœr, -nøz] *n* 1 : donor 2 : (card) dealer
dont [dɔ̃] *pron* : of which, of whom, whose
doré, -rée [dɔre] *adj* 1 : gilt 2 : golden
dorénavant [dɔrenavã] *adv* : henceforth
dorer [dɔre] *vt* : gild 2 BRUNIR : tan — *vi* : brown (in cooking)
dorloter [dɔrlɔte] *vi* : pamper
dormir [dɔrmir] {30} *vi* : sleep, be asleep
dortoir [dɔrtwar] *nm* : dormitory
dorure [dɔryr] *nf* : gilding, gilt
dos [do] *nms & pl* : back
dose [doz] *nf* : dose — **doser** [doze] *vt* : measure out (a dose of medicine)
dossier [dosje] *nm* 1 : file, record 2 : back (of a chair)
doter [dɔte] *vt* 1 : endow 2 ÉQUIPER : equip

douane [dwan] *nf* 1 : customs 2 : (import) duty — **douanier, -nière** [dwanje, -njɛr] *adj* : customs — **douanier** *nm* : customs officer
double [dubl] *adj & adj* : double — ~ *nm* 1 : double 2 : copy, duplicate — **doublement** [dubləmã] *adv* : doubly — **doubler** [duble] *vt* 1 : double 2 : line (fabric) 3 : dub (a film, etc.) 4 DÉPASSER : pass, overtake — *vi* : double — **doublure** [dublyr] *nf* 1 : lining 2 : understudy
douce → **doux** — **doucement** [dusmã] *adv* 1 : gently, softly 2 LENTEMENT : slowly — **douceur** [dusœr] *nf* 1 : softness, smoothness 2 : gentleness, mildness
douche [duʃ] *nf* : shower — **doucher** [duʃe] *se doucher* *vr* : take a shower
doué, douée [dwe] *adj* 1 : gifted, talented 2 ~ **de** : endowed with
douille [duj] *nf* : electric socket
douillet, -lette [dujɛ, -jɛt] *adj* CONFORTABLE : cozy
douleur [dulœr] *nf* 1 : pain 2 CHAGRIN : grief — **douloureux, -reuse** [dulurø, -røz] *adj* : painful
douter [dute] *vt* 1 : doubt 2 ~ **de** : question — **se douter** *vr* ~ **de** : suspect — **doute** [dut] *nm* : doubt — **douteux, -teuse** [dutø, -tøz] *adj* : doubtful
doux, douce [du, dus] *adj* 1 : sweet 2 : soft (of skin) 3 : mild, gentle
douze [duz] *adj* 1 : twelve 2 : twelfth (in dates) — ~ *nms & pl* : twelve — **douzaine** [duzɛn] *nf* : dozen — **douzième** [duzjɛm] *adj & nmf & nm* : twelfth
doyen, doyenne [dwajɛ̃, -jɛn] *n* : dean
dragon [dragɔ̃] *nm* : dragon
draguer [drage] *vt* : dredge
drainer [drene] *vt* : drain — **drainage** [drenaʒ] *nm* : drainage, draining
drame [dram] *nm* 1 : drama 2 : tragedy — **dramatique** [dramatik] *adj* : dramatic — **dramatiser** [dramatize] *vt* : dramatize — **dramaturge** [dramatyrʒ] *nmf* : playwright
drap [dra] *nm* 1 : sheet 2 : woolen fabric
drapeau [drapo] *nm, pl* -**peaux** : flag
draper [drape] *vt* : drape
drastique [drastik] *adj* : drastic
dresser [drese] *vt* 1 LEVER : raise 2 ÉRIGER : put up, erect 3 ÉTABLIR : draft, draw up 4 : train (an animal) 5 ~ **les oreilles** : cock one's ears — **se dresser** *vr* 1 : stand up 2 : rise up, tower
dribbler [drible] *vi* : dribble (in sports)
drogue [drɔg] *nf* : drug — **drogué, -guée** [drɔge] *n* : drug addict — **droguer** [drɔge] *vt* : drug — **se droguer** *vr* : take drugs
droit [drwa] *nm* 1 : right 2 : fee, tax, duty 3 **le** ~ : law 4 ~**s d'auteur** : copyright — ~ *adv* : straight, directly — **droit, droite**

[drwa, drwat] *adj* **1** : right, right-hand **2** : straight, direct **3** VERTICAL : upright, vertical **4** HONNÊTE : honest — **droite** *nf* **1** : right, right-hand side **2 la ~** : the right (in politics) **droitier, tière** [drwatje, -tjɛr] *adj* : right-handed — **droiture** [drwatyr] *nf* : uprightness, integrity

drôle [drol] *adj* : funny — **drôlement** [drolmɑ̃] *adv* **1** : amusingly **2** BIZARREMENT : strangely, oddly **3** *fam* : really, awfully

dru, drue [dry] *adj* : thick (of hair, etc.)

du → de, le

dû, due [dy] *adj* **1** : due, owing **2 ~ à** : due to — **dû** *nm* : due

duc [dyk] *nm* : duke — **duchesse** [dyʃɛs] *nf* : duchess

duel [dɥɛl] *nm* : duel

dûment [dymɑ̃] *adv* : duly

dune [dyn] *nf* : dune

duo [dyo] *nm* **1** : duet **2** : duo, pair

dupe [dyp] *nf* : dupe — **duper** [dype] *vt* : dupe, deceive

duplex [dyplɛks] *nm* : duplex (apartment)

duplicata [dyplikata] *nms & pl* : duplicate

duquel → lequel

dur, dure [dyr] *adj* **1** : hard, stiff **2** DIFFICILE : difficult **3** SÉVÈRE : harsh — **dur** *adv* : hard

durable [dyrabl] *adj* : durable, lasting

durant [dyrɑ̃] *prep* **1** : for (a period of time) **2** : during

durcir [dyrsir] *v* : harden — **se durcir** *vr* : harden — **durcissement** [dyrsismɑ̃] *nm* : hardening

durée [dyre] *nf* : duration, length

durement [dyrmɑ̃] *adv* : harshly, severely

durer [dyre] *vi* : last, go on

dureté [dyrte] *nf* **1** : hardness **2** SÉVÉRITÉ : harshness

duvet [dyvɛ] *nm* **1** : down (fabric) **2** : sleeping bag

dynamique [dinamik] *adj* : dynamic

dynamite [dinamit] *nf* : dynamite — **dynamiter** [dinamite] *vt* : dynamite, blast

dynastie [dinasti] *nf* : dynasty

E

e [ø] *nm* : e, fifth letter of the alphabet

eau [o] *nf, pl* **eaux 1** : water **2 ~ de Cologne** : cologne **3 ~ douce** : freshwater **4 ~ de Javel** : bleach **5 ~ oxygénée** : hydrogen peroxide — **eau–de–vie** *nf, pl* **eaux–de–vie** : brandy

ébahir [ebair] *vt* : astound, dumbfound

ébaucher [eboʃe] *vt* : sketch out, outline — **s'ébaucher** *vr* : form, take shape — **ébauche** [eboʃ] *nf* : outline, sketch

ébène [ebɛn] *nf* : ebony — **ébéniste** [ebenist] *nmf* : cabinetmaker

éblouir [ebluir] *vt* : dazzle, stun

ébouler [ebule] *v* **s'ébouler** *vr* : cave in, collapse

ébouriffer [eburife] *vt* : tousle, ruffle

ébranler [ebrɑ̃le] *vt* **1** : shake **2** : weaken, undermine

ébrécher [ebreʃe] {87} *vt* : chip, nick — **ébréchure** [ebreʃyr] *nf* : chip, nick

ébriété [ebrijete] *nf* : inebriation, drunkenness

ébullition [ebylisjɔ̃] *nf* : boil, boiling

écailler [ekaje] *vt* **1** : scale (fish) **2** : open (a shell) **3** : chip (paint) — **s'écailler** *vr* : flake off — **écaille** [ekaj] *nf* **1** : scale (of a fish) **2** : tortoiseshell **3** FRAGMENT : flake, chip

écarlate [ekarlat] *adj & nf* : scarlet

écarquiller [ekarkije] *vt* **~ les yeux** : open one's eyes wide

écarter [ekarte] *vt* **1** : spread, open **2** ÉLOIGNER : move apart **3** EXCLURE : rule out **4** DÉTOURNER : divert, distract — **s'écarter** *vr* **1** : move away **2** SE SÉPARER : part, open — **écart** [ekar] *nm* **1** : distance, gap **2** VARIATION : difference **3** : lapse (of conduct) **4** DÉVIATION : swerve **5 à l'~** : apart, away — **écarté, -tée** [ekarte] *adj* **1** ISOLÉ : remote **2** : wide apart — **écartement** [ekartəmɑ̃] *nm* : gap

ecclésiastique [eklezjastik] *nm* : clergyman

écervelé, -lée [esɛrvəle] *adj* : scatterbrained

échafaud [eʃafo] *nm* : scaffold — **échafaudage** [eʃafodaʒ] *nm* : scaffolding

échalote [eʃalɔt] *nf* **1** : shallot **2** *Can* : scallion

échanger [eʃɑ̃ʒe] {17} *vt* : exchange — **échange** [eʃɑ̃ʒ] *nm* **1** : exchange **2** : trade, commerce — **échangeur** [eʃɑ̃ʒœr] *nm* : (highway) interchange

échantillon [eʃɑ̃tijɔ̃] *nm* : sample

échapper [eʃape] *vi* **1 ~ à** : escape (from) **2 laisser ~** : let out **3 l'~ belle** : have a narrow escape — *vt Can* : drop — **s'échapper** *vr* : escape

écharde [eʃard] *nf* : splinter

écharpe [eʃarp] *nf* **1** : scarf **2 en ~** : in a sling

échasse [eʃas] *nf* : stilt

échauffer [eʃofe] *v* **s'échauffer** *vr* : warm up

échéance [eʃeãs] *nf* **1** : due date **2** OBLIGATION : financial obligation, payment **3 à longue ~** : in the long run — **échéant** [eʃeã] **le cas ~** *adv phr* : if need be

échec [eʃɛk] *nm* **1** : failure, setback **2 ~s** *nmpl* : chess **3 ~ et mat** : checkmate **4 en ~** : in check

échelle [eʃɛl] *nf* **1** : ladder **2** MESURE : scale — **échelon** [eʃlɔ̃] *nm* **1** : rung **2** NIVEAU : level — **échelonner** [eʃlɔne] *vt* : space out, spread out

échevelé, -lée [eʃəvle] *adj* : disheveled

échiquier [eʃikje] *nm* : chessboard

écho [eko] *nm* : echo — **échographie** [ekografi] *nf* : ultrasound

échoir [eʃwar] {31} *vi* **1** : fall due **2 ~ à qqn** : fall to s.o.

échouer [eʃwe] *vi* : fail (of an exam) — **s'échouer** *vr* : run aground

éclabousser [eklabuse] *vt* : splash, spatter — **éclaboussure** [eklabusyr] *nf* : splash

éclairer [eklere] *vt* **1** : light (up) **2** INFORMER : enlighten **3** EXPLIQUER : clarify — *vi* : give light — **s'éclairer** *vr* **1** : light up **2** : become clearer — **éclair** [eklɛr] *nm* **1** ÉCLAT : flash **2** : (flash of) lightning — **éclairage** [eklɛraʒ] *nm* : lighting, illumination — **éclaircie** [eklɛrsi] *nf* **1** : sunny spell **2** : clearing, glade — **éclaircir** [eklɛrsir] *vt* **1** : lighten **2** CLARIFIER : clarify **3** : thin (in cooking) — **s'éclaircir** *vr* : clear (up) — **éclaircissement** [eklɛrsismã] *nm* : explanation, clarification

éclaireur, -reuse [eklɛrœr, -røz] *n* : boy scout *m*, girl scout *f* — **éclaireur** *nm* : (military) scout

éclater [eklate] *vi* **1** : burst, explode **2** : break up, splinter — **éclat** [ekla] *nm* **1** : splinter, chip **2** : brilliance, shine **3** : splendor **4 ~ de rire** : burst (of laughter) — **éclatant, -tante** [eklatã, -tãt] *adj* **1** BRILLANT : brilliant **2 un succès éclatant** : a resounding success — **éclatement** [eklatmã] *nm* **1** : explosion, bursting **2** : rupture, split

éclipse [eklips] *nf* : eclipse — **éclipser** [eklipse] *v* **s'éclipser** *vr* : slip away

éclore [eklɔr] {32} *vi* **1** : hatch **2** : open out, blossom — **éclosion** [eklozjɔ̃] *nf* **1** : hatching **2** : blossoming

écluse [eklyz] *nf* : lock (of a canal)

écœurer [ekœre] *vt* : sicken, disgust — **écœurant, -rante** [ekœrã, -rãt] *adj* **1** : cloying, sickening **2** DÉGUEULASSE : disgusting

école [ekɔl] *nf* **1** : school **2 ~ secondaire** *Can* : high school **3 ~ maternelle** *Can* : kindergarten — **écolier, -lière** [ekɔlje, -ljɛr] *n* : schoolboy *m*, schoolgirl *f*

écologie [ekɔlɔʒi] *nf* : ecology — **écologique** [ekɔlɔʒik] *adj* : ecological

économie [ekɔnɔmi] *nf* **1** : economy **2** : economics **3 ~s** *nfpl* : savings — **économe** [ekɔnɔm] *adj* : thrifty, economical — **~** *nmf* : bursar — **économique** [ekɔnɔmik] *adj* : economic — **économiser** [ekɔnɔmize] *v* : save — **économiste** [ekɔnɔmist] *nmf* : economist

écorce [ekɔrs] *nf* **1** : bark (of a tree) **2** : peel (of a fruit)

écorcher [ekɔrʃe] *vt* **1** DÉPOUILLER : skin **2** ÉGRATIGNER : scratch, graze — **écorchure** [ekɔrʃyr] *nf* : graze, scratch

écossais, -saise [ekɔsɛ, -sɛz] *adj* **1** : Scottish **2** : tartan, plaid

écosser [ekɔse] *vt* : shell (peas, etc.)

écosystème [ekɔsistɛm] *nm* : ecosystem

écouler [ekule] *vt* : sell, dispose of — **s'écouler** *vr* **1** : flow (out) **2** PASSER : pass, elapse — **écoulement** [ekulmã] *nm* : flow

écourter [ekurte] *vt* : cut short, curtail

écouter [ekute] *vt* : listen to — *vi* : listen — **écouteur** [ekutœr] *nm* **1** : (telephone) receiver **2 ~s** *nmpl* : headphones

écoutille [ekutij] *nf* : hatch (of a ship)

écran [ekrã] *nm* : screen

écraser [ekraze] *vt* **1** : crush, squash, mash **2** : run over (an animal, etc.) **3** ACCABLER : overwhelm — **s'écraser** *vr* : crash (of a plane, etc.) — **écrasant, -sante** [ekrazã, -zãt] *adj* : crushing, overwhelming

écrémé, -mée [ekreme] *adj* **lait écrémé** : skim milk

écrevisse [ekrəvis] *nf* : crayfish

écrier [ekrije] {96} *v* **s'écrier** *vr* : exclaim

écrin [ekrɛ̃] *nm* : case, box

écrire [ekrir] {33} *v* : write — **s'écrire** *vr* : be spelled — **écrit** [ekri] *nm* **1** : writing(s) **2** : document **3 par ~** : in writing — **écriteau** [ekrito] *nm, pl* **-teaux** : notice, sign — **écriture** [ekrityr] *nf* : writing — **écrivain** [ekrivɛ̃] *nm* : writer — **écrivaillon** [ekrivajɔ̃] *nm fam* : hack writer

écrou [ekru] *nm* : (metal) nut

écrouler [ekrule] *v* **s'écrouler** *vr* : collapse — **écroulement** [ekrulmã] *nm* : collapse

écueil [ekœj] *nm* RÉCIF : reef

écume [ekym] *nf* **1** : foam, froth **2** : scum (in cooking) — **écumer** [ekyme] *vi* : foam, froth — **écumeux, -meuse** [ekymø, -møz] *adj* : foamy

écureuil [ekyrœj] *nm* : squirrel

écurie [ekyri] *nf* : stable

écusson [ekysɔ̃] *nm* : badge

édenté, -tée [edãte] *adj* : toothless

édifice [edifis] *nm* : building — **édifier** [edifje] {96} *vt* CONSTRUIRE : build

éditer [edite] *vt* **1** : publish **2** : edit — **éditeur, -trice** [editœr, -tris] *n* **1** : publisher **2** : editor — **édition** [edisjɔ̃] *nf* **1** : publishing **2** : édition (of a book) — **éditorial** [editorjal] *nm, pl* **-riaux** [-rjo] : editorial

édredon [edrədɔ̃] *nm* : comforter

éducation [edykasjɔ̃] *nf* **1** ENSEIGNEMENT : education **2** : upbringing (of children) **3** avoir de l'~ : have good manners — **éducatif, -tive** [edykatif, -tiv] *adj* : educational — **éduquer** [edyke] *vt* **1** : educate **2** ÉLEVER : bring up

effacer [efase] {6} *vt* : erase, delete — **s'effacer** *vr* **1** : fade **2** S'ÉCARTER : stand aside

effectif, -tive [efɛktif, -tiv] *adj* : real, actual — **effectivement** [efɛktivmã] *adv* **1** : indeed, in fact **2** RÉELLEMENT : really

effectuer [efɛktɥe] *vt* EXÉCUTER : carry out, make

efféminé, -née [efemine] *adj* : effeminate

effervescent, -cente [efɛrvesɑ, -sãt] *adj* : effervescent

effet [efɛ] *nm* **1** RÉSULTAT : effect, result **2** en ~ : indeed, actually **3** faire bon ~ : make a good impression

efficace [efikas] *adj* : efficient — **efficacité** [efikasite] *nf* **1** : efficiency **2** : effectiveness

effilocher [efilɔʃe] *vt* : shred, fray — **s'effilocher** *vr* : fray

effleurer [eflœre] *vt* **1** FRÔLER : touch lightly, graze **2** ça m'a effleuré l'esprit : it crossed my mind

effondrer [efɔ̃dre] *v* **s'effondrer** *vr* : collapse — **effondrement** [efɔ̃drəmã] *nm* : collapse

efforcer [efɔrse] {6} *v* **s'efforcer** *vr* : strive, endeavor

effort [efɔr] *nm* : effort

effrayer [efreje] {11} *vt* : frighten — **effrayant, -frayante** [efrɛjã, -jãt] *adj* : frightening

effréné, -née [efrene] *adj* : wild, unrestrained

effriter [efrite] *vt* : crumble — **s'effriter** *vr* : crumble

effroi [efrwa] *nm* : terror, dread

effronté, -tée [efrɔ̃te] *adj* : impudent

effroyable [efrwajabl] *adj* : dreadful

égal, -gale [egal] *adj, mpl* **égaux** [ego] **1** : equal **2** RÉGULIER : regular, even **3** ça m'est ~ : it makes no difference to me — **~** *n* : equal — **également** [egalmã] *adv* **1** : equally **2** AUSSI : also, as well — **égaler** [egale] *vt* : equal — **égaliser** [egalize] *vt* **1** : equalize **2** : level (out) — **égalité** [egalite] *nf* : equality

égard [egar] *nm* **1** : regard, consideration **2** à cet ~ : in this respect **3** à l'~ de : with regard to

égarer [egare] *vt* **1** : lead astray **2** PERDRE : lose, misplace — **s'égarer** *vr* **1** : lose one's way **2** : be misplaced

égayer [egeje] {11} *vt* : cheer up

églefin [egləfɛ̃] *nm* : haddock

église [egliz] *nf* : church

ego [ego] *nm* : ego — **égoïsme** [egɔism] *nm* : selfishness — **égoïste** [egɔist] *adj* : selfish

égorger [egɔrʒe] {17} *vt* : cut the throat of

égotisme [egɔtism] *nm* : egotism — **égotiste** [egɔtist] *adj* : egotistic(al)

égoutter [egute] *vt* : allow to drip, drain — **s'égoutter** *vr* : drain — **égout** [egu] *nm* : sewer — **égouttoir** [egutwar] *nm* : (dish) drainer

égratigner [egratiɲe] *vt* : scratch, graze — **égratignure** [egratiɲyr] *nf* : scratch

eh [e] *interj* **1** : hey! **2** ~ bien : well

éhonté, -tée [eɔ̃te] *adj* : shameless, brazen

éjaculer [eʒakyle] *v* : ejaculate

éjecter [eʒɛkte] *vt* **1** : eject **2** *fam* : kick out

élaborer [elabɔre] *vt* : develop, put together — **élaboration** [elabɔrasjɔ̃] *nf* : elaboration, development

élan¹ [elɑ̃] *nm* **1** : momentum **2** : rush, surge (of energy, etc.)

élan² *nm* : elk

élancé, -cée [elɑ̃se] *adj* : slender

élancer [elɑ̃se] {6} *v* **s'élancer** *vr* SE PRÉCIPITER : dash, rush — **élancement** [elɑ̃smã] *nm* : shooting pain

élargir [elarʒir] *vt* : widen, broaden — **s'élargir** *vr* : expand, become broader — **élargissement** [elarʒismã] *nm* : widening, expanding

élastique [elastik] *adj* : elastic, flexible — **~** *nm* **1** : elastic **2** : rubber band

électeur, -trice [elɛktœr, -tris] *n* : voter — **élection** [elɛksjɔ̃] *nf* : election — **électoral, -rale** [elɛktɔral] *adj, mpl* **-raux** [-ro] : electoral, election — **électorat** [elɛktɔra] *nm* : electorate

électricité [elɛktrisite] *nf* : electricity — **électricien, -cienne** [elɛktrisjɛ̃, -sjɛn] *n* : electrician — **électrique** [elɛktrik] *adj* : electric(al)

électrocuter [elɛktrɔkyte] *vt* : electrocute

électron [elɛktrɔ̃] *nm* : electron — **électronique** [elɛktrɔnik] *adj* : electronic — **~** *nf* : electronics

élégance [elegɑ̃s] *nf* : elegance — **élégant, -gante** [elegã, -gãt] *adj* : elegant

élément [elemã] *nm* **1** : element **2** COMPOSANT : component, part — **élémentaire** [elemãter] *adj* : elementary, basic

éléphant [elefã] *nm* : elephant

élevage [ɛlvaʒ] *nm* : breeding

élévation

56

élévation [elevasjɔ̃] *nf* **1** : elevation **2** AUG-
MENTATION : rise, increase
élève [elɛv] *nmf* : pupil, student
élever [elve] {52} *vt* **1** : raise **2** ÉRIGER
: erect **3** ÉDUQUER : bring up (a child) —
s'élever *vr* **1** : rise (up) **2** ~ **à** : amount to
— **élevé, -vée** [elve] *adj* **1** : high, elevated
2 bien ~ : well-mannered — **éleveur,**
-veuse [elvœr, -vøz] *n* : breeder
éligible [eliʒibl] *adj* : eligible
éliminer [elimine] *vt* : eliminate — **élimina-**
tion [eliminasjɔ̃] *nf* : elimination
élire [elir] {51} *vt* : elect
élite [elit] *nf* : elite
elle [ɛl] *pron* **1** : she, it **2** : her **3 elles** *pron*
pl : they, them — **elle–même** [ɛlmɛm] *pron*
1 : herself, itself **2 elles–mêmes** *pron pl*
: themselves
éloge [elɔʒ] *nm* : eulogy, praise
éloigner [elwaɲe] *vt* **1** ÉCARTER : push
aside, move away **2** DÉTOURNER : divert,
turn away — **s'éloigner** *vr* : move or go
away — **éloigné, -gnée** [elwaɲe] *adj* : distant, remote — **éloignement** [elwaɲmã] *nm*
: distance, remoteness
éloquence [elɔkãs] *nf* : eloquence — **élo-**
quent, -quente [elɔkã, -kãt] *adj* : eloquent
élu, -lue [ely] *adj* : elected — ~ *n* : elected
representative
élucider [elyside] *vt* : elucidate
éluder [elyde] *vt* : elude
émacié, -ciée [emasje] *adj* : emaciated
émail [emaj] *nm, pl* **émaux** [emo] : enamel
émanciper [emãsipe] *vt* : emancipate —
émancipation [emãsipasjɔ̃] *nf* : emancipa-
tion
émaner [emane] *vi* ~ **de** : emanate from
emballer [ãbale] *vt* **1** EMPAQUETER : pack,
wrap **2** *fam* : thrill — **s'emballer** *vr* **1**
: race (of an engine), bolt (of a horse) **2** *fam*
: get carried away — **emballage** [ãbalaʒ]
nm : packing, wrapping
embarcadère [ãbarkadɛr] *nm* : wharf, pier
embarcation [ãbarkasjɔ̃] *nf* : small boat
embardée [ãbarde] *nf* : swerve (of a car)
embargo [ãbargo] *nm* : embargo
embarquer [ãbarke] *vt* **1** : embark **2**
CHARGER : load — *vi* : board — **s'em-**
barquer *vr* : board — **embarquement**
[ãbarkəmã] *nm* **1** : boarding **2** : loading
(on board)
embarrasser [ãbarase] *vt* **1** ENCOMBRER
: clutter **2** ENTRAVER : hinder **3** GÊNER
: embarrass — **s'embarrasser** *vr* ~ **de**
: burden oneself with — **embarras** [ãbara]
nms & pl **1** : difficulty **2** : embarrassment
— **embarrassant, -sante** [ãbarasã, -sãt]
adj **1** : embarrassing, awkward **2** ENCOM-
BRANT : cumbersome

embaucher [ãboʃe] *vt* : hire — **embauche**
[ãboʃ] *nf* : hiring, employment
embaumer [ãbome] *vt* **1** : embalm **2**
: scent, make fragrant
embellir [ãbelir] *vt* **1** ENJOLIVER : beautify
2 EXAGÉRER : embellish
embêter [ãbete] *vt* **1** : annoy, bother **2**
LASSER : bore — **s'embêter** *vr* : be bored —
embêtant, -tante [ãbetã, -tãt] *adj* : annoying — **embêtement** [ãbetmã] *nm* : hassle,
bother
emblée [ãble] **d'**~ *adv phr* : right away
emblème [ãblɛm] *nm* : emblem
embobiner [ãbɔbine] *vt fam* : bamboozle,
trick
emboîter [ãbwate] *vt* : fit together — **s'em-**
boîter *vr* ~ **dans** : fit into
embonpoint [ãbɔ̃pwɛ̃] *nm* : stoutness, cor-
pulence
embouchure [ãbuʃyr] *nf* **1** : mouth (of a
river) **2** : mouthpiece
embourber [ãburbe] *v* **s'embourber** *vr*
: get bogged down
embouteillage [ãbutejaʒ] *nm* : traffic jam
emboutir [ãbutir] *vt* HEURTER : crash into,
ram
embranchement [ãbrãʃmã] *nm* : junction,
fork
embraser [ãbraze] *vt* : set on fire — **s'em-**
braser *vr* : catch fire
embrasser [ãbrase] *vt* **1** : kiss **2** ÉTREIN-
DRE : embrace, hug — **s'embrasser** *vr*
: kiss
embrasure [ãbrazyr] *nf* : doorway
embrayage [ãbrejaʒ] *nm* : clutch (of an automobile) — **embrayer** [ãbreje] {11} *vi*
: engage the clutch
embrocher [ãbrɔʃe] *vt* : skewer (meat on a
spit)
embrouiller [ãbruje] *vt* **1** : tangle up **2**
COMPLIQUER : confuse — **s'embrouiller** *vr*
: get mixed up
embryon [ãbrijɔ̃] *nm* : embryo
embûche [ãbyʃ] *nf* : trap, pitfall
embuer [ãbɥe] *vt* : mist up
embuscade [ãbyskad] *nf* : ambush
éméché, -chée [emeʃe] *adj fam* : tipsy
émeraude [emrod] *nf* : emerald
émerger [emɛrʒe] {17} *vi* : emerge — **émer-**
gence [emɛrʒãs] *nf* : emergence
émeri [emri] *nm* : emery
émerveiller [emɛrveje] *vt* : amaze —
s'émerveiller *vr* ~ **de** : marvel at — **émer-**
veillement [emɛrvejmã] *nm* : amazement,
wonder
émettre [emɛtr] {53} *vt* **1** : produce, give
out **2** : issue (a check) **3** TRANSMETTRE
: transmit, broadcast **4** EXPRIMER : express
— **émetteur** [emetœr] *nm* **1** : transmitter **2**
: issuer

émeute [emøt] *nf* : riot — **émeutier, -tière** [emøtje] *n* : rioter

émietter [emjete] *vt* : crumble, break up — **s'émietter** *vr* : crumble

émigrer [emigre] *vi* 1 : emigrate 2 : migrate — **émigrant, -grante** [emigrã, -grãt] *n* : emigrant — **émigration** [emigrasjɔ̃] *nf* : emigration — **émigré, -grée** [emigre] *n* : emigrant, émigré

éminence [eminãs] *nf* : eminence — **éminent, -nente** [eminã, -nãt] *adj* : eminent

émission [emisjɔ̃] *nf* 1 : emission 2 : transmission (of a message) 3 : program, broadcast 4 : issue (of a magazine, etc.)

emmagasiner [ãmagazine] *vt* : store (up)

emmêler [ãmele] *vt* 1 : tangle 2 EM-BROUILLER : muddle, mix up

emménager [ãmenaʒe] {17} *vi* : move in

emmener [ãmne] {52} *vt* : take

emmitoufler [ãmitufle] *vt* : wrap up, bundle up — **s'emmitoufler** *vr* : bundle (up)

émoi [emwa] *nm* : excitement, turmoil

émotif, -tive [emɔtif, -tiv] *adj* : emotional — **émotion** [emosjɔ̃] *nf* : emotion — **émotionnel, -nelle** [emosjɔnɛl] *adj* : emotional

émousser [emuse] *vt* : blunt, dull

émouvoir [emuvwar] {56} *vt* : move, affect — **s'émouvoir** *vr* 1 : be moved 2 ~ **de** : be concerned about — **émouvant, -vante** [emuvã, -vãt] *adj* : moving

empailler [ãpaje] *vt* : stuff

empaqueter [ãpakte] {8} *vt* : package, wrap up

emparer [ãpare] *v* **s'emparer** *vr* ~ **de** : seize, take hold of

empathie [ãpati] *nf* : empathy

empêcher [ãpeʃe] *vt* 1 : prevent, stop 2 **il n'empêche que** : nevertheless — **s'empêcher** *vr* : refrain, stop oneself — **empêchement** [ãpɛʃmã] *nm* : hitch, difficulty

empereur [ãprœr] *nm* : emperor

empester [ãpɛste] *vt* : stink up — *vi* : stink

empêtrer [ãpetre] *v* **s'empêtrer** *vr* : become entangled

emphase [ãfaz] *nf* : pomposity

empiéter [ãpjete] {87} *vi* ~ **sur** : infringe on

empiffrer [ãpifre] *v* **s'empiffrer** *vr fam* : stuff oneself

empiler [ãpile] *vt* : pile, stack — **s'empiler** *vr* : pile up

empire [ãpir] *nm* 1 : empire 2 **sous l'**~ **de** : under the influence of

empirer [ãpire] *v* : worsen

emplacement [ãplasmã] *nm* : site, location

emplette [ãplɛt] *nf* 1 ACHAT : purchase 2 **faire ses** ~**s** : go shopping

emplir [ãplir] *vt* : fill — **s'emplir** *vr* : fill up

employer [ãplwaje] {58} *vt* 1 UTILISER : use 2 : employ, provide a job for — **s'employer**

vr : be used — **emploi** [ãplwa] *nm* 1 : use 2 TRAVAIL : employment, job 3 ~ **du temps** : schedule, timetable — **employé, -ployée** [ãplwaje] *n* : employee — **employeur, -ployeuse** [ãplwajœr, -plwajøz] *n* : employer

empocher [ãpɔʃe] *vt* : pocket

empoigner [ãpwaɲe] *vt* : grasp, seize

empoisonner [ãpwazɔne] *vt* : poison — **empoisonnement** [ãpwazɔnmã] *nm* : poisoning

emporter [ãpɔrte] *vt* 1 : take (away) 2 EN-TRAÎNER : carry away 3 **l'**~ **sur** : beat, get the better of — **s'emporter** *vr* : lose one's temper

empreinte [ãprɛ̃t] *nf* 1 : print, imprint 2 ~ **digitale** : fingerprint

empresser [ãprese] *v* **s'empresser** *vr* 1 ~ **auprès de** : be attentive toward 2 ~ **de** : be in a hurry to — **empressé, -sée** [ãprese] *adj* : attentive, eager (to please) — **empressement** [ãprɛsmã] *nm* 1 : attentiveness 2 : eagerness

emprise [ãpriz] *nf* : influence, hold

emprisonner [ãprizɔne] *vt* : imprison — **emprisonnement** [ãprizɔnmã] *nm* : imprisonment

emprunter [ãprœ̃te] *vt* 1 : borrow 2 PREN-DRE : take, follow — **emprunt** [ãprœ̃] *nm* : loan

ému, -mue [emy] *adj* : moved, touched

en [ã] *prep* 1 : in, into 2 **aller** ~ **Belgique** : go to Belgium 3 ~ **guerre** : at war 4 ~ **vacances** : on vacation 5 ~ **voiture** : by car 6 **fait** ~ **plastique** : made of plastic — ~ *pron* 1 (*expressing quantity*) : some, any 2 (*representing a noun governed by* de) : it, them 3 **qu'**~ **ferons-nous?** : what will we do of it? 4 **j'**~ **viens** : I've just come from there

encadrer [ãkadre] *vt* 1 : frame 2 ENTOURER : surround 3 SURVEILLER : supervise — **encadrement** [ãkadrəmã] *nm* : frame

encaisser [ãkese] *vt* 1 : cash (a check), collect (money) 2 *fam* : take, tolerate

encastrer [ãkastre] *vt* : embed, build in

enceinte [ãsɛ̃t] *adj* : pregnant — ~ *nf* 1 : wall, enclosure 2 ~ **acoustique** : speaker

encens [ãsã] *nm* : incense

encercler [ãsɛrkle] *vt* : surround, encircle

enchaîner [ãʃene] *vt* 1 : chain (up) 2 LIER : link, connect — **s'enchaîner** *vr* : be connected — **enchaînement** [ãʃɛnmã] *nm* 1 SÉRIE : series, sequence 2 LIEN : chain, link

enchanter [ãʃãte] *vt* 1 ENSORCELER : enchant, bewitch 2 RAVIR : delight — **enchanté, -tée** [ãʃãte] *adj* 1 : enchanted 2 ~ **de vous connaître** : delighted/pleased to meet you — **enchantement** [ãʃãtmã] *nm* 1

enchère

: enchantment **2** : delight — **enchanteur, -teresse** [ɑ̃ʃɑ̃tœr, -trɛs] *adj* : enchanting
enchère [ɑ̃ʃɛr] *nf* **1** : bid, bidding **2 vente aux ~s** : auction
enchevêtrer [ɑ̃ʃəvɛtre] *vt* **1** : tangle — **s'enchevêtrer** *vr* : become tangled
enclencher [ɑ̃klɑ̃ʃe] *vt* : engage (a mechanism) — **s'enclencher** *vr* : engage, interlock
enclin, -cline [ɑ̃klɛ̃, -klin] *adj* **~ à** : inclined to
enclore [ɑ̃klɔr] {34} *vt* : enclose
enclos [ɑ̃klo] *nm* : enclosure
enclume [ɑ̃klym] *nf* : anvil
encoche [ɑ̃kɔʃ] *nf* : notch
encolure [ɑ̃kɔlyr] *nf* : neck (of a dress, etc.)
encombrer [ɑ̃kɔ̃bre] *vt* **1** : clutter (up) **2** OBSTRUER : block, hamper — **s'encombrer** *vr* **de** : burden oneself with — **encombrant, -brante** [ɑ̃kɔ̃brɑ̃, -brɑ̃t] *adj* : cumbersome — **encombre** [ɑ̃kɔ̃br] **sans ~** *adv phr* : without a hitch — **encombrement** [ɑ̃kɔ̃brəmɑ̃] *nm* **1** : clutter, congestion **2** EMBOUTEILLAGE : traffic jam
encontre [ɑ̃kɔ̃tr] **à l'~ de** *prep phr* : against, contrary to
encore [ɑ̃kɔr] *adv* **1** TOUJOURS : still **2** : more, again **3 ~ que** : although **4 pas ~** : not yet **5 si ~** : if only
encourager [ɑ̃kuraʒe] {17} *vt* : encourage — **encouragement** [ɑ̃kuraʒmɑ̃] *nm* : encouragement
encourir [ɑ̃kurir] {23} *vt* : incur
encrasser [ɑ̃krase] *vt* **1** SALIR : dirty **2** OBSTRUER : clog up
encre [ɑ̃kr] *nf* : ink — **encrer** [ɑ̃kre] *vt* : ink — **encrier** [ɑ̃krije] *nm* : inkwell
encyclopédie [ɑ̃siklɔpedi] *nf* : encyclopedia
endetter [ɑ̃dete] *v* **s'endetter** *vr* : get into debt
endeuillé, -lée [ɑ̃dœje] *adj* : in mourning, bereaved
endive [ɑ̃div] *nf* : endive, chickory
endoctriner [ɑ̃dɔktrine] *vt* : indoctrinate — **endoctrinement** [ɑ̃dɔktrinmɑ̃] *nm* : indoctrination
endommager [ɑ̃dɔmaʒe] {17} *vt* : damage
endormir [ɑ̃dɔrmir] {30} *vt* : put to sleep — **s'endormir** *vr* : fall asleep — **endormi, -mie** [ɑ̃dɔrmi] *adj* **1** : asleep **2** : sleepy
endosser [ɑ̃dose] *vt* **1** : take on, assume **2** : endorse (a check)
endroit [ɑ̃drwa] *nm* **1** : place, spot **2 à l'~** : right side up
enduire [ɑ̃dɥir] {49} *vt* : coat, cover — **enduit** [ɑ̃dɥi] *nm* : coating
endurance [ɑ̃dyrɑ̃s] *nf* : endurance
endurcir [ɑ̃dyrsir] *vt* : toughen, harden — **s'endurcir** *vr* : harden
endurer [ɑ̃dyre] *vt* : endure

énergie [enɛrʒi] *nf* : energy — **énergique** [enɛrʒik] *adj* : energetic
énerver [enɛrve] *vt* : irritate, annoy — **s'énerver** *vr* : get worked up
enfance [ɑ̃fɑ̃s] *nf* : childhood — **enfant** [ɑ̃fɑ̃] *nmf* : child — **enfanter** [ɑ̃fɑ̃te] *v* : give birth to — **enfantillage** [ɑ̃fɑ̃tijaʒ] *nm* : childishness — **enfantin, -tine** [ɑ̃fɑ̃tɛ̃, -tin] *adj* **1** : childlike **2** : childish
enfer [ɑ̃fɛr] *nm* : hell
enfermer [ɑ̃fɛrme] *vt* : shut up, lock up — **s'enfermer** *vr* **1** : shut oneself away **2 ~ dans** : retreat into
enfiler [ɑ̃file] *vt* **1** : slip on, put on (a garment) **2** : string, thread (a needle)
enfin [ɑ̃fɛ̃] *adv* **1** : finally, at last **2** : lastly **3 ~, je crois** : at least I think so **4 mais ~, donne-le-moi!** : come on, give it to me!
enflammer [ɑ̃flame] *vt* **1** : ignite, set fire to **2** : inflame (in medicine) — **s'enflammer** *vr* : catch fire
enfler [ɑ̃fle] *v* : swell — **s'enfler** *vr* : swell up — **enflure** [ɑ̃flyr] *nf* : swelling
enfoncer [ɑ̃fɔse] {6} *vt* **1** : drive or push in **2** DÉFONCER : break down — *vi* : sink — **s'enfoncer** *vr* **1** : sink in **2** CÉDER : give way
enfouir [ɑ̃fwir] *vt* **1** : bury **2** CACHER : hide
enfreindre [ɑ̃frɛdr] {37} *vt* : infringe
enfuir [ɑ̃fɥir] {46} *v* **s'enfuir** *vr* : flee
engager [ɑ̃gaʒe] {17} *vt* **1** OBLIGER : bind, commit **3** RECRUTER : hire **3** COMMENCER : start **4 ~ qqn à** : urge s.o. to **5 ~ une vitesse** : put a car in gear — **s'engager** *vr* **1** : commit oneself **2** : enlist (in the army) **3 ~ dans** : enter, turn onto (a street) — **engagé, -gée** [ɑ̃gaʒe] *adj* **1** : committed **2** *Can fam* : busy — **engageant, -geante** [ɑ̃gaʒɑ̃, -ʒɑ̃t] *adj* : engaging — **engagement** [ɑ̃gaʒmɑ̃] *nm* **1** PROMESSE : commitment **2** PARTICIPATION : involvement
engin [ɑ̃ʒɛ̃] *nm* : machine, device
engloutir [ɑ̃glutir] *vt* **1** : gobble up, devour **2** : engulf, swallow up
engorger [ɑ̃gɔrʒe] {17} *vt* : block, jam up
engouement [ɑ̃gumɑ̃] *nm* : infatuation
engouffrer [ɑ̃gufre] *vt* : devour
engourdir [ɑ̃gurdir] *vt* : numb — **s'engourdir** *vr* : go numb — **engourdi, -die** [ɑ̃gurdi] *adj* : numb
engraisser [ɑ̃grese] *vt* : fatten — *vi* : put on weight — **engrais** [ɑ̃grɛ] *nm* : fertilizer, manure
engrenage [ɑ̃grənaʒ] *nm* : gears *pl*
engueuler [ɑ̃gœle] *vt fam* : yell at, bawl out
énième [enjɛm] *adj* : nth, umpteenth
enivrer [ɑ̃nivre] *vt* : intoxicate, make drunk — **s'enivrer** *vr* : get drunk
enjamber [ɑ̃ʒɑ̃be] *vt* **1** : step over **2** : span — **enjambée** [ɑ̃ʒɑ̃be] *nf* : stride

enjeu [ãʒø] *nm, pl* **-jeux** : stake (in games)
enjôler [ãʒole] *vt* : cajole, wheedle
enjoliver [ãʒɔlive] *vt* : embellish — **enjoliveur** [ãjɔlivœr] *nm* : hubcap
enjoué, -jouée [ãʒwe] *adj* : cheerful
enlacer [ãlase] {6} *vt* : embrace, hug
enlaidir [ãledir] *vt* : make ugly — *vi* : grow ugly
enlever [ãlve] {52} *vt* **1** : remove, take away **2** KIDNAPPER : abduct — **enlèvement** [ãlɛvmã] *nm* **1** : removal **2** : abduction
enliser [ãlize] *v* **s'enliser** *vr* : sink, get stuck
ennemi, -mie [ɛnmi] *n* : enemy
ennui [ãnɥi] *nm* **1** PROBLÈME : trouble, problem **2** : boredom — **ennuyant, -nuyante** [ãnɥijã, ãnɥijãt] *adj Can* **1** : annoying **2** : boring — **ennuyer** [ãnɥije] {58} *vt* **1** AGACER : annoy **2** : bore — **s'ennuyer** *vr* : be bored — **ennuyeux, -nuyeuse** [ãnɥijø, ãnɥijøz] *adj* **1** : annoying **2** : boring
énoncer [enɔ̃se] {6} *vt* : express, state — **énoncé** [enɔ̃se] *nm* **1** : statement **2** LIBELLÉ : wording
énorme [enɔrm] *adj* : enormous, huge — **énormément** [enɔrmemã] *adv* **~ de** : a great number of
enquête [ãkɛt] *nf* **1** INVESTIGATION : investigation, inquiry **2** SONDAGE : survey — **enquêter** [ãkete] *vi* : investigate
enraciner [ãrasine] *vt* : root — **s'enraciner** *vr* : take root
enrager [ãraʒe] {17} *vi* : be furious — **enragé, -gée** [ãraʒe] *adj* **1** : rabid (of an animal) **2** : furious (of a person)
enrayer [ãreje] {11} *vt* **1** : check, curb **2** BLOQUER : jam
enregistrer [ãrəʒistre] *vt* **1** : record **2** INSCRIRE : register **3** : check in (baggage) — **enregistrement** [ãrəʒistrəmã] *nm* **1** : registration **2** : (tape) recording
enrhumer [ãryme] *v* **s'enrhumer** *vr* : catch a cold
enrichir [ãriʃir] *vt* : enrich — **s'enrichir** *vr* : grow rich — **enrichissement** [ãriʃismã] *nm* : enrichment
enrober [ãrɔbe] *vt* : coat
enrôler [ãrole] *vt* : enroll, enlist — **s'enrôler** *vr* : enlist
enroué, -rouée [ãrwe] *adj* : hoarse
enrouler [ãrule] *vt* : wind, coil — **s'enrouler** *vr* **~ dans** : wrap oneself in (a blanket)
ensanglanté, -tée [ãsãglãte] *adj* : bloody, bloodstained
enseignant, -gnante [ãsɛɲã, -ɲãt] *adj* : teaching — **~** *n* : teacher
enseigne [ãsɛɲ] *nf* : sign
enseigner [ãsɛɲe] *v* : to teach — **enseignement** [ãsɛɲmã] *nm* **1** : teaching **2** : education

ensemble [ãsãbl] *adv* : together — **~** *nm* **1** : group, set **2** TOTALITÉ : whole **3** : (musical) ensemble **4** : suit, outfit **5 dans l'~** : on the whole
ensemencer [ãsəmãse] {6} *vt* : sow
ensoleillé, -lée [ãsɔleje] *adj* : sunny
ensorceler [ãsɔrsəle] {8} *vt* : bewitch, charm
ensuite [ãsɥit] *adv* **1** : then, next **2** : afterwards, later
ensuivre [ãsɥivr] {35} *v* **s'ensuivre** *vr* : ensue, follow
entailler [ãtaje] *vt* : gash, cut — **entaille** [ãtaj] *nf* **1** : cut, gash **2** ENCOCHE : notch
entamer [ãtame] *vt* **1** : cut into, eat into **2** : start, enter into (negotiations)
entasser [ãtase] *vt* **1** : pile (up) **2** SERRER : cram — **s'entasser** *vr* : pile up
entendre [ãtãdr] {63} *vt* **1** : hear **2** COMPRENDRE : understand **3** VOULOIR : intend — **s'entendre** *vr* **1** : agree **2 ~ avec** : get along with — **entendement** [ãtãdmã] *nm* : understanding — **entendu, -due** [ãtãdy] *adj* **1** : agreed, understood **2 bien ~** : of course — **entente** [ãtãt] *nf* **1** : harmony **2** ACCORD : agreement, understanding
entériner [ãterine] *vt* : ratify
enterrer [ãtere] *vt* : bury — **enterrement** [ãtermã] *nm* **1** : burial **2** FUNÉRAILLES : funeral
en-tête [ãtɛt] *nm, pl* **en-têtes** : heading
entêter [ãtete] *v* **s'entêter** *vr* : be obstinate, persist — **entêté, -tée** [ãtete] *adj* : stubborn, obstinate — **entêtement** [ãtɛtmã] *nm* : stubbornness
enthousiasme [ãtuzjasm] *nm* : enthusiasm — **enthousiasmer** [ãtuzjasme] *vt* : fill with enthusiasm, excite — **enthousiaste** [ãtuzjast] *adj* : enthusiastic — **~** *nmf* : enthusiast, fan
entier, -tière [ãtje, -tjɛr] *adj* : entire, whole — **entier** *nm* **en ~** : totally, in its entirety — **entièrement** [ãtjɛrmã] *adv* : entirely, wholly
entité [ãtite] *nf* : entity
entonnoir [ãtɔnwar] *nm* : funnel (utensil)
entorse [ãtɔrs] *nf* : sprain
entortiller [ãtɔrtije] *vt* : twist, wind
entourer [ãture] *vt* : surround — **entourage** [ãturaʒ] *nm* : circle (of friends or family)
entracte [ãtrakt] *nm* : intermission
entraide [ãtrɛd] *nf* : mutual aid
entrailles [ãtraj] *nfpl* **1** : entrails **2** PROFONDEURS : depths
entrain [ãtrɛ̃] *nm* : liveliness, spirit
entraîner [ãtrene] *vt* **1** EMPORTER : carry away **2** OCCASIONNER : lead to, involve **3** FORMER : train, coach — **s'entraîner** *vr* : train, practice — **entraînant, -nante** [ãtrɛnã, -nãt] *adj* : lively — **entraînement**

[ɑ̃trɛnmɑ̃] *nm* **1** : training, coaching **2** PRATIQUE : practice — **entraîneur, -neuse** [ɑ̃trɛnœr, -nøz] *n* : trainer, coach

entraver [ɑ̃trave] *vt* : hinder — **entrave** [ɑ̃trav] *nf* : hindrance

entre [ɑ̃tr] *prep* **1** : between **2** PARMI : among

entrecôte [ɑ̃trəkot] *nf* : rib steak

entrecroiser [ɑ̃trəkrwaze] *v* **s'entrecroiser** *vr* : intersect

entrée [ɑ̃tre] *nf* **1** : entrance, entry **2** ACCÈS : admission **3** BILLET : ticket **4** : first course (of a meal) **5** : entry (in a text), input (of information)

entre-jambes [ɑ̃trəʒɑ̃b] *nms & pl* : crotch (of clothing)

entrelacer [ɑ̃trəlase] {6} *vt* : intertwine

entremêler [ɑ̃trəmele] *vt* : mix together

entremets [ɑ̃trəmɛ] *nms & pl* : dessert

entreposer [ɑ̃trəpoze] *vt* : store — **entrepôt** [ɑ̃trəpo] *nm* : warehouse

entreprendre [ɑ̃trəprɑ̃dr] {70} *vt* : undertake, start — **entreprenant, -nante** [ɑ̃trəprənɑ̃, -nɑ̃t] *adj* : enterprising — **entrepreneur, -neuse** [ɑ̃trəprənœr, -nøz] *n* : contractor — **entreprise** [ɑ̃trəpriz] *nf* **1** : enterprise, undertaking **2** : business, firm

entrer [ɑ̃tre] *vi* **1** : enter, go in, come in **2** ça n'entre pas : it doesn't fit **3** ~ dans : join, go into — *vt* **1** : bring in, take in **2** : enter, input (data, etc.)

entre-temps [ɑ̃trətɑ̃] *adv* : meanwhile

entretenir [ɑ̃trətnir] {92} *vt* **1** MAINTENIR : maintain **2** ~ qqn de : speak to s.o. about — **s'entretenir** *vr* **1** ~ avec : consult with, converse with **2** ~ de : discuss, talk about — **entretenu, -nue** [ɑ̃trətny] *adj* : kept, maintained — **entretien** [ɑ̃trətjɛ̃] *nm* **1** : maintenance **2** CONVERSATION : talk, interview

entrevoir [ɑ̃trəvwar] {99} *vt* **1** : glimpse, make out **2** PRÉSAGER : foresee, anticipate — **entrevue** [ɑ̃trəvy] *nf* : meeting, interview

entrouvert, -verte [ɑ̃truvɛr, -vɛrt] *adj & adv* : half open, ajar

énumérer [enymere] {87} *vt* : enumerate — **énumération** [-merasjɔ̃] *nf* : enumeration

envahir [ɑ̃vair] *vt* **1** : invade **2** : overcome (fear, etc.)

envelopper [ɑ̃vlɔpe] *vt* **1** : envelop **2** RECOUVRIR : wrap up, cover — **enveloppe** [ɑ̃vlɔp] *nf* : envelope

envergure [ɑ̃vɛrgyr] *nf* **1** : wingspan **2** IMPORTANCE : breadth, scope

envers [ɑ̃vɛr] *prep* : toward, to — ~ *nm* **1** REVERS : back, reverse **2** à l'~ : inside out, upside down, backward

envie [ɑ̃vi] *nf* **1** : envy **2** DÉSIR : desire, wish — **envier** [ɑ̃vje] {96} *vt* : envy — **envieux, -vieuse** [ɑ̃vjø, -vjøz] *adj* : envious

environ [ɑ̃virɔ̃] *adv* : about, approximately — **environnement** [ɑ̃virɔnmɑ̃] *nm* : environment, surroundings — **environnant, -nante** [ɑ̃virɔnɑ̃, -nɑ̃t] *adj* : surrounding — **environs** [ɑ̃virɔ̃] *nmpl* **1** : surroundings **2** aux ~ de : around, about

envisager [ɑ̃vizaʒe] {17} *vt* : consider, imagine

envoi [ɑ̃vwa] *nm* **1** : sending, dispatching **2** COLIS : parcel, package

envoler [ɑ̃vɔle] *v* **s'envoler** *vr* **1** : take off (of a plane) **2** : fly away (of a bird) — **envol** [ɑ̃vɔl] *nm* : takeoff — **envolée** [ɑ̃vɔle] *nf* **1** : flight **2** AUGMENTATION : rise, surge

envoyer [ɑ̃vwaje] {36} *vt* **1** : send (out) **2** LANCER : throw **3** ~ par la poste : mail — **envoyé, -voyée** [ɑ̃vwaje] *n* : envoy

enzyme [ɑ̃zim] *nf* : enzyme

épagneul, -gneule [epaɲœl] *n* : spaniel

épais, -paisse [epɛ, -pɛs] *adj* : thick — **épaisseur** [epɛsœr] *nf* **1** : thickness **2** : layer — **épaissir** [epesir] *v* **s'épaissir** *vr* : thicken

épancher [epɑ̃ʃe] *vt* : give vent to — **s'épancher** *vr* : pour one's heart out

épanouir [epanwir] *v* **s'épanouir** *vr* **1** : bloom **2** S'ÉCLAIRER : light up **3** SE DÉVELOPPER : develop, flourish — **épanouissement** [epanwismɑ̃] *nm* : blossoming

épargner [eparɲe] *vt* **1** ÉCONOMISER : save **2** : spare (s.o.'s life, etc.) — **s'épargner** *vr* : spare oneself — **épargne** [eparɲ] *nf* **1** : saving **2** : savings *pl*

éparpiller [eparpije] *vt* : scatter, disperse — **s'éparpiller** *vr* : dissipate — **épars, -parse** [epar, -pars] *adj* : scattered

épater [epate] *vt fam* : amaze — **épatant, -tante** [epatɑ̃, -tɑ̃t] *adj fam* : amazing

épaule [epol] *nf* : shoulder — **épaulette** [epolɛt] *nf* : shoulder strap

épave [epav] *nf* : wreck (of a ship)

épée [epe] *nf* : sword

épeler [eple] {8} *vt* : spell

éperdu, -due [epɛrdy] *adj* **1** : intense, passionate **2** ~ de peur : overcome with fear — **éperdument** [epɛrdymɑ̃] *adv* : frantically, desperately

éperon [eprɔ̃] *nm* : spur — **éperonner** [eprɔne] *vt* : spur (on)

éphémère [efemɛr] *adj* : ephemeral

épi [epi] *nm* **1** : ear, cob **2** : tuft (of hair)

épice [epis] *nf* : spice — **épicé, -cée** [epise] *adj* : spicy — **épicer** [epise] {6} *vt* : spice — **épicerie** [episri] *nf* **1** : grocery store **2** ~s *nfpl* : groceries *pl* — **épicier, -cière** [episje, -sjɛr] *n* : grocer

épidémie [epidemi] *nf* : epidemic — **épidémique** [-demik] *adj* : epidemic

épiderme [epidɛrm] *nm* : skin

épier [epje] {96} *vt* **1** : spy on **2** ATTENDRE : watch out for

épilepsie [epilɛpsi] *nf* : epilepsy — **épileptique** [epilɛptik] *adj & nmf* : epileptic

~~epiler lepilel *vt* : remove hair from, pluck~~

épilogue [epilɔg] *nm* **1** : epilogue **2** : conclusion, outcome

épinards [epinar] *nmpl* : spinach

épine [epin] *nf* **1** : thorn **2** ~ **dorsale** : spine, backbone — **épineux, -neuse** [epinø, -nøz] *adj* : thorny

épingle [epɛ̃gl] *nf* **1** : pin **2** ~ **à cheveux** : hairpin **3** ~ **de sûreté** : safety pin

épique [epik] *adj* : epic

épisode [epizɔd] *nm* : episode

épitaphe [epitaf] *nf* : epitaph

épithète [epitɛt] *nf* : epithet

éplucher [eplyʃe] *vt* **1** PELER : peel **2** EXAMINER : scrutinize

éponge [epɔ̃ʒ] *nf* : sponge — **éponger** [epɔ̃ʒe] {17} *vt* : sponge up, mop up

épopée [epɔpe] *nf* : epic

époque [epɔk] *nf* **1** : age, era **2** : time, period

épouse [epuz] *nf* → **époux** — **épouser** [epuze] *vt* : marry, wed

épousseter [epuste] {8} *vt* : dust

époustouflant, -flante [epustuflɑ̃, -flɑ̃t] *adj fam* : amazing

épouvantable [epuvɑ̃tabl] *adj* : dreadful, horrible

épouvantail [epuvɑ̃taj] *nm* : scarecrow

épouvanter [epuvɑ̃te] *vt* : terrify — **épouvante** [epuvɑ̃t] *nf* : horror

époux, -pouse [epu, -puz] *n* : spouse, husband *m*, wife *f*

éprendre [eprɑ̃dr] {70} *v* **s'éprendre** *vr* ~ **de** : fall in love with

épreuve [eprœv] *nf* **1** ESSAI : test **2** : ordeal, trial **3** : event (in sports) **4** : proof, print (in printing)

éprouver [epruve] *vt* **1** : test, try **2** RESSENTIR : feel, experience **3** AFFECTER : distress

épuiser [epɥize] *vt* : exhaust — **épuisé, -sée** [epɥize] *adj* **1** : exhausted **2** : out of stock — **épuisement** [epɥizmɑ̃] *nm* : exhaustion

épurer [epyre] *vt* **1** : purify, refine **2** : purge (in politics) — **épuration** [epyrasjɔ̃] *nf* **1** : purification **2** : purge

équateur [ekwatœr] *nm* : equator

équation [ekwasjɔ̃] *nf* : equation

équerre [ekɛr] *nf* **1** : square **2** **d'**~ : square, straight

équestre [ekɛstr] *adj* : equestrian

équilibre [ekilibr] *nm* : equilibrium, balance — **équilibré, -brée** [ekilibre] *adj* : well-balanced — **équilibrer** [ekilibre] *vt* : balance

équinoxe [ekinɔks] *nm* : equinox

équipage [ekipaʒ] *nm* : crew

équiper [ekipe] *vt* : equip, outfit — **équipe**

[ekip] *nf* : team — **équipement** [ekipmɑ̃] *nm* : equipment — **équipier, -pière** [ekipje, -pjɛr] *n* : team member

équitable [ekitabl] *adj* : fair, equitable — **équitablement** [-tabləmɑ̃] *adv* : fairly

équitation [ekitasjɔ̃] *nf* : horseback riding

équité [ekite] *nf* : equity, fairness

équivalence [ekivalɑ̃s] *nf* : equivalence — **équivalent, -lente** [ekivalɑ̃, -lɑ̃t] *adj* : equivalent — **équivalent** *nm* : equivalent — **équivaloir** [ekivalwar] {95} *vi* ~ **à** : be equivalent to

équivoque [ekivɔk] *adj* **1** : equivocal, ambiguous **2** DOUTEUX : questionable

érable [erabl] *nm* : maple

éradiquer [eradike] *vt* : eradicate

érafler [erafle] *vt* : scratch — **éraflure** [eraflyr] *nf* : scratch, scrape

ère [ɛr] *nf* : era

érection [erɛksjɔ̃] *nf* : erection

éreinter [erɛ̃te] *vt* **1** ÉPUISER : exhaust **2** CRITIQUER : criticize — **s'éreinter** *vr* : wear oneself out — **éreintant, -tante** [erɛ̃tɑ̃, -tɑ̃t] *adj* : exhausting

ergoter [ɛrgote] *vi* : quibble

ériger [eriʒe] {17} *vt* : erect — **s'ériger** *vr* ~ **en** : set oneself up as

ermite [ɛrmit] *nm* : hermit

éroder [erɔde] *vt* : erode — **érosion** [erozjɔ̃] *nf* : erosion

érotique [erɔtik] *adj* : erotic — **érotisme** [erɔtism] *nm* : eroticism

errer [ere] *vi* : wander, roam — **erreur** [erœr] *nf* : error, mistake — **erroné, -née** [erɔne] *adj* : erroneous

érudit, -dite [erydi, -dit] *adj* : scholarly — ~ *n* : scholar — **érudition** [erydisjɔ̃] *nf* : learning, scholarship

éruption [erypsjɔ̃] *nf* **1** : eruption **2** : rash (in medicine)

escabeau [eskabo] *nm, pl* **-beaux 1** : stool **2** ÉCHELLE : stepladder

escadre [eskadr] *nf* : squadron — **escadrille** [eskadrij] *nf* : squadron — **escadron** [eskadrɔ̃] *nm* : squadron, squad

escalader [ɛskalade] *vt* : climb — **escalade** [ɛskalad] *nf* : (rock) climbing

escale [ɛskal] *nf* : stopover

escalier [ɛskalje] *nm* **1** : stairs *pl*, steps *pl* **2** ~ **de secours** : fire escape **3** ~ **mécanique** : escalator

escalope [ɛskalɔp] *nf* : cutlet

escamoter [ɛskamɔte] *vt* **1** : fold away, retract **2** ÉVITER : evade — **escamotable** [ɛskamɔtabl] *adj* : retractable, foldaway

escargot [ɛskargo] *nm* : snail

escarmouche [ɛskarmuʃ] *nf* : skirmish

escarpé, -pée [ɛskarpe] *adj* : steep

esclaffer [ɛsklafe] *v* **s'esclaffer** *vr* : burst out laughing

esclave [ɛsklav] *adj & nmf* : slave — **esclavage** [ɛsklavaʒ] *nm* : slavery

escompter [ɛskɔ̃te] *vt* **1** : discount **2** ESPÉRER : count on, expect — **escompte** [ɛskɔ̃t] *nm* : discount

escorter [ɛskɔrte] *vt* : escort — **escorte** [ɛskɔrt] *nf* : escort

escrime [ɛskrim] *nf* : fencing

escroc [ɛskro] *nm* : swindler, crook — **escroquer** [ɛskrɔke] *vt* : swindle, defraud — **escroquerie** [ɛskrɔkri] *nf* : swindle, fraud

eskimo [ɛskimo] → **esquimau**

ésotérique [ezɔterik] *adj* : esoteric

espace [ɛspas] *nm* : space — **espacer** [ɛspase] {6} *vt* : space (out)

espadon [ɛspadɔ̃] *nm* : swordfish

espadrilles [ɛspadrij] *nfpl Can* : sneakers *pl*

espagnol, -gnole [ɛspaɲɔl] *adj* : Spanish — **espagnol** *nm* : Spanish (language)

espèce [ɛspɛs] *nf* **1** : species **2** SORTE : sort, kind **3** ~**s** *nfpl* : cash

espérer [ɛspere] {87} *vt* **1** : hope for **2** ESCOMPTER : expect — **espérance** [ɛsperɑ̃s] *nf* : hope

espiègle [ɛspjɛgl] *adj* : mischievous

espion, -pionne [ɛspjɔ̃, -pjɔn] *n* : spy — **espionnage** [ɛspjɔnaʒ] *nm* : espionage — **espionner** [ɛspjɔne] *vt* : spy on

espoir [ɛspwar] *nm* : hope

esprit [ɛspri] *nm* **1** : mind **2** ATTITUDE : spirit **3** HUMOUR : wit **4** FANTÔME : ghost

esquimau, -maude [ɛskimo, -mod] *adj, mpl* **-maux** [-mo] : Eskimo

esquisse [ɛskis] *nf* : sketch — **esquisser** [ɛskise] *vt* : sketch

esquiver [ɛskive] *vt* : avoid, dodge — **esquive** [ɛskiv] *nf* : dodge

essai [ɛse] *nm* **1** TENTATIVE : attempt, try **2** ÉPREUVE : trial, test **3** : (literary) essay

essaim [ɛsɛ̃] *nm* : swarm

essayer [eseje] {11} *vt* : try

essence [ɛsɑ̃s] *nf* : gasoline — **essentiel, -tielle** [ɛsɑ̃sjɛl] *adj* : essential — **essentiel** *nm* : main part, essentials *pl* — **essentiellement** [-sjɛlmɑ̃] *adv* : essentially

essieu [esjø] *nm, pl* **-sieux** : axle

essor [esɔr] *nm* **1** : flight (of a bird) **2** : expansion, growth

essouffler [esufle] *vt* : make breathless — **s'essouffler** *vr* : get out of breath

essuyer [esɥije] {58} *vt* **1** : wipe, dry **2** SUBIR : suffer, endure — **essuie—glace** [esɥiglas] *nm, pl* **essuie—glaces** : windshield wiper — **essuie—mains** [esɥimɛ̃] *nms & pl* : hand towel — **essuie—tout** [esɥitu] *nms & pl* : paper towel

est [ɛst] *adj* : east, eastern — ~ *nm* **1** : east **2 l'Est** : the East

estampe [ɛstɑ̃p] *nf* : engraving, print — **estampille** [ɛstɑ̃pij] *nf* : stamp

esthétique [ɛstetik] *adj* : aesthetic — **esthéticien, -cienne** [ɛstetisjɛ̃, -sjɛn] *n* : beautician

estimer [ɛstime] *vt* **1** : assess, evaluate **2** ~~CALCULER : estimate 3 RESPECTER : esteem~~ **4** CONSIDÉRER : consider — **estimation** [ɛstimasjɔ̃] *nf* : estimate — **estime** [ɛstim] *nf* : esteem, respect

estival, -vale [ɛstival] *adj, mpl* **-vaux** [-vo] : summer

estomac [ɛstɔma] *nm* : stomach

estrade [ɛstrad] *nf* : platform, stage

estragon [ɛstragɔ̃] *nm* : tarragon

estropié, -piée [ɛstrɔpje] *adj* : crippled, maimed

estuaire [ɛstɥɛr] *nm* : estuary

esturgeon [ɛstyrʒɔ̃] *nm* : sturgeon

et [e] *conj* : and

étable [etabl] *nf* : cowshed

établi [etabli] *nm* : workbench

établir [etablir] *vt* **1** : establish, set up **2** : draw up (a list, etc.) — **s'établir** *vr* : become established, get set up — **établissement** [etablismɑ̃] *nm* : establishment

étage [etaʒ] *nm* **1** : story, floor **2** : tier, level — **étagère** [etaʒɛr] *nf* : shelf, bookshelf

étai [etɛ] *nm* : prop, support

étain [etɛ̃] *nm* **1** : tin **2** : pewter

étaler [etale] *vt* **1** : display **2** ÉTENDRE : spread (out) **3** ÉCHELONNER : space out, stagger — **s'étaler** *vr* **1** S'ÉTENDRE : spread out **2** *fam* : fall flat, sprawl — **étalage** [etalaʒ] *nm* **1** : display. **2** DEVANTURE : shopwindow **3 faire** ~ **de** : flaunt

étalon [etalɔ̃] *nm* **1** : stallion **2** MODÈLE : standard

étancher [etɑ̃ʃe] *vt* **1** : stem, staunch **2** : quench (thirst) — **étanche** [etɑ̃ʃ] *adj* : watertight, waterproof

étang [etɑ̃] *nm* : pond

étape [etap] *nf* **1** ARRÊT : stop, halt **2** : stage (of development)

état [eta] *nm* **1** : state, condition **2** : statement (of expenses, etc.) **3** : (social) status **4** MÉTIER : profession, trade

étau [eto] *nm, pl* **-taux** : vise

étayer [eteje] {11} *vt* : prop up

été [ete] *nm* : summer

éteindre [etɛ̃dr] {37} *vt* **1** : put out, extinguish **2** : turn off, switch off — **s'éteindre** *vr* **1** : go out, die out **2** MOURIR : die

étendard [etɑ̃dar] *nm* : standard, flag

étendre [etɑ̃dr] {63} *vt* **1** ÉTALER : spread (out) **2** : hang up (laundry) **3** ALLONGER : stretch (out) **4** ACCROÎTRE : extend — **s'étendre** *vr* **1** : stretch **2** SE COUCHER : lie down **3** CROÎTRE : spread — **étendu, -due** [etɑ̃dy] *adj* : extensive, wide — **étendue** *nf* **1** : area **2** : extent

éternel, -nelle [etɛrnɛl] *adj* : eternal — **éter-**

nellement [-nɛlmɑ̃] *adv* : eternally, forever — **éternité** [etɛrnite] *nf* : eternity

éternuer [etɛrnɥe] *vi* : sneeze — **éternuement** [etɛrnymɑ̃] *nm* : sneeze

éther [etɛr] *nm* : ether

éthique [etik] *adj* : ethical — ~ *nf* : ethics

ethnique [ɛtnik] *adj* : ethnic

étincelle [etɛ̃sɛl] *nf* : spark — **étinceler** [etɛ̃sle] {8} *vi* : sparkle

étiquette [etikɛt] *nf* 1 : label 2 PROTOCOLE : etiquette — **étiqueter** [etikte] {8} *vt* : label

étirer [etire] *vt* : stretch — **s'étirer** *vr* : stretch (out)

étoffe [etɔf] *nf* : material, fabric

étoile [etwal] *nf* : star — **étoilé, -lée** [etwale] *adj* : starry

étonner [etɔne] *vt* : astonish — **s'étonner** *vr* : be surprised — **étonnant, -nante** [etɔnɑ̃, -nɑ̃t] *adj* : astonishing — **étonnement** [etɔnmɑ̃] *nm* : surprise, astonishment

étouffer [etufe] *vt* 1 : stifle 2 ASPHYXIER : smother 3 : deaden (sound, etc.) — **s'étouffer** *vr* 1 : choke 2 : suffocate

étourderie [eturdəri] *nf* : thoughtlessness

étourdir [eturdir] *vt* 1 ASSOMMER : stun 2 : make dizzy — **étourdi, -die** [eturdi] *adj* : absentminded, scatterbrained — **étourdissant, -sante** [eturdisɑ̃, -sɑ̃t] *adj* 1 BRUYANT : deafening 2 : stunning — **étourdissement** [eturdismɑ̃] *nm* VERTIGE : dizziness

étourneau [eturno] *nm*, *pl* **-neaux** [-no] : starling

étrange [etrɑ̃ʒ] *adj* : strange — **étrangement** [etrɑ̃ʒmɑ̃] *adv* : oddly, strangely — **étrangeté** [etrɑ̃ʒte] *nf* : strangeness, oddity — **étranger, -gère** [etrɑ̃ʒe, -ʒɛr] *adj* 1 : foreign (of a country, etc.) 2 : unfamiliar, strange — ~ *n* 1 : foreigner 2 : stranger 3 **à l'étranger** : abroad

étrangler [etrɑ̃gle] *vt* 1 : strangle 2 SERRER : constrict — **s'étrangler** *vr* : choke

être [ɛtr] {38} *vi* 1 : be, exist 2 ~ **à** : belong to — *v aux* : have — ~ *nm* 1 : being 2 PERSONNE : person

étreindre [etrɛ̃dr] {37} *vt* 1 : embrace, hug 2 SERRER : grip — **étreinte** [etrɛ̃t] *nf* 1 : embrace, hug 2 **sous l'~ de** : in the grip of

étrenner [etrene] *vt* : use for the first time

étrier [etrije] *nm* : stirrup

étriqué, -quée [etrike] *adj* 1 : skimpy 2 MESQUIN : petty

étroit, -troite [etrwa, -trwat] *adj* 1 : narrow 2 SERRÉ : tight — **étroitesse** [etrwatɛs] *nf* : narrowness

étude [etyd] *nf* 1 : study, studying 2 BUREAU : office — **étudiant, -diante** [etydjɑ̃, -djɑ̃t] *adj & n* : student — **étudier** [etydje] {96} *v* : study

étui [etɥi] *nm* : case

euphémisme [øfemism] *nm* : euphemism

euphorie [øfɔri] *nf* : euphoria

euro [øro] *nm* : euro (monetary unit)

européen, -péenne [ørɔpeɛ̃, -peɛn] *adj* : European

eux [ø] *pron* : they, them — **eux-mêmes** [ømɛm] *pron pl* : themselves

évacuer [evakɥe] *vt* : evacuate — **évacuation** [evakɥasjɔ̃] *nf* : evacuation

évader [evade] *v* **s'évader** *vr* : escape — **évadé, -dée** [evade] *n* : fugitive

évaluer [evalɥe] *vt* : evaluate, assess — **évaluation** [evalɥasjɔ̃] *nf* : evaluation, assessment

évangile [evɑ̃ʒil] *nm* 1 : gospel 2 **l'Évangile** : the Gospel

évanouir [evanwir] *v* **s'évanouir** *vr* : faint — **évanouissement** [evanwismɑ̃] *nm* : fainting, faint

évaporer [evapɔre] *v* **s'évaporer** *vr* : evaporate — **évaporation** [evapɔrasjɔ̃] *nf* : evaporation

évasif, -sive [evazif, -ziv] *adj* : evasive — **évasion** [evazjɔ̃] *nf* : escape

éveiller [eveje] *vt* 1 RÉVEILLER : awaken 2 : arouse (curiosity, etc.) — **s'éveiller** *vr* 1 : wake up 2 : be aroused — **éveil** [evɛj] *nm* 1 : awakening 2 **en ~** : on the alert — **éveillé, -lée** [eveje] *adj* 1 : awake 2 ALERTE : alert

événement [evɛnmɑ̃] *nm* : event

éventail [evɑ̃taj] *nm* 1 : fan 2 GAMME : range, spread

éventaire [evɑ̃tɛr] *nm* : stall, stand

éventé, -tée [evɑ̃te] *adj* : stale, flat

éventrer [evɑ̃tre] *vt* : tear open

éventualité [evɑ̃tɥalite] *nf* : eventuality, possibility — **éventuel, -tuelle** [evɑ̃tɥɛl] *adj* : possible — **éventuellement** [-tɥɛlmɑ̃] *adv* : possibly

évêque [evɛk] *nm* : bishop

évertuer [evɛrtɥe] *v* **s'évertuer** *vr* : strive, do one's best

éviction [eviksjɔ̃] *nf* : eviction

évidemment [evidamɑ̃] *adv* : obviously, of course

évidence [evidɑ̃s] *nf* : obviousness — **évident, -dente** [evidɑ̃, -dɑ̃t] *adj* : obvious, evident

évider [evide] *vt* : hollow out

évier [evje] *nm* : sink

évincer [evɛ̃se] {6} *vt* : oust

éviter [evite] *vt* 1 : avoid 2 ~ **à qqn de faire qqch** : save s.o. from (doing) sth

évoluer [evɔlɥe] *vi* 1 : evolve, develop 2 SE DÉPLACER : maneuver, move about — **évolution** [evɔlysjɔ̃] *nf* 1 : evolution 2 CHANGEMENT : development, change

évoquer [evɔke] *vt* : evoke, call to mind

exacerber [ɛgzasɛrbe] *vt* : exacerbate

exact, exacte [ɛgzakt] *adj* 1 : exact 2 JUSTE

: correct **3** PONCTUEL : punctual — **exactement** [ɛgzaktəmɑ̃] *adv* : exactly — **exactitude** [ɛgzaktityd] *nf* **1** : accuracy **2** PONC-
TUALITÉ : punctuality

ex aequo [ɛgzɛko] *adv* : equal

exagérer [ɛgzaʒere] {87} *vt* : exaggerate —
vi : go too far, overdo it — **exagération**
[ɛgzaʒerasjɔ̃] *nf* : exaggeration — **exagéré,
-rée** [ɛgzaʒere] *adj* : exaggerated, excessive
exalter [ɛgzalte] *vt* **1** : excite, stir **2** GLORI-
FIER : exalt — **s'exalter** *vr* : get excited
examiner [ɛgzamine] *vt* : examine — **examen** [ɛgzamɛ̃] *nm* : examination
exaspérer [ɛgzaspere] {87} *vt* : exasperate
— **exaspération** [ɛgzasperasjɔ̃] *nf* : exasperation
exaucer [ɛgzose] {6} *vt* : grant
excaver [ɛkskave] *vt* : excavate — **excavation** [ɛkskavasjɔ̃] *nf* : excavation
excéder [ɛksede] {87} *vt* **1** : exceed **2**
EXASPÉRER : exasperate — **excédent**
[ɛksedɑ̃] *nm* : surplus, excess — **excédentaire** [ɛksedatɛr] *adj* : surplus, excess
exceller [ɛksele] *vi* : excel — **excellence**
[ɛkselɑ̃s] *nf* : excellence — **excellent,
-lente** [ɛkselɑ̃, -lɑ̃t] *adj* : excellent
excentrique [ɛksɑ̃trik] *adj & nmf* : eccentric
— **excentricité** [ɛksɑ̃trisite] *nf* : eccentricity
excepter [ɛksɛpte] *vt* : except, exclude —
excepté [ɛksɛpte] *prep* SAUF : except, apart
from — **exception** [ɛksɛpsjɔ̃] *nf* **1** : exception **2 à l'~ de** : except for — **exceptionnel, -nelle** [ɛksɛpsjɔnɛl] *adj* : exceptional
excès [ɛksɛ] *nm* **1** : excess **2 ~ de vitesse**
: speeding — **excessif, -sive** [ɛksɛsif, -siv]
adj : excessive
exciter [ɛksite] *vt* **1** : excite **2** STIMULER
: stimulate — **s'exciter** *vr* : get excited —
excitant, -tante [ɛksitɑ̃, -tɑ̃t] *adj* : exciting
— **excitation** [ɛksitasjɔ̃] *nf* : excitement
exclamer [ɛksklame] *v* **s'exclamer** *vr* : exclaim — **exclamation** [ɛksklamasjɔ̃] *nf*
: exclamation
exclure [ɛksklyr] {39} *vt* **1** : exclude **2** EX-
PULSER : expel — **exclusif, -sive** [ɛksklyzif,
-ziv] *adj* : exclusive — **exclusivement**
[-sivmɑ̃] *adv* : exclusively — **exclusion**
[ɛksklyzjɔ̃] *nf* **1** : exclusion **2** EXPULSION
: expulsion — **exclusivité** [ɛksklyzivite] *nf*
1 : exclusive rights *pl* **2 en ~** : exclusively
excréments [ɛkskremɑ̃] *nmpl* : excrement,
feces
excroissance [ɛkskrwasɑ̃s] *nf* : outgrowth
excursion [ɛkskyrsjɔ̃] *nf* : excursion, trip
excuser [ɛkskyze] *vt* : excuse — **s'excuser**
vr : apologize — **excuse** [ɛkskyz] *nf* **1**
: excuse **2 ~s** *nfpl* : apology
exécrer [ɛgzekre] {87} *vt* : abhor, loathe —

exécrable [ɛgzekrabl] *adj* : atrocious,
awful
exécuter [ɛgzekyte] *vt* **1** : execute **2** EF-
FECTUER : perform — **s'exécuter** *vr* : comply — **exécutant, -tante** [ɛgzekytɑ̃, -tɑ̃t] *n*
: performer — **exécutif, -tive** [ɛgzekytif,
-tiv] *adj* : executive — **exécution**
[ɛgzekysjɔ̃] *nf* : execution
exemple [ɛgzɑ̃pl] *nm* **1** : example **2 par ~**
: for example, for instance — **exemplaire**
[ɛgzɑ̃plɛr] *adj* : exemplary — **~** *nm* **1**
: copy **2** : specimen, example
exempt, exempte [ɛgzɑ̃, ɛgzɑ̃t] *adj* : exempt — **exempter** [ɛgzɑ̃te] *vt* : exempt —
exemption [ɛgzɑ̃psjɔ̃] *nf* : exemption
exercer [ɛgzɛrse] {6} *vt* **1** : exercise, train **2**
: exert (control, influence, etc.) **3** : practice
(a profession) — **s'exercer** *vr* : practice —
exercice [ɛgzɛrsis] *nm* **1** : exercise **2 en
~** : in office
exhaler [ɛgzale] *vt* **1** : exhale **2** ÉMETTRE
: utter, breathe
exhaustif, -tive [ɛgzostif, -tiv] *adj* : exhaustive
exhiber [ɛgzibe] *vt* : exhibit, show off — **exhibition** [ɛgzibisjɔ̃] *nf* : display, exhibition
exhorter [ɛgzɔrte] *vt* : exhort, urge
exiger [ɛgziʒe] {17} *vt* : demand, require —
exigeant, -geante [ɛgziʒɑ̃, -ʒɑ̃t] *adj* : demanding, choosy — **exigence** [ɛgziʒɑ̃s] *nf*
: demand, requirement
exigu, -guë [ɛgzigy] *adj* : cramped, tiny
exil [ɛgzil] *nm* : exile — **exilé, -lée** [ɛgzile] *n*
: exile — **exiler** [ɛgzile] *vt* : exile — **s'exiler**
vr : go into exile, isolate oneself
exister [ɛgziste] *vi* : exist — **existant, -tante**
[ɛgzistɑ̃, -tɑ̃t] *adj* : existing — **existence**
[ɛgzistɑ̃s] *nf* : existence
exode [ɛgzɔd] *nm* : exodus
exonérer [ɛgzɔnere] {87} *vt* : exempt —
exonération [ɛgzɔnerasjɔ̃] *nf* : exemption
exorbitant, -tante [ɛgzɔrbitɑ̃, -tɑ̃t] *adj* : exorbitant
exotique [ɛgzɔtik] *adj* : exotic
expansion [ɛkspɑ̃sjɔ̃] *nf* : expansion — **ex-
pansif, -sive** [ɛkspɑ̃sif, -siv] *adj* : expan-
sive
expatrier [ɛkspatrije] {96} *vt* : expatriate —
s'expatrier *vr* : emigrate — **expatrié, -triée**
[ɛkspatrije] *adj & n* : expatriate
expédient, -diente [ɛkspedjɑ̃, -djɑ̃t] *adj*
: expedient — **expédient** *nm* : expedient
expédier [ɛkspedje] {96} *vt* : send, dispatch
— **expéditeur, -trice** [ɛkspeditœr, -tris] *n*
: sender — **expéditif, -tive** [ɛkspeditif,
-tiv] *adj* : quick — **expédition** [ɛkspedisjɔ̃]
nf **1** : sending, shipment **2** VOYAGE : expedition
expérience [ɛksperjɑ̃s] *nf* **1** : experience **2**
ESSAI : experiment — **expérimental, -tale**

[ɛksperimɑ̃tal] *adj, mpl* -**taux** [-to] : experimental — **expérimentation** [ɛksperimɑ̃tasjɔ̃] *nf* : experimentation — **expérimenté, -tée** [ɛksperimɑ̃te] *adj* : experienced — **expérimenter** [ɛksperimɑ̃te] *vt* : test, experiment with

expert, -perte [ɛkspɛr, -pɛrt] *adj & n* : expert — **expertise** [ɛkspɛrtiz] *nf* **1** : expert appraisal **2** COMPÉTENCE : expertise

expier [ɛkspje] {96} *vt* : atone for

expirer [ɛkspire] *vi* **1** : breathe out **2** : expire (of a contract) — *vt* : exhale — **expiration** [ɛkspirasjɔ̃] *nf* **1** ÉCHÉANCE : expiration **2** : exhalation (of breath)

explication [ɛksplikasjɔ̃] *nf* : explanation — **explicatif, -tive** [ɛksplikatif, -tiv] *adj* : explanatory

explicite [ɛksplisit] *adj* : explicit

expliquer [ɛksplike] *vt* : explain — **s'expliquer** *vr* **1** : explain oneself **2** : be explained

exploiter [ɛksplwate] *vt* **1** : exploit **2** : work (a field, a mine, etc.), run (a business, etc.) — **exploit** [ɛksplwa] *nm* : exploit — **exploitation** [ɛksplwatasjɔ̃] *nf* **1** : exploitation **2** : running, management (of a farm, mine, etc.) **3** ~ **agricole** : (small) farm

explorer [ɛksplɔre] *vt* : explore — **explorateur, -trice** [ɛksplɔratœr, -tris] *n* : explorer — **exploration** [ɛksplɔrasjɔ̃] *nf* : exploration

exploser [ɛksploze] *vi* **1** : explode **2** : burst out, flare up (with anger, etc.) — **explosif, -sive** [ɛksplozif, -ziv] *adj* : explosive — **explosif** *nm* : explosive — **explosion** [ɛksplozjɔ̃] *nf* **1** : explosion **2** : outburst (of anger, joy, etc.)

exporter [ɛkspɔrte] *vt* : export — **exportateur, -trice** [ɛkspɔrtatœr, -tris] *adj* : exporting — ~ *n* : exporter — **exportation** [ɛkspɔrtasjɔ̃] *nf* : export, exportation

exposer [ɛkspoze] *vt* **1** : exhibit **2** EXPLIQUER : explain **3** ORIENTER : orient **4** : expose (to danger), risk (one's life, reputation, etc.) — **s'exposer** *vr* : expose oneself — **exposant, -sante** [ɛkspozɑ̃, -zɑ̃t] *n* : exhibitor — **exposé** [ɛkspoze] *nm* **1** : lecture, talk **2** : account, report — **exposition** [ɛkspozisjɔ̃] *nf* **1** : exhibition **2** PRÉSENTATION : exposition **3** ORIENTATION : orientation, aspect

exprès [ɛksprɛ] *adv* **1** : on purpose, intentionally **2** SPÉCIALEMENT : specially — **exprès, -presse** [ɛksprɛs] *adj* **1** : express, explicit **2** : special delivery — **express** [ɛksprɛs] *adj* : express — ~ *nm* **1** : express (train) **2** *or* **café** ~ : espresso — **expressément** [ɛksprɛsemɑ̃] *adv* : expressly — **expressif, -sive** [ɛksprɛsif, -siv] *adj* : expressive — **expression** [ɛksprɛsjɔ̃] *nf* : expression

exprimer [ɛksprime] *vt* **1** : express **2** EXTRAIRE : squeeze, extract — **s'exprimer** *vr* : express oneself

expulser [ɛkspylse] *vt* : expel, evict — **expulsion** [ɛkspylsjɔ̃] *nf* : expulsion, eviction

exquis, -quise [ɛkski, -kiz] *adj* : exquisite

extase [ɛkstaz] *nf* : ecstasy — **extasier** [ɛkstazje] {96} *v* **s'extasier** *vr* : be in ecstasy — **extatique** [ɛkstatik] *adj* : ecstatic

extension [ɛkstɑ̃sjɔ̃] *nf* **1** : stretching (of a muscle, etc.) **2** ÉLARGISSEMENT : extension, expansion — **extensif, -sive** [ɛkstɑ̃sif, -siv] *adj* : extensive

exténuer [ɛkstenɥe] *vt* : exhaust, tire out — **exténuant, -ante** [ɛkstenɥɑ, -ɥɑ̃t] *adj* : exhausting

extérieur, -rieure [ɛksterjœr] *adj* **1** : exterior, outside **2** APPARENT : apparent **3** ÉTRANGER : foreign — **extérieur** *nm* **1** : exterior **2 à l'**~ : abroad — **extérieurement** [ɛksterjœrmɑ̃] *adv* **1** : externally **2** APPAREMMENT : outwardly — **extérioriser** [ɛksterjɔrize] *vt* : show, express

exterminer [ɛkstɛrmine] *vt* : exterminate — **extermination** [ɛkstɛrminasjɔ̃] *nf* : extermination

externe [ɛkstɛrn] *adj* : external

extinction [ɛkstɛ̃ksjɔ̃] *nf* **1** : extinction **2** : extinguishing — **extincteur** [ɛkstɛ̃ktœr] *nm* : fire extinguisher

extirper [ɛkstirpe] *vt* : eradicate

extorquer [ɛkstɔrke] *vt* : extort — **extorsion** [ɛkstɔrsjɔ̃] *nf* : extortion

extra [ɛkstra] *adj* **1** : first-rate **2** *fam* : fantastic — ~ *nms & pl* **1** : extra person **2** : extra thing or amount

extraction [ɛkstraksjɔ̃] *nf* : extraction

extrader [ɛkstrade] *vt* : extradite

extraire [ɛkstrɛr] {40} *vt* : extract — **extrait** [ɛkstrɛ] *nm* **1** : extract, essence **2** : excerpt (of a speech, etc.)

extraordinaire [ɛkstraɔrdinɛr] *adj* : extraordinary

extraterrestre [ɛkstratɛrɛstr] *adj & nmf* : extraterrestrial

extravagant, -gante [ɛkstravagɑ̃, -gɑ̃t] *adj* : extravagant — **extravagance** [-vagɑ̃s] *nf* : extravagance

extraverti, -tie [ɛkstravɛrti] *adj* : extroverted — ~ *n* : extrovert

extrême [ɛkstrɛm] *adj* : extreme — ~ *nm* : extreme — **extrêmement** [ɛkstrɛmmɑ̃] *adv* : extremely — **extrémité** [ɛkstremite] *nf* : extremity

exubérant, -rante [ɛgzyberɑ̃, -rɑ̃t] *adj* : exuberant — **exubérance** [-berɑ̃s] *nf* : exuberance

exulter [ɛgzylte] *vi* : exult

exutoire [ɛgzytwar] *nm* : outlet

F

f [ɛf] *nm* : f, sixth letter of the alphabet
fable [fabl] *nf* : fable
fabriquer [fabrike] *vt* **1** : make, manufacture **2** INVENTER : fabricate — **fabricant, -cante** [fabrikᾰ, -kᾰt] *n* : manufacturer — **fabrication** [fabrikasjɔ̃] *nf* : manufacture, making — **fabrique** [fabrik] *nf* : factory
fabuleux, -leuse [fabylø, -løz] *adj* : fabulous
façade [fasad] *nf* : façade, front
face [fas] *nf* **1** VISAGE : face **2** CÔTÉ : side **3** en ~ : opposite **4** à ~ : face-to-face **5** faire ~ à : face — **facette** [fasɛt] *nf* : facet
facétieux, -tieuse [fasesjø, -sjøz] *adj* : facetious
fâcher [faʃe] *vt* : anger — **se fâcher** *vr* : get angry — **fâché, -chée** [faʃe] *adj* : angry — **fâcheux, -cheuse** [faʃø, -ʃøz] *adj* : unfortunate
facile [fasil] *adj* **1** : easy **2** : easygoing — **facilement** [fasilmᾰ] *adv* : easily — **facilité** [fasilite] *nf* **1** : easiness **2** APTITUDE : aptitude — **faciliter** [fasilite] *vt* : facilitate
façon [fasɔ̃] *nf* **1** : way, manner **2** ~s *nfpl* : behavior, manners **3** de ~ à : so as to **4** de toute ~ : in any case **5** faire des ~s : put on airs — **façonner** [fasɔne] *vt* **1** FORMER : shape **2** FABRIQUER : manufacture
fac-similé [faksimile] *nm, pl* **fac-similés** : facsimile, copy
facteur[1], **-trice** [faktœr, -tris] *n* : mailman
facteur[2] *nm* : factor
faction [faksjɔ̃] *nf* **1** GROUPE : faction **2** : guard (duty)
factuel, -tuelle [faktɥɛl] *adj* : factual
facture [faktyr] *nf* : bill, invoice — **facturer** [faktyre] *vt* : bill
facultatif, -tive [fakyltatif, -tiv] *adj* : optional
faculté [fakylte] *nf* **1** : faculty, ability **2** LIBERTÉ : option **3** : faculty (of a university)
fade [fad] *adj* : bland
faible [fɛbl] *adj* **1** : weak, feeble **2** : small (in quantity) **3** PÂLE : faint, light — ~ *nmf* : weakling — ~ *nm* : weakness — **faiblesse** [fɛblɛs] *nf* : weakness — **faiblir** [feblir] *vi* **1** : weaken **2** DIMINUER : die down
faïence [fajᾰs] *nf* : earthenware
faillir [fajir] {41} *vi* ~ à : fail to — *vt* **1** : narrowly miss **2** ~ faire qqch : nearly do sth — **faille** [faj] *nf* **1** : fault (in geology) **2** FAIBLESSE : flaw — **faillible** [fajibl] *adj* : fallible — **faillite** [fajit] *nf* **1** ÉCHEC : failure **2** faire ~ : go bankrupt

faim [fɛ̃] *nf* **1** : hunger **2** avoir ~ : be hungry
fainéant, -néante [feneᾰ, -neᾰt] *adj* : lazy — ~ *n* : loafer, idler
faire [fɛr] {42} *vt* **1** : do **2** : make **3** : equal, amount to **4** DIRE : say **5** cela ne fait rien : it doesn't matter **6** ~ du football : play football **7** ~ mal à : hurt **8** ~ soleil : be sunny **9** ~ un rêve : have a dream — **se faire** *vr* **1** ~ à : get used to **2** s'en faire : worry — **faire-part** [fɛrpar] *nms & pl* : announcement (of marriage, etc.) — **faisable** [fəzabl] *adj* : feasible
faisan, -sane [fəzᾰ] *n* : pheasant
faisceau [fɛso] *nm, pl* **-ceaux** : beam (of light)
fait, faite [fɛ, fɛt] *adj* **1** : made, done **2** : ripe (of cheese) **3** tout fait : ready-made — **fait** *nm* **1** : fact **2** ÉVÉNEMENT : event **3** au ~ : by the way **4** sur le ~ : red-handed
faîte [fɛt] *nm* **1** SOMMET : summit, top **2** APOGÉE : pinnacle
falaise [falɛz] *nf* : cliff
falloir [falwar] {43} *v impers* **1** comme il faut : proper(ly) **2** il fallait le faire : it had to be done **3** il fallait me le dire! : you should have said so! **4** il faut partir : we must go **5** il faut que je ... : I need to ... — **s'en falloir** *vr* **1** peu s'en faut : very nearly **2** tant s'en faut : far from it
falsifier [falsifje] {96} *vt* : falsify
famé, -mée [fame] *adj* mal famé : disreputable
famélique [famelik] *adj* : starving
fameux, -meuse [famø, -møz] *adj* **1** CÉLÈBRE : famous **2** *fam* : first-rate
familial, -liale [familjal] *adj, mpl* **-liaux** [-ljo] : family — **familiale** *nf* : station wagon
familiariser [familjarize] *v* **se familiariser** *vr* : familiarize oneself — **familiarité** [familjarite] *nf* : familiarity — **familier, -lière** [familje, -ljɛr] *adj* **1** : familiar **2** : informal
famille [famij] *nf* : family
famine [famin] *nf* : famine
fanatique [fanatik] *adj* : fanatic(al) — ~ *nmf* : fanatic — **fanatisme** [-natism] *nm* : fanaticism
faner [fane] *v* **se faner** *vr* : fade
fanfare [fᾰfar] *nf* **1** : fanfare **2** : brass band
fanfaron, -ronne [fᾰfarɔ̃, -rɔn] *adj* : boastful — ~ *n* : braggart
fantaisie [fᾰtezi] *nf* **1** : fantasy **2** CAPRICE : whim — **fantaisiste** [fᾰtezist] *adj* : fanciful
fantasme [fᾰtasm] *nm* : fantasy — **fantas-**

mer [fɑ̃tasme] *vi* : fantasize — **fantasque** [fɑ̃task] *adj* **1** CAPRICIEUX : whimsical **2** BIZARRE : strange, weird — **fantastique** [fɑ̃tastik] *adj* : fantastic

fantoche [fɑ̃tɔʃ] *adj & nm* : puppet

fantôme [fɑ̃tom] *nm* : ghost

faon [fɑ̃] *nm* : fawn

farce [fars] *nf* **1** : practical joke **2** : farce (in theater) — **farceur, -ceuse** [farsœr, -søz] *n* : prankster

farcir [farsir] *vt* : stuff (in cooking)

fard [far] *nm* : makeup

fardeau [fardo] *nm, pl* **-deaux** : load, burden

farfelu, -lue [farfəly] *adj fam* : wacky

farine [farin] *nf* : flour

farouche [faruʃ] *adj* **1** SAUVAGE : wild **2** TIMIDE : shy **3** ACHARNÉ : fierce

fascicule [fasikyl] *nm* **1** : section (of a book) **2** LIVRET : booklet

fasciner [fasine] *vt* : fascinate — **fascinant, -nante** [fasinɑ̃, -nɑ̃t] *adj* : fascinating — **fascination** [fasinasjɔ̃] *nf* : fascination

fascisme [faʃism] *nm* : fascism — **fasciste** [faʃist] *adj & nmf* : fascist

faste[1] [fast] *adj* : lucky

faste[2] *nm* : pomp, splendor

fastidieux, -dieuse [fastidjø, -djøz] *adj* : tedious

fatal, -tale [fatal] *adj, mpl* **-tals 1** MORTEL : fatal **2** INÉVITABLE : inevitable — **fatalement** [fatalmɑ̃] *adv* : inevitably — **fatalité** [fatalite] *nf* **1** SORT : fate **2** : inevitability

fatidique [fatidik] *adj* : fateful

fatiguer [fatige] *vt* **1** : fatigue, tire **2** ENNUYER : annoy **3** : strain (an engine, etc.) — *vi* : grow tired — **se fatiguer** *vr* : wear oneself out — **fatigant, -gante** [fatigɑ̃, -gɑ̃t] *adj* **1** : tiring **2** ENNUYEUX : tiresome — **fatigue** [fatig] *nf* : fatigue — **fatigué, -guée** [fatige] *adj* : tired

faubourg [fobur] *nm* : suburb

faucher [foʃe] *vt* **1** : mow, cut **2** *fam* : swipe, pinch — **fauché, -chée** [foʃe] *adj fam* : broke, penniless

faucille [fosij] *nf* : sickle

faucon [fokɔ̃] *nm* : falcon, hawk

faufiler [fofile] *vt* : baste (in sewing) — **se faufiler** *vr* : weave one's way

faune [fon] *nf* : fauna, wildlife

faussaire [fosɛr] *nmf* : forger

fausse → **faux**[2]

fausser [fose] *vt* **1** : distort **2** DÉFORMER : bend — **faussement** [fosmɑ̃] *adv* **1** : falsely **2** : wrongfully — **fausseté** [foste] *nf* **1** : falseness **2** DUPLICITÉ : duplicity

faute [fot] *nf* **1** : fault **2** ERREUR : mistake **3** **~ de** : for lack of

fauteuil [fotœj] *nm* **1** : armchair **2** **~ roulant** : wheelchair

fautif, -tive [fotif, -tiv] *adj* **1** COUPABLE : at fault **2** ERRONÉ : faulty

fauve [fov] *nm* : big cat

faux[1] [fo] *nfs & pl* : scythe

faux[2], **fausse** [fo] *adj* **1** : false **2** INCORRECT : wrong **3** FALSIFIÉ : counterfeit, fake **4 fausse couche** : miscarriage **5 faire un faux pas** : stumble **6 faux nom** : alias — **~** *nm* : forgery — **~** *adv* : out of tune — **faux–filet** [fofilɛ] *nm, pl* **faux–filets** : sirloin — **faux–monnayeur** [fomɔnɛjœr] *nm, pl* **faux–monnayeurs** : forger

faveur [favœr] *nf* **1** : favor **2 en ~ de** : in favor of — **favorable** [favorabl] *adj* : favorable — **favori, -rite** [favori, -rit] *adj & n* : favorite — **favoris** [favori] *nmpl* : sideburns — **favoriser** [favorize] *vt* **1** : favor **2** ENCOURAGER : promote — **favoritisme** [favoritism] *nm* : favoritism

fax [faks] *nm* : fax — **faxer** [fakse] *vt* : fax

fébrile [febril] *adj* : feverish

fécond, -conde [fekɔ̃, -kɔ̃d] *adj* : fertile — **féconder** [fekɔ̃de] *vt* : fertilize, impregnate — **fécondité** [fekɔ̃dite] *nf* : fertility

fécule [fekyl] *nf* : starch — **féculent, -lente** [fekylɑ̃, -lɑ̃t] *adj* : starchy — **féculent** [fekylɑ̃] *nm* : starchy food

fédéral, -rale [federal] *adj, mpl* **-raux** [-ro] : federal — **fédération** [federasjɔ̃] *nf* : federation

fée [fe] *nf* : fairy — **féerie** [fe(e)ri] *nf* : enchantment — **féerique** [fe(e)rik] *adj* : magical, enchanting

feindre [fɛ̃dr] {37} *vt* : feign — *vi* : pretend — **feinte** [fɛ̃t] *nf* : trick, ruse

fêler [fele] *vt* : crack

féliciter [felisite] *vt* : congratulate — **félicitations** [felisitasjɔ̃] *nfpl* : congratulations

félin, -line [felɛ̃, -lin] *adj & nm* : feline

fêlure [felyr] *nf* : crack

femelle [fəmɛl] *adj & nf* : female

féminin, -nine [feminɛ̃, -nin] *adj* : feminine — **féminisme** [feminism] *nm* : feminism — **féministe** [feminist] *adj & nmf* : feminist — **féminité** [feminite] *nf* : femininity

femme [fam] *nf* **1** : woman **2** ÉPOUSE : wife **3** **~ au foyer** : homemaker **4** **~ d'affaires** : businesswoman

fendre [fɑ̃dr] {63} *vt* : split, break — **se fendre** *vr* : crack

fenêtre [fənɛtr] *nf* : window

fenouil [fənuj] *nm* : fennel

fente [fɑ̃t] *nf* **1** : slit, slot **2** FISSURE : crack

féodal, -dale [feodal] *adj, mpl* **-daux** [-do] : feudal

fer [fɛr] *nm* **1** : iron **2** **~ à cheval** : horseshoe **3** **~ à repasser** : iron (for clothes)

férié, -riée [ferje] *adj* **jour férié** : holiday

ferme [fɛrm] *adj* : firm — **~** *adv* : firmly,

fermé

hard — ~ *nf* : farm — **fermement** [fɛrmǝmɑ̃] *adv* : firmly

fermé, -mée [fɛrme] *adj* **1** : closed, shut (off) **2** EXCLUSIF : exclusive

fermenter [fɛrmɑ̃te] *vi* : ferment — **fermentation** [fɛrmɑ̃tasjɔ̃] *nf* : fermentation

fermer [fɛrme] *vt* **1** : close, shut **2** : close down (a factory, etc.) **3** ÉTEINDRE : turn off **4** ~ **à clef** : lock up — **se fermer** *vr* : close (up)

fermeté [fɛrmǝte] *nf* : firmness

fermeture [fɛrmǝtyr] *nf* **1** : closing, shutting **2** ~ **à glissière** : zipper

fermier, -mière [fɛrmje, -mjɛr] *n* : farmer

fermoir [fɛrmwar] *nm* : clasp

féroce [feros] *adj* : ferocious — **férocité** [ferosite] *nf* : ferocity, ferociousness

ferraille [fɛraj] *nf* : scrap iron

ferronnerie [fɛrɔnri] *nf* **1** : ironworks **2** : wrought iron

ferroviaire [fɛrɔvjɛr] *adj* : rail, railroad

ferry-boat [fɛribot] *nm, pl* **ferry-boats** : ferry

fertile [fɛrtil] *adj* : fertile — **fertiliser** [fɛrtilize] *vt* : fertilize — **fertilité** [fɛrtilite] *nf* : fertility

fervent, -vente [fɛrvɑ̃, -vɑ̃t] *adj* : fervent — ~ *n* : enthusiast — **ferveur** [fɛrvœr] *nf* : fervor

fesses [fɛs] *nfpl* : buttocks — **fessée** [fese] *nf* : spanking — **fesser** [fese] *vt* : spank

festin [fɛstɛ̃] *nm* : feast

festival [fɛstival] *nm, pl* **-vals** : festival — **festivités** [fɛstivite] *nfpl* : festivities

fête [fɛt] *nf* **1** : holiday **2** : party **3** FOIRE : fair **4 de** ~ : festive **5 faire la** ~ : have a good time — **fêter** [fete] *vt* : celebrate

fétiche [fetiʃ] *nm* : fetish

fétide [fetid] *adj* : fetid

feu¹ [fø] *nm, pl* **feux 1** : fire **2** *or* ~ **de circulation** : traffic light **3** : burner (of a stove) **4** : light (for a cigarette, etc.) **5** TIR : fire, shooting **6** ~ **de joie** : bonfire **7 feux d'artifice** : fireworks **8 mettre le** ~ **à** : set fire to **9 prendre** ~ : catch fire

feu², feue [fø] *adj* : late, deceased

feuille [fœj] *nf* **1** : leaf **2** : sheet (of paper, etc.) — **feuillage** [fœjaʒ] *nm* : foliage — **feuillet** [fœjɛ] *nm* : page, leaf — **feuilleter** [fœjte] {8} *vt* : leaf through — **feuilleton** [fœjtɔ̃] *nm* : series, serial

feutre [føtr] *nm* : felt — **feutré, -trée** [føtre] *adj* : muffled, hushed

fève [fɛv] *nf* : broad bean

février [fevrije] *nm* : February

fiable [fjabl] *adj* : reliable — **fiabilité** [fjabilite] *nf* : reliability

fiancer [fijɑ̃se] {6} *v* **se fiancer** *vr* : get engaged — **fiançailles** [fijɑ̃saj] *nfpl* : engagement — **fiancé, -cée** [fijɑ̃se] *n* : fiancé *m*, fiancée *f*

fibre [fibr] *nf* **1** : fiber **2** ~ **de verre** : fiberglass — **fibreux, -breuse** [fibrø, -brøz] *adj* : fibrous

ficelle [fisɛl] *nf* : string, twine — **ficeler** [fisle] {8} *vt* : tie up

fiche [fiʃ] *nf* **1** : index card **2** FORMULAIRE : form **3** : (electric) plug

ficher [fiʃe] *vt* **1** : drive (in) **2** *fam* : do **3** *fam* : give — ~ **qqn dehors** *fam* : kick s.o. out — **se ficher** *vr* **1** ~ **de** *fam* : make fun of **2 je m'en fiche** *fam* : I don't give a damn

fichier [fiʃje] *nm* : file, index

fichu¹, -chue [fiʃy] *adj fam* **1** : lousy, awful **2** CONDAMNÉ : done for

fichu² *nm* : scarf, kerchief

fiction [fiksjɔ̃] *nf* : fiction — **fictif, -tive** [fiktif, -tiv] *adj* : fictional, fictitious

fidèle [fidɛl] *adj* : faithful — ~ *nmf* **1** : follower **2** : regular (customer) **3 les** ~**s** : the faithful — **fidèlement** [-dɛlmɑ̃] *adv* : faithfully — **fidélité** [fidelite] *nf* : fidelity

fier¹ [fje] *v* **se fier** *vr* ~ **à** : trust, rely on

fier², fière [fjɛr] *adj* : proud — **fièrement** [fjɛrmɑ̃] *adv* : proudly — **fierté** [fjɛrte] *nf* : pride

fièvre [fjɛvr] *nf* : fever — **fiévreux, -vreuse** [fjɛvrø, -vrøz] *adj* : feverish

figer [fiʒe] {17} *v* **se figer** *vr* : coagulate

figue [fig] *nf* : fig

figure [figyr] *nf* **1** VISAGE : face **2** PERSONNAGE : figure **3** ILLUSTRATION : illustration — **figurant, -rante** [figyrɑ̃, -rɑ̃t] *n* : extra (in theater) — **figurer** [figyre] *vi* : appear — *vt* : represent — **se figurer** *vr* : imagine

fil [fil] *nm* **1** : thread **2** : wire **3 au** ~ **de** : in the course of **4 coup de** ~ *fam* : phone call **5** ~ **dentaire** : dental floss — **file** [fil] *nf* **1** : line, file, row **2** : lane (of a highway) **3 en** ~ *or* **à la** ~ : one after another — **filer** [file] *vt* **1** : spin (yarn) **2** SUIVRE : shadow **3** *fam* : give — *vi* **1** : run (of stockings) **2** *fam* : dash off **3** *fam* : fly by, slip away **4** ~ **bien** *Can fam* : be doing fine

filet [filɛ] *nm* **1** : net **2** : fillet (of beef, etc.) **3** : trickle (of water)

filiale [filjal] *nf* : subsidiary (company)

filière [filjɛr] *nf* : (official) channels *pl*

filigrane [filigran] *nm* : watermark

fille [fij] *nf* **1** : girl **2** : daughter — **fillette** [fijɛt] *nf* : little girl

filleul, -leule [fijœl] *n* : godchild, godson *m*, goddaughter *f*

film [film] *nm* : film — **filmer** [filme] *vt* : film

filon [filɔ̃] *nm* : vein, lode

fils [fis] *nm* : son

filtre [filtr] *nm* : filter — **filtrer** [filtre] *vt* **1** : filter **2** : screen (visitors, etc.) — *vi* : filter through

fin¹, fine [fɛ̃, fin] *adj* **1** : fine **2** MINCE : thin **3** : excellent (in quality) **4** : sharp, keen **5** *Can* : nice — **fin** *adv* : finely

fin² *nf* **1** : end **2 à la ~** : in the end **3 prendre ~** : come to an end **4 sans ~** : endless(ly)

final, -nale [final] *adj, mpl* **-nals** *or* **-naux** [fino] : final — **finale** *nf* : finals *pl* (in sports) — **finalement** [finalmã] *adv* **1** : finally **2** : after all — **finaliste** [finalist] *nmf* : finalist

finance [finɑ̃s] *nf* **1** : finance **2 ~s** *nfpl* : finances — **financer** [finɑ̃se] {6} *vt* : finance — **financier, -cière** [finɑ̃sje, -sjɛr] *adj* : financial

finesse [finɛs] *nf* **1** : finesse, delicacy **2** PERSPICACITÉ : shrewdness

finir [finir] *vt* : finish — *vi* **1** : finish **2 en ~ avec** : be done with **3 ~ par faire** : end up doing — **fini, -nie** [fini] *adj* **1** : finished **2** : finite — **finition** [finisjɔ̃] *nf* : finish

fiole [fjɔl] *nf* : vial

firme [firm] *nf* : firm

fisc [fisk] *nm* : tax collection agency — **fiscal, -cale** [fiskal] *adj, mpl* **-caux** [fisko] : fiscal — **fiscalité** [fiskalite] *nf* : tax system

fissure [fisyr] *nf* : crack

fiston [fistɔ̃] *nm fam* : son, youngster

fixe [fiks] *adj* **1** IMMOBILE : fixed **2** INVARIABLE : invariable, set — **fixer** [fikse] *vt* **1** ATTACHER : fix, fasten **2** DÉCIDER : determine **3** ÉTABLIR : establish **4 ~ son regard sur** : stare at — **se fixer** *vr* **1** : settle down **2** SE DÉCIDER : decide

flacon [flakɔ̃] *nm* : small bottle

flageller [flaʒele] *vt* : flog, whip

flagrant [flagrã] *adj* **1** : flagrant **2 en ~ délit** : red-handed

flairer [flɛre] *vt* **1** : sniff, smell **2** DISCERNER : detect, sense — **flair** [flɛr] *nm* **1** : sense of smell **2** INTUITION : intuition

flamand, -mande [flamã, -mãd] *adj* : Flemish

flamant [flamã] *nm* : flamingo

flambant, -bante [flãbã, -bãt] *adj* **flambant neuf** : brand-new

flambeau [flãbo] *nm, pl* **-beaux** : torch

flamber [flãbe] *vi* : burn, blaze — **flambée** [flãbe] *nf* **1** : blaze, fire **2** : outburst (of anger, etc.)

flamboyer [flãbwaje] {58} *vi* : blaze, flame — **flamboyant, -boyante** [flãbwajã, -bwajãt] *adj* : blazing

flamme [flam] *nf* **1** : flame **2** FERVEUR : passion, fervor **3 en ~s** : on fire

flan [flã] *nm* : baked custard

flanc [flã] *nm* : side, flank

flancher [flãʃe] *vi fam* **1** : give in **2** : give out, fail

flanelle [flanɛl] *nf* : flannel

flâner [flane] *vi* **1** SE BALADER : stroll **2** PARESSER : loaf around

flanquer [flãke] *vt* **1** : flank **2 ~ par terre** : fling to the ground **3 ~ un coup à** *fam* : punch

flaque [flak] *nf* : puddle, pool

flash [flaʃ] *nm, pl* **flashs** *or* **flashes** [flaʃ] **1** : flash (in photography) **2** : news flash

flasque [flask] *adj* : flabby, limp

flatter [flate] *vt* **1** : flatter **2** CARESSER : stroke — **se flatter** *vr* : pride oneself — **flatterie** [flatri] *nf* : flattery — **flatteur, -teuse** [flatœr, -tøz] *adj* : flattering — **~** *n* : flatterer

fléau [fleo] *nm, pl* **fléaux** : calamity, scourge

flèche [flɛʃ] *nf* **1** : arrow **2** : spire (of a church) — **fléchette** [fleʃɛt] *nf* : dart

fléchir [fleʃir] *vt* PLIER : bend, flex — *vi* **1** : bend, give way **2** FAIBLIR : weaken

flegme [flɛgm] *nm* : composure — **flegmatique** [flɛgmatik] *adj* : phlegmatic

flemme [flɛm] *nf France fam* : laziness

flétan [fletã] *nm* : halibut

flétrir [fletrir] *v* **se flétrir** *vr* : wither, fade

fleur [flœr] *nf* **1** : flower **2 en ~** : in blossom — **fleuri, -rie** [flœri] *adj* **1** : flowered **2** : flowery — **fleurir** [flœrir] *vi* **1** : flower, blossom **2** PROSPÉRER : flourish — **fleuriste** [flœrist] *nmf* : florist

fleuve [flœv] *nm* : river

flexible [flɛksibl] *adj* : flexible — **flexibilité** [flɛksibilite] *nf* : flexibility — **flexion** [flɛksjɔ̃] *nf* : bending, flexing

flic [flik] *nm fam* : cop

flirter [flœrte] *vi* : flirt

flocon [flɔkɔ̃] *nm* **1** : flake **2 ~ de neige** : snowflake **3 ~s de maïs** : cornflakes

floraison [flɔrɛzɔ̃] *nf* : flowering, blossoming — **floral, -rale** [flɔral] *adj, mpl* **-raux** [flɔro] : floral — **flore** [flɔr] *nf* : flora — **florissant, -sante** [flɔrisã, -sãt] *adj* : flourishing

flot [flo] *nm* **1** : flood, stream **2 à ~** : afloat

flotter [flɔte] *vi* **1** : float **2** : flutter (of a flag) — **flotte** [flɔt] *nf* : fleet — **flotteur** [flɔtœr] *nm* : float

flou, floue [flu] *adj* **1** : blurred **2** : vague, hazy (of ideas, etc.)

fluctuer [flyktɥe] *vi* : fluctuate — **fluctuation** [flyktɥasjɔ̃] *nf* : fluctuation

fluide [flɥid] *adj* **1** : fluid **2** : flowing freely — **~** *nm* : fluid — **fluidité** [flɥidite] *nf* : fluidity

fluor [flyɔr] *nm* : fluorine

fluorescent, -cente [flyɔresã, -sãt] *adj* : fluorescent — **fluorescence** [-sãs] *nf* : fluorescence

flûte [flyt] *nf* **1** : flute **2** : baguette — **~** *interj* **~ alors!** : nonsense!

fluvial, -viale [flyvjal] *adj, mpl* **-viaux** [-vjo]
: river

flux [fly] *nm* **1** : flow **2** MARÉE : flood tide **3**
le ~ et le reflux : the ebb and flow

fœtus [fetys] *nms & pl* : fetus

foi [fwa] *nf* **1** : faith **2 bonne ~** : honesty,
sincerity **3 digne de ~** : reliable **4 ma**
~ ! : well!

foie [fwa] *nm* : liver

foin [fwɛ̃] *nm* : hay

foire [fwar] *nf* : fair, market

fois [fwa] *nf* **1** : time, occasion **2 à la ~** : at
the same time, together **3 des ~** : some-
times **4 il était une ~** : once upon a time

foison [fwazɔ̃] **à ~** *adv phr* : in abundance
— **foisonner** [fwazɔne] *vi* : abound

fol → **fou**

folâtrer [fɔlatre] *vi* : frolic — **folâtre** [fɔlatr]
adj : playful, frisky

folie [fɔli] *nf* **1** : craziness, madness **2 à la**
~ : madly

folklore [fɔlklɔr] *nm* : folklore — **folk-**
lorique [fɔlklɔrik] *adj* : folk (of music,
dance, etc.)

folle → **fou** — **follement** [fɔlmɑ̃] *adv*
: madly, wildly

foncer [fɔ̃se] {6} *vt* : darken — *vi* **~ sur**
: rush at — **foncé, -cée** [fɔ̃se] *adj* : dark (of
colors)

foncier, -cière [fɔ̃sje, -sjɛr] *adj* **1** : land,
property **2** FONDAMENTAL : fundamental —
foncièrement [fɔ̃sjɛrmɑ̃] *adv* : fundamen-
tally

fonction [fɔ̃ksjɔ̃] *nf* **1** : function **2** EMPLOI
: job, post **3 faire ~ de** : serve as **4 en ~**
de : according to **5 ~ publique** : civil
service — **fonctionnaire** [fɔ̃ksjɔnɛr] *nmf*
: official, civil servant — **fonctionnel,**
-nelle [fɔ̃ksjɔnɛl] *adj* : functional — **fonc-**
tionnement [fɔ̃ksjɔnmɑ̃] *nm* : functioning,
working — **fonctionner** [fɔ̃ksjɔne] *vi*
: function, work

fond [fɔ̃] *nm* **1** : bottom, back **2** CŒUR
: heart, root **3** ARRIÈRE-PLAN : background
4 à ~ : thoroughly **5 au ~** : in fact **6 au**
~ de : at the bottom of, in the depths of

fondamental, -tale [fɔ̃damɑ̃tal] *adj, mpl*
-taux [-to] : fundamental — **fondamentale-**
ment [-talmɑ̃] *adv* : basically

fonder [fɔ̃de] *vt* **1** : found **2** BASER : base —
se fonder *vr* **~ sur** : be based on — **fon-**
dateur, -trice [fɔ̃datœr, -tris] *n* : founder
— **fondation** [fɔ̃dasjɔ̃] *nf* : foundation —
fondé, -dée [fɔ̃de] *adj* : well-founded —
fondement [fɔ̃dmɑ̃] *nm* **1** : foundation **2**
sans ~ : groundless

fondre [fɔ̃dr] {63} *vt* **1** : melt, smelt **2** : cast
(a statue, etc.) — *vi* **1** : melt **2 ~ en**
larmes : dissolve into tears

fonds [fɔ̃] *nms & pl* **1** : fund **2 ~** *nmpl*

: funds, capital **3** *or* **~ de commerce**
: business

fontaine [fɔ̃tɛn] *nf* **1** : fountain **2** SOURCE
: spring

fonte [fɔ̃t] *nf* **1** : melting, smelting **2** : thaw-
ing (of snow) **3** : cast iron

football [futbol] *nm* **1** : soccer **2** *Can* : football **3 ~ américain** *France* : football —
footballeur, -leuse [futbolœr, -løz] *n* : soccer player, football player

footing [futiŋ] *nm France* : jogging

forage [fɔraʒ] *nm* : drilling

forçat [fɔrsa] *nm* : convict

force [fɔrs] *nf* **1** : force **2** PUISSANCE
: strength **3 à ~ de** : as a result of **4 les**
~s armées : the armed forces — **forcé,**
-cée [fɔrse] *adj* **1** : forced **2** INÉVITABLE
: inevitable — **forcément** [fɔrsemɑ̃] *adv*
: inevitably — **forcer** [fɔrse] {6} *vt* **1**
: force, compel **2** : force open **3** : strain,
overtax (one's voice, etc.) — *vi* : overdo it
— **se forcer** *vr* : force oneself

forer [fɔre] *vt* : drill, bore

forêt [fɔrɛ] *nf* : forest — **foresterie**
[fɔrɛstəri] *nf* : forestry — **forestier, -tière**
[fɔrɛstje, -tjɛr] *adj* : forest

forfaire [fɔrfɛr] {44} *vi* **~ à** : fail in

forfait [fɔrfɛ] *nm* **1** : fixed price **2 déclarer**
~ : withdraw — **forfaitaire** [fɔrfɛtɛr] *adj*
: inclusive

forge [fɔrʒ] *nf* : forge — **forger** [fɔrʒe] {16}
vt : forge — **forgeron** [fɔrʒərɔ̃] *nm* : blacksmith

formaliser [fɔrmalize] *v* **se formaliser** *vr*
: take offense

formalité [fɔrmalite] *nf* : formality

format [fɔrma] *nm* : format — **formater**
[fɔrmate] *vt* : format (a computer disk)

formation [fɔrmasjɔ̃] *nf* **1** : formation **2** AP-
PRENTISSAGE : education, training — **forme**
[fɔrm] *nf* **1** : form, shape **2 ~s** *nfpl*
: (human) figure **3 ~s** *nfpl* : proprieties **4**
en ~ : fit, in shape — **formel, -melle**
[fɔrmɛl] *adj* **1** : formal **2** CATÉGORIQUE
: definitive — **formellement** [-mɛlmɑ̃] *adv*
: strictly, absolutely — **former** [fɔrme] *vt* **1**
: form **2** : train, educate, develop

formidable [fɔrmidabl] *adj* **1** : tremendous **2**
fam : great, terrific

formulaire [fɔrmylɛr] *nm* : form, questionnaire

formule [fɔrmyl] *nf* **1** : formula **2** MÉTHODE
: way, method **3** FORMULAIRE : form **4 ~**
de politesse : polite phrase, closing (of a
letter) — **formuler** [fɔrmyle] *vt* : formulate,
express

fort, forte [fɔr, fɔrt] *adj* **1** PUISSANT : strong
2 : loud **3** CONSIDÉRABLE : large **4** DOUÉ
: gifted — **fort** [fɔr] *adv* **1** : strongly, loudly,
hard **2** TRÈS : very — **fort** *nm* **1** : fort,

fortress **2** : strong point — **forteresse** [fɔrtərɛs] *nf* : fortress — **fortifier** [fɔrtifje] {96} *vt* : fortify, strengthen — **fortification** [fɔrtifikasjɔ̃] *nf* : fortification

fortuit, -tuite [fɔrtɥi, -tɥit] *adj* : fortuitous, chance

fortune [fɔrtyn] *nf* : fortune — **fortuné, -née** [fɔrtyne] *adj* : wealthy

forum [fɔrɔm] *nm* : forum

fosse [fos] *nf* **1** : pit **2** TOMBE : grave **3** ~ **septique** : septic tank — **fossé** [fose] *nm* **1** : ditch, trench **2** ~ **de générations** : generation gap — **fossette** [fosɛt] *nf* : dimple

fossile [fosil] *nm* : fossil

fou [fu] (**fol** [fɔl] *before a vowel or mute h*), **folle** [fɔl] *adj* **1** : mad, crazy **2** *fam* : tremendous — ~ *n* : crazy person, lunatic — **fou** *nm* **1** : fool, jester **2** : bishop (in chess)

foudre [fudr] *nf* : lightning — **foudroyant, -droyante** [fudrwajɑ̃, fudrwajɑ̃t] *adj* **1** : overwhelming **2** SOUDAIN : sudden — **foudroyer** [fudrwaje] {58} *vt* : strike down

fouet [fwɛ] *nm* **1** : whip **2** : whisk **3 de plein** ~ : head-on — **fouetter** [fwete] *vt* : whip

fougère [fuʒɛr] *nf* : fern

fougue [fug] *nf* : ardor, spirit — **fougueux, -geuse** [fugø, -gøz] *adj* : fiery

fouiller [fuje] *vt* **1** : search **2** CREUSER : excavate, dig — *vi* ~ **dans** : rummage through — **fouille** [fuj] *nf* **1** : search **2** ~**s** *nfpl* : excavations — **fouillis** [fuji] *nm* : jumble

fouiner [fwine] *vi fam* : snoop around

foulard [fular] *nm* : scarf

foule [ful] *nf* **1** : crowd **2 une** ~ **de** : masses of, lots of

fouler [fule] *vt* : press, tread on — **se fouler** *vr* : sprain (one's ankle, etc.) — **foulée** [fule] *nf* **dans la** ~ **de** : in the aftermath of — **foulure** [fulyr] *nf* : sprain

four [fur] *nm* **1** : oven **2** *fam* : flop (in theater, etc.)

fourbu, -bue [furby] *adj* : exhausted

fourche [furʃ] *nf* **1** : pitchfork **2** : fork (of a road) — **fourchette** [furʃet] *nf* : fork

fourgon [furgɔ̃] *nm* : van, truck — **fourgonnette** [furgɔnɛt] *nf* : minivan

fourmi [furmi] *nf* : ant — **fourmilière** [furmiljɛr] *nf* : anthill — **fourmiller** [furmije] *vi* **1** : swarm **2** ~ **de** : be teeming with

fourneau [furno] *nm, pl* **-neaux** [furno] **1** : stove **2** CUISINIÈRE : furnace

fournée [furne] *nf* : batch

fournir [furnir] *vt* **1** : supply, provide (with) **2** ~ **un effort** : make an effort — **fourni, -nie** [furni] *adj* : thick, bushy — **fournisseur, -seuse** [furnisœr, -søz] *n* : supplier — **fournitures** [furnityr] *nfpl* : equipment, supplies

fourrage [furaʒ] *nm* : fodder — **fourrager** [furaʒe] {17} *vi* : forage

fourré [fure] *nm* : thicket

fourreau [furo] *nm, pl* **-reaux** : sheath

fourrer [fure] *vt* **1** : stuff, fill **2** *fam* : thrust, stick — **fourre-tout** [furtu] *nms & pl* : tote bag, carryall

fourrière [furjɛr] *nf* : pound (for animals or vehicles)

fourrure [furyr] *nf* : fur

fourvoyer [furvwaje] {58} *v* **se fourvoyer** *vr* **1** : lead astray **2** ~ **dans** : get involved in

foyer [fwaje] *nm* **1** : hearth **2** DOMICILE : home **3** RÉSIDENCE : residence, hall **4** : foyer (of a theater) **5 lunettes à double** ~ : bifocals

fracas [fraka] *nms & pl* : crash, din — **fracasser** [frakase] *vt* : shatter, smash

fraction [fraksjɔ̃] *nf* : fraction

fracture [fraktyr] *nf* : fracture — **fracturer** [fraktyre] *vt* : fracture

fragile [fraʒil] *adj* **1** : fragile **2** FAIBLE : frail — **fragilité** [fraʒilite] *nf* **1** : fragility **2** FAIBLESSE : frailty

fragment [fragmɑ̃] *nm* : fragment

frais, fraîche [frɛ, frɛʃ] *adj* **1** : fresh **2** : cool (of weather) **3 peinture fraîche** : wet paint — **frais** *nm* **1 mettre au** ~ : put in a cool place **2 prendre le** ~ : take a breath of fresh air **3 frais** *nmpl* : expenses, fees — ~ [frɛ] *adv* **1** : freshly **2 il fait** ~ : it's cool outside — **fraîcheur** [frɛʃœr] *nf* **1** : freshness **2** : coolness — **fraîchir** [frɛʃir] *vi* : cool off (of weather)

fraise [frɛz] *nf* : strawberry

framboise [frɑ̃bwaz] *nf* : raspberry

franc, franche [frɑ̃, frɑ̃ʃ] *adj* **1** HONNÊTE : frank **2** VÉRITABLE : utter, downright — **franc** [frɑ̃] *nm* : franc

français, -çaise [frɑ̃sɛ, -sɛz] *adj* : French — **français** *nm* : French (language)

franchement [frɑ̃ʃmɑ̃] *adv* **1** SINCÈREMENT : frankly **2** NETTEMENT : clearly **3** VRAIMENT : downright, really

franchir [frɑ̃ʃir] *vt* **1** : cross (over) **2** : cover (a distance)

franchise [frɑ̃ʃiz] *nf* **1** SINCÉRITÉ : frankness **2** EXONÉRATION : exemption, allowance **3** : franchise

franco-canadien, -dienne [frɑ̃kokanadjɛ̃, -djɛn] *adj* : French-Canadian

francophone [frɑ̃kɔfɔn] *adj* : French-speaking

frange [frɑ̃ʒ] *nf* **1** : fringe **2** : bangs (of hair)

frapper [frape] *vt* **1** : strike, hit **2** IMPRESSIONNER : impress — *vi* : bang, knock — **frappant, -pante** [frapɑ̃, -pɑ̃t] *adj* : striking

fraternel, -nelle [fratɛrnɛl] *adj* : fraternal, brotherly — **fraterniser** [fratɛrnize] *vi*

: fraternize — **fraternité** [fratɛrnite] *nf* : fraternity, brother-hood
fraude [frod] *nf* : fraud — **frauder** [frode] *v* : cheat — **fraudeur, -deuse** [frodœr, -døz] *n* : cheat, swindler — **frauduleux, -leuse** [frodylø, -løz] *adj* : fraudulent
frayer [frɛje] {11} *v* **se frayer** *vr* ～ **un chemin** : make one's way
frayeur [frɛjœr] *nf* : fright
fredonner [frədɔne] *vt* : hum
frégate [fregat] *nf* : frigate
frein [frɛ̃] *nm* **1** : brake **2 mettre un ～ à** : curb, block — **freiner** [frene] *vt* : slow down, check — *vi* : brake
frêle [frɛl] *adj* : frail
frelon [frəlɔ̃] *nm* : hornet
frémir [fremir] *vi* **1** FRISSONNER : shiver **2** TREMBLER : quiver, flutter **3** : simmer (in cooking)
frêne [frɛn] *nm* : ash (tree or wood)
frénésie [frenezi] *nf* : frenzy — **frénétique** [frenetik] *adj* : frantic, frenzied
fréquenter [frekɑ̃te] *vt* **1** : frequent **2** : attend (school, etc.) **3** COTOYER : associate with, see — **fréquemment** [frekamɑ̃] *adv* : frequently — **fréquence** [frekɑ̃s] *nf* : frequency — **fréquent, -quente** [frekɑ̃, -kɑ̃t] *adj* : frequent — **fréquentation** [frekɑ̃tasjɔ̃] *nf* **1** : frequenting **2** PRÉSENCE : attendance **3** RELATION : acquaintance
frère [frɛr] *nm* **1** : brother **2** : friar
fresque [frɛsk] *nf* : fresco
fret [frɛ] *nm* : freight
fretin [frətɛ̃] *nm* **menu ～** : small fry
friable [frijabl] *adj* : crumbly
friand, friande [frijɑ̃, -jɑ̃d] *adj* ～ **de** : fond of
friandise [frijɑ̃diz] *nf* **1** : delicacy **2** ～**s** *nfpl* : sweets
fric [frik] *nm fam* : dough, cash
friction [friksjɔ̃] *nf* **1** : friction **2** MASSAGE : massage — **frictionner** [friksjɔne] *vt* : rub, massage
frigide [friʒid] *adj* : frigid
frigo [frigo] *nm fam* : fridge
frileux, -leuse [frilø, -løz] *adj* **1** : sensitive to cold **2** PRUDENT : cautious
frimer [frime] *vi fam* : show off
fringale [frɛ̃gal] *nf* **avoir la ～** *fam* : be ravenous
fringant, -gante [frɛ̃gɑ̃, -gɑ̃t] *adj* : dashing
fripon, -ponne [fripɔ̃, -pɔn] *adj* : mischievous — ～ *n* : rascal
fripouille [fripuj] *nf fam* : scoundrel
frire [frir] {45} *v* : fry
friser [frize] *vt* **1** BOUCLER : curl **2** : border on, be close to — *vi* : curl — **frisé, -sée** [frize] *adj* : curly, curly-haired
frisquet, -quette [friskɛ, -kɛt] *adj* : chilly, nippy

frisson [frisɔ̃] *nm* : shiver, shudder — **frissonner** [frisɔne] *vi* : shiver, shudder
friture [frityr] *nf* **1** : frying **2** : deep fat, oil **3** : fried food — **frites** [frit] *nfpl* : french fries
frivole [frivɔl] *adj* : frivolous — **frivolité** [frivɔlite] *nf* : frivolity
froid, froide [frwa, frwad] *adj* : cold — **froid** [frwa] *adv* **il fait ～** : it's cold (outside) — ～ *nm* **1** : cold **2 être en ～ avec** : be on bad terms with **3 prendre ～** : catch cold — **froidement** [frwadmɑ̃] *adv* : coldly, coolly — **froideur** [frwadœr] *nf* : coldness, coolness
froisser [frwase] *vt* **1** : crumple, crease **2** BLESSER : offend — **se froisser** *vr* **1** : crease, crumple (up) **2** ～ **un muscle** : strain a muscle
frôler [frole] *vt* : brush against, touch lightly
fromage [frɔmaʒ] *nm* **1** : cheese **2** ～ **blanc** : cottage cheese — **fromagerie** [frɔmaʒri] *nf* : cheese shop
fronce [frɔ̃s] *nf* : gather, crease — **froncement** [frɔ̃smɑ̃] *nm* ～ **de sourcils** : frown
froncer [frɔ̃se] {6} *vt* **1** : gather (fabric) **2** ～ **les sourcils** : frown
fronde [frɔ̃d] *nf* **1** : rebellion, revolt **2** LANCE-PIERRES : slingshot
front [frɔ̃] *nm* **1** : forehead **2** : front (in politics, war, etc.) **3** AUDACE : audacity, cheek **4 de ～** : head-on **5 faire ～ à** : confront — **frontal, -tale** [frɔ̃tal] *adj, mpl* **-taux** [frɔ̃to] : frontal — **frontalier, -lière** [frɔ̃talje, -ljɛr] *adj* : frontier — **frontière** [frɔ̃tjɛr] *nf* : frontier, border
frotter [frɔte] *vt* **1** : rub **2** NETTOYER : polish, scrub — *vi* : rub — **frottement** [frɔtmɑ̃] *nm* **1** : rubbing **2** ～**s** *nmpl* : friction, disagreement
frousse [frus] *nf fam* : scare, fright
fructueux, -tueuse [fryktɥø, -tɥøz] *adj* : fruitful
frugal, -gale [frygal] *adj, mpl* **-gaux** [frygo] : frugal — **frugalité** [frygalite] *nf* : frugality
fruit [frɥi] *nm* **1** : fruit **2** ～**s de mer** : seafood — **fruité, -tée** [frɥite] *adj* : fruity — **fruitier, -tière** [frɥitje, -tjɛr] *adj* : fruit
frustrer [frystre] *vt* **1** : frustrate **2** ～ **de** : deprive of — **frustrant, -trante** [frystrɑ̃, -trɑ̃t] *adj* : frustrating — **frustration** [frystrasjɔ̃] *nf* : frustration
fugace [fygas] *adj* : fleeting
fugitif, -tive [fyʒitif, -tiv] *n* : fugitive, runaway
fugue [fyg] *nf* **1 faire une ～** : run away **2** ～ **amoureuse** : elopement
fuir [fɥir] {46} *vi* **1** : flee **2** SUINTER : leak — *vt* : avoid, shun — **fuite** [fɥit] *nf* **1** : flight, escape **2** : leak (of water, information, etc.)

fulgurant, -rante [fylgyrᾰ, -rᾰt] *adj* : dazzling, vivid
fulminer [fylmine] *vi* : be enraged
fumer [fyme] *vt* : smoke — *vi* **1** : smoke **2** : give off steam — **fumé, -mée** [fyme] *adj* **1** : smoked **2** : tinted (of glass, etc.) — **fumée** *nf* **1** : smoke **2** VAPEUR : steam — **fumeur, -meuse** [fymœr, -møz] *n* : smoker
fumier [fymje] *nm* : dung, manure
fumigation [fymigasjɔ̃] *nf* : fumigation
funambule [fynᾰbyl] *nmf* : tightrope walker
funèbre [fynɛbr] *adj* **1** : funeral **2** LUGUBRE : gloomy — **funérailles** [fy-neraj] *nfpl* : funeral — **funéraire** [fynerɛr] *adj* : funeral
funeste [fynɛst] *adj* DÉSASTREUX : disastrous
fur [fyr] **au ~ et à mesure** *adv phr* : little by little
furet [fyrɛ] *nm* : ferret
fureter [fyrte] {20} *vi* : pry
fureur [fyrœr] *nf* **1** : rage, fury **2 faire ~** : be all the rage
furibond, -bonde [fyribɔ̃, -bɔ̃d] *adj* : furious

— **furie** [fyri] *nf* : fury, rage — **furieux, -rieuse** [fyrjø, -jøz] *adj* : furious
furoncle [fyrɔ̃kl] *nm* : boil
furtif, -tive [fyrtif, -tiv] *adj* : furtive, sly — **furtivement** *adv* : stealthily
fuseau [fyzo] *nm, pl* **-seaux 1** : spindle **2 ~ horaire** : time zone
fusée [fyze] *nf* **1** : rocket **2 ~ éclairante** : flare
fuselé, -lée [fyzle] *adj* : slender, tapering
fusible [fyzibl] *nm* : fuse
fusil [fyzi] *nm* : gun, rifle — **fusillade** [fyzijad] *nf* : gunfire — **fusiller** [fyzije] *vt* : shoot
fusion [fyzjɔ̃] *nf* : fusion — **fusionner** [fyzɔnje] *v* : merge
fût [fy] *nm* : barrel, cask
futé, -tée [fyte] *adj* : cunning, crafty
futile [fytil] *adj* : futile — **futilité** [fytilite] *nf* : futility
futur, -ture [fytyr] *adj & nm* : future
fuyant, fuyante [fɥijᾰ, fɥijᾰt] *adj* : elusive, shifty

G

g [ʒe] *nm* : g, seventh letter of the alphabet
gabarit [gabari] *nm* **1** : size, dimensions *pl* **2** *fam* : caliber, type
gâcher [gaʃe] *vt* : spoil, ruin
gâchette [gaʃɛt] *nf* : trigger
gâchis [gaʃi] *nm* **1** DÉSORDRE : mess **2** GASPILLAGE : waste
gadget [gadʒɛt] *nm* : gadget
gadoue [gadu] *nf* : mud, muck
gaffe [gaf] *nf fam* : blunder — **gaffer** [gafe] *vi fam* : blunder, goof (up)
gage [gaʒ] *nm* **1** : security **2** GARANTIE : pledge, guarantee **3 ~s** *nmpl* : wages, pay **4 en ~ de** : as a token of **5 mettre en ~** : pawn — **gager** [gaʒe] {17} *vt* **1** : bet, wager **2** : guarantee (a loan, etc.) — **gageure** [gaʒœr] *nf* **1** : challenge **2** *Can* : bet, wager
gagner [gaɲe] *vt* **1** : win **2** : earn (one's living, etc.) **3** : gain (speed, etc.) **4** : save (time, space, etc.) **5** ATTEINDRE : reach — *vi* **1** : win **2 ~ en** : increase in **3 y ~** : be better off — **gagnant, -gnante** [gaɲᾰ, -ɲᾰt] *adj* : winning — **~** *n* : winner — **gagne–pain** [gaɲpɛ̃] *nms & pl* : job, livelihood
gai, gaie [gɛ] *adj* : cheerful, merry — **gaieté** [gete] *nf* : cheerfulness
gaillard, -larde [gajar, -jard] *adj* **1** : spright-ly **2** GRIVOIS : ribald — **~** *nmf* : vigorous person
gain [gɛ̃] *nm* **1** : earnings *pl* **2** PROFIT : gain **3** ÉCONOMIE : saving
gaine [gɛn] *nf* **1** : girdle **2** : sheath (of a dagger)
gala [gala] *nm* : gala, reception
galant, -lante [galᾰ, -lᾰt] *adj* : courteous, gallant
galaxie [galaksi] *nf* : galaxy
galbe [galb] *nm* : curve, shapeliness
galerie [galri] *nf* **1** : gallery **2** : balcony (in a theater) **3** : roof rack (of an automobile)
galet [galɛ] *nm* : pebble
galette [galɛt] *nf* : flat round cake
gallois, -loise [galwa, -lwaz] *adj* : Welsh — **gallois** *nm* : Welsh (language)
gallon [galɔ̃] *nm* : gallon
galoper [galɔpe] *vi* : gallop — **galop** [galo] *nm* : gallop
galopin [galɔpɛ̃] *nm* : rascal
galvaniser [galvanize] *vt* : galvanize
galvauder [galvode] *vt* : sully, tarnish
gambade [gᾱbad] *nf* : leap, skip — **gambader** [gᾱbade] *vi* : leap about
gamelle [gamɛl] *nf* : mess kit
gamin, -mine [gamɛ̃, -min] *adj* : mischievous — **~** *n* : kid, youngster

gamme [gam] *nf* **1** : scale (in music) **2** SÉRIE : range, gamut

ganglion [gɑ̃glijɔ̃] *nm* **avoir des ~s** : have swollen glands

gangrène [gɑ̃grɛn] *nf* : gangrene

gangster [gɑ̃gstɛr] *nm* : gangster

gant [gɑ̃] *nm* **1** : glove **2 ~ de toilette** : washcloth

garage [garaʒ] *nm* : garage — **garagiste** [garaʒist] *nmf* **1** : garage owner **2** : (garage) mechanic

garant, -rante [garɑ̃, -rɑ̃t] *n* : guarantor — **garant** *nm* : guarantee (in law) — **garantie** [garɑ̃ti] *nf*: guarantee, warranty — **garantir** [garɑ̃tir] *vt* **1** : guarantee **2 ~ de** : protect from

garçon [garsɔ̃] *nm* **1** : boy, young man **2** SERVEUR : waiter **3 ~ manqué** : tomboy

garder [garde] *vt* **1** : keep **2** SURVEILLER : watch over **3 ~ de** : protect from — **se garder** *vr* **1** : keep **2 ~ de** : be careful not to — **garde** [gard] *nm* **1** : guard **2 ~ du corps** : bodyguard — **~** *nf* **1** : nurse **2** : (military) guard **3** : custody, care **4 de ~** : on duty **5 mettre en ~** : warn **6 prendre ~** : be careful — **garde-fou** [gardəfu] *nm, pl* **garde-fous** : railing — **garde-manger** [gardəmɑ̃ʒe] *nms & pl* : pantry — **garderie** [gardəri] *nf* : day-care center — **garde-robe** [gardərɔb] *nf, pl* **garde-robes** : wardrobe, closet — **gardien, -dienne** [gardjɛ̃, -djɛn] *n* **1** : warden, custodian **2** PROTECTEUR : guardian — **gardien** *nm* **1 ~ de but** : goalkeeper **2 ~ de la paix** *France* : police officer — **gardienne** *nf* **~ d'enfants** : day-care worker

gare¹ [gar] *nf* **1** : station **2 ~ routière** *France or* **~ d'autobus** *Can* : bus station

gare² *interj* **1 ~ à toi!** : watch out! **2 sans crier ~** : without warning

garer [gare] *vt* STATIONNER : park — **se garer** *vr* **1** : park **2** S'ÉCARTER : move away

gargariser [gargarize] *v* **se gargariser** *vr* : gargle

gargouiller [garguje] *vi* : gurgle, rumble

garnement [garnəmɑ̃] *nm* : rascal

garnir [garnir] *vt* **1** REMPLIR : fill **2** COUVRIR : cover **3** DÉCORER : decorate, trim — **garni, -nie** [garni] *adj* : served with vegetables

garnison [garnizɔ̃] *nf* : garrison

garniture [garnityr] *nf* **1** : filling (in cooking) **2** DÉCORATION : trimming, garnish

gars [ga] *nm fam* **1** : boy, lad **2** TYPE : guy, fellow

gaspiller [gaspije] *vt* : waste, squander — **gaspillage** [gaspijaʒ] *nm* : waste

gastrique [gastrik] *adj* : gastric

gastronomie [gastrɔnɔmi] *nf* : gastronomy

gâteau [gato] *nm, pl* **-teaux 1** : cake **2 ~ sec** *France* : cookie

gâter [gate] *vt* **1** : pamper **2** ABÎMER : spoil, ruin — **se gâter** *vr* **1** : go bad **2** SE DÉTÉRIORER : deteriorate

gâterie [gatri] *nf* : little treat, delicacy

gâteux, -teuse [gatø, -tøz] *adj* : senile

gauche [goʃ] *adj* **1** : left **2** MALADROIT : clumsy — **~** *nf* **1** : left **2 la ~** : the left (wing) — **gaucher, -chère** [goʃe, -ʃɛr] *adj* : left-handed — **gaucherie** [goʃri] *nf*: awkwardness

gaufre [gofr] *nf* : waffle — **gaufrette** [gofrɛt] *nf*: wafer

gausser [gose] *v* **se gausser** *vr* **~ de** : deride, make fun of

gaver [gave] *v* **se gaver** *vr* : stuff oneself

gay [gɛ] *adj* : gay (homosexual)

gaz [gaz] *nms & pl* : gas

gaze [gaz] *nf* : gauze

gazer [gaze] *vi fam* **ça gaze?** : how are things going?

gazette [gazɛt] *nf* : newspaper

gazeux, -zeuse [gazø, -zøz] *adj* : fizzy, carbonated

gazon [gazɔ̃] *nm* **1** : grass, turf **2** PELOUSE : lawn

gazouiller [gazuje] *vi* **1** : chirp **2** : gurgle, babble (of a baby)

geai [ʒɛ] *nm* : jay

géant, géante [ʒeɑ̃, -ɑ̃t] *adj* : giant, gigantic — **~** *n* : giant

geler [ʒəle] {20} *v* : freeze — *v impers* **on gèle!** : it's freezing! — **gel** [ʒɛl] *nm* **1** : frost **2** : gel **3** : freezing (of prices, etc.) — **gélatine** [ʒelatin] *nf* : gelatin — **gelée** *nf* **1** : (hoar)frost **2** : jelly — **gelure** [ʒəlyr] *nf* : frostbite

gémir [ʒemir] *vi* : groan, moan — **gémissement** [ʒemismɑ̃] *nm* : groan(ing), moan(ing)

gemme [ʒɛm] *nf*: gem

gênant, -nante [ʒenɑ̃, -nɑ̃t] *adj* **1** : embarrassing **2** ENCOMBRANT : cumbersome **3** ENNUYEUX : annoying

gencives [ʒɑ̃siv] *nfpl* : gums

gendarme [ʒɑ̃darm] *nm* : police officer — **gendarmerie** [ʒɑ̃darməri] *nf* **1** *France* : police force **2** *France* : police station **3** *Can* : federal police force

gendre [ʒɑ̃dr] *nm* : son-in-law

gène [ʒɛn] *nm* : gene

généalogie [ʒenealɔʒi] *nf*: genealogy

gêner [ʒene] *vt* **1** : embarrass, make uncomfortable **2** DÉRANGER : bother **3** ENCOMBRER : hamper — **se gêner** *vr* : put oneself out — **gêne** [ʒɛn] *nf* **1** : inconvenience **2** : embarrassment **3** : (physical) discomfort — **gêné, -née** [ʒene] *adj* **1** : embarrassed **2** *Can* : shy

général, -rale [ʒeneral] *adj, mpl* **-raux** [-ro] : general — **général** *nm, pl* **-raux** : general — **généralement** [-ralmã] *adv* : generally, usually — **généraliser** [ʒeneralize] *v* : generalize — **se généraliser** *vr* : become widespread — **généraliste** [ʒeneralist] *nmf* : general practitioner — **généralité** [ʒeneralite] *nf* : majority

générateur [ʒeneratœr] *nm* : generator

génération [ʒenerasjɔ̃] *nf* : generation

génératrice [ʒeneratris] *nf* : (electric) generator

générer [ʒenere] {87} *vt* : generate

généreux, -reuse [ʒenerø, -røz] *adj* : generous — **généreusement** [-røzmã] *adv* : generously

générique [ʒenerik] *adj* : generic — ~ *nm* : credits *pl* (in movies)

générosité [ʒenerozite] *nf* : generosity

génétique [ʒenetik] *adj* : genetic — ~ *nf* : genetics

génie [ʒeni] *nm* **1** : genius **2** INGÉNIERIE : engineering — **génial, -niale** [ʒenjal] *adj, mpl* **-niaux** [-njo] **1** : brilliant **2** *fam* : fantastic, great

génisse [ʒenis] *nf* : heifer

génital, -tale [ʒenital] *adj, mpl* **-taux** [-to] : genital

genou [ʒənu] *nm, pl* **-noux 1** : knee **2 se mettre à ~x** : kneel down

genre [ʒãr] *nm* **1** SORTE : kind, type **2** ATTITUDE : style, manner **3** : gender (in grammar)

gens [ʒã] *nmfpl* **1** : people **2 ~ d'affaires** : businesspeople **3 jeunes ~** : teenagers

gentil, -tille [ʒãti, -tij] *adj* **1** : kind, nice **2** SAGE : well-behaved — **gentillesse** [ʒãtijɛs] *nf* : kindness, niceness — **gentiment** [ʒãtimã] *adv* : nicely, kindly

géographie [ʒeɔgrafi] *nf* : geography — **géographique** [ʒeɔgrafik] *adj* : geographic(al)

geôlier, -lière [ʒolje, -ljɛr] *n* : jailer

géologie [ʒeɔlɔʒi] *nf* : geology — **géologique** [ʒeɔlɔʒik] *adj* : geologic(al)

géométrie [ʒeɔmetri] *nf* : geometry — **géométrique** [ʒeɔmetrik] *adj* : geometric(al)

géranium [ʒeranjɔm] *nm* : geranium

gérant, -rante [ʒerã, -rãt] *n* : manager

gerbe [ʒɛrb] *nf* **1** : sheaf (of wheat) **2** : bunch (of flowers, etc.)

gercer [ʒɛrse] {6} *v* **se gercer** *vr* : chap, crack — **gerçure** [ʒɛrsyr] *nf* : crack (in the skin)

gérer [ʒere] {87} *vt* : manage

germain, -maine [ʒɛrmɛ̃, -mɛn] *adj* **cousin germain** : first cousin

germe [ʒɛrm] *nm* **1** : germ **2** POUSSE : sprout

germer [ʒɛrme] *vi* **1** : sprout, germinate **2** : form (of ideas, etc.)

gésier [ʒezje] *nm* : gizzard

gésir [ʒezir] {47} *vi* : lie, be lying

gestation [ʒɛstasjɔ̃] *nf* : gestation

geste [ʒɛst] *nm* : gesture, movement

gestion [ʒɛstjɔ̃] *nf* : management — **gestionnaire** [ʒɛstjɔner] *nmf* : administrator

geyser [ʒezɛr] *nm* : geyser

gibet [ʒibɛ] *nm* : gallows

gibier [ʒibje] *nm* **1** : game (animals) **2** *fam* : prey

giboulée [ʒibule] *nf* : sudden shower

gicler [ʒikle] *vi* : spurt, squirt, spatter — **giclée** [ʒikle] *nf* : spurt, squirt

gifle [ʒifl] *nf* : slap (in the face) — **gifler** [ʒifle] *vt* : slap

gigantesque [ʒigãtɛsk] *adj* : gigantic, huge

gigot [ʒigo] *nm* : leg (of lamb) — **gigoter** [ʒigɔte] *vi fam* : wriggle, fidget

gilet [ʒile] *nm* **1** : vest **2** : cardigan (sweater) **3 ~ de sauvetage** : life jacket

gin [dʒin] *nm* : gin

gingembre [ʒɛ̃ʒãbr] *nm* : ginger

girafe [ʒiraf] *nf* : giraffe

giratoire [ʒiratwar] *adj* **sens ~** : rotary, traffic circle

girofle [ʒirɔfl] *nm* **clou de ~** : clove

girouette [ʒirwɛt] *nf* : weather vane

gisement [ʒizmã] *nm* : deposit (in geology)

gitan, -tane [ʒitã, -tan] *n* : Gypsy

gîte [ʒit] *nm* **1** : shelter, lodging **2 le ~ et le couvert** : room and board

givre [ʒivr] *nm* : frost — **givrer** [ʒivre] *v* **se givrer** *vr* : frost (up)

glabre [glabr] *adj* : hairless

glacer [glase] {6} *vt* **1** : freeze, chill **2** : frost (a cake) — **glaçage** [glasaʒ] *nm* : frosting — **glace** [glas] *nf* **1** : ice **2** *France* : ice cream **3** MIROIR : mirror **4** VITRE : glass — **glacé, -cée** [glase] *adj* **1** : icy, chilly **2** : iced — **glacial, -ciale** [glasjal] *adj, mpl* **-cials** *or* **-ciaux** [-sjo] : icy, frigid — **glacier** [glasje] *nm* : glacier — **glacière** [glasjɛr] *nf* : cooler, icebox — **glaçon** [glasɔ̃] *nm* **1** : block of ice **2** : icicle **3** : ice cube

glaise [glɛz] *nf* : clay

gland [glã] *nm* **1** : acorn **2** : tassel (ornament)

glande [glãd] *nf* : gland

glapir [glapir] *vi* : yelp

glas [gla] *nm* **sonner le ~** : toll the bell

glauque [glok] *adj* : gloomy, dreary

glisser [glise] *vi* **1** : slide, slip **2** DÉRAPER : skid — *vt* : slip, slide — **se glisser** *vr* **~ dans** : slip into, creep into — **glissant, -sante** [glisã, -sãt] *adj* : slippery — **glissement** [glismã] *nm* **1** : sliding, gliding **2** ÉVOLUTION : shift — **glissière** [glisjɛr] *nf* **1**

: slide, groove, chute **2 à ~** : sliding —
glissoire [gliswar] *nf* : slide
globe [glɔb] *nm* **1** : globe **2 ~ oculaire**
: eyeball **3 le ~ terrestre** : the earth —
global, -bale [glɔbal] *adj, mpl* **-baux**
[glɔbo] : overall, total — **globalement**
[glɔbalmã] *adv* : as a whole
gloire [glwar] *nf* **1** : glory, fame **2** MÉRITE
: credit — **glorieux, -rieuse** [glɔrjø, -rjøz]
adj : glorious — **glorifier** [glɔrifje] {96} *vt*
: glorify
glossaire [glɔsɛr] *nm* : glossary
glousser [gluse] *vi* **1** : cluck **2** : chuckle —
gloussement [glusmã] *nm* **1** : cluck,
clucking **2** : chuckling
glouton, -tonne [glutɔ̃, -tɔn] *adj* : gluttonous, greedy — **~** *n* : glutton — **gloutonnerie** [glutɔnri] *nf* : gluttony
gluant, gluante [glɥã, glɥãt] *adj* : sticky
glucose [glykoz] *nm* : glucose
gobelet [gɔblɛ] *nm* : tumbler, beaker
gober [gɔbe] *vt* **1** : swallow whole **2** *fam*
: swallow, fall for
godasse [gɔdas] *nf fam* : shoe
goéland [gɔelã] *nm* : gull
goguenard, -narde [gognar, -nard] *adj*
: mocking
goinfre [gwɛ̃fr] *nm fam* : pig, glutton
golf [gɔlf] *nm* : golf
golfe [gɔlf] *nm* : gulf, bay
gomme [gɔm] *nf* **1** : gum, resin **2** : eraser **3**
~ à mâcher : chewing gum — **gommer**
[gɔme] *vt* : erase
gond [gɔ̃] *nm* : hinge
gondole [gɔ̃dɔl] *nf* : gondola
gondoler [gɔ̃dɔle] *v* **se gondoler** *vr* : warp,
buckle
gonfler [gɔ̃fle] *vt* **1** : swell **2** : blow up, inflate (a balloon, etc.) **3** GROSSIR : exaggerate — *vi* : swell — **se gonfler** *vr* **1** : swell
up **2 ~ de** : swell up with, be filled with —
gonflé, -flée [gɔ̃fle] *adj* : swollen, bloated
— **gonflement** [gɔ̃fləmã] *nm* : swelling
gorge [gɔrʒ] *nf* **1** : throat **2** POITRINE
: bosom, chest **3** : gorge (in geography) —
gorgée [gɔrʒe] *nf* : mouthful, sip — **gorger**
[gɔrʒe] {17} *v* **se gorger** *vr* : gorge oneself
gorille [gɔrij] *nm* : gorilla
gosier [gozje] *nm* : throat
gosse [gɔs] *nmf France fam* : kid, youngster
gothique [gɔtik] *adj* : Gothic
goudron [gudrɔ̃] *nm* : tar — **goudronner**
[gudrɔne] *vt* : tar (a road)
gouffre [gufr] *nm* : gulf, abyss
goujat [guʒa] *nm* : boor
goulot [gulo] *nm* **1** : neck (of a bottle) **2 ~
d'étranglement** : bottleneck
goulu, -lue [guly] *adj* : greedy
gourde [gurd] *nf* **1** : flask **2** : gourd **3** *fam*
: dope, dumbbell

gourdin [gurdɛ̃] *nm* : cudgel, club
gourmand, -mande [gurmã, -mãd] *adj*
GLOUTON : greedy — **~** *n* : glutton —
gourmandise [gurmãdiz] *nf* **1** : greed **2**
~s *nfpl* : sweets, delicacies
gousse [gus] *nf* **~ d'ail** : clove of garlic
goût [gu] *nm* **1** : taste **2** SAVEUR : flavor **3**
GRÉ : fondness, liking **4 de bon ~** : tasteful — **goûter** [gute] *vt* : taste — *vi* **1** : have
an afternoon snack **2 ~ à** *or* **~ de** : try
out, sample — **~** *nm* : afternoon snack
goutte [gut] *nf* : drop (of water, etc.) —
gouttelette [gutlɛt] *nf* : droplet — **goutter**
[gute] *vi* : drip — **gouttière** [gutjɛr] *nf*
: gutter (on a roof)
gouvernail [guvɛrnaj] *nm* **1** : rudder **2**
BARRE : helm
gouverner [guvɛrne] *vt* : govern, rule —
gouvernante [guvɛrnãt] *nf* **1** : governess
2 : housekeeper — **gouvernement** [gu-
vɛrnəmã] *nm* : government — **gouvernemental, -tale** [-mãtal] *adj* : governmental
— **gouverneur** [guvɛrnœr] *nm* : governor
grâce [gras] *nf* **1** : gracefulness **2** FAVEUR
: favor **3** PARDON : mercy, pardon **4 de
bonne ~** : willingly **5 ~ à** : thanks to
— **gracier** [grasje] {96} *vt* : pardon —
gracieux, -cieuse [grasjø, -sjøz] *adj* **1**
: graceful **2** AIMABLE : gracious **3** GRATUIT
: free
grade [grad] *nm* **1** : rank **2 monter en ~**
: be promoted
gradin [gradɛ̃] *nm* **1** : tier **2 ~s** *nmpl*
: bleachers, stands
graduel, -duelle [gradɥɛl] *adj* : gradual —
graduellement [-dɥɛlmã] *adv* : gradually
graduer [gradɥe] *vt* **1** : graduate (a measur-
ing instrument) **2** : increase gradually
graffiti [grafiti] *nmpl* : graffiti
grain [grɛ̃] *nm* **1** : (cereal) grain **2** : speck,
particle (of sand, salt, dust, etc.) **3 ~ de
café** : coffee bean **4 ~ de poivre** : pep-
percorn **5 ~ de beauté** : mole — **graine**
[grɛn] *nf* : seed
graisse [grɛs] *nf* **1** : fat **2** LUBRIFIANT
: grease — **graisser** [grɛse] *vt* : lubricate,
grease — **graisseux, -seuse** [grɛsø, -søz]
adj : greasy
grammaire [gramɛr] *nf* : grammar — **grammatical, -cale** [gramatikal] *adj, mpl* **-caux**
[-ko] : grammatical
gramme [gram] *nm* : gram
grand, grande [grã, grãd] *adj* **1** : tall **2**
GROS : big, large **3** IMPORTANT : great, important **4** : elder, older, grown-up — **grand**
[grã] *adv* : wide **2 ~ ouvert** : wide-
open — **grand–chose** [grãʃoz] *pron* **pas
~** : not much — **grandeur** [grãdœr] *nf* **1**
DIMENSION : size **2** : greatness —
grandiose [grãdjoz] *adj* : grandiose —

grandir [grᾰdir] *vt* **1** : make (look) taller **2** EXAGÉRER : exaggerate — *vi* **1** : grow **2** AUGMENTER : increase — **grand–mère** [grᾰmɛr] *nf, pl* **grands–mères** : grandmother — **grand père** [grᾰpɛr] *nm, pl* **grands–pères** : grandfather — **grands–parents** [grᾰparᾱ] *nmpl* : grandparents

grange [grᾱʒ] *nf* : barn

granit *or* **granite** [granit] *nm* : granite

granulé [granyle] *nm* : tablet (in medicine) — **granuleux, -leuse** [granylø, -løz] *adj* : granular

graphique [grafik] *adj* : graphic — ∼ *nm* : graph, chart

grappe [grap] *nf* : cluster (of grapes, etc.)

grappin [grapɛ̃] *nm* **1** : grapnel **2 mettre le** ∼ **sur** : get one's hooks into

gras, grasse [gra, gras] *adj* **1** : fatty **2** GROS : fat (of persons) **3** HUILEUX : greasy, oily **4** VULGAIRE : crude, coarse **5** : bold (of type) — **gras** *nm* **1** : (animal) fat **2** : grease — **grassouillet, -lette** [grasuje, -jɛt] *adj* : pudgy, plump

gratifier [gratifje] {96} *vt* ∼ **de** : reward with — **gratification** [gratifikasjɔ̃] *nf* : bonus

gratin [gratɛ̃] *nm* : dish baked with cheese or crumb topping

gratis [gratis] *adv* : free

gratitude [gratityd] *nf* : gratitude

gratte–ciel [gratsjɛl] *nms & pl* : skyscraper

gratter [grate] *vt* : scratch, scrape — **se gratter** *vr* : scratch oneself

gratuit, -tuite [gratɥi, -tɥit] *adj* **1** : free **2** : gratuitous — **gratuitement** [-tɥitmᾱ] *adv* : free (of charge)

gravats [grava] *nmpl* : rubble

grave [grav] *adj* **1** : serious, grave **2** SOLENNEL : solemn **3 voix** ∼ : deep voice — **gravement** [gravmᾱ] *adv* : seriously

graver [grave] *vt* **1** : engrave **2** : carve **3** ENREGISTRER : cut, record

gravier [gravje] *nm* : gravel

gravillon [gravijɔ̃] *nm* : (fine) gravel, grit

gravir [gravir] *vt* : climb (up)

gravité [gravite] *nf* **1** : gravity (in physics) **2** IMPORTANCE : seriousness — **graviter** [gravite] *vi* : gravitate

gravure [gravyr] *nf* **1** : engraving **2** : print (of a picture), plate (in a book)

gré [gre] *nm* **1** VOLONTÉ : will **2** GOÛT : taste, liking **3 à votre** ∼ : as you wish

grec, grecque [grɛk] *adj* : Greek — **grec** *nm* : Greek (language)

greffe [grɛf] *nf* **1** : graft (in botany) **2** : graft, transplant (in medicine) — **greffer** [grɛfe] *vt* **1** : graft **2** : transplant (an organ)

greffier, -fière [grɛfje, -fjɛr] *n* : clerk of court

grêle¹ [grɛl] *adj* **1** : lanky, lean **2** AIGU : shrill

grêle² *nf* : hail — **grêler** [grele] *v impers* **il grêle** : it's hailing — **grêlon** [grɛlɔ̃] *nm* : hailstone

grelot [grəlo] *nm* : small bell — **grelotter** [grələte] *vi* : shiver

grenade [grənad] *nf* **1** : pomegranate **2** : grenade (weapon)

grenier [grənje] *nm* : attic, loft

grenouille [grənuj] *nf* : frog

grès [grɛ] *nm* **1** : sandstone **2** POTERIE : stoneware

grésiller [grezije] *vi* : crackle, sizzle

grève [grɛv] *nf* **1** RIVAGE : shore **2** : strike — **gréviste** [grevist] *nmf* : striker

gribouiller [gribuje] *v* : scribble — **gribouillage** [gribujaʒ] *nm* : scribble, scrawl

grief [grijɛf] *nm* : grievance — **grièvement** [grijɛvmᾱ] *adv* : seriously, severely

griffe [grif] *nf* **1** : claw **2** : signature, label (of a product) — **griffer** [grife] *vt* : scratch — **griffonner** [grifɔne] *vt* : scribble, jot down

grignoter [griɲɔte] *vt* **1** : nibble **2** AMOINDRIR : erode, eat away (at)

gril [gril] *nm* **1** : broiler **2** : grill (for cooking) — **grillade** [grijad] *nf* : grilled meat, grill

grille [grij] *nf* **1** : metal fencing, gate, bars *pl* **2** : grate (of a sewer, etc.) **3** : grid (in games) — **grillage** [grijaʒ] *nm* : wire fencing

griller [grije] *vt* **1** : toast, grill, broil **2** : burn out (a fuse, etc.) — *vi* : broil — **grille–pain** [grijpɛ̃] *nms & pl* : toaster

grillon [grijɔ̃] *nm* : cricket

grimace [grimas] *nf* : grimace — **grimacer** [grimase] {6} *vi* : grimace

grimper [grɛ̃pe] *v* : climb

grincer [grɛ̃se] {6} *vi* **1** : creak, grate **2** ∼ **des dents** : grind one's teeth — **grincement** [grɛ̃smᾱ] *nm* : creak, squeak

grincheux, -cheuse [grɛ̃ʃø, -ʃøz] *adj* : grumpy

grippe [grip] *nf* **1** : flu, influenza **2 prendre qqn en** ∼ : take a sudden dislike to s.o. — **grippé, -pée** [gripe] *adj* **être** ∼ : have the flu

gris, grise [gri, griz] *adj* **1** : gray **2** MORNE : dull, dreary **3** *fam* : tipsy — **gris** *nm* : gray — **grisaille** [grizaj] *nf* **1** : grayness (of weather) **2** MONOTONIE : dullness

griser [grize] *vt* : intoxicate — **grisant, -sante** [grizᾰ, -zᾱt] *adj* : intoxicating, heady

grisonner [grizɔne] *vi* : turn gray, go gray

grive [griv] *nf* : thrush

grivois, -voise [grivwa, -waz] *adj* : bawdy

grogner [grɔɲe] *vi* **1** : growl **2** : grumble — **grognement** [grɔɲmᾱ] *nm* **1** : growling **2** : rumbling, roar — **grognon, -gnonne** [grɔɲɔ̃, -ɲɔn] *adj* : grumpy, grouchy

groin [grwɛ̃] *nm* : snout
grommeler [grɔmle] {8} *v* : mutter
gronder [grɔ̃de] *vt* : scold — *vi* **1** : rumble, roar **2** GROGNER : growl — **grondement** [grɔ̃dəmɑ̃] *nm* **1** : rumble, rumbling **2** GROGNEMENT : growling

gros, grosse [gro, gros] *adj* **1** : big, large **2** ÉPAIS : thick **3** CORPULENT : fat **4** GRAVE : serious **5** LOURD : heavy **6** ~ **lot** : jackpot — **gros** [gro] *adv* BEAUCOUP : a lot — ~ *nm* **1 en** ~ : roughly, in general **2 le** ~ **de** : the bulk of

groseille [grozɛj] *nf* **1** : currant **2** ~ **à maquereau** : gooseberry

grossir [grosir] *vt* **1** AUGMENTER : increase **2** EXAGÉRER : exaggerate **3** AGRANDIR : magnify — *vi* **1** : put on weight **2** : grow larger — **grossesse** [grosɛs] *nf* : pregnancy — **grosseur** [grosœr] *nf* **1** : fatness **2** VOLUME : size **3** : lump (in medicine) — **grossier, -sière** [grosje, -sjɛr] *adj* **1** APPROXIMATIF : coarse, rough **2** VULGAIRE : crude, vulgar **3** FLAGRANT : gross, glaring — **grossièrement** [grosjɛrmɑ̃] *adv* **1** APPROXIMATIVEMENT : roughly **2** VULGAIREMENT : crudely — **grossièreté** [grosjɛrte] *nf* **1** : coarseness **2** : rudeness — **grossiste** [grosist] *nmf* : wholesaler

grosso modo [grosomodo] *adv* : more or less, roughly

grotesque [grɔtɛsk] *adj* **1** : grotesque **2** RIDICULE : absurd, ridiculous

grotte [grɔt] *nf* : cave

grouiller [gruje] *vi* ~ **de** : swarm with — **se grouiller** *vr fam* : hurry, get a move on

groupe [grup] *nm* **1** : group **2** ~ **sanguin** : blood type — **groupement** [grupmɑ̃] *nm* : grouping, group — **grouper** [grupe] *vt* : group — **se grouper** *vr* : gather, get together

gruau [gryo] *nm Can* : oatmeal

grue [gry] *nf* : crane

grumeau [grymo] *nm, pl* **-meaux** : lump (in sauce, etc.)

gruyère [gryjɛr] *nm* : Gruyère (cheese)

gué [ge] *nm* : ford, crossing

guenilles [gənij] *nfpl* : rags and tatters

guenon [gənɔ̃] *nf* : female monkey

guépard [gepar] *nm* : cheetah

guêpe [gɛp] *nf* : wasp — **guêpier** [gepje] *nm* **1** : wasps' nest **2** : tight spot, trap

guère [gɛr] *adv* **ne . . . guère** : hardly, scarcely, rarely

guérilla [gerija] *nf* : guerilla warfare — **guérillero** [gerijero] *nm* : guerilla

guérir [gerir] *vt* : cure, heal — *vi* : get better, heal — **guérison** [gerizɔ̃] *nf* **1** : cure, healing **2** RÉTABLISSEMENT : recovery

guérite [gerit] *nf* : sentry box

guerre [gɛr] *nf* : war — **guerrier, -rière** [gɛrje, -jɛr] *adj* : warlike — ~ *n* : warrior

guetter [gete] *vt* **1** : watch (intently) **2** ATTENDRE : watch out for **3** MENACER : threaten — **guet** [gɛ] *nm* **faire le** ~ : be on the lookout — **guet-apens** [gɛtapɑ̃] *nm, pl* **guets-apens** : ambush

gueule [gœl] *nf* **1** : mouth (of an animal, a tunnel, etc.) **2** *fam* : face **3 ta** ~! *fam* : shut up! **4** ~ **de bois** : hangover — **gueuler** [gœle] *v fam* : bawl, bellow

gui [gi] *nm* : mistletoe

guichet [giʃɛ] *nm* **1** : window, counter **2** : box office **3** ~ **automatique** : automatic teller machine — **guichetier, -tière** [giʃtje, -tjɛr] *n* : counter clerk, teller

guide [gid] *nm* **1** : guide **2** : guidebook — **guider** [gide] *vt* : guide — **guides** *nfpl* : reins

guidon [gidɔ̃] *nm* : handlebars *pl*

guignol [giɲɔl] *nm* **1** : puppet show **2 faire le** ~ : clown around

guillemets [gijmɛ] *nmpl* : quotation marks

guilleret, -rette [gijrɛ, -rɛt] *adj* : sprightly, perky

guillotine [gijɔtin] *nf* : guillotine

guimauve [gimov] *nf* : marshmallow

guindé, -dée [gɛ̃de] *adj* : stiff, prim

guirlande [girlɑ̃d] *nf* **1** : garland **2** ~**s de Noël** : tinsel

guise [giz] *nf* **1 à ta** ~ : as you wish **2 en** ~ **de** : by way of

guitare [gitar] *nf* : guitar — **guitariste** [gitarist] *nmf* : guitarist

gymnase [ʒimnaz] *nm* : gymnasium — **gymnaste** [ʒimnast] *nmf* : gymnast

gymnastique [ʒimnastik] *nf* : gymnastics

gynécologie [ʒinekɔlɔʒi] *nf* : gynecology — **gynécologue** [ʒinekɔlɔg] *nmf* : gynecologist

H

h [aʃ] *nm* : h, eighth letter of the alphabet

habile [abil] *adj* : skillful, clever — **habilement** [abilmɑ̃] *adv* : skillfully, cleverly — **habileté** [abilte] *nf* : skill, cleverness

habilité, -tée [abilite] *adj* ～ **à** : entitled to

habiller [abije] *vt* : dress, clothe — **s'habiller** *vr* 1 : get dressed 2 ～ **en** : dress up as — **habillé, -lée** [abije] *adj* 1 : dressed 2 ÉLÉGANT : dressy — **habillement** [abijmɑ̃] *nm* : clothes *pl*, clothing

habit [abi] *nm* 1 : outfit, costume 2 : (religious) habit 3 *or* ～ **de soirée** : evening dress, tails *pl* 4 ～**s** *nmpl* : clothes

habiter [abite] *vt* : live in, inhabit — *vi* : live, reside — **habitant, -tante** [abitɑ̃, -tɑ̃t] *n* 1 : inhabitant 2 : occupant — **habitat** [abita] *nm* 1 : habitat 2 : housing — **habitation** [abitasjɔ̃] *nf* 1 : house, home 2 **conditions d'**～ : living conditions

habitude [abityd] *nf* 1 : habit 2 COUTUME : custom 3 **comme d'**～ : as usual 4 **d'**～ : usually — **habitué, -tuée** [abitɥe] *n* : regular (customer) — **habituel, -tuelle** [abitɥɛl] *adj* : usual, regular — **habituellement** [-tɥɛlmɑ̃] *adv* : usually — **habituer** [abitɥe] *vt* : accustom — **s'habituer** *vr* ～ **à** : get used to

hache [ˈaʃ] *nf* : ax — **haché, -chée** [ˈaʃe] *adj* 1 : chopped, minced, ground 2 SACCADÉ : jerky — **hacher** [ˈaʃe] *vt* : chop, mince, grind — **hachette** [aʃɛt] *nf* : hatchet — **hachis** [ˈaʃi] *nms & pl* : ground or minced food — **hachoir** [ˈaʃwar] *nm* 1 : meat grinder 2 : chopper, cleaver 3 : cutting board

hagard, -garde [ˈagar, -gard] *adj* : distraught, wild

haie [ˈɛ] *nf* 1 : hedge 2 : hurdle (in sports) 3 : line, row (of persons)

haillons [ˈajɔ̃] *nmpl* : rags, tatters

haïr [ˈair] {48} *vt* : hate — **haine** [ˈɛn] *nf* : hatred, hate — **haineux, -neuse** [ˈɛnø, -nøz] *adj* : full of hatred

haïtien, -tienne [aisjɛ̃, -sjɛn] *adj* : Haitian

hâle [ˈal] *nm* : suntan — **hâlé, -lée** [ˈale] *adj* : (sun)tanned

haleine [alɛn] *nf* 1 : breath 2 **hors d'**～ : out of breath

haleter [ˈalte] {20} *vi* : pant, gasp — **haletant, -tante** [ˈaltɑ̃, -tɑ̃t] *adj* : panting, breathless — **halètement** [ˈalɛtmɑ̃] *nm* : gasp

hall [ˈol] *nm* : hall, lobby

halle [ˈal] *nf France* : covered market

hallucination [alysinasjɔ̃] *nf* : hallucination

halte [ˈalt] *nf* 1 ARRÊT : stop, halt 2 : stopping place 3 ～ **routière** *Can* : rest area (on a highway)

haltère [altɛr] *nm* : dumbbell — **haltérophilie** [alterɔfili] *nf* : weightlifting

hamac [ˈamak] *nm* : hammock

hamburger [ˈɑ̃bœrgœr] *nm* : hamburger (cooked)

hameçon [amsɔ̃] *nm* : fishhook

hamster [ˈamstɛr] *nm* : hamster

hanche [ˈɑ̃ʃ] *nf* : hip

handball [ˈɑ̃dbal] *nm* : handball

handicap [ˈɑ̃dikap] *nm* : handicap — **handicapé, -pée** [ˈɑ̃dikape] *adj* : handicapped — ～ *n* : handicapped person — **handicaper** [ˈɑ̃dikape] *vt* : handicap

hangar [ˈɑ̃gar] *nm* 1 : (large) shed 2 *or* ～ **d'aviation** : hangar

hanter [ˈɑ̃te] *vt* : haunt — **hantise** [ˈɑ̃tiz] *nf* : dread

happer [ˈape] *vt* 1 : seize, snatch 2 **être happé par** : be hit by (a car, etc.)

harceler [ˈarsəle] {8 *and* 20} *vt* : harass — **harcèlement** [ˈarsɛlmɑ̃] *nm* : harassment

hardi, -die [ˈardi] *adj* : bold, daring — **hardiesse** [ˈardjɛs] *nf* : boldness, audacity — **hardiment** [ˈardimɑ̃] *adv* : boldly

hareng [ˈarɑ̃] *nm* : herring

hargne [ˈarɲ] *nf* : aggressiveness — **hargneux, -neuse** [ˈarɲø, -ɲøz] *adj* : aggressive, bad-tempered

haricot [ˈariko] *nm* 1 : bean 2 ～ **vert** : string bean

harmonica [armɔnika] *nm* : harmonica

harmonie [armɔni] *nf* : harmony — **harmonieux, -nieuse** [armɔnjø, -njøz] *adj* : harmonious — **harmoniser** [armɔnize] *vt* : harmonize — **s'harmoniser** *vr* : go well together

harnais [ˈarnɛ] *nm* : harness — **harnacher** [ˈarnaʃe] *vt* : harness (an animal)

harpe [ˈarp] *nf* : harp

harpon [ˈarpɔ̃] *nm* : harpoon — **harponner** [ˈarpɔne] *vt fam* : nab, collar

hasard [ˈazar] *nm* 1 : chance, luck 2 ～**s** *nmpl* : hazards, danger 3 **au** ～ : at random — **hasarder** [ˈazarde] *vt* : risk, venture — **se hasarder** *vr* ～ **à faire** : risk doing — **hasardeux, -deuse** [ˈazardø, -døz] *adj* : risky

hâte [ˈat] *nf* 1 : haste, hurry 2 **avoir** ～ **de** : be eager to — **hâter** [ˈate] *vt* : hasten, hurry — **se hâter** *vr* : hurry — **hâtif, -tive** [ˈatif, -tiv] *adj* 1 : hasty, rash 2 PRÉCOCE : early

hausser [ˈose] *vt* 1 : raise 2 ～ **les épaules**

haut

80

: shrug one's shoulders — **se hausser** *vr*
: stand up, reach up — **hausse** ['os] *nf* 1
: rise, increase 2 **à la ~** *or* **en ~** : rising,
up

haut, haute ['o, 'ot] *adj* 1 : high 2 : high
ranking — **haut** ['o] *adv* 1 : high 2 FORT
: loud, loudly — **~** *nm* 1 SOMMET : top 2
des ~s et des bas : ups and downs 3 **en
~** : upstairs 4 **en ~ de** : on top of 5 **un
mètre de ~** : one meter high — **hautain,
-taine** ['otɛ̃, -tɛn] *adj* : haughty — **hautbois**
['obwa] *nms & pl* : oboe — **hautement**
['otmɑ̃] *adv* : highly — **hauteur** ['otœr] *nf*
1 : height 2 ARROGANCE : haughtiness —
haut-le-cœur ['olkœr] *nms & pl* **avoir des
~** : retch, gag — **haut-parleur** ['oparlœr]
nm, *pl* **haut-parleurs** : loudspeaker
hâve ['av] *adj* : gaunt
havre ['avr] *nm* : haven
hayon ['ajɔ̃] *nm* : tailgate
hé ['e] *interj* : hey
hebdomadaire [ɛbdɔmadɛr] *adj & nm*
: weekly
héberger [ebɛrʒe] {17} *vt* : accommodate,
put up — **hébergement** [ebɛrʒəmɑ̃] *nm*
: accommodations *pl*
hébété, -tée [ebete] *adj* : dazed — **hébétude**
[ebetyd] *nf* : stupor
hébreu [ebrø] *adj m, pl* **-breux** : Hebrew —
~ *nm* : Hebrew (language) — **hébraïque**
[ebraik] *adj* : Hebrew, Hebraic
hein ['ɛ̃] *interj* : eh?, what?
hélas ['elas] *interj* : alas!
héler ['ele] {87} *vt* : hail, summon
hélice [elis] *nf* : propeller
hélicoptère [elikɔptɛr] *nm* : helicopter
hémisphère [emisfɛr] *nm* : hemisphere
hémorragie [emɔraʒi] *nf* : bleeding, hemorrhage
hémorroïdes [emɔrɔid] *nfpl* : hemorrhoids
hennir ['enir] *vi* : neigh — **hennissement**
['enismɑ̃] *nm* : neighing
hépatite [epatit] *nf* : hepatitis
herbe [ɛrb] *nf* 1 : grass 2 : herb (in cooking)
3 **en ~** : budding 4 **mauvaise ~** : weed
— **herbage** [ɛrbaʒ] *nm* : pasture — **her-
beux, -beuse** [ɛrbø, -bøz] *adj* : grassy —
herbicide [ɛrbisid] *nm* : weed killer
héréditaire [ereditɛr] *adj* : hereditary —
hérédité [eredite] *nf* : heredity
hérésie [erezi] *nf* : heresy
hérisser ['erise] *vt* 1 : ruffle up (fur, feathers, etc.) 2 **~ qqn** *fam* : irritate s.o. — **se
hérisser** *vr* 1 : stand on end 2 *fam* : bristle
(with annoyance) — **hérisson** ['erisɔ̃] *nm*
: hedgehog
hériter [erite] *vi* **~ de** : inherit — *vt* : inherit
— **héritage** [eritaʒ] *nm* 1 : inheritance 2
: (cultural) heritage — **héritier, -tière** [er-
itje, -tjɛr] *n* : heir, heiress *f*

hermétique [ɛrmetik] *adj* 1 ÉTANCHE : airtight, watertight 2 OBSCUR : obscure
hernie ['ɛrni] *nf* : hernia
héroïne [erɔin] *nf* 1 : heroine 2 : heroin —
héroïque [erɔik] *adj* : heroic — **héroïsme**
[erɔism] *nm* : heroism
héron ['erɔ̃] *nm* : heron
héros ['ero] *nm* : hero
hésiter [ezite] *vi* : hesitate — **hésitant,
-tante** [ezitɑ̃, -tɑ̃t] *adj* : hesitant — **hésitation** [ezitasjɔ̃] *nf* : hesitation
hétérogène [eterɔʒɛn] *adj* : heterogeneous
hétérosexuel, -sexuelle [eterɔsɛksyɛl] *adj
& n* : heterosexual
hêtre ['ɛtr] *nm* : beech
heure [œr] *nf* 1 : time 2 : hour 3 **~ de
pointe** : rush hour 4 **~s supplémentaires** : overtime 5 **quelle ~ est-il?** : what
time is it? 6 **tout à l'~** : later on
heureux, -reuse [œrø, -røz] *adj* 1 : happy
2 SATISFAIT : glad, pleased 3 CHANCEUX
: fortunate, lucky — **heureusement**
[œrøzmɑ̃] *adv* : fortunately, luckily
heurter ['œrte] *vt* 1 : strike, collide with 2
OFFENSER : offend, go against — *vi* : hit,
collide — **se heurter** *vr* **~ à** : come up
against — **heurt** ['œr] *nm* 1 : collision,
crash 2 CONFLIT : conflict
hexagone [ɛgzagɔn] *nm* : hexagon
hiberner [ibɛrne] *vi* : hibernate
hibou ['ibu] *nm, pl* **-boux** [ibu] : owl
hic ['ik] *nm fam* 1 : snag 2 **voilà le ~**
: that's the trouble
hideux, -deuse ['idø, -døz] *adj* : hideous
hier [ijɛr] *adv* : yesterday
hiérarchie ['jerarʃi] *nf* : hierarchy — **hiérarchique** ['jerarʃik] *adj* : hierarchical
hilarité [ilarite] *nf* : hilarity, mirth — **hilarant, -rante** [ilarɑ̃, -rɑ̃t] *adj* : hilarious —
hilare [ilar] *adj* : mirthful, merry
hindou, -doue [ɛ̃du] *adj* : Hindu
hippie *or* **hippy** ['ipi] *nmf, pl* **-pies** : hippie
hippique [ipik] *adj* : equestrian, horse —
hippodrome [ipɔdrom] *nm* : racecourse
hippopotame [ipɔpɔtam] *nm* : hippopotamus
hirondelle [irɔ̃dɛl] *nf* : swallow
hirsute [irsyt] *adj* : hairy, shaggy
hispanique [ispanik] *adj* : Hispanic
hisser ['ise] *vt* : hoist, haul up — **se hisser**
vr : raise oneself up
histoire [istwar] *nf* 1 : history 2 RÉCIT
: story 3 AFFAIRE : affair, matter 4 **~s** *nfpl*
: trouble, problems — **historien, -rienne**
[istɔrjɛ̃, -rjɛn] *n* : historian — **historique**
[istɔrik] *adj* : historical, historic
hiver [ivɛr] *nm* : winter — **hivernal, -nale**
[ivɛrnal] *adj, mpl* **-naux** [-no] : winter, wintry

hocher [ɔʃe] *vt* ~ **la tête** : nod, shake one's head

hochet [ɔʃɛ] *nm* : rattle

hockey [ɔkɛ] *nm* : hockey

hollandais, -daise [ɔlɑdɛ, -dɛz] *adj* : Dutch

holocauste [ɔlɔkost] *nm* : holocaust

homard [ɔmar] *nm* : lobster

homélie [ɔmeli] *nf* : homily

homéopathie [ɔmeɔpati] *nf* : homeopathy

homicide [ɔmisid] *nm* : homicide

hommage [ɔmaʒ] *nm* **1** : homage **2 rendre** ~ **à** : pay tribute to

homme [ɔm] *nm* **1** : man **2 l'**~ : man, mankind **3** ~ **d'affaires** : businessman

homme–grenouille [ɔmgrənuj] *nm, pl* **hommes–grenouilles** : frogman

homogène [ɔmɔʒɛn] *adj* : homogeneous

homologue [ɔmɔlɔg] *nmf* : counterpart

homologuer [ɔmɔlɔge] *vt* : ratify, approve

homonyme [ɔmɔnim] *nm* **1** : homonym **2** : namesake

homosexuel, -sexuelle [ɔmɔsɛksɥɛl] *adj & n* : homosexual — **homosexualité** [ɔmɔsɛksɥalite] *nf* : homosexuality

honnête [ɔnɛt] *adj* **1** : honest **2** JUSTE : reasonable, fair — **honnêtement** [ɔnɛtmɑ̃] *adv* **1** : honestly **2** DÉCEMMENT : fairly, decently — **honnêteté** [ɔnɛtte] *nf* : honesty

honneur [ɔnœr] *nm* **1** : honor **2** MÉRITE : credit

honorer [ɔnɔre] *vt* **1** : honor **2** : be a credit to **3** PAYER : pay (a debt) — **honorable** [ɔnɔrabl] *adj* **1** : honorable **2** CONVENABLE : respectable, decent — **honorablement** [-rabləmɑ̃] *adv* **1** : honorably **2** SUFFISAMMENT : respectably, decently — **honoraire** [ɔnɔrɛr] *adj* : honorary — **honoraires** *nmpl* : fees — **honorifique** [ɔnɔrifik] *adj* : honorary

honte [ɔ̃t] *nf* **1** : shame **2 avoir** ~ : be ashamed — **honteux, -teuse** [ɔ̃tø, -tøz] *adj* **1** : ashamed **2** DÉSHONORANT : shameful

hôpital [ɔpital] *nm, pl* **-taux** [-to] : hospital

hoquet [ɔkɛ] *nm* **1** : hiccup **2 avoir le** ~ : have the hiccups — **hoqueter** [ɔkte] {8} *vi* : hiccup

horaire [ɔrɛr] *adj* : hourly — ~ *nm* : timetable, schedule

horizon [ɔrizɔ̃] *nm* **1** : horizon **2** : view, vista — **horizontal, -tale** [ɔrizɔ̃tal] *adj, mpl* **-taux** [-to] : horizontal

horloge [ɔrlɔʒ] *nf* : clock — **horloger, -gère** [ɔrlɔʒe, -ʒɛr] *n* : watchmaker

hormone [ɔrmɔn] *nf* : hormone

horoscope [ɔrɔskɔp] *nm* : horoscope

horreur [ɔrœr] *nf* **1** : horror **2 avoir** ~ **de** : detest — **horrible** [ɔribl] *adj* : horrible — **horrifiant, -fiante** [ɔrifjɑ̃, -fjɑ̃t] *adj* : horrifying — **horrifier** [ɔrifje] {96} *vt* : horrify

hors [ɔr] *prep* **1** : except for, save **2** ~ **de**

: out of, outside, beyond **3 être** ~ **de soi** : be beside oneself — **hors–bord** [ɔrbɔr] *nms & pl* **1** : outboard motor **2** : speedboat — **hors–d'œuvre** [ɔrdœvr] *nms & pl* : hors d'œuvre — **hors–la–loi** [ɔrlalwa] *nms & pl* : outlaw

horticulture [ɔrtikyltyr] *nf* : horticulture

hospice [ɔspis] *nm France* **1** : home (for the elderly, etc.) **2** : hospice

hospitalier, -lière [ɔspitalje, -jɛr] *adj* **1** : hospital **2** ACCUEILLANT : hospitable — **hospitaliser** [ɔspitalize] *vt* : hospitalize — **hospitalité** [ɔspitalite] *nf* : hospitality

hostie [ɔsti] *nf* : host (in religion)

hostile [ɔstil] *adj* : hostile — **hostilité** [ɔstilite] *nf* **1** : hostility **2** ~**s** *nfpl* : hostilities, war

hot-dog [ɔtdɔg] *nm, pl* **hot–dogs** : hot dog

hôte, hôtesse [ot, otɛs] *n* : host, hostess *f* — **hôte** *nmf* : guest

hôtel [otɛl] *nm* **1** : hotel **2** ~ **de ville** : town hall — **hôtelier, -lière** [otəlje, -jɛr] *adj* : hotel — ~ *n* : hotel manager, innkeeper — **hôtellerie** [otɛlri] *nf* : hotel business

hôtesse [otɛs] *nf* **1** → **hôte 2** : receptionist **3** ~ **de l'air** : stewardess

hotte [ɔt] *nf* **1** : basket (carried on the back) **2** : hood (of a chimney or stove)

houblon [ublɔ̃] *nm* : hops *pl*

houe [u] *nf* : hoe

houille [uj] *nf* : coal — **houiller, -lère** [uje, -jɛr] *adj* : coal, coal-mining — **houillère** *nf* : coal mine

houle [ul] *nf* : swell, surge

houlette [ulɛt] *nf* **sous la** ~ **de** : under the guidance of

houleux, -leuse [ulø, -løz] *adj* : stormy

houppe [up] *or* **houppette** [upɛt] *nf* : powder puff

hourra [ura] *nm & interj* : hurrah

housse [us] *nf* : cover, dust cover

houx [u] *nms & pl* : holly

huard *or* **huart** [yar] *nm Can* : loon

hublot [yblo] *nm* : porthole

huche [yʃ] *nf* ~ **à pain** : bread box

huer [ɥe] *vt* : boo — *vi* : hoot — **huées** [ɥe] *nfpl* : boos, booing

huile [ɥil] *nf* **1** : oil **2** : oil painting — **huiler** [ɥile] *vt* : oil — **huileux, -leuse** [ɥilø, -løz] *adj* : oily — **huilier** [ɥilje] *nm* : cruet

huis [ɥi] *nm* **à** ~ **clos** : behind closed doors

huissier [ɥisje] *nm* **1** : usher **2** *or* ~ **de justice** : bailiff

huit [ɥit, *before consonant* ɥi] *adj* **1** : eight **2** : eighth (in dates) — ~ *nms & pl* : eight — **huitaine** [ɥitɛn] *nf* **une** ~ **(de jours)** : about a week — **huitième** [ɥitjɛm] *adj & nmf & nm* : eighth

huître [ɥitr] *nf* : oyster

hululer ['ylyle] *vi* : hoot — **hululement** ['ylylmɑ̃] *nm* : hoot (of an owl)

humain, -maine [ymɛ̃, -mɛn] *adj* 1 : human 2 BIENVEILLANT : humane — **humain** *nm* i human being humanitaire [ymanitɛr] *adj* : humanitarian — **humanité** [ymanite] *nf* : humanity

humble [œ̃bl] *adj* : humble — **humblement** [œ̃bləmɑ̃] *adv* : humbly

humecter [ymɛkte] *vt* : dampen, moisten

humer ['yme] *vt* 1 : breathe in, inhale 2 : smell

humeur [ymœr] *nf* 1 : mood, humor 2 CA-RACTÈRE : temperament

humide [ymid] *adj* 1 : moist, damp 2 : humid — **humidité** [ymidite] *nf* 1 : dampness 2 : humidity

humilier [ymilje] {96} *vt* : humiliate — **s'humilier** *vr* : humble oneself — **humiliant, -liante** [ymiljɑ̃, -jɑ̃t] *adj* : humiliating — **humiliation** [ymiljasjɔ̃] *nf* : humiliation — **humilité** [ymilite] *nf* : humility

humour [ymur] *nm* 1 : humor, wit 2 **avoir de l'~** : have a sense of humor — **humoriste** [ymɔrist] *nmf* : humorist — **humoristique** [ymɔristik] *adj* : humorous

huppé, -pée ['ype] *adj fam* : posh, high-class

hurler ['yrle] *vt* : yell out — *vi* 1 : howl, roar 2 CRIER : yell, shout — **hurlement** ['yrləmɑ̃] *nm* : howl, yell

hutte ['yt] *nf* : hut

hybride [ibrid] *adj & nm* : hybrid

hydratant, -tante [idratɑ̃, -tɑ̃t] *adj* : moisturizing — **hydratant** *nm* : moisturizer

hydrate [idrat] *nm* **~ de carbon** : carbohydrate

hydraulique [idrolik] *adj* : hydraulic

hydroélectrique *or* **hydro–électrique** [idroelɛktrik] *adj* : hydroelectric

hydrogène [idrɔʒɛn] *nm* : hydrogen

hyène [jɛn] *nf* : hyena

hygiène [iʒjɛn] *nf* : hygiene — **hygiénique** [iʒjenik] *adj* : hygienic

hymne [imn] *nm* 1 : hymn 2 **~ nationale** : national anthem

hyperactif, -tive [iperaktif, tiv] *adj* : hyperactive

hypermétrope [ipɛrmetrɔp] *adj* : farsighted

hypertension [ipɛrtɑ̃sjɔ̃] *nf* : high blood pressure

hypnotiser [ipnɔtize] *vt* : hypnotize — **hypnose** [ipnoz] *nf* : hypnosis

hypocrisie [ipɔkrizi] *nf* : hypocrisy — **hypocrite** [ipɔkrit] *adj* : hypocritical — **~** *nmf* : hypocrite

hypothèque [ipɔtɛk] *nf* : mortgage — **hypothéquer** [ipɔteke] {87} *vt* : mortgage

hypothèse [ipɔtɛz] *nf* : hypothesis — **hypothétique** [ipɔtetik] *adj* : hypothetical

hystérie [isteri] *nf* : hysteria — **hystérique** [isterik] *adj* : hysterical

i [i] *nm* : i, ninth letter of the alphabet

iceberg [ajsbɛrg] *nm* : iceberg

ici [isi] *adv* 1 : here 2 : now 3 **d'~ là** : by then 4 **par ~** : this way

icône [ikon] *nf* : icon

idéal, idéale [ideal] *adj, mpl* **idéals** *or* **idéaux** [ideo] : ideal — **idéal** *nm* : ideal — **idéaliser** [idealize] *vt* : idealize — **idéaliste** [idealist] *adj* : idealistic — **~** *nmf* : idealist

idée [ide] *nf* : idea

identifier [idɑ̃tifje] {96} *vt* : identify — **s'identifier** *vr* **~ à** : identify with — **identification** [idɑ̃tifikasjɔ̃] *nf* : identification — **identique** [idɑ̃tik] *adj* : identical — **identité** [idɑ̃tite] *nf* : identity

idéologie [ideɔlɔʒi] *nf* : ideology — **idéologique** [ideɔlɔʒik] *adj* : ideological

idiome [idjom] *nm* : idiom (language) — **idiomatique** [idjɔmatik] *adj* : idiomatic

idiot, -diote [idjo, -djɔt] *adj* : idiotic — **~** *n* : idiot, fool — **idiotie** [idjɔsi] *nf* : idiocy

idole [idɔl] *nf* : idol — **idolâtrer** [idɔlatre] *vt* : idolize

idyllique [idilik] *adj* : idyllic

igloo [iglu] *nm* : igloo

ignifuge [iɲifyʒ] *adj* : fireproof

ignoble [iɲɔbl] *adj* : base, vile

ignorance [iɲɔrɑ̃s] *nf* : ignorance — **ignorant, -rante** [iɲɔrɑ̃, -rɑ̃t] *adj* : ignorant — **ignorer** [iɲɔre] *vt* 1 : be unaware of 2 : ignore

il [il] *pron* 1 : he, it 2 (*as subject of an impersonal verb*) : it 3 **ils** *pron pl* : they 4 **il y a** : there is, there are

île [il] *nf* : island, isle

illégal, -gale [ilegal] *adj, mpl* **-gaux** [-go] : illegal — **illégalité** [ilegalite] *nf* : illegality

illégitime [ileʒitim] *adj* : illegitimate — **illégitimité** [ileʒitimite] *nf* : illegitimacy

illettré, -trée [iletre] *adj & n* : illiterate

illicite [ilisit] *adj* : illicit

illimité, -tée [ilimite] *adj* : unlimited

illisible [ilizibl] *adj* : illegible

illogique [iloʒik] *adj* : illogical

illuminer [ilymine] *vt* : illuminate, light up — **illumination** [ilyminasjɔ̃] *nf* : illumination

illusion [ilyzjɔ̃] *nf* : illusion — **illusoire** [ilyzwar] *adj* : illusory

illustration [ilystrasjɔ̃] *nf* : illustration — **illustre** [ilystr] *adj* : illustrious, renowned — **illustré, -trée** [ilystre] *adj* : illustrated — **illustrer** [ilystre] *vt* : illustrate

îlot [ilo] *nm* **1** : small island **2** : block (of houses)

ils [il] → **il**

image [imaʒ] *nf* **1** : image **2** DESSIN : picture

imaginer [imaʒine] *vt* **1** : imagine **2** INVENTER : devise, think up — **s'imaginer** *vr* : picture oneself — **imaginaire** [imaʒinɛr] *adj* : imaginary — **imaginatif, -tive** [imaʒinatif, -tiv] *adj* : imaginative — **imagination** [imaʒinasjɔ̃] *nf* : imagination

imbattable [ɛ̃batabl] *adj* : unbeatable

imbécile [ɛ̃besil] *adj* : stupid, idiotic — ~ *nmf* : fool, idiot — **imbécillité** [ɛ̃besilite] *nf* : idiocy, stupidity

imbiber [ɛ̃bibe] *vt* : soak — **s'imbiber** *vr* : get soaked

imbuvable [ɛ̃byvabl] *adj* : undrinkable

imiter [imite] *vt* **1** COPIER : imitate, mimic **2** : look (just) like — **imitateur, -trice** [imitatœr, -tris] *n* **1** : imitator **2** : impersonator — **imitation** [imitasjɔ̃] *nf* **1** : imitation **2** : impersonation

immaculé, -lée [imakyle] *adj* : immaculate

immangeable [ɛ̃mɑ̃ʒabl] *adj* : inedible

immanquable [ɛ̃mɑ̃kabl] *adj* **1** : impossible to miss **2** INÉVITABLE : inevitable

immatriculer [imatrikyle] *vt* : register — **immatriculation** [imatrikylasjɔ̃] *nf* **1** : registration **2 plaque d'~** : license plate

immature [imatyr] *adj* : immature — **immaturité** [imatyrite] *nf* : immaturity

immédiat, -diate [imedja, -djat] *adj* : immediate — **immédiatement** [-djatmɑ̃] *adv* : immediately

immense [imɑ̃s] *adj* : immense — **immensité** [imɑ̃site] *nf* : immensity

immerger [imɛrʒe] {17} *vt* : immerse, submerge — **immersion** [imɛrsjɔ̃] *nf* : immersion

immeuble [imœbl] *nm* : building

immigrer [imigre] *vi* : immigrate — **immigrant, -grante** [imigrɑ̃, -grɑ̃t] *adj & n* : immigrant — **immigration** [imigrasjɔ̃] *nf* : immigration — **immigré, -grée** [imigre] *n* : immigrant

imminent, -nente [iminɑ̃, -nɑ̃t] *adj* : imminent — **imminence** [iminɑ̃s] *nf* : imminence

immiscer [imise] {6} *v* **s'immiscer** *vr* ~ **dans** : interfere with

immobile [imɔbil] *adj* : motionless

immobilier, -lière [imɔbilje, -ljɛr] *adj* : real estate, property

immobiliser [imɔbilize] *vt* **1** : immobilize **2** ARRÊTER : bring to a halt — **s'immobiliser** *vr* : stop — **immobilité** [imɔbilite] *nf* : immobility, stillness

immodéré, -rée [imɔdere] *adj* : immoderate, excessive

immonde [imɔ̃d] *adj* : foul, filthy

immoral, -rale [imɔral] *adj, mpl* **-raux** [-ro] : immoral — **immoralité** [imɔralite] *nf* : immorality

immortalité [imɔrtalite] *nf* : immortality — **immortel, -telle** [imɔrtɛl] *adj* : immortal

immuable [imɥabl] *adj* : unchanging

immuniser [imynize] *vt* : immunize — **immunisation** [-nizasjɔ̃] *nf* : immunization — **immunité** [imynite] *nf* : immunity

impact [ɛ̃pakt] *nm* : impact

impair, -paire [ɛ̃pɛr] *adj* : odd, uneven — **impair** *nm* : blunder

impardonnable [ɛ̃pardɔnabl] *adj* : unforgivable

imparfait, -faite [ɛ̃parfɛ, -fɛt] *adj* : imperfect — **imparfait** *nm* : imperfect (tense)

impartial, -tiale [ɛ̃parsjal] *adj, mpl* **-tiaux** [-sjo] : unbiased, impartial — **impartialité** [ɛ̃parsjalite] *nf* : impartiality

impartir [ɛ̃partir] *vt* : grant, bestow

impasse [ɛ̃pas] *nf* **1** : impasse, deadlock **2** CUL-DE-SAC : dead end

impassible [ɛ̃pasibl] *adj* : impassive

impatient, -tiente [ɛ̃pasjɑ̃, -sjɑ̃t] *adj* : impatient — **impatiemment** [ɛ̃pasjamɑ̃] *adv* : impatiently — **impatience** [-sjɑ̃s] *nf* : impatience — **impatienter** [ɛ̃pasjɑ̃te] *vt* : annoy — **s'impatienter** *vr* : lose patience

impeccable [ɛ̃pekabl] *adj* : impeccable, faultless

impénétrable [ɛ̃penetrabl] *adj* **1** : impenetrable **2** : inscrutable

impénitent, -tente [ɛ̃penitɑ̃, -tɑ̃t] *adj* : unrepentant

impensable [ɛ̃pɑ̃sabl] *adj* : unthinkable

impératif, -tive [ɛ̃peratif, -tiv] *adj* : imperative — **impératif** *nm* : imperative (mood)

impératrice [ɛ̃peratris] *nf* : empress

imperceptible [ɛ̃pɛrsɛptibl] *adj* : imperceptible

imperfection [ɛ̃pɛrfɛksjɔ̃] *nf* : imperfection

impérial, -riale [ɛ̃perjal] *adj, mpl* **-riaux** [-rjo] : imperial — **impérialisme** [ɛ̃perjalism] *nm* : imperialism

impérieux, -rieuse [ɛ̃perjø, -jøz] *adj* **1** : imperious **2** PRESSANT : urgent

impérissable [ɛ̃perisabl] *adj* : imperishable

imperméable [ɛ̃pɛrmeabl] *adj* : waterproof — ~ *nm* : raincoat

impersonnel, -nelle [ɛ̃pɛrsɔnɛl] *adj* : impersonal

impertinent, -nente [ɛ̃pɛrtinɑ̃, -nɑ̃t] *adj* : impertinent — **impertinence** [-tinɑ̃s] *nf* : impertinence

imperturbable [ɛ̃pɛrtyrbabl] *adj* : unflappable

impétueux, -tueuse, [ɛ̃petɥø, -tɥøz] *adj* : impetuous

impitoyable [ɛ̃pitwajabl] *adj* : merciless, pitiless

implacable [ɛ̃plakabl] *adj* : implacable

implanter [ɛ̃plɑ̃te] *vt* 1 : establish 2 : implant (in medicine) — **s'implanter** *vr* : be set up — **implantation** [ɛ̃plɑ̃tasjɔ̃] *nf* : establishment

implication [ɛ̃plikasjɔ̃] *nf* : implication

implicite [ɛ̃plisit] *adj* : implicit

impliquer [ɛ̃plike] *vt* 1 : implicate 2 SUPPOSER : imply 3 ENTRAÎNER : entail, involve — **s'impliquer** *vr* : become involved

implorer [ɛ̃plɔre] *vt* : implore

imploser [ɛ̃ploze] *vi* : implode

impoli, -lie [ɛ̃pɔli] *adj* : impolite, rude — **impolitesse** [ɛ̃pɔlitɛs] *nf* : rudeness

impopulaire [ɛ̃pɔpylɛr] *adj* : unpopular

importer[1] [ɛ̃pɔrte] *vi* 1 : matter, be important 2 **n'importe qui** : anyone, anybody 3 **n'importe quoi** : anything 4 **peu importe** : no matter — **importance** [ɛ̃pɔrtɑ̃s] *nf* : importance — **important, -tante** [ɛ̃pɔrtɑ̃, -tɑ̃t] *adj* 1 : important 2 LARGE : considerable — **important** *nm* l'~ : the important thing, the main thing

importer[2] *vt* : import — **importateur, -trice** [ɛ̃pɔrtatœr, -tris] *n* : importer — **importation** [ɛ̃pɔrtasjɔ̃] *nf* 1 : importing 2 : import

importun, -tune [ɛ̃pɔrtœ̃, -tyn] *adj* : troublesome, unwelcome — ~ *n* : nuisance, pest — **importuner** [ɛ̃pɔrtyne] *vt* : pester

imposer [ɛ̃poze] *vt* 1 : impose 2 TAXER : tax — **s'imposer** *vr* 1 : be essential 2 : stand out — **imposable** [ɛ̃pozabl] *adj* : taxable — **imposant, -sante** [ɛ̃pozɑ̃, -zɑ̃t] *adj* : imposing

impossible [ɛ̃posibl] *adj* : impossible — ~ *nm* l'~ : the impossible — **impossibilité** [ɛ̃posibilite] *nf* : impossibility

imposteur [ɛ̃postœr] *nm* : impostor

impôt [ɛ̃po] *nm* : tax, duty

impotent, -tente [ɛ̃potɑ̃, -tɑ̃t] *adj* : infirm, disabled

impraticable [ɛ̃pratikabl] *adj* : impassable (of a road, etc.)

imprécis, -cise [ɛ̃presi, -siz] *adj* : imprecise — **imprécision** [ɛ̃presizjɔ̃] *nf* : imprecision

imprégner [ɛ̃preɲe] {87} *vt* IMBIBER : impregnate, soak — **s'imprégner** *vr* ~ **de** : become filled with

impression [ɛ̃presjɔ̃] *nf* 1 : impression 2 : printing — **impressionnable** [ɛ̃presjɔnabl] *adj* : impressionable — **impressionnant, -nante** [ɛ̃presjɔnɑ̃, -nɑ̃t] *adj* : impressive — **impressionner** [ɛ̃presjɔne] *vt* : impress

imprévisible [ɛ̃previzibl] *adj* : unpredictable

imprévoyance [ɛ̃prevwajɑ̃s] *nf* : lack of foresight — **imprévu, -vue** [ɛ̃prevy] *adj* : unforeseen, unexpected

imprimer [ɛ̃prime] *vt* 1 : print 2 : imprint — **imprimante** [ɛ̃primɑ̃t] *nf* : printer — **imprimé, -mée** [ɛ̃prime] *adj* : printed (of fabric, etc.) — **imprimerie** [ɛ̃primri] *nf* 1 : printing 2 : print shop — **imprimeur, -meuse** [ɛ̃primœr, -møz] *n* : printer

improbable [ɛ̃prɔbabl] *adj* : improbable, unlikely — **improbabilité** [-babilite] *nf* : unlikelihood

impromptu, -tue [ɛ̃prɔ̃pty] *adj* : impromptu

impropre [ɛ̃prɔpr] *adj* 1 INCORRECT : incorrect 2 INADAPTÉ : unsuitable

improviser [ɛ̃prɔvize] *v* : improvise — **improvisation** [ɛ̃prɔvizasjɔ̃] *nf* : improvisation

improviste [ɛ̃prɔvist] **à l'~** *adv phr* : unexpectedly

imprudent, -dente [ɛ̃prydɑ̃, -dɑ̃t] *adj* : rash, careless — **imprudemment** [ɛ̃prydamɑ̃] *adv* : carelessly — **imprudence** [ɛ̃prydɑ̃s] *nf* : carelessness

impudent, -dente [ɛ̃pydɑ̃, -dɑ̃t] *adj* : impudent — **impudence** [ɛ̃pydɑ̃s] *nf* : impudence

impudique [ɛ̃pydik] *adj* : immodest, indecent

impuissance [ɛ̃pɥisɑ̃s] *nf* 1 : helplessness 2 : (physical) impotence — **impuissant, -sante** [ɛ̃pɥisɑ̃, -sɑ̃t] *adj* 1 : helpless 2 : impotent (in medicine)

impulsion [ɛ̃pylsjɔ̃] *nf* 1 : impulse 2 POUSSÉE : impetus — **impulsif, -sive** [ɛ̃pylsif, -siv] *adj* : impulsive — **impulsivité** [ɛ̃pylsivite] *nf* : impulsiveness

impuni, -nie [ɛ̃pyni] *adj* : unpunished — **impunément** [ɛ̃pynemɑ̃] *adv* : with impunity — **impunité** [ɛ̃pynite] *nf* : impunity

impur, -pure [ɛ̃pyr] *adj* : impure — **impureté** [ɛ̃pyrte] *nf* : impurity

imputer [ɛ̃pyte] *vt* : impute

inabordable [inabɔrdabl] *adj* : inaccessible

inacceptable [inaksɛptabl] *adj* : unacceptable

inaccessible [inaksesibl] *adj* : inaccessible

inaccoutumé, -mée [inakutyme] *adj* : unaccustomed

inachevé, -vée [inaʃve] *adj* : unfinished

inaction [inaksjɔ̃] *nf* : inaction, inactivity — **inactif, -tive** [inaktif, -tiv] *adj* : inactive — **inactivité** [inaktivite] *nf* : inactivity

inadapté, -tée [inadapte] *adj* 1 : maladjusted 2 ~ **à** : unsuited to, unsuitable for

inadéquat, -quate [inadekwa, -kwat] *adj* : inadequate

inadmissible [inadmisibl] *adj* : unacceptable

inadvertance [inadvɛrtɑ̃s] *nf* par ~ : inadvertently

inaltérable [inalterabl] *adj* : stable, unchanging

inamovible [inamɔvibl] *adj* : fixed, permanent

inanimé, -mée [inanime] *adj* 1 : inanimate 2 INCONSCIENT : unconscious

inaperçu, -çue [inapɛrsy] *adj* : unseen, unnoticed

inapplicable [inaplikabl] *adj* : inapplicable

inapte [inapt] *adj* : unfit, unsuited

inarticulé, -lée [inartikyle] *adj* : inarticulate

inassouvi, -vie [inasuvi] *adj* : unsatisfied, unfulfilled

inattaquable [inatakabl] *adj* 1 : irreproachable 2 IRRÉFUTABLE : irrefutable

inattendu, -due [inatɑ̃dy] *adj* : unexpected

inattention [inatɑ̃sjɔ̃] *nf* 1 : inattention 2 faute d'~ : careless error — **inattentif, -tive** [inatɑ̃tif, -tiv] *adj* : inattentive, distracted

inaudible [inodibl] *adj* : inaudible

inaugurer [inogyre] *vt* : inaugurate — **inaugural, -rale** [inogyral] *adj, mpl* -raux [-ro] : inaugural — **inauguration** [inogyrasjɔ̃] *nf* : inauguration

incalculable [ɛ̃kalkylabl] *adj* : incalculable, countless

incapable [ɛ̃kapabl] *adj* : incapable, unable — **incapacité** [ɛ̃kapasite] *nf* : incapacity, inability

incarcérer [ɛ̃karsere] {87} *vt* : incarcerate

incarner [ɛ̃karne] *vt* : play (a role)

incassable [ɛ̃kasabl] *adj* : unbreakable

incendie [ɛ̃sɑ̃di] *nm* : fire — **incendiaire** [ɛ̃sɑ̃djɛr] *adj* : inflammatory

incendier [ɛ̃sɑ̃dje] {96} *vt* : set on fire

incertain, -taine [ɛ̃sɛrtɛ̃, -tɛn] *adj* 1 : uncertain 2 VAGUE : indistinct — **incertitude** [ɛ̃sɛrtityd] *nf* : uncertainty

incessant, -sante [ɛ̃sesɑ̃, -sɑ̃t] *adj* : incessant

inceste [ɛ̃sɛst] *nm* : incest — **incestueux, -tueuse** [ɛ̃sɛstɥø, -tɥøz] *adj* : incestuous

inchangé, -gée [ɛ̃ʃɑ̃ʒe] *adj* : unchanged

incidence [ɛ̃sidɑ̃s] *nf* : effect, impact

incident [ɛ̃sidɑ̃] *nm* : incident

incinérer [ɛ̃sinere] {87} *vt* 1 : incinerate 2 : cremate — **incinérateur** [ɛ̃sineratœr] *nm* : incinerator — **incinération** [ɛ̃sinerasjɔ̃] *nf* 1 : incineration 2 : cremation

incision [ɛ̃sizjɔ̃] *nf* : incision

inciter [ɛ̃site] *vt* : incite

incliner [ɛ̃kline] *vt* 1 PENCHER : tilt, bend 2 INCITER : incline, prompt — *vi* ~ à : be inclined to — **s'incliner** *vr* 1 : tilt, lean 2 ~ devant : bow to — **inclinaison** [ɛ̃klinɛzɔ̃] *nf* : incline, slope — **inclination** [ɛ̃klinasjɔ̃] *nf* 1 : nod, bow 2 TENDANCE : inclination, tendency

inclure [ɛ̃klyr] {39} *vt* 1 : include 2 JOINDRE : enclose — **inclus, -cluse** [ɛ̃kly, -klyz] *adj* : inclusive — **inclusion** [ɛ̃klyzjɔ̃] *nf* : inclusion

incognito [ɛ̃kɔɲito] *adv & adj* : incognito

incohérent, -rente [ɛ̃kɔerɑ̃, -rɑ̃t] *adj* : incoherent — **incohérence** [ɛ̃kɔerɑ̃s] *nf* : incoherence

incolore [ɛ̃kɔlɔr] *adj* : colorless

incommensurable [ɛ̃kɔmɑ̃syrabl] *adj* : immeasurable

incommode [ɛ̃kɔmɔd] *adj* 1 : inconvenient 2 INCONFORTABLE : uncomfortable — **incommoder** [ɛ̃kɔmɔde] *vt* : inconvenience

incomparable [ɛ̃kɔ̃parabl] *adj* : incomparable

incompatible [ɛ̃kɔ̃patibl] *adj* : incompatible

incompétent, -tente [ɛ̃kɔ̃petɑ̃, -tɑ̃t] *adj* : incompetent — **incompétence** [ɛ̃kɔ̃petɑ̃s] *nf* : incompetence

incomplet, -plète [ɛ̃kɔ̃plɛ, -plɛt] *adj* : incomplete

incompréhensible [ɛ̃kɔ̃preɑ̃sibl] *adj* : incomprehensible — **incompréhension** [ɛ̃kɔ̃preɑ̃sjɔ̃] *nf* : lack of understanding — **incompris, -prise** [ɛ̃kɔ̃pri, -priz] *adj* : misunderstood

inconcevable [ɛ̃kɔ̃svabl] *adj* : inconceivable

inconciliable [ɛ̃kɔ̃siljabl] *adj* : irreconcilable

inconditionnel, -nelle [ɛ̃kɔ̃disjɔnɛl] *adj* : unconditional — ~ *n* : enthusiast

inconduite [ɛ̃kɔ̃dɥit] *nf* : misconduct

inconfort [ɛ̃kɔ̃fɔr] *nm* : discomfort — **inconfortable** [ɛ̃kɔ̃fɔrtabl] *adj* : uncomfortable

incongru, -grue [ɛ̃kɔ̃gry] *adj* 1 : incongruous 2 : unseemly, inappropriate

inconnu, -nue [ɛ̃kɔny] *adj* : unknown — ~ *n* 1 : unknown (person) 2 ÉTRANGER : stranger

inconscient, -ciente [ɛ̃kɔ̃sjɑ̃, -sjɑ̃t] *adj* 1 : unaware 2 : unconscious — **inconsciemment** [ɛ̃kɔ̃sjamɑ̃] *adv* 1 : unconsciously 2 : thoughtlessly — **inconscience** [ɛ̃kɔ̃sjɑ̃s] *nf* 1 : unconsciousness 2 : thoughtlessness

inconsidéré, -rée [ɛ̃kɔ̃sidere] *adj* : thoughtless

inconsistant, -tante [ɛ̃kɔ̃sistɑ̃, -tɑ̃t] *adj* : flimsy, weak

inconsolable [ɛ̃kɔ̃sɔlabl] *adj* : inconsolable

inconstant, -stante [ɛ̃kɔ̃stɑ̃, -stɑ̃t] *adj* : fickle

incontestable [ɛ̃kɔ̃tɛstabl] *adj* : unquestionable, indisputable — **incontesté, -tée** [ɛ̃kɔ̃tɛste] *adj* : undisputed

incontournable

incontournable [ɛ̃kɔ̃turnabl] *adj* : essential, that cannot be ignored

inconvenant, -nante [ɛ̃kɔ̃vnã, -nãt] *adj* : improper, unseemly — **inconvenance** [ɛ̃kɔ̃vnãs] *nf* : impropriety

inconvénient [ɛ̃kɔ̃venjã] *nm* : disadvantage, drawback

incorporer [ɛ̃kɔrpɔre] *vt* : incorporate

incorrect, -recte [ɛ̃kɔrɛkt] *adj* **1** ERRONÉ : incorrect **2** INCONVENANT : improper — **incorrectement** [ɛ̃kɔrɛktəmã] *adv* : wrongly

incorrigible [ɛ̃kɔriʒibl] *adj* : incorrigible

incrédule [ɛ̃kredyl] *adj* : incredulous

incriminer [ɛ̃krimine] *vt* : incriminate — **incrimination** [ɛ̃kriminasjɔ̃] *nf* : incrimination

incroyable [ɛ̃krwajabl] *adj* : unbelievable, incredible — **incroyant, -croyante** [ɛ̃krwajã, -jãt] *n* : unbeliever

inculper [ɛ̃kylpe] *vt* : indict, charge — **inculpation** [ɛ̃kylpasjɔ̃] *nf* : indictment, charge — **inculpé, -pée** [ɛ̃kylpe] *n* : accused, defendant

inculquer [ɛ̃kylke] *vt* : instill

inculte [ɛ̃kylt] *adj* **1** : uncultivated **2** : uneducated

incurable [ɛ̃kyrabl] *adj* : incurable

incursion [ɛ̃kyrsjɔ̃] *nf* : incursion, foray

indécent, -cente [ɛ̃desã, -sãt] *adj* : indecent — **indécence** [ɛ̃desãs] *nf* : indecency

indéchiffrable [ɛ̃deʃifrabl] *adj* : indecipherable

indécis, -cise [ɛ̃desi, -siz] *adj* **1** : indecisive **2** INCERTAIN : undecided — **indécision** [ɛ̃desizjɔ̃] *nf* : indecision

indéfini, -nie [ɛ̃defini] *adj* **1** : indefinite **2** VAGUE : ill-defined — **indéfinissable** [ɛ̃definisabl] *adj* : indefinable

indélébile [ɛ̃delebil] *adj* : indelible

indélicat, -cate [ɛ̃delika, -kat] *adj* **1** : indelicate **2** MALHONNÊTE : dishonest

indemne [ɛ̃dɛmn] *adj* : unharmed

indemnité [ɛ̃dɛmnite] *nf* **1** : indemnity **2** ALLOCATION : allowance — **indemniser** [ɛ̃dɛmnize] *vt* : indemnify, compensate

indéniable [ɛ̃denjabl] *adj* : undeniable

indépendant, -dante [ɛ̃depãdã, -dãt] *adj* : independent — **indépendamment** [ɛ̃depãdamã] *adv* : independently — **indépendance** [-pãdãs] *nf* : independence

indescriptible [ɛ̃dɛskriptibl] *adj* : indescribable

indésirable [ɛ̃dezirabl] *adj* : undesirable

indestructible [ɛ̃dɛstryktibl] *adj* : indestructible

indéterminé, -née [ɛ̃detɛrmine] *adj* : indeterminate, unspecified

index [ɛ̃dɛks] *nm* **1** : index **2** : forefinger, index finger — **indexer** [ɛ̃dekse] *vt* : index

indication [ɛ̃dikasjɔ̃] *nf* **1** : indication **2** RENSEIGNEMENT : information **3** ~s *nfpl* : instructions, directions — **indicateur, -trice** [ɛ̃dikatœr, -tris] *adj* → **panneau, poteau** — ~ *n* **1** : informer — **indicateur** *nm* **1** GUIDE : guide, directory **2** : gauge, meter — **indicatif, -tive** [ɛ̃dikatif, -tiv] *adj* : indicative — **indicatif** *nm* : indicative (mood)

indice [ɛ̃dis] *nm* **1** SIGNE : sign, indication **2** : clue **3** : index (of prices, etc.) **4** ÉVALUATION : rating

indicible [ɛ̃disibl] *adj* : inexpressible

indien, -dienne [ɛ̃djɛ̃, -djɛn] *adj* : Indian

indifférent, -rente [ɛ̃diferã, -rãt] *adj* : indifferent — **indifférence** [ɛ̃diferãs] *nf* : indifference

indigène [ɛ̃diʒɛn] *adj* : indigenous, native — ~ *nmf* : native

indigent, -gente [ɛ̃diʒã, -ʒãt] *adj* : destitute

indigestion [ɛ̃diʒɛstjɔ̃] *nf* : indigestion — **indigeste** [ɛ̃diʒɛst] *adj* : indigestible

indignation [ɛ̃diɲasjɔ̃] *nf* : indignation — **indigne** [ɛ̃diɲ] *adj* **1** : unworthy **2** MÉPRISABLE : shameful — **indigné, -gnée** [ɛ̃diɲe] *adj* : indignant — **indigner** [ɛ̃diɲe] *vr* : outrage — **s'indigner** *vr* : be indignant — **indignité** [ɛ̃diɲite] *nf* **1** : unworthiness **2** : indignity

indigo [ɛ̃digo] *adj & nm* : indigo

indiquer [ɛ̃dike] *vt* **1** : indicate, point out **2** DIRE : give, state — **indiqué, -quée** [ɛ̃dike] *adj* **1** : given, specified **2** RECOMMANDÉ : advisable **3** APPROPRIÉ : appropriate

indirect, -recte [ɛ̃dirɛkt] *adj* : indirect — **indirectement** [-rɛktəmã] *adv* : indirectly

indiscipliné, -née [ɛ̃disipline] *adj* : undisciplined, unruly

indiscrétion [ɛ̃diskresjɔ̃] *nf* : indiscretion — **indiscret, -crète** [ɛ̃diskrɛ, -krɛt] *adj* : indiscreet

indispensable [ɛ̃dispãsabl] *adj* : indispensable

indisponible [ɛ̃dispɔnibl] *adj* : unavailable

indisposer [ɛ̃dispoze] *vt* : upset, make ill — **indisposé, -sée** [ɛ̃dispoze] *adj* : unwell — **indisposition** [ɛ̃dispozisjɔ̃] *nf* : ailment, indisposition

indissociable [ɛ̃disɔsjabl] *adj* : inseparable

indistinct, -tincte [ɛ̃distɛ̃(kt), -tɛ̃kt] *adj* : indistinct

individu [ɛ̃dividy] *nm* : individual — **individualité** [ɛ̃dividɥalite] *nf* : individuality — **individuel, -duelle** [ɛ̃dividɥɛl] *adj* **1** : individual **2** PARTICULIER : personal, private — **individuellement** [ɛ̃dividɥɛlmã] *adv* : individually

indolent, -lente [ɛ̃dɔlã, -lãt] *adj* : lazy — **indolence** [ɛ̃dɔlãs] *nf* : laziness

indolore [ɛ̃dɔlɔr] *adj* : painless

infrarouge

indomptable [ɛ̃dɔ̃tabl] *adj* : indomitable

indu, -due [ɛ̃dy] *adj* : unseemly, ungodly

induire [ɛ̃dɥir] {49} *vt* **1** INCITER : incite, induce **2** CONCLURE : infer, conclude

indulgence [ɛ̃dylʒɑ̃s] *nf* : indulgence — **indulgent, -gente** [ɛ̃dylʒɑ̃, -ʒɑ̃t] *adj* : indulgent

indûment [ɛ̃dymɑ̃] *adv* : unduly

industrie [ɛ̃dystri] *nf* : industry — **industrialiser** [ɛ̃dystrijalize] *vt* : industrialize — **industriel, -trielle** [ɛ̃dystrijɛl] *adj* : industrial — **industrieux, -trieuse** [ɛ̃dystrijø, -trijøz] *adj* : industrious

inébranlable [inebrɑ̃labl] *adj* : unshakeable

inédit, -dite [inedi, -dit] *adj* **1** : unpublished **2** ORIGINAL : novel, original

inefficace [inefikas] *adj* **1** : inefficient **2** : ineffective — **inefficacité** [inefikasite] *nf* **1** : inefficiency **2** : ineffectiveness

inégal, -gale [inegal] *adj, mpl* **-gaux** [-go] **1** : unequal **2** IRRÉGULIER : uneven — **inégalé, -lée** [inegale] *adj* : unequaled — **inégalité** [inegalite] *nf* **1** : inequality **2** IRRÉGULARITÉ : unevenness, irregularity

inéligible [ineliʒibl] *adj* : ineligible

inéluctable [inelyktabl] *adj* : inescapable

inepte [inɛpt] *adj* : inept

inépuisable [inepɥizabl] *adj* : inexhaustible

inerte [inɛrt] *adj* **1** : inert, lifeless **2** APATHIQUE : apathetic — **inertie** [inɛrsi] *nf* **1** : inertia **2** APATHIE : apathy

inespéré, -rée [inɛspere] *adj* : unhoped for, unexpected

inestimable [inɛstimabl] *adj* : inestimable

inévitable [inevitabl] *adj* : inevitable — **inévitablement** [-tabləmɑ̃] *adv* : inevitably

inexact, -exacte [inɛgza(kt), -ɛgzakt] *adj* : inaccurate, incorrect

inexcusable [inɛkskyzabl] *adj* : inexcusable

inexistant, -tante [inɛgzistɑ̃, -tɑ̃t] *adj* : non-existent

inexpérience [inɛksperjɑ̃s] *nf* : inexperience — **inexpérimenté, -tée** [inɛksperimɑ̃te] *adj* : inexperienced

inexplicable [inɛksplikabl] *adj* : inexplicable — **inexpliqué, -quée** [inɛksplike] *adj* : unexplained

inexprimable [inɛksprimabl] *adj* : inexpressible

infaillible [ɛ̃fajibl] *adj* : infallible

infâme [ɛ̃fam] *adj* : vile — **infamie** [ɛ̃fam] *adj* : infamy

infanterie [ɛ̃fɑ̃tri] *nf* : infantry

infantile [ɛ̃fɑ̃til] *adj* : infantile, childish

infarctus [ɛ̃farktys] *nm or* ~ **myocarde** : heart attack

infatigable [ɛ̃fatigabl] *adj* : tireless

infect, -fecte [ɛ̃fɛkt] *adj* : revolting, foul — **infecter** [ɛ̃fɛkte] *vt* **1** : infect **2** : contami-

nate — **s'infecter** *vr* : become infected — **infectieux, -tieuse** [ɛ̃fɛksjø, -tjøz] *adj* : infectious — **infection** [ɛ̃fɛksjɔ̃] *nf* **1** : infection **2** PUANTEUR : stench

inférieur, -rieure [ɛ̃ferjœr] *adj & n* : inferior — **intériorité** [ɛ̃ferjɔrite] *nf* : inferiority

infernal, -nale [ɛ̃fɛrnal] *adj, mpl* **-naux** [-no] : infernal

infertile [ɛ̃fɛrtil] *adj* : infertile — **infertilité** [-tilite] *nf* : infertility

infester [ɛ̃fɛste] *vt* : infest

infidèle [ɛ̃fidɛl] *adj* : unfaithful — **infidélité** [ɛ̃fidelite] *nf* : infidelity

infiltrer [ɛ̃filtre] *vt* : infiltrate — **s'infiltrer** *vr* ~ **dans** : seep into, penetrate — **infiltration** [ɛ̃filtrasjɔ̃] *nf* : infiltration

infime [ɛ̃fim] *adj* : minute, tiny

infini, -nie [ɛ̃fini] *adj* : infinite — **infini** *nm* **1** : infinity **2 à l'**~ : endlessly — **infinité** [ɛ̃finite] *nf* **1** : infinity **2** : infinite number

infinitif [ɛ̃finitif] *nm* : infinitive

infirme [ɛ̃firm] *adj* : disabled, infirm — ~ *nmf* : disabled person — **infirmerie** [ɛ̃firmɔri] *nf* : infirmary — **infirmier, -mière** [ɛ̃firmje, -mjɛr] *n* : nurse — **infirmité** [ɛ̃firmite] *nf* : disability

inflammable [ɛ̃flamabl] *adj* : inflammable, flammable — **inflammation** [ɛ̃flamasjɔ̃] *nf* : inflammation

inflation [ɛ̃flasjɔ̃] *nf* : inflation — **inflationniste** [ɛ̃flasjɔnist] *adj* : inflationary

inflexible [ɛ̃flɛksibl] *adj* : inflexible, unbending — **inflexion** [ɛ̃flɛksjɔ̃] *nf* **1** : inflection (of the voice) **2** : nod (of the head)

infliger [ɛ̃fliʒe] {17} *vt* **1** : inflict **2** : impose (a penalty, etc.)

influence [ɛ̃flyɑ̃s] *nf* : influence — **influencer** [ɛ̃flyɑ̃se] {6} *vt* : influence — **influent, -fluente** [ɛ̃flyɑ̃, -flyɑ̃t] *adj* : influential — **influer** [ɛ̃flye] *vi* ~ **sur** : have an influence on

informateur, -trice [ɛ̃fɔrmatœr, -tris] *n* : informant, informer

informaticien, -cienne [ɛ̃fɔrmatisjɛ̃, -sjɛn] *n* : computer programmer

information [ɛ̃fɔrmasjɔ̃] *nf* **1** : information **2** ~**s** *nfpl* : news — **informatif, -tive** [ɛ̃fɔrmatif, -tiv] *adj* : informative

informatique [ɛ̃fɔrmatik] *adj* : computer — ~ *nf* : computer science — **informatiser** [ɛ̃fɔrmatize] *vt* : computerize

informe [ɛ̃fɔrm] *adj* : shapeless

informer [ɛ̃fɔrme] *vt* : inform — **s'informer** *vr* : inquire

infortune [ɛ̃fɔrtyn] *nf* : misfortune — **infortuné, -née** [ɛ̃fɔrtyne] *adj* : unfortunate

infraction [ɛ̃fraksjɔ̃] *nf* : breach (in law)

infranchissable [ɛ̃frɑ̃ʃisabl] *adj* **1** : insurmountable **2** IMPRACTICABLE : impassable

infrarouge [ɛ̃fraruʒ] *adj* : infrared

infrastructure [ɛ̃frastryktyr] *nf* : infrastructure

infructueux, -tueuse [ɛ̃fryktɥø, -tɥøz] *adj* : fruitless

infuser [ɛ̃fyze] *v* **1** : infuse **2** : brew (tea etc.) — **infusion** [ɛ̃tyzjɔ̃] *nf* : infusion

ingénieur, -nieure [ɛ̃ʒenjœr] *n* : engineer — **ingénierie** [ɛ̃ʒeniri] *nf* : engineering

ingénieux, -nieuse [ɛ̃ʒenjø, -njøz] *adj* : ingenious — **ingéniosité** [ɛ̃ʒenjozite] *nf* : ingenuity

ingénu, -nue [ɛ̃ʒeny] *adj* : ingenuous, naive

ingérence [ɛ̃ʒerɑ̃s] *nf* : interference

ingratitude [ɛ̃gratityd] *nf* : ingratitude — **ingrat, -grate** [ɛ̃gra, -grat] *adj* **1** : ungrateful **2** : thankless

ingrédient [ɛ̃gredjɑ̃] *nm* : ingredient

inhabitable [inabitabl] *adj* : uninhabitable — **inhabité, -tée** [inabite] *adj* : uninhabited

inhabituel, -tuelle [inabitɥɛl] *adj* : unusual

inhaler [inale] *vt* : inhale — **inhalation** [-alasjɔ̃] *nf* : inhaling

inhérent, -rente [inerɑ̃, -rɑ̃t] *adj* : inherent

inhiber [inibe] *vt* : inhibit — **inhibition** [inibisjɔ̃] *nf* : inhibition

inhumain, -maine [inymɛ̃, -mɛn] *adj* : inhuman — **inhumanité** [inymanite] *nf* : inhumanity

inhumer [inyme] *vt* : bury — **inhumation** [inymasjɔ̃] *nf* : burial

initial, -tiale [inisjal] *adj, mpl* **-tiaux** [-sjo] : initial — **initiale** *nf* : initial

initiative [inisjativ] *nf* : initiative

initier [inisje] {96} *vt* : initiate — **initiateur, -trice** [inisjatœr, -tris] *n* **1** : initiator **2** NOVATEUR : innovator — **initiation** [inisjasjɔ̃] *nf* : initiation

injecter [ɛ̃ʒɛkte] *vt* : inject — **injection** [ɛ̃ʒɛksjɔ̃] *nf* : injection

injonction [ɛ̃ʒɔ̃ksjɔ̃] *nf* : order, injunction

injure [ɛ̃ʒyr] *nf* : insult, abuse — **injurier** [ɛ̃ʒyrje] {96} *vt* : insult — **injurieux, -rieuse** [ɛ̃ʒyrjø, -rjøz] *adj* : insulting, abusive

injuste [ɛ̃ʒyst] *adj* : unjust, unfair — **injustice** [ɛ̃ʒystis] *nf* : injustice

injustifié, -fiée [ɛ̃ʒystifje] *adj* : unjustified

inlassable [ɛ̃lasabl] *adj* : tireless

inné, -née [ine] *adj* : innate, inborn

innocent, -cente [inɔsɑ̃, -sɑ̃t] *adj & n* : innocent — **innocence** [inɔsɑ̃s] *nf* : innocence — **innocenter** [inɔsɑ̃te] *vt* : clear, exonerate

innombrable [inɔ̃brabl] *adj* : innumerable, countless

innover [inɔve] *v* : innovate — **innovateur, -trice** [inɔvatœr, -tris] *adj* : innovative — *~ n* : innovator — **innovation** [inɔvasjɔ̃] *nf* : innovation

inoccupé, -pée [inɔkype] *adj* : unoccupied

inoculer [inɔkyle] *vt* : inoculate — **inoculation** [-kylasjɔ̃] *nf* : inoculation

inodore [inɔdɔr] *adj* : odorless

inoffensif, -sive [inɔfɑ̃sif, -siv] *adj* : inoffensive, harmless

inonder [inɔ̃de] *vt* : flood, inundate — **inondation** [inɔ̃dɑsjɔ̃] *nf* : flood

inopiné, -née [inɔpine] *adj* : unexpected

inopportun, -tune [inɔpɔrtœ̃, -tyn] *adj* : untimely

inoubliable [inublijabl] *adj* : unforgettable

inouï, inouïe [inwi] *adj* : incredible, unheard of

inquiet, -quiète [ɛ̃kjɛ, -kjɛt] *adj* : anxious, worried — **inquiétant, -tante** [ɛ̃kjetɑ̃, -tɑ̃t] *adj* : worrisome — **inquiéter** [ɛ̃kjete] {87} *vt* **1** : worry **2** DÉRANGER : bother, disturb — **s'inquiéter** *vr* : be worried — **inquiétude** [ɛ̃kjetyd] *nf* : worry, anxiety

inquisition [ɛ̃kizisjɔ̃] *nf* : inquisition

insaisissable [ɛ̃sezizabl] *adj* : elusive

insalubre [ɛ̃salybr] *adj* : unhealthy

insanité [ɛ̃sanite] *nf* : insanity

insatiable [ɛ̃sasjabl] *adj* : insatiable

insatisfait, -faite [ɛ̃satisfɛ, -fɛt] *adj* : dissatisfied — **insatisfaction** [ɛ̃satisfaksjɔ̃] *nf* : dissatisfaction

inscrire [ɛ̃skrir] {33} *vt* **1** ÉCRIRE : write down **2** ENREGISTRER : register, enroll — **s'inscrire** *vr* : register, enroll — **inscription** [ɛ̃skripsjɔ̃] *nf* **1** : inscription **2** : registration, enrollment

insecte [ɛ̃sɛkt] *nm* : insect — **insecticide** [ɛ̃sɛktisid] *nm* : insecticide

insécurité [ɛ̃sekyrite] *nf* : insecurity

insensé, -sée [ɛ̃sɑ̃se] *adj* : crazy, foolish

insensible [ɛ̃sɑ̃sibl] *adj* : insensitive — **insensibilité** [ɛ̃sɑ̃sibilite] *nf* : insensitivity

inséparable [ɛ̃separabl] *adj* : inseparable

insérer [ɛ̃sere] {87} *vt* : insert

insidieux, -dieuse [ɛ̃sidjø, -djøz] *adj* : insidious

insigne [ɛ̃siɲ] *nm* **1** : badge **2** *or* *~s nmpl* : insignia

insignifiant, -fiante [ɛ̃siɲifjɑ̃, -fjɑ̃t] *adj* : insignificant — **insignifiance** [-ɲifjɑ̃s] *nf* : insignificance

insinuation [ɛ̃sinɥasjɔ̃] *nf* : insinuation — **insinuer** [ɛ̃sinɥe] *vt* : insinuate — **s'insinuer** *vr* *~ dans* : insinuate oneself into, penetrate

insipide [ɛ̃sipid] *adj* : insipid

insister [ɛ̃siste] *vi* **1** : insist **2** *~ sur* : emphasize, stress — **insistance** [ɛ̃sistɑ̃s] *nf* : insistence — **insistant, -tante** [ɛ̃sistɑ̃, -tɑ̃t] *adj* : insistent

insociable [ɛ̃sɔsjabl] *adj* : unsociable

insolation [ɛ̃sɔlasjɔ̃] *nf* : sunstroke

insolent, -lente [ɛ̃sɔlɑ̃, -lɑ̃t] *adj* : insolent — **insolence** [ɛ̃sɔlɑ̃s] *nf* : insolence

insolite [ɛ̃sɔlit] *adj* : unusual, bizarre

insoluble [ɛ̃sɔlybl] *adj* : insoluble

insolvable [ɛ̃sɔlvabl] *adj* : insolvent
insomnie [ɛ̃sɔmni] *nf* : insomnia
insondable [ɛ̃sɔ̃dabl] *adj* **1** : bottomless **2** IMPÉNÉTRABLE : unfathomable
insonoriser [ɛ̃sɔnɔrize] *vt* : soundproof
insouciant, -ciante [ɛ̃susjɑ̃, -sjɑ̃t] *adj* : carefree — **insouciance** [ɛ̃susjɑ̃s] *nf* : carefree attitude
insoutenable [ɛ̃sutnabl] *adj* **1** : untenable **2** INTOLÉRABLE : unbearable
inspecter [ɛ̃spɛkte] *vt* : inspect — **inspecteur, -trice** [ɛ̃spɛktœr, -tris] *n* : inspector — **inspection** [ɛ̃spɛksjɔ̃] *nf* : inspection
inspirer [ɛ̃spire] *vt* : inspire — *vi* : inhale — **s'inspirer** *vr* ~ **de** : be inspired by — **inspirant, -rante** [ɛ̃spirɑ̃, -rɑ̃t] *adj* : inspirational — **inspiration** [ɛ̃spirasjɔ̃] *nf* **1** : inspiration **2** : breathing in
instable [ɛ̃stabl] *adj* **1** BRANLANT : unsteady **2** : unstable, unsettled — **instabilité** [ɛ̃stabilite] *nf* : instability
installer [ɛ̃stale] *vt* : install, set up — **s'installer** *vr* : settle (in) — **installation** [ɛ̃stalasjɔ̃] *nf* **1** : installation **2** ~s *nfpl* : installations, facilities
instance [ɛ̃stɑ̃s] *nf* **1** AUTORITÉ : authority **2** : legal proceedings **3 en** ~ : pending
instant [ɛ̃stɑ̃] *nm* : instant, moment — **instantané, -née** [ɛ̃stɑ̃tane] *adj* : instantaneous, instant — **instantané** *nm* : snapshot
instar [ɛ̃star] **à l'**~ **de** *prep phr* : following the example of, like
instaurer [ɛ̃store] *vt* : institute, establish — **instauration** [ɛ̃storasjɔ̃] *nf* : institution
instigateur, -trice [ɛ̃stigatœr, -tris] *n* : instigator — **instigation** [ɛ̃stigasjɔ̃] *nf* : instigation
instinct [ɛ̃stɛ̃] *nm* : instinct — **instinctif, -tive** [ɛ̃stɛ̃ktif, -tiv] *adj* : instinctive, instinctual
instituer [ɛ̃stitɥe] *vt* **1** : institute, establish **2** NOMMER : appoint — **institut** [ɛ̃stity] *nm* : institute — **instituteur, -trice** [ɛ̃stitytœr, -tris] *n* : schoolteacher — **institution** [ɛ̃stitysjɔ̃] *nf* : institution
instruction [ɛ̃stryksjɔ̃] *nf* **1** : instruction, education **2** ~s *nfpl* : instructions — **instruire** [ɛ̃strɥir] {49} *vt* **1** : instruct **2** ~ **de** : inform of — **s'instruire** *vr* **1** : educate oneself **2** ~ **de** : find out about — **instruit, -truite** [ɛ̃strɥi, -trɥit] *adj* : learned, educated
instrument [ɛ̃strymɑ̃] *nm* : instrument — **instrumental, -tale** [ɛ̃strymɑ̃tal] *adj, mpl* **-taux** [-to] : instrumental
insu [ɛ̃sy] **à l'**~ **de** *prep phr* : without the knowledge of, unknown to
insuffisant, -sante [ɛ̃syfizɑ̃, -zɑ̃t] *adj* : insufficient, inadequate — **insuffisance** [ɛ̃syfizɑ̃s] *nf* : inadequacy

insulaire [ɛ̃sylɛr] *adj* : island, insular — ~ *nmf* : islander
insuline [ɛ̃sylin] *nf* : insulin
insulter [ɛ̃sylte] *vt* : insult — **insulte** [ɛ̃sylt] *nf* : insult
insupportable [ɛ̃sypɔrtabl] *adj* : unbearable
insurger [ɛ̃syrʒe] {17} *v* **s'insurger** *vr* : rebel, rise up — **insurgé, -gée** [ɛ̃syrʒe] *n* : insurgent, rebel
insurmontable [ɛ̃syrmɔ̃tabl] *adj* : insurmountable
insurrection [ɛ̃syrɛksjɔ̃] *nf* : insurrection
intact, -tacte [ɛ̃takt] *adj* : intact
intangible [ɛ̃tɑ̃ʒibl] *adj* : intangible
intarissable [ɛ̃tarisabl] *adj* : inexhaustible
intégral, -grale [ɛ̃tegral] *adj, mpl* **-graux** [-gro] **1** : complete **2** : unabridged — **intégralité** [ɛ̃tegralite] *nf* : whole — **intégrant, -grante** [ɛ̃tegrɑ̃, -grɑ̃t] *adj* **faire partie intégrante de** : be an integral part of
intègre [ɛ̃tɛgr] *adj* : honest, upright
intégrer [ɛ̃tegre] {87} *vt* : integrate — **s'intégrer** *vr* : integrate
intégrité [ɛ̃tegrite] *nf* : integrity
intellect [ɛ̃telɛkt] *nm* : intellect — **intellectuel, -tuelle** [ɛ̃telɛktɥel] *adj & n* : intellectual
intelligent, -gente [ɛ̃teliʒɑ̃, -ʒɑ̃t] *adj* : intelligent — **intelligence** [ɛ̃teliʒɑ̃s] *nf* **1** : intelligence **2** COMPRÉHENSION : understanding — **intelligible** [ɛ̃teliʒibl] *adj* : intelligible, comprehensible
intempéries [ɛ̃tɑ̃peri] *nfpl* : bad weather
intempestif, -tive [ɛ̃tɑ̃pɛstif, -tiv] *adj* : untimely
intense [ɛ̃tɑ̃s] *adj* : intense — **intensément** [ɛ̃tɑ̃semɑ̃] *adv* : intensely — **intensif, -sive** [ɛ̃tɑ̃sif, -siv] *adj* : intensive — **intensifier** [ɛ̃tɑ̃sifje] {96} *vt* : intensify — **intensité** [ɛ̃tɑ̃site] *nf* : intensity
intenter [ɛ̃tɑ̃te] *vt* : initiate, pursue (legal action)
intention [ɛ̃tɑ̃sjɔ̃] *nf* : intention, intent — **intentionnel, -nelle** [ɛ̃tɑ̃sjɔnɛl] *adj* : intentional
interactif, -tive [ɛ̃tɛraktif, -tiv] *adj* : interactive — **interaction** [ɛ̃tɛraksjɔ̃] *nf* : interaction
intercaler [ɛ̃tɛrkale] *vt* : insert
intercéder [ɛ̃tɛrsede] {87} *vi* : intercede
intercepter [ɛ̃tɛrsɛpte] *vt* : intercept
interchangeable [ɛ̃tɛrʃɑ̃ʒabl] *adj* : interchangeable
intercontinental, -tale [ɛ̃tɛrkɔ̃tinɑ̃tal] *adj, mpl* **-taux** [-to] : intercontinental
interdire [ɛ̃tɛrdir] {29} *vt* **1** : ban, prohibit **2** EMPÊCHER : prevent — **interdiction** [ɛ̃tɛrdiksjɔ̃] *nf* : ban, prohibition — **interdit, -dite** [ɛ̃tɛrdi, -dit] *adj* **1** : prohibited **2** STUPÉFAIT : dumbfounded

intéresser

intéresser [ɛterese] *vt* **1** : interest **2** CON-CERNER : concern — **s'intéresser** *vr* ~ **à** : be interested in — **intéressant, -sante** [ɛteresã, -sãt] *adj* **1** : interesting **2** AVAN-TAGEUX : attractive, worthwhile — **in-téressé, -sée** *adj* **1** : self-interested **2** CONCERNÉ : concerned — ~ *n* : interested party — **intérêt** [ɛtere] *nm* : interest

interface [ɛterfas] *nf* : interface

interférence [ɛterferãs] *nf* : interference — **interférer** [ɛterfere] {87} *vi* : interfere

intérieur, -rieure [ɛterjœr] *adj* **1** : inner, inside **2** : internal, domestic (in politics) — **intérieur** *nm* **1** : inside (of a drawer, etc.) **2** : interior, home **3 à l'~** : indoors **4 d'~** : indoor — **intérieurement** [ɛterjœrmã] *adv* : inwardly, internally

intérim [ɛterim] *nm* **1** : interim (period) **2** : temporary activity — **intérimaire** [ɛterimɛr] *adj* : temporary, acting — ~ *nmf* : temporary employee

interjection [ɛterʒɛksjɔ̃] *nf* : interjection

interlocuteur, -trice [ɛterlɔkytœr, -tris] *n* : speaker

intermède [ɛtermɛd] *nm* : interlude

intermédiaire [ɛtermedjɛr] *adj* : intermediate — ~ *nmf* : intermediary, go-between

interminable [ɛterminabl] *adj* : interminable

intermittent, -tente [ɛtermitã, -tãt] *adj* : intermittent, sporadic — **intermittence** [ɛtermitãs] *nf* **par** ~ : intermittently

international, -nale [ɛternasjonal] *adj, mpl* **-naux** [-no] : international

interne [ɛtern] *adj* : internal

interner [ɛterne] *vt* **1** : intern (in politics) **2** : confine (in medicine)

interpeller [ɛterpəle] *vt* **1** : shout at, call out to **2** INTERROGER : question

interphone [ɛterfɔn] *nm* : intercom

interposer [ɛterpoze] *v* **s'interposer** *vr* : intervene

interpréter [ɛterprete] {87} *vt* **1** : interpret **2** : perform, play (a role) — **interprétation** [ɛterpretasjɔ̃] *nf* : interpretation — **interprète** [ɛterprɛt] *nmf* **1** : interpreter **2** REPRÉSENTANT : spokesperson **3** : performer (in theater, etc.)

interroger [ɛterɔʒe] {17} *vt* : interrogate, question — **s'interroger** *vr* ~ **sur** : wonder about — **interrogateur, -trice** [ɛterɔgatœr, -tris] *adj* : questioning — **interrogatif, -tive** [ɛterɔgatif, -tiv] *adj* : interrogative — **interrogation** [ɛterɔgasjɔ̃] *nf* **1** : interrogation **2** : test (in school) — **interrogatoire** [ɛterɔgatwar] *nm* : interrogation, questioning

interrompre [ɛterɔ̃pr] {77} *v* : interrupt — **s'interrompre** *vr* : break off — **interrupteur** [ɛteryptœr] *nm* : switch — **interrup-**

-tion [ɛterypsjɔ̃] *nf* **1** : interruption **2 sans** ~ : continuously

intersection [ɛtersɛksjɔ̃] *nf* : intersection

interurbain, -baine [ɛteryrbɛ̃, -bɛn] *adj* : long-distance — **interurbain** *nm* : long-distance telephone service

intervalle [ɛterval] *nm* **1** : space, gap **2** : interval (of time) **3 dans l'~** : in the meantime

intervenir [ɛtervənir] {92} *vi* **1** : intervene **2** SURVENIR : take place **3** : operate (in medicine) — **intervention** [ɛtervãsjɔ̃] *nf* **1** : intervention **2** OPERATION : (medical) operation

intervertir [ɛtervertir] *vt* : invert, reverse

interview [ɛtervju] *nf* : interview — **interviewer** [ɛtervjuve] *vt* : interview

intestin [ɛtestɛ̃] *nm* : intestine — **intestinal, -nale** [ɛtestinal] *adj, mpl* **-naux** [-no] : intestinal

intime [ɛtim] *adj* **1** : intimate **2** PERSONNEL : private — ~ *nmf* : close friend

intimider [ɛtimide] *vt* : intimidate — **intimidant, -dante** [ɛtimidã, -dãt] *adj* : intimidating — **intimidation** [-midasjɔ̃] *nf* : intimidation

intimité [ɛtimite] *nf* : intimacy

intituler [ɛtityle] *vt* : call, title — **s'intituler** *vr* : be called

intolérable [ɛtɔlerabl] *adj* : intolerable, unbearable — **intolérant, -rante** [ɛtɔlerã, -rãt] *adj* : intolerant — **intolérance** [-rãs] *nf* : intolerance

intonation [ɛtɔnasjɔ̃] *nf* : intonation

intoxiquer [ɛtɔksike] *vt* EMPOISONNER : poison — **intoxication** [ɛtɔksikasjɔ̃] *nf* : poisoning

intransigeant, -geante [ɛtrãziʒɑ, -ʒãt] *adj* : uncompromising

intransitif, -tive [ɛtrãzitif, -tiv] *adj* : intransitive

intraveineux, -neuse [ɛtravɛnø, -nøz] *adj* : intravenous

intrépide [ɛtrepid] *adj* : intrepid, fearless

intriguer [ɛtrige] *vt* : intrigue, puzzle — *vi* : plot, scheme — **intrigue** [ɛtrig] *nf* **1** : intrigue **2** : plot (of a story)

intrinsèque [ɛtrɛ̃sɛk] *adj* : intrinsic

introduire [ɛtrɔdɥir] {49} *vt* **1** : introduce **2** : show in, bring in **3** INSÉRER : insert **4** : enter, input (data) — **s'introduire** *vr* : penetrate, get in — **introduction** [ɛtrɔdyksjɔ̃] *nf* **1** : introduction **2** : insertion

introuvable [ɛtruvabl] *adj* : unobtainable, nowhere to be found

introverti, -tie [ɛtrɔverti] *adj* : introverted — ~ *n* : introvert

intrusion [ɛtryzjɔ̃] *nf* : intrusion — **intrus, -truse** [ɛtry, -tryz] *n* : intruder

intuition [ɛ̃tɥisjɔ̃] *nf* : intuition — **intuitif, -tive** [ɛ̃tɥitif, -tiv] *adj* : intuitive

Inuit [inɥi] *adj* : Inuit

inusable [inyzabl] *adj* : durable

inusité, -tée [inyzite] *adj* : unusual, uncommon

inutile [inytil] *adj* **1** : useless **2** SUPERFLU : pointless — **inutilement** [inytilmã] *adv* : needlessly — **inutilisable** [inytilizabl] *adj* : unusable — **inutilité** [inytilite] *nf* : uselessness

invalide [ɛ̃valid] *adj* : disabled — ~ *nmf* : disabled person — **invalidité** [ɛ̃validite] *nf* : disability

invariable [ɛ̃varjabl] *adj* : invariable

invasion [ɛ̃vazjɔ̃] *nf* : invasion

inventaire [ɛ̃vɑ̃ter] *nm* **1** : inventory **2 faire l'**~ : take stock

invention [ɛ̃vɑ̃sjɔ̃] *nf* : invention — **inventer** [ɛ̃vɑ̃te] *vt* : invent — **inventeur, -trice** [ɛ̃vɑ̃tœr, -tris] *n* : inventor — **inventif, -tive** [ɛ̃vɑ̃tif, -tiv] *adj* : inventive

inverse [ɛ̃vers] *adj* : reverse, opposite — ~ *nm* : reverse, opposite — **inversement** [ɛ̃versəmã] *adv* : conversely — **inverser** [ɛ̃verse] *vt* : reverse, invert

invertébré, -brée [ɛ̃vertebre] *adj* : invertebrate — **invertébré** *nm* : invertebrate

investigation [ɛ̃vestigasjɔ̃] *nf* : investigation

investir [ɛ̃vestir] *v* : invest — **investissement** [ɛ̃vestismã] *nm* : investment — **investisseur, -seuse** [ɛ̃vestisœr, -søz] *n* : investor

invétéré, -rée [ɛ̃vetere] *adj* : inveterate

invincible [ɛ̃vɛ̃sibl] *adj* : invincible

invisible [ɛ̃vizibl] *adj* : invisible

inviter [ɛ̃vite] *vt* : invite — **invitation** [ɛ̃vitasjɔ̃] *nf* : invitation — **invité, -tée** [ɛ̃vite] *n* : guest

involontaire [ɛ̃vɔlɔ̃ter] *adj* : involuntary

invoquer [ɛ̃vɔke] *vt* : invoke

invraisemblable [ɛ̃vrɛsɑ̃blabl] *adj* : improbable, unlikely

invulnérable [ɛ̃vylnerabl] *adj* : invulnerable

iode [jɔd] *nm* : iodine

ion [jɔ̃] *nm* : ion

iris [iris] *nm* : iris

irlandais, -daise [irlɑ̃dɛ, -dɛz] *adj* : Irish

ironie [irɔni] *nf* : irony — **ironique** [irɔnik] *adj* : ironic(al)

irradier [iradje] {96} *vt* : irradiate — *vi* : radiate

irrationnel, -nelle [irasjɔnɛl] *adj* : irrational

irréalisable [irealizabl] *adj* : unworkable

irréconciliable [irekɔ̃siljabl] *adj* : irreconcilable

irrécupérable [irekyperabl] *adj* : irretrievable, beyond repair

irréel, -réelle [ireel] *adj* : unreal

irréfléchi, -chie [irefleʃi] *adj* : thoughtless, rash

irréfutable [irefytabl] *adj* : irrefutable

irrégulier, -lière [iregylje, -ljɛr] *adj* : irregular — **irrégularité** [iregylarite] *nf* : irregularity

irrémédiable [iremedjabl] *adj* : irreparable

irremplaçable [irɑ̃plasabl] *adj* : irreplaceable

irréparable [ireparabl] *adj* : irreparable

irréprochable [ireprɔʃabl] *adj* : irreproachable, blameless

irrésistible [irezistibl] *adj* : irresistible

irrésolu, -lue [irezɔly] *adj* **1** INDÉCIS : irresolute **2** : unresolved (of a problem)

irrespectueux, -tueuse [irespɛktɥø, -tɥøz] *adj* : disrespectful

irresponsable [irespɔ̃sabl] *adj* : irresponsible — **irresponsabilité** [irespɔ̃sabilite] *nf* : irresponsibility

irrigation [irigasjɔ̃] *nf* : irrigation — **irriguer** [irige] *vt* : irrigate

irriter [irite] *vt* : irritate — **s'irriter** *vr* : get irritated — **irritable** [iritabl] *adj* : irritable — **irritation** [iritasjɔ̃] *nf* : irritation

irruption [irypsjɔ̃] *nf* : bursting in

islam [islam] *nm* : Islam — **islamique** [islamik] *adj* : Islamic

isoler [izɔle] *vt* **1** : isolate **2** : insulate — **s'isoler** *vr* : isolate oneself — **isolation** [izɔlasjɔ̃] *nf* : insulation — **isolement** [izɔlmã] *nm* **1** : isolation **2** ISOLATION : insulation — **isolément** [izɔlemã] *adv* : separately, individually

israélien, -lienne [israeljɛ̃, -ljɛn] *adj* : Israeli

issu, -sue [isy] *adj* ~ **de 1** : descended from **2** : resulting from

issue *nf* **1** SORTIE : exit **2** SOLUTION : solution **3** FIN : ending, outcome

isthme [ism] *nm* : isthmus

italien, -lienne [italjɛ̃, -ljɛn] *adj* : Italian — **italien** *nm* : Italian (language)

italique [italik] *nf* : italics *pl*

itinéraire [itinerɛr] *nm* : itinerary

itinérant, -rante [itinerɑ̃, -rɑ̃t] *adj* : itinerant

ivoire [ivwar] *adj & nm* : ivory

ivre [ivr] *adj* : drunk — **ivresse** [ivrɛs] *nf* : drunkenness — **ivrogne, ivrognesse** [ivrɔɲ, -ɲɛs] *n* : drunkard

J

j [ʒi] *nm* : j, 10th letter of the alphabet
jacasser [ʒakase] *vi* : chatter, jabber
jachère [ʒaʃɛr] *nf* : fallow land
jacinthe [ʒasɛ̃t] *nf* : hyacinth
jadis [ʒadis] *adv* : in times past, formerly
jaillir [ʒajir] *vi* **1** : spurt out, gush (out) **2** APPARAÎTRE : spring up, emerge
jais [ʒɛ] *nms & pl* **1** : jet (stone) **2 de ~** : jet-black
jalon [ʒalɔ̃] *nm* : marker, milestone — **jalonner** [ʒalɔne] *vt* **1** : mark out (a route, etc.) **2** LONGER : line
jaloux, -louse [ʒalu, -luz] *adj* : jealous — **jalouser** [ʒaluze] *vt* : be jealous of — **jalousie** [ʒaluzi] *nf* **1** : jealousy **2** : venetian blind
jamais [ʒamɛ] *adv* **1** : ever **2 ne ... ~** : never **3 à ~** *or* **pour ~** : forever
jambe [ʒɑ̃b] *nf* : leg
jambon [ʒɑ̃bɔ̃] *nm* : ham
jante [ʒɑ̃t] *nf* : rim (of a wheel)
janvier [ʒɑ̃vje] *nm* : January
japonais, -naise [ʒapɔnɛ, -nɛz] *adj* : Japanese — **japonais** *nm* : Japanese (language)
japper [ʒape] *vi* : yap, yelp
jaquette [ʒakɛt] *nf* **1** : dust jacket **2** : jacket (for women)
jardin [ʒardɛ̃] *nm* **1** : garden **2 ~ d'enfants** *France* : kindergarten **3 ~ zoologique** : zoo — **jardinage** [ʒardinaʒ] *nm* : gardening — **jardiner** [ʒardine] *vi* : garden — **jardinier, -nière** [ʒardinje, -njɛr] *n* : gardener — **jardinière** *nf* : plant stand, window box
jargon [ʒargɔ̃] *nm* **1** : jargon **2** CHARABIA : gibberish
jarre [ʒar] *nf* : (earthenware) jar
jarret [ʒarɛ] *nm* **1** : back of the knee **2** : shank (in cooking) — **jarretelle** [ʒartɛl] *nf* : garter belt — **jarretière** [ʒartjɛr] *nf* : garter
jaser [ʒaze] *vi* **1** : chatter, prattle **2** MÉDIRE : gossip
jatte [ʒat] *nf* : bowl, basin
jauge [ʒoʒ] *nf* **1** : capacity **2** INDICATEUR : gauge — **jauger** [ʒoʒe] {17} *vt* : gauge
jaune [ʒon] *adj* : yellow — **~** *nm* **1** : yellow **2** *or* **~ d'œuf** : egg yolk — **jaunir** [ʒonir] *v* : turn yellow — **jaunisse** [ʒonis] *nf* : jaundice
Javel [ʒavɛl] *nf* → **eau**
javelot [ʒavlo] *nm* : javelin
jazz [dʒaz] *nm* : jazz
je [ʒə] (**j'** *before vowel or mute h*) *pron* : I
jean [dʒin] *nm* **1** : denim **2** : (blue) jeans *pl*
jeep [dʒip] *nf* : jeep
jersey [ʒɛrzɛ] *nm* : jersey (fabric)

Jésus [ʒezy] *nm* : Jesus
jeter [ʒəte] {8} *vt* **1** LANCER : throw **2** : throw away **3** ÉMETTRE : give off **4 ~ l'éponge** : throw in the towel **5 ~ un coup d'œil** : take a look at **6 ~ un sort** : cast a spell — **se jeter** *vr* **1 ~ dans** : flow into **2 ~ sur** : pounce on — **jet** [ʒɛ] *nm* **1** : jet, spurt **2** LANCER : throw, throwing **3** : jet (airplane) **4 ~ d'eau** : fountain — **jetable** [ʒətabl] *adj* : disposable — **jetée** [ʒəte] *nf* : pier, jetty
jeton [ʒətɔ̃] *nm* : token, counter
jeu [ʒø] *nm, pl* **jeux 1** DIVERTISSEMENT : play **2** : game **3** : set (of chess, etc.), deck (of playing cards) **4 ~ de dames** : checkers **5 ~ de mots** : pun **6 en ~** : at stake **7 le ~** : gambling
jeudi [ʒødi] *nm* : Thursday
jeun [ʒœ̃] **à ~** *adv phr* : on an empty stomach
jeune [ʒœn] *adj* **1** : young **2** CADET : younger **3** RÉCENT : new, recent — **~** *nmf* **1** : young person **2 les ~s** : young people
jeûner [ʒøne] *vi* : fast — **jeûne** [ʒøn] *nm* : fast
jeunesse [ʒœnɛs] *nf* **1** : youth **2** : youthfulness **3** JEUNES : young people
joaillier, -lière [ʒɔaje, -jɛr] *n* : jeweler — **joaillerie** [ʒɔajri] *nf* **1** : jewelry store **2** : jewelry
job [dʒɔb] *nm fam* : job
jockey [ʒɔkɛ] *nm* : jockey
jogging [dʒɔgiŋ] *nm* **1** : jogging **2** : sweat suit
joie [ʒwa] *nf* : joy
joindre [ʒwɛ̃dr] {50} *vt* **1** : join, link, combine **2** INCLURE : enclose, attach **3** CONTACTER : reach, contact — **se joindre** *vr* **1** : join together **2 ~ à** : join in — **joint** [ʒwɛ̃] *nm* **1** : joint **2** : seal, washer
joker [ʒɔkɛr] *nm* : joker (in playing cards)
joli, -lie [ʒɔli] *adj* **1** BEAU : pretty, attractive **2** : nice — **joliment** [ʒɔlimɑ̃] *adv* **1** : nicely **2** *fam* : really, awfully
jonc [ʒɔ̃] *nm* **1** : reed, rush **2** : (wedding) band
joncher [ʒɔ̃ʃe] *vt* **~ de** : strew with, litter with
jonction [ʒɔ̃ksjɔ̃] *nf* : junction
jongler [ʒɔ̃gle] *vi* : juggle — **jongleur, -gleuse** [ʒɔ̃glœr, -gløz] *n* : juggler
jonquille [ʒɔ̃kij] *nf* : daffodil
joue [ʒu] *nf* : cheek
jouer [ʒwe] *vi* **1** : play **2** : act, perform **3** PARIER : gamble **4 faire ~** : flex — *vt* **1** : play **2** PARIER : bet, wager **3** : perform —

jouet [ʒwɛ] *nm* : toy, plaything — **joueur, joueuse** [ʒwœr, ʒwøz] *n* **1** : player **2** : gambler

jouffflu, -flue [ʒuflУ] *adj* : chubby-cheeked

joug [ʒu] *nm* : yoke

jouir [ʒwir] *vi* ~ **de** : enjoy — **jouissance** [ʒwisãs] *nf* **1** : pleasure **2** : use, (legal) possession

jour [ʒur] *nm* **1** : day **2** : daylight, daytime **3** ASPECT : aspect, light **4** ~ **de l'An** : New Year's Day **5 de nos** ~**s** : nowadays **6 donner le** ~ **à** : give birth to **7 mettre à** ~ : update

journal [ʒurnal] *nm, pl* **-naux 1** : diary, journal **2** : newspaper **3** ~ **télévisé** : television news

journalier, -lière [ʒurnalje, -ljɛr] *adj* : daily — ~ *n* : day worker, laborer

journaliste [ʒurnalist] *nmf* : journalist — **journalisme** [ʒurnalism] *nm* : journalism

journée [ʒurne] *nf* **1** : day **2 toute la** ~ : all day long

jovial, -viale [ʒɔvjal] *adj, mpl* **-vials** *or* **-viaux** [-vjo] : jovial

joyau [ʒwajo] *nm, pl* **joyaux** : jewel, gem

joyeux, joyeuse [ʒwajø, -jøz] *adj* **1** : joyful, happy **2 Joyeux Noël!** : Merry Christmas!

jubiler [ʒybile] *vi* : rejoice, be jubilant — **jubilé** [ʒybile] *nm* : jubilee — **jubilation** [ʒybilasjõ] *nf* : jubilation

jucher [ʒyʃe] *v* **se jucher** *vr* ~ **sur** : perch on

judaïque [ʒydaik] *adj* : Judaic — **judaïsme** [ʒydaism] *nm* : Judaism

judiciaire [ʒydisjɛr] *adj* : judicial — **judicieux, -cieuse** [ʒydisjø, -sjøz] *adj* : judicious

judo [ʒydo] *nm* : judo

juger [ʒyʒe] {17} *vt* **1** ÉVALUER : judge **2** CONSIDÉRER : think, consider **3** : try (in law) **4** ~ **de** : assess — **se juger** *vr* : consider oneself — **juge** [ʒyʒ] *nm* : judge — **jugement** [ʒyʒmã] *nm* **1** : judgment, opinion **2** VERDICT : verdict, sentence

juguler [ʒygyle] *vt* : stifle, suppress

juif, juive [ʒɥif, ʒɥiv] *adj* : Jewish

juillet [ʒɥijɛ] *nm* : July

juin [ʒɥɛ̃] *nm* : June

jumeau, -melle [ʒymo, -mɛl] *adj & n, mpl* **-meaux** : twin — **jumeler** [ʒymle] {8} *vt* : twin, couple — **jumelles** [ʒymɛl] *nfpl* : binoculars, field glasses

jument [ʒymã] *nf* : mare

jungle [ʒœ̃gl] *nf* : jungle

junior [ʒynjɔr] *adj & nmf* : junior

jupe [ʒyp] *nf* : skirt — **jupon** [ʒypõ] *nm* : slip, petticoat

jurer [ʒyre] *vt* : swear, vow — *vi* **1** : swear, curse **2** ~ **avec** : clash with **3** ~ **de** : swear to — **juré, -rée** [ʒyre] *n* : juror

juridiction [ʒyridiksjõ] *nf* : jurisdiction

juridique [ʒyridik] *adj* : legal

juriste [ʒyrist] *nmf* : legal expert, lawyer

juron [ʒyrõ] *nm* : swearword

jury [ʒyri] *nm* : jury

jus [ʒy] *nms & pl* **1** : juice **2** : gravy

jusque [ʒyskə] (**jusqu'** [ʒysk] *before a vowel*) *prep* **1** : even **2** *or* **jusqu'à** : up to, as far as **3 jusqu'à** *or* **jusqu'en** : until **4 jusqu'à présent** : up to now **5 jusqu'où?** : how far?

justaucorps [ʒystokɔr] *nms & pl* : leotard

juste [ʒyst] *adj* **1** ÉQUITABLE : just, fair **2** EXACT : correct, accurate **3** SERRÉ : tight **4 au** ~ : exactly, precisely — ~ *adv* **1** : just, exactly **2** : in tune **3** *or* **tout** ~ : only just, barely — **justement** [ʒystəmã] *adv* **1** EXACTEMENT : exactly, precisely **2** ÉQUITABLEMENT : justly **3** : just now — **justesse** [ʒystɛs] *nf* **1** PRÉCISION : accuracy **2** : soundness (of reasoning, etc.) **3 de** ~ : just barely

justice [ʒystis] *nf* **1** ÉQUITÉ : fairness **2** : law, justice

justifier [ʒystifje] {96} *vt* : justify — *vi* ~ **de** : give proof of — **se justifier** *vr* : justify oneself — **justification** [ʒystifikasjõ] *nf* : justification

juteux, -teuse [ʒytø, -tøz] *adj* : juicy

juvénile [ʒyvenil] *adj* : youthful, juvenile

juxtaposer [ʒykstapoze] *vt* : juxtapose

K

k [ka] *nm* : k, 11th letter of the alphabet

kaki [kaki] *adj* : khaki

kangourou [kãguru] *nm* : kangaroo

karaté [karate] *nm* : karate

kascher [kaʃɛr] *adj* : kosher

kayak *or* **kayac** [kajak] *nm* : kayak

kermesse [kɛrmɛs] *nf* : fair, bazaar

kérosène [kerozɛn] *nm* : kerosene

ketchup [kɛtʃœp] *nm* : ketchup

kidnapper [kidnape] *vt* : kidnap — **kidnappeur, -peuse** [kidnapœr, -pøz] *n* : kidnapper

kilo [kilo] *nm* : kilo — **kilogramme** [kilɔgram] *nm* : kilogram — **kilomètre** [kilɔmɛtr] *nm* : kilometer — **kilométrage** [kilɔmetraʒ] *nm* : distance in kilometers, mileage — **kilowatt** [kilowat] *nm* : kilowatt

kimono [kimɔno] *nm* : kimono

kinésithérapie [kinezjterapi] *nf* : physical therapy

kiosque [kjɔsk] *nm* **1** : kiosk, stall **2** ~ **à musique** : bandstand

kiwi [kiwi] *nm* : kiwi

klaxon [klaksɔn] *nm* : horn — **klaxonner** [klaksone] *vi* : honk

kyrielle [kirjɛl] *nf* **une** ~ **de** : a string of

kyste [kist] *nm* : cyst

L

l [ɛl] *nm* : l, 12th letter of the alphabet

l' *pron & art* → **le**

la *pron & art* → **le**

là [la] *adv* **1** (*indicating a place*) : there, here **2** : then **3** (*indicating a situation or a certain point*) : when **4 de** ~ : hence **5** ~ **où** : where **6 par** ~ : over there, that way — **là‑bas** [laba] *adv* : over there

label [labɛl] *nm* : label

labeur [labœr] *nm* : toil, labor

laboratoire [labɔratwar] *nm* : laboratory

laborieux, -rieuse [labɔrjø, -rjøz] *adj* **1** : laborious **2** INDUSTRIEUX : hardworking

labourer [labure] *vt* : plow — **labour** [labur] *nm* : plowing

labyrinthe [labirɛ̃t] *nm* : labyrinth, maze

lac [lak] *nm* : lake

lacer [lase] {6} *vt* : lace up

lacérer [lasere] {87} *vt* : tear up, shred

lacet [lasɛ] *nm* **1** : shoelace **2** : sharp bend (in a road)

lâcher [laʃe] *vt* **1** RELÂCHER : loosen **2** LIBÉRER : release **3** : let out (a word, etc.) **4** *fam* : drop (someone) — *vi* : give way — **lâche** [laʃ] *adj* **1** : loose, slack **2** POLTRON : cowardly — ~ *nmf* : coward — **lâcheté** [laʃte] *nf* : cowardice

laconique [lakɔnik] *adj* : laconic

lacrymogène [lakrimɔʒɛn] *adj* **gaz** ~ : tear gas

lacune [lakyn] *nf* : gap

là‑dedans [laddɑ̃] *adv* : in here, in there

là‑dessous [ladsu] *adv* : under here, under there

là‑dessus [ladsy] *adv* **1** : on here, on there **2 il n'y a aucun doute** ~ : there's no doubt about it

ladite → **ledit**

lagune [lagyn] *nf* : lagoon

là‑haut [lao] *adv* **1** : up there **2** : upstairs

laïc [laik] *nm* **les** ~**s** : the laity

laid, laide [lɛ, lɛd] *adj* **1** : ugly **2** : despicable (of an action) — **laideur** [lɛdœr] *nf* : ugliness

laine [lɛn] *nf* : wool — **lainage** [lɛnaʒ] *nm* **1** : woolen fabric **2** : woolen garment

laïque [laik] *adj* : lay, secular — ~ *nmf* : layman, laywoman

laisse [lɛs] *nf* : lead, leash

laisser [lese] *vt* : leave — *v aux* **1** : let, allow **2** ~ **faire** : not interfere — **se laisser** *vr* : allow oneself **2** ~ **aller** : let oneself go — **laisser–aller** [leseale] *nms & pl* : carelessness — **laissez–passer** [lesepase] *nms & pl* : pass, permit

lait [lɛ] *nm* : milk — **laiterie** [lɛtri] *nf* **1** : dairy industry **2** : dairy — **laiteux, -teuse** [lɛtø, -tøz] *adj* : milky — **laitier, -tière** [lɛtje, -tjɛr] *adj* : dairy — ~ *n* **1** : milkman **2** : dairyman

laiton [lɛtɔ̃] *nm* : brass

laitue [lety] *nf* : lettuce

lambeau [lɑ̃bo] *nm, pl* **-beaux 1** : rag, scrap **2 en** ~**x** : in tatters

lambiner [lɑ̃bine] *vi fam* : dawdle

lambris [lɑ̃bri] *nms & pl* : paneling

lame [lam] *nf* **1** : strip, slat **2** ~ **de razoir** : razor blade — **lamelle** [lamɛl] *nf* : thin strip

lamenter [lamɑ̃te] *v* **se lamenter** *vr* : lament — **lamentable** [lamɑ̃tabl] *adj* **1** : deplorable **2** PITOYABLE : pitiful, pathetic

lampe [lɑ̃p] *nf* **1** : lamp **2** ~ **de poche** : flashlight — **lampadaire** [lɑ̃padɛr] *nm* **1** : floor lamp **2** : streetlight — **lampion** [lɑ̃pjɔ̃] *nm* : Chinese lantern

lance [lɑ̃s] *nf* **1** : spear, lance **2** *or* ~ **à eau** : hose

lancée [lɑ̃se] *nf* **1** : momentum **2 continuer sur sa** ~ : keep going

lancer [lɑ̃se] {6} *vt* **1** : throw, hurl **2** : launch **3** ÉMETTRE : issue, give out **4** : start up (a motor) — **se lancer** *vr* ~ **dans** : launch into — ~ *nm* : throw, throwing — **lancement** [lɑ̃smɑ̃] *nm* **1** : throwing **2** : launching — **lance–pierres** [lɑ̃spjɛr] *nms & pl* : slingshot

lanciner [lɑ̃sine] *vi* : throb — *vt* : haunt, obsess — **lancinant, -nante** [lɑ̃sinɑ̃, -nɑ̃t] *adj* : shooting, throbbing

landau [lɑ̃do] *nm France* : baby carriage

lande [lɑ̃d] *nf* : moor, heath

langage [lɑ̃gaʒ] *nm* : language

lange [lɑ̃ʒ] *nm* : baby blanket

langouste [lɑ̃gust] *nf* : crayfish — **langoustine** [lɑ̃gustin] *nf* : prawn

langue [lɑ̃g] *nf* **1** : tongue **2** : language — **languette** [lɑ̃gɛt] *nf* **1** : tongue (of a shoe) **2** : strip

langueur [lɑ̃gœr] *nf* : languor, lethargy — **languir** [lɑ̃gir] *vi* **1** : languish, pine **2** : flag (of conversation, etc.) — **languissant, -sante** [lɑ̃gisɑ̃, -sɑ̃t] *adj* : languid, listless

lanière [lanjɛr] *nf* : strap, lash, thong

lanterne [lɑ̃tɛrn] *nf* **1** LAMPE : lantern **2** : parking light

laper [lape] *vt* : lap up

lapider [lapide] *vt* : stone

lapin, -pine [lapɛ̃, -pin] *n* **1** : rabbit **2 poser un ~ à qqn** : stand s.o. up

laps [laps] *nms & pl* : lapse (of time) — **lapsus** [lapsys] *nms & pl* : slip, error

laque [lak] *nf* **1** : lacquer **2** : hair spray

laquelle → **lequel**

larcin [larsɛ̃] *nm* : petty theft

lard [lar] *nm* **1** : fat, lard **2** : bacon

large [larʒ] *adj* **1** : wide, broad **2** CONSIDÉRABLE : extensive **3** AMPLE : loose-fitting **4** GÉNÉREUX : generous — **~** *nm* **1 de ~** : wide, in width **2 le ~** : the open sea — **~** *adv* : on a large scale, generously — **largement** [larʒəmɑ̃] *adv* **1** : widely **2** DE BEAUCOUP : greatly, by far **3** GÉNÉREUSEMENT : generously **4** AU MOINS : easily — **largesse** [larʒɛs] *nf* : generosity — **largeur** [larʒœr] *nf* : width, breadth **2 ~ d'esprit** : broad-mindedness

larguer [large] *vt* **1** : release, drop **2** *fam* : ditch, get rid of

larme [larm] *nf* **1** : tear **2** *fam* : drop, small quantity — **larmoyant, -moyante** [larmwajɑ̃, -mwajɑ̃t] *adj* : tearful

larve [larv] *nf* : larva

larynx [larɛ̃ks] *nms & pl* : larynx — **laryngite** [larɛ̃ʒit] *nf* : laryngitis

las, lasse [la, las] *adj* : weary

lasagne [lazaɲ] *nf* : lasagna

laser [lazɛr] *nm* : laser

lasser [lase] *vt* **1** : weary, tire out **2** ENNUYER : bore — **se lasser** *vr* **~ de** : grow weary of — **lassitude** [lasityd] *nf* : weariness

latent, -tente [latɑ̃, -tɑ̃t] *adj* : latent

latéral, -rale [lateral] *adj, mpl* **-raux** [-ro] : side, lateral

latex [latɛks] *nms & pl* : latex

latin, -tine [latɛ̃, -tin] *adj* : Latin — **latin** *nm* : Latin (language)

latitude [latityd] *nf* : latitude

latte [lat] *nf* : lath, floorboard

lauréat, -réate [lɔrea, -reat] *n* : prizewinner

laurier [lɔrje] *nm* **1** : laurel **2 feuille de ~** : bay leaf

lavable [lavabl] *adj* : washable

lavabo [lavabo] *nm* **1** : (bathroom) sink **2 ~s** *nmpl France* : toilets

lavage [lavaʒ] *nm* **1** : wash, washing **2 ~ de cerveau** : brainwashing

lavande [lavɑ̃d] *nf* : lavender

lave [lav] *nf* : lava

laver [lave] *vt* : wash — **se laver** *vr* **1** : wash oneself **2 ~ les mains** : wash one's hands — **lave–linge** [lavlɛ̃ʒ] *nms & pl France* : washing machine — **laverie** [lavri] *nf* : self-service laundry — **lavette** [lavɛt] *nf* : dishcloth — **laveur, -veuse** [lavœr, -vøz] *n* : washer, cleaner — **lave–vaisselle** [lavvesɛl] *nms & pl* : dishwasher — **lavoir** [lavwar] *nm Can* : self-service laundry

laxatif [laksatif] *nm* : laxative

le, la [lə, la] (**l'** [l] *before a vowel or mute h*) *pron, pl* **les** [le] : him, her, it, them — **~** *art* **1** : the **2** : a, an, per

lécher [leʃe] {87} *vt* : lick, lap — **se lécher** *vr* : lick (one's fingers, etc.) — **lèche-vitrines** [lɛʃvitrin] *nms & pl* **faire du ~** : window-shop

leçon [ləsɔ̃] *nf* : lesson

lecteur, -trice [lɛktœr, -tris] *n* : reader — **lecteur** *nm* **1 ~ de disquettes** : disk drive **2 ~ laser** : CD player — **lecture** [lɛktyr] *nf* : reading

ledit, ladite [lədi, ladit] *adj, pl* **lesdits, lesdites** [ledi, ledit] : the aforesaid

légal, -gale [legal] *adj, mpl* **-gaux** [lego] : legal, lawful — **légaliser** [legalize] *vt* : legalize — **légalité** [legalite] *nf* : lawfulness

légende [leʒɑ̃d] *nf* **1** : legend, tale **2** : caption (of an illustration) — **légendaire** [leʒɑ̃dɛr] *adj* : legendary

léger, -gère [leʒe, -ʒɛr] *adj* **1** : light **2** FAIBLE : slight, faint **3** IMPRUDENT : thoughtless **4 à la légère** : rashly — **légèrement** [leʒɛrmɑ̃] *adv* **1** : lightly **2** : slightly — **légèreté** [leʒɛrte] *nf* **1** : lightness **2** : thoughtlessness

légiférer [leʒifere] *vi* : legislate

légion [leʒiɔ̃] *nf* : legion

législation [leʒislasjɔ̃] *nf* : legislation — **législateur, -trice** [leʒislatœr, -tris] *n* : legislator, lawmaker — **législatif, -tive** [leʒislatif, -tiv] *adj* : legislative — **législatif** *nm* : legislature — **législature** [leʒislatyr] *nf* : term (of office)

légitime [leʒitim] *adj* **1** LÉGAL : lawful **2**

: rightful, legitimate **3 ~ défense** : self-defense

legs [lɛg] *nms & pl* : legacy — **léguer** [lege] {87} *vt* **1** : bequeath **2** TRANSMETTRE : pass ▪▪

légume [legym] *nm* : vegetable

lendemain [lɑ̃dmɛ̃] *nm* **1** : next day **2 au ~ de** : just after, following **3 du jour au ~** : in a very short time **4 le ~ matin** : the next morning

lent, lente [lɑ̃, lɑ̃t] *adj* : slow — **lenteur** [lɑ̃tœr] *nf* : slowness

lentille [lɑ̃tij] *nf* **1** : lentil **2** : (optical) lens

léopard [leɔpar] *nm* : leopard

lèpre [lɛpr] *nf* : leprosy

lequel, laquelle [ləkɛl, lakɛl] *pron, pl* **lesquels, lesquelles** [lekɛl] (*with* **à** *and* **de** *contracted to* **auquel, auxquels, auxquelles; duquel, desquels, desquelles**) **1** : which **2** : who, whom **3 lequel préférez-vous?** : which one do you prefer?

les → le

lesbienne [lɛsbjɛn] *nf* : lesbian

lesdits, lesdites → ledit

léser [leze] {87} *vt* **1** : wrong **2** BLESSER : injure

lésiner [lezine] *vi* **~ sur** : skimp on

lésion [lezjɔ̃] *nf* : lesion

lesquels, lesquelles → lequel

lessive [lɛsiv] *nf* **1** LAVAGE : washing, wash **2** : laundry detergent — **lessiver** [lɛsive] *vt* **1** : wash, scrub **2 être lessivé** *fam* : be exhausted

lest [lɛst] *nm* : ballast

leste [lɛst] *adj* : nimble

léthargie [letarʒi] *nf* : lethargy — **léthargique** [letarʒik] *adj* : lethargic

lettre [lɛtr] *nf* **1** : letter (of the alphabet) **2** CORRESPONDANCE : letter **3 ~s** *nfpl* : arts, humanities **4 à la ~** : exactly **5 en toutes ~s** : in full — **lettré, -trée** [lɛtre] *adj* : well-read

leucémie [løsemi] *nf* : leukemia

leur [lœr] *adj, pl* **leurs** : their — **~** *pron* **1** : (to) them **2 le ~, la ~, les ~s** : theirs

leurre [lœr] *nm* **1** : (fishing) lure **2** ILLUSION : illusion, deception — **leurrer** [lœre] *vt* : deceive, delude — **se leurrer** *vr* : delude oneself

levain [ləvɛ̃] *nm* **1** : leaven **2 sans ~** : unleavened

lever [ləve] {52} *vt* **1** : lift **2** : raise **3** : close (a meeting), lift (a ban) — *vi* **1** : come up (of plants) **2** : rise (in cooking) — **se lever** *vr* **1** : get up **2** : stand up **3** : rise (of the sun) **4 le jour se lève** : day is breaking — **~** *nm* **1** : rising, rise **2 ~ du soleil** : sunrise — **levée** [ləve] *nf* **1** SUPPRESSION : lifting **2** : collection (of mail, etc.)

levier [ləvje] *nm* **1** : lever **2 ~ de vitesse** : gearshift

lèvre [lɛvr] *nf* : lip

lévrier [levrije] *nm* : greyhound

levure [ləvyr] *nf* **1** : yeast **2 ~ chimique** : baking powder

lexique [lɛksik] *nm* **1** : glossary, lexicon **2** VOCABULAIRE : vocabulary

lézard [lezar] *nm* : lizard

lézarder [lezarde] *v* **se lézarder** *vr* : crack

liaison [ljɛzɔ̃] *nf* : liaison

liant, liante [ljɑ̃, ljɑ̃t] *adj* : sociable

liasse [ljas] *nf* : bundle, wad

libanais, -naise [libanɛ, -nɛz] *adj* : Lebanese

libeller [libele] *vt* : draw up (a document), make out (a check)

libellule [libelyl] *nf* : dragonfly

libéral, -rale [liberal] *adj & n, mpl* **-raux** [-ro] : liberal

libérer [libere] {87} *vt* : free, release, liberate — **se libérer** *vr* : free oneself — **libération** [liberasjɔ̃] *nf* : liberation, freeing — **libéré, -rée** [libere] *adj* **~ de** : free from

liberté [libɛrte] *nf* **1** : freedom, liberty **2 en ~ conditionnelle** : on probation **3 mettre en ~** : set free

libido [libido] *nf* : libido

libraire [librɛr] *nmf* : bookseller — **librairie** [libreri] *nf* : bookstore

libre [libr] *adj* **1** : free **2** DISPONIBLE : available, unoccupied **3** DÉGAGÉ : clear, free **4 ~ arbitre** : free will — **libre-échange** [libreʃɑ̃ʒ] *nm, pl* **libres-échanges** [librəzeʃɑ̃ʒ] : free trade — **librement** [librəmɑ̃] *adv* : freely — **libre-service** [librəsɛrvis] *nm, pl* **libres-services** : self-service

licence [lisɑ̃s] *nf* **1** : (bachelor's) degree **2** : license, permit **3 prendre des ~s avec** : take liberties with — **licencié, -ciée** [lisɑ̃sje] *n* : (university) graduate

licencier [lisɑ̃sje] {96} *vt* : lay off, dismiss — **licenciement** [lisɑ̃simɑ̃] *nm* : layoff, dismissal

lichen [likɛn] *nm* : lichen

licite [lisit] *adj* : lawful

lie [li] *nf* : sediment, dregs

liège [ljɛʒ] *nm* : cork

lien [ljɛ̃] *nm* **1** ATTACHE : bond, strap **2** RAPPORT : link **3** RELATION : tie, relationship — **lier** [lje] {96} *vt* **1** : bind, tie up **2** RELIER : link up **3** : strike up (a friendship, etc.) **4** UNIR : unite — **se lier** *vr* **~ avec** : become friends with

lierre [ljɛr] *nm* : ivy

liesse [ljɛs] *nf* : jubilation

lieu [ljø] *nm, pl* **lieux 1** ENDROIT : place **2 au ~ de** : instead of **3 avoir ~** : take place **4 avoir ~ de** : have reason to **5 en premier ~** : in the first place **6 tenir ~ de** : serve as **7 ~x** *nmpl* : premises — **lieu-dit** *or*

lieudit [ljødi] *nm, pl* **lieux–dits** *or* **lieudits** : locality

lieutenant [ljøtnã] *nm* : lieutenant

lièvre [ljɛvr] *nm* : hare

ligament [ligamãl] *nm* : ligament

ligne [liɲ] *nf* **1** : line **2** PARCOURS : route **3** en ~ : online (in computers) **4** ~ **droite** : beeline — **lignée** [liɲe] *nf* **1** : line, lineage **2** DESCENDANTS : descendants *pl*

ligoter [ligɔte] *vt* : tie up, bind

ligue [lig] *nf* : league, alliance — **liguer** [lige] *v* **se liguer** *vr* **1** : join forces **2** ~ **contre** : conspire against

lilas [lila] *nms & pl* : lilac

limace [limas] *nf* : slug (mollusk)

lime [lim] *nf* **1** : file **2** ~ **à ongles** : nail file — **limer** [lime] *vt* : file — **se limer** *vr* ~ **les ongles** : file one's nails

limiter [limite] *vt* : limit — **limitation** [limitasjɔ̃] *nf* : limitation — **limite** [limit] *adj* **cas** ~ : borderline case **2 date** ~ : deadline **3 vitesse** ~ : speed limit — ~ *nf* **1** : limit **2** : border, boundary

limitrophe [limitrɔf] *adj* : bordering, adjacent

limoger [limɔʒe] {17} *vt* : dismiss

limon [limɔ̃] *nm* : silt

limonade [limɔnad] *nf* : lemonade

limousine [limuzin] *nf* : limousine

limpide [lɛ̃pid] *adj* : (crystal) clear — **limpidité** [lɛ̃pidite] *nf* : clearness

lin [lɛ̃] *nm* **1** : flax **2** : linen

linceul [lɛ̃sœl] *nm* : shroud

linéaire [lineɛr] *adj* : linear

linge [lɛ̃ʒ] *nm* **1** : (household) linen **2** LESSIVE : wash, washing **3** CHIFFON : cloth **4** *or* ~ **de corps** : underwear **5** *Can fam* : clothes *pl*, clothing — **lingerie** [lɛ̃ʒri] *nf* **1** : lingerie **2** *Can* : linen closet

lingot [lɛ̃go] *nm* : ingot

linguistique [lɛ̃gɥistik] *adj* : linguistic — ~ *nf* : linguistics — **linguiste** [lɛ̃gɥist] *nmf* : linguist

linoléum [linɔleɔm] *nm* : linoleum

lion, lionne [ljɔ̃, ljɔn] *n* : lion, lioness *f* — **lionceau** [ljɔ̃so] *nm, pl* -**ceaux** : lion cub

liqueur [likœr] *nf* **1** : liqueur **2** *Can* : soft drink

liquide [likid] *adj* : liquid — ~ *nm* **1** : liquid **2** ARGENT : cash — **liquidation** [likidasjɔ̃] *nf* **1** : liquidation **2** : clearance sale — **liquider** [likide] *vt* **1** : liquidate **2** : eliminate — **liquidités** [likidite] *nfpl* : liquid assets

lire [lir] {51} *vt* : read

lis *or* **lys** [lis] *nms & pl* : lily

lisible [lizibl] *adj* : legible — **lisibilité** [-zibilite] *nf* : legibility

lisière [lizjɛr] *nf* : edge, outskirts *pl*

lisse [lis] *adj* : smooth, sleek

liste [list] *nf* : list

lit [li] *nm* **1** : bed **2** ~ **de camp** : cot — **literie** [litri] *nf* : bedding — **litière** [litjɛr] *nf* : litter

litige [litiʒ] *nm* : dispute

litre [litr] *nm* : liter

littérature [literatyr] *nf* : literature — **littéraire** [literɛr] *adj* : literary — **littéral, -rale** [literal] *adj, mpl* -**raux** [-ro] : literal

littoral [litɔral] *nm* : coast(line) — ~ *adj* : coastal

liturgie [lityrʒi] *nf* : liturgy — **liturgique** [lityrʒik] *adj* : liturgical

livide [livid] *adj* : pallid, pale

livraison [livrɛzɔ̃] *nf* : delivery

livre[1] [livr] *nm* **1** : book **2** ~ **de poche** : paperback **3** ~ **de recettes** : cookbook

livre[2] *nf* **1** : pound **2** *or* ~ **sterling** : pound (monetary unit)

livrer [livre] *vt* **1** : deliver **2** REMETTRE : hand over — **se livrer** *vr* **1** ~ **à** : devote oneself to **2** ~ **à** : surrender to **3** ~ **à** : confide in

livret [livrɛ] *nm* : booklet

livreur, -vreuse [livrœr, -vrøz] *n* : deliveryman *m*, delivery woman *f*

lobe [lɔb] *nm* : lobe

local, -cale [lɔkal] *adj, mpl* -**caux** [lɔko] : local — **local** *nm, pl* -**caux** : place, premises *pl* — **localiser** [lɔkalize] *vt* **1** SITUER : locate **2** LIMITER : localize — **localité** [lɔkalite] *nf* : locality

location [lɔkasjɔ̃] *nf* **1** : renting, leasing **2** : rented property — **locataire** [lɔkatɛr] *nmf* : tenant

locomotive [lɔkɔmɔtiv] *nf* : locomotive, engine

locution [lɔkysjɔ̃] *nf* : phrase, idiom

loge [lɔʒ] *nf* **1** : dressing room **2** : box (at the theater) **3** : lodge

loger [lɔʒe] {17} *vt* **1** : lodge **2** CONTENIR : accommodate — **se loger** *vr* **1** : find accommodations **2** ~ **dans** : lodge itself in — **logement** [lɔʒmã] *nm* **1** : accommodation **2** : apartment **3** HABITAT : housing

logiciel [lɔʒisjɛl] *nm* : software

logique [lɔʒik] *adj* : logical — ~ *nf* : logic

logis [lɔʒi] *nms & pl* : dwelling, abode

logistique [lɔʒistik] *nf* : logistics

loi [lwa] *nf* : law

loin [lwɛ̃] *adv* **1** : far **2** : a long time ago **3** ~ **de** : far from **4 plus** ~ : further — ~ *nm* **1 au** ~ : in the distance **2 de** ~ : from a distance **3 de** ~ : by far — **lointain, -taine** [lwɛ̃tɛ̃, -tɛn] *adj* : distant — **lointain** *nm* : distance

loisir [lwazir] *nm* **1** : leisure **2** ~**s** *nmpl* : leisure activities

long, longue [lɔ̃, lɔ̃g] *adj* : long — **long** [lɔ̃] *adv* : much, a lot — ~ *nm* **1** : length **2 de**

~ : long, in length **3 le ~ de** : along — **à la longue** *adv phr* : in the long run

longer [lɔ̃ʒe] {17} *vt* **1** : walk along, follow **2** LIMITER : border

longévité [lɔ̃ʒevite] *nf* : longevity

longitude [lɔ̃ʒityd] *nf* : longitude

longtemps [lɔ̃tã] *adv* **1** : a long time **2 avant ~** : before long

longue → **long** — **longuement** [lɔ̃gmã] *adv* **1** : for a long time **2** : at length — **longueur** [lɔ̃gœr] *nf* **1** : length **2 à ~ de journée** : all day long **3 ~ d'onde** : wavelength **4 ~s** *nfpl* : tedious parts (of a film, etc.) — **longue–vue** [lɔ̃gvy] *nf, pl* **longues–vues** : telescope

lopin [lɔpɛ̃] *nm* **~ de terre** : plot of land

loquace [lɔkas] *adj* : talkative

loque [lɔk] *nf* **1** : wreck (person) **2 ~s** *nfpl* : rags

loquet [lɔkɛ] *nm* : latch

lorgner [lɔrɲe] *vt* : eye, ogle

lors [lɔr] *adv* **~ de 1** : at the time of **2** : during

lorsque [lɔrskə] (**lorsqu'** [lɔrsk] *before a vowel or mute h) conj* : when

losange [lɔzãʒ] *nm* **1** : lozenge, diamond shape **2** *Can* : (baseball) diamond

lot [lo] *nm* **1** SORT : fate, lot **2** PRIX : prize **3** PART : share

loterie [lɔtri] *nf* : lottery

lotion [lɔsjɔ̃] *nf* : lotion

lotissement [lɔtismã] *nm* : (housing) development

louange [lwãʒ] *nf* : praise — **louable** [lwabl] *adj* : praiseworthy

louche[1] [luʃ] *nf* : ladle

louche[2] *adj* : shady, suspicious — **loucher** [luʃe] *vi* **1** : be cross-eyed **2** : squint

louer[1] [lwe] *vt* : praise — **se louer** *vr* **~ de** : be satisfied about

louer[2] *vt* : rent, lease — **se louer** *vr* : be for rent

loufoque [lufɔk] *adj fam* : crazy, zany

loup [lu] *nm* : wolf

loupe [lup] *nf* : magnifying glass

louper [lupe] *vt fam* **1** : bungle, mess up **2** : miss (a train, etc.)

lourd, lourde [lur, lurd] *adj* : heavy — **lourd** *adv* **peser ~** : be heavy — **lourdement** [lurdəmã] *adv* : heavily — **lourdeur** [lurdœr] *nf* : heaviness

loutre [lutr] *nf* : otter

louvoyer [luvwaje] {58} *vi* : hedge, equivocate

loyal, loyale [lwajal] *adj, mpl* **loyaux** [lwajo] **1** : loyal **2** HONNÊTE : fair — **loyauté** [lwajote] *nf* **1** : loyalty **2** : fairness

loyer [lwaje] *nm* : rent

lu [ly] *pp* → **lire**

lubie [lybi] *nf* : whim

lubrifier [lybrifje] {96} *vt* : lubricate — **lubrifiant** [lybrifjã] *nm* : lubricant

lucarne [lykarn] *nf* : skylight

lucide [lysid] *adj* : lucid — **lucidité** [lysidite] *nf* : lucidity

lucratif, -tive [lykratif, -tiv] *adj* : lucrative, profitable

ludique [lydik] *adj* : play, playing

lueur [lɥœr] *nf* **1** : faint light **2** : glimmer (of hope, etc.)

luge [lyʒ] *nf* : sled

lugubre [lygybr] *adj* : gloomy, dismal

lui [lɥi] *pron* **1** (*used as indirect object*) : (to) him, (to) her, (to) it **2** (*used as object of a preposition*) : him, it **3** (*used as subject or for emphasis*) : he **4** (*used as a reflexive pronoun*) : himself — **lui–même** [lɥimɛm] *pron* : himself, itself

luire [lɥir] {49} *vi* : shine, gleam — **luisant, -sante** [lɥizã, -zãt] *adj* : shining, gleaming

lumière [lymjɛr] *nf* : light — **luminaire** [lyminɛr] *nm* : lamp, light — **lumineux, -neuse** [lyminø, -nøz] *adj* **1** : luminous **2** RADIEUX : radiant, bright

lunaire [lynɛr] *adj* : lunar, moon

lunatique [lynatik] *adj* : whimsical

lunch [lœ̃ʃ] *nm, pl* **lunchs** *or* **lunches 1** BUFFET : buffet **2** *Can* : lunch

lundi [lœ̃di] *nm* : Monday

lune [lyn] *nf* **1** : moon **2 ~ de miel** : honeymoon

lunette [lynɛt] *nf* **1** : telescope **2 ~ arrière** : rear window (of an automobile) **3 ~s** *nfpl* : glasses **4 ~s bifocales** : bifocals

lurette [lyrɛt] *nf* **il y a belle ~** *fam* : ages ago

lustre [lystr] *nm* **1** : luster, sheen **2** : chandelier — **lustré, -trée** [lystre] *adj* : shiny, glossy

luth [lyt] *nm* : lute

lutin [lytɛ̃] *nm* : imp, goblin

lutrin [lytrɛ̃] *nm* : lectern

lutte [lyt] *nf* **1** : fight, struggle **2** : wrestling — **lutter** [lyte] *vi* **1** SE BATTRE : fight, struggle **2** : wrestle — **lutteur, -teuse** [lytœr, -tøz] *n* **1** : fighter **2** : wrestler

luxation [lyksasjɔ̃] *nf* : dislocation (of a joint)

luxe [lyks] *nm* : luxury

luxer [lykse] *v* **se luxer** *vr* : dislocate (one's shoulder, etc.)

luxueux, -xueuse [lyksɥø, -sɥøz] *adj* : luxurious

luxure [lyksyr] *nf* : lust — **luxurieux, -rieuse** [lyksyrjø, -rjøz] *adj* : lustful

luzerne [lyzɛrn] *nf* : alfalfa

lycée [lise] *nm France* : high school — **lycéen, -céenne** [liseɛ̃, -seɛn] *n France* : high school student

lynx [lɛ̃ks] *nm* : lynx

lyrique [lirik] *adj* : lyric(al)

lys → **lis**

M

m [ɛm] *nm* : m, 13th letter of the alphabet

ma → **mon**

macabre [makabr] *adj* : macabre

macaron [makarɔ̃] *nm* **1** : macaroon **2** INSIGNE : badge, sticker

macaronis [makarɔni] *nmpl* : macaroni

macédoine [masedwan] *nf* : mixture (of fruits or vegetables)

macérer [masere] {87} *v* : steep, soak

mâcher [maʃe] *vt* : chew

machin [maʃɛ̃] *nm fam* : thingamajig, thing

machine [maʃin] *nf* **1** : machine **2** : engine (of a ship, a train, etc.) **3** ~ **à écrire** : typewriter **4** ~ **à laver** : washing machine — **machiniste** [maʃinist] *nmf* : (bus) driver

mâchoire [maʃwar] *nf* : jaw

mâchonner [maʃɔne] *vt* : chew

maçon [masɔ̃] *nm* : bricklayer, mason — **maçonnerie** [masɔnri] *nf* : masonry

maculer [makyle] *vt* : stain

madame [madam] *nf, pl* **mesdames** [medam] **1** : Mrs., Ms., Madam **2** : lady — **mademoiselle** [madmwazɛl] *nf, pl* **mesdemoiselles** [medmwazɛl] **1** : Miss, Ms. **2** : young lady

mafia *or* **maffia** [mafja] *nf* : Mafia

magasin [magazɛ̃] *nm* **1** : shop, store **2** ENTREPÔT : warehouse **3** : magazine (of a gun or camera) **4 grand** ~ : department store

magazine [magazin] *nm* REVUE : magazine

magie [maʒi] *nf* : magic — **magicien, -cienne** [maʒisjɛ̃, -sjɛn] *n* : magician — **magique** [maʒik] *adj* : magic(al)

magistral, -trale [maʒistral] *adj, mpl* **-traux** [-tro] **1** : brilliant, masterly **2 cours magistral** : lecture

magistrat [maʒistra] *nm* : magistrate

magnanime [maɲanim] *adj* : magnanimous

magnat [maɲa] *nm* : magnate, tycoon

magnétique [maɲetik] *adj* : magnetic — **magnétiser** [maɲetize] *vt* : magnetize — **magnétisme** [maɲetism] *nm* : magnetism

magnétophone [maɲetɔfɔn] *nm* : tape recorder

magnétoscope [maɲetɔskɔp] *nm* : videocassette recorder, VCR

magnifique [maɲifik] *adj* : magnificent

magnolia [maɲɔlja] *nm* : magnolia

mai [mɛ] *nm* : May

maigre [mɛgr] *adj* **1** MINCE : thin **2** INSUFFISANT : meager **3** : low-fat, lean (of meat) — **maigrir** [mɛgrir] *vi* : lose weight, reduce

maille [maj] *nf* **1** : stitch (in knitting) **2** : mesh (of a net)

maillot [majo] *nm* **1** : jersey **2** ~ **de bain** : bathing suit

main [mɛ̃] *nf* **1** : hand **2** SAVOIR-FAIRE : know-how, skill **3 de première** ~ : firsthand **4 donner un coup de** ~ **à** : lend a helping hand to **5** ~ **courante** : handrail — **main-d'œuvre** [mɛ̃dœvr] *nf, pl* **mains-d'œuvre** : manpower, workforce

maint, mainte [mɛ̃, mɛ̃t] *adj* : many a

maintenant [mɛ̃tnɑ̃] *adv* **1** : now **2** : nowadays

maintenir [mɛ̃tnir] {92} *vt* **1** : maintain **2** SOUTENIR : support — **se maintenir** *vr* : remain, persist — **maintien** [mɛ̃tjɛ̃] *nm* **1** : maintaining, maintenance **2** PORT : bearing, deportment

maire, mairesse [mɛr, mɛrɛs] *n* : mayor — **mairie** [meri] *nf* : town hall, city hall

mais [mɛ] *conj* **1** : but **2** ~ **oui** : certainly, of course

maïs [mais] *nm* : corn, maize

maison [mezɔ̃] *nf* **1** : house, home **2** SOCIÉTÉ : firm — ~ *adj* **1** : homemade **2** : in-house (of an employee) — **maisonnée** [mɛzɔne] *nf* : household

maître, -tresse [mɛtr, -trɛs] *n* **1** : master, mistress **2** ~ **d'école** : schoolteacher — ~ *adj* **1** : main, key — **maître** [mɛtr] *nm* **1** : master (of a pet, etc.) **2** EXPERT : expert — **maîtrise** [metriz] *nf* **1** : skill, mastery **2** : master's degree **3** ~ **de soi** : self-control — **maîtriser** [metrize] *vt* **1** : master **2** CONTENIR : control, restrain

majesté [maʒɛste] *nf* : majesty — **majestueux, -tueuse** [maʒɛstɥø, -tɥøz] *adj* : majestic

majeur, -jeure [maʒœr] *adj* **1** : major, main **2** : of age (in law) — **majeur** *nm* : middle finger — **majorité** [maʒɔrite] *nf* : majority

majuscule [maʒyskyl] *adj* : capital, uppercase — ~ *nf* : capital letter

mal [mal] *adv* **1** : poorly, badly **2** INCORRECTEMENT : wrongly **3 aller** ~ : be unwell — ~ *adj* **1** : wrong **2** MAUVAIS : bad — ~ *nm, pl* **maux** [mo] **1** DOULEUR : pain **2** MALADIE : sickness **3** DOMMAGE : harm **4** : evil **5** PEINE : trouble, difficulty

malade [malad] *adj* : sick, ill — ~ *nmf* : sick person, patient — **maladie** [maladi] *nf* : illness, disease — **maladif, -dive** [maladif, -div] *adj* : sickly

maladresse [maladrɛs] *nf* **1** : clumsiness **2** BÉVUE : blunder — **maladroit, -droite** [maladrwa, -drwat] *adj* : clumsy, awkward

malaise [malɛz] *nm* **1** : dizziness **2** GÊNE : uneasiness, malaise

malaxer [malakse] *vt* **1** : knead **2** MÉLANGER : mix

malchance [malʃɑ̃s] *nf* : bad luck, misfortune — **malchanceux, -ceuse** [malʃɑ̃søø, -søz] *adj* : unfortunate

mâle [mal] *adj* **1** : male **2** : manly — **~** *nm* : male

malédiction [malediksjɔ̃] *nf* : curse

maléfique [malefik] *adj* : evil

malencontreux, -treuse [malɑ̃kɔ̃trø, -trøz] *adj* : unfortunate, untoward

malentendu [malɑ̃tɑ̃dy] *nm* : misunderstanding

malfaçon [malfasɔ̃] *nf* : fault, defect

malfaisant, -sante [malfəzɑ̃, -zɑ̃t] *adj* : evil, harmful — **malfaiteur** [malfɛtœr] *nm* : criminal

malgré [malgre] *prep* **1** : in spite of, despite **2 ~ tout** : nevertheless, even so

malheur [malœr] *nm* : misfortune — **malheureux, -reuse** [malœrø, -røz] *adj* **1** : unhappy **2** MALCHANCEUX : unfortunate — **~** *n* : unfortunate person — **malheureusement** [malœrøzmɑ̃] *adv* : unfortunately

malhonnête [malɔnɛt] *adj* : dishonest — **malhonnêteté** [malɔnɛtte] *nf* : dishonesty

malice [malis] *nf* : mischief, mischievousness — **malicieux, -cieuse** [malisjø, -sjøz] *adj* : mischievous

malin, -ligne [malɛ̃, -liɲ] *adj* **1** : clever **2** *fam* : difficult **3** MÉCHANT : malicious **4** : malignant (in medicine)

malle [mal] *nf* : trunk

malléable [maleabl] *adj* : malleable

mallette [malɛt] *nf* : small suitcase, valise

malnutrition [malnytrisjɔ̃] *nf* : malnutrition

malodorant, -rante [malɔdɔrɑ̃, -rɑ̃t] *adj* : foul-smelling, smelly

malpropre [malprɔpr] *adj* : dirty — **malpropreté** [malprɔprəte] *nf* : dirtiness

malsain, -saine [malsɛ̃, -sɛn] *adj* : unhealthy

malt [malt] *nm* : malt

maltraiter [maltrete] *vt* : mistreat

malveillance [malvɛjɑ̃s] *nf* : spite, malevolence — **malveillant, -lante** [malvɛjɑ̃, -jɑ̃t] *adj* : spiteful

maman [mamɑ̃] *nf* : mom, mommy

mamelle [mamɛl] *nf* **1** : teat **2** PIS : udder — **mamelon** [mamɛlɔ̃] *nm* : nipple

mammifère [mamifɛr] *nm* : mammal

mammouth [mamut] *nm* : mammoth

manche [mɑ̃ʃ] *nf* **1** : sleeve (of a shirt) **2** : round (in sports), set (in tennis) **3** *Can* : inning (in baseball) **4 la Manche** : the English Channel — **~** *nm* **1** : handle, neck, shaft **2 ~ à balai** : broomstick — **manchette** [mɑ̃ʃɛt] *nf* **1** : cuff **2** : headline (in the press)

manchot [mɑ̃ʃo] *nm* : penguin

mandarine [mɑ̃darin] *nf* : tangerine, mandarin orange

mandat [mɑ̃da] *nm* **1** : mandate **2** *or* **~ d'arrêt** : (arrest) warrant **3** *or* **~ postal** : money order — **mandataire** [mɑ̃datɛr] *nmf* **1** REPRÉSENTANT : representative, agent **2** : proxy (in politics)

manège [manɛʒ] *nm* **1** : riding school **2** : merry-go-round

manette [manɛt] *nf* : lever

manger [mɑ̃ʒe] {17} *vt* **1** : eat **2** DÉPENSER : consume, use up — *vi* : eat — **~** *nm* : food — **mangeable** [mɑ̃ʒabl] *adj* : edible — **mangeoire** [mɑ̃ʒwar] *nf* : feeding trough

mangue [mɑ̃g] *nf* : mango

maniable [manjabl] *adj* : easy to handle, manageable

maniaque [manjak] *adj* : fussy — **~** *nmf* **1** : fussy person **2** : fanatic — **manie** [mani] *nf* **1** HABITUDE : habit **2** : quirk, obsession

manier [manje] {96} *vt* **1** MANIPULER : handle **2** UTILISER : use — **maniement** [manimɑ̃] *nm* : handling, use, operation

manière [manjɛr] *nf* **1** : manner, way **2 de ~ à** : so as to **3 de toute ~** : in any case, anyway **4 ~s** *nfpl* : manners — **maniéré, -rée** [manjere] *adj* : affected, mannered

manifester [manifɛste] *vt* **1** : express **2** RÉVÉLER : reveal, show — *vi* : demonstrate — **se manifester** *vr* : appear — **manifestation** [manifɛstasjɔ̃] *nf* **1** : (political) demonstration **2** MARQUE : indication **3** : appearance (of an illness, etc.) — **manifestant, -tante** [manifɛstɑ̃, -tɑ̃t] *n* : demonstrator — **manifeste** [manifɛst] *adj* : obvious — **~** *nm* : manifesto

manigance [manigɑ̃s] *nf* : scheme, trick — **manigancer** [manigɑ̃se] {6} *vt* : plot

manipuler [manipyle] *vt* **1** MANIER : handle **2** : manipulate — **manipulation** [manipylasjɔ̃] *nf* **1** MANIEMENT : handling **2** : manipulation

manivelle [manivɛl] *nf* : crank

mannequin [mankɛ̃] *nm* **1** : dummy, mannequin **2** : (fashion) model

manœuvre [manœvr] *nf* : maneuver — **manœuvrer** [manœvre] *vt* **1** : maneuver **2** : operate (a machine, etc.) **3** MANIPULER : manipulate — *vi* : maneuver

manoir [manwar] *nm* : manor

manquer [mɑ̃ke] *vt* : miss (an opportunity, etc.) — *vi* **1** : lack, be missing **2** ÉCHOUER : fail **3** : be absent (of a student, etc.) **4 ~ de** : be short of — **manque** [mɑ̃k] *nm* **1** : lack **2** LACUNE : gap — **manqué, -quée** [mɑ̃ke] *adj* **1** : failed **2** : missed

mansarde [mɑ̃sard] *nf* : attic

manteau [mɑ̃to] *nm, pl* **-teaux** [-to] : coat

manucure [manykyr] *nf* : manicure — ~ *nmf* : manicurist

manuel, -elle [manɥɛl] *adj* : manual — **manuel** *nm* : manual, handbook

manufacture [manyfaktyr] *nf* : factory — **manufacturer** [manyfaktyre] *vt* : manufacture

manuscrit, -scrite [manyskri, -skrit] *adj* : handwritten — **manuscrit** *nm* : manuscript

manutention [manytɑ̃sjɔ̃] *nf* 1 : handling 2 **frais de ~** : handling charges

maquereau [makro] *nm, pl* **-reaux** [-ro] : mackerel

maquette [makɛt] *nf* : (scale) model

maquiller [makije] *vt* : make up (one's face) — **se maquiller** *vr* : put on makeup — **maquillage** [makijaʒ] *nm* : makeup

maquis [maki] *nm France* : brush, undergrowth

marais [marɛ] *nm* : marsh, swamp

marasme [marasm] *nm* 1 : dejection, depression 2 : (economic) stagnation

marathon [maratɔ̃] *nm* : marathon

marauder [marode] *vi* VOLER : pilfer, thieve

marbre [marbr] *nm* 1 : marble 2 *Can* : home plate (in baseball)

marchand, -chande [marʃɑ̃, -ʃɑ̃d] *n* : storekeeper, merchant — ~ *adj* : market — **marchander** [marʃɑ̃de] *vt* : haggle over — *vi* : haggle, bargain — **marchandises** [marʃɑ̃diz] *nfpl* : goods, merchandise

marche [marʃ] *nf* 1 : step, stair 2 PROMENADE : walk, walking 3 RYTHME : pace 4 : march (in music) 5 ~ **arrière** : reverse 6 **en ~** : running, operating 7 **mettre en ~** : start up

marché [marʃe] *nm* 1 : market 2 ACCORD : deal 3 **bon ~** : cheap 4 ~ **noir** : black market

marchepied [marʃəpje] *nm* : step, steps *pl*

marcher [marʃe] *vi* 1 : walk, march 2 ~ **sur** : step on, tread on 3 FONCTIONNER : work, go, run — **marcheur, -cheuse** [marʃœr, -ʃøz] *n* : walker

mardi [mardi] *nm* 1 : Tuesday 2 ~ **gras** : Mardi Gras

mare [mar] *nf* 1 : pond 2 ~ **de** : pool of

marécage [marekaʒ] *nm* : marsh, swamp — **marécageux, -geuse** [marekaʒø, -ʒøz] *adj* : marshy, swampy

maréchal [mareʃal] *nm, pl* **-chaux** [-ʃo] : marshal

marée [mare] *nf* 1 : tide 2 ~ **noire** : oil slick

marelle [marɛl] *nf* : hopscotch

margarine [margarin] *nf* : margarine

marge [marʒ] *nf* : margin — **marginal, -nale** [marʒinal] *adj, mpl* **-naux** [-no] : marginal

marguerite [margərit] *nf* : daisy

marier [marje] {96} *vt* 1 : marry 2 : blend (colors, etc.) — **se marier** *vr* : get married — **mari** [mari] *nm* : husband — **mariage** [marjaʒ] *nm* 1 : marriage 2 : wedding — **marié, -riée** [marje] *adj* : married — ~ *n* 1 : groom *m*, bride *f* 2 **les mariés** : the newlyweds

marin, -rine [marɛ̃, -rin] *adj* : sea, marine — **marin** *nm* : sailor — **marine** *nf* : navy

mariner [marine] *v* : marinate

marionnette [marjɔnɛt] *nf* 1 : puppet 2 ~ **à fils** : marionette

maritime [maritim] *adj* : maritime, coastal

marmelade [marməlad] *nf* 1 : stewed fruit 2 : marmalade

marmite [marmit] *nf* : cooking pot

marmonner [marmɔne] *v* : mutter, mumble

marmot [marmo] *nm fam* : kid, brat

marmotte [marmɔt] *nf* : woodchuck

marmotter [marmɔte] *v* : mutter, mumble

marocain, -caine [marɔkɛ̃, -kɛn] *adj* : Moroccan

marotte [marɔt] *nf* : craze, fad

marquer [marke] *vt* 1 : mark 2 INDIQUER : show, indicate 3 ÉCRIRE : note (down) 4 : score (in sports) — *vi* 1 : leave a mark 2 : stand out (of an event, etc.) — **marquant, -quante** [markɑ̃, -kɑ̃t] *adj* : memorable, outstanding — **marque** [mark] *nf* 1 : mark, trace 2 : brand, make 3 : score (in sports) 4 ~ **déposée** : registered trademark — **marqué, -quée** [marke] *adj* : marked, distinct

marquisse [markiz] *nf* : canopy, marquee

marraine [marɛn] *nf* : godmother

marrant, -rante [marɑ̃, -rɑ̃t] *adj fam* : amusing, funny

marre [mar] *adv* **en avoir ~** *fam* : be fed up

marron, -ronne [marɔ̃, -rɔn] *adj* : brown — **marron** *nm* 1 : chestnut 2 : brown — **marronnier** [marɔnje] *nm* : chestnut tree

mars [mars] *nm* : March

Mars *nf* : Mars (planet)

marsouin [marswɛ̃] *nm* : porpoise

marteau [marto] *nm, pl* **-teaux** [marto] 1 : hammer 2 ~ **pneumatique** : pneumatic drill — **marteau–piqueur** [martopikœr] *nm, pl* **marteaux–piqueurs** : jackhammer — **marteler** [martəle] {20} *vt* : hammer

martial, -tiale [marsjal] *adj, mpl* **-tiaux** [-sjo] : martial

martyr, -tyre [martir] *n* : martyr — **martyriser** [martirize] *vt* : martyr

mascarade [maskarad] *nf* : masquerade

mascotte [maskɔt] *nf* : mascot

masculin, -line [maskylɛ̃, -lin] *adj* : male, masculine — **masculin** *nm* : masculine

masque [mask] *nm* : mask — **masquer** [maske] *vt* : mask, conceal

massacrer [masakre] *vt* : massacre — **massacre** [masakr] *nm* : massacre

massage [masaʒ] *nm* : massage

masse [mas] *nf* 1 : mass, body (of water, etc.) 2 : sledgehammer 3 les ∼s : the masses

masser [mase] *vt* 1 : massage 2 ASSEMBLER : gather — **masseur, -seuse** [masœr, -søz] *n* : masseur *m*, masseuse *f*

massif, -sive [masif, -siv] *adj* 1 : massive 2 : solid (of gold, silver, etc.) — **massif** *nm* : clump (of trees)

massue [masy] *nf* : club, bludgeon

mastic [mastik] *nm* : putty — **mastiquer** [mastike] *vt* : chew

masturber [mastyrbe] *v* **se masturber** *vr* : masturbate — **masturbation** [mastyrbasjɔ̃] *nf* : masturbation

mat, mate [mat] *adj* 1 : dull, matte (of a finish, etc.) 2 : checkmated (in chess)

mât [ma] *nm* 1 : mast 2 POTEAU : pole, post

match [matʃ] *nm* : match, game

matelas [matla] *nm* : mattress — **matelasser** [matlase] *vt* REMBOURRER : pad

matelot [matlo] *nm* : sailor, seaman

mater [mate] *vt* DOMPTER : subdue, curb

matériaux [materjo] *nmpl* : materials

matériel, -rielle [materjɛl] *adj* : material — **matériel** *nm* 1 : equipment, material(s) 2 : computer hardware — **matérialiser** [materjalize] *vt* : realize, make happen — **se matérialiser** *vr* : materialize — **matérialiste** [materjalist] *adj* : materialistic

maternel, -nelle [matɛrnɛl] *adj* : maternal, motherly — **maternelle** *nf or* **école** ∼ : nursery school — **maternité** [maternite] *nf* 1 : maternity 2 GROSSESSE : pregnancy

mathématique [matematik] *adj* : mathematical — **mathématicien, -cienne** [matematisjɛ̃, -sjɛn] *n* : mathematician — **mathématiques** [matematik] *nfpl* : mathematics — **maths or math** [mat] *nfpl fam* : math

matière [matjɛr] *nf* 1 : matter, substance 2 SUJET : subject 3 ∼s premières : raw materials

matin [matɛ̃] *nm* : morning — **matinal, -nale** [matinal] *adj, mpl* **-naux** [-no] 1 : morning 2 être ∼ : be up early — **matinée** [matine] *nf* 1 : morning 2 : matinee

matraque [matrak] *nf* : club — **matraquer** [matrake] *vt* 1 : club, bludgeon 2 : plug (a product)

matrice [matris] *nf* : matrix

matricule [matrikyl] *nf* : register, roll

matrimonial, -niale [matrimɔnjal] *adj, mpl* **-niaux** [-njo] : matrimonial

maturité [matyrite] *nf* : maturity

maudire [modir] *vt* : curse, damn — **maudit, -dite** [modi, -dit] *adj* : damned

maugréer [mogree] {89} *vi* GROGNER : grumble

maussade [mosad] *adj* 1 MOROSE : sullen 2 temps ∼ : dismal weather

mauvais, -vaise [movɛ, -vɛz] *adj* 1 : bad (of a grade, etc.) 2 : wrong (of an answer, etc.) 3 DÉPLAISANT : nasty, unpleasant

mauve [mov] *adj & nm* : mauve

mauviette [movjɛt] *nf* : weakling

maux → mal

maxillaire [maksilɛr] *nm* : jawbone

maxime [maksim] *nf* ADAGE : maxim, proverb

maximum [maksimɔm] *adj & nm, pl* **-mums** [-mɔm] *or* **-ma** [-ma] : maximum

mayonnaise [majɔnɛz] *nf* : mayonnaise

mazout [mazut] *nm* : heating oil

me [mə] *pron* (m' [m] *before a vowel or mute h*) 1 : me, to me 2 : myself, to myself

mec [mɛk] *nm fam* : guy

mécanique [mekanik] *nf* 1 : mechanics 2 : mechanism — ∼ *adj* : mechanical — **mécanicien, -cienne** [mekanisjɛ̃, -sjɛn] *n* 1 : mechanic 2 : (railway or flight) engineer — **mécanisme** [mekanism] *nm* : mechanism

méchant, -chante [meʃɑ̃, -ʃɑ̃t] *adj* 1 : nasty, malicious 2 : naughty, bad (of a child) 3 : vicious (of a dog) — ∼ *n* 1 : villain (in a book or film) 2 : naughty child — **méchamment** [meʃamɑ̃] *adv* : nastily — **méchanceté** [meʃɑ̃ste] *nf* : nastiness

mèche [mɛʃ] *nf* 1 : wick (of a candle) 2 : lock (of hair) 3 : bit (of a drill)

méconnaissable [mekɔnɛsabl] *adj* : unrecognizable

mécontent, -tente [mekɔ̃tɑ̃, -tɑ̃t] *adj* : discontented, dissatisfied — **mécontentement** [mekɔ̃tɑ̃tmɑ̃] *nm* : discontent, dissatisfaction

médaille [medaj] *nf* : medal — **médaillé, -lée** [medaje] *n* : medalist — **médaillon** [medajɔ̃] *nm* 1 : medallion 2 : locket

médecin [medsɛ̃] *nm* : doctor, physician — **médecine** [medsin] *nf* : medicine

média [medja] *nm* 1 : medium 2 les ∼s : the media

médian, -diane [medjɑ̃, -djan] *adj* : median

médiation [medjasjɔ̃] *nf* : mediation, arbitration — **médiateur, -trice** [medjatœr, -tris] *n* : mediator, arbitrator

médical, -cale [medikal] *adj, mpl* **-caux** [-ko] : medical — **médicament** [medikamɑ̃] *nm* : medicine, drug — **médication** [medikasjɔ̃] *nf* : medication — **médicinal, -nale** [medisinal] *adj, mpl* **-naux** [-no] : medicinal

médiéval, -vale [medjeval] *adj, mpl* **-vaux** [-vo] : medieval

médiocre [medjɔkr] *adj* : mediocre — **médiocrité** [medjɔkrite] *nf* : mediocrity

méditer [medite] *vt* : reflect on, think over

— *vi* : meditate — **méditation** [meditasjɔ̃] *nf* : meditation

médium [medjɔm] *nm* : medium, psychic

méduse [medyz] *nf* : jellyfish

meeting [miltiŋ] *nm* **1** : meeting **2** : meet (in sports)

méfait [mefɛ] *nm* **1** : misdeed, misdemeanour **2 ~s** *nmpl* : ravages

méfier [mefje] {96} *v* **se méfier** *vr* **1** : be careful, beware **2 ~ de** : distrust — **méfiance** [mefjɑ̃s] *nf* : distrust — **méfiant, -fiante** [mefjɑ̃, -fjɑ̃t] *adj* : distrustful

mégarde [megard] *nf* **par ~** : inadvertently

mégot [mego] *nm* : cigarette butt

meilleur, -leure [mɛjœr] *adj* **1** : better **2** : best — **~** *n* : best (one) — **meilleur** *adv* : better

mélancolie [melɑ̃kɔli] *nf* : melancholy — **mélancolique** [melɑ̃kɔlik] *adj* : melancholy

mélanger [melɑ̃ʒe] {17} *vt* **1** : mix, blend **2** CONFONDRE : mix up, confuse — **se mélanger** *vr* **1** : blend (with) **2** : get mixed up — **mélange** [melɑ̃ʒ] *nm* **1** : mixing, blending **2** : mixture, blend

mélasse [melas] *nf* : molasses

mêlée [mele] *nf* **~ générale** : free-for-all

mêler [mele] *vt* : mix — **se mêler** *vr* **1** : mix, mingle **2 mêlez-vous de vos affaires** : mind your own business

mélodie [melɔdi] *nf* : melody

mélomane [melɔman] *nmf* : music lover

melon [melɔ̃] *nm* : melon

membrane [mɑ̃bran] *nf* : membrane

membre [mɑ̃br] *nm* **1** : limb **2** : member (of a group)

même [mɛm] *adj* **1** : same, identical **2** (*used as an intensifier*) : very, actual **3** → **elle-même, lui-même, eux-mêmes** — **~ pron le ~, la ~, les ~s** : the same (one, ones) — **~** *adv* **1** : even **2 de ~** : likewise, the same

mémère [memɛr] *nf fam* **1** : grandma **2** *Can* : gossip

mémoire [memwar] *nf* : memory — **~** *nm* **1** : dissertation, thesis **2 ~s** *nmpl* : memoirs

mémorable [memɔrabl] *adj* : memorable

mémorandum [memɔrɑ̃dɔm] *nm* : memorandum

mémoriser [memɔrize] *vt* : memorize

menacer [mənase] {6} *v* : threaten — **menaçant, -çante** [mənasɑ̃, -sɑ̃t] *adj* : threatening — **menace** [mənas] *nf* : threat

ménage [menaʒ] *nm* **1** : household, family **2 faire le ~** : do the housework **3 un heureux ~** : a happy couple — **ménagement** [menaʒmɑ̃] *nm* : consideration, care — **ménager** [menaʒe] {17} *vt* **1** ÉPARGNER : save **2** : handle or treat with care — **se**

ménager *vr* : take it easy — **ménager, -gère** [menaʒe, -ʒɛr] *adj* : household, domestic — **ménagère** [menaʒɛr] *nf* : housewife

mendier [mɑ̃dje] {96} *v* : beg — **mendiant, -diante** [mɑ̃djɑ̃, -djɑ̃t] *n* : beggar

menées [məne] *nfpl* : scheming, intrigues

mener [məne] {52} *vt* **1** : lead **2** DIRIGER : conduct, run **3 ~ qqch à terme** : see sth through — **meneur, -neuse** [mənœr, -nøz] *n* **1** : leader **2 meneuse de claque** *Can* : cheerleader

méningite [menɛ̃ʒit] *nf* : meningitis

ménopause [menɔpoz] *nf* : menopause

menottes [mənɔt] *nfpl* : handcuffs

mensonge [mɑ̃sɔ̃ʒ] *nm* **1** : lie **2 le ~** : lying — **mensonger, -gère** [mɑ̃sɔ̃ʒe, -ʒɛr] *adj* : false, misleading

menstruation [mɑ̃stryasjɔ̃] *nf* RÈGLES : menstruation — **menstruel, -struelle** [mɑ̃stryɛl] *adj* : menstrual

mensuel, -suelle [mɑ̃sɥɛl] *adj* : monthly — **mensuel** *nm* : monthly (magazine)

mensurations [mɑ̃syrasjɔ̃] *nfpl* : measurements

mental, -tale [mɑ̃tal] *adj, mpl* **-taux** [-to] : mental — **mentalité** [mɑ̃talite] *nf* : mentality

menteur, -teuse [mɑ̃tœr, -tøz] *adj* : untruthful, false — **~** *n* : liar

menthe [mɑ̃t] *nf* : mint

mention [mɑ̃sjɔ̃] *nf* **1** : mention **2** : (academic) distinction — **mentionner** [mɑ̃sjɔne] *vt* : mention

mentir [mɑ̃tir] {82} *vi* : lie

menton [mɑ̃tɔ̃] *nm* : chin

menu, -nue [məny] *adj* **1** PETIT : tiny **2** : minor, trifling — **menu** *adv* : finely — **~** *nm* : menu

menuiserie [mənɥizri] *nf* : woodworking, carpentry — **menuisier** [mənɥizje] *nm* : woodworker, carpenter

méprendre [meprɑ̃dr] {70} *v* **se méprendre** *vr* **~ sur** : be mistaken about

mépris [mepri] *nm* **1** DÉDAIN : contempt **2 au ~ de** : regardless of — **méprisable** [meprizabl] *adj* : despicable, contemptible — **méprisant, -sante** [meprizɑ̃, -zɑ̃t] *adj* : contemptuous, scornful — **mépriser** [meprize] *vt* : despise, scorn

mer [mɛr] *nf* **1** : sea **2** MARÉE : tide

mercenaire [mɛrsənɛr] *adj & nmf* : mercenary

mercerie [mɛrsəri] *nf* : notions *pl*

merci [mɛrsi] *interj* : thank you!, thanks! — **~** *nm* : thank-you — **~** *nf* : mercy

mercredi [mɛrkrədi] *nm* : Wednesday

mercure [mɛrkyr] *nm* : mercury

Mercure *nf* : Mercury (planet)

mère [mɛr] *nf* : mother

méridional, -nale [meridjɔnal] *adj, mpl* **-naux** [-no] : southern

meringue [mərɛ̃g] *nf* : meringue

mérite [merit] *nm* : merit, credit — **mériter** [merite] *vt* : deserve, merit — **méritoire** [meritwar] *adj* : commendable

merle [mɛrl] *nm* : blackbird

merveille [mɛrvɛj] *nf* **1** : wonder, marvel **2** **à ~** : wonderfully — **merveilleux, -leuse** [mɛrvɛjø, -jøz] *adj* : wonderful, marvelous

mes → mon

mésaventure [mezavɑ̃tyr] *nf* : misfortune, mishap

mesdames → madame

mesdemoiselles → mademoiselle

mésentente [mezɑ̃tɑ̃t] *nf* DÉSACCORD : misunderstanding, disagreement

mesquin, -quine [mɛskɛ̃, -kin] *adj* **1** : mean, petty **2** : cheap, stingy — **mesquinerie** [mɛskinri] *nf* **1** : pettiness **2** AVARICE : stinginess

message [mɛsaʒ] *nm* : message — **messager, -gère** [mɛsaʒe, -ʒɛr] *n* : messenger — **messagerie** [mɛsaʒri] *nf* : parcel delivery service

messe [mɛs] *nf* : Mass

mesure [məzyr] *nf* **1** : measure, measurement **2** RETENUE : moderation **3 à la ~ de** : worthy of **4 à ~ que** : as **5 dans la ~ où** : insofar as — **mesuré, -rée** [məzyre] *adj* : measured, restrained — **mesurer** [məzyre] *vt* **1** : measure **2** ÉVALUER : assess

métabolisme [metabɔlism] *nm* : metabolism

métal [metal] *nm, pl* **-taux** [meto] : metal — **métallique** [metalik] *adj* : metallic

métamorphose [metamɔrfoz] *nf* : metamorphosis

métaphore [metafɔr] *nf* : metaphor

météo [meteo] *nf fam* : weather forecast

météore [meteɔr] *nm* : meteor

météorologie [meteɔrɔlɔʒi] *nf* : meteorology — **météorologique** [meteɔrɔlɔʒik] *adj* : meteorological, weather — **météorologiste** [meteɔrɔlɔʒist] *nmf* : meteorologist

méthode [metɔd] *nf* **1** : method, system **2** MANUEL : primer — **méthodique** [metɔdik] *adj* : methodical

méticuleux, -leuse [metikylø, -løz] *adj* : meticulous

métier [metje] *nm* **1** : job, profession **2** : experience, skill **3** *or* **~ à tisser** : loom

métis, -tisse [metis] *adj & n* : half-breed, half-caste

métrage [metraʒ] *nm* **1** : length (of an object) **2** : footage (of a film)

mètre [mɛtr] *nm* **1** : meter **2 ~ ruban** : tape measure — **métrique** [metrik] *adj* : metric

métro [metro] *nm* : subway

métropole [metrɔpɔl] *nf* : city, metropolis — **métropolitain, -taine** [metrɔpɔlitɛ̃, -tɛn] *adj* : metropolitan

mets [mɛ] *nm* PLAT : dish

metteur [metœr] *nm* **~ en scène** : producer, director

mettre [mɛtr] {53} *vt* **1** PLACER : put, place **2** : put on, wear **3** AJOUTER : add (in), put in **4** DISPOSER : prepare, arrange **5 ~ au point** : develop, finalize **6 ~ en marche** : turn on, switch on — **se mettre** *vr* **1** : become, get **2** : put on, wear **3 ~ à faire** : start doing **4 ~ à table** : sit down at the table

meuble [mœbl] *nm* **1** : piece of furniture **2** **~s** *nmpl* : furniture — **meublé, -blée** [mœble] *adj* : furnished — **meubler** [mœble] *vt* : furnish

meugler [møgle] *vi* : moo, low — **meuglement** [møgləmɑ̃] *nm* : mooing, lowing

meule [møl] *nf* **1** : millstone **2 ~ de foin** : haystack

meurtre [mœrtr] *nm* : murder — **meurtrier, -trière** [mœrtrije, -trijɛr] *adj* : deadly — **~** *n* ASSASSIN : murderer

meurtrir [mœrtrir] *vt* : bruise — **meurtrissure** [mœrtrisyr] *nf* : bruise

meute [møt] *nf* : pack (of hounds)

mexicain, -caine [mɛksikɛ̃, -kɛn] *adj* : Mexican

miaou [mjau] *nm* : meow — **miauler** [mjole] *vi* : meow

mi-bas [miba] *nms & pl* : kneesock

miche [miʃ] *nf* : round loaf of bread

mi-chemin [miʃmɛ̃] **à ~** *adv phr* : halfway, midway

microbe [mikrɔb] *nm* : germ, microbe

microfilm [mikrɔfilm] *nm* : microfilm

micro-ondes [mikrɔɔ̃d] *nms & pl* : microwave oven

microphone [mikrɔfɔn] *nm* : microphone

microscope [mikrɔskɔp] *nm* : microscope — **microscopique** [mikrɔskɔpik] *adj* : microscopic

microsillon [mikrɔsijɔ̃] *nm* : long-playing record

midi [midi] *nm* **1** : midday, noon **2** : lunchtime **3** SUD : south

mie [mi] *nf* : inside, soft part (of a loaf of bread)

miel [mjɛl] *nm* : honey — **mielleux, -leuse** [mjɛlø, -løz] *adj* : sickly sweet

mien, mienne [mjɛ̃, mjɛn] *adj* : mine, my own — **~** *pron* **le mien, la mienne, les miens, les miennes** : mine

miette [mjɛt] *nf* **1** : crumb **2 en ~s** : in pieces

mieux [mjø] *adv & adj* **1** (*comparative of* **bien**) : better **2** (*superlative of* **bien**) **le ~**, la ~, les ~ : the best — ~ *nm* 1 : best 2 il y a du ~ : there's some improvement

mignon, -gnonne [miɲɔ̃, -ɲɔn] *adj* 1 : sweet, cute 2 GENTIL : nice, kind

migraine [migrɛn] *nf* : headache, migraine

migration [migrasjɔ̃] *nf* : migration — **migrateur, -trice** [migratœr, -tris] *adj* : migratory

mijoter [miʒɔte] *vt* 1 : simmer 2 MANIGANCER : plot, cook up — *vi* : simmer, stew

mil [mil] → **mille**

mile [majl] *nm* : mile

milice [milis] *nf* : militia

milieu [miljø] *nm, pl* **-lieux** 1 CENTRE : middle 2 ENTOURAGE : environment 3 au ~ de : among, in the midst of

militaire [militɛr] *adj* : military — ~ *nm* SOLDAT : soldier, serviceman

militant, -tante [militɑ̃, -tɑ̃t] *adj & n* : militant

millage [milaʒ] *nm Can* : mileage (of a motor vehicle)

mille [mil] *adj* : one thousand — ~ *nm or* ~ **marin** : nautical mile

millénaire [milenɛr] *nm* : millennium

mille-pattes [milpat] *nms & pl* 1 : centipede 2 : millipede

millésime [milezim] *nm* 1 : year (of manufacture) 2 : vintage year

millet [mijɛ] *nm* : millet

milliard [miljar] *nm* : billion — **milliardaire** [miljardɛr] *nmf* : billionaire

millier [milje] *nm* : thousand

milligramme [miligram] *nm* : milligram

millimètre [milimetr] *nm* : millimeter

million [miljɔ̃] *nm* : million — **millionnaire** [miljɔnɛr] *nmf* : millionaire

mime [mim] *nmf* : mime — **mimer** [mime] *vt* : mimic

mimique [mimik] *nf* GRIMACE : face

minable [minabl] *adj* : shabby

mince [mɛ̃s] *adj* 1 : thin, slender 2 INSIGNIFIANT : meager, scanty — **minceur** [mɛ̃sœr] *nf* : thinness, slenderness

mine[1] [min] *nf* : appearance, look

mine[2] *nf* 1 : (coal) mine 2 : (pencil) lead — **miner** [mine] *vt* : undermine, weaken — **minerai** [minrɛ] *nm* : ore

minéral, -rale [mineral] *adj, mpl* **-raux** [-ro] : mineral — **minéral** *nm* : mineral

minet, -nette [minɛ, -nɛt] *n fam* : pussycat

mineur[1], **-neure** [minœr] *adj & nmf* : minor

mineur[2] *nm* : miner

miniature [minjatyr] *adj & nf* : miniature

minimal, -male [minimal] *adj, mpl* **-maux** [-mo] : minimal, minimum — **minime** [minim] *adj* : minimal, negligible — **minimiser** [minimize] *vt* : minimize — **minimum** [minimɔm] *adj & nm, pl* **-mums** [-mɔm] *or* **-ma** [-ma] : minimum

ministère [ministɛr] *nm* 1 : department, ministry 2 CABINET : government — **ministériel, -rielle** [ministerjɛl] *adj* : governmental — **ministre** [ministr] *nm* : minister, secretary

minorité [minɔrite] *nf* : minority — **minoritaire** [minɔritɛr] *adj* : minority

minou [minu] *nm fam* : pussycat

minuit [minɥi] *nm* : midnight

minuscule [minyskyl] *adj* : minute, tiny — ~ *nf* : small (lowercase) letter

minute [minyt] *nf* : minute — **minuter** [minyte] *vt* : time — **minuterie** [minytri] *nf* : timer

minutieux, -tieuse [minysjø, -sjøz] *adj* 1 MÉTICULEUX : meticulous 2 : detailed (of work, etc.) — **minutie** [minysi] *nf* : meticulousness

miracle [mirakl] *nm* : miracle — **miraculeux, -leuse** [mirakylø, -løz] *adj* : miraculous

mirage [miraʒ] *nm* : mirage

mire [mir] *nf* **point de** ~ : target

miroir [mirwar] *nm* : mirror

miroiter [mirwate] *vi* BRILLER : sparkle, shimmer — **miroitement** [mirwatmɑ̃] *nm* : sparkling, shimmering

mis, mise [mi, miz] *adj* 1 : clad 2 **bien** ~ : well-dressed

mise [miz] *nf* 1 : putting, placing 2 : stake (in games of chance) 3 TENUE : dress, attire — **miser** [mize] *vt* : bet — *vi* ~ **sur** : bet on, count on

misérable [mizerabl] *adj* 1 PITOYABLE : wretched, pitiful 2 INSIGNIFIANT : meager, paltry — ~ *nmf* 1 : wretch 2 : scoundrel — **misère** [mizɛr] *nf* 1 : poverty 2 : misery — **miséricorde** [mizerikɔrd] *nf* : mercy, forgiveness

missile [misil] *nm* : missile

mission [misjɔ̃] *nf* : mission — **missionnaire** [misjɔnɛr] *adj & nmf* : missionary

mitaine [mitɛn] *nf Can, Switz* : mitten

mite [mit] *nf* : clothes moth

mi-temps [mitɑ̃] *nms & pl* : part-time job — ~ *nfs & pl* : halftime (in sports)

miteux, -teuse [mitø, -tøz] *adj* : seedy, shabby

mitigé, -gée [mitiʒe] *adj* 1 : lukewarm, reserved 2 **sentiments mitigés** : mixed feelings

mitoyen, -toyenne [mitwajɛ̃, -jɛn] *adj* : common, dividing

mitrailleuse [mitrajøz] *nf* : machine gun

mi-voix [mivwa] à ~ *adv phr* : in a low voice

mixeur [miksœr] *or* **mixer** [miksɛr] *nm* : mixer, blender

mixte [mikst] *adj* 1 : mixed 2 **école** ~ : coeducational school

mobile [mɔbil] *adj* **1** : mobile, moving **2 feuilles ~s** : loose-leaf paper — **~** *nm* **1** : motive (of a crime) **2** : (paper) mobile —
mobilier [mɔbilje] *nm* MEUBLES : furniture
mobiliser [mɔbilize] *vt* : mobilize
mobilité [mɔbilite] *nf* : mobility
mocassin [mɔkasɛ̃] *nm* : moccasin
moche [mɔʃ] *adj fam* **1** : ugly **2** MAUVAIS : lousy
modalité [mɔdalite] *nf* : form, mode
mode [mɔd] *nm* **1** : mode, method **2 ~ d'emploi** : directions for use — **~** *nf* : fashion
modèle [mɔdɛl] *nm* : model — **~** *adj* : model, exemplary — **modeler** [mɔdle] {20} *vt* : mold, shape
modem [mɔdɛm] *nm* : modem
modérer [mɔdere] {87} *vt* : moderate, restrain — **modérateur, -trice** [mɔderatœr, -tris] *adj* : moderating — **modération** [mɔderasjɔ̃] *nf* MESURE : moderation, restraint — **modéré, -rée** [mɔdere] *adj* : moderate
moderne [mɔdɛrn] *adj* : modern — **moderniser** [mɔdɛrnize] *vt* : modernize
modeste [mɔdɛst] *adj* : modest — **modestie** [mɔdɛsti] *nf* : modesty
modifier [mɔdifje] {96} *vt* : modify — **se modifier** *vr* : change — **modification** [mɔdifikasjɔ̃] *nf* : modification
modique [mɔdik] *adj* : modest, low
moduler [mɔdyle] *vt* : modulate, adjust
moelle [mwal] *nf* **1** : marrow **2 ~ épinière** : spinal cord — **moelleux, -leuse** [mwalø, -løz] *adj* **1** DOUX : soft **2** : moist (of a cake)
mœurs [mœr(s)] *nfpl* **1** : morals **2** USAGES : customs, habits
moi [mwa] *pron* **1** : I **2** : me **3 à ~** : mine — **~** *nm* **le ~** : the self, the ego — **moi-même** [mwamɛm] *pron* : myself
moindre [mwɛ̃dr] *adj* **1** : lesser, smaller, lower **2 le ~, la ~** : the least, the slightest
moine [mwan] *nm* : monk
moineau [mwano] *nm, pl* **-neaux** : sparrow
moins [mwɛ̃] *adv* **1** : less **2 le ~** : least, the least **3 ~ de** : less than, fewer **4 à ~ que** : unless **5 en ~** : missing — **~** *nm* **1** : minus (sign) **2 au ~** *or* **du ~** : at least **3 pour le ~** : at (the very) least — **~** *prep* **1** : minus **2** (*in expressions of time*) : to, of **3** (*in expressions of temperature*) : below
mois [mwa] *nm* : month
moisi, -sie [mwazi] *adj* : moldy — **moisi** *nm* : mold, mildew — **moisir** [mwazir] *vi* **1** : become moldy **2** *fam* : stagnate — **moisissure** [mwazisyr] *nf* : mold, mildew
moisson [mwasɔ̃] *nf* : harvest, crop — **moissonner** [mwasɔne] *vt* : harvest, reap — **moissonneuse** [mwasɔnøz] *nf* : harvester, reaper — **moissonneuse-batteuse** [mwasɔnøzbatøz] *nf, pl* **moissonneuses-batteuses** : combine (harvester)
moite [mwat] *adj* : damp, clammy
moitié [mwatje] *nf* **1** : half **2 à ~** : half, halfway — **moitié-moitié** *adv* : fifty-fifty
moka [mɔka] *nm* : mocha
mol → mou
molaire [mɔlɛr] *nf* : molar
molécule [mɔlekyl] *nf* : molecule
molle → mou — mollesse [mɔlɛs] *adj* **1** : softness **2** INDOLENCE : indolence, apathy — **mollement** [mɔlmɑ̃] *adv* **1** DOUCEMENT : softly, gently **2** : weakly, feebly
mollet [mɔlɛ] *nm* : calf (of the leg)
mollir [mɔlir] *vi* **1** : soften, go soft **2** FAIBLIR : weaken, slacken
mollusque [mɔlysk] *nm* : mollusk
môme [mom] *nmf France fam* : kid, youngster
moment [mɔmɑ̃] *nm* **1** : moment, while **2** INSTANT : minute, instant **3** OCCASION : time, occasion **4** : present (time) **5 du ~ que** : since — **momentané, -née** [mɔmɑ̃tane] *adj* : momentary, temporary — **momentanément** [-nemɑ̃] *adv* **1** : momentarily **2** : at the moment
momie [mɔmi] *nf* : mummy
mon [mɔ̃], **ma** [ma] *adj, pl* **mes** [mɛ] : my
monarchie [mɔnarʃi] *nf* : monarchy — **monarque** [mɔnark] *nm* : monarch
monastère [mɔnaster] *nm* : monastery
monceau [mɔ̃so] *nm, pl* **-ceaux** [mɔ̃so] : heap, pile
mondain, -daine [mɔ̃dɛ̃, -dɛn] *adj* **1** : society, social **2** RAFFINÉ : fashionable
monde [mɔ̃d] *nm* **1** : world **2** : society, people *pl* **3 tout le ~** : everyone — **mondial, -diale** [mɔ̃djal] *adj, mpl* **-diaux** [-djo] **1** : world **2** : worldwide, global — **mondialement** [mɔ̃djalmɑ̃] *adv* : throughout the world
monétaire [mɔnetɛr] *adj* : monetary
moniteur, -trice [mɔnitœr, -tris] *n* : instructor, coach — **moniteur** *nm* : monitor, screen
monnaie [mɔnɛ] *nf* **1** : money, currency **2** PIÈCE : coin — **monnayer** [mɔneje] {11} *vt* **1** : convert into cash **2** : capitalize on (experience, etc.) — **monnayeur** [mɔnejœr] *nm* → **faux-monnayeur**
monocorde [mɔnɔkɔrd] *adj* : droning, monotonous
monogramme [mɔnɔgram] *nm* : monogram
monologue [mɔnɔlɔg] *nm* : monologue, soliloquy
monopole [mɔnɔpɔl] *nm* : monopoly — **monopoliser** [mɔnɔpɔlize] *vt* : monopolize
monotone [mɔnɔtɔn] *adj* : monotonous, dull — **monotonie** [mɔnɔtɔni] *nf* : monotony
monsieur [məsjø] *nm, pl* **messieurs** [mɛsjø] **1** : Mr., sir **2** : man, gentleman

monstre [mɔ̃str] *nm* : monster — ~ *adj* : huge, colossal — **monstrueux, -trueuse** [mɔ̃stryø, -tryøz] *adj* **1** : monstrous, huge **2** TERRIBLE : hideous — **monstruosité** [mɔ̃stryozite] *nf* : monstrosity

mont [mɔ̃] *nm* : mount, mountain

montage [mɔ̃taʒ] *nm* **1** : editing (of a film) **2 chaîne de** ~ : assembly line

montagne [mɔ̃taɲ] *nf* **1** : mountain **2 la** ~ : the mountains **3** ~**s russes** : roller coaster — **montagneux, -gneuse** [mɔ̃taɲø, -ɲøz] *adj* : mountainous

montant, -tante [mɔ̃tã, -tãt] *adj* : uphill, rising — **montant** *nm* **1** : upright, post **2** SOMME : total, sum

mont–de–piété [mɔ̃dpjete] *nm, pl* **monts–de–piété** *France* : pawnshop

monte–charge [mɔ̃tʃarʒ] *nms & pl* : freight elevator

monter [mɔ̃te] *vi* **1** : go up, come up, climb (up) **2** : rise (of temperature, etc.) **3** ~ **à** : ride (a bicycle, etc.) **4** ~ **dans** : get into, board **5** ~ **sur** : mount, get on (a horse) — *vt (with auxiliary verb* avoir*)* **1** : take up, bring up **2** : raise, turn up (volume, etc.) **3** : go up, climb (up) **4** : assemble, put together **5** ~ **à cheval** : ride a horse — **se monter** *vr* ~ **à** : amount to — **montée** [mɔ̃te] *nf* **1** : rise, rising **2** : ascent, climb **3** PENTE : slope

montre [mɔ̃tr] *nf* **1** : watch **2 faire** ~ **de** : show, display

montréalais, -laise [mɔ̃reale, -lɛz] *adj* : of or from Montreal

montre–bracelet [mɔ̃trəbraslɛ] *nf, pl* **montres–bracelets** : wristwatch

montrer [mɔ̃tre] *vt* **1** : show, reveal **2** INDIQUER : point out — **se montrer** *vr* **1** : show oneself **2** : prove to be

monture [mɔ̃tyr] *nf* **1** : mount, horse **2** : setting (for jewelry) **3** : frames *pl* (for eyeglasses)

monument [mɔnymã] *nm* : monument — **monumental, -tale** [mɔnymãtal] *adj, mpl* **-taux** [-to] : monumental

moquer [mɔke] *v* **se moquer** *vr* **1** ~ **de** : make fun of, mock **2 je m'en moque** : I couldn't care less — **moquerie** [mɔkri] *nf* : mockery

moquette [mɔkɛt] *nf* : wall-to-wall carpeting

moqueur, -queuse [mɔkœr, -køz] *adj* : mocking

moral, -rale [mɔral] *adj, mpl* **-raux** [mɔro] : moral — **moral** *nm* : morale, spirits *pl* — **morale** *nf* **1** : morals *pl*, morality **2** : moral (of a story) — **moralisateur, -trice** [mɔralizatœr, -tris] *adj* : moralizing — **moralité** [mɔralite] *nf* : morality

morbide [mɔrbid] *adj* : morbid

morceau [mɔrso] *nm, pl* **-ceaux** : piece, bit — **morceler** [mɔrsəle] {8} *vt* : break up, divide

mordant, -dante [mɔrdã, -dãt] *adj* : biting, scathing — **mordant** *nm* : bite, punch

mordiller [mɔrdije] *vt* : nibble at

mordre [mɔrdr] {63} *v* : bite — **se mordre** *vr* ~ **la langue** : bite one's tongue — **mordu, -due** *adj* : smitten (with love) — ~ *n fam* : fan, buff

morfondre [mɔrfɔ̃dr] {63} *v* **se morfondre** *vr* **1** : mope **2** *Can* : wear oneself out

morgue [mɔrg] *nf* **1** : morgue, mortuary **2** ARROGANCE : arrogance

morille [mɔrij] *nf* : type of mushroom

morne [mɔrn] *adj* **1** SOMBRE : gloomy, glum **2** MAUSSADE : dismal, dreary

morose [mɔroz] *adj* : morose, sullen

morphine [mɔrfin] *nf* : morphine

mors [mɔr] *nm* : bit (of a bridle)

morse [mɔrs] *nm* **1** : walrus **2** : Morse code

morsure [mɔrsyr] *nf* : bite

mort, morte [mɔr, mɔrt] *adj* : dead — ~ *n* **1** : dead person, corpse **2** VICTIME : fatality — **mort** *nf* : death — **mortalité** [mɔrtalite] *nf* : mortality — **mortel, -telle** [mɔrtɛl] *adj* **1** : mortal **2** FATAL : fatal — ~ *n* : mortal

mortier [mɔrtje] *nm* : mortar

mortifier [mɔrtifje] {96} *vt* : mortify

mortuaire [mɔrtɥɛr] *adj* **1** FUNÈBRE : funeral **2 salon** — *Can* : funeral home

morue [mɔry] *nf* : cod

mosaïque [mɔzaik] *adj & nf* : mosaic

mosquée [mɔske] *nf* : mosque

mot [mo] *nm* **1** : word **2** : note, line **3** ~ **de passe** : password **4** ~**s croisés** : crossword puzzle

motel [mɔtɛl] *nm* : motel

moteur [mɔtœr] *nm* : engine, motor — **moteur, -trice** [mɔtœr, -tris] *adj* **1** : motor **2 force motrice** : driving force

motif [mɔtif] *nm* **1** RAISON : motive, grounds *pl* **2** DESSIN : pattern, design

motion [mɔsjɔ̃] *nf* : motion (in politics)

motiver [mɔtive] *vt* **1** : motivate **2** EXPLIQUER : justify, explain — **motivation** [mɔtivasjɔ̃] *nf* : motivation, incentive

moto [mɔto] *nf* : bike, motorbike — **moto-cyclette** [mɔtɔsiklɛt] *nf* : motorcycle

motoriser [mɔtɔrize] *vt* : motorize

motte [mɔt] *nf* : clod, lump (of earth, etc.)

mou [mu] (**mol** [mɔl] *before vowel or mute h*), **molle** [mɔl] *adj* **1** : soft **2** FLASQUE : flabby, limp **3** LÂCHE : slack **4 avoir les jambes molles** : be weak in the knees

mouchard, -charde [muʃar, -ʃard] *n fam* : informer, stool pigeon

mouche [muʃ] *nf* : fly

moucher [muʃe] *v* **se moucher** *vr* : blow one's nose

moucheron [muʃrɔ̃] *nm* : gnat
moucheté [muʃte] *adj* : speckled, flecked
mouchoir [muʃwar] *nm* : handkerchief
moudre [mudr] {54} *vt* : grind
moue [mu] *nf* 1 : pout 2 faire la ~ : pout
mouette [mwɛt] *nf* : gull, seagull
mouffette *or* moufette [mufɛt] *nf* : skunk
moufle [mufl] *nf* : mitten
mouiller [muje] *vt* 1 : wet, moisten 2 ~ l'ancre : drop anchor — se mouiller *vr* 1 : get wet 2 *fam* : become involved — mouillage [mujaʒ] *nm* : anchorage, berth — mouillé, -lée [muje] *adj* : wet
moulage [mulaʒ] *nm* 1 : molding, casting 2 faire un ~ de : take a cast of
moulant, -lante [mulɑ̃, -lɑ̃t] *adj* : tight-fitting (of clothes, etc.)
moule[1] [mul] *nf* : mussel
moule[2] *nm* 1 : mold, matrix 2 ~ à gâteaux : cake pan — mouler [mule] *vt* 1 : mold 2 : cast (a statue)
moulin [mulɛ̃] *nm* 1 : mill 2 ~ à café : coffee grinder 3 ~ à paroles *fam* : chatterbox — moulinet [mulinɛ] *nm* : reel, winch
moulu, -lue [muly] *adj* 1 : ground (of coffee, etc.) 2 *fam* : worn-out
moulure [mulyr] *nf* : molding
mourir [murir] {55} *vi* 1 : die 2 : die out (of a sound, etc.) 3 ~ de faim : be dying of hunger — mourant, -rante [murɑ̃, -rɑ̃t] *n* : dying person
mousquet [muskɛ] *nm* : musket — mousquetaire [muskətɛr] *nm* : musketeer
mousse [mus] *nf* 1 : moss (in botany) 2 : foam, lather 3 : mousse (in cooking) — moussant, -sante [musɑ̃, -sɑ̃t] *adj* : foaming — mousser [muse] *vi* : foam, froth, lather — mousseux, -seuse [musø, -søz] *adj* 1 : foaming, frothy 2 vin ~ : sparkling wine
moustache [mustaʃ] *nf* 1 : mustache 2 ~s *nfpl* : whiskers (of an animal)
moustique [mustik] *nm* : mosquito — moustiquaire [mustikɛr] *nf* 1 : mosquito net 2 : screen (for a window, etc.)
moutarde [mutard] *nf* : mustard
mouton [mutɔ̃] *nm* 1 : sheep, sheepskin 2 : mutton (in cooking)
mouvement [muvmɑ̃] *nm* 1 : movement 2 ACTIVITÉ : activity, bustle 3 IMPULSION : impulse, reaction — mouvementé, -tée [muvmɑ̃te] *adj* 1 : eventful, hectic 2 ACCIDENTÉ : rough, uneven — mouvoir [muvwar] {56} *vt* : move, prompt
moyen, moyenne [mwajɛ̃, -jɛn] *adj* 1 : medium 2 : average 3 Moyen Âge : Middle Ages *pl* — moyen *nm* 1 : way, means *pl* 2 : possibility 3 ~s *nmpl* : means, resources — moyenne *nf* : average —

moyennement [mwajɛnmɑ̃] *adv* MODÉRÉMENT : fairly, moderately
moyeu [mwajø] *nm*, *pl* moyeux : hub (of a wheel)
muer [mɥe] *vi* 1 : molt, shed 2 : change, break (of the voice) — mue [my] *nf* : molting, shedding
muet, muette [mɥɛ, mɥɛt] *adj* 1 : dumb 2 SILENCIEUX : silent — ~ *n* : mute, dumb person
muffin [mɔfœn] *nm Can* : muffin
muguet [mygɛ] *nm* : lily of the valley
mule [myl] *nf* : female mule — mulet [mylɛ] *nm* : male mule
multicolore [myltikɔlɔr] *adj* : multicolored
multimédia [myltimedja] *adj* : multimedia
multinational, -nale [myltinasjɔnal] *adj*, *mpl* -naux [-no] : multinational
multiple [myltipl] *adj* 1 : multiple 2 DIVERS : many — ~ *nm* : multiple — multiplication [myltiplikasjɔ̃] *nf* : multiplication — multiplier [myltiplije] {96} *vt* : multiply — se multiplier *vr* : proliferate
multitude [myltityd] *nf* : multitude, mass
municipal, -pale [mynisipal] *adj*, *mpl* -paux [-po] : municipal, town — municipalité [mynisipalite] *nf* 1 : municipality, town 2 : town council
munir [mynir] *vt* : equip, provide — se munir *vr* ~ de : equip oneself with
munitions [mynisjɔ̃] *nfpl* : ammunition, munitions
mur [myr] *nm* : wall
mûr, mûre [myr] *adj* 1 : ripe (of a fruit) 2 : mature (of a person)
muraille [myraj] *nf* : (high) wall — mural, -rale [myral] *adj*, *mpl* -raux [myro] : wall, mural — murale [myral] *nf* : mural
mûre [myr] *nf* : blackberry
mûrir [myrir] *v* 1 : ripen 2 ÉVOLUER : mature, develop
murmure [myrmyr] *nm* : murmur — murmurer [myrmyre] *v* : murmur
muscade [myskad] *nf or* noix ~ : nutmeg
muscle [myskl] *nm* : muscle — musclé, -clée [myskle] *adj* : muscular, powerful — musculaire [myskylɛr] *adj* : muscular — musculature [myskylatyr] *nf* : muscles *pl*
muse [myz] *nf* : muse
museau [myzo] *nm*, *pl* -seaux : muzzle, snout
musée [myze] *nm* : museum
museler [myzle] {8} *vt* : muzzle — muselière [myzəljɛr] *nf* : muzzle
musique [myzik] *nf* : music — musical, -cale [myzikal] *adj* -caux [-ko] : musical — musicien, -cienne [myzisjɛ̃, -sjɛn] *n* : musician
musulman, -mane [myzylmɑ̃, -man] *adj & n* : Muslim

mutant, -tante [mytɑ̃, -tɑ̃t] *adj & n* : mutant — **mutation** [mytasjɔ̃] *nf* **1** : transformation **2** : transfer (of an employee) — **muter** [myte] *vt* : transfer (an employee)

mutiler [mytile] *vt* : mutilate

mutiner [mytine] *v* **se mutiner** *vr* : mutiny, rebel — **mutinerie** [mytinri] *nf* RÉBELLION : mutiny, rebellion

mutuel, -tuelle [mytɥɛl] *adj* : mutual

myope [mjɔp] *adj* : nearsighted — **myopie** [mjɔpi] *nf* : myopia, nearsightedness

myrtille [mirtil] *nf France* : blueberry

mystère [mistɛr] *nm* : mystery — **mystérieux, -rieuse** [misterjø, -rjøz] *adj* : mysterious

mystifier [mistifje] {96} *vt* DUPER : deceive, dupe

mystique [mistik] *adj* : mystic, mystical

mythe [mit] *nm* : myth — **mythique** [mitik] *adj* : mythic(al) — **mythologie** [mitɔlɔʒi] *nf* : mythology

N

n [ɛn] *nm* : n, 14th letter of the alphabet

nacre [nakr] *nf* : mother-of-pearl — **nacré, -crée** [nakre] *adj* : pearly

nager [naʒe] {17} *v* : swim — **nage** [naʒ] *nf* **1** : swimming **2** : stroke (in swimming) **3 en ~** : dripping with sweat — **nageoire** [naʒwar] *nf* : fin, flipper — **nageur, -geuse** [naʒœr, -ʒøz] *n* : swimmer

naguère [nagɛr] *adv* **1** RÉCEMMENT : recently **2** AUTREFOIS : formerly

naïf, naïve [naif, naiv] *adj* **1** INGÉNU : naive **2** CRÉDULE : gullible

nain, naine [nɛ̃, nɛn] *n* : dwarf, midget

naître [nɛtr] {57} *vi* **1** : be born **2** : rise, originate — **naissance** [nɛsɑ̃s] *nf* **1** : birth **2 donner ~ à** : give rise to — **naissant, -sante** [nɛsɑ̃, -sɑ̃t] *adj* : incipient

naïveté [naivte] *nf* : naïveté

nantir [nɑ̃tir] *vt* **~ de** : provide with — **nanti, -tie** [nɑ̃ti] *adj* : affluent, well-to-do — **nantissement** [nɑ̃tismɑ̃] *nm* : collateral

nappe [nap] *nf* **1** : tablecloth **2** : layer, sheet (of water, oil, etc.) — **napper** [nape] *vt* : coat, cover — **napperon** [naprɔ̃] *nm* : mat, doily

narcotique [narkɔtik] *nm* : narcotic

narguer [narge] *vt* : mock, taunt

narine [narin] *nf* : nostril

narquois, -quoise [narkwa, -kwaz] *adj* : sneering, derisive

narrer [nare] *vt* : narrate, tell — **narrateur, -trice** [naratœr, -tris] *n* : narrator — **narration** [narasjɔ̃] *nf* : narration, narrative

nasal, -sale [nazal] *adj, mpl* **-saux** [nazo] : nasal — **naseau** [nazo] *nm, pl* **-seaux** : nostril (of an animal) — **nasillard, -larde** [nazijar, -jard] *adj* : nasal (in tone)

natal, -tale [natal] *adj, mpl* **-tals** : native (of a country, etc.) — **natalité** [natalite] *nf* : birthrate

natation [natasjɔ̃] *nf* : swimming

natif¹, -tive [natif, -tiv] *adj* **~ de** : be born in

natif², -tive *n* : native

nation [nasjɔ̃] *nf* : nation — **national, -nale** [nasjɔnal] *adj, mpl* **-naux** [-no] : national — **nationale** *nf France* : highway — **nationaliser** [nasjɔnalize] *vt* : nationalize — **nationalisme** [nasjɔnalism] *nm* : nationalism — **nationalité** [nasjɔnalite] *nf* : nationality

nativité [nativite] *nf* : nativity

natte [nat] *nf* **1** : (straw) mat **2** : braid (of hair) — **natter** [nate] *vt* : braid, plait

naturaliser [natyralize] *vt* : naturalize

nature [natyr] *nf* **1** : nature **2 ~ morte** : still life — **~** *adj* : plain (of yogurt, etc.) — **naturel, -relle** [natyrɛl] *adj* : natural — **naturel** *nm* **1** : nature, disposition **2** AISANCE : naturalness — **naturellement** [natyrɛlmɑ̃] *adv* **1** : naturally **2** : of course

naufrage [nofraʒ] *nm* : shipwreck — **naufragé, -gée** [nofraʒe] *adj & n* : castaway

nausée [noze] *nf* : nausea — **nauséabond, -bonde** [nozeabɔ̃, -bɔ̃d] *adj* : nauseating, revolting

nautique [notik] *adj* : nautical

naval, -vale [naval] *adj, mpl* **-vals** : naval

navet [navɛ] *nm* **1** : turnip **2** *fam* : third-rate film, novel, etc.

navette [navɛt] *nf* **1** : shuttle **2 faire la ~** : shuttle back and forth, commute

naviguer [navige] *vi* : sail, navigate — **navigable** [navigabl] *adj* : navigable — **navigateur, -trice** [navigatœr, -tris] *n* : navigator — **navigation** [navigasjɔ̃] *nf* : navigation

navire [navir] *nm* : ship, vessel

navrant, -vrante [navrɑ̃, -vrɑ̃t] *adj* **1** : upsetting, distressing **2** REGRETTABLE : unfortunate — **navré, -vrée** [navre] *adj* **être ~ de** : be sorry about

ne [nə] (**n'** *before a vowel or mute h*) *adv* **1**
∼ **pas** : not **2** ∼ **jamais** : never **3** ∼
plus : no longer **4** ∼ **que** : only
né, née [ne] *adj* : born
néanmoins [neãmwɛ̃] *adv* : nevertheless,
yet
néant [neã] *nm* : emptiness, nothingness
nébuleux, -leuse [nebylø, -løz] *adj* **1**
: cloudy (of the sky) **2** VAGUE : nebulous
nécessaire [nesesɛr] *adj* : necessary — ∼
nm **1** : necessity, need **2** TROUSSE : bag, kit
— **nécessairement** [nesesɛrmã] *adv* : necessarily — **nécessité** [nesesite] *nf* : necessity, need — **nécessiter** [nesesite] *vt* EX-
IGER : require, call for
nécrologie [nekrɔlɔʒi] *nf* : obituary
nectar [nɛktar] *nm* : nectar
nectarine [nɛktarin] *nf* : nectarine
nef [nɛf] *nf* : nave
néfaste [nefast] *adj* NUISIBLE : harmful
négatif, -tive [negatif, -tiv] *adj* : negative —
négatif *nm* : negative (in photography) —
négative *nf* **répondre par la** ∼ : reply in
the negative — **négation** [negasjɔ̃] *nf* : negative (in grammar)
négliger [negliʒe] {17} *vt* **1** : neglect **2**
IGNORER : disregard — **négligé, -gée**
[negliʒe] *adj* : untidy (of appearance, etc.)
— **négligé** *nm* : negligee — **négligeable**
[negliʒabl] *adj* : negligible — **négligence**
[negliʒãs] *nf* : negligence, carelessness —
négligent, -gente [negliʒã, -ʒãt] *adj* : negligent
négoce [negɔs] *nm* : business, trade — **négociant, -ciante** [negɔsjã, -sjãt] *n* : merchant
négocier [negɔsje] {96} *v* : negotiate — **négociable** [negɔsjabl] *adj* : negotiable —
négociateur, -trice [negɔsjatœr, -tris] *n*
: negotiator — **négociation** [negɔsjasjɔ̃] *nf*
: negotiation
nègre, négresse [nɛgr, negrɛs] *adj & n*
(*sometimes considered offensive*) : Negro
neige [nɛʒ] *nf* **1** : snow **2** ∼ **fondue** : slush
— **neiger** [neʒe] {17} *v impers* : snow —
neigeux, -geuse [nɛʒø, -ʒøz] *adj* : snowy
nénuphar [nenyfar] *nm* : water lily
néon [neɔ̃] *nm* : neon
néophyte [neɔfit] *nmf* : novice, beginner
Neptune [nɛptyn] *nf* : Neptune (planet)
nerf [nɛr] *nm* **1** : nerve **2** VIGUEUR : vigor,
spirit — **nerveux, -veuse** [nɛrvø, -vøz] *adj*
: nervous, tense — **nervosité** [nɛrvozite] *nf*
: nervousness
nervure [nɛrvyr] *nf* : vein (of a leaf)
n'est–ce pas [nɛspa] *adv* : no?, isn't that
right?, isn't it?
net, nette [nɛt] *adj* **1** PROPRE : clean, tidy **2**
CLAIR : clear, distinct — **net** *adv* : plainly,
flatly — **nettement** [nɛtmã] *adv* **1** : clearly,

distinctly **2** : definitely — **netteté** [nɛtte] *nf*
1 : cleanness **2** : clearness, sharpness
nettoyer [nɛtwaje] {58} *vt* **1** : clean (up) **2**
∼ **à sec** : dry-clean — **nettoyage** [nɛtwa-
jaʒ] *nm* : cleaning — **nettoyant** [nɛtwajã]
nm : cleaning agent
neuf[1] [nœf] *adj* **1** : nine **2** : ninth (in dates)
— ∼ *nms & pl* : nine
neuf[2]**, neuve** [nœf, nœv] *adj* : new — **neuf**
nm **quoi de** ∼? : what's new?
neurologie [nørɔlɔʒi] *nf* : neurology
neutre [nøtr] *adj* **1** : neuter (in grammar) **2**
: neutral — **neutraliser** [nøtralize] *vt* : neutralize — **neutralité** [nøtralite] *nf* : neutrality
neutron [nøtrɔ̃] *nm* : neutron
neuvième [nœvjɛm] *adj & nmf & nm* : ninth
neveu [nəvø] *nm, pl* **-veux** : nephew
névrosé, -sée [nevroze] *adj & n* : neurotic
— **névrotique** [nevrɔtik] *adj* : neurotic
nez [ne] *nm* : nose
ni [ni] *conj* **1** ∼ . . . ∼ : neither . . . nor **2**
∼ **plus** ∼ **moins** : no more, no less
niais, niaise [njɛ, njɛz] *adj* : simple, foolish
— **niaiserie** [njɛzri] *nf* : foolishness
niche [niʃ] *nf* **1** : niche, recess **2** : kennel —
nicher [niʃe] *vi* : nest
nickel [nikɛl] *nm* : nickel
nicotine [nikɔtin] *nf* : nicotine
nid [ni] *nm* **1** : nest **2** ∼ **de brigands** : den
of thieves
nièce [njɛs] *nf* : niece
nier [nje] {96} *vt* : deny
nigaud, -gaude [nigo, -god] *n* : simpleton,
fool
niveau [nivo] *nm, pl* **-veaux** [nivo] **1** : level
2 ∼ **de vie** : standard of living — **niveler**
[nivle] {8} *vt* : level
noble [nɔbl] *adj* : noble — ∼ *nmf* : noble,
nobleman *m*, noblewoman *f* — **noblesse**
[nɔblɛs] *nf* : nobility
noce [nɔs] *nf* **1** : wedding, wedding party **2**
∼**s** *nfpl* : wedding
nocif, -cive [nɔsif, -siv] *adj* : noxious, harmful
nocturne [nɔktyrn] *adj* : nocturnal, night
Noël [nɔɛl] *nm* **1** : Christmas **2 père** ∼
: Santa Claus
nœud [nø] *nm* **1** : knot, tie **2** : knot (nautical
speed) **3** ∼ **coulant** : noose **4** ∼ **papillon** : bow tie
noir, noire [nwar] *adj* **1** : black **2** SALE
: dirty, grimy **3** OBSCUR : dark — **noir** *nm*
1 : black **2 dans le** ∼ : in the dark, in
darkness — **Noir, Noire** *n* : black man,
black woman — **noirceur** [nwarsœr] *nf* **1**
: blackness **2** *Can* : darkness — **noircir**
[nwarsir] *vi* : grow dark, darken — *vt*
: blacken
noisette [nwazɛt] *nf* : hazelnut

numéral

noix [nwa] *nfs & pl* **1** : nut, walnut **2** : piece, lump (of butter, etc.) **3** ~ **de cajou** : cashew (nut)

nom [nõ] *nm* **1** : name **2** : (proper) noun

nomade [nɔmad] *nmf* : nomad — ~ *adj* : nomadic

nombre [nõbr] *nm* : number — **nombreux, -breuse** [nõbrø, -brøz] *adj* : numerous

nombril [nõbril] *nm* : navel

nominal, -nale [nɔminal] *adj, mpl* **-naux** [-no] : nominal

nommer [nɔme] *vt* **1** : name, call **2** : appoint, nominate **3** CITER : mention — **se nommer** *vr* **1** S'APPELER : be named **2** : introduce oneself — **nommément** [nɔmemã] *adv* : by name, namely

non [nõ] *adv* **1** : no **2 je pense que** ~ : I don't think so **3** ~ **plus** : neither, either — ~ *nm* : no

nonchalance [nõʃalãs] *nf* : nonchalance — **nonchalant, -lante** [nõʃalã, -lãt] *adj* : nonchalant

non-sens [nõsãs] *nms & pl* ABSURDITÉ : nonsense, absurdity

nord [nɔr] *adj* : north, northern — ~ *nm* **1** : north **2 le Nord** : the North

nord-est [nɔrɛst] *adj s & pl* : northeast, northeastern — ~ *nm* : northeast

nord-ouest [nɔrwɛst] *adj s & pl* : northwest, northwestern — ~ *nm* : northwest

normal, -male [nɔrmal] *adj, mpl* **-maux** [nɔrmo] : normal — **normale** *nf* **1** : average **2** NORME : norm — **normalement** [nɔrmalmã] *adv* : normally, usually — **normaliser** [nɔrmalize] *vt* : normalize, standardize — **normalité** [nɔrmalite] *nf* : normality — **norme** [nɔrm] *nf* : norm, standard

nos → **notre**

nostalgie [nɔstalʒi] *nf* : nostalgia — **nostalgique** [nɔstalʒik] *adj* : nostalgic

notable [nɔtabl] *adj & nm* : notable

notaire [nɔtɛr] *nm* : notary public

notamment [nɔtamã] *adv* : especially, particularly

notation [nɔtasjõ] *nf* : notation

note [nɔt] *nf* **1** : note **2** ADDITION : bill, check **3** : mark, grade (in school) — **noter** [nɔte] *vt* **1** REMARQUER : note, notice **2** MARQUER : mark, write (down) **3** : mark, grade (an exam)

notice [nɔtis] *nf* : instructions *pl*

notifier [nɔtifje] {96} *vt* : notify

notion [nɔsjõ] *nf* : notion, idea

notoire [nɔtwar] *adj* **1** CONNU : well-known **2** : notorious (of a criminal) — **notoriété** [nɔtɔrjete] *nf* : notoriety

notre [nɔtr] *adj, pl* **nos** [no] : our

nôtre [notr] *pron* **le** ~**, la** ~**, les** ~**s** : ours

nouer [nwe] *vt* : tie, knot — **noueux, noueuse** [nwø, nwøz] *adj* : gnarled

nougat [nuga] *nm* : nougat

nouille [nuj] *nf* **1** *fam* : nitwit, idiot **2** ~**s** *nfpl* : noodles, pasta

nourrir [nurir] *vt* **1** ALIMENTER : feed, nourish **2** : provide for (a family, etc.) **3** : nurse, harbor (a grudge, etc.) — **se nourrir** *vr* : eat — **nourrice** [nuris] *nf* : wet nurse — **nourrissant, -sante** [nurisã, -sãt] *adj* : nourishing, nutritious — **nourrisson** [nurisõ] *nm* : infant — **nourriture** [nurityr] *nf* : food

nous [nu] *pron* **1** : we **2** : us **3** ~**-mêmes** : ourselves

nouveau [nuvo] (**-vel** [-vɛl] *before a vowel or mute h*), **-velle** [-vɛl] *adj, mpl* **-veaux** [nuvo] **1** : new **2 de** ~ *or* **à** ~ : again, once again **3** ~ **venu** : newcomer — **nouveau** *nm* **1 du** ~ : something new **2 le** ~ : the new — **nouveau-né, -née** [nuvone] *adj & n, mpl* **nouveau-nés** : newborn — **nouveauté** [nuvote] *nf* **1** : newness, novelty **2** INNOVATION : innovation

nouvelle [nuvɛl] *nf* **1** : piece of news **2** : short story **3** ~**s** *nfpl* : news — **nouvellement** [nuvɛlmã] *adv* : newly, recently

novateur, -trice [nɔvatœr, -tris] *adj* : innovative — ~ *n* : innovator

novembre [nɔvãbr] *nm* : November

novice [nɔvis] *adj* : inexperienced — ~ *nmf* : novice, beginner

noyau [nwajo] *nm, pl* **noyaux** [nwajo] **1** : pit, stone (of a fruit) **2** : nucleus, core (in science)

noyauter [nwajote] *vt* : infiltrate

noyer[1] [nwaje] {58} *vt* **1** : drown **2** : flood (an engine) — **se noyer** *vr* : drown — **noyé, noyée** [nwaje] *n* : drowning victim

noyer[2] *nm* : walnut tree

nu, nue [ny] *adj* **1** : naked, nude **2** : plain, bare (of a wall) — **nu** *nm* **1** : nude **2 à** ~ : bare, exposed

nuage [nɥaʒ] *nm* : cloud — **nuageux, -geuse** [nɥaʒø, -ʒøz] *adj* : cloudy

nuance [nɥãs] *nf* **1** TON : hue, shade **2** SUBTILITÉ : nuance — **nuancer** [nɥãse] {6} *vt* : qualify (opinions, etc.)

nucléaire [nykleɛr] *adj* : nuclear

nudité [nydite] *nf* : nudity, nakedness

nuée [nɥe] *nf* : horde, swarm

nuire [nɥir] {49} *vi* ~ **à** : harm, injure — **nuisible** [nɥizibl] *adj* : harmful

nuit [nɥi] *nf* **1** : night, nighttime **2 faire** ~ : be dark out

nul, nulle [nyl] *adj* **1** AUCUN : no **2** : null, invalid **3 être nul en maths** : be hopeless in math **5 nulle part** : nowhere — **nul** *pron* : no one, nobody — **nullement** [nylmã] *adv* : by no means

numéraire [nymerɛr] *nm* : cash

numéral, -rale [nymeral] *adj, mpl* **-raux** [-ro] : numeral — **numéral** *nm, pl* **-raux** : numeral — **numérique** [nymerik] *adj* **1** : numerical **2** : digital — **numéro** [nymero] *nm* **1** : number **2** : issue (of a periodical) — **numéroter** [nymerɔte] *vt* : number

nuptial, -tiale [nypsjal] *adj, mpl* **-tiaux** [-sjo] : nuptial, wedding

nuque [nyk] *nf* : nape of the neck
nutrition [nytrisjɔ̃] *nf* : nutrition — **nutritif, -tive** [nytritif, -tiv] *adj* **1** : nutritious **2** : nutritional
nylon [nilɔ̃] *nm* : nylon
nymphe [nɛ̃f] *nf* : nymph

O

o [o] *nm* : o, 15th letter of the alphabet
oasis [ɔazis] *nf* : oasis
obéir [ɔbeir] *vi* ~ **à 1** : obey **2** : respond to — **obéissance** [ɔbeisɑ̃s] *nf* : obedience — **obéissant, -sante** [ɔbeisɑ̃, -sɑ̃t] *adj* : obedient
obélisque [ɔbelisk] *nm* : obelisk
obèse [ɔbez] *adj* : obese — **obésité** [ɔbezite] *nf* : obesity
objecter [ɔbʒɛkte] *vt* **1** : raise as an objection **2** PRÉTEXTER : plead (as an excuse) — **objectif, -tive** [ɔbʒɛktif, -tiv] *adj* : objective — **objectif** *nm* **1** BUT : objective, goal **2** : lens (of an optical instrument) — **objectivité** [ɔbʒɛktivite] *nf* : objectivity — **objection** [ɔbʒɛksjɔ̃] *nf* : objection — **objet** [ɔbʒɛ] *nm* **1** : object, thing **2** : subject, topic **3** BUT : aim, purpose **4 complément d'**~ : object (in grammar)
obligation [ɔbligasjɔ̃] *nf* **1** : obligation **2** : (savings) bond — **obligatoire** [ɔbligatwar] *adj* : compulsory, obligatory — **obligatoirement** [ɔbligatwarmɑ̃] *adv* : necessarily
obliger [ɔbliʒe] {17} *vt* **1** : oblige **2** CONTRAINDRE : force, compel — **obligé, -gée** [ɔbliʒe] *adj* **1 c'est obligé** *fam* : it's bound to happen, it's inevitable **2 être obligé de** : have to — **obligeance** [ɔbliʒɑ̃s] *nf* AMABILITÉ : kindness — **obligeant, -geante** [ɔbliʒɑ̃, -ʒɑ̃t] *adj* : obliging, kind
oblique [ɔblik] *adj* **1** : oblique **2 en** ~ : crosswise, diagonally — **obliquer** [ɔblike] *vi* : bear, turn (off)
oblitérer [ɔblitere] {87} *vt* : cancel (a stamp)
oblong, oblongue [ɔblɔ̃, ɔblɔ̃g] *adj* : oblong
obscène [ɔpsɛn] *adj* : obscene — **obscénité** [ɔpsenite] *nf* : obscenity
obscur, -cure [ɔpskyr] *adj* **1** SOMBRE : dark **2** VAGUE : obscure — **obscurcir** [ɔpskyrsir] *vt* **1** ASSOMBRIR : darken **2** : obscure, blur — **s'obscurcir** *vr* **1** : grow dark **2** : become obscure — **obscurité** [ɔpskyrite] *nf* **1** : darkness **2** : obscurity

obséder [ɔpsede] {87} *vt* : obsess — **obsédant, -dante** [ɔpsedɑ̃, -dɑ̃t] *adj* : haunting, obsessive — **obsédé, -dée** [ɔpsede] *n* : obsessive, fanatic
obsèques [ɔpsɛk] *nfpl* : funeral
observer [ɔpsɛrve] *vt* : observe — **observateur, -trice** [ɔpsɛrvatœr, -tris] *adj* : observant, perceptive — ~ *n* : observer — **observation** [ɔpsɛrvasjɔ̃] *nf* **1** : observance **2** : observation — **observatoire** [ɔpsɛrvatwar] *nm* **1** : observatory **2** : observation post
obsession [ɔpsesjɔ̃] *nf* : obsession — **obsessionnel, -nelle** [ɔpsesjɔnɛl] *adj* : obsessive
obsolète [ɔpsɔlɛt] *adj* : obsolete
obstacle [ɔpstakl] *nm* : obstacle
obstétrique [ɔpstetrik] *nf* : obstetrics
obstiner [ɔpstine] *v* **s'obstiner** *vr* ~ **à** : persist in — **obstiné, -née** [ɔpstine] *adj* ENTÊTÉ : obstinate, stubborn
obstruction [ɔpstryksjɔ̃] *nf* : obstruction — **obstruer** [ɔpstrye] *vt* : obstruct
obtenir [ɔptənir] {92} *vt* : obtain, get — **obtention** [ɔptɑ̃sjɔ̃] *nf* : obtaining
obturer [ɔptyre] *vt* **1** : seal, stop up **2** : fill (a tooth)
obtus, -tuse [ɔpty, -tyz] *adj* : obtuse
obus [ɔby] *nm* **1** : (mortar) shell **2 éclats d'**~ : shrapnel
occasion [ɔkazjɔ̃] *nf* **1** : opportunity **2** CIRCONSTANCE : occasion **3** : bargain **4 d'**~ : secondhand — **occasionnel, -nelle** [ɔkazjɔnɛl] *adj* : occasional — **occasionnel, -nelle** *n Can* : temp, temporary employee — **occasionner** [ɔkazjɔne] *vt* CAUSER : cause
occident [ɔksidɑ̃] *nm* **1** : west **2 l'Occident** : the West — **occidental, -tale** [ɔksidɑ̃tal] *adj, mpl* **-taux** [-to] : western, Western
occulte [ɔkylt] *adj* : occult
occuper [ɔkype] *vt* **1** : occupy **2** REMPLIR : take up, fill **3** ~ **un poste** : hold a job — **s'occuper** *vr* **1** : keep busy **2** ~ **de** : han-

dle, take care of — **occupant, -pante** [ɔkypɑ̃,-pɑ̃t] *n* : occupant — **occupation** [ɔkypasjɔ̃] *nf* **1** : occupation **2** : occupancy — **occupé, -pée** [ɔkype] *adj* **1** : busy **2 zone occupée** : occupied zone

occurrence [ɔkyrɑ̃s] *nf* **1** : instance, occurrence **2 en l'~** : in this case

océan [ɔseɑ̃] *nm* : ocean — **océanique** [ɔseanik] *adj* : oceanic, ocean

ocre [ɔkr] *nmf* : ocher, ochre

octave [ɔktav] *nf* : octave

octet [ɔktɛt] *nm* : byte

octobre [ɔktɔbr] *nm* : October

octogone [ɔktɔgon] *nm* : octagon

octroyer [ɔktrwaje] {58} *vt* : grant, bestow

oculaire [ɔkylɛr] *adj* : ocular, eye — **oculiste** [ɔkylist] *nmf* : oculist

ode [ɔd] *nf* : ode

odeur [ɔdœr] *nf* : odor, smell

odieux, -dieuse [ɔdjø, -djøz] *adj* EXÉCRABLE : odious, hateful

odorant, -rante [ɔdɔrɑ̃, -rɑ̃t] *adj* PARFUMÉ : fragrant

odorat [ɔdɔra] *nm* : sense of smell

œil [œj] *nm, pl* **yeux** [jø] **1** : eye **2 coup d'~** : glance — **œillade** [œjad] *nf* : wink — **œillères** [œjɛr] *nfpl* : blinders — **œillet** [œjɛ] *nm* : carnation

œsophage [ezɔfaʒ] *nm* : esophagus

œstrogène [ɛstrɔʒɛn] *nm* : estrogen

œuf [œf] *nm, pl* **œufs** [ø] : egg

œuvre [œvr] *nm* : (body of) work — **~** *nf* **1** : work, undertaking, task **2 ~ d'art** : work of art — **œuvrer** [œvre] *vi* : work

offense [ɔfɑ̃s] *nf* : insult, offense — **offenser** [ɔfɑ̃se] *vt* : offend — **s'offenser** *vr* **~ de** : take offense at — **offensif, -sive** [ɔfɑ̃sif, -siv] *adj* : offensive, attacking — **offensive** *nf* : offensive

office [ɔfis] *nm* **1** : service (in religion) **2 faire ~ de** : act as

officiel, -cielle [ɔfisjɛl] *adj & n* : official — **officialiser** [ɔfisjalize] *vt* : make official — **officier** [ɔfisje] *nm* : officer (in the armed forces) — **officieux, -cieuse** [ɔfisjø, -sjøz] *adj* : unofficial, informal

offrande [ɔfrɑ̃d] *nf* : offering

offre [ɔfr] *nf* **1** : offer, bid **2 l'~ et la demande** : supply and demand

offrir [ɔfrir] {83} *vt* : offer, give — **s'offrir** *vr* **1** : treat oneself to **2** SE PRÉSENTER : present itself

offusquer [ɔfyske] *vt* : offend — **s'offusquer** *vr* : take offense

ogive [ɔʒiv] *nf* : warhead

ogre, ogresse [ɔgr, ɔgrɛs] *n* : ogre

oh [o] *interj* : oh — **ohé** [ɔe] *interj* : hey

oie [wa] *nf* : goose

oignon [ɔɲɔ̃] *nm* **1** : onion **2** : bulb (of a tulip, etc.) **3** : bunion (in medicine)

oindre [wɛ̃dr] {59} *vt* : anoint

oiseau [wazo] *nm, pl* **oiseaux** : bird

oisif, -sive [wazif, -ziv] *adj* : idle — **oisiveté** [wazivte] *nf* : idleness

oisillon [wazijɔ̃] *nm* : fledgling

oléoduc [ɔleɔdyk] *nm* : (oil) pipeline

olfactif, -tive [ɔlfaktif, -tiv] *adj* : olfactory

olive [ɔliv] *nf* : olive

olympique [ɔlɛ̃pik] *adj* : Olympic

ombilical, -cale [ɔ̃bilikal] *adj, mpl* **-caux** [-ko] : umbilical

ombrage [ɔ̃braʒ] *nm* **1** OMBRE : shade **2 porter ~ à** : offend — **ombragé, -gée** [ɔ̃braʒe] *adj* : shady, shaded — **ombre** [ɔ̃br] *nf* **1** : shadow **2** SOUPÇON : hint, trace **3 à l'~** : in the shade

omelette [ɔmlɛt] *nf* : omelet

omettre [ɔmɛtr] {53} *vt* : omit, leave out — **omission** [ɔmisjɔ̃] *nf* : omission

omnibus [ɔmnibys] *nm* : local train

omnipotent, -tente [ɔmnipɔtɑ̃, -tɑ̃t] *adj* : omnipotent

omoplate [ɔmɔplat] *nf* : shoulder blade

on [ɔ̃] *pron* **1** : one, we, you **2** : they, people **3** QUELQU'UN : someone

once [ɔ̃s] *nf* : ounce

oncle [ɔ̃kl] *nm* : uncle

onctueux, -tueuse [ɔ̃ktɥø, -tɥøz] *adj* : smooth, creamy

onde [ɔ̃d] *nf* : wave

on–dit [ɔ̃di] *nms & pl* : rumor

onduler [ɔ̃dyle] *vi* **1** : undulate, sway **2** : be wavy (of hair) — **ondulation** [ɔ̃dylasjɔ̃] *nf* : undulation, wave — **ondulé, -lée** [ɔ̃dyle] *adj* **1** : wavy **2 carton ondulé** : corrugated cardboard

onéreux, -reuse [ɔnerø, -røz] *adj* COÛTEUX : costly

ongle [ɔ̃gl] *nm* : nail, fingernail

onguent [ɔ̃gɑ̃] *nm* : ointment

onyx [ɔniks] *nm* : onyx

onze [ɔ̃z] *adj* **1** : eleven **2** : eleventh (in dates) — **~** *nms & pl* : eleven — **onzième** [ɔ̃zjɛm] *adj & nmf & nm* : eleventh

opale [ɔpal] *nf* : opal

opaque [ɔpak] *adj* : opaque

opéra [ɔpera] *nm* **1** : opera **2** : opera house

opération [ɔperasjɔ̃] *nf* **1** : operation **2** : transaction (in banking, etc.) — **opérateur, -trice** [ɔperatœr, -tris] *n* : operator — **opérationnel, -nelle** [ɔperasjɔnɛl] *adj* : operational — **opérer** [ɔpere] {87} *vt* : operate on (a patient) — *vi* **1** : take effect, work **2** INTERVENIR : act

opiner [ɔpine] *vi* **~ de la tête** : nod in agreement

opiniâtre [ɔpinjatr] *adj* OBSTINÉ : stubborn, persistent

opinion [ɔpinjɔ̃] *nf* : opinion, belief

opium [ɔpjɔm] *nm* : opium

opportun, -tune [ɔpɔrtœ̃, -tyn] *adj* : opportune, timely — **opportunisme** [ɔpɔrtynism] *nm* : opportunism — **opportuniste** [ɔpɔrtynist] *adj* : opportunist, opportunistic — **~** *nmf* : opportunist

opposer [ɔpoze] *vt* 1 : put up (an objection, etc.) 2 : contrast (ideas, etc.) 3 DIVISER : divide — **s'opposer** *vr* 1 : clash, conflict 2 **~ à** : be opposed to — **opposant, -sante** [ɔpozɑ̃, -zɑ̃t] *n* ADVERSAIRE : opponent — **opposé, -sée** [ɔpoze] *adj* 1 : opposing 2 : opposite 3 **~ à** : opposed to — **opposé** *nm* 1 : opposite 2 **à l'~ de** : contrary to — **opposition** [ɔpozisjɔ̃] *nf* 1 : opposition 2 : objection (in law)

oppresser [ɔprese] *vt* : oppress, burden — **oppressif, -sive** [ɔpresif, -siv] *adj* : oppressive — **oppresseur** [ɔprescœr] *nm* : oppressor — **oppression** [ɔpresjɔ̃] *nf* : oppression

opprimer [ɔprime] *vt* : oppress

opter [ɔpte] *vi* **~ pour** : opt for, choose

opticien, -cienne [ɔptisjɛ̃, -sjɛn] *n* : optician

optimisme [ɔptimism] *nm* : optimism — **optimiste** [ɔptimist] *adj* : optimistic — **~** *nmf* : optimist

optimum [ɔptimɔm] *adj & nm* : optimum

option [ɔpsjɔ̃] *nf* : option, choice — **optionnel, -nelle** [ɔpsjɔnɛl] *adj* FACULTATIF : optional

optique [ɔptik] *adj* : optic(al) — **~** *nf* 1 : optics 2 PERSPECTIVE : viewpoint

opulent, -lente [ɔpylɑ̃, -lɑ̃t] *adj* : opulent — **opulence** [-lɑ̃s] *nf* : opulence

or[1] [ɔr] *nm* : gold

or[2] *conj* 1 : but, yet 2 : now

oracle [ɔrakl] *nm* : oracle

orage [ɔraʒ] *nm* : storm, thunderstorm — **orageux, -geuse** [ɔraʒø, -ʒøz] *adj* : stormy

oral, -rale [ɔral] *adj, mpl* **oraux** [ɔro] : oral

orange [ɔrɑ̃ʒ] *adj* : orange — **~** *nf* : orange (fruit) — **~** *nm* : orange (color) — **oranger** [ɔrɑ̃ʒe] *nm* : orange tree

orateur, -trice [ɔratœr, -tris] *n* : orator, speaker

orbite [ɔrbit] *nf* 1 : orbit 2 : eye socket

orchestre [ɔrkɛstr] *nm* : orchestra

orchidée [ɔrkide] *nf* : orchid

ordinaire [ɔrdinɛr] *adj* 1 : ordinary, common 2 HABITUEL : usual — **~** *nm* 1 **l'~** : the ordinary 2 **d'~** : usually, as a rule — **ordinairement** [-nɛrmɑ̃] *adv* : usually

ordinateur [ɔrdinatœr] *nm* : computer

ordonnance [ɔrdɔnɑ̃s] *nf* 1 : order 2 : (medical) prescription

ordonner [ɔrdɔne] *vt* 1 : put in order, arrange 2 COMMANDER : order 3 : ordain (in religion) — **ordonné, -née** [ɔrdɔne] *adj* : tidy, orderly

ordre [ɔrdr] *nm* 1 : order 2 PROPRETÉ : tidiness 3 NATURE : nature, sort 4 **~ du jour** : agenda

ordure [ɔrdyr] *nf* 1 : filth 2 **~s** *nfpl* : trash, garbage — **ordurier, -rière** [ɔrdyrje] *adj* : filthy

oreille [ɔrej] *nf* 1 : ear 2 OUÏE : hearing

oreiller [ɔreje] *nm* : pillow

oreillons [ɔrejɔ̃] *nmpl* : mumps

orfèvre [ɔrfɛvr] *nm* : goldsmith

organe [ɔrgan] *nm* : organ (of the body) — **organique** [ɔrganik] *adj* : organic

organiser [ɔrganize] *vt* : organize — **s'organiser** *vr* : get organized — **organisateur, -trice** [ɔrganizatœr, -tris] *n* : organizer — **organisation** [ɔrganizasjɔ̃] *nf* : organization

organisme [ɔrganism] *nm* 1 : organism (in biology) 2 : organization, body

organiste [ɔrganist] *nmf* : organist

orgasme [ɔrgasm] *nm* : orgasm

orge [ɔrʒ] *nf* : barley

orgelet [ɔrʒəlɛ] *nm* : sty (in medicine)

orgie [ɔrʒi] *nf* : orgy

orgue [ɔrg] *nm* : organ (musical instrument)

orgueil [ɔrgœj] *nm* : pride — **orgueilleux, -leuse** [ɔrgœjø, -jøz] *adj* : proud

orient [ɔrjɑ̃] *nm* 1 : east 2 **l'Orient** : the Orient, the East — **oriental, -tale** [ɔrjɑ̃tal] *adj, mpl* **-taux** [-to] 1 : eastern 2 : oriental

orienter [ɔrjɑ̃te] *vt* 1 : position, orient 2 GUIDER : guide, direct — **s'orienter** *vr* : find one's bearings — **orientation** [ɔrjɑ̃tasjɔ̃] *nf* 1 : orientation, direction, aspect 2 : guidance, (career) counseling

orifice [ɔrifis] *nm* : orifice

originaire [ɔriʒinɛr] *adj* **être ~ de** : be a native of

original, -nale [ɔriʒinal, -nal] *adj, mpl* **-naux** [-no] 1 : original 2 EXCENTRIQUE : eccentric — **~** *n* : character, eccentric — **original** *nm, pl* **-naux** : original — **originalité** [ɔriʒinalite] *nf* 1 : originality 2 : eccentricity — **origine** [ɔriʒin] *nf* 1 : origin 2 **à l'~** : originally — **originel, -nelle** [ɔriʒinɛl] *adj* : original, primary

orignal [ɔriɲal] *nm, pl* **-naux** [-ɲo] : moose

orme [ɔrm] *nm* : elm

orner [ɔrne] *vt* DÉCORER : decorate, adorn — **orné, -née** [ɔrne] *adj* : ornate, flowery — **ornement** [ɔrnəmɑ̃] *nm* : ornament, adornment — **ornemental, -tale** [ɔrnəmɑ̃tal] *adj, mpl* **-taux** [-to] : ornamental

ornière [ɔrnjɛr] *nf* : rut

ornithologie [ɔrnitɔlɔʒi] *nf* : ornithology

orphelin, -line [ɔrfəlɛ̃, -lin] *n* : orphan

orteil [ɔrtɛj] *nm* : toe

orthodoxe [ɔrtɔdɔks] *adj* : orthodox — **orthodoxie** [ɔrtɔdɔksi] *nf* : orthodoxy

orthographe [ɔrtɔgraf] *nf* : spelling, orthography — **orthographier** [ɔrtɔgrafje] {96} *vt* : spell

orthopédie [ɔrtɔpedi] *nf* : orthopedics — **orthopédique** [ɔrtɔpedik] *adj* : orthopedic

ortie [ɔrti] *nf* : nettle

os [ɔs] *nm* : bone

osciller [ɔsile] *vi* 1 : oscillate 2 HESITATE : vacillate, waver — **oscillation** [ɔsilasjɔ̃] *nf* : oscillation

oser [oze] *vt* 1 : dare 2 **si j'ose dire** : if I may say so — **osé, -sée** [oze] *adj* : daring, bold

osier [ozje] *nm* 1 : willow (tree) 2 : wicker (furniture)

osmose [ɔsmoz] *nf* : osmosis

ossature [ɔsatyr] *nf* 1 : skeleton, bone structure 2 : frame(work) — **ossements** [ɔsmɑ̃] *nmpl* : remains, bones — **osseux, -seuse** [ɔsø, -søz] *adj* : bony

ostensible [ɔstɑ̃sibl] *adj* : conspicuous, obvious — **ostentation** [ɔstɑ̃tasjɔ̃] *nf* : ostentation

ostéopathe [ɔsteopat] *nmf* : osteopath

ostracisme [ɔstrasism] *nm* : ostracism

otage [ɔtaʒ] *nm* : hostage

ôter [ote] *vt* 1 RETIRER : remove, take away 2 SOUSTRAIRE : subtract

otite [ɔtit] *nf* : ear infection

ou [u] *conj* 1 : or 2 **ou ... ou ...** : either ... or ...

où [u] *adv* 1 : where, wherever 2 **d'~** : from which, from where — **~** *pron* : where, that, in which, on which, to which

ouate [wat] *nf* 1 : absorbent cotton 2 BOURRE : padding, wadding — **ouaté, -tée** [wate] *adj* : padded, quilted

oublier [ublije] {96}*vt* : forget — **s'oublier** *vr* 1 : be forgotten 2 : forget oneself — **oubli** [ubli] *nm* 1 : forgetfulness 2 : oversight — **oublieux, -blieuse** [ublijø, -blijøz] *adj* : forgetful

ouest [west] *adj* : west, western — **~** *nm* 1 : west 2 **l'Ouest** : the West

oui [wi] *adv* & *nms* & *pl* : yes

ouïe [wi] *nf* 1 : (sense of) hearing 2 **~s** *nfpl* : gills — **ouï–dire** [widir] *nms* & *pl* : hearsay

ouïr [wir] {60} *vt* : hear

ouragan [uragɑ̃] *nm* : hurricane

ourler [urle] *vt* : hem — **ourlet** [urlɛ] *nm* : hem

ours [urs] *nm* 1 : bear 2 **~ blanc** *or* **~ polaire** : polar bear — **ourse** [urs] *nf* : she-bear

outil [uti] *nm* : tool — **outillage** [utijaʒ] *nm* 1 : set of tools 2 : equipment — **outiller** [utije] *vt* ÉQUIPER : equip

outrager [utraʒe] {17} *vt* INSULTER : offend, insult — **outrage** [utraʒ] *nm* : insult

outrance [utrɑ̃s] *nf* : excess — **outrancier, -cière** [utrɑ̃sje, -sjɛr] *adj* : excessive, extreme

outre [utr] *adv* 1 **en ~** : in addition, besides 2 **~ mesure** : overly, unduly 3 **passer ~ à** : disregard — **~** *prep* : besides, in addition to — **outre–mer** [utrəmɛr] *adv* : overseas — **outrepasser** [utrəpase] *vt* : exceed, overstep

outrer [utre] *vt* 1 EXAGÉRER : exaggerate 2 INDIGNER : outrage

ouvert, -verte [uvɛr, -vɛrt] *adj* 1 : open 2 : on, running (of a light, a faucet, etc.) — **ouverture** [uvɛrtyr] *nf* 1 : opening 2 : overture (in music) 3 **~ d'esprit** : open-mindedness

ouvrable [uvrabl] *adj* 1 **jour ~** : weekday, working day 2 **heures ~s** : business hours

ouvrage [uvraʒ] *nm* : work

ouvre–boîtes [uvrəbwat] *nms* & *pl* : can opener — **ouvre–bouteilles** [uvrəbutɛj] *nms* & *pl* : bottle opener

ouvreur, -vreuse [uvrœr, -vrøz] *n* : usher, usherette *f*

ouvrier, -vrière [uvrije, -vrijɛr] *n* : worker — **~** *adj* : working-class

ouvrir [uvrir] {83} *vt* 1 : open 2 : turn on (a light, a radio, etc.) — *vi* : open — **s'ouvrir** *vr* : open (up)

ovaire [ɔvɛr] *nm* : ovary

ovale [ɔval] *adj* & *nm* : oval

ovation [ɔvasjɔ̃] *nf* : ovation

overdose [ɔvœrdoz] *nf* : overdose

oxyde [ɔksid] *nm* **~ de carbone** : carbon monoxide — **oxyder** [ɔkside] *v* **s'oxyder** *vr* : rust

oxygène [ɔksiʒɛn] *nm* : oxygen

ozone [ozɔn] *nm* : ozone

P

p [pe] *nm* : p, 16th letter of the alphabet

pacifier [pasifje] {96} *vt* : pacify, calm — **pacifique** [pasifik] *adj* **1** : peaceful **2** l'océan Pacifique : the Pacific Ocean — **pacifiste** [pasifist] *nmf* : pacifist

pacotille [pakɔtij] *nf* **1** : shoddy goods **2 de ~** : cheap

pacte [pakt] *nm* ACCORD : pact, agreement

pagaie [pagɛ] *nf* : paddle

pagaille *or* **pagaïe** [pagaj] *nf fam* **1** : mess, chaos **2 en ~** : in great quantities

pagayer [pagaje] {11} *vi* : paddle

page [paʒ] *nf* : page

paie [pɛ] *nf* : pay, wages *pl* — **paiement** [pɛmã] *nm* : payment

païen, païenne [pajɛ̃, pajɛn] *adj & n* : pagan, heathen

paillard, -larde [pajar, -jard] *adj* : bawdy

paillasson [pajasɔ̃] *nm* : doormat

paille [paj] *nf* **1** : (piece of) straw **2** : (drinking) straw

paillette [pajɛt] *nf* : sequin

pain [pɛ̃] *nm* **1** : bread **2** : loaf (of bread) **3** : cake, bar (of soap, etc.)

pair, paire [pɛr] *adj* : even — **pair** *nm* **1** : peer **2 aller de ~** : go hand in hand **3 hors ~** : without equal — **paire** [pɛr] *nf* : pair

paisible [pezibl] *adj* : peaceful, quiet

paître [pɛtr] {61} *vi* : graze

paix [pɛ] *nf* : peace

palace [palas] *nm* : luxury hotel

palais [palɛ] *nms & pl* **1** : palace **2** : palate **3 ~ de justice** : courts of law

palan [palã] *nm* : hoist

pale [pal] *nf* : blade (of a propeller, etc.)

pâle [pal] *adj* **1** BLÊME : pale **2** CLAIR : light, pale

palet [palɛ] *nm* : puck (in ice hockey)

paletot [palto] *nm* : short coat

palette [palɛt] *nf* **1** : palette **2** : shoulder (of pork, etc.)

pâleur [palœr] *nf* : paleness

palier [palje] *nm* **1** : landing, floor **2** NIVEAU : level, stage

pâlir [palir] *vi* : turn pale

palissade [palisad] *nf* : fence

pallier [palje] {96} *vt* : alleviate, compensate for

palmarès [palmarɛs] *nms & pl* : list of winners

palme [palm] *nf* **1** : palm leaf **2** NAGEOIRE : flipper **3 remporter la ~** : be victorious

palmé, -mée [palme] *adj* : webbed

palmier [palmje] *nm* : palm tree

palourde [palurd] *nf* : clam

palper [palpe] *vt* : feel, finger — **palpable** [palpabl] *adj* : tangible

palpiter [palpite] *vi* : palpitate, throb — **palpitant, -tante** [palpitã, -tãt] *adj* : thrilling, exciting

paludisme [palydism] *nm* : malaria

pâmer [pame] *v* **se pâmer** *vr* : be ecstatic, swoon

pamphlet [pãflɛ] *nm* : lampoon

pamplemousse [pãpləmus] *nmf* : grapefruit

pan [pã] *nm* **1** : section, piece **2** : tail (of a garment)

panacée [panase] *nf* : panacea

panais [panɛ] *nm* : parsnip

pancarte [pãkart] *nf* : sign, placard

pancréas [pãkreas] *nm* : pancreas

panda [pãda] *nm* : panda

paner [pane] *vt* : coat with breadcrumbs

panier [panje] *nm* : basket

panique [panik] *nf* : panic — **paniquer** [panike] *vi* : panic

panne [pan] *nf* **1** : breakdown **2 ~ d'électricité** : power failure, blackout

panneau [pano] *nm, pl* **-neaux 1** : panel **2** : sign, signpost **3 ~ de signalisation** : road sign **4 ~ publicitaire** : billboard

panoplie [panɔpli] *nf* **1** GAMME : array, range **2** DÉGUISEMENT : outfit, costume

panorama [panɔrama] *nm* : panorama — **panoramique** [panɔramik] *adj* : panoramic

panser [pãse] *vt* **1** : groom (a horse) **2** : dress, bandage (a wound) — **pansement** [pãsmã] *nm* : dressing, bandage

pantalon [pãtalɔ̃] *nm* : pants *pl*, trousers *pl*

panthère [pãtɛr] *nf* : panther

pantin [pãtɛ̃] *nm* FANTOCHE : puppet (person)

pantomime [pãtɔmim] *nf* : pantomime

pantoufle [pãtufl] *nf* : slipper

panure [panyr] *nf* : bread crumbs *pl*

paon [pã] *nm* : peacock

papa [papa] *nm fam* : dad, daddy

pape [pap] *nm* : pope

paperasse [papras] *nf* : papers *pl*, paperwork

papeterie [papɛtri] *nf* : stationery

papier [papje] *nm* **1** : paper **2** : document, paper **3 ~ d'aluminium** : aluminum foil, tinfoil **4 ~ hygiénique** : toilet paper **5 ~ mouchoir** *Can* : tissue **6 ~ peint** : wallpaper **7 ~s** *nmpl* : (identification) papers

papillon [papijɔ̃] *nm* **1** : butterfly **2 ~ de nuit** : moth

papoter [papɔte] *vi* : gab, chatter

Pâque [pak] *nf* : Passover

paquebot [pakbo] *nm* : liner, ship
pâquerette [pakrɛt] *nf* : daisy
Pâques [pak] *nm & nfpl* : Easter
paquet [pakɛ] *nm* **1** : package, parcel **2** : pack (of cigarettes, etc.) **3** un ~ de : a heap of, a pile of
par [par] *prep* **1** : through **2** : by, by means of **3** : as, for **4** : at, during **5** ~ **avion** : by airmail **6** ~ **exemple** : for example **7** ~ **ici** : around here **8** ~ **moments** : at times **9** ~ **personne** : per person **10** de ~ : throughout
parabole [parabɔl] *nf* : parable
parachever [paraʃve] {52} *vt* : complete, perfect
parachute [paraʃyt] *nm* : parachute — **parachutiste** [paraʃytist] *nmf* : paratrooper
parade [parad] *nf* : parade — **parader** [parade] *vi* : strut, show off
paradis [paradi] *nm* : paradise, heaven
paradoxe [paradɔks] *nm* : paradox — **paradoxal, -xale** [paradɔksal] *adj, mpl* **-xaux** [-kso] : paradoxical
paraffine [parafin] *nf* : paraffin (wax)
parages [paraʒ] *nmpl* **dans les** ~ : in the vicinity
paragraphe [paragraf] *nm* : paragraph
paraître [parɛtr] {7} *vi* **1** : appear **2** : show, be visible **3** SEMBLER : seem, look **4** à ~ : forthcoming — *v impers* il **paraît que** : it seems that, apparently
parallèle [paralɛl] *adj* : parallel — ~ *nm* **1** : parallel **2 mettre en** ~ : compare — ~ *nf* : parallel (line)
paralyser [paralyze] *vt* : paralyze — **paralysie** [paralizi] *nf* : paralysis
paramètre [paramɛtr] *nm* : parameter
paranoïa [paranɔja] *nf* : paranoia
parapet [parapɛ] *nm* : parapet
paraphe [paraf] *nm* **1** : initials *pl* **2** : signature — **parapher** [parafe] *vt* : initial
paraphrase [parafraz] *nf* : paraphrase
parapluie [paraplɥi] *nm* : umbrella
parascolaire [paraskɔlɛr] *adj* : extracurricular
parasite [parazit] *nm* **1** : parasite **2** ~**s** *nmpl* : (radio) interference
parasol [parasɔl] *nm* : parasol, sunshade
paravent [paravɑ̃] *nm* : screen, partition
parc [park] *nm* **1** : park **2** : grounds *pl* **3** ENCLOS : pen, playpen **4** : fleet (of automobiles) **5** ~ **d'attractions** : amusement park
parcelle [parsɛl] *nf* **1** : fragment **2** : plot (of land)
parce que [parskə] *conj* : because
parchemin [parʃəmɛ̃] *nm* : parchment
parcimonieux, -nieuse [parsimɔnjø, -njøz] *adj* : parsimonious
par-ci, par-là [parsiparla] *adv* : here and there

parcmètre [parkmɛtr] *nm France* : parking meter
parcomètre [parkɔmɛtr] *nm Can* : parking meter
parcourir [parkurir] {23} *vt* **1** : cover (a distance), travel through **2** : leaf through (a text)
parcours [parkur] *nm* **1** : course (of a river), route (of a bus, etc.) **2** : course (in sports)
par-delà *or* **par delà** [pardəla] *prep* : beyond
par-dessous [pardəsu] *adv & prep* : underneath
pardessus [pardəsy] *nms & pl* : overcoat
par-dessus [pardəsy] *adv* : over, above, on top — ~ *prep* **1** : over, above **2** ~ **bord** : overboard **3** ~ **tout** : above all
par-devant [pardəvɑ̃] *adv* : in front, at the front
pardonner [pardɔne] *vt* **1** : forgive, pardon **2 pardonnez-moi** : excuse me — **pardon** [pardɔ̃] *nm* **1** : forgiveness, pardon **2** ~? : pardon?, what did you say? **3** ~ : pardon me, sorry
pare-balles [parbal] *adj s & pl* : bulletproof
pare-brise [parbriz] *nms & pl* : windshield
pare-chocs [parʃɔk] *nms & pl* : bumper
pareil, -reille [parɛj] *adj* **1** SEMBLABLE : similar, alike **2** TEL : such — ~ *n* **1** ÉGAL : equal, peer **2 sans pareil** : unequaled — **pareil** [parɛj] *adv fam* : in the same way
parent, -rente [parɑ̃, -rɑ̃t] *adj* : similar, related — ~ *n* **1** : relative, relation **2 parents** *nmpl* : parents — **parenté** [parɑ̃te] *nf* **1** : relationship **2** : family, relations *pl*
parenthèse [parɑ̃tɛz] *nf* : parenthesis, bracket
parer [pare] *vt* **1** : adorn, array **2** : ward off, parry — *vi* ~ à : deal with
paresser [parɛse] *vi* : laze around — **paresse** [parɛs] *nf* : laziness, idleness — **paresseux, -seuse** [parəsø, -søz] *adj* : lazy — **paresseux** *nm* : sloth (animal)
parfaire [parfɛr] {62} *vt* : perfect, refine — **parfait, -faite** [parfɛ, -fɛt] *adj* **1** : perfect **2** TOTAL : absolute, complete — **parfaitement** [-fɛtmɑ̃] *adv* **1** : perfectly **2** ABSOLUMENT : definitely
parfois [parfwa] *adv* : sometimes
parfumer [parfyme] *vt* **1** : scent, perfume **2** : flavor (ice cream, etc.) — **se parfumer** *vr* : wear perfume — **parfum** [parfœ̃] *nm* **1** : scent, fragrance **2** : perfume **3** GOÛT : flavor — **parfumé, -mée** [parfyme] *adj* **1** : fragrant, scented **2** : flavored — **parfumerie** [parfymri] *nf* : perfume shop
pari [pari] *nm* : bet, wager — **parier** [parje] {96} *vt* : bet, wager
paria [parja] *nm* : outcast
parisien, -sienne [parizjɛ̃, -zjɛn] *adj* : Parisian

parjurer [parʒyre] *v* **se parjurer** *vr* : perjure oneself

parking [parkiŋ] *nm* : parking lot

parlant, -lante [parlɑ̃, -lɑ̃t] *adj* : vivid, eloquent

parlement [parləmɑ̃] *nm* : parliament — **parlementaire** [parləmɑ̃tɛr] *adj* : parliamentary — **parlementer** [parləmɑ̃te] *vi* : negotiate

parler [parle] *vt* : talk, speak — *vi* **1** : talk, speak **2** ~ **à** : talk to **3** ~ **de** : mention, refer to — **se parler** *vr* **1** : speak to each other **2** : be spoken (of a language) — ~ *nm* : speech, way of speaking

parloir [parlwar] *nm* : parlor

parmi [parmi] *prep* : among

parodie [parɔdi] *nf* : parody — **parodier** [parɔdje] {96} *vt* : parody, mimic

paroi [parwa] *nf* **1** : partition **2** : wall (in anatomy, etc.) **3** ~ **rocheuse** : rock face

paroisse [parwas] *nf* : parish — **paroissien, -sienne** [parwasjɛ̃, -sjɛn] *n* : parishioner

parole [parɔl] *nf* **1** : (spoken) word **2** PROMESSE : word, promise **3** : speech **4** ~**s** *nfpl* : lyrics **5 prendre la** ~ : speak

paroxysme [parɔksism] *nm* : height, climax

parquer [parke] *vt* **1** : pen (cattle, etc.) **2** GARER : park

parquet [parke] *nm* : parquet (floor)

parrain [parɛ̃] *nm* **1** : godfather **2** : sponsor, patron — **parrainer** [parɛne] *vt* : sponsor

parsemer [parsəme] {52} *vt* ~ **de** : scatter with, strew with

part [par] *nf* **1** : portion, piece **2** : part, share **3** : side, position **4** **à** ~ : apart from **5** **de la** ~ **de** : on behalf of **6** **de toutes** ~**s** : from all sides **7** **d'une** ~ : on (the) one hand **8** **faire sa** ~ : do one's share **9** **prendre** ~ **à** : take part in

partager [partaʒe] {17} *vt* **1** : divide up **2** RÉPARTIR : share — **se partager** *vr* : share — **partage** [partaʒ] *nm* : sharing, dividing

partance [partɑ̃s] *nf* **1 en** ~ : ready to depart **2 en** ~ **pour** : bound for — **partant, -tante** [partɑ̃, -tɑ̃t] *adj* : ready, willing

partenaire [partənɛr] *nmf* : partner

parterre [partɛr] *nm* **1** : flower bed **2** : orchestra section (in a theater)

parti [parti] *nm* **1** : group, camp **2** : (political) party **3** ~ **pris** : bias **4 prendre** ~ : take a stand **5 prendre son** ~ : make up one's mind **6 tirer** ~ **de** : take advantage of — **parti, -tie** [parti] *adj fam* : intoxicated, high

partial, -tiale [parsjal] *adj, mpl* **-tiaux** [-sjo] : biased, partial

participe [partisip] *nm* : participle

participer [partisipe] *vi* ~ **à 1** : participate in **2** : contribute to — **participant, -pante** [partisipɑ̃, -pɑ̃t] *n* : participant — **partici-**

pation [partisipasjɔ̃] *nf* **1** : participation **2** : contribution

particule [partikyl] *nf* : particle

particulier, -lière [partikylje, -ljɛr] *adj* **1** : particular, specific **2** DISTINCTIF : peculiar **3** PRIVÉ : private, personal **4 en** ~ : especially, in particular — **particularité** [partikylarite] *nf* : idiosyncrasy — **particulier** [partikylje] *nm* : individual — **particulièrement** [partikyljɛrmɑ̃] *adv* : especially, particularly

partie [parti] *nf* **1** : part **2** : game, match **3** : party, participant **4** SORTIE : outing **5 en** ~ : partly, in part **6 faire** ~ **de** : be a part of — **partiel, -tielle** [parsjɛl] *adj* : partial

partir [partir] {82} *vi* **1** : leave, depart **2** : start up, go off **3** COMMENCER : start **4** S'ENLEVER : come out (of a stain, etc.) **5 à** ~ **de** : from

partisan, -sane [partizɑ̃, -zan] *adj & n* : partisan

partition [partisjɔ̃] *nf* : score (in music)

partout [partu] *adv* **1** : everywhere **2** : all (in sports)

parure [paryr] *nf* **1** : finery **2** ENSEMBLE : set

parution [parysjɔ̃] *nf* : publication, launch

parvenir [parvənir] {92} *vi* **1** ~ **à** : reach, arrive at **2** ~ **à faire** : manage to do

parvis [parvi] *nm* : square (in front of a church)

pas¹ [pa] *adv* **1** → **ne 2** : not **3** ~ **du tout** : not at all **4** ~ **mal de** : quite a lot of

pas² *nms & pl* **1** : step, footstep **2** : footprint **3** : pace, gait **4** : step (in dancing) **5 de ce** ~ : right away **6** ~ **de la porte** : doorstep

passable [pasabl] *adj* : passable, fair — **passablement** [pasabləmɑ̃] **1** : quite, rather **2** : reasonably well

passage [pasaʒ] *nm* **1** : passing, crossing **2** SÉJOUR : stay, visit **3** CHEMIN : route, way **4** : passage (in a text) **5** ~ **pour piétons** : pedestrian crossing **6** ~ **interdit** : do not enter — **passager, -gère** [pasaʒe, -ʒɛr] *adj* : passing, temporary — *n* **1** : passenger **2** ~ **clandestin** : stowaway — **passant, -sante** [pasɑ̃, -sɑ̃t] *adj* : busy, crowded — ~ *n* : passerby

passe [pas] *nf* **1** : pass (in sports) **2 mauvaise** ~ : difficult time

passé, -sée [pase] *adj* **1** : last, past **2** DÉCOLORÉ : faded — **passé** *nm* **1** : past **2** : past tense — ~ *prep* : after, beyond

passe–partout [paspartu] *nms & pl* : master key

passeport [paspɔr] *nm* : passport

passer [pase] *vt* **1** : cross, go over **2** : pass, go past **3** : hand over **4** : put through to (on the telephone) **5** : take (an exam, etc.) **6** : spend (time) **7** : skip, pass over **8** ENFILER

: slip on **9** : show (a film), play (a cassette, etc.) — *vi* **1** : pass, go past, go by **2** : drop by **3** ALLER : go **4 en passant** : incidentally **5 laissez-moi passer** : let me through — **se passer** *vr* **1** : take place **2** SE DÉROULER : turn out **3** : pass, go by (of time) **4 ~ de** : dispense with, do without
passereau [pasro] *nm, pl* **-reaux** : sparrow
passerelle [pasrɛl] *nf* **1** : footbridge **2** : gangplank
passe–temps [pastã] *nms & pl* : hobby, pastime
passeur, -seuse [pasœr, -søz] *n* : smuggler
passible [pasibl] *adj* **~ de** : liable to
passif, -sive [pasif, -siv] *adj* : passive — **passif** *nm* **1** : passive voice **2** : liabilities *pl*
passionner [pasjone] *vt* : fascinate, captivate — **se passionner** *vr* **~ pour** : have a passion for — **passion** [pasjɔ̃] *nf* : passion — **passionnant, -nante** [pasjonã, -nãt] *adj* : exciting, fascinating — **passionné, -née** [pasjone] *adj* : passionate — **~** *n* : enthusiast
passoire [paswar] *nf* : sieve, colander
pastel [pastɛl] *adj & nm* : pastel
pastèque [pastɛk] *nf* : watermelon
pasteur [pastœr] *nm* : minister, pastor
pasteuriser [pastœrize] *vt* : pasteurize
pastille [pastij] *nf* : lozenge
patate [patat] *nf* **1** *fam* : potato **2** *or* **~ douce** : sweet potato
patauger [patoʒe] {17} *vi* : splash about, paddle
pâte [pat] *nf* **1** : dough, batter **2 ~ à modeler** : modeling clay **3 ~ dentifrice** : toothpaste **4 ~s** *nfpl* : pasta
pâté [pate] *nm* **1** : pâté **2** *or* **~ de maisons** : block (of houses)
patelin [patlɛ̃] *nm fam* : little village
patent, -tente [patã, -tãt] *adj* : obvious, patent
patère [patɛr] *nf* : peg, hook
paternel, -nelle [patɛrnɛl] *adj* : paternal, fatherly — **paternité** [patɛrnite] *nf* : fatherhood
pâteux, -teuse [patø, -tøz] *adj* **1** : pasty, doughy **2 avoir la langue pâteuse** : have a coated tongue
pathologie [patɔlɔʒi] *nf* : pathology
patience [pasjãs] *nf* **1** : patience **2 jeu de ~** : solitaire — **patient, -tiente** [pasjã, -sjãt] *adj & n* : patient — **patiemment** [pasjamã] *adv* : patiently — **patienter** [pasjãte] *vi* : wait
patin [patɛ̃] *nm* **1** : skate **2 ~s à glace** : ice skates **3 ~s à roulettes** : roller skates — **patinage** [patinaʒ] *nm* : skating — **patiner** [patine] *vi* **1** : skate **2** : skid — **patineur, -neuse** [patinœr, -nøz] *n* : skater — **patinoire** [patinwar] *nf* : skating rink

pâtisserie [patisri] *nf* **1** : cake, pastry **2** : pastry shop, bakery
patrie [patri] *nf* : homeland
patrimoine [patrimwan] *nm* **1** : inheritance **2** HÉRITAGE : heritage
patriote [patrijɔt] *adj* : patriotic — **~** *nmf* : patriot — **patriotique** [patrijɔtik] *adj* : patriotic
patron, -tronne [patrɔ̃, -trɔn] *n* : boss, manager — **patron** *nm* : pattern (in sewing) — **patronner** [patrɔne] *vt* : support, sponsor
patrouille [patruj] *nf* : patrol — **patrouiller** [patruje] *vi* : patrol
patte [pat] *nf* **1** : paw, hoof, foot **2** *fam* : leg, foot (of a person) **3** : tab, flap
pâturage [patyraʒ] *nm* : pasture
paume [pom] *nf* : palm (of the hand)
paumer [pome] *v fam* : lose — **se paumer** *vr fam* : get lost
paupière [popjɛr] *nf* : eyelid
pause [poz] *nf* **1** : pause **2** : break (from work)
pauvre [povr] *adj* : poor — **~** *nmf* : poor man, poor woman — **pauvreté** [povrəte] *nf* : poverty
pavaner [pavane] *v* **se pavaner** *vr* : strut about
paver [pave] *vt* : pave — **pavé** [pave] *nm* **1** : pavement **2** : cobblestone
pavillon [pavijɔ̃] *nm* **1** : pavilion **2** *France* : (detached) house **3** : ward, wing (in a hospital) **4** : flag (on a ship)
pavoiser [pavwaze] *vi fam* : rejoice
pavot [pavo] *nm* : poppy
paye [pɛj] *nf* → **paie**
payement [pɛmã] → **paiement**
payer [peje] {11} *vt* : pay (for) — *vi* : pay — **se payer** *vr* : treat oneself
pays [pei] *nm* **1** : country **2** : region, area **3 du ~** : local — **paysage** [peizaʒ] *nm* : scenery, landscape — **paysan, -sanne** [peizã, -zan] *adj* **1** : agricultural, farming **2** : rural, rustic — **~** *n* **1** : small farmer **2** : peasant
péage [peaʒ] *nm* **1** : toll **2** : tollbooth
peau [po] *nf, pl* **peaux 1** : (human) skin **2** : hide, pelt **3** : peel, skin (of a fruit) **4 petites peaux** : cuticle
pêche [pɛʃ] *nf* **1** : peach **2** : fishing
péché [peʃe] *nm* : sin — **pécher** [peʃe] {87} *vi* : sin
pêcher[1] [peʃe] *vt* **1** : fish for **2** *fam* : get, dig up — *vi* : fish
pêcher[2] [peʃe] *nm* : peach tree
pécheur[1] **, -cheresse** [peʃœr, -ʃrɛs] *n* : sinner
pêcheur[2] **, -cheuse** [pɛʃœr, -ʃøz] *n* **1** : fisherman **2 pêcheur à la ligne** : angler
pécule [pekyl] *nm* : savings *pl*
pécuniaire [pekynjɛr] *adj* : financial

pédagogie [pedagɔʒi] *nf* : education — **pédagogique** [pedagɔʒik] *adj* : educational

pédale [pedal] *nf* : pedal — **pédaler** [pedale] *vi* : pedal — **pédalo** [pedalo] *nm* : pedal boat

pédant, -dante [pedɑ̃, -dɑ̃t] *adj* : pedantic — ~ *n* : pedant

pédestre [pedɛstr] *adj* **randonnée** ~ : hike

pédiatre [pedjatr] *nmf* : pediatrician

pédicure [pedikyr] *nmf* : chiropodist

pègre [pɛgr] *nf* : (criminal) underworld

peigne [pɛɲ] *nm* : comb — **peigner** [peɲe] *vt* : comb — **se peigner** *vr* : comb one's hair — **peignoir** [pɛɲwar] *nm* : bathrobe

peindre [pɛ̃dr] {37} *vt* **1** : paint **2** DÉCRIRE : depict, portray

peine [pɛn] *nf* **1** : sorrow, sadness **2** EFFORT : trouble **3** : punishment **4** à ~ : hardly, barely — **peiner** [pene] *vt* ATTRISTER : sadden, distress — *vi* **1** : struggle **2** : labor (of an engine, etc.)

peintre [pɛ̃tr] *nm* : painter — **peinture** [pɛ̃tyr] *nf* **1** : paint **2** : painting

péjoratif, -tive [peʒɔratif, -tiv] *adj* : derogatory

pelage [pəlaʒ] *nm* : coat, fur (of an animal)

pêle-mêle [pɛlmɛl] *adv* : every which way

peler [pəle] {20} *v* : peel

pèlerin, -rine [pɛlrɛ̃] *n* : pilgrim — **pèlerinage** [pɛlrinaʒ] *nm* : pilgrimage — **pèlerine** [pɛlrin] *nf* : cape

pélican [pelikɑ̃] *nm* : pelican

pelle [pɛl] *nf* **1** : shovel **2** ~ à poussière : dustpan — **pelletée** [pɛlte] *nf* : shovelful — **pelleter** [pɛlte] {8} *vt* : shovel

pellicule [pelikyl] *nf* **1** : (photographic) film **2** : thin layer, film **3** ~s *nfpl* : dandruff

pelote [pəlɔt] *nf* : ball (of string, etc.) — **peloton** [plɔtɔ̃] *nm* **1** : pack, group **2** : squad, platoon **3** ~ de tête : front runners — **pelotonner** [pələtɔne] *v* **se pelotonner** *vr* : curl up (into a ball)

pelouse [pəluz] *nf* **1** : lawn, grass **2** : field (in sports)

peluche [pəlyʃ] *nf* **1** : plush **2** ~s *nfpl* : fluff, lint **3** *or* **animal en** ~ : stuffed animal

pelure [pəlyr] *nf* : peel, skin

pénal, -nale [penal] *adj, mpl* **-naux** [peno] : penal — **pénaliser** [penalize] *vt* : penalize — **pénalité** [penalite] *nf* : penalty

penaud, -naude [pəno, -nod] *adj* : sheepish

penchant [pɑ̃ʃɑ̃] *nm* : tendency, inclination

pencher [pɑ̃ʃe] *vt* INCLINER : tilt, tip — *vi* **1** : slant, lean **2** ~ pour : favor — **se pencher** *vr* : hunch over

pendaison [pɑ̃dɛzɔ̃] *nf* **1** : hanging **2** ~ de crémaillère : housewarming

pendant, -dante [pɑ̃dɑ̃, -dɑ̃t] *adj* : hanging, dangling — **pendant** *nm* **1** *or* ~ d'oreille : drop earring **2** CONTREPARTIE : counterpart — ~ *prep* **1** : during, for **2** ~ que : while — **pendentif** [pɑ̃dɑ̃tif] *nm* : pendant

penderie [pɑ̃dri] *nf* : closet, wardrobe

pendre [pɑ̃dr] {63} *v* : hang — **se pendre** *vr* : hang oneself

pendule [pɑ̃dyl] *nm* : pendulum — ~ *nf* : clock

pêne [pɛn] *nm* : bolt (of a lock)

pénétrer [penetre] {87} *vt* : penetrate — *vi* ~ **dans** : enter

pénible [penibl] *adj* **1** : painful, distressing **2** ARDU : difficult — **péniblement** [peniblǝmɑ̃] *adv* : with difficulty

péniche [peniʃ] *nf* **1** : barge **2** ~ aménagée : houseboat

pénicilline [penisilin] *nf* : penicillin

péninsule [penɛ̃syl] *nf* : peninsula

pénis [penis] *nm* : penis

pénitent, -tente [penitɑ̃, -tɑ̃t] *adj* : repentant — **pénitencier** [penitɑ̃sje] *nm* : penitentiary

pénombre [penɔ̃br] *nf* : half-light

pensée [pɑ̃se] *nf* **1** IDÉE : thought **2** ESPRIT : mind **3** : pansy — **penser** [pɑ̃se] *vt* **1** : think **2** CROIRE : believe, suppose **3** ~ **faire** : plan on doing — *vi* ~ à : think about — **pensif, -sive** [pɑ̃sif, -siv] *adj* : pensive

pension [pɑ̃sjɔ̃] *nf* **1** : pension **2** : boarding-house **3** : room and board **4** ~ **alimentaire** : alimony — **pensionnaire** [pɑ̃sjɔnɛr] *nmf* : boarder, roomer — **pensionnat** [pɑ̃sjɔna] *nm* : boarding school

pentagone [pɛ̃tagɔn] *nm* : pentagon

pente [pɑ̃t] *nf* **1** : slope **2 en** ~ : sloping

pénurie [penyri] *nf* : shortage, scarcity

pépé [pepe] *nm France fam* : grandpa

pépier [pepje] {96} *vi* : chirp, tweet — **pépiement** [pepimɑ̃] *nm* : peep (of a bird)

pépin [pepɛ̃] *nm* **1** : seed (of a fruit) **2** *fam* : snag, hitch — **pépinière** [pepinjɛr] *nf* : (tree) nursery

pépite [pepit] *nf* : nugget

perçant, -çante [pɛrsɑ̃, -sɑ̃t] *adj* **1** : piercing **2** : sharp, keen (of vision)

percée [pɛrse] *nf* **1** : opening, gap **2** DÉCOUVERTE : breakthrough

percepteur [pɛrsɛptœr] *nm* : tax collector

perceptible [pɛrsɛptibl] *adj* : perceptible, noticeable

perception [pɛrsɛpsjɔ̃] *nf* **1** : perception **2** RECOUVREMENT : collection (of taxes)

percer [pɛrse] {6} *vt* **1** : pierce, puncture **2** PÉNÉTRER : penetrate **3** ~ **ses dents** : be teething — *vi* **1** : break through **2** : come through (of a tooth) — **perceuse** [pɛrsøz] *nf* : drill

percevoir [pɛrsǝvwar] {26} *vt* **1** : perceive **2** : collect (taxes)

perche [pɛrʃ] *nf* **1** : pole, rod **2** : perch, bass (fish)

percher [pɛrʃe] *v* **se percher** *vr* : perch, roost — **perchoir** [pɛrʃwar] *nm* : perch, roost

percussion [pɛrkysjɔ̃] *nf* : percussion

percuter [pɛrkyte] *vt* : strike, crash into — **percutant, -tante** [pɛrkytɑ̃, -tɑ̃t] *adj* : forceful, striking

perdre [pɛrdr] {63} *vt* **1** : lose **2** GASPILLER : waste **3** MANQUER : miss **4** : ruin (one's reputation, etc.) — *vi* : lose — **se perdre** *vr* : get lost — **perdant, -dante** [pɛrdɑ̃, -dɑ̃t] *adj* : losing — ~ *n* : loser

perdrix [pɛrdri] *nfs & pl* : partridge

perdu, -due [pɛrdy] *adj* **1** : lost **2 temps perdu** : wasted time

père [pɛr] *nm* **1** : father **2** ~**s** *nmpl* : ancestors

perfectionner [pɛrfɛksjɔne] *vt* : perfect, improve — **se perfectionner** *vr* : improve — **perfection** [pɛrfɛksjɔ̃] *nf* **1** : perfection **2 à la** ~ : perfectly — **perfectionné, -née** [pɛrfɛksjɔne] *adj* : sophisticated — **perfectionnement** [pɛrfɛksjɔnmɑ̃] *nm* : improvement

perforer [pɛrfɔre] *vt* : perforate, pierce

performance [pɛrfɔrmɑ̃s] *nf* **1** : performance **2** RÉUSSITE : achievement — **performant, -mante** [pɛrfɔrmɑ̃, -mɑ̃t] *adj* : high-performance

péril [peril] *nm* : peril, danger — **périlleux, -leuse** [perijø, -jøz] *adj* : perilous

périmé, -mée [perime] *adj* : out-of-date, expired

périmètre [perimɛtr] *nm* : perimeter

période [perjɔd] *nf* **1** : period, time **2 par** ~**s** : periodically — **périodique** [perjɔdik] *adj* : periodic, periodical — ~ *nm* : periodical

péripétie [peripesi] *nf* : incident, event

périphérie [periferi] *nf* **1** : periphery, circumference **2** : outskirts *pl* (of a city) — **périphérique** [periferik] *adj* **1** : peripheral **2** : outlying (areas)

périple [peripl] *nm* : journey

périr [perir] *vi* : perish

périssable [perisabl] *adj* : perishable

perle [pɛrl] *nf* **1** : pearl **2** : gem, treasure (of a person)

permanent, -nente [pɛrmanɑ̃, -nɑ̃t] *adj* : permanent — **permanente** *nf* : perm, permanent — **permanence** [pɛrmanɑ̃s] *nf* : permanence

permettre [pɛrmɛtr] {53} *vt* **1** : allow, permit **2** : enable, make possible — **se permettre** *vr* **1** : allow oneself **2** ~ **de** : take the liberty of — **permis** [pɛrmi] *nm* : license, permit — **permission** [pɛrmisjɔ̃] *nf* **1** : permission **2** : leave (in the military)

permuter [pɛrmyte] *vt* : switch around — *vi* : switch places

pernicieux, -cieuse [pɛrnisjø, -sjøz] *adj* : pernicious

peroxyde [pɛrɔksid] *nm* : peroxide

perpendiculaire [pɛrpɑ̃dikylɛr] *adj* : perpendicular

perpétrer [pɛrpetre] {87} *vt* : perpetrate, commit

perpétuer [pɛrpetɥe] *vt* : perpetuate — **perpétuel, -tuelle** [pɛrpetɥɛl] *adj* **1** : perpetual **2** : permanent — **perpétuité** [pɛrpetɥite] *nf* **à** ~ : for life

perplexe [pɛrplɛks] *adj* : perplexed, puzzled — **perplexité** [pɛrplɛksite] *nf* : perplexity

perquisition [pɛrkizisjɔ̃] *nf* : (police) search

perron [pɛrɔ̃] *nm* : (front) steps

perroquet [pɛrɔkɛ] *nm* : parrot

perruche [peryʃ] *nf* : parakeet

perruque [peryk] *nf* : wig

persécuter [pɛrsekyte] *vt* **1** : persecute **2** HARCELER : harass — **persécution** [pɛrsekysjɔ̃] *nf* : persecution

persévérer [pɛrsevere] {87} *vi* : persevere, persist — **persévérance** [pɛrseverɑ̃s] *nf* : perseverance

persienne [pɛrsjɛn] *nf* : shutter

persil [pɛrsi] *nm* : parsley

persister [pɛrsiste] *vi* : persist — **persistant, -tante** [pɛrsistɑ̃, -tɑ̃t] *adj* : persistent — **persistance** [-tɑ̃s] *nf* : persistence

personnage [pɛrsɔnaʒ] *nm* **1** : (fictional) character **2** : character, individual

personnalité [pɛrsɔnalite] *nf* **1** : personality **2** : celebrity

personne [pɛrsɔn] *nf* : person — ~ *pron* **1** : no one, nobody **2** : anyone, anybody — **personnel, -nelle** [pɛrsɔnɛl] *adj* : personal, private — **personnel** *nm* : personnel, staff

perspective [pɛrspɛktiv] *nf* **1** : perspective (in art) **2** : point of view **3** POSSIBILITÉ : outlook, prospect

perspicace [pɛrspikas] *adj* : insightful, shrewd — **perspicacité** [pɛrspikasite] *nf* : shrewdness

persuader [pɛrsɥade] *vt* : persuade, convince — **persuasion** [pɛrsɥazjɔ̃] *nf* : persuasion

perte [pɛrt] *nf* **1** : loss **2** GASPILLAGE : waste **3 à** ~ **de vue** : as far as the eye can see

pertinent, -nente [pɛrtinɑ̃, -nɑ̃t] *adj* : pertinent — **pertinence** [pɛrtinɑ̃s] *nf* : pertinence

perturber [pɛrtyrbe] *vt* **1** INTERROMPRE : disrupt **2** DÉRANGER : disturb, upset — **perturbation** [pɛrtyrbasjɔ̃] *nf* : disruption

pervertir [pɛrvɛrtir] *vt* : pervert, corrupt — **pervers, -verse** [pɛrvɛr, -vɛrs] *adj* : perverse

peser [pəze] {52} *vt* **1** : weigh **2** EXAMINER

: consider — *vi* **1** : weigh **2** INFLUER : carry weight **3 ~ sur** : press, push — **pesament** [pəzamɑ̃] *adv* : heavily — **pesant, -sante** [pəzɑ̃, -zɑ̃t] *adj* **1** : heavy **2** : burdensome — **pesanteur** [pəzɑ̃tœr] *nf* **1** : gravity (in physics) **2** LOURDEUR : heaviness, weight — **pesée** [pəze] *nf* : weighing

pèse-personne [pɛzpɛrsɔn] *nm, pl* **pèse-personnes** : (bathroom) scales

pessimiste [pesimist] *adj* : pessimistic — **~** *nmf* : pessimist — **pessimisme** [pesimism] *nm* : pessimism

peste [pɛst] *nf* **1** : plague **2** : pest (person)

pesticide [pɛstisid] *nm* : pesticide

pétale [petal] *nm* : petal

pétarader [petarade] *vi* : backfire — **pétard** [petar] *nm* : firecracker

péter [pete] {87} *vi fam* : go off, explode — *vt fam* : bust, break

pétiller [petije] *vi* **1** : sparkle **2** : bubble, fizz **3** : crackle (of fire) — **pétillant, -lante** [petijɑ̃, -jɑ̃t] *adj* **1** : sparkling **2** : bubbly

petit, -tite [p(ə)ti, -tit] *adj* **1** : small, little **2** COURT : short **3** : young (of an animal) **4 ma petite sœur** : my little sister **5 petit ami, petite amie** : boyfriend, girlfriend **6 petit déjeuner** : breakfast — **~** *n* : little boy *m*, little girl *f* — **petit** *nm* : cub

petit-fils, petite-fille [p(ə)tifis, p(ə)titfij] *n* : grandson *m*, granddaughter *f*

pétition [petisjɔ̃] *nf* : petition

petits-enfants [p(ə)tizɑ̃fɑ̃] *nmpl* : grandchildren

pétrifier [petrifje] {96} *vt* : petrify

pétrin [petrɛ̃] *nm fam* : fix, jam

pétrir [petrir] *vt* : knead

pétrole [petrɔl] *nm* **1** : oil, petroleum **2** *or* **~ lampant** : kerosene — **pétrolier, -lière** [petrɔlje, -ljɛr] *adj* : oil, petroleum — **pétrolier** *nm* **1** : oil tanker **2** : oilman

pétulant, -lante [petylɑ̃, -lɑ̃t] *adj* : vivacious

peu [pø] *adv* **1** : little, not much **2** : not very **3 ~ après** : shortly after — **~** *nm* **1 ~ à ~** : little by little **2 le ~ de** : the few, the little **3 un ~** : a little, a bit — **~** *pron* **1** : few (people) **2 ~ de** : few

peupler [pœple] *vt* : populate, inhabit — **se peupler** *vr* : become populated — **peuple** [pœpl] *nm* : people *pl*

peuplier [pøplije] *nm* : poplar

peur [pœr] *nf* **1** : fear **2 avoir ~ de** : be afraid of **3 de ~ que** : lest **4 faire ~ à** : frighten — **peureux, -reuse** [pœrø, -røz] *adj* : fearful, afraid

peut-être [pøtɛtr] *adv* : perhaps, maybe

pharaon [faraɔ̃] *nm* : pharaoh

phare [far] *nm* **1** : lighthouse **2** : headlight

pharmacie [farmasi] *nf* : pharmacy, drugstore — **pharmacien, -cienne** [farmasjɛ̃, -sjɛn] *n* : pharmacist

phase [faz] *nf* : phase, stage

phénomène [fenɔmɛn] *nm* : phenomenon

philanthrope [filɑ̃trɔp] *nmf* : philanthropist

philatélie [filateli] *nf* : stamp collecting

philosophe [filɔzɔf] *nmf* : philosopher — **philosophie** [filɔzɔfi] *nf* : philosophy

phobie [fɔbi] *nf* : phobia

phonétique [fɔnetik] *adj* : phonetic — **~** *nf* : phonetics

phoque [fɔk] *nm* : seal

phosphore [fɔsfɔr] *nm* : phosphorous

photo [fɔto] *nf* : photo

photocopie [fɔtɔkɔpi] *nf* : photocopy — **photocopier** [fɔtɔkɔpje] {96} *vt* : photocopy — **photocopieur** [fɔtɔkɔpjœr] *nm or* **photocopieuse** [fɔtɔkɔpjøz] *nf* : photocopier

photographie [fɔtɔgrafi] *nf* **1** : photography **2** : photograph — **photographe** [fɔtɔgraf] *nmf* : photographer — **photographier** [fɔtɔgrafje] {96} *vt* : photograph

phrase [fraz] *nf* : sentence

physicien, -cienne [fizisjɛ̃, -sjɛn] *n* : physicist

physiologie [fizjɔlɔʒi] *nf* : physiology

physionomie [fizjɔnɔmi] *nf* : face

physique [fizik] *adj* : physical — **~** *nm* : physique — **~** *nf* : physics

piailler [pjaje] *vi* : squawk

piano [pjano] *nm* **1** : piano **2 ~ à queue** : grand piano — **pianiste** [pjanist] *nmf* : pianist

pic [pik] *nm* **1** : woodpecker **2** CIME : peak **3** : pick(ax)

pichet [piʃɛ] *nm* : pitcher, jug

pickpocket [pikpɔkɛt] *nm* : pickpocket

picorer [pikɔre] *v* : peck

picoter [pikɔte] *vi* : prickle, sting — **picotement** [pikɔtmɑ̃] *nm* : prickling, stinging

pie [pi] *nf* **1** : magpie **2** *fam* : chatterbox

pièce [pjɛs] *nf* **1** : piece, bit **2** : part, item **3** : room, bedroom **4** : piece (in music) **5 ~ de théâtre** : play **6** *or* **~ de monnaie** : coin **7 ~ jointe** : enclosure (in correspondence)

pied [pje] *nm* **1** : foot **2** : base, bottom, leg (of a table, etc.) **3** : stalk, head (of lettuce) **4 aux ~s nus** : barefoot **5 coup de ~** : kick **6 mettre sur ~** : set up, get off the ground — **piédestal** [pjedɛstal] *nm, pl* **-taux** [-to] : pedestal

piège [pjɛʒ] *nm* **1** : trap, snare **2** : pitfall **3 prendre au ~** : entrap — **piéger** [pjeʒe] {64} *vt* **1** : trap **2** : booby-trap

pierre [pjɛr] *nf* **1** : stone **2 ~ de touche** : touchstone **3 ~ tombale** : tombstone — **pierreries** [pjɛrri] *nfpl* : precious stones, gems — **pierreux, -reuse** [pjɛrø, -røz] *adj* : stony

piété [pjete] *nf* : piety

piétiner [pjetine] *vt* : trample on — *vi* **1** : stamp one's feet **2** STAGNER : make no headway

piéton, -tonne [pjetɔ̃, -tɔn] *n* : pedestrian — **piétonnier, -nière** [pjetɔnje, -njɛr] *adj* : pedestrian

piètre [pjɛtr] *adj* : poor, wretched

pieu [pjø] *nm, pl* **pieux** : post, stake

pieuvre [pjœvr] *nf* : octopus

pieux, pieuse [pjø, pjøz] *adj* : pious

pige [piʒ] *nf* à la ~ : freelance

pigeon [piʒɔ̃] *nm* : pigeon

piger [piʒe] {17} *vt fam* **1** : understand **2** *Can* : to pick (a card, a number, etc.) **3 tu piges?** : get it?

pigment [pigmã] *nm* : pigment

pignon [piɲɔ̃] *nm* **1** : gable **2** : cogwheel

pile [pil] *nf* **1** : pile, heap **2** : (storage) battery **3** ~ ou face? : heads or tails? — ~ *adv fam* **1** : abruptly **2** JUSTE : exactly, right **3** à l'heure ~ : on the dot

piler [pile] *vt* **1** : crush, pound **2** *Can* : mash (potatoes, etc.)

pilier [pilje] *nm* : pillar, column

piller [pije] *vt* : loot, pillage — **pillage** [pijaʒ] *nm* : looting — **pillard, -larde** [pijar, -jard] *n* : looter

pilon [pilɔ̃] *nm* **1** : pestle **2** : (chicken) drumstick — **pilonner** [pilɔne] *vt* **1** : crush, pound **2** : bombard, shell

pilote [pilɔt] *adj* : pilot, test — ~ *nm* **1** : pilot, driver **2** GUIDE : guide — **pilotage** [pilɔtaʒ] *nm* : piloting, flying — **piloter** [pilɔte] *vt* **1** : pilot, fly, drive **2** GUIDER : show around

pilule [pilyl] *nf* : pill

piment [pimã] *nm* **1** : pepper **2** ~ **rouge** : hot pepper **3** ~ **doux** : sweet pepper

pin [pɛ̃] *nm* : pine

pinard [pinar] *nm fam* : (cheap) wine

pince [pɛ̃s] *nf* **1** : pliers *pl* **2** : tongs *pl* **3** : pincer, claw **4** : dart, fold **5** ~ à épiler : tweezers *pl* **6** ~ à linge : clothespin

pinceau [pɛ̃so] *nm, pl* **-ceaux** : paintbrush

pincer [pɛ̃se] {6} *vt* **1** : pinch **2** : nip at, sting (of wind, etc.) **3** *fam* : nab — *vi* **1** : be nippy (of weather) — **pincé, -cée** [pɛ̃se] *adj* : forced, stiff — **pincée** [pɛ̃se] *nf* : pinch, small amount — **pincement** [pɛ̃smã] *nm* **1** : pinch **2** : twinge — **pincettes** [pɛ̃sɛt] *nfpl* **1** : small tweezers **2** : (fire) tongs

pinède [pinɛd] *nf* : pine forest

pingouin [pɛ̃gwɛ̃] *nm* : auk

pingre [pɛ̃gr] *adj* : stingy

pintade [pɛ̃tad] *nf* : guinea fowl

pinte [pɛ̃t] *nf* : pint

pioche [pjɔʃ] *nf* : pickax, pick — **piocher** [pjɔʃe] *vt* : dig (up)

pion, pionne [pjɔ̃, pjɔn] *n France fam* : stu-

dent monitor — **pion** *nm* **1** : pawn (in chess) **2** : piece (in checkers)

pionnier, -nière [pjɔnje, -njɛr] *n* : pioneer

pipe [pip] *nf* : pipe

pipeline [pajplajn] *nm* : pipeline

piquant, -quante [pikã, -kãt] *adj* **1** : prickly, bristly **2** ÉPICÉ : hot, spicy — **piquant** *nm* **1** : prickle, thorn **2** : spine, quill

pique [pik] *nm* : spade (in playing cards) — ~ *nf* : cutting remark

pique-assiette [pikasjɛt] *nmfs & pl* : freeloader

pique-nique [piknik] *nm, pl* **pique-niques** : picnic

piquer [pike] *vt* **1** : prick, puncture **2** : sting, bite **3** : stick (into) **4** ÉVEILLER : arouse (interest, etc.) **5** *fam* : pinch, swipe **6** *fam* : nab, catch — *vi* **1** : sting, burn **2** : dive, swoop down — **se piquer** *vr* ~ **de** : pride oneself on — **piquet** [pikɛ] *nm* **1** : post, stake, peg **2** ~ **de grève** : picket line —

piqûre [pikyr] *nf* **1** : prick **2** : sting, bite **3** : injection, shot

pirate [pirat] *nm* **1** : pirate **2** ~ **de l'air** : hijacker

pire [pir] *adj* **1** : worse **2 le ~, la ~, les ~s** : the worst — ~ *nm* **1 le ~** : the worst **2 au ~** : at the worst

pis [pi] *adv* **1** : worse **2 de mal en ~** : from bad to worse — ~ *adj* : worse — ~ *nms & pl* **1** : udder **2 le ~** : the worst

pis-aller [pizale] *nms & pl* : last resort

piscine [pisin] *nf* : swimming pool

pissenlit [pisãli] *nm* : dandelion

pistache [pistaʃ] *nf* : pistachio

piste [pist] *nf* **1** TRACE : track, trail **2** : path, route **3** : (ski) slope **4** : racetrack **5** INDICE : lead, clue **6** *or* ~ **d'atterrissage** : runway, airstrip

pistolet [pistɔlɛ] *nm* **1** : pistol, handgun **2** : spray gun

piston [pistɔ̃] *nm* : piston

pitié [pitje] *nf* : pity, mercy — **piteux, -teuse** [pitø, -tøz] *adj* : pitiful

piton [pitɔ̃] *nm* **1** : eye, hook **2** *Can fam* : button, switch

pitoyable [pitwajabl] *adj* : pitiful

pitre [pitr] *nm* : clown

pittoresque [pitɔrɛsk] *adj* : picturesque

pivot [pivo] *nm* : pivot — **pivoter** [pivɔte] *vi* : pivot, revolve

pizza [pidza] *nf* : pizza — **pizzeria** [pidzerja] *nf* : pizzeria

placage [plakaʒ] *nm* : veneer

placard [plakar] *nm* **1** : cupboard, closet **2** AFFICHE : poster — **placarder** [plakarde] *vt* : post, put up

placer [plase] {6} *vt* **1** : place, set, put **2** : seat (s.o.) **3** : put in, interject **4** : invest (money, etc.) — **se placer** *vr* **1** : position oneself **2** : get a job **3 ~ premier** : finish first — **place** [plas] *nf* **1** : place, spot **2** : room, space **3** : seat (at the theater) **4** : rank, position **5** : (public) square **6** EMPLOI : job, position **7 à la ~ de** : instead of **8 mettre en ~** : set up — **placement** [plasmã] *nm* **1** : investment **2 bureau de ~** : placement agency

placide [plasid] *adj* : placid, calm

plafond [plafɔ̃] *nm* : ceiling — **plafonner** [plafɔne] *vi* : reach a maximum, peak

plage [plaʒ] *nf* **1** : beach, shore **2** : seaside resort

plagier [plaʒje] {96} *vt* : plagiarize — **plagiat** [plaʒja] *nm* : plagiarism

plaider [plede] *vi* : plead, litigate — *vt* : plead (a case)

plaie [plɛ] *nf* : wound, cut

plaignant, -gnante [plɛɲɑ̃, -ɲɑ̃t] *n* : plaintiff

plaindre [plɛ̃dr] {65} *vt* : pity — **se plaindre** *vr* **1** : moan **2 ~ de** : complain about — **plainte** [plɛ̃t] *nf* **1** : moan **2** : complaint

plaire [plɛr] {66} *vi* **1** : be pleasing **2 ~ à** : please, suit — *v impers* **1** : please **2 s'il vous plaît** : please — **se plaire** *vr* **~ à** : like, enjoy — **plaisance** [plɛzɑ̃s] *nf or* **navigation de ~** : sailing, boating — **plaisant, -sante** [plɛzɑ̃, -zɑ̃t] *adj* **1** AGRÉABLE : pleasant **2** AMUSANT : amusing, funny — **plaisanter** [plɛzɑ̃te] *vi* : joke, jest — **plaisanterie** [plɛzɑ̃tri] *nf* **1** BLAGUE : joke, jest **2** FARCE : prank — **plaisantin** [plɛzɑ̃tɛ̃] *nm* : practical joker — **plaisir** [plezir] *nm* **1** : pleasure **2 au ~** : see you soon **3 avec ~!** : of course! **4 faire ~ à** : please

plan, plane [plã, plan] *adj* : flat, level — **plan** *nm* **1** : plane (in geometry) **2** : plan, strategy **3** : map, diagram **4 premier ~** : foreground

planche [plãʃ] *nf* **1** : board, plank **2 ~ à repasser** : ironing board **3 ~ à roulettes** : skateboard — **plancher** [plãʃe] *nm* : floor

planer [plane] *vi* **1** : glide, soar **2 ~ sur** : hover over

planète [planɛt] *nf* : planet — **planétaire** [planeter] *adj* : planetary

planeur [planœr] *nm* : glider

planifier [planifje] {96} *vt* : plan — **planification** [planifikasjɔ̃] *nf* : planning

planque [plãk] *nf fam* : hideout — **planquer** [plãke] *vt fam* : hide away, stash

planter [plãte] *vt* **1** : plant **2** ENFONCER : drive in **3** INSTALLER : put up, set up **4** *fam* : ditch, drop — **se planter** *vr* **1** *fam* : stand, plant oneself **2** *fam* : get it wrong, mess up — **plant** [plã] *nm* : seedling, young plant — **plantation** [plãtasjɔ̃] *nf* **1** : planting **2** : plantation — **plante** [plãt] *nf* **1** : sole (of the foot) **2** : plant

plaquer [plake] *vt* **1** : veneer, plate **2** APLATIR : stick (down), flatten **3** : tackle (in football) **4** *fam* : ditch, get rid of — **plaque** [plak] *nf* **1** : plate, sheet **2** : plaque, nameplate **3** : patch (of ice, etc.) **4 ~ chauffante** : hotplate **5 ~ d'immatriculation** : license plate — **plaqué, -quée** [plake] *adj* : plated — **plaquette** [plakɛt] *nf* **1** : slab (of butter, etc.) **2** : pamphlet

plastique [plastik] *adj & nm* : plastic

plat, plate [pla, plat] *adj* **1** : flat, level **2** : dull, bland — **plat** *nm* **1** : plate, dish **2** : course (of a meal) **3 à ~** : flat down **4 à ~** : dead (of a battery) **5 ~ de résistance** : main course

platane [platan] *nm* : plane tree

plateau [plato] *nm, pl* **-teaux 1** : tray, platter **2** : plateau (in geography) **3** : stage, set (in theater)

plate-bande [platbãd] *nf, pl* **plates-bandes** : flower bed

plate-forme [platfɔrm] *nf, pl* **plates-formes** : platform

platine[1] [platin] *nm* : platinum

platine[2] *nf* : turntable

platitude [platityd] *nf* : trite remark

platonique [platɔnik] *adj* : platonic

plâtre [platr] *nm* **1** : plaster **2** : plaster cast — **plâtrer** [platre] *vt* **1** : plaster **2** : put in a (plaster) cast

plausible [plozibl] *adj* : plausible, likely

plein, pleine [plɛ̃, plɛn] *adj* **1** REMPLI : full, filled (up) **2** : rounded, full **3** : pregnant (of an animal) **4 en plein jour** : in broad daylight **5 le plein air** : the outdoors — **plein** *nm* **1 à ~** : fully, totally **2 faire le ~** : fill up — **plénitude** [plenityd] *nf* : fullness

pleurer [plœre] *vt* **1** : weep for, mourn **2** : shed (tears) — *vi* **1** : cry, weep **2** : water (of eyes) **3 ~ sur** : bemoan — **pleurnicher** [plœrniʃe] *vi fam* : whine, snivel — **pleurs** [plœr] *nfpl* **en ~** : in tears

pleuvoir [pløvwar] {67} *v impers* **1** : rain **2 il pleut** : it's raining — *vi* : rain down, pour down

plier [plije] {96} *vt* **1** : fold (up) **2** : bend — *vi* **1** : bend, sag **2** : yield, give in — **se plier** *vr* **1** : fold **2 ~ à** : submit to — **pli** [pli] *nm* **1** : fold, pleat, crease **2** HABITUDE : habit **3 sous ce ~** : enclosed — **pliant, pliante** [plijã, plijãt] *adj* : folding, collapsible

plinthe [plɛ̃t] *nf* : baseboard

plisser [plise] *vt* **1** : pleat, fold, crease **2** FRONCER : wrinkle (one's brow), pucker (one's lips)

plomb [plɔ̃] *nm* **1** : lead **2** : (lead) pellet **3** FUSIBLE : fuse — **plombage** [plɔ̃baʒ] *nm* : filling (of a tooth) — **plomber** [plɔ̃be] *vt* **1** : weight with lead **2** : fill (a tooth) —

plomberie [plɔ̃bri] *nf* : plumbing — **plombier** [plɔ̃bje] *nm* : plumber

plonger [plɔ̃ʒe] {17} *vt* : thrust, plunge — *vi* **1** : dive **2 ~ dans** : plunge into — **se plonger** vr ~ dans : immerse oneself into — **plongeant, -geante** [plɔ̃ʒɑ̃, -ʒɑ̃t] *adj* **1** : plunging **2 vue plongeante** : bird's-eye view — **plongée** [plɔ̃ʒe] *nf* **1** : diving **2 ~ sous–marine** : skin diving — **plongeoir** [plɔ̃ʒwar] *nm* : diving board — **plongeon** [plɔ̃ʒɔ̃] *nm* **1** : dive **2** : loon (bird) — **plongeur, -geuse** [plɔ̃ʒœr, -ʒøz] *n* **1** : diver **2** : dishwasher (person)

plouf [pluf] *nm* : splash

ployer [plwaje] {58} *v* : bow, bend

pluie [plɥi] *nf* **1** : rain, rainfall **2 une ~ de** : a stream of

plume [plym] *nf* **1** : feather **2** : quill pen — **plumage** [plymaʒ] *nm* : feathers *pl* — **plumeau** [plymo] *nm, pl* **-meaux** [plymo] : feather duster — **plumer** [plyme] *vt* : pluck

plupart [plypar] *nf* **1 la ~ des** : most, the majority of **2 pour la ~** : for the most part, mostly

pluriel, -rielle [plyrjɛl] *adj & nm* : plural — **pluriel** *nm* : plural

plus [ply(s)] *adv* **1** : more **2** (*used with* ne) : no more, no longer **3 ~ de** : more (than) **4 de ~** : in addition, furthermore **5 de ~ en ~** : increasingly **6 en ~** : as well **7 le ~** : the most **8 non ~** : neither, either — **~** *nm* **1** : plus (sign) **2** *fam* : plus, advantage — **~** *conj* : plus (in calculations)

plusieurs [plyzjœr] *adj & pron* : several

plutôt [plyto] *adv* **1** : rather, instead **2 ~ que** : rather than

pluvieux, -vieuse [plyvjø, -vjøz] *adj* : rainy, wet

pneu [pnø] *nm, pl* **pneus** : tire — **pneumatique** [pnømatik] *adj* : inflatable

pneumonie [pnømɔni] *nf* : pneumonia

poche [pɔʃ] *nf* **1** : pocket (in clothing) **2 ~s** *nfpl* CERNES : bags (under the eyes) — **pocher** [pɔʃe] *vt* : poach (in cooking) — **pochette** [pɔʃɛt] *nf* **1** : folder, case, sleeve **2** : book (of matches) **3** : pocket handkerchief

poêle [pwal] *nm* : stove — **~** *nf or* **~ à frire** : frying pan

poème [pɔɛm] *nm* : poem — **poésie** [pɔezi] *nf* **1** : poetry **2** : poem — **poète** [pɔɛt] *nmf* : poet — **poétique** [pɔetik] *adj* : poetic(al)

poids [pwa] *nms & pl* **1** : weight, heaviness **2** FARDEAU : burden **3** IMPORTANCE : meaning, influence **4 ~ et mesures** : weights and measures **5 ~ et haltères** : weight lifting

poignant, -gnante [pwaɲɑ̃, -ɲɑ̃t] *adj* : moving, poignant

poignard [pwaɲar] *nm* : dagger — **poignarder** [pwaɲarde] *vt* : stab

poigne [pwaɲ] *nf* **1** : grip, grasp **2 à ~** : firm, forceful

poignée [pwaɲe] *nf* **1** : handful **2** : handle, knob **3 ~ de main** : handshake

poignet [pwaɲɛ] *nm* **1** : wrist **2** : cuff

poil [pwal] *nm* **1** : hair **2** : fur, coat **3** : bristle (of a brush) **4 à ~** *fam* : stark naked — **poilu, -lue** [pwaly] *adj* : hairy

poinçon [pwɛ̃sɔ̃] *nm* **1** : awl, punch **2** MARQUE : hallmark, stamp — **poinçonner** [pwɛ̃sɔne] *vt* : punch, perforate

poing [pwɛ̃] *nm* **1** : fist **2 coup de ~** : punch

point [pwɛ̃] *nm* **1** : point, position **2** DEGRÉ : degree, extent **3** : period (in punctuation) **4** QUESTION : matter **5** : point (in sports) **6** : stitch (in sewing) **7 à ~** : just right, just in time **8 mettre au ~** : adjust, perfect **9 ~ culminant** : highlight **10 ~ de vue** : point of view **11 ~ du jour** : daybreak **12 ~ mort** : neutral (gear) **13 ~s cardinaux** : points of the compass — **~** *adv* **1** (*used with* **ne**) : not **2 ~ du tout** : not at all

pointe [pwɛ̃t] *nf* **1** : point, tip **2** SOUPÇON : touch, hint **3 de ~** : state-of-the-art **4 heures de ~** : rush hour **5 sur la ~ des pieds** : on tiptoe

pointer [pwɛ̃te] *vt* **1** COCHER : check, mark off **2** : aim (a rifle at), point (a finger at) — *vi* **1** : clock in **2** : break, dawn (of a new day) — **se pointer** *vr fam* : show up

pointillé [pwɛ̃tije] *nm* : dotted line

pointilleux, -leuse [pwɛ̃tijø, -jøz] *adj* : finicky, fussy

pointu, -tue [pwɛ̃ty] *adj* : pointed, sharp

pointure [pwɛ̃tyr] *nf* : size (of clothing)

point–virgule [pwɛ̃virgyl] *nm, pl* **points–virgules** : semicolon

poire [pwar] *nf* : pear

poireau [pwaro] *nm, pl* **-reaux** : leek — **poireauter** [pwarote] *vi fam* : hang around

poirier [pwarje] *nm* : pear tree

pois [pwa] *nms & pl* **1** : pea **2 à ~** : spotted, polka-dot

poison [pwazɔ̃] *nm* : poison

poisse [pwas] *nf fam* : bad luck

poisseux, -seuse [pwasø, -søz] *adj* : sticky

poisson [pwasɔ̃] *nm* **1** : fish **2 ~ d'avril!** : April fool! — **poissonnerie** [pwasɔnri] *nf* : fish market — **poissonnier, -nière** [pwasɔnje, -njɛr] *n* : fish merchant

poitrine [pwatrin] *nf* **1** : chest **2** : breasts *pl*, bosom **3** : breast (in cooking)

poivre [pwavr] *nm* : pepper — **poivré, -vrée** [pwavre] *adj* : peppery — **poivrer** [pwavre] *vt* : pepper — **poivrier** [pwavrije] *nm or* **poivrière** [pwavrijɛr] *nf* : pepper shaker — **poivron** [pwavrɔ̃] *nm* : pepper (vegetable) poker [pɔkɛr] *nm* : poker

pôle [pol] *nm* : pole — polaire [pɔlɛr] *adj* : polar

polémique [pɔlemik] *adj* : controversial — *nf* : debate, controversy

poli, -lie [pɔli] *adj* 1 COURTOIS : polite 2 LISSE : polished, smooth

police [pɔlis] *nf* 1 : police, police force 2 ～ d'assurance : insurance policy — policier, -cière [pɔlisje, -sjɛr] *adj* 1 : police 2 roman policier : detective novel — policier *nm* : police officer

poliomyélite [pɔljɔmjelit] *nf* : poliomyelitis

polir [pɔlir] *vt* : polish, shine

polisson, -sonne [pɔlisɔ̃, -sɔn] *n* : naughty child, rascal

politesse [pɔlitɛs] *nf* 1 : politeness 2 : polite remark

politique [pɔlitik] *adj* : political — ～ *nf* 1 : politics 2 : policy, procedure — politicien, -cienne [pɔlitisjɛ̃, -sjɛn] *n* : politician

pollen [pɔlɛn] *nm* : pollen

polluer [pɔlɥe] *vt* : pollute — polluant [pɔlɥɑ̃] *nm* : pollutant — pollution [pɔlysjɔ̃] *nf*

polo [pɔlo] *nm* 1 : polo 2 : polo shirt

poltron, -tronne [pɔltrɔ̃, -trɔn] *adj* : cowardly — ～ *n* : coward

polyester [pɔliɛstɛr] *nm* : polyester

polyvalent, -lente [pɔlivalɑ̃, -lɑ̃t] *adj* : versatile, multipurpose

pommade [pɔmad] *nf* : ointment

pomme [pɔm] *nf* 1 : apple 2 ～ d'Adam : Adam's apple 3 ～ de pin : pinecone 4 ～ de terre : potato 5 ～s frites : French fries — pommeau [pɔmo] *nm* : knob (of a cane) — pommette [pɔmɛt] *nf* : cheekbone — pommier [pɔmje] *nm* : apple tree

pompe [pɔ̃p] *nf* 1 : pump 2 APPARAT : pomp, ceremony 3 ～s funèbres : funeral home — pomper [pɔ̃pe] *vt* : pump

pompette [pɔ̃pɛt] *adj fam* : tipsy

pompeux, -peuse [pɔ̃pø, -pøz] *adj* : pompous

pompier [pɔ̃pje] *nm* : firefighter, fireman

pompiste [pɔ̃pist] *nmf* : service station attendant

pompon [pɔ̃pɔ̃] *nm* : pompom

pomponner [pɔ̃pɔne] *v* se pomponner *vr* : get all dressed up

poncer [pɔ̃se] {6} *vt* : sand (down)

ponctualité [pɔ̃ktɥalite] *nf* : punctuality

ponctuation [pɔ̃ktɥasjɔ̃] *nf* : punctuation

ponctuel, -tuelle [pɔ̃ktɥɛl] *adj* 1 : prompt, punctual 2 : limited, selective

ponctuer [pɔ̃ktɥe] *vt* : punctuate

pondéré, -rée [pɔ̃dere] *adj* : levelheaded, sensible

pondre [pɔ̃dr] {63} *vt* : lay (eggs)

poney [pɔnɛ] *nm* : pony

pont [pɔ̃] *nm* 1 : bridge 2 : deck (of a ship)

ponte [pɔ̃t] *nf* : laying (of eggs)

pont–levis [pɔ̃ləvi] *nm, pl* ponts–levis : drawbridge

ponton [pɔ̃tɔ̃] *nm* : pontoon

pop [pɔp] *adj s & pl* : pop

pop–corn [pɔpkɔrn] *nms & pl* : popcorn

popote [pɔpɔt] *nf* 1 : mess (in the military) 2 *fam* : cooking

populaire [pɔpylɛr] *adj* 1 : popular 2 : working-class — popularité [pɔpylarite] *nf* : popularity

population [pɔpylasjɔ̃] *nf* : population — populeux, -leuse [pɔpylø, -løz] *adj* : densely populated

porc [pɔr] *nm* 1 : pig, hog 2 : pork (in cooking)

porcelaine [pɔrsəlɛn] *nf* 1 : porcelain 2 : china, chinaware

porc–épic [pɔrkepik] *nm, pl* porcs–épics : porcupine

porche [pɔrʃ] *nm* : porch

porcherie [pɔrʃəri] *nf* : pigpen, pigsty

pore [pɔr] *nm* : pore — poreux, -reuse [pɔrø, -røz] *adj* : porous

pornographie [pɔrnɔgrafi] *nf* : pornography — pornographique [-grafik] *adj* : pornographic

port [pɔr] *nm* 1 : port, harbor 2 : wearing, carrying (of arms, etc.) 3 MAINTIEN : bearing 4 ～ payé : postpaid

portable [pɔrtabl] *adj* : portable

portail [pɔrtaj] *nm* : gate

portant, -tante [pɔrtɑ̃, -tɑ̃t] *adj* bien portant : in good health

portatif, -tive [pɔrtatif, -tiv] *adj* : portable

porte [pɔrt] *nf* 1 : door, doorway 2 : gate (at an airport, etc.) 3 ～ de sortie : exit, way out

porte–avions [pɔrtavjɔ̃] *nms & pl* : aircraft carrier

porte–bagages [pɔrtbagaʒ] *nms & pl* : luggage rack

porte–bonheur [pɔrtbɔnœr] *nms & pl* : lucky charm

porte–clés *or* porte–clefs [pɔrtəkle] *nms & pl* : key ring

porte–documents [pɔrtdɔkymɑ̃] *nms & pl* : briefcase

portée [pɔrte] *nf* 1 : range 2 : impact, significance 3 : litter (of kittens, etc.) 4 à ～ de : within reach of

portefeuille [pɔrtəfœj] *nm* 1 : wallet 2 : portfolio (in finance or politics)

portemanteau [pɔrtmɑ̃to] *nm, pl* -teaux [-to] : coat rack

porte–monnaie [pɔrtmɔnɛ] *nms & pl* : change purse

porte–parole [pɔrtparɔl] *nms & pl* : spokesperson

porter [pɔrte] *vt* **1** TRANSPORTER : carry **2** : wear, have on **3** APPORTER : bring **4** : bear (responsibility, etc.) **5 être porté à** : be inclined to — *vi* **1** : carry (of a voice) **2** ~ **sur** CONCERNER : be about — **se porter** *vr* **1** : be worn **2** ~ **bien** : be (feel, go) well

porte–savon [pɔrtsavɔ̃] *nms & pl* : soap dish

porte–serviettes [pɔrtsɛrvjɛt] *nms & pl* : towel rack

porteur, -teuse [pɔrtœr, -tøz] *n* **1** : porter **2** : holder, bearer (of news, etc.) **3** : carrier (of disease)

porte–voix [pɔrtəvwa] *nms & pl* : megaphone

portier, -tière [pɔrtje, -tjɛr] *n* : doorman

portière *nf* : door (of an automobile)

portillon [pɔrtijɔ̃] *nm* : gate

portion [pɔrsjɔ̃] *nf* : portion

porto [pɔrto] *nm* : port (wine)

portrait [pɔrtrɛ] *nm* : portrait

portuaire [pɔrtɥɛr] *adj* : harbor, port

portugais, -gaise [pɔrtygɛ, -gɛz] *adj* : Portuguese — **portugais** *nm* : Portuguese (language)

poser [poze] *vt* **1** : put (down), place **2** INSTALLER : put up, install **3** : pose (a problem) **4** ~ **sa candidature** : apply (for a job) — *vi* : pose, sit — **se poser** *vr* **1** : land, alight **2** : arise, come up — **pose** [poz] *nf* **1** : installing **2** : pose, posture — **posé, -sée** [poze] *adj* : composed, calm

positif, -tive [pozitif, -tiv] *adj* : positive

position [pozisjɔ̃] *nf* **1** : position **2 prendre** ~ : take a stand — **positionner** [pozisjɔne] *vt* : position, place

posologie [pozɔlɔʒi] *nf* : dosage

posséder [posede] {87} *vt* **1** AVOIR : possess, have **2** MAÎTRISER : know thoroughly — **possesseur** [posesœr] *nm* : owner, possessor — **possessif, -sive** [posesif, -siv] *adj* : possessive — **possession** [posesjɔ̃] *nf* : ownership, possession

possible [posibl] *adj* : possible — ~ *nm* **1 dans la mesure du** ~ : as far as possible **2 faire son** ~ : do one's utmost — **possibilité** [posibilite] *nf* **1** : possibility **2** ~**s** *nfpl* : means, resources

poste [pɔst] *nm* **1** : job, position **2** : post, station **3** : (telephone) extension **4** ~ **d'essence** : gas station **5** ~ **de pilotage** : cockpit **6** ~ **de pompiers** *Can* : fire station **7** ~ **de télévision** : television set — ~ *nf* **1** : mail service **2** : post office — **postal, -tale** [pɔstal] *adj, mpl* -**taux** [pɔsto] : postal, mail — **poster** [pɔste] *vt* **1** : post, station **2** : mail

postérieur, -rieure [pɔsterjœr] *adj* **1** : later (of a date, etc.) **2** : rear, back — **postérieur** *nm fam* : bottom, buttocks *pl*

postérité [pɔsterite] *nf* : posterity

posthume [pɔstym] *adj* : posthumous

postiche [pɔstiʃ] *adj* : false, fake

postier, -tière [pɔstje, -tjɛr] *n* : postal worker

post–scriptum [pɔstskriptɔm] *nms & pl* : postscript

postuler [pɔstyle] *vt* : apply for (a position) — **postulant, -lante** [pɔstylɑ̃, -lɑ̃t] *n* : candidate, contestant

posture [pɔstyr] *nf* : posture

pot [po] *nm* **1** : pot, jar, container **2** *fam* : drink, glass **3** ~ **d'échappement** : muffler (of an automobile)

potable [pɔtabl] *adj* **1** : drinkable **2** *fam* : fair, passable

potage [pɔtaʒ] *nm* : soup — **potager** [pɔtaʒe] *adj* **jardin** ~ : vegetable garden

pot–au–feu [pɔtofø] *nms & pl* : beef stew

pot–de–vin [podvɛ̃] *nm, pl* **pots–de–vin** : bribe

pote [pɔt] *nm fam* : pal, buddy

poteau [pɔto] *nm, pl* -**teaux 1** : post, pole **2** ~ **indicateur** : signpost

potelé, -lée [pɔtle] *adj* : chubby, plump

potence [pɔtɑ̃s] *nf* : gallows

potentiel, -tielle [pɔtɑ̃sjɛl] *adj & nm* : potential

poterie [pɔtri] *nf* : pottery

potin [pɔtɛ̃] *nm fam* **1** *France* : noise, racket **2** ~**s** *nmpl* : gossip

potion [pɔsjɔ̃] *nf* : potion

potiron [pɔtirɔ̃] *nm* : large pumpkin

pot–pourri [popuri] *nm, pl* **pots–pourris** : potpourri

pou [pu] *nm, pl* **poux** : louse

poubelle [pubɛl] *nf* : garbage can

pouce [pus] *nm* **1** : thumb **2** : big toe **3** : inch (measurement) **4 faire du** ~ *Can* : hitchhike

poudre [pudr] *nf* : powder — **poudrer** [pudre] *vt* : powder — **poudrerie** [pudrəri] *nf Can* : (snow) flurries *pl* — **poudreux, -dreuse** [pudrø, -drøz] *adj* : powdery — **poudrier** [pudrije] *nm* : (powder) compact

pouffer [pufe] *vi* ~ **de rire** : burst out laughing

pouilleux, -leuse [pujø, -jøz] *adj* **1** : lousy, flea-ridden **2** : seedy (of a neighborhood)

poulailler [pulaje] *nm* : henhouse, chicken coop

poulain [pulɛ̃] *nm* **1** : colt, foal **2** PROTÉGÉ : protégé

poule [pul] *nf* **1** : hen **2** : fowl (in cooking) — **poulet** [pulɛ] *nm* : chicken

pouliche [puliʃ] *nf* : filly

poulie [puli] *nf* : pulley

pouls [pu] *nm* : pulse

poumon [pumɔ̃] *nm* : lung

poupe [pup] *nf* : stern

poupée [pupe] *nf* : doll

poupon [pupɔ̃] *nm* **1** : tiny baby **2** : baby doll — **pouponnière** [pupɔnjɛr] *nf* : nursery (for babies)

pour [pur] *prep* **1** : for **2** : to, in order to **3** ~~sont : pourconf~~ **4** ~~: que : in order that,~~ so that — ~ *nm* **le** ~ **et le contre** : the pros and cons

pourboire [purbwar] *nm* : tip

pourcentage [pursɑ̃taʒ] *nm* : percentage

pourchasser [purʃase] *vt* : pursue, hunt down

pourparlers [purparle] *nmpl* : talks, negotiations

pourquoi [purkwa] *adv & conj* : why — ~ *nms & pl* : reason, cause

pourrir [purir] *v* : rot, decay — **pourri, -rie** [puri] *adj* : rotten — **pourriture** [purityr] *nf* : rot, decay

poursuivre [pursɥivr] {88} *vt* **1** : pursue, chase **2** CONTINUER : carry on with **3** ~ **en justice** : sue, prosecute **4** HARCELER : hound — *vi* : continue — **poursuite** [pursɥit] *nf* **1** : pursuit **2** ~**s** *nfpl* : legal proceedings, lawsuit — **poursuivant, -vante** [pursɥivɑ̃, -vɑ̃t] *n* **1** : pursuer **2** : plaintiff

pourtant [purtɑ̃] *adv* : however, yet

pourtour [purtur] *nm* : perimeter

pourvoir [purvwar] {68} *vt* ~ **de** : provide with — *vi* ~ **à** : provide for — **pourvu** [purvy] *conj* ~ **que 1** : provided that **2** : let's hope (that)

pousser [puse] *vt* **1** : push, shove **2** INCITER : encourage, urge **3** POURSUIVRE : pursue, continue (with) **4** : let out (a scream) — *vi* **1** : push **2** CROÎTRE : grow — **se pousser** *vr* : move over — **pousse** [pus] *nf* **1** : growth **2** BOURGEON : shoot, sprout — **poussé, -sée** [puse] *adj* : advanced, extensive — **poussée** [puse] *nf* **1** : pressure **2** IMPULSION : push **3** AUGMENTATION : upsurge **4** ACCÈS : attack, outbreak (in medicine) — **poussette** [pusɛt] *nf* : stroller

poussière [pusjɛr] *nf* : dust — **poussiéreux, -reuse** [pusjerø, -røz] *adj* : dusty

poussin [pusɛ̃] *nm* : chick

poutre [putr] *nf* : beam, girder

pouvoir [puvwar] {69} *v aux* **1** : be able to **2** : be permitted to — *v impers* : be possible — *vt* **1** : be able to do **2 je n'en peux plus!** : I can't take anymore! — **se pouvoir** *v impers* : be possible — ~ *nm* : power

pragmatique [pragmatik] *adj* : pragmatic

prairie [preri] *nf* : meadow

pratiquer [pratike] *vt* **1** : practice **2** : play (a sport) **3** : use, apply **4** EFFECTUER : carry out — **praticable** [pratikabl] *adj* **1** : feasible **2** : passable (of a road, etc.) — **praticien, -cienne** [pratisjɛ̃, -sjɛn] *n* : practitioner — **pratiquant, -quante** [pratikɑ̃,

-kɑ̃t] *adj* : practicing — ~ *n* : churchgoer, follower — **pratique** [pratik] *adj* : practical — ~ *nf* : practice

pré [pre] *nm* : meadow

préalable [prealabl] *adj* **1** : preliminary **2 sans avis** ~ : without prior notice — ~ *nm* **1** : prerequisite **2 au** ~ : beforehand

préambule [preɑ̃byl] *nm* **1** : preamble **2 sans** ~ : without warning

préau [preo] *nm, pl* **préaux** [preo] : (covered) playground, courtyard

préavis [preavi] *nm* : (prior) notice

précaire [prekɛr] *adj* : precarious

précaution [prekosjɔ̃] *nf* **1** : precaution **2** PRUDENCE : caution, care

précéder [presede] {87} *vt* : precede — **précédemment** [presedamɑ̃] *adv* : previously — **précédent, -dente** [presedɑ̃, -dɑ̃t] *adj* : previous, prior — **précédent** *nm* : precedent

prêcher [preʃe] *v* : preach

précieux, -cieuse [presjø, -sjøz] *adj* **1** : precious **2** UTILE : valuable

précipice [presipis] *nm* : abyss, chasm

précipiter [presipite] *vt* **1** : hurl, throw **2** HÂTER : hasten, speed up — **se précipiter** *vr* **1** : hasten, rush **2** ~ **sur** : throw oneself on — **précipitation** [presipitasjɔ̃] *nf* **1** : hurry, haste **2** ~**s** *nfpl* : precipitation (in meteorology) — **précipité, -tée** [presipite] *adj* **1** : rapid **2** HÂTIF : hasty, rash

préciser [presize] *vt* : specify, make clear — **se préciser** *vr* : become clearer — **précis, -cise** [presi, -siz] *adj* **1** : precise, accurate **2** : clear, specific — **précis** *nms & pl* **1** : summary **2** MANUEL : handbook — **précisément** [presizemɑ̃] *adv* : precisely, exactly — **précision** [presizjɔ̃] *nf* **1** : precision **2** : clarity

précoce [prekɔs] *adj* **1** : early **2** : precocious (of a child, etc.)

préconçu, -cue [prekɔ̃sy] *adj* : preconceived

préconiser [prekɔnize] *vt* : recommend, advocate

précurseur [prekyrsœr] *nm* : forerunner

prédateur [predatœr] *nm* : predator

prédécesseur [predesɛsœr] *nm* : predecessor

prédilection [predilɛksjɔ̃] *nf* **1** : partiality **2 de** ~ : favorite

prédire [predir] {29} *vt* : predict — **prédiction** [prediksjɔ̃] *nf* : prediction

prédisposer [predispoze] *vt* : predispose

prédominant, -nante [predɔminɑ̃, -nɑ̃t] *adj* : predominant

préfabriqué, -quée [prefabrike] *adj* : prefabricated

préface [prefas] *nf* : preface

préfecture [prefɛktyr] *nf* ~ **de police** *France* : police headquarters

préférer [prefere] {87} *vt* : prefer — **préférable** [preferabl] *adj* : preferable — **préféré, -rée** [prefere] *adj* & *n* : favorite — **préférence** [preferãs] *nf* : preference

préfet [prɛfɛ] *nm* ~ **de police** *France* : police commissioner

préfixe [prefiks] *nm* : prefix

préhistorique [preistɔrik] *adj* : prehistoric

préjudice [preʒydis] *nm* 1 : harm, damage 2 **porter** ~ **à** : cause harm to — **préjudiciable** [preʒydisjabl] *adj* : harmful, detrimental

préjugé [preʒyʒe] *nm* : prejudice

prélasser [prelase] *v* **se prélasser** *vr* : lounge (around)

prélever [preləve] {52} *vt* 1 : withdraw, deduct 2 : take (a sample of) — **prélèvement** [prelɛvmã] *nm* 1 : withdrawal, deduction 2 : (blood) sample

préliminaire [preliminɛr] *adj* : preliminary

prélude [prelyd] *nm* : prelude

prématuré, -rée [prematyre] *adj* : premature

prémédité [premedite] *adj* : premeditated

premier, -mière [prəmje, -mjɛr] *adj* 1 : first 2 : top, leading 3 **premier ministre** : prime minister — ~ *n* : first (one) — **premier** *nm* : first (in dates) — **première** *nf* 1 : first class 2 : premiere (of a show) — **premièrement** [prəmjɛrmã] *adv* : in the first place, firstly

prémunir [premynir] *v* **se prémunir** *vr* ~ **contre** : protect oneself against

prendre [prãdr] {70} *vt* 1 : take 2 ACHETER : get, pick up 3 : take on (responsibility) 4 ATTRAPER : catch, capture 5 : put on, gain (weight) 6 : have (a meal) — *vi* 1 : set, thicken 2 : break out (of fire) 3 ~ **à droite** : bear right 4 ~ **sur soi** : take upon oneself — **se prendre** *vr* 1 : be taken 2 : get caught 3 ~ **les doigts dans** : catch one's fingers in 4 ~ **pour** : consider oneself 5 **s'en** ~ **à** : attack — **preneur, -neuse** [prənœr, -nøz] *n* : buyer, taker

prénom [prenɔ̃] *nm* : given name, first name

préoccuper [preɔkype] *vt* : worry, preoccupy — **préoccupation** [preɔkypasjɔ̃] *nf* : worry, concern

préparer [prepare] *vt* 1 : prepare, make ready 2 ~ **qqn à** : prepare s.o. for — **se préparer** *vr* : prepare oneself, get ready — **préparatifs** [preparatif] *nmpl* : preparations — **préparation** [preparasjɔ̃] *nf* : preparation

prépondérant, -rante [prepɔ̃derã, -rãt] *adj* : predominant

préposer [prepoze] *vt* ~ **à** : put in charge of — **préposé, -sée** [prepoze] *n* 1 : employee, clerk 2 *France* : mailman

préposition [prepozisjɔ̃] *nf* : preposition

prérogative [prerɔgativ] *nf* : prerogative

près [prɛ] *adv* 1 : close, near(by) 2 : near, soon 3 **à ...** ~ : more or less, within about 4 **à peu** ~ : almost, just about 5 **de** ~ : closely 6 ~ **de** : near

présage [prezaʒ] *nm* : omen — **présager** [prezaʒe] {17} *vt* 1 : foresee 2 : portend, bode

presbyte [prɛsbit] *adj* : farsighted

presbytère [prɛsbitɛr] *nm* : rectory

prescrire [prɛskrir] {33} *vt* : prescribe — **prescription** [prɛskripsjɔ̃] *nf* : prescription

préséance [preseãs] *nf* : precedence

présent, -sente [prezã, -zãt] *adj* : present — ~ *nm* : present (time) — **présence** [prezãs] *nf* 1 : presence 2 **en** ~ : face to face 3 ~ **d'esprit** : presence of mind — **présentement** [prezãtmã] *adv* : at the moment, now

présenter [prezãte] *vt* 1 MONTRER : present, show 2 : introduce (to) 3 : pay, offer (one's condolences) 4 : submit (a proposal, etc.) — **se présenter** *vr* 1 : go, come, appear 2 : introduce oneself 3 ~ **à** : run for (an office) — **présentateur, -trice** [prezãtatœr, -tris] *n* : newscaster, anchor — **présentation** [prezãtasjɔ̃] *nf* 1 : presentation 2 : introduction — **présentoir** [prezãtwar] *nm* : display shelf

préserver [prezɛrve] *vt* 1 : protect 2 CONSERVER : preserve — **préservatif** [prezɛrvatif] *nm* : condom — **préservation** [prezɛrvasjɔ̃] *nf* : protection, preservation

présider [prezide] *vt* : preside over, chair — *vi* ~ **à** : rule over, govern — **président, -dente** [prezidã, -dãt] *n* 1 : president 2 : chairperson — **présidence** [prezidãs] *nf* 1 : presidency 2 : chairmanship — **présidentiel, -tielle** [prezidãsjɛl] *adj* : presidential

présomption [prezɔ̃psjɔ̃] *nf* : presumption — **présomptueux, -tueuse** [prezɔ̃ptɥø, -tɥøz] *adj* : presumptuous

presque [prɛsk] *adv* : almost, nearly

presqu'île [prɛskil] *nf* : peninsula

pressant, -sante [prɛsã, -sãt] *adj* : urgent, pressing

presse [prɛs] *nf* : press

pressé, -sée [prese] *adj* 1 : hurried 2 : urgent 3 : freshly squeezed

pressentir [presãtir] {82} *vt* : sense, have a premonition about — **pressentiment** [presãtimã] *nm* : premonition

presse–papiers [prɛspapje] *nms* & *pl* : paperweight

presser [prese] *vt* 1 : press, squeeze 2 INCITER : urge 3 HÂTER : hurry, rush — *vi* : be pressing, be urgent — **se presser** *vr* 1 SE HÂTER : hurry up 2 ~ **contre** *or* ~ **sur** : snuggle up against — **pression** [prɛsjɔ̃] *nf* : pressure

prestance [prɛstɑ̃s] *nf* : (imposing) presence
prestation [prɛstasjɔ̃] *nf* : benefit, allowance
— **prestataire** [prɛstatɛr] *nm* : recipient
prestidigitateur, -trice [prɛstidiʒitatœr, -tris] *n* : magician, conjurer
prestige [prɛstiʒ] *nm* : prestige — **prestigieux, -gieuse** [prɛstiʒjø, -ʒjøz] *adj* : prestigious
présumer [prezyme] *vt* : presume, suppose — *vi* ~ **de** : overestimate, overrate
prêt¹, prête [prɛ, prɛt] *adj* **1** : ready, prepared **2** DISPOSÉ : willing
prêt² *nm* : loan
prêt-à-porter [prɛtaporte] *nm, pl* **prêts-à-porter** : ready-to-wear (clothing)
prétendre [pretɑ̃dr] {63} *vt* **1** : claim, maintain **2** VOULOIR : intend — **prétendant, -dante** [pretɑ̃dɑ̃, -dɑ̃t] *n* : pretender (to a throne) — **prétendant** *nm* : suitor — **prétendu, -due** [pretɑ̃dy] *adj* : so-called, alleged
prétention [pretɑ̃sjɔ̃] *nf* : pretentiousness — **prétentieux, -tieuse** [pretɑ̃sjø, -sjøz] *adj* : pretentious
prêter [prete] *vt* **1** : lend **2** ~ **à** : attribute to **3** ~ **attention** : pay attention **4** ~ **l'oreille** — *vi* ~ **à** : give rise to, cause — **se prêter** *vr* ~ **à** : lend itself to, suit — **prêteur, -teuse** [pretœr, -tøz] *n* **prêteur sur gages** : pawnbroker
prétexte [pretɛkst] *nm* : pretext, excuse — **prétexter** [pretɛkste] *vt* : use as an excuse
prêtre [prɛtr] *nm* : priest
preuve [prœv] *nf* **1** : proof, evidence **2 faire** ~ **de** : show
prévaloir [prevalwar] {71} *vi* : prevail — **se prévaloir** *vr* **1** ~ **de** : take advantage of **2** ~ **de** : boast of
prévenant, -nante [prevnɑ̃, -nɑ̃t] *adj* : considerate, thoughtful
prévenir [prevnir] {92} *vt* **1** ÉVITER : prevent **2** AVISER : tell, inform **3** AVERTIR : warn **4** ANTICIPER : anticipate — **prévention** [prevɑ̃sjɔ̃] *nf* : prevention — **prévenu, -nue** [prevny] *n* : defendant, accused
prévoir [prevwar] {99} *vt* **1** : predict, anticipate **2** : plan (on), schedule **3** : provide for, allow (for) — **prévisible** [previzibl] *adj* : foreseeable — **prévision** [previzjɔ̃] *nf* **1** : prediction **2** ~**s** *nfpl* : forecast — **prévoyant, -voyante** [prevwajɑ̃, -vwajɑ̃t] *adj* : provident, farsighted — **prévoyance** [prevwajɑ̃s] *nf* : foresight
prier [prije] {96} *vi* : pray — *vt* **1** ~ **de** : ask to, request to **2 je vous en prie** : please **3 je vous en prie** : don't mention it, you're welcome — **prière** [prijɛr] *nf* : prayer
primaire [primɛr] *adj* : primary, elementary
prime¹ [prim] *adj* **1** : early, first **2 de** ~ **abord** : at first

prime² *nf* **1** : premium, allowance **2** RÉCOMPENSE : bonus, gift
primer [prime] *vt* : prevail over — *vi* : be of primary importance
primeurs [primœr] *nfpl* : early produce
primevère [primvɛr] *nf* : primrose
primitif, -tive [primitif, -tiv] *adj* : primitive
primordial, -diale [primordjal] *adj, mpl* **-diaux** [-djo] : essential, vital
prince [prɛ̃s] *nm* : prince — **princesse** [prɛ̃sɛs] *nf* : princess
principal, -pale [prɛ̃sipal] *adj, mpl* **-paux** [-po] : main, principal — **principal** *nm* ESSENTIEL : main thing — **principalement** [prɛ̃sipalmɑ̃] *adv* : primarily, mainly
principe [prɛ̃sip] *nm* : principle, rule
printemps [prɛ̃tɑ̃] *nm* : spring
priorité [prijorite] *nf* **1** : priority **2** : right-of-way **3 en** ~ : first
pris¹ [pri] *pp* → **prendre**
pris², prise [pri, priz] *adj* **1** : taken, sold **2** OCCUPÉ : busy **3** ~ **de** : afflicted with
prise [priz] *nf* **1** : capture, catch **2** : hold, grip **3** *Can* : strike (in baseball) **4** ~ **de courant** : (electrical) outlet **5** ~ **de sang** : blood test
priser [prize] *vt* : prize, value
prison [prizɔ̃] *nf* : prison — **prisonnier, -nière** [prizɔnje, -njɛr] *adj* : captive — ~ *n* : prisoner
priver [prive] *vt* : deprive — **se priver** *vr* ~ **de** : go without — **privé, -vée** [prive] *adj* : private — **privé** *nm* **1** : private sector **2 en** ~ : in private
privilégier [privileʒje] {96} *vt* : privilege, favor — **privilège** [privilɛʒ] *nm* : privilege
prix [pri] *nms & pl* **1** : price, cost **2** : prize **3 à tout** ~ : at all costs
probable [probabl] *adj* : probable, likely — **probabilité** [probabilite] *nf* : probability — **probablement** [probabləmɑ̃] *adv* : probably
problème [problɛm] *nm* : problem
procéder [prosede] {87} *vi* **1** : proceed **2** ~ **à** : carry out — **procédé** [prosede] *nm* : process, procedure — **procédure** [prosedyr] *nf* **1** : procedure **2** : proceedings *pl* (in law)
procès [prosɛ] *nm* **1** : lawsuit **2** : (criminal) trial
procession [prosesjɔ̃] *nf* : procession
processus [prosesys] *nms & pl* : process, system
procès-verbal [prosɛvɛrbal] *nm, pl* **procès-verbaux** [-vɛrbo] **1** : minutes *pl* (of a meeting) **2** *France* : (parking) ticket
prochain, -chaine [prɔʃɛ̃, -ʃɛn] *adj* **1** SUIVANT : next, following **2** PROCHE : imminent, forthcoming **3 à la prochaine!** *fam*

: see you!, until next time! — **prochain** *nm* : fellowman — **prochainement** [prɔ-ʃɛnmɑ̃] *adv* : soon, shortly

proche [prɔʃ] *adj* **1** : near(by) **2** : imminent, near **3** ~ **de** : close to — **proches** [prɔʃ] *nmpl* : close relatives

proclamer [prɔklame] *vt* : proclaim, declare — **proclamation** [prɔklamasjɔ̃] *nf* : proclamation, declaration

procuration [prɔkyrasjɔ̃] *nf* : proxy (in an election)

procurer [prɔkyre] *vt* : provide, give — **se procurer** *vr* : get, obtain — **procureur** [prɔkyrœr] *nm or* ~ **général** : prosecutor

prodige [prɔdiʒ] *nm* : prodigy — **prodigieux, -gieuse** [prɔdiʒjø, -ʒjøz] *adj* : prodigious, extraordinary

prodigue [prɔdig] *adj* **1** : extravagant **2** GÉNÉREUX : lavish — **prodiguer** [prɔdige] *vt* : lavish

produire [prɔdɥir] {49} *vt* **1** : produce **2** CAUSER : bring about — **se produire** *vr* **1** : occur, happen **2** : perform (on stage) — **producteur** [prɔdyktœr] *nm* : producer — **production** [prɔdyksjɔ̃] *nf* : production — **produit** [prɔdɥi] *nm* : product

profaner [prɔfane] *vt* : defile, desecrate — **profane** [prɔfan] *adj* : secular — ~ *nmf* : layperson

proférer [prɔfere] {87} *vt* : utter

professer [prɔfese] *vt* : profess

professeur [prɔfesœr] *nm* **1** : (school)-teacher **2** : professor

profession [prɔfesjɔ̃] *nf* : occupation, trade — **professionnel, -nelle** [prɔfesjɔnɛl] *adj & n* : professional

profil [prɔfil] *nm* : profile

profit [prɔfi] *nm* **1** : profit **2** AVANTAGE : benefit — **profiter** [prɔfite] *vi* **1** ~ **à** : be of benefit to **2** ~ **de** : take advantage of

profond, -fonde [prɔfɔ̃, -fɔ̃d] *adj* **1** : deep **2** : profound — **profondément** [prɔfɔ̃demɑ̃] *adv* : profoundly, deeply — **profondeur** [prɔfɔ̃dœr] *nf* : depth

profusion [prɔfyzjɔ̃] *nf* : profusion

progéniture [prɔʒenityr] *nf* : offspring

programme [prɔgram] *nm* **1** : program **2** : plan, schedule **3** : curriculum, syllabus (in academics) — **programmer** [prɔgrame] *vt* **1** : program (a computer) **2** : plan, schedule — **programmeur, -meuse** [prɔgramœr, -møz] *n* : (computer) programmer

progrès [prɔgrɛ] *nm* : progress — **progresser** [prɔgrese] *vi* : make progress — **progressif, -sive** [prɔgresif, -siv] *adj* : progressive — **progressivement** [-sivmɑ̃] *adv* : progressively, gradually

prohiber [prɔibe] *vt* : prohibit — **prohibition** [prɔibisjɔ̃] *nf* : prohibition

proie [prwa] *nf* : prey

projecteur [prɔʒɛktœr] *nm* **1** : projector **2** : spotlight — **projectile** [prɔʒɛktil] *nm* : missile, projectile — **projection** [prɔʒɛksjɔ̃] *nf* : projection, showing

projeter [prɔʃte] {8} *vt* **1** LANCER : throw **2** : project, show (a film, etc.) **3** : cast, project (light) **4** PRÉVOIR : plan — **projet** [prɔʒɛ] *nm* **1** : plan, project **2** ÉBAUCHE : draft, outline

proliférer [prɔlifere] {87} *vi* : proliferate — **prolifération** [-ferasjɔ̃] *nf* : proliferation — **prolifique** [prɔlifik] *adj* : prolific

prologue [prɔlɔg] *nm* : prologue

prolonger [prɔlɔ̃ʒe] {17} *vt* : prolong, extend — **se prolonger** *vr* : continue — **prolongation** [prɔlɔ̃gasjɔ̃] *nf* : extension (of time) — **prolongement** [prɔlɔ̃ʒmɑ̃] *nm* : extension (of a road, etc.)

promener [prɔmne] {52} *vt* : take for a walk — **se promener** *vr* : go for a walk — **promenade** [prɔmnad] *nf* **1** : walk, stroll **2** : trip, ride (in a car, etc.) **3** : walkway, promenade — **promeneur, -neuse** [prɔmnœr, -nøz] *n* : walker

promettre [prɔmɛtr] {53} *v* : promise — **se promettre** *vr* ~ **de** : resolve to — **promesse** [prɔmɛs] *nf* : promise — **prometteur, -teuse** [prɔmɛtœr, -tøz] *adj* : promising

promontoire [prɔmɔ̃twar] *nm* : headland

promouvoir [prɔmuvwar] {56} *vt* : promote — **promotion** [prɔmɔsjɔ̃] *nf* : promotion

prompt, prompte [prɔ̃, prɔ̃t] *adj* : prompt, quick

prôner [prone] *vt* : advocate

pronom [prɔnɔ̃] *nm* : pronoun

prononcer [prɔnɔ̃se] {6} *vt* : pronounce — *vi* : hand down a decision (in law) — **se prononcer** *vr* : give one's opinion — **prononciation** [prɔnɔ̃sjasjɔ̃] *nf* : pronunciation

pronostic [prɔnɔstik] *nm* **1** : prognosis **2** PRÉVISION : forecast

propagande [prɔpagɑ̃d] *nf* : propaganda

propager [prɔpaʒe] {17} *vt* : propagate, spread — **se propager** *vr* : spread — **propagation** [prɔpagasjɔ̃] *nf* : propagation

prophète [prɔfɛt] *nm* : prophet — **prophétie** [prɔfesi] *nf* : prophecy — **prophétique** [prɔfetik] *adj* : prophetic — **prophétiser** [prɔfetize] *vt* : prophesy

propice [prɔpis] *adj* : favorable

proportion [prɔpɔrsjɔ̃] *nf* **1** : proportion, ratio **2** ~**s** *nfpl* : dimensions, size — **proportionnel, -nelle** [prɔpɔrsjɔnɛl] *adj* : proportional

proposer [prɔpoze] *vt* **1** : suggest, propose **2** OFFRIR : offer **3** : nominate (for election) — **se proposer** *vr* ~ **de** : intend to — **propos** [prɔpo] *nms & pl* **1** : subject **2** BUT : intention, point **3** ~ *nmpl* : comments, talk **4 à ~** : appropriate **5 à ~ de** : regarding, about — **proposition** [prɔpozisjɔ̃] *nf* **1** : suggestion **2** OFFRE : offer, proposal

propre [prɔpr] *adj* **1** : clean, neat **2** : proper, correct (if a word) **3** ~ **à** : characteristic of **4** ~ **à** : suitable for **5 par sa ~ faute** : through his own fault — **proprement** [prɔprəmɑ̃] *adv* **à ~ parler** : strictly speaking — **propreté** [prɔprəte] *nf* : cleanliness, neatness

propriété [prɔprijete] *nf* **1** : property **2** : ownership — **propriétaire** [prɔprijetɛr] *nmf* **1** : owner **2** : landlord, landlady *f*

propulser [prɔpylse] *vt* : propel

prorata [prɔrata] *nms & pl* **au ~ de** : in proportion to

proscrire [prɔskrir] {33} *vt* **1** INTERDIRE : ban, prohibit **2** BANNIR : banish — **proscrit, -scrite** [prɔskri, -skrit] *n* : outcast

prose [proz] *nf* : prose

prospectus [prɔspɛktys] *nms & pl* : leaflet

prospérer [prɔspere] {87} *vi* : flourish, thrive — **prospérité** [prɔsperite] *nf* : prosperity

prosterner [prɔstɛrne] *v* **se prosterner** *vr* : bow down

prostituée [prɔstitɥe] *nf* : prostitute — **prostitution** [prɔstitysjɔ̃] *nf* : prostitution

prostré, -trée [prɔstre] *adj* : prostrate

protagoniste [prɔtagɔnist] *nmf* : protagonist

protéger [prɔteʒe] {64} *vt* **1** : protect **2** PATRONNER : support — **se protéger** *vr* ~ **de** : protect oneself from — **protecteur, -trice** [prɔtɛktœr, -tris] *adj* : protective — **~** *n* **1** : protector **2** : patron — **protection** [prɔtɛksjɔ̃] *nf* : protection

protéine [prɔtein] *nf* : protein

protestant, -tante [prɔtɛstɑ̃, -tɑ̃t] *adj & n* : Protestant

protester [prɔtɛste] *vi* : protest — **protestation** [prɔtɛstasjɔ̃] *nf* : protest

prothèse [prɔtɛz] *nf* **1** : prosthesis **2** ~ **dentaire** : denture

protocole [prɔtɔkɔl] *nm* : protocol

protubérant, -rante [prɔtyberɑ̃, -rɑ̃t] *adj* : protruding — **protubérance** [prɔtyberɑ̃s] *nf* : protuberance

proue [pru] *nf* : prow, bow (of a ship)

prouesse [pruɛs] *nf* : feat

prouver [pruve] *vt* **1** ÉTABLIR : prove **2** MONTRER : show, demonstrate

provenance [prɔvnɑ̃s] *nf* **1** : source, origin **2 en ~ de** : from

provenir [prɔvnir] {92} *vi* **~ de 1** : come from **2** : result from

proverbe [prɔvɛrb] *nm* : proverb

providence [prɔvidɑ̃s] *nf* : providence

province [prɔvɛ̃s] *nf* : province — **provincial, -ciale** [-vɛ̃sjal] *adj, mpl* **-ciaux** [-sjo] : provincial

proviseur [prɔvizœr] *nm France* : principal (of a school)

provision [prɔvizjɔ̃] *nf* **1** : stock, supply **2** ~**s** *nfpl* : provisions, food

provisoire [prɔvizwar] *adj* : temporary

provoquer [prɔvɔke] *vt* **1** : give rise to **2** DÉFIER : provoke — **provocant, -cante** [prɔvɔkɑ̃, -kɑ̃t] *adj* : provocative — **provocation** [prɔvɔkasjɔ̃] *nf* : provocation

proximité [prɔksimite] *nf* : closeness, proximity

prude [pryd] *nf* : prude

prudent, -dente [prydɑ̃, -dɑ̃t] *adj* : careful, cautious — **prudemment** [prydamɑ̃] *adv* : carefully, cautiously — **prudence** [prydɑ̃s] *nf* : care, caution

prune [pryn] *nf* : plum — **pruneau** [pryno] *nm, pl* **-neaux** : prune

prunelle [prynɛl] *nf* : pupil (of the eye)

psaume [psom] *nm* : psalm

pseudonyme [psødɔnim] *nm* : pseudonym

psychanalyser [psikanalize] *vt* : psychoanalyze — **psychanalyse** [psikanaliz] *nf* : psychoanalysis — **psychanalyste** [-list] *nmf* : psychoanalyst

psychiatrie [psikjatri] *nf* : psychiatry — **psychiatre** [psikjatr] *nmf* : psychiatrist — **psychiatrique** [psikjatrik] *adj* : psychiatric

psychologie [psikɔlɔʒi] *nf* : psychology — **psychologique** [psikɔlɔʒik] *adj* : psychological — **psychologue** [psikɔlɔg] *nmf* : psychologist

puant, puante [pɥɑ̃, -ɑ̃t] *adj* : foul, stinking — **puanteur** [pɥɑ̃tœr] *nf* : stink, stench

puberté [pybɛrte] *nf* : puberty

public, -blique [pyblik] *adj* : public — **public** *nm* **1** : public **2** : audience, spectators *pl*

publication [pyblikasjɔ̃] *nf* : publication

publicité [pyblisite] *nf* **1** : publicity **2** : (television) commercial — **publicitaire** [pyblisitɛr] *adj* : advertising

publier [pyblije] {96} *vt* : publish

puce [pys] *nf* **1** : flea **2** : computer chip

pudeur [pydœr] *nf* : modesty — **pudique** [pydik] *adj* : modest, decent

puer [pɥe] *vi* : smell, stink — *vt* : reek of

puéril, -rile [pɥeril] *adj* : childish

puis [pɥi] *adv* : then, afterwards

puiser [pɥize] *vt* ~ **dans** : draw from, dip into

puisque [pɥiskə] *conj* : since, as, because

puissant, -sante [pɥisɑ̃, -sɑ̃t] *adj* : powerful — **puissance** [pɥisɑ̃s] *nf* : power

puits [pɥi] *nm* **1** : well **2** : (mine) shaft

pull *or* **pull-over** [pyl, pylɔvɛr] *nm France* : pullover sweater

pulpe [pylp] *nf* : pulp

pulsation [pylsasjɔ̃] *nf* BATTEMENT : beat

pulsion [pylsjɔ̃] *nf* : drive, urge

pulvériser [pylverize] *vt* **1** : pulverize **2** VA-PORISER : spray
punaise [pynɛz] *nf* **1** : (bed)bug **2** : thumbtack
punch [pɔʃ] *nm* : punch (drink)
punir [pynir] *vt* : punish — **punition** [pynisjɔ̃] *nf* : punishment
pupille[1] [pypij] *nmf* : ward (of the court)
pupille[2] *nf* : pupil (of the eye)
pupitre [pypitr] *nm* **1** : music stand **2** BUREAU : desk
pur, pure [pyr] *adj* : pure — **pureté** [pyrte] *nf* : purity
purée [pyre] *nf* **1** : puree **2** ~ **de pommes de terre** : mashed potatoes
purgatoire [pyrgatwar] *nm* : purgatory

purger [pyrʒe] {17} *vt* **1** : drain (a radiator, etc.) **2** : rid of, purge **3** : serve (a sentence) — **purge** [pyrʒ] *nf* : purge
purifier [pyrifje] {96} *vt* : purify — **purification** [pyrifikasjɔ̃] *nf* : purification
puritain, -taine [pyritɛ̃, -tɛn] *n* : puritan — ~ *adj* : puritanical
pur–sang [pyrsɑ̃] *nms & pl* : Thoroughbred
pus [py] *nm* : pus
putride [pytrid] *adj* : rotten
puzzle [pœzl] *nm* : (jigsaw) puzzle
pyjama [piʒama] *nm* : pajamas *pl*
pylône [pilon] *nm* : pylon
pyramide [piramid] *nf* : pyramid
pyromane [piroman] *nmf* : arsonist
python [pitɔ̃] *nm* : python

Q

q [ky] *nm* : q, 17th letter of the alphabet
quadriller [kadrije] *vt* : surround, take control of — **quadrillage** [kadrijaʒ] *nm* : crisscross pattern, grid — **quadrillé, -lée** [kadrije] *adj* : squared
quadrupède [k(w)adrypɛd] *nm* : quadruped
quadruple [k(w)adrypl] *adj* : quadruple
quai [kɛ] *nm* **1** : quay, wharf **2** : platform (at a railway station)
qualifier [kalifje] {96} *vt* **1** : qualify **2** DÉCRIRE : describe — **qualification** [kalifikasjɔ̃] *nf* : qualification
qualité [kalite] *nf* **1** : quality, excellence **2** : quality, property **3 en ~ de** : in one's role as
quand [kɑ̃] *adv & conj* **1** : when **2** ~ **même** : all the same, even so
quant [kɑ̃] ~ **à** *prep phr* : as for, as to, regarding
quantité [kɑ̃tite] *nf* : quantity
quarantaine [karɑ̃tɛn] *nf* **1** : quarantine **2 une ~ de** : about forty
quarante [karɑ̃t] *adj & nms & pl* : forty — **quarantième** [karɑ̃tjɛm] *adj & nmf & nm* : fortieth
quart [kar] *nm* **1** : quarter, fourth **2 un ~ d'heure** : fifteen minutes
quartier [kartje] *nm* **1** : piece, segment, quarter **2** : area, district **3** ~ **général** : (military) headquarters
quartz [kwarts] *nm* : quartz
quasi [kazi] *adv* : nearly, almost
quatorze [katɔrz] *adj* **1** : fourteen **2** : fourteenth (in dates) — ~ *nms & pl* : fourteen

— **quatorzième** [katɔrzjɛm] *adj & nmf & nm* : fourteenth
quatre [katr] *adj* **1** : four **2** : fourth (in dates) — ~ *nms & pl* : four
quatre–vingt–dix [katrəvɛ̃dis] *adj & nms & pl* : ninety
quatre–vingts [katrəvɛ̃] (**quatre-vingt** *with another numeral adjective*) *adj & nms & pl* : eighty
quatrième [katrijɛm] *adj & nmf* : fourth
quatuor [kwatɥɔr] *nm* : quartet
que [kə] *conj* **1** : that **2 plus** ~ **nécessaire** : more than necessary **3 qu'il fasse soleil ou non** : whether it's sunny or not **4** → **ne** — ~ *pron* **1** : who, whom, that **2** : which **3** ~ **faire?** : what should we do? — ~ *adv* : how (much), how (many)
québécois, -coise [kebekwa, -kwaz] *adj* : Quebecer, Quebecois
quel, quelle [kɛl] *adj* **1** : what, which **2** : whatever, whichever, whoever — ~ *pron* : who, which one
quelconque [kɛlkɔ̃k] *adj* **1** : some sort of, any **2 un être** ~ : an ordinary person
quelque [kɛlk(ə)] *adj* **1** : a few, several, some **2** ~ **chose** : something **3** ~ **part** : somewhere **4** ~ **peu** : somewhat — ~ *adv* : about, approximately
quelquefois [kɛlkəfwa] *adv* : sometimes
quelques–uns, quelques–unes [kɛlkəzœ̃, kɛlkəzyn] *pron* : some, a few
quelqu'un [kɛlkœ̃] *pron* **1** : someone, somebody **2** : anyone, anybody **3 y a-t-il quelqu'un?** : is anybody there?
quémander [kemɑ̃de] *vt* : beg for

qu'en–dira–t–on [kɑ̃diratɔ̃] *nms & pl* : gossip

querelle [kərɛl] *nf* : quarrel — **quereller** [kərele] *v* **se quereller** *vr* : quarrel — **querelleur, -leuse** [kərelœr, -løz] *adj* : quarrelsome

question [kɛstjɔ̃] *nf* **1** : question **2** : matter, issue — **questionnaire** [kɛstjɔnɛr] *nm* : questionnaire — **questionner** [kɛstjɔne] *vt* : question

quête [kɛt] *nf* **1** : quest, search **2** : collection (of money) — **quêter** [kete] *vt* : look for, seek — *vi* : take a collection

queue [kø] *nf* **1** : tail **2** : tail end, rear, bottom **3** : handle (of a pot) **4** ~ **de billard** : cue (stick) **5** ~ **de cheval** : ponytail **6** **faire la** ~ : stand in line

qui [ki] *pron* **1** : who, whom **2** : which, that **3** ~ **que** : whoever, whomever

quiconque [kikɔ̃k] *pron* **1** : whoever, whomever **2** : anyone, anybody

quiétude [kjetyd] *nf* : quiet, tranquility

quille [kij] *nf* **1** : keel **2** ~**s** *nfpl* : ninepins

quincaillerie [kɛ̃kajri] *nf* **1** : hardware **2** : hardware store

quinte [kɛ̃t] *nf or* ~ **de toux** : coughing fit

quintuple [kɛ̃typl] *adj* : fivefold

quinzaine [kɛ̃zɛn] *nf* **1 une** ~ **de** : about fifteen **2 une** ~ **de jours** : two weeks

quinze [kɛ̃z] *adj* **1** : fifteen **2** : fifteenth (in dates) — ~ *nms & pl* : fifteen — **quinzième** [kɛ̃zjɛm] *adj & nmf & nm* : fifteenth

quiproquo [kiprɔko] *nm* : misunderstanding

quittance [kitɑ̃s] *nf* : receipt

quitte [kit] *adj* **1** : even, quits **2** ~ **à** : even if, at the risk of

quitter [kite] *vt* **1** : leave, depart from **2** : take off (a hat, etc.) **3 ne quittez pas** : hold the (telephone) line — **se quitter** *vr* : part, separate

qui–vive [kiviv] *nms & pl* **être sur le** ~ : be on the alert

quoi [kwa] *pron* **1** : what **2** (*after a pronoun*) : which **3** ~ **que** : whatever

quoique [kwakə] *conj* : although, though

quota [kɔta] *nm* : quota

quotidien, -dienne [kɔtidjɛ̃, -djɛn] *adj* **1** : daily **2** : everyday, routine — **quotidien** *nm* **1** : daily (newspaper) **2 au** ~ : on a daily basis — **quotidiennement** [kɔtidjɛnmɑ̃] *adv* : daily

quotient [kɔsjɑ̃] *nm* : quotient

R

r [ɛr] *nm* : r, 18th letter of the alphabet

rabâcher [rabaʃe] *vt* : repeat over and over

rabaisser [rabɛse] *vt* **1** : reduce **2** DÉPRÉCIER : belittle, degrade — **rabais** [rabɛ] *nms & pl* RÉDUCTION : reduction, discount

rabat [raba] *nm* : flap

rabat–joie [rabaʒwa] *nms & pl* : killjoy, spoilsport

rabattre [rabatr] {12} *vt* **1** : reduce, diminish **2** : bring down, pull down — **se rabattre** *vr* **1** : fold up, shut **2** ~ **sur** : make do with

rabbin [rabɛ̃] *nm* : rabbi

rabot [rabo] *nm* : plane (tool) — **raboter** [rabɔte] *vt* : plane

raboteux, -teuse [rabɔtø, -tøz] *adj* INÉGAL : rough, uneven

rabougri, -grie [rabugri] *adj* **1** : stunted **2** : shriveled (up)

rabrouer [rabrue] *vt* : snub

raccommoder [rakɔmɔde] *vt* : mend, patch up

raccompagner [rakɔ̃paɲe] *vt* : take (someone) back, see home

raccorder [rakɔrde] *vt* : connect, link up — **raccord** [rakɔr] *nm* : link, connection — **raccordement** [rakɔr-dəmɑ̃] *nm* : linking, connection

raccourcir [rakursir] *vt* : shorten — *vi* : become shorter, shrink — **raccourci** [rakursi] *nm* **1** : shortcut **2 en** ~ : in short, briefly

raccrocher [rakrɔʃe] *vt* ~ **le récepteur** : hang up (a telephone receiver) — *vi* : hang up (on s.o.) — **se raccrocher** *vr* ~ **à** : hang on to

race [ras] *nf* **1** : (human) race **2** : breed (of animals) **3 de** ~ : thoroughbred

racheter [raʃte] {20} *vt* **1** : buy back **2** : buy more of **3** : redeem (in religion) **4** COMPENSER : make up for — **rachat** [raʃa] *nm* : buying back

racial, -ciale [rasjal] *adj, mpl* **-ciaux** [rasjo] : racial

racine [rasin] *nf* : root

racisme [rasism] *nm* : racism — **raciste** [rasist] *adj & nmf* : racist

racler [rakle] *vt* : scrape (off) — **raclée** [rakle] *nf fam* : beating, thrashing

racoler [rakɔle] *vt* : solicit

raconter [rakɔ̃te] vt 1 CONTER : tell, relate 2 : say, talk about — **racontars** [rakɔ̃tar] nmpl : gossip — **raconteur, -teuse** [rakɔ̃tœr, -tøz] n : storyteller

radar [radar] nm : radar

rade [rad] nf en ~ : stranded

radeau [rado] nm, pl **-deaux** : raft

radiateur [radjatœr] nm 1 : radiator 2 : heater

radical, -cale [radikal] adj, mpl **-caux** [-ko] : radical — ~ n : radical

radier [radje] {96} vt : cross off

radieux, -dieuse [radjø, -djøz] adj : radiant, dazzling

radin, -dine [radɛ̃] adj fam : stingy — ~ n fam : cheapskate

radio [radjo] nf 1 : radio 2 RADIOGRAPHIE : X ray

radioactif, -tive [radjoaktif, -tiv] adj : radioactive

radiodiffuser [radjodifyze] vt : broadcast — **radiodiffusion** [radjodifyzjɔ̃] nf : broadcasting

radiographie [radjografi] nf : X ray — **radiographier** [radjografje] {96} vt : X-ray

radis [radi] nm : radish

radoter [radɔte] vi : ramble on

radoucir [radusir] vt : soften (up) — **se radoucir** vr : grow milder

rafale [rafal] nf 1 : gust (of wind, etc.) 2 : burst (of gunfire)

raffermir [rafɛrmir] vt : firm up, tone up

raffiner [rafine] vt : refine — **raffinage** [rafinaʒ] nm : refining — **raffiné, -née** [rafine] adj : refined — **raffinement** [rafinmɑ̃] nm : refinement — **raffinerie** [rafinri] nf : refinery

raffoler [rafɔle] vi ~ de : adore, be crazy about

rafistoler [rafistɔle] vt fam : patch up, fix up

rafler [rafle] vt fam : swipe, steal — **rafle** [rafl] nf : (police) raid

rafraîchir [rafrɛʃir] vt : refresh, cool — **se rafraîchir** vr 1 : get cooler 2 : freshen up — **rafraîchissant, -sante** [rafrɛʃisɑ̃, -sɑ̃t] adj : refreshing — **rafraîchissement** [rafrɛʃismɑ̃] nm 1 : cooling 2 ~s nmpl : cool drinks, refreshments

rage [raʒ] nf 1 : rabies 2 FUREUR : rage — **rager** [raʒe] {17} vi : rage, fume

ragot [rago] nm fam : gossip

ragoût [ragu] nm : ragout, stew

raide [rɛd] adj 1 : stiff (of muscles) 2 : tight, taut (of a rope) 3 : steep (of a hill) 4 : straight (of hair) — ~ adv : steeply — **raideur** [rɛdœr] nf 1 : stiffness 2 : steepness — **raidir** [rɛdir] vt : stiffen, tighten — **se raidir** vr : tighten, tense up

raie [rɛ] nf 1 : stripe 2 : part (in hair)

raifort [rɛfɔr] nm : horseradish

rail [raj] nm : rail, track

railler [raje] vt : make fun of — **raillerie** [rajri] nf : mockery — **railleur, -leuse** [rajœr, -jøz] adj MOQUEUR : mocking

rainure [renyr] nf : groove, slot

raisin [rɛzɛ̃] nm 1 : grape 2 ~ de Corinthe : currant 3 ~ sec : raisin

raison [rɛzɔ̃] nf 1 : reason 2 avoir ~ : be right 3 en ~ de : because of 4 perdre la ~ : lose one's mind — **raisonnable** [rɛzɔnabl] adj : sensible, reasonable — **raisonnement** [rɛzɔnmɑ̃] nm 1 : reasoning 2 : argument — **raisonner** [rɛzɔne] vi : reason — vt : reason with

rajeunir [raʒœnir] vt : make look younger — vi : look younger

rajouter [raʒute] vt 1 : add 2 en ~ : exaggerate — **rajout** [raʒu] nm : addition

rajuster [raʒyste] vt : (re)adjust

râle [ral] nm : groan

ralentir [ralɑ̃tir] v : slow down — **ralenti, -tie** [ralɑ̃ti] adj : slow — **ralenti** nm 1 : slow motion 2 : idling speed (of a car) — **ralentissement** [ralɑ̃tismɑ̃] nm : slowing down

râler [rale] vi 1 : groan 2 fam : grumble

rallier [ralje] {96} vt : rally (troops) — **se rallier** vr : rally

rallonger [ralɔ̃ʒe] {17} vt : lengthen — vi : get longer — **rallonge** [ralɔ̃ʒ] nf : extension (cord)

rallumer [ralyme] vt 1 : turn back on 2 RANIMER : revive

ramasser [ramase] vt 1 : pick up, collect 2 CUEILLIR : pick, gather — **se ramasser** vr : crouch — **ramassage** [ramasaʒ] nm : picking up, collection

rambarde [rɑ̃bard] nf : guardrail

rame [ram] nf 1 AVIRON : oar 2 : (subway) train 3 : ream (of paper)

rameau [ramo] nm, pl **-meaux** : branch, bough

ramener [ramne] {52} vt 1 : bring back, take back 2 RÉDUIRE : reduce

ramer [rame] vi : row

ramification [ramifikasjɔ̃] nf : offshoot

ramollir [ramɔlir] vt : soften — **se ramollir** vr : soften

ramoner [ramɔne] vt : sweep (a chimney), clean out (pipes) — **ramoneur** [ramɔnœr] nm : chimney sweep

rampe [rɑ̃p] nf 1 : (access) ramp 2 : banister, handrail 3 : footlights pl 4 ~ de lancement : launching pad

ramper [rɑ̃pe] vi 1 : crawl, creep 2 S'ABAISSER : grovel

rancart [rɑ̃kar] nm mettre au ~ fam : discard, scrap

rance [rɑ̃s] adj : rancid — **rancir** [rɑ̃sir] vi : turn rancid

rancœur [rᾶkœr] *nf* RESSENTIMENT : rancor, resentment

rançon [rᾶsɔ̃] *nf* : ransom — **rançonner** [rᾶsɔne] *vt* : hold to ransom

rancune [rᾶkyn] *nf* **1** : rancor, resentment **2** garder **~** à : hold a grudge against

randonnée [rᾶdɔne] *nf* **1** : ride, trip **2** : walk, hike — **randonneur, -neuse** [rᾶdɔnœr, -nøz] *n* : hiker

rang [rᾶ] *nm* **1** RANGÉE : row **2** : rank (in a hierarchy) — **rangée** [rᾶʒe] *nf* : row, line — **rangement** [rᾶʒmᾶ] *nm* **1** : tidying up **2** : storage space — **ranger** [rᾶʒe] {17} *vt* **1** : tidy up CLASSER : put in order **3** : put away (objects), park (a vehicle) — **se ranger** *vr* **1** : line up **2** SE GARER : park **3** S'ASSAGIR : settle down **4 ~** à : go along with

ranimer [ranime] *vt* **1** : revive **2** : rekindle (a fire)

rapace [rapas] *adj* : rapacious — **~** *nm* : bird of prey

rapatrier [rapatrije] {96} *vt* : repatriate, send home

râper [rape] *vt* : grate (cheese, etc.) — **râpe** [rap] *nf* : grater

rapetisser [raptise] *vt* : shorten — *vi* : shrink — **se rapetisser** *vr* : shrink

râpeux, -peuse [rapø, -pøz] *adj* : rough

rapide [rapid] *adj* **1** : quick, rapid **2** : steep — **~** *nm* **1** : rapids *pl* **2** : express train — **rapidement** [rapidmᾶ] *adv* : rapidly, swiftly — **rapidité** [rapidite] *nf* : rapidity, speed

rapiécer [rapjese] {6} *vt* : patch (up)

rappeler [raple] {8} *vt* **1** : remind **2** : call back — **se rappeler** *vr* : remember, recall — **rappel** [rapɛl] *nm* **1** : reminder **2** : recall

rapporter [rapɔrte] *vt* **1** : bring back, take back **2** : yield (in finance) **3** RELATER : tell, report — *vi* **1** : yield a profit **2** *fam* : tell tales — **se rapporter** *vr* **~** à : relate to — **rapport** [rapɔr] *nm* **1** : report **2** LIEN : connection **3** RENDEMENT : return, yield **4** PROPORTION : ratio **5 ~s** *nmpl* : relations **6 ~s** *nmpl* : sexual intercourse — **rapporteur, -teuse** [rapɔrtœr, -tøz] *n* : tattletale

rapprocher [raprɔʃe] *vt* **1** : bring closer **2** COMPARER : compare — **se rapprocher** *vr* **1 ~** de : approach, come closer to **2 ~** de : resemble — **rapproché, -chée** [raprɔʃe] *adj* : close

raquette [rakɛt] *nf* **1** : (tennis) racket **2** : snowshoe

rare [rar] *adj* **1** : rare, uncommon **2** : infrequent **3** CLAIRSEMÉ : sparse — **rarement** [rarmᾶ] *adv* : seldom, rarely — **rareté** [rarte] *nf* : rarity, scarcity

ras [ra] *adv* : short — **ras, rase** [ra, raz] *adj* : short (of hair)

raser [raze] {87} *vt* **1** : shave **2** DÉTRUIRE : raze **3** FRÔLER : graze, skim — **se raser** *vr* : shave — **rasage** [razaʒ] *nm* : shaving — **rasoir** [razwar] *nm* : razor

raseur, -seuse [razœr, -zøz] *n fam* : bore

rassasier [rasazje] {96} *vt* : satisfy — **se rassasier** *vr* : eat one's fill

rassembler [rasᾶble] *vt* : gather, collect — **se rassembler** *vr* : gather, assemble — **rassemblement** [rasᾶbləmᾶ] *nm* : gathering, assembly

rasseoir [raswar] {9} *v* **se rasseoir** *vr* : sit down again

rassir [rasir] {72} *vi* : go stale

rassis, -sise [rasi, -siz] *adj* : stale

rassurer [rasyre] *vt* : reassure — **rassurant, -rante** [rasyrᾶ, -rᾶt] *adj* : reassuring

rat [ra] *nm* : rat

ratatiner [ratatine] *v* **se ratatiner** *vr* : shrivel up

rate [rat] *nf* : spleen

râteau [rato] *nm, pl* **-teaux** : rake

rater [rate] *vt* **1** MANQUER : miss **2** : fail (an exam, etc.) — *vi* ÉCHOUER : fail, go wrong

ratifier [ratifje] {96} *vt* : ratify — **ratification** [-tifikasjɔ̃] *nf* : ratification

ration [rasjɔ̃] *nf* : share, ration

rationaliser [rasjonalize] *vt* : rationalize — **rationnel, -nelle** [rasjonɛl] *adj* : rational

rationner [rasjone] *vt* : ration

ratisser [ratise] *vt* : rake

raton [ratɔ̃] *nm* **~ laveur** : raccoon

rattacher [rataʃe] *vt* **1** : tie up again **2** RELIER : link, connect

rattraper [ratrape] *vt* **1** : recapture **2** : catch up with (s.o.) **3 ~ le temps perdu** : make up for lost time

raturer [ratyre] *vt* BIFFER : delete — **rature** [ratyr] *nf* : deletion

rauque [rok] *adj* ENROUÉ : hoarse

ravager [ravaʒe] {17} *vt* : ravage, devastate — **ravages** [ravaʒ] *nmpl* **faire des ~** : wreak havoc

ravaler [ravale] *vt* **1** : restore (a building) **2** : stifle (one's anger)

ravi, -vie [ravi] *adj* ENCHANTÉ : delighted

ravin [ravɛ̃] *nm* : ravine

ravir [ravir] *vt* : delight

raviser [ravize] *v* **se raviser** *vr* : change one's mind

ravisseur, -seuse [ravisœr, -søz] *n* : kidnapper

ravitailler [ravitaje] *vt* **1** : supply (with food) **2** : refuel

raviver [ravive] *vt* : revive

ravoir [ravwar] {73} *vt* : get back

rayer [reje] {11} *vt* **1** ÉRAFLER : scratch **2** BARRER : cross out, erase — **rayé, rayée** [reje] *adj* : striped

rayon [rejɔ̃] *nm* **1** : ray **2** : radius (of a circle) **3** : range, scope **4** ÉTAGÈRE : shelf **5**

: department (in a store) **6 ~ de miel** · honeycomb

rayonnant, -nante [rɛjɔnɑ̃, nɑ̃t] *adj* : radiant

rayonne [rɛjɔn] *nf* : rayon

rayonner [rɛjɔne] *vi* **1** : radiate **2** BRILLER : shine **3** : tour around **4 ~ sur** : exert influence on — **rayonnement** [rɛjɔnmɑ̃] *nm* : radiation

rayure [rɛjyr] *nf* **1** : stripe **2** ÉRAFLURE : scratch

raz–de–marée [radmare] *nms & pl* : tidal wave

réagir [reaʒir] *vi* : react — **réacteur** [reaktœr] *nm* **1** : jet engine **2** : (nuclear) reactor — **réaction** [reaksjɔ̃] *nf* **1** : reaction **2 à ~** : jet-propelled — **réactionnaire** [reaksjɔnɛr] *adj & nmf* : reactionary

réaliser [realize] *vt* **1** : carry out, execute **2** ACCOMPLIR : achieve **3** : direct (a film) **4** : realize (a profit) — **se réaliser** *vr* : materialize, come true — **réalisateur, -trice** [realizatœr, -tris] *n* : director (in movies, television, etc.) — **réalisation** [realizasjɔ̃] *nf* **1** EXÉCUTION : execution, carrying out **2** : accomplishment **3** : production (of a film)

réaliste [realist] *adj* : realistic

réalité [realite] *nf* **1** : reality **2 en ~** : in fact, actually

réanimer [reanime] *vt* : resuscitate

réapparaître [reaparɛtr] {7} *vi* : reappear

rébarbatif, -tive [rebarbatif, -tiv] *adj* : forbidding, daunting

rebâtir [rəbatir] *vt* : rebuild

rebattu, -tue [rəbaty] *adj* : hackneyed

rebelle [rəbɛl] *nmf* : rebel — *adj* : rebellious — **rebeller** [rəbɛle] *v* **se rebeller** *vr* : rebel — **rébellion** [rebɛljɔ̃] *nf* : rebellion

rebondir [rəbɔ̃dir] *vi* **1** : bounce, rebound **2** : start (up) again — **rebond** [rəbɔ̃] *nm* : bounce, rebound

rebord [rəbɔr] *nm* : edge, sill (of a window)

rebours [rəbur] **à ~** *adv phr* : the wrong way

rebrousse–poil [rəbruspwal] **à ~** *adv phr* : the wrong way

rebrousser [rəbruse] *vt* **1** : brush back **2 ~ chemin** : turn back

rebuffade [rəbyfad] *nf* : rebuff, snub

rebut [rəby] *nm* **1** : trash, scrap **2 mettre au ~** : discard — **rebutant, -tante** [rəbytɑ̃, -tɑ̃t] *adj* : repellent, disagreeable — **rebuter** [rəbyte] *vt* : put off, discourage

récalcitrant, -trante [rekalsitrɑ̃, -trɑ̃t] *adj* : stubborn

récapituler [rekapityle] *vt* RÉSUMER : recapitulate, sum up

recel [rəsɛl] *nm* : possession of stolen goods

récemment [resamɑ̃] *adv* DERNIÈREMENT : recently

recensement [rəsɑ̃smɑ̃] *nm* : census

récent, -cente [resɑ̃, -sɑ̃t] *adj* : recent

récépissé [resepise] *nm* : receipt

récepteur [reseptœr] *nm* : receiver

réception [resɛpsjɔ̃] *nf* : reception — **réceptionniste** [resɛpsjɔnist] *nmf* : receptionist

récession [resesjɔ̃] *nf* : recession

recette [rəsɛt] *nf* **1** : recipe (in cooking) **2** : take, receipts *pl*

recevoir [rəsəvwar] {26} *vt* **1** : receive, get **2** ACCUEILLIR : welcome **3** : see (a client, etc.) **4** : accommodate, hold — **receveur, -veuse** [rəsəvœr, -vøz] *n* **1** *Can* : catcher (in sports) **2 ~ des contributions** : tax collector

rechange [rəʃɑ̃ʒ] *nm* **de ~ 1** : spare, extra **2** : alternative

réchapper [reʃape] *vi* **~ de** : come through, survive

recharger [rəʃarʒe] {17} *vt* **1** : refill **2** : recharge — **recharge** [rəʃarʒ] *nf* **1** : refill **2** : recharging

réchaud [reʃo] *nm* : (portable) stove

réchauffer [reʃofe] *vt* : reheat — **se réchauffer** *vr* : warm up, get warmer

rêche [rɛʃ] *adj* : rough, prickly

rechercher [rəʃɛrʃe] *vt* : search for, seek — **recherche** [rəʃɛrʃ] *nf* **1** : search **2** : (academic) research — **recherché, -chée** [rəʃɛrʃe] *adj* : sought-after, in demand

rechigner [rəʃiɲe] *vi* **1** : grumble **2 ~ à** : balk at

rechute [rəʃyt] *nf* : relapse

récif [resif] *nm* : reef

récipient [resipjɑ̃] *nm* : container

réciproque [resiprɔk] *adj* : reciprocal

réciter [resite] *vt* : recite — **récit** [resi] *nm* : account, story — **récital** [resital] *nm, pl* **-tals** : recital

réclamer [reklame] *vt* **1** : call for, demand **2** REVENDIQUER : claim — **réclamation** [reklamasjɔ̃] *nf* PLAINTE : complaint — **réclame** [reklam] *nf* **1** : advertisement **2** : advertising

reclus, -cluse [rəkly, -klyz] *n* : recluse

recoin [rəkwɛ̃] *nm* : nook, corner

récolte [rekɔlt] *nf* **1** : harvesting **2** : harvest, crop — **récolter** [rekɔlte] *vt* **1** : harvest **2** RAMASSER : gather, collect

recommander [rəkɔmɑ̃de] *vt* **1** : recommend **2** : register (a letter, etc.) — **recommandation** [rəkɔmɑ̃dasjɔ̃] *nf* : recommendation

recommencer [rəkɔmɑ̃se] {6} *v* : begin again

récompenser [rekɔ̃pɑ̃se] *vt* : reward — **récompense** [rekɔ̃pɑ̃s] *nf* : reward

réconcilier [rekɔ̃silje] {96} *vt* : reconcile — **réconciliation** [rekɔ̃siljasjɔ̃] *nf* : reconciliation

reconduire [rəkɔ̃dɥir] {49} *vt* RACCOMPA-GNER : see home, accompany

réconforter [rekɔ̃fɔrte] *vt* : comfort — **réconfort** [rekɔ̃fɔr] *nm* : comfort — **réconfortant, -tante** [rekɔ̃fɔrtɑ̃, -tɑ̃t] *adj* : comforting, heartwarming

reconnaître [rəkɔnɛtr] {7} *vt* **1** : recognize **2** ADMETTRE : acknowledge — **reconnaissance** [rəkɔnɛsɑ̃s] *nf* **1** : recognition **2** GRATITUDE : gratitude — **reconnaissable** [rəkɔnɛsabl] *adj* : recognizable — **reconnaissant, -sante** [rəkɔnɛsɑ̃, -sɑ̃t] *adj* : grateful — **reconnu, -nue** [rəkɔny] *adj* : well-known

reconsidérer [rəkɔ̃sidere] {87} *vt* : reconsider

reconstituer [rəkɔ̃stitɥe] *vt* : recreate, reconstruct

reconstruire [rəkɔ̃strɥir] {49} *vt* : reconstruct, rebuild

record [rəkɔr] *nm* : record

recouper [rəkupe] *v* **se recouper** *vr* : tally, match up

recourbé, -bée [rəkurbe] *adj* : curved, hooked

recourir [rəkurir] {23} *vi* ~ **à** : resort to — **recours** [rəkur] *nm* : recourse, resort

recouvrer [rəkuvre] *vt* : recover, regain

recouvrir [rəkuvrir] {83} *vt* : cover (up)

récréation [rekreasjɔ̃] *nf* **1** LOISIRS : recreation **2** : recess, break — **récréatif, -tive** [rekreatif, -tiv] *adj* : recreational

recréer [rəkree] {89} *vt* : re-create

récrier [rekrije] {96} *v* **se récrier** *vr* : exclaim

récrimination [rekriminasjɔ̃] *nf* : reproach

récrire [rekrir] {33} *vt* : rewrite

recroqueviller [rəkrɔkvije] *v* **se recroqueviller** *vr* **1** : curl up **2** : shrivel up

recruter [rəkryte] *vt* : recruit — **recrue** [rəkry] *nf* : recruit — **recrutement** [rəkrytmɑ̃] *nm* : recruitment

rectangle [rɛktɑ̃gl] *nm* : rectangle — **rectangulaire** [-tɑ̃gyler] *adj* : rectangular

rectifier [rɛktifje] {96} *vt* : rectify, correct — **rectification** [rɛktifikasjɔ̃] *nf* : correction

recto [rɛkto] *nm* : right side (of a page)

rectum [rɛktɔm] *nm* : rectum

reçu, -cue [rəsy] *adj* : accepted, approved — **reçu** *nm* : receipt

recueillir [rəkœjir] {3} *vt* **1** : collect, gather **2** : obtain (information) — **se recueillir** *vr* : meditate — **recueil** [rəkœj] *nm* : collection

reculer [rəkyle] *vt* **1** REPOUSSER : move back, push back **2** DIFFÉRER : postpone — *vi* **1** : move back, back up **2** ~ **devant** : shrink from — **recul** [rəkyl] *nm* **1** : recoil (of a fire arm) **2 avec le** ~ : with hindsight — **reculons** [rəkylɔ̃] **à** ~ *adv phr* : backward

récupérer [rekypere] {87} *vt* **1** : recover, get back **2** : salvage **3** : make up (hours of work, etc.) — *vi* SE RÉTABLIR : recover, recuperate

récurer [rekyre] *vt* : scour

recycler [rəsikle] *vt* **1** : retrain (personnel) **2** : recycle — **se recycler** *vr* : retrain

rédacteur, -trice [redaktœr, -tris] *n* : editor — **rédaction** [redaksjɔ̃] *nf* **1** : writing, editing **2** : editorial staff

reddition [redisjɔ̃] *nf* : surrender

rédemption [redɑ̃psjɔ̃] *nf* : redemption

redevable [rədəvabl] *adj* **être** ~ **à** : be indebted to — **redevance** [rədəvɑ̃s] *nf* : dues *pl*, fees *pl*

rédiger [rediʒe] {17} *vt* : draw up, write

redire [rədir] {29} *vt* RÉPÉTER : repeat

redondant, -dante [rədɔ̃dɑ̃, -dɑ̃t] *adj* SUPERFLU : redundant

redonner [rədɔne] *vt* **1** RENDRE : give back **2** RÉTABLIR : restore (confidence)

redoubler [rəduble] *vt* **1** DOUBLER : double **2** : repeat (a year in school) **3** ~ **ses efforts** : intensify one's efforts

redouter [rədute] *vt* : fear — **redoutable** [rədutabl] *adj* : formidable

redresser [rədrɛse] *vt* **1** : straighten (up) **2** : rectify, redress (wrongs, etc.) — **se redresser** *vr* : straighten up

réduction [redyksjɔ̃] *nf* : reduction

réduire [redɥir] {49} *vt* **1** : reduce **2** ~ **en** : crush to — **réduit, -duite** [redɥi, -dɥit] *adj* **1** : reduced (of speed) **2** : small, limited — **réduit** *nm* : recess, nook

rééduquer [reedyke] *vt* : rehabilitate — **rééducation** [reedykasjɔ̃] *nf* : rehabilitation

réel, -elle [reɛl] *adj* : real — **réel** *nm* : reality — **réellement** [reɛlmɑ̃] *adv* : really

refaire [rəfɛr] {42} *vt* : do again, redo — **réfection** [refɛksjɔ̃] *nf* : repair

référence [referɑ̃s] *nf* : reference

référendum [referɛ̃dɔm] *nm* : referendum

référer [refere] {87} *v* **se référer** *vr* ~ **à** : refer to

réfléchir [refleʃir] *vt* : reflect — *vi* PENSER : think — **réfléchi, -chie** [refleʃi] *adj* **1** : thoughtful **2** : reflexive (of a verb)

refléter [rəflete] {87} *vt* : reflect, mirror — **reflet** [rəflɛ] *nm* : reflection, image

réflexe [reflɛks] *adj & nm* : reflex

réflexion [reflɛksjɔ̃] *nf* **1** : reflection (of light, etc.) **2** PENSÉE : thought

refluer [rəflye] *vi* **1** : ebb, flow back **2** : surge back (of crowds, etc.) — **reflux** [rəflys] *nm* : ebb

réformer [rəfɔrme] *vt* : reform — **réformateur, -trice** [reformatœr, -tris] *n* : reformer — **réforme** [reform] *nf* : reform

refouler [rəfule] *vt* **1** : drive back (a crowd) **2** ~ **ses larmes** : hold back tears

réfractaire [refraktɛr] *adj* ~ **à** : resistant to

refrain [rəfrɛ̃] *nm* : refrain, chorus

refréner [rəfrene] *or* **réfréner** [refrene] {87} *vt* : curb, check

réfrigérer [refriʒere] {87} *vt* : refrigerate — **réfrigérateur** [refriʒeratœr] *nm* : refrigerator

refroidir [rəfrwadir] *v* : cool (down) — **refroidissement** [rəfrwadismɑ̃] *nm* **1** : cooling **2** RHUME : cold, chill

refuge [rəfyʒ] *nm* : refuge — **réfugié, -giée** [refyʒje] *n* : refugee — **réfugier** [refyʒje] {96} *v* **se réfugier** *vr* : take refuge

refuser [rəfyze] *vt* : refuse — **refus** [rəfy] *nm* : refusal

réfuter [refyte] *vt* : refute

regagner [rəgaɲe] *vt* **1** : win back **2** ~ **son domicile** : return home

régal [regal] *nm, pl* **-gals** DÉLICE : delight, treat — **régaler** [regale] *vt* : treat — **se régaler** *vr* **1** : enjoy oneself **2** ~ **de** : feast on

regard [rəgar] *nm* **1** : look **2 au** ~ **de** : in regard to — **regarder** [rəgarde] *vt* **1** : look at, watch **2** CONSIDÉRER : consider **3** CONCERNER : concern — *vi* : look — **se regarder** *vr* **1** : look at oneself **2** : look at each other

régénérer [reʒenere] {87} *vt* : regenerate

régie [reʒi] *nf* **1** *France* : public corporation **2** *Can* : provincial public-service agency

régime [reʒim] *nm* **1** : (political) regime **2** : system **3** : cluster, bunch (of bananas) **4 au** ~ : on a diet

région [reʒjɔ̃] *nf* : region, area — **régional, -nale** [reʒjonal] *adj, mpl* **-naux** [-no] : regional

régir [reʒir] *vt* : govern

registre [rəʒistr] *nm* : register

réglable [reglabl] *adj* **1** : adjustable **2** : payable — **réglage** [reglaʒ] *nm* : adjustment

règle [rɛgl] *nf* **1** : ruler (instrument) **2** LOI : rule **3** ~**s** *nfpl* : menstrual period **4 en** ~ : in order, valid — **réglé, -glée** [regle] *adj* ORGANISÉ : orderly, organized — **règlement** [rɛgləmɑ̃] *nm* **1** : regulations *pl* **2** RÉSOLUTION : settlement — **réglementation** [rɛgləmɑ̃tasjɔ̃] *nf* : regulation — **régler** [regle] {87} *vt* **1** : adjust, regulate **2** : settle (a dispute)

réglisse [reglis] *nf* : licorice

régner [reɲe] {87} *vi* : reign — **règne** [rɛɲ] *nm* : reign, rule

regorger [rəgorʒe] {17} *vi* ~ **de** : overflow with

regretter [rəgrɛte] *vt* **1** : regret, be sorry about **2** : miss (s.o.) — **regret** [rəgrɛ] *nm* : regret

régularité [regylarite] *nf* : regularity — **régulier, -lière** [regylje, -ljɛr] *adj* **1** : regular **2** CONSTANT : even, steady

réhabiliter [reabilite] *vt* **1** : rehabilitate **2** RÉNOVER : renovate — **réhabilitation** [reabilitasjɔ̃] *nf* : rehabilitation

rein [rɛ̃] *nm* **1** : kidney **2** ~**s** *nmpl* DOS : back

reine [rɛn] *nf* : queen

réinsérer [reẽsere] {87} *vt* : rehabilitate

réitérer [reitere] {87} *vt* : reiterate, repeat

rejeter [rəʒte] {8} *vt* **1** RENVOYER : throw back **2** REFUSER : reject — **rejet** [rəʒɛ] *nm* : rejection

rejoindre [rəʒwɛ̃dr] {50} *vt* **1** RENCONTRER : join, meet **2** RATTRAPER : catch up with **3** REGAGNER : return to — **se rejoindre** *vr* : meet

réjouir [reʒwir] *vt* : delight — **se réjouir** *vr* : rejoice, be delighted — **réjouissance** [reʒwisɑ̃s] *nf* **1** : rejoicing **2** ~**s** *nfpl* : festivities — **réjouissant, -sante** [reʒwisɑ̃, -sɑ̃t] *adj* : cheering, delightful

relâcher [rəlɑʃe] *vt* **1** DESSERRER : loosen (up), slacken **2** LIBÉRER : release — **se relâcher** *vr* **1** : loosen **2** : become lax — **relâche** [rəlɑʃ] *nf* : respite

relais [rəlɛ] *nm* **1** : relay **2** ~ **routier** : truck stop

relancer [rəlɑ̃se] {6} *vt* **1** : throw back **2** : revive, boost (the economy, etc.) — **relance** [rəlɑ̃s] *nf* : boost

relatif, -tive [rəlatif, -tiv] *adj* : relative — **relativité** [rəlativite] *nf* : relativity

relation [rəlasjɔ̃] *nf* **1** : connection, relation **2** : relationship **3** CONNAISSANCE : acquaintance **4** ~**s** *nfpl* : relations

relaxer [rəlakse] *vt* : relax — **relaxation** [rəlaksasjɔ̃] *nf* : relaxation

relayer [rəlɛje] {11} *vt* : relieve — **se relayer** *vr* : take turns

reléguer [rəlege] {87} *vt* : relegate

relent [rəlɑ̃] *nm* : stench

relève [rəlɛv] *nf* **1** : relief **2 prendre la** ~ : take over

relever [rəlve] {52} *vt* **1** : pick up, raise (up) **2** AUGMENTER : increase **3** RELAYER : relieve **4** : bring out, enhance — **se relever** *vr* : get up (again) — **relevé** [rəlɛve] *nm* **1** : (bank) statement **2** : reading (of a meter)

relief [rəljɛf] *nm* **1** : relief **2 mettre en** ~ : highlight

relier [rəlje] {96} *vt* **1** : link, join **2** : bind (a book)

religion [rəliʒjɔ̃] *nf* : religion — **religieux, -gieuse** [rəliʒjø, -ʒjøz] *adj* : religious — ~ *n* : monk *m*, nun *f*

relique [rəlik] *nf* : relic

reliure [rəljyr] *nf* : binding

reluire [rəlɥir] {49} *vi* BRILLER : glisten,

shine — **reluisant, -sante** [rəlɥizɑ̃, -zɑ̃t] *adj* : gleaming

remanier [rəmanje] {96} *vt* : revise, modify

remarquer [rəmarke] *vt* **1** : remark, observe **2** CONSTATER : notice — **remarquable** [rəmarkabl] *adj* : remarkable — **remarque** [rəmark] *nf* : remark

remblai [rɑ̃blɛ] *nm* : embankment

rembobiner [rɑ̃bɔbine] *vt* : rewind

rembourrer [rɑ̃bure] *vt* : pad

rembourser [rɑ̃burse] *vt* **1** : repay (a debt) **2** : refund, reimburse — **remboursement** [rɑ̃bursəmɑ̃] *nm* : refund, reimbursement

remède [rəmɛd] *nm* : remedy, cure — **remédier** [rəmedje] {96} *vi* ~ **à** : remedy, cure

remercier [rəmɛrsje] {96} *vt* **1** : thank **2** CONGÉDIER : dismiss, fire — **remerciement** [rəmɛrsimɑ̃] *nm* **1** : thanking **2** ~**s** *nmpl* : thanks

remettre [rəmɛtr] {53} *vt* **1** REMPLACER : replace **2** RAJOUTER : add **3** : put back (on) **4** DONNER : deliver, hand over **5** : postpone **6** RECONNAÎTRE : recognize, place — **se remettre** *vr* **1** : go back, get back **2** : put on again **3** : recover, get better **4** ~ **à** : begin again **5** ~ **de** : get over — **remise** [rəmiz] *nf* **1** : postponement **2** LIVRAISON : delivery **3** : remission (of a debt, etc.) **4** RABAIS : discount **5** : shed — **rémission** [remisjɔ̃] *nf* : remission

remonter [rəmɔ̃te] *vt* **1** : take back up, bring back up, raise up (again) **2** : go back up (the stairs, etc.) **3** : cheer up, invigorate — *vi* **1** : go back up, rise (again) **2** ~ **à** : date back to — **remontée** [rəmɔ̃te] *nf* **1** : climb, ascent **2** ~ **mécanique** : ski lift — **remonte–pente** [rəmɔ̃tpɑ̃t] *nm, pl* **remonte–pentes** : ski lift

remords [rəmɔr] *nm* : remorse

remorquer [rəmɔrke] *vt* : tow — **remorque** [rəmɔrk] *nf* : trailer — **remorqueuse** [rəmɔrkøz] *nf Can* : tow truck

remous [rəmu] *nm* : (back)wash

remplacer [rɑ̃plase] {6} *vt* : replace — **remplaçant, -çante** [rɑ̃plasɑ̃, -sɑ̃t] *n* : substitute — **remplacement** [rɑ̃-plasmɑ̃] *nm* : replacement

remplir [rɑ̃plir] *vt* **1** : fill (up) **2** : fill out (a form, etc.) **3** : carry out, fulfill — **remplissage** [rɑ̃plisaʒ] *nm* : filling, filler

remporter [rɑ̃pɔrte] *vt* **1** REPRENDRE : take back **2** : win (a prize, etc.)

remue–ménage [rəmymenaʒ] *nms & pl* : commotion, fuss

remuer [rəmɥe] *vt* **1** MÉLANGER : stir, mix **2** ~ **la queue** : wag its tail — *vi* : fidget, squirm

rémunérer [remynere] {87} *vt* : pay (for) — **rémunération** [remynerasjɔ̃] *nf* : payment

renâcler [rənakle] *vi* **1** : snort **2** ~ **à** : balk at

renaître [rənɛtr] {57} *vi* : be reborn — **renaissance** [rənɛsɑ̃s] *nf* : rebirth, revival

renard [rənar] *nm* : fox

renchérir [rɑ̃ʃerir] *vi* **1** : become more expensive **2** ~ **sur** : go (one step) further than

rencontrer [rɑ̃kɔ̃tre] *vt* **1** : meet **2** TROUVER : come across, encounter — **se rencontrer** *vr* **1** : meet **2** SE TROUVER : be found — **rencontre** [rɑ̃kɔ̃tr] *nf* **1** : meeting, encounter **2** : match, game

rendement [rɑ̃dmɑ̃] *nm* **1** : output **2** RAPPORT : yield

rendez–vous [rɑ̃devu] *nms & pl* **1** : appointment, meeting **2** : meeting place

rendre [rɑ̃dr] {63} *vt* **1** : give back, return **2** : pronounce (a verdict) **3** EXPRIMER : convey **4** ~ **grâces** : give thanks — *vi* VOMIR : vomit — **se rendre** *vr* **1** : surrender **2** ~ **à** : go to **3** ~ **compte de** : realize, be aware of

rêne [rɛn] *nf* : rein

renfermer [rɑ̃fɛrme] *vt* : contain — **se renfermer** *vr* : withdraw (into oneself) — **renfermé** [rɑ̃fɛrme] *nm* : mustiness

renfler [rɑ̃fle] *v* **se renfler** *vr* : bulge, swell — **renflement** [rɑ̃fləmɑ̃] *nm* : bulge

renforcer [rɑ̃fɔrse] {6} *vt* : reinforce — **renfort** [rɑ̃fɔr] *nm* : reinforcement

renfrogné, -gnée [rɑ̃frɔɲe] *adj* : sullen, scowling

rengaine [rɑ̃gɛn] *nf* **la même** ~ : the same old story

renier [rənje] {96} *vt* : deny, disown

renifler [rənifle] *v* : sniff

renne [rɛn] *nm* : reindeer

renom [rənɔ̃] *nm* : renown, fame — **renommé, -mée** [rənɔme] *adj* : renowned — **renommée** *nf* : fame, renown

renoncer [rənɔ̃se] {6} *vi* ~ **à** : renounce, give up — **renonciation** [rənɔ̃sjasjɔ̃] *nf* : renunciation

renouer [rənwe] *vt* REPRENDRE : renew, resume

renouveau [rənuvo] *nm, pl* **-veaux** : revival

renouveler [rənuvle] {8} *vt* : renew — **renouvellement** [rənuvɛlmɑ̃] *nm* : renewal

rénover [renɔve] *vt* : renovate — **rénovation** [renɔvasjɔ̃] *nf* : renovation

renseigner [rɑ̃sɛɲe] *vt* : inform — **se renseigner** *vr* : ask, make inquiries — **renseignement** [rɑ̃sɛɲəmɑ̃] *nm* : information

rentable [rɑ̃tabl] *adj* : profitable

rente [rɑ̃t] *nf* **1** : (private) income **2** ~ **viagère** : annuity

rentrer [rɑ̃tre] *vi* **1** : go in, get in **2** : go back in **3** RETOURNER : return — *vt* **1** : bring in, take in **2** : pull in (one's stomach) — **ren-**

réputation

trée [rɑ̃tre] *nf* **1** : return (to work, etc.) **2** ~ **scolaire** : start of the new school year

renverser [rɑ̃verse] *vt* **1** : knock down, overturn **2** RÉPANDRE : spill **3** : overthrow (a regime) **4** STUPÉFIER : astonish — **se renverser** *vr* : fall over, overturn — **renversement** [rɑ̃vɛrsəmɑ̃] *nm* : reversal

renvoyer [rɑ̃vwaje] {36} *vt* **1** : send back, throw back **2** CONGÉDIER : dismiss **3** REMETTRE : postpone **4** ~ **à** : refer to **5** *Can fam* : throw up — **renvoi** [rɑ̃vwa] *nm* **1** : return (of a package) **2** LICENCIEMENT : dismissal **3** : cross-reference **4** REMISE : postponement **5** : belch, burp

réorganiser [reɔrganize] *vt* : reorganize

repaire [rəpɛr] *nm* : den, lair

répandre [repɑ̃dr] {63} *vt* **1** : spill **2** : shed (blood, tears, etc.) **3** : spread (the news) **4** : give off, emit — **se répandre** *vr* **1** : spill **2** SE PROPAGER : spread — **répandu, -due** [repɑ̃dy] *adj* : widespread

réparer [repare] *vt* **1** : repair **2** : make up for (an error) — **réparation** [reparasjɔ̃] *nf* : repair, repairing

repartir [rəpartir] {82} *vt* : retort — *vi* **1** : leave again **2** : start again

répartir [repartir] *vt* **1** : divide up, distribute **2** : spread (out) — **se répartir** *vr* : divide — **répartition** [repartisjɔ̃] *nf* : distribution

repas [rəpa] *nm* : meal

repasser [rəpase] *vt* **1** : pass again, take again, show again **2** : iron, press **3** : go (back) over — *vi* : pass by again, come again — **repassage** [rəpasaʒ] *nm* : ironing

repentir [rəpɑ̃tir] {82} *v* **se repentir** *vr* : repent — ~ *nm* : repentance

répercuter [repɛrkyte] *v* **se répercuter** *vr* **1** : echo **2** ~ **sur** : have repercussions on — **répercussion** [repɛrkysjɔ̃] *nf* : repercussion

repère [rəpɛr] *nm* **1** : line, mark **2 point de** ~ : landmark — **repérer** [rəpere] {87} *vt* **1** : mark **2** SITUER : locate — **se repérer** *vr* : find one's way

répertoire [repɛrtwar] *nm* **1** : list, index **2** : repertoire (in theater) **3** ~ **d'adresses** : address book **4** ~ **téléphonique** : telephone directory

répéter [repete] {87} *vt* **1** : repeat **2** : rehearse (in theater) — **répétitif, -tive** [repetitif, -tiv] *adj* : repetitive, repetitious — **répétition** [repetisjɔ̃] *nf* **1** : repetition **2** : rehearsal

répit [repi] *nm* : respite

replacer [rəplase] {6} *vt* : replace

replier [rəplije] {96} *vt* : fold up, fold over — **se replier** *vr* **1** : fold up **2** ~ **sur soi-même** : withdraw into oneself

répliquer [replike] *vt* RÉPONDRE : reply — *vi* **1** : respond **2** RIPOSTER : retort — **réplique**

[replik] *nf* **1** : reply **2** : line (in a play) **3** : replica (in art)

répondre [repɔ̃dr] {63} *v* : answer, reply — **répondeur** [repɔ̃dœr] *nm* : answering machine — **réponse** [repɔ̃s] *nf* : answer, response

report [rəpɔr] *nm* RENVOI : postponement

reportage [rəpɔrtaʒ] *nm* : report

reporter¹ [rəpɔrte] *vt* **1** : take back **2** REMETTRE : postpone **3** : carry forward (a calculation, etc.)

reporter² [rəpɔrtɛr] *nm* : reporter

reposer [rəpoze] *v* : rest — **se reposer** *vr* **1** : rest **2** ~ **sur** : rely on — **repos** [rəpo] *nm* : rest — **reposant, -sante** [rəpozɑ̃, -zɑ̃t] *nm* : restful

repousser [rəpuse] *vi* : grow back — *vt* **1** : push back **2** DÉGOÛTER : disgust **3** : turn down (an offer) **4** REPORTER : postpone — **repoussant, -sante** [rəpusɑ̃, -sɑ̃t] *adj* DÉGOÛTANT : repulsive

reprendre [rəprɑ̃dr] {70} *vt* **1** : take (up) again **2** : take back, return **3** RETROUVER : regain **4** RECOMMENCER : resume **5** : repair, alter (a garment) — *vi* **1** : pick up, improve **2** : resume

représailles [rəprezaj] *nfpl* : reprisals

représenter [rəprezɑ̃te] *vt* **1** : represent **2** JOUER : perform — **représentant, -tante** [rəprezɑ̃tɑ̃, -tɑ̃t] *n* : representative — **représentatif, -tive** [rəprezɑ̃tatif, -tiv] *adj* : representative — **représentation** [rəprezɑ̃tasjɔ̃] *nf* **1** : representation **2** : performance (in theater)

réprimander [reprimɑ̃de] *vt* : reprimand — **réprimande** [reprimɑ̃d] *nf* : reprimand

réprimer [reprime] *vt* : repress, suppress

reprise [rəpriz] *nf* **1** : recapture **2** : resumption **3** : repeat, revival **4** : recovery **5** : trade-in (of goods) **6** : round (in sports) **7** : darn, mend — **repriser** [rəprize] *vt* : darn, mend

reprocher [rəprɔʃe] *vt* ~ **à** : reproach — **reproche** [rəprɔʃ] *nm* : reproach

reproduire [rəprɔdɥir] {49} *vt* : reproduce — **se reproduire** *vr* **1** : reproduce **2** SE RÉPÉTER : recur — **reproduction** [rəprɔdyksjɔ̃] *nf* : reproduction

réprouver [repruve] *vt* : condemn

reptile [rɛptil] *nm* : reptile

repu, -pue [rəpy] *adj* : satiated, full

république [repyblik] *nf* : republic — **républicain, -caine** [repyblikɛ̃, -kɛn] *adj & n* : republican

répudier [repydje] {96} *vt* : repudiate

répugner [repyɲe] *vt* : disgust — *vi* ~ **à** : be averse to — **répugnance** [repyɲɑ̃s] *nf* **1** : repugnance **2** : reluctance — **répugnant, -gnante** [repyɲɑ̃, -ɲɑ̃t] *adj* : repugnant

réputation [repytasjɔ̃] *nf* : reputation —

réputé, -tée [repyte] *adj* : renowned, famous

requérir [rəkerir] {21} *vt* : require

requête [rəkɛt] *nf* : request

requin [rəkɛ̃] *nm* : shark

requis, -quise [rəki, -kiz] *adj* : required

rescapé, -pée [rɛskape] *n* : survivor

rescousse [rɛskus] *nf* : rescue, aid

réseau [rezo] *nm*, *pl* **-seaux** : network

réserver [rezɛrve] *vt* : reserve — **réservation** [rezɛrvasjɔ̃] *nf* : reservation — **réserve** [rezɛrv] *nf* **1** PROVISION : stock **2** RETENUE : reserve **3** : (Indian) reservation **4** : (game) preserve **5 sous ~ de** : subject to — **réservé, -vée** [rezɛrve] *adj* : reserved

réservoir [rezɛrvwar] *nm* **1** : tank **2** : reservoir

résidence [rezidɑ̃s] *nf* : residence — **résident, -dente** [rezidɑ̃, -dɑ̃t] *n* : resident — **résidentiel, -tielle** [rezidɑ̃sjɛl] *adj* : residential — **résider** [rezide] *vi* : reside

résidu [rezidy] *nm* : residue

résigner [reziɲe] *vt* : resign — **se résigner** *vr* **~ à** : resign oneself to — **résignation** [reziɲasjɔ̃] *nf* : resignation

résilier [rezilje] {96} *vt* : terminate

résine [rezin] *nf* : resin

résister [reziste] *vi* **~ à** : resist — **résistance** [rezistɑ̃s] *nf* : resistance — **résistant, -tante** [rezistɑ̃, -tɑ̃t] *adj* : tough, durable

résolu, -lue [rezɔly] *adj* : resolute, resolved — **résolution** [rezɔlysjɔ̃] *nf* **1** : resolution **2** DÉTERMINATION : resolve

résonner [rezɔne] *vi* : resound — **résonance** [rezɔnɑ̃s] *nf* : resonance — **résonnant, -nante** [rezɔnɑ̃, -nɑ̃t] *adj* : resonant

résorber [rezɔrbe] *vt* : absorb, reduce

résoudre [rezudr] {74} *vt* : solve, resolve — **se résoudre** *vr* **~ à** : decide to

respect [rɛspɛ] *nm* : respect — **respectable** [rɛspɛktabl] *adj* : respectable — **respecter** [rɛspɛkte] *vt* : respect

respectif, -tive [rɛspɛktif, -tiv] *adj* : respective

respectueux, -tueuse [rɛspɛktyø, -tyøz] *adj* : respectful

respirer [rɛspire] *v* : breathe — **respiration** [rɛspirasjɔ̃] *nf* : breathing

resplendir [rɛsplɑ̃dir] *vi* : shine — **resplendissant, -sante** [rɛsplɑ̃disɑ̃, -sɑ̃t] *adj* : radiant

responsable [rɛspɔ̃sabl] *adj* : responsible — **responsabilité** [rɛspɔ̃sabilite] *nf* **1** : responsibility **2** : liability

resquiller [rɛskije] *vi fam* **1** : sneak in (without paying) **2** : cut in line

ressaisir [rəsezir] *v* **se ressaisir** *vr* : pull oneself together

ressasser [rəsase] *vt* : keep going over

ressembler [rəsɑ̃ble] *vi* **~ à** : resemble —

se ressembler *vr* : resemble each other, look alike — **ressemblance** [rəsɑ̃blɑ̃s] *nf* **1** : resemblance, likeness **2** SIMILITUDE : similarity

ressentir [rəsɑ̃tir] {82} *vt* : feel — **se ressentir** *vr* : feel the effects of — **ressentiment** [rəsɑ̃timɑ̃] *nm* : resentment

resserrer [rəsere] *vt* : tighten (a knot, etc.) — **se resserrer** *vr* **1** : tighten (up) **2** : narrow

ressortir [rəsɔrtir] {82} *vt* : take out again, bring out again — *vi* **1** : go out again **2** : stand out — *v impers* : emerge, be evident — **ressort** [rəsɔr] *nm* **1** : spring (of a mattress, etc.) **2** : impulse, motivation **3 en dernier ~** : as a last resort — **ressortissant, -sante** [rəsɔrtisɑ̃, -sɑ̃t] *n* : national

ressource [rəsurs] *nf* : resource

ressusciter [resysite] *vt* : resuscitate — *vi* : come back to life, revive

restant, -tante [rɛstɑ̃, -tɑ̃t] *adj* : remaining — **restant** *nm* : remainder

restaurant [rɛstɔrɑ̃] *nm* : restaurant

restaurer [rɛstɔre] *vt* : restore

rester [rɛste] *vi* **1** : stay, remain **2** : be left — *v impers* **il reste** : there remains — **reste** [rɛst] *nm* **1** : remainder, rest **2 au ~** *or* **du ~** : besides, moreover **3 ~s** *nmpl* : leftovers **4 ~s** *nmpl* : remains

restituer [rɛstitɥe] *vt* **1** : restore, return **2** : reproduce (sound, etc.)

restreindre [rɛstrɛ̃dr] {37} *vt* : restrict — **restrictif, -tive** [rɛstriktif, -tiv] *adj* : restrictive — **restriction** [rɛstriksjɔ̃] *nf* : restriction

résultat [rezylta] *nm* : result — **résulter** [rezylte] {75} *vi* **~ de** : result from — *v impers* **il résulte** : it follows

résumer [rezyme] *vt* : summarize, sum up — **résumé** [rezyme] *nm* **1** : summary **2 en ~** : in short

résurrection [rezyrɛksjɔ̃] *nf* : resurrection

rétablir [retablir] *vt* : restore — **se rétablir** *vr* **1** : be restored **2** GUÉRIR : recover — **rétablissement** [reta-blismɑ̃] *nm* **1** : restoration **2** GUÉRISON : recovery

retarder [rətarde] *vt* **1** : delay **2** REPORTER : postpone **3** : set back (a clock, etc.) — *vi* : be slow — **retard** [rətar] *nm* **1** : lateness, delay **2** : backwardness — **retardataire** [rətardatɛr] *nmf* : latecomer

retenir [rətənir] {92} *vt* **1** : hold back, stop **2** RETARDER : keep, detain **3** GARDER : retain **4** RÉSERVER : reserve, book **5** SE RAPPELER : remember **6** : carry (in mathematics) — **se retenir** *vr* **1** : restrain oneself **2** **~ à** : hold on to

retentir [rətɑ̃tir] *vi* : ring, resound — **retentissant, -sante** [rətɑ̃tisɑ̃, -sɑ̃t] *adj* : resounding — **retentissement** [rətɑ̃tismɑ̃] *nm* : effect, impact

retenue [rətəny] *nf* **1** : deduction **2** : detention (in school) **3** RÉSERVE : reserve, restraint

réticent, -cente [retisã, -sãt] *adj* : reticent, reluctant — **réticence** [retisãs] *nf* : reticence, reluctance

rétine [retin] *nf* : retina

retiré, -rée [rətire] *adj* : remote, secluded

retirer [rətire] *vt* **1** : take off (clothing, etc.) **2** : take away, remove **3** : withdraw (money, support, etc.) **4** : collect (baggage, etc.) **5** *Can* : retire, put out (in baseball) — **se retirer** *vr* : withdraw, retreat

retomber [rətɔ̃be] *vi* : fall again, fall back — **retombées** [rətɔ̃be] *nfpl* : repercussions, consequences

rétorquer [retɔrke] *vt* : retort

rétorsion [retɔrsjɔ̃] *nf* : retaliation

retoucher [rətuʃe] *vt* **1** : touch up **2** : alter (a dress, etc.) — **retouche** [rətuʃ] *nf* **1** : touching up **2** : alteration

retour [rətur] *nm* **1** : return **2** de ~ : back

retourner [rəturne] *vt* **1** : turn over **2** : return (a compliment, etc.) — *vi* REVENIR : return — **se retourner** *vr* **1** : turn around **2** : overturn (of a boat, etc.) **3** ~ **contre** : turn against

retrait [rətrɛ] *nm* **1** : withdrawal **2** en ~ : set back **3** *Can* : out (in baseball)

retraite [rətrɛt] *nf* **1** : retirement **2** : retreat (in religion, etc.) **3** PENSION : pension

retransmettre [rətrãsmɛtr] {53} *vt* : broadcast — **retransmission** [rətrãsmisjɔ̃] *nf* : broadcast

rétrécir [retresir] *vi* : shrink

rétribuer [retribɥe] *vt* : pay — **rétribution** [retribysjɔ̃] *nf* RÉMUNÉRATION : payment

rétroactif, -tive [retrɔaktif, -tiv] *adj* : retroactive

rétrograder [retrɔgrade] *vt* : demote — *vi* : downshift (of a gear)

retrousser [rətruse] *vt* : turn up, roll up

retrouvailles [rətruvaj] *nfpl* : reunion

retrouver [rətruve] *vt* **1** : find (again) **2** REVOIR : see again **3** SE RAPPELER : remember — **se retrouver** *vr* **1** : meet again **2** : find one's way

rétroviseur [retrɔvizœr] *nm* : rearview mirror

réunir [reynir] *vt* RASSEMBLER : gather, collect — **se réunir** *vr* : meet — **réunion** [reynjɔ̃] *nf* : meeting

réussir [reysir] *vi* : succeed — *vt* **1** : make a success of **2** : pass (an exam) — **réussi, -sie** [reysi] *adj* : successful — **réussite** [reysit] *nf* : success

revanche [rəvãʃ] *nf* **1** : revenge **2** en ~ : on the other hand

rêve [rɛv] *nm* : dream

réveiller [reveje] *vt* **1** : wake up **2** : awaken

— **se réveiller** *vr* : wake up — **réveil** [revɛj] *nm* **1** : waking up, awakening **2** : alarm clock — **réveille–matin** [revɛjmatɛ̃] *nms & pl* : alarm clock

révéler [revele] {87} *vt* **1** : reveal **2** INDIQUER : show — **se révéler** *vr* : prove to be — **révélation** [revelasjɔ̃] *nf* : revelation

revendiquer [rəvãdike] *vt* **1** : claim **2** EXIGER : demand — **revendication** [rəvãdikasjɔ̃] *nf* : claim

revendre [rəvãdr] {63} *vt* : sell

revenir [rəvnir] {92} *vi* **1** : come back, return **2** ~ **à** : return to, go back to **3** ~ **à** : come down to, amount to **4** ~ **de** : get over

revente [rəvãt] *nf* : resale

revenu [rəvəny] *nm* : revenue, income

rêver [reve] *v* : dream

réverbère [reverbɛr] *nm* : streetlight

révérence [reverãs] *nf* **1** VÉNÉRATION : reverence **2** : bow, curtsy

révérend, -rende [reverã, -rãd] *adj* : reverend

rêverie [rɛvri] *nf* : daydreaming

revers [rəvɛr] *nm* **1** ENVERS : back, reverse **2** : lapel (of a jacket), cuff (of trousers) **3** : backhand (in tennis) **4** ÉCHEC : setback

réversible [reversibl] *adj* : reversible

revêtement [rəvɛtmã] *nm* **1** : facing (in construction) **2** : surface (of a road)

rêveur, -veuse [rɛvœr, -vøz] *adj* : dreamy — ~ *n* : dreamer

revirement [rəvirmã] *nm* : reversal, turnabout

réviser [revize] *vt* **1** : revise, review **2** : overhaul (a vehicle) — **révision** [revizjɔ̃] *nf* **1** : review, revision **2** : service (of a vehicle)

révocation [revɔkasjɔ̃] *nf* **1** : dismissal **2** : repeal

revoir [rəvwar] {99} *vt* **1** : see again **2** RÉVISER : review — **se revoir** *vr* : meet (each other) again — ~ *nm* au ~ : goodbye

révolter [revɔlte] *vt* : revolt, outrage — **se révolter** *vr* : rebel — **révolte** [revɔlt] *nf* : revolt

révolu, -lue [revɔly] *adj* : past

révolution [revɔlysjɔ̃] *nf* : revolution — **révolutionnaire** [revɔlysjɔnɛr] *adj & nmf* : revolutionary — **révolutionner** [revɔlysjɔne] *vt* : revolutionize

revolver [revɔlvɛr] *nm* : revolver

révoquer [revɔke] *vt* **1** : dismiss **2** : revoke (a privilege, etc.)

revue [rəvy] *nf* **1** : magazine **2** passer en ~ : go over

rez–de–chaussée [redʃose] *nms & pl* : first floor, ground floor

rhabiller [rabije] *v* **se rhabiller** *vr* : get dressed again

rhétorique [retɔrik] *adj* : rhetorical — ~ *nf* : rhetoric

rhinocéros [rinɔserɔs] *nm* : rhinoceros

rhubarbe [rybarb] *nf* : rhubarb

rhum [rɔm] *nm* : rum

rhumatisme [rymatism] *nm* : rheumatism

rhume [rym] *nm* : cold

ricaner [rikane] *vi* : snicker, giggle

riche [riʃ] *adj* : rich — ~ *nmf* : rich person — **richesse** [riʃɛs] *nf* **1** : wealth **2** : richness

ricocher [rikɔʃe] *vi* : ricochet — **ricochet** [rikɔʃɛ] *nm* : ricochet

ride [rid] *nf* **1** : wrinkle **2** : ripple (on water)

rideau [rido] *nm, pl* **-deaux** : curtain

rider [ride] *vt* **1** : wrinkle **2** : ripple (water)

ridicule [ridikyl] *adj* ABSURDE : ridiculous — ~ *nm* : ridicule — **ridiculiser** [ridikylize] *vt* : ridicule

rien [rjɛ̃] *pron* **1** : nothing **2** : anything **3 de** ~ : don't mention it, you're welcome **4** ~ **que** : only, just — ~ *nm* : trifle

rigide [riʒid] *adj* **1** : rigid **2** RIGOUREUX : strict — **rigidité** [riʒidite] *nf* : rigidity

rigoler [rigɔle] *vi fam* **1** : have fun **2** PLAISANTER : laugh, joke — **rigolo, -lote** [rigɔlɔ, -lɔt] *adj fam* : funny, comical

rigueur [rigœr] *nf* **1** SÉVÉRITÉ : rigor, harshness **2** : precision **3 à la** ~ : if absolutely necessary **4 de** ~ : obligatory — **rigoureux, -reuse** [rigurø, -røz] *adj* **1** : rigorous **2** : harsh (of climate)

rimer [rime] *vi* : rhyme — **rime** [rim] *nf* : rhyme

rincer [rɛ̃se] {6} *vt* : rinse — **rinçage** [rɛ̃saʒ] *nm* : rinsing, rinse

riposte [ripɔst] *nf* **1** RÉPLIQUE : retort **2** CONTRE-ATTAQUE : counterattack — **riposter** [ripɔste] *vt* : retort — *vi* : counter, retaliate

rire [rir] {76} *vi* **1** : laugh **2** S'AMUSER : joke, have fun **3** ~ **de** : mock, make fun of — ~ *nm* : laugh, laughter

risque [risk] *nm* **1** : risk — **risqué, -quée** [riske] *adj* : risky — **risquer** [riske] *vt* **1** : risk **2 ça risque d'arriver** : it may very well happen — **se risquer** *vr* : venture

rissoler [risɔle] *v* : brown (in cooking)

ristourne [risturn] *nf* REMISE : discount

rite [rit] *nm* : rite, ritual — **rituel, -tuelle** [rituɛl] *adj* : ritual — **rituel** *nm* : rite, ritual

rivage [rivaʒ] *nm* : shore

rival, -vale [rival] *adj & n, mpl* **-vaux** [rivo] : rival — **rivaliser** [rivalize] *vi* ~ **avec** : compete with, rival — **rivalité** [rivalite] *nf* : rivalry

rive [riv] *nf* : bank, shore

river [rive] *vt* : rivet

riverain, -raine [rivrɛ̃, -rɛn] *n* : resident (on a street)

rivet [rivɛ] *nm* : rivet

rivière [rivjɛr] *nf* : river

rixe [riks] *nf* BAGARRE : brawl, fight

riz [ri] *nm* : rice — **rizière** [rizjɛr] *nf* : (rice) paddy

robe [rɔb] *nf* **1** : dress **2** PELAGE : coat **3** ~ **de mariée** : wedding gown **4** ~ **de nuit** *Can* : nightgown

robinet [rɔbinɛ] *nm* : faucet

robot [rɔbo] *nm* : robot

robuste [rɔbyst] *adj* : robust

roc [rɔk] *nm* : rock — **roche** [rɔʃ] *nf* : rock — **rocher** [rɔʃe] *nm* : rock — **rocheux, -cheuse** [rɔʃø, -ʃøz] *adj* : rocky

roder [rɔde] *vt* **1** : break in (a vehicle) **2** *fam* : polish up (a performance, etc.)

rôder [rode] *vi* **1** : prowl **2** ERRER : wander about — **rôdeur, -deuse** [rodœr, -døz] *n* : prowler

rogne [rɔɲ] *nf fam* : anger

rognon [rɔɲɔ̃] *nm* : kidney (in cooking)

roi [rwa] *nm* : king

rôle [rol] *nm* : role, part

roman [rɔmã] *nm* : novel — **romancier, -cière** [rɔmãsje, -sjɛr] *n* : novelist

romantique [rɔmãtik] *adj* : romantic

rompre [rɔ̃pr] {77} *vt* : break (off) — *vi* : break up

ronce [rɔ̃s] *nf* : bramble

rond, ronde [rɔ̃, rɔ̃d] *adj* : round — **rond** *nm* **1** : circle, ring **2** : (round) slice **3** *Can* : burner (of a stove) — **ronde** *nf* : rounds *pl*, patrol

rondelet, -lette [rɔ̃dlɛ, -lɛt] *adj fam* : plump

rondelle [rɔ̃dɛl] *nf* **1** : washer **2** TRANCHE : slice **3** *Can* : (hockey) puck

rondeur [rɔ̃dœr] *nf* : roundness

rondin [rɔ̃dɛ̃] *nm* : log

rond-point [rɔ̃pwɛ̃] *nm, pl* **ronds-points** : traffic circle, rotary

ronfler [rɔ̃fle] *vi* : snore — **ronflement** [rɔ̃fləmã] *nm* : snore, snoring

ronger [rɔ̃ʒe] {17} *vt* **1** : gnaw, nibble **2** : eat away at — **se ronger** *vr* ~ **les ongles** : bite one's nails — **rongeur** [rɔ̃ʒœr] *nm* : rodent

ronronner [rɔ̃rɔne] *vi* **1** : purr **2** : hum (of an engine, etc.)

rosbif [rɔzbif] *nm* : roast beef

rose [roz] *nf* : rose — ~ *adj & nm* : rose, pink (color) — **rosé, -sée** [roze] *adj* : rosy, pinkish

roseau [rozo] *nm, pl* **-seaux** : reed

rosée [roze] *nf* : dew

rosier [rozje] *nm* : rosebush

rosser [rɔse] *vt* : beat, thrash

rossignol [rɔsiɲɔl] *nm* : nightingale

rotatif, -tive [rɔtatif, -tiv] *adj* : rotary — **rotation** [rɔtasjɔ̃] *nf* : rotation

roter [rote] *vi fam* : burp, belch

rôti [roti] *nm* : roast (meat)

rotin [rɔtɛ̃] *nm* : rattan

rôtir [rotir] *v* : roast — **rôtissoire** [rotiswar] *nf* : rotisserie

rotule [rɔtyl] *nf* : kneecap

rouage [rwaʒ] *nm* **1** : cogwheel **2** ～**s** *nmpl* : workings

roucouler [rukule] *vi* : coo

roue [ru] *nf* **1** : wheel **2 grande ～** : Ferris wheel

rouer [rwe] *vt* ～ **de coups** : thrash, beat

rouet [rwɛ] *nm* : spinning wheel

rouge [ruʒ] *adj* : red — ～ *n* **1** : red **2** ～ **à lèvres** : lipstick — **rougeâtre** [ruʒatr] *adj* : reddish — **rougeaud, -geaude** [ruʒo, -ʒod] *adj* : ruddy

rouge–gorge [ruʒgɔrʒ] *nm, pl* **rouges–gorges** : robin

rougeole [ruʒɔl] *nf* : measles

rougeoyer [ruʒwaje] {58} *vi* : turn red, glow

rougeur [ruʒœr] *nf* **1** : redness **2** ～**s** *nfpl* : red blotches (on skin)

rougir [ruʒir] *vt* : make red — *vi* **1** : redden, turn red **2** : blush (with shame, etc.)

rouille [ruj] *nf* : rust — **rouillé, -lée** [ruje] *adj* : rusty — **rouiller** [ruje] *v* : rust

rouler [rule] *vt* : roll (up) — *vi* **1** : roll **2** : go, run (of a car) **3** CONDUIRE : drive — **roulant, -lante** [rulɑ̃, -lɑ̃t] *adj* : on wheels — **rouleau** [rulo] *nm, pl* **-leaux 1** : roller **2** : roll (of paper) — **roulement** [rulmɑ̃] *nm* **1** : roll, rolling **2** : rumble (of thunder) **3** : turnover (in finance) **4** ～ **à billes** : ball bearing **5** ～ **de tambour** : drum roll

roulette [rulɛt] *nf* : roulette

roulotte [rulɔt] *nf Can* : trailer, camper

rouspéter [ruspete] {87} *vi fam* RONCHONNER : grumble — **rouspéteur, -teuse** [ruspetœr, -tøz] *n* : grouch

roussir [rusir] *vt* : scorch, singe

route [rut] *nf* **1** : road **2** : route, highway **3** CHEMIN : way, path **4 bonne ～ !** : have a good trip! **5 se mettre en ～** : set out, get going

routier, -tière [rutje, -tjɛr] *adj* : road — **routier** *nm* **1** : truck driver **2** : truck stop

routine [rutin] *nf* : routine — **routinier, -nière** [rutinje, -njɛr] *adj* : routine

roux, rousse [ru, rus] *adj* : russet, red — ～ *n* : redhead

royal, royale [rwajal] *adj, mpl* **royaux** [rwajo] : royal, regal — **royaume** [rwajom] *nm* : kingdom, realm — **royauté** [rwajote] *nf* : royalty

ruban [rybɑ̃] *nm* **1** : ribbon **2** ～ **adhésif** : adhesive tape

rubéole [rybeɔl] *nf* : German measles

rubis [rybi] *nms & pl* : ruby

rubrique [rybrik] *nf* **1** : column (in a newspaper) **2** : heading

ruche [ryʃ] *nf* : hive, beehive

rude [ryd] *adj* **1** : rough (of a surface, etc.) **2** PÉNIBLE : hard, tough **3** : severe, harsh (of winter) — **rudement** [rydmɑ̃] *adv* **1** : roughly, harshly **2** *fam* DRÔLEMENT : awfully, terribly

rudimentaire [rydimɑ̃tɛr] *adj* : rudimentary — **rudiments** [rydimɑ̃] *nmpl* : rudiments

rue [ry] *nf* : street

ruée [rɥe] *nf* : rush

ruelle [rɥɛl] *nf* : alley(way)

ruer [rɥe] *vi* : buck (of a horse) — **se ruer** *vr* **1** ～ **sur** : fling oneself at **2** ～ **vers** : rush toward

rugir [ryʒir] *vt* : bellow out — *vi* : roar — **rugissement** [ryʒismɑ̃] *nm* **1** : roar **2** : howling

ruine [rɥin] *nf* **1** : ruin **2 tomber en ～** : fall into ruin — **ruiner** [rɥine] *vt* **1** : ruin **2** DÉTRUIRE : wreck

ruisseau [rɥiso] *nm, pl* **-seaux** : stream, creek

ruisseler [rɥisle] {8} *vi* : stream, flood

rumeur [rymœr] *nf* : rumor

ruminer [rymine] *vt* : ponder — *vi* : brood

rupture [ryptyr] *nf* **1** : break, breaking **2** : breakup (of a relationship) **3** : breach (of contract)

rural, -rale [ryral] *adj, mpl* **-raux** [ryro] : rural

ruse [ryz] *nf* **1** : trick **2** : cunning — **rusé, -sée** [ryze] *adj* MALIN : cunning

russe [rys] *adj* : Russian — ～ *nm* : Russian (language)

rustique [rystik] *adj* : rustic

rythme [ritm] *nm* **1** : rhythm, beat **2** : rate, pace — **rythmique** [ritmik] *adj* : rhythmic, rhythmical

S

s [ɛs] *nm* : s, 19th letter of the alphabet

sa → son

sabbat [saba] *nm* : Sabbath

sable [sabl] *nm* 1 : sand 2 ~s mouvants : quicksand — sablé [sable] *nm* : shortbread (cookie) — sabler [sable] *vt* : sand — sablonneux, -neuse [sablɔnø, -nøz] *adj* : sandy

saborder [sabɔrde] *vt* : scuttle (a ship)

sabot [sabo] *nm* 1 : clog, wooden shoe 2 : hoof

saboter [sabɔte] *vt* 1 : sabotage 2 : botch up — sabotage [sabɔtaʒ] *nm* : sabotage — saboteur, -teuse [sabɔtœr, -tøz] *n* : saboteur

sabre [sabr] *nm* : saber

sac [sak] *nm* 1 : sack, bag 2 ~ à dos : backpack, knapsack 3 ~ à main : handbag, purse

saccade [sakad] *nf* : jerk, jolt — saccadé, -dée [sakade] *adj* : jerky

saccager [sakaʒe] {17} *vt* 1 : sack 2 DÉVASTER : devastate, wreck

sacerdoce [sasɛrdɔs] *nm* 1 : priesthood 2 : vocation

sachet [saʃɛ] *nm* 1 : packet, small bag 2 : sachet

sacoche [sakɔʃ] *nf* : bag, satchel

sacrer [sakre] *vt* 1 : crown 2 : consecrate — sacre [sakr] *nm* 1 : coronation 2 : consecration — sacré, -crée [sakre] *adj* 1 : sacred, holy 2 *fam* : damned, heck of a — sacrement [sakrəmã] *nm* : sacrament

sacrifier [sakrifje] {96} *vt* : sacrifice — *vi* ~ à : conform to — se sacrifier *vr* : sacrifice oneself — sacrifice [sakrifis] *nm* : sacrifice

sacrilège [sakrilɛʒ] *nm* : sacrilege — ~ *adj* : sacrilegious

sadique [sadik] *adj* : sadistic — sadisme [sadism] *nm* : sadism

safari [safari] *nm* : safari

sagace [sagas] *adj* : shrewd

sage [saʒ] *adj* 1 : wise 2 DOCILE : well-behaved — ~ *n* : wise person, sage — sage-femme [saʒfam] *nf, pl* sages–femmes : midwife — sagesse [saʒɛs] *nf* : wisdom

saigner [seɲe] *v* : bleed — saignant, -gnante [seɲã, -ɲãt] *adj* : rare, undercooked — saignement [seɲmã] *nm* : bleeding

saillir [sajir] {78} *vi* : project — saillant, -lante [sajã, -jãt] *adj* 1 : projecting 2 : salient — saillie [saji] *nf* 1 : projection 2 faire ~ : project

sain, saine [sɛ̃, sɛn] *adj* 1 : healthy, sound 2 : wholesome

saindoux [sɛ̃du] *nm* : lard

saint, sainte [sɛ̃, sɛ̃t] *adj* : holy — ~ *n* : saint

saisir [sezir] *vt* 1 : seize, grab 2 COMPRENDRE : grasp 3 IMPRESSIONNER : strike, impress 4 : enter (data) — se saisir *vr* ~ de : seize — saisie [sezi] *nf* : seizure (of property) — saisissant, -sante [sezisã, -sãt] *adj* : striking

saison [sɛzɔ̃] *nf* : season — saisonnier, -nière [sɛzɔnje, -njɛr] *adj* : seasonal

salade [salad] *nf* : salad — saladier [saladje] *nm* : salad bowl

salaire [salɛr] *nm* : salary, wages — salarié, -riée [salarje] *n* : salaried employee

salaud [salo] *nm usu vulgar* : bastard

sale [sal] *adj* : dirty — saleté [salte] *nf* 1 : dirt 2 : dirtiness 3 *fam* : dirty trick

saler [sale] *vt* : salt — salé, -lée [sale] *adj* 1 : salty 2 : salted 3 *fam* : steep — salière [saljɛr] *nf* : saltshaker

salir [salir] *vt* : soil — se salir *vr* : get dirty

salive [saliv] *nf* : saliva

salle [sal] *nf* 1 : room 2 : auditorium, hall 3 ~ à manger : dining room 4 ~ de bains : bathroom

salon [salɔ̃] *nm* 1 : living room 2 : (beauty) salon 3 EXPOSITION : exhibition, show

salopette [salɔpɛt] *nf* : overalls *pl*

salubre [salybr] *adj* : healthy

saluer [salɥe] *vt* 1 : greet 2 : say goodbye to 3 : salute — salut [saly] *nm* 1 : greeting 2 : salute 3 : safety 4 : salvation 5 ~! : hello!, good-bye! — salutation [salytasjɔ̃] *nf* : greeting

samedi [samdi] *nm* : Saturday

sanction [sãksjɔ̃] *nf* : sanction — sanctionner [sãksjɔne] *vt* 1 : sanction 2 : punish

sanctuaire [sãktɥɛr] *nm* : sanctuary

sandale [sãdal] *nf* : sandal

sandwich [sãdwitʃ] *nm, pl* -wiches *or* -wichs [-witʃ] : sandwich

sang [sã] *nm* : blood — sang–froid [sãfrwa] *nms & pl* 1 : composure, calm 2 de ~ : in cold blood — sanglant, -glante [sãglã, -glãt] *adj* 1 : bloody 2 : cruel

sangle [sãgl] *nf* : strap

sanglot [sãglo] *nm* : sob — sangloter [sãglɔte] *vi* : sob

sangsue [sãsy] *nf* : leech

sanguin, -guine [sãgɛ̃, -gin] *adj* 1 : blood 2 : sanguine

sanitaire [saniter] *adj* **1** : sanitary **2** : health — **~s** *nmpl* : bathroom

sans [sã] *adv & prep* **1** : without **2** **~ que** . without

santé [sãte] *nf* **1** : health **2 à votre ~ !** : to your health!, cheers!

saper [sape] *vt* MINER : undermine

sapeur–pompier [sapœrpɔ̃pje] *nm*, *pl* **sapeurs–pompiers** *France* : firefighter

saphir [safir] *nm* : sapphire

sapin [sapɛ̃] *nm* : fir

sarcastique [sarkastik] *adj* : sarcastic — **sarcasme** [sarkasm] *nm* : sarcasm

sarcler [sarkle] *vt* : weed

sardine [sardin] *nf* : sardine

satellite [satelit] *nm* : satellite

satin [satɛ̃] *nm* : satin

satire [satir] *nf* : satire — **satirique** [satirik] *adj* : satirical

satisfaire [satisfɛr] {42} *vt* : satisfy — *vi* **~ à** : satisfy — **se satisfaire** *vr* **~ de** : be content with — **satisfaction** [satisfaksjɔ̃] *nf* : satisfaction — **satisfaisant, -sante** [satisfəzã, -zãt] *adj* **1** : satisfactory **2** : satisfying — **satisfait, -faite** [satisfɛ, -fɛt] *adj* : satisfied

saturer [satyre] *vt* : saturate

Saturne [satyrn] *nf* : Saturn

sauce [sos] *nf* : sauce

saucisse [sosis] *nf* : sausage — **saucisson** [sosisɔ̃] *nm* : sausage, cold cut

sauf, sauve [sof, sov] *adj* : safe — **sauf** *prep* **1** : except (for), apart from **2** **~ si** : unless

sauge [soʒ] *nf* : sage (herb)

saugrenu, -nue [sogrəny] *adj* : preposterous

saule [sol] *nm* : willow

saumon [somɔ̃] *nm* : salmon

sauna [sona] *nm* : sauna

saupoudrer [sopudre] *vt* : sprinkle

saut [so] *nm* **1** : jump, leap **2 faire un ~ chez qqn** : drop in on s.o. — **sauter** [sote] *vt* **1** : jump over **2** OMETTRE : skip — *vi* **1** BONDIR : jump, leap **2** EXPLOSER : blow up — **sauterelle** [sotrɛl] *nf* : grasshopper — **sauteur, -teuse** [sotœr, -tøz] *n* : jumper — **sautiller** [sotije] *vi* : hop

sauvage [sovaʒ] *adj* **1** CRUEL : savage **2** : wild **3** FAROUCHE : shy — **~** *nmf* : savage — **sauvagerie** [sovaʒri] *nf* **1** : savagery **2** : unsociability

sauvegarde [sovgard] *nf* **1** : safeguard **2** : backup (of a computer file) — **sauvegarder** [sovgarde] *vt* **1** : safeguard **2** : save (a computer file)

sauver [sove] *vt* : save, rescue — **se sauver** *vr* **1** : escape **2** *fam* : leave, rush off — **sauve-qui-peut** [sovkipø] *nms & pl* : stampede, panic — **sauvetage** [sovtaʒ] *nm* : rescue — **sauveteur** [sovtœr] *nm* : rescuer, lifesaver — **sauvette** [sovɛt] **à la ~** *adv phr* : hastily — **sauveur** [sovœr] *nm* : savior

savant, -vante [savã, -vãt] *adj* : learned, scholarly — **~** *n* : scholar — **savant** *nm* : scientist

saveur [savœr] *nf* : flavor, savor

savoir [savwar] {79} *vt* **1** : know **2** : be able to, know how to — **~** *nm* **1** : learning, knowledge **2 à ~** : namely — **savoir–faire** [savwarfɛr] *nms & pl* : know-how, expertise

savon [savɔ̃] *nm* : soap — **savonner** [savɔne] *vt* : soap (up), lather — **savonnette** [savɔnɛt] *nf* : bar of soap — **savonneux, -neuse** [savɔnø, -nøz] *adj* : soapy

savourer [savure] *vt* : savor — **savoureux, -reuse** [savurø, -røz] *adj* : savory, tasty

saxophone [saksofɔn] *nm* : saxophone

scandale [skãdal] *nf* **1** : scandal **2** SCÈNE : scene, row — **scandaleux, -leuse** [skãdalø, -løz] *adj* : scandalous — **scandaliser** [skãdalize] *vt* : scandalize

scandinave [skãdinav] *adj* : Scandinavian

scarabée [skarabe] *nm* : beetle

scarlatine [skarlatin] *nf* : scarlet fever

sceau [so] *nm* **1** : seal **2** : hallmark, stamp

scélérat, -rate [selera, -rat] *n* : villain

sceller [sele] *vt* : seal — **scellé** [sele] *nm* : seal

scène [sɛn] *nf* **1** : scene **2** : stage (in theater) — **scénario** [senarjo] *nm* : scenario

sceptique [sɛptik] *adj* : skeptical — **~** *nmf* : skeptic

schéma [ʃema] *nm* : diagram — **schématique** [ʃematik] *adj* : schematic

schisme [ʃism] *nm* : schism

scie [si] *nf* : saw

sciemment [sjamã] *adv* : knowingly

science [sjãs] *nf* **1** : science **2** SAVOIR : learning, knowledge — **scientifique** [sjãtifik] *adj* : scientific — **~** *nmf* : scientist

scier [sje] {96} *vt* : saw — **scierie** [siri] *nf* : sawmill

scinder [sɛ̃de] *vt* : split, divide — **se scinder** *vr* : be divided, split up

scintiller [sɛ̃tije] *vi* : sparkle — **scintillement** [sɛ̃tijmã] *nm* : sparkling, twinkling

scission [sisjɔ̃] *nf* : split

scolaire [skɔlɛr] *adj* : school — **scolarité** [skɔlarite] *nf* : schooling

score [skɔr] *nm* : score

scotch [skɔtʃ] *nm* : Scotch whiskey

scrupule [skrypyl] *nm* : scruple — **scrupuleux, -leuse** [skrypylø, -løz] *adj* : scrupulous

scruter [skryte] *vt* : scrutinize — **scrutin** [skrytɛ̃] *nm* **1** : ballot **2** : polls *pl*

sculpter [skylte] *vt* : sculpt, sculpture — **sculpteur** [skyltœr] *nm* : sculptor — **sculpture** [skyltyr] *nf* : sculpture

se [sə] (**s'** *before a vowel or mute h*) *pron* **1**

: oneself, himself, herself, themselves, itself **2** : each other, one another

séance [seɑ̃s] *nf* **1** : session, meeting **2** : performance

seau [so] *nm, pl* **seaux** : bucket, pail

sec, sèche [sɛk, sɛʃ] *adj* **1** : dry **2** : dried (of fruit) **3** DUR : harsh, sharp — **sec** [sɛk] *adv* BRUSQUEMENT : abruptly, hard — ~ *nm* **1** : dryness **2** à ~ : dried up **3** à ~ *fam* : broke — **sèche–cheveux** [sɛʃʃəvø] *nms & pl* : hairdryer — **sécher** [seʃe] {87} *vt* **1** : dry **2** *France fam* : skip (a class, etc.) — *vi* : dry (up), dry out — **sécheresse** [seʃrɛs] *nf* **1** : drought **2** : dryness — **séchoir** [seʃwar] *nm* : dryer

second, -conde [səgɔ̃, -gɔ̃d] *adj & nmf* : second — **second** *nm* **1** : assistant, helper **2** : third floor — **secondaire** [səgɔ̃dɛr] *adj* : secondary — **seconde** [səgɔ̃d] *nf* : second — **seconder** [səgɔ̃de] *vt* : assist

secouer [səkwe] *vt* **1** : shake (one's head, etc.) **2** : shake off

secourir [səkurir] {23} *vt* **1** : help, aid **2** : rescue — **secouriste** [səkurist] *nmf* : first aid worker — **secours** [səkur] *nms & pl* **1** : help, aid **2** au ~! : help! **3** de ~ : (for) emergency **4** premiers ~ : first aid **5** secours *nmpl* : rescuers

secousse [səkus] *nf* **1** SACCADE : jolt, jerk **2** CHOC : shock **3** : tremor

secret, -crète [səkrɛ, -krɛt] *adj* : secret — **secret** *nm* **1** : secret **2** : secrecy

secrétaire [səkretɛr] *nmf* : secretary — **secrétariat** [səkretarjat] *nm* : secretary's office

sécréter [sekrete] {87} *vt* : secrete — **sécrétion** [-resjɔ̃] *nf* : secretion

secte [sɛkt] *nm* : sect

secteur [sɛktœr] *nm* : sector, area

section [sɛksjɔ̃] *nf* : section — **sectionner** [sɛksjɔne] *vt* **1** DIVISER : divide **2** : sever

séculaire [sekylɛr] *adj* : age-old

sécurité [sekyrite] *nf* **1** : security **2** : safety — **sécuriser** [sekyrize] *vt* : reassure

sédatif, -tive [sedatif, -tiv] *adj* : sedative — **sédatif** *nm* : sedative

sédentaire [sedɑ̃tɛr] *adj* : sedentary

sédiment [sedimɑ̃] *nm* : sediment

séduire [sedɥir] {49} *vt* **1** : seduce **2** : charm **3** : appeal to — **séducteur, -trice** [sedyktœr, -tris] *adj* : seductive — ~ *n* : seducer — **séduction** [sedyksjɔ̃] *nf* **1** : seduction **2** : charm, appeal — **séduisant, -sante** [sedɥizɑ̃, -zɑ̃t] *adj* : seductive, attractive

segment [sɛgmɑ̃] *nm* : segment

ségrégation [segregasjɔ̃] *nf* : segregation

seigle [sɛgl] *nm* : rye

seigneur [sɛɲœr] *nm* **1** : lord **2** le Seigneur : the Lord

sein [sɛ̃] *nm* **1** : breast, bosom **2** au ~ de : within

séisme [seism] *nm* : earthquake

seize [sɛz] *adj* **1** : sixteen **2** : sixteenth (in dates) — ~ *nms & pl* : sixteen — **seizième** [sɛzjɛm] *adj & nmf & nm* : sixteenth

séjour [seʒur] *nm* : stay — **séjourner** [seʒurne] *vi* : stay (at a hotel, etc.)

sel [sɛl] *nm* : salt

sélection [selɛksjɔ̃] *nf* : selection — **sélectionner** [selɛksjɔne] *vt* : select, choose

selle [sɛl] *nf* : saddle

sellette [selɛt] *nf* être sur la ~ : be in the hot seat

selon [səlɔ̃] *prep* **1** : according to **2** ~ que : depending on whether

semaine [səmɛn] *nf* : week

sémantique [semɑ̃tik] *adj* : semantic — ~ *nf* : semantics

sembler [sɑ̃ble] *vi* : seem — *v impers* il semble que : it seems that — **semblable** [sɑ̃blabl] *adj* **1** : similar, like **2** TEL : such — ~ *nmf* : fellow creature — **semblant** [sɑ̃blɑ̃] *nm* **1** : semblance, appearance **2** faire ~ : pretend

semelle [səmɛl] *nf* : sole

semer [səme] {52} *vt* **1** : sow, seed **2** RÉPANDRE : scatter — **semence** [səmɑ̃s] *nf* : seed

semestre [səmɛstr] *nm* : semester — **semestriel, -trielle** [səmɛstrijɛl] *adj* : semiannual

séminaire [seminɛr] *nm* **1** : seminary **2** : seminar

semi–remorque [səmirəmɔrk] *nm, pl* **semi–remorques** : semitrailer

semis [səmi] *nm* **1** : seedling **2** : seedbed

semonce [səmɔ̃s] *nf* RÉPRIMANDE : reprimand

semoule [səmul] *nf* : semolina

sénat [sena] *nm* : senate — **sénateur** [senatœr] *nm* : senator

sénile [senil] *adj* : senile — **sénilité** [senilite] *nf* : senility

sens [sɑ̃s] *nms & pl* **1** : sense **2** SIGNIFICATION : meaning **3** DIRECTION : direction, way **4** à mon ~ : in my opinion **5** ~ dessus dessous : upside down

sensation [sɑ̃sasjɔ̃] *nf* : sensation — **sensationnel, -nelle** [sɑ̃sasjɔnɛl] *adj* : sensational

sensé, -sée [sɑ̃se] *adj* : sensible

sensibiliser [sɑ̃sibilize] *vt* ~ à : make sensitive to — **sensibilité** [sɑ̃sibilite] *nf* : sensitivity — **sensible** [sɑ̃sibl] *adj* **1** : sensitive **2** APPRÉCIABLE : noticeable — **sensiblement** [sɑ̃sibləmɑ̃] *adv* **1** : noticeably **2** : approximately

sensoriel, -rielle [sɑ̃sɔrjɛl] *adj* : sensory

sensuel, -suelle [sɑ̃sɥɛl] *adj* : sensual, sensuous — **sensualité** [sɑ̃sɥalite] *nf* : sensuality

sentence [sãtãs] *nf* JUGEMENT : sentence

senteur [sãtœr] *nf* : scent

sentier [sãtje] *nm* : path

sentiment [sãtimã] *nm* **1** : sentiment, feeling **2** recevez l'expression de mes **~s** respectueux : yours truly — **sentimental, -tale** [sãtimãtal] *adj, mpl* **-taux** [-to] : sentimental — **sentimentalité** [-talite] *nf* : sentimentality

sentinelle [sãtinɛl] *nf* : sentinel

sentir [sãtir] {82} *vt* **1** : smell, taste **2** : feel **3** : appreciate **4** PRESSENTIR : sense — *vi* : smell — **se sentir** *vr* : feel (tired, sick, etc.)

seoir [swar] {80} *vi* — **à** : suit

séparer [separe] *vt* **1** DÉTACHER : separate **2** : divide — **se séparer** *vr* **1** : separate **2** **~ de** : part with, be without — **séparation** [separasjɔ̃] *nf* : separation — **séparé, -rée** [separe] *adj* **1** : separate **2** : separated — **séparément** [separemã] *adv* : separately

sept [sɛt] *adj* **1** : seven **2** : seventh (in dates) — **~** *nms & pl* : seven

septante [sɛptãt] *adj Bel, Switz* **1** : seventy **2** : seventieth — **~** *nms & pl Bel, Switz* : seventy

septembre [sɛptãbr] *nm* : September

septième [sɛtjɛm] *adj & nmf & nm* : seventh

sépulture [sepyltyr] *nf* TOMBE : grave

séquelle [sekɛl] *nf* **1** : consequence **2 ~s** *nfpl* : aftereffects

séquence [sekãs] *nf* : sequence

séquestrer [sekɛstre] *nm* : confine, sequester

serein, -reine [sərɛ̃, -rɛn] *adj* CALME : serene, calm — **sérénité** [serenite] *nf* : serenity

sergent [sɛrʒã] *nm* : sergeant

série [seri] *nf* **1** : series **2** : set **3 de ~** : mass-produced, standard **4** fabrication en **~** : mass production

sérieux, -rieuse [serjø, -rjøz] *adj* : serious — **sérieux** *nm* **1** : seriousness **2** prendre au **~** : take seriously — **sérieusement** [serjøzmã] *adv* : seriously

serin [sərɛ̃] *nm* : canary

seringue [sərɛ̃g] *nf* : syringe

serment [sɛrmã] *nm* **1** : oath **2** : vow, promise

sermon [sɛrmɔ̃] *nm* : sermon

serpent [sɛrpã] *nm* **1** : snake **2 ~ à son-nettes** : rattlesnake — **serpenter** [sɛrpãte] *vi* : meander — **serpentin** [sɛrpãtɛ̃] *nm* : streamer

serre [sɛr] *nf* **1** : greenhouse, hothouse **2 ~s** *nfpl* : claws

serré, -rée [sere] *adj* **1** : tight **2** : crowded, cramped, dense

serrer [sere] *vt* **1** : squeeze, grip **2** : clench (one's fists, etc.) **3** : tighten (a knot, etc.) **4** : stay close to **5** : push closer together — **se**

serrer *vr* **1** : huddle up **2** : tighten (up) **3** **~ la main** : shake hands

serrure [sɛryr] *nf* : lock — **serrurier** [sɛryrje] *nm* : locksmith

sérum [serɔm] *nm* : scrum

serveur, -veuse [sɛrvœr, -vøz] *n* : waiter *m*, waitress *f* — **serveur** *nm* : (computer) server

serviable [sɛrvjabl] *adj* : helpful, obliging

service [sɛrvis] *nm* **1** : service **2** FAVEUR : favor **3** : serving, course **4** : department **5** : (coffee) set **6** : serve (in sports) **7 hors ~** : out of order

serviette [sɛrvjɛt] *nf* **1** : napkin **2** : towel **3** : briefcase **4 ~ hygiénique** : sanitary napkin

servir [sɛrvir] {81} *vt* **1** : serve **2** : wait on, attend to — *vi* **1** : be useful, serve **2 ~ de** : serve as — **se servir** *vr* **1** : serve oneself, help oneself **2 ~ de** : make use of

serviteur [sɛrvitœr] *nm* : servant

ses → **son**

session [sesjɔ̃] *nf* : session

seuil [sœj] *nm* : threshold

seul, seule [sœl] *adj* **1** : alone **2** : lonely **3** UNIQUE : only, sole — **~** *pron* : only one, single one — **seulement** [sœlmã] *adv* **1** : only **2** MÊME : even — **~** *conj* : but, only

sève [sɛv] *nf* : sap

sévère [sevɛr] *adj* : severe — **sévérité** [severite] *nf* : severity

sévir [sevir] *vi* **1** : rage **2 ~ contre** : punish

sevrer [səvre] *vt* : wean

sexe [sɛks] *nm* **1** : sex **2** : sex organs, genitals — **sexisme** [sɛksism] *nm* : sexism — **sexiste** [sɛksist] *adj & nmf* : sexist — **sexualité** [sɛksɥalite] *nf* : sexuality — **sexuel, sexuelle** [sɛksɥɛl] *adj* : sexual

seyant, seyante [sɛjã, -jãt] *adj* : becoming, flattering

shampooing [ʃãpwɛ̃] *nm* : shampoo

shérif [ʃerif] *nm* : sheriff

short [ʃɔrt] *nm* : shorts *pl*

si¹ [si] *adv* **1** TELLEMENT : so, such, as **2** : yes **3 ~ bien que** : with the result that, so

si² *conj* : if, whether

sida [sida] *nm* : AIDS

sidérer [sidere] {87} *vt fam* : stagger, amaze

sidérurgie [sideryrʒi] *nf* : steel industry

siècle [sjɛkl] *nm* : century

siège [sjɛʒ] *nm* **1** : seat **2** : siege **3** *or* **~ social** : headquarters — **siéger** [sjeʒe] {64} *vi* **1** : sit (in an assembly) **2** : have its headquarters

sien, sienne [sjɛ̃, sjɛn] *adj* : his, hers, its, one's — **~** *pron* **le sien, la sienne, les siens, les siennes** : his, hers, its, one's, theirs

sieste [sjɛst] *nf* : siesta, nap

siffler [sifle] *vt* **1** : whistle **2** : whistle for, whistle at **3** : boo — *vi* **1** : whistle **2** : hiss **3** : wheeze — **sifflement** [sifləmã] *nm* : whistling — **sifflet** [siflɛ] *nm* **1** : whistle **2** ~s *nmpl* : boos — **siffloter** [siflɔte] *v* : whistle

sigle [sigl] *nm* : acronym

signaler [siɲale] *vt* **1** : signal **2** : point out — **se signaler** *vr* : distinguish oneself — **signal** [siɲal] *nm, pl* **-gnaux** [-ɲo] : signal — **signalement** [siɲalmã] *nm* : description — **signalisation** [siɲalizasjɔ̃] *nf* : signals *pl*, signs *pl*

signature [siɲatyr] *nf* **1** : signature **2** : signing

signe [siɲ] *nm* **1** : sign **2** : (punctuation) mark — **signer** [siɲe] *vt* : sign — **se signer** *vr* : cross oneself

signifier [siɲifje] {96} *vt* : signify, mean — **significatif, -tive** [siɲifikatif, -tiv] *adj* : significant — **signification** [siɲifikasjɔ̃] *nf* : significance, meaning

silence [silãs] *nm* **1** : silence **2** : rest (in music) — **silencieux, -cieuse** [silãsjø, -sjøz] *adj* : silent, quiet — **silencieux** *nm* : muffler

silex [silɛks] *nm* : flint

silhouette [silwɛt] *nf* : silhouette, outline

silicium [silisjɔm] *nm* : silicon

sillage [sijaʒ] *nm* : wake (of a ship)

sillon [sijɔ̃] *nm* **1** : furrow **2** : groove (of a disc, etc.) — **sillonner** [sijɔne] *vt* **1** CREUSER : furrow **2** : crisscross

silo [silo] *nm* : silo

simagrée [simagre] *nf* **faire des** ~**s** : put on airs

similaire [similɛr] *adj* : similar — **similitude** [similityd] *nf* : similarity

simple [sɛ̃pl] *adj* **1** : simple **2** : mere **3** **aller** ~ : one-way ticket — ~ *nm* : singles (in tennis) — **simplement** [sɛ̃pləmã] *adv* : simply — **simplicité** [sɛ̃plisite] *nf* : simplicity — **simplifier** [sɛ̃plifje] {96} *vt* : simplify

simulacre [simylakr] *nm* : sham, pretense

simuler [simyle] *vt* : simulate — **simulation** [simylasjɔ̃] *nf* : simulation

simultané, -née [simyltane] *adj* : simultaneous

sincère [sɛ̃sɛr] *adj* : sincere — **sincèrement** [-sɛrmã] *adv* : sincerely — **sincérité** [sɛ̃serite] *nf* : sincerity

singe [sɛ̃ʒ] *nm* : monkey — **singer** [sɛ̃ʒe] {17} *vt* **1** IMITER : mimic **2** FEINDRE : feign — **singeries** [sɛ̃ʒri] *nfpl* : antics

singulariser [sɛ̃gylarize] *vt* : draw attention to — **se singulariser** *vr* : call attention to oneself

singularité [sɛ̃gylarite] *nf* : peculiarity

singulier, -lière [sɛ̃gylje, -ljɛr] *adj* : singular — **singulier** *nm* : singular (in grammar) —

singulièrement [sɛ̃gyljɛrmã] *nm* **1** : strangely **2** NOTAMMENT : particularly

sinistre [sinistr] *adj* : sinister — ~ *nm* DÉSASTRE : disaster — **sinistré, -trée** [sinistre] *adj* : damaged, stricken — ~ *n* : disaster victim

sinon [sinɔ̃] *conj* **1** : or else **2** : if not **3** ~ **que** : except that

sinueux, -nueuse [sinɥø, -nɥøz] *adj* : winding, meandering

siphon [sifɔ̃] *nm* : siphon

sirène [sirɛn] *nf* **1** : mermaid **2** : siren, alarm

sirop [siro] *nm* : syrup

siroter [sirɔte] *vt fam* : sip

sis, sise [si, siz] *adj* : located (in law)

site [sit] *nm* **1** : site **2** : setting

sitôt [sito] *adv* **1** : as soon as **2** ~ **après** : immediately after

situer [sitɥe] *vt* : situate, locate — **situation** [sitɥasjɔ̃] *nf* **1** : situation **2** ~ **de famille** : marital status

six [sis, *before consonant* si, *before vowel* siz] *adj* **1** : six **2** : sixth (in dates) — ~ *nms & pl* : six — **sixième** [sizjɛm] *adj & nmf & nm* : sixth

ski [ski] *nm* **1** : ski **2** : skiing **3** ~ **nautique** : waterskiing — **skier** [skje] {96} *vi* : ski — **skieur, skieuse** [skjœr, skjøz] *n* : skier

slip [slip] *nm* **1** : briefs *pl* **2** : panties *pl*

smoking [smɔkiŋ] *nm* : tuxedo

snob [snɔb] *adj* : snobbish — ~ *nmf* : snob — **snober** [snɔbe] *vt* : snub — **snobisme** [snɔbism] *nm* : snobbery

sobre [sɔbr] *adj* : sober — **sobriété** [sɔbrijete] *nf* : sobriety

soccer [sɔkɛr] *nm Can* : soccer

sociable [sɔsjabl] *adj* : sociable

social, -ciale [sɔsjal] *adj, mpl* **-ciaux** [-sjo] : social — **socialisme** [sɔsjalism] *nm* : socialism — **socialiste** [-sjalist] *adj & nmf* : socialist — **société** [sɔsjete] *nf* **1** : society **2** COMPAGNIE : company, firm

sociologie [sɔsjɔlɔʒi] *nf* : sociology — **sociologique** [sɔsjɔlɔʒik] *adj* : sociological — **sociologue** [sɔsjɔlɔg] *nmf* : sociologist

socle [sɔkl] *nm* : base, pedestal

soda [sɔda] *nm* : soda, soft drink

sodium [sɔdjɔm] *nm* : sodium

sœur [sœr] *nf* **1** : sister **2** : nun

sofa [sɔfa] *nm* : sofa

soi [swa] *pron* : oneself, himself, herself, itself — **soi–disant** [swadizã] *adv* : supposedly — ~ *adj* : so-called

soie [swa] *nf* **1** : silk **2** : bristle

soif [swaf] *nf* **1** : thirst **2** **avoir** ~ : be thirsty

soigner [swaɲe] *vt* **1** : treat, nurse, look after **2** : do with care — **se soigner** *vr* : take care of oneself — **soigné, -gnée** [swaɲe] *adj* **1** : carefully done **2** : neat — **soigneux, -gneuse** [swaɲø, -ɲøz] *adj* **1** : careful **2** : neat, tidy

soi–même [swamɛm] *pron* : oneself

soin [swɛ̃] *nm* **1** : care **2** ~**s** *nmpl* : care **3 premiers** ~**s** : first aid **4 prendre** ~ **de** : take care of

soir [swar] *nm* : evening, night — **soirée** [sware] *nf* **1** : evening **2** FÊTE : party

soit [swa] *adv* : so be it, very well — ~ *conj* **1** : that is, in other words **2 soit . . . soit . . .** : either . . . or . . .

soixante [swasãt] *adj & nms & pl* : sixty — **soixante–dix** [swasãtdis] *adj & nms & pl* : seventy — **soixante–dixième** [swasãtdizjɛm] *adj & nmf & nm* : seventieth — **soixantième** [swasãtjɛm] *adj & nmf & nm* : sixtieth

soja [sɔʒa] *nm* : soybean

sol [sɔl] *nm* **1** : ground, floor **2** PLANCHER : flooring **3** TERRE : soil

solaire [sɔlɛr] *adj* **1** : solar **2** : sun

soldat [sɔlda] *nm* : soldier

solde[1] [sɔld] *nf* : pay

solde[2] *nm* **1** : balance (in finance) **2** *or* ~**s** *nmpl* : sale — **solder** [sɔlde] *vt* **1** : settle (an account, etc.) **2** : sell off, put on sale — **se solder** *vr* ~ **par** : end in

sole [sɔl] *nf* : sole (fish)

soleil [sɔlɛj] *nm* **1** : sun **2** : sunshine, sunlight

solennel, -nelle [sɔlanɛl] *adj* **1** : solemn **2** : formal — **solennité** [sɔlanite] *nf* : solemnity

solidaire [sɔlidɛr] *adj* **1** : united **2** : interdependent — **solidarité** [sɔlidarite] *nf* : solidarity

solide [sɔlid] *adj* : solid — ~ *nm* : solid — **solidement** [sɔlidmã] *adv* : solidly — **solidifier** [sɔlidifje] {96} *v* **se solidifier** *vr* : solidify — **solidité** [sɔlidite] *nf* : solidity

solitaire [sɔlitɛr] *adj* : solitary — ~ *nmf* **1** : loner, recluse — ~ *nm* : solitaire — **solitude** [sɔlityd] *nf* **1** : solitude **2** : loneliness

solliciter [sɔlisite] *vt* **1** : solicit, seek **2** : appeal to, approach — **sollicitude** [sɔlisityd] *nf* : solicitude, concern

solo [sɔlo] *nm, pl* **solos** *or* **soli** : solo

soluble [sɔlybl] *adj* : soluble — **solution** [sɔlysjɔ̃] *nf* : solution

solvable [sɔlvabl] *adj* : solvent

sombre [sɔ̃br] *adj* **1** OBSCUR : dark **2** TRISTE : gloomy

sombrer [sɔ̃bre] *vi* COULER : sink

sommaire [sɔmɛr] *adj* **1** : brief, concise **2** : summary — ~ *nm* : summary

somme[1] [sɔm] *nf* **1** : sum **2 en** ~ : in short, all in all

somme[2] *nm* : short nap, catnap

sommeil [sɔmɛj] *nm* : sleep — **sommeiller** [sɔmɛje] *vi* **1** : doze **2** : lie dormant

sommer [sɔme] *vt* : summon

sommet [sɔmɛ] *nm* : summit, top

sommier [sɔmje] *nm* : base (of a bed), bed springs *pl*

somnambule [sɔmnãbyl] *nmf* : sleepwalker

somnifère [sɔmnifɛr] *nm* : sleeping pill

somnolence [sɔmnɔlãs] *nf* : drowsiness — **somnolent, -lente** [sɔmnɔlã, -lãt] *adj* : drowsy — **somnoler** [sɔmnɔle] *vi* : doze

somptueux, -tueuse [sɔ̃ptɥø, -tɥøz] *adj* : sumptuous

son[1], **sa** [sɔ̃, sa] *adj, pl* **ses** [se] : his, her, its, one's

son[2] *nm* **1** : sound **2** : volume **3** : (wheat) bran

sonde [sɔ̃d] *nf* **1** : probe **2** : sounding line — **sondage** [sɔ̃daʒ] *nm* : poll, survey — **sonder** [sɔ̃de] *vt* **1** : survey, poll **2** : sound, probe

songe [sɔ̃ʒ] *nm* : dream — **songer** [sɔ̃ʒe] {17} *vt* : consider, imagine — *vi* **1** : dream **2** ~ **à** : think about — **songeur, -geuse** [sɔ̃ʒœr, -ʒøz] *adj* : pensive

sonner [sɔne] *v* **1** : strike, sound — **sonnant, -nante** [sɔnã, -nãt] *adj* **à cinq heures sonnantes** : at five o'clock sharp — **sonné, -née** [sɔne] *adj* **1** *fam* : groggy **2** *fam* : crazy, nuts **3 il est minuit sonné** : it's past midnight — **sonnerie** [sɔnri] *nf* **1** : ringing, ring **2** : alarm (bell)

sonnet [sɔnɛ] *nm* : sonnet

sonnette [sɔnɛt] *nf* : bell, doorbell

sonore [sɔnɔr] *adj* **1** : resonant **2** : sound — **sonorisation** [sɔnɔrizasjɔ̃] *nf* : sound system — **sonorité** [sɔnɔrite] *nf* **1** : tone **2** : resonance, acoustics

sophistiqué, -quée [sɔfistike] *adj* : sophisticated

soporifique [sɔpɔrifik] *adj* : soporific

soprano [sɔprano] *nmf* : soprano

sorbet [sɔrbɛ] *nm* : sorbet

sorcier, -cière [sɔrsje, -sjɛr] *n* : sorcerer, witch — **sorcellerie** [sɔrsɛlri] *nf* : sorcery, witchcraft

sordide [sɔrdid] *adj* **1** : sordid **2** : squalid

sornettes [sɔrnɛt] *nfpl* : nonsense

sort [sɔr] *nm* **1** : fate, lot **2** : spell, hex

sortant, -tante [sɔrtã, -tãt] *adj* : outgoing, resigning

sorte [sɔrt] *nf* **1** ESPÈCE : sort, kind **2 de** ~ **que** : so that **3 en quelque** ~ : in a way

sortie [sɔrti] *nf* **1** : exit **2** DÉPART : departure **3** : launch, release (of a book, etc.) **4** EXCURSION : outing

sortilège [sɔrtilɛʒ] *nm* : spell

sortir [sɔrtir] {82} *vt* **1** : take out, bring out **2** : launch, release — *vi* **1** : go out, come out **2** PARTIR : leave, exit **3** ~ **de** : come from, come out of — **se sortir** *vr* **1** ~ **de** : get out of **2 s'en sortir** : get by, pull through

sosie [sɔzi] *nm* : double

sot, sotte [so, sɔt] *adj* : foolish, silly — ~ ⟨illegible⟩ ⟨illegible⟩ **sottise** [sɔtiz] *nf* **1** : foolishness **2** : foolish act or remark

sou [su] *nm* **être sans le** ~ : be penniless

soubresaut [subrəso] *nm* : jolt, start

souche [suʃ] *nf* **1** : stump (of a tree) **2** : stock, descent

soucier [susje] {96} *v* **se soucier** *vr* : worry, be concerned — **souci** [susi] *nm* : worry, concern — **soucieux, -cieuse** [susjø, -sjøz] *adj* : anxious, concerned

soucoupe [sukup] *nf* **1** : saucer **2** ~ **volante** : flying saucer

soudain, -daine [sudɛ̃, -dɛn] *adj* : sudden — **soudainement** [-dɛnmɑ̃] *adv* : suddenly

soude [sud] *nf* : soda

souder [sude] *vt* : weld, solder

soudoyer [sudwaje] {58} *vt* : bribe

soudure [sudyr] *nf* **1** : solder **2** : soldering

souffler [sufle] *vt* **1** : blow **2** ÉTEINDRE : blow out **3** CHUCHOTER : whisper — *vi* **1** : blow **HALETER** : pant, puff — **souffle** [sufl] *nm* **1** : breath, breathing **2** : puff, gust — **soufflé** [sufle] *nm* : soufflé — **soufflet** [suflɛ] *nm* : bellows

souffrir [sufrir] {83} *vt* **1** SUPPORTER : tolerate **2** PERMETTRE : allow — *vi* : suffer — **souffrance** [sufrɑ̃s] *nf* **1** : suffering **2** en ~ : pending — **souffrant, -frante** [sufrɑ̃, -frɑ̃t] *adj* : unwell

soufre [sufr] *nm* : sulfur

souhait [swɛ] *nm* **1** : wish **2** à vos ~s! : bless you! — **souhaitable** [swɛtabl] *adj* : desirable — **souhaiter** [swete] *vt* : wish, hope for

souiller [suje] *vt* : soil

soûl, soûle [su, sul] *adj* : drunk

soulager [sulaʒe] {17} *vt* : relieve — **soulagement** [sulaʒmɑ̃] *nm* : relief

soûler [sule] *vt* : make drunk, intoxicate — **se soûler** *vr* : get drunk

soulever [sulve] {52} *vt* **1** : lift, raise **2** PROVOQUER : stir up — **se soulever** *vr* **1** : rise up **2** : lift oneself up — **soulèvement** [sulɛvmɑ̃] *nm* : uprising

soulier [sulje] *nm* : shoe

souligner [suliɲe] *vt* **1** : underline **2** : emphasize

soumettre [sumɛtr] {53} *vt* **1** : subjugate **2** PRÉSENTER : submit **3** ~ **à** : subject to — **se soumettre** *vr* : submit — **soumis, -mise** [sumi, -miz] *adj* : submissive — **soumission** [sumisjɔ̃] *nf* : submission

soupape [supap] *nf* : valve

soupçon [supsɔ̃] *nm* **1** : suspicion **2** : hint, touch — **soupçonner** [supsɔne] *vt* : suspect

— **soupçonneux, -neuse** [supsɔnø, -nøz] *adj* : suspicious

soupe [sup] *nf* : soup

souper [supe] *vi Can* : have supper — *nm Can* : supper

soupeser [supəze] {52} *vt* **1** : feel the weight of **2** PESER : weigh, consider

soupière [supjɛr] *nf* : tureen

soupirer [supire] *vi* : sigh — **soupir** [supir] *nm* : sigh

souple [supl] *adj* : supple, flexible — **souplesse** [suplɛs] *nf* : suppleness, flexibility

source [surs] *nf* **1** : source **2** : spring (of water)

sourcil [sursi] *nm* : eyebrow — **sourciller** [sursije] *vi* **sans** ~ : without batting an eyelid — **sourcilleux, -leuse** [sursijø, -jøz] *adj* **1** : finicky **2** : supercilious

sourd, sourde [sur, surd] *adj* : deaf — ~ *nmf* : deaf person — **sourd–muet, sourde–muette** [surmɥɛ, surdmɥɛt] *n* : deaf-mute

sourdre [surdr] {84} *vi* MONTER : well up

sourire [surir] {76} *vi* : smile — ~ *nm* : smile — **souriant, -riante** [surjɑ̃, -rjɑ̃t] *adj* : smiling, cheerful

souris [suri] *nf* : mouse

sournois, -noise [surnwa, -nwaz] *adj* : sly, underhanded

sous [su] *prep* **1** : under, beneath **2** : during **3** ~ **peu** : shortly

sous–alimenté, -tée [suzalimɑ̃te] *adj* : malnourished

sous–bois [subwa] *nms & pl* : undergrowth

souscrire [suskrir] {33} *vi* ~ **à** : subscribe to — **souscription** [suskripsjɔ̃] *nf* : subscription

sous–développé, -pée [sudevlɔpe] *adj* : underdeveloped

sous–entendre [suzɑ̃tɑ̃dr] {63} *vt* : imply, infer — **sous–entendu** [suzɑ̃tɑ̃dy] *nm* : insinuation

sous–estimer [suzɛstime] *vt* : underestimate

sous–jacent, -cente [suʒasɑ̃, -sɑ̃t] *adj* : underlying

sous–louer [sulwe] *vt* : sublet

sous–marin, -rine [sumarɛ̃, -rin] *adj* : underwater — **sous–marin** *nm* : submarine

sous–officier [suzɔfisje] *nm* : noncommissioned officer

sous–produit [suprɔdɥi] *nm* : by-product

sous–sol [susɔl] *nm* : basement, cellar

sous–titre [sutitr] *nm* : subtitle

soustraire [sustrɛr] {40} *vt* **1** : subtract **2** : remove, take away — **se soustraire** *vr* ~ **à** : escape from — **soustraction** [sustraksjɔ̃] *nf* : subtraction

sous–vêtement [suvɛtmɑ̃] *nm* **1** : undergarment **2** ~s *nmpl* : underwear

soutane [sutan] *nf* : cassock

soute [sut] *nf* : hold (of a ship)
soutenir [sutnir] {92} *vt* **1** MAINTENIR : support, hold up **2** RÉSISTER : withstand **3** : sustain — **soutenu, -nue** [sutny] *adj* **1** : formal **2** : sustained
souterrain, -raine [suterɛ̃, -rɛn] *adj* : underground — **souterrain** *nm* : underground passage
soutien [sutjɛ̃] *nm* : support
soutien–gorge [sutjɛ̃gɔrʒ] *nm, pl* **soutiens–gorge** : bra, brassiere
soutirer [sutire] *vt* ∼ **à** : extract from
souvenir [suvnir] {92} *v* **se souvenir** *vr* **1** ∼ **de** : remember **2** ∼ **que** : remember that — ∼ *nm* **1** : memory **2** : souvenir **3** **mes meilleurs** ∼**s à** : my best regards to
souvent [suvɑ̃] *adv* : often
souverain, -raine [suvrɛ̃, -rɛn] *adj* **1** : supreme **2** : sovereign — ∼ *n* : sovereign — **souveraineté** [suvrɛnte] *nf* : sovereignty
soviétique [sɔvjetik] *adj* : Soviet
soyeux, soyeuse [swajø, swajøz] *adj* : silky
spacieux, -cieuse [spasjø, -sjøz] *adj* : spacious
spaghetti [spagɛti] *nmpl* : spaghetti
sparadrap [sparadra] *nm* : adhesive tape
spasme [spasm] *nm* : spasm
spatial, -tiale [spasjal] *adj, mpl* **-tiaux 1** : spatial **2 vaisseau spatial** : spaceship
speaker, -kerine [spikœr, -krin] *n France* : announcer (on radio, TV, etc.)
spécial, -ciale [spesjal] *adj, mpl* **-ciaux** [-sjo] **1** : special **2** BIZARRE : odd, peculiar — **spécialement** [spesjalmɑ̃] *adv* **1** EXPRÈS : specially **2** : especially — **spécialiser** [spesjalize] *v* **se spécialiser** *vr* : specialize — **spécialiste** [spesjalist] *nmf* : specialist — **spécialité** [spesjalite] *nf* : specialty
spécifier [spesifje] {96} *vt* : specify — **spécifique** [spesifik] *adj* : specific
spécimen [spesimɛn] *nm* : specimen
spectacle [spɛktakl] *nm* **1** : spectacle, sight **2** : show — **spectaculaire** [spɛktakylɛr] *adj* : spectacular — **spectateur, -trice** [spɛktatœr, -tris] *n* **1** : spectator **2** : observer, onlooker
spectre [spɛktr] *nm* **1** : specter, ghost **2** : spectrum
spéculer [spekyle] *vi* : speculate — **spéculation** [spekylasjɔ̃] *nf* : speculation
sperme [spɛrm] *nm* : sperm
sphère [sfɛr] *nf* : sphere — **sphérique** [sferik] *adj* : spherical
spirale [spiral] *nf* : spiral
spirituel, -tuelle [spiritɥɛl] *adj* : spiritual — **spiritualité** [spiritɥalite] *nf* : spirituality
splendeur [splɑ̃dœr] *nf* : splendor — **splendide** [splɑ̃did] *adj* : splendid
spongieux, -gieuse [spɔ̃ʒjø, -ʒjøz] *adj* : spongy

spontané, -née [spɔ̃tane] *adj* : spontaneous — **spontanéité** [spɔ̃taneite] *nf* : spontaneity — **spontanément** [-nemɑ̃] *adv* : spontaneously
sporadique [spɔradik] *adj* : sporadic
sport [spɔr] *adj* : sport, sports — ∼ *nm* **1** : sport **2** ∼**s d'équipes** : team sports — **sportif, -tive** [spɔrtif, -tiv] *adj* **1** : sport, sports **2** : sportsmanlike **3** : athletic — ∼ *n* : sportsman *m*, sportswoman *f*
spot [spɔt] *nm* **1** : spotlight **2** PUBLICITÉ : commercial
sprint [sprint] *nm* : sprint
square [skwar] *nm France* : small public garden
squelette [skəlɛt] *nm* : skeleton
stabiliser [stabilize] *vt* : stabilize — **stabilité** [stabilite] *nf* : stability — **stable** [stabl] *adj* : stable, steady
stade [stad] *nm* **1** : stadium **2** ÉTAPE : stage, phase
stage [staʒ] *nm* **1** : internship **2** : (training) course — **stagiaire** [staʒjɛr] *nmf* : trainee, intern
stagner [stagne] *vi* : stagnate — **stagnant, -gnante** [stagnɑ̃, -gnɑ̃t] *adj* : stagnant
stalle [stal] *nf* : stall
stand [stɑ̃d] *nm* **1** : stand, stall, booth **2** ∼ **de tir** : shooting range
standard [stɑ̃dar] *adj* : standard — ∼ *nm* **1** : standard **2** : (telephone) switchboard — **standardiste** [stɑ̃dardist] *nmf* : switchboard operator
standing [stɑ̃diŋ] *nm* : standing, status
star [star] *nf* VEDETTE : star
station [stasjɔ̃] *nf* **1** : station **2** ∼ **d'autobus** : bus stop **3** ∼ **balnéaire** : seaside resort — **stationnaire** [stasjɔnɛr] *adj* : stationary — **stationner** [stasjɔne] *vi* : park — **stationnement** [stasjɔnmɑ̃] *nm* : parking — **station–service** [stasjɔ̃sɛrvis] *nf, pl* **stations–service** : gas station, service station
statistique [statistik] *adj* : statistical — ∼ *nf* **1** : statistic **2** : statistics
statue [staty] *nf* : statue
statuer [statɥe] *vi* : decree, ordain
stature [statyr] *nf* : stature
statut [staty] *nm* **1** : statute **2** : status — **statutaire** [statytɛr] *adj* : statutory
steak [stɛk] *nm* : steak
stéréo [stereo] *adj & nf* : stereo
stéréotype [stereɔtip] *nm* **1** : stereotype **2** : cliché
stérile [steril] *adj* : sterile — **stérilisation** [-lizasjɔ̃] *nf* : sterilization — **stériliser** [sterilize] *vt* : sterilize — **stérilité** [sterilite] *nf* : sterility
stéthoscope [stetɔskɔp] *nm* : stethoscope
stigmate [stigmat] *nm* : mark, stigma — **stigmatiser** [stigmatize] *vt* : stigmatize

stimuler [stimyle] *vt* : stimulate — **stimulation** [-mylasjɔ̃] *nf* : stimulation — **stimulant, -lante** [stimylɑ̃, -lɑ̃t] *adj* : stimulating — **stimulant** *nm* 1 : stimulant 2 : stimulus

stipuler [stipyle] *vt* : stipulate

stock [stɔk] *nm* : stock, goods — **stocker** [stɔke] *vt* : stock

stoïque [stɔik] *adj* : stoic, stoical — ~ *nmf* : stoic

stop [stɔp] *nm* 1 : stop sign 2 : brake light — ~ *interj* : stop — **stopper** [stɔpe] *vt* 1 : stop, halt 2 : mend — *vi* : stop

store [stɔr] *nm* 1 : awning 2 : blind, window shade

strapontin [strapɔ̃tɛ̃] *nm* : folding seat

stratagème [strataʒɛm] *nm* : stratagem — **stratégie** [strateʒi] *nf* : strategy — **stratégique** [strateʒik] *adj* : strategic

stress [strɛs] *nms & pl* : stress — **stressant, -sante** [strɛsɑ̃, -sɑ̃t] *adj* : stressful

strict, stricte [strikt] *adj* 1 : strict 2 : austere, plain

strident, -dente [stridɑ̃, -dɑ̃t] *adj* : strident, shrill

strier [strije] {96} *vt* : streak

strophe [strɔf] *nf* : stanza

structure [stryktyr] *nf* : structure — **structural, -rale** [stryktyral] *adj, mpl* **-raux** [-ro] : structural — **structurer** [stryktyre] *vt* : structure

studieux, -dieuse [stydjø, -djøz] *adj* : studious

studio [stydjo] *nm* 1 : studio 2 : studio apartment

stupéfier [stypefje] {96} *vt* : astonish, stun — **stupéfaction** [stypefaksjɔ̃] *nf* : astonishment — **stupéfait, -faite** [stypefɛ, -fɛt] *adj* : amazed, astounded — **stupéfiant, -fiante** [stypefjɑ̃, -fjɑ̃t] *adj* : amazing, astounding — **stupéfiant** *nm* : drug, narcotic

stupeur [stypœr] *nf* 1 : astonishment 2 : stupor

stupide [stypid] *adj* : stupid — **stupidité** [stypidite] *nf* : stupidity

style [stil] *nm* : style

stylo [stilo] *nm* 1 : pen 2 ~ **à bille** : ballpoint (pen)

suave [sɥav] *adj* 1 : sweet 2 : smooth, suave

subalterne [sybaltɛrn] *adj & nmf* : subordinate

subconscient, -ciente [sybkɔ̃sjɑ̃, -sjɑ̃t] *adj & nm* : subconscious

subdiviser [sybdivize] *vt* : subdivide

subir [sybir] *vt* 1 : undergo 2 : suffer 3 SUPPORTER : put up with 4 : take (an exam)

subit, -bite [sybi, -bit] *adj* : sudden — **subitement** [-bitmɑ̃] *adv* : suddenly

subjectif, -tive [sybʒɛktif, -tiv] *adj* : subjective — **subjectivité** [sybʒɛktivite] *nf* : subjectivity

subjonctif [sybʒɔ̃ktif] *nm* : subjunctive

subjuguer [sybʒyge] *vt* : captivate

sublime [syblim] *adj* : sublime

submerger [sybmɛrʒe] {17} *vt* 1 : submerge, flood 2 : overwhelm

subordonner [sybɔrdɔne] *vt* : subordinate — **subordonné, -née** [sybɔrdɔne] *adj & n* : subordinate

subreptice [sybrɛptis] *adj* : surreptitious

subséquent, -quente [sybsekɑ̃, -kɑ̃t] *adj* : subsequent

subside [sypsid] *nm* : grant, subsidy

subsidiaire [sybzidjɛr] *adj* : subsidiary

subsister [sybziste] *vi* 1 SURVIVRE : subsist, survive (on) 2 DURER : remain

substance [sypstɑ̃s] *nf* : substance — **substantiel, -tielle** [sypstɑ̃sjɛl] *adj* : substantial

substantif [sypstɑ̃tif] *nm* : noun

substituer [sypstitɥe] *vt* : substitute — **se substituer** *vr* ~ **à** : substitute for, replace — **substitut** [sypstity] *nm* : substitute — **substitution** [sypstitysjɔ̃] *nf* : substitution

subterfuge [sybtɛrfyʒ] *nm* : ploy, subterfuge

subtil, -tile [syptil] *adj* : subtle — **subtilité** [syptilite] *nf* : subtlety

subvenir [sybvənir] {92} *vi* ~ **à** : provide for, meet — **subvention** [sybvɑ̃sjɔ̃] *nf* : subsidy — **subventionner** [sybvɑ̃sjɔne] *vt* : subsidize

subversif, -sive [sybvɛrsif, -siv] *adj* : subversive — **subversion** [sybvɛrsjɔ̃] *nf* : subversion

suc [syk] *nm* 1 : juice 2 : sap

succédané [syksedane] *nm* : substitute

succéder [syksede] {87} *vi* ~ **à** : succeed, follow — **se succéder** *vr* : follow one another

succès [syksɛ] *nm* : success

successeur [syksesœr] *nm* : successor — **successif, -sive** [syksesif, -siv] *adj* : successive — **succession** [syksesjɔ̃] *nf* : succession

succinct, -cincte [syksɛ̃, -sɛ̃t] *adj* : succinct

succion [syksjɔ̃, sysjɔ̃] *nf* : suction, sucking

succomber [sykɔ̃be] *vi* 1 : die 2 ~ **à** : succumb to

succulent, -lente [sykylɑ̃, -lɑ̃t] *adj* : succulent

succursale [sykyrsal] *nf* : branch (of a bank, etc.)

sucer [syse] {6} *vt* : suck

sucette [sysɛt] *nf* 1 : lollipop 2 : pacifier

sucre [sykr] *nm* : sugar — **sucré, -crée** [sykre] *adj* : sweet, sweetened — **sucrer** [sykre] *vt* : sweeten, add sugar to

sud [syd] *adj* : south, southern, southerly — ~ *nm* 1 : south 2 **le Sud** : the South

sud–africain, -caine [sydafrikɛ̃, -kɛn] *adj* : South African

sud–américain, -caine [sydamerikɛ̃, -kɛn] *adj* : South American
sud–est [sydɛst] *adj s & pl* : southeast, southeastern — **~** *nm* : southeast
sud–ouest [sydwɛst] *adj s & pl* : southwest, southwestern — **~** *nm* : southwest
suédois, -doise [sɥedwa, -dwaz] *adj* : Swedish — **suédois** *nm* : Swedish (language)
suer [sɥe] *vi* : sweat — *vt* : sweat, ooze — **sueur** [sɥœr] *nf* : sweat
suffire [syfir] {86} *vi* : suffice — **se suffire** *vr or* **~ à soi–même** : be self-sufficient — **suffisamment** [syfizamɑ̃] *adv* : sufficiently — **suffisance** [syfizɑ̃s] *nf* : self-importance — **suffisant, -sante** [syfizɑ̃, -zɑ̃t] *adj* 1 : sufficient 2 : conceited
suffixe [syfiks] *nm* : suffix
suffoquer [syfɔke] *v* : suffocate, choke
suffrage [syfraʒ] *nm* : suffrage, vote
suggérer [syɡʒere] {86} *vt* : suggest — **suggestion** [syɡʒɛstjɔ̃] *nf* : suggestion
suicide [sɥisid] *nm* : suicide — **suicider** [sɥiside] *v* **se suicider** *vr* : commit suicide
suie [sɥi] *nf* : soot
suinter [sɥɛ̃te] *vi* : ooze, seep
suisse [sɥis] *adj* : Swiss
suite [sɥit] *nf* 1 : suite 2 : continuation, sequel 3 SÉRIE : series, sequence 4 CONSÉQUENCE : result 5 **par la ~** : later, afterwards 6 **par ~ de** : due to, as a result of
suivre [sɥivr] {88} *vt* 1 : follow 2 : take (a course) 3 : keep up with — *vi* 1 : follow 2 : keep up 3 **faire ~** : forward (mail) — **se suivre** *vr* : follow one another — **suivant, -vante** [sɥivɑ̃, -vɑ̃t] *adj* : following, next — **~** *n* : next one, following one — **suivant** *prep* : according to — **suivi, -vie** [sɥivi] *adj* 1 : regular, steady 2 : coherent
sujet, -jette [syʒɛ, -ʒɛt] *adj* **~ à** : subject to, prone to — **~** *n* : subject (of a state or country) — **sujet** *nm* 1 : subject, topic 2 RAISON : cause
summum [sɔmɔm] *nm* : height, peak
super [sypɛr] *adj s & pl fam* : great, super
superbe [sypɛrb] *adj* : superb
supercherie [sypɛrʃəri] *nf* TROMPERIE : deception
superficie [sypɛrfisi] *nf* : area, surface — **superficiel, -cielle** [sypɛrfisjɛl] *adj* : superficial
superflu, -flue [sypɛrfly] *adj* : superfluous
supérieur, -rieure [sypɛrjœr] *adj* 1 : superior 2 : upper, top 3 **~ à** : higher than — **~** *n* : superior — **supériorité** [sypɛrjɔrite] *nf* : superiority
superlatif [sypɛrlatif] *nm* : superlative
supermarché [sypɛrmarʃe] *nm* : supermarket
superstitieux, -tieuse [sypɛrstisjø, -sjøz]

adj : superstitious — **superstition** [sypɛrstisjɔ̃] *nf* : superstition
superviser [sypɛrvize] *vt* : supervise
supplanter [syplɑ̃te] *vt* : supplant
suppléer [syplee] {89} *vt* 1 REMPLACER : replace, fill in for 2 : supplement — *vi* **~ à** : make up for — **suppléant, -pléante** [syplẽɑ̃, -pleɑ̃t] *adj & n* : substitute, replacement
supplément [syplemɑ̃] *nm* 1 : supplement 2 : extra charge — **supplémentaire** [syplemɑ̃tɛr] *adj* : additional, extra
supplication [syplikasjɔ̃] *nf* : plea
supplice [syplis] *nm* : torture — **supplicier** [syplisje] {96} *vt* TORTURER : torture
supplier [syplije] {96} *vt* : implore, beg
supporter[1] [sypɔrte] *vt* 1 SOUTENIR : support, hold up 2 ENDURER : tolerate, bear — **support** [sypɔr] *nm* : support, prop — **supportable** [sypɔrtabl] *adj* : bearable, tolerable
supporter[2] [sypɔrtɛr] *nm* : supporter, fan
supposer [sypoze] *vt* 1 : suppose, assume 2 IMPLIQUER : imply — **supposition** [sypozisjɔ̃] *nf* : supposition
suppositoire [sypozitwar] *nm* : suppository
supprimer [syprime] *vt* 1 : abolish 2 : take out, delete — **suppression** [sypresjɔ̃] *nf* 1 : removal, elimination 2 : deletion
suppurer [sypyre] *vi* : fester
suprême [syprɛm] *adj* : supreme — **suprématie** [syprematsi] *nf* : supremacy
sur[1] [syr] *prep* 1 : on, upon 2 : over, above 3 : about, on 4 PARMI : out of 5 : by (in measurements)
sur[2], **sure** [syr] *adj* : sour
sûr, sûre [syr] *adj* 1 CERTAIN : sure, certain 2 FIABLE : reliable 3 : safe, secure 4 : sound 5 **~ de soi** : self-confident
surabondance [syrabɔ̃dɑ̃s] *nf* : overabundance
suranné, -née [syrane] *adj* : outdated
surcharger [syrʃarʒe] {17} *vt* 1 : overload 2 : alter — **surcharge** [syrʃarʒ] *nf* : overload
surchauffer [syrʃofe] *vt* : overheat
surclasser [syrklase] *vt* : outclass
surcroît [syrkrwa] *nm* 1 : increase 2 **de ~** : in addition
surdité [syrdite] *nf* : deafness
surélever [syrelve] {52} *vt* : raise, heighten
sûrement [syrmɑ̃] *adv* 1 : surely 2 : safely 3 **~ pas** : certainly not
surenchérir [syrɑ̃ʃerir] *vi* : bid higher
surestimer [syrestime] *vt* : overestimate, overrate
sûreté [syrte] *nf* 1 SÉCURITÉ : safety 2 : surety, guarantee (in law)
surexcité, -tée [syrɛksite] *adj* : overexcited
surf [sœrf] *nm* : surfing

surface [syrfas] *nf* : surface
surgelé [syrʒəle] *adj* : frozen (of food)
surgir [syrʒir] *vi* : appear suddenly, arise
surhumain, -maine [syrymɛ̃, -mɛn] *adj* : superhuman
sur–le–champ [syrləʃɑ̃] *adv* : immediately
surlendemain [syrlɑ̃dmɛ̃] *nm* **le ~** : two days later
surmener [syrməne] {52} *vt* : overwork — **surmenage** [syrmənaʒ] *nm* : overwork
surmonter [syrmɔ̃te] *vt* **1** : overcome **2** : surmount, top
surnager [syrnaʒe] {17} *vi* : float
surnaturel, -relle [syrnatyrɛl] *adj & nm* : supernatural
surnom [syrnɔ̃] *nm* : nickname
surnombre [syrnɔ̃br] *nm* **en ~** : excess, too many
surnommer [syrnɔme] *vt* : nickname
surpasser [syrpase] *vt* : surpass, outdo
surpeuplé, -plée [syrpœple] *adj* : overpopulated
surplomber [syrplɔ̃be] *v* : overhang
surplus [syrply] *nm* : surplus
surprendre [syrprɑ̃dr] {70} *vt* **1** ÉTONNER : surprise **2** : catch, take by surprise **3** : overhear — **surprenant, -nante** [syrprənɑ̃, -nɑ̃t] *adj* : surprising — **surprise** [syrpriz] *nf* : surprise
sursaut [syrso] *nm* : start, jump — **sursauter** [syrsote] *vi* : start, jump
surseoir [syrswar] {90} *vi* **~ à** : postpone, defer
sursis [syrsi] *nm* : reprieve
surtaxe [syrtaks] *nf* : surcharge
surtout [syrtu] *adv* **1** : above all **2** : especially, particularly
surveiller [syrvɛje] *vt* **1** : watch (over) **2** : supervise — **surveillance** [syrvɛjɑ̃s] *nf* **1** : supervision **2** : watch, surveillance — **surveillant, -lante** [syrvɛjɑ̃, -jɑ̃t] *n* **1** : supervisor, overseer **2 ~ de prison** : prison guard
survenir [syrvənir] {92} *vi* : occur, take place
survivre [syrvivr] {98} *vi* **1** : survive **2 ~ à** : outlive — **survie** [syrvi] *nf* : survival — **survivant, -vante** [syrvivɑ̃, -vɑ̃t] *n* : survivor

survoler [syrvɔle] *vi* **1** : fly over **2** : skim through
sus [sy(s)] *adv* **1 en ~** : extra **2 en ~ de** : in addition to
susceptible [sysɛptibl] *adj* **1** : sensitive, touchy **2 ~ de** : likely to — **susceptibilité** [sysɛptibilite] *nf* : susceptibility
susciter [sysite] *vt* : arouse, give rise to
suspect, -pecte [syspɛ, -pɛkt] *adj* : suspicious, suspect — **~** *n* : suspect — **suspecter** [syspɛkte] *vt* : suspect
suspendre [syspɑ̃dr] {63} *vt* **1** INTERROMPRE : suspend, interrupt **2** PENDRE : hang up — **se suspendre** *vr* **~ à** : hang from — **suspens** [syspɑ̃] *nm* **en ~** : unresolved, uncertain
suspense [syspɑ̃s] *nm* : suspense
suspicion [syspisjɔ̃] *nf* : suspicion
suture [sytyr] *nf* **1** : suture **2 point de ~** : stitch
svelte [zvɛlt] *adj* : slender, svelte
syllabe [silab] *nf* : syllable
symbole [sɛ̃bɔl] *nm* : symbol — **symbolique** [sɛ̃bɔlik] *adj* : symbolic — **symboliser** [sɛ̃bɔlize] *vt* : symbolize — **symbolisme** [sɛ̃bɔlism] *nm* : symbolism
symétrie [simetri] *nf* : symmetry — **symétrique** [simetrik] *adj* : symmetrical, symmetric
sympathie [sɛ̃pati] *nf* **1** : liking **2** CONDOLÉANCES : condolences — **sympathique** [sɛ̃patik] *adj* : nice, likeable — **sympathiser** [sɛ̃patize] *vi* **~ avec** : get along with
symphonie [sɛ̃fɔni] *nf* : symphony — **symphonique** [sɛ̃fɔnik] *adj* : symphonic
symptôme [sɛ̃ptom] *nm* : symptom
synagogue [sinagɔg] *nf* : synagogue
syndicat [sɛ̃dika] *nm* : union, labor union — **syndiquer** [sɛ̃dike] *vt* : unionize — **se syndiquer** *vr* : join a union
syndrome [sɛ̃drom] *nm* : syndrome
synonyme [sinɔnim] *nm* : synonym — **~** *adj* : synonymous
syntaxe [sɛ̃taks] *nf* : syntax
synthèse [sɛ̃tɛz] *nf* : synthesis — **synthétique** [sɛ̃tetik] *adj* : synthetic
système [sistɛm] *nm* : system — **systématique** [sistematik] *adj* : systematic

T

t [te] *nm* : t, 20th letter of the alphabet

tabac [taba] *nm* **1** : tobacco **2** ~ **à priser** : snuff **3** *France* : tobacco shop

table [tabl] *nf* **1** : table **2 se mettre à** ~ : sit down to eat **3** ~ **de matières** : table of contents

tableau [tablo] *nm, pl* **-bleaux 1** PEINTURE : painting **2** : picture, scene **3** : table, chart **4** ~ **d'affichage** : bulletin board **5** ~ **de bord** : dashboard **6** ~ **noir** : blackboard

tabler [table] *vt* ~ **sur** : count on

tablette [tablɛt] *nf* **1** : shelf **2** : bar (of candy), stick (of gum)

tablier [tablije] *nm* : apron

tabou, -boue [tabu] *adj* : taboo — **tabou** *nm* : taboo

tabouret [tabure] *nm* : stool

tache [taʃ] *nf* **1** : stain, spot **2** ~ **de rousseur** : freckle — **tacher** [taʃe] *vt* SALIR : stain, spot

tâche [taʃ] *nf* : task — **tâcher** [taʃe] *vi* ~ **de** : try to

tacheté [taʃte] *adj* : speckled

tacite [tasit] *adj* : tacit

tact [takt] *nm* : tact

tactique [taktik] *adj* : tactical — ~ *nf* STRATÉGIE : tactics *pl*

taie [tɛ] *nf or* ~ **d'oreiller** : pillowcase

tailler [taje] *vt* **1** : cut, prune, trim **2** : sharpen (a pencil) — **taille** [taj] *nf* **1** : cutting, pruning **2** : size (of clothing, etc.) **3** HAUTEUR : height **4** : waist — **tailleur** [tajœr] *nm* **1** : woman's suit **2** : tailor

taire [tɛr] {91} *vt* **1** : hush up, keep secret — **se taire** *vr* **1** : be quiet **2** : fall silent

talc [talk] *nm* : talcum powder

talent [talɑ̃] *nm* : talent — **talentueux, -tueuse** [talɑ̃tɥø, -tɥøz] *adj* : talented

talon [talɔ̃] *nm* **1** : heel **2** : stub (of a check) — **talonner** [talɔne] *vt* **1** : follow closely **2** : harass

talus [taly] *nms & pl* : embankment, slope

tambour [tɑ̃bur] *nm* : drum — **tambouriner** [tɑ̃burine] *vt* : drum

tamia [tamja] *nm* : chipmunk

tamis [tami] *nms & pl* : sieve, sifter — **tamiser** [tamize] *vt* **1** : sift **2** : filter

tampon [tɑ̃pɔ̃] *nm* **1** BOUCHON : plug **2** : buffer (of a railway car) **3** : rubber stamp **4** ~ **encreur** : ink pad **5** ~ **hygiénique** : tampon — **tamponner** [tɑ̃pɔne] *vt* **1** : dab **2** HEURTER : crash into **3** : stamp (a document)

tandis [tɑ̃di] ~ **que** *conj phr* **1** : while **2** : whereas

tangente [tɑ̃ʒɑ̃t] *nf* : tangent

tangible [tɑ̃ʒibl] *adj* : tangible

tango [tɑ̃go] *nm* : tango

tanguer [tɑ̃ge] *vi* : pitch (of a ship, etc.)

tanière [tanjɛr] *nf* : lair, den

tanner [tane] *vt* **1** : tan (leather, etc.) **2** *fam* : pester, annoy

tant [tɑ̃] *adv* **1** : so much, so many **2 en** ~ **que** : as, in so far as **3** ~ **mieux!** : so much the better! **4** ~ **pis!** : too bad! **5** ~ **que** : as much as, as long as

tante [tɑ̃t] *nf* : aunt

tantôt [tɑ̃to] *adv* **1** : sometimes **2** *Can* : later **3** *France* : this afternoon

tapage [tapaʒ] *nm* **1** : uproar, din **2** SCANDALE : scandal — **tapageur, -geuse** [tapaʒœr, -ʒøz] *adj* **1** : rowdy **2** TAPE-À-L'ŒIL : flashy

tape [tap] *nf* : slap — **tape-à-l'œil** [tapalœj] *adj* : flashy

taper [tape] *vt* **1** : hit, slap **2** : type — *vi* **1** : hit, bang **2** : beat down (of the sun)

tapir [tapir] *v* **se tapir** *vr* : crouch

tapis [tapi] *nms & pl* **1** : carpet **2** ~ **roulant** : moving walkway, conveyor belt — **tapisser** [tapise] *vt* **1** : wallpaper **2** ~ **de** : cover with — **tapisserie** [tapisri] *nf* **1** : tapestry **2** : wallpaper

tapoter [tapɔte] *vt* : tap, pat

taquiner [takine] *vt* : tease — **taquinerie** [takinri] *nf* : teasing

tarabiscoté, -tée [tarabiskɔte] *adj* : fussy, overelaborate

tard [tar] *adv* : late — **tarder** [tarde] *vi* : take a long time — **tardif, -dive** [tardif, -div] *adj* : late

tare [tar] *nf* DÉFAUT : defect

tarif [tarif] *nm* **1** : rate, fare **2** : price, schedule of prices **3** ~ **douanier** : tariff, customs duty

tarir [tarir] *v* : dry up

tarte [tart] *nf* : tart, pie

tartine [tartin] *nf* : slice of bread (and butter) — **tartiner** [tartine] *vt* : spread (with butter, etc.)

tartre [tartr] *nm* : tartar

tas [ta] *nms & pl* **1** : heap, pile **2 des** ~ **de** : a lot of, piles of

tasse [tas] *nf* : cup

tasser [tase] *vt* **1** : pack down **2** ENTASSER : cram, squeeze **3** *Can* : move over — **se tasser** *vr* **1** : shrink **2** : cram (into a car)

tâter [tate] *vt* **1** : feel **2** ~ **le terrain** : check out the lay of the land — *vi* ~ **de** : try one's hand at

tatillon, -lonne [tatijɔ̃, -jɔn] *adj* : fussy, finicky

tâtonner [tatɔne] *vi* : grope about — **tâtons** [tatɔ̃] **à ~** *adv phr* **avancer à ~** : feel one's way

tatouer [tatwe] *vt* : tattoo — **tatouage** [tatwaʒ] *nm* **1** : tattoo **2** : tattooing

taudis [todi] *nms & pl* : hovel, slum

taule [tol] *nf fam* : prison

taupe [top] *nf* : mole

taureau [tɔro] *nm, pl* **-reaux** : bull

taux [to] *nms & pl* **1** : rate **2** : level **3 ~ de change** : exchange rate **4 ~ de cholestérol** : cholesterol level

taverne [tavɛrn] *nf* : inn, tavern

taxe [taks] *nf* : tax — **taxer** [takse] *vt* : tax

taxi [taksi] *nm* : taxi, taxicab

te [tə] (**t'** *before a vowel or mute h*) *pron* **1** : you, to you **2** (*used as a reflexive pronoun*) : yourself

technique [tɛknik] *nf* : technique — **~** *adj* : technical — **technicien, -cienne** [tɛknisjɛ̃, -sjɛn] *n* : technician

technologie [tɛknɔlɔʒi] *nf* : technology — **technologique** [tɛknɔlɔʒik] *adj* : technological

tee-shirt [tiʃœrt] *nm, pl* **tee-shirts** : T-shirt

teindre [tɛ̃dr] {37} *vt* : dye — **teint** [tɛ̃] *nm* : complexion — **teinte** [tɛ̃t] *nf* **1** : shade, hue **2 une ~ de** : a tinge of — **teinter** [tɛ̃te] *vt* : tint, stain — **teinture** [tɛ̃tyr] *nf* **1** : dye **2** : dyeing — **teinturerie** [tɛ̃tyrri] *nf* **1** : dyeing **2** : dry cleaner's — **teinturier, -rière** [tɛ̃tyrje, -rjɛ] *n* : dry cleaner

tel, telle [tɛl] *adj* **1** : such **2** : such and such, a certain **3 ~ que** : such as, like **4 tel quel** : as (it) is — **~** *pron* **1** : a certain one, someone **2 un tel, une telle** : so-and-so

télé [tele] *nf fam* : TV

télécommande [telekɔmɑ̃d] *nf* : remote control

télécommunication [telekɔmynikas-jɔ̃] *nf* : telecommunication

télécopie [telekɔpi] *nf* : fax — **télécopieur** [telekɔpjœr] *nm* : fax machine

télégramme [telegram] *nm* : telegram

télégraphe [telegraf] *nm* : telegraph

téléphone [telefɔn] *nm* : telephone — **téléphoner** [telefɔne] *vt* : telephone, call — **téléphonique** [telefɔnik] *adj* : telephone

télescope [teleskɔp] *nm* : telescope — **télescoper** [teleskɔpe] *v* **se télescoper** *vr* **1** : collide **2** : overlap — **télescopique** [teleskɔpik] *adj* : telescopic

télésiège [telesjɛʒ] *nm* : chairlift

téléski [teleski] *nm* : ski lift

téléviser [televize] *vt* : televise — **téléviseur** [televizœr] *nm* : television set — **télévision** [televizjɔ̃] *nf* **1** : television **2** TÉLÉVISEUR : television set

tellement [tɛlmɑ̃] *adv* **1** : so, so much **2 ~ de** : so many, so much

téméraire [temerɛr] *adj* : rash, reckless — **témérité** [temerite] *nf* : rashness, recklessness

témoin [temwɛ̃] *nm* **1** : witness **2** : baton (in a relay race) — **témoignage** [temwaɲaʒ] *nm* **1** RÉCIT : account, story **2** : testimony (in court) **3** PREUVE : evidence — **témoigner** [temwaɲe] *vt* **1** : testify, attest **2** MONTRER : show — *vi* : testify

tempe [tɑ̃p] *nf* : temple

tempérament [tɑ̃peramɑ̃] *nm* CARACTÈRE : temperament

température [tɑ̃peratyr] *nf* : temperature

tempéré, -rée [tɑ̃pere] *adj* : temperate

tempête [tɑ̃pɛt] *nf* : storm

temple [tɑ̃pl] *nm* **1** : temple **2** : (protestant) church

temporaire [tɑ̃pɔrɛr] *adj* : temporary

temporel, -relle [tɑ̃pɔrɛl] *adj* : temporal, worldly

temps [tɑ̃] *nms & pl* **1** : time **2** : weather **3** : tense (in grammar) **4 à plein ~** : fulltime **5 de ~ à autre** : from time to time **6 quel ~ fait-il?** : what's the weather like?

tenace [tənas] *adj* : tenacious, stubborn — **ténacité** [tənasite] *nf* : tenacity

tenailles [tənaj] *nfpl* : pincers, tongs

tendance [tɑ̃dɑ̃s] *nf* **1** : tendency **2** COURANT : trend

tendon [tɑ̃dɔ̃] *nm* : tendon, sinew

tendre[1] [tɑ̃dr] {63} *vt* **1** : tense, tighten (a rope, etc.) **2 ~ la main** : hold out one's hand **3 ~ un piège à** : set a trap for — *vi* **1 ~ à** : tend to **2 ~ vers** : strive for — **se tendre** *vr* **1** : tighten **2** : become strained — **tendu, -due** [tɑ̃dy] *adj* **1** : tight, taut **2** : tense, strained **3** : outstretched (of a hand)

tendre[2] *adj* **1** : tender, soft **2** : gentle, loving — **tendresse** [tɑ̃drɛs] *nf* : tenderness, affection

ténèbres [tenɛbr] *nfpl* : darkness — **ténébreux, -breuse** [tenebrø, -brøz] *adj* OBSCUR : dark

teneur [tənœr] *nf* : content

tenir [tənir] {92} *vt* **1** : hold, keep **2** : have, catch **3** : run, manage (a hotel, store, etc.) **4** : take up (a space) **5** CONSIDÉRER : hold, regard — *vi* **1** : hold, stay in place **2** DURER : hold up, last **3** : fit (into a space) **4 ~ à** : be fond of **5 ~ à** : be anxious to **6 ~ de** : take after — *v impers* : depend — **se tenir** *vr* **1** : hold, hold up, hold onto **2** RESTER : remain **3** : behave (oneself) **4 ~ debout** : stand still

tennis [tenis] *nm* **1** : tennis **2 ~** *nmpl France* : sneakers

ténor [tenɔr] *nm* : tenor

tension [tɑ̃sjɔ̃] *nf* : tension

tentacule [tɑ̃takyl] *nm* : tentacle
tentation [tɑ̃tasjɔ̃] *nf* : temptation
tentative [tɑ̃tativ] *nf* : attempt
tente [tɑ̃t] *nf* : tent
tenter [tɑ̃te] *vt* **1** : tempt **2** ESSAYER : attempt
tenu, -nue [təny] *adj* **1** : obliged **2 bien ~** : well-kept, tidy
ténu, -nue [teny] *adj* : tenuous
tenue *nf* **1** : conduct, manners *pl* **2** MAINTIEN : posture **3** : clothes *pl*, dress **4 ~ de livres** : bookkeeping
terme [tɛrm] *nm* **1** : term, word **2** ÉCHÉANCE : deadline **3 mettre un ~ à** : put an end to
terminer [tɛrmine] *v* FINIR : finish — **se terminer** *vr* : end — **terminaison** [tɛrminɛzɔ̃] *nf* : ending — **terminal, -nale** [tɛrminal] *adj, mpl* **-naux** [-no] : final, terminal — **terminal** *nm, pl* **-naux** : terminal
terminologie [tɛrminɔlɔʒi] *nf* : terminology
terminus [tɛrminys] *nms & pl* : terminus
terne [tɛrn] *adj* **1** FADE : drab **2** ENNUYEUX : dull
ternir [tɛrnir] *vt* : tarnish
terrain [tɛrɛ̃] *nm* **1** : ground **2** PARCELLE : plot (of land) **3** : land, terrain **4 ~ d'aviation** : airfield **5 ~ de camping** : campsite
terrasse [tɛras] *nf* : terrace — **terrasser** [terase] *vt* : knock down, floor
terre [tɛr] *nf* **1** TERRAIN : land **2** : dirt, soil **3** : earth, world **4 aller à ~** : go ashore **5 la Terre** : the Earth **6 par ~** : on the ground, on the floor **7 sous ~** : underground **8 terre-à-terre** : down-to-earth, matter-of-fact
terrestre [tɛrɛstr] *adj* **1** : earth, terrestrial **2** : earthly, worldly
terreur [tɛrœr] *nf* : terror
terreux, -reuse [tɛrø, -røz] *adj* : earthy
terrible [tɛribl] *adj* **1** : terrible **2** *fam* FORMIDABLE : terrific, great
terrier [tɛrje] *nm* **1** : hole, burrow **2** CHIEN : terrier
terrifier [tɛrifje] {96} *vt* ÉPOUVANTER : terrify
territoire [tɛritwar] *nm* : territory — **territorial, -riale** [tɛritɔrjal] *adj, mpl* **-riaux** [-rjo] : territorial
terroriser [tɛrɔrize] *vt* : terrorize — **terrorisme** [tɛrɔrism] *nm* : terrorism — **terroriste** [-rɔrist] *adj & nmf* : terrorist
tes → ton[1]
tesson [tɛsɔ̃] *nm* : fragment, shard
test [tɛst] *nm* : test
testament [tɛstamɑ̃] *nm* **1** : will, testament **2 Ancien Testament** : Old Testament
tester [tɛste] *vt* : test
testicule [tɛstikyl] *nm* : testicle
tétanos [tetanos] *nms & pl* : tetanus
têtard [tɛtar] *nm* : tadpole

tête [tɛt] *nf* **1** : head **2** VISAGE : face **3** MENEUR : leader **4** : top (of a class, etc.) **5** ESPRIT : mind, brain **6 faire la ~** : sulk **7 tenir ~ à** : stand up to — **tête-à-queue** [tɛtakø] *nms & pl* : spin (of an automobile) — **tête-à-tête** [tɛtatɛt] *nms & pl* : tête-à-tête
téter [tete] {87} *vt* : suck (at) — *vi* : suckle, nurse — **tétine** [tetin] *nf* **1** : teat **2** : nipple (on a baby's bottle), pacifier
têtu, -tue [tety] *adj* : stubborn
texte [tɛkst] *nm* : text
textile [tɛkstil] *nm* : textile
texture [tɛkstyr] *nf* : texture
thé [te] *nm* : tea
théâtre [teatr] *nm* : theater — **théâtral, -trale** [teatral] *adj, mpl* **-traux** [-tro] : theatrical
théière [tejɛr] *nf* : teapot
thème [tɛm] *nm* : theme
théologie [teɔlɔʒi] *nf* : theology
théorie [teɔri] *nf* : theory — **théorique** [teɔrik] *adj* : theoretical
thérapie [terapi] *nf* : therapy — **thérapeute** [terapøt] *nmf* : therapist — **thérapeutique** [terapøtik] *adj* : therapeutic
thermal, -male [tɛrmal] *adj, mpl* **-maux** [tɛrmo] : thermal — **thermique** [tɛrmik] *adj* : thermal
thermomètre [tɛrmɔmɛtr] *nm* : thermometer
thermos [tɛrmos] *nmfs & pl* : thermos
thermostat [tɛrmosta] *nm* : thermostat
thèse [tɛz] *nf* : thesis
thon [tɔ̃] *nm* : tuna
thym [tɛ̃] *nm* : thyme
tibia [tibja] *nm* : shin(bone)
tic [tik] *nm* **1** : tic, twitch **2** HABITUDE : mannerism
ticket [tikɛ] *nm* BILLET : ticket
tiède [tjɛd] *adj* : lukewarm — **tiédir** [tjedir] *vi* : warm up, cool down
tien, tienne [tjɛ̃, tjɛn] *adj* : yours, of yours — **~** *pron* **le tien, la tienne, les tiens, les tiennes** : yours
tiers, tierce [tjɛr, tjɛrs] *adj* : third — **tiers** *nm* **1** : third **2** : third party
tige [tiʒ] *nf* **1** : stem, stalk **2** : (metal) rod
tigre [tigr] *nm* : tiger — **tigresse** [tigrɛs] *nf* : tigress
tilleul [tijœl] *nm* : linden (tree)
timbale [tɛ̃bal] *nf* : tumbler, cup
timbre [tɛ̃br] *nm* **1** : (postage) stamp **2** SONNETTE : bell **3** TON : timbre, tone — **timbrer** [tɛ̃bre] *vt* : stamp, postmark
timide [timid] *adj* : timid, shy — **timidité** [timidite] *nf* : shyness
tintamarre [tɛ̃tamar] *nm* : din, racket
tinter [tɛ̃te] *vt* : ring, toll — *vi* **1** : ring, chime **2** : jingle, tinkle — **tintement** [tɛ̃tmɑ̃] *nm* : ringing, chiming

tir [tir] *nm* : shooting, firing

tirage [tiraʒ] *nm* **1** : printing, printout **2** : circulation (of a newspaper, etc.) **3** : drawing (in a lottery)

tirailler [tiraje] *vt* : pull at, tug at

tiré, -rée [tire] *adj* : drawn, haggard

tire–bouchon [tirbuʃɔ̃] *nm, pl* **tire–bouchons** : corkscrew

tirelire [tirlir] *nf* : piggy bank

tirer [tire] *vt* **1** : pull, tug **2** : fire, shoot **3** ~ **de** : pull out of, draw away from **4** ~ **la langue** : stick out one's tongue **5** ~ **une ligne** : draw a line — *vi* **1** : pull **2** : fire, shoot **3** ~ **au sort** : draw lots — **se tirer** *vr* **1** ~ **de** : get through, escape from **2** **s'en tirer** *fam* : cope, manage

tiret [tire] *nm* : dash, hyphen

tireur, -reuse [tirœr, -røz] *n* : gunman

tiroir [tirwar] *nm* : drawer

tisane [tizan] *nf* : herbal tea

tisonnier [tizɔnje] *nm* : poker

tisser [tise] *vt* : weave — **tissage** [tisaʒ] *nm* **1** : weaving **2** : weave

tissu [tisy] *nm* **1** : material, fabric **2** : tissue (in biology)

titre [titr] *nm* **1** : title (of a book, etc.) **2** : rank, qualification **3** *or* **gros** ~ : headline **4** : security, bond **5 à** ~ **d'exemple** : as an example

tituber [titybe] *vi* : stagger

titulaire [tityler] *adj* : tenured, permanent — ~ *nmf* **1** : holder **2** : tenured professor

toast [tost] *nm* : toast

toboggan [tɔbɔgɑ̃] *nm* : toboggan, sleigh

toge [tɔʒ] *nf* : gown, robe (of a judge, etc.)

toi [twa] *pron* **1** : you **2 TOI-MÊME** : yourself

toile [twal] *nf* **1** : cloth, fabric **2 TABLEAU** : canvas, painting **3** ~ **d'araignée** : spiderweb, cobweb

toilette [twalɛt] *nf* **1** : washing up **2 TENUE** : clothing, outfit **3** *Can* : toilet, bathroom **4** ~**s** *nfpl* : toilet, bathroom

toi–même [twamɛm] *pron* : yourself

toison [twazɔ̃] *nf* : fleece

toit [twa] *nm* : roof — **toiture** [twatyr] *nf* : roofing

tôle [tol] *nf* **1** : sheet metal **2** ~ **ondulée** : corrugated iron

tolérer [tɔlere] {87} *vt* : tolerate — **tolérance** [tɔlerɑ̃s] *nf* : tolerance — **tolérant, -rante** [tɔlerɑ̃, -rɑ̃t] *adj* : tolerant

tollé [tɔle] *nm* : outcry

tomate [tɔmat] *nf* : tomato

tombant, -bante [tɔ̃bɑ̃, -bɑ̃t] *adj* : sloping, drooping

tombe [tɔ̃b] *nf* SÉPULTURE : grave, tomb — **tombeau** [tɔ̃bo] *nm, pl* **-beaux** : tomb, mausoleum

tomber [tɔ̃be] *vi* **1** : fall, drop **2** : die down, subside **3** : droop, sag **4** ~ **amoureux** : fall in love **5** ~ **malade** : fall ill **6** ~ **sur** : run into, come across **7 laisser** ~ : give up — **tombée** [tɔ̃be] *nf* **à la** ~ **du jour** *or* **à la** ~ **de la nuit** : at nightfall, at the close of day

tome [tɔm] *nm* : volume (of a book)

ton[1] [tɔ̃] [tɔ̃ (tɔn *before a vowel or mute h*)], **ta** [ta] *adj, pl* **tes** [te] : your

ton[2] *nm* **1** : tone, pitch **2** : hue, shade — **tonalité** [tɔnalite] *nf* **1** : tone **2** : tonality, key (in music) **3** : dial tone

tondre [tɔ̃dr] {63} *vt* **1** : mow (the lawn) **2** : shear, clip (hair) — **tondeuse** [tɔ̃døz] *nf* **1** *or* ~ **à gazon** : lawn mower **2** : clippers *pl*, shears *pl*

tonifier [tɔnifje] {96} *vt* REVIGORER : tone up, invigorate — **tonique** [tɔnik] *nm* : tonic

tonne [tɔn] *nf* : ton

tonneau [tɔno] *nm, pl* **-neaux 1** : barrel, cask **2** : rollover (of an automobile) — **tonnelet** [tɔnlɛ] *nm* : keg

tonner [tɔne] *vi* : thunder — **tonnerre** [tɔnɛr] *nm* : thunder

tonton [tɔ̃tɔ̃] *nm fam* : uncle

tonus [tɔnys] *nms & pl* **1** : (muscle) tone **2** : energy, vigor

toqué, -quée [tɔke] *adj fam* : crazy

torche [tɔrʃ] *nf* : torch

torchon [tɔrʃɔ̃] *nm* **1** CHIFFON : rag **2** ~ **à vaisselle** : dishcloth — **torcher** [tɔrʃe] *vt fam* : wipe

tordre [tɔrdr] {63} *vt* : twist, wring — **se tordre** *vr* **1** : twist **2** : double up (with pain, laughter, etc.) — **tordu, -due** [tɔrdy] *adj* : twisted, warped

torero [tɔrero] *nm* : bullfighter

tornade [tɔrnad] *nf* : tornado

torpeur [tɔrpœr] *nf* : lethargy

torpille [tɔrpij] *nf* : torpedo

torrent [tɔrɑ̃] *nm* : torrent

torride [tɔrid] *adj* : torrid

torsade [tɔrsad] *nf* : twist, coil

torse [tɔrs] *nm* : torso, chest

tort [tɔr] *nm* **1** : wrong **2 à** ~ : wrongly **3 avoir** ~ : be wrong **4 faire du** ~ **à** : harm

torticolis [tɔrtikɔli] *nms & pl* : stiff neck

tortiller [tɔrtije] *vt* : twist — **se tortiller** *vr* : wriggle, squirm

tortue [tɔrty] *nf* : turtle, tortoise

tortueux, -euse [tɔrtɥø, -øz] *adj* **1** : winding (of a road) **2** : convoluted, tortuous

torture [tɔrtyr] *nf* : torture — **torturer** [tɔrtyre] *vt* : torture

tôt [to] *adv* **1** : soon **2** : early **3** ~ **ou tard** : sooner or later

total, -tale [tɔtal] *adj, mpl* **-taux** [tɔto] : total — **total** *nm, pl* **-taux** : total — **totaliser** [tɔtalize] *vt* : total — **totalitaire** [tɔtalitɛr] *adj* : totalitarian — **totalité** [tɔtalite] *nf* **1 en** ~ : completely **2 la** ~ **de** : all of

toucher [tuʃe] *vt* **1** : touch, handle **2** : hit, strike **3** CONCERNER : affect **4** ÉMOUVOIR : move, touch **5** : receive, earn (a salary) — *vi* ~ **à 1** : touch upon, bring up **2** : relate to — **se toucher** *vr* : touch each other — ~ *nm* **1** : sense of touch **2** SENSATION : feel

touchant, -chante [tuʃɑ̃, -ʃɑ̃t] *adj* ÉMOUVANT : touching — **touche** [tuʃ] *nf* **1** : key (on a keyboard) **2** TRACE : trace, hint

touffe [tuf] *nf* : tuft, clump — **touffu, -fue** [tufy] *adj* : bushy

toujours [tuʒur] *adv* **1** : always, forever **2** ENCORE : still

toupet [tupɛ] *nm fam* : nerve, cheek

toupie [tupi] *nf* : top (toy)

tour[1] [tur] *nm* **1** : tour, circuit **2** : walk, ride **3** ~ **de taille** : girth (of a person) **4** **attendre son** ~ : wait one's turn **5** **jouer un** ~ **à qqn** : play a trick on s.o. **6** : lathe (in carpentry)

tour[2] *nf* **1** : tower **2** : castle (in chess)

tourbe [turb] *nf* : peat

tourbillon [turbijɔ̃] *nm* **1** : whirlwind, whirlpool **2** : whirl, bustle — **tourbillonner** [turbijɔne] *vi* : whirl, swirl

tourelle [turɛl] *nf* : turret

touriste [turist] *nmf* : tourist — **tourisme** [turism] *nm* : tourism — **touristique** [turistik] *adj* : tourist

tourment [turmɑ̃] *nm* : torment — **tourmenter** [turmɑ̃te] *vt* : torment — **se tourmenter** *vr* S'INQUIÉTER : worry

tourner [turne] *vt* **1** : turn, rotate **2** : stir (a sauce), toss (a salad) **3** : shoot, film — *vi* **1** : turn, revolve, spin **2** : run (of an engine, etc.) **3** : make a film **4** : go bad, sour (of milk) **5** **bien** ~ : turn out well — **se tourner** *vr* : turn around — **tournant, -nante** [turnɑ̃, -nɑ̃t] *adj* : turning, revolving — **tournant** *nm* **1** : bend **2** : turning point — **tournée** [turne] *nf* **1** : tour **2** *fam* : round (of drinks)

tournesol [turnəsɔl] *nm* : sunflower

tournevis [turnəvis] *nms & pl* : screwdriver

tourniquet [turnikɛ] *nm* : turnstile

tournoi [turnwa] *nm* : tournament

tournoyer [turnwaje] {58} *vi* : whirl, spin

tournure [turnyr] *nf* **1** : turn (of events) **2** : expression

tourterelle [turtərɛl] *nf* : turtledove

tousser [tuse] *vi* : cough

tout [tu] (**toute(s)**) [tut] *before feminine adjectives beginning with a consonant or an aspirate h*) *adv* **1** COMPLÈTEMENT : completely **2** : quite, very, all **3** ~ **à coup** : suddenly **4** ~ **à fait** : completely, entirely **5** ~ **de suite** : immediately — **tout, toute** *adj, pl* **tous, toutes 1** : all **2** : each, every **3** **à tout âge** : at any age **4** **à toute vitesse** : at full speed **5** **tout le monde** : everyone, every-body — **tout** *nm* **1** **le** ~ : the whole **2** **pas du** ~ : not at all — **tout** *pron, pl* **tous, toutes 1** : all, everything **2** : anyone, every-one

toutefois [tutfwa] *adv* : however

toux [tu] *nfs & pl* : cough

toxicomane [tɔksikɔman] *nmf* : drug addict

toxique [tɔksik] *adj* : toxic, poisonous

trac [trak] *nm* : stage fright, jitters *pl*

tracasser [trakase] *vt* : worry, bother — **se tracasser** *vr* : worry, fret — **tracas** [traka] *nms & pl* **1** : worry **2** ~ *nmpl* ENNUIS : troubles, problems

tracer [trase] {6} *vt* **1** : trace **2** DESSINER : draw **3** ~ **le chemin** : pave the way — **trace** [tras] *nf* **1** : track, trail **2** : trace, vestige **3** ~ **s de pas** : footprints **4** **suivre les** ~ **s de qqn** : follow in s.o.'s footsteps — **tracé** [trase] *nm* PLAN : plan, layout

trachée [traʃe] *nf* : trachea, windpipe

tract [trakt] *nm* : leaflet

tractations [traktasjɔ̃] *nfpl* : negotiations

tracteur [traktœr] *nm* : tractor

traction [traksjɔ̃] *nf* **1** : traction **2** ~ **avant** : front-wheel drive

tradition [tradisjɔ̃] *nf* : tradition — **traditionnel, -nelle** [tradisjɔnɛl] *adj* : traditional

traduire [tradɥir] {49} *vt* : translate — **traducteur, -trice** [tradyktœr, -tris] *n* : translator — **traduction** [tradyksjɔ̃] *nf* : translation

trafic [trafik] *nm* **1** : traffic **2** : (drug) trafficking — **trafiquant, -quante** [trafikɑ̃, -kɑ̃t] *n* : dealer, trafficker — **trafiquer** [trafike] *vt* : doctor, tamper with — *vi* : traffic, trade

tragédie [traʒedi] *nf* : tragedy — **tragique** [traʒik] *adj* : tragic

trahir [trair] *vt* : betray — **trahison** [traizɔ̃] *nf* **1** : betrayal **2** : treason

train [trɛ̃] *nm* **1** : (passenger) train **2** : pace, rate **3** : set, series **4** **en** ~ **de** : in the process of **5** ~ **de vie** : lifestyle

traîner [trene] *vt* **1** : pull, drag **2** ~ **les pieds** : drag one's feet — *vi* **1** : drag **2** : dawdle, lag behind **3** : be lying around (of clothes, etc.) — **se traîner** *vr* : drag oneself, crawl — **traîne** [trɛn] *nf* **1** : train (of a dress) **2** *Can* : toboggan, sled — **traîneau** [treno] *nm, pl* **-neaux** : sled, sleigh — **traînée** [trene] *nf* **1** : streak **2** TRACE : trail **3** : drag (of an airplane, etc.)

train–train [trɛ̃trɛ̃] *nms & pl* ROUTINE : routine

traire [trɛr] {40} *vt* : milk (an animal)

trait [trɛ] *nm* **1** : (character) trait **2** : stroke, line **3** **avoir** ~ **à** : relate to **4** **d'un** ~ : in one gulp **5** ~ **d'union** : hyphen **6** ~ **s** *nmpl* : features

traite [trɛt] *nf* **1** : milking **2 d'une ~** : in one go **3 ~ bancaire** : bank draft

traité [trete] *nm* **1** : treaty **2** : treatise

traiter [trete] *vt* **1** : treat **2** : process (data) **3 ~ qqn de menteur** : call s.o. a liar — *vi ~* **de** : deal with — **traitement** [trɛtmã] *nm* **1** : treatment **2 ~ de texte** : word processing

traiteur [trɛtœr] *nm* : caterer

traître, -tresse [trɛtr, -trɛs] *n* : traitor — *~ adj* : treacherous

trajectoire [traʒɛktwar] *nf* : trajectory

trajet [traʒɛ] *nm* **1** PARCOURS : route **2** VOYAGE : journey

trancher [trãʃe] *vt* **1** COUPER : cut **2** : resolve (an issue) — *vi* **1** : stand out **2** : come to a decision — **tranchant, -chante** [trãʃã, -ʃãt] *adj* : sharp, cutting — **tranchant** *nm* : cutting edge — **tranche** [trãʃ] *nf* **1** : slice (of bread) **2** PARTIE : portion, section **3** : edge (of a book) — **tranchée** *nf* : trench

tranquille [trãkil] *adj* **1** : calm, quiet **2 tiens-toi ~!** : sit still! — **tranquillisant** [trãkilizɑ] *nm* : tranquilizer — **tranquilliser** [trãkilize] *vt* RASSURER : reassure — **tranquillité** [trãkilite] *nf* CALME : peacefulness, tranquillity

transaction [trãzaksjõ] *nf* : transaction

transcrire [trãskrir] {33} *vt* : transcribe — **transcription** [trãskripsjõ] *nf* : transcription

transe [trãs] *nf* : trance

transférer [trãsfere] *vt* : transfer — **transfert** [trãsfɛr] *nm* : transfer

transformer [trãsfɔrme] *vt* : transform, change — **se transformer** *vr ~* **en** : turn into — **transformateur** [trãsfɔrmatœr] *nm* : transformer — **transformation** [trãsfɔrmasjõ] *nf* : transformation

transfusion [trãsfyzjõ] *nf* : transfusion

transgresser [trãsgrese] *vt* ENFREINDRE : infringe, violate

transir [trãzir] *vt* **1** : chill (to the bone) **2** : paralyse (with fear)

transistor [trãzistɔr] *nm* : transistor

transit [trãzit] *nm* : transit

transitif, -tive [trãzitif, -tiv] *adj* : transitive

transition [trãzisjõ] *nf* : transition — **transitoire** [trãzitwar] *adj* : transitory, transient

translucide [trãslysid] *adj* : translucent

transmettre [trãsmɛtr] {53} *vt* **1** : transmit (signals, data, etc.) **2** : pass on, convey **3** : broadcast (a show) — **transmission** [trãsmisjõ] *nf* **1** : transmission **2** : broadcasting

transparent, -rente [trãsparã, -rãt] *adj* : transparent — **transparence** [trãsparãs] *nf* : transparency

transpercer [trãspɛrse] {6} *vt* : pierce

transpirer [trãspire] *vt* : perspire — **transpiration** [trãspirasjõ] *nf* : perspiration

transplanter [trãsplãte] *vt* : transplant — **transplantation** [trãsplãtasjõ] *nm* : transplant

transporter [trãspɔrte] *vt* : transport, carry — **transport** [trãspɔr] *nm* : transport — **transporteur** [trãspɔrtœr] *nm* : carrier, transporter

transposer [trãspoze] *vt* : transpose

transversal, -sale [trãsversal] *adj, mpl* **-saux** [-so] : cross (of a beam)

trapèze [trapɛz] *nm* **1** : trapezoid **2** : trapeze

trappe [trap] *nf* **1** PIÈGE : trap **2** : trapdoor

trapu, -pue [trapy] *adj* : stocky, squat

traquer [trake] *vt* POURSUIVRE : track down

traumatiser [tromatize] *vt* : traumatize — **traumatisant, -sante** [tromatizã, -zãt] *adj* : traumatic — **traumatisme** [tromatism] *nm* : trauma

travailler [travaje] *vt* **1** : work **2** PRATIQUER : work on **3** TRACASSER : worry — *vi* : work — **travail** [travaj] *nm, pl* **-vaux** [travo] **1** : work **2** TÂCHE : task, job **3** EMPLOI : work, employment **4 travaux** *nmpl* : works, work — **travailleur, -leuse** [travajœr, -jøz] *adj* : hardworking, industrious — *~ n* : worker

travée [trave] *nf* **1** : row (of seats) **2** : span (of a bridge)

travers [travɛr] *nms & pl* **1 à ~** *or* **au ~** : through **2 de ~** : askew, wrongly **3 en ~** : across, sideways — **traverser** [travɛrse] *vt* **1** : cross (the road, etc.) **2** : run through, pass through — **traversée** [traverse] *nf* : crossing

trébucher [trebyʃe] *vi* : stumble

trèfle [trɛfl] *nm* **1** : clover, shamrock **2** : clubs *pl* (in playing cards)

treillis [treji] *nms & pl* : trellis, lattice

treize [trɛz] *adj* **1** : thirteen **2** : thirteenth (in dates) — *~ nms & pl* : thirteen — **treizième** [trɛzjɛm] *adj & nmf & nm* : thirteenth

trembler [trãble] *vi* **1** : shake, tremble **2** : quiver (of the voice) — **tremblement** [trãbləmã] *nm* **1** : trembling **2** FRISSON : shiver **3 ~ de terre** : earthquake — **trembloter** [trãblɔte] *vi* : quaver

trémousser [tremuse] *v* **se trémousser** *vr* : wriggle around

tremper [trãpe] *vt* **1** : soak **2** : dip, dunk — **trempe** [trãp] *nf* : caliber, quality — **trempé, -pée** [trãpe] *adj* : soaked

tremplin [trãplɛ] *nm* **1** : springboard **2** *or* **~ à ski** : ski jump

trente [trãt] *adj* **1** : thirty **2** : thirtieth (in dates) — *~ nms & pl* : thirty — **trentième** [trãtjɛm] *adj & nmf & nm* : thirtieth

trépied [trepje] *nm* : tripod

trépigner [trepiɲe] *vi* : stamp one's feet

très [trɛ] *adv* : very

trésor [trezɔr] *nm* : treasure

tressaillir [tresajir] {93} *vi* **1** : start (with surprise, etc.), wince (with pain) **2** TREMBLER : quiver, tremble — **tressaillement** [tresajmɑ̃] *nm* : start, wince

tresse [trɛs] *nf* : braid, plait — **tresser** [trese] *vt* **1** : braid, plait **2** : weave (a basket, etc.)

treuil [trœj] *nm* : winch

trêve [trɛv] *nf* **1** : truce **2** : respite

tri [tri] *nm* : sorting (out)

triangle [trijɑ̃gl] *nm* : triangle — **triangulaire** [trijɑ̃gylɛr] *adj* : triangular

tribal, -bale [tribal] *adj, mpl* **-baux** [tribo] : tribal

tribord [tribɔr] *nm* : starboard

tribu [triby] *nf* : tribe

tribulations [tribylasjɔ̃] *nfpl* : tribulations

tribunal [tribynal] *nm, pl* **-naux** [-no] : court

tribune [tribyn] *nf* **1** : gallery, grandstand **2** : rostrum, platform **3** DÉBAT : forum

tribut [triby] *nm* : tribute

tributaire [tribytɛr] *adj* être ~ de : be dependent on

tricher [triʃe] *vi* : cheat — **tricherie** [triʃri] *nf* : cheating — **tricheur, -cheuse** [triʃœr, -ʃøz] *n* : cheat

tricoter [trikɔte] *v* : knit — **tricot** [triko] *nm* **1** : knitting **2** : knitted fabric **3** CHANDAIL : sweater

tricycle [trisikl] *nm* : tricycle

trier [trije] {96} *vt* **1** : sort (out) **2** CHOISIR : select

trimbaler *or* **trimballer** [trɛ̃bale] *vt fam* : cart around

trimestre [trimɛstr] *nm* **1** : quarter (in economics, etc.) **2** : term (in school) — **trimestriel, -trielle** [trimɛstrijɛl] *adj* : quarterly

tringle [trɛ̃gl] *nf* : rod

trinité [trinite] *nf* : trinity

trinquer [trɛ̃ke] *vi* : clink glasses, drink (a toast)

trio [trijo] *nm* : trio

triomphe [trijɔ̃f] *nm* : triumph — **triompher** [trijɔ̃fe] *vi* : triumph

tripes [trip] *nfpl* **1** : tripe **2** *fam* : guts

triple [tripl] *adj & nm* : triple, treble — **tripler** [triple] *v* : triple — **triplés, -plées** [triple] *npl* : triplets

tripoter [tripɔte] *vt* : fiddle with

trique [trik] *nf* : cudgel

triste [trist] *adj* **1** : sad **2** : dismal **3** LAMENTABLE : deplorable, sorry — **tristesse** [tristɛs] *nf* : sadness, gloominess

triton [tritɔ̃] *nm* : newt

troc [trɔk] *nm* : swap

trognon [trɔɲɔ̃] *nm* : core (of an apple, etc.)

trois [trwa] *adj* **1** : three **2** : third (in dates)

— ~ *nms & pl* : three — **troisième** [trwazjɛm] *adj & nmf* : third

trombe [trɔ̃b] *nf* **1** : waterspout **2** ~s d'eau : downpour

trombone [trɔ̃bɔn] *nm* **1** : trombone **2** : paper clip

trompe [trɔ̃p] *nf* **1** : horn **2** : trunk (of an elephant)

tromper [trɔ̃pe] *vt* **1** DUPER : deceive **2** : be unfaithful to (one's spouse) — **se tromper** *vr* : make a mistake — **tromperie** [trɔ̃pri] *nf* : deception, deceit

trompette [trɔ̃pɛt] *nf* : trumpet

trompeur, -peuse [trɔ̃pœr, -pøz] *adj* **1** : deceitful **2** : misleading

tronc [trɔ̃] *nm* **1** : trunk (of a tree) **2** TORSE : torso

tronçon [trɔ̃sɔ̃] *nm* : section — **tronçonneuse** [trɔ̃sɔnøz] *nf* : chain saw

trône [tron] *nm* : throne

tronquer [trɔ̃ke] *vt* : truncate

trop [tro] *adv* **1** : too **2** ~ de : too many, too much **3** de ~ *or* en ~ : too many, extra

trophée [trɔfe] *nm* : trophy

tropique [trɔpik] *nm* **1** : tropic **2** ~s *nmpl* : tropics — **tropical, -cale** [trɔpikal] *adj, mpl* **-caux** [-ko] : tropical

trop-plein [trɔplɛ̃] *nm, pl* **trop-pleins** : overflow **2** SURPLUS : excess, surplus

troquer [trɔke] *vt* : trade, barter

trotter [trɔte] *vi* : trot

trotteuse [trɔtøz] *nf* : second hand (of a watch)

trottiner [trɔtine] *vi* : scurry along

trottinette [trɔtinɛt] *nf* : scooter

trottoir [trɔtwar] *nm* : sidewalk

trou [tru] *nm* **1** : hole **2** : gap (of time) **3** ~ de mémoire : memory lapse **4** ~ de (la) serrure : keyhole

troubler [truble] *vt* **1** : disturb **2** BROUILLER : blur, cloud **3** INQUIÉTER : trouble — **trouble** [trubl] *adj* **1** : cloudy **2** FLOU : blurred, unclear — ~ *nm* **1** : confusion **2** : trouble **3** ~s *nmpl* : disorder (in medicine) **4** ~s *nmpl* : unrest

trouer [true] *vt* : make a hole in, pierce — **trouée** [true] *nf* : gap

trouille [truj] *nf fam* : fear, fright

troupe [trup] *nf* **1** : troop **2** ~ de théâtre : theater company

troupeau [trupo] *nm, pl* **-peaux** : herd, flock

trousse [trus] *nf* **1** : kit, case **2** aux ~s de : on the heels of

trousseau [truso] *nm, pl* **-seaux** **1** : trousseau **2** ~ de clefs : bunch of keys

trouver [truve] *vt* **1** : find **2** ESTIMER : think — **se trouver** *vr* **1** : be (found) **2** : find oneself **3** SE SENTIR : feel — *v impers* **il se**

trouve que : it turns out that — **trouvaille** [truvaj] *nf* DÉCOUVERTE : find
truand [tryɑ̃] *nm* : gangster, crook
truc [tryk] *nm* **1** : trick **2** *fam* MACHIN : thing, thingamajig
truelle [tryɛl] *nf* : trowel
truffe [tryf] *nf* : truffle
truite [trɥit] *nf* : trout
truquer [tryke] *vt* : fix, rig
trust [trœst] *nm* : trust, cartel
tsar [tsar, dzar] *nm* : czar
t–shirt [tiʃœrt] *nm* → **tee–shirt**
tu [ty] *pron* : you
tuba [tyba] *nm* **1** : tuba **2** : snorkel
tube [tyb] *nm* **1** : tube **2** *fam* : hit (song)
tuberculose [tybɛrkyloz] *nf* : tuberculosis
tuer [tɥe] *vt* **1** : kill **2** ÉPUISER : exhaust — **se tuer** *vr* **1** : be killed, die **2** : kill oneself — **tuerie** [tyri] *nf* CARNAGE : slaughter — **tueur, tueuse** [tɥœr, tɥøz] *n* : killer
tue–tête [tytɛt] **à ～** *adv phr* : at the top of one's lungs
tuile [tɥil] *nf* **1** : tile **2** *fam* : bad luck
tulipe [tylip] *nf* : tulip
tumeur [tymœr] *nf* : tumor
tumulte [tymylt] *nm* : tumult, commotion — **tumultueux, -tueuse** [tymyltɥø, -tɥøz] *adj* : stormy, turbulent

tunique [tynik] *nf* : tunic
tunnel [tynɛl] *nm* : tunnel
tuque [tyk] *nf Can* : stocking cap
turban [tyrbɑ̃] *nm* : turban
turbine [tyrbin] *nf* : turbine
turbulence [tyrbylɑ̃s] *nf* : turbulence — **turbulent, -lente** [tyrbylɑ̃, -lɑ̃t] *adj* **1** : unruly **2** : turbulent
turc, turque [tyrk] *adj* : Turkish — **turc** *nm* : Turkish (language)
turquoise [tyrkwaz] *adj* : turquoise
tutelle [tytɛl] *nf* **1** : guardianship **2** : care, protection
tuteur, -trice [tytœr, -tris] *n* **1** : guardian **2** : tutor — **tuteur** *nm* : stake
tutoyer [tytwaje] {58} *vt* : address someone as *tu*
tuyau [tɥijo] *nm, pl* **tuyaux 1** : pipe, tube **2** *fam* : tip, advice — **tuyauterie** [tɥijotri] *nf* : pipes *pl*, plumbing
tympan [tɛ̃pɑ̃] *nm* : eardrum
type [tip] *nm* **1** : type, kind **2** : example, model **3** : (physical) type **4** *fam* : guy, fellow
typhon [tifɔ̃] *nm* : typhoon
typique [tipik] *adj* : typical
tyran [tirɑ̃] *nm* : tyrant — **tyrannie** [tirani] *nf* : tyranny

U

u [y] *nm* : u, 21st letter of the alphabet
ulcère [ylsɛr] *nm* : ulcer
ultérieur, -rieure [ylterjœr] *adj* : later, subsequent — **ultérieurement** [ylterjœrmɑ̃] *adv* : subsequently
ultimatum [yltimatɔm] *nm* : ultimatum — **ultime** [yltim] *adj* : ultimate, final
ultraviolet, -lette [yltravjolɛ, -lɛt] *adj* : ultraviolet
un, une [œ̃ (œn *before a vowel or mute* h), yn] *adj* : a, an, one — **～** *n & pron* **1** : one **2 une par une** : one by one — **～** *art, pl* **des 1** (*used in the singular*) : a, an **2** (*used in the plural*) : some — **un** *nm* : (number) one
unanime [ynanim] *adj* : unanimous — **unanimité** [ynanimite] *nf* : unanimity
uni, -nie [yni] *adj* **1** : united **2** LISSE : smooth **3** : solid (of a color) **4** : close-knit (of a family)
unifier [ynifje] {96} *vt* : unite, unify — **unification** [ynifikasjɔ̃] *nf* : unification
uniforme [ynifɔrm] *adj* : uniform, even —

～ *nm* : uniform — **uniformiser** *vt* : make uniform, standardize — **uniformité** [yniformite] *nf* : uniformity
unilatéral, -rale [ynilateral] *adj, pl* **-raux** [-ro] : unilateral
union [ynjɔ̃] *nf* : union
unique [ynik] *adj* **1** : unique **2 enfant ～** : only child **3 sens ～** : one-way — **uniquement** [ynikmɑ̃] *adv* : only, solely
unir [ynir] *vt* **1** : unite, connect **2** COMBINER : combine — **s'unir** *vr* : unite
unisson [ynisɔ̃] *nm* : unison
unité [ynite] *nf* **1** : unity **2** : unit
univers [ynivɛr] *nm* : universe — **universel, -selle** [ynivɛrsɛl] *vt* : universal
universitaire [ynivɛrsitɛr] *adj* : university, academic — **université** [ynivɛrsite] *nf* : university
uranium [yranjɔm] *nm* : uranium
Uranus [yranys] *nm* : Uranus
urbain, -baine [yrbɛ̃, -bɛn] *adj* : urban, city — **urbanisme** [yrbanism] *nm* : city planning

urgence [yrʒɑ̃s] *nf* **1** : urgency **2** : emergency **3** d'∼ : urgently, immediately — **urgent, -gente** [yrʒɑ̃, -ʒɑ̃t] *adj* : urgent

urine [yrin] *nf* : urine — **uriner** [yrine] *vi* : urinate — **urinoir** [yrinwar] *nm* : urinal

urne [yrn] *nf* **1** : urn **2** : ballot box

urticaire [yrtikɛr] *nf* : hives

usage [yzaʒ] *nm* **1** : use **2** : usage (of a word) **3** COUTUME : habit, custom — **usagé, -gée** [yzaʒe] *adj* **1** : used, secondhand — **usager** [yzaʒe] *nm* : user

user [yze] *vt* **1** CONSOMMER : use **2** : wear out, to use up — *vi* **1** ∼ **de** : exercise (one's rights, etc.) **2** ∼ **de** : make use of — **usé, -sée** [yze] *adj* **1** : worn-out **2** : hackneyed, trite

usine [yzin] *nf* : factory

usité, -tée [yzite] *adj* : commonly used

ustensile [ystɑ̃sil] *nm* : utensil

usuel, -suelle [yzɥɛl] *adj* : common, usual — **usuellement** [yzɥɛlmɑ̃] *adv* : usually, ordinarily

usure [yzyr] *nm* : wear (and tear)

usurper [yzyrpe] *vt* : usurp

utérus [yterys] *nms & pl* : uterus

utile [ytil] *adj* : useful — **utilisable** [ytilizabl] *adj* : usable — **utiliser** [ytilize] *vt* : use — **utilisateur, -trice** [ytilizatœr, -tris] *n* : user — **utilisation** [ytilizasjɔ̃] *nf* : use — **utilité** [ytilite] *nf* : usefulness

utopie [ytɔpi] *nf* : utopia — **utopique** [ytɔpik] *adj* : utopian

V

v [ve] *nm* : v, 22d letter of the alphabet

va [va], *etc.* → **aller**

vacances [vakɑ̃s] *nfpl* : vacation — **vacancier, -cière** [vakɑ̃sje, -sjɛr] *n* : vacationer — **vacant, -cante** [vakɑ̃, -kɑ̃t] *adj* : vacant

vacarme [vakarm] *nm* : racket, din

vaccin [vaksɛ̃] *nm* : vaccine — **vacciner** [vaksine] *vt* : vaccinate — **vaccination** [vaksinasjɔ̃] *nf* : vaccination

vache [vaʃ] *nf* : cow — ∼ *adj fam* : mean, nasty — **vachement** [vaʃmɑ̃] *adv fam* : really, very — **vacherie** [vaʃri] *nf fam* **1** : nastiness **2** : dirty trick

vaciller [vasije] *vi* **1** : stagger, sway **2** : flicker (of a light) **3** : falter, fail — **vacillant, -lante** [vasijɑ̃, -jɑ̃t] *adj* **1** : unsteady, shaky **2** : wavering, faltering — **vacillement** [vasijmɑ̃] *nm* **1** : flicker **2** : faltering

va–et–vient [vaevjɛ̃] *nms & pl* **1** : comings and goings **2** : to-and-fro motion

vagabond, -bonde [vagabɔ̃, -bɔ̃d] *n* : vagrant, tramp — **vagabonder** [vagabɔ̃de] *vi* : roam, wander

vagin [vaʒɛ̃] *nm* : vagina

vague[1] [vag] *adj* : vague, indistinct — ∼ *nm* : vagueness — **vaguement** [vagmɑ̃] *adv* : vaguely, slightly

vague[2] *nf* : wave

vaillant, -lante [vajɑ̃, -jɑ̃t] *adj* **1** : valiant, brave **2** : healthy, robust — **vaillamment** [vajamɑ̃] *adv* : courageously

vain, vaine [vɛ̃, vɛn] *adj* **1** : vain, futile **2 en** ∼ : in vain

vaincre [vɛ̃kr] {94} *vt* **1** BATTRE : defeat **2**
SURMONTER : overcome — **vaincu, -cue** [vɛ̃ky] *adj* : defeated — **vainqueur** [vɛ̃kœr] *nm* : victor, winner

vaisseau [vɛso] *nm, pl* **-seaux 1** : (blood) vessel **2** : vessel, ship **3** ∼ **spatial** : spaceship

vaisselle [vɛsɛl] *nf* : crockery, dishes *pl*

valable [valabl] *adj* **1** VALIDE : valid **2** BON : good, worthwhile

valet [valɛ] *nm* **1** : servant **2** : jack (in playing cards)

valeur [valœr] *nf* **1** : value **2** MÉRITE : merit, worth **3 objets de** ∼ : valuables **4** ∼**s** *nfpl* : stocks, securities

valide [valid] *adj* : valid — **valider** [valide] *vt* : validate — **validité** [validite] *nf* : validity

valise [valiz] *nf* : suitcase

vallée [vale] *nf* : valley — **vallon** [valɔ̃] *nm* : small valley — **vallonné, -née** [valɔne] *adj* : hilly

valoir [valwar] {95} *vi* **1** : have a (certain) cost **2** : be worth **3** : apply, be valid **4 ça vaut combien?** : how much is it worth? **5 faire** ∼ : point out, assert — *vt* **1** PROCURER : earn, bring (to) **2** ∼ **la peine** : be worth the trouble — *v impers* **il vaut mieux** : it's better (to) — **se valoir** *vr* : be equivalent

valoriser [valɔrize] *vt* : increase the value of

valse [vals] *nf* : waltz — **valser** [valse] *vi* : waltz

valve [valv] *nf* : valve

vampire [vɑ̃pir] *nm* : vampire

vandale [vɑ̃dal] *nmf* : vandal — **vandalisme** [vɑ̃dalism] *nm* : vandalism

vanille [vanij] *nf* : vanilla
vanité [vanite] *nf* : vanity — **vaniteux, -teuse** [vanitø, -tøz] *adj* : conceited, vain
vanne [van] *nf* **1** : floodgate **2** *fam* : dig, gibe
vanter [vɑ̃te] *vt* : vaunt, praise — **se vanter** *vr* **1** : boast **2** ~ **de** : pride oneself on — **vantard, -tarde** [vɑ̃tar, -tard] *adj* : boastful — ~ *n* : braggart — **vantardise** [vɑ̃tardiz] *nf* : boast
va–nu–pieds [vanypje] *nmfs & pl* : beggar
vapeur [vapœr] *nf* **1** : steam **2** ~**s** *nfpl* : fumes
vaporiser [vaporize] *vt* : spray — **vaporisateur** [vaporizatœr] *nm* : spray, atomizer
vaquer [vake] *vi* — **à** : attend to, see to
varappe [varap] *nf* : rock climbing
variable [varjabl] *adj* : variable, changeable — **variante** [varjɑ̃t] *nf* : variant — **variation** [varjasjɔ̃] *nf* : variation
varice [varis] *nf* : varicose vein
varicelle [varisɛl] *nf* : chicken pox
varier [varje] {96} *v* : vary — **varié, -riée** [varje] *adj* **1** : varied, varying **2** : various, diverse — **variété** [varjete] *nf* : variety
variole [varjol] *nf* : smallpox
vase[1] [vaz] *nm* : vase
vase[2] *nf* BOUE : mud, silt — **vaseux, -seuse** [vazø, -zøz] *adj* BOUEUX : muddy
vaste [vast] *adj* : vast, immense
vaurien, -rienne [vorjɛ̃, -rjɛn] *n* : good-for-nothing
vautour [votur] *nm* : vulture
vautrer [votre] *v* **se vautrer** *vr* ~ **dans** : wallow in
veau [vo] *nm, pl* **veaux 1** : calf **2** : veal
vécu [veky] *pp* → **vivre** — **vécu, -cue** [veky] *adj* : real, true
vedette [vədɛt] *nf* **1** : star, celebrity **2 mettre en** ~ : put in the spotlight, feature
végétal, -tale [veʒetal] *adj, mpl* **-taux** : vegetable, plant — **végétal** *nm* : vegetable, plant — **végétarien, -rienne** [veʒetarjɛ̃, -rjɛn] *adj & n* : vegetarian — **végéter** [veʒete] {87} *vi* : vegetate — **végétation** [veʒetasjɔ̃] *nf* : vegetation
véhément, -mente [veemɑ̃, -mɑ̃t] *adj* : vehement — **véhémence** [veemɑ̃s] *nf* : vehemence
véhicule [veikyl] *nm* : vehicle
veiller [veje] *vt* : sit up with, watch over — *vi* **1** : stay awake **2** : keep watch **3** : be vigilant **4** ~ **à** : see to — **veille** [vɛj] *nf* **1** : day before, eve **2** : watch, vigil — **veillée** [veje] *nf* **1** SOIRÉE : evening **2** ~ **funèbre** : wake — **veilleur, -leuse** [vejœr, -jøz] *n* **1** : lookout, sentry **2** ~ **de nuit** : night watchman — **veilleuse** *nf* **1** : night-light **2** : pilot light
veine [vɛn] *nf* **1** : vein **2** *fam* : luck
vélo [velo] *nm* : bike, bicycle

vélomoteur [velɔmɔtœr] *nm* : moped
velours [vəlur] *nm* **1** : velvet, velour **2** ~ **côtelé** : corduroy — **velouté, -tée** [vəlute] *adj* : velvety, smooth
velu, -lue [vəly] *adj* : hairy
venaison [vənɛzɔ̃] *nf* : venison
vendange [vɑ̃dɑ̃ʒ] *nf* : grape harvest
vendre [vɑ̃dr] {63} *vt* **1** : sell **2 à** ~ : for sale — **se vendre** : sell — **vendeur, -deuse** [vɑ̃dœr, -døz] *n* : salesperson
vendredi [vɑ̃drədi] *nm* : Friday
vénéneux, -neuse [venenø, -nøz] *adj* : poisonous
vénérer [venere] {87} *vt* : venerate — **vénérable** [venerabl] *adj* : venerable
vénérien, -rienne [venerjɛ̃, -rjɛn] *adj* : venereal
venger [vɑ̃ʒe] {17} *vt* : avenge — **se venger** *vr* : take revenge — **vengeance** [vɑ̃ʒɑ̃s] *nf* : vengeance, revenge — **vengeur, -geresse** [vɑ̃ʒœr, -ʒrɛs] *adj* : vengeful — ~ *n* : avenger
venin [vənɛ̃] *nm* : venom, poison — **venimeux, -meuse** [vənimø, -møz] *adj* : poisonous
venir [vənir] {92} *vi* **1** : come **2** ~ **de** : come from **3 en** ~ **à** : come to (a conclusion, etc.) **4 faire** ~ : send for — *v aux* **1** : come and, come to **2** ~ **de** : have just
vent [vɑ̃] *nm* **1** : wind **2 il y a du** ~ *or* **il fait du** ~ : it's windy — **venteux, -teuse** [vɑ̃tø, -tøz] *adj* : windy
vente [vɑ̃t] *nf* **1** : sale, selling **2 en** ~ : for sale
ventiler [vɑ̃tile] *vt* : ventilate — **ventilateur** [vɑ̃tilatœr] *nm* : (electric) fan, ventilator — **ventilation** [vɑ̃tilasjɔ̃] *nf* : ventilation
ventouse [vɑ̃tuz] *nf* **1** : suction cup **2** : plunger
ventre [vɑ̃tr] *nm* **1** : stomach, belly **2** : womb **3 avoir mal au** ~ : have a stomachache
ventriloque [vɑ̃trilɔk] *nmf* : ventriloquist
venu [vəny] *pp* → **venir** — **venu, -nue** [vəny] *adj* **1 bien venu** : timely **2 mal venu** : ill-advised, unwelcome — **venue** *nf* : coming, arrival
Vénus [venys] *nf* : Venus (planet)
ver [vɛr] *nm* **1** : worm **2** ~ **de terre** : earthworm
véranda [verɑ̃da] *nf* : veranda, porch
verbe [vɛrb] *nm* : verb — **verbal, -bale** [vɛrbal] *adj, mpl* **-baux** [-bo] : verbal
verdeur [vɛrdœr] *nf* : vigor, vitality
verdict [vɛrdikt] *nm* : verdict
verdir [vɛrdir] *v* : turn green — **verdoyant, -doyante** [vɛrdwajɑ̃, -dwajɑ̃t] *adj* : green, verdant — **verdure** [vɛrdyr] *nf* : greenery
verge [vɛrʒ] *nf* : rod, stick
verger [vɛrʒe] *nm* : orchard

verglacé, -cée [vɛrglase] *adj* : icy — **verglas** [vɛrgla] *nm* : black ice

vergogne [vɛrgɔɲ] *nf* **sans ~** : shamelessly

véridique [veridik] *adj* : truthful

vérifier [verifje] {96} *vt* : verify, check — **vérification** [verifikasjɔ̃] *nf* : verification, check

vérité [verite] *nf* **1** : truth **2 en ~** : in fact — **véritable** [veritabl] *adj* **1** RÉEL : true, actual **2** AUTHENTIQUE : genuine **3** (*used as an intensive*) : real — **véritablement** [-tabləmɑ̃] *adv* : actually, really

vermine [vɛrmin] *nf* : vermin

vernis [vɛrni] *nms & pl* **1** : varnish **2** : glaze (on pottery) **3** : veneer, facade **4 ~ à ongles** : nail polish — **vernir** [vɛrnir] *vt* : varnish — **vernissage** [vɛrnisaʒ] *nm* **1** : varnishing **2** : opening (of an art exhibition) — **vernisser** [vɛrnise] *vt* : glaze (ceramics)

verre [vɛr] *nm* **1** : glass **2** : (drinking) glass **3 ~s** *nmpl* : eyeglasses, lenses **4 prendre un ~** : have a drink — **verrerie** [vɛrri] *nf* : glassware — **verrière** [vɛrjɛr] *nf* **1** : glass roof **2** : glass wall

verrou [vɛru] *nm* : bolt — **verrouiller** [vɛruje] *vt* : bolt, lock

verrue [vɛry] *nf* : wart

vers[1] [vɛr] *nms & pl* : line, verse (of poetry)

vers[2] *prep* **1** : toward, towards **2** : about, around, near

versant [vɛrsɑ̃] *nm* : slope, side (of a hill, etc.)

versatile [vɛrsatil] *adj* : fickle

verser [vɛrse] *vt* **1** : pour, serve **2** PAYER : pay **3** RÉPANDRE : shed (tears, etc.) — *vi* **1** : overturn **2 ~ dans** : lapse into — **verse** [vɛrs] *nf* **pleuvoir à ~** : pour (rain) — **versé, -sée** [vɛrse] *adj* **~ dans** : (well-) versed in — **versement** [vɛrsəmɑ̃] *nm* **1** : payment **2** : installment

verset [vɛrsɛ] *nm* : verse

version [vɛrsjɔ̃] *nf* : version

verso [vɛrso] *nm* : back (of a page)

vert, verte [vɛr, vɛrt] *adj* **1** : green **2** : unripe **3** GAILLARD : sprightly, vigorous — **vert** *nm* : green

vertèbre [vɛrtɛbr] *nf* : vertebra — **vertébral, -brale** [vɛrtebral] *adj, mpl* **-braux** [-bro] : vertebral

vertement [vɛrtəmɑ̃] *adv* : sharply, severely

vertical, -cale [vɛrtikal] *adj, mpl* **-caux** [-ko] : vertical — **verticale** *nf* **à la ~** : vertically — **verticalement** [-kalmɑ̃] *adv* : vertically

vertige [vɛrtiʒ] *nm* : dizziness — **vertigineux, -neuse** [vɛrtiʒinø, -nøz] *adj* **1** : dizzy **2** : breathtaking

vertu [vɛrty] *nf* **1** : virtue **2 en ~ de** : by virtue of — **vertueux, -tueuse** [vɛrtɥø, -tɥøz] *adj* : virtuous

verve [vɛrv] *nf* : humor, wit

vésicule [vezikyl] *nf* **~ biliaire** : gallbladder

vessie [vesi] *nf* : bladder

veste [vɛst] *nf* **1** : jacket **2** *Can* : vest

vestiaire [vɛstjɛr] *nm* : locker room

vestibule [vɛstibyl] *nm* : hall

vestige [vɛstiʒ] *nm* **1** : vestige **2** : relic, remains

veston [vɛstɔ̃] *nm* : (man's) jacket

vêtement [vɛtmɑ̃] *nm* **1** : garment, article of clothing **2 ~s** *nmpl* : clothes, clothing

vétéran [veterɑ̃] *nm* : veteran

vétérinaire [veterinɛr] *nmf* : veterinarian

vêtir [vetir] {97} *vt* HABILLER : dress — **se vêtir** *vr* : get dressed — **vêtu, -tue** [vɛty] *adj* : dressed

veto [veto] *nms & pl* : veto

veuf, veuve [vœf, vœv] *adj* : widowed — **~** *n* : widower *m*, widow *f*

vexer [vɛkse] *vt* : vex, upset — **se vexer** *vr* : take offense — **vexant, -ante** [vɛksɑ̃, -sɑ̃t] *adj* : hurtful

via [vja] *prep* : via

viable [vjabl] *adj* : viable

viaduc [vjadyk] *nm* : viaduct

viande [vjɑ̃d] *nf* **1** : meat **2 ~ hachée** : hamburger

vibrer [vibre] *vi* : vibrate — **vibrant, -brante** [vibrɑ̃, -brɑ̃t] *adj* : vibrant — **vibration** [vibrɑsjɔ̃] *nf* : vibration

vicaire [vikɛr] *nm* : vicar, curate

vice [vis] *nm* **1** DÉBAUCHE : vice **2** DÉFAUT : defect

vice–président, -dente [visprezidɑ̃, -dɑ̃t] *n* : vice president

vice versa *or* **vice–versa** [vis(e)vɛrsa] *adv* : vice versa

vicier [visje] {96} *vt* : pollute, taint

vicieux, -cieuse [visjø, -sjøz] *adj* : perverse, depraved

victime [viktim] *nf* : victim

victoire [viktwar] *nf* : victory — **victorieux, -rieuse** [viktɔrjø, -rjøz] *adj* : victorious

vidange [vidɑ̃ʒ] *nf* **1** : emptying, draining **2** : oil change — **vidanger** [vidɑ̃ʒe] {17} *vt* : empty, drain

vide [vid] *adj* : empty — **~** *nm* **1** : emptiness, void **2** LACUNE : gap

vidéo [video] *adj s & pl* : video — **~** *nf* : video

vidéocassette [videokasɛt] *nf* : videocassette, videotape

vider [vide] *vt* **1** : empty **2** : vacate (the premises) **3** : clean (a fowl), gut (a fish) — **videur** [vidœr] *nm* : bouncer

vie [vi] *nf* **1** : life **2** : lifetime **3** : livelihood, living **4 à ~** : for life **5 être en ~** : be alive **6 jamais de la ~!** : never!

vieil → vieux

viellard [vjɛjar] *nm* : old man

vieille → **vieux**

vieillir [vjejir] *vt* : make (someone) old, age
— *vi* **1** : grow old, age **2** : become outdated
— **vieillesse** [vjɛjɛs] *nf* : old age

vierge [vjɛrʒ] *adj* **1** : virgin **2** : empty, blank
(of a tape, etc.) — ～ *nf* : virgin

vieux [vjø] (**vieil** [vjɛj] *before a vowel or mute
h*), **vieille** [vjɛj] *adj, mpl* **vieux 1** : old **2
vieille fille** : old maid **3 vieux jeu** : old-
fashioned — ～ *n* : old man *m*, old woman *f*

vif, vive [vif, viv] *adj* **1** : lively, animated **2**
AIGU : sharp, keen **3** : vivid (of a color) **4**
: brisk, bracing (of the wind) — **vif** *nm* **1 à**
～ : open, exposed **2 le** ～ **du sujet** : the
heart of the matter **3 sur le** ～ : on the spot,
from life

vigilant, -lante [viʒilɑ̃, -lɑ̃t] *adj* : vigilant —
vigilance [viʒilɑ̃s] *nf* : vigilance

vigne [viɲ] *nf* **1** : grapevine **2** : vineyard —
vigneron, -ronne [viɲrɔ̃, -rɔn] *n* : wine-
grower

vignette [viɲɛt] *nf* : label, sticker

vignoble [viɲɔbl] *nm* : vineyard

vigueur [vigœr] *nf* **1** : vigor **2 en** ～ : in
force — **vigoureux, -reuse** [vigurø, -røz]
adj **1** : vigorous, sturdy **2** : forceful, energetic

VIH [veiaʃ] *nm* (*Virus de l'Immunodéficience
Humaine*) : HIV

vil, vile [vil] *adj* : vile, base

vilain, -laine [vilɛ̃, -lɛn] *adj* **1** LAID : ugly **2**
MÉCHANT : naughty

villa [vila] *nf* : villa

village [vilaʒ] *nm* : village — **villageois,
-geoise** [vilaʒwa, -ʒwaz] *n* : villager

ville [vil] *nf* **1** : city, town **2 en** ～ : downtown

villégiature [vileʒjatyr] *nf* **1** : vacation **2** *or*
lieu de ～ : resort

vin [vɛ̃] *nm* : wine

vinaigre [vinɛgr] *nm* : vinegar — **vinaigrette** [vinɛgrɛt] *nf* : vinaigrette

vindicatif, -tive [vɛ̃dikatif, -tiv] *adj* : vindictive

vingt [vɛ̃ (vɛ̃t *before a vowel, mute h, and
the numbers 22-29*)] *adj* **1** : twenty **2**
: twentieth (in dates) — ～ *nms & pl*
: twenty — **vingtaine** [vɛ̃tɛn] *nf* : about
twenty — **vingtième** [vɛ̃tjɛm] *adj & nmf &
nm* : twentieth

vinicole [vinikɔl] *adj* : wine, wine-growing

vinyle [vinil] *nm* : vinyl

viol [vjɔl] *nm* : rape — **violation** [vjɔlasjɔ̃] *nf*
: violation

violent, -lente [vjɔlɑ̃, -lɑ̃t] *adj* : violent —
violemment [vjɔlamɑ̃] *adv* : violently —
violence [vjɔlɑ̃s] *nf* : violence

violer [vjɔle] *vt* **1** : rape **2** : violate, break (a
law, etc.)

violet, -lette [vjɔlɛ, -lɛt] *adj* : purple, violet
— **violet** *nm* : purple, violet — **violette** *nf*
: violet (flower)

violon [vjɔlɔ̃] *nm* : violin — **violoncelle**
[vjɔlɔ̃sɛl] *nm* : cello — **violoniste**
[vjɔlɔnist] *nmf* : violinist

vipère [vipɛr] *nf* : adder, viper

virer [vire] *vt* **1** : transfer (funds) **2** *fam*
: fire, expel — *vi* **1** : veer, turn **2** : change
color — **virage** [viraʒ] *nm* **1** COURBE
: bend, turn **2** : change, shift (in direction)
— **virée** [vire] *nf fam* : outing, trip — **virement** [virmɑ̃] *nm* : (bank) transfer

virevolter [virvɔlte] *vi* : twirl

virginité [virʒinite] *nf* : virginity

virgule [virgyl] *nf* **1** : comma **2** : (decimal)
point

viril, -rile [viril] *adj* : virile, manly — **virilité**
[virilite] *nf* : virility

virtuel, -tuelle [virtɥɛl] *adj* : virtual

virtuose [virtɥoz] *nmf* : virtuoso

virulent, -lente [virylɑ̃, -lɑ̃t] *adj* : virulent —
virus [virys] *nms & pl* : virus

vis [vi] *nfs & pl* : screw

visa [viza] *nm* : visa

visage [vizaʒ] *nm* : face

vis-à-vis [vizavi] *adv* ～ **de 1** : opposite,
facing **2** : towards, with respect to — ～
nms & pl **en** ～ : facing each other

viscères [visɛr] *nmpl* : innards

viser [vize] *vt* : aim for, aim at — *vi* **1** : aim
2 ～ **à** : aim at, intend to — **visée** [vize] *nf*
: aim, design

visible [vizibl] *adj* **1** : visible **2** : obvious —
visibilité [vizibilite] *nf* : visibility

visière [vizjɛr] *nf* : visor (of a cap, etc.)

vision [vizjɔ̃] *nf* : vision — **visionnaire**
[vizjɔnɛr] *adj & nmf* : visionary — **vision-
ner** [vizjɔne] *vt* : view

visite [vizit] *nf* **1** : visit **2** VISITEUR : visitor
3 : examination, inspection **4 rendre** ～ **à
qqn** : visit s.o. — **visiter** [vizite] *vt* **1** : visit
2 EXAMINER : examine, inspect — **visiteur,
-teuse** [vizitœr, -tøz] *n* : visitor

vison [vizɔ̃] *nm* : mink

visqueux, -queuse [viskø, -køz] *adj* : viscous

visser [vise] *vt* : screw (on)

visuel, -suelle [vizɥɛl] *adj* : visual — **visualiser** [vizɥalize] *vt* : visualize

vital, -tale [vital] *adj, mpl* **-taux** [vito] : vital
— **vitalité** [vitalite] *nf* : vitality

vitamine [vitamin] *nf* : vitamin

vite [vit] *adv* **1** RAPIDEMENT : fast, quickly **2**
TÔT : soon — **vitesse** [vitɛs] *nf* **1** : speed **2**
: gear (of a car)

viticole [vitikɔl] *adj* : wine, wine-growing —
viticulture [vitikyltyr] *nf* : wine growing

vitre [vitr] *nf* **1** : pane, windowpane **2** : window (of a car, train, etc.) — **vitrail** [vitraj]

nm, pl **-traux** [vitro] : stained-glass window
— **vitré, -trée** [vitre] *adj* : glass, glazed —
vitrer [vitre] *vt* : glaze — **vitreux, -treuse**
[vitrø, -trøz] *adj* : glassy — **vitrine** [vitrin]
nf **1** : shop window **2** : display case
vivable [vivabl] *adj* : bearable
vivacité [vivasite] *nf* **1** : vivacity, liveliness
2 AGILITÉ : quickness **3** : sharpness, vivid-
ness
vivant, -vante [vivɑ̃, -vɑ̃t] *adj* **1** : alive, living **2** ANIMÉ : lively — **vivant** *nm* **1 du ~
de** : during the lifetime of **2 les ~s** : the
living
vivats [viva] *nmpl* : cheers
vive → vif — **~** [viv] *interj* : long live, three
cheers for — **vivement** [vivmɑ̃] *adv* **1**
: quickly **2** : greatly
vivier [vivje] *nm* : fishpond
vivifier [vivifje] {96} *vt* : invigorate — **vivifiant, -fiante** [vivifjɑ̃, -fjɑ̃t] *adj* : invigorating
vivre [vivr] {98} *vt* : live through, experience
— *vi* **1** : live **2 ~ de** : live on, live by —
vivres [vivr] *nmpl* : provisions, food
vocabulaire [vokabylɛr] *nm* : vocabulary
vocation [vokasjɔ̃] *nf* : vocation, calling
vociférer [vosifere] {87} *v* : shout, scream
vodka [vodka] *nf* : vodka
vœu [vø] *nm, pl* **vœux 1** SOUHAIT : wish **2**
SERMENT : vow **3 meilleurs ~x** : best
wishes
vogue [vog] *nf* : vogue, fashion
voici [vwasi] *prep* **1** : here is, here are **2**
: this is, these are **3 me ~** : here I am **4 ~
trois jours** : three days ago
voie [vwa] *nf* **1** : road, route, way **2** : lane
(of a highway) **3** : way, course **4** *or* **~ ferrée** : railroad track, railroad **5 en ~ de** : in
the process of **6 la Voie lactée** : the Milky
Way
voilà [vwala] *prep* **1** : there is, there are **2**
: that is, those are **3** VOICI : here is, here are
4 ~ tout! : that's all! **5 ~ un an** : a year
ago
voile [vwal] *nm* : veil — **~** *nf* **1** : sail **2**
: sailing — **voiler** [vwale] *vt* **1** : veil **2** DIS-
SIMULER : conceal — **se voiler** *vr* : warp (of
wood) — **voilier** [vwalje] *nm* : sailboat —
voilure [vwalyr] *nf* : sails *pl*
voir [vwar] {99} *vt* **1** : see **2 faire ~** *or*
laisser ~ : show — *vi* **1** : see **2 ~ à** : see
to, make sure that **3 voyons** : let's see — **se
voir** *vr* **1** : see oneself **2** : see each other **3
ça se voit** : that's obvious, it shows
voire [vwar] *adv* : indeed, or even
voirie [vwari] *nf* : highway department
voisin, -sine [vwazɛ̃, -zin] *adj* **1** : neighboring, adjoining **2 ~ de** : similar to — **~** *n*
: neighbor — **voisinage** [vwazinaʒ] *nm* **1**
: neighborhood **2** ENVIRONS : vicinity

voiture [vwatyr] *nf* **1** AUTOMOBILE : car, automobile **2** WAGON : (railroad) car, coach **3
~ d'enfant** : baby carriage
voix [vwa] *nfs & pl* **1** : voice **2** VOTE : vote **3
à haute ~** : out loud
vol [vol] *nm* **1** : (plane) flight **2** : flock (of
birds) **3** : theft, robbery
volage [volaʒ] *adj* : fickle, flighty
volaille [volaj] *nf* **1** : poultry **2** : fowl
volant [volɑ̃] *nm* **1** : steering wheel **2** : shuttlecock **3** : flounce (of a skirt)
volcan [volkɑ̃] *nm* : volcano — **volcanique**
[volkanik] *adj* : volcanic
volée [vole] *nf* **1** : volley **2** VOL : flock,
flight
voler[1] [vole] *vt* **1** : steal **2** : rob **3 ~ à
l'étalage** : shoplift
voler[2] *vi* : fly — **volet** [volɛ] *nm* **1** : shutter,
flap **2** : (detachable) section — **voleter**
[volte] {8} *vi* : flutter, flit
voleur, -leuse [volœr, -løz] *adj* : dishonest
— **~** *n* : thief, robber
volière [voljɛr] *nf* : aviary
volley [volɛ] *or* **volley–ball** [volɛbol] *nm*
: volleyball
volontaire [volɔ̃tɛr] *adj* **1** : voluntary **2** : deliberate **3** DÉTERMINÉ : willful — **~** *nmf*
: volunteer — **volontairement** [volɔ̃tɛrmɑ̃]
adv **1** : voluntarily **2** : deliberately —
volonté [volɔ̃te] *nf* **1** : will **2** : willpower **3
à ~** : at will **4 bonne ~** : goodwill —
volontiers [volɔ̃tje] *adv* : willingly, gladly
volt [volt] *nm* : volt — **voltage** [voltaʒ] *nm*
: voltage
volte–face [voltəfas] *nfs & pl* : about-face
voltiger [voltiʒe] {17} *vi* : flutter about —
voltige [voltiʒ] *nf* : acrobatics
volubile [volybil] *adj* : voluble
volume [volym] *nm* : volume — **volumineux, -neuse** [volyminø, -nøz] *adj*
: bulky
volupté [volypte] *nf* : sensual pleasure —
voluptueux, -tueuse [volyptɥø, -tɥøz] *adj*
: voluptuous
volute [volyt] *nf* : coil (of smoke, etc.)
vomir [vomir] *vt* : vomit — *vi* : vomit
vorace [voras] *adj* : voracious
vote [vot] *nm* **1** : vote **2** : voting — **voter**
[vote] *vi* : vote — *vt* : vote for
votre [votr] *adj, pl* **vos** [vo] : your
vôtre [votr] *pron* **le ~, la ~, les ~s**
: yours, your own
vouer [vwe] *vt* **1** PROMETTRE : vow, pledge
2 CONSACRER : dedicate, devote **3 voué à**
: doomed to
vouloir [vulwar] {100} *vt* **1** : want, wish for
2 CONSENTIR À : agree to, be willing to **3
~ dire** : mean **4 en ~ à** : bear a grudge
against **5 veuillez patienter** : please wait

— **voulu, -lue** [vuly] *adj* **1** DÉLIBÉRÉ : intentional **2** REQUIS : required
vous [vu] *pron* **1** (*as subject or direct object*) : you **2** (*as indirect object*) : you, to you **3** : yourself **4** à ~ : yours — **vous-même** [vumɛm] *pron, pl* **vous-mêmes** : yourself
voûte [vut] *nf* : vault, arch — **voûté, -tée** [vute] *adj* **1** : arched **2** : stooped, bent over
vouvoyer [vuvwaje] {58} *vt* : address as *vous*
voyage [vwajaʒ] *nm* **1** : trip, voyage **2 avoir son** ~ *Can fam* : to be fed up — **voyager** [vwajaʒe] {17} *vi* : travel — **voyageur, -geuse** [vwajaʒœr, -ʒøz] *n* **1** : traveler **2** : passenger
voyance [vwajɑ̃s] *nf* : clairvoyance — **voyant, voyante** [vwajɑ̃, vwajɑ̃t] *adj* : loud, gaudy — ~ *n* : clairvoyant — **voyant** *nm* : warning light
voyelle [vwajɛl] *nf* : vowel
voyou [vwaju] *nm* : thug, hoodlum
vrac [vrak] *adv* **1 en** ~ : loose, in bulk **2 en** ~ : haphazardly

vrai, vraie [vrɛ] *adj* **1** : true **2** : real **3 à vrai dire** : to tell the truth — **vraiment** [vrɛmɑ̃] *adv* : really
vraisemblable [vrɛzɑ̃blabl] *adj* : likely, probable — **vraisemblance** [vrɛzɑ̃blɑ̃s] *nf* : likelihood, probability
vrombir [vrɔ̃bir] *vi* **1** : hum, buzz **2** : roar (of an engine) — **vrombissement** [vrɔ̃bismɑ̃] *nm* : humming, buzzing, roaring
vu [vy] *pp* → **voir** — ~ *prep* : in view of, considering — **vu, vue** [vy] *adj* **1** : seen, regarded **2 bien vu** : well thought of — **vue** *nf* **1** : sight, eyesight **2** : view, vista **3** IDÉE : opinion, view — **vu que** *conj phr* : seeing that, inasmuch as
vulgaire [vylgɛr] *adj* **1** GROSSIER : vulgar **2** ORDINAIRE : common — **vulgariser** [vylgarize] *vt* : popularize — **vulgarité** [vylgarite] *nf* : vulgarity
vulnérable [vylnerabl] *adj* : vulnerable — **vulnérabilité** [vylnerabilite] *nf* : vulnerability

W

w [dublǝve] *nm* : w, 23d letter of the alphabet
wagon [vagɔ̃] *nm* : car (of a train)
wagon-lit [vagɔ̃li] *nm, pl* **wagons-lits** : sleeping car
wagon-restaurant [vagɔ̃rɛstorɑ̃] *nm, pl* **wagons-restaurants** : dining car

wallon, -lonne [walɔ̃, -lɔn] *adj* : Walloon
watt [wat] *nm* : watt
w-c [vese] *nmpl* : toilet
week-end [wikɛnd] *nm, pl* **week-ends** : weekend
western [wɛstɛrn] *nm* : western
whisky [wiski] *nm, pl* **-kies** : whiskey

XYZ

x [iks] *nm* : x, 24th letter of the alphabet
xénophobie [gzenɔfɔbi] *nf* : xenophobia
xérès [gzerɛs, kserɛs] *nm* : sherry
xylophone [ksilɔfɔn] *nm* : xylophone
y [igrɛk] *nm* : y, 25th letter of the alphabet
y [i] *adv* **1** : there **2 ça** ~ **est !** : finally! **3 il** ~ **a** : there is, there are — ~ *pron* **1** : it, about it, on it, in it **2** : them, about them, on them, in them **3 j'y suis!** : I've got it!
yacht [jɔt] *nm* : yacht
yaourt [jaurt] *nm* : yogurt
yeux [jø] → **œil**
yoga [jɔga] *nm* : yoga

yogourt *or* **yoghourt** [jɔgurt] → **yaourt**
yo-yo *or* **yoyo** [jojo] *nm* : yo-yo
z [zɛd] *nm* : z, 26th letter of the alphabet
zèbre [zɛbr] *nm* : zebra — **zébrure** [zebryr] *nf* **1** : stripe **2** : welt
zèle [zɛl] *nm* : zeal — **zélé, -lée** [zele] *adj* : zealous
zénith [zenit] *nm* : zenith
zéro [zero] *adj* **1** : zero **2** : nil, worthless — ~ *nm* : zero, naught
zézayer [zezeje] *vi* : lisp
zigzag [zigzag] *nm* : zigzag — **zigzaguer** [zigzage] *vi* : zigzag

zinc [zɛ̃g] *nm* : zinc
zizanie [zizani] *nf* : discord, conflict
zodiaque [zɔdjak] *nm* : zodiac
zona [zona] *nm* : shingles
zone [zon] *nf* : zone, area — **zonage** [zonaʒ] *nm* : zoning

zoo [zo(o)] *nm* : zoo — **zoologie** [zɔɔlɔʒi] *nf* : zoology
zoom [zum] *nm* **1** : zoom lens **2** faire un ~ : zoom in
zut [zyt] *interj fam* : darn!, damn it!

English-French
Dictionary

A

a¹ [ˈeɪ] *n, pl* **a's** *or* **as** [ˈeɪz] : a *m*, première lettre de l'alphabet

a² [ə, ˈeɪ] *art* (**an** [ən, ˈæn] *before a vowel or silent h*) **1** : un *m*, une *f* **2** PER : par

aback [əˈbæk] *adv* **taken ~** : déconcerté

abandon [əˈbændən] *vt* : abandonner — **~** *n* : abandon *m*

abashed [əˈbæʃt] *adj* : décontenancé

abate [əˈbeɪt] *vi* **abated; abating** : s'apaiser, se calmer

abbey [ˈæbi] *n, pl* **-beys** : abbaye *f* — **abbot** [ˈæbət] *n* : abbé *m*

abbreviate [əˈbriːviˌeɪt] *vt* **-ated; -ating** : abréger — **abbreviation** [əˌbriːviˈeɪʃən] *n* : abréviation *f*

abdicate [ˈæbdɪˌkeɪt] *v* **-cated; -cating** : abdiquer

abdomen [ˈæbdəmən, æbˈdoːmən] *n* : abdomen *m* — **abdominal** [æbˈdɑmənəl] *adj* : abdominal

abduct [æbˈdʌkt] *vt* : enlever — **abduction** [æbˈdʌkʃən] *n* : enlèvement *m*

aberration [ˌæbəˈreɪʃən] *n* : aberration *f*

abhor [əbˈhɔr, æb-] *vt* **-horred; -horring** : abhorrer, détester

abide [əˈbaɪd] *v* **abode** [əˈboːd] *or* **abided; abiding** *vt* : supporter — *vi* **~ by** : respecter, se conformer à

ability [əˈbɪləti] *n, pl* **-ties 1** : aptitude *f* **2** SKILL : habileté *f*, talent *m*

ablaze [əˈbleɪz] *adj* : en feu

able [ˈeɪbəl] *adj* **abler; ablest 1** CAPABLE : capable **2** SKILLED : habile — **ably** [ˈeɪbəli] *adv* : habilement

abnormal [æbˈnɔrməl] *adj* : anormal — **abnormality** [ˌæbnɔrˈmæləti, -nɔr-] *n, pl* **-ties** : anormalité *f*, anomalie *f*

aboard [əˈbord] *adv* : à bord — **~** *prep* : à bord de, dans

abode [əˈboːd] *n* : demeure *f*, domicile *m*

abolish [əˈbɑlɪʃ] *vt* : abolir — **abolition** [ˌæbəˈlɪʃən] *n* : abolition *f*

abominable [əˈbɑmənəbəl] *adj* : abominable

aborigine [ˌæbəˈrɪdʒəni] *n* : aborigène *mf*

abort [əˈbɔrt] *vt* : faire avorter — **abortion** [əˈbɔrʃən] *n* : avortement *m*

abound [əˈbaʊnd] *vi* **~ in** : abonder en

about [əˈbaʊt] *adv* **1** APPROXIMATELY : vers, environ **2** AROUND : autour **3** NEARBY : près **4 be ~ to** : être sur le point de — **~** *prep* **1** AROUND : autour de **2** CONCERNING : sur, de

above [əˈbʌv] *adv* **1** OVERHEAD : au-dessus, en haut **2** PREVIOUSLY : ci-dessus — **~**

prep **1** OVER : au-dessus de **2** EXCEEDING : plus de **3 ~ all** : surtout

abrasive [əˈbreɪsɪv] *adj* : abrasif

abreast [əˈbrɛst] *adv* **1** : de front, côte à côte **2 ~ of** : au courant de

abridge [əˈbrɪdʒ] *vt* **abridged; abridging** : abréger

abroad [əˈbrɔd] *adv* **1** : à l'étranger **2** WIDELY : de tous côtés

abrupt [əˈbrʌpt] *adj* **1** SUDDEN : brusque **2** STEEP : abrupt

abscess [ˈæbˌsɛs] *n* : abcès *m*

absence [ˈæbsənts] *n* **1** : absence *f* **2** LACK : manque *m* — **absent** [ˈæbsənt] *adj* : absent — **absentee** [ˌæbsənˈtiː] *n* : absent *m*, -sente *f* — **absentminded** [ˌæbsəntˈmaɪndəd] *adj* : distrait

absolute [ˈæbsəˌluːt, ˌæbsəˈluːt] *adj* : absolu — **absolutely** [ˈæbsəˌluːtli, ˌæbsəˈluːtli] *adv* : absolument

absolve [əbˈzɑlv, æb-, -ˈsɑlv] *vt* **-solved; -solving** : absoudre

absorb [əbˈzɔrb, æb-, -ˈsɔrb] *vt* : absorber — **absorbent** [əbˈzɔrbənt, æb-, -ˈsɔr-] *adj* : absorbant — **absorption** [əbˈzɔrpʃən, æb-, -ˈsɔrp-] *n* : absorption *f*

abstain [əbˈsteɪn, æb-] *vi* **~ from** : s'abstenir de — **abstinence** [ˈæbstənənts] *n* : abstinence *f*

abstract [æbˈstrækt, ˈæbˌ-] *adj* : abstrait — **~** *n* SUMMARY : résumé *m*

absurd [əbˈsərd, -ˈzərd] *adj* : absurde — **absurdity** [əbˈsərdəti, -ˈzər-] *n, pl* **-ties** : absurdité *f*

abundant [əˈbʌndənt] *adj* : abondant — **abundance** [əˈbʌndənts] *n* : abondance *f*

abuse [əˈbjuːz] *vt* **abused; abusing 1** MISUSE : abuser de **2** MISTREAT : maltraiter **3** INSULT : injurier — **~** [əˈbjuːs] *n* **1** MISUSE : abus *m* **2** MISTREATMENT : mauvais traitement *m* **3** INSULTS : insultes *fpl*, injures *fpl* — **abusive** [əˈbjuːsɪv] *adj* : injurieux

abut [əˈbʌt] *vi* **abutted; abutting ~ on** : être contigu à

abyss [əˈbɪs, ˈæbɪs] *n* : abîme *m*

academy [əˈkædəmi] *n, pl* **-mies 1** SCHOOL : école *f*, collège *m* **2** SOCIETY : académie *f* — **academic** [ˌækəˈdɛmɪk] *adj* **1** : universitaire **2** THEORETICAL : théorique

accelerate [ɪkˈsɛləˌreɪt, æk-] *v* **-ated; -ating** : accélérer — **acceleration** [ɪkˌsɛləˈreɪʃən, æk-] *n* : accélération *f*

accent [ˈækˌsɛnt, ækˈsɛnt] *vt* : accentuer — **~** [ˈækˌsɛnt, -sənt] *n* : accent *m* — **accen-**

tuate [ɪkˈsɛntʃʊˌeɪt, æk-] *vt* **-ated; -ating** : accentuer

accept [ɪkˈsɛpt, æk-] *vt* : accepter — **acceptable** [ɪkˈsɛptəbəl, æk-] *adj* : acceptable — **acceptance** [ɪkˈsɛptən/s, æk-] *n* **1** : acceptation *f* **2** APPROVAL : approbation *f*

access [ˈækˌsɛs] *n* : accès *m* — **accessible** [ɪkˈsɛsəbəl, æk-] *adj* : accessible

accessory [ɪkˈsɛsəri, æk-] *n, pl* **-ries 1** : accessoire *m* **2** ACCOMPLICE : complice *mf*

accident [ˈæksədənt] *n* **1** : accident *m* **2 by** ~ : par hasard — **accidental** [ˌæksəˈdɛntəl] *adj* : accidentel — **accidentally** [ˌæksəˈdɛntəli, -ˈdɛntli] *adv* : accidentellement, par hasard

acclaim [əˈkleɪm] *vt* : acclamer — ~ *n* : acclamation *f*

acclimate [ˈækləˌmeɪt, əˈklaɪmət] *vt* **-mated; -mating** : acclimater

accommodate [əˈkɑməˌdeɪt] *vt* **-dated; -dating 1** ADAPT : accommo-der **2** SATISFY : satisfaire **3** LODGE : loger **4** HOLD : contenir — **accommodation** [əˌkɑməˈdeɪʃən] *n* **1** : accommodation *f* **2** ~**s** *npl* LODGING : logement *m*

accompany [əˈkʌmpəni, -ˈkɑm-] *vt* **-nied; -nying** : accompagner

accomplice [əˈkɑmpləs, -ˈkʌm-] *n* : complice *mf*

accomplish [əˈkɑmplɪʃ, -ˈkʌm-] *vt* **1** : accomplir **2** REALIZE : réaliser — **accomplishment** [əˈkɑmplɪʃmənt, -ˈkʌm-] *n* : accomplissement *m*

accord [əˈkɔrd] *n* **1** AGREEMENT : accord *m* **2 of one's own** ~ : de son plein gré — **accordance** [əˈkɔrdən/s] *n* **in** ~ **with** : conformément à — **accordingly** [əˈkɔrdɪŋli] *adv* : en conséquence — **according to** [əˈkɔrdɪŋ] *prep* : selon, d'après

accordion [əˈkɔrdiən] *n* : accordéon *m*

account [əˈkaʊnt] *n* **1** : compte *m* **2** REPORT : compte *m* rendu **3** WORTH : importance *f* **4 on** ~ **of** : à cause de **5 on no** ~ : en aucun cas **6 take into** ~ : tenir compte de — ~ *vi* — **for** : expliquer — **accountable** [əˈkaʊntəbəl] *adj* : responsable — **accountant** [əˈkaʊntənt] *n* : comptable *mf* — **accounting** [əˈkaʊntɪŋ] *n* : comptabilité *f*

accrue [əˈkruː] *vi* **-crued; -cruing** : s'accumuler

accumulate [əˈkjuːmjəˌleɪt] *v* **-lated; -lating** *vt* : accumuler — *vi* s'accumuler — **accumulation** [əˌkjuːmjəˈleɪʃən] *n* : accumulation *f*

accurate [ˈækjərət] *adj* : exact, précis — **accurately** *adv* : exactement, avec précision — **accuracy** [ˈækjərəsi] *n, pl* **-cies** : exactitude *f*, précision *f*

accuse [əˈkjuːz] *vt* **-cused; -cusing** : ac-

cuser — **accusation** [akyzasjɔ̃] *n* : accusation *f*

accustom [əˈkʌstəm] *vt* : accoutumer — **accustomed** [əˈkʌstəmd] *adj* **1** CUSTOMARY : habituel **2** **be** ~ **to** : avoir l'habitude à

ace [ˈeɪs] *n* : as *m*

ache [ˈeɪk] *vi* **ached; aching** : faire mal — ~ *n* : douleur *f*

achieve [əˈtʃiːv] *vt* **achieved; achieving** : accomplir, atteindre — **achievement** [əˈtʃiːvmənt] *n* : accomplissement *m*, réussite *f*

acid [ˈæsəd] *adj* : acide — ~ *n* : acide *m*

acknowledge [ɪkˈnɑlɪʤ, æk-] *vt* **-edged; -edging 1** ADMIT : admettre **2** RECOGNIZE : reconnaître **3** ~ **receipt of** : accuser réception de — **acknowledgment** [ɪkˈnɑlɪʤmənt, æk-] *n* **1** : reconnaissance *f* **2** ~ **of receipt** : accusé *m* de réception

acne [ˈækni] *n* : acné *f*

acorn [ˈeɪˌkɔrn, -kərn] *n* : gland *m*

acoustic [əˈkuːstɪk] *or* **acoustical** [əˈkuːstɪkəl] *adj* : acoustique — **acoustics** [əˈkuːstɪks] *ns & pl* : acoustique *f*

acquaint [əˈkweɪnt] *vt* **1** ~ **s.o. with** : mettre qqn au courant de **2 be** ~**ed with** : connaître (une personne) — **acquaintance** [əˈkweɪntən/s] *n* : connaissance *f*

acquire [əˈkwaɪr] *vt* **-quired; -quiring** : acquérir — **acquisition** [ˌækwəˈzɪʃən] *n* : acquisition *f*

acquit [əˈkwɪt] *vt* **-quitted; -quitting** : acquitter

acre [ˈeɪkər] *n* : acre *f* — **acreage** [ˈeɪkərɪʤ] *n* : superficie *f*

acrid [ˈækrəd] *adj* : âcre

acrobat [ˈækrəˌbæt] *n* : acrobate *mf* — **acrobatic** [ˌækrəˈbætɪk] *adj* : acrobatique — **acrobatics** [ˌækrəˈbætɪks] *ns & pl* : acrobatie *f*

across [əˈkrɔs] *adv* **1** : de large, d'un côté à l'autre **2** ~ **from** : en face de **3 go** ~ : traverser — ~ *prep* **1** ~ **the street** : de l'autre côté de la rue **2 lie** ~ **sth** : être en travers de qqch

acrylic [əˈkrɪlɪk] *n* : acrylique *m*

act [ˈækt] *vi* **1** : agir **2** PERFORM : jouer, faire du théâtre **3** ~ **as** : servir de — *vt* : jouer (un rôle) — ~ *n* **1** ACTION : acte *m* **2** DECREE : loi *f* **3** : acte *m* (d'une pièce de théâtre), numéro *m* (de variétés) **4 put on an** ~ : jouer la comédie — **acting** *adj* : intérimaire

action [ˈækʃən] *n* **1** : action *f* **2** DEED : acte *m* **2** LAWSUIT : procès *m*, action *f*

activate [ˈæktəˌveɪt] *vt* **-vated; -vating** : activer

active [ˈæktɪv] *adj* : actif — **activity** [ækˈtɪvəti] *n, pl* **-ties** : activité *f*

actor [ˈæktər] *n* : acteur *m*, -trice *f* — **actress** [ˈæktrəs] *n* : actrice *f*

actual [ˈæktʃʊəl] *adj* **1** : réel, véritable **2**

VERY : même — **actually** [ˈæktʃuəli, -ʃəli] *adv* **1** REALLY : vraiment **2** IN FACT : en fait
acupuncture [ˈækjuˌpʌŋktʃər] *n* : acupuncture *f*
acute [əˈkjuːt] *adj* **acuter; acutest 1** : aigu **2** KEEN : fin
ad [ˈæd] *n* → advertisement
adamant [ˈædəmənt, -ˌmænt] *adj* : inflexible
adapt [əˈdæpt] *vt* : adapter — *vi* : s'adapter — **adaptable** [əˌdæptəbəl] *adj* : adaptable — **adaptation** [ˌæˌdæpˈteɪʃən, -dəp-] *n* : adaptation *f* — **adapter** [əˈdæptər] *n* : adapteur *m*
add [ˈæd] *vt* **1** : ajouter **2** ~ **up** : additionner — *vi* : additionner
addict [ˈædɪkt] *n or* **drug** ~ : toxicomane *mf*; drogué *m*, -guée *f* — **addiction** [əˈdɪkʃən] *n* **1** : dépendance *f* **2 drug** ~ : toxicomanie *f*
addition [əˈdɪʃən] *n* **1** : addition *f* **2 in** ~ : en plus — **additional** [əˈdɪʃənəl] *adj* : additionnel, supplémentaire — **additive** [ˈædətɪv] *n* : additif *m*
address [əˈdrɛs] *vt* **1** : adresser (une lettre, etc.) **2** : s'adresser à (une personne), aborder (un problème) — ~ [əˈdrɛs, ˈæˌdrɛs] *n* **1** : adresse *f* **2** SPEECH : discours *m*
adept [əˈdɛpt] *adj* : habile
adequate [ˈædɪkwət] *adj* : adéquat, suffisant — **adequately** [ˈædɪkwətli] *adv* : suffisamment
adhere [ædˈhir, əd-] *vi* **-hered; -hering 1** STICK : adhérer **2** ~ **to** KEEP : adhé-rer à, observer — **adherence** [ædˈhirənts, əd-] *n* : adhésion *f* — **adhesion** [ædˈhiʒən, əd-] *n* : adhésion *f*, adhérence *f* — **adhesive** [ædˈhiːsɪv, əd-, -zɪv] *adj* : adhésif — ~ *n* : adhésif *m*
adjacent [əˈdʒeɪsənt] *adj* : adjacent, contigu
adjective [ˈædʒɪktɪv] *n* : adjectif *m*
adjoining [əˈdʒɔɪnɪŋ] *adj* : contigu
adjourn [əˈdʒərn] *vt* : ajourner — *vi* : suspendre la séance
adjust [əˈdʒʌst] *vt* : ajuster — *vi* ADAPT : s'adapter — **adjustable** [əˈdʒʌstəbəl] *adj* : réglable, ajustable — **adjustment** [əˈdʒʌstmənt] *n* **1** : ajustement *m* **2** ADAPTATION : adaptation *f*
ad-lib [ˈædˈlɪb] *vt* **ad-libbed; ad-libbing** : improviser
administer [ædˈmɪnəstər, əd-] *vt* : administrer — **administration** [ædˌmɪnəˈstreɪʃən, əd-] *n* : administration *f* — **administrative** [ædˈmɪnəˌstreɪtɪv, əd-] *adj* : administratif — **administrator** [ædˈmɪnəˌstreɪtər, əd-] *n* : admi-nistrateur *m*, -trice *f*
admirable [ˈædmərəbəl] *adj* : admirable
admiral [ˈædmərəl] *n* : amiral *m*
admire [ædˈmaɪr] *vt* **-mired; -miring** : ad-

mirer — **admiration** [ˌædməˈreɪʃən] *n* : ad-miration *f* — **admirer** [ædˈmaɪrər] *n* : admi-rateur *m*, -trice *f* — **admiring** [ædˈmaɪrɪŋ] *adj* : admiratif
admit [ædˈmɪt, əd-] *vt* **-mitted; mitting 1** : admettre **2** ACKNOWLEDGE : reconnaître **3** CONFESS : avouer — **admission** [ædˈmɪʃən] *n* **1** ADMITTANCE : admission *f* **2** FEE : entrée *f* **3** CONFESSION : aveu *m* — **admittance** [ædˈmɪtənts, əd-] *n* : entrée *f*
admonish [ædˈmɑnɪʃ, əd-] *vt* : réprimander
ado [əˈduː] *n* **1** : agitation *f* **2 without further** ~ : sans plus de cérémonie
adolescent [ˌædəlˈɛsənt] *n* : adolescent *m*, -cente *f* — **adolescence** [ˌædəlˈɛsənts] *n* : adolescence *f*
adopt [əˈdɑpt] *vt* : adopter — **adoption** [əˈdɑpʃən] *n* : adoption *f*
adore [əˈdor] *vt* **adored; adoring** : adorer — **adorable** [əˈdorəbəl] *adj* : adorable — **adoration** [ˌædəˈreɪʃən] *n* : adoration *f*
adorn [əˈdorn] *vt* : orner
adrift [əˈdrɪft] *adv & adj* : à la dérive
adroit [əˈdrɔɪt] *adj* : adroit, habile
adult [əˈdʌlt, ˈæˌdʌlt] *adj* : adulte — ~ *n* : adulte *mf*
adultery [əˈdʌltəri] *n, pl* **-teries** : adultère *m*
advance [ædˈvænts, əd-] *v* **-vanced; -vancing** *vt* : avancer — *vi* **1** : avancer **2** IMPROVE : progresser — ~ *n* **1** : avance *f* **2 in** ~ : à l'avance, d'avance — **advancement** [ædˈvæntsmənt, əd-] *n* : avancement *m*
advantage [ədˈvæntɪdʒ, æd-] *n* **1** : avantage *m* **2 take** ~ **of** : profiter de — **advantageous** [ˌædˌvænˈteɪdʒəs, -vən-] *adj* : avantageux
advent [ˈædˌvɛnt] *n* **1** : avènement *m* **2 Advent** : Avent *m*
adventure [ædˈvɛntʃər, əd-] *n* : aventure *f* — **adventurous** [ædˈvɛntʃərəs, əd-] *adj* : aventureux
adverb [ˈædˌvərb] *n* : adverbe *m*
adversary [ˈædvərˌsɛri] *n, pl* **-saries** : adversaire *mf*
adverse [ædˈvɛrs, ˈæˌd-] *adj* : défavorable — **adversity** [ædˈvərsəti, əd-] *n, pl* **-ties** : adversité *f*
advertise [ˈædvərˌtaɪz] *v* **-tised; -tising** *vt* : faire de la publicité pour — *vi* : passer une annonce (dans un journal) — **advertisement** [ˈædvərˌtaɪzmənt, ædˈvərtəzmənt] *n* : publicité *f*, annonce *f* — **advertiser** [ˈædvərˌtaɪzər] *n* : annonceur *m* — **advertising** [ˈædvərˌtaɪzɪŋ] *n* : publicité *f*
advice [ædˈvaɪs] *n* : conseils *mpl*
advise [ædˈvaɪz, əd-] *vt* **-vised; -vising 1** : conseiller **2** RECOMMEND : recommander **3** INFORM : aviser — **advisable** [ædˈvaɪzəbəl, əd-] *adj* : recommandé, prudent — **adviser** [ædˈvaɪzər, əd-] *n* : conseiller *m*,

-lère *f* — **advisory** [æd'vaɪzəri, əd-] *adj* : consultatif

advocate ['ædvə,keɪt] *vt* **-cated; -cating** : préconiser — ~ ['ædvəkət] *n* **1** SUPPORTER : défenseur *m* **2** LAWYER : avocat *m*, -cate *f*

aerial ['æriəl] *adj* : aérien — ~ *n* : antenne *f*

aerobics [ˌær'o:bɪks] *ns & pl* : aérobic *m*

aerodynamic [ˌæro:daɪ'næmɪk] *adj* : aérodynamique

aerosol ['ærə,sɔl] *n* : aérosol *m*

aesthetic [ɛs'θɛtɪk] *adj* : esthétique

afar [ə'fɑr] *adv* **from ~** : de loin

affable ['æfəbəl] *adj* : affable

affair [ə'fær] *n* **1** : affaire *f* **2 or love ~** : liaison *f*, affaire *f* de cœur

affect [ə'fɛkt, æ-] *vt* : affecter — **affection** [ə'fɛkʃən] *n* : affection *f* — **affectionate** [ə'fɛkʃənət] *adj* : affectueux

affirm [ə'fərm] *vt* : affirmer — **affirmative** [ə'fərmətɪv] *adj* : affirmatif

affix [ə'fɪks] *vt* : apposer (une signature), coller (un timbre)

afflict [ə'flɪkt] *vt* : affliger — **affliction** [ə'flɪkʃən] *n* : affliction *f*

affluent ['æ,flu:ənt; æ'flu:-, ə-] *adj* : riche

afford [ə'ford] *vt* **1** : avoir les moyens d'acheter **2 ~ to do** : se permettre de faire

afloat [ə'flo:t] *adj & adv* : à flot

afoot [ə'fʊt] *adv & adj* : en train, en cours

afraid [ə'freɪd] *adj* **1 be ~ of** : avoir peur de, craindre **2 be ~ that** : regretter que **3 I'm ~ not** : hélas, non

African ['æfrɪkən] *adj* : africain

after ['æftər] *adv* **1** AFTERWARD : après **2** BEHIND : en arrière — ~ *conj* : après que — ~ *prep* **1** : après **2 ~ all** : après tout **3 it's ten ~ five** : il est cinq heures dix

aftereffect ['æftərɪˌfɛkt] *n* : répercussion *f*

aftermath ['æftərˌmæθ] *n* : suites *fpl*

afternoon [ˌæftər'nu:n] *n* : après-midi *mf*

afterward ['æftərwərd] *or* **afterwards** [-wərdz] *adv* : après, ensuite

again [ə'gɛn, -gɪn] *adv* **1** : encore (une fois), de nouveau **2 ~ and ~** : maintes et maintes fois **3 then ~** : d'autre part

against [ə'gɛntst, -'gɪntst] *prep* **1** : contre **2 go ~** : aller à l'encontre

age ['eɪdʒ] *n* **1** : âge *m* **2** ERA : ère *f*, époque *f* **3 come of ~** : atteindre la majorité **4 for ~s** : depuis longtemps **5 old ~** : vieillesse *f* — ~ *v* **age; aging** : vieillir — **aged** ['eɪdʒəd, 'eɪdʒd] *adj* **1** : âgé de **2** ['eɪdʒd] OLD : vieux, âgé

agency ['eɪdʒəntsi] *n, pl* **-cies** : agence *f*

agenda [ə'dʒɛndə] *n* : ordre *m* du jour, programme *m*

agent ['eɪdʒənt] *n* : agent *m*

aggravate ['ægrə,veɪt] *vt* **-vated; -vating 1**

WORSEN : aggraver **2** ANNOY : agacer, énerver

aggregate ['ægrɪgət] *adj* : total, global — ~ *n* : ensemble *m*, total *m*

aggression [ə'grɛʃən] *n* : agression *f* — **aggressive** [ə'grɛsɪv] *adj* : agressif — **aggressor** [ə'grɛsər] *n* : agresseur *m*

aghast [ə'gæst] *adj* : horrifié

agile ['ædʒəl] *adj* : agile — **agility** [ə'dʒɪləti] *n, pl* **-ties** : agilité *f*

agitate ['ædʒə,teɪt] *vt* **-tated; -tating 1** SHAKE : agiter **2** TROUBLE : inquiéter — **agitation** [ˌædʒə'teɪʃən] *n* : agitation *f*

ago [ə'go:] *adv* **1** : il y a **2 long ~** : il y a longtemps

agony ['ægəni] *n, pl* **-nies** : angoisse *f*, souffrance *f* — **agonize** ['ægə,naɪz] *vi* **-nized; -nizing** : se tourmenter — **agonizing** ['ægə,naɪzɪŋ] *adj* : déchirant

agree [ə'gri:] *v* **agreed; agreeing** *vt* **1** ADMIT : convenir **2 ~ that** : reconnaître que — *vi* **1** : être d'accord **2** CORRESPOND : concorder **3 ~ to** : consentir à — **agreeable** [ə'gri:əbəl] *adj* **1** PLEASING : agréable **2** WILLING : consentant — **agreement** [ə'gri:mənt] *n* : accord *m*

agriculture ['ægrɪ,kʌltʃər] *n* : agriculture *f* — **agricultural** [ˌægrɪ'kʌltʃərəl] *adj* : agricole

aground [ə'graʊnd] *adv* **run ~** : s'échouer

ahead [ə'hɛd] *adv* **1** IN FRONT : en avant, devant **2** BEFOREHAND : à l'avance **3** LEADING : en avance **4 go ~!** : allez-y! — **ahead of** *prep* **1** IN FRONT OF : devant **2 ~ time** : avant l'heure

aid ['eɪd] *vt* : aider — ~ *n* : aide *f*, secours *m*

AIDS ['eɪdz] *n (acquired immunodeficiency syndrome)* : sida *m*

ail ['eɪl] *vi* : être souffrant — **ailment** ['eɪlmənt] *n* : maladie *f*

aim ['eɪm] *vt* : braquer (une arme à feu), diriger (une remarque, etc.) — *vi* **1 ~ to** : avoir l'intention de **2 ~ at** *or* **~ for** : viser — ~ *n* : but *m* — **aimless** ['eɪmləs] *adj* : sans but

air ['ær] *vt* **1** : aérer **2** EXPRESS : exprimer **3** BROADCAST : diffuser — ~ *n* **1** : air *m* **2 on the ~** : à l'antenne — **air-conditioned** [ˌærkən'dɪʃənd] *adj* : climatisé — **air-conditioning** [ˌærkən'dɪʃənɪŋ] *n* : climatisation *f* — **aircraft** ['ær,kræft] *ns & pl* : avion *m* — **air force** *n* : armée *f* de l'air — **airline** ['ær,laɪn] *n* : compagnie *f* aérienne — **airmail** ['ær,meɪl] *n* **1** : poste *f* aérienne **2 by ~** : par avion — **airplane** ['ær,pleɪn] *n* : avion *m* — **airport** ['ær,port] *n* : aéroport *m* — **airstrip** ['ær,strɪp] *n* : piste *f* d'atterrissage — **airtight** ['ær'taɪt] *adj* : hermétique — **airy** ['æri] *adj* **airier; -est** : aéré

aisle ['aɪl] *n* : allée *f* (d'un théâtre, etc.), couloir *m* (d'un avion)

ajar [ə'dʒɑr] *adj & adv* : entrouvert

akin [ə'kɪn] *adj* ~ **to** : semblable à

alarm [ə'lɑrm] *n* **1** : alarme *f* **2** ANXIETY : inquiétude *f* — ~ *vt* : alarmer — **alarm clock** *n* : réveille-matin *m*

alas [ə'læs] *interj* : hélas!

album ['ælbəm] *n* : album *m*

alcohol ['ælkə,hɔl] *n* : alcool *m* — **alcoholic** [,ælkə'hɔlɪk] *adj* : alcoolisé, alcoolique — ~ *n* : alcoolique *mf* — **alcoholism** ['ælkəhɔ,lɪzəm] *n* : alcoolisme *m*

alcove ['æl,ko:v] *n* : alcôve *f*

ale ['eɪl] *n* : bière *f*

alert [ə'lərt] *adj* **1** WATCHFUL : vigilant **2** LIVELY : alerte, éveillé — ~ *n* : alerte *f* — ~ *vt* : alerter — **alertness** [ə'lərtnəs] *n* **1** : vigilance *f* **2** : vivacité *f*

alfalfa [æl'fælfə] *n* : luzerne *f*

alga ['ælgə] *n, pl* **-gae** ['æl,dʒiː] : algue *f*

algebra ['ældʒəbrə] *n* : algèbre *f*

Algerian [æl'dʒɪriən] *adj* : algérien

alias ['eɪliəs] *adv* : alias — ~ *n* : nom *m* d'emprunt, faux nom *m*

alibi ['ælə,baɪ] *n* : alibi *m*

alien ['eɪliən] *adj* : étranger — ~ *n* **1** FOREIGNER : étranger *m*, -gère *f* **2** EXTRATERRESTRIAL : extraterrestre *mf* — **alienate** ['eɪliə,neɪt] *vt* **-ated; -ating** : aliéner — **alienation** [,eɪliə'neɪʃən] *n* : aliénation *f*

alight [ə'laɪt] *vi* : descendre, se poser

align [ə'laɪn] *vt* : aligner — **alignment** [ə'laɪnmənt] *n* : alignement *m*

alike [ə'laɪk] *adv* : de la même façon — ~ *adj* **1** : semblable **2 be** ~ : se ressembler

alimony ['ælə,mo:ni] *n, pl* **-nies** : pension *f* alimentaire

alive [ə'laɪv] *adj* **1** LIVING : vivant, en vie **2** LIVELY : vif, animé

all ['ɔl] *adv* **1** COMPLETELY : tout, complètement **2** ~ **at once** : tout d'un coup **3** ~ **the better** : tant mieux — ~ *adj* : tout — ~ *pron* **1** EVERYTHING : tout **2** EVERYONE : tous, toutes **3** ~ **in** ~ : tout compte fait — **all–around** [,ɔlə'raʊnd] *adj* VERSATILE : complet

allay [ə'leɪ] *vt* : calmer, apaiser

allege [ə'lɛdʒ] *vt* **-leged; -leging** : alléguer, prétendre — **allegation** [,ælɪ'geɪʃən] *n* : allégation *f* — **alleged** [ə'lɛdʒd, ə'lɛdʒəd] *adj* : présumé, prétendu — **allegedly** [ə'lɛdʒədli] *adv* : prétendument

allegiance [ə'liːdʒənts] *n* : allégeance *f*

allergy ['ælərdʒi] *n, pl* **-gies** : allergie *f* — **allergic** [ə'lərdʒɪk] *adj* : allergique

alleviate [ə'liːvi,eɪt] *vt* **-ated; -ating** : soulager, alléger

alley ['æli] *n, pl* **-leys** : ruelle *f*, allée *f*

alliance [ə'laɪənts] *n* : alliance *f*

alligator ['ælə,geɪtər] *n* : alligator *m*

allocate ['ælə,keɪt] *vt* **-cated; -cating** : allouer, assigner

allot [ə'lɑt] *vt* **allotted; allotting 1** ASSIGN : attribuer **2** DISTRIBUTE : répartir — **allotment** [ə'lɑtmənt] *n* : allocation *f*

allow [ə'laʊ] *vt* **1** PERMIT : permettre **2** CONCEDE : admettre **3** GRANT : accorder — *vi* ~ **for** : tenir compte de — **allowance** [ə'laʊənts] *n* **1** : allocation *f* **2** : argent *m* de poche (pour les enfants) **3 make** ~**s for** : tenir compte de

alloy ['æ,lɔɪ] *n* : alliage *m*

all right *adv* **1** YES : d'accord **2** WELL : bien **3** CERTAINLY : bien, sans doute — ~ *adj* : pas mal, bien

allude [ə'luːd] *vi* **-luded; -luding** ~ **to** : faire allusion à

allure [ə'lʊr] *vt* **-lured; -luring** : attirer

allusion [ə'luːʒən] *n* : allusion *f*

ally [ə'laɪ, 'æ,laɪ] *vt* **-lied; -lying 1** : allier **2** ~ **oneself with** : s'allier avec — ~ ['æ,laɪ, ə'laɪ] *n, pl* **allies** : allié *m*, -liée *f*

almanac ['ɔlmə,næk, 'æl-] *n* : almanach *m*

almighty [ɔl'maɪti] *adj* : tout puissant, formidable

almond ['ɑmənd, 'ɑl-, 'æ-, 'æl-] *n* : amande *f*

almost ['ɔl,mo:st, ɔl'mo:st] *adv* : presque

alms ['ɑmz, 'ɑlmz, 'ælmz] *ns & pl* : aumône *f*

alone [ə'lo:n] *adv* **1** : seul **2 leave** ~ : laisser tranquille — ~ *adj* : seul

along [ə'lɔŋ] *adv* **1 all** ~ : tout le temps **2** ~ **with** : avec, accompagné de — ~ *prep* **1** : le long de **2** ON : sur — **alongside** [ə,lɔŋ'saɪd] *adv* : à côté — ~ *or* ~ **of** *prep* : à côté de

aloof [ə'luːf] *adj* : distant

aloud [ə'laʊd] *adv* : à haute voix

alphabet ['ælfə,bɛt] *n* : alphabet *m* — **alphabetic** [,ælfə'bɛtɪk] *or* **alphabetical** [-tɪkəl] *adj* : alphabétique

already [ɔl'rɛdi] *adv* : déjà

also ['ɔl,so:] *adv* : aussi

altar ['ɔltər] *n* : autel *m*

alter ['ɔltər] *vt* **1** : changer, modifier **2** : retoucher (un vêtement) — **alteration** [,ɔltə'reɪʃən] *n* **1** : changement *m*, modification *f* **2** ~**s** *npl* : retouches *fpl*

alternate ['ɔltərnət] *adj* : alternatif — ~ ['ɔltər,neɪt] *v* **-nated; -nating** *vt* : faire alterner — *vi* : alterner — **alternating current** ['ɔltər,neɪtɪŋ] *n* : courant *m* alternatif — **alternative** [ɔl'tərnətɪv] *adj* : alternatif — ~ *n* : alternative *f*

although [ɔl'ðo:] *conj* : bien que, quoique

altitude ['æltə,tuːd, -,tjuːd] *n* : altitude *f*

altogether [,ɔltə'gɛðər] *adv* **1** COMPLETELY : entièrement, tout à fait **2** ON THE WHOLE

: dans l'ensemble **3 how much ~?** : combien en tout?

aluminum [ə'lu:mənəm] *n* : aluminium *m*

always ['ɔlwiz, -ˌweɪz] *adv* **1** : toujours **2** FOREVER : pour toujours

am → **be**

amass [ə'mæs] *vt* : amasser

amateur ['æmətʃər, -tər, -ˌtʊr, -ˌtjʊr] *adj* : amateur — **~** *n* : amateur *m*

amaze [ə'meɪz] *vt* **amazed; amazing** : étonner, stupéfier — **amazement** [ə'meɪzmənt] *n* : stupéfaction *f* — **amazing** [ə'meɪzɪŋ] *adj* : étonnant

ambassador [æm'bæsəˌdər] *n* : ambassadeur *m*, -drice *f*

amber ['æmbər] *n* : ambre *m*

ambiguous [æm'bɪgjuəs] *adj* : ambigu — **ambiguity** [ˌæmbə'gju:əti] *n, pl* -**ties** : ambiguïté *f*

ambition [æm'bɪʃən] *n* : ambition *f* — **ambitious** [æm'bɪʃəs] *adj* : ambitieux

ambivalence [æm'bɪvələnts] *n* : ambivalence *f* — **ambivalent** [æm'bɪvələnt] *adj* : ambivalent

amble ['æmbəl] *vi* -**bled; -bling** : déambuler

ambulance ['æmbjələnts] *n* : ambulance *f*

ambush ['æmbʊʃ] *vt* : tendre une embuscade à — **~** *n* : embuscade *f*

amenable [ə'mi:nəbəl, -'mɛ-] *adj* **1** : accommodant **2 ~ to** : disposé à

amend [ə'mɛnd] *vt* : amender, modifier — **amendment** [ə'mɛndmənt] *n* : amendement *m* — **amends** [ə'mɛndz] *ns & pl* **make ~** : réparer ses torts

amenities [ə'mɛnəˌtis, -'mi:-] *npl* : équipements *mpl*, aménagements *mpl*

American [ə'mɛrɪkən] *adj* : américain

amiable ['eɪmiˌəbəl] *adj* : aimable

amicable ['æmɪkəbəl] *adj* : amical

amid [ə'mɪd] *or* **amidst** [ə'mɪdst] *prep* : au milieu de, parmi

amiss [ə'mɪs] *adv* **1** : mal **2 take sth ~** : prendre qqch de travers — **~** *adj* **something is ~** : quelque chose ne va pas

ammonia [ə'mo:njə] *n* : ammoniaque *f*

ammunition [ˌæmjə'nɪʃən] *n* : munitions *fpl*

amnesia [æm'ni:ʒə] *n* : amnésie *f*

amnesty ['æmnəsti] *n, pl* -**ties** : amnistie *f*

amoeba [ə'mi:bə] *n, pl* -**bas** *or* -**bae** [-bi:] : amibe *f*

among [e'mʌŋ] *prep* : parmi, entre

amount [ə'maʊnt] *vi* **1 ~ to** TOTAL : s'élever à **2 that ~s to the same thing** : cela revient au même — **~** *n* **1** : quantité *f* **2** SUM : somme *f*, montant *m*

amphibian [æm'fɪbiən] *n* : amphibien *m* — **amphibious** [æm'fɪbiəs] *adj* : amphibie

amphitheater ['æmfəˌθi:ətər] *n* : amphithéâtre *m*

ample ['æmpəl] *adj* -**pler; -plest 1** SPACIOUS : ample **2** PLENTIFUL : abondant

amplify ['æmpləˌfaɪ] *vt* -**fied; -fying** : amplifier — **amplifier** ['æmpləˌfaɪər] *n* ; amplificateur *m*

amputate ['æmpjəˌteɪt] *v* -**tated; -tating** : amputer — **amputation** [ˌæmpjə'teɪʃən] *n* : amputation *f*

amuse [ə'mju:z] *vt* **amused; amusing** : amuser — **amusement** [ə'mju:zmənt] *n* **1** ENJOYMENT : amusement *m* **2** DIVERSION : divertissement *m*

an → **a²**

analgesic [ˌænəl'ʤi:zɪk, -sɪk] *n* : analgésique *m*

analogy [ə'nælədʒi] *n, pl* -**gies** : analogie *f* — **analogous** [ə'næləgəs] *adj* : analogue

analysis [ə'næləsəs] *n, pl* -**yses** [-ˌsi:z] : analyse *f* — **analyst** [ˈænəlɪstɪk] *or* **analytical** [-tɪkəl] *adj* : analytique — **analyze** *or Brit* **analyse** ['ænəˌlaɪz] *vt* -**lyzed; -lyzing** *or Brit* -**lysed; -lysing** : analyser

anarchy ['ænərki, -ˌnɑr-] *n* : anarchie *f*

anatomy [ə'næṭəmi] *n, pl* -**mies** : anatomie *f* — **anatomic** [ˌænə'ṭɑmɪk] *or* **anatomical** [-mɪkəl] *adj* : anatomique

ancestor ['ænˌsɛstər] *n* : ancêtre *mf* — **ancestral** [æn'sɛstrəl] *adj* : ancestral — **ancestry** ['ænˌsɛstri] *n* **1** LINEAGE : ascendance *f* **2** ANCESTORS : ancêtres *mpl*

anchor ['æŋkər] *n* **1** : ancre *f* **2** : présentateur *m*, -trice *f* (à la télévision) — **~** *vt* : ancrer — *vi* : jeter l'ancre

anchovy ['ænˌtʃo:vi, æn'tʃo:-] *n, pl* -**vies** *or* -**vy** : anchois *m*

ancient ['eɪntʃənt] *adj* : ancien

and ['ænd] *conj* **1** : et **2 come ~ see** : venez voir **3 more ~ more** : de plus en plus **4 try ~ finish it soon** : tâchez de l'achever bientôt

anecdote ['ænɪkˌdo:t] *n* : anecdote *f*

anemia [ə'ni:miə] *n* : anémie *f* — **anemic** [ə'ni:mɪk] *adj* : anémique

anesthesia [ˌænəs'θi:ʒə] *n* : anesthésie *f* — **anesthetic** ['ænəs'θɛtɪk] *adj* : anesthésique — **~** *n* : anesthésique *m*

anew [ə'nu:, -'nju:] *adv* : encore, de nouveau

angel ['eɪnʤəl] *n* : ange *m* — **angelic** [æn'ʤɛlɪk] *or* **angelical** [-lɪkəl] *adj* : angélique

anger ['æŋgər] *vt* : fâcher, mettre en colère — **~** *n* : colère *f*

angle ['æŋgəl] *n* **1** : angle *m* **2 at an ~** : de biais — **angler** ['æŋglər] *n* : pêcheur *m*, -cheuse *f* à la ligne

Anglo–Saxon [ˌæŋglo'sæksən] *adj* : anglo-saxon

angry ['æŋgri] *adj* -**grier; -est** : fâché, en colère — **angrily** ['æŋgrəli] *adv* : avec colère

anguish ['æŋgwɪʃ] *n* : angoisse *f*

angular ['æŋgjələr] *adj* : anguleux

animal ['ænəməl] *n* : animal *m*

animate ['ænə,meɪt] *vt* **-mated; -mating** : animer, stimuler — **~** ['ænəmət] *adj* ALIVE : vivant — **animated** ['ænə,meɪtəd] *adj* **1** : animé **2 ~ cartoon** : dessin *m* animé — **animation** [,ænə'meɪʃən] *n* : animation *f*

animosity [,ænə'masəti] *n, pl* **-ties** : animosité *f*

anise ['ænəs] *n* : anis *m*

ankle ['æŋkəl] *n* : cheville *f*

annex [ə'nɛks, 'æ,nɛks] *vt* : annexer — **~** ['æ,nɛks, -nɪks] *n* : annexe *f*

annihilate [ə'naɪə,leɪt] *vt* **-lated; -lating** : anéantir, annihiler — **annihilation** [ə,naɪə-'leɪʃən] *n* : anéantissement *m*

anniversary [,ænə'vərsəri] *n, pl* **-ries** : anniversaire *m*

annotate ['ænə,teɪt] *vt* **-tated; -tating** : annoter

announce [ə'naʊnts] *vt* **-nounced; -nouncing** : annoncer — **announcement** [ə-'naʊntsmənt] *n* **1** : annonce *f* **2** NOTIFICATION : avis *m* **3** : faire-part *m* (de mariage, etc.) — **announcer** [ə'naʊntsər] *n* : présentateur *m*, -trice *f*; speaker *m*, -kerine *f* *France*

annoy [ə'nɔɪ] *vt* : agacer, ennuyer — **annoyance** [ə'nɔɪənts] *n* : contrariété *f* — **annoying** [ə'nɔɪɪŋ] *adj* : agaçant

annual ['ænjuəl] *adj* : annuel

annuity [ə'nu:əti] *n, pl* **-ties** : rente *f* (viagère)

annul [ə'nʌl] *vt* **anulled; anulling** : annuler — **annulment** [ə'nʌlmənt] *n* : annulation *f*

anoint [ə'nɔɪnt] *vt* : oindre

anomaly [ə'naməli] *n, pl* **-lies** : anomalie *f*

anonymous [ə'nanəməs] *adj* : anonyme — **anonymity** [,ænə'nɪməti] *n* : anonymat *m*

another [ə'nʌðər] *adj* **1** : un(e) autre **2 ~ beer** : encore une bière **3 in ~ year** : dans un an — **~ pron 1** : un autre *m*, une autre *f* **2 one after ~** : l'un après l'autre

answer ['æntsər] *n* **1** REPLY : réponse *f* **2** SOLUTION : solution *f* — **~ vt 1** : répondre à **2 ~ the door** : aller ouvrir la porte — *vi* : répondre

ant ['ænt] *n* : fourmi *f*

antagonize [æn'tægə,naɪz] *vt* **-nized; -nizing** : éveiller l'hostilité de, contrarier — **antagonistic** [æn,tægə'nɪstɪk] *adj* : antagoniste

antarctic [ænt'ɑrktɪk, -'ɑrtɪk] *adj* : antarctique

antelope ['æntəl,o:p] *n, pl* **-lope** *or* **-lopes** : antilope *f*

antenna [æn'tɛnə] *n, pl* **-nae** *or* **-nas** : antenne *f*

anthem ['ænθəm] *n* : hymne *m*

anthology [æn'θalədʒi] *n, pl* **-gies** : anthologie *f*

anthropology [,ænθrə'palədʒi] *n* : anthropologie *f*

antibiotic [,æntibaɪ'ɑtɪk, ,æn,taɪ-, -bɪ] *adj* : antibiotique — **~** *n* : antibiotique *m*

antibody ['ænti,badi] *n, pl* **-bodies** : anticorps *m*

anticipate [æn'tɪsə,peɪt] *vt* **-pated; -pating 1** FORESEE : anticiper **2** EXPECT : s'attendre à — **anticipation** [æn,tɪsə'peɪʃən] *n* : anticipation *f*

antics ['æntɪks] *npl* : singeries *fpl*

antidote ['ænti,do:t] *n* : antidote *m*

antifreeze ['ænti,fri:z] *n* : antigel *m*

antipathy [æn'tɪpəθi] *n, pl* **-thies** : antipathie *f*

antiquated ['æntə,kweɪtəd] *adj* : dépassé

antique [æn'ti:k] *adj* : ancien, antique — **~** *n* : antiquité *f* — **antiquity** [æn'tɪkwəti] *n, pl* **-ties** : antiquité *f*

anti–Semitic [,æntisə'mɪtɪk, ,æn,taɪ-] *adj* : antisémite

antiseptic [,æntə'sɛptɪk] *adj* : antiseptique — **~** *n* : antiseptique *m*

antisocial [,ænti'so:ʃəl, ,æn,taɪ-] *adj* UNSOCIABLE : peu sociable

antlers ['æntlərz] *npl* : bois *mpl*, ramure *f*

antonym ['æntə,nɪm] *n* : antonyme *m*

anus ['eɪnəs] *n* : anus *m*

anvil ['ænvəl, -vɪl] *n* : enclume *f*

anxiety [æŋk'zaɪəti] *n, pl* **-ties 1** APPREHENSION : anxiété *f* **2** EAGERNESS : impatience *f* — **anxious** ['æŋkʃəs] *adj* **1** WORRIED : inquiet, anxieux **2** EAGER : impatient — **anxiously** ['æŋkʃəsli] *adv* **1** : anxieusement **2** : avec impatience

any ['ɛni] *adv* **1** SOMEWHAT : un peu **2** AT ALL : du tout **3 do you want ~ more tea?** : voulez-vous encore du thé? **4 she doesn't smoke ~ longer** : elle ne fume plus — **~ adj 1** : de, de la, du, des **2** WHICHEVER : quelconque, n'importe quel **3 at ~ moment** : à tout moment **4 we don't have ~ money** : nous n'avons pas d'argent — **~ pron 1** WHICHEVER : n'importe lequel **2 do you have ~** : est-ce que vous en avez?

anybody ['ɛni,badi, -,bʌdi, -,bɑ-] → **anyone**

anyhow ['ɛni,haʊ] *adv* **1** : de toute façon, en tout cas **2** HAPHAZARDLY : n'importe comment

anymore [,ɛni'mɔr] *adv* **not ~** : ne plus

anyone ['ɛni,wʌn] *pron* **1** SOMEONE : quelqu'un **2** (*in negative constructions*) : personne **3 ~ can play** : tout le monde peut jouer, n'importe qui peut jouer

anyplace ['ɛni,pleɪs] → **anywhere**

anything ['ɛni,θɪŋ] *pron* **1** WHATEVER : n'importe quoi **2** SOMETHING : quelque chose **3** (*in negative constructions*) : rien **4**

~ **but** : tout sauf **5 hardly** ~ : presque rien

anytime ['ɛni,taɪm] *adv* : n'importe quand

anyway ['ɛni,weɪ] → **anyhow**

anywhere ['ɛni,hwɛr] *adv* **1** : n'importe où **2** SOMEWHERE : quelque part **3** (*in negative constructions*) : nulle part **4** ~ **else** : partout ailleurs

apart [ə'pɑrt] *adv* **1** ASIDE : à part, à l'écart **2** SEPARATED : éloigné **3** ~ **from** : en dehors de **4 five minutes** ~ : à cinq minutes d'intervalle **5 take** ~ : démonter **6 tell** ~ : distinguer

apartment [ə'pɑrtmənt] *n* : appartement *m*

apathy ['æpəθi] *n* : apathie *f* — **apathetic** [,æpə'θɛtɪk] *adj* : apathique

ape ['eɪp] *n* : grand singe *m*

aperture ['æpərtʃər, -,tʃʊr] *n* : ouverture *f*

apex ['eɪ,pɛks] *n, pl* **apexes** *or* **apices** ['eɪpə,siːz, 'æ-] : sommet *m*

apiece [ə'piːs] *adv* **1** : chacun **2 two dollars** ~ : deux dollars la pièce

aplomb [ə'plɑm, -'plʌm] *n* : aplomb *m*

apology [ə'pɑlədʒi] *n, pl* **-gies** : excuses *fpl* — **apologetic** [ə'pɑlə'dʒɛtɪk] *adj* **1** : d'excuse **2 be** ~ : s'excuser — **apologize** [ə'pɑlə,dʒaɪz] *vi* **-gized; -gizing** : s'excuser, faire des excuses

apostle [ə'pɑsəl] *n* : apôtre *m*

apostrophe [ə'pɑstrə,fiː] *n* : apostrophe *f*

appall *or Brit* **appal** [ə'pɔl] *vt* **-palled; -palling** : épouvanter — **appalling** [ə'pɔlɪŋ] *adj* : épouvantable

apparatus [,æpə'rætəs, -'reɪ-] *n, pl* **-tuses** *or* **-tus** : appareil *m*

apparel [ə'pærəl] *n* : habillement *m*

apparent [ə'pærənt] *adj* **1** OBVIOUS : évident **2** SEEMING : apparent — **apparently** [ə'pærəntli] *adv* : apparemment

apparition [,æpə'rɪʃən] *n* : apparition *f*

appeal [ə'piːl] *vt* : faire appel contre (un jugement) — *vi* **1** ~ **for** : lancer un appel à **2** ~ **to** ATTRACT : plaire à **3** ~ **to** INVOKE : faire appel à — ~ *n* **1** REQUEST : appel *m* **2** ATTRACTION : attrait *m* — **appealing** [ə'piːlɪŋ] *adj* : attrayant, séduisant

appear [ə'pɪr] *vi* **1** : apparaître **2** SEEM : paraître, sembler **3** COME OUT : paraître, sortir — **appearance** [ə'pɪrənts] *n* **1** LOOK : apparence *f* **2** ARRIVAL : apparition *f* **3** ~**s** *npl* : apparences *fpl*

appease [ə'piːz] *vt* **-peased; -peasing** : apaiser

appendix [ə'pɛndɪks] *n, pl* **-dixes** *or* **-dices** [-də,siːz] : appendice *m* — **appendicitis** [ə-,pɛndə'saɪtəs] *n* : appendicite *f*

appetite ['æpə,taɪt] *n* : appétit *m* — **appetizer** ['æpə,taɪzər] *n* : amuse-gueule *m* — **appetizing** ['æpə,taɪzɪŋ] *adj* : appétissant

applaud [ə'plɔd] *v* : applaudir — **applause** [ə'plɔz] *n* : applaudissements *mpl*

apple ['æpəl] *n* : pomme *f*

appliance [ə'plaɪənts] *n* : appareil *m*

apply [ə'plaɪ] *v* **-plied; -plying** *vt* **1** : appliquer **2** EXERT : exercer **3** ~ **oneself** : s'appliquer — *vi* **1** : s'appliquer **2** ~ **for** : poser sa candidature pour — **applicant** ['æplɪkənt] *n* : candidat *m*, -date *f* — **application** [,æplə'keɪʃən] *n* **1** USE : application *f* **2** : demande *f* (d'emploi)

appoint [ə'pɔɪnt] *vt* **1** SET : fixer **2** NAME : nommer — **appointment** [ə'pɔɪntmənt] *n* **1** : nomination *f* **2** MEETING : rendez-vous *m*

apportion [ə'pɔrʃən] *vt* : répartir

appraise [ə'preɪz] *vt* **-praised; -praising** : évaluer — **appraisal** [ə'preɪzəl] *n* : évaluation *f*

appreciate [ə'priːʃi,eɪt, -'prɪ-] *vt* **-ated; -ating** **1** VALUE : apprécier **2** REALIZE : comprendre, se rendre compte de **3 I** ~ **your help** : je vous suis reconnaissant de m'avoir aidé — **appreciation** [ə,priːʃi-'eɪʃən, -,prɪ-] *n* **1** EVALUATION : appréciation *f* **2** GRATITUDE : reconnaissance *f* — **appreciative** [ə'priːʃətɪv, -'prɪ-; ə'priːʃi-,eɪ-] *adj* : reconnaissant

apprehend [,æprɪ'hɛnd] *vt* **1** ARREST : appréhender **2** UNDERSTAND : comprendre **3** DREAD : appréhender — **apprehension** [,æprɪ'hɛntʃən] *n* : appréhension *f* — **apprehensive** [,æprɪ'hɛntsɪv] *adj* : inquiet

apprentice [ə'prɛntɪs] *n* : apprenti *m*, -tie *f* — **apprenticeship** [ə'prɛntɪs,ʃɪp] *n* : apprentissage *m*

approach [ə'proːtʃ] *vt* **1** NEAR : s'approcher de **2** : s'adresser à (quelqu'un), aborder (un problème, etc.) — *vi* : s'approcher — ~ *n* : approche *f* — **approachable** [ə'proːtʃəbəl] *adj* : abordable, accessible

appropriate [ə'proːpri,eɪt] *vt* **-ated; -ating** **1** SEIZE : s'approprier **2** ALLOCATE : affecter — ~ [ə'proːpriət] *adj* : approprié

approve [ə'pruːv] *vt* **-proved; -proving** *or* ~ **of** : approuver — **approval** [ə'pruːvəl] *n* : approbation *f*

approximate [ə'prɑksəmət] *adj* : approximatif — ~ [ə'prɑksə,meɪt] *vt* **-mated; -mating** : se rapprocher de — **approximately** [ə'prɑksəmətli] *adv* : à peu près, environ

apricot ['æprə,kɑt, 'eɪ-] *n* : abricot *m*

April ['eɪprəl] *n* : avril *m*

apron ['eɪprən] *n* : tablier *m*

apt ['æpt] *adj* **1** : approprié **2 be** ~ **to** : avoir tendance à — **aptitude** ['æptə,tuːd, -,tjuːd] *n* : aptitude *f*

aquarium [ə'kwæriəm] *n, pl* **-iums** *or* **-ia** [-iə] : aquarium *m*

aquatic [ə'kwɑṭɪk, -'kwæ-] *adj* **1** : aquatique **2** : nautique (se dit des sports)
aqueduct ['ækwə₁dʌkt] *n* : aqueduc *m*
Arab ['ærəb] *or* **Arabic** ['ærəbɪk] *adj* : arabe — **Arabic** *n* : arabe *m* (langue)
arbitrary ['ɑrbə₁trɛri] *adj* : arbitraire
arbitrate ['ɑrbə₁treɪt] *v* -**trated; -trating** : arbitrer — **arbitration** [₁ɑrbə'treɪʃən] *n* : arbitrage *m*
arc ['ɑrk] *n* : arc *m*
arcade [ɑr'keɪd] *n* **1** : arcade *f* **2 shopping ~** : galerie *f* marchande
arch ['ɑrtʃ] *n* : voûte *f*, arc *m* — **~** *vt* : arquer, courber
archaeology *or* **archeology** [₁ɑrki'ɑlədʒi] *n* : archéologie *f* — **archaeological** [₁ɑrkiə-'lɑdʒɪkəl] *adj* : archéologique — **archaeologist** [₁ɑrki'ɑlədʒɪst] *n* : archéologue *mf*
archaic [ɑr'keɪɪk] *adj* : archaïque
archbishop [ɑrtʃ'bɪʃəp] *n* : archevêque *m*
archery ['ɑrtʃəri] *n* : tir *m* à l'arc
archipelago [₁ɑrkə'pelə₁goː, ₁ɑrtʃə-] *n, pl* -**goes** *or* -**gos** [-goːz] : archipel *m*
architecture ['ɑrkə₁tɛktʃər] *n* : architecture *f* — **architect** ['ɑrkə₁tɛkt] *n* : architecte *mf* — **architectural** [₁ɑrkə'tɛktʃərəl] *adj* : architectural
archives ['ɑr₁kaɪvz] *npl* : archives *fpl*
archway ['ɑrtʃ₁weɪ] *n* : voûte *f*, arcade *f*
arctic ['ɑrktɪk, 'ɑrt-] *adj* : arctique
ardent ['ɑrdənt] *adj* : ardent — **ardently** ['ɑrdəntli] *adv* : ardemment — **ardor** ['ɑrdər] *n* : ardeur *f*
arduous ['ɑrdʒuəs] *adj* : ardu
are → be
area ['æriə] *n* **1** REGION : région *f* **2** SURFACE : aire *f* **3** FIELD : domaine *m* **4 ~ code** : indicatif *m* de zone, indicatif *m* régional *Can*
arena [ə'riːnə] *n* : arène *f*, aréna *m Can*
aren't ['ɑrnt, 'ɑrənt] (*contraction of* **are not**) → **be**
argue ['ɑr₁gjuː] *v* -**gued; -guing** *vi* **1** QUARREL : se disputer **2** DEBATE : argumenter — *vt* DEBATE : discuter — **argument** ['ɑrgjəmənt] *n* **1** QUARREL : dispute *f* **2** DEBATE : discussion *f* **3** REASONING : argument *m*
arid ['ærəd] *adj* : aride
arise [ə'raɪz] *vi* **arose** [ə'roːz]; **arisen** [ə-'rɪzən]; **arising 1** : se présenter **2 ~ from** : résulter de
aristocracy [₁ærə'stɑkrəsi] *n, pl* -**cies** : aristocratie *f* — **aristocrat** [ə'rɪstə₁kræt] *n* : aristocrate *mf* — **aristocratic** [ə₁rɪstə-'krætɪk] *adj* : aristocratique
arithmetic [ə'rɪθmə₁tɪk] *n* : arithmétique *f*
ark ['ɑrk] *n* : arche *f*
arm ['ɑrm] *n* **1** : bras *m* **2** WEAPON : arme *f* — **~** *vt* : armer — **armament** ['ɑrməmənt]

n : armement *m* — **armchair** ['ɑrm₁tʃɛr] *n* : fauteuil *m* — **armed** ['ɑrmd] *adj* **1** : armé **2 ~ forces** : forces *fpl* armées **3 ~ robbery** : vol *m* à main armée
armistice ['ɑrməstɪs] *n* : armistice *m*
armor *or Brit* **armour** ['ɑrmər] *n* **1** : armure *f* **2** *or* **~ plating** : blindage *m* — **armored** *or Brit* **armoured** ['ɑrmərd] *adj* : blindé — **armory** *or Brit* **armoury** ['ɑrməri] *n, pl* -**mories** : arsenal *m*
armpit ['ɑrm₁pɪt] *n* : aisselle *f*
army ['ɑrmi] *n, pl* -**mies** : armée *f*
aroma [ə'roːmə] *n* : arôme *m* — **aromatic** [₁ærə'mæṭɪk] *adj* : aromatique
around [ə'raund] *adv* **1** : de circonférence **2** NEARBY : là, dans les parages **3** APPROXIMATELY : environ, à peu près **4 all ~** : tout autour — **~** *prep* **1** SURROUNDING : autour de **2** THROUGHOUT : partout dans **3 ~ here** : par ici **4 ~ noon** : vers midi
arouse [ə'rauz] *vt* **aroused; arousing 1** AWAKE : réveiller **2** STIMULATE : éveiller
arrange [ə'reɪndʒ] *v* -**ranged; -ranging** *vt* : arranger — *vi* **~ for** : prendre des dispositions pour — **arrangement** [ə'reɪndʒmənt] *n* **1** ORDER : arrangement *m* **2 ~s** *npl* : dispositions *fpl*
array [ə'reɪ] *n* : sélection *f*
arrears [ə'rɪrz] *npl* **1** : arriéré *m* **2 be in ~** : avoir du retard
arrest [ə'rɛst] *vt* : arrêter — **~** *n* : arrestation *f*
arrive [ə'raɪv] *vi* -**rived; -riving 1** : arriver **2 ~ at** : parvenir à, atteindre — **arrival** [ə-'raɪvəl] *n* : arrivée *f*
arrogance ['ærəgənts] *n* : arrogance *f* — **arrogant** ['ærəgənt] *adj* : arrogant
arrow ['æro] *n* : flèche *f*
arsenal ['ɑrsənəl] *n* : arsenal *m*
arsenic ['ɑrsənɪk] *n* : arsenic *m*
arson ['ɑrsən] *n* : incendie *m* criminel
art ['ɑrt] *n* : art *m*
artefact *Brit* → **artifact**
artery ['ɑrṭəri] *n, pl* -**teries** : artère *f*
artful ['ɑrtfəl] *adj* : rusé, astucieux
arthritis [ɑr'θraɪṭəs] *n, pl* -**thritides** [-'θrɪṭə-₁diːz] : arthrite *f* — **arthritic** [ɑr'θrɪṭɪk] *adj* : arthritique
artichoke ['ɑrṭə₁tʃoːk] *n* : artichaut *m*
article ['ɑrtɪkəl] *n* : article *m*
articulate [ɑr'tɪkjə₁leɪt] *v* -**lated; -lating** : articuler — **~** [ɑr'tɪkjələt] *adj* **be ~** : s'exprimer bien
artifact *or Brit* **artefact** ['ɑrṭə₁fækt] *n* : objet *m* fabriqué
artificial [₁ɑrṭə'fɪʃəl] *adj* : artificiel
artillery [ɑr'tɪləri] *n, pl* -**leries** : artillerie *f*
artist ['ɑrṭɪst] *n* : artiste *mf* — **artistic** [ɑr-'tɪstɪk] *adj* : artistique
as ['æz] *adv* **1 ~ much** : autant **2 ~ tall**

~ : aussi grand que **3** ~ **well** : aussi —
~ *conj* **1** LIKE : comme **2** WHILE : tandis
que, alors que **3** SINCE : puisque, comme **4**
~ **is** : tel quel — ~ *prep* : en tant que,
comme — ~ *pron* **1** : que **2** ~ **you know**
: comme vous savez

asbestos [æz'bɛstəs, æs-] *n* : amiante *m*

ascend [ə'sɛnd] *vt* : monter (à), gravir — *vi*
: monter — **ascent** [ə'sɛnt] *n* : ascension *f*

ascertain [ˌæsər'teɪn] *vt* : établir

ascribe [ə'skraɪb] *vt* -**cribed; -cribing** ~
to: attribuer à

as for *prep* : quant à

ash[1] ['æʃ] *n* : cendre *f*

ash[2] *n* : frêne *m* (arbre)

ashamed [ə'ʃeɪmd] *adj* **1** : honteux **2 be** ~
: avoir honte

ashore [ə'ʃor] *adv* : à terre

ashtray ['æʃˌtreɪ] *n* : cendrier *m*

Asian ['eɪʒən, -ʃən] *adj* : asiatique

aside [ə'saɪd] *adv* : de côté, à part — **aside
from** *prep* **1** BESIDES : à part **2** EXCEPT
: sauf

as if *conj* : comme si

ask ['æsk] *vt* **1** : demander **2** INVITE : inviter **3** ~ **a question** : poser une question
4 ~ **s.o.** : demandez à qqn — *vi* : demander

askance [ə'skænts] *adv* **look** ~ : regarder
du coin de l'œil

askew [ə'skju:] *adv & adj* : de travers

asleep [ə'sli:p] *adj* **1** : endormi **2 fall** ~
: s'endormir

as of *prep* : dès, à partir de

asparagus [ə'spærəgəs] *ns & pl* : asperges
fpl

aspect ['æˌspɛkt] *n* : aspect *m*

asphalt ['æsˌfɔlt] *n* : asphalte *m*

asphyxiate [æ'sfɪksiˌeɪt] *vt* -**ated; -ating**
: asphyxier — **asphyxiation** [æˌsfɪksi-
'eɪʃən] *n* : asphyxie *f*

aspire [ə'spaɪr] *vi* -**pired; -piring** ~ **to** : aspirer à — **aspiration** [ˌæspə'reɪʃən] *n* : aspiration *f*

aspirin ['æsprən, 'æspə-] *n, pl* **aspirin** *or* **as-
pirins** : aspirine *f*

ass ['æs] *n* **1** : âne *m* **2** FOOL : idiot *m*,
-diote *f*

assail [ə'seɪl] *vt* : assaillir — **assailant** [ə-
'seɪlənt] *n* : assaillant *m*, -lante *f*

assassin [ə'sæsən] *n* : assassin *m* — **assassinate** [ə'sæsənˌeɪt] *vt* -**nated; -nating** : assassiner — **assassination** [əˌsæsən'eɪʃən]
n : assassinat *m*

assault [ə'sɔlt] *vt* : agresser — ~ *n* : agression *f*, assaut *m* (militaire)

assemble [ə'sɛmbəl] *v* -**bled; -bling** *vt* **1**
CONSTRUCT : assembler **2** GATHER : rassembler — *vi* CONVENE : se rassembler — **assembly** [ə'sɛmbli] *n, pl* -**blies 1** MEETING

: assemblée *f*, réunion *f* **2** ~ **line** : chaîne *f*
de montage

assent [ə'sɛnt] *vi* : consentir — ~ *n* : assentiment *m*

assert [ə'sərt] *vt* **1** : affirmer **2** ~ **oneself**
: s'imposer — **assertion** [ə'sərʃən] *n* : assertion *f* — **assertive** [ə'sərtɪv] *adj* : assuré

assess [ə'sɛs] *vt* : évaluer — **assessment**
[ə'sɛsmənt] *n* : évaluation *f*

asset ['æˌsɛt] *n* **1** : avantage *m*, atout *m* **2**
~**s** *npl* : biens *mpl*, actif *m*

assiduous [ə'sɪdʒuəs] *adj* : assidu

assign [ə'saɪn] *vt* **1** ALLOT : assigner **2** AP-
POINT : nommer — **assignment** [ə-
'saɪnmənt] *n* **1** TASK : mission *f* **2** HOME-
WORK : devoir *m*

assimilate [ə'sɪməˌleɪt] *vt* -**lated; -lating**
: assimiler

assist [ə'sɪst] *vt* : aider, assister — **assistance** [ə'sɪstənts] *n* : aide *f*, assistance *f* —
assistant [ə'sɪstənt] *n* : assistant *m*, -tante *f*;
adjoint *m*, -jointe *f*

associate [ə'so:ʃiˌeɪt, -si-] *v* -**ated; -ating** *vt*
: associer — *vi* ~ **with** : fréquenter — ~
[ə'so:ʃiət, -siət] *n* : associé *m*, -ciée *f* — **association** [əˌso:ʃi'eɪʃən, -si-] *n* : association *f*

as soon as *conj* : aussitôt que

assorted [ə'sɔrtəd] *adj* : assorti — **assortment** [ə'sɔrtmənt] *n* : assortiment *m*

assume [ə'su:m] *vt* -**sumed; -suming 1**
: assumer **2** SUPPOSE : supposer, présumer
— **assumption** [ə'sʌmpʃən] *n* : supposition *f*

assure [ə'ʃur] *vt* -**sured; -suring** : assurer
— **assurance** [ə'ʃurənts] *n* : assurance *f*

asterisk ['æstəˌrɪsk] *n* : astérisque *m*

asthma ['æzmə] *n* : asthme *m*

as though → as if

as to *prep* : sur, concernant

astonish [ə'stanɪʃ] *vt* : étonner — **astonishing** [ə'stanɪʃɪŋ] *adj* : étonnant — **astonishment** [ə'stanɪʃmənt] *n* : étonnement *m*

astound [ə'staund] *vt* : stupéfier — **astounding** [ə'staundɪŋ] *adj* : stupéfiant

astray [ə'streɪ] *adv* **1 go** ~ : s'égarer **2
lead** ~ : égarer

astrology [ə'stralədʒi] *n* : astrologie *f*

astronaut ['æstrəˌnɔt] *n* : astronaute *mf*

astronomy [ə'stranəmi] *n, pl* -**mies** : astronomie *f* — **astronomer** [ə'stranəmər] *n*
: astronome *mf* — **astronomical** [ˌæstrə-
'namɪkəl] *adj* : astronomique

astute [ə'stu:t, -'stju:t] *adj* : astucieux — **as-
tuteness** [ə'stu:tnəs, -'stju:t-] *n* : astuce *f*

as well as *conj* : en plus de — ~ *prep*
: ainsi que, à part

asylum [ə'saɪləm] *n* : asile *m*

at ['æt] *prep* **1** : à **2** ~ **the dentist's** : chez
le dentiste **3** ~ **three o'clock** : à trois

heures **4 ~ war** : en guerre **5 be angry ~** : être fâché contre **6 laugh ~** : rire de **7 shoot ~** : tirer sur — **at all** *adv* : du tout

ate ['eɪt] → **eat**

atheist ['eɪθiːɪst] *n* : athée *mf* — **atheism** ['eɪθiˌɪzəm] *n* : athéisme *m*

athlete ['æθˌliːt] *n* : athlète *mf* — **athletic** [æθ'lɛtɪk] *adj* : athlétique — **athletics** [æθ'lɛtɪks] *ns & pl* : athlétisme *m*

atlas ['ætləs] *n* : atlas *m*

atmosphere ['ætməˌsfɪr] *n* : atmosphère *f* — **atmospheric** [ˌætmə'sfɪrɪk, -'sfɛr-] *adj* : atmosphérique

atom ['ætəm] *n* : atome *m* — **atomic** [ə'tɑmɪk] *adj* : atomique

atomizer ['ætəˌmaɪzər] *n* : atomiseur *m*

atone [ə'toːn] *vi* **atoned; atoning ~ for** : expier — **atonement** [ə'toːnmənt] *n* : expiation *f*

atrocious [ə'troːʃəs] *adj* : atroce — **atrocity** [ə'trɑsəti] *n, pl* **-ties** : atrocité *f*

atrophy ['ætrəfi] *vi* **-phied; phying** : s'atrophier

attach [ə'tætʃ] *vt* **1** : attacher **2 become ~ed to** : s'attacher à — *vi* ADHERE : s'attacher — **attachment** [ə'tætʃmənt] *n* **1** AFFECTION : attachement *m* **2** ACCESSORY : accessoire *m*

attack [ə'tæk] *v* : attaquer — **~** *n* **1** : attaque *f* **2 heart ~** : crise *f* cardiaque — **attacker** [ə'tækər] *n* : agresseur *m*

attain [ə'teɪn] *vt* : atteindre — **attainment** [ə'teɪnmənt] *n* : réalisation *f*

attempt [ə'tɛmpt] *vt* : tenter — **~** *n* : tentative *f*

attend [ə'tɛnd] *vt* **1** : assister à **2 ~ church** : aller à l'église — *vi* **1 ~ to** : s'occuper de **2 ~ to** HEED : prêter attention à — **attendance** [ə'tɛndənts] *n* **1** : présence *f* **2** TURNOUT : assistance *f* — **attendant** [ə'tɛndənt] *n* **1** : gardien *m*, -dienne *f* **2 service station ~** : pompiste *mf*

attention [ə'tɛntʃən] *n* **1** : attention *f* **2 pay ~ to** : prêter attention à — **attentive** [ə'tɛntɪv] *adj* : attentif

attest [ə'tɛst] *vt* : attester — *vi* **~ to** : témoigner de

attic ['ætɪk] *n* : grenier *m*

attitude ['ætəˌtuːd, -ˌtjuːd] *n* : attitude *f*

attorney [ə'tərni] *n, pl* **-neys** : avocat *m*, -cate *f*

attract [ə'trækt] *vt* : attirer — **attraction** [ə'trækʃən] *n* **1** : attrait *f* **2** : attraction *f* (en science) — **attractive** [ə'træktɪv] *adj* : attirant, attrayant

attribute ['ætrəˌbjuːt] *n* : attribut *m* — **~** [ə'trɪˌbjuːt] *vt* **-uted; -uting** : attribuer

auburn ['ɔbərn] *adj* : auburn

auction ['ɔkʃən] *vt* : vendre aux enchères — **~** *n* : vente *f* aux enchères

audacious [ɔ'deɪʃəs] *adj* : audacieux — **audacity** [ɔ'dæsəti] *n, pl* **-ties** : audace *f*

audible ['ɔdəbəl] *adj* : audible

audience ['ɔdiənts] *n* : assistance *f*, public *m*

audio ['ɔdiˌoː] *adj* : audio — **audiovisual** [ˌɔdioˈvɪʒuəl] *adj* : audiovisuel

audition [ɔ'dɪʃən] *n* : audition *f* — **~** *v* : auditionner

auditor ['ɔdətər] *n* : auditeur *m*, -trice *f*

auditorium [ˌɔdə'toriəm] *n, pl* **-riums** *or* **-ria** [-riə] : salle *f*

augment [ɔg'mɛnt] *vt* : augmenter

augur ['ɔgər] *vi* **~ well** : être de bon augure

August ['ɔgəst] *n* : août *m*

aunt ['ænt, 'ɑnt] *n* : tante *f*

aura ['ɔrə] *n* : aura *f*, atmosphère *f*

auspices ['ɔspəsəz, -ˌsiːz] *npl* : auspices *mpl*

auspicious [ɔ'spɪʃəs] *adj* : favorable

austere [ɔ'stɪr] *adj* : austère — **austerity** [ɔ'stɛrəti] *n, pl* **-ties** : austérité *f*

Australian [ɔ'streɪljən] *adj* : australien

authentic [ə'θɛntɪk, ɔ-] *adj* : authentique

author ['ɔθər] *n* : auteur *m*

authority [ə'θɔrəti, ɔ-] *n, pl* **-ties** : autorité *f* — **authoritarian** [ə,θɔrə'tɛriən, ə-] *adj* : autoritaire — **authoritative** [ə'θɔrəˌteɪtɪv, ɔ-] *adj* **1** DICTATORIAL : autoritaire **2** DEFINITIVE : qui fait autorité — **authorization** [ˌɔθərə'zeɪʃən] *n* : autorisation *f* — **authorize** ['ɔθəˌraɪz] *vt* **-rized; -rizing** : autoriser

autobiography [ˌɔtoˌbaɪ'ɑgrəfi] *n, pl* **-phies** : autobiographie *f* — **autobiographical** [ˌɔtobaɪə'græfɪkəl] *adj* : autobiographique

autograph ['ɔtəˌgræf] *n* : autographe *m*

automate ['ɔtəˌmeɪt] *v* **-mated; -mating** : automatiser — **automatic** [ˌɔtə'mætɪk] *adj* : automatique — **automation** [ˌɔtə'meɪʃən] *n* : automatisation *f*

automobile [ˌɔtəmo'biːl, -'moːˌbiːl] *n* : automobile *f*, voiture *f*

autonomy [ɔ'tɑnəmi] *n, pl* **-mies** : autonomie *f* — **autonomous** [ɔ'tɑnəməs] *adj* : autonome

autopsy ['ɔˌtɑpsi, -təp-] *n, pl* **-sies** : autopsie *f*

autumn ['ɔtəm] *n* : automne *m*

auxiliary [ɔg'zɪljəri, -'zɪləri] *adj* : auxiliaire — **~** *n, pl* **-ries** : auxiliaire *mf*

avail [ə'veɪl] *vt* **~ oneself of** : profiter de — **~ n to no ~** : en vain, sans résultat

available [ə'veɪləbəl] *adj* : disponible — **availability** [əˌveɪlə'bɪləti] *n, pl* **-ties** : disponibilité *f*

avalanche ['ævəˌlæntʃ] *n* : avalanche *f*

avarice ['ævərəs] *n* : avarice *f*

avenge [ə'vɛndʒ] *vt* **avenged; avenging** : venger

avenue ['ævəˌnuː, -ˌnjuː] *n* : avenue *f*

average ['ævrɪdʒ, 'ævə-] *vt* **-aged; -aging**

: faire en moyenne — **~** *adj* : moyen — **~**
n : moyenne *f*
averse [ə'vərs] *adj* be **~** to : répugner à —
aversion [ə'vərʒən] *n* : aversion *f*
avert [ə'vərt] *vt* **1** PREVENT : éviter **2** ~ one's
eyes : détourner les yeux
aviation [ˌeɪvi'eɪʃən] *n* : aviation *f*
avid ['ævɪd] *adj* **1** be **~** for : être avide de
2 ENTHUSIASTIC : passionné — **avidly**
['ævɪdli] *adv* : avidement
avocado [ˌævə'kɑdo, ˌɑvə-] *n, pl* -**dos** : avocat *m*
avoid [ə'vɔɪd] *vt* : éviter
await [ə'weɪt] *vt* : attendre
awake [ə'weɪk] *v* **awoke** [ə'wo:k]; **awoken**
[ə'wo:kən] *or* **awaked** [ə'weɪkt]; **awaking**
vt : réveiller, éveiller — *vi* WAKE UP : se
réveiller — **~** *adj* : éveillé, réveillé —
awaken [ə'weɪkən] → **awake**
award [ə'wɔrd] *vt* **1** GRANT : accorder **2**
CONFER : décerner — **~** *n* : prix *m*
aware [ə'wær] *adj* **1** : au courant **2** be **~** of
: être conscient de — **awareness** [ə-
'wærnəs] *n* : conscience *f*

awash [ə'wɔʃ] *adj* **~** with : inondé de
away [ə'weɪ] *adv* **1** chatter **~** : bavarder
sans arrêt **2** give **~** : donner **3** go **~**!
: allez-vous en! **4** take **~** : enlever **5** ten
kilometers **~** : à dix kilomètres d'ici **6**
turn **~** : se détourner — **~** *adj* **1** ABSENT
: absent **2** **~** game : match *m* à l'extérieur
awe ['ɔ] *n* : crainte *f* mêlée de respect —
awesome ['ɔsəm] *adj* : impressionnant
awful ['ɔfəl] *adj* **1** : affreux **2** an **~** lot of
: énormément de — **awfully** ['ɔfəli] *adv* : extrêmement
awhile [ə'hwaɪl] *adv* : un moment
awkward ['ɔkwərd] *adj* **1** : gauche, maladroit **2** EMBARRASSING : gênant **3** DIFFI-
CULT : difficile — **awkwardly** ['ɔkwərdli]
adv : maladroitement
awning ['ɔnɪŋ] *n* : auvent *m*
awoke, awoken → **awake**
awry [ə'raɪ] *adv* go **~** : mal tourner
ax *or* **axe** ['æks] *n* : hache *f*
axiom ['æksiəm] *n* : axiome *m*
axis ['æksɪs] *n, pl* **axes** [-si:z] : axe *m*
axle ['æksəl] *n* : essieu *m*

B

b ['bi:] *n, pl* **b's** *or* **bs** ['bi:z] : b *m*, deu-xième
lettre de l'alphabet
babble ['bæbəl] *vi* -**bled; -bling 1** : babiller,
gazouiller **2** MURMUR : murmurer — **~** *n*
: babillage *m*
baboon [bæ'bu:n] *n* : babouin *m*
baby ['beɪbi] *n, pl* -**bies** : bébé *m* — **~** *vt*
-**bied; -bying** : dorloter — **baby carriage** *n*
: voiture *f* d'enfant, landau *m* *France* —
babyish ['beɪbiɪʃ] *adj* : enfantin —
baby–sit ['beɪbiˌsɪt] *vi* -**sat** [-ˌsæt]; -**sitting**
: garder des enfants, faire du baby-sitting
France — **baby–sitter** ['beɪbiˌsɪtər] *n* : gardienne *f* d'enfants, baby-sitter *mf France*
bachelor ['bætʃələr] *n* **1** : célibataire *m* **2**
GRADUATE : licencié *m*, -ciée *f*
back ['bæk] *n* **1** : dos *m* **2** REVERSE : revers
m, dos *m* **3** REAR : derrière *m*, arrière *m*,
fond *m* **4** : arrière *m* (aux sports) — **~** *adv*
1 : en arrière, vers l'arrière **2** be **~** : être
de retour **3** go **~** : retourner **4** two years
~ : il y a deux ans — **~** *adj* **1** REAR : arrière, de derrière **2** OVERDUE : arriéré —
vt **1** SUPPORT : soutenir, appuyer **2** *or* **~**
up : mettre en marche arrière (un véhicule)
— *vi* **1** **~** down : céder **2** **~** up : reculer
— **backache** ['bækˌeɪk] *n* : mal *m* de dos —

backbone ['bækˌbo:n] *n* : colonne *f*
vertébrale — **backfire** ['bækˌfaɪr] *vi* -**fired;
-firing** : pétarader — **background** ['bæk-
ˌgraʊnd] *n* **1** : arrière-plan *m*, fond *m* (d'un
tableau) **2** EXPERIENCE : formation *f* —
backhand ['bækˌhænd] *adj* : de revers —
backhanded ['bækˌhændəd] *adj* : équivoque — **backing** ['bækɪŋ] *n* : soutien *m*,
appui *m* — **backlash** ['bækˌlæʃ] *n* : contre-
coup *m*, répercussion *f* — **backlog** ['bæk-
ˌlɔg] *n* : accumulation *f* (de travail, etc.)
— **backpack** ['bækˌpæk] *n* : sac *m* à dos —
backstage [ˌbæk'steɪdʒ, 'bækˌ-] *adv* : dans
les coulisses — **backtrack** ['bækˌtræk] *vi*
: revenir sur ses pas — **backup** ['bækˌʌp] *n*
1 SUPPORT : soutien *m*, appui *m* **2** : sauvegarde *f* (en informatique) — **backward**
['bækwərd] *or* **backwards** [-wərdz] *adv* **1**
: en arrière **2** bend over **~s** : faire tout
son possible **3** do it **~** : fais-le à l'envers
4 fall **~** : tomber à la renverse — **backward** *adj* : en arrière
bacon [beɪkən] *n* : lard *m*, bacon *m*
bacteria [bæk'tɪriə] *npl* : bactéries *fpl*
bad ['bæd] *adj* **worse** ['wərs]; **worst** ['wərst]
1 : mauvais **2** ROTTEN : pourri **3** SEVERE
: grave, aigu **4** from **~** to worse : de mal

bargain

en pis **5 too ~**! : quel dommage! **— ~**
adv → **badly**

badge [ˈbædʒ] *n* : insigne *m*, plaque *f*

badger [ˈbædʒər] *n* : blaireau *m* **— ~** *vt*
: harceler

badly [ˈbædli] *adv* **1** : mal **2** SEVERELY
: gravement **3 need ~** : avoir grand besoin
de

baffle [ˈbæfəl] *vt* **-fled; -fling** : déconcerter

bag [ˈbæg] *n* **1** : sac *m* **2** HANDBAG : sac *m* à
main **3** SUITCASE : valise *f* **— ~** *vt*
bagged; bagging : mettre en sac

baggage [ˈbægɪdʒ] *n* : bagages *mpl*

baggy [ˈbægi] *adj* **-gier; -est** : ample, trop
grand

bagpipes [ˈbægˌpaɪps] *npl* : cornemuse *f*

bail [ˌbeɪl] *n* : caution *f* **— ~** *vt* **1** *or* **~ out**
: vider, écoper (un bateau) **2** *or* **~ out** RE-
LEASE : mettre en liberté sous caution **3 ~
out** EXTRICATE : tirer d'affaire

bailiff [ˈbeɪlif] *n* : huissier *m*

bait [ˈbeɪt] *vt* **1** : appâter **2** HARASS : tourmenter **— ~** *n* : appât *m*

bake [ˈbeɪk] *v* **baked; baking** *vt* : faire cuire
au four **—** *vi* : cuire (au four) **— baker**
[ˈbeɪkər] *n* : boulanger *m*, -gère *f* **— bakery**
[ˈbeɪkəri] *n*, *pl* **-ries** : boulangerie *f* **— baking soda** *n* : bicarbonate *m* de soude

balance [ˈbæləns] *n* **1** SCALES : balance *f* **2**
COUNTERBALANCE : contrepoids *m* **3** EQUI-
LIBRIUM : équilibre *m* **4** REMAINDER : reste
m **5** *or* **bank ~** : solde *m* **— ~** *v* **-anced;
-ancing** *vt* **1** : faire ses comptes **2** EQUAL-
IZE : équilibrer **3** WEIGH : peser **—** *vi* : être
en équilibre

balcony [ˈbælkəni] *n*, *pl* **-nies** : balcon *m*

bald [ˈbɔld] *adj* **1** : chauve **2** WORN : usé

balk [ˈbɔk] *vi* **~ at** : reculer devant

ball [ˈbɔl] *n* **1** : balle *f*, ballon *m*, boule *f* **2**
DANCE : bal *m* **3 ~ of string** : pelote *f* de
ficelle

ballad [ˈbæləd] *n* : ballade *f*

ballast [ˈbæləst] *n* : lest *m*, ballast *m*

ballerina [ˌbæləˈrinə] *n* : ballerine *f*

ballet [bæˈleɪ, ˈbæˌleɪ] *n* : ballet *m*

ballistic [bəˈlɪstɪk] *adj* : balistique

balloon [bəˈluːn] *n* : ballon *m*, balloune *f* *Can*

ballot [ˈbælət] *n* **1** : bulletin *m* de vote **2**
VOTING : scrutin *m*

ballpoint pen [ˈbɔlˌpɔɪnt] *n* : stylo *m* à bille

ballroom [ˈbɔlˌruːm, -ˌrʊm] *n* : salle *f* de
danse, salle *f* de bal

balm [ˈbam, ˈbalm] *n* : baume *m* **— balmy**
[ˈbami, ˈbal-] *adj* **balmier; -est** : doux,
agréable

baloney [bəˈloːni] *n* NONSENSE : balivernes
fpl

bamboo [bæmˈbuː] *n* : bambou *m*

bamboozle [bæmˈbuːzəl] *vt* **-zled; -zling**
: embobiner *fam*

ban [ˈbæn] *vt* **banned; banning** : interdire
— ~ *n* : interdiction *f*

banana [bəˈnænə] *n* : banane *f*

band [ˈbænd] *n* **1** STRIP : bande *f* **2** GROUP
: groupe *m*, orchestre *m* **— ~** *vi* **~ together** : se réunir, se grouper

bandage [ˈbændɪdʒ] *n* : pansement *m*, bandage *m* **— ~** *vt* : bander, panser

bandy [ˈbændi] *vt* **-died; -dying ~ about**
: faire circuler

bang [ˈbæŋ] *vt* **1** STRIKE : frapper **2** SLAM
: claquer **—** *vi* **~ on** : cogner sur **— ~** *n* **1**
BLOW : coup *m* **2** EXPLOSION : détonation *f*
3 SLAM : claquement *m*

bangs [ˈbæŋz] *npl* : frange *f*

banish [ˈbænɪʃ] *vt* : bannir

banister [ˈbænəstər] *n* : rampe *f*

bank [ˈbæŋk] *n* **1** : banque *f* **2** : talus *m*, rive
f (d'un fleuve) **3** EMBANKMENT : terre-plein
m **— ~** *vt* : déposer **—** *vi* **1** : avoir un
compte en banque **2 ~ on** : compter sur **—
banker** [ˈbæŋkər] *n* : banquier *m* **— banking** [ˈbæŋkɪŋ] *n* : opérations *fpl* bancaires

bankrupt [ˈbæŋkˌrʌpt] *adj* : en faillite **—
bankruptcy** [ˈbæŋkˌrʌptsi] *n*, *pl* **-cies** : faillite *f*

banner [ˈbænər] *n* : bannière *f*

banquet [ˈbæŋkwət] *n* : banquet *m*

banter [ˈbæntər] *n* : plaisanteries *fpl* **— ~**
vi : plaisanter

baptize [ˈbæpˌtaɪz, ˈbæpˌtaɪz] *vt* **-tized; -tiz-
ing** : baptiser **— baptism** [ˈbæpˌtɪzəm] *n*
: baptême *m*

bar [ˈbar] *n* **1** : barre *f* (de métal), barreau *m*
(d'une fenêtre) **2** BARRIER : obstacle *m*,
barrière *f* **3** TAVERN : bar *m* **4 behind ~s**
: sous les verrous **5 ~ of soap** : pain *m* de
savon **— ~** *vt* **barred; barring 1** OB-
STRUCT : barrer, bloquer **2** EXCLUDE : exclure **3** PROHIBIT : interdire **— ~** *prep* **1**
: sauf **2 ~ none** : sans exception

barbarian [barˈbæriən] *n* : barbare *mf* **—
barbaric** [barˈbærɪk] *adj* : barbare

barbecue [ˈbarbɪˌkjuː] *vt* **-cued; -cuing**
: griller au charbon de bois **— ~** *n* : barbecue *m*

barbed wire [ˈbarbdˈwaɪr] *n* : fil *m* de fer
barbelé

barber [ˈbarbər] *n* : coiffeur *m*, -feuse *f*; barbier *m* *Can*

bare [ˈbær] *adj* **barer; barest 1** : dénudé **2**
EMPTY : vide **3** MINIMUM : essentiel **—
barefaced** [ˈbærˌfeɪst] *adj* : éhonté **—
barefoot** [ˈbærˌfʊt] *or* **barefooted** [-ˌfʊtəd]
adv : pieds nus **— ~** *adj* **be ~** : être nu-
pieds **— barely** [ˈbærli] *adv* : à peine, tout
juste

bargain [ˈbargən] *n* **1** AGREEMENT : marché
m **2** BUY : aubaine *f* **— ~** *vi* **1** : négocier,
marchander **2 ~ for** : s'attendre à

barge [ˈbɑrdʒ] *n* : chaland *m* — ~ *vi*
 barged; barging ~ **in** : interrompre
baritone [ˈbærə,toːn] *n* : baryton *m*
bark[1] [ˈbɑrk] *vi* : aboyer — ~ *n* : aboiement
 m (d'un chien)
bark[2] *n* : écorce *f* (d'un arbre)
barley [ˈbɑrli] *n* : orge *f*
barn [ˈbɑrn] *n* : grange *f*
barometer [bəˈrɑmətər] *n* : baromètre *m*
baron [ˈbærən] *n* : baron *m* — **baroness**
 [ˈbærənɪs, -nəs, -ˈnɛs] *n* : baronne *f*
barracks [ˈbærəks] *npl* : caserne *f*
barrage [bəˈrɑʒ, -ˈrɑdʒ] *n* 1 : tir *m* de barrage 2 : déluge *m* (de questions, etc.)
barrel [ˈbærəl] *n* 1 : tonneau *m*, fût *m*, baril
 m 2 : canon *m* (d'une arme à feu)
barren [ˈbærən] *adj* : stérile
barricade *vt* [ˈbærə,keɪd, ,bærəˈ-] **-caded;
 -cading** : barricader — ~ *n* : barricade *f*
barrier [ˈbæriər] *n* : barrière *f*
barring [ˈbɑrɪŋ] *prep* : excepté, sauf
bartender [ˈbɑr,tɛndər] *n* : barman *m*
barter [ˈbɑrtər] *vt* : échanger, troquer — ~
 n : échange *m*, troc *m*
base [ˈbeɪs] *n*, *pl* **bases** : base *f* — ~ *vt*
 based; basing : baser, fonder — ~ *adj*
 baser; basest : bas, vil
baseball [ˈbeɪs,bɔl] *n* : baseball *m*, base-ball
 m
basement [ˈbeɪsmənt] *n* : sous-sol *m*
bash [ˈbæʃ] *vt* : cogner, frapper — ~ *n* 1
 BLOW : coup *m* 2 PARTY : fête *f*
bashful [ˈbæʃfəl] *adj* : timide, gêné *Can*
basic [ˈbeɪsɪk] *adj* : fondamental, de base —
 basically [ˈbeɪsɪkli] *adv* : au fond, fondamentalement
basil [ˈbeɪzəl, ˈbæzəl] *n* : basilic *m*
basin [ˈbeɪsən] *n* : bassin *m* (d'un fleuve)
basis [ˈbeɪsəs] *n*, *pl* **bases** [-,siːz] : base *f*
bask [ˈbæsk] *vi* ~ **in the sun** : se chauffer
 au soleil
basket [ˈbæskət] *n* : corbeille *f*, panier *m* —
 basketball [ˈbæskət,bɔl] *n* : basket *m*, basket-ball *m*, ballon-panier *m* *Can*
bass[1] [ˈbæs] *n*, *pl* **bass** *or* **basses** : perche *f*,
 bar *m* (poisson)
bass[2] [ˈbeɪs] *n* : basse *f* (voix, instrument)
bassoon [bəˈsuːn, bæ-] *n* : basson *m*
bastard [ˈbæstərd] *n* : bâtard *m*, -tarde *f*
baste [ˈbeɪst] *vt* **basted; basting** 1 STITCH
 : faufiler, bâtir 2 : arroser (un rôti, etc.)
bat[1] [ˈbæt] *n* : chauve-souris *f* (animal)
bat[2] *n* : batte *f*, bâton *m* *Can* — ~ *vt* **batted;
 batting** : frapper
batch [ˈbætʃ] *n* : liasse *f* (de papiers, etc.), lot
 m (de marchandises), fournée *f* (de pain,
 etc.)
bath [ˈbæθ] *n*, *pl* **baths** [ˈbæðz, ˈbæθs] 1
 : bain *m* 2 BATHROOM : salle *f* de bains 3
 take a ~ : prendre un bain — **bathe** [ˈbeɪð]

v **bathed; bathing** *vt* : baigner — *vi* : se
 baigner, prendre un bain — **bathrobe**
 [ˈbæθ,roːb] *n* : peignoir *m* (de bain), robe *f*
 de chambre — **bathroom** [ˈbæθ,ruːm,
 -,rʊm] *n* : salle *f* de bains — **bathtub** [ˈbæθ-
 ,tʌb] *n* : baignoire *f*
baton [bəˈtɑn] *n* : bâton *m*
battalion [bəˈtæljən] *n* : bataillon *m*
batter [ˈbætər] *vt* 1 BEAT : battre 2 MIS-
TREAT : maltraiter — ~ *n* 1 : pâte *f* (à
 cuire) 2 HITTER : batteur *m* (au baseball)
battery [ˈbætəri] *n*, *pl* **-teries** : batterie *f*, pile
 f (d'une radio, etc.)
battle [ˈbætəl] *n* 1 : bataille *f* 2 STRUGGLE
 : lutte *f* — ~ *vi* **-tled; -tling** : lutter — **battlefield** [ˈbætəl,fiːld] *n* : champ *m* de bataille
 — **battleship** [ˈbætəl,ʃɪp] *n* : cuirassé *m*
bawdy [ˈbɔdi] *adj* **bawdier; -est** : paillard,
 grivois
bawl [ˈbɔl] *vi* : brailler *fam*
bay[1] [ˈbeɪ] *n* INLET : baie *f*
bay[2] *n* *or* ~ **leaf** : laurier *m*
bay[3] *vi* : aboyer — ~ *n* : aboiement *m*
bayonet [,beɪəˈnɛt, ˈbeɪə,nɛt] *n* : baïonnette *f*
bay window *n* : fenêtre *f* en saillie
bazaar [bəˈzɑr] *n* 1 : bazar *m* 2 SALE : vente
 f (de charité)
be [ˈbiː] *v* **was** [ˈwəz, ˈwɑz]; **were** [ˈwər];
 been [ˈbɪn]; **being; am** [ˈæm]; **is** [ˈɪz]; **are**
 [ˈɑr] *vi* 1 : être 2 (*expressing a state*) : être,
 avoir 3 (*expressing age*) : avoir 4 (*expressing equality*) : faire, égaler 5 (*expressing
 health or well-being*) : aller, se porter — *v
 aux* 1 : être en train de 2 (*indicating obligation*) : devoir 3 (*used in passive constructions*) : être — *v impers* 1 (*indicating
 weather*) : faire 2 (*indicating time*) : être
beach [ˈbiːtʃ] *n* : plage *f*
beacon [ˈbiːkən] *n* : phare *m*, signal *m* lumineux
bead [ˈbiːd] *n* 1 : perle *f* 2 DROP : goutte *f* 3
 ~**s** *npl* NECKLACE : collier *m*
beak [ˈbiːk] *n* : bec *m*
beaker [ˈbiːkər] *n* : gobelet *m*
beam [ˈbiːm] *n* 1 : poutre *f* (de bois) 2 RAY
 : rayon *m* — ~ *vi* SHINE : rayonner — ~ *vt*
 BROADCAST : diffuser, transmettre
bean [ˈbiːn] *n* 1 : haricot *m* 2 *or* **coffee** ~
 : grain *m* (de café)
bear[1] [ˈbær] *n*, *pl* **bears** *or* **bear** : ours *m*,
 ourse *f*
bear[2] *v* **bore** [ˈbor]; **borne** [ˈbɔrn]; **bearing**
 vt 1 CARRY : porter 2 ENDURE : supporter
 — *vi* 1 ~ **in mind** : tenir compte de 2 ~
 left/right : prendre à gauche, à droite —
 bearable [ˈbærəbəl] *adj* : supportable
beard [ˈbɪrd] *n* : barbe *f*
bearer [ˈbærər] *n* : porteur *m*, -teuse *f*
bearing [ˈbærɪŋ] *n* 1 MANNER : maintien *m*

bend

2 SIGNIFICANCE : rapport *m* **3 get one's ~s** : s'orienter

beast ['bi:st] *n* : bête *f*

beat ['bi:t] *v* **beat; beaten** ['bi:tən] *or* **beat; beating** : battre — **~** *n* **1** : battement *m* **2** RHYTHM : rythme *m*, temps *m* — **beating** ['bi:tɪŋ] *n* **1** : raclée *f fam* **2** DEFEAT : défaite *f*

beauty ['bju:ti] *n, pl* **-ties** : beauté *f* — **beautician** [bju:'tɪʃən] *n* : esthéticien *m*, -cienne *f* — **beautiful** ['bju:tɪfəl] *adj* **1** : beau **2** WONDERFUL : merveilleux — **beautifully** ['bju:tɪfəli] *adv* WONDERFULLY : merveilleusement — **beautify** ['bju:tɪ,faɪ] *vt* **-fied; -fying** : embellir

beaver ['bi:vər] *n* : castor *m*

because [bi'kʌz, -'kɔz] *conj* : parce que — **because of** *prep* : à cause de

beckon ['bɛkən] *vt* : faire signe à, attirer — *vi* : faire signe

become [bi'kʌm] *v* **-came** [-'keɪm]; **-come; -coming** *vi* : devenir — *vt* SUIT : aller à, convenir à — **becoming** [bi'kʌmɪŋ] *adj* **1** SUITABLE : convenable **2** FLATTERING : seyant

bed ['bɛd] *n* **1** : lit *m* **2** BOTTOM : fond *m* (de la mer) **3 go to ~** : se coucher — **bedclothes** ['bɛd,klo:z, -,klo:ðz] *npl* : draps *mpl* et couvertures *fpl*

bedridden ['bɛd,rɪdən] *adj* : alité

bedroom ['bɛd,ru:m, -,rʊm] *n* : chambre *f* (à coucher)

bedspread ['bɛd,sprɛd] *n* : couvre-lit *m*

bedtime ['bɛd,taɪm] *n* : heure *f* du coucher

bee ['bi:] *n* : abeille *f*

beech ['bi:ʧ] *n, pl* **beeches** *or* **beech** : hêtre *m*

beef ['bi:f] *n* : bœuf *m* — **beefsteak** ['bif-,steɪk] *n* : bifteck *m*

beehive ['bi:,haɪv] *n* : ruche *f*

beeline ['bi:,laɪn] *n* **make a ~ for** : se diriger droit vers

been → **be**

beep ['bi:p] *n* : coup *m* de klaxon, bip *m* — **~** *vi* : klaxonner, faire bip — **beeper** ['bi:pər] *n* : récepteur *m* de radiomessagerie

beer ['bɪr] *n* : bière *f*

beet ['bi:t] *n* : betterave *f*

beetle ['bi:ţəl] *n* : scarabée *m*

before [bi'for] *adv* **1** : avant, auparavant **2 the month ~** : le mois dernier — **~** *prep* **1** (*in space*) : devant **2** (*in time*) : avant **3 ~ my eyes** : sous mes yeux — **~** *conj* : avant de, avant que — **beforehand** [bi'for-,hænd] *adv* : à l'avance

befriend [bi'frɛnd] *vt* : offrir son amitié à

beg ['bɛg] *v* **begged; begging** *vt* **1** : mendier **2** ENTREAT : supplier, prier — *vi* : mendier — **beggar** ['bɛgər] *n* : mendiant *m*, -diante *f*

begin [bi'gɪn] *v* **-gan** [-'gæn]; **-gun** [-'gʌn]; **-ginning** : commencer — **beginner** [bi-'gɪnər] *n* : débutant *m*, -tante *f* — **beginning** [bi'gɪnɪŋ] *n* : début *m*, commencement *m*

begrudge [bi'grʌʤ] *vt* **-grudged; -grudging 1** : accorder à regret **2** ENVY : envier

behalf [bi'hæf, -haf] *n* **on ~ of** : de la part de, au nom de

behave [bi'heɪv] *vi* **-haved; -having** : se conduire, se comporter — **behavior** *or Brit* **behaviour** [bi'heɪvjər] *n* : conduite *f*, comportement *m*

behind [bi'haɪnd] *adv* **1** : derrière, en arrière **2 fall ~** : prendre du retard — **~** *prep* **1** : derrière, en arrière de **2** : en retard sur (l'horaire, etc.) **3 her friends are ~ her** : elle a l'appui de ses amis

behold [bi'ho:ld] *vt* **-held; -holding** : contempler

beige ['beɪʒ] *adj & nm* : beige

being ['bi:ɪŋ] *n* **1** : être *m*, créature *f* **2 come into ~** : prendre naissance

belated [bi'leɪtəd] *adj* : tardif

belch ['bɛlʧ] *vi* : roter *fam* — **~** *n* : renvoi *m*

belfry ['bɛlfri] *n, pl* **-fries** : beffroi *m*, clocher *m*

Belgian ['bɛlʤən] *adj* : belge

belie [bi'laɪ] *vt* **-lied; -lying** : démentir, contredire

belief [bə'li:f] *n* **1** TRUST : confiance *f* **2** CONVICTION : croyance *f* **3** FAITH : foi *f* — **believable** [bə'li:vəbəl] *adj* : croyable — **believe** [bə'li:v] *v* **-lieved; -lieving** : croire — **believer** [bə'li:vər] *n* : croyant *m*, croyante *f*

belittle [bi'lɪţəl] *vt* **-tled; -tling** : rabaisser

bell ['bɛl] *n* **1** : cloche *f*, clochette *f* **2** : sonnette *f* (d'une porte, etc.)

belligerent [bə'lɪʤərənt] *adj* : belligérant

bellow ['bɛ,lo:] *vi* **1** : beugler **2** HOWL : brailler *fam*, hurler

belly ['bɛli] *n, pl* **-lies** : ventre *m*

belong [bi'lɔŋ] *vi* **1 ~ to** : appartenir à, être à **2 ~ to** : être membre de (un club, etc.) **3 where does it ~ ?** : où va-t-il? — **belongings** [bi'lɔŋɪŋz] *npl* : affaires *fpl*, effets *mpl* personnels

beloved [bi'lʌvəd, -'lʌvd] *adj* : bien-aimé — **~** *n* : bien-aimé *m*, -mée *f*

below [bi'lo:] *adv* : en dessous, en bas — **~** *prep* : sous, au-dessous de, en dessous de

belt ['bɛlt] *n* **1** : ceinture *f* **2** STRAP : courroie *f* (d'une machine) **3** AREA : zone *f*, région *f* — **~** *vt* THRASH : donner un coup à

bench ['bɛnʧ] *n* **1** : banc *m* **2** WORKBENCH : établi *m* **3** COURT : cour *f*, tribunal *m*

bend ['bɛnd] *v* **bent** ['bɛnt]; **bending** *vt* : plier, courber — *vi* **1** : se plier, se courber **2** *or* **~ over** : se pencher — **~** *n* : virage *m*, coude *m*

beneath [bɪˈniːθ] *adv* : au-dessous, en bas — ~ *prep* : sous, en dessous de

benediction [ˌbɛnəˈdɪkʃən] *n* : bénédiction *f*

benefactor [ˈbɛnəˌfæktər] *n* : bienfaiteur *m*, -trice *f*

benefit [ˈbɛnəfɪt] *n* **1** : avantage *m*, bénéfice *m* **2** AID : allocation *f*, prestation *f* — ~ *vt* : profiter à, bénéficier à — *vi* : profiter, tirer avantage — **beneficial** [ˌbɛnəˈfɪʃəl] *adj* : avantageux — **beneficiary** [ˌbɛnəˈfɪʃiˌɛri, -ˈfɪʃəri] *n, pl* **-ries** : bénéficiaire *mf*

benevolent [bəˈnɛvələnt] *adj* : bienveillant

benign [bɪˈnaɪn] *adj* **1** KIND : bienveillant, aimable **2** : bénin (en médecine)

bent [ˈbɛnt] *adj* **1** : tordu, courbé **2 be ~ on doing** : être décidé à faire — ~ *n* : aptitude *f*, penchant *m*

bequeath [bɪˈkwiːθ, -ˈkwiːð] *vt* : léguer — **bequest** [bɪˈkwɛst] *n* : legs *m*

berate [bɪˈreɪt] *vt* **-rated; -rating** : réprimander

bereaved [bɪˈriːvd] *adj* : endeuillé, attristé — **bereavement** [bɪˈriːvmənt] *n* : deuil *m*

beret [bəˈreɪ] *n* : béret *m*

berry [ˈbɛri] *n, pl* **-ries** : baie *f*

berserk [bərˈsərk, -ˈzərk] *adj* **1** : fou, enragé **2 go ~** : devenir fou furieux

berth [ˈbərθ] *n* **1** MOORING : mouillage *m* **2** BUNK : couchette *f*

beset [bɪˈsɛt] *vt* **-set; -setting 1** HARASS : assaillir **2** SURROUND : encercler

beside [bɪˈsaɪd] *prep* **1** : à côté de, près de **2 be ~ oneself** : être hors de soi — **besides** [bɪˈsaɪdz] *adv* : en plus — ~ *prep* **1** : en plus de **2** EXCEPT : sauf

besiege [bɪˈsiːdʒ] *vt* **-sieged; -sieging** : assiéger

best [ˈbɛst] *adj* (*superlative of* **good**) **1** : meilleur **2** : plus beau — ~ *adv* (*superlative of* **well**) : le mieux, le plus — ~ *n* **1 at ~** : au mieux **2 do one's ~** : faire de son mieux **3 the ~** : le meilleur — **best man** *n* : garçon *m* d'honneur, témoin *n*

bestow [bɪˈstoː] *vt* : accorder, concéder

bet [ˈbɛt] *n* : pari *m*, gageure *f Can* — ~ *v* **bet; betting** *vt* : parier, gager *Can* — *vi* ~ **on sth** : parier sur qqch

betray [bɪˈtreɪ] *vt* : trahir — **betrayal** [bɪˈtreɪəl] *n* : trahison *f*

better [ˈbɛtər] *adj* (*comparative of* **good**) **1** : meilleur **2 get ~** : s'améliorer — ~ *adv* (*comparative of* **well**) **1** : mieux **2 all the ~** : tant mieux — ~ *n* **1 the ~** : le meilleur, la meilleure **2 get the ~ of** : l'emporter sur — ~ *vt* **1** IMPROVE : améliorer **2** SURPASS : surpasser, faire mieux que

between [bɪˈtwiːn] *prep* : entre — ~ *adv or* **in ~** : au milieu

beverage [ˈbɛvrɪdʒ, ˈbɛvə-] *n* : boisson *f*

beware [bɪˈwær] *vi* ~ **of** : prendre garde à, se méfier de

bewilder [bɪˈwɪldər] *vt* : rendre perplexe, déconcerter — **bewilderment** [bɪˈwɪldərmənt] *n* : perplexité *f*, confusion *f*

bewitch [bɪˈwɪtʃ] *vt* : enchanter

beyond [biˈjɑnd] *adv* : au-delà, plus loin — ~ *prep* : au-delà de

bias [ˈbaɪəs] *n* **1** PREJUDICE : préjugé *m* **2** TENDENCY : penchant *m* — **biased** [ˈbaɪəst] *adj* : partial

bib [ˈbɪb] *n* : bavoir *m* (d'un bébé)

Bible [ˈbaɪbəl] *n* : Bible *f* — **biblical** [ˈbɪblɪkəl] *adj* : biblique

bibliography [ˌbɪbliˈɑgrəfi] *n, pl* **-phies** : bibliographie *f*

biceps [ˈbaɪˌsɛps] *ns & pl* : biceps *m*

bicker [ˈbɪkər] *vi* : se chamailler

bicycle [ˈbaɪsɪkəl, -ˌsɪ-] *n* : bicyclette *f*, vélo *m* — ~ *vi* **-cled; -cling** : faire de la bicyclette, faire du vélo

bid [ˈbɪd] *vt* **bade** [ˈbæd, ˈbeɪd] *or* **bid; bidden** [ˈbɪdən] *or* **bid; bidding 1** OFFER : offrir **2** ~ **farewell** : dire adieu — ~ *n* **1** OFFER : offre *f*, enchère *f* **2** ATTEMPT : tentative *f*

bide [ˈbaɪd] *vt* **bode** [ˈboːd] *or* **bided; bided; biding** ~ **one's time** : attendre le bon moment

bifocals [baɪˌfoːkəlz] *npl* : lunettes *fpl* bifocales

big [ˈbɪg] *adj* **bigger; biggest** : grand, gros

bigot [ˈbɪgət] *n* : fanatique *mf* — **bigotry** [ˈbɪgətri] *n, pl* **-tries** : fanatisme *m*

bike [ˈbaɪk] *n* **1** BICYCLE : vélo *m* **2** MOTORCYCLE : moto *f*

bikini [bəˈkiːni] *n* : bikini *m*

bile [ˈbaɪl] *n* : bile *f*

bilingual [baɪˈlɪŋgwəl] *adj* : bilingue

bill [ˈbɪl] *n* **1** BEAK : bec *m* (d'un oiseau) **2** INVOICE : facture *f*, compte *m*, addition *f* (au restaurant) **3** LAW : projet *m* de loi **4** BANKNOTE : billet *m* (de banque) — ~ *vt* : facturer, envoyer la facture à

billiards [ˈbɪljərdz] *n* : billard *m*

billion [ˈbɪljən] *n, pl* **billions** *or* **billion** : milliard *m*

billow [ˈbɪloː] *vi* : onduler (se dit d'un drapeau)

bin [ˈbɪn] *n* : coffre *m*, boîte *f*

binary [ˈbaɪnəri, -ˌnɛri] *adj* : binaire

bind [ˈbaɪnd] *vt* **bound** [ˈbaʊnd]; **binding 1** TIE : lier **2** OBLIGE : obliger **3** UNITE : unir **4** : relier (un livre) — **binder** [ˈbaɪndər] *n* FOLDER : classeur *m* — **binding** [ˈbaɪndɪŋ] *n* : reliure *f* (d'un livre)

binge [ˈbɪndʒ] *n* : bringue *f fam*

bingo [ˈbɪŋˌgoː] *n, pl* **-gos** : bingo *m*

binoculars [bəˈnɑkjələrz, baɪ-] *npl* : jumelles *fpl*

biochemistry [ˌbaɪoˈkɛməstri] *n* : biochimie *f*

biography [baɪˈɑgrəfi, bi:-] *n, pl* **-phies** : biographie *f* — **biographer** [baɪˈɑgrəfər] *n* : biographe *mf* — **biographical** [ˌbaɪəˈgræfɪkəl] *adj* : biographique

biology [baɪˈɑləʤi] *n* : biologie *f* — **biological** [-ʤɪkəl] *adj* : biologique — **biologist** [baɪˈɑləʤɪst] *n* : biologiste *mf*

birch [ˈbərʧ] *n* : bouleau *m*

bird [ˈbərd] *n* : oiseau *m*

birth [ˈbərθ] *n* **1** : naissance *f* **2 give ~ to** : accoucher de — **birthday** [ˈbərθˌdeɪ] *n* : anniversaire *m* — **birthmark** [ˈbərθˌmɑrk] *n* : tache *f* de vin — **birthplace** [ˈbərθˌpleɪs] *n* : lieu *m* de naissance — **birthrate** [ˈbərθˌreɪt] *n* : natalité *f*

biscuit [ˈbɪskət] *n* : petit pain *m* au lait

bisexual [ˌbaɪˈsɛkʃəwəl, -ˈsɛkʃəl] *adj* : bisexuel

bishop [ˈbɪʃəp] *n* **1** : évêque *m* **2** : fou *m* (aux échecs)

bison [baɪzən, -sən] *ns & pl* : bison *m*

bit[1] [ˈbɪt] *n* : mors *m* (d'une bride)

bit[2] *n* **1** : morceau *m*, bout *m* **2** : bit *m* (en informatique) **3 a ~** : un peu

bitch [ˈbɪʧ] *n* : chienne *f* — **~** *vi* COMPLAIN : râler *fam*

bite [ˈbaɪt] *v* **bit** [ˈbɪt]; **bitten** [ˈbɪtən]; **biting** *vt* **1** : mordre — *vi* STING : piquer — *vi* : mordre — **~** *n* **1** : piqûre *f* (d'insecte), morsure *f* (de chien, etc.) **2** MOUTHFUL : bouchée *f* — **biting** *adj* **1** PENETRATING : pénétrant **2** SCATHING : mordant

bitter [ˈbɪtər] *adj* **1** : amer **2 it's ~ cold** : il fait un froid glacial — **bitterness** [ˈbɪtərnəs] *n* : amertume *f*

bizarre [bəˈzɑr] *adj* : bizarre

black [ˈblæk] *adj* **1** : noir — **~** *n* **1** : noir *m* (couleur) **2** : Noir *m*, Noire *f* (personne) — **black–and–blue** [ˌblækənˈblu:] *adj* : couvert de bleus — **blackberry** [ˈblækˌbɛri] *n, pl* **-ries** : mûre *f* — **blackboard** [ˈblækˌbord] *n* : tableau *m* (noir) — **blacken** [ˈblækən] *vt* : noircir — **blackmail** [ˈblækˌmeɪl] *n* : chantage *m* — **~** *vi* : faire chanter — **black market** *n* : marché *m* noir — **blackout** [ˈblækˌaʊt] *n* **1** : panne *f* d'électricité **2** FAINT : évanouissement *m* — **blacksmith** [ˈblækˌsmɪθ] *n* : forgeron *m* — **blacktop** [ˈblækˌtɑp] *n* : asphalte *m*

bladder [ˈblædər] *n* : vessie *f*

blade [ˈbleɪd] *n* **1** : lame *f* (de couteau) **2** : pale *f* (d'hélice, de rame, etc.) **3 ~ of grass** : brin *m* d'herbe

blame [ˈbleɪm] *vt* **blamed; blaming** : blâmer, reprocher — **~** *n* : faute *f*, responsabilité *f* — **blameless** [ˈbleɪmləs] *adj* : irréprochable

bland [ˈblænd] *adj* : fade, insipide

blank [ˈblæŋk] *adj* **1** : blanc (se dit d'une page, etc.) **2** EMPTY : vide — **~** *n* : blanc *m*, vide *m*

blanket [ˈblæŋkət] *n* **1** : couverture *f* (d'un lit) **2 ~ of snow** : couche *f* de neige — **~** *vt* : recouvrir

blare [ˈblær] *vi* **blared; blaring** : beugler

blasé [blɑˈzeɪ] *adj* : blasé

blasphemy [ˈblæsfəmi] *n, pl* **-mies** : blasphème *m*

blast [ˈblæst] *n* **1** GUST : rafale *f*, souffle *m* **2** EXPLOSION : explosion *f* **3 at full ~** : à plein volume — **~** *vt* BLOW UP : faire sauter — **blast–off** [ˈblæstˌɔf] *n* : lancement *m*

blatant [ˈbleɪtənt] *adj* : flagrant

blaze [ˈbleɪz] *n* **1** FIRE : incendie *f* **2** BRIGHTNESS : éclat *m* — **~** *v* **blazed; blazing** : flamber

blazer [ˈbleɪzər] *n* : blazer *m*

bleach [ˈbli:ʧ] *vt* : blanchir, décolorer — **~** *n* : décolorant *m*, eau *f* de Javel

bleachers [ˈbli:ʧərz] *npl* : gradins *mpl*

bleak [ˈbli:k] *adj* **1** DESOLATE : désolé **2** GLOOMY : triste, sombre

bleat [ˈbli:t] *vi* : bêler — **~** *n* : bêlement *m*

bleed [ˈbli:d] *v* **bled** [ˈblɛd]; **bleeding** : saigner

blemish [ˈblɛmɪʃ] *vt* : tacher, ternir — **~** *n* : tache *f*, défaut *m*

blend [ˈblɛnd] *vt* : mélanger — **~** *n* : mélange *m*, combinaison *f* — **blender** [ˈblɛndər] *n* : mixer *m*

bless [ˈblɛs] *vt* **blessed** [ˈblɛst]; **blessing** : bénir — **blessed** [ˈblɛsəd] *or* **blest** [ˈblɛst] *adj* : bénit, saint — **blessing** [ˈblɛsɪŋ] *n* : bénédiction *f*

blew → **blow**

blind [ˈblaɪnd] *adj* : aveugle — **~** *vt* **1** : aveugler **2** DAZZLE : éblouir — **~** *n* **1** : store *m* (d'une fenêtre) **2 the ~** : les non-voyants *mpl* — **blindfold** [ˈblaɪndˌfo:ld] *vt* : bander les yeux à — **~** *n* : bandeau *m* — **blindly** [ˈblaɪndli] *adv* : aveuglément — **blindness** [ˈblaɪndnəs] *n* : cécité *f*

blink [ˈblɪŋk] *vi* **1** : cligner des yeux **2** FLICKER : clignoter — **~** *n* : battement *m* des paupières — **blinker** [ˈblɪŋkər] *n* : clignotant *m*

bliss [ˈblɪs] *n* : félicité *f* — **blissful** [ˈblɪsfəl] *adj* : bienheureux

blister [ˈblɪstər] *n* **1** : ampoule *f*, cloque *f* (sur la peau) **2** : boursouflure *f* (sur une surface peinte) — **~** *vi* **1** : se couvrir d'ampoules *fpl* (se dit de la peau) **2** : se boursoufler (se dit de la peinture, etc.)

blitz [ˈblɪts] *n* : bombardement *m*

blizzard [ˈblɪzərd] *n* : tempête *f* de neige

bloated [ˈblo:təd] *adj* : boursouflé, gonflé

blob [ˈblɑb] *n* **1** DROP : goutte *f* **2** SPOT : tache *f*

block ['blɑk] n 1 : bloc m 2 OBSTRUCTION : obstruction f 3 : pâté m de maisons, bloc m Can 4 or building ~ : cube m — ~ vt : bloquer, boucher — **blockade** [blɑ'keɪd] n . bɪocus m — **blockage** ['blɑkɪdʒ] n : obstruction f

blond or **blonde** ['blɑnd] adj : blond — ~ n : blond m, blonde f

blood ['blʌd] n : sang m — **blood pressure** n : tension f artérielle — **bloodshed** ['blʌd-ʃed] n : carnage m — **bloodshot** ['blʌd-ʃɑt] adj : injecté de sang — **bloodstained** ['blʌd,steɪnd] adj : taché de sang — **bloodstream** ['blʌd,stri:m] n : sang m, système m sanguin — **bloodthirsty** ['blʌd,θərsti] adj : sanguinaire — **bloody** ['blʌdi] adj **bloodier; -est** : ensanglanté

bloom ['blu:m] n 1 : fleur f 2 **in full ~** : en pleine floraison — ~ vi : fleurir, éclore

blossom ['blɑsəm] n : fleur f — ~ vi 1 : fleurir 2 MATURE : s'épanouir

blot ['blɑt] n : tache f (d'encre, etc.) — ~ vt **blotted; blotting** 1 : tacher 2 DRY : sécher

blotch ['blɑtʃ] n : tache f — **blotchy** ['blɑ'tʃi] adj **blotchier; -est** : tacheté

blouse ['blaʊs, 'blaʊz] n : chemisier m

blow ['blo:] v **blew** ['blu:]; **blown** ['blo:n]; **blowing** vi 1 : souffler 2 SOUND : sonner 3 or ~ **out** : éclater (se dit d'un pneu), s'éteindre (se dit d'une bougie) — vt 1 : souffler 2 SOUND : jouer de (la trompette, etc.) 3 BUNGLE : rater 4 ~ **one's nose** : se moucher — ~ n : coup m — **blowout** ['blo:,aʊt] n : éclatement m — **blow up** vi : exploser, sauter — vt 1 EXPLODE : faire sauter 2 INFLATE : gonfler

blubber ['blʌbər] n : graisse f de baleine

bludgeon ['blʌdʒən] n : matraque f — ~ vt : matraquer

blue ['blu:] adj **bluer; bluest** 1 : bleu 2 MELANCHOLY : triste — ~ n : bleu m — **blueberry** ['blu:,beri] n, pl **-ries** : myrtille f France, bleuet m Can — **bluebird** ['blu:-,bərd] n : oiseau m bleu — **blue cheese** n : (fromage m) bleu m — **blueprint** ['blu:-,prɪnt] n : plan m (de travail) — **blues** ['blu:z] ns & pl 1 : cafard m 2 : blues m (musique)

bluff ['blʌf] v : bluffer — ~ n 1 : falaise f, escarpement m 2 DECEPTION : bluff m —

blunder ['blʌndər] vi : faire une gaffe — ~ n : gaffe f fam

blunt ['blʌnt] adj 1 DULL : émoussé 2 DIRECT : brusque, franc — ~ vt : émousser

blur ['blər] n : image f floue — ~ vt **blurred; blurring** : brouiller, rendre flou

blurb ['blərb] n : notice f publicitaire

blurt ['blərt] vt or ~ **out** : laisser échapper

blush ['blʌʃ] n : rougeur f — ~ vi : rougir

blustery ['blʌstəri] adj : venteux, orageux

boar ['bor] n : sanglier m

board ['bord] n 1 PLANK : planche f 2 COMMITTEE : conseil m 3 : tableau m (d'un jeu) 4 **room and ~** : pension f complète — ~ vt 1 : monter à bord de (un avion, un navire), monter dans (un train) 2 LODGE : prendre en pension 3 ~ **up** : couvrir de planches — **boarder** ['bordər] n : pensionnaire mf

boast ['bo:st] n : vantardise f — ~ vi : se vanter — **boastful** ['bo:stfəl] adj : vantard

boat ['bo:t] n : bateau m, barque f

bob ['bɑb] vi **bobbed; bobbing** or ~ **up and down** : monter et descendre

bobbin ['bɑbən] n : bobine f

body ['bɑdi] n, pl **bodies** 1 : corps m 2 CORPSE : cadavre m 3 : carrosserie f (d'une voiture) 4 ~ **of water** : masse f d'eau — **bodily** ['bɑdəli] adj : physique, corporel — **bodyguard** ['bɑdi,gɑrd] n : garde m du corps

bog ['bɑg, 'bɔg] n : marais m, marécage m — ~ vi **bogged; bogging** or ~ **down** : s'embourber

bogus ['bo:gəs] adj : faux

bohemian [bo:'hi:miən] adj : bohème

boil ['bɔɪl] v : faire bouillir — ~ vi : bouillir — ~ n 1 : ébullition f 2 : furoncle m (en médecine) — **boiler** ['bɔɪlər] n : chaudière f

boisterous ['bɔɪstərəs] adj : bruyant, tapageur

bold ['bo:ld] adj 1 DARING : hardi, audacieux 2 IMPUDENT : effronté — **boldness** ['bo:ldnəs] n : hardiesse f, audace f

bologna [bə'lo:ni] n : gros m saucisson

bolster ['bo:lstər] n : traversin m — ~ vt **-stered; -stering** or ~ **up** : soutenir

bolt ['bo:lt] n 1 LOCK : verrou m 2 SCREW : boulon m 3 ~ **of lightning** : éclair m, coup m de foudre — ~ vt LOCK : verrouiller — vi FLEE : se sauver

bomb ['bɑm] n : bombe f — ~ vt : bombarder — **bombard** [bɑm'bɑrd, bəm-] vt : bombarder — **bombardment** [bɑm-'bɑrdmənt] n : bombardement m — **bomber** ['bɑmər] n : bombardier m

bond ['bɑnd] n 1 TIE : lien m 2 SECURITY : bon m — ~ vi or ~ **with** : s'attacher à

bondage ['bɑndɪdʒ] n : esclavage m

bone ['bo:n] n : os m, arête f — ~ vt **boned; boning** : désosser

bonfire ['bɑn,faɪr] n : feu m de joie

bonus ['bo:nəs] n : gratification f, prime f

bony ['bo:ni] adj **bonier; -est** : plein d'os, plein d'arêtes

boo ['bu:] n, pl **boos** : huée f — ~ vt : huer, siffler

book ['bʊk] n 1 : livre m 2 NOTEBOOK : cahier m — ~ vt : réserver — **bookcase** ['bʊk,keɪs] n : bibliothèque f — **bookkeep-**

ing ['bʊk,ki:pɪŋ] *n* : comptabilité *f* — **booklet** ['bʊklət] *n* : brochure *f* — **bookmark**
['bʊk,mark] *n* : signet *m* — **bookseller**
['bʊk,sɛlər] *n* : libraire *mf* — **bookshelf**
['bʊk,ʃɛlf] *n, pl* **-shelves** : rayon *m*, étagère
f (à livres) — **bookstore** ['bʊk,stor] *n* : librairie *f*

boom ['bu:m] *vi* **1** : gronder, retentir **2**
PROSPER : prospérer — **~** *n* **1** : grondement *m* **2** : boom *m* (économique)

boon ['bu:n] *n* : bienfait *m*

boost ['bu:st] *vt* **1** LIFT : soulever **2** IN-
CREASE : augmenter — **~** *n* **1** INCREASE
: augmentation *f* **2** ENCOURAGEMENT : encouragement *m*

boot ['bu:t] *n* : botte *f* — **~** *vt* **1** : donner un
coup de pied à **2** *or* **~ up** : amorcer (en informatique)

booth ['bu:θ] *n, pl* **booths** ['bu:ðz, 'bu:θs]
: baraque *f* (d'un marché), cabine *f* (téléphonique)

booze ['bu:z] *n* : alcool *m*, boissons *fpl* alcoolisées

border ['bɔr,dər] *n* **1** EDGE : bord *m* **2**
BOUNDARY : frontière *f* **3** : bordure *f* (d'un
vêtement, etc.)

bore¹ ['bor] *vt* **bored; boring** DRILL : percer,
forer

bore² *vt* TIRE : ennuyer — **~** *n* : raseur *m*,
-seuse *f fam* — **boredom** ['bordəm] *n*
: ennui *m* — **boring** ['borɪŋ] *adj* : ennuyeux,
ennuyant *Can*

born ['bɔrn] *adj* **1** : né **2 be ~** : naître

borough ['bəro] *n* : arrondissement *m* urbain

borrow ['baro] *vt* : emprunter

bosom ['buzəm, 'bʊ-] *n* BREAST : poitrine *f*
— **~** *adj* **~ friend** : ami intime

boss ['bɔs] *n* : patron *m*, -tronne *f*; chef *m* —
~ *vt* SUPERVISE : diriger — **bossy** ['bɔsi]
adj **bossier; -est** : autoritaire

botany ['batəni] *n* : botanique *f* — **botanical**
[bə'tænɪkəl] *adj* : botanique

botch ['batʃ] *vt or* **~ up** : bousiller *fam*,
saboter

both ['bo:θ] *adj* : les deux — **~** *conj* : à la
fois — **~** *pron* : tous les deux, l'un et
l'autre

bother ['baðər] *vt* **1** TROUBLE : préoccuper
2 PESTER : harceler — *vi* **~ to** : se donner
la peine de — **~** *n* : ennui *m*

bottle ['batəl] *n* **1** : bouteille *f* **2** *or* **baby ~**
: biberon *m* — **~** *vt* **-tled; -tling** : mettre en
bouteille — **bottleneck** ['batəl,nɛk] *n* : embouteillage *m*

bottom ['batəm] *n* **1** : bas *m* (d'une page,
etc.), fond *m* (d'une bouteille, d'un lac,
etc.), pied *m* (d'un escalier) **2** BUTTOCKS
: derrière *m fam* — **~** *adj* : du bas, inférieur
— **bottomless** ['batəmləs] *adj* : insondable

bough ['baʊ] *n* : rameau *m*

bought → **buy**

boulder ['bo:ldər] *n* : rocher *m*

boulevard ['bʊlə,vard, 'bu:-] *n* : boulevard
m

bounce ['baʊnts] *v* **bounced; bouncing** *vt*
: faire rebondir — *vi* : rebondir — **~** *n*
: bond *m*, rebond *m*

bound¹ ['baʊnd] *adj* **~ for** : à destination de

bound² *adj* **1** OBLIGED : obligé **2 be ~ to**
: être certain de

bound³ *n* **out of ~s** : interdit — **boundary**
['baʊndri, -dəri] *n, pl* **-aries** : limite *f*, frontière *f* — **boundless** ['baʊndləs] *adj* : sans
bornes

bouquet [bo:'keɪ, bu:-] *n* : bouquet *m*

bourbon ['bərbən, 'bʊr-] *n* : bourbon *m*

bourgeois ['bʊrʒ,wa, bʊrʒ'wa] *adj* : bourgeois

bout ['baʊt] *n* **1** : combat *m* (aux sports) **2**
: accès *m* (de fièvre)

bow¹ ['baʊ] *vi* : s'incliner — *vt* **1** : incliner **2**
~ one's head : baisser la tête — **~** ['baʊ]
n : révérence *f*, salut *m*

bow² ['bo:] *n* **1** : arc *m* **2 tie a ~** : faire un
nœud

bow³ ['baʊ] *n* : proue *f* (d'un bateau)

bowels ['baʊəlz] *npl* **1** : intestins *mpl* **2**
DEPTHS : entrailles *fpl*

bowl¹ ['bo:l] *n* : bol *m*, cuvette *f*

bowl² *vi* : jouer au bowling — **bowling**
['bo:lɪŋ] *n* : bowling *m*

box¹ ['baks] *vi* FIGHT : boxer, faire de la boxe
— **boxer** ['baksər] *n* : boxeur *m* — **boxing**
['baksɪŋ] *n* : boxe *f*

box² *n* **1** : boîte *f*, caisse *f*, coffre *m* **2** : loge
f (au théâtre) — **~** *vt* : mettre en boîte —
box office *n* : guichet *m*, billetterie *f*

boy ['bɔɪ] *n* : garçon *m*

boycott ['bɔɪ,kat] *vt* : boycotter — **~** *n*
: boycott *m*, boycottage *m*

boyfriend ['bɔɪ,frɛnd] *n* : petit ami *m*

bra ['bra] → **brassiere**

brace ['breɪs] *n* **1** SUPPORT : support *m* **2**
~s *npl* : appareil *m* orthodontique — **~** *vi*
~ oneself for : se préparer pour

bracelet ['breɪslət] *n* : bracelet *m*

bracket ['brækət] *n* **1** SUPPORT : support *m*
2 : parenthèse *f*, crochet *m* (signe de ponctuation) **3** CATEGORY : catégorie *f* — **~** *vt*
: mettre entre parenthèses, mettre entre cro-
chets

brag ['bræg] *vi* **bragged; bragging** : se vanter

braid ['breɪd] *vt* : tresser — **~** *n* : tresse *f* (de
cheveux)

braille ['breɪl] *n* : braille *m*

brain ['breɪn] *n* **1** : cerveau *m* **2** *or* **~s** *npl*
: intelligence *f* — **brainstorm** ['breɪn-
,stɔrm] *n* : idée *f* géniale — **brainwash**
['breɪn,waʃ, -,wɑʃ] *vt* : faire un lavage de

cerveau à — **brainy** ['breɪni] *adj* **brainier; -est** : intelligent, calé *fam*

brake ['breɪk] *n* : frein *m* — ~ *vi* **braked; braking** : freiner

bramble ['bræmbəl] *n* : ronce *f*

bran ['bræn] *n* : son *m*

branch ['bræntʃ] *n* **1** : branche *f* (d'un arbre) **2** DIVISION : succursale *f* — ~ *vi or* ~ **off** : bifurquer

brand ['brænd] *n* **1** : marque *f* (sur un animal) **2** *or* ~ **name** : marque *f* déposée — ~ *vt* **1** : marquer (au fer rouge) **2** LABEL : étiqueter

brandish ['brændɪʃ] *vt* : brandir

brand-new ['brænd'nu:, -'nju:] *adj* : tout neuf

brandy ['brændi] *n, pl* **-dies** : cognac *m*, eau-de-vie *f*

brash ['bræʃ] *adj* : impertinent

brass ['bræs] *n* **1** : cuivre *m* (jaune), laiton *m* **2** : cuivres *mpl* (d'un orchestre)

brassiere [brə'zɪr, brɑ-] *n* : soutien-gorge *m*, brassière *f* *Can*

brat ['bræt] *n* : môme *mf* *France fam;* gosse *mf* *France fam*

bravado [brə'vɑ'do] *n, pl* **-does** *or* **-dos** : bravade *f*

brave ['breɪv] *adj* **braver; bravest** : courageux, brave — ~ *vt* **braved; braving** : braver, défier — **bravery** ['breɪvəri] *n, pl* **-eries** : courage *m*

brawl ['brɔl] *n* : bagarre *f*

brawn ['brɔn] *n* : muscles *mpl* — **brawny** ['brɔni] *adj* **brawnier; -est** : musclé

bray ['breɪ] *vi* : braire

brazen ['breɪzən] *adj* : effronté

Brazilian [brə'zɪljən] *adj* : brésilien

breach ['bri:tʃ] *n* **1** VIOLATION : infraction *f* **2** GAP : brèche *f*

bread ['brɛd] *n* **1** : pain *m* **2** ~ **crumbs** : chapelure *f*

breadth ['brɛtθ] *n* : largeur *f*

break ['breɪk] *v* **broke** ['bro:k]; **broken** ['bro:kən]; **breaking** *vt* **1** : casser, briser **2** VIOLATE : violer (la loi) **3** INTERRUPT : interrompre **4** SURPASS : battre (un record, etc.) **5** ~ **a habit** : se défaire d'une habitude **6** ~ **the news** : annoncer la nouvelle — *vi* **1** : se casser, se briser **2** ~ **away** : s'évader **3** ~ **down** : tomber en panne (se dit d'une voiture) **4** ~ **into** : entrer par effraction **5** ~ **up** SEPARATE : rompre, se quitter — ~ *n* **1** : cassure *f*, rupture *f* **2** GAP : trouée *f*, brèche *f* **3** REST : pause *f*, break *m* *Can* **4 a lucky** ~ : un coup de veine — **breakable** ['breɪkəb'l] *adj* : cassable — **breakdown** ['breɪk,daʊn] *n* **1** : panne *f* (d'une machine), rupture *f* (des négociations) **2** *or* **nervous** ~ : dépression *f* nerveuse

breakfast ['brɛkfəst] *n* : petit déjeuner *m* *France*, déjeuner *Can*

breast ['brɛst] *n* **1** : sein *m* (d'une femme) **2** CHEST : poitrine *f* — **breast-feed** ['brɛst-,fi:d] *vt* **-fed** [-,fɛd], **-feeding** : allaiter

breath ['brɛθ] *n* : souffle *m*, haleine *f*, respiration *f* — **breathe** ['bri:ð] *v* **breathed; breathing** : respirer — **breathless** ['brɛθləs] *adj* : à bout de souffle, hors d'haleine — **breathtaking** ['brɛθ,teɪkɪŋ] *adj* : à couper le souffle

breed ['bri:d] *v* **bred** ['brɛd]; **breeding** *vt* **1** : élever (du bétail) **2** CAUSE : engendrer — *vi* : se reproduire — ~ *n* **1** : race *f* **2** CLASS : espèce *f*, sorte *f*

breeze ['bri:z] *n* : brise *f* — **breezy** ['bri:zi] *adj* **breezier; -est 1** WINDY : venteux **2** NONCHALANT : désinvolte

brevity ['brɛvəti] *n, pl* **-ties** : brièveté *f*

brew ['bru:] *vt* : brasser (de la bière), faire infuser (du thé) — *vi* : fermenter (se dit de la bière), infuser (se dit du thé, etc.) — **brewery** ['bru:əri, 'brʊri] *n, pl* **-eries** : brasserie *f*

bribe ['braɪb] *n* : pot-de-vin *m* — ~ *vt* **bribed; bribing** : soudoyer — **bribery** ['braɪbəri] *n, pl* **-eries** : corruption *f*

brick ['brɪk] *n* : brique *f* — **bricklayer** ['brɪk,leɪər] *n* : maçon *m*

bride ['braɪd] *n* : mariée *f* — **bridal** ['braɪdəl] *adj* : nuptial — **bridegroom** ['braɪd,gru:m] *n* : marié *m* — **bridesmaid** ['braɪdz,meɪd] *n* : demoiselle *f* d'honneur

bridge ['brɪdʒ] *n* **1** : pont *m* **2** : arête *f* (du nez) **3** : bridge *m* (jeu de cartes) — ~ *vt* **bridged; bridging 1** : construire un pont sur **2** ~ **the gap** : combler une lacune

bridle ['braɪdəl] *n* : bride *f* — ~ *vt* **-dled; -dling** : brider

brief ['bri:f] *adj* : bref — ~ *n* **1** : résumé *m* **2** ~**s** *npl* UNDERPANTS : slip *m* — ~ *vt* : donner des instructions à — **briefcase** ['bri:f,keɪs] *n* : serviette *f*, porte-documents *m* — **briefly** ['bri:fli] *adv* : brièvement

brigade [brɪ'geɪd] *n* : brigade *f*

bright ['braɪt] *adj* **1** : brillant, éclatant **2** CHEERFUL : joyeux **3** INTELLIGENT : intelligent — **brighten** ['braɪtən] *vi* **1** : s'éclaircir (se dit du temps) **2** *or* ~ **up** : s'animer — *vt* ENLIVEN : égayer

brilliant ['brɪljənt] *adj* : brillant — **brilliance** ['brɪljənts] *n* **1** BRIGHTNESS : éclat *m* **2** INTELLIGENCE : intelligence *f*

brim ['brɪm] *n* : bord *m* (d'un chapeau, etc.) — ~ *vi* **brimmed; brimming** *or* ~ **over** : être plein jusqu'à déborder

brine ['braɪn] *n* : saumure *f*

bring ['brɪŋ] *vt* **brought** ['brɔt]; **bringing 1** : amener (une personne ou un animal), apporter (une chose) **2** ~ **about** : occasionner **3** ~ **around** PERSUADE : convaincre **4**

~ **back** : rapporter **5** ~ **down** : faire tomber **6** ~ **on** CAUSE : provoquer **7** ~ **out** : sortir **8** ~ **to an end** : mettre fin à **9** ~ **up** REAR. : élever **10** ~ **up** MENTION : mentionner

brink ['brɪŋk] *n* **1** EDGE : bord *m* **2 on the** ~ **of** : au bord de

brisk ['brɪsk] *adj* **1** FAST : rapide **2** LIVELY : vif

bristle ['brɪsəl] *n* **1** : soie *f* (d'un animal) **2** : poil *m* (d'une brosse) — ~ *vi* -**tled; -tling** : se hérisser

British ['brɪṭɪʃ] *adj* : britannique

brittle ['brɪṭəl] *adj* -**tler; -tlest** : fragile

broach ['broːʧ] *vt* : entamer

broad ['broːd] *adj* **1** WIDE : large **2** GENERAL : grand **3 in** ~ **daylight** : en plein jour

broadcast ['broːd,kæst] *v* -**cast; -casting** *vt* : diffuser, téléviser — *vi* : émettre — ~ *n* : émission *f*

broaden ['broːdən] *vt* : élargir — *vi* : s'élargir — **broadly** ['broːdli] *adv* : en général — **broad–minded** ['broːd'maɪndəd] *adj* : large d'esprit, tolérant

broccoli ['brɑkəli] *n* : brocoli *m*

brochure [bro'ʃʊr] *n* : brochure *f*, dépliant *m*

broil ['broɪl] *v* : griller

broke ['broːk] → **break** — ~ *adj* : fauché *fam*, cassé *Can fam* — **broken** ['broːkən] *adj* : cassé, brisé — **brokenhearted** [,broː-kən'hɑrṭəd] *adj* : au cœur brisé

broker ['broːkər] *n* : courtier *m*, -tière *f*

bronchitis [brɑn'kaɪṭəs, brɑŋ-] *n* : bronchite *f*

bronze ['brɑnz] *n* : bronze *m*

brooch ['broːʧ, 'bruːʧ] *n* : broche *f*

brood ['bruːd] *n* : couvée *f* (d'oiseaux) — ~ *vi* **1** INCUBATE : couver **2** ~ **about** : ressasser, ruminer

brook ['brʊk] *n* : ruisseau *m*

broom ['bruːm, 'brʊm] *n* : balai *m* — **broomstick** ['bruːm,stɪk, 'brʊm-] *n* : manche *m* à balai

broth ['brɔθ] *n, pl* **broths** ['brɔθs, 'brɔðz] : bouillon *m*

brothel ['brɑθəl, 'brɔ-] *n* : bordel *m fam*

brother ['brʌðər] *n* : frère *m* — **brotherhood** ['brʌðər,hʊd] *n* : fraternité *f* — **brother–in–law** ['brʌðərɪn,lɔ] *n, pl* **brothers–in–law** : beau-frère *m* — **brotherly** ['brʌðərli] *adj* : fraternel

brought → **bring**

brow ['braʊ] *n* **1** EYEBROW : sourcil *m* **2** FOREHEAD : front *m* **3** : sommet *m* (d'une colline)

brown ['braʊn] *adj* : brun, marron — ~ *n* : brun *m*, marron *m* — ~ *vt* : faire dorer (en cuisine)

browse ['braʊz] *vi* **browsed; browsing** : regarder, jeter un coup d'œil

browser ['braʊzər] *n* : navigateur *m* (en informatique)

bruise ['bruːz] *vt* **bruised; bruising 1** : faire un bleu à, contusionner **2** : taler (un fruit) — ~ *n* : bleu *m*, contusion *f*, prune *f Can*

brunch ['brʌnʧ] *n* : brunch *m*

brunet *or* **brunette** [bru'nɛt] *n* : brun *m*, brune *f*

brunt ['brʌnt] *n* **bear the** ~ **of** : subir le plus gros de

brush ['brʌʃ] *n* **1** : brosse *f* (à cheveux), pinceau *m* (de peintre) **2** UNDERGROWTH : brousses *fpl* — ~ *vt* **1** : brosser **2** GRAZE : effleurer **3** ~ **off** DISREGARD : écarter — *vi* ~ **up on** : réviser — **brush–off** ['brʌʃ,ɔf] *n* **give s.o. the** ~ : envoyer promener qqn

brusque ['brʌsk] *adj* : brusque

brutal ['bruːṭəl] *adj* : brutal — **brutality** [bru'tæləṭi] *n, pl* -**ties** : brutalité *f*

brute ['bruːt] *adj* : brutal — ~ *n* : brute *f*

bubble ['bʌbəl] *n* : bulle *f* — ~ *vi* -**bled; -bling** : bouillonner

buck ['bʌk] *n, pl* **bucks 1** *or pl* **buck** : mâle *m* (animal) **2** DOLLAR : dollar *m* — ~ *vi* **1** : ruer (se dit d'un cheval) **2** ~ **up** : ne pas se laisser abattre — *vt* OPPOSE : résister

bucket ['bʌkət] *n* : seau *m*

buckle ['bʌkəl] *n* : boucle *f* — ~ *v* -**led; -ling** *vt* **1** FASTEN : boucler **2** WARP : gauchir — *vi* BEND : se courber, se voiler

bud ['bʌd] *n* : bourgeon *m* (d'une feuille), bouton *m* (d'une fleur) — ~ *vi* **budded; budding** : bourgeonner

Buddhism ['buː,dɪzəm, 'bʊ-] *n* : bouddhisme *m* — **Buddhist** ['buː,dɪst, 'bʊ-] *adj* : bouddhiste — ~ *n* : bouddhiste *mf*

buddy ['bʌdi] *n, pl* -**dies** : copain *m*, -pine *f*

budge ['bʌʤ] *vi* **budged; budging 1** MOVE : bouger **2** YIELD : céder

budget ['bʌʤət] *n* : budget *m* — ~ *vt* : budgétiser — *vi* : dresser un budget — **budgetary** ['bʌʤə,tɛri] *adj* : budgétaire

buff ['bʌf] *n* **1** : chamois *m* (couleur) **2** ENTHUSIAST : mordu *m*, -due *f fam;* fanatique *mf* — ~ *adj* : chamois, beige — ~ *vt* POLISH : polir

buffalo ['bʌfə,loː] *n, pl* -**lo** *or* -**loes** : buffle *m*, bison *m* (d'Amérique)

buffer ['bʌfər] *n* : tampon *m*

buffet [,bʌ'feɪ, ,buː-] *n* : buffet *m* (repas ou meuble)

buffoon [,bʌ'fuːn] *n* : bouffon *m*

bug ['bʌg] *n* **1** INSECT : insecte *m*, bestiole *f* **2** FLAW : défaut *m* **3** GERM : microbe *m* **4** : bogue *m* (en informatique) — ~ *vt* **bugged; bugging 1** : installer un microphone dans (une maison, etc.) **2** PESTER : embêter

buggy ['bʌgi] *n, pl* -**gies 1** CARRIAGE

: calèche f **2** or **baby ~** : voiture f d'enfant, landau m *France*

bugle ['bju:ˌgəl] n **1** : clairon m

build ['bɪld] v **built** ['bɪlt] **building** vt **1**
: construire, bâtir **2** DEVELOP : établir — vi
1 or **~ up** INTENSIFY : augmenter, intensifier **2** or **~ up** ACCUMULATE : s'accumuler
— **~** n PHYSIQUE : carrure f, charpente f —
builder ['bɪldər] n : entrepreneur m —
building ['bɪldɪŋ] n **1** : bâtiment m, immeuble m **2** CONSTRUCTION : construction f —
built–in ['bɪlt'ɪn] adj : encastré

bulb ['bʌlb] n **1** : bulbe m **2** LIGHTBULB
: ampoule f

bulge ['bʌldʒ] vi **bulged; bulging** : être gonflé, se renfler — **~** n : renflement m

bulk ['bʌlk] n **1** : masse f, volume m **2 in ~**
: en gros — **bulky** ['bʌlki] adj **bulkier; -est**
: volumineux

bull ['bʊl] n **1** : taureau m **2** MALE : mâle m

bulldog ['bʊlˌdɔg] n : bouledogue m

bulldozer ['bʊlˌdo:zər] n : bulldozer m

bullet ['bʊlət] n : balle f (d'un fusil)

bulletin ['bʊlətən, -lətɩn] n : bulletin m —
bulletin board n : tableau m d'affichage,
babillard m *Can*

bulletproof ['bʊlətˌpru:f] adj : pare-balles

bullfight ['bʊlˌfaɪt] n : corrida f — **bullfighter** ['bʊlˌfaɪtər] n : torero m

bull's–eye ['bʊlzˌaɪ] n, pl **bull's–eyes** : centre m (de la cible)

bully ['bʊli] n, pl **-lies** : tyran m — **~** vt
-lied; -lying : malmener, maltraiter

bum ['bʌm] n : clochard m, -charde f

bumblebee ['bʌmbəlˌbi:] n : bourdon m

bump ['bʌmp] n **1** BULGE : bosse f, protubérance f **2** IMPACT : coup m, choc m **3**
JOLT : secousse f — **~** vt : heurter, cogner —
vi **~ into** MEET : tomber sur — **bumper**
['bʌmpər] n : pare-chocs m — **~** adj : exceptionnel — **bumpy** ['bʌmpi] adj
bumpier; -est 1 : cahoteux (se dit d'un
chemin) **2 a ~ flight** : un vol agité

bun ['bʌn] n : petit pain m (au lait)

bunch ['bʌntʃ] n **1** : bouquet m (de fleurs),
grappe f (de raisins), botte f (de légumes,
etc.) **2** GROUP : groupe m — **~** vt **~ together** : mettre ensemble — vi **~ up**
: s'entasser

bundle ['bʌndəl] n **1** : liasse f (de papiers,
etc.) **2** PARCEL : paquet m — **~** vi **-dled;
-dling ~ up** : s'emmitoufler

bungalow ['bʌŋgəˌlo:] n : maison f sans
étage

bungle ['bʌŋgəl] vt **-gled; -gling** : gâcher

bunion ['bʌnjən] n : oignon m

bunk ['bʌŋk] n **1** : couchette f **2 ~ bed**
: lits mpl superposés

bunny ['bʌni] n, pl **-nies** : lapin m

buoy ['bu:i, 'bɔɪ] n : bouée f — **~** vt or **~**

up : revigorer — **buoyant** ['bɔɪənt,
'bu:jənt] adj **1** : qui flotte **2** LIGHTHEARTED
: allègre, optimiste

burden ['bərdən] n : fardeau m — **~** vt **~
sth with** : accabler qqn de — **burdensome**
['bərdənsəm] adj : lourd

bureau ['bjʊro] n **1** : commode f (meuble) **2**
: service m (gouvernemental) **3** AGENCY
: agence f — **bureaucracy** [bjʊ'rakrəsi] n,
pl **-cies** : bureaucratie f — **bureaucrat**
['bjʊrəˌkræt] n : bureaucrate mf — **bureaucratic** [ˌbjʊrəˈkrætɩk] adj : bureaucratique

burglar ['bərglər] n : cambrioleur m, -leuse f
— **burglarize** ['bərgləˌraɪz] vt **-ized; -izing**
: cambrioler — **burglary** ['bərgləri] n, pl
-glaries : cambriolage m

Burgundy ['bərgəndi] n, pl **-dies** : bourgogne m (vin)

burial ['bɛriəl] n : enterrement m

burly ['bərli] adj **-lier; -est** : costaud fam

burn ['bərn] v **burned** ['bərnd, 'bərnt] or
burnt ['bərnt]; **burning** : brûler — **~** n
: brûlure f — **burner** ['bərnər] n : brûleur m
(d'une cuisinière), rond m *Can*

burnish ['bərnɩʃ] vt : polir

burp ['bərp] vi : avoir des renvois, roter fam
— **~** n : renvoi m

burrow ['bəro] n : terrier m — **~** vt : creuser
— vi **~ into** : fouiller dans

burst ['bərst] v **burst** or **bursted; bursting**
vi **1** : crever, éclater **2 ~ into tears** : fondre en larmes **3 ~ out laughing** : éclater
de rire — **~** vt : crever, faire éclater —
n **1** EXPLOSION : explosion f **2** OUTBURST
: élan m (d'enthousiasme), éclat m (de rire)

bury ['bɛri] vt **buried; burying 1** : enterrer
2 HIDE : enfouir, cacher

bus ['bʌs] n, pl **buses** or **busses** : bus m, autobus m — **~** v **bused** or **bussed** ['bʌst];
busing or **bussing** ['bʌsɩŋ] vt : transporter
en autobus — vi : voyager en autobus

bush ['bʊʃ] n SHRUB : buisson m

bushel ['bʊʃəl] n : boisseau m

bushy ['bʊʃi] adj **bushier; -est** : touffu

busily ['bɩzəli] adv : activement

business ['bɩznəs, -nəz] n **1** COMMERCE
: affaires fpl **2** COMPANY : ent-reprise f **3**
it's none of your ~ : ce n'est pas de vos
affaires — **businessman** ['bɩznəsˌmæn,
-nəz-] n, pl **-men** : homme m d'affaires —
businesswoman ['bɩznəsˌwʊmən, -nəz-]
n, pl **-women** : femme f d'affaires

bust¹ ['bʌst] vt BREAK : briser

bust² n **1** : buste m (en sculpture) **2**
BREASTS : seins fpl, poitrine f

bustle ['bʌsəl] vi **-tled; -tling** or **~ about**
: s'affairer — **~** n or **hustle and ~** : agitation f, activité f

busy ['bɩzi] adj **busier; -est 1** : occupé **2**
BUSTLING : animé

but ['bʌt] *conj* : mais — ~ *prep* : sauf, excepté

butcher ['butʃər] *n* : boucher *m*, -chère *f* — ~ *vt* **1** : abattre **2** BOTCH : bousiller *fam*

butler ['bʌtlər] *n* : maître *m* d'hôtel

butt ['bʌt] *vi* ~ **in** : interrompre — ~ *n* **1** : crosse *f* (d'un fusil) **2** : mégot *m fam* (de cigarette)

butter ['bʌtər] *n* : beurre *m* — ~ *vt* : beurrer

butterfly ['bʌtər,flaɪ] *n, pl* **-flies** : papillon *m*

buttermilk ['bʌtər,mɪlk] *n* : babeurre *m*

buttocks ['bʌtəks, -,tɑks] *npl* : fesses *fpl*

button ['bʌtən] *n* : bouton *m* — ~ *vt* : boutonner — *vi or* ~ **up** : se boutonner — **buttonhole** ['bʌtən,ho:l] *n* : boutonnière *f*

buttress ['bʌtrəs] *n* : contrefort *m*

buy ['baɪ] *vt* **bought** ['bɔt]; **buying** : acheter — ~ *n* : achat *m* — **buyer** ['baɪər] *n* : acheteur *m*, -teuse *f*

buzz ['bʌz] *vi* : bourdonner — ~ *n* : bourdonnement *m*

buzzer ['bʌzər] *n* : sonnette *f*

by ['baɪ] *prep* **1** NEAR : près de, à côté de **2** VIA : par, en **3** PAST : devant, à côté de **4** DURING : pendant **5** (*in expressions of time*) : avant **6** (*indicating cause or agent*) : par — ~ *adv* **1** ~ **and** ~ : bientôt **2** ~ **and large** : en général **3** **go** ~ : passer **4** **stop** ~ : arrêter

bygone ['baɪ,gɔn] *adj* **1** : passé, d'autrefois **2** **let** ~**s be** ~**s** : enterrer le passé

bypass ['baɪ,pæs] *n* : route *f* de contournement — ~ *vt* : contourner

by–product ['baɪ,prɑdəkt] *n* : sous-produit *m*, dérivé *m*

bystander ['baɪ,stændər] *n* : spectateur *m*, -trice *f*

byte ['baɪt] *n* : octet *m*

C

c ['si:] *n, pl* **c's** *or* **cs** : c *m*, troisième lettre de l'alphabet

cab ['kæb] *n* **1** : taxi *m* **2** : cabine *f* (d'un camion, etc.)

cabbage ['kæbɪʤ] *n* : chou *m*

cabin ['kæbən] *n* **1** : cabane *f* **2** : cabine *f* (d'un navire, d'un avion, etc.)

cabinet ['kæbnət] *n* **1** CUPBOARD : armoire *f* **2** : cabinet *m* (en politique) **3** *or* **medicine** ~ : pharmacie *f*

cable ['keɪbəl] *n* : câble *m* — **cable television** *n* : câble *m*

cackle ['kækəl] *vi* **-led; -ling** : caqueter, glousser

cactus ['kæktəs] *n, pl* **cacti** [-,taɪ] *or* **-tuses** : cactus *m*

cadence ['keɪdənts] *n* : cadence *f*, rythme *m*

cadet [kə'dɛt] *n* : élève *mf* officier

café [kæ'feɪ, kə-] *n* : café *m*, bistrot *m* — **cafeteria** [,kæfə'tɪriə] *n* : cafétéria *f*

caffeine [kæ'fi:n] *n* : caféine *f*

cage ['keɪʤ] *n* : cage *f*

cajole [kə'ʤo:l] *vt* **-joled; -joling** : cajoler, enjôler

Cajun ['keɪʤən] *adj* : acadien, cajun

cake ['keɪk] *n* **1** : gâteau *m* **2** BAR : pain *m* (de savon) — **caked** ['keɪkt] *adj* ~ **with** : couvert de

calamity [kə'læməti] *n, pl* **-ties** : calamité *f*

calcium ['kælsiəm] *n* : calcium *m*

calculate ['kælkjə,leɪt] *v* **-lated; -lating** : calculer — **calculating** ['kælkjə,leɪtɪŋ] *adj* : calculateur — **calculation** [,kælkjə'leɪʃən] *n* : calcul *m* — **calculator** ['kælkjə,leɪtər] *n* : calculatrice *f*

calendar ['kæləndər] *n* : calendrier *m*

calf¹ ['kæf] *n, pl* **calves** ['kævz] : veau *m* (de bovin)

calf² *n, pl* **calves** : mollet *m* (de la jambe)

caliber *or* **calibre** ['kæləbər] *n* : calibre *m*

call ['kɔl] *vi* **1** : appeler **2** VISIT : passer, faire une visite **3** ~ **for** : demander — *vt* **1** : appeler **2** ~ **back** : rappeler **3** ~ **off** : annuler — ~ *n* **1** : appel *m* **2** SHOUT : cri *m* **3** VISIT : visite *f* **4** NEED : demande *f* — **calling** ['kɔlɪŋ] *n* : vocation *f*

callous ['kæləs] *adj* : dur, sans cœur

calm ['kɑm, 'kɑlm] *n* : calme *m*, tranquillité *f* — ~ *vt* : calmer, apaiser — *vi or* ~ **down** : se calmer — ~ *adj* : calme, tranquille

calorie ['kæləri] *n* : calorie *f*

came → **come**

camel ['kæməl] *n* : chameau *m*

camera ['kæmrə, 'kæmərə] *n* : appareil *m* photo, caméra *f*

camouflage ['kæmə,flɑʒ, -,flɑʤ] *n* : camouflage *m* — ~ *vt* **-flaged; -flaging** : camoufler

camp ['kæmp] *n* **1** : camp *m* **2** FACTION : parti *m* — ~ *vi* : camper, faire du camping

campaign [kæm'peɪn] *n* : campagne *f* — ~ *vi* : faire campagne

camping [ˈkæmpɪŋ] *n* : camping *m*
campus [ˈkæmpəs] *n* : campus *m*, cité *f* universitaire *Can*
can[1] [ˈkæn] *v aux, past* **could** [ˈkʊd]; *present s u pl* **can** 1 *(expressing possibility or permission)* : pouvoir 2 *(expressing knowledge or ability)* : savoir 3 **that cannot be** : cela n'est pas possible
can[2] *n* : boîte *f* (d'aliments), canette *f* (de boisson gazeuse), bidon *m* (d'essence, etc.) — ~ *vt* **canned; canning** : mettre en boîte
Canadian [kəˈneɪdiən] *adj* : canadien
canal [kəˈnæl] *n* : canal *m*
canary [kəˈnɛri] *n, pl* **-naries** : canari *m*, serin *m*
cancel [ˈkænt̬səl] *vt* **-celed** *or* **-celled; -celing** *or* **-celling** : annuler — **cancellation** [ˌkænt̬səˈleɪʃən] *n* : annulation *f*
cancer [ˈkænt̬sər] *n* : cancer *m* — **cancerous** [ˈkænt̬sərəs] *adj* : cancéreux
candid [ˈkændɪd] *adj* : franc, sincère
candidate [ˈkændəˌdeɪt, -dət] *n* : candidat *m*, -date *f* — **candidacy** [ˈkændədəsi] *n, pl* **-cies** : candidature *f*
candle [ˈkændəl] *n* : bougie *f*, chandelle *f* — **candlestick** [ˈkændəlˌstɪk] *n* : chandelier *m*, bougeoir *m*
candor *or Brit* **candour** [ˈkændər] *n* : franchise *f*
candy [ˈkændi] *n, pl* **-dies** 1 : bonbon *m* 2 ~ **store** : confiserie *f*
cane [ˈkeɪn] *n* : canne *f* — ~ *vt* **caned; caning** FLOG : fouetter
canine [ˈkeɪˌnaɪn] *n or* ~ **tooth** : canine *f* — ~ *adj* : canin
canister [ˈkænəstər] *n* : boîte *f*
cannibal [ˈkænəbəl] *n* : cannibale *mf*
cannon [ˈkænən] *n, pl* **-nons** *or* **-non** : canon *m*
cannot (**can not**) [ˈkænˌɑt, kəˈnɑt] → **can**[1]
canoe [kəˈnuː] *n* : canoë *m*, canot *m Can*
canon [ˈkænən] *n* : canon *m*, règle *f*
can opener *n* : ouvre-boîtes *m*
canopy [ˈkænəpi] *n, pl* **-pies** : auvent *m*, baldaquin *m*
can't [ˈkænt, ˈkɑnt] *(contraction of* **can not**) → **can**[1]
cantaloupe [ˈkæntəlˌoːp] *n* : cantaloup *m*
cantankerous [kænˈtæŋkərəs] *adj* : acariâtre
canteen [kænˈtiːn] *n* CAFETERIA : cantine *f*
canter [ˈkæntər] *vi* : aller au petit galop — ~ *n* : petit galop *m*
canvas [ˈkænvəs] *n* : toile *f*
canvass [ˈkænvəs] *vt* : solliciter les voix de (les électeurs) — ~ *n* : démarchage *m* électoral
canyon [ˈkænjən] *n* : canyon *m*
cap [ˈkæp] *n* 1 : casquette *f* 2 : capsule *f* (d'une bouteille), capuchon *m* (d'un stylo,

etc.) — ~ *vt* **capped; capping** COVER : couvrir
capable [ˈkeɪpəbəl] *adj* : capable — **capability** [ˌkeɪpəˈbɪləti] *n, pl* **-ties** : aptitude *f*, capacité *f*
capacity [kəˈpæsəti] *n, pl* **-ties** 1 : capacité *f* 2 ROLE : qualité *f*
cape[1] [ˈkeɪp] *n* : cap *m* (en géographie)
cape[2] *n* CLOAK : cape *f*, pèlerine *f*
caper [ˈkeɪpər] *n* : câpre *f*
capital [ˈkæpətəl] *adj* 1 : capital, principal 2 : majuscule (se dit d'une lettre) — ~ *n* 1 *or* ~ **city** : capitale *f* 2 WEALTH : capital *m*, fonds *mpl* 3 *or* ~ **letter** : majuscule *f* — **capitalism** [ˈkæpətəlˌɪzəm] *n* : capitalisme *m* — **capitalist** [ˈkæpətəlɪst] *or* **capitalistic** [ˈkæpətəlˈɪstɪk] *adj* : capitaliste — **capitalize** [ˈkæpətəlˌaɪz] *v* **-ized; -izing** *vt* : écrire avec une majuscule — *vi* ~ **on** : tirer profit de
capitol [ˈkæpətᵊl] *n* : capitole *m*
capsize [ˈkæpˌsaɪz, kæpˈsaɪz] *v* **-sized; -sizing** *vt* : faire chavirer — *vi* : chavirer
capsule [ˈkæpsəl, -ˌsuːl] *n* : capsule *f*
captain [ˈkæptən] *n* : capitaine *m*
caption [ˈkæpʃən] *n* 1 : légende *f* (d'une illustration) 2 SUBTITLE : sous-titre *m*
captivate [ˈkæptəˌveɪt] *vt* **-vated; -vating** : captiver, fasciner
captive [ˈkæptɪv] *adj* : captif — ~ *n* : captif *m*, -tive *f* — **captivity** [kæpˈtɪvəti] *n* : captivité *f*
capture [ˈkæpʃər] *n* : capture *f*, prise *f* — ~ *vt* **-tured; -turing** 1 SEIZE : capturer 2 : captiver (l'imagination), capter (l'attention)
car [ˈkɑr] *n* 1 : voiture *f*, automobile *f* 2 *or* **railroad** ~ : wagon *m*
carafe [kəˈræf, -ˈrɑf] *n* : carafe *f*
caramel [ˈkɑrməl; ˈkærəməl, -ˌmɛl] *n* : caramel *m*
carat [ˈkærət] *n* : carat *m*
caravan [ˈkærəˌvæn] *n* : caravane *f*
carbohydrate [ˌkɑrboˈhaɪˌdreɪt, -drət] *n* : hydrate *m* de carbone
carbon [ˈkɑrbən] *n* : carbone *m*
carburetor [ˈkɑrbəˌreɪtər, -bjə-] *n* : carburateur *m*
carcass [ˈkɑrkəs] *n* : carcasse *f*
card [ˈkɑrd] *n* : carte *f* — **cardboard** [ˈkɑrdˌbord] *n* : carton *m*
cardiac [ˈkɑrdiˌæk] *adj* : cardiaque
cardigan [ˈkɑrdɪgən] *n* : cardigan *m*
cardinal [ˈkɑrdᵊnəl] *n* : cardinal *m* — ~ *adj* : cardinal, essentiel
care [ˈkær] *n* 1 : soin *m* 2 WORRY : préoccupation *f* — ~ *vi* **cared; caring** 1 : se préoccuper, se soucier 2 ~ **for** TEND : prendre soin de 3 ~ **for** LIKE : aimer 4 **I don't** ~ : ça m'est égal

career [kə'rɪr] *n* : carrière *f*, profession *f*

carefree ['kær,fri:, ,kær'-] *adj* : insouciant

careful ['kærfəl] *adj* **1** : prudent **2** be ~! : fais attention! — **carefully** ['kærfəli] *adv* : prudemment, avec soin — **careless** ['kærləs] *adj* : négligent — **carelessness** ['kærləsnəs] *n* : négligence *f*

caress [kə'rɛs] *n* : caresse *f* — ~ *vt* : caresser

cargo ['kɑr,go:] *n, pl* **-goes** *or* **-gos** : chargement *m*, cargaison *f*

Caribbean [,kærə'bi:ən, kə'rɪbiən] *adj* : des Caraïbes

caricature ['kærɪkə,tʃur] *n* : caricature *f*

caring ['kærɪŋ] *adj* : aimant, affectueux

carnage ['kɑrnɪdʒ] *n* : carnage *m*

carnation [kɑr'neɪʃən] *n* : œillet *m*

carnival ['kɑrnəvəl] *n* : carnaval *m*

carol ['kærəl] *n* : chant *m* de Noël

carpenter ['kɑrpəntər] *n* : charpentier *m*, menuisier *m* — **carpentry** ['kɑrpəntri] *n* : charpenterie *f*, menuiserie *f*

carpet ['kɑrpət] *n* : tapis *m*

carriage ['kærɪdʒ] *n* **1** : transport *m* (de marchandises) **2** BEARING : maintien *m* **3** → **baby carriage 4** *or* **horse-drawn** ~ : calèche *f*, carrosse *m*

carrier ['kæriər] *n* **1** : transporteur *m* **2** : porteur *m*, -teuse *f* (d'une maladie)

carrot ['kærət] *n* : carotte *f*

carry ['kæri] *v* **-ried; -rying** *vt* **1** : porter **2** TRANSPORT : transporter **3** STOCK : vendre **4** ENTAIL : comporter **5** ~ **oneself** : se présenter — *vi* : porter (se dit de la voix) — **carry away** *vt* **get carried away** : s'emballer — **carry on** *vt* CONDUCT : réaliser — *vi* **1** : mal se comporter **2** CONTINUE : continuer — **carry out** *vt* **1** : réaliser, effectuer **2** FULFILL : accomplir

cart ['kɑrt] *n* : charrette *f* — ~ *vt or* ~ **around** : trimbaler *fam*

carton ['kɑrtən] *n* : boîte *f* de carton

cartoon [kɑr'tu:n] *n* **1** : dessin *m* humoristique **2** COMIC STRIP : bande *f* dessinée **3** *or* **animated** ~ : dessin *m* animé

cartridge ['kɑrtrɪdʒ] *n* : cartouche *f*

carve ['kɑrv] *vt* **carved; carving 1** : tailler (le bois, etc.) **2** : découper (de la viande)

case ['keɪs] *n* **1** : boîte *f*, caisse *f* **2** **in any** ~ : en tout cas **3** **in** ~ **of** : au cas de **4** **just in** ~ : au cas où

cash ['kæʃ] *n* : espèces *fpl*, argent *m* liquide — ~ *vt* : encaisser

cashew ['kæ,ʃu:, kə'ʃu:] *n* : noix *f* de cajou

cashier [kæ'ʃɪr] *n* : caissier *m*, -sière *f*

cashmere ['kæʒ,mɪr, 'kæʃ-] *n* : cachemire *m*

cash register *n* : caisse *f* enregistreuse

casino [kə'si:,no:] *n, pl* **-nos** : casino *m*

cask ['kæsk] *n* : fût *m*, tonneau *f*

casket ['kæskət] *n* : cercueil *m*

casserole ['kæsə,ro:l] *n* : ragoût *m*

cassette [kə'sɛt, kæ-] *n* : cassette *f*

cast ['kæst] *vt* **cast; casting 1** THROW : jeter, lancer **2** : donner un rôle à (au cinéma, etc.) **3** MOLD : couler (du métal) **4** ~ **one's vote** : voter — ~ *n* **1** : distribution *f* (d'acteurs) **2** *or* **plaster** ~ : plâtre *m*

cast iron *n* : fonte *f*

castle ['kæsəl] *n* : château *m*

castrate ['kæs,treɪt] *vt* **-trated; -trating** : châtrer

casual ['kæʒuəl] *adj* **1** : nonchalant **2** INFORMAL : décontracté — **casually** ['kæʒuəli, 'kæʒəli] *adv* **1** : nonchalamment **2** ~ **dressed** : habillé simplement

casualty ['kæʒuəlti, 'kæʒəl-] *n, pl* **-ties 1** : accident *m* grave, désastre *m* **2** VICTIM : blessé *m*, -sée *f*; accidenté *m*, -tée *f*; mort *m*, morte *f*

cat ['kæt] *n* : chat *m*, chatte *f*

catalog *or* catalogue ['kætə,lɔg] *n* : catalogue *m*

cataract ['kætə,rækt] *n* : cataracte *f*

catastrophe [kə'tæstrə,fi:] *n* : catastrophe *f*

catch ['kætʃ, 'kɛtʃ] *v* **caught** ['kɔt]; **catching** *vt* **1** CAPTURE, TRAP : attraper **2** SURPRISE : surprendre **3** GRASP : saisir **4** SNAG : accrocher **5** : prendre (le train, etc.) **6** ~ **one's breath** : reprendre son souffle — *vi* **1** SNAG : s'accrocher **2** ~ **fire** : prendre feu — ~ *n* **1** : prise *f*, capture *f* **2** PITFALL : piège *f* — **catching** ['kætʃɪŋ, 'kɛ-] *adj* : contagieux — **catchy** ['kætʃi, 'kɛ-] *adj* **catchier; -est** : entraînant

category ['kætə,gori] *n, pl* **-ries** : catégorie *f*, classe *f* — **categorical** [,kætə'gorɪkəl] *adj* : catégorique

cater ['keɪtər] *vi* **1** : fournir des repas **2** ~ **to** : pourvoir à — **caterer** ['keɪtərər] *n* : traiteur *m*

caterpillar ['kætər,pɪlər] *n* : chenille *f*

cathedral [kə'θi:drəl] *n* : cathédrale *f*

catholic ['kæθəlɪk] *adj* **1** : universel **2 Catholic** : catholique — **catholicism** [kə'θɑlə,sɪzəm] *n* : catholicisme *m*

cattle ['kætəl] *npl* : bétail *m*, bovins *mpl*

caught → **catch**

cauldron ['kɔldrən] *n* : chaudron *m*

cauliflower ['kɑlɪ,flaʊər, 'kɔ-] *n* : chou-fleur *m*

cause ['kɔz] *n* **1** : cause *f* **2** REASON : raison *f*, motif *m* — ~ *vt* **caused; causing** : causer, occasionner

caution ['kɔʃən] *n* **1** WARNING : avertissement *m* **2** CARE : prudence *f* — ~ *vt* : avertir, mettre en garde — **cautious** ['kɔʃəs] *adj* : prudent, avisé — **cautiously** ['kɔʃəsli] *adv* : prudemment

cavalier [,kævə'lɪr] *adj* : cavalier, désinvolte

cavalry ['kævəlri] *n, pl* **-ries** : cavalerie *f*
cave ['keɪv] *n* : grotte *f*, caverne *f* — *vi*
caved; caving *or* ∼ **in** : s'affaisser, s'effondrer
cavern ['kævərn] *n* : caverne *f*
caviar *or* **caviare** ['kævi,ɑr, 'kɑ-] *n* : caviar *m*
cavity ['kævəti] *n, pl* **-ties** 1 : cavité *f* 2 : carie *f* (dentaire)
CD [,si:'di:] *n* : CD *m*, disque *m* compact
cease ['si:s] *v* **ceased; ceasing** : cesser — **cease-fire** ['si:s'faɪr] *n* : cessez-le-feu *m* — **ceaseless** ['si:sləs] *adj* : incessant, continuel
cedar ['si:dər] *n* : cèdre *m*
cedilla [sɪ'dɪlə] *n* : cédille *nf*
ceiling ['si:lɪŋ] *n* : plafond *m*
celebrate ['sɛlə,breɪt] *v* **-brated; -brating** *vt* : fêter, célébrer — *vi* : faire le fête — **celebrated** ['sɛlə,breɪtəd] *adj* : célèbre — **celebration** [,sɛlə'breɪʃən] *n* 1 : célébration *f* 2 FESTIVITY : fête *f* — **celebrity** [sə'lɛbrəti] *n, pl* **-ties** : célébrité *f*
celery ['sɛləri] *n, pl* **-eries** : céleri *m*
cell ['sɛl] *n* : cellule *f*
cellar ['sɛlər] *n* : cave *f*
cello ['tʃɛ,lo:] *n, pl* **-los** : violoncelle *m*
cellular ['sɛljələr] *adj* : cellulaire
cement [sɪ'mɛnt] *n* : ciment *m*
cemetery ['sɛmə,tɛri] *n, pl* **-teries** : cimetière *m*
censor ['sɛntsər] *vt* : censurer — **censorship** ['sɛntsər,ʃɪp] *n* : censure *f* — **censure** ['sɛntʃər] *n* : censure *f*, blâme *m* — ∼ *vt* **-sured; -suring** : critiquer, blâmer
census ['sɛntsəs] *n* : recensement *m*
cent ['sɛnt] *n* : cent *m*
centennial [sɛn'tɛniəl] *n* : centenaire *m*
center *or Brit* **centre** ['sɛntər] *n* : centre *m* — ∼ *v* **centered** *or Brit* **centred; centering** *or Brit* **centring** *vt* : centrer — *vi* ∼ **on** : se concentrer sur
centigrade ['sɛntə,greɪd, 'sɑn-] *adj* : centigrade
centimeter ['sɛntə,mi:tər, 'sɑn-] *n* : centimètre *m*
centipede ['sɛntə,pi:d] *n* : mille-pattes *m*
central ['sɛntrəl] *adj* : central — **centralize** ['sɛntrə,laɪz] *vt* **-ized; -izing** : centraliser
centre → **center**
century ['sɛntʃəri] *n, pl* **-ries** : siècle *m*
ceramics [sə'ræmɪks] *n* : céramique *f*
cereal ['sɪriəl] *n* : céréale *f*
ceremony ['sɛrə,mo:ni] *n, pl* **-nies** : cérémonie *f*
certain ['sərtən] *adj* 1 : certain 2 **be** ∼ **of** : être assuré de 3 **for** ∼ : au juste — **certainly** ['sərtənli] *adv* : certainement, bien sûr — **certainty** ['sərtənti] *n, pl* **-ties** : certitude *f*

certify ['sərtə,faɪ] *vt* **-fied; -fying** : certifier — **certificate** [sər'tɪfɪkət] *n* : certificat *m*
chafe ['tʃeɪf] *vi* **chafed; chafing** 1 RUB : frotter 2 ∼ **at** : s'irriter de
chain ['tʃeɪn] *n* 1 : chaîne *f* 2 ∼ **of events** : série *f* d'événements — ∼ *vt* : enchaîner
chair ['tʃɛr] *n* 1 : chaise *f* 2 : chaire *f* (d'une université) — ∼ *vt* : présider — **chairman** ['tʃɛrmən] *n, pl* **-men** [-mən, -,mɛn] : président *m* — **chairperson** ['tʃɛr,pərsən] *n* : presidente *m*, -dente *f*
chalk ['tʃɔk] *n* : craie *f*
challenge ['tʃælɪndʒ] *vt* **-lenged; -lenging** 1 DISPUTE : contester 2 DARE : défier — ∼ *n* : défi *m* — **challenging** ['tʃælɪndʒɪŋ] *adj* : stimulant
chamber ['tʃeɪmbər] *n* : chambre *f* (de commerce, etc.)
champagne [ʃæm'peɪn] *n* : champagne *m*
champion ['tʃæmpiən] *n* : champion *m*, -pionne *f* — **championship** ['tʃæmpiən,ʃɪp] *n* : championnat *m*
chance ['tʃænts] *n* 1 LUCK : hasard *m* 2 OPPORTUNITY : occasion *f* 3 LIKELIHOOD : chances *fpl* 4 **by** ∼ : par hasard 5 **take a** ∼ : prendre un risque — ∼ *vt* **chanced; chancing** : hasarder, risquer — ∼ *adj* : fortuit
chandelier [,ʃændə'lɪr] *n* : lustre *m*
change ['tʃeɪndʒ] *v* **changed; changing** *vt* 1 : changer 2 SWITCH : changer de — *vi* 1 : changer 2 *or* ∼ **clothes** : se changer — ∼ *n* 1 : changement *m* 2 COINS : monnaie *f* — **changeable** ['tʃeɪndʒəbəl] *adj* : changeant
channel ['tʃænəl] *n* 1 : canal *m* 2 : chenal *m* (dans un fleuve, etc.) 3 : chaîne *f* (de télévision)
chant ['tʃænt] *n* : chant *m*
chaos ['keɪ,ɑs] *n* : chaos *m* — **chaotic** [keɪ'ɑtɪk] *adj* : chaotique
chap[1] ['tʃæp] *vi* **chapped; chapping** : se gercer
chap[2] *n* : type *m fam*, bonhomme *m fam*
chapel ['tʃæpəl] *n* : chapelle *f*
chaperon *or* **chaperone** ['ʃæpə,ro:n] *n* : chaperon *m*
chaplain ['tʃæplɪn] *n* : aumônier *m*
chapter ['tʃæptər] *n* : chapitre *m*
char ['tʃɑr] *vt* **charred; charring** : carboniser
character ['kærɪktər] *n* 1 : caractère *m* 2 : personnage *m* (d'un roman, etc.) — **characteristic** [,kærɪktə'rɪstɪk] *adj* : caractéristique — ∼ *n* : caractéristique *f* — **characterize** ['kærɪktə,raɪz] *vt* **-ized; -izing** : caractériser
charcoal ['tʃɑr,ko:l] *n* : charbon *m* de bois
charge ['tʃɑrdʒ] *n* 1 : charge *f* (électrique) 2 COST : prix *m*, frais *mpl* 3 ACCUSATION : inculpation *f* 4 **be in** ∼ : être responsable —

~ *v* charged; charging *vt* **1** : charger (une batterie) **2** ENTRUST : charger, confier **3** ACCUSE : inculper **4** : payer par carte de crédit — *vi* **1** : se précipiter, foncer **2 ~ too much** : demander trop (d'argent)

charisma [kə'rızmə] *n* : charisme *m* — **charismatic** [ˌkærəz'mætık] *adj* : charismatique

charity ['tʃærəti] *n, pl* **-ties 1** : organisation *f* caritative **2** GOODWILL : charité *f*

charlatan ['ʃɑrlətən] *n* : charlatan *m*

charm ['tʃɑrm] *n* : charme *m* — **~** *vt* : charmer, captiver — **charming** ['tʃɑrmıŋ] *adj* : charmant

chart ['tʃɑrt] *n* : graphique *m*, tableau *m*

charter ['tʃɑrtər] *n* : charte *f* — **~** *vt* : affréter (un vol, etc.)

chase ['tʃeıs] *n* : poursuite *f* — **~** *vt* **chased; chasing 1** : poursuivre, courir après **2** *or* **~ away** : chasser

chasm ['kæzəm] *n* : gouffre *m*, abîme *m*

chaste ['tʃeıst] *adj* **chaster; chastest** : chaste — **chastity** ['tʃæstəti] *n* : chasteté *f*

chat ['tʃæt] *vi* **chatted; chatting** : bavarder, causer — **~** *n* : causerie *f* — **chatter** ['tʃætər] *vi* **1** : bavarder **2** : claquer (se dit des dents) — **~** *n* : bavardage *m* — **chatterbox** ['tʃætərˌbɑks] *n* : moulin *m* à paroles *fam* — **chatty** ['tʃæti] *adj* **chattier; -est** : bavard

chauffeur ['ʃoːfər, ʃo'fər] *n* : chauffeur *m*

chauvinist ['ʃoːvənıst] *or* **chauvinistic** [ˌʃoːvə'nıstık] *adj* : chauvin

cheap ['tʃiːp] *adj* **1** INEXPENSIVE : bon marché **2** SHODDY : de mauvaise qualité — **~** *adv* : à bon marché

cheat ['tʃiːt] *vt* : frauder, tromper — *vi* **1** : tricher **2 ~ on s.o.** : tromper qqn — **~** *or* **cheater** ['tʃiːtər] *n* : tricheur *m*, -cheuse *f*

check ['tʃɛk] *n* **1** HALT : arrêt *m* **2** RESTRAINT : limite *f*, frein *m* **3** INSPECTION : contrôle *m* **4** *or Brit* **cheque** DRAFT : chèque *m* **5** BILL : addition *f* — **~** *vt* **1** HALT : freiner, arrêter **2** RESTRAIN : retenir, contenir **3** VERIFY : vérifier **4 ~ in** : se présenter à la réception (à l'hôtel) **5** *or* **~ off** MARK : cocher **6 ~ out** : quitter (l'hôtel) **7 ~ out** VERIFY : vérifier — **checkbook** ['tʃɛkˌbʊk] *n* : carnet *m* de chèques

checkers ['tʃɛkərz] *n* : jeu *m* de dames

checkmate ['tʃɛkˌmeıt] *n* : échec *m* et mat

checkpoint ['tʃɛkˌpɔınt] *n* : poste *m* de contrôle

checkup ['tʃɛkˌʌp] *n* : examen *m* médical

cheek ['tʃik] *n* : joue *f*

cheer ['tʃır] *n* **1** : gaieté *f* **2** APPLAUSE : acclamation *f* **3 ~s!** : à votre santé! — **~** *vt* **1** COMFORT : encourager **2** APPLAUD : acclamer — **cheerful** ['tʃırfəl] *adj* : de bonne humeur

cheese ['tʃiːz] *n* : fromage *m*

cheetah ['tʃiːt̬ə] *n* : guépard *m*

chef ['ʃɛf] *n* : cuisinier *m*, -nière *f*; chef *m* (cuisinier)

chemical ['kɛmıkəl] *adj* : chimique — **~** *n* : produit *m* chimique — **chemist** ['kɛmıst] *n* : chimiste *mf* — **chemistry** ['kɛmıstri] *n, pl* **-tries** : chimie *f*

cheque *Brit* → **check**

cherish ['tʃɛrıʃ] *vt* **1** : chérir, aimer **2** HARBOR : caresser, nourrir (un espoir, etc.)

cherry ['tʃɛri] *n, pl* **-ries** : cerise *f*

chess ['tʃɛs] *n* : échecs *mpl*

chest ['tʃɛst] *n* **1** BOX : coffre *m* **2** : poitrine *f* (du corps) **3** *or* **~ of drawers** : commode *f*

chestnut ['tʃɛstˌnʌt] *n* : marron *m*, châtaigne *f*

chew ['tʃuː] *vt* : mastiquer, mâcher — **chewing gum** *n* : chewing-gum *m France*, gomme *f* à mâcher

chick ['tʃık] *n* : poussin *m* — **chicken** ['tʃıkən] *n* : poulet *m* — **chicken pox** *n* : varicelle *f*

chicory ['tʃıkəri] *n, pl* **-ries 1** : endive *f* **2** : chicorée *f*

chief ['tʃiːf] *adj* : principal, en chef — **~** *n* : chef *m* — **chiefly** ['tʃiːfli] *adv* : principalement, surtout

child ['tʃaıld] *n, pl* **children** ['tʃıldrən] **1** : enfant *mf* **2** OFFSPRING : fils *m*, fille *f* — **childbirth** ['tʃaıldˌbərθ] *n* : accouchement *m* — **childhood** ['tʃaıldˌhʊd] *n* : enfance *f* — **childish** ['tʃaıldıʃ] *adj* : puéril, enfantin — **childlike** ['tʃaıldˌlaık] *adj* : innocent, d'enfant — **childproof** ['tʃaıldˌpruːf] *adj* : de sécurité pour enfants

chili *or* **chile** *or* **chilli** ['tʃıli] *n, pl* **chilies** *or* **chiles** *or* **chillies 1** *or* **~ pepper** : piment *m* fort **2** : chili *m* con carne

chill ['tʃıl] *n* **1** : froid *m* **2 catch a ~** : attraper un coup de froid **3 there's a ~ in the air** : il fait un peu froid — **~** *vt* : refroidir, réfrigérer — **chilly** ['tʃıli] *adj* **chillier; -est** : frais, froid

chime ['tʃaım] *v* **chimed; chiming** : carillonner — **~** *n* : carillon *m*

chimney ['tʃımni] *n, pl* **-neys** : cheminée *f*

chimpanzee ['tʃımˌpæn'ziː, ˌtʃım-; tʃım'pænzi, ʃım-] *n* : chimpanzé *m*

chin ['tʃın] *n* : menton *m*

china ['tʃaınə] *n* : porcelaine *f*

Chinese ['tʃaı'niːz, -niːs] *adj* : chinois — **~** *n* : chinois *m* (langue)

chip ['tʃıp] *n* **1** : éclat *m* (de verre), copeau *m* (de bois) **2** : jeton *m* (de poker, etc.) **3** NICK : ébréchure *f* **4** *or* **computer ~** : puce *f* — **~** *v* **chipped; chipping** *vt* : ébrécher (de la vaisselle, etc.), écailler (de la peinture) — *vi* **~ in** : contribuer

chipmunk ['tʃıpˌmʌŋk] *n* : tamia *m*

chiropodist [kə'rapədɪst, ʃə-] *n* : pédicure *mf*

chiropractor ['kaɪrə,præktər] *n* : chiropracteur *m*

chirp ['tʃərp] *vi* : pépier

chisel ['tʃɪzəl] *n* : ciseau *m* — ~ *vt* **-eled** *or* **-elled**; **-eling** *or* **-elling** : ciseler

chitchat ['tʃɪt,tʃæt] *n* : bavardage *m*

chivalry ['ʃɪvəlri] *n, pl* **-ries** : chevalerie *f*

chive ['tʃaɪv] *n* : ciboulette *f*

chlorine ['klor,iːn] *n* : chlore *m*

chock–full ['tʃak'fʊl, 'tʃʌk-] *adj* : bondé, plein à craquer

chocolate ['tʃakələt, 'tʃɔk-] *n* : chocolat *m*

choice ['tʃɔɪs] *n* : choix *m* — ~ *adj* **choicer**; **choicest** : de choix, de première qualité

choir ['kwaɪr] *n* : chœur *m*

choke ['tʃoːk] *v* **choked**; **choking** *vt* **1** : étrangler, étouffer **2** BLOCK : boucher — *vi* : s'étouffer (en mangeant) — ~ *n* : starter *m* (d'une voiture)

cholesterol [kə'lɛstə,rol] *n* : cholestérol *m*

choose ['tʃuːz] *v* **chose** ['tʃoːz]; **chosen** ['tʃoːzən]; **choosing** *vt* **1** SELECT : choisir **2** DECIDE : décider — *vi* : choisir — **choosy** *or* **choosey** ['tʃuːzi] *adj* **choosier**; **-est** : exigeant

chop ['tʃap] *vt* **chopped**; **chopping 1** : couper (du bois), hacher (des légumes, etc.) **2** ~ **down** : abattre — ~ *n* : côtelette *f* (de porc, etc.) — **choppy** ['tʃapi] *adj* **-pier**; **-est** : agité (se dit de la mer)

chopsticks ['tʃap,stɪks] *npl* : baguettes *fpl*

chord ['kɔrd] *n* : accord *m* (en musique)

chore ['tʃor] *n* **1** : corvée *f* **2 household** ~**s** : travaux *mpl* ménagers

choreography [,kori'agrəfi] *n, pl* **-phies** : chorégraphie *f*

chorus ['korəs] *n* **1** : chœur *m* (de chanteurs) **2** REFRAIN : refrain *m*

chose, chosen → **choose**

christen ['krɪsən] *vt* : baptiser — **christening** ['krɪsənɪŋ] *n* : baptême *m*

Christian ['krɪstʃən] *adj* : chrétien — ~ *n* : chrétien *m*, -tienne *f* — **Christianity** [,krɪstʃi'ænəti, ,krɪs'tʃæ-] *n* : christianisme *m*

Christmas ['krɪsməs] *n* : Noël *m*

chrome ['kroːm] *n* : chrome *m* — **chromium** ['kroːmiəm] *n* : chrome *m*

chronic ['kranɪk] *adj* : chronique

chronicle ['kranɪkəl] *n* : chronique *f*

chronology [krə'nalədʒi] *n, pl* **-gies** : chronologie *f* — **chronological** [,kranəl-'adʒɪkəl] *adj* : chronologique

chrysanthemum [krɪ'sæntθəməm] *n* : chrysanthème *m*

chubby ['tʃʌbi] *adj* **-bier**; **-est** : potelé, dodu

chuck ['tʃʌk] *vt* : tirer, lancer

chuckle ['tʃʌkəl] *vi* **-led**; **-ling** : glousser, rire tout bas — ~ *n* : petit rire *m*

chum ['tʃʌm] *n* : copain *m*, -pine *f*; camarade *mf*

chunk ['tʃʌŋk] *n* (gros) morceau *m*

church ['tʃərtʃ] *n* : église *f*

churn ['tʃərn] *vt* **1** : battre (du beurre) **2** STIR : agiter, remuer **3** ~ **out** : produire en série

cider ['saɪdər] *n* : cidre *m*

cigar [sɪ'gar] *n* : cigare *m* — **cigarette** [,sɪgə'rɛt, 'sɪgə,rɛt] *n* : cigarette *f*

cinch ['sɪntʃ] *n* **it's a** ~ : c'est du gâteau

cinema ['sɪnəmə] *n* : cinéma *m*

cinnamon ['sɪnəmən] *n* : cannelle *f*

cipher ['saɪfər] *n* **1** ZERO : zéro *m* **2** CODE : chiffre *m*

circa ['sərkə] *prep* : environ, vers

circle ['sərkəl] *n* : cercle *m* — ~ *vt* **-cled**; **-cling 1** : faire le tour de **2** SURROUND : entourer, encercler

circuit ['sərkət] *n* : circuit *m* — **circuitous** [,sər'kjuːətəs] *adj* : détourné, indirect

circular ['sərkjələr] *adj* : circulaire — ~ *n* LEAFLET : circulaire *f*

circulate ['sərkjə,leɪt] *v* **-lated**; **-lating** : circuler — **circulation** [,sərkjə'leɪʃən] *n* **1** FLOW : circulation *f* **2** : tirage *m* (d'un journal)

circumcise ['sərkəm,saɪz] *vt* **-cised**; **-cising** : circoncire — **circumcision** [,sərkəm-'sɪʒn, 'sərkəm,-] *n* : circoncision *f*

circumference [sər'kʌmpfrənts] *n* : circonférence *f*

circumflex ['sərkəm,flɛks] *n* : accent *m* circonflexe

circumspect ['sərkəm,spɛkt] *adj* : circonspect, prudent

circumstance ['sərkəm,stænts] *n* **1** : circonstance *f* **2 under no** ~**s** : en aucun cas

circus ['sərkəs] *n* : cirque *m*

cistern ['sɪstərn] *n* TANK : citerne *f*

cite ['saɪt] *vt* **cited**; **citing** : citer — **citation** [saɪ'teɪʃən] *n* : citation *f*

citizen ['sɪtəzən] *n* : citoyen *m*, -toyenne *f* — **citizenship** ['sɪtəzən,ʃɪp] *n* : citoyenneté *f*

citrus ['sɪtrəs] *n, pl* **-rus** *or* **-ruses** *or* ~ **fruit** : agrumes *mpl*

city ['sɪti] *n, pl* **-ties** : ville *f* — **city hall** *n* : hôtel *m* de ville

civic ['sɪvɪk] *adj* : civique — **civics** ['sɪvɪks] *ns & pl* : instruction *f* civique

civil ['sɪvəl] *adj* **1** : civil **2** ~ **rights** : droits *mpl* civiques **3** ~ **service** : fonction *f* publique — **civilian** [sə'vɪljən] *n* : civil *m*, -vile *f* — **civility** [sə'vɪləti] *n, pl* **-ties** : civilité *f*, courtoisie *f* — **civilization** [,sɪvələ-'zeɪʃən] *n* : civilisation *f* — **civilize** ['sɪvə,laɪz] *vt* **-lized**; **-lizing** : civiliser

clad ['klæd] *adj* ~ **in** : vêtu de, habillé de

claim ['kleɪm] *vt* **1** DEMAND : revendiquer,

réclamer **2** MAINTAIN : prétendre — ⁓ *n*
1 : revendication *f* **2** ASSERTION : affirmation *f*

clam [ˈklæm] *n* : palourde *f*

clamber [ˈklɑmbər] *vi* : grimper (avec difficulté)

clammy [ˈklæmi] *adj* -**mier; -est** : moite

clamor *or Brit* **clamour** [ˈklæmər] *n*
: clameur *f*, cris *mpl* — ⁓ *vi* : vociférer

clamp [ˈklæmp] *n* : crampon *m* — ⁓ *vt* : attacher, fixer

clan [ˈklæn] *n* : clan *m*

clandestine [klænˈdɛstɪn] *adj* : clandestin, secret

clang [ˈklæŋ] *n* : bruit *m* métallique

clap [ˈklæp] *v* **clapped; clapping** : applaudir — ⁓ *n* : applaudissement *m*

clarify [ˈklærəˌfaɪ] *vt* -**fied; -fying** : clarifier, éclaircir — **clarification** [ˌklærəfəˈkeɪʃən] *n* : clarification *f*

clarinet [ˌklærəˈnɛt] *n* : clarinette *f*

clarity [ˈklærəti] *n* : clarté *f*

clash [ˈklæʃ] *vi* : s'opposer, se heurter — ⁓ *n* : conflit *m*

clasp [ˈklæsp] *n* : fermoir *m*, boucle *f* — ⁓ *vt* **1** FASTEN : attacher **2** HOLD : serrer

class [ˈklæs] *n* **1** : classe *f* **2** COURSE : cours *m* — ⁓ *vt* : classer, classifier

classic [ˈklæsɪk] *or* **classical** [ˈklæsɪkəl] *adj*
: classique — **classic** *n* : classique *m*

classify [ˈklæsəˌfaɪ] *vt* -**fied; -fying** : classer, classifier — **classification** [ˌklæsəfəˈkeɪʃən] *n* : classification *f* — **classified** [ˈklæsəˌfaɪd] *adj* **1** : confidentiel **2** ⁓ **ads** : petites annonces *fpl*

classmate [ˈklæsˌmeɪt] *n* : compagnon *m*, compagne *f* de classe

classroom [ˈklæsˌruːm] *n* : salle *f* de classe

clatter [ˈklætər] *vi* : cliqueter — ⁓ *n* : bruit *m*, cliquetis *m*

clause [ˈklɔz] *n* : clause *f*

claustrophobia [ˌklɔstrəˈfoːbiə] *n* : claustrophobie *f*

claw [ˈklɔ] *n* : griffe *f* (d'un chat, etc.), pince *f* (d'un crustacé)

clay [ˈkleɪ] *n* : argile *f*

clean [ˈkliːn] *adj* **1** : propre **2** UNADULTERATED : pur — ⁓ *vt* : nettoyer, laver — **cleanliness** [ˈklɛnlinəs] *n* : propreté *f* — **cleanse** [ˈklɛnz] *vt* **cleansed; cleansing** : nettoyer, purifier

clear [ˈkliːr] *adj* **1** : clair **2** TRANSPARENT : transparent **3** OPEN : libre, dégagé — ⁓ *vt* **1** : débarrasser (un espace, etc.), dégager (une voie) **2** ⁓ **a check** : encaisser un chèque **3** ⁓ **up** RESOLVE : résoudre — *vi* **1** ⁓ **up** BRIGHTEN : s'éclaircir (se dit du temps, etc.) **2** ⁓ **up** VANISH : disparaître (se dit d'un symptôme, etc.) — ⁓ *adv* **1** **hear loud and** ⁓ : entendre très clairement

2 make oneself ⁓ : s'expliquer — **clearance** [ˈklɪrənts] *n* **1** SPACE : espace *m* libre **2** AUTHORIZATION : autorisation *f* **3** ⁓ **sale** : liquidation *f* — **clearing** [ˈklɪrɪŋ] *n* : clairière *f* — **clearly** [ˈklɪrli] *adv* **1** DISTINCTLY : clairement **2** OBVIOUSLY : évidemment

cleaver [ˈkliːvər] *n* : couperet *m*

clef [ˈklɛf] *n* : clé *f* (en musique)

clement [ˈklɛmənt] *adj* : doux, clément — **clemency** [ˈklɛməntsi] *n, pl* -**cies** : clémence *f*

clench [ˈklɛntʃ] *vt* : serrer

clergy [ˈklərdʒi] *n, pl* -**gies** : clergé *m* — **clergyman** [ˈklərdʒimən] *n, pl* -**men** [-mən, -ˌmɛn] : ecclésiastique *m* — **clerical** [ˈklɛrɪkəl] *adj* **1** : clérical, du clergé **2** ⁓ **work** : travail *m* de bureau

clerk [ˈklərk, *Brit* ˈklɑrk] *n* **1** : employé *m*, -ployée *f* de bureau **2** SALESPERSON : vendeur *m*, -deuse *f*

clever [ˈklɛvər] *adj* **1** SKILLFUL : habile, adroit **2** SMART : astucieux — **cleverly** [ˈklɛvərli] *adv* **1** : habilement **2** : astucieusement — **cleverness** [ˈklɛvərnəs] *n* **1** SKILL : habileté *f* **2** INTELLIGENCE : intelligence *f*

cliché [kliˈʃeɪ] *n* : cliché *m*

click [ˈklɪk] *vt* : faire claquer — *vi* **1** : faire un déclic **2** : cliquer (en informatique) — ⁓ *n* : déclic *m*

client [ˈklaɪənt] *n* : client *m*, cliente *f* — **clientele** [ˌklaɪənˈtɛl, ˌkliː-] *n* : clientèle *f*

cliff [ˈklɪf] *n* : falaise *f*

climate [ˈklaɪmət] *n* : climat *m*

climax [ˈklaɪˌmæks] *n* : point *m* culminant, apogée *m*

climb [ˈklaɪm] *vt* : monter, gravir — *vi* RISE : monter, augmenter — ⁓ *n* : montée *f*, ascension *f*

cling [ˈklɪŋ] *vi* **clung** [ˈklʌŋ]; **clinging** ⁓ **to** : s'accrocher à

clinic [ˈklɪnɪk] *n* : clinique *f* — **clinical** [ˈklɪnɪkəl] *adj* : clinique

clink [ˈklɪŋk] *vi* : cliqueter

clip [ˈklɪp] *vt* **clipped; clipping 1** : couper, tailler **2** FASTEN : attacher (avec un trombone) — ⁓ *n* FASTENER : attache *f*, pince *f* — **clippers** [ˈklɪpərz] *npl* **1** *or* **nail** ⁓ : coupe-ongles *m* **2** SHEARS : tondeuse *f*

cloak [ˈkloːk] *vt* : cape *f*

clock [ˈklɑk] *n* **1** : horloge *f*, pendule *f* **2 around the** ⁓ : d'affilée — **clockwise** [ˈklɑkˌwaɪz] *adv & adj* : dans le sens des aiguilles d'une montre

clog [ˈklɑg] *n* : sabot *m* — ⁓ *v* **clogged; clogging** *vt* : boucher, bloquer — *vi or* ⁓ **up** : se boucher

cloister [ˈklɔɪstər] *n* : cloître *m*

close[1] [ˈkloːz] *v* **closed; closing** *vt* : fermer — *vi* **1** : fermer, se fermer **2** TERMINATE

: prendre fin, se terminer **3 ~ in** : se rapprocher — **~** n : fin f, conclusion f

close² [ˈkloːs] adj **closer; closest 1** NEAR : proche **2** INTIMATE : intime **3** STRICT : rigoureux, étroit **4** ~ **= game** : une partie serrée — **~** adv : de près — **closely** [ˈkloːsli] adv : de près — **closeness** [ˈkloːsnəs] n **1** : proximité f **2** INTIMACY : intimité f

closet [ˈklɑzət] n : placard m, garde-robe f

closure [ˈkloːʒər] n : fermeture f, clôture f

clot [ˈklɑt] n : caillot m — **~** vi **clotted; clotting** : cailler, (se) coaguler

cloth [ˈklɔːθ] n, pl **cloths** [ˈklɔːðz, ˈklɔːθs] : tissu m

clothe [ˈkloːð] vt **clothed** or **clad** [ˈklæd]; **clothing** : habiller, vêtir — **clothes** [ˈkloːz, ˈkloːðz] npl **1** : vêtements mpl **2 put on one's ~** : s'habiller — **clothespin** [ˈkloːz-ˌpɪn] n : pince f (à linge) — **clothing** [ˈkloːðɪŋ] n : vêtements mpl

cloud [ˈklaʊd] n : nuage m — **~** vi or **~ over** : se couvrir de nuages — **cloudy** [ˈklaʊdi] adj **cloudier; -est** : nuageux, couvert

clout [ˈklaʊt] n : influence m, poids m

clove [ˈkloːv] n **1** : clou m de girofle **2** or **garlic ~** : gousse f d'ail

clover [ˈkloːvər] n : trèfle m

clown [ˈklaʊn] n : clown m — **~** vi or **~ around** : faire le clown

cloying [ˈklɔɪɪŋ] adj : mièvre

club [ˈklʌb] n **1** : massue f, matraque f **2** ASSOCIATION : club m, groupe m **3 ~s** npl : trèfle m (aux cartes) — **~** vt **clubbed; clubbing** : matraquer

cluck [ˈklʌk] vi : glousser

clue [ˈkluː] n **1** : indice m **2 I haven't got a ~** : je n'ai aucune idée

clump [ˈklʌmp] n : massif m (d'arbres), touffe f (d'herbe)

clumsy [ˈklʌmzi] adj **-sier; -est** : maladroit, gauche

cluster [ˈklʌstər] n : groupe m (de personnes), grappe f (de raisins, etc.) — vi : se rassembler, se grouper

clutch [ˈklʌtʃ] vt : saisir, étreindre — vi **~ at** : s'agripper à — **~** n : embrayage m (d'une voiture)

clutter [ˈklʌtər] vt : encombrer — **~** n : désordre m, fouillis m

coach [ˈkoːtʃ] n **1** CARRIAGE : carrosse m **2** : voiture f, wagon m (d'un train) **3** BUS : autocar m **4** : billet m d'avion de deuxième classe **5** TRAINER : entraîneur m, -neuse f — **~** vt **1** : entraîner (une équipe sportive) **2** TUTOR : donner des leçons à

coagulate [koˈægjəˌleɪt] v **-lated; -lating** vt : coaguler — vi : se coaguler

coal [ˈkoːl] n : charbon m

coalition [ˌkoːəˈlɪʃən] n : coalition f

coarse [ˌkors] adj **coarser; coarsest 1** : gros (se dit du sable, du sel, etc.) **2** CRUDE : grossier, vulgaire — **coarseness** [ˈkorsnəs] n **1** ROUGHNESS : rudesse f **2** CRUDENESS : grossièreté f

coast [ˈkoːst] n : côte f — **coastal** [ˈkoːstəl] adj : côtier, littoral

coaster [ˈkoːstər] n : dessous-de-verre m

coast guard n : gendarmerie f maritime France, garde f côtière Can

coastline [ˈkoːstˌlaɪn] n : littoral m

coat [ˈkoːt] n **1** : manteau m **2** : pelage m (d'un animal) **3** : couche f (de peinture) — **~** vt **with** : couvrir de, recouvrir de — **coat hanger** n : cintre m — **coating** [ˈkoːt̬ɪŋ] n : couche f, revêtement m — **coat of arms** n : blason m, armoiries fpl

coax [ˈkoːks] vt : amadouer, cajoler

cob [ˈkɑb] → **corncob**

cobblestone [ˈkɑbəlˌstoːn] n : pavé m

cobweb [ˈkɑbˌwɛb] n : toile f d'araignée

cocaine [koˈkeɪn, ˈkoːˌkeɪn] n : cocaïne f

cock [ˈkɑk] n ROOSTER : coq m — **~** vt **1** : armer (un fusil) **2** TILT : pencher (la tête, etc.) — **cockeyed** [ˈkɑkˌaɪd] adj **1** ASKEW : de travers **2** ABSURD : insensé

cockpit [ˈkɑkˌpɪt] n : poste m de pilotage

cockroach [ˈkɑkˌroːtʃ] n : cafard m

cocktail [ˈkɑkˌteɪl] n : cocktail m

cocoa [ˈkoːˌkoː] n : cacao m

coconut [ˈkoːkəˌnʌt] n : noix f de coco

cocoon [kəˈkuːn] n : cocon m

cod [ˈkɑd] ns & pl : morue f

coddle [ˈkɑdəl] vt **-dled; -dling** : dorloter

code [ˈkoːd] n : code m — **~** vt : coder

coeducational [ˌkoːˌɛdʒəˈkeɪʃənəl] adj : mixte

coerce [koˈərs] vt **-erced; -ercing** : contraindre — **coercion** [koˈərʒən, -ʃən] n : contrainte f

coffee [ˈkɔfi] n : café m — **coffeepot** [ˈkɔfiˌpɑt] n : cafetière f

coffer [ˈkɔfər] n : coffre m, caisse f

coffin [ˈkɔfən] n : cercueil m, bière f

cog [ˈkɑg] n : dent f (d'une roue)

cogent [ˈkoːdʒənt] adj : convaincant, persuasif

cognac [ˈkoːnˌjæk] n : cognac m

cogwheel [ˈkɑgˌʍiːl] n : pignon m

coherent [koˈhɪrənt] adj : cohérent

coil [ˈkɔɪl] vt : enrouler — vi : s'enrouler — **~** n **1** : rouleau m **2** : volute f (de fumée)

coin [ˈkɔɪn] n : pièce f de monnaie

coincide [ˌkoːɪnˈsaɪd, ˈkoːɪnˌsaɪd] vi **-cided; -ciding** : coïncider — **coincidence** [koˈɪntsədənts] n : coïncidence f

colander [ˈkɑləndər, ˈkʌ-] n : passoire f

cold [ˈkoːld] adj **1** : froid **2 be ~** : avoir froid **3 it's ~ today** : il fait froid aujour-

　　　　　　　　　　　　　　　　　　　　　　　commit

d'hui — **~** *n* **1** : froid *m* **2** : rhume *m* (en médecine) **3 catch a ~** : s'enrhumer

coleslaw ['ko:l,slɔ] *n* : salade *f* de chou cru

colic ['kalik] *n* : coliques *fpl*

collaborate [kə'læbə,reɪt] *vi* **-rated; -rating** : collaborer, coopérer — **collaboration** [kə-,læbə'reɪʃən] *n* : collaboration *f*

collapse [kə'læps] *vi* **-lapsed; -lapsing** : s'effondrer, s'écrouler — **~** *n* : effondrement *m*, écroulement *m* — **collapsible** [kə'læpsəbəl] *adj* : pliant

collar ['kalər] *n* : col *m* — **collarbone** ['kalər,bo:n] *n* : clavicule *f*

collateral [kə'lætərəl] *n* : nantissement *m*

colleague ['ka,li:g] *n* : collègue *mf*

collect [kə'lɛkt] *vt* **1** GATHER : ramasser, recueillir **2** : percevoir (des impôts), encaisser (une somme d'argent) **3** : collectionner (des objets) — *vi* **1** ASSEMBLE : se rassembler, se réunir **2** ACCUMULATE : s'accumuler — **~** *adv* **call ~** : téléphoner en PCV *France*, téléphoner à frais virés *Can* — **collection** [kə'lɛkʃən] *n* **1** : collection *f* (de livres, etc.) **2** : quête *f* (à l'église) — **collective** [kə'lɛktɪv] *adj* : collectif

college ['kalɪdʒ] *n* : établissement *m* d'enseignement supérieur

collide [kə'laɪd] *vi* **-lided; -liding** : se heurter, entrer en collision — **collision** [kə'lɪʒən] *n* : collision *f*

colloquial [kə'lo:kwiəl] *adj* : familier

cologne [kə'lo:n] *n* : eau *f* de Cologne

colon[1] ['ko:lən] *n*, *pl* **colons** *or* **cola** [-lə] : côlon *m* (en anatomie)

colon[2] *n*, *pl* **colons** : deux-points *m*

colonel ['kərnəl] *n* : colonel *m*

colony ['kaləni] *n*, *pl* **-nies** : colonie *f* — **colonial** [kə'lo:niəl] *adj* : colonial — **colonize** ['kalə,naɪz] *vt* **-nized; -nizing** : coloniser

color *or Brit* **colour** ['kʌlər] *n* : couleur *f* — **~** *vt* : colorer — **color–blind** *or Brit* **colour–blind** ['kʌlər,blaɪnd] *adj* : daltonien — **colored** *or Brit* **coloured** ['kʌlərd] *adj* : coloré — **colorful** *or Brit* **colourful** ['kʌlərfəl] *adj* : coloré — **colorless** *or Brit* **colourless** ['kʌlərləs] *adj* : incolore

colossal [kə'lasəl] *adj* : colossal

colt ['ko:lt] *n* : poulain *m*

column ['kaləm] *n* **1** : colonne *f* **2** : rubrique *f* (dans la presse) — **columnist** ['kaləmnɪst, -ləmɪst] *n* : chroniqueur *m*, -queuse *f*

coma ['ko:mə] *n* : coma *m*

comb ['ko:m] *n* **1** : peigne *m* **2** : crête *f* (d'un coq) — **~** *vt* : (se) peigner

combat ['kam,bæt] *n* : combat *m* — **~** [kəm'bæt, 'kam,bæt] *vt* **-bated** *or* **-batted; -bating** *or* **-batting** : combattre — **combatant** [kəm'bætənt] *n* : combattant *m*, -tante *f*

combine [kəm'baɪn] *vt* **-bined; -bining** : combiner — **~** ['kam,baɪn] *n* HARVESTER : moissonneuse-batteuse *f* — **combination** [,kambə'neɪʃən] *n* : combinaison *f*

combustion [kəm'bʌstʃən] *n* : combustion *f*

come ['kʌm] *vi* **came** ['keɪm]; **come; coming 1** : venir **2** ARRIVE : arriver **3 ~ about** : se produire **4 ~ back** : revenir **5 ~ from** : provenir de **6 ~ in** : entrer **7 ~ out** : sortir **8 ~ to** REVIVE : revenir à soi **9 ~ on!** : allez! **10 ~ up** OCCUR : se présenter **11 how ~?** : comment ça se fait? — **comeback** ['kʌm,bæk] *n* **1** RETURN : rentrée *f* **2** RETORT : réplique *f*

comedy ['kamədi] *n*, *pl* **-dies** : comédie *f* — **comedian** [kə'mi:diən] *n* : comique *mf*

comet ['kamət] *n* : comète *f*

comfort ['kʌmpfərt] *vt* : consoler, réconforter — **~** *n* **1** : confort *m* **2** SOLACE : consolation *f*, réconfort *m* — **comfortable** ['kʌmpfərtəbəl, 'kʌmpftə-] *adj* : confortable

comic ['kamɪk] *or* **comical** ['kamɪkəl] *adj* : comique — **~** *n* : comique *mf* — **comic strip** *n* : bande *f* dessinée

coming ['kʌmɪŋ] *adj* : à venir

comma ['kamə] *n* : virgule *f*

command [kə'mænd] *vt* **1** ORDER : ordonner, commander **2 ~ respect** : inspirer le respect — *vi* : donner des ordres — **~** *n* **1** ORDER : ordre *m* **2** MASTERY : maîtrise *f* — **commander** [kə'mændər] *n* : commandant *m* — **commandment** [kə'mændmənt] *n* : commandement *m* (en religion)

commemorate [kə'mɛmə,reɪt] *vt* **-rated; -rating** : commémorer — **commemoration** [kə,mɛmə'reɪʃən] *n* : commémoration *f*

commence [kə'mɛnts] *v* **-menced; -mencing** : commencer — **commencement** [kə'mɛntsmənt] *n* : remise *f* des diplômes

commend [kə'mɛnd] *vt* : louer — **commendable** [kə'mɛndəbəl] *adj* : louable

comment ['ka,mɛnt] *n* : commentaire *m*, remarque *f* — **~** *vi* : faire des commentaires — **commentary** ['kamən,tɛri] *n*, *pl* **-taries** : commentaire *m* — **commentator** ['kamən,teɪtər] *n* : commentateur *m*, -trice *f*

commerce ['kamərs] *n* : commerce *m* — **commercial** [kə'mɛrʃəl] *adj* : commercial — **~** *n* : annonce *f* publicitaire — **commercialize** [kə'mərʃə,laɪz] *vt* **-ized; -izing** : commercialiser

commiserate [kə'mɪzə,reɪt] *vi* **-ated; -ating** : compatir

commission [kə'mɪʃən] *n* : commission *f*, comité *m* — **~** *vt* : commander (une œuvre d'art) — **commissioner** [kə'mɪʃənər] *n* : commissaire *m*

commit [kə'mɪt] *vt* **-mitted; -mitting 1** ENGAGE : confier **2** : commettre (un crime, etc.) **3 ~ oneself** : s'engager — **commitment** [kə'mɪtmənt] *n* **1** PROMISE : engagement *m* **2** OBLIGATION : obligation *f*

committee [kə'mɪti] *n* : comité *m*

commodity [kə'madəti] *n*, *pl* **-ties** : marchandise *f*, denrée *f*

common ['kamən] *adj* **1** : commun **2** WIDESPREAD : universel — **~** *n* **in ~** : en commun — **commonly** ['kamənli] *adv* : communément — **commonplace** ['kamən,pleɪs] *adj* : commun, banal — **common sense** *n* : bon sens *m*

commotion [kə'mo:ʃən] *n* : vacarme *m*, brouhaha *m*

commune ['ka,mju:n, kə'mju:n] *n* : communauté *f* — **communal** [kə'mju:nəl] *adj* : communautaire

communicate [kə'mju:nə,keɪt] *v* **-cated; -cating** : communiquer — **communication** [kə,mju:nə'keɪʃən] *n* : communication *f*

communion [kə'mju:njən] *n* : communion *f*

Communism ['kamjə,nɪzəm] *n* : communisme *m* — **Communist** ['kamjə,nɪst] *adj* : communiste

community [kə'mju:nəti] *n*, *pl* **-ties** : communauté *f*

commute [kə'mju:t] *vi* **-muted; -muting** : faire la navette, faire un trajet journalier

compact [kəm'pækt, 'kam,pækt] *adj* : compact — **~** ['kam,pækt] *n* **1** *or* **~ car** : voiture *f* compacte **2** *or* **powder ~** : poudrier *m* — **compact disc** ['kam,pækt-'dɪsk] *n* : disque *m* compact, compact *m*

companion [kəm'pænjən] *n* : compagnon *m*, compagne *f* — **companionship** [kəm-'pænjən,ʃɪp] *n* : compagnie *f*

company ['kʌmpəni] *n*, *pl* **-nies** **1** : compagnie *f*, société *f* **2** : troupe *f* (de théâtre) **3** GUESTS : invités *mpl*

compare [kəm'pær] *v* **-pared; -paring** *vt* : comparer — *vi* **~ with** : être comparable à — **comparative** [kəm'pærətɪv] *adj* : comparatif, relatif — **comparison** [kəm-'pærəsən] *n* : comparaison *f*

compartment [kəm'partmənt] *n* : compartiment *m*

compass ['kʌmpəs, 'kam-] *n* **1** : boussole *f* **2 points of the ~** : points *mpl* cardinaux

compassion [kəm'pæʃən] *n* : compassion *f* — **compassionate** [kəm'pæʃənət] *adj* : compatissant

compatible [kəm'pætəbəl] *adj* : compatible — **compatibility** [kəm,pætə'bɪləti] *n* : compatibilité *f*

compel [kəm'pɛl] *vt* **-pelled; -pelling** : contraindre, obliger — **compelling** [kəm-'pɛlɪŋ] *adj* : irrésistible

compensate ['kampən,seɪt] *v* **-sated; -sating** *vi* **~ for** : compenser — *vt* : indemniser

— **compensation** [,kampən'seɪʃən] *n* : compensation *f*

compete [kəm'pi:t] *vi* **-peted; -peting** : faire concurrence, rivaliser — **competent** ['kampətənt] *adj* : compétent — **competition** [,kampə'tɪʃən] *n* **1** : concurrence *f* **2** CONTEST : compétition *f* — **competitor** [kəm'pɛtətər] *n* : concurrent *m*, -rente *f*

compile [kəm'paɪl] *vt* **-piled; -piling** : dresser (une liste, etc.)

complacency [kəm'pleɪsəntsi] *n* : satisfaction *f* de soi, suffisance *f* — **complacent** [kəm'pleɪsənt] *adj* : content de soi

complain [kəm'pleɪn] *vi* : se plaindre — **complaint** [kəm'pleɪnt] *n* : plainte *f*

complement ['kampləmənt] *n* : complément *m* — **~** ['kamplə,mɛnt] *vt* : aller bien avec — **complementary** [,kamplə-'mɛntəri] *adj* : complémentaire

complete [kəm'pli:t] *adj* **-pleter; -est 1** WHOLE : complet, intégral **2** FINISHED : achevé **3** TOTAL : complet, absolu — **~** *vt* **-pleted; -pleting 1** : compléter (un puzzle, etc.), remplir (un questionnaire) **2** FINISH : achever — **completely** [kəm'pli:tli] *adv* : complètement — **completion** [kəm-'pli:ʃən] *n* : achèvement *m*

complex [kam'plɛks, kəm-; 'kam,plɛks] *adj* : complexe — **~** ['kam,plɛks] *n* : complexe *m*

complexion [kəm'plɛkʃən] *n* : teint *m*

complexity [kəm'plɛksəti, kam-] *n*, *pl* **-ties** : complexité *f*

compliance [kəm'plaɪənts] *n* **1** : conformité *f* **2 in ~ with** : conformément à — **compliant** [kəm'plaɪənt] *adj* : soumis

complicate ['kamplə,keɪt] *vt* **-cated; -cating** : compliquer — **complicated** ['kamplə-,keɪtəd] *adj* : compliqué — **complication** [,kamplə'keɪʃən] *n* : complication *f*

compliment ['kampləmənt] *n* : compliment *m* — **~** ['kamplə,mɛnt] *vt* : complimenter — **complimentary** [,kamplə'mɛntəri] *adj* **1** FLATTERING : flatteur **2** FREE : gratuit

comply [kəm'plaɪ] *vi* **-plied; -plying ~ with** : se conformer à, respecter

component [kəm'po:nənt, 'kam,po:-] *n* : composant *m*, élément *m*

compose [kəm'po:z] *vt* **-posed; -posing 1** : composer **2 ~ oneself** : retrouver son calme — **composer** [kəm'po:zər] *n* : compositeur *m*, -trice *f* — **composition** [,kampə'zɪʃən] *n* : composition *f* — **composure** [kəm'po:ʒər] *n* : calme *m*, sang-froid *m*

compound¹ [kam'paʊnd,kəm-; 'kam,paʊnd] *adj* : composé — **~** ['kam,paʊnd] *n* : composé *m* (en chimie)

compound² ['kam,paʊnd] *n* ENCLOSURE : enceinte *f*, enclos *m*

comprehend [ˌkɑmprɪˈhɛnd] *vt* : comprendre — **comprehension** [ˌkɑmprɪˈhɛntʃən] *n* : compréhension *f* — **comprehensive** [ˌkɑmprɪˈhɛntsɪv] *adj* : complet, détaillé

compress [kəmˈprɛs] *vt* : comprimer — **compression** [kəmˈprɛʃən] *n* : compression *f*

comprise [kəmˈpraɪz] *vt* **-prised; -prising** : comprendre

compromise [ˈkɑmprəˌmaɪz] *n* : compromis *m* — ~ *v* **-mised; -mising** *vi* : faire un compromis — *vt* : compromettre

compulsion [kəmˈpʌlʃən] *n* URGE : envie *f* — **compulsory** [kəmˈpʌlsəri] *adj* : obligatoire

compute [kəmˈpjuːt] *vt* **-puted; -puting** : calculer — **computer** [kəmˈpjuːtə̯r] *n* **1** : ordinateur *m* **2** ~ **science** : informatique *f* — **computerize** [kəmˈpjuːtə̯ˌraɪz] *vt* **-ized; -izing** : informatiser

con [ˈkɑn] *vt* **conned; conning** : duper, escroquer — ~ *n* **the pros and** ~**s** : le pour et le contre

concave [kɑnˈkeɪv, ˈkɑnˌkeɪv] *adj* : concave

conceal [kənˈsiːl] *vt* : dissimuler, cacher

concede [kənˈsiːd] *vt* **-ceded; -ceding** : accorder, concéder

conceit [kənˈsiːt] *n* : suffisance *f*, vanité *f* — **conceited** [kənˈsiːtəd] *adj* : suffisant, vaniteux

conceive [kənˈsiːv] *v* **-ceived; -ceiving** *vt* : concevoir — *vi* ~ **of** : concevoir

concentrate [ˈkɑntsənˌtreɪt] *v* **-trated; -trating** *vt* : concentrer — *vi* : se concentrer — **concentration** [ˌkɑntsənˈtreɪʃən] *n* : concentration *f*

concept [ˈkɑnˌsɛpt] *n* : concept *m* — **conception** [kənˈsɛpʃən] *n* : conception *f*

concern [kənˈsərn] *vt* **1** : concerner **2** ~ **oneself about** : s'inquiéter de — ~ *n* **1** BUSINESS : affaire *f* **2** WORRY : inquiétude *f* — **concerned** [kənˈsərnd] *adj* **1** ANXIOUS : inquiet **2 as far as I'm** ~ : en ce qui me concerne — **concerning** [kənˈsərnɪŋ] *prep* : concernant

concert [ˈkɑnˌsərt] *n* : concert *m* — **concerted** [kənˈsərtəd] *adj* : concerté

concession [kənˈsɛʃən] *n* : concession *f*

concise [kənˈsaɪs] *adj* : concis

conclude [kənˈkluːd] *v* **-cluded; -cluding** *vt* : conclure — *vi* : s'achever, se terminer — **conclusion** [kənˈkluːʒən] *n* : conclusion *f* — **conclusive** [kənˈkluːsɪv] *adj* : concluant

concoct [kənˈkɑkt, kɑn-] *vt* **1** PREPARE : confectionner **2** DEVISE : fabriquer — **concoction** [kənˈkɑkʃən] *n* : mélange *m*

concrete [kɑnˈkriːt, ˈkɑnˌkriːt] *adj* **1** : de béton **2** REAL : concret, réel — ~ [ˈkɑnˌkriːt, kɑnˈkriːt] *n* : béton *m*

concur [kənˈkər] *vi* **-curred, -curring** : être d'accord

concussion [kənˈkʌʃən] *n* : commotion *f* cérébrale

condemn [kənˈdɛm] *vt* : condamner — **condemnation** [ˌkɑnˌdɛmˈneɪʃən] *n* : condamnation *f*

condense [kənˈdɛnts] *vt* **-densed; -densing** : condenser — **condensation** [ˌkɑnˌdɛnˈseɪʃən, -dən-] *n* : condensation *f*

condescending [ˌkʼndɪˈsɛndɪŋ] *adj* : condescendant

condiment [ˈkɑndəmənt] *n* : condiment *m*

condition [kənˈdɪʃən] *n* **1** : condition *f* **2 in good** ~ : en bon état— **conditional** [kənˈdɪʃənəl] *adj* : conditionnel

condolences [kənˈdoːləntsəz] *npl* : condoléances *fpl*

condom [ˈkɑndəm] *n* : préservatif *m*

condominium [ˌkɑndəˈmɪniəm] *n, pl* **-ums** : immeuble *m* en copropriété

condone [kənˈdoːn] *vt* **-doned; -doning** : excuser

conducive [kənˈduːsɪv, -ˈdjuː-] *adj* : propice, favorable

conduct [ˈkɑnˌdʌkt] *n* : comportement *m*, conduite *f* — ~ [kənˈdʌkt] *vt* **1** : conduire, diriger **2** ~ **oneself** : se comporter — **conductor** [kənˈdʌktər] *n* **1** : conducteur *m* (d'électricité) **2** : chef *m* d'orchestre **3** : contrôleur *m* (de train, etc.)

cone [ˈkoːn] *n* **1** : cône *m* **2** *or* **ice-cream** ~ : cornet *m* (de crème glacée)

confection [kənˈfɛkʃən] *n* : confiserie *f*, bonbon *m*

confederation [kənˌfɛdəˈreɪʃən] *n* : confédération *f*

confer [kənˈfər] *v* **-ferred; -ferring** *vt* : conférer — *vi* ~ **with** : conférer avec, s'entretenir avec — **conference** [ˈkɑnfrənts, -fərənts] *n* : conférence *f*

confess [kənˈfɛs] *vt* : confesser, avouer — *vi* ~ **to** : admettre — **confession** [kənˈfɛʃən] *n* : confession *f*

confetti [kənˈfɛti] *n* : confettis *mpl*

confide [kənˈfaɪd] *v* **-fided; -fiding** *vt* : confier — *vi* ~ **in** : se confier à — **confidence** [ˈkɑnfədənts] *n* **1** TRUST : confiance *f* **2** SELF-ASSURANCE : confiance *f* en soi, assurance *f* **3** SECRET : confidence *f* — **confident** [ˈkɑnfədənt] *adj* **1** SURE : confiant, sûr **2** SELF-ASSURED : sûr de soi — **confidential** [ˌkɑnfəˈdɛntʃəl] *adj* : confidentiel

confine [kənˈfaɪn] *vt* **-fined; -fining 1** LIMIT : confiner, limiter **2** IMPRISON : enfermer — **confines** [ˈkɑnˌfaɪnz] *npl* : confins *mpl*, limites *fpl*

confirm [kənˈfərm] *vt* : confirmer — **confirmation** [ˌkɑnfərˈmeɪʃən] *n* : confirmation *f*

confiscate ['kɑnfə,skeɪt] *vt* **-cated; -cating** : confisquer

conflict ['kɑn,flɪkt] *n* : conflit *m* — ~ [kən-'flɪkt] *vi* : être en conflit, s'opposer

conform [kən-'fɔrm] *vi* ~ **with** : se conformer à, être conforme à — **conformity** [kən'fɔrməti] *n, pl* **-ties** : conformité *f*

confound [kən'faʊnd, kɑn-] *vt* : confondre, déconcerter

confront [kən'frʌnt] *vt* : affronter, faire face à — **confrontation** [,kɑnfrən'teɪʃən] *n* : confrontation *f*

confuse [kən'fju:z] *vt* **-fused; -fusing** : troubler, déconcerter — **confusing** [kən-'fju:zɪŋ] *adj* : déroutant — **confusion** [kən-'fju:ʒən] *n* : confusion *f*

congenial [kən'ʤi:niəl] *adj* : sympathique

congested [kən'ʤɛstəd] *adj* **1** : congestionné (en médecine) **2** OBSTRUCTED : encombré — **congestion** [kən'ʤɛstʃən] *n* : congestion *f*

Congolese [,kɑŋɡə'li:z,-'li:s] *adj* : congolais

congratulate [kən'ɡræʤə,leɪt, -'ɡrætʃə-] *vt* **-lated; -lating** : féliciter — **congratulations** [kən,ɡræʤə'leɪʃənz, -,ɡrætʃə-] *npl* : félicitations *fpl*

congregate ['kɑŋɡrɪ,ɡeɪt] *vi* **-gated; -gating** : se rassembler, se réunir — **congregation** [,kɑŋɡrɪ'ɡeɪʃən] *n* : assemblée *f* (de fidèles)

congress ['kɑŋɡrəs] *n* : congrès *m* — **congressman** ['kɑŋɡrəsmən] *n, pl* **-men** [-mən, -,mɛn] : membre *m* d'un congrès

conjecture [kən'ʤɛktʃər] *n* : conjecture *f*, supposition *f* — ~ *vt* **-tured; -turing** : conjecturer, présumer

conjugate ['kɑnʤə,ɡeɪt] *vt* **-gated; -gating** : conjuguer — **conjugation** [,kɑnʤə-'ɡeɪʃən] *f*

conjunction [kən'ʤʌŋkʃən] *n* : conjonction *f* (en grammaire)

conjure ['kɑnʤər, 'kʌn-] *vt* **-jured; -juring** ~ **up** : invoquer, évoquer

connect [kə'nɛkt] *vi* : assurer la correspondance (avec un train, etc.) — *vt* **1** JOIN : relier **2** ASSOCIATE : associer **3** : brancher (en électricité) — **connection** [kə'nɛkʃən] *n* **1** : lien *m*, rapport *m* **2** : correspondance *f* (de train, etc.) **3** ~**s** *npl* : relations *fpl* (sociales)

connote [kə'no:t] *vt* **-noted; -noting** : évoquer, indiquer

conquer ['kɑŋkər] *vt* : conquérir, vaincre — **conqueror** ['kɑŋkərər] *n* : conquérant *m*, -rante *f* — **conquest** ['kɑn,kwɛst, 'kɑŋ-] *n* : conquête *f*

conscience ['kɑntʃənts] *n* : conscience *f* — **conscientious** [,kɑntʃi'ɛntʃəs] *adj* : consciencieux

conscious ['kɑntʃəs] *adj* **1** AWARE : conscient **2** INTENTIONAL : délibéré — **consciously** ['kɑntʃəsli] *adv* : consciemment — **consciousness** ['kɑntʃəsnəs] *n* **1** AWARENESS : conscience *f* **2** lose ~ : perdre connaissance

consecrate ['kɑntsə,kreɪt] *vt* **-crated; -crating** : consacrer

consecutive [kən'sɛkjətɪv] *adj* : consécutif

consensus [kən'sɛntsəs] *n* : consensus *m*

consent [kən'sɛnt] *vi* : consentir — ~ *n* : consentement *m*, accord *m*

consequence ['kɑntsə,kwɛnts, -kwənts] *n* **1** : conséquence *f* **2 of no** ~ : sans importance — **consequently** ['kɑntsəkwəntli, -,kwɛnt-] *adv* : par conséquent

conserve [kən'sərv] *vt* **-served; -serving** : conserver, préserver — **conservation** [,kɑntsər'veɪʃən] *n* : conservation *f* — **conservative** [kən'sərvətɪv] *adj* **1** : conservateur **2** CAUTIOUS : modéré, prudent — ~ *n* : conservateur *m*, -trice *f* — **conservatory** [kən'sərvə,tori] *n, pl* **-ries** : conservatoire *m*

consider [kən'sɪdər] *vt* : considérer — **considerable** [kən'sɪdərəbəl] *adj* : considérable — **considerate** [kən'sɪdərət] *adj* : attentionné, prévenant — **consideration** [kən,sɪdə'reɪʃən] *n* : considération *f* — **considering** [kən'sɪdərɪŋ] *prep* : étant donné, vu

consign [kən'saɪn] *vt* SEND : expédier, envoyer — **consignment** [kən'saɪnmənt] *n* : envoi *m*

consist [kən'sɪst] *vi* **1** ~ **in** : consister à **2** ~ **of** : se composer de, consister en — **consistency** [kən'sɪstəntsi] *n, pl* **-cies 1** TEXTURE : consistance *f* **2** COHERENCE : cohérence *f* — **consistent** [kən'sɪstənt] *adj* **1** : constant, régulier **2** ~ **with** : en accord avec

console [kən'so:l] *vt* **-soled; -soling** : consoler, réconforter — **consolation** [,kɑntsə-'leɪʃən] *n* : consolation *f*

consolidate [kən'sɑlə,deɪt] *vt* **-dated; -dating** : consolider — **consolidation** [kən-,sɑlə'deɪʃən] *n* : consolidation *f*

consonant ['kɑntsənənt] *n* : consonne *f*

conspicuous [kən'spɪkjuəs] *adj* **1** OBVIOUS : évident, visible **2** STRIKING : voyant

conspire [kən'spaɪr] *vi* **-spired; -spiring** : conspirer, comploter — **conspiracy** [kən-'spɪrəsi] *n, pl* **-cies** : conspiration *f*

constant ['kɑntstənt] *adj* : constant — **constantly** ['kɑntstəntli] *adv* : constamment

constellation [,kɑntstə'leɪʃən] *n* : constellation *f*

constipated ['kɑntstə,peɪtəd] *adj* : constipé — **constipation** [,kɑntstə'peɪʃən] *n* : constipation *f*

constituent [kən'stɪtʃuənt] *n* **1** COMPONENT : composant *m* **2** VOTER : électeur *m*, -trice *f*

constitute ['kɑntstə,tu:t, -tju:t] *vt* **-tuted;**

-tuting : constituer — **constitution** [ˌkɑntstəˈtuːʃən, -ˈtjuː-] *n* : constitution *f* — **constitutional** [ˌkɑntstəˈtuːʃənəl, -ˈtjuː-] *adj* : constitutionnel

constraint [kənˈstreɪnt] *n* : contrainte *f*

construct [kənˈstrʌkt] *vt* : construire, bâtir — **construction** [kənˈstrʌkʃən] *n* : construction *f* — **constructive** [kənˈstrʌktɪv] *adj* : constructif

construe [kənˈstruː] *vt* **-strued; -struing** : interpréter

consulate [ˈkɑntsələt] *n* : consulat *m*

consult [kənˈsʌlt] *vt* : consulter — **consultant** [kənˈsʌltənt] *n* : consultant *m*, -tante *f* — **consultation** [ˌkɑntsəlˈteɪʃən] *n* : consultation *f*

consume [kənˈsuːm] *vt* **-sumed; -suming** : consommer — **consumer** [kənˈsuːmər] *n* : consommateur *m*, -trice *f* — **consumption** [kənˈsʌmpʃən] *n* : consommation *f*

contact [ˈkɑnˌtækt] *n* **1** TOUCHING : contact *m* **2 be in ~ with** : être en rapport avec **3 business ~** : relation *f* de travail — **~** [ˈkɑnˌtækt, kənˈ-] *vt* : contacter — **contact lens** [ˈkʼnˌtæktˈlɛnz] *n* : lentille *f* (de contact), verre *m* de contact

contagious [kənˈteɪdʒəs] *adj* : contagieux

contain [kənˈteɪn] *vt* **1** : contenir **2 ~ oneself** : se contenir, se maîtriser — **container** [kənˈteɪnər] *n* : récipient *m*

contaminate [kənˈtæmə̩neɪt] *vt* **-nated; -nating** : contaminer — **contamination** [kənˌtæmə̩neɪʃən] *n* : contamination *f*

contemplate [ˈkɑntəm̩pleɪt] *v* **-plated; -plating** *vt* **1** : contempler **2** CONSIDER : envisager, considérer — *vi* : réfléchir — **contemplation** [ˌkɑntəm̩pleɪʃən] *n* : contemplation *f*, réflexion *f*

contemporary [kənˈtɛmpəˌrɛri] *adj* : contemporain — **~** *n, pl* **-raries** : contemporain *m*, -raine *f*

contempt [kənˈtɛmpt] *n* : mépris *m*, dédain *m* — **contemptible** [kənˈtɛmptəbəl] *adj* : méprisable — **contemptuous** [kənˈtɛmptʃuəs] *adj* : méprisant

contend [kənˈtɛnd] *vi* **1** COMPETE : rivaliser **2 ~ with** : faire face à — *vt* : soutenir, maintenir — **contender** [kənˈtɛndər] *n* : concurrent *m*, -rente *f*

content[1] [ˈkɑnˌtɛnt] *n* **1** : contenu *m* **2 table of ~s** : table *f* des matières

content[2] [kənˈtɛnt] *adj* : content — **~** *vt* **~ oneself with** : se contenter de, être satisfait de — **contented** [kənˈtɛntəd] *adj* : content, satisfait

contention [kənˈtɛntʃən] *n* **1** ARGUMENT : dispute *f*, discussion *f* **2** OPINION : affirmation *f*, assertion *f*

contentment [kənˈtɛntmənt] *n* : contentement *m*

contest [kənˈtɛst] *vt* : contester, disputer — **~** [ˈkɑnˌtɛst] *n* **1** STRUGGLE : lutte *f* **2** COMPETITION : concours *m*, compétition *f* — **contestant** [kənˈtɛstənt] *n* : concurrent *m*, -rente *f*

context [ˈkɑnˌtɛkst] *n* : contexte *m*

continent [ˈkɑntənənt] *n* : continent *m* — **continental** [ˌkɑntənˈɛntəl] *adj* : continental

contingency [kənˈtɪndʒəntsi] *n, pl* **-cies** : éventualité *f*

continue [kənˈtɪnjuː] *v* **-ued; -uing** *vt* **1** KEEP UP : continuer (à) **2** RESUME : reprendre — *vi* : continuer — **continual** [kəˈtɪnjuəl] *adj* : continuel — **continuation** [kənˌtɪnjuˈeɪʃən] *n* : continuation *f* — **continuity** [ˌkɑntənˈuːəti, -ˈjuː-] *n, pl* **-ties** : continuité *f* — **continuous** [kənˈtɪnjuəs] *adj* : continu

contort [kənˈtɔrt] *vt* : tordre — **contortion** [kənˈtɔrʃən] *n* : contorsion *f*

contour [ˈkɑnˌtʊr] *n* : contour *m*

contraband [ˈkɑntrəˌbænd] *n* : contrebande *f*

contraception [ˌkɑntrəˈsɛpʃən] *n* : contraception *f* — **contraceptive** [ˌkɑntrəˈsɛptɪv] *adj* : contraceptif — **~** *n* : contraceptif *m*

contract [ˈkɑnˌtrækt] *n* : contrat *m* — **~** [kənˈtrækt] *vt* : contracter — *vi* : se contracter — **contraction** [kənˈtrækʃən] *n* : contraction *f* — **contractor** [ˈkɑnˌtræktər, kənˈtræk-] *n* : entrepreneur *m*, -neuse *f*

contradiction [ˌkɑntrəˈdɪkʃən] *n* : contradiction *f* — **contradict** [ˌkɑntrəˈdɪkt] *vt* : contredire — **contradictory** [ˌkɑntrəˈdɪktəri] *adj* : contradictoire

contraption [kənˈtræpʃən] *n* : truc *m fam*, machin *m fam*

contrary [ˈkɑnˌtrɛri] *n, pl* **-traries 1** : contraire *m* **2 on the ~** : au contraire — **~** *adj* **1** : contraire, opposé **2 ~ to** : contrairement à

contrast [kənˈtræst] *vi* : contraster — **~** [ˈkɑnˌtræst] *n* : contraste *m*

contribute [kənˈtrɪbjət] *v* **-uted; -uting** *vi* : contribuer — *vt* : apporter, donner — **contribution** [ˌkɑntrəˈbjuːʃən] *n* : contribution *f* — **contributor** [kənˈtrɪbjətər] *n* : collaborateur *m*, -trice *f*

contrite [ˈkɑnˌtraɪt, kənˈtraɪt] *adj* : contrit

contrive [kənˈtraɪv] *vt* **-trived; -triving 1** DEVISE : inventer, imaginer **2 ~ to** : parvenir à, réussir à

control [kənˈtroːl] *vt* **-trolled; -trolling 1** RULE, RUN : diriger **2** REGULATE : contrôler, régler **3** RESTRAIN : maîtriser — **~** *n* **1** : contrôle *m*, régulation *f* **2** RESTRAINT : maîtrise *f* **3 remote ~** : commande *f* à distance

controversy [ˈkɑntrəˌvərsi] *n, pl* **-sies**

: controverse f — **controversial** [ˌkɑntrə-ˈvərʃəl, -siəl] adj : controversé

convalescence [ˌkɑnvəˈlɛsənts] n : convalescence f

convene [kənˈviːn] v -vened; -vening vt : convoquer — vi : se réunir

convenience [kənˈviːnjənts] n 1 : commodité f, confort m 2 at your ~ : quand cela vous conviendra — **convenient** [kənˈviːnjənt] adj : commode

convent [ˈkɑnvənt, -ˌvɛnt] n : couvent m

convention [kənˈvɛntʃən] n 1 : convention f 2 CUSTOM : usage m — **conventional** [kənˈvɛntʃənəl] adj : conventionnel

converge [kənˈvərdʒ] vi -verged; -verging : converger

converse[1] [kənˈvərs] vi -versed; -versing ~ with : s'entretenir avec — **conversation** [ˌkɑnvərˈseɪʃən] n : conversation f

converse[2] [kənˈvərs, ˈkɑnˌvərs] n : contraire m, inverse m — **conversely** [kənˈvərsli, ˈkɑnˌvərs-] adv : inversement

conversion [kənˈvərʒən] n : conversion f — **convert** [kənˈvərt] vt : convertir — **convertible** [kənˈvərtəbəl] n : décapotable f

convex [kɑnˈvɛks, ˈkɑnˌ-, kənˈ-] adj : convexe

convey [kənˈveɪ] vt -veyed; -veying : transmettre, exprimer

convict [kənˈvɪkt] vt : déclarer coupable — ~ [ˈkɑnˌvɪkt] n : détenu m, -nue f — **conviction** [kənˈvɪkʃən] n 1 : condamnation f 2 BELIEF : conviction f

convince [kənˈvɪnts] vt -vinced; -vincing : convaincre, persuader — **convincing** [kənˈvɪntsɪŋ] adj : convaincant

convoluted [ˈkɑnvəˌluːtəd] adj : compliqué

convulsion [kənˈvʌlʃən] n : convulsion f

cook [ˈkʊk] n : cuisinier m, -nière f — ~ vi : cuisiner, faire la cuisine — vt : préparer (de la nourriture) — **cookbook** [ˈkʊkˌbʊk] n : livre m de recettes

cookie or **cooky** [ˈkʊki] n, pl -ies : biscuit m, gâteau m sec

cooking [ˈkʊkɪŋ] n : cuisine f

cool [ˈkuːl] adj 1 : frais 2 CALM : calme 3 UNFRIENDLY : indifférent, froid — ~ vt : refroidir — vi or ~ down : se refroidir — ~ n 1 : fraîcheur m 2 lose one's ~ : perdre son sang-froid — **cooler** [ˈkuːlər] n : glacière f — **coolness** [ˈkuːlnəs] n : fraîcheur f

coop [ˈkuːp, ˈkʊp] n or **chicken** ~ : poulailler m — ~ vt or ~ up : enfermer

cooperate [koˈɑpəˌreɪt] vi -ated; -ating : coopérer — **cooperation** [koˌɑpəˈreɪʃən] n : coopération f — **cooperative** [koˈɑpərətɪv, -ˈɑpəˌreɪtɪv] adj : coopératif

coordinate [koˈɔrdənˌeɪt] vt -nated; -nating : coordonner — **coordination** [koˌɔrdənˈeɪʃən] n : coordination f

cop [ˈkɑp] n 1 : flic m fam 2 the ~s : la police fam

cope [ˈkoːp] vi coped, coping 1 : se débrouiller 2 ~ with : faire face à

copious [ˈkoːpiəs] adj : copieux

copper [ˈkɑpər] n : cuivre m

copy [ˈkɑpi] n, pl **copies** 1 : copie f, reproduction f 2 : exemplaire m (d'un livre, etc.) — ~ **copied; copying** 1 : faire une copie de 2 IMITATE : copier — **copyright** [ˈkɑpiˌraɪt] n : droits mpl d'auteur

coral [ˈkɔrəl] n : corail m

cord [ˈkɔrd] n : corde f, cordon m

cordial [ˈkɔrdʒəl] adj : cordial, amical

corduroy [ˈkɔrdəˌrɔɪ] n : velours m côtelé

core [ˈkor] n 1 : trognon m (d'un fruit) 2 CENTER : cœur m, centre m

cork [ˈkɔrk] n 1 : liège m 2 : bouchon m (d'une bouteille) — **corkscrew** [ˈkɔrkˌskruː] n : tire-bouchon m

corn [ˈkɔrn] n 1 : grain m (de blé, etc.) 2 or **Indian** ~ : maïs m 3 : cor m (sur le pied) — **corncob** [ˈkɔrnˌkɑb] n : épi m de maïs

corner [ˈkɔrnər] n 1 : coin m, angle m 2 **around the** ~ : à deux pas d'ici — **cornerstone** [ˈkɔrnərˌstoːn] n : pierre f angulaire

cornmeal [ˈkɔrnˌmiːl] n : farine f de maïs — **cornstarch** [ˈkɔrnˌstɑrtʃ] n : fécule f de maïs

corny [ˈkɔrni] adj cornier; -est : banal, à l'eau de rose

coronary [ˈkɔrəˌnɛri] n, pl -naries : infarctus m

coronation [ˌkɔrəˈneɪʃən] n : couronnement m

corporal [ˈkɔrpərəl] n : caporal-chef m

corporation [ˌkɔrpəˈreɪʃən] n : compagnie f commerciale, société f — **corporate** [ˈkɔrpərət] adj : d'entreprise

corps [ˈkor] n, pl **corps** [ˈkorz] : corps m

corpse [ˈkɔrps] n : cadavre m

corpulent [ˈkɔrpjələnt] adj : corpulent, gras

corral [kəˈræl] n : corral m

correct [kəˈrɛkt] vt : corriger — ~ adj 1 : juste, correct 2 **that's** ~ : c'est exact — **correction** [kəˈrɛkʃən] n : correction f

correlation [ˌkɔrəˈleɪʃən] n : corrélation f

correspond [ˌkɔrəˈspɑnd] vi : correspondre — **correspondence** [ˌkɔrəˈspɑndənts] n : correspondance f — **correspondent** [ˌkɔrəˈspɑndənt] n 1 : correspondant m, -dante f 2 REPORTER : journaliste mf

corridor [ˈkɔrədər, -ˌdɔr] n : corridor m

corroborate [kəˈrɑbəˌreɪt] vt -rated; -rating : corroborer

corrode [kəˈroːd] vt -roded; -roding : corroder — **corrosion** [kəˈroɪʒn] n : corrosion f

corrugated [ˈkɔrəˌgeɪtəd] *adj* : ondulé

corrupt [kəˈrʌpt] *vt* : corrompre — ~ *adj* : corrumpu — **corruption** [kəˈrʌpʃən] *n* : corruption *f*

cosmetic [kʊzˈmɛtɪk] *n* : cosmétique *f* — ~ *adj* : cosmétique

cosmic [ˈkʊzmɪk] *adj* : cosmique

cosmopolitan [ˌkʊzməˈpɑlətən] *adj* : cosmopolite

cosmos [ˈkʊzməs, -ˌmoːs, -ˌmɑs] *n* : cosmos *m*, univers *m*

cost [ˈkɔst] *n* : coût *m*, prix *m* — ~ *vi* **cost; costing 1** : coûter **2 how much does it ~?** : combien ça coûte? — **costly** [ˈkɔstli] *adj* **-lier; -est** : coûteux, cher

costume [ˈkɑsˌtuːm, -ˌtjuːm] *n* : costume *m*

cot [ˈkɑt] *n* : lit *m* de camp

cottage [ˈkɑtɪʤ] *n* : petite maison *f* — **cottage cheese** *n* : fromage *m* blanc

cotton [ˈkɑtən] *n* : coton *m*

couch [ˈkaʊtʃ] *n* : canapé *m*, sofa *m*

cough [ˈkɔf] *vi* : tousser — ~ *n* : toux *f*

could [ˈkʊd] → **can**[1]

council [ˈkaʊntsəl] *n* : conseil *m*, assemblée *f* — **councillor** *or* **councilor** [ˈkaʊntsələr] *n* : conseiller *m*, -lère *f*

counsel [ˈkaʊntsəl] *n* **1** ADVICE : conseil *m* **2** LAWYER : avocat *m*, -cate *f* — ~ *vt* **-seled** *or* **-selled; -seling** *or* **-selling** : conseiller, guider — **counselor** *or* **counsellor** [ˈkaʊntsələr] *n* **1** : conseiller *m*, -lère *f* **2** *or* **camp ~** : moniteur *m*, -trice *f*

count[1] [ˈkaʊnt] *vt* : compter, énumérer — *vi* **1** : compter **2 ~ on** : compter sur — ~ *n* : compte *m*, décompte *m*

count[2] *n* : comte *m* (noble)

counter[1] [ˈkaʊntər] *n* **1** : comptoir *m* **2** TOKEN : jeton *m*

counter[2] *vt* : s'opposer à, contrecarrer — *vi* : riposter — ~ *adv* **~ to** : à l'encontre de — **counteract** [ˌkaʊntərˈækt] *vt* : neutraliser — **counterattack** [ˈkaʊntərəˌtæk] *n* : contre-attaque *f* — **counterbalance** [ˌkaʊntərˈbælənts] *n* : contrepoids *m* — **counterclockwise** [ˌkaʊntərˈklɑkˌwaɪz] *adv & adj* : dans le sens contraire des aiguilles d'une montre — **counterfeit** [ˈkaʊntərˌfɪt] *vt* : contrefaire — ~ *adj* : faux — **counterpart** [ˈkaʊntərˌpɑrt] *n* : homologue *mf* (d'une personne), équivalent *m* (d'une chose)

countess [ˈkaʊntɪs] *n* : comtesse *f*

countless [ˈkaʊntləs] *adj* : innombrable, incalculable

country [ˈkʌntri] *n*, *pl* **-tries 1** NATION : pays *m*, patrie *f* **2** COUNTRYSIDE : campagne *f* — ~ *adj* : champêtre, rural — **countryside** [ˈkʌntriˌsaɪd] *n* : campagne *f*

county [ˈkaʊnti] *n*, *pl* **-ties** : comté *m*

coup [ˈkuː] *n*, *pl* **coups** [ˈkuːz] *or* **~ d'état** : coup *m* d'état

couple [ˈkʌpəl] *n* **1** : couple *m* **2 a ~ of** : deux ou trois — ~ *v* **-pled; -pling** *vt* : accoupler — *vi* : s'accoupler

coupon [ˈkuːˌpɑn, ˈkjuː-] *n* : coupon *m*

courage [ˈkərɪʤ] *n* : courage *m* — **courageous** [kəˈreɪʤəs] *adj* : courageux

courier [ˈkʊriər, ˈkəriər] *n* : messager *m*, -gère *f*

course [ˈkors] *n* **1** : cours *m* **2** : service *m*, plat *m* (au restaurant) **3 ~ of action** : ligne *f* de conduite **4 golf ~** : terrain *m* de golf **5 in the ~ of** : au cours de **6 of ~** : bien sûr

court [ˈkort] *n* **1** : cour *f* (d'un souverain, etc.) **2** : court *m*, terrain *m* (de sports) **3** TRIBUNAL : cour *f*, tribunal *m* — ~ *vt* : courtiser, faire la cour à

courteous [ˈkərtiəs] *adj* : courtois, poli — **courtesy** [ˈkərtəsi] *n*, *pl* **-sies** : courtoisie *f*

courthouse [ˈkortˌhaʊs] *n* : palais *m* de justice — **courtroom** [ˈkortˌruːm] *n* : salle *f* de tribunal

courtship [ˈkortˌʃɪp] *n* : cour *f*

courtyard [ˈkortˌjard] *n* : cour *f*, patio *m*

cousin [ˈkʌzən] *n* : cousin *m*, -sine *f*

cove [ˈkoːv] *n* : anse *f*

covenant [ˈkʌvənənt] *n* : contrat *m*, convention *f*

cover [ˈkʌvər] *vt* **1** : couvrir, recouvrir **2** *or* **~ up** : cacher **3** DEAL WITH : traiter **4** : parcourir (une distance) **5** INSURE : assurer — ~ *n* **1** LID : couvercle *m* **2** SHELTER : abri *m*, refuge *m* **3** : couverture *f* (d'un livre) **4 ~s** *npl* BEDCLOTHES : couvertures *fpl* — **coverage** [ˈkʌvərɪʤ] *n* : reportage *m*, couverture *f* — **covert** [ˈkoːˌvərt, ˈkʌvərt] *adj* : voilé, secret — **cover-up** [ˈkʌvərˌʌp] *n* : opération *f* de camouflage

covet [ˈkʌvət] *vt* : convoiter — **covetous** [ˈkʌvətəs] *adj* : avide, cupide

cow [ˈkaʊ] *n* : vache *f*

coward [ˈkaʊərd] *n* : lâche *mf*; poltron *m*, -tronne *f* — **cowardice** [ˈkaʊərdɪs] *n* : lâcheté *f* — **cowardly** [ˈkaʊərdli] *adj* : lâche

cowboy [ˈkaʊˌbɔɪ] *n* : cow-boy *m*

cower [ˈkaʊər] *vi* : se recroqueviller

coy [ˈkɔɪ] *adj* : faussement timide

coyote [kaɪˈoːti, ˈkaɪˌoːt] *n*, *pl* **coyotes** *or* **coyote** : coyote *m*

cozy [ˈkoːzi] *adj* **-zier; -est** : douillet, confortable

crab [ˈkræb] *n* : crabe *m*

crack [ˈkræk] *vt* **1** SPLIT : fêler, fendre **2** : casser (un œuf, etc.) **3** : faire claquer (un fouet) **4 ~ down on** : sévir contre — *vi* **1** SPLIT : se fêler, se fendre **2** BREAK : se casser, muer (se dit de la voix) — ~ *n* **1**

: craquement *m*, bruit *m* sec **2** CREVICE : crevasse *f*, fissure *f*

cracker ['krækər] *n* : biscuit *m* salé

crackle ['krækəl] *vi* **-led; -ling** : crépiter, pétiller — **~** *n* : crépitement *m*

cradle ['kreɪdəl] *n* : berceau *m* — **~** *vt* **-dled; -dling** : bercer (un enfant)

craft ['kræft] *n* **1** TRADE : métier *m*, art *m* **2** CUNNING : ruse *f* **3** *pl usu* **craft** BOAT : embarcation *f* — **craftsman** ['kræftsmən] *n, pl* **-men** [-mən, -ˌmɛn] : artisan *m*, -sane *f* — **craftsmanship** ['kræftsmənˌʃɪp] *n* : artisanat *m* — **crafty** ['kræfti] *adj* **craftier; -est** : astucieux, rusé

cram ['kræm] *v* **crammed; cramming** *vt* : fourrer, entasser — *vi* : étudier à la dernière minute

cramp ['kræmp] *n* : crampe *f*

cranberry ['krænˌbɛri] *n, pl* **-ries** : canneberge *f*

crane ['kreɪn] *n* : grue *f* — **~** *vt* **craned; craning** : tendre (le cou, etc.)

crank ['kræŋk] *n* **1** : manivelle *f* **2** ECCENTRIC : excentrique *mf* — **cranky** ['kræŋki] *adj* **crankier; -est** : irritable

crash ['kræʃ] *vi* **1** : se fracasser, s'écraser **2** : faire faillite (se dit d'une banque), s'effondrer (se dit du marché) — *vt* **~** one's car : avoir un accident de voiture — **~** *n* **1** : fracas *m*, bruit *m* sourd **2** COLLISION : accident *m*

crass ['kræs] *adj* : grossier

crate ['kreɪt] *n* : cageot *m*, caisse *f*

crater ['kreɪtər] *n* : cratère *m*

crave ['kreɪv] *vt* **craved; craving** : désirer, avoir très envie de — **craving** ['kreɪvɪŋ] *n* : envie *f* (incontrôlable), soif *f*

crawl ['krɔl] *vi* : ramper, marcher à quatre pattes — **~** *n* at a **~** : à un pas de tortue

crayon ['kreɪˌɑn, -ən] *n* : crayon *m* de cire

craze ['kreɪz] *n* : mode *f* passagère

crazy ['kreɪzi] *adj* **-zier; -est 1** : fou **2** go **~** : devenir fou — **craziness** ['kreɪzinəs] *n* : folie *f*

creak ['kri:k] *vi* : grincer, craquer — **~** *n* : grincement *m*

cream ['kri:m] *n* : crème *f* — **creamy** ['kri:mi] *adj* **creamier; -est** : crémeux

crease ['kri:s] *n* : (faux) pli *m* — **~** *v* **creased; creasing** *vt* : froisser — *vi* : se froisser

create [kri'eɪt] *vt* **-ated; -ating** : créer — **creation** [kri'eɪʃən] *n* : création *f* — **creative** [kri'eɪtɪv] *adj* : créateur — **creator** [kri'eɪtər] *n* : créateur *m*, -trice *f*

creature ['kri:tʃər] *n* : créature *f*

credence ['kri:dənts] *n* give **~** to : accorder du crédit à

credentials [krɪ'dɛntʃəlz] *npl* : références *fpl*

credible ['krɛdəbəl] *adj* : crédible — **credibility** [ˌkrɛdə'bɪləti] *n* : crédibilité *f*

credit ['krɛdɪt] *n* **1** : crédit *m* **2** RECOGNITION : mérite *m* **3** to his **~** : à son honneur — **~** *vt* **1** : créditer (un compte de banque) **2** **with** : attribuer à — **credit card** *n* : carte *f* de crédit — **creditor** ['krɛdɪtər] *n* : créancier *m*, -cière *f*

credulous ['krɛdʒələs] *adj* : crédule

creed ['kri:d] *n* : credo *m*

creek ['kri:k, 'krɪk] *n* : ruisseau *m*

creep ['kri:p] *vi* **crept** ['krɛpt]; **creeping 1** CRAWL : ramper **2** : avancer sans un bruit — **~** *n* **1** **~s** *npl* : frissons *mpl*, chair *f* de poule **2** **move at a ~** : avancer au ralenti

cremate ['kri:ˌmeɪt] *vt* **-mated; -mating** : incinérer

crescent ['krɛsənt] *n* : croissant *m*

cress ['krɛs] *n* : cresson *m*

crest ['krɛst] *n* : crête *f*

crevice ['krɛvɪs] *n* : fissure *f*, fente *f*

crew ['kru:] *n* **1** : équipage *m* (d'un navire) **2** TEAM : équipe *f*

crib ['krɪb] *n* : lit *m* d'enfant

cricket ['krɪkət] *n* **1** : grillon *m* (insecte) **2** : cricket *m* (jeu)

crime ['kraɪm] *n* : crime *m*, délit *m* — **criminal** ['krɪmənəl] *adj* : criminel — **~** *n* : criminel *m*, -nelle *f*

cringe ['krɪndʒ] *vi* **cringed; cringing** : reculer (devant)

crinkle ['krɪŋkəl] *vt* **-kled; -kling** : froisser, chiffonner

cripple ['krɪpəl] *vt* **-pled; -pling 1** DISABLE : estropier **2** INCAPACITATE : paralyser

crisis ['kraɪsɪs] *n, pl* **-ses** [-ˌsi:z] : crise *f*

crisp ['krɪsp] *adj* : croustillant, croquant — **crispy** ['krɪspi] *adj* **crispier; -est** : croustillant, croquant

crisscross ['krɪsˌkrɔs] *vt* : entrecroiser

criterion [kraɪ'tɪriən] *n, pl* **-ria** [-riə] : critère *m*

critic ['krɪtɪk] *n* : critique *mf* — **critical** ['krɪtɪkəl] *adj* : critique — **criticism** ['krɪtəˌsɪzəm] *n* : critique *f* — **criticize** ['krɪtəˌsaɪz] *vt* **-cized; -cizing** : critiquer

croak ['kro:k] *vi* : coasser

crockery ['krɑkəri] *n* : faïence *f*

crocodile ['krɑkəˌdaɪl] *n* : crocodile *m*

crony ['kro:ni] *n, pl* **-nies** : copain *m*, -pine *f*

crook ['krʊk] *n* **1** STAFF : houlette *f* (d'un berger) **2** THIEF : escroc *m* **3** BEND : courbe *f* — **crooked** ['krʊkəd] *adj* **1** BENT : crochu, courbé **2** DISHONEST : malhonnête

crop ['krɑp] *n* **1** HARVEST : récolte *f*, moisson *f* **2** PRODUCE : culture *f* — **~** *v* **cropped; cropping** *vt* TRIM : tailler — *vi* **~** **up** : surgir, se présenter

cross ['krɔs] *n* : croix *f* — **~** *vt* **1** : traverser (la rue, etc.) **2** CROSSBREED : croiser **3** OP-POSE : contrarier **4** : croiser (les bras, etc.) **5** ~ **out** : rayer — ~ *adj* **1** ANGRY : fâché, contrarié **2** ~ **street** : rue *f* transversale — ~~crossbreed~~ ['krɔs,briːd] *vt* ~~-bred~~ [-bred]; **-breeding** : croiser (deux espèces) — **cross-eyed** ['krɔs,aɪd] *adj* : qui louche — **cross fire** *n* : feux *mpl* croisés — **crossing** ['krɔsɪŋ] *n* **1** : croisement *m* **2** → **crosswalk** — **cross-reference** [,krɔs'refrən/s, -'refərən/s] *n* : renvoi *m* — **crossroads** ['krɔs,roːdz] *n* : carrefour *m* — **cross section** *n* **1** : coupe *f* transversale **2** SAMPLE : échantillon *m* — **crosswalk** ['krɔs,wɔk] *n* : passage *m* pour piétons — **crossword puzzle** ['krɔs,wərd] *n* : mots *mpl* croisés

crotch ['krɑʧ] *n* : entre-jambes *m*

crouch ['krauʧ] *vi* : s'accroupir

crow ['kroː] *n* : corbeau *m* — ~ *vi* **crowed** *or Brit* **crew; crowing** : chanter (se dit du coq)

crowbar ['kroː,bɑr] *n* : (pince à) levier *m*

crowd ['kraud] *vi* : se presser, s'entasser — *vt* : serrer, entasser — ~ *n* : foule *f*

crown ['kraun] *n* : couronne *f* — ~ *vt* : couronner

crucial ['kruːʃəl] *adj* : crucial

crucify ['kruːsə,faɪ] *vt* **-fied; -fying** : crucifier — **crucifix** ['kruːsə,fɪks] *n* : crucifix *m* — **crucifixion** [,kruːsə'fɪkʃən] *n* : crucifixion *f*

crude ['kruːd] *adj* **cruder; crudest 1** RAW : brut **2** VULGAR : grossier **3** ROUGH : rudimentaire

cruel ['kruːəl] *adj* **-eler** *or* **-eller; -elest** *or* **-ellest** : cruel — **cruelty** ['kruːəlti] *n, pl* **-ties** : cruauté *f*

cruet ['kruːɪt] *n* : huilier *m*, vinaigrier *m*

cruise ['kruːz] *vi* **cruised; cruising** : rouler à sa vitesse de croisière — ~ *n* : croisière *f* — **cruiser** ['kruːzər] *n* **1** WARSHIP : croiseur *m* **2** *or* **police** ~ : véhicule *m* de police

crumb ['krʌm] *n* : miette *f*

crumble ['krʌmbəl] *v* **-bled; -bling** *vt* : émietter — *vi* : s'émietter, s'effriter

crumple ['krʌmpəl] *vt* **-pled; -pling** : froisser, chiffonner

crunch ['krʌnʧ] *vt* : croquer — **crunchy** ['krʌnʧi] *adj* **crunchier; -est** : croquant

crusade [kruː'seɪd] *n* : croisade *f*, campagne *f*

crush ['krʌʃ] *vt* : écraser, aplatir — ~ *n* **have a** ~ **on s.o.** : avoir le béguin pour qqn

crust ['krʌst] *n* : croûte *f*

crutch ['krʌʧ] *n* : béquille *f*

crux ['krʌks, kruks] *n* : point *m* crucial, cœur *m*

cry ['kraɪ] *vi* **cried; crying 1** SHOUT : crier,

pousser un cri **2** WEEP : pleurer — ~ *n, pl* **cries** : cri *m*

crypt ['krɪpt] *n* : crypte *f*

crystal ['krɪstəl] *n* : cristal *m*

cub ['kʌb] *n* : petit *m* (d'un animal)

cube ['kjuːb] *n* : cube *m* — **cubic** ['kjuːbɪk] *adj* : cube, cubique

cubicle ['kjuːbɪkəl] *n* : box *m*

cuckoo ['kuːˌkuː, 'kuː-] *n, pl* **-oos** : coucou *m* (oiseau)

cucumber ['kjuːˌkʌmbər] *n* : concombre *m*

cuddle ['kʌdəl] *v* **-dled; -dling** *vt* : caresser, câliner — *vi* : se câliner

cudgel ['kʌʤəl] *n* : gourdin *m*, trique *f*

cue[1] ['kjuː] *n* SIGNAL : signal *m*

cue[2] *n or* ~ **stick** : queue *f* de billard

cuff ['kʌf] *n* : poignet *m* (de chemise), revers *m* (de pantalon)

cuisine [kwɪ'ziːn] *n* : cuisine *f*

culinary ['kʌləˌneri, 'kjuːlə-] *adj* : culinaire

cull ['kʌl] *vt* : choisir, sélectionner

culminate ['kʌlməˌneɪt] *vi* **-nated; -nating** : culminer — **culmination** [,kʌlmə'neɪʃən] *n* : point *m* culminant

culprit ['kʌlprɪt] *n* : coupable *mf*

cult ['kʌlt] *n* : culte *m*

cultivate ['kʌltəˌveɪt] *vt* **-vated; -vating** : cultiver — **cultivation** [,kʌltə'veɪʃən] *n* : culture *f* (de la terre)

culture ['kʌlʧər] *n* : culture *f* — **cultural** ['kʌlʧərəl] *adj* : culturel — **cultured** ['kʌltlərd] *adj* : cultivé

cumbersome ['kʌmbərsəm] *adj* : encombrant

cumulative ['kjuːmjələtɪv, -ˌleɪtɪv] *adj* : cumulatif

cunning ['kʌnɪŋ] *adj* : astucieux — ~ *n* : ruse *f*, astuce *f*

cup ['kʌp] *n* **1** : tasse *f* **2** TROPHY : coupe *f*

cupboard ['kʌbərd] *n* : placard *m*, armoire *f*

curator ['kjurˌeɪtər, kju'reɪtər] *n* : conservateur *m*, -trice *f*

curb ['kərb] *n* **1** RESTRAINT : contrainte *f*, frein *m* **2** : bord *m* du trottoir — ~ *vt* : mettre un frein à

curdle ['kərdəl] *vi* **-dled; -dling** : (se) cailler

cure ['kjur] *n* : remède *m* — ~ *vt* **cured; curing** : guérir

curfew ['kərˌfjuː] *n* : couvre-feu *m*

curious ['kjuriəs] *adj* : curieux — **curiosity** [,kjuri'ɑsəti] *n, pl* **-ties** : curiosité *f*

curl ['kərl] *vt* **1** : friser, boucler **2** COIL : enrouler — *vi* **1** : boucler (se dit des cheveux) **2** ~ **up** : se pelotonner — ~ *n* : boucle *f* (de cheveux) — **curler** ['kərlər] *n* : bigoudi *m* — **curly** ['kərli] *adj* **curlier; -est** : bouclé, frisé

currant ['kərənt] *n* **1** BERRY : groseille *f* **2** RAISIN : raisin *m* de Corinthe

currency [ˈkərəntsi] *n, pl* **-cies 1** : monnaie *f*, devise *f* **2 gain** ~ : se répandre

current [ˈkərənt] *adj* **1** PRESENT : en cours **2** PREVALENT : courant, commun — ~ *n* **1** ⌶⌶⌶⌶⌶ *⌶⌶*

curriculum [kəˈrɪkjələm] *n, pl* **-la** [-lə] : programme *m* (scolaire)

curry [ˈkəri] *n, pl* **-ries** : curry *m*

curse [ˈkərs] *n* : malédiction *f* — ~ *v* **cursed; cursing** *vt* : maudire — *vi* SWEAR : sacrer, jurer

cursor [ˈkərsər] *n* : curseur *m*

cursory [ˈkərsəri] *adj* : superficiel, hâtif

curt [ˈkərt] *adj* : brusque

curtail [kərˈteɪl] *vt* : écourter

curtain [ˈkərtən] *n* : rideau *m*

curtsy [ˈkərtsi] *vi* **-sied;** *or* **-seyed;** *or* **-sying** *or* **-seying** : faire une révérence — ~ *n* : révérence *f*

curve [ˈkərv] *v* **curved; curving** *vt* : courber — *vi* : se courber, faire une courbe — ~ *n* : courbe *f*

cushion [ˈkʊʃən] *n* : coussin *m* — ~ *vt* : amortir

custard [ˈkʌstərd] *n* : flan *m*

custody [ˈkʌstədi] *n, pl* **-dies 1** CARE : garde *f* **2 be in** ~ : être en détention

custom [ˈkʌstəm] *n* : coutume *f*, tradition *f* — ~ *adj* : fait sur commande — **custom-**

ary [ˈkʌstəˌmɛri] *adj* : habituel, coutumier — **customer** [ˈkʌstəmər] *n* : client *m*, cliente *f* — **customs** [ˈkʌstˈmz] *npl* : douane *f*

cut [ˈkʌt] *v* **cut; cutting** *vt* **1** ⌶⌶⌶⌶⌶ **2** REDUCE : réduire **3** ~ **oneself** : se couper (le doigt, etc.) **4** *or* ~ **up** : découper — *vi* **1** : couper **2** ~ **in** : interrompre — ~ *n* **1** : coupure *f* **2** REDUCTION : réduction *f*

cute [ˈkjuːt] *adj* **cuter; cutest** : mignon, joli

cutlery [ˈkʌtləri] *n* : couverts *mpl*

cutlet [ˈkʌtlət] *n* : escalope *f*

cutting [ˈkʌtɪŋ] *adj* **1** : cinglant (se dit du vent) **2** CURT : mordant, tranchant

cyanide [ˈsaɪəˌnaɪd, -nɪd] *n* : cyanure *m*

cycle [ˈsaɪkəl] *n* : cycle *m* — ~ *vi* **-cled; -cling** : faire de la bicyclette — **cyclic** [ˈsaɪklɪk, ˈsɪ-] *or* **cyclical** [-klɪkəl] *adj* : cyclique — **cyclist** [ˈsaɪklɪst] *n* : cycliste *mf*

cyclone [ˈsaɪˌkloːn] *n* : cyclone *m*

cylinder [ˈsɪləndər] *n* : cylindre *m* — **cylindrical** [səˈlɪndrɪkəl] *adj* : cylindrique

cymbal [ˈsɪmbəl] *n* : cymbale *f*

cynic [ˈsɪnɪk] *n* : cynique *mf* — **cynical** [ˈsɪnɪkəl] *adj* : cynique — **cynicism** [ˈsɪnəˌsɪzəm] *n* : cynisme *m*

cypress [ˈsaɪprəs] *n* : cyprès *m*

cyst [ˈsɪst] *n* : kyste *m*

czar [ˈzɑr, ˈsɑr] *n* : tsar *m*

D

d [ˈdiː] *n, pl* **d's** *or* **ds** [ˈdiːz] : d *m*, quatrième lettre de l'alphabet

dab [ˈdæb] *n* : touche *f*, petite quantité *f* — ~ *vt* **dabbed; dabbing** : appliquer délicatement

dabble [ˈdæbəl] *vi* **-bled; -bling** ~ **in** : s'intéresser superficiellement à

dad [ˈdæd] *n* : papa *m fam* — **daddy** [ˈdædi] *n, pl* **-dies** : papa *m fam*

daffodil [ˈdæfəˌdɪl] *n* : jonquille *f*

dagger [ˈdægər] *n* : poignard *m*

daily [ˈdeɪli] *adj* : quotidien — ~ *adv* : quotidiennement

dainty [ˈdeɪnti] *adj* **-tier; -est** : délicat

dairy [ˈdæri] *n, pl* **dairies** : laiterie *f*, crémerie *f France*

daisy [ˈdeɪzi] *n, pl* **-sies** : marguerite *f*

dam [ˈdæm] *n* : barrage *m*

damage [ˈdæmɪdʒ] *n* **1** : dégâts *mpl* **2** ~**s** *npl* : dommages *mpl* et intérêts *mpl* — ~ *vt* **-aged; -aging** : endommager (des objets), abîmer (sa santé)

damn [ˈdæm] *vt* **1** CONDEMN : condamner **2** CURSE : maudire — ~ *n* **not give a** ~ : s'en ficher *fam* — ~ *or* **damned** [ˈdæmd] *adj* : fichu *fam*, sacré *fam*

damp [ˈdæmp] *adj* : humide, moite — **dampen** [ˈdæmpən] *vt* **1** MOISTEN : humecter **2** DISCOURAGE : décourager — **dampness** [ˈdæmpnəs] *n* : humidité *f*

dance [ˈdænts] *v* **danced; dancing** : danser — ~ *n* : danse *f* — **dancer** [ˈdæntsər] *n* : danseur *m*, -seuse *f*

dandelion [ˈdændlˌaɪən] *n* : pissenlit *m*

dandruff [ˈdændrəf] *n* : pellicules *fpl*

danger [ˈdeɪndʒər] *n* : danger *m* — **dangerous** [ˈdeɪndʒərəs] *adj* : dangereux

dangle [ˈdæŋɡəl] *v* **-gled; -gling** *vi* HANG : pendre — *vt* : balancer, laisser pendre

dank [ˈdæŋk] *adj* : froid et humide

dare [ˈdær] *v* **dared; daring** *vt* : défier — *vi* : oser — ~ *n* : défi *m* — **daring** [ˈdeɪrɪŋ] *adj* : audacieux, hardi

dark [ˈdɑrk] *adj* **1** : noir **2** : foncé (se dit des

cheveux, etc.) **3** GLOOMY : sombre **4 get ~** : faire nuit — **darken** ['dɑrkən] *vt* : obscurcir — *vi* : s'obscurcir — **darkness** ['dɑrknəs] *n* : obscurité *f*, noirceur *f Can*

darling ['dɑrlɪŋ] *n* BELOVED : chéri *m*, -rie *f* — *~ adj* : chéri

darn ['dɑrn] *vt* : repriser (en couture) — *~ adj* : sacré

dart ['dɑrt] *n* **1** : fléchette *f*, dard *m Can* **2 ~s** *npl* : fléchettes *fpl* (jeu) — *~ vi* : se précipiter, s'élancer

dash ['dæʃ] *vt ~* **off** : terminer à la hâte — *vi* : se précipiter — *~ n* **1** : tiret *m* (signe de ponctuation) **2** PINCH : pincée *f*, soupçon *m* **3** RUSH : course *f* folle — **dashboard** ['dæʃ,bord] *n* : tableau *m* de bord — **dashing** ['dæʃɪŋ] *adj* : fringant, élégant

data ['deɪt̬ə, 'dæ-, 'dɑ-] *ns & pl* : données *fpl* — **database** ['deɪt̬ə,beɪs, 'dæ-, 'dɑ-] *n* : base *f* de données

date[1] ['deɪt] *n* : datte *f* (fruit)

date[2] *n* **1** : date *f* **2** APPOINTMENT : rendez-vous *m* — *~ vt* **dated; dating** *vt* **1** : dater (un chèque, etc.) **2** : sortir avec (qqn) — *vi ~* **from** : dater de, remonter à — **dated** ['deɪt̬əd] *adj* : démodé

daughter ['dɔt̬ər] *n* : fille *f* — **daughter–in-law** ['dɔt̬ərɪn,lɔ] *n, pl* **daughters–in–law** : belle-fille *f*, bru *f*

daunt ['dɔnt] *vt* : décourager

dawdle ['dɑdəl] *vi* **-dled; -dling** : lambiner *fam*, traîner

dawn ['dɔn] *vi* **1** : se lever (se dit du jour) **2 it ~ed on him that** : il s'est rendu compte que — *~ n* : aube *f*

day ['deɪ] *n* **1** : jour *m* **2** *or* **working ~** : journée *f* (de travail) **3 the ~ before** : la veille **4 the ~ before yesterday** : avant-hier **5 the ~ after** : le lendemain **6 the ~ after tomorrow** : après-demain — **daybreak** ['deɪ,breɪk] *n* : aube *f* — **daydream** ['deɪ,dri:m] *n* : rêve *m*, rêverie *f* — *~ vi* : rêver — **daylight** ['deɪ,laɪt] *n* : lumière *f* du jour — **daytime** ['deɪ,taɪm] *n* : jour *m*, journée *f*

daze ['deɪz] *vt* **dazed; dazing** : abasourdir — *~ n* **in a ~** : hébété

dazzle ['dæzəl] *vt* **-zled; -zling** : éblouir

dead ['dɛd] *adj* : mort — *~ n* **the ~** : les morts — *~ adv* COMPLETELY : complètement — **deaden** ['dɛdən] *vt* **1** : calmer (une douleur) **2** MUFFLE : assourdir — **dead end** ['dɛd'ɛnd] *n* : cul-de-sac *m*, impasse *f* — **deadline** ['dɛd,laɪn] *n* : date *f* limite — **deadly** ['dɛdli] *adj* **-lier; -est** : mortel — **dealings** ['di:lɪŋz] *npl* : transactions *fpl*, affaires *fpl*

deaf ['dɛf] *adj* : sourd — **deafen** ['dɛfən] *vt* : assourdir — **deafness** ['dɛfnəs] *n* : surdité *f*

deal ['di:l] *n* **1** TRANSACTION : affaire *f*, marché *m* **2** : donne *f* (aux cartes) — *~ v* **dealt; dealing** *vt* **1** : donner **2** : distribuer (des cartes) **3 ~ a blow** : assener un coup — *vi ~* **with** CONCERN : traiter de — **dealer** ['di:lər] *n* : marchand *m*, -chande *f*; négociant *m*, -ciante *f*

dean ['di:n] *n* : doyen *m*, doyenne *f*

dear ['dɪr] *adj* : cher — *~ n* : chéri *m*, -rie *f* — **dearly** ['dɪrli] *adv* : beaucoup

death ['dɛθ] *n* : mort *f*

debate [dɪ'beɪt] *n* : débat *m*, discussion *f* — *~ v* **-bated; -bating** : discuter

debit ['dɛbɪt] *vt* : débiter — *~ n* : débit *m*

debris [də'bri:, deɪ-; 'deɪ,bri:] *n, pl* **-bris** [-'bri:z, -,bri:z] : décombres *mpl*

debt ['dɛt] *n* : dette *f*

debug [,di:'bʌg] *vt* : déboguer

debut [deɪ'bju:, 'deɪ,bju:] *n* : débuts *mpl* — *~ vi* : débuter

decade ['dɛ,keɪd, dɛ'keɪd] *n* : décennie *f*

decadence ['dɛkədənts] *n* : décadence *f* — **decadent** ['dɛkədənt] *adj* : décadent

decanter [dɪ'kæntər] *n* : carafe *f*

decay [dɪ'keɪ] *vi* **1** DECOMPOSE : se décomposer, pourrir **2** : se carier (se dit d'une dent) — *~ n* **1** : pourriture *f* **2** *or* **tooth ~** : carie *f* (dentaire)

deceased [dɪ'si:st] *adj* : décédé, défunt — *~ n* **the ~** : le défunt, la défunte

deceive [dɪ'si:v] *v* **-ceived; -ceiving** : tromper — **deceit** [dɪ'si:t] *n* : tromperie *f* — **deceitful** [dɪ'si:tfəl] *adj* : trompeur

December [dɪ'sɛmbər] *n* : décembre *m*

decent ['di:sənt] *adj* **1** : décent, convenable **2** KIND : bien, aimable — **decency** ['di:səntsi] *n, pl* **-cies** : décence *f*

deception [dɪ'sɛpʃən] *n* : tromperie *f* — **deceptive** [dɪ'sɛptɪv] *adj* : trompeur

decide [dɪ'saɪd] *v* **-cided; -ciding** *vt* : décider — *vi* : se décider — **decided** [dɪ'saɪdəd] *adj* RESOLUTE : décidé

decimal ['dɛsəməl] *adj* : décimal — *~ n* : décimale *f* — **decimal point** *n* : virgule *f*

decipher [dɪ'saɪfər] *vt* : déchiffrer

decision [dɪ'sɪʒən] *n* : décision *f* — **decisive** [dɪ'saɪsɪv] *adj* **1** RESOLUTE : décidé **2** CONCLUSIVE : décisif

deck ['dɛk] *n* **1** : pont *m* (d'un navire) **2** *or* **~ of cards** : jeu *m* de cartes

declare [dɪ'klær] *vt* **-clared; -claring** : déclarer — **declaration** [,dɛklə'reɪʃən] *n* : déclaration *f*

decline [dɪ'klaɪn] *v* **-clined; -clining** : décliner — *~ n* **1** DETERIORATION : déclin *m* **2** DECREASE : baisse *f*

decompose [,di:kəm'po:z] *vt* **-posed; -posing** : décomposer — *vi* : se décomposer

decongestant [,di:kən'dʒɛstənt] *n* : décongestif *m*

decorate ['dɛkə,reɪt] vt -rated; -rating : décorer — **decor** or **décor** [deɪ'kɔr, 'deɪ,kɔr] n : décor m — **decoration** [,dɛkə'reɪʃən] n : décoration f — **decorative** ['dɛkərətɪv, -,reɪtɪv] adj : décoratif — **decorator** ['dɛkə,reɪtər] n : décorateur m, -trice f

decoy ['di:,kɔɪ, di'-] n : appeau m

decrease [di'kri:s] v -creased; -creasing : diminuer — ~ ['di:,kri:s] n : diminution f

decree [di'kri:] n : décret m — ~ vt -creed; -creeing : décréter

decrepit [di'krɛpɪt] adj 1 FEEBLE : décrépit 2 DILAPIDATED : délabré

dedicate ['dɛdɪ,keɪt] vt -cated; -cating 1 : dédier 2 ~ **oneself to** : se consacrer à — **dedication** [dɛdɪ'keɪʃən] n 1 DEVOTION : dévouement m 2 INSCRIPTION : dédicace f

deduce [di'du:s, -'dju:s] vt -duced; -ducing : déduire — **deduct** [di'dʌkt] vt : déduire — **deduction** [di'dʌkʃən] n : déduction f

deed ['di:d] n : action f, acte m

deem ['di:m] vt : juger, considérer

deep ['di:p] adj : profond — ~ adv 1 DEEPLY : profondément 2 ~ **down** : au fond — **deepen** ['di:pən] vt : approfondir — vi : devenir plus profond — **deeply** ['di:pli] adv : profondément

deer ['dɪr] ns & pl : cerf m

default [di'fɔlt, 'di:,fɔlt] n by ~ : par défaut — ~ vi 1 : ne pas s'acquitter (d'une dette) 2 : déclarer forfait (aux sports)

defeat [di'fi:t] vt : battre, vaincre — ~ n : défaite f

defect ['di:,fɛkt, di'fɛkt] n : défaut m — **defective** [di'fɛktɪv] adj : défectueux

defence Brit → **defense**

defend [di'fɛnd] vt : défendre — **defendant** [di'fɛndənt] n : défendeur m, -deresse f; accusé m, -sée f — **defense** or Brit **defence** [di'fɛnts, 'di:,fɛnts] n : défense f — **defensive** [di'fɛntsɪv] adj : défensif — ~ n **on the** ~ : sur la défensive

defer [di'fər] v -ferred; -ferring vt : différer — vi ~ **to** : s'en remettre à

defiance [di'faɪənts] n 1 : défi m 2 **in** ~ **of** : au mépris de — **defiant** [di'faɪənt] adj : de défi

deficient [di'fɪʃənt] adj 1 INADEQUATE : insuffisant 2 FAULTY : défectueux — **deficiency** [di'fɪʃəntsi] n, pl -cies 1 LACK : carence f 2 FLAW : défaut m

deficit ['dɛfəsɪt] n : déficit m

defile [di'faɪl] vt -filed; -filing DESECRATE : profaner

define [di'faɪn] vt -fined; -fining : définir — **definite** ['dɛfənɪt] adj 1 : défini, précis 2 CERTAIN : certain, sûr — **definitely** ['dɛfənɪtli] adv : certainement — **definition** [,dɛfə'nɪʃən] n : définition f — **definitive** [də'fɪnətɪv] adj : définitif

deflate [di'fleɪt] v -flated; -flating vt : dégonfler (un pneu, etc.) — vi : se dégonfler

deflect [di'flɛkt] vt : faire dévier — vi : dévier

deform [di'fɔrm] v : déformer — **deformity** [di'fɔrməti] n, pl -ties : difformité f

defraud [di'frɔd] vt : frauder, escroquer

defrost [di'frɔst] vt THAW : décongeler

defy [di'faɪ] vt -fied; -fying 1 CHALLENGE : défier 2 RESIST : résister à

degenerate [di'dʒɛnə,reɪt] vi -ated; -ating : dégénérer

degrade [di'greɪd] vt -graded; -grading : dégrader — **degrading** adj : dégradant

degree [di'gri:] n 1 : degré m 2 or **academic** ~ : diplôme m

dehydrate [di'haɪ,dreɪt] vt -drated; -drating : déshydrater

deign ['deɪn] vi ~ **to** : daigner

deity ['di:əti, 'deɪ-] n, pl -ties : dieu m, déesse f

dejected [di'dʒɛktəd] adj : abattu — **dejection** [di'dʒɛkʃən] n : abattement m

delay [di'leɪ] n : retard m, délai m — ~ vt 1 POSTPONE : différer 2 HOLD UP : retarder

delectable [di'lɛktəbəl] adj : délicieux

delegate ['dɛlɪgət, -,geɪt] n : délégué m, -guée f — ~ ['dɛlɪ,geɪt] v -gated; -gating : déléguer — **delegation** [,dɛlɪ'geɪʃən] n : délégation f

delete [di'li:t] vt -leted; -leting : supprimer, effacer

deliberate [dɪ'lɪbə,reɪt] v -ated; -ating vt : délibérer sur — vi : délibérer — ~ [dɪ'lɪbərət] adj : délibéré — **deliberately** [dɪ'lɪbərətli] adv : exprès

delicacy ['dɛlɪkəsi] n, pl -cies 1 : délicatesse f 2 FOOD : mets m fin — **delicate** ['dɛlɪkət] adj : délicat

delicatessen [,dɛlɪkə'tɛsən] n : charcuterie f

delicious [di'lɪʃəs] adj : délicieux

delight [di'laɪt] n : plaisir m, joie f — ~ vt : réjouir — vi ~ **in** : prendre plaisir à — **delightful** [di'laɪtfəl] adj : charmant, ravissant

delinquent [di'lɪŋkwənt] adj : délinquant — ~ n : délinquant m, -quante f

delirious [di'lɪriəs] adj : délirant, en délire — **delirium** [di'lɪriəm] n : délire m

deliver [di'lɪvər] vt 1 DISTRIBUTE : livrer 2 FREE : libérer 3 : mettre au monde (un enfant) 4 : prononcer (un discours, etc.) 5 DEAL : asséner (un coup, etc.) — **delivery** [di'lɪvəri] n, pl -eries 1 DISTRIBUTION : livraison f, distribution f 2 LIBERATION : délivrance f 3 CHILDBIRTH : accouchement m

delude [di'lu:d] vt -luded; -luding 1 : tromper 2 ~ **oneself** : se faire des illusions

deluge ['dɛl,ju:dʒ, -ju:ʒ] n : déluge m

delusion [dɪˈluːʒən] *n* : illusion *f*

deluxe [dɪˈlʌks, -ˈʊks] *adj* : de luxe

delve [ˈdɛlv] *vi* **delved; delving 1** : creuser **2 ~ into** PROBE : fouiller dans

demand [dɪˈmænd] *n* **1** REQUEST : demande *f* **2** CLAIM : réclamation *f* **3** → **supply** — **~** *vt* : exiger — **demanding** [dɪˈmændɪŋ] *adj* : exigeant

demean [dɪˈmiːn] *vt* **~ oneself** : s'abaisser

demeanor *or Brit* **demeanour** [dɪˈmiːnər] *n* : comportement *m*

demented [dɪˈmɛntəd] *adj* : dément, fou

democracy [dɪˈmɑkrəsi] *n, pl* **-cies** : démocratie *f* — **democrat** [ˈdɛməˌkræt] *n* : démocrate *mf* — **democratic** [ˌdɛməˈkrætɪk] *adj* : démocratique

demolish [dɪˈmɑlɪʃ] *vt* : démolir — **demolition** [ˌdɛməˈlɪʃən, ˌdiː-] *n* : démolition *f*

demon [ˈdiːmən] *n* : démon *m*

demonstrate [ˈdɛmənˌstreɪt] *v* **-strated; -strating** *vt* : démontrer — *vi* RALLY : manifester — **demonstration** [ˌdɛmənˈstreɪʃən] *n* **1** : démonstration *f* **2** RALLY : manifestation *f* — **demonstrative** [dɪˈmɑnstrətɪv] *adj* : démonstratif — **demonstrator** [ˈdɛmənˌstreɪtər] *n* PROTESTOR : manifestant *m*, -tante *f*

demoralize [dɪˈmɔrəˌlaɪz] *vt* **-ized; -izing** : démoraliser

demote [dɪˈmoːt] *vt* **-moted; -moting** : rétrograder

demure [dɪˈmjʊr] *adj* : modeste, réservé

den [ˈdɛn] *n* LAIR : antre *m*, tanière *f*

denial [dɪˈnaɪəl] *n* **1** : démenti *m*, dénégation *f* **2** REFUSAL : refus *m*

denim [ˈdɛnəm] *n* : jean *m*

denomination [dɪˌnɑməˈneɪʃən] *n* **1** : confession *f* (religieuse) **2** : valeur *f* (monétaire)

denote [dɪˈnoːt] *vt* **-noted; -noting** : dénoter

denounce [dɪˈnaʊnts] *vt* **-nounced; -nouncing** : dénoncer

dense [ˈdɛnts] *adj* **denser; -est 1** THICK : dense **2** STUPID : bête, obtus — **density** [ˈdɛntsəti] *n, pl* **-ties** : densité *f*

dent [ˈdɛnt] *vt* : cabosser — **~** *n* : bosse *f*

dental [ˈdɛntəl] *adj* : dentaire — **dental floss** *n* : fil *m* dentaire — **dentist** [ˈdɛntɪst] *n* : dentiste *mf* — **dentures** [ˈdɛntʃərz] *npl* : dentier *m*

denunciation [dɪˌnʌntsiˈeɪʃən] *n* : dénonciation *f*

deny [dɪˈnaɪ] *vt* **-nied; -nying 1** : nier **2** REFUSE : refuser

deodorant [dɪˈoːdərənt] *n* : déodorant *m*

depart [dɪˈpɑrt] *vi* **1** : partir **2 ~ from** : s'écarter de

department [dɪˈpɑrtmənt] *n* : ministère *m* (gouvernemental), service *m* (d'un hôpital, etc.), rayon *m* (d'un magasin) — **department store** *n* : grand magasin *m*

departure [dɪˈpɑrtʃər] *n* **1** : départ *m* **2** DEVIATION : écart *m*

depend [dɪˈpɛnd] *vi* **1 ~ on** : dépendre de, compter sur **2 ~ on s.o.** : compter sur qqn **3 that ~s** : tout dépend — **dependable** [dɪˈpɛndəbəl] *adj* : digne de confiance — **dependence** [dɪˈpɛndənts] *n* : dépendance *f* — **dependent** [dɪˈpɛndənt] *adj* : dépendant

depict [dɪˈpɪkt] *vt* **1** PORTRAY : représenter **2** DESCRIBE : dépeindre

deplete [dɪˈpliːt] *vt* **-pleted; -pleting** : épuiser, réduire

deplore [dɪˈplor] *vt* **-plored; -ploring** : déplorer — **deplorable** [dɪˈplorəbəl] *adj* : déplorable

deploy [dɪˈplɔɪ] *vt* : déployer

deport [dɪˈport] *vt* : expulser (d'un pays) — **deportation** [ˌdiˌporˈteɪʃən] *n* : expulsion *f*

deposit [dɪˈpɑzət] *vt* **-ited; -iting** : déposer — **~** *n* **1** : dépôt *m* **2** DOWN PAYMENT : acompte *m*, arrhes *fpl France*

depreciate [dɪˈpriːʃiˌeɪt] *vi* **-ated; -ating** : se déprécier — **depreciation** [dɪˌpriːʃiˈeɪʃən] *n* : dépréciation *f*

depress [dɪˈprɛs] *vt* **1** PRESS : appuyer sur **2** SADDEN : déprimer — **depressed** [dɪˈprɛst] *adj* : déprimé — **depressing** [dɪˈprɛsɪŋ] *adj* : déprimant — **depression** [dɪˈprɛʃən] *n* : dépression *f*

deprive [dɪˈpraɪv] *vt* **-prived; -priving** : priver

depth [ˈdɛpθ] *n, pl* **depths** : profondeur *f*

deputy [ˈdɛpjuti] *n, pl* **-ties** : adjoint *m*, -jointe *f*

derail [dɪˈreɪl] *vi* : dérailler — **derailment** [dɪˈreɪlmənt] *n* : déraillement *m*

deride [dɪˈraɪd] *vt* **-rided; -riding** : railler — **derision** [dɪˈrɪʒən] *n* : dérision *f*

derive [dɪˈraɪv] *vi* **-rived; -riving ~ from** : provenir de

derogatory [dɪˈrɑgəˌtori] *adj* : désobligeant

descend [dɪˈsɛnd] *v* : descendre — **descendant** [dɪˈsɛndənt] *n* : descendant *m*, -dante *f* — **descent** [dɪˈsɛnt] *n* **1** : descente *f* **2** LINEAGE : descendance *f*

describe [dɪˈskraɪb] *vt* **-scribed; -scribing** : décrire — **description** [dɪˈskrɪpʃən] *n* : description *f* — **descriptive** [dɪˈskrɪptɪv] *adj* : descriptif

desecrate [ˈdɛsɪˌkreɪt] *vt* **-crated; -crating** : profaner

desert [ˈdɛzərt] *n* : désert *m* — **~** *adj* **~ island** : île *f* déserte — **~** [dɪˈzərt] *vt* : abandonner — *vi* : déserter — **deserter** [dɪˈzərtər] *n* : déserteur *m*

deserve [dɪˈzərv] *vt* **-served; -serving** : mériter

design [dɪˈzaɪn] *vt* **1** DEVISE : concevoir **2** DRAW : dessiner — **~** *n* **1** : conception *f* **2**

PLAN : plan *m* **3** SKETCH : dessin *m* **4** PATTERN : motif *m*
designate ['dɛzɪg,neɪt] *vt* **-nated; -nating** : désigner
designer [ar'zainer] *n* : dessinateur *m*, -trice *f*
desire [di'zaɪr] *vt* **-sired; -siring** : désirer — ~ *n* : désir *m*
desk ['dɛsk] *n* : bureau *m*, pupitre *m* (d'un élève)
desolate ['dɛsələt, -zə-] *adj* : désolé
despair [di'spær] *vi* : désespérer — ~ *n* : désespoir *m*
desperate ['dɛspərət] *adj* : désespéré —. **desperation** [,dɛspə'reɪʃən] *n* : désespoir *m*
despise [di'spaɪz] *vt* **-spised; -spising** : mépriser — **despicable** [di'spɪkəbəl, 'dɛspɪ-] *adj* : méprisable
despite [də'spaɪt] *prep* : malgré
dessert [di'zərt] *n* : dessert *m*
destination [,dɛstɪ'neɪʃən] *n* : destination *f* — **destined** ['dɛstənd] *adj* **1** : destiné **2** ~ **for** : à destination de — **destiny** ['dɛstəni] *n, pl* **-nies** : destin *m*, destinée *f*
destitute ['dɛstə,tu:t, -,tju:t] *adj* : indigent
destroy [di'strɔɪ] *vt* : détruire — **destruction** [di'strʌkʃən] *n* : destruction *f* — **destructive** [di'strʌktɪv] *adj* : destructeur
detach [di'tætʃ] *vt* : détacher — **detached** [di'tætʃt] *adj* : détaché
detail [di'teɪl, 'di:,teɪl] *n* : détail *m* — ~ *vt* : détailler — **detailed** [di'teɪld, 'di:,teɪld] *adj* : détaillé
detain [di'teɪn] *vt* **1** : détenir (un prisonnier) **2** DELAY : retenir
detect [di'tɛkt] *vt* : détecter, déceler — **detection** [di'tɛkʃən] *n* : détection *f* — **detective** [di'tɛktɪv] *n* : détective *m*
detention [di'tɛnʃən] *n* : détention *f*
deter [di'tər] *vt* **-terred; -terring** : dissuader
detergent [di'tərdʒənt] *n* : détergent *m*
deteriorate [di'tɪriə,reɪt] *vi* **-rated; -rating** : se détériorer — **deterioration** [di,tɪriə'reɪʃən] *n* : détérioration *f*
determine [di'tərmən] *vt* **-mined; -mining** **1** : déterminer **2** RESOLVE : décider — **determined** [di'tərmənd] *adj* RESOLUTE : déterminé — **determination** [di,tərmə'neɪʃən] *n* : détermination *f*
detest [di'tɛst] *vt* : détester
detour ['di:,tur, di'tur] *n* : détour *m* — ~ *vi* : faire un détour
devastate ['dɛvə,steɪt] *vt* **-tated; -tating** : dévaster — **devastating** ['dɛvə,steɪtɪŋ] *adj* : accablant — **devastation** [,dɛvə'steɪʃən] *n* : dévastation *f*
develop [di'vɛləp] *vt* **1** : développer **2** ~ **an illness** : contracter une maladie — *vi* **1** GROW : se développer **2** HAPPEN : se manifester — **developing** [di'vɛləpɪŋ] *adj* **1** : en

expansion **2** ~ **country** : pays en voie de développement — **development** [di'vɛləpmənt] *n* : développement *m*
deviate ['di:vi,eɪt] *vi* **-ated; -ating** : dévier, s'écarter
device [di'vaɪs] *n* : appareil *m*, mécanisme *m*
devil ['dɛvəl] *n* : diable *m* — **devilish** ['dɛvəlɪʃ] *adj* : diabolique
devious ['di:viəs] *adj* CRAFTY : sournois
devise [di'vaɪz] *vt* **-vised; -vising** : inventer, concevoir
devoid [di'vɔɪd] *adj* ~ **of** : dépourvu de
devote [di'vo:t] *vt* **-voted; -voting** : consacrer, dédier — **devoted** [di'vo:təd] *adj* : dévoué — **devotion** [di'vo:ʃən] *n* **1** DEDICATION : dévouement *m* **2** PIETY : dévotion *f*
devour [di'vauər] *vt* : dévorer
devout [di'vaut] *adj* **1** PIOUS : dévot **2** EARNEST : fervent
dew ['du:, 'dju:] *n* : rosée *f*
dexterity [dɛk'stɛrəti] *n, pl* **-ties** : dextérité *f*
diabetes [,daɪə'bi:tiz] *n* : diabète *m* — **diabetic** [,daɪə'bɛtɪk] *adj* : diabétique — ~ *n* : diabétique *mf*
diabolic [,daɪə'bɑlɪk] *or* **diabolical** [-lɪkəl] *adj* : diabolique
diagnosis [,daɪɪg'no:sɪs] *n, pl* **-ses** [-'no:,si:z] : diagnostic *m* — **diagnose** ['daɪɪg,no:s, ,daɪɪg'no:s] *vt* **-nosed; -nosing** : diagnostiquer
diagonal [daɪ'ægənəl] *adj* : diagonal — **diagonally** [daɪ'ægənəli] *adv* : en diagonale
diagram ['daɪə,græm] *n* : diagramme *m*
dial ['daɪl] *n* : cadran *m* (d'une horloge), bouton *m* (d'une radio) — ~ *vt* **-aled** *or* **-alled; -aling** *or* **-alling** : faire, composer (un numéro de téléphone)
dialect ['daɪə,lɛkt] *n* : dialecte *m*
dialogue ['daɪə,lɔg] *n* : dialogue *m*
diameter [daɪ'æmətər] *n* : diamètre *m*
diamond ['daɪmənd, 'daɪə-] *n* **1** : diamant *m* **2** : losange *m* (forme géométrique) **3** : carreau *m* (aux cartes) **4** *or* **baseball** ~ : terrain *m* de baseball, losange *m* Can
diaper ['daɪpər, 'daɪə-] *n* : couche *f* (de bébé)
diaphragm ['daɪə,fræm] *n* : diaphragme *m*
diarrhea *or Brit* **diarrhoea** [,daɪə'ri:ə] *n* : diarrhée *f*
diary ['daɪəri:] *n, pl* **-ries** : journal *m* intime
dice ['daɪs] *ns & pl* : dé *m* (à jouer)
dictate ['dɪk,teɪt, dɪk'teɪt] *vt* **-tated; -tating** : dicter — **dictation** [dɪk'teɪʃən] *n* : dictée *f* — **dictator** ['dɪk,teɪtər] *n* : dictateur *m*
dictionary ['dɪkʃə,nɛri] *n, pl* **-naries** : dictionnaire *m*
did → **do**
die[1] ['daɪ] *vi* **died** ['daɪd]; **dying** ['daɪɪŋ] **1** : mourir, décéder **2** *or* ~ **down** SUBSIDE

: diminuer **3 be dying to** : mourir d'envie de

die² ['daɪ] *n, pl* **dice** ['daɪs] : dé *m* (à jouer)

diesel ['di:zəl, -səl] *n* : diesel *m*

diet ['daɪət] *n* **1** FOOD : alimentation *f* **2 go on a** ~ : être au régime — ~ *vi* : suivre un régime

differ ['dɪfər] *vi* **-ferred; -ferring** : différer — **difference** ['dɪfrənts, 'dɪfərənts] *n* : différence *f* — **different** ['dɪfrənt, 'dɪfərənt] *adj* : différent — **differentiate** [dɪfə'rɛntʃi,eɪt] *v* **-ated; -ating** *vt* : différencier — *vi* ~ **between** : faire la différence entre — **differently** ['dɪfrəntli, 'dɪfərəntli] *adv* : différemment

difficult ['dɪfɪˌkʌlt] *adj* : difficile — **difficulty** ['dɪfɪˌkʌlti] *n, pl* **-ties** : difficulté *f*

dig ['dɪg] *v* **dug** ['dʌg]; **digging 1** : creuser **2** ~ **up** : déterrer

digest ['daɪˌdʒɛst] *n* : résumé *m* — ~ ['daɪˌdʒɛst] *vt* **1** : digérer **2** SUMMARIZE : résumer — **digestion** [daɪ'dʒɛstʃən, dɪ-] *n* : digestion *f* — **digestive** [daɪ'dʒɛstɪv, dɪ-] *adj* : digestif

digit ['dɪdʒət] *n* NUMERAL : chiffre *m* — **digital** ['dɪdʒətəl] *adj* : digital

dignity ['dɪgnəti] *n, pl* **-ties** : dignité *f* — **dignified** ['dɪgnəˌfaɪd] *adj* : digne

digress [daɪ'grɛs, də-] *vi* : s'écarter (du sujet)

dike ['daɪk] *n* : digue *f*

dilapidated [də'læpəˌdeɪtəd] *adj* : délabré

dilate [daɪ'leɪt, 'daɪˌleɪt] *v* **-lated; -lating** *vt* : dilater — *vi* : se dilater

dilemma [dɪ'lɛmə] *n* : dilemme *m*

diligence ['dɪlədʒənts] *n* : assiduité *f* — **diligent** ['dɪlədʒənt] *adj* : assidu, appliqué

dilute [daɪ'lu:t, də-] *vt* **-luted; -luting** : diluer

dim ['dɪm] *v* **dimmed; dimming** *vt* : baisser — *vi* : baisser, s'affaiblir — ~ *adj* **dimmer; dimmest 1** DARK : sombre **2** FAINT : faible, vague

dime ['daɪm] *n* : pièce *f* de dix cents

dimension [də'mɛntʃən, daɪ-] *n* : dimension *f*

diminish [də'mɪnɪʃ] *v* : diminuer

diminutive [də'mɪnjətɪv] *adj* : minuscule

dimple ['dɪmpəl] *n* : fossette *f*

din ['dɪn] *n* : vacarme *m*, tapage *m*

dine ['daɪn] *vi* **dined; dining** : dîner — **diner** ['daɪnər] *n* **1** : dîneur *m*, -neuse *f* **2** : petit restaurant *m* — **dining room** *n* : salle *f* à manger — **dinner** ['dɪnər] *n* : dîner *m*

dinosaur ['daɪnəˌsɔr] *n* : dinosaure *m*

dip ['dɪp] *v* **dipped; dipping** *vt* : plonger, tremper — *vi* : baisser, descendre — ~ *n* **1** DROP : déclivité *f* **2** SWIM : petite baignade *f* **3** SAUCE : sauce *f*

diploma [də'plo:mə] *n* : diplôme *m*

diplomacy [də'plo:məsi] *n* : diplomatie *f* — **diplomat** ['dɪpləˌmæt] *n* : diplomate *mf* — **diplomatic** [ˌdɪplə'mætɪk] *adj* **1** : diplomatique **2** TACTFUL : diplomate

dire ['daɪr] *adj* **direr; direst 1** : grave, terrible **2** EXTREME : extrême

direct [də'rɛkt, daɪ-] *vt* **1** : diriger **2** ORDER : ordonner — ~ *adj* **1** STRAIGHT : direct **2** FRANK : franc — ~ *adv* : directement — **direct current** *n* : courant *m* continu — **direction** [də'rɛkʃən, daɪ-] *n* **1** : direction *f* **2 ask for** ~**s** : demander des indications — **directly** [də'rɛktli, daɪ-] *adv* **1** STRAIGHT : directement **2** IMMEDIATELY : tout de suite — **director** [də'rɛktər, daɪ-] *n* **1** : directeur *m*, -trice *f* **2 board of** ~**s** : conseil *m* d'administration — **directory** [də'rɛktəri, daɪ-] *n, pl* **-ries** : annuaire *m* (téléphonique)

dirt ['dərt] *n* **1** : saleté *f* **2** SOIL : terre *f* — **dirty** ['dərti] *adj* **dirtier; -est 1** : sale **2** INDECENT : obscène, cochon *fam* — ~ *vt* **dirtied; dirtying** : salir

disability [ˌdɪsə'bɪləti] *n, pl* **-ties** : infirmité *f* — **disable** [dɪs'eɪbəl] *vt* **-abled; -abling** : rendre infirme — **disabled** [dɪs'eɪbəld] *adj* : handicapé, infirme

disadvantage [ˌdɪsəd'væntɪdʒ] *n* : désavantage *m*

disagree [ˌdɪsə'gri:] *vi* **1** : ne pas être d'accord (avec qqn) **2** CONFLICT : ne pas convenir — **disagreeable** [ˌdɪsə'gri:əbəl] *adj* : désagréable — **disagreement** [ˌdɪsə'gri:mənt] *n* **1** : désaccord *m* **2** ARGUMENT : différend *m*

disappear [ˌdɪsə'pɪr] *vi* : disparaître — **disappearance** [ˌdɪsə'pi:rənts] *n* : disparition *f*

disappoint [ˌdɪsə'pɔɪnt] *vt* : décevoir — **disappointment** [ˌdɪsə'pɔɪntmənt] *n* : déception *f*

disapprove [ˌdɪsə'pru:v] *vi* **-proved; -proving** ~ **of** : désapprouver — **disapproval** [ˌdɪsə'pru:vəl] *n* : désapprobation *f*

disarm [dɪs'ɑrm] *v* : désarmer — **disarmament** [dɪs'ɑrməmənt] *n* : désarmement *m*

disarray [ˌdɪsə'reɪ] *n* : désordre *m*

disaster [dɪ'zæstər] *n* : désastre *m* — **disastrous** [dɪ'zæstrəs] *adj* : désastreux

disbelief [ˌdɪsbɪ'li:f] *n* : incrédulité *f*

disc → **disk**

discard [dɪs'kɑrd, 'dɪsˌkɑrd] *vt* : se débarrasser de

discern [dɪ'sərn, -'zərn] *vt* : discerner — **discernible** [dɪ'sərnəbəl, -'zər-] *adj* : perceptible

discharge [dɪs'tʃɑrdʒ, 'dɪsˌ-] *vt* **-charged; -charging 1** UNLOAD : décharger **2** DISMISS : renvoyer **3** RELEASE : libérer — ~ ['dɪsˌtʃɑrdʒ, dɪs'-] *n* **1** : décharge *f* (électrique) **2** FLOW : écoulement *m* **3** DISMISSAL : renvoi *m* **4** RELEASE : libération *f*

disciple [dɪˈsaɪpəl] *n* : disciple *mf*
discipline [ˈdɪsəplən] *n* : discipline *f* — ~
vt **-plined; -plining 1** PUNISH : punir **2**
CONTROL : discipliner
disclose [dɪsˈkloːz] *vt* **-closed; -closing**
: révéler
discomfort [dɪsˈkʌmfərt] *n* **1** : malaise *m* **2**
UNEASINESS : gêne *f*
disconcert [ˌdɪskənˈsərt] *vt* : déconcerter
disconnect [ˌdɪskəˈnɛkt] *vt* : débrancher (un
appareil électrique), couper (l'électricité,
etc.)
discontinue [ˌdɪskənˈtɪnˌjuː] *vt* **-ued; -uing**
: cesser, interrompre
discord [ˈdɪsˌkɔrd] *n* STRIFE : discorde *m*
discount [ˈdɪsˌkaunt, dɪsˈ-] *n* : rabais *m*,
remise *f* — ~ *vt* : faire une remise de
discourage [dɪsˈkərɪdʒ] *vt* **-aged; -aging**
: décourager — **discouragement** [dɪsˈkərɪdʒmənt] *n* : découragement *m*
discover [dɪsˈkʌvər] *vt* : découvrir — **discovery** [dɪsˈkʌvəri] *n, pl* **-eries** : découverte *f*
discredit [dɪsˈkrɛdət] *vt* : discréditer
discreet [dɪˈskriːt] *adj* : discret
discrepancy [dɪsˈkrɛpəntsi] *n, pl* **-cies** : divergence *f*
discretion [dɪsˈkrɛʃən] *n* : discrétion *f*
discriminate [dɪsˈkrɪməˌneɪt] *vi* **-nated;
-nating 1 ~ against** : être l'objet de discriminations **2 ~ between** : distinguer
entre — **discrimination** [dɪsˌkrɪməˈneɪʃən]
n discrimination *f*, préjugés *mpl*
discuss [dɪsˈkʌs] *vt* : discuter de, parler de
— **discussion** [dɪsˈkʌʃən] *n* : discussion *f*
disdain [dɪsˈdeɪn] *n* : dédain *m* — ~ *vt* : dédaigner
disease [dɪˈziːz] *n* : maladie *f*
disembark [ˌdɪsɪmˈbark] *vi* : débarquer
disengage [ˌdɪsɪnˈgeɪdʒ] *vt* **-gaged; -gaging
1** RELEASE : dégager **2 ~ the clutch**
: débrayer
disentangle [ˌdɪsɪnˈtæŋgəl] *vt* **-gled; -gling**
: démêler
disfigure [dɪsˈfɪɡjər] *vt* **-ured; -uring** : défigurer
disgrace [dɪsˈskreɪs] *vt* **-graced; -gracing**
: déshonorer — ~ *n* **1** DISHONOR : disgrâce *f* **2** SHAME : honte *f* — **disgraceful**
[dɪˈskreɪsfəl] *adj* : honteux
disgruntled [dɪsˈgrʌntəld] *adj* : mécontent
disguise [dɪsˈkaɪz] *vt* **-guised; -guising**
: déguiser — ~ *n* : déguisement *m*
disgust [dɪsˈkʌst] *n* : dégoût *m* — ~ *vt* : dégoûter — **disgusting** [dɪsˈkʌstɪn] *adj*
: écœurant, dégoûtant
dish [ˈdɪʃ] *n* **1** : assiette *f* **2** *or* **serving ~**
: plat *m* de service **3 ~es** *npl* : vaisselle *f* —
~ *vt or* **~ out** : servir — **dishcloth** [ˈdɪʃˌklɔθ] *n* : torchon *m* (à vaisselle), lavette *f*

dishearten [dɪsˈhartən] *vt* : décourager
disheveled *or* **dishevelled** [dɪˈʃɛvəld] *adj*
: en désordre (se dit des vêtements, etc.)
dishonest [dɪsˈanəst] *adj* : malhonnête —
dishonesty [dɪsˈanəsti] *n, pl* **-ties** : malhonnêteté *f*
dishonor [dɪsˈanər] *n* : déshonneur *m* — ~
vt : déshonorer — **dishonorable** [dɪsˈanərəbəl] *adj* : déshonorant
dishwasher [ˈdɪʃˌwɔʃər] *n* : lave-vaisselle *m*
disillusion [dɪsəˈluːʒən] *vt* : désillusionner
— **disillusionment** [dɪsəˈluːʒənmənt] *n*
: désillusion *f*
disinfect [ˌdɪsɪnˈfɛkt] *vt* : désinfecter — **disinfectant** [ˌdɪsɪnˈfɛktənt] *n* : désinfectant *m*
disintegrate [dɪsˈɪntəˌgreɪt] *vi* **-grated;
-grating** : se désagréger, se désintégrer
disinterested [dɪsˈɪntərəstəd, -ˌrɛs-] *adj*
: désintéressé
disjointed [dɪsˈdʒɔɪntəd] *adj* : décousu, incohérent
disk *or* **disc** [ˈdɪsk] *n* : disque *m*
dislike [dɪsˈlaɪk] *n* : aversion *f*, antipathie *f* —
~ *vt* **-liked; -liking** : ne pas aimer
dislocate [ˈdɪsloˌkeɪt, dɪsˈloː-] *vt* **-cated;
-cating** : se démettre, se luxer
dislodge [dɪsˈladʒ] *vt* **-lodged; -lodging**
: déplacer, déloger
disloyal [dɪsˈlɔɪəl] *adj* : déloyal — **disloyalty** [dɪsˈlɔɪəlti] *n, pl* **-ties** : déloyauté *f*
dismal [ˈdɪzməl] *adj* : sombre, triste
dismantle [dɪsˈmæntəl] *vt* **-tled; -tling** : démonter
dismay [dɪsˈmeɪ] *vt* : consterner — ~ *n*
: consternation *f*
dismiss [dɪsˈmɪs] *vt* **1** DISCHARGE : renvoyer, congédier **2** REJECT : ne pas tenir
compte de — **dismissal** [dɪsˈmɪsəl] *n* : renvoi *m*, licenciement *m*
disobey [ˌdɪsəˈbeɪ] *vt* : désobéir à — *vi* : désobéir — **disobedience** [ˌdɪsəˈbiːdiənts] *n*
: désobéissance *f* — **disobedient** [-ənt] *adj*
: désobéissant
disorder [dɪsˈɔrdər] *n* **1** : désordre *m* **2** AILMENT : troubles *mpl*, maladie *f* — **disorderly** [dɪsˈɔrdərli] *adj* : désordonné
disorganize [dɪsˈɔrɡəˌnaɪz] *vt* **-nized; -nizing** : désorganiser
disown [dɪsˈoːn] *vt* : renier
disparage [dɪsˈpærɪdʒ] *vt* **-aged; -aging**
: dénigrer
disparity [dɪsˈpærəti] *n, pl* **-ties** : disparité *f*
dispatch [dɪsˈpætʃ] *vt* : envoyer, expédier
dispel [dɪsˈpɛl] *vt* **-pelled; -pelling** : dissiper
dispense [dɪsˈpɛnts] *v* **-pensed; -pensing**
vt : distribuer — *vi* **~ with** : se passer de
disperse [dɪsˈpərs] *v* **-persed; -persing** *vt*
: disperser — *vi* : se disperser
display [dɪsˈpleɪ] *vt* PRESENT : exposer — ~
n : exposition *f*, étalage *m*

dispose [dɪs'po:z] v **-posed; -posing** vt : disposer — vi ~ **of** : se débarrasser de — **disposable** [dɪs'po:zəbəl] adj : jetable — **disposal** [dɪs'po:zəl] n **1** : élimination f (de déchets) **2 have at one's** ~ : avoir à sa disposition — **disposition** [ˌdɪspə'zɪʃən] n : TEMPERAMENT : caractère m

dispute [dɪs'pju:t] vt **-puted; -puting** : contester — ~ n : dispute f, conflit m

disqualify [dɪs'kwalə,faɪ] vt **-fied; -fying** : disqualifier

disregard [ˌdɪsrɪ'gard] vt : ne pas tenir compte de — ~ n : indifférence f

disreputable [dɪs'repjʊtəbəl] adj : mal famé

disrespect [ˌdɪsrɪ'spɛkt] n : manque m de respect — **disrespectful** [ˌdɪsrɪ'spɛktfəl] adj : irrespectueux

disrupt [dɪs'rʌpt] vt : perturber, déranger — **disruption** [dɪs'rʌpʃən] n : perturbation f

dissatisfied [dɪs'sætəs,faɪd] adj : mécontent

disseminate [dɪ'sɛmə,neɪt] vt **-nated; -nating** : disséminer

dissent [dɪ'sɛnt] vi : différer, être en désaccord — ~ n : dissentiment m

dissertation [ˌdɪsər'teɪʃən] n THESIS : thèse f

dissipate ['dɪsə,peɪt] v **-pated; -pating** vt DISPERSE : dissiper — vi : se dissiper

dissolve [dɪ'zalv] v **-solved; -solving** vt : dissoudre — vi : se dissoudre

dissuade [dɪ'sweɪd] vt **-suaded; -suading** : dissuader

distance ['dɪstənts] n **1** : distance f **2 in the** ~ : au loin — **distant** ['dɪstənt] adj : distant

distaste [dɪs'teɪst] n : dégoût m — **distasteful** [dɪs'teɪstfəl] adj : déplaisant, répugnant

distill or Brit **distil** [dɪ'stɪl] vt **-tilled; -tilling** : distiller

distinct [dɪ'stɪŋkt] adj **1** CLEAR : distinct **2** DEFINITE : net — **distinction** [dɪ'stɪŋkʃən] n : distinction f — **distinctive** [dɪ'stɪŋktɪv] adj : distinctif

distinguish [dɪ'stɪŋgwɪʃ] vt : distinguer — **distinguished** [dɪ'stɪŋgwɪʃt] adj : distingué

distort [dɪ'stɔrt] vt : déformer — **distortion** [dɪ'stɔrʃən] n : déformation f

distract [dɪ'strækt] vt : distraire — **distraction** [dɪ'strækʃən] n : distraction f

distraught [dɪ'strɔt] adj : éperdu

distress [dɪ'strɛs] n **1** : angoisse f, affliction f **2 in** ~ : en détresse f — ~ vt : affliger — **distressing** [dɪ'strɛsɪŋ] adj : pénible

distribute [dɪ'strɪ,bju:t, -bjʊt] vt **-uted; -uting** : distribuer, répartir — **distribution** [ˌdɪstrə'bju:ʃən] n : distribution f — **distributor** [dɪ'strɪbjʊtər] n : distributeur m

district ['dɪs,trɪkt] n **1** AREA : région f **2** : quartier m (d'une ville) **3** : district m (administratif)

distrust [dɪs'trʌst] n : méfiance f — ~ vt : se méfier de

disturb [dɪ'stərb] vt **1** BOTHER : déranger **2** WORRY : troubler, inquiéter

disturbance [dɪ'stərbənts] n **to cause a** ~ : faire du tapage

disuse [dɪs'ju:s] n **fall into** ~ : tomber en désuétude

ditch ['dɪtʃ] n : fossé m

dive ['daɪv] vi **dived** or **dove** ['do:v]; **dived; diving** : plonger — ~ n **1** : plongeon m **2** DESCENT : piqué m — **diver** ['daɪvər] n : plongeur m, -geuse f

diverge [də'vərdʒ, daɪ-] vi **-verged; -verging** : diverger

diverse [daɪ'vərs, də-, 'daɪˌvərs] adj : divers — **diversify** [daɪ'vərsə,faɪ, də-] vt **-fied; -fying** : diversifier

diversion [daɪ'vərʒən, də-] n **1** DEVIATION : déviation f **2** AMUSEMENT : divertissement m

diversity [daɪ'vərsəti, də-] n, pl **-ties** : diversité f

divert [də'vərt, daɪ-] vt **1** DEFLECT : détourner **2** AMUSE : divertir

divide [də'vaɪd] v **-vided; -viding** vt : diviser — vi : se diviser

dividend ['dɪvɪˌdɛnd, -dənd] n : dividende m

divine [də'vaɪn] adj **diviner; -est** : divin — **divinity** [də'vɪnəti] n, pl **-ties** : divinité f

division [dɪ'vɪʒən] n : division f

divorce [də'vors] n : divorce m — ~ vi **-vorced; -vorcing** : divorcer

divulge [də'vʌldʒ, daɪ-] vt **-vulged; -vulging** : divulguer

dizzy ['dɪzi] adj **dizzier; -est** : vertigineux — **dizziness** ['dɪzinəs] n : vertige m, étourdissement m

DNA [ˌdi:ˌɛn'eɪ] n (deoxyribonucleic acid) : ADN m

do ['du:] v **did** ['dɪd]; **done** ['dʌn]; **doing; does** ['dʌz] vt **1** : faire **2** PREPARE : préparer **3** ~ **one's hair** : se coiffer — vi **1** BEHAVE : faire **2** MANAGE : s'en sortir **3** SUFFICE : suffire **4** ~ **away with** : éliminer **5 how are you doing?** : comment-vas-tu? — v aux **1 does he work?** : travaille-t-il? **2 I don't know** : je ne sais pas **3** ~ **be careful** : fais attention, je t'en prie **4 he reads more than I** ~ : il lit plus que moi **5 you know him, don't you?** : vous le connaissez, n'est-ce pas?

dock ['dak] n : dock m — ~ vi : se mettre à quai

doctor ['daktər] n **1** : docteur m (de droit, etc.) **2** PHYSICIAN : médecin m, docteur m

doctrine ['daktrɪn] n : doctrine f

document ['dakjʊmənt] n : document m — **documentary** [ˌdakjʊ'mɛntəri] n, pl **-ries** : documentaire m

dodge ['dadʒ] n : ruse f, truc m — ~ vt **dodged; dodging** : esquiver

doe [ˈdo:] *n, pl* **does** *or* **doe** : biche *f*
does → **do**
doesn't [ˈdʌzɪnt] (*contraction of* **do not**) → **do**
dog [ˈdɔg, ˈdɑg] *n* **1** CHIEN *m* — **~** *vt* **dogged; dogging** : poursuivre — **dogged** [ˈdɔgəd] *adj* : tenace
dogma [ˈdɔgmə] *n* : dogme *m*
doldrums [ˈdo:ldrəmz, ˈdɑl-] *npl* **be in the ~** : être dans le marasme
doll [ˈdɑl, ˈdɔl] *n* : poupée *f*
dollar [ˈdɑlər] *n* : dollar *m*
dolphin [ˈdɑlfən, ˈdɔl-] *n* : dauphin *m*
domain [doˈmeɪn, də-] *n* : domaine *m*
dome [ˈdo:m] *n* : dôme *m*
domestic [dəˈmɛstɪk] *adj* **1** FAMILY : familial **2** HOUSEHOLD : ménager, domestique **3** INTERNAL : intérieur, du pays — **~** *n* SERVANT : domestique *mf* — **domesticate** [dəˈmɛstɪˌkeɪt] *vt* **-cated; -cating** : domestiquer
dominant [ˈdɑmənənt] *adj* : dominant — **dominate** [ˈdɑməˌneɪt] *v* **-nated; -nating** : dominer — **domineer** [ˌdɑməˈnɪr] *vi* : se montrer autoritaire
donate [ˈdo:ˌneɪt, do:ˈ-] *vt* **-nated; -nating** : faire (un) don — **donation** [do:ˈneɪʃən] *n* : don *m*, donation *f*
done [ˈdʌn] → **do** — **~** *adj* **1** FINISHED : fini, terminé **2** COOKED : cuit
donkey [ˈdɑŋki, ˈdʌŋ] *n, pl* **-keys** : âne *m*
donor [ˈdo:nər] *n* **1** : donateur *m*, -trice *f* **2 blood ~** : donneur *m*, -neuse *f* de sang
don't [ˈdo:nt] (*contraction of* **do not**) → **do**
doodle [ˈdu:dəl] *v* **-dled; -dling** : gribouiller
doom [ˈdu:m] *n* : perte *f*, ruine *f* — **~** *vt* : vouer, condamner
door [ˈdor] *n* **1** : porte *f* **2** : portière *f* (d'une voiture) **3** ENTRANCE : entrée *f* — **doorbell** [ˈdorˌbɛl] *n* : sonnette *f* — **doorknob** [ˈdorˌnɑb] *n* : bouton *m* de porte — **doormat** [ˈdorˌmæt] *n* : paillasson *m* — **doorstep** [ˈdorˌstɛp] *n* : pas *m* de la porte — **doorway** [ˈdorˌweɪ] *n* : porte *f*, embrasure *f* (de la porte)
dope [ˈdo:p] *n* **1** DRUG : drogue *f* **2** IDIOT : imbécile *mf*
dormitory [ˈdorməˌtori] *n, pl* **-ries** : dortoir *m*
dose [ˈdo:s] *n* : dose *f* — **dosage** [ˈdo:sɪʤ] *n* : posologie *f*
dot [ˈdɑt] *n* **1** POINT : point *m* **2 on the ~** : pile *fam*
dote [ˈdo:t] *vi* **doted; doting ~ on** : adorer
double [ˈdʌbəl] *adj* : double — **~** *v* **-bled; -bling** *vt* **1** : doubler **2** FOLD : plier (en deux) — *vi* : doubler — **~** *adv* **1** : deux fois **2 see ~** : voir double — **~** *n* : double *m* — **double bass** *n* : contrebasse *f* — **doubly** [ˈdʌbli] *adv* : doublement, deux fois plus

doubt [ˈdaʊt] *vt* **1** : douter **2** DISTRUST : douter de — **~** *n* : doute *m* — **doubtful** [ˈdaʊtfəl] *adj* : douteux
dough [ˈdo:] *n* : pâte *f* (en cuisine) — **doughnut** [ˈdo:ˌnʌt] *n* : beignet *m*, beigne *m* Can
douse [ˈdaʊs, ˈdaʊz] *vt* **doused; dousing 1** DRENCH : tremper **2** EXTINGUISH : éteindre
dove[1] [ˈdo:v] → **dive**
dove[2] [ˈdʌv] *n* : colombe *f*
down [ˈdaʊn] *adv* **1** DOWNWARD : en bas, vers le bas **2 fall ~** : tomber **3 go ~** : descendre — **~** *prep* **1** : en bas de **2** ALONG : le long de — **~** *adj* **1** : qui descend **2** DOWNCAST : déprimé, abattu — **~** *n* : duvet *m* — **downcast** [ˈdaʊnˌkæst] *adj* : abattu — **downfall** [ˈdaʊnˌfɔl] *n* : chute *f* — **downhearted** [ˌdaʊnˈhɑrtəd] *adj* : découragé — **downhill** [ˈdaʊnˈhɪl] *adv* **go ~** : descendre — **download** [ˈdaʊnˌlo:d] *vt* : télécharger (en informatique) — **down payment** *n* : acompte *m* — **downpour** [ˈdaʊnˌpor] *n* : averse *f* — **downright** [ˈdaʊnˌraɪt] *adv* : carrément — **~** *adj* : véritable, catégorique — **downstairs** [*adv* ˈdaʊnˈstærz, *adj* ˈdaʊnˌstærz] *adv & adj* : en bas — **downstream** [ˈdaʊnˈstri:m] *adv* : en aval — **down-to-earth** [ˌdaʊntuˈərθ] *adj* : terre à terre — **downtown** [ˌdaʊnˈtaʊn, ˈdaʊnˌtaʊn] *n* : centre-ville *m* — **~** [ˌdaʊnˈtaʊn] *adv* : en ville — **downward** [ˈdaʊnwərd] *or* **downwards** [-wərdz] *adv* : en bas, vers le bas — **downward** *adv* : vers le bas
doze [ˈdo:z] *vi* **dozed; dozing** : sommeiller, somnoler
dozen [ˈdʌzən] *n, pl* **-ens** *or* **-en** : douzaine *f*
drab [ˈdræb] *adj* **drabber; drabbest** : terne
draft [ˈdræft, ˈdrɑft] *n* **1** : courant *m* d'air **2** *or* **rough ~** : brouillon *m* **3** : conscription *f* (militaire) **4** *or* **bank ~** : traite *f* bancaire **5** *or* **~ beer** : bière *f* pression — **~** *vt* **1** OUTLINE : faire le brouillon de **2** : appeler (des soldats) sous les drapeaux — **drafty** [ˈdræfti] *adj* **draftier; -est** : plein de courants d'air
drag [ˈdræg] *v* **dragged; dragging** *vt* **1** HAUL : tirer **2** : traîner (les pieds, etc.) **3** : glisser (en informatique) — *vi* TRAIL : traîner — **~** *n* **1** RESISTANCE : résistance *f* (aérodynamique) **2 what a ~!** : quelle barbe!
dragon [ˈdrægən] *n* : dragon *m* — **dragonfly** [ˈdrægənˌflaɪ] *n, pl* **-flies** : libellule *f*
drain [ˈdreɪn] *vt* **1** EMPTY : vider, drainer **2** EXHAUST : épuiser — *vi* : s'écouler, s'égoutter (se dit de la vaisselle) — **~** *n* **1** : tuyau *m* d'écoulement **2** SEWER : égout *m* **3** DEPLETION : épuisement *m* — **drainage** [ˈdreɪnɪʤ] *n* : drainage *m* — **drainpipe** [ˈdreɪnˌpaɪp] *n* : tuyau *m* d'écoulement
drama [ˈdrɑmə, ˈdræ-] *n* : drame *m* — **dra-**

matic [drə'mætɪk] *adj* : dramatique — **dramatize** ['dræmə,taɪz, 'drɑ-] *vt* **-tized; -tizing** : dramatiser

drank → **drink**

drape ['dreɪp] *vt* **draped; draping** : draper — **drapes** *npl* CURTAINS : rideaux *mpl*

drastic ['dræstɪk] *adj* : sévère, énergique

draught ['dræft, 'drɑft] → **draft**

draw ['drɔ] *v* **drew** ['dru:]; **drawn** ['drɔn]; **drawing** ['drɔɪŋ] *vt* **1** PULL : tirer **2** ATTRACT : attirer **3** SKETCH : dessiner **4** MAKE : faire (une distinction, etc.) **5** *or* ~ **up** FORMULATE : rédiger — *vi* **1** SKETCH : dessiner **2** ~ **near** : approcher — ~ *n* **1** DRAWING : tirage *m* (au sort) **2** TIE : match *m* nul **3** ATTRACTION : attraction *f* — **drawback** ['drɔ,bæk] *n* : inconvénient *m* — **drawer** ['drɔr, 'drɔər] *n* : tiroir *m* — **drawing** ['drɔɪŋ] *n* **1** SKETCH : dessin *m* **2** LOTTERY : tirage *m* (au sort)

drawl ['drɔl] *n* : voix *f* traînante

dread ['drɛd] *vt* : redouter, craindre — ~ *n* : crainte *f*, terreur *f* — **dreadful** ['drɛdfəl] *adj* : affreux, épouvantable

dream ['dri:m] *n* : rêve *m* — ~ *v* **dreamed** ['dri:md] *or* **dreamt** ['drɛmpt]; **dreaming** : rêver — **dreamer** ['dri:mər] *n* : rêveur *m*, -veuse *f* — **dreamy** ['dri:mi] *adj* **dreamier; -est** : rêveur

dreary ['drɪri] *adj* **drearier; -est** : morne, sombre

dredge ['drɛʤ] *vt* **dredged; dredging** : draguer

dregs ['drɛgz] *npl* : lie *f*

drench ['drɛntʃ] *vt* : tremper

dress ['drɛs] *vt* **1** CLOTHE : habiller, vêtir **2** : assaisonner (une salade) **3** BANDAGE : panser (une blessure) — *vi* **1** : s'habiller **2** *or* ~ **up** : se mettre en grande toilette **3** ~ **up as** : se déguiser en — ~ *n* **1** CLOTHING : tenue *f* **2** : robe *f* (de femme) — **dresser** ['drɛsər] *n* : commode *f* à miroir — **dressing** ['drɛsɪŋ] *n* **1** SAUCE : sauce *f*, vinaigrette *f* **2** BANDAGE : pansement *m* — **dressmaker** ['drɛs,meɪkər] *n* : couturière *f* — **dressy** ['drɛsi] *adj* **dressier; -est** : habillé, élégant

drew → **draw**

dribble ['drɪbəl] *vi* **-bled; -bling 1** TRICKLE : tomber goutte à goutte **2** DROOL : baver **3** : dribbler (aux sports) — ~ *n* **1** TRICKLE : filet *m* **2** DROOL : bave *f*

drier, driest → **dry**

drift ['drɪft] *n* **1** MOVEMENT : mouvement *m* **2** HEAP : banc *m* (de neige) *Can* — ~ *vi* **1** : dériver (sur l'eau), être emporté (par le vent) **2** ACCUMULATE : s'amonceler

drill ['drɪl] *n* **1** : perceuse *f* (outil) **2** EXERCISE : exercice *m* — ~ *vt* **1** : percer, forer **2** TRAIN : entraîner

drink ['drɪŋk] *v* **drank** ['dræŋk]; **drunk** ['drʌŋk] *or* **drank; drinking** : boire — ~ *n* : boisson *f*

drip ['drɪp] *vi* **dripped; dripping** : tomber goutte à goutte, dégoutter — ~ *n* DROP : goutte *f*

drive ['draɪv] *v* **drove** ['dro:v]; **driven** ['drɪvən]; **driving** *vt* **1** : conduire **2** COMPEL : inciter — *vi* : conduire, rouler — ~ *n* **1** : promenade *f* (en voiture) **2** CAMPAIGN : campagne *f* **3** VIGOR : énergie *f* **4** NEED : besoin *m* fondamental

driver ['draɪvər] *n* **1** : conducteur *m*, -trice *f* **2** CHAUFFEUR : chauffeur *m*

driveway ['draɪv,weɪ] *n* : allée *f*, entrée *f* (de garage)

drizzle ['drɪzəl] *n* : bruine *f* — ~ *vi* **-zled; -zling** : bruiner

drone ['dro:n] *n* **1** BEE : abeille *f* mâle **2** HUM : bourdonnement *m* — ~ *vi* **droned; droning 1** BUZZ : bourdonner **2** *or* ~ **on** : parler d'un ton monotone

drool ['dru:l] *vi* : baver — ~ *n* : bave *f*

droop ['dru:p] *vi* : pencher, tomber

drop ['drɑp] *n* **1** : goutte *f* (de liquide) **2** DECLINE, FALL : baisse *f* **3** DESCENT : chute *f* — ~ *v* **dropped; dropping** *vt* **1** : laisser tomber **2** LOWER : baisser **3** ABANDON : abandonner **4** ~ **off** LEAVE : déposer — *vi* **1** FALL : tomber **2** DECREASE : baisser **3** ~ **by** : passer

drought ['draʊt] *n* : sécheresse *f*

drove ['dro:v] → **drive**

droves ['dro:vz] *npl* **in** ~ : en masse

drown ['draʊn] *vt* : noyer — *vi* : se noyer

drowsy ['draʊzi] *adj* **drowsier; -est** : somnolent — **drowsiness** ['draʊzinəs] *n* : somnolence *f*

drudgery ['drʌʤəri] *n, pl* **-eries** : corvée *f*

drug ['drʌg] *n* **1** MEDICATION : médicament *m* **2** NARCOTIC : drogue *f*, stupéfiant *m* — ~ *vt* **drugged; drugging** : droguer — **drugstore** ['drʌg,stor] *n* : pharmacie *f*

drum ['drʌm] *n* **1** : tambour *m* **2** *or* **oil** ~ : bidon *m* — ~ *v* **drummed; drumming** *vi* : jouer du tambour — *vt* : tambouriner — **drumstick** ['drʌm,stɪk] *n* **1** : baguette *f* de tambour **2** : pilon *m* (de poulet)

drunk ['drʌŋk] → **drink** — ~ *adj* : ivre — ~ *or* **drunkard** ['drʌŋkərd] *n* : ivrogne *m*, ivrognesse *f* — **drunken** ['drʌŋkən] *adj* : ivre

dry ['draɪ] *adj* **drier; driest** : sec — ~ *v* **dried; drying** *vt* **1** : sécher **2** WIPE : essuyer — *vi* : sécher — **dry-clean** ['draɪ,kli:n] *vt* : nettoyer à sec — **dry cleaner** *n* : teinturerie *f* — **dryer** ['draɪər] *n* : séchoir *m* — **dryness** ['draɪnəs] *n* : sécheresse *f*

dual ['du:əl, 'dju:-] *adj* : double

dub ['dʌb] *vt* **dubbed; dubbing** : doubler (un film, etc.)

dubious ['du:biəs, 'dju:-] *adj* **1** DOUBTFUL : douteux **2** QUESTIONABLE : suspect

duck ['dʌk] *n, pl* **ducks** *or* **duck** : canard *m* — ~ *vt* **1** PLUNGE : plonger **2** LOWER : baisser **3** AVOID, DODGE : éviter, esquiver — **duckling** ['dʌklɪŋ] *n* : caneton *m*

duct ['dʌkt] *n* : conduit *m*

due ['du:, 'dju:] *adj* **1** PAYABLE : dû, payable **2** APPROPRIATE : qui convient **3** EXPECTED : attendu **4** ~ **to** : en raison de — ~ *n* **1** : dû *m* **2** ~**s** *npl* FEE : cotisation *f* — ~ *adv* : plein, droit vers

duel ['du:əl, 'dju:-] *n* : duel *m*

duet [du:'ɛt, dju:-] *n* : duo *m*

dug → **dig**

duke ['du:k, 'dju:k] *n* : duc *m*

dull ['dʌl] *adj* **1** STUPID : stupide **2** BLUNT : émoussé **3** BORING : ennuyeux **4** LACKLUSTER : terne — ~ *vt* **1** BLUNT : émousser **2** DIM, TARNISH : ternir

duly ['du:li] *adv* **1** PROPERLY : dûment **2** EXPECTEDLY : comme prévu

dumb ['dʌm] *adj* **1** MUTE : muet **2** STUPID : bête

dumbfound *or* **dumfound** [ˌdʌm'faʊnd] *vt* : abasourdir

dummy ['dʌmi] *n, pl* **-mies** **1** FOOL : imbécile *mf* **2** MANNEQUIN : mannequin *m* — ~ *adj* : faux

dump ['dʌmp] *vt* : déposer, jeter — ~ *n* **1** : décharge *f* (publique) **2 down in the** ~**s** : déprimé

dune ['du:n, 'dju:n] *n* : dune *f*

dung ['dʌŋ] *n* : fumier *m*

dungeon ['dʌndʒən] *n* : cachot *m*

dunk ['dʌŋk] *vt* : tremper

duo ['du:o:, 'dju:-] *n, pl* **duos** : duo *m*

dupe ['du:p, 'dju:p] *n* : dupe *f* — ~ *vt* **duped; duping** : duper

duplex ['du:ˌplɛks, 'dju:-] *n* : duplex *m*, maison *f* jumelée

duplicate ['du:plɪkət, 'dju:-] *adj* : en double — ~ ['du:plɪˌkeɪt, 'dju:-] *vt* **-cated; -cating** : faire un double de, copier — ~ ['du:plɪkət, 'dju:-] *n* : double *m*

durable ['dʊrəbəl, 'djʊr-] *adj* : durable, résistant

duration [dʊ'reɪʃən, djʊ-] *n* : durée *f*

during ['dʊrɪŋ, 'djʊr-] *prep* : pendant

dusk ['dʌsk] *n* : crépuscule *m*

dust ['dʌst] *n* : poussière *f* — ~ *vt* **1** : épousseter **2** SPRINKLE : saupoudrer — **dustpan** ['dʌstˌpæn] *n* : pelle *f* à poussière — **dusty** ['dʌsti] *adj* **dustier; -est** : poussiéreux

duty ['du:ti, 'dju:-] *n, pl* **-ties** **1** TASK : fonction *f* **2** OBLIGATION : devoir *m* **3** TAX : taxe *f*, droit *m* — **dutiful** ['du:tɪfəl, 'dju:-] *adj* : obéissant

dwarf ['dwɔrf] *n* : nain *m*, naine *f*

dwell ['dwɛl] *vi* **dwelled** *or* **dwelt** ['dwɛlt]; **dwelling 1** RESIDE : demeurer **2** ~ **on** : penser sans cesse à — **dweller** ['dwɛlər] *n* : habitant *m*, -tante *f* — **dwelling** ['dwɛlɪŋ] *n* : habitation *f*

dwindle ['dwɪndəl] *vi* **-dled; -dling** : diminuer

dye ['daɪ] *n* : teinture *f* — ~ *vt* **dyed; dyeing** : teindre

dying → **die¹**

dynamic [daɪ'næmɪk] *adj* : dynamique

dynamite ['daɪnəˌmaɪt] *n* : dynamite *f* — ~ *vt* **-mited; -miting** : dynamiter

dynasty ['daɪnəsti, -næs-] *n, pl* **-ties** : dynastie *f*

E

e ['i:] *n, pl* **e's** *or* **es** ['i:z] : e *m*, cinquième lettre de l'alphabet

each ['i:tʃ] *adj* : chaque — ~ *pron* **1** : chacun *m*, -cune *f* **2** ~ **other** : l'un l'autre **3 they love** ~ **other** : ils s'aiment — ~ *adv* : chacun, par personne

eager ['i:gər] *adj* **1** ENTHUSIASTIC : avide **2** IMPATIENT : impatient — **eagerness** ['i:gərnəs] *n* : enthousiasme *m*, empressement *m*

eagle ['i:gəl] *n* : aigle *m*

ear ['ɪr] *n* **1** : oreille *f* **2** ~ **of corn** : épi *m* de maïs — **eardrum** ['ɪrˌdrʌm] *n* : tympan *m*

earl ['ərl] *n* : comte *m*

earlobe ['ɪrˌlo:b] *n* : lobe *m* de l'oreille

early ['ərli] *adv* **-lier; -est 1** : tôt, de bonne heure **2 as** ~ **as possible** : le plus tôt possible **3 ten minutes** ~ : en avance de dix minutes — ~ *adj* **-lier; -est 1** FIRST : premier **2** ANCIENT : ancien **3 in the** ~ **afternoon** : au début de l'après-midi

earmark ['ɪrˌmɑrk] *vt* : réserver, désigner

earn ['ərn] *vt* **1** : gagner **2** DESERVE : mériter

earnest ['ərnəst] *adj* : sérieux — ~ *n* **in** ~ : sérieusement

earnings ['ərnɪŋz] *npl* **1** WAGES : salaire *m* **2** PROFITS : gains *mpl*

earphone ['ɪr,fo:n] *n* : écouteur *m*

earring ['ɪr,rɪŋ] *n* : boucle *f* d'oreille

earshot ['ɪr,ʃɑt] *n* within ~ : à portée de voix

earth ['ərθ] *n* **1** GROUND : terre *f*, sol *m* **2 the Earth** : la terre — **earthly** ['ərθli] *adj* : terrestre — **earthquake** ['ərθ,kweɪk] *n* : tremblement *m* de terre — **earthworm** ['ərθ,wərm] *n* : ver *m* de terre — **earthy** ['ərθi] *adj* **earthier; earthiest** : terreux

ease ['i:z] *n* **1** FACILITY : facilité *f* **2** COMFORT : bien-être *m* **3 feel at** ~ : être à l'aise — ~ *v* **eased; easing** *vt* **1** FACILITATE : faciliter **2** ALLEVIATE : soulager, réduire — *vi* ~ **up** : s'atténuer

easel ['i:zəl] *n* : chevalet *m*

easily ['i:zəli] *adv* **1** : facilement **2** UNQUESTIONABLY : de loin

east ['i:st] *adv* : vers l'est, à l'est — ~ *adj* : est — ~ *n* **1** : est *m* **2 the East** : l'Est *m*, l'Orient *m*

Easter ['i:stər] *n* : Pâques *m*, Pâques *fpl*

easterly ['i:stərli] *adv* : vers l'est — ~ *adj* : d'est, de l'est

eastern ['i:stərn] *adj* **1** : est, de l'est **2 Eastern** : de l'Est, oriental

easy ['i:zi] *adj* **easier; easiest 1** : facile, aisé **2** RELAXED : décontracté — **easygoing** [,i:zi'go:ɪŋ] *adj* : accommodant

eat ['i:t] *v* **ate** ['eɪt]; **eaten** ['i:tən]; **eating** : manger

eaves ['i:vz] *npl* : avant-toit *m* — **eavesdrop** ['i:vz,drɑp] *vi* **-dropped; -dropping** : écouter aux portes

ebb ['ɛb] *n* : reflux *m* — ~ *vi* **1** : refluer **2** DECLINE : décliner

ebony ['ɛbəni] *n, pl* **-nies** : ébène *f*

eccentric [ɪk'sɛntrɪk] *adj* : excentrique — ~ *n* : excentrique *mf* — **eccentricity** [,ɛk,sɛn'trɪsəti] *n, pl* **-ties** : excentricité *f*

echo ['ɛ,ko:] *n, pl* **echoes** : écho *m* — ~ *v* **echoed; echoing** *vt* : répéter — *vi* : se répercuter, résonner

eclipse [ɪ'klɪps] *n* : éclipse *f*

ecology [i'kɑləʤi, ɛ-] *n, pl* **-gies** : écologie *f* — **ecological** [,i:kə'lɑʤɪkəl, ,ɛkə-] *adj* : écologique

economy [i'kɑnəmi] *n, pl* **-mies** : économie *f* — **economic** [,i:kə'nɑmɪk, ,ɛkə-] *adj* : économique — **economical** [,i:kə'nɑmɪkəl, ,ɛkə-] *adj* THRIFTY : économe — **economics** [,i:kə'nɑmɪks, ,ɛkə-] *ns & pl* : sciences *fpl* économiques, économie *f* — **economist** [i'kɑnəmɪst] *n* : économiste *mf* — **economize** [i'kɑnə,maɪz] *v* **-mized; -mizing** : économiser

ecstasy ['ɛkstəsi] *n, pl* **-sies** : extase *f* — **ecstatic** [ɛk'stætɪk, ɪk-] *adj* : extatique

edge ['ɛʤ] *n* **1** BORDER : bord *m* **2** : tranchant *m* (d'un couteau, etc.) **3** ADVANTAGE : avantage *m* — ~ *vi* : avancer lentement — **edgewise** ['ɛʤ,waɪz] *adv* : de côté — **edgy** ['ɛʤi] *adj* **edgier; edgiest** : énervé

edible ['ɛdəbəl] *adj* : comestible

edit ['ɛdɪt] *vt* **1** : réviser, corriger **2** ~ **out** : couper — **edition** [ɪ'dɪʃən] *n* : édition *f* — **editor** ['ɛdɪtər] *n* : rédacteur *m*, -trice *f* (d'un journal); éditeur *m*, -trice *f* (d'un livre) — **editorial** [,ɛdɪ'toriəl] *n* : éditorial *m*

educate ['ɛʤə,keɪt] *vt* **-cated; -cating** : instruire, éduquer — **education** [,ɛʤə'keɪʃən] *n* **1** : éducation *f*, études *fpl* **2** TEACHING : enseignement *m*, instruction *f* — **educational** [,ɛʤə'keɪʃənəl] *adj* **1** : éducatif **2** TEACHING : pédagogique — **educator** ['ɛʤə,keɪtər] *n* : éducateur *m*, -trice *f*

eel ['i:l] *n* : anguille *f*

eerie ['ɪri] *adj* **eerier, -est** : étrange

effect [ɪ'fɛkt] *n* **1** : effet *m* **2 go into** ~ : entrer en vigueur — ~ *vt* : effectuer, réaliser — **effective** [ɪ'fɛktɪv] *adj* **1** : efficace **2 become** ~ : entrer en vigueur — **effectiveness** [ɪ'fɛktɪvnəs] *n* : efficacité *f*

effeminate [ə'fɛmənət] *adj* : efféminé

efficient [ɪ'fɪʃənt] *adj* : efficace — **efficiency** [ɪ'fɪʃəntsi] *n pl* **-cies** : efficacité *f*

effort ['ɛfərt] *n* **1** : effort *m* **2 it's not worth the** ~ : ça ne vaut pas la peine — **effortless** ['ɛfərtləs] *adj* : facile

egg ['ɛg] *n* : œuf *m* — **eggplant** ['ɛg,plænt] *n* : aubergine *f* — **eggshell** ['ɛg,ʃɛl] *n* : coquille *f* d'œuf

ego ['i:,go:] *n, pl* **egos 1** SELF : moi *m* **2** SELF-ESTEEM : amour-propre *m* — **egotism** ['i:gə'tɪzəm] *n* : égotisme *m* — **egotistic** [,i:gə'tɪstɪk] *or* **egotistical** [-'tɪstɪkəl] *adj* : égocentrique

Egyptian [i'ʤɪpʃən] *adj* : égyptien

eight ['eɪt] *n* : huit *m* — ~ *adj* : huit — **eighteen** [eɪt'ti:n] *n* : dix-huit *m* — ~ *adj* : dix-huit — **eighteenth** [eɪt'ti:nθ] *n* **1** : dix-huitième *mf* **2 October** ~ : le dix-huit octobre — ~ *adj* : dix-huitième — **eighth** ['eɪtθ] *n* **1** : huitième *mf* **2 February** ~ : le huit février — ~ *adj* : huitième — **eight hundred** *adj* : huit cents — **eightieth** [eɪtiəθ] *n* : quatre-vingtième *mf* — ~ *adj* : quatre-vingtième — **eighty** [eɪti] *n, pl* **eighties** : quatre-vingts *m* — ~ *adj* : quatre-vingts

either ['i:ðər, 'aɪ-] *adj* **1** : l'un ou l'autre **2** EACH : chaque — ~ *pron* : l'un ou l'autre, n'importe lequel — ~ *conj* **1** : ou, soit **2** (*in negative constructions*) : ni

eject [i'ʤɛkt] *vt* : éjecter, expulser

elaborate [i'læbərət] *adj* **1** DETAILED : détaillé **2** COMPLEX : compliqué — ~ [i'læbə,reɪt] *v* **-rated; -rating** *vt* : élaborer — *vi* ~ **on** : donner des détails sur

elapse [i'læps] *vi* **elapsed; elapsing**
: s'écouler

elastic [i'læstɪk] *adj* : élastique — **~** *n*
: élastique *m* — **elasticity** [i‚læs'tɪsəti,
i‚lmo] *n, pl* **-ties** : élasticité *f*

elated [i'leɪtəd] *adj* : fou de joie — **elation**
[i'leɪʃən] *n* : allégresse *f*, joie *f*

elbow ['ɛl‚bo:] *n* : coude *m*

elder ['ɛldər] *adj* : aîné, plus âgé — **~** *n*
: aîné *m*, aînée *f* — **elderly** ['ɛldərli] *adj* : âgé

elect [i'lɛkt] *vt* : élire — **~** *adj* : élu, futur —
election [i'lɛkʃən] *n* : élection *f* — **electoral** [i'lɛktərəl] *adj* : électoral — **electorate** [i'lɛktərət] *n* : électorat *m*

electricity [i‚lɛk'trɪsəti] *n, pl* **-ties** : électricité *f* — **electric** [i'lɛktrɪk] *or* **electrical**
[-trɪkəl] *adj* : électrique — **electrician**
[i‚lɛk'trɪʃən] *n* : électricien *m*, -cienne *f* —
electrocute [i'lɛktrə‚kju:t] *vt* **-cuted; -cut-
ing** : électrocuter

electron [i'lɛk‚trɑn] *n* : électron *m* — **electronic** [i‚lɛk'trɑnɪk] *adj* : électronique —
electronic mail : courrier *m* électronique
— **electronics** [i‚lɛk'trɑnɪks] *n* : électronique *f*

elegant ['ɛligənt] *adj* : élégant — **elegance**
['ɛligənts] *n* : élégance *f*

element ['ɛlə‚mənt] *n* **1** : élément *m* **2 ~s**
npl BASICS : rudiments *mpl* — **elementary**
[‚ɛlə'mɛntri] *adj* : élémentaire — **elementary school** *n* : école *f* primaire

elephant ['ɛləfənt] *n* : éléphant *m*

elevate ['ɛlə‚veɪt] *vt* **-vated; -vating** : élever
— **elevator** ['ɛlə‚veɪtər] *n* : ascenseur *m*

eleven [ɪ'lɛvən] *n* : onze *m* — **~** *adj* : onze
— **eleventh** [ɪ'lɛvənθ] *n* **1** : onzième *mf* **2**
March ~ : le onze mars — **~** *adj* : onzième

elf ['ɛlf] *n, pl* **elves** ['ɛlvz] : lutin *m*

elicit [ɪ'lɪsət] *vt* : provoquer

eligible ['ɛlədʒəbəl] *adj* : éligible, admissible

eliminate [ɪ'lɪmə‚neɪt] *vt* **-nated; -nating**
: éliminer — **elimination** [ɪ‚lɪmə'neɪʃən] *n*
: élimination *f*

elite [eɪ'li:t, i-] *n* : élite *f*

elk ['ɛlk] *n* : élan *m* (d'Europe), wapiti *m*
(d'Amérique)

elm ['ɛlm] *n* : orme *m*

elongate [i'lɔŋ‚geɪt] *vt* **-gated; -gating** : allonger

elope [i'lo:p] *vi* **eloped; eloping** : s'enfuir
(pour se marier) — **elopement** [i'lo:pmənt]
n : fugue *f* amoureuse

eloquence ['ɛlə‚kwənts] *n* : éloquence *f* —
eloquent ['ɛlə‚kwənt] *adj* : éloquent

else ['ɛls] *adv* **or ~** : sinon, autrement — **~**
adj **1 everyone ~** : tous les autres **2 what
~** : quoi d'autre — **elsewhere** ['ɛls‚hwɛr]
adv : ailleurs

elude [i'lu:d] *vt* **eluded; eluding** : échapper
à, éluder — **elusive** [i'lu:sɪv] *adj* : insaisissable

elves → elf

e-mail ['i:‚meɪl] *n* : courriel *m*, e-mail *m*
France

emanate ['ɛmə‚neɪt] *vi* **-nated; -nating**
: émaner

emancipate [i'mæntsə‚peɪt] *vt* **-pated; -pat-
ing** : émanciper

embalm [ɪm'bɑm, ɛm-, -'bɑlm] *vt* : embaumer

embankment [ɪm'bæŋkmənt, ɛm-] *n*
: digue *f* (d'une rivière), remblai *m* (d'une
route)

embargo [ɪm'bɑrgo, ɛm-] *n, pl* **-goes** : embargo *m*

embark [ɪm'bɑrk, ɛm-] *vt* : embarquer — *vi*
~ on : entreprendre

embarrass [ɪm'bærəs, ɛm-] *vt* : gêner, embarrasser — **embarrassing** [ɪm'bærəsɪŋ,
ɛm-] *adj* : embarrassant — **embarrassment**
[ɪm'bærəsmənt, ɛm-] *n* : gêne *f*, embarras *m*

embassy ['ɛmbəsi] *n, pl* **-sies** : ambassade *f*

embed [ɪm'bɛd, ɛm-] *vt* **-bedded; -bedding**
: enfoncer

embellish [ɪm'bɛlɪʃ, ɛm-] *vt* : embellir —
embellishment [ɪm'bɛlɪʃmənt, ɛm-] *n*
: ornement *m*

embers ['ɛmbərz] *npl* : braise *f*

embezzle [ɪm'bɛzəl, ɛm-] *vt* **-zled; -zling**
: détourner — **embezzlement** [ɪm'bɛzəl-
mənt, ɛm-] *n* : détournement *m* de fonds

emblem ['ɛmbləm] *n* : emblème *m*

embody [ɪm'bɑdi, ɛm-] *vt* **-bodied; -body-
ing** : incarner

embrace [ɪm'breɪs, ɛm-] *v* **-braced; -brac-
ing** *vt* : embrasser — *vi* : s'embrasser — **~**
n : étreinte *f*

embroider [ɪm'brɔɪdər, ɛm-] *vt* : broder —
embroidery [ɪm'brɔɪdəri, ɛm-] *n, pl*
-deries : broderie *f*

embryo ['ɛmbri‚o:] *n* : embryon *m*

emerald ['ɛmrəld, 'ɛmə-] *n* : émeraude *f*

emerge [i'mərdʒ] *vi* **emerged; emerging 1**
APPEAR : apparaître **2 ~ from** : émerger
de — **emergence** [i'mərdʒənts] *n* : apparition *f*

emergency [i'mərdʒəntsi] *n, pl* **-cies 1** : urgence *f* **2 ~ exit** : sortie *f* de secours **3 ~
room** : salle *f* des urgences

emery ['ɛməri] *n, pl* **-eries 1** : émeri *m* **2 ~
board** : lime *f* à ongles

emigrant ['ɛmɪgrənt] *n* : émigrant *m*,
-grante *f* — **emigrate** ['ɛmə‚greɪt] *vi*
-grated; -grating : émigrer

eminence ['ɛmənənts] *n* : éminence *f* — **eminent** ['ɛmənənt] *adj* : éminent

emission [i'mɪʃən] *n* : émission *f* — **emit**
[i'mɪt] *vt* **emitted; emitting** : émettre

emotion [i'moːʃən] *n* : émotion *f* — **emotional** [i'moːʃənəl] *adj* **1** : émotif **2** MOVING : émouvant

emperor ['ɛmpərər] *n* : empereur *m*

emphasis ['ɛmfəsɪs] *n, pl* **-ses** [-ˌsiːz] : accent — **emphasize** ['ɛmfəˌsaɪz] *vt* **-sized; -sizing** : insister sur — **emphatic** [ɪm'fætɪk, ɛm-] *adj* : énergique, catégorique

empire ['ɛmˌpaɪr] *n* : empire *m*

employ [ɪm'plɔɪ, ɛm-] *vt* : employer — **employee** [ɪmˌplɔɪ'iː, ɛm-, -'plɔɪˌiː] *n* : employé *m*, -ployée *f* — **employer** [ɪm'plɔɪər, ɛm-] *n* : employeur *m*, -ployeuse *f* — **employment** [ɪm'plɔɪmənt, ɛm-] *n* : emploi *m*, travail *m*

empower [ɪm'paʊər, ɛm-] *vt* : autoriser

empress ['ɛmprəs] *n* : impératrice *f*

empty ['ɛmpti] *adj* **-tier; -est 1** : vide **2** MEANINGLESS : vain — ~ *v* **-tied; -tying** *vt* : vider — *vi* : se vider — **emptiness** ['ɛmptinəs] *n* : vide *m*

emulate ['ɛmjəˌleɪt] *vt* **-lated; -lating** : imiter

enable [ɪ'neɪbəl, ɛ-] *vt* **-abled; -abling** : permettre

enact [ɪ'nækt, ɛ-] *vt* : promulguer (une loi, etc.)

enamel [ɪ'næməl] *n* : émail *m*

enchant [ɪn'tʃænt, ɛn-] *vt* : enchanter — **enchanting** [ɪn'tʃæntɪŋ, ɛn-] *adj* : enchanteur

encircle [ɪn'sərkəl, ɛn-] *vt* **-cled; -cling** : entourer, encercler

enclose [ɪn'kloːz, ɛn-] *vt* **-closed; -closing 1** SURROUND : entourer **2** INCLUDE : joindre (à une lettre) — **enclosure** [ɪn'kloːʒər, ɛn-] *n* **1** : enceinte *f* **2** : pièce *f* jointe (à une lettre)

encompass [ɪn'kʌmpəs, ɛn-, -'kɑm-] *vt* **1** ENCIRCLE : entourer **2** INCLUDE : inclure

encore ['ɑŋˌkor] *n* : bis *m*

encounter [ɪn'kaʊntər, ɛn-] *vt* : rencontrer — ~ *n* : rencontre *f*

encourage [ɪn'kərɪdʒ, ɛn-] *vt* **-aged; -aging** : encourager — **encouragement** [ɪn'kərɪdʒmənt, ɛn-] *n* : encouragement *m*

encroach [ɪn'kroːtʃ, ɛn-] *vi* ~ **on** : empiéter sur

encyclopedia [ɪnˌsaɪklə'piːdiə, ɛn-] *n* : encyclopédie *f*

end ['ɛnd] *n* **1** : fin *f* **2** EXTREMITY : bout *m* **3 come to an** ~ : prendre fin **4 in the** ~ : finalement— ~ *vt* : terminer, mettre fin à — *vi* : se terminer

endanger [ɪn'deɪndʒər, ɛn-] *vt* : mettre en danger

endearing [ɪn'dɪrɪŋ, ɛn-] *adj* : attachant

endeavor *or Brit* **endeavour** [ɪn'dɛvər, ɛn-] *vt* ~ **to** : s'efforcer de — ~ *n* : effort *m*

ending ['ɛndɪŋ] *n* : fin *f*, dénouement *m*

endive ['ɛnˌdaɪv, ˌɑn'diːv] *n* : endive *f*

endless ['ɛndləs] *adj* **1** INTERMINABLE : interminable **2** INNUMERABLE : innombrable **3** ~ **possibilities** : possibilités *fpl* infinies

endorse [ɪn'dors, ɛn-] *vt* **-dorsed; -dorsing 1** SIGN : endosser **2** APPROVE : approuver — **endorsement** [ɪn'dorsmənt, ɛn-] *n* APPROVAL : approbation *f*

endow [ɪn'dau, ɛn-] *vt* : doter

endure [ɪn'dur, ɛn-, -'djur-] *v* **-dured; -during** *vt* : supporter, endurer — *vi* LAST : durer — **endurance** [ɪn'durənts, ɛn-, -'djur-] *n* : endurance *f*

enemy ['ɛnəmi] *n, pl* **-mies** : ennemi *m*, -mie *f*

energy ['ɛnərdʒi] *n, pl* **-gies** : énergie *f* — **energetic** [ˌɛnər'dʒɛtɪk] *adj* : énergique

enforce [ɪn'fors, ɛn-] *vt* **-forced; -forcing 1** : faire respecter (une loi) **2** IMPOSE : imposer — **enforcement** [ɪn'forsmənt, ɛn-] *n* : exécution *f*, application *f*

engage [ɪn'geɪdʒ, ɛn-] *v* **-gaged; -gaging** *vt* **1** : engager (une conversation) **2** ~ **the clutch** : embrayer — *vi* ~ **in** : prendre part à, s'occuper de — **engaged** [ɪn'geɪdʒd, ɛn-] *adj* **get** ~ **to** : se fiancer à — **engagement** [ɪn'geɪdʒmənt, ɛn-] *n* **1** : fiançailles *fpl* **2** APPOINTMENT : rendez-vous *m* — **engaging** [ɪn'geɪdʒɪŋ, ɛn-] *adj* : engageant, attirant

engine ['ɛndʒən] *n* **1** : moteur *m* **2** LOCOMOTIVE : locomotive *f* — **engineer** [ˌɛndʒə'nɪr] *n* : ingénieur *m*, -nieure *f* — **engineering** [ˌɛndʒə'nɪrɪŋ] *n* : ingénierie *f*

English ['ɪŋglɪʃ, 'ɪŋlɪʃ] *adj* : anglais — ~ *n* : anglais *m* (langue) — **Englishman** ['ɪŋglɪʃmən, 'ɪŋlɪʃ-] *n* : Anglais *m* — **Englishwoman** ['ɪŋglɪʃˌwumən, 'ɪŋlɪʃ-] *n* : Anglaise *f*

engrave [ɪn'greɪv, ɛn-] *vt* **-graved; -graving** : graver — **engraving** [ɪn'greɪvɪŋ, ɛn-] *n* : gravure *f*

engross [ɪn'groːs, ɛn-] *vt* : absorber, occuper

engulf [ɪn'gʌlf, ɛn-] *vt* : engloutir

enhance [ɪn'hænts, ɛn-] *vt* **-hanced; -hancing** : améliorer, rehausser

enjoy [ɪn'dʒɔɪ, ɛn-] *vt* **1** LIKE : aimer **2** POSSESS : jouir de **3** ~ **oneself** : s'amuser — **enjoyable** [ɪn'dʒɔɪəbəl, ɛn-] *adj* : agréable — **enjoyment** [ɪn'dʒɔɪmənt, ɛn-] *n* : plaisir *m*

enlarge [ɪn'lɑrdʒ, ɛn-] *vt* **-larged; -larging** : agrandir — **enlargement** [ɪn'lɑrdʒmənt, ɛn-] *n* : agrandissement *m*

enlighten [ɪn'laɪtən, ɛn-] *vt* : éclairer

enlist [ɪn'lɪst, ɛn-] *vt* **1** ENROLL : enrôler **2** OBTAIN : obtenir — *vi* : s'engager, s'enrôler

enliven [ɪn'laɪvən, ɛn-] *vt* : animer

enormous [ɪ'nɔrməs] *adj* : énorme

enough [i'nʌf] *adj* : assez de — ~ *adv*

: assez — ~ *pron* have ~ of : en avoir assez de

enquire [ɪnˈkwaɪr, ɛn-], **enquiry** [ˈɪnˌkwaɪri, ˈɛn-, -kwəri; ɪnˈkwaɪri, ɛnˈ-] → inquire, inquiry

enrage [ɪnˈreɪdʒ, ɛn-] *vt* **-raged; -raging** : rendre furieux

enrich [ɪnˈrɪtʃ, ɛn-] *vt* : enrichir

enroll *or* **enrol** [ɪnˈroːl, ɛn-] *v* **-rolled; -rolling** *vt* 1 : inscrire (à l'école, etc.) 2 ENLIST : enrôler — *vi* : s'inscrire

ensue [ɪnˈsuː, ɛn-] *vi* **-sued; -suing** : s'ensuivre

ensure [ɪnˈʃʊr, ɛn-] *vt* **-sured; -suring** : assurer

entail [ɪnˈteɪl, ɛn-] *vt* : entraîner, comporter

entangle [ɪnˈtæŋɡəl, ɛn-] *vt* **-gled; -gling** : emmêler

enter [ˈɛntər] *vt* 1 : entrer dans 2 RECORD : inscrire — *vi* 1 : entrer 2 ~ **into** : entamer

enterprise [ˈɛntərˌpraɪz] *n* 1 : entreprise *f* 2 INITIATIVE : initiative *f* — **enterprising** [ˈɛntərˌpraɪzɪŋ] *adj* : entreprenant

entertain [ˌɛntərˈteɪn] *vt* 1 AMUSE : amuser, divertir 2 CONSIDER : considérer 3 : recevoir (des invités) — **entertainment** [ˌɛntərˈteɪnmənt] *n* : divertissement *m*

enthrall *or* **enthral** [ɪnˈθrɔl, ɛn-] *vt* **-thralled; -thralling** : captiver

enthusiasm [ɪnˈθuːziˌæzəm, ɛn-, -ˈθjuː-] *n* : enthousiasme *m* — **enthusiast** [ɪnˈθuːziˌæst, ɛn-, -ˈθjuː-, -əst] *n* : enthousiaste *mf*; passionné *m*, -née *f* — **enthusiastic** [ɪnˌθuːziˈæstɪk, ɛn-, -ˈθjuː-] *adj* : enthousiaste

entice [ɪnˈtaɪs, ɛn-] *vt* **-ticed; -ticing** : attirer, entraîner

entire [ɪnˈtaɪr, ɛn-] *adj* : entier, complet — **entirely** [ɪnˈtaɪrli, ɛn-] *adv* : entièrement — **entirety** [ɪnˈtaɪrti, ɛn-, -taɪrəti] *n, pl* **-ties** 1 : totalité *f* 2 **in its** ~ : dans son ensemble

entitle [ɪnˈtaɪtəl, ɛn-] *vt* **-tled; -tling** 1 NAME : intituler 2 AUTHORIZE : autoriser, donner droit à — **entitlement** [ɪnˈtaɪtəlmənt, ɛn-] *n* : droit *m*

entity [ˈɛntəti] *n, pl* **-ties** : entité *f*

entrails [ˈɛnˌtreɪlz, -trəlz] *npl* : entrailles *fpl*

entrance[1] [ɪnˈtrænts, ɛn-] *vt* **-tranced; -trancing** : transporter, ravir

entrance[2] [ˈɛntrənts] *n* : entrée *f*

entreat [ɪnˈtriːt, ɛn-] *vt* : supplier

entrée *or* **entree** [ˈɑnˌtreɪ, ˌɑnˈ-] *n* : entrée *f*, plat *m* principal

entrust [ɪnˈtrʌst, ɛn-] *vt* : confier

entry [ˈɛntri] *n, pl* **-tries** ENTRANCE : entrée *f*

enumerate [ɪˈnuːməˌreɪt, ɛ-, -ˈnjuː-] *vt* **-ated; -ating** : énumérer

enunciate [iˈnʌntsiˌeɪt, ɛ-] *vt* **-ated; -ating** 1 STATE : énoncer 2 PRONOUNCE : articuler

envelop [ɪnˈvɛləp, ɛn-] *vt* : envelopper — **envelope** [ˈɛnvəˌloːp, ˈɑn-] *n* : enveloppe *f*

envious [ˈɛnviəs] *adj* : envieux, jaloux — **enviously** [ˈɛnviəsli] *adv* : avec envie

environment [ɪnˈvaɪrənmənt, ɛn-, -ˈvaɪərn-] *n* : environnement *m*, milieu *m* — **environmental** [ɪnˌvaɪrənˈmɛntəl, ɛn-, -ˌvaɪərn-] *adj* : de l'environnement — **environmentalist** [ɪnˌvaɪrənˈmɛntəlɪst, ɛn-, -ˌvaɪərn-] *n* : écologiste *mf*

envision [ɪnˈvɪʒən, ɛn-] *vt* : envisager

envoy [ˈɛnˌvɔɪ, ˈɑn-] *n* : envoyé *m*, -voyée *f*

envy [ˈɛnvi] *n* : envie *f*, jalousie *f* — ~ *vt* **-vied; -vying** : envier

enzyme [ˈɛnˌzaɪm] *n* : enzyme *f*

epic [ˈɛpɪk] *adj* : épique — ~ *n* : épopée *f*

epidemic [ˌɛpəˈdɛmɪk] *n* : épidémie *f* — ~ *adj* : épidémique

epilepsy [ˈɛpəˌlɛpsi] *n, pl* **-sies** : épilepsie *f* — **epileptic** [ˌɛpəˈlɛptɪk] *adj* : épileptique — ~ *n* : épileptique *mf*

episode [ˈɛpəˌsoːd] *n* : épisode *m*

epitaph [ˈɛpəˌtæf] *n* : épitaphe *f*

epitome [ɪˈpɪtəmi] *n* : exemple *m* même, modèle *m* — **epitomize** [ɪˈpɪtəˌmaɪz] *vt* **-mized; -mizing** : incarner

equal [ˈiːkwəl] *adj* 1 SAME : égal 2 **be** ~ **to** : être à la hauteur de — ~ *n* : égal *m*, -gale *f* — ~ *vt* **equaled** *or* **equalled; equaling** *or* **equalling** : égaler — **equality** [ɪˈkwɑləti] *n, pl* **-ties** : égalité *f* — **equalize** [ˈiːkwəˌlaɪz] *vt* **-ized; -izing** : égaliser — **equally** [ˈiːkwəli] *adv* 1 : également 2 ~ **important** : tout aussi important

equate [ɪˈkweɪt] *vt* **equated; equating** ~ **with** : assimiler à — **equation** [ɪˈkweɪʒən] *n* : équation *f*

equator [ɪˈkweɪtər] *n* : équateur *m*

equilibrium [ˌiːkwəˈlɪbriəm, ˌɛ-] *n, pl* **-riums** *or* **-ria** : équilibre *m*

equinox [ˈiːkwəˌnɑks, ˈɛ-] *n* : équinoxe *m*

equip [ɪˈkwɪp] *vt* **equipped; equipping** : équiper — **equipment** [ɪˈkwɪpmənt] *n* : équipement *m*, matériel *m*

equity [ˈɛkwəti] *n, pl* **-ties** 1 FAIRNESS : équité *f* 2 **equities** *npl* STOCKS : actions *fpl* ordinaires

equivalent [ɪˈkwɪvələnt] *adj* : équivalent — ~ *n* : équivalent *m*

era [ˈɪrə, ˈɛrə, ˈiːrə] *n* : ère *f*, époque *f*

eradicate [ɪˈrædəˌkeɪt] *vt* **-cated; -cating** : éradiquer

erase [ɪˈreɪs] *vt* **erased; erasing** : effacer — **eraser** [ɪˈreɪsər] *n* : gomme *f*, efface *f Can*

erect [ɪˈrɛkt] *adj* : droit — ~ *vt* 1 BUILD : construire 2 RAISE : ériger — **erection** [ɪˈrɛkʃən] *n* 1 BUILDING : construction *f* 2 : érection *f* (en physiologie)

erode [ɪˈroːd] *vt* **eroded; eroding** : éroder, ronger — **erosion** [ɪˈroːʒən] *n* : érosion *f*

erotic [ɪˈrɑtɪk] *adj* : érotique

err [ˈɛr, ˈər] *vi* : se tromper

errand ['ɛrənd] *n* : course *f*, commission *f*

erratic [ɪ'rætɪk] *adj* : irrégulier

error ['ɛrər] *n* : erreur *f* — **erroneous** [ɪ-'ro:niəs, ɛ-] *adj* : erroné

erupt [ɪ'rʌpt] *vi* **1** : entrer en éruption (se dit d'un volcan) **2** : éclater (se dit de la guerre, etc.) — **eruption** [ɪ'rʌpʃən] *n* : éruption *f*

escalate ['ɛskə‚leɪt] *vi* **-lated; -lating 1** : s'intensifier **2** : monter en flèche (se dit des prix, etc.)

escalator ['ɛskə‚leɪtər] *n* : escalier *m* mécanique

escape [ɪ'skeɪp, ɛ-] *v* **-caped; -caping** *vt* : échapper à, éviter — *vi* : s'échapper, s'évader — **~** *n* : fuite *f*, évasion *f*

escort ['ɛs‚kɔrt] *n* GUARD : escorte *f* — **~** [ɪ'skɔrt, ɛ-] *vt* : escorter

Eskimo ['ɛskə‚mo:] *adj* : esquimau

especially [ɪ'spɛʃəli] *adv* : particulièrement

espionage ['ɛspiə‚naʒ, -‚naʤ] *n* : espionnage *m*

espresso [ɛ'sprɛ‚so:] *n*, *pl* **-sos** : express *m*, café *m* express

essay ['ɛ‚seɪ] *n* : essai *m* (littéraire), dissertation *f* (académique)

essence ['ɛsənts] *n* : essence *f* — **essential** [ɪ'sɛntʃəl] *adj* : essentiel — **~** *n* **1** : objet *m* essentiel **2 the ~s** : l'essentiel *m*

establish [ɪ'stæblɪʃ, ɛ-] *vt* : établir — **establishment** [ɪ'stæblɪʃmənt, ɛ-] *n* : établissement *m*

estate [ɪ'steɪt, ɛ-] *n* **1** POSSESSIONS : biens *mpl* **2** LAND, PROPERTY : propriété *f*, domaine *m*

esteem [ɪ'sti:m, ɛ-] *n* : estime *f* — **~** *vt* : estimer

esthetic [ɛs'θɛtɪk] → **aesthetic**

estimate ['ɛstə‚meɪt] *vt* **-mated; -mating** : estimer — **~** ['ɛstəmət] *n* : estimation *f* — **estimation** [‚ɛstə'meɪʃən] *n* **1** JUDGMENT : jugement *m* **2** ESTEEM : estime *f*

estuary ['ɛstʃu‚weri] *n*, *pl* **-aries** : estuaire *m*

eternal [ɪ'tərnəl, i:-] *adj* : éternel — **eternity** [ɪ'tərnəti, i:-] *n*, *pl* **-ties** : éternité *f*

ether ['i:θər] *n* : éther *m*

ethical ['ɛθɪkəl] *adj* : éthique, moral — **ethics** ['ɛθɪks] *ns & pl* : éthique *f*, morale *f*

ethnic ['ɛθnɪk] *adj* : ethnique

etiquette ['ɛtɪkət, -‚kɛt] *n* : étiquette *f*, convenances *fpl*

Eucharist ['ju:kərɪst] *n* : Eucharistie *f*

eulogy ['ju:ləʤi] *n*, *pl* **-gies** : éloge *m*

euphemism ['ju:fə‚mɪzəm] *n* : euphémisme *m*

euphoria [ju'foriə] *n* : euphorie *f*

European [‚jurə'pi:ən, -pi:n] *adj* : européen

evacuate [ɪ'vækju‚eɪt] *vt* **-ated; -ating** : évacuer — **evacuation** [ɪ‚vækju'eɪʃən] *n* : évacuation *f*

evade [ɪ'veɪd] *vt* **evaded; evading** : éviter, esquiver

evaluate [ɪ'vælju‚eɪt] *vt* **-ated; -ating** : évaluer

evaporate [ɪ'væpə‚reɪt] *vi* **-rated; -rating** : s'évaporer

evasion [ɪ'veɪʒən] *n* : évasion *f* — **evasive** [ɪ'veɪsɪv] *adj* : évasif

eve ['i:v] *n* : veille *f*

even ['i:vən] *adj* **1** REGULAR, STEADY : régulier **2** LEVEL : uni, plat **3** EQUAL : égal **4 ~ number** : nombre *m* pair **5 get ~ with** : se venger de — **~** *adv* **1** : même **2 ~ better** : encore mieux **3 ~ so** : quand même — **~** *vt* : égaliser — *vi or* **~ out** : s'égaliser

evening ['i:vnɪŋ] *n* : soir *m*, soirée *f*

event [ɪ'vɛnt] *n* **1** : événement *m* **2** : épreuve *f* (aux sports) **3 in the ~ of** : en cas de — **eventful** [ɪ'vɛntfəl] *adj* : mouvementé

eventual [ɪ'vɛntʃuəl] *adj* : final — **eventuality** [ɪ‚vɛntʃu'æləti] *n*, *pl* **-ties** : éventualité *f* — **eventually** [ɪ'vɛntʃuəli] *adv* : finalement, en fin de compte

ever ['ɛvər] *adv* **1** ALWAYS : toujours **2 ~ since** : depuis **3 hardly ~** : presque jamais

evergreen ['ɛvər‚gri:n] *n* : plante *f* à feuilles persistantes

everlasting [‚ɛvər'læstɪŋ] *adj* : éternel

every ['ɛvri] *adj* **1** EACH : chaque **2 ~ month** : tous les mois — **everybody** ['ɛvri‚bʌdi, -'bɑ-] *pron* : tout le monde — **everyday** [‚ɛvri'deɪ, 'ɛvri‚-] *adj* : quotidien, de tous les jours — **everyone** ['ɛvri‚wʌn] → **everybody** — **everything** ['ɛvri‚θɪŋ] *pron* : tout — **everywhere** ['ɛvri‚hwɛr] *adv* : partout

evict [ɪ'vɪkt] *vt* : expulser — **eviction** [ɪ'vɪkʃən] *n* : expulsion *f*

evidence ['ɛvədənts] *n* **1** PROOF : preuve *f* **2** TESTIMONY : témoignage *m* — **evident** ['ɛvɪdənt] *adj* : évident — **evidently** ['ɛvɪdəntli, ‚ɛvɪ'dɛntli] *adv* **1** OBVIOUSLY : évidemment, manifestement **2** APPARENTLY : apparemment

evil ['i:vəl, -vɪl] *adj* **eviler** *or* **eviller; evilest** *or* **evillest** : mauvais, méchant — **~** *n* : mal *m*

evoke [i'vo:k] *vt* **evoked; evoking** : évoquer

evolution [‚ɛvə'lu:ʃən, ‚i:-] *n* : évolution *f* — **evolve** [i'vɑlv] *vi* **evolved; evolving** : évoluer, se développer

exact [ɪg'zækt, ɛg-] *adj* : exact, précis — **~** *vt* : exiger — **exacting** [ɪg'zæktɪŋ, ɛg-] *adj* : exigeant — **exactly** [ɪg'zæktli, ɛg-] *adv* : exactement

exaggerate [ɪg'zæʤə‚reɪt, ɛg-] *v* **-ated; -ating** : exagérer — **exaggeration** [ɪg-'zæʤə'reɪʃən, ɛg-] *n* : exagération *f*

examine [ɪgˈzæmən, ɛg-] vt -ined; -ining 1 : examiner 2 QUESTION : interroger —
exam [ɪgˈzæm, ɛg-] n : examen m — **examination** [ɪgˌzæməˈneɪʃən, ɛg-] n : examen m

exasperate [ɪgˈzæspəˌreɪt, ɛg-] vt -ated; -ating : exaspérer — **exasperation** [ɪgˌzæspəˈreɪʃən, ɛg-] n : exaspération f

excavate [ˈɛkskəˌveɪt] vt -vated; -vating : creuser, excaver

exceed [ɪkˈsiːd, ɛk-] vt : dépasser — **exceedingly** [ɪkˈsiːdɪŋli, ɛk-] adv : extrêmement

excel [ɪkˈsɛl, ɛk-] vi -celled; -celling : exceller — **excellence** [ˈɛksələnts] n : excellence f — **excellent** [ˈɛksələnt] adj : excellent

except [ɪkˈsɛpt] prep 1 : sauf, excepté 2 ~ **for** : à part — vt : excepter — **exception** [ɪkˈsɛpʃən] n : exception f — **exceptional** [ɪkˈsɛpʃənəl] adj : exceptionnel

excerpt [ɛkˈsərpt, ˈɛgˌzərpt] n : extrait m

excess [ɪkˈsɛs, ˈɛkˌsɛs] n : excès m — ~ [ˈɛkˌsɛs, ɪkˈsɛs] adj : excédentaire, en trop — **excessive** [ɪkˈsɛsɪv, ɛk-] adj : excessif

exchange [ɪksˈtʃeɪndʒ, ɛks-; ˈɛksˌtʃeɪndʒ] n 1 : échange m 2 : change m (en finances) — ~ vt -changed; -changing : échanger

excise [ˈɪkˌsaɪz, ɛk-] n or ~ **tax** : contribution f indirecte

excite [ɪkˈsaɪt, ɛk-] vt -cited; -citing : exciter — **excited** [ɪkˈsaɪtəd, ɛk-] adj : excité, enthousiaste — **excitement** [ɪkˈsaɪtmənt, ɛk-] n : enthousiasme m — **exciting** [ɪkˈsaɪtɪŋ, ɛk-] adj : passionnant

exclaim [ɪksˈkleɪm, ɛk-] vi : s'exclamer — **exclamation** [ˌɛkskləˈmeɪʃən] n : exclamation f — **exclamation point** n : point m d'exclamation

exclude [ɪksˈkluːd, ɛks-] vt -cluded; -cluding : exclure — **excluding** [ɪksˈkluːdɪŋ, ɛks-] prep : à part, à l'exclusion de — **exclusion** [ɪksˈkluːʃn, ɛks-] n : exclusion f — **exclusive** [ɪksˈkluːsɪv, ɛks-] adj : exclusif

excrement [ˈɛkskrəmənt] n : excréments mpl

excruciating [ɪkˈskruːʃiˌeɪtɪŋ, ɛk-] adj : atroce, insupportable

excursion [ɪkˈskərʒən, ɛk-] n : excursion f

excuse [ɪkˈskjuːz, ɛk-] vt -cused; -cusing 1 : excuser 2 ~ **me** : excusez-moi, pardon — ~ [ɪkˈskjuːs, ɛk-] n : excuse f

execute [ˈɛksɪˌkjuːt] vt -cuted; -cuting : exécuter — **execution** [ˌɛksɪˈkjuːʃən] n : exécution f — **executioner** [ˌɛksɪˈkjuːʃənər] n : bourreau m

executive [ɪgˈzɛkjətɪv, ɛg-] adj : exécutif — ~ n 1 MANAGER : cadre m 2 or ~ **branch** : executif m, pouvoir m exécutif

exemplify [ɪgˈzɛmpləˌfaɪ, ɛg-] vt -fied; -fying : illustrer — **exemplary** [ɪgˈzɛmpləri, ɛg-] adj : exemplaire

exempt [ɪgˈzɛmpt, ɛg-] adj : exempt — ~ vt : exempter — **exemption** [ɪgˈzɛmpʃən, ɛg-] n : exemption f

exercise [ˈɛksərˌsaɪz] n : exercice m — ~ v -cised; -cising vt : exercer — vi : faire de l'exercice

exert [ɪgˈzərt, ɛg-] vt 1 : exercer 2 ~ **oneself** : se donner de la peine — **exertion** [ɪgˈzərʃən, ɛg-] n : effort m

exhale [ɛksˈheɪl] v -haled; -haling : expirer

exhaust [ɪgˈzɔst, ɛg-] vt : épuiser — ~ n 1 or ~ **fumes** : gaz m d'échappement 2 or ~ **pipe** : tuyau m d'échappement — **exhaustion** [ɪgˈzɔstʃən, ɛg-] n : épuisement m — **exhaustive** [ɪgˈzɔstɪv, ɛg-] adj : exhaustif

exhibit [ɪgˈzɪbət, ɛg-] vt 1 DISPLAY : exposer 2 SHOW : montrer — ~ n 1 : objet m exposé 2 EXHIBITION : exposition f — **exhibition** [ˌɛksəˈbɪʃən] n : exposition f

exhilarate [ɪgˈzɪləˌreɪt, ɛg-] vt -rated; -rating : animer — **exhilaration** [ɪgˌzɪləˈreɪʃən, ɛg-] n : joie f

exile [ˈɛgˌzaɪl, ˈɛkˌsaɪl] n 1 : exil m 2 OUTCAST : exilé m, -lée f — ~ vt **exiled; exiling** : exiler

exist [ɪgˈzɪst, ɛg-] vi : exister — **existence** [ɪgˈzɪstənts, ɛg-] n : existence f

exit [ˈɛgzət, ˈɛksət] n : sortie f — ~ vi : sortir

exodus [ˈɛksədəs] n : exode m

exonerate [ɪgˈzɑnəˌreɪt, ɛg-] vt -ated; -ating : disculper

exorbitant [ɪgˈzɔrbətənt, ɛg-] adj : exorbitant, excessif

exotic [ɪgˈzɑtɪk, ɛg-] adj : exotique

expand [ɪkˈspænd, ɛk-] vt : étendre, élargir — vi : s'étendre, s'agrandir — **expanse** [ɪkˈspænts, ɛk-] n : étendue f — **expansion** [ɪkˈspænʧən, ɛk-] n : expansion f

expatriate [ɛksˈpeɪtriət, -ˌeɪt] n : expatrié m, -triée f — ~ adj : expatrié

expect [ɪkˈspɛkt, ɛk-] vt 1 ANTICIPATE : s'attendre à 2 AWAIT : attendre 3 REQUIRE : exiger, demander — vi **be expecting** : attendre un bébé, être enceinte — **expectancy** [ɪkˈspɛktənsi, ɛk-] n, pl -cies : attente f, espérance f — **expectant** [ɪkˈspɛktənt, ɛk-] adj 1 : qui attend 2 ~ **mother** : future mère f — **expectation** [ˌɛkˌspɛkˈteɪʃən] n : attente f

expedient [ɪkˈspiːdiənt, ɛk-] adj : opportun — ~ n : expédient m

expedition [ˌɛkspəˈdɪʃən] n : expédition f

expel [ɪkˈspɛl, ɛk-] vt -pelled; -pelling : expulser, renvoyer (un élève)

expend [ɪkˈspɛnd, ɛk-] vt : dépenser — **expendable** [ɪkˈspɛndəbəl, ɛk-] adj : remplaçable — **expenditure** [ɪk'spɛndɪtʃər, ɛk-, -,tʃʊr] *n* : dépense *f* — **expense** [ɪk'spɛnts, ɛk-] *n* 1 : dépense *f* 2 **~s** *npl* : frais *mpl* 3 **at the ~ of** : aux dépens de — **expensive** [ɪk'spɛntsɪv, ɛk-] *adj* : cher, coûteux

experience [ɪk'spɪriənts, ɛk-] *n* : expérience *f* — **~** *vt* **-enced; -encing** : éprouver, connaître — **experienced** [ɪk'spɪriəntst, ɛk-] *adj* : expérimenté — **experiment** [ɪk'spɛrəmənt, ɛk-, -'spɪr-] *n* : expérience *f* — **~** *vi* : expérimenter — **experimental** [ɪk-,spɛrə'mɛntəl, ɛk-, -,spɪr-] *adj* : expérimental

expert ['ɛk,spərt, ɪk'spərt] *adj* : expert — **~** ['ɛk,spərt] *n* : expert *m*, -perte *f* — **expertise** [,ɛkspər'tiːz] *n* : compétence *f*

expire [ɪk'spaɪr, ɛk-] *vi* **-pired; -piring** : expirer — **expiration** [,ɛkspə'reɪʃən] *n* : expiration *f*

explain [ɪk'spleɪn, ɛk-] *vt* 1 : expliquer 2 **~ oneself** : s'expliquer — **explanation** [,ɛksplə'neɪʃən] *n* : explication *f* — **explanatory** [ɪk'splænə,tori, ɛk-] *adj* : explicatif

explicit [ɪk'splɪsət, ɛk-] *adj* : explicite

explode [ɪk'sploːd, ɛk-] *v* **-ploded; -ploding** *vt* : faire exploser — *vi* : exploser

exploit ['ɛk,splɔɪt] *n* : exploit *m* — **~** [ɪk-'splɔɪt, ɛk-] *vt* : exploiter — **exploitation** [,ɛk,splɔɪ'teɪʃən] *n* : exploitation *f*

exploration [,ɛksplə'reɪʃən] *n* : exploration *f* — **explore** [ɪk'splor, ɛk-] *v* **-plored; -ploring** : explorer — **explorer** [ɪk'splorər, ɛk-] *n* : explorateur *m*, -trice *f*

explosion [ɪk'sploːʒən, ɛk-] *n* : explosion *f* — **explosive** [ɪk'sploːsɪv, ɛk-] *adj* : explosif — **~** *n* : explosif *m*

export [ɛk'sport, 'ɛk,sport] *vt* : exporter — **~** ['ɛk,sport] *n* : exportation *f*

expose [ɪk'spoːz, ɛk-] *vt* **-posed; -posing** 1 : exposer 2 REVEAL : révéler — **exposure** [ɪk'spoːʒər, ɛk-] *n* : exposition *f*

express [ɪk'sprɛs, ɛk-] *adj* 1 SPECIFIC : exprès, formel 2 FAST : express — **~** *adv* **send ~** : envoyer en exprès — **~** *n or* **~ train** : rapide *m*, express *m* — **~** *vt* : exprimer — **expression** [ɪk'sprɛʃən, ɛk-] *n* : expression *f* — **expressive** [ɪk'sprɛsɪv, ɛk-] *adj* : expressif — **expressly** [ɪk'sprɛsli, ɛk-] *adv* : expressément — **expressway** [ɪk-'sprɛs,weɪ, ɛk-] *n* : autoroute *f*

expulsion [ɪk'spʌlʃən, ɛk-] *n* : expulsion *f*, renvoi *m* (d'un élève)

exquisite [ɛk'skwɪzət, 'ɛk,skwɪ-] *adj* : exquis

extend [ɪk'stɛnd, ɛk-] *vt* 1 STRETCH : étendre 2 LENGTHEN : prolonger 3 ENLARGE : agrandir 4 **~ one's hand** : tendre la main — *vi* : s'étendre — **extension** [ɪk'stɛntʃən, ɛk-] *n* 1 : extension *f* 2 LENGTHENING : pro-

longation *f* 3 ANNEX : annexe *f* 4 : poste *m* (de téléphone) 5 **~ cord** : rallonge *f* — **extensive** [ɪk'stɛntsɪv, ɛk-] *adj* : étendu, vaste — **extent** [ɪk'stɛnt, ɛk-] *n* 1 : étendue *f*, ampleur *f* 2 DEGREE : mesure *f*, degré *m*

exterior [ɛk'stɪriər] *adj* : extérieur — **~** *n* : extérieur *m*

exterminate [ɪk'stərmə,neɪt, ɛk-] *vt* **-nated; -nating** : exterminer — **extermination** [ɪk-,stərmə'neɪʃən, ɛk-] *n* : extermination *f*

external [ɪk'stərnəl, ɛk-] *adj* : externe — **externally** [ɪk'stərnəli, ɛk-] *adv* : extérieurement

extinct [ɪk'stɪŋkt, ɛk-] *adj* : disparu — **extinction** [ɪk'stɪŋkʃən, ɛk-] *n* : extinction *f*

extinguish [ɪk'stɪŋgwɪʃ, ɛk-] *vt* : éteindre — **extinguisher** [ɪk'stɪŋgwɪʃər, ɛk-] *n* : extincteur *m*

extol [ɪk'stoːl, ɛk-] *vt* **-tolled; -tolling** : louer

extort [ɪk'stort, ɛk-] *vt* : extorquer — **extortion** [ɪk'storʃən, ɛk-] *n* : extorsion *f*

extra ['ɛkstrə] *adj* : supplémentaire, de plus — **~** *n* : supplément *m* — **~** *adv* 1 : plus (que d'habitude) 2 **cost ~** : coûter plus cher

extract [ɪk'strækt, ɛk-] *vt* : extraire, arracher — **~** ['ɛk,strækt] *n* : extrait *m* — **extraction** [ɪk'strækʃən, ɛk-] *n* : extraction *f*

extracurricular [,ɛkstrəkə'rɪkjələr] *adj* : parascolaire

extraordinary [ɪk'strordən,ɛri, ,ɛkstrə-'ord-] *adj* : extraordinaire

extraterrestrial [,ɛkstrətə'rɛstriəl] *adj* : extraterrestre — **~** *n* : extraterrestre *mf*

extravagant [ɪk'strævɪgənt, ɛk-] *adj* 1 : extravagant 2 WASTEFUL : prodigue — **extravagance** [ɪk'strævɪgənts, ɛk-] *n* 1 : extravagance *f* 2 WASTEFULNESS : prodigalité *f*

extreme [ɪk'striːm, ɛk-] *adj* : extrême — **~** *n* : extrême *m* — **extremity** [ɪk'strɛməti, ɛk-] *n, pl* **-ties** : extrémité *f*

extricate ['ɛkstrə,keɪt] *vt* **-cated; -cating** 1 : dégager 2 **~ oneself from** : s'extirper de

extrovert ['ɛkstrə,vərt] *n* : extraverti *m*, -tie *f* — **extroverted** ['ɛkstrə,vərtəd] *adj* : extraverti

exuberant [ɪg'zuːbərənt, ɛg-] *adj* : exubérant — **exuberance** [ɪg'zuːbərənts, ɛg-] *n* : exubérance *f*

exult [ɪg'zʌlt, ɛg-] *vi* : exulter

eye ['aɪ] *n* 1 : œil *m* 2 VISION : vision *f* 3 GLANCE : regard *m* 4 **~ of a needle** : chas *m* — **~** *vt* **eyed; eyeing** *or* **eying** : regarder — **eyeball** ['aɪ,bɔl] *n* : globe *m* oculaire — **eyebrow** ['aɪ,braʊ] *n* : sourcil *m* — **eyeglasses** ['aɪ,glæsəz] *npl* : lunettes *fpl* — **eyelash** ['aɪ,læʃ] *n* : cil *m* — **eyelid** ['aɪ,lɪd] *n* : paupière *f* — **eyesight** ['aɪ,saɪt] *n* : vue *f*, vision *f* — **eyewitness** ['aɪ'wɪtnəs] *n* : témoin *m* oculaire

F

f ['ɛf] n, pl **f's** or **fs** ['ɛfs] : f m, sixième lettre de l'alphabet

fable ['feɪbəl] n : fable f

fabric ['fæbrɪk] n : tissu m, étoffe f

fabulous ['fæbjələs] adj : fabuleux

facade [fə'sɑd] n : façade f

face ['feɪs] n **1** : visage m, figure f **2** EXPRESSION : mine f **3** SURFACE : face f (d'une monnaie), façade f (d'un bâtiment) **4** ~ **value** : valeur f nominale **5 in the ~ of** DESPITE : en dépit de **6 lose ~** : perdre la face **7 make a ~** : faire la grimace — ~ vt **faced; facing 1** CONFRONT : faire face à **2** OVERLOOK : être en face de, donner sur — **faceless** ['feɪsləs] adj : anonyme

facet ['fæsət] n : facette f

face–to–face adv : face à face

facial ['feɪʃəl] adj : du visage

facetious [fə'si:ʃəs] adj : facétieux

facility [fə'sɪləti] n, pl **-ties 1** : facilité f **2 facilities** npl : installations fpl — **facilitate** [fə'sɪlə,teɪt] vt **-tated; -tating** : faciliter

facsimile [fæk'sɪməli] n : fac-similé m

fact ['fækt] n **1** : fait m **2 in ~** : en fait

faction ['fækʃən] n : faction f

factor ['fæktər] n : facteur m

factory ['fæktəri] n, pl **-ries** : usine f, fabrique f

factual ['fæktʃʊəl] adj : factuel, basé sur les faits

faculty ['fækəlti] n, pl **-ties** : faculté f

fad ['fæd] n : mode f passagère, manie f

fade ['feɪd] v **faded; fading** vi **1** WITHER : se flétrir, se faner **2** DISCOLOR : se décolorer **3** DIM : s'affaiblir, diminuer **4** VANISH : disparaître — vt : décolorer

fail ['feɪl] vi **1** : échouer **2** WEAKEN : faiblir, baisser **3** BREAK DOWN : tomber en panne **4** ~ **in** : manquer à — vt **1** DISAPPOINT : décevoir **2** NEGLECT : manquer, négliger **3** : échouer à (un examen) — ~ n **without ~** : à coup sûr — **failing** ['feɪlɪŋ] n : défaut m — **failure** ['feɪljər] n **1** : échec m **2** BREAKDOWN : panne f

faint ['feɪnt] adj **1** WEAK : faible **2** INDISTINCT : vague **3 feel ~** : se sentir mal — vi **1** : s'évanouir — **fainthearted** ['feɪnt-'hɑrtəd] adj : timide — **faintly** ['feɪntli] adv **1** WEAKLY : faiblement **2** SLIGHTLY : légèrement

fair[1] ['fær] n : foire f

fair[2] adj **1** BEAUTIFUL : beau **2** : blond (se dit des cheveux), clair (se dit de la peau) **3** JUST : juste, équitable **4** ADEQUATE : passable **5** LARGE : grand — **fairly** ['færli] adv

1 HONESTLY : équitablement **2** QUITE : assez — **fairness** ['færnəs] n : équité f

fairy ['færi] n, pl **fairies 1** : fée f **2** ~ **tale** n : conte m de fées

faith ['feɪθ] n, pl **faiths** ['feɪθs, 'feɪðz] : foi f — **faithful** ['feɪθfəl] adj : fidèle — **faithfully** adv : fidèlement — **faithfulness** ['feɪθfəlnəs] n : fidélité f

fake ['feɪk] v **faked; faking** vt **1** FALSIFY : falsifier **2** FEIGN : simuler — vi PRETEND : faire semblant — ~ adj : faux — ~ n **1** IMITATION : faux m **2** IMPOSTER : imposteur m

falcon ['fælkən, 'fɔl-] n : faucon m

fall ['fɔl] vi **fell** ['fɛl]; **fallen** ['fɔlən]; **falling 1** : tomber **2** ~ **asleep** : s'endormir **3** ~ **back** : se retirer **4** ~ **back on** : avoir recours à **5** ~ **behind** : prendre du retard **6** ~ **in love** : tomber amoureux **7** ~ **out** QUARREL : se disputer — ~ n **1** : chute f **2** AUTUMN : automne m **3** ~**s** npl WATERFALL : chute f (d'eau), cascade f

fallacy ['fæləsi] n, pl **-cies** : erreur f

fallible ['fæləbəl] adj : faillible

fallow ['fælo] adj : en jachère

false ['fɔls] adj **falser; falsest 1** : faux **2** ~ **alarm** : fausse alerte f **3** ~ **teeth** : dentier m — **falsehood** ['fɔls,hʊd] n : mensonge m — **falsely** ['fɔlsli] adv : faussement — **falseness** ['fɔlsnəs] n : fausseté f — **falsify** ['fɔlsə,faɪ] vt **-fied; -fying** : falsifier

falter ['fɔltər] vi **1** STUMBLE : chanceler **2** WAVER : hésiter

fame ['feɪm] n : renommée f

familiar [fə'mɪljər] adj **1** : familier **2 be ~ with** : bien connaître — **familiarity** [fə,mɪli-'ærəti, -,mɪl'jær-] n, pl **-ties** : familiarité f — **familiarize** [fə'mɪljə,raɪz] vt **-ized; -izing** ~ **oneself** : se familiariser

family ['fæmli, 'fæmə-] n, pl **-lies** : famille f

famine ['fæmən] n : famine f

famished ['fæmɪʃt] adj : affamé

famous ['feɪməs] adj : célèbre

fan ['fæn] n **1** : éventail m, ventilateur m (électrique) **2** ENTHUSIAST : enthousiaste mf — ~ vt **fanned; fanning 1** : attiser (un feu) **2** ~ **oneself** : s'éventer (le visage)

fanatic [fə'nætɪk] n : fanatique mf — or **fanatical** [-tɪkəl] adj : fanatique — **fanaticism** [fə'nætə,sɪzəm] n : fanatisme m

fancy ['fæntsi] vt **-cied; -cying 1** LIKE : aimer **2** WANT : avoir envie de **3** IMAGINE : s'imaginer — ~ adj **fancier; -est 1** ELABORATE : recherché **2** LUXURIOUS : fin, de luxe — ~ n, pl **-cies 1** LIKING : goût m **2**

WHIM : fantaisie *f* **3 take a ~ to** : se prendre d'affection pour — **fanciful** [ˈfæn*t*sɪfəl] *adj* : fantaisiste

fanfare [ˈfænˌfær] *n* : fanfare *f*

fang [ˈfæŋ] *n* : croc *m*, crochet *m* (d'un serpent)

fantasy [ˈfæntəsi] *n, pl* **-sies 1** DREAM : fantasme *m* **2** IMAGINATION : fantaisie *f* — **fantasize** [ˈfæntəˌsaɪz] *vi* **-sized; -sizing** : fantasmer — **fantastic** [fænˈtæstɪk] *adj* : fantastique

far [ˈfɑr] *adv* **farther** [ˈfɑrðər] *or* **further** [ˈfər-]; **farthest** *or* **furthest** [-ðəst] **1** : loin **2 as ~ as** : jusqu'à **3 as ~ as possible** : autant que possible **4 by ~** : de loin **5 ~ away** : au loin **6 ~ from it!** : pas du tout! **7 ~ worse** : bien pire **8 so ~** : jusqu'ici — ~ *adj* **farther** *or* **further**; **farthest** *or* **furthest 1** : lointain **2 the ~ right** : l'extrême droite **3 the ~ side** : l'autre côté — **faraway** [ˈfɑrəˌweɪ] *adj* : éloigné, lointain

farce [ˈfɑrs] *n* : farce *f*

fare [ˈfær] *vi* **fared; faring** : aller — ~ *n* **1** : tarif *m*, prix *m* **2** FOOD : nourriture *f*

farewell [færˈwɛl] *n* : adieu *m* — ~ *adj* : d'adieu

far-fetched [ˈfɑrˈfɛtʃt] *adj* : improbable, bizarre

farm [ˈfɑrm] *n* : ferme *f* — ~ *vt* : cultiver — *vi* : être fermier — **farmer** [ˈfɑrmər] *n* : fermier *m*, -mière *f* — **farmhand** [ˈfɑrmˌhænd] *n* : ouvrier *m*, -vrière *f* agricole — **farmhouse** [ˈfɑrmˌhaʊs] *n* : ferme *f* — **farming** [ˈfɑrmɪŋ] *n* : agriculture *f*, élevage (des animaux) — **farmyard** [ˈfɑrmˌjɑrd] *n* : cour *f* de ferme

far-off [ˈfɑrˌɔf, -ˈɔf] *adj* : lointain

far-reaching [ˈfɑrˈriːtʃɪŋ] *adj* : d'une grande portée

farsighted [ˈfɑrˌsaɪtəd] *adj* **1** : presbyte **2** SHREWD : prévoyant

farther [ˈfɑrðər] *adv* **1** : plus loin **2** MORE : de plus — ~ *adj* : plus éloigné, plus lointain — **farthest** [ˈfɑrðəst] *adv* : le plus loin — ~ *adj* : le plus éloigné

fascinate [ˈfæsənˌeɪt] *vt* **-nated; -nating** : fasciner — **fascination** [ˌfæsənˈeɪʃən] *n* : fascination *f*

fascism [ˈfæʃˌɪzəm] *n* : fascisme *m* — **fascist** [ˈfæʃɪst] *adj* : fasciste — ~ *n* : fasciste *mf*

fashion [ˈfæʃən] *n* **1** MANNER : façon *f* **2** STYLE : mode *f* **3 out of ~** : démodé — **fashionable** [ˈfæʃənəbəl] *adj* : à la mode

fast[1] [ˈfæst] *vi* : jeûner — ~ *n* : jeûne *m*

fast[2] *adj* **1** SWIFT : rapide **2** SECURE : ferme **3 my watch is ~** : ma montre avance — ~ *adv* **1** SECURELY : solidement, ferme **2** SWIFTLY : rapidement, vite **3 ~ asleep** : profondément endormi

fasten [ˈfæsən] *vt* : attacher, fermer — *vi* : s'attacher, se fermer — **fastener** [ˈfæsənər] *n* : attache *f*, fermeture *f*

fastidious [fæsˈtɪdiəs] *adj* : méticuleux

fat [ˈfæt] *adj* **fatter; fattest 1** : gros, gras **2** THICK : épais — ~ *n* : gras *m* (de la viande), graisse *f* (du corps)

fatal [ˈfeɪtəl] *adj* **1** DEADLY : mortel **2** FATEFUL : fatal — **fatality** [feɪˈtæləti, fə-] *n, pl* **-ties** : mort *m*

fate [ˈfeɪt] *n* **1** DESTINY : destin *m* **2** LOT : sort *m* — **fateful** [ˈfeɪtfəl] *adj* : fatidique

father [ˈfɑðər] *n* : père *m* — **fatherhood** [ˈfɑðərˌhʊd] *n* : paternité *f* — **father-in-law** [ˈfɑðərɪnˌlɔ] *n, pl* **fathers-in-law** : beau-père *m* — **fatherly** [ˈfɑðərli] *adj* : paternel

fathom [ˈfæðəm] *vt* : comprendre

fatigue [fəˈtiːg] *vt* **-tigued; -tiguing** : fatiguer — ~ *n* : fatigue *f*

fatten [ˈfætən] *vt* : engraisser — **fattening** [ˈfætənɪŋ] *adj* : qui fait grossir

fatty [ˈfæti] *adj* **fattier; -est** : gras

faucet [ˈfɔsət] *n* : robinet *m*

fault [ˈfɔlt] *n* **1** FLAW : défaut *m* **2** RESPONSIBILITY : faute *f* **3** : faille *f* (géologique) — ~ *vt* : trouver des défauts à, critiquer — **faultless** [ˈfɔltləs] *adj* : irréprochable — **faulty** [ˈfɔlti] *adj* **faultier; -est** : fautif, défectueux

fauna [ˈfɔnə] *n* : faune *f*

favor *or Brit* **favour** [ˈfeɪvər] *n* **1** APPROVAL : faveur *f* **2 do s.o. a ~** : rendre un service à qqn **3 in ~ of** : en faveur de, pour — ~ *vt* **1** : favoriser **2** PREFER : préférer — **favorable** *or Brit* **favourable** [ˈfeɪvərəbəl] *adj* : favorable — **favorite** *or Brit* **favourite** [ˈfeɪvərət] *adj* : favori, préféré — ~ *n* : favori *m*, -rite *f*; préféré *m*, -rée *f* — **favoritism** *or Brit* **favouritism** [ˈfeɪvərəˌtɪzəm] *n* : favoritisme *m*

fawn[1] [ˈfɔn] *vi* **~ upon** : flatter servilement

fawn[2] *n* : faon *m*

fax [ˈfæks] *n* : fax *m*, télécopie *f* — ~ *vt* : faxer, envoyer par télécopie

fear [ˈfɪr] *vt* : craindre, avoir peur de — *vi* **~ for** : craindre pour — ~ *n* : crainte *f*, peur *f* — **fearful** [ˈfɪrfəl] *adj* **1** FRIGHTENING : effrayant **2** AFRAID : craintif, peureux

feasible [ˌfiːzəbəl] *adj* : faisable

feast [ˈfiːst] *n* : banquet *m*, festin *m* — ~ *vi* : se régaler de

feat [ˈfiːt] *n* : exploit *m*, prouesse *f*

feather [ˈfɛðər] *n* : plume *f*

feature [ˈfiːtʃər] *n* **1** : trait *m* (du visage) **2** CHARACTERISTIC : caractéristique *f* — ~ *vt* : mettre en vedette — *vi* : figurer

February [ˈfɛbjuˌɛri, ˈfɛbu-, ˈfɛbru-] *n* : février *m*

feces [ˈfiːˌsiːz] *npl* : fèces *fpl*

federal [ˈfɛdrəl, -dərəl] *adj* : fédéral —

federation [ˌfɛdəˈreɪʃən] n : fédération f
fed up [ˈfɛd] adj be ~ : en avoir assez, en avoir marre fam
fee [ˈfiː] n 1 : frais mpl (de scolarité), honoraires mpl (médicaux) 2 or entrance ~ : droit m d'entrée
feeble [ˈfiːbəl] adj -bler; -blest 1 : faible 2 a ~ **excuse** : une piètre excuse
feed [ˈfiːd] v fed [ˈfɛd]; feeding vt 1 : nourrir, donner à manger à 2 SUPPLY : alimenter — vi EAT : manger, se nourrir — ~ n : fourrage m
feel [ˈfiːl] v felt [ˈfɛlt]; feeling vt 1 : sentir 2 TOUCH : toucher 3 EXPERIENCE : ressentir (un sentiment) 4 BELIEVE : croire — vi 1 : se sentir 2 SEEM : sembler 3 ~ **cold/thirsty** : avoir froid, soif 4 ~ **like** WANT : avoir envie de — ~ n : toucher m, sensation f — **feeling** [ˈfiːlɪŋ] n 1 SENSATION : sensation f 2 EMOTION : sentiment m 3 OPINION : avis m 4 ~s npl : sentiments mpl
feet → **foot**
feign [ˈfeɪn] vt : feindre
feline [ˈfiːˌlaɪn] adj : félin — ~ n : félin m
fell¹ → **fall**
fell² [ˈfɛl] vt : abattre (un arbre)
fellow [ˈfɛˌloː] n 1 COMPANION : compagnon m 2 MAN : gars m fam, type m fam — **fellowship** [ˈfɛloːˌʃɪp] n 1 COMPANIONSHIP : camaraderie f 2 GRANT : bourse f universitaire
felon [ˈfɛlən] n : criminel m, -nelle f — **felony** [ˈfɛləni] n, pl -nies : crime m
felt¹ → **feel**
felt² [ˈfɛlt] n : feutre m
female [ˈfiːˌmeɪl] adj : femelle (se dit des animaux), féminin (se dit des personnes) — ~ n 1 : femelle f (animal) 2 WOMAN : femme f
feminine [ˈfɛmənən] adj : féminin — **femininity** [ˌfɛməˈnɪnəti] n : féminité f — **feminism** [ˈfɛməˌnɪzəm] n : féminisme m — **feminist** [ˈfɛmənɪst] adj : féministe — ~ n : féministe mf
fence [ˈfɛnts] n : clôture f, barrière f — ~ v **fenced; fencing** vt : clôturer — vi : faire de l'escrime — **fencing** [ˈfɛntsɪŋ] n : escrime f
fend [ˈfɛnd] vt or ~ **off** : parer (un coup) — vi ~ **for oneself** : se débrouiller tout seul
fender [ˈfɛndər] n : aile f (d'une voiture)
fennel [ˈfɛnəl] n : fenouil m
ferment [fərˈmɛnt] vi : fermenter — **fermentation** [ˌfərmənˈteɪʃən, -ˌmɛn-] n : fermentation f
fern [ˈfərn] n : fougère f
ferocious [fəˈroːʃəs] adj : féroce — **ferocity** [fəˈrasəti] n : férocité f

ferret [ˈfɛrət] n : furet m — ~ vt ~ **out** : dénicher
Ferris wheel [ˈfɛrɪs] n : grande roue f
ferry [ˈfɛri] vt -ried; -rying : transporter — ~ n, pl -ries : ferry m, transbordeur m
fertile [ˈfərtəl] adj : fertile — **fertility** [fərˈtɪləti] n : fertilité f, fécondité f — **fertilize** [ˈfərtəlˌaɪz] vt -ized; -izing : fertiliser (une terre), féconder (un œuf, etc.) — **fertilizer** [ˈfərtəlˌaɪzər] n : engrais m
fervent [ˈfərvənt] adj : fervent — **fervor** or Brit **fervour** [ˈfərvər] n : ferveur f
fester [ˈfɛstər] vi : suppurer
festival [ˈfɛstəvəl] n : festival m — **festive** [ˈfɛstɪv] adj : joyeux, de fête — **festivities** [fɛsˈtɪvətiz] npl : réjouissances fpl
fetch [ˈfɛtʃ] vt 1 BRING : aller chercher 2 REALIZE : rapporter (de l'argent)
fetid [ˈfɛtəd] adj : fétide
fetish [ˈfɛtɪʃ] n : fétiche m
fetter [ˈfɛtər] vt : enchaîner — **fetters** [ˈfɛtərz] npl : fers mpl, chaînes fpl
fetus [ˈfiːtəs] n : fœtus m
feud [ˈfjuːd] n : querelle f — ~ vi : se quereller
feudal [ˈfjuːdəl] adj : féodal
fever [ˈfiːvər] n : fièvre f — **feverish** [ˈfiːvərɪʃ] adj : fiévreux
few [ˈfjuː] adj 1 : peu de 2 a ~ : quelques — ~ pron 1 : peu, quelques-uns, quelques-unes 2 quite a ~ : un assez grand nombre de — **fewer** [ˈfjuːər] adj : moins de — ~ pron : moins
fiancé, fiancée [ˌfiːˌɑnˈseɪ, ˌfiːˈɑnˌseɪ] n : fiancé m, -cée f
fiasco [fiˈæsˌkoː] n, pl -coes : fiasco m
fib [ˈfɪb] n : petit mensonge m — ~ vi **fibbed; fibbing** : raconter des histoires
fiber or Brit **fibre** [ˈfaɪbər] n : fibre f — **fiberglass** [ˈfaɪbərˌglæs] n : fibre f de verre — **fibrous** [ˈfaɪbrəs] adj : fibreux
fickle [ˈfɪkəl] adj : volage, inconstant
fiction [ˈfɪkʃən] n : fiction f — **fictional** [ˈfɪkʃənəl] or **fictitious** [fɪkˈtɪʃəs] adj : fictif
fiddle [ˈfɪdəl] n : violon m — ~ vi -**dled; -dling** ~ **with** : tripoter
fidelity [fəˈdɛləti, faɪ-] n, pl -ties : fidélité f
fidget [ˈfɪdʒət] vi : remuer — **fidgety** [ˈfɪdʒəti] adj : agité
field [ˈfiːld] n 1 : champ m 2 : terrain m (de sport) 3 SPECIALTY : domaine m — **field glasses** npl : jumelles fpl — **field trip** : sortie f éducative
fiend [ˈfiːnd] n 1 : diable m 2 FANATIC : mordu m — **fiendish** [ˈfiːndɪʃ] adj : diabolique
fierce [ˈfɪrs] adj **fiercer; -est** 1 FEROCIOUS : féroce 2 INTENSE : violent — **fierceness** [ˈfɪrsnəs] n : férocité f

fiery ['faɪəri] *adj* **fierier; -est 1** BURNING : brûlant **2** SPIRITED : ardent

fifteen [fɪf'ti:n] *n* : quinze *m* — ~ *adj* : quinze — **fifteenth** [fɪf'ti:nθ] *n* **1** : quinzième *mf* **2 November** ~ : le 15 novembre — ~ *adj* : quinzième

fifth ['fɪfθ] *n* **1** : cinquième *mf* **2 June** ~ : le cinq juin — ~ *adj* : cinquième

fiftieth ['fɪftiəθ] *n* : cinquantième *mf* — ~ *adj* : cinquantième

fifty ['fɪfti] *n, pl* **-ties** : cinquante *m* — ~ *adj* : cinquante — **fifty-fifty** [,fɪfti'fɪfti] *adv* : moitié-moitié — ~ *adj* **a** ~ **chance** : une chance sur deux

fig ['fɪg] *n* : figue *f*

fight ['faɪt] *v* **fought** ['fɔt]; **fighting** *vi* **1** BATTLE : se battre **2** QUARREL : se disputer **3** STRUGGLE : lutter — *vt* : se battre contre, combattre — ~ *n* **1** BATTLE : combat *m* **2** BRAWL : bagarre *f* **3** QUARREL : dispute *f* **4** STRUGGLE : lutte *f* — **fighter** ['faɪtər] *n* **1** : combattant *m*, -tante *f* **2** *or* ~ **plane** : avion *m* de chasse

figment ['fɪgmənt] *n* ~ **of the imagination** : produit *m* de l'imagination

figurative ['fɪgjərətɪv, -gə-] *adj* : figuré

figure ['fɪgjər, -gər] *n* **1** : figure *f* **2** NUMBER : chiffre *m* **3** SHAPE : forme *f* **4** ~ **of speech** : façon *f* de parler **5 watch one's** ~ : surveiller sa ligne — ~ *v* **-ured; -uring** *vt* : penser, supposer — *vi* **1** APPEAR : figurer **2 that** ~ **s!** : ça se comprend! — **figurehead** ['fɪgjər,hɛd, -gər-] *n* **1** : figure *f* de proue (d'un navire) **2** : homme *m* de paille — **figure out** *vt* : comprendre

file¹ ['faɪl] *n* : lime *f* (outil) — ~ *vt* **filed; filing** : limer

file² *v* **filed; filing** *vt* **1** CLASSIFY : classer **2** ~ **charges** : déposer une plainte — ~ *n* **1** : dossier *m* **2** *or* ~ **computer** : fichier *m*

file³ ROW : file *f* — ~ *vi* ~ **past** : défiler devant

fill ['fɪl] *vt* **1** : remplir **2** PLUG : boucher (un trou) **3** : plomber (une dent) **4** ~ **in** INFORM : mettre au courant — *vi* **1** *or* ~ **up** : se remplir **2** ~ **in for** : remplacer — ~ *n* **1 eat one's** ~ : se rassasier **2 have had one's** ~ **of** : en avoir assez de

fillet [fɪ'leɪ, 'fɪ,leɪ, 'fɪlət] *n* : filet *m*

filling ['fɪlɪŋ] *n* **1** : garniture *f* (d'une tarte, etc.) **2** : plombage *m* (d'une dent) **3** ~ **station** → **service station**

filly ['fɪli] *n, pl* **-lies** : pouliche *f*

film ['fɪlm] *n* **1** : pellicule *f* **2** MOVIE : film *m* — ~ *vt* : filmer

filter ['fɪltər] *n* : filtre *m* — ~ *v* : filtrer

filth ['fɪlθ] *n* : saleté *f* — **filthiness** ['fɪlθinəs] *n* : saleté *f* — **filthy** ['fɪlθi] *adj* **filthier; -est** : sale, dégoûtant

fin ['fɪn] *n* : nageoire *f*

final ['faɪnəl] *adj* **1** LAST : dernier **2** CONCLUSIVE : définitif **3** ULTIMATE : final — ~ *n* **1** *or* ~ **s** : finale *f* (d'une compétition) **2** ~ **s** *npl* : examens *mpl* de fin de semestre — **finalist** ['faɪnəlɪst] *n* : finaliste *mf* — **finalize** ['faɪnəl,aɪz] *vt* **-ized; -izing** : mettre au point — **finally** ['faɪnəli] *adv* : enfin, finalement

finance [fə'næns, 'faɪ,næns] *n* **1** : finance *f* **2** ~ **s** *npl* RESOURCES : finances *fpl* — ~ *vt* **-nanced; -nancing** : financer — **financial** [fə'næntʃəl, faɪ-] *adj* : financier

find ['faɪnd] *vt* **found** ['faʊnd]; **finding 1** LOCATE : trouver **2** REALIZE : s'apercevoir **3** ~ **out** : découvrir **4** ~ **guilty** : prononcer coupable — ~ *n* : trouvaille *f* — **finding** ['faɪndɪŋ] *n* **1** FIND : découverte *f* **2** ~ **s** *npl* : conclusions *fpl*

fine¹ ['faɪn] *n* : amende *f* — ~ *vt* **fined; fining** : condamner à une amende

fine² *adj* **finer; -est 1** DELICATE : fin **2** SUBTLE : subtil **3** EXCELLENT : excellent **4** : beau (se dit du temps) **5 be** ~ : aller bien **6 that's** ~ **with me** : ça me va — ~ *adv* OK : très bien — **fine arts** *npl* : beaux-arts *mpl* — **finely** ['faɪnli] *adv* **1** EXCELLENTLY : exceptionellement **2** PRECISELY : délicatement **3** MINUTELY : finement

finesse [fə'nɛs] *n* : finesse *f*

finger ['fɪŋgər] *n* : doigt *m* — ~ *vt* : toucher, palper — **fingernail** ['fɪŋgər,neɪl] *n* : ongle *m* — **fingerprint** ['fɪŋgər,prɪnt] *n* : empreinte *f* digitale — **fingertip** ['fɪŋgər,tɪp] *n* : bout *m* du doigt

finicky ['fɪnɪki] *adj* : pointilleux

finish ['fɪnɪʃ] *vt* : finir, terminer — *vi* : finir, terminer — ~ *n* **1** END : fin *f* **2** *or* ~ **line** : arrivée *f* **3** SURFACE : finition *f*, fini *m Can*

finite ['faɪ,naɪt] *adj* : fini

fir ['fər] *n* : sapin *m*

fire ['faɪr] *n* **1** : feu *m* **2** BLAZE : incendie *m* **3 catch** ~ : prendre feu **4 on** ~ : en feu **5 open** ~ **on** : ouvrir le feu sur — ~ *vt* **fired; firing 1** IGNITE : incendier **2** DISMISS : renvoyer, virer **3** SHOOT : tirer — **fire alarm** *n* : avertisseur *m* d'incendie — **firearm** ['faɪr,ɑrm] *n* : arme *f* à feu — **firecracker** ['faɪr,krækər] *n* : pétard *m* — **fire engine** : pompe *f* à incendie — **fire escape** *n* : escalier *m* de secours — **fire extinguisher** *n* : extincteur *m* — **firefighter** ['faɪr,faɪtər] *n* : pompier *m*, sapeur-pompier *m France* — **fireman** ['faɪrmən] *n, pl* **-men** [-mən, -,mɛn] → **firefighter** — **fireplace** ['faɪr,pleɪs] *n* : cheminée *f*, foyer *m* — **fireproof** ['faɪr,pru:f] *adj* : ignifuge — **fireside** ['faɪr,saɪd] *n* : coin *m* du feu — **fire station** *n* : caserne *f* de pompiers *France*, poste *m* de pompiers *Can* — **firewood** ['faɪr,wʊd] *n* : bois *m* de chauffage — **fireworks** ['faɪr,wərks] *npl* : feux *mpl* d'artifice

firm

firm[1] ['fərm] *n* : entreprise *f*, firme *f*

firm[2] *adj* **1** : ferme **2** STEADY : solide **3** **stand** ~ : tenir bon — **firmly** ['fərmli] *adv* : fermement — **firmness** ['fərmnəs] *n* : fermeté *f*

first ['fərst] *adj* **1** : premier **2 at ~ sight** : à première vue — ~ *adv* **1** : d'abord **2 for the ~ time** : pour la première fois **3 ~ of all** : tout d'abord — ~ *n* **1** : premier *m*, -mière *f* **2 or ~ gear** : première *f* **3 at ~** : au début — **first aid** *n* : premiers secours *mpl* — **first–class** ['fərst'klæs] *adv* : en première — ~ *adj* : de première qualité, de première classe — **firstly** ['fərstli] *adv* : premièrement

fiscal ['fɪskəl] *adj* : fiscal

fish ['fɪʃ] *n*, *pl* **fish** *or* **fishes** : poisson *m* — ~ *vi* **1** : pêcher **2** ~ **for** SEEK : chercher **3 go** ~**ing** : aller à la pêche — **fisherman** ['fɪʃərmən] *n*, *pl* **-men** [-mən, -mɛn] : pêcheur *m*, -cheuse *f* — **fishhook** ['fɪʃ-ˌhʊk] *n* : hameçon *m* — **fishing** ['fɪʃɪŋ] *n* : pêche *f* — **fishing pole** *n* : canne *f* à la pêche — **fishy** ['fɪʃi] *adj* **fishier; -est 1** : de poisson **2** SUSPICIOUS : louche

fist ['fɪst] *n* : poing *m*

fit[1] ['fɪt] *n* : crise *f* (épileptique), accès *m* (de colère, etc.)

fit[2] *adj* **fitter; fittest 1** APPROPRIATE : convenable **2** HEALTHY : en forme **3 see ~ to** : trouver bon de — ~ *v* **fitted; fitting** *vt* **1** (*relating to clothing*) : aller à **2** MATCH : correspondre à **3** INSTALL : poser, insérer **4** EQUIP : équiper — *vi* **1** : être de la bonne taille **2 or ~ in** BELONG : s'intégrer — ~ *n* : coupe *f* (d'un vêtement) — **fitful** ['fɪtfəl] *adj* **1** : intermittent **2** : agité (se dit du sommeil) — **fitness** ['fɪtnəs] *n* **1** HEALTH : forme *f* physique **2** SUITABILITY : aptitude *f* — **fitting** ['fɪtɪŋ] *adj* : approprié, convenable

five ['faɪv] *n* : cinq *m* — ~ *adj* : cinq — **five hundred** *adj* : cinq cents

fix ['fɪks] *vt* **1** ATTACH : fixer **2** REPAIR : réparer **3** PREPARE : préparer **4** RIG : truquer — ~ *n* **be in a ~** : être dans le pétrin *m* — **fixed** ['fɪkst] *adj* : fixe — **fixture** ['fɪkstʃər] *n* : installation *f*

fizz ['fɪz] *vi* : pétiller — ~ *n* : pétillement *m*

fizzle ['fɪzəl] *vi* ~ **out** : s'éteindre

flabbergasted ['flæbərˌgæstəd] *adj* : sidéré

flabby ['flæbi] *adj* **flabbier; -est** : mou

flaccid ['flæksəd, 'flæsəd] *adj* : flasque

flag[1] ['flæg] *vi* WEAKEN : faiblir

flag[2] *n* : drapeau *m* — ~ *vt* **flagged; flagging** : faire signe à (un taxi, etc.) — **flagpole** [ˌflæg'poːl] *n* : mât *m*

flagrant ['fleɪgrənt] *adj* : flagrant

flair ['flær] *n* **1** TALENT : don *m* **2** STYLE : style *m*

flake ['fleɪk] *n* : flocon *m* (de neige), écaille *f* (de peinture) — ~ *vi* **flaked; flaking** *or* ~ **off** : s'écailler

flamboyant [flæm'bɔɪənt] *adj* : extravagant

flame ['fleɪm] *n* **1** : flamme *f* **2 burst into** ~**s** : s'embraser, s'enflammer

flamingo [flə'mɪŋgo] *n*, *pl* **-gos** : flamant *m*

flammable ['flæməbəl] *adj* : inflammable

flank ['flæŋk] *n* : flanc *m* — ~ *vt* : flanquer

flannel ['flænəl] *n* : flanelle *f*

flap ['flæp] *n* : rabat *m* — ~ *v* **flapped; flapping** *vt* : battre (des ailes) — *vi* ~ **in the wind** : claquer au vent

flare ['flær] *vi* **flared; flaring** ~ **up 1** BLAZE : s'embraser **2** ERUPT : s'emporter (se dit d'une personne), éclater (se dit d'une dispute, etc.) — ~ *n* : fusée *f* éclairante

flash ['flæʃ] *vi* **1** SPARKLE : briller **2** BLINK : clignoter **3** ~ **past** : passer comme un éclair — *vt* **1** PROJECT : projeter **2** SHOW : montrer **3** ~ **a smile** : lancer un sourire — ~ *n* **1** éclat *m* **2** : flash *m* (d'un appareil photographique) **3** ~ **of lightning** : éclair *m* **4 in a** ~ : dans un instant — **flashlight** ['flæʃˌlaɪt] *n* : lampe *f* de poche — **flashy** ['flæʃi] *adj* **flashier; -est** : tape-à-l'œil, tapageur

flask ['flæsk] *n* : flacon *m*

flat ['flæt] *adj* **flatter; flattest 1** LEVEL : plat **2** DOWNRIGHT : catégorique **3** FIXED : fixe **4** MONOTONOUS : monotone **5** : éventé (se dit d'une boisson) **6** : bémol (en musique) **7** ~ **tire** : crevé, à plat — ~ *n* **1** : bémol *m* (en musique) **2** *Brit* APARTMENT : appartement *m* **3 or** ~ **tire** : crevaison *f* — ~ *adv* **1** : à plat **2** ~ **broke** : complètement fauché **3 in one hour** ~ : dans une heure pile *fam* — **flatly** ['flætli] *adv* : catégoriquement — **flatten** ['flætən] *vt* : aplatir — *vi or* ~ **out** : s'aplanir

flatter ['flætər] *vt* : flatter — **flatterer** ['flætərər] *n* : flatteur *m*, -teuse *f* — **flattering** ['flætərɪŋ] *adj* : flatteur — **flattery** ['flætəri] *n*, *pl* **-ries** : flatterie *f*

flaunt ['flɔnt] *vt* : faire étalage de

flavor *or Brit* **flavour** ['fleɪvər] *n* **1** : goût *m* **2** FLAVORING : parfum *m* — ~ *vt* : parfumer — **flavorful** *or Brit* **flavourful** ['fleɪvərfəl] *adj* : savoureux — **flavoring** *or Brit* **flavouring** ['fleɪvərɪŋ] *n* : parfum *m*

flaw ['flɔ] *n* : défaut *m* — **flawless** ['flɔləs] *adj* : sans défaut, parfait

flax ['flæks] *n* : lin *m*

flea ['fliː] *n* : puce *f*

fleck ['flɛk] *n* : petite tache *f*, moucheture *f*

flee ['fliː] *v* **fled** ['flɛd]; **fleeing** : fuir

fleece ['fliːs] *n* : toison *f* — ~ *vt* **fleeced; fleecing** : escroquer

fleet ['fliːt] *n* : flotte *f*

fleeting ['fliːtɪŋ] *adj* : bref

Flemish ['flɛmɪʃ] *adj* : flamand

flesh ['flɛʃ] *n* : chair *f* — **fleshy** ['flɛʃi] *adj* **fleshier; -est** : charnu

flew ▸ **fly**[1]

flex ['flɛks] *vt* : fléchir — **flexible** ['flɛksəbəl] *adj* : flexible — **flexibility** ['flɛksə'bɪləti] *n* : flexibilité *f*

flick ['flɪk] *n* : petit coup *m* — ∼ *vt* ∼ **a switch** : appuyer sur un bouton — *vi* ∼ **through** : feuilleter

flicker ['flɪkər] *vi* : vaciller — ∼ *n* **1** : vacillement *m* **2 a** ∼ **of hope** : une lueur d'espoir

flier ['flaɪər] *n* **1** PILOT : aviateur *m*, -trice *f* **2** *or* **flyer** LEAFLET : prospectus *m*

flight[1] ['flaɪt] *n* **1** FLYING : vol *m* **2** ∼ **of stairs** : escalier *m*

flight[2] *n* ESCAPE : fuite *f*

flimsy ['flɪmzi] *adj* **flimsier; -est 1** LIGHT : léger **2** SHAKY : peu solide **3 a** ∼ **excuse** : une pauvre excuse

flinch ['flɪntʃ] *vi* **1** WINCE : tressaillir **2** ∼ **from** : reculer devant

fling ['flɪŋ] *vt* **flung** ['flʌŋ]; **flinging 1** THROW : lancer **2** ∼ **open** : ouvrir brusquement — ∼ *n* **1** AFFAIR : affaire *f*, aventure *f* **2 have a** ∼ **at** : essayer de faire

flint ['flɪnt] *n* : silex *m*

flip ['flɪp] *v* **flipped; flipping** *vt* **1** *or* ∼ **over** : faire sauter **2** ∼ **a coin** : jouer à pile ou face — *vi* **1** *or* ∼ **over** : se retourner **2** ∼ **through** : feuilleter — ∼ *n* : saut *m* périlleux

flippant ['flɪpənt] *adj* : désinvolte

flipper ['flɪpər] *n* : nageoire *f*

flirt ['flərt] *vi* : flirter — ∼ *n* : flirteur *m*, -teuse *f* — **flirtatious** [,flər'teɪʃəs] *adj* : charmeur

flit ['flɪt] *vi* **flitted; flitting** : voleter

float ['flo:t] *n* **1** RAFT : radeau *m* **2** CORK : flotteur *m* **3** : char *m* (de carnaval) — ∼ *vi* : flotter — *vt* : faire flotter

flock ['flɑk] *n* **1** : volée *f* (d'oiseaux), troupeau *m* (de moutons) **2** CROWD : foule *f* — ∼ *vi* : affluer, venir en foule

flog ['flɑg] *vt* **flogged; flogging** : flageller

flood ['flʌd] *n* **1** : inondation *f* **2** : déluge *m* (de paroles, de larmes, etc.) — ∼ *vt* : inonder — *vi* : déborder (se dit d'une rivière) — **floodlight** ['flʌd,laɪt] *n* : projecteur *m*

floor ['flor] *n* **1** : plancher *m* **2** GROUND : sol *m* **3** STORY : étage *m* **4** **dance** ∼ : piste *f* de danse **5** **ground** ∼ : rez-de-chaussée *m* — ∼ *vt* **1** KNOCK DOWN : terrasser **2** ASTOUND : stupéfier — **floorboard** ['flor,bord] *n* : planche *f*

flop ['flɑp] *vi* **flopped; flopping 1** : s'agiter mollement **2** *or* ∼ **down** COLLAPSE : s'affaler **3** FAIL : échouer — ∼ *n* : fiasco *m* —

floppy ['flɑpi] *adj* **floppier; -est** : mou — **floppy disk** *n* : disquette *f*

flora ['florə] *n* : flore *f* — **floral** ['florəl] *adj* : floral — **florid** ['florɪd] *adj* **1** FLOWERY : fleuri **2** RUDDY : rougeaud — **florist** ['florɪst] *n* : fleuriste *mf*

floss ['flɔs] → **dental floss**

flounder[1] ['flaʊndər] *n, pl* **flounder** *or* **flounders** : flet *m*

flounder[2] *vi* **1** *or* ∼ **about** : patauger **2** FALTER : bredouiller

flour ['flaʊər] *n* : farine *f*

flourish ['flərɪʃ] *vi* **1** PROSPER : prospérer **2** THRIVE : s'épanouir — *vt* BRANDISH : brandir — ∼ *n* : grand geste *m* — **flourishing** ['flərɪʃɪŋ] *adj* : florissant

flout ['flaʊt] *vt* : bafouer

flow ['flo:] *vi* **1** : couler **2** MOVE : s'écouler **3** CIRCULATE : circuler **4** BILLOW : flotter — ∼ *n* **1** : écoulement *m* (d'un liquide) **2** MOVEMENT : circulation *f* **3** : flux *m* (de la marée)

flower ['flaʊər] *n* : fleur *f* — ∼ *vi* : fleurir — **flowering** ['flaʊərɪŋ] *n* : floraison *f* — **flowerpot** ['flaʊər,pɑt] *n* : pot *m* de fleurs — **flowery** ['flaʊəri] *adj* : fleuri

flown → **fly**[1]

flu ['flu:] *n* : grippe *f*

fluctuate ['flʌktʃu,eɪt] *vi* **-ated; -ating** : fluctuer — **fluctuation** [,flʌktʃu'eɪʃən] *n* : fluctuation *f*

fluency ['flu:əntsi] *n* : aisance *f* — **fluent** ['flu:ənt] *adj* **1** : coulant, aisé **2 be** ∼ **in** : parler couramment — **fluently** ['flu:əntli] *adv* : couramment

fluff ['flʌf] *n* **1** DOWN : duvet *m* **2** FUZZ : peluches *fpl* — **fluffy** ['flʌfi] *adj* **fluffier; -est** : duveteux

fluid ['flu:ɪd] *adj* : fluide — ∼ *n* : fluide *m*

flunk ['flʌŋk] *vt* FAIL : rater

fluorescent [,flʊr'ɛsənt, ,flɔr-] *adj* : fluorescent

flurry ['fləri] *n, pl* **-ries 1** GUST : rafale *f* **2** *or* **snow** ∼ : poudrerie *f Can* **3** : tourbillon *m* (d'activité)

flush ['flʌʃ] *vi* BLUSH : rougir — *vt* ∼ **the toilet** : tirer la chasse d'eau — ∼ *n* **1** : chasse *f* (d'eau) **2** BLUSH : rougeur *f* — ∼ *adj* : au même niveau — ∼ *adv* : de niveau

fluster ['flʌstər] *vt* : troubler

flute ['flu:t] *n* : flûte *f*

flutter ['flʌtər] *vi* **1** FLAP : battre (se dit des ailes) **2** FLIT : voleter **3** ∼ **about** : s'agiter — ∼ *n* **1** : battement *m* (d'ailes) **2** STIR : agitation *f*, émoi *m*

flux ['flʌks] *n* **in a state of** ∼ : dans un état de perpétuel changement

fly[1] ['flaɪ] *v* **flew** ['flu:]; **flown** ['flo:n]; **flying** *vi* **1** : voler **2** TRAVEL : prendre l'avion **3** : flotter (se dit d'un drapeau) **4** RUSH : filer

5 FLEE : s'enfuir — *vt* : faire voler — ~ *n*, *pl* **flies** : braguette *f* (d'un pantalon)

fly² *n*, *pl* **flies** : mouche *f* (insecte)

flyer → **flier**

flying saucer *n* : soucoupe *f* volante

foal ['fo:l] *n* : poulain *m*

foam ['fo:m] *n* : mousse *f*, écume *f* — ~ *vi* : mousser, écumer — **foamy** ['fo:mi] *adj* **foamier; -est** : mousseux, écumeux (se dit de la mer)

focus ['fo:kəs] *n*, *pl* **foci** ['fo:ˌsaɪ, -ˌkaɪ] 1 : foyer *m* 2 **be in** ~ : être au point 3 ~ **of attention** : centre *m* d'attention — ~ *v* **-cused** *or* **-cussed; -cusing** *or* **-cussing** *vt* 1 : mettre au point (un instrument) 2 : fixer (les yeux) — *vi* ~ **on** : se concentrer sur

fodder ['fadər] *n* : fourrage *m*

foe ['fo:] *n* : ennemi *m*, -mie *f*

fog ['fɔg, 'fag] *n* : brouillard *m* — ~ *vi* **fogged; fogging** *or* ~ **up** : s'embuer — **foggy** ['fɔgi, 'fa-] *adj* **foggier; -est** : brumeux — **foghorn** ['fɔg,hɔrn, 'fag-] *n* : corne *f* de brume

foil¹ ['fɔɪl] *vt* : déjouer

foil² *n* : feuille *f* (d'aluminium, etc.)

fold¹ ['fo:ld] *n* 1 : parc *m* à moutons 2 **return to the** ~ : rentrer au bercail

fold² *vt* 1 : plier 2 ~ **one's arms** : croiser les bras — *vi* 1 *or* ~ **up** : se plier 2 FAIL : échouer — ~ *n* CREASE : pli *m* — **folder** ['fo:ldər] *n* 1 FILE : chemise *f* 2 PAMPHLET : dépliant *m*

foliage ['fo:liɪʤ, -lɪʤ] *n* : feuillage *m*

folk ['fo:k] *n*, *pl* **folk** *or* **folks** 1 PEOPLE : gens *mfpl* 2 ~ **s** *npl* PARENTS : famille *f*, parents *mpl* — ~ *adj* : populaire, folklorique — **folklore** ['fo:k,lor] *n* : folklore *m*

follow ['falo] *vt* 1 : suivre 2 PURSUE : poursuivre 3 ~ **up** : donner suite à — *vi* 1 : suivre 2 ENSUE : s'ensuivre — **follower** ['faloər] *n* : partisan *m*, -sane *f* — **following** ['faloɪŋ] *adj* : suivant — ~ *n* : partisans *mpl* — ~ *prep* : après

folly ['fali] *n*, *pl* **-lies** : folie *f*

fond ['fand] *adj* 1 : affectueux 2 **be** ~ **of** : aimer beaucoup

fondle ['fandəl] *vt* **-dled; -dling** : caresser

fondness ['fandnəs] *n* 1 : affection *f* 2 **have a** ~ **for** : avoir une prédilection pour

food ['fu:d] *n* : nourriture *f* — **foodstuffs** ['fu:d,stʌfs] *npl* : denrées *fpl* alimentaires

fool ['fu:l] *n* 1 : idiot *m*, -diote *f* 2 JESTER : fou *m* — ~ *vt* DECEIVE : duper — *vi* 1 JOKE : plaisanter 2 ~ **around** : perdre son temps — **foolhardy** ['fu:l,hardi] *adj* : téméraire — **foolish** ['fu:lɪʃ] *adj* : bête, idiot — **foolishness** ['fu:lɪʃnəs] *n* : bêtise *f*, sottise *f* — **foolproof** ['fu:l,pru:f] *adj* : infaillible

foot ['fut] *n*, *pl* **feet** ['fi:t] : pied *m* — **footage** ['futɪʤ] *n* : métrage *m* — **football** ['fut,bɔl] *n* : football *m* américain, football *m Can* — **footbridge** ['fut,brɪʤ] *n* : passerelle *f* — **foothills** ['fut,hɪlz] *npl* : contreforts *mpl* — **foothold** ['fut,ho:ld] *n* : prise *f* de pied — **footing** ['futɪŋ] *n* 1 → **foothold** 2 STATUS : position *f* 3 **on equal** ~ : sur pied d'égalité — **footlights** ['fut,laɪts] *npl* : rampe *f* — **footnote** ['fut,no:t] *n* : note *f* (en bas de la page) — **footpath** ['fut,pæθ] *n* : sentier *m* — **footprint** ['fut,prɪnt] *n* : empreinte *f* (de pied) — **footstep** ['fut,stɛp] *n* : pas *m* — **footwear** ['fut,wær] *n* : chaussures *fpl*

for ['fɔr] *prep* 1 : pour 2 BECAUSE OF : de, à cause de 3 (*indicating duration*) : pour, pendant 4 (*indicating destination*) : pour, à destination de 5 **a cure** ~ **cancer** : un remède contre le cancer 6 ~ **sale** : à vendre — ~ *conj* BECAUSE : car

forage ['fɔrɪʤ] *vi* **-aged; -aging** : fourrager

foray ['fɔr,eɪ] *n* : incursion *f*

forbid [fər'bɪd] *vt* **-bade** [-'bæd, -'beɪd] *or* **-bad** [-'bæd]; **-bidden** [-'bɪdən]; **-bidding** : interdire, défendre — **forbidding** [fər'bɪdɪŋ] *adj* : menaçant

force ['fors] *n* 1 : force *f* 2 *or* ~ **s** *npl* : forces *fpl* 3 **by** ~ : de force 4 **in** ~ : en vigueur — ~ *vt* **forced; forcing** 1 : forcer 2 IMPOSE : imposer — **forceful** ['forsfəl] *adj* : vigoureux

forceps ['forsəps, -ˌsɛps] *ns & pl* : forceps *m*

forcibly ['forsəbli] *adv* : de force

ford ['ford] *n* : gué *m* — ~ *vt* : passer à gué

fore ['for] *n* 1 : avant *m* (d'un navire) 2 **come to the** ~ : se mettre en évidence

forearm ['for,arm] *n* : avant-bras *m*

foreboding [for'bo:dɪŋ] *n* : pressentiment *m*

forecast ['for,kæst] *vt* **-cast; -casting** : prévoir — ~ *n or* **weather** ~ : prévisions *fpl* météorologiques, météo *f fam*

forefathers ['for,faðərz] *npl* : ancêtres *mfpl*, aïeux *mpl*

forefinger ['for,fɪŋgər] *n* : index *m*

forefront ['for,frʌnt] *n* : premier rang *m*

forego [for'go:] → **forgo**

foregone [for'gɔn] *adj* **it's a** ~ **conclusion** : c'est gagné d'avance

foreground ['for,graund] *n* : premier plan *m*

forehead ['fɔrəd, 'for,hɛd] *n* : front *m*

foreign ['fɔrən] *adj* 1 : étranger (se dit d'une langue, etc.) 2 ~ **trade** : commerce *m* extérieur — **foreigner** ['fɔrənər] *n* : étranger *m*, -gère *f*

foreman ['formən] *n*, *pl* **-men** [-mən, -ˌmɛn] : contremaître *m*

foremost ['for,mo:st] *adj* : principal — ~ *adv* **first and** ~ : tout d'abord

forensic [fə'rɛntsɪk] *adj* : médico-légal

forerunner ['for,rʌnər] *n* : précurseur *m*

foresee [for'si:] *vt* **-saw; -seen; -seeing**

: prévoir — **foreseeable** [for'si:əbəl] *adj*
: prévisible

foreshadow [for'ʃædo:] *vt* : présager

foresight ['for,saɪt] *n* : prévoyance *f*

forest ['forəst] *n* : forêt *f* — **forestry**
['forəstri] *n* : sylviculture *f*

foretaste ['for,teɪst] *n* : avant-goût *m*

foretell [for'tɛl] *vt* **-told; -telling** : prédire

forethought ['for,θɔt] *n* : prévoyance *f*

forever [fər'ɛvər] *adv* **1** ETERNALLY : toujours **2** CONTINUALLY : sans cesse

forewarn [for'wɔrn] *vt* : avertir, prévenir

foreword ['forwərd] *n* : avant-propos *m*

forfeit ['fɔrfət] *n* **1** PENALTY : peine *f* **2 pay
a ~** : avoir un gage — **~** *vt* : perdre

forge ['fɔrdʒ] *n* : forge *f* — **~** *v* **forged;
forging** *vt* **1** : forger (un métal, etc.) **2**
COUNTERFEIT : contrefaire, falsifier — *vi*
~ ahead : prendre de l'avance — **forger**
['fɔrdʒər] *n* : faussaire *mf*, faux-monnayeur
m — **forgery** ['fɔrdʒəri] *n*, *pl* **-eries** : faux
m, contrefaçon *f*

forget [fər'gɛt] *v* **-got** [-'gɑt]; **-gotten**
[-'gɑtən] *or* **-got; -getting** : oublier — **forgetful** [fər'gɛtfəl] *adj* : distrait

forgive [fər'gɪv] *vt* **-gave** [-'geɪv]; **-given**
[-'gɪvən]; **-giving** : pardonner — **forgiveness** [fər'gɪvnəs] *n* : pardon *m*

forgo *or* **forego** [for'go:] *vt* **-went; -gone;
-going** : renoncer à, se priver de

fork ['fɔrk] *n* **1** : fourchette *f* **2** PITCHFORK
: fourche *f* **3** JUNCTION : bifurcation *f*
(d'une route) — **~** *vt or* **~ over** : allonger
fam — *vi* : bifurquer

forlorn [fər'lɔrn] *adj* : triste

form ['fɔrm] *n* **1** : forme *f* **2** DOCUMENT
: formulaire *m* — **~** *vt* : former — *vi* : se
former, prendre forme

formal ['fɔrməl] *adj* **1** : officiel, solennel **2**
: soigné, soutenu (se dit du langage) — **~** *n*
1 *or* **~ dance** : bal *m* **2** *or* **~ dress**
: tenue *f* de soirée — **formality** [fɔr'mæləti]
n, *pl* **-ties** : formalité *f*

format ['fɔr,mæt] *n* : format *m* — **~** *vt*
-matted; -matting : formater (une diskette,
etc.)

formation [fɔr'meɪʃən] *n* : formation *f*

former ['fɔrmər] *adj* **1** PREVIOUS : ancien **2**
FIRST : premier — **formerly** ['fɔrmərli] *adv*
: autrefois

formidable ['fɔrmədəbəl, fɔr'mɪdə-] *adj*
: redoutable

formula ['fɔrmjələ] *n*, *pl* **-las** *or* **-lae** [-,li:,
-,laɪ] **1** : formule *f* **2** *or* **baby ~** : lait *m* re-
constitué — **formulate** ['fɔrmjə,leɪt] *vt*
-lated; -lating : formuler

forsake [fər'seɪk] *vt* **-sook** [-'sʊk]; **-saken**
[-'seɪkən]; **-saking** : abandonner

fort ['fɔrt] *n* : fort *m*

forth ['forθ] *adv* **1 and so ~** : et ainsi de

suite **2 from this day ~** : dorénavant **3 go
back and ~** : aller et venir — **forthcoming** [forθ'kʌmɪŋ, 'forθ-] *adj* **1** COMING
: prochain, à venir **2** OPEN : communicatif
— **forthright** ['forθ,raɪt] *adj* : franc, direct

fortieth ['fɔrtiəθ] *n* : quarantième *mf* — **~**
adj : quarantième

fortify ['fɔrtə,faɪ] *vt* **-fied; -fying** : fortifier —
fortification [,fɔrtəfə'keɪʃən] *n* : fortification *f*

fortitude ['fɔrtə,tu:d, -,tju:d] *n* : force *f*
d'âme

fortnight ['fort,naɪt] *n* : quinzaine *f*, quinze
jours *mpl*

fortress ['fɔrtrəs] *n* : forteresse *f*

fortunate ['fɔrtʃənət] *adj* : heureux — **fortunately** ['fɔrtʃənətli] *adv* : heureusement —
fortune ['fɔrtʃən] *n* **1** : fortune *f* **2** LUCK
: chance *f* — **fortune-teller** ['fɔrtʃən,tɛlər]
n : diseuse *f* de bonne aventure

forty ['fɔrti] *n*, *pl* **forties** : quarante *m* — **~**
adj : quarante

forum ['forəm] *n*, *pl* **-rums** : forum *m*

forward ['forwərd] *adj* **1** : avant, en avant **2**
BRASH : effronté — **~** *adv* : en avant, vers
l'avant — **~** *n* : avant *m* (aux sports) — **~**
vt : expédier (des marchandises), faire
suivre (du courrier) — **forwards**
['forwərdz] *adv* → **forward**

fossil ['fɑsəl] *n* : fossile *m*

foster ['fɔstər] *adj* : adoptif, d'accueil — **~**
vt **1** NURTURE : nourrir **2** ENCOURAGE : encourager

fought → **fight**

foul ['faʊl] *adj* **1** : infect (se dit d'une odeur,
etc.) **2 ~ language** : langage *m* ordurier **3
~ play** : jeu *m* irrégulier **4 ~ weather**
: sale temps *m* — **~** *n* : faute *f* (aux sports)
— **~** *vt* : salir, souiller

found[1] ['faʊnd] → **find**

found[2] *vt* : fonder, établir — **foundation**
[faʊn'deɪʃən] *n* **1** : fondation *f* **2** BASIS
: base *f*, fondement *m*

founder[1] ['faʊndər] *n* : fondateur *m*, -trice *f*

founder[2] *vi* **1** SINK : sombrer **2** COLLAPSE
: s'effondrer

fountain ['faʊntən] *n* : fontaine *f*

four ['for] *n* : quatre *m* — **~** *adj* : quatre —
fourfold ['for,fo:ld, -'fo:ld] *adj* : quadruple
— **four hundred** *adj* : quatre cents

fourteen [for'ti:n] *n* : quatorze *m* — **~** *adj*
: quatorze — **fourteenth** [for'ti:nθ] *n* **1**
: quatorzième *mf* **2 June ~** : le quatorze
juin — **~** *adj* : quatorzième

fourth ['forθ] *n* **1** : quatrième *mf* (dans une
série) **2** : quart *m* (en mathématiques) **3
August ~** : le quatre août — **~** *adj* : quatrième

fowl ['faʊl] *n*, *pl* **fowl** *or* **fowls** : volaille *f*

fox ['fɑks] *n*, *pl* **foxes** : renard *m* — **~** *vt*

TRICK : tromper, berner — **foxy** ['fɑksi] *adj*
foxier; -est SHREWD : rusé

foyer ['fɔɪər, 'fɔɪˌjeɪ] *n* : vestibule *m*, foyer *m*
(d'un théâtre)

fraction ['frækʃən] *n* : fraction *f*

fracture ['fræktʃər] *n* : fracture *f* — ~ *vt*
-tured; -turing : fracturer

fragile ['frædʒəl, -ˌdʒaɪl] *adj* : fragile —
fragility [frə'dʒɪləti] *n* : fragilité *f*

fragment ['frægmənt] *n* : fragment *m*

fragrance ['freɪgrənts] *n* : parfum *m* — **fragrant** ['freɪgrənt] *adj* : parfumé

frail ['freɪl] *adj* : frêle, fragile

frame ['freɪm] *vt* **framed; framing 1** EN-
CLOSE : encadrer **2** DEVISE : élaborer **3**
FORMULATE : formuler **4** INCRIMINATE
: monter un coup contre — ~ *n* **1** : cadre *m*
(d'un tableau, etc.) **2** : charpente *f* (d'un édifice, etc.) **3** ~**s** *npl* : monture *f* (de
lunettes) **4** ~ **of mind** : état *m* d'esprit —
framework ['freɪmˌwərk] *n* : structure *f*,
cadre *m*

franchise ['frænˌtʃaɪz] *n* **1** : franchise *f* (en
commerce) **2** SUFFRAGE : droit *m* de vote

frank ['fræŋk] *adj* : franc — **frankly**
['fræŋkli] *adv* : franchement — **frankness**
['fræŋknəs] *n* : franchise *f*

frantic ['fræntɪk] *adj* : frénétique

fraternal [frə'tərnəl] *adj* : fraternel — **fraternity** [frə'tərnəti] *n, pl* **-ties** : fraternité *f* —
fraternize ['frætərˌnaɪz] *vi* **-nized; -nizing**
: fraterniser

fraud ['frɔd] *n* **1** DECEIT : fraude *f* **2** IMPOS-
TOR : imposteur *m* — **fraudulent**
['frɔdʒələnt] *adj* : frauduleux

fraught ['frɔt] *adj* ~ **with** : chargé de

fray[1] ['freɪ] *n* : bagarre *f*

fray[2] *vt* : mettre (les nerfs) à vif — *vi* : s'effilocher

freak ['fri:k] *n* **1** ODDITY : phénomène *m* **2**
ENTHUSIAST : fana *mf fam* — ~ *adj* : anormal — **freakish** ['fri:kɪʃ] *adj* : anormal,
bizarre

freckle ['frɛkəl] *n* : tache *f* de rousseur

free ['fri:] *adj* **freer; freest 1** : libre **2** *or* ~
of charge : gratuit **3** ~ **from** : dépourvu
de — ~ *vt* **freed; freeing 1** RELEASE
: libérer **2** DISENGAGE : dégager — ~ *adv*
1 : librement **2 for** ~ : gratuitement —
freedom ['fri:dəm] *n* : liberté *f* — **freelance** ['fri:ˌlænts] *adv* : à la pige — **freely**
['fri:li] *adv* **1** : librement **2** LAVISHLY
: largement — **freeway** ['fri:ˌweɪ] *n* : autoroute *f* — **free will** ['fri:ˌwɪl] *n* **1** : libre arbitre *m* **2 of one's own** ~ : de sa propre
volonté

freeze ['fri:z] *v* **froze** ['fro:z]; **frozen**
['fro:zən]; **freezing** *vt* **1** : geler (de l'eau),
congeler (des aliments, etc.) **2** FIX : bloquer
— *vi* : geler — ~ *n* **1** : gel *m* **2** : blocage *m*

(des prix, etc.) — **freeze-dry** ['fri:z'draɪ] *vt*
-dried; -drying : lyophiliser — **freezer**
['fri:zər] *n* : congélateur *m* — **freezing**
['fri:zɪŋ] *adj* **1** : glacial **2 it's** ~ : on gèle

freight ['freɪt] *n* **1** SHIPPING : transport *m* **2**
GOODS : fret *m*, marchandises *fpl*

French ['frɛntʃ] *adj* : français — ~ *n* **1**
: français *m* (langue) **2 the** ~ : les Français

French Canadian *adj* : canadien français —
~ *n* : Canadien *m* français, Canadienne *f*
française

french fries ['frɛntʃˌfraɪz] *npl* : frites *fpl*

Frenchman ['frɛntʃmən] *n, pl* **-men** [-mən,
-ˌmɛn] : Français *m* — **Frenchwoman**
['frɛntʃˌwʊmən] *n, pl* **-women** [-ˌwɪmən]
: Française *f*

frenzy ['frɛnzi] *n, pl* **-zies** : frénésie *f* —
frenzied ['frɛnzid] *adj* : frénétique

frequency ['fri:kwəntsi] *n, pl* **-cies**
: fréquence *f* — **frequent** [fri'kwɛnt,
'fri:kwənt] *vt* : fréquenter — ~ ['fri:kwənt]
adj : fréquent — **frequently** ['fri:kwəntli]
adv : fréquemment

fresco ['frɛsˌko:] *n, pl* **-coes** : fresque *f*

fresh ['frɛʃ] *adj* **1** : frais **2** NEW : nouveau **3**
IMPUDENT : insolent **4** ~ **water** : eau *f*
douce — **freshen** ['frɛʃən] *vt* : rafraîchir —
vi ~ **up** : se rafraîchir — **freshly** ['frɛʃli]
adv : récemment — **freshman** ['frɛʃmən] *n,
pl* **-men** [-mən, -ˌmɛn] : étudiant *m*, -diante
f de première année — **freshness** ['frɛʃnəs]
n : fraîcheur *f*

fret ['frɛt] *vi* **fretted; fretting** : s'inquiéter —
fretful ['frɛtfəl] *adj* : irritable

friar ['fraɪər] *n* : frère *m*

friction ['frɪkʃən] *n* : friction *f*

Friday ['fraɪˌdeɪ, -di] *n* : vendredi *m*

friend ['frɛnd] *n* : ami *m*, amie *f* — **friendli-
ness** ['frɛndlinəs] *n* : gentillesse *f* —
friendly ['frɛndli] *adj* **friendlier; -est** : gentil, amical — **friendship** ['frɛndˌʃɪp] *n*
: amitié *f*

frigate ['frɪgət] *n* : frégate *f*

fright ['fraɪt] *n* : peur *f*, frayeur *f* — **frighten**
['fraɪtən] *vt* : faire peur à, effrayer — **frightened** ['fraɪtnd] *adj* : apeuré, effrayé —
frightening ['fraɪtnɪŋ] *adj* : effrayant —
frightful ['fraɪtfəl] *adj* : terrible, affreux

frigid ['frɪdʒɪd] *adj* : glacial

frill ['frɪl] *n* **1** RUFFLE : volant *m* (d'une jupe),
jabot *m* (d'une chemise) **2** LUXURY : luxe *m*

fringe ['frɪndʒ] *n* **1** : frange *f* **2** EDGE : bordure *f* **3** ~ **benefits** : avantages *mpl* sociaux

frisk ['frɪsk] *vt* SEARCH : fouiller — **frisky**
['frɪski] *adj* **friskier; -est** : vif, folâtre

fritter ['frɪtər] *n* : beignet *m* — ~ *vt or* ~
away : gaspiller

frivolous ['frɪvələs] *adj* : frivole — **frivolity**
[frɪ'vɑləti] *n, pl* **-ties** : frivolité *f*

frizzy ['frɪzi] *adj* **frizzier; -est** : crépu

fro ['fro:] *adv* → **to**

frock ['frɑk] *n* : robe *f*

frog ['frɔg, 'frɑg] *n* **1** : grenouille *f* **2 have a ~ in one's throat** : avoir un chat dans la gorge — **frogman** ['frɔg,mæn, 'frɑg-, -mən] *n, pl* **-men** [-mən, -,mɛn] : homme-grenouille *m*

frolic ['frɑlɪk] *vi* **-icked; -icking** : folâtrer

from ['frʌm, 'frɑm] *prep* **1** (*indicating a starting point*) : de, à partir de **2** (*indicating a source or cause*) : de, par, à **3 ~ now on** : à partir de maintenant **4 protection ~ the sun** : protection contre le soleil **5 drink ~ a glass** : boire dans un verre

front ['frʌnt] *n* **1** : avant *m*, devant *m* **2** APPEARANCE : air *m*, contenance *f* **3** : front *m* (militaire) **4** : façade *f* (d'un bâtiment) **5 in ~** : à l'avant **6 in ~ of** : devant — ~ *vi* **~ on** : donner sur — ~ *adj* **1** : de devant, (en) avant **2 ~ row** : premier rang *m*

frontier [,frʌn'tɪr] *n* : frontière *f*

frost ['frɔst] *n* **1** : givre *m* **2** FREEZING : gel *m*, gelée *f* — ~ *vt* : glacer (un gâteau) — **frostbite** ['frɔst,baɪt] *n* : gelure *f* — **frosting** ['frɔstɪŋ] *n* ICING : glaçage *m* — **frosty** ['frɔsti] *adj* **frostier; -est 1** : couvert de givre **2** FRIGID : glacial

froth ['frɔθ] *n, pl* **froths** ['frɔθs, 'frɔðz] : écume *f*, mousse *f* — **frothy** ['frɔθi, -ði] *adj* **frothier; -est** : écumeux, mousseux

frown ['fraʊn] *vi* : froncer les sourcils — ~ *n* : froncement *m* de sourcils

froze, frozen → **freeze**

frugal ['fru:gəl] *adj* : économe

fruit ['fru:t] *n* : fruit *m* — **fruitcake** ['fru:t-,keɪk] *n* : cake *m* — **fruitful** ['fru:tfəl] *adj* : fructueux — **fruition** [fru:'ɪʃən] *n* **come to ~** : se réaliser — **fruity** ['fru:ti] *adj* **fruitier; -est** : fruité

frustrate ['frʌs,treɪt] *vt* **-trated; -trating** : frustrer — **frustrating** ['frʌs,treɪtɪŋ] *adj* : frustrant — **frustration** [,frʌs'treɪʃən] *n* : frustration *f*

fry ['fraɪ] *v* **fried; frying** : frire — ~ *n, pl* **fries 1** *or* **small ~** : menu fretin *m* **2 fries** → **french fries** — **frying pan** *n* : poêle *f*

fudge ['fʌʤ] *n* : caramel *m* mou — ~ *vt* FALSIFY : truquer

fuel ['fju:əl] *n* : combustible *m*, carburant *m* — ~ *vt* **-eled** *or* **-elled; -eling** *or* **-elling 1** : alimenter en combustible **2** STIMULATE : aviver

fugitive ['fju:ʤətɪv] *n* : fugitif *m*, -tive *f*

fulfill *or* **fulfil** [fʊl'fɪl] *vt* **-filled; -filling 1** EXECUTE : accomplir, réaliser **2** FILL, MEET : remplir — **fulfillment** [fʊl'fɪlmənt] *n* **1** ACCOMPLISHMENT : réalisation *f* **2** SATISFACTION : contentement *m*

full ['fʊl, 'fʌl] *adj* **1** FILLED : plein **2** COMPLETE : entier, total **3** : ample (se dit d'une jupe), rond (se dit d'un visage) **4** : complet (se dit d'un hotel, etc.) — ~ *adv* **1** DIRECTLY : carrément **2 know ~ well** : savoir très bien — ~ *n* **in ~** : entièrement — **full-fledged** ['fʊl'flɛʤd] *adj* : à part entière — **fully** ['fʊli] *adv* : complètement

fumble ['fʌmbəl] *vi* **-bled; -bling** : tâtonner, fouiller

fume ['fju:m] *vi* **fumed; fuming** RAGE : rager, fulminer — **fumes** ['fju:mz] *npl* : vapeurs *fpl*

fumigate ['fju:mə,geɪt] *vt* **-gated; -gating** : désinfecter par fumigation

fun ['fʌn] *n* **1** : amusement *m* **2 have ~** : s'amuser **3 for ~** : pour rire **4 make ~ of** : se moquer de

function ['fʌŋkʃən] *n* **1** : fonction *f* **2** GATHERING : réception *f*, cérémonie *f* — ~ *vi* **1** : fonctionner **2 ~ as** : servir de — **functional** ['fʌŋkʃənəl] *adj* : fonctionnel

fund ['fʌnd] *n* **1** : fonds *m* **2 ~s** *npl* RESOURCES : fonds *mpl* — ~ *vt* : financer

fundamental [,fʌndə'mɛntəl] *adj* : fondamental — **fundamentals** *npl* : principes *mpl* de base

funeral ['fju:nərəl] *n* : enterrement *m*, funérailles *fpl* — ~ *adj* : funèbre — **funeral home** *or* **funeral parlor** *n* : entreprise *f* de pompes funèbres

fungus ['fʌŋgəs] *n, pl* **fungi** ['fʌn,ʤaɪ, 'fʌŋ-,gaɪ] **1** MUSHROOM : champignon *m* **2** MOLD : moisissure *f*

funnel ['fʌnəl] *n* **1** : entonnoir *m* **2** SMOKESTACK : cheminée *f*

funny ['fʌni] *adj* **funnier; -est 1** : drôle, amusant **2** PECULIAR : bizarre — **funnies** ['fʌniz] *npl* : bandes *fpl* dessinées

fur ['fər] *n* : fourrure *f* — ~ *adj* : de fourrure

furious ['fjʊriəs] *adj* : furieux

furnace ['fərnəs] *n* : fourneau *m*

furnish ['fərnɪʃ] *vt* **1** SUPPLY : fournir **2** : meubler (un appartement, etc.) — **furnishings** ['fərnɪʃɪŋz] *npl* : ameublement *m*, meubles *mpl* — **furniture** ['fərnɪʧər] *n* : meubles *mpl*

furrow ['fəro:] *n* : sillon *m*

furry ['fəri] *adj* **furrier; -est** : au poil touffu (se dit d'un animal), en peluche (se dit d'un jouet, etc.)

further ['fərðər] *adv* **1** FARTHER : plus loin **2** MORE : davantage, plus **3** MOREOVER : de plus — ~ *adj* **1** FARTHER : plus éloigné **2** ADDITIONAL : supplémentaire **3 until ~ notice** : jusqu'à nouvel ordre — **furthermore** ['fərðər,mor] *adv* : en outre, de plus — **furthest** ['fərðəst] *adv & adj* → **farthest**

furtive ['fərtɪv] *adj* : furtif

fury ['fjʊri] *n, pl* **-ries** : fureur *f*

fuse¹ *or* **fuze** [ˈfjuːz] *n* : amorce *f*, détonateur *m* (d'une bombe, etc.)

fuse² *v* **fused; fusing** *vt* **1** MELT : fondre **2** UNITE : fusionner — ~ *n* **1** : fusible *m*, plomb *m* (en electricite) **2** blow a ~ : faire sauter un plomb — **fusion** [ˈfjuːʒən] *n* : fusion *f*

fuss [ˈfʌs] *n* **1** : agitation *f*, remuemenage *m* **2 make a ~** : faire des histoires — ~ *vi* **1** : s'agiter **2** WORRY : s'inquiéter — **fussy**

fussier; -est 1 FINICKY : tatillon, pointilleux **2** ELABORATE : tarabiscoté

futile [ˈfjuːt̬əl, ˈfjuːˌtaɪl] *adj* : futile, vain — **futility** [fjuːˈtɪlət̬i] *n* : futilité *f*

future [ˈfjuːtʃər] *adj* ; futur — ~ *n* : avenir *m*, futur *m*

fuze *n* → **fuse¹**

fuzz [ˈfʌz] *n* FLUFF : peluches *fpl* — **fuzzy** [ˈfʌzi] *adj* **fuzzier; -est 1** FURRY : duveteux **2** INDISTINCT : flou **3** VAGUE : confus

G

g [ˈdʒiː] *n, pl* **g's** *or* **gs** [ˈdʒiːz] : g *m*, septième lettre de l'alphabet

gab [ˈgæb] *vi* **gabbed; gabbing** : bavarder — ~ *n* CHATTER : bavardage *m*

gable [ˈgeɪbəl] *n* : pignon *m*

gadget [ˈgædʒət] *n* : gadget *m*

gag [ˈgæg] *v* **gagged; gagging** *vt* : bâillonner — *vi* CHOKE : avoir des haut-le-cœur — ~ *n* **1** : bâillon *m* **2** JOKE : blague *f*

gage → **gauge**

gaiety [ˈgeɪət̬i] *n, pl* **-eties** : gaieté *f*

gain [ˈgeɪn] *n* **1** PROFIT : profit *m* **2** INCREASE : augmentation *f* — ~ *vt* **1** OBTAIN : gagner **2 ~ weight** : prendre du poids — *vi* **1** PROFIT : gagner **2** : avancer (se dit d'une horloge) — **gainful** [ˈgeɪnfəl] *adj* : rémunéré

gait [ˈgeɪt] *n* : démarche *f*

gala [ˈgeɪlə, ˈgæ-, ˈgɑ-] *n* : gala *m*

galaxy [ˈgæləksi] *n, pl* **-axies** : galaxie *f*

gale [ˈgeɪl] *n* : coup *m* de vent

gall [ˈgɔl] *n* **have the ~ to** : avoir le culot de

gallant [ˈgælənt] *adj* : galant

gallbladder [ˈgɔlˌblædər] *n* : vesicule *f* biliaire

gallery [ˈgæləri] *n, pl* **-leries** : galerie *f*

gallon [ˈgælən] *n* : gallon *m*

gallop [ˈgæləp] *vi* : galoper — ~ *n* : galop *m*

gallows [ˈgæˌloːz] *n, pl* **-lows** *or* **-lowses** [-ˌloːzəz] : gibet *m*, potence *f*

gallstone [ˈgɔlˌstoːn] *n* : calcul *m* biliaire

galore [gəˈlor] *adv* : en abondance

galoshes [gəˈlɑʃəz] *npl* : caoutchoucs *mpl*, claques *fpl Can*

galvanize [ˈgælvənˌaɪz] *vt* **-nized; -nizing** : galvaniser

gamble [ˈgæmbəl] *v* **-bled; -bling** *vi* : jouer — *vt* WAGER : parier — ~ *n* **1** BET : pari *m* **2** RISK : entreprise *f* risquée — **gambler** [ˈgæmbələr] *n* : joueur *m*, joueuse *f*

game [ˈgeɪm] *n* **1** : jeu *m* **2** MATCH : match *m*, partie *f* **3** *or* **~ animals** : gibier *m* — ~ *adj* READY : partant, prêt

gamut [ˈgæmət] *n* : gamme *f*

gang [ˈgæŋ] *n* : bande *f* — ~ *vi* **~ up on** : se liguer contre

gangplank [ˈgæŋˌplæŋk] *n* : passerelle *f*

gangrene [ˈgæŋˌgriːn, ˈgæn-; gæŋˈ-, gæn-ˈ] *n* : gangrène *f*

gangster [ˈgæŋstər] *n* : gangster *m*

gangway [ˈgæŋˌweɪ] → **gangplank**

gap [ˈgæp] *n* **1** OPENING : trou *m* **2** INTERVAL : intervalle *m* **3** DIFFERENCE : écart *m* **4** DEFICIENCY : lacune *f*

gape [ˈgeɪp] *vi* **gaped; gaping 1** OPEN : bâiller **2** STARE : rester bouche bée

garage [gəˈrɑʒ, -ˈrɑdʒ] *n* : garage *m*

garb [ˈgɑrb] *n* : costume *m*, mise *f*

garbage [ˈgɑrbɪdʒ] *n* : ordures *fpl* — **garbage can** *n* : poubelle *f*

garble [ˈgɑrbəl] *vt* **-bled; -bling** : embrouiller — **garbled** [ˈgɑrbəld] *adj* : confus

garden [ˈgɑrdən] *n* : jardin *m* — ~ *vi* : jardiner — **gardener** [ˈgɑrdənər] *n* : jardinier *m*, -nière *f*

gargle [ˈgɑrgəl] *vi* **-gled; -gling** : se gargariser

garish [ˈgærɪʃ] *adj* : criard, voyant

garland [ˈgɑrlənd] *n* : guirlande *f*

garlic [ˈgɑrlɪk] *n* : ail *m*

garment [ˈgɑrmənt] *n* : vêtement *m*

garnish [ˈgɑrnɪʃ] *vt* : garnir — ~ *n* : garniture *f*

garret [ˈgærət] *n* : mansarde *f*

garrison [ˈgærəsən] *n* : garnison *f*

garter [ˈgɑrtər] *n* : jarretière *f*

gas [ˈgæs] *n, pl* **gases 1** : gaz *m* **2** GASOLINE : essence *f* — ~ *v* **gassed; gassing** *vt* : asphyxier au gaz — *vi* **~ up** : faire le plein d'essence — **gas station** *n* : station-service *f*

gash ['gæʃ] *n* : entaille *f* — **~** *vt* : entailler
gasket ['gæskət] *n* : joint *m* (d'étanchéité)
gasoline ['gæsə,li:n, ,gæsə'-] *n* : essence *f*
gasp ['gæsp] *vi* **1** : avoir le souffle coupé **2** PANT : haleter — **~** *n* : halètement *m*
gastric ['gæstrɪk] *adj* : gastrique
gastronomy [gæs'tranəmi] *n* : gastronomie *f*
gate ['geɪt] *n* **1** DOOR : porte *f* **2** BARRIER : barrière *f*, grille *f* — **gateway** ['geɪt,weɪ] *n* : porte *f*, entrée *f*
gather ['gæðər] *vt* **1** ASSEMBLE : rassembler **2** COLLECT : ramasser **3** CONCLUDE : déduire — *vi* ASSEMBLE : se rassembler — **gathering** ['gæðərɪŋ] *n* : rassemblement *m*
gaudy ['gɔdi] *adj* -**dier; -est** : criard, tape-à-l'œil
gauge ['geɪdʒ] *n* **1** INDICATOR : jauge *f*, indicateur *m* **2** CALIBER : calibre *m* — **~** *vt* **gauged; gauging 1** MEASURE : jauger **2** ESTIMATE : évaluer
gaunt ['gɔnt] *adj* : décharné, émacié
gauze ['gɔz] *n* : gaze *f*
gave → give
gawky ['gɔki] *adj* **gawkier; gawkiest** : gauche, maladroit
gay ['geɪ] *adj* **1** : gai **2** HOMOSEXUAL : gay
gaze ['geɪz] *vi* **gazed; gazing** : regarder (fixement) — **~** *n* : regard *m*
gazette [gə'zet] *n* : journal *m* officiel
gear ['gɪr] *n* **1** EQUIPMENT : équipement *m* **2** POSSESSIONS : effets *mpl* personnels **3** SPEED : vitesse *f* **4** *or* **~ wheel** : roue *f* dentée — **~** *vt* : adapter — *vi* **~ up** : se préparer — **gearshift** ['gɪr,ʃɪft] *n* : levier *m* de vitesse
geese → goose
gelatin ['dʒelətən] *n* : gélatine *f*
gem ['dʒem] *n* : pierre *f* précieuse, gemme *f* — **gemstone** ['dʒem,sto:n] *n* : pierre *f* précieuse
gender ['dʒendər] *n* **1** SEX : sexe *m* **2** : genre *m* (en grammaire)
gene ['dʒi:n] *n* : gène *m*
genealogy [,dʒi:ni'alədʒi, ,dʒe-, -'æ-] *n, pl* -**gies** : généalogie *f*
general ['dʒenrəl, 'dʒenə-] *adj* : général — **~** *n* **1** : général *m* (militaire) **2 in ~** : en général — **generalize** ['dʒenrə,laɪz, 'dʒenərə-] *v* -**ized; -izing** : généraliser — **generally** ['dʒenrəli, 'dʒenərə-] *adv* : généralement, en général — **general practitioner** *n* : généraliste *mf*
generate ['dʒenə,reɪt] *vt* -**ated; -ating** : générer — **generation** [,dʒenə'reɪʃən] *n* : génération *f* — **generator** ['dʒenə,reɪtər] *n* **1** : générateur *m* **2** : génératrice *f* (d'énergie électrique)
generous ['dʒenərəs] *adj* **1** : généreux **2**

AMPLE : copieux — **generosity** [,dʒenə'rasəti] *n, pl* -**ties** : générosité *f*
genetic [dʒə'netɪk] *adj* : génétique — **genetics** [dʒə'netɪks] *n* : génétique *f*
genial ['dʒi:niəl] *adj* : affable
genital ['dʒenətəl] *adj* : génital — **genitals** ['dʒenətəlz] *npl* : organes *mpl* génitaux
genius ['dʒi:njəs] *n* : génie *m*
genocide ['dʒenə,saɪd] *n* : génocide *m*
genteel [dʒen'ti:l] *adj* : distingué
gentle ['dʒentəl] *adj* -**tler; -tlest 1** MILD : doux **2** LIGHT : léger — **gentleman** ['dʒentəlmən] *n, pl* -**men** [-mən, -,men] **1** MAN : monsieur *m* **2 act like a ~** : agir en gentleman — **gentleness** ['dʒentəlnəs] *n* : douceur *f*
genuine [,dʒenjuwən] *adj* **1** AUTHENTIC : authentique, véritable **2** SINCERE : sincère
geography [dʒi'agrəfi] *n, pl* -**phies** : géographie *f* — **geographic** [,dʒi:ə'græfɪk] *or* **geographical** [-fɪkəl] *adj* : géographique
geology [dʒi'alədʒi] *n* : géologie *f* — **geologic** [,dʒi:ə'ladʒɪk] *or* **geological** [-dʒɪkəl] *adj* : géologique
geometry [dʒi'amətri] *n, pl* -**tries** : géométrie *f* — **geometric** [,dʒi:ə'metrɪk] *or* **geometrical** [-trɪkəl] *adj* : géométrique
geranium [dʒə'reɪniəm] *n* : géranium *m*
geriatric [,dʒeri'ætrɪk] *adj* : gériatrique — **geriatrics** [,dʒeri'ætrɪks] *n* : gériatrie *f*
germ ['dʒərm] *n* **1** : germe *m* **2** MICROBE : microbe *m*
German ['dʒərmən] *adj* : allemand — **~** *n* : allemand *m* (langue)
germinate ['dʒərmə,neɪt] *v* -**nated; -nating** *vi* : germer — *vt* : faire germer
gestation [dʒe'steɪʃən] *n* : gestation *f*
gesture ['dʒestʃər] *n* : geste *m* — **~** *vi* -**tured; -turing 1** : faire des gestes **2 ~ to** : faire signe à
get ['get] *v* **got** ['gat]; **got** *or* **gotten** ['gatən]; **getting** *vt* **1** OBTAIN : obtenir, trouver **2** RECEIVE : recevoir, avoir **3** EARN : gagner **4** FETCH : aller chercher **5** CATCH : attraper (une maladie) **6** UNDERSTAND : comprendre **7** PREPARE : préparer **8 ~ one's hair cut** : se faire couper les cheveux **9 have got to** : devoir — *vi* **1** BECOME : devenir **2** GO, MOVE : aller, arriver **3** PROGRESS : avancer **4 ~ ahead** : progresser **5 ~ at** MEAN : vouloir dire **6 ~ away** : s'échapper **7 ~ back at** : se venger de **8 ~ by** : s'en sortir **9 ~ out** : sortir **10 ~ over** : se remettre de **11 ~ together** MEET : se réunir **12 ~ up** : se lever — **get along** *vi* **1** MANAGE : aller **2 get along with** : bien s'entendre avec — **getaway** ['getə,weɪ] *n* : fuite *f* — **get-together** ['gettə,geðər] *n* : réunion *f*
geyser ['gaɪzər] *n* : geyser *m*

ghastly ['gæstli] *adj* **-lier; -est** : épouvantable

ghetto ['gɛṭo:] *n, pl* **-tos** *or* **-toes** : ghetto *m*

ghost ['go:st] *n* : fantôme *m*, spectre *m* — **ghastly** ['gæstli] *adj* lier : épouvantable

giant ['dʒaɪənt] *n* : géant *m*, géante *f* — ~ *adj* : géant, gigantesque

gibberish ['dʒɪbərɪʃ] *n* : baragouin *m*, charabia *m fam*

gibe ['dʒaɪb] *vi* **gibed; gibing** ~ **at** : se moquer de — ~ *n* : moquerie *f*

giblets ['dʒɪbləts] *npl* : abats *mpl* (de volaille)

giddy ['gɪdi] *adj* **-dier; -est** : vertigineux — **giddiness** ['gɪdinəs] *n* : vertige *m*

gift ['gɪft] *n* **1** PRESENT : cadeau *m* **2** TALENT : don *m* — **gifted** ['gɪftəd] *adj* : doué

gigantic [dʒaɪ'gæntɪk] *adj* : gigantesque

giggle ['gɪgəl] *vi* **-gled; -gling** : rire bêtement — ~ *n* : petit rire *m*

gild ['gɪld] *vt* **gilded** ['gɪldəd] *or* **gilt** ['gɪlt]; **gilding** : dorer

gill ['gɪl] *n* : branchie *f*, ouïe *f*

gilt ['gɪlt] *adj* : doré

gimmick ['gɪmɪk] *n* : truc *m*, gadget *m*

gin ['dʒɪn] *n* : gin *m*

ginger ['dʒɪndʒər] *n* : gingembre *m* — **ginger ale** *n* : boisson *f* gazeuse au gingembre — **gingerbread** ['dʒɪndʒər,brɛd] *n* : pain *m* d'épice — **gingerly** ['dʒɪndʒərli] *adv* : avec précaution

giraffe [dʒə'ræf] *n* : girafe *f*

girdle ['gərdəl] *n* : gaine *f*

girl ['gərl] *n* : fille *f*, jeune fille *f* — **girlfriend** ['gərl,frɛnd] *n* : copine *f*, petite amie *f*

girth ['gərθ] *n* : circonférence *f*

gist ['dʒɪst] *n* **the** ~ : l'essentiel *m*

give ['gɪv] *v* **gave** ['geɪv]; **given** ['gɪvən]; **giving** *vt* **1** : donner **2** ~ **out** DISTRIBUTE : distribuer **3** ~ **up smoking** : arrêter de fumer — *vi* **1** YIELD : céder **2** ~ **in** *or* ~ **up** : se rendre — ~ *n* : élasticité *f*, souplesse *f* — **given** ['gɪvən] *adj* **1** SPECIFIED : donné **2** INCLINED : enclin — **given name** *n* : prénom *m*

glacier ['gleɪʃər] *n* : glacier *m*

glad ['glæd] *adj* **gladder; gladdest 1** : content **2 be** ~ **to** : être heureux de **3** ~ **to meet you** : enchanté — **gladden** ['glædən] *vt* : réjouir — **gladly** ['glædli] *adv* : avec plaisir, volontiers

glade ['gleɪd] *n* : clairière *f*

glamour *or* **glamor** ['glæmər] *n* : charme *m* — **glamorous** ['glæmərəs] *adj* : séduisant

glance ['glænts] *vi* **glanced; glancing** ~ **at** : jeter un coup d'œil à — ~ *n* : coup *m* d'œil

gland ['glænd] *n* : glande *f*

glare ['glær] *vi* **glared; glaring 1** : briller d'un éclat éblouissant **2** ~ **at** : lancer un regard furieux à — ~ *n* **1** : lumière *f* éblouissante **2** STARE : regard *m* furieux — **glaring** ['glærɪŋ] *adj* **1** BRIGHT : éblouissant **2** FLAGRANT : flagrant

glass ['glæs] *n* **1** : verre *m* **2** ~ **es** *npl* SPECTACLES : lunettes *fpl* — ~ *adj* : en verre — **glassware** ['glæs,wær] *n* : verrerie *f* — **glassy** ['glæsi] *adj* **glassier; glassiest** : vitreux

glaze ['gleɪz] *vt* **glazed; glazing** : vernisser (des céramiques) — ~ *n* **1** : vernis *m* **2** FROSTING : glaçage *m*

gleam ['gli:m] *n* : lueur *f* — ~ *vi* : luire, reluire

glee ['gli:] *n* : joie *f* — **gleeful** ['gli:fəl] *adj* : joyeux

glib ['glɪb] *adj* **glibber; glibbest** : désinvolte

glide ['glaɪd] *vi* **glided; gliding** : glisser (sur une surface), planer (en l'air) — **glider** ['glaɪdər] *n* : planeur *m*

glimmer ['glɪmər] *vi* : jeter une faible lueur — ~ *n* : lueur *f*

glimpse ['glɪmps] *vt* **glimpsed; glimpsing** : entrevoir — ~ *n* **1** : aperçu *m* **2 catch a** ~ **of** : entrevoir

glint ['glɪnt] *vi* : étinceler — ~ *n* : reflet *m*

glisten ['glɪsən] *vi* : briller

glitter ['glɪṭər] *vi* : scintiller, étinceler — ~ *n* : scintillement *m*

gloat ['glo:t] *vi* : jubiler

globe ['glo:b] *n* : globe *m* — **global** ['glo:bəl] *adj* : mondial

gloom ['glu:m] *n* **1** DARKNESS : obscurité *f* **2** SADNESS : tristesse *f* — **gloomy** ['glu:mi] *adj* **gloomier; gloomiest 1** DARK : sombre **2** DISMAL : lugubre

glory ['glori] *n, pl* **-ries** : gloire *f* — **glorify** ['glorə,faɪ] *vt* **-fied; -fying** : glorifier — **glorious** ['gloriəs] *adj* : glorieux

gloss ['glɔs, 'glɑs] *n* : brillant *m*, lustre *m*

glossary ['glɔsəri, 'glɑ-] *n, pl* **-ries** : glossaire *m*

glossy ['glɔsi, 'glɑ-] *adj* **glossier; glossiest** : brillant

glove ['glʌv] *n* : gant *m*

glow ['glo:] *vi* **1** : luire **2** ~ **with health** : rayonner de santé — ~ *n* : lueur *f*

glue ['glu:] *n* : colle *f* — ~ *vt* **glued; gluing** *or* **glueing** : coller

glum ['glʌm] *adj* **glummer; glummest** : morne, triste

glut ['glʌt] *n* : surabondance *f*

glutton ['glʌtən] *n* : glouton *m*, -tonne *f* — **gluttonous** ['glʌtənəs] *adj* : glouton — **gluttony** ['glʌtəni] *n, pl* **-tonies** : gloutonnerie *f*

gnarled ['nɑrld] *adj* : noueux

gnash ['næʃ] *vt* ~ **one's teeth** : grincer des dents

gnat ['næt] *n* : moucheron *m*

gnaw ['nɔ] *vt* : ronger

go ['goː] *v* **went** ['wɛnt]; **gone** ['gɔn, 'gʌn]; **going; goes** ['goːz] *vi* **1** : aller **2** LEAVE : partir, s'en aller **3** EXTEND : s'étendre **4** SELL : se vendre **5** FUNCTION : marcher **6** DISAPPEAR : disparaître **7** ~ **back on** : revenir sur **8** ~ **for** FAVOR : aimer **9** ~ **off** EXPLODE : exploser **10** ~ **out** : sortir **11** ~ **with** MATCH : aller avec **12** ~ **without** : se passer de — *v aux* **be going to do** : aller faire — ~ *n, pl* **goes 1** ATTEMPT : essai *m*, tentative *f* **2 be on the** ~ : ne jamais s'arrêter

goad ['goːd] *vt* : aiguillonner (un animal), provoquer (une personne)

goal ['goːl] *n* : but *m* — **goalie** ['goːli] → **goalkeeper** — **goalkeeper** ['goːl,kiːpər] *n* : gardien *m* de but

goat ['goːt] *n* : chèvre *f*

goatee [goː'tiː] *n* : barbiche *f*

gobble ['gabəl] *vt* **-bled; -bling** *or* ~ **up** : engloutir

goblet ['gablət] *n* : verre *m* à pied

goblin ['gablən] *n* : lutin *m*

god ['gad, 'gɔd] *n* **1** : dieu *m* **2 God** : Dieu *m* — **goddess** ['gadəs, 'gɔ-] *n* : déesse *f* — **godchild** ['gad,tʃaɪld, 'gɔd-] *n, pl* **-children** : filleul *m*, -leule *f* — **godfather** ['gad,faðər, 'gɔd-] *n* : parrain *m* — **godmother** ['gad,mʌðər, 'gɔd-] *n* : marraine *f*

goes → **go**

goggles ['gagəlz] *npl* : lunettes *fpl* (protectrices)

gold ['goːld] *n* : or *m* — **golden** ['goːldən] *adj* **1** : en or, d'or **2** : doré, couleur *f* d'or — **goldfish** ['goːld,fɪʃ] *n* : poisson *m* rouge — **goldsmith** ['goːld,smɪθ] *n* : orfèvre *m*

golf ['galf, 'gɔlf] *n* : golf *m* — ~ *vi* : jouer au golf — **golf ball** *n* : balle *f* de golfe — **golf course** *n* : terrain *m* de golf — **golfer** ['galfər, 'gɔl-] *n* : joueur *m*, joueuse *f* de golf

gone ['gɔn] *adj* **1** PAST : passé **2** DEPARTED : parti

good ['gʊd] *adj* **better** ['bɛtər]; **best** ['bɛst] **1** : bon **2** OBEDIENT : sage **3 be** ~ **at** : être bon en **4 feel** ~ : se sentir bien **5** ~ **evening** : bonsoir **6** ~ **morning** : bonjour **7** ~ **night** : bonsoir, bonne nuit **8 have a** ~ **time** : s'amuser — ~ *n* **1** : bien *m* **2** GOODNESS : bonté *f* **3** ~**s** *npl* PROPERTY : biens *mpl* **4** ~**s** *npl* WARES : marchandises *fpl* **5 for** ~ : pour de bon — ~ *adv* : bien — **good–bye** *or* **good–by** [gʊd'baɪ] *n* : au revoir *m* — **good–looking** [gʊd-'lʊkɪŋ] *adj* : beau — **goodness** ['gʊdnəs] *n* **1** : bonté *f* **2 thank** ~ **!** : Dieu merci! — **goodwill** [gʊd'wɪl] *n* : bienveillance *f* — **goody** ['gʊdi] *n, pl* **goodies 1** ~**!** : chouette! *fam* **2 goodies** *npl* : friandises *fpl*

goof ['guːf] *n* : gaffe *f fam* — ~ *vi* **1** *or* ~ **up** : gaffer *fam* **2** ~ **around** : faire l'imbécile

goose ['guːs] *n, pl* **geese** ['giːs] : oie *f* — **goose bumps** *npl* : chair *f* de poule

gopher ['goːfər] *n* : gaufre *m*

gore ['goːr] *n* BLOOD : sang *m*

gorge ['gɔrdʒ] *n* RAVINE : gorge *f*, défilé *m* — ~ *vt* **gorged; gorging** ~ **oneself** : se gorger

gorgeous ['gɔrdʒəs] *adj* : magnifique, splendide

gorilla [gə'rɪlə] *n* : gorille *m*

gory ['gori] *adj* **gorier; goriest** : sanglant

gospel ['gaspəl] *n* **1** : évangile *m* **2 the Gospel** : l'Évangile

gossip ['gasɪp] *n* : commérages *mpl fam*, ragots *mpl fam* — ~ *vi* : bavarder — **gossipy** ['gasɪpi] *adj* : bavard

got → **get**

Gothic ['gaθɪk] *adj* : gothique

gotten → **get**

gourmet ['gʊr,meɪ, gʊr'meɪ] *n* : gourmet *m*

govern ['gʌvərn] *v* : gouverner — **governess** ['gʌvərnəs] *n* : gouvernante *f* — **government** ['gʌvərmənt] *n* : gouvernement *m* — **governor** ['gʌvənər, 'gʌvərnər] *n* : gouverneur *m*

gown ['gaʊn] *n* **1** : robe *f* **2** : toge *f* (de juge, etc.)

grab ['græb] *vt* **grabbed; grabbing** : saisir

grace ['greɪs] *n* : grâce *f* — ~ *vt* **graced; gracing 1** HONOR : honorer **2** ADORN : orner — **graceful** ['greɪsfəl] *adj* : gracieux — **gracious** ['greɪʃəs] *adj* : courtois, gracieux

grade ['greɪd] *n* **1** QUALITY : catégorie *f*, qualité *f* **2** RANK : grade *m*, rang *m* (militaire) **3** YEAR : classe *f* (à l'école) **4** MARK : note *f* **5** SLOPE : pente *f* — ~ *vt* **graded; grading 1** CLASSIFY : classer **2** MARK : noter (un examen, etc.) — **grade school** → **elementary school**

gradual ['grædʒʊəl] *adj* : graduel, progressif — **gradually** ['grædʒʊəli, 'grædʒəli] *adv* : petit à petit

graduate ['grædʒuət] *n* : diplômé *m*, -mée *f* — ~ ['grædʒu,eɪt] *vi* **-ated; -ating** : recevoir son diplôme — **graduation** [,grædʒu'eɪʃən] *n* : remise *f* des diplômes

graffiti [grə'fiːti, græ-] *npl* : graffiti *mpl*

graft ['græft] *n* : greffe *f* — ~ *vt* : greffer

grain ['greɪn] *n* **1** : grain *m* **2** CEREAL : céréales *fpl*

gram ['græm] *n* : gramme *m*

grammar ['græmər] *n* : grammaire *f* — **grammar school** → **elementary school**

grand ['grænd] *adj* **1** : grand, magnifique **2** FABULOUS : formidable *fam* — **grandchild** ['grænd,tʃaɪld] *n, pl* **-children** [-,tʃɪldrən]

: petit-fils *m*, petite-fille *f* — **granddaughter** ['grænd,dɔtər] *n* : petite-fille *f* — **grandeur** ['grændʒər] *n* : grandeur *f* — **grandfather** ['grænd,faðər] *n* : grand-père *m* — **grandiose** ['grændi,oːs, ,grændiˈ] *adj* : grandiose — **grandmother** ['grænd,mʌðər] *n* : grand-mère *f* — **grandparents** ['grænd,pærənts] *npl* : grands-parents *mpl* — **grandson** ['grænd,sʌn] *n* : petit-fils *m* — **grandstand** ['grænd,stænd] *n* : tribune *f*

granite ['grænɪt] *n* : granit *m*, granite *m*

grant ['grænt] *vt* **1** : accorder **2** ADMIT : admettre **3 take for granted** : prendre pour acquis — ~ *n* **1** SUBSIDY : subvention *f* **2** SCHOLARSHIP : bourse *f*

grape ['greɪp] *n* : raisin *m*

grapefruit ['greɪp,fruːt] *n* : pamplemousse *mf*

grapevine ['greɪp,vaɪn] *n* : vigne *f*

graph ['græf] *n* : graphique *m* — **graphic** ['græfɪk] *adj* : graphique

grapnel ['græpnəl] *n* : grappin *m*

grapple ['græpəl] *vi* **-pled; -pling** ~ **with** : lutter avec

grasp ['græsp] *vt* **1** : saisir **2** UNDERSTAND : comprendre — ~ *n* **1** : prise *f* **2** UNDERSTANDING : compréhension *f* **3 within s.o.'s** ~ : à la portée de qqn

grass ['græs] *n* **1** : herbe *f* **2** LAWN : gazon *m*, pelouse *f* — **grasshopper** ['græs,hapər] *n* : sauterelle *f*

grate¹ ['greɪt] *v* **grated; grating** *vt* : râper (du fromage, etc.) — *vi* : grincer

grate² *n* : grille *f*

grateful ['greɪtfəl] *adj* : reconnaissant — **gratefully** ['greɪtfəli] *adv* : avec reconnaissance — **gratefulness** ['greɪtfəlnəs] *n* : gratitude *f*, reconnaissance *f*

grater ['greɪtər] *n* : râpe *f*

gratify ['grætə,faɪ] *vt* **-fied; -fying 1** PLEASE : faire plaisir à **2** SATISFY : satisfaire

grating ['greɪtɪŋ] *n* : grille *f*

gratitude ['grætə,tuːd, -,tjuːd] *n* : gratitude *f*

gratuitous [grəˈtuːətəs] *adj* : gratuit

gratuity [grəˈtuːəti] *n, pl* **-ities** TIP : pourboire *m*

grave¹ ['greɪv] *n* : tombe *f*

grave² *adj* **graver; gravest** : grave, sérieux

gravel ['grævəl] *n* : gravier *m*

gravestone ['greɪv,stoːn] *n* : pierre *f* tombale — **graveyard** ['greɪv,jɑrd] *n* : cimetière *m*

gravity ['grævəti] *n, pl* **-ties 1** SERIOUSNESS : gravité *f* **2** : pesanteur *f* (en physique)

gravy ['greɪvi] *n, pl* **-vies** : sauce *f* (au jus de viande)

gray ['greɪ] *adj* **1** : gris **2** GLOOMY : morne — ~ *n* : gris *m* — ~ *vi or* **turn** ~ : grisonner

graze¹ ['greɪz] *vi* **grazed; grazing** : paître

graze² *vt* **1** TOUCH : frôler **2** SCRATCH : écorcher

grease ['griːs] *n* : graisse *f* — ~ ['griːs, 'griːz] *vt* **greased; greasing** : graisser — **greasy** ['griːsi, -zi] *adj* **greasier; greasiest 1** : graisseux **2** OILY : huileux

great ['greɪt] *adj* **1** : grand **2** FANTASTIC : génial *fam*, formidable *fam* — **great-grandchild** [,greɪtˈgrænd,tʃaɪld] *n, pl* **-children** [-,tʃɪldrən] : arrière-petit-enfant *m*, arrière-petite-enfant *f* — **great-grandfather** [,greɪtˈgrænd,faðər] *n* : arrière-grand-père *m* — **great-grandmother** [,greɪtˈgrænd,mʌðər] *n* : arrière-grand-mère *f* — **greatly** ['greɪtli] *adv* **1** MUCH : beaucoup **2** VERY : énormément — **greatness** ['greɪtnəs] *n* : grandeur *f*

greed ['griːd] *n* **1** : avarice *f*, avidité *f* **2** GLUTTONY : gloutonnerie *f* — **greedily** ['griːdəli] *adv* : avidement — **greedy** ['griːdi] *adj* **greedier; greediest 1** : avare, avide **2** GLUTTONOUS : glouton

Greek ['griːk] *adj* : grec — ~ *n* : grec *m* (langue)

green ['griːn] *adj* **1** : vert **2** INEXPERIENCED : inexpérimenté — ~ *n* **1** : vert *m* (couleur) **2** ~**s** *npl* : légumes *mpl* verts — **greenery** ['griːnəri] *n, pl* **-eries** : verdure *f* — **greenhouse** ['griːn,haʊs] *n* : serre *f*

greet ['griːt] *vt* **1** : saluer **2** WELCOME : accueillir — **greeting** ['griːtɪŋ] *n* **1** : salutation *f* **2** ~**s** *npl* REGARDS : salutations *fpl* **3 birthday** ~**s** : vœux *mpl* d'anniversaire

grenade [grəˈneɪd] *n* : grenade *f*

grew → **grow**

grey → **gray**

greyhound ['greɪ,haʊnd] *n* : lévrier *m*

grid [grɪd] *n* **1** GRATING : grille *f* **2** : quadrillage *m* (d'une carte, etc.)

griddle ['grɪdəl] *n* : plaque *f* chauffante

grief ['griːf] *n* : chagrin *m*, douleur *f* — **grievance** ['griːvənts] *n* : grief *m* — **grieve** ['griːv] *v* **grieved; grieving** *vt* DISTRESS : peiner, chagriner — *vi* ~ **for** : pleurer — **grievous** ['griːvəs] *adj* : grave, sérieux

grill ['grɪl] *vt* **1** : griller (en cuisine) **2** INTERROGATE : cuisiner *fam* — ~ *n* : gril *m* (de cuisine) — **grille** *or* **grill** ['grɪl] *n* GRATING : grille *f*

grim ['grɪm] *adj* **grimmer; grimmest 1** STERN : sévère **2** GLOOMY : sinistre

grimace ['grɪməs, grɪˈmeɪs] *n* : grimace *f* — ~ *vi* **-maced; -macing** : grimacer

grime ['graɪm] *n* : saleté *f*, crasse *f* — **grimy** ['graɪmi] *adj* **grimier; grimiest** : sale, crasseux

grin ['grɪn] *vi* **grinned; grinning** : sourire — ~ *n* : (grand) sourire *m*

grind ['graɪnd] *v* **ground** ['graʊnd]; **grind-**

ing *vt* **1** : moudre (du café, etc.) **2** SHARPEN
: aiguiser **3** ~ **one's teeth** : grincer des
dents — *vi* : grincer — ~ *n* **the daily** ~
: le train-train quotidien — **grinder**
['graɪndər] *n* : moulin *m*

grip ['grɪp] *vt* **gripped; gripping 1** : serrer,
empoigner **2** CAPTIVATE : captiver — ~ *n*
1 : prise *f*, étreinte *f* **2** TRACTION : adhérence *f* **3 come to** ~**s with** : en venir
aux prises avec

gripe ['graɪp] *vi* **griped; griping** : rouspéter
fam, ronchonner *fam* — ~ *n* : plainte *f*

grisly ['grɪzli] *adj* **-lier; -est** : horrible,
macabre

gristle ['grɪsəl] *n* : cartilage *m*

grit ['grɪt] *n* **1** : sable *m*, gravillon *m* **2** ~**s**
npl : gruau *m* de maïs — ~ *vt* **gritted; grit-
ting** ~ **one's teeth** : serrer les dents

groan ['groːn] *vi* : gémir — ~ *n* : gémissement *m*

grocery ['groːsəri, -ʃəri] *n, pl* **-ceries 1** *or*
~ **store** : épicerie *f* **2 groceries** *npl*
: épiceries *fpl*, provisions *fpl* — **grocer**
['groːsər] *n* : épicier *m*, -cière *f*

groggy ['groːgi] *adj* **-gier; -est** : chancelant,
sonné *fam*

groin ['groɪn] *n* : aine *f*

groom ['gruːm, 'grʊm] *n* BRIDEGROOM
: marié *m* — ~ *vt* : panser (un animal)

groove ['gruːv] *n* : rainure *f*, sillon *m*

grope ['groːp] *vi* **groped; groping 1** : tâtonner **2** ~ **for** : chercher à tâtons

gross ['groːs] *adj* **1** SERIOUS : flagrant **2**
TOTAL : brut **3** VULGAR : grossier — ~ *n*
~ **income** : recettes *fpl* brutes — **grossly**
['groːsli] *adv* : extrêmement

grotesque [groː'tɛsk] *adj* : grotesque

grouch ['graʊtʃ] *n* : rouspéteur *m*, -teuse *f*
fam — **grouchy** ['graʊtʃi] *adj* **grouchier;
grouchiest** : grognon

ground[1] ['graʊnd] → **grind**

ground[2] *n* **1** : sol *m*, terre *f* **2** *or* ~**s** LAND
: terrain *m* **3** ~**s** *npl* REASON : raison *f* —
~ *vt* BASE : baser, fonder — **groundhog**
['graʊnd,hɔg] *n* : marmotte *f* d'Amérique —
groundwork ['graʊnd,wərk] *n* : travail *m*
préparatoire

group ['gruːp] *n* : groupe *m* — ~ *vt*
: grouper, réunir — *vi or* ~ **together** : se
grouper

grove ['groːv] *n* : bosquet *m*

grovel ['grɑvəl, 'grʌ-] *vi* **-eled** *or* **-elled;
-eling** *or* **-elling** : ramper

grow ['groː] *v* **grew** ['gruː]; **grown** ['groːn];
growing *vi* **1** : pousser (se dit des plantes),
grandir (se dit des personnes) **2** INCREASE
: croître **3** BECOME : devenir — *vt* **1** CULTI-
VATE : cultiver **2** : laisser pousser (la barbe,
etc.) — **grower** ['groːər] *n* : cultivateur *m*,
-trice *f*

growl ['graʊl] *vi* : grogner, gronder — ~ *n*
: grognement *m*, grondement *m*

grown–up ['groːn,əp] *adj* : adulte — ~ *n*
: adulte *mf*

growth ['groːθ] *n* **1** : croissance *f* **2** IN-
CREASE : augmentation *f* **3** TUMOR : tumeur
f

grub ['grʌb] *n* FOOD : bouffe *f fam*

grubby ['grʌbi] *adj* **-bier; -est** : sale

grudge ['grʌdʒ] *n* **1** : rancune *f* **2 hold a** ~
: en vouloir à

grueling *or* **gruelling** ['gruːlɪŋ, gruːə-] *adj*
: exténuant, épuisant

gruesome ['gruːsəm] *adj* : horrible

gruff ['grʌf] *adj* : bourru, brusque

grumble ['grʌmbəl] *vi* **-bled; -bling** : ronchonner *fam*

grumpy ['grʌmpi] *adj* **grumpier; grumpi-
est** : grincheux, grognon

grunt ['grʌnt] *vi* : grogner — ~ *n* : grognement *m*

guarantee [ˌgærən'tiː] *n* : garantie *f* — ~ *vt*
-teed; -teeing : garantir

guarantor [ˌgærən'tɔr] *n* : garant *m*, -rante *f*

guard ['gɑrd] *n* **1** : garde *m* (personne) **2 be
on one's** ~ : être sur ses gardes — ~ *vt*
: garder, surveiller — *vi* ~ **against** : se
garder de — **guardian** ['gɑrdiən] *n* **1** : tuteur *m*, -trice *f* (d'un mineur) **2** PROTECTOR
: gardien *m*, -dienne *f*

guerrilla *or* **guerilla** [gə'rɪlə] *n* **1** : guérillero
m **2** ~ **warfare** : guérilla *f*

guess ['gɛs] *vt* **1** : deviner **2** SUPPOSE
: penser — *vi* : deviner — ~ *n* : conjecture
f

guest ['gɛst] *n* **1** VISITOR : invité *m*, -tée *f* **2**
: client *m*, cliente *f* (d'un hôtel)

guide ['gaɪd] *n* **1** : guide *mf* (personne) **2**
: guide *m* (livre, etc.) — ~ *vt* **guided;
guiding** : guider — **guidance** ['gaɪdənts] *n*
: conseils *mpl*, direction *f* — **guidebook**
['gaɪd,bʊk] *n* : guide *m* — **guideline** ['gaɪd-
,laɪn] *n* : ligne *f* directrice

guild ['gɪld] *n* : association *f*

guile ['gaɪl] *n* : ruse *f*

guilt ['gɪlt] *n* : culpabilité *f* — **guilty** ['gɪlti]
adj **guiltier; guiltiest** : coupable

guinea pig ['gɪni-] *n* : cobaye *m*

guise ['gaɪz] *n* : apparence *f*

guitar [gə'tɑr, gɪ-] *n* : guitare *f*

gulf ['gʌlf] *n* : golfe *m*

gull ['gʌl] *n* : mouette *f*

gullible ['gʌlɪbəl] *adj* : crédule

gully ['gʌli] *n, pl* **-lies** : ravin *m*

gulp ['gʌlp] *vt or* ~ **down** : avaler — ~ *n*
: gorgée *f*, bouchée *f*

gum[1] ['gʌm] *n* : gencive *f*

gum[2] *n* CHEWING GUM : chewing-gum *m*
France, gomme *f* à mâcher

gun ['gʌn] *n* **1** FIREARM : arme *f* à feu, fusil

m **2** *or* **spray** ~ : pistolet *m* — ~ *vt*
gunned; gunning *or* ~ **down** : abattre —
gunfire ['gʌn,faɪr] *n* : fusillade *f*, coups *mpl*
de feu — **gunman** ['gʌnmən] *n, pl* **-men**
[,mɛn , ,mən] : personne *f* armée — **gun-**
powder ['gʌn,paʊdər] *n* : poudre *f* (à
canon) — **gunshot** ['gʌn,ʃɑt] *n* : coup *m* de
feu

gurgle ['gərgəl] *vi* **-gled; -gling 1** : gargouiller **2** : gazouiller (se dit d'un bébé)
gush ['gʌʃ] *vi* **1** SPOUT : jaillir **2** ~ **over**
: s'extasier devant
gust ['gʌst] *n* : rafale *f*
gusto ['gʌs,to:] *n, pl* **-toes** : enthousiasme *m*
gut ['gʌt] *n* **1** : intestin *m* **2** ~s *npl* IN-
NARDS : entrailles *fpl* **3** ~s *npl* COURAGE

: cran *m fam* — ~ *vt* **gutted; gutting**
: détruire l'intérieur de (un édifice)
gutter ['gʌtər] *n* **1** : gouttière *f* (d'un toit) **2**
: caniveau *m* (d'une rue)
guy ['gaɪ] *n* : type *m fam*
guzzle ['gʌzəl] *vt* **-zled; -zling** : bâfrer *fam*,
engloutir
gym ['dʒɪm] *or* **gymnasium** [dʒɪm'neɪziəm,
-ʒəm] *n, pl* **-siums** *or* **-sia** [-zi:ə, -ʒə] : gymnase *m* — **gymnast** ['dʒɪmnəst, -,næst] *n*
: gymnaste *mf* — **gymnastics** [dʒɪm-
'næstɪks] *n* : gymnastique *f*
gynecology [,gaɪnə'kɑlədʒi] *n* : gynécologie *f* — **gynecologist** [,gaɪnə'kɑlədʒɪst] *n*
: gynécologue *mf*
Gypsy ['dʒɪpsi] *n, pl* **-sies** : gitan *m*, -tane *f*

H

h ['eɪtʃ] *n, pl* **h's** *or* **hs** ['eɪtʃəz] : h *m*, huitième
lettre de l'alphabet
habit ['hæbɪt] *n* **1** CUSTOM : habitude *f*, coutume *f* **2** : habit *m* (religieux)
habitat ['hæbɪ,tæt] *n* : habitat *m*
habitual [hə'bɪtʃʊəl] *adj* **1** CUSTOMARY
: habituel **2** INVETERATE : invétéré
hack¹ ['hæk] *n* **1** : cheval *m* de louage **2** *or*
~ **writer** : écrivaillon *m*
hack² *vt* CUT : tailler — *vi* ~ **into** : entrer
dans (en informatique)
hackneyed ['hæknɪd] *adj* : rebattu
hacksaw ['hæk,sɔ] *n* : scie *f* à métaux
had → **have**
haddock ['hædək] *ns & pl* : églefin *m*
hadn't ['hædənt] (*contraction of* **had not**) →
have
hag ['hæg] *n* : vieille sorcière *f*
haggard ['hægərd] *adj* : hâve, exténué
haggle ['hægəl] *vi* **-gled; -gling** : marchander
hail¹ ['heɪl] *vt* **1** ACCLAIM : acclamer **2**
: héler (un taxi)
hail² ['heɪl] *n* : grêle *f* (en météorologie) —
~ *vi* : grêler — **hailstone** ['heɪl,sto:n] *n*
: grêlon *m*
hair ['hær] *n* **1** : cheveux *mpl* (sur la tête) **2**
: poil *m* (de chien, sur les jambes, etc.) —
hairbrush ['hær,brʌʃ] *n* : brosse *f* à cheveux
— **haircut** ['hær,kʌt] *n* : coupe *f* de cheveux
— **hairdo** ['hær,du:] *n, pl* **-dos** : coiffure *f* —
hairdresser ['hær,drɛsər] *n* : coiffeur *m*,
-feuse *f* — **hairless** ['hærləs] *adj* : sans
cheveux, glabre — **hairpin** ['hær,pɪn] *n*
: épingle *f* à cheveux — **hair–raising** ['hær-

,reɪzɪŋ] *adj* : à vous faire dresser les cheveux
sur la tête — **hair spray** *n* : laque *f* — **hairy**
['hæri] *adj* **hairier, -est** : poilu, velu
Haitian ['heɪʃən, 'heɪtiən] *adj* : haïtien
half ['hæf] *n, pl* **halves** ['hævz] **1** : moitié *f*,
demi *m*, -mie *f* **2** : en deux **3** *or* **half-**
time : mi-temps *f* (aux sports) — ~ *adj* **1**
: demi **2** ~ **an hour** : une demi-heure **3 in**
~ : en deux — ~ *adv* : à demi, à moitié —
halfhearted ['hæf'hɑrtəd] *adj* : sans enthousiasme — **halfway** ['hæf'weɪ] *adv & adj*
: à mi-chemin
halibut ['hælɪbət] *ns & pl* : flétan *m*
hall ['hɔl] *n* **1** HALLWAY : couloir *m* **2** AUDI-
TORIUM : salle *f* **3** LOBBY : entrée *f*,
vestibule *m* **4** DORMITORY : résidence *f* universitaire
hallmark ['hɔl,mark] *n* : marque *f*, sceau *m*
Halloween [,hælə'wi:n, ,hɑ-] *n* : Halloween *f*
hallucination [hə,lu:sən'eɪʃən] *n* : hallucination *f*
hallway ['hɔl,weɪ] *n* **1** ENTRANCE : entrée *f*,
vestibule *m* **2** CORRIDOR : couloir *m*
halo ['heɪ,lo:] *n, pl* **-los** *or* **-loes** : auréole *f*
halt ['hɔlt] *n* **1** : halte *f* **2 come to a** ~
: s'arrêter — ~ *vi* : s'arrêter — *vt* : arrêter
halve ['hæv] *vt* **halved; halving 1** DIVIDE
: couper en deux **2** REDUCE : réduire de
moitié — **halves** → **half**
ham ['hæm] *n* : jambon *m*
hamburger ['hæm,bərgər] *or* **hamburg**
[-,bərg] *n* **1** : viande *f* hachée (crue) **2**
: hamburger *m* (cuit)
hammer ['hæmər] *n* : marteau *m* — ~ *vt*
: marteler, enfoncer (à coups de marteau)

hammock [ˈhæmək] *n* : hamac *m*

hamper[1] [ˈhæmpər] *vt* : gêner

hamper[2] *n* : panier *m* (à linge)

hamster [ˈhæmˌstər] *n* : hamster *m*

hand [ˈhænd] *n* **1** : main *f* **2** : aiguille *f* (d'une montre, etc.) **3** HANDWRITING : écriture *f* **4** : main *f*, jeu *m* (aux cartes) **5** WORKER : ouvrier *m*, -vrière *f* **6 by ~** : à la main **7 give s.o. a ~** : donner un coup de main à qqn **8 on ~** : disponible **9 on the other ~** : d'autre part — **~** *vt* **1** : donner, passer **2 ~ out** : distribuer — **handbag** [ˈhændˌbæg] *n* : sac *m* à main — **handbook** [ˈhændˌbʊk] *n* : manuel *m*, guide *m* — **handcuffs** [ˈhændˌkʌfs] *npl* : menottes *fpl* — **handful** [ˈhændˌfʊl] *n* : poignée *f* — **handgun** [ˈhændˌgʌn] *n* : pistolet *m*, revolver *m*

handicap [ˈhændiˌkæp] *n* : handicap *m* — **~** *vt* **-capped; -capping** : handicaper — **handicapped** [ˈhændiˌkæpt] *adj* : handicapé

handicrafts [ˈhændiˌkræfts] *npl* : objets *mpl* artisanaux

handiwork [ˈhændiˌwərk] *n* : ouvrage *m*

handkerchief [ˈhæŋkərˌtʃəf, -ˌtʃiːf] *n, pl* **-chiefs** : mouchoir *m*

handle [ˈhændəl] *n* : manche *m* (d'un ustensile), poignée *f* (de porte), anse *f* (d'un panier, etc.) — **~** *vt* **-dled; -dling 1** TOUCH : toucher à, manipuler **2** MANAGE : s'occuper de — **handlebars** [ˈhændəlˌbarz] *npl* : guidon *m*

handmade [ˈhændˌmeɪd] *adj* : fait à la main

handout [ˈhændˌaʊt] *n* **1** ALMS : aumône *f* **2** LEAFLET : prospectus *m*

handrail [ˈhændˌreɪl] *n* : rampe *f*

handshake [ˈhændˌʃeɪk] *n* : poignée *f* de main

handsome [ˈhæntsəm] *adj* **handsomer; -est 1** ATTRACTIVE : beau **2** GENEROUS : généreux **3** LARGE : considérable

handwriting [ˈhændˌraɪtɪŋ] *n* : écriture *f* — **handwritten** [ˈhændˌrɪtən] *adj* : écrit à la main

handy [ˈhændi] *adj* **handier; -est 1** NEARBY : à portée de la main, proche **2** USEFUL : commode, pratique **3** CLEVER : adroit — **handyman** [ˈhændimən] *n, pl* **-men** [-mən, -ˌmɛn] : bricoleur *m*

hang [ˈhæŋ] *v* **hung** [ˈhʌŋ]; **hanging** *vt* **1** : suspendre, accrocher **2** (*past tense often* **hanged**) EXECUTE : pendre **3 ~ one's head** : baisser la tête — *vi* **1** : être accroché, pendre **2 ~ up** : raccrocher — **~** *n* **get the ~ of** : piger *fam*

hangar [ˈhæŋər, ˈhæŋɡər] *n* : hangar *m*

hanger [ˈhæŋər] *n or* **coat ~** : cintre *m*

hangover [ˈhæŋˌoːvər] *n* : gueule *f* de bois

hanker [ˈhæŋkər] *vi* **~ for** : désirer, avoir envie de — **hankering** [ˈhæŋkərɪŋ] *n* : désir *m*, envie *f*

haphazard [hæpˈhæzərd] *adj* : fait au hasard

happen [ˈhæpən] *vi* **1** OCCUR : arriver, se passer **2** CHANCE : arriver par hasard **3 it so happens that ...** : il se trouve que ... — **happening** [ˈhæpənɪŋ] *n* : événement *m*

happy [ˈhæpi] *adj* **happier; -est 1** : heureux **2 be ~ with** : être satisfait de — **happily** [ˈhæpəli] *adv* : heureusement — **happiness** [ˈhæpinəs] *n* : bonheur *m* — **happy-go-lucky** [ˈhæpiɡoːˈlʌki] *adj* : insouciant

harass [həˈræs, ˈhærəs] *vt* : harceler — **harassment** [həˈræsmənt, ˈhærəsmənt] *n* : harcèlement *m*

harbor *or Brit* **harbour** [ˈharbər] *n* : port *m* — **~** *vt* **1** SHELTER : héberger **2 ~ a grudge against** : garder rancune à

hard [ˈhard] *adj* **1** : dur **2** DIFFICULT : difficile **3 ~ water** : eau *f* calcaire — **~** *adv* **1** : dur **2** FORCEFULLY : fort **3 take sth ~** : mal prendre qqch — **harden** [ˈhardən] *vt* : durcir, endurcir — *vi* : s'endurcir — **hard-headed** [ˈhardˈhɛdəd] *adj* : têtu, entêté — **hard-hearted** [ˈhardˈhartəd] *adj* : dur, insensible — **hardly** [ˈhardli] *adv* **1** BARELY : à peine, ne . . . guère **2 it's ~ surprising** : ce n'est pas surprenant — **hardness** [ˈhardnəs] *n* : dureté *f* — **hardship** [ˈhardˌʃɪp] *n* : épreuves *fpl* — **hardware** [ˈhardˌwær] *n* **1** : quincaillerie *f* **2** : matériel *m* (en informatique) — **hardworking** [ˈhardˈwərkɪŋ] *adj* : travailleur, travaillant *Can*

hardy [ˈhardi] *adj* **hardier; -est 1** BOLD : hardi, intrépide **2** ROBUST : résistant

hare [ˈhær] *n, pl* **hare** *or* **hares** : lièvre *m*

harm [ˈharm] *n* **1** INJURY : mal *m* **2** DAMAGE : dommage *m* **3** WRONG : tort *m* — *vt* : faire du mal à, nuire à — **harmful** [ˈharmfəl] *adj* : nuisible — **harmless** [ˈharmləs] *adj* : inoffensif

harmonica [harˈmanɪkə] *n* : harmonica *m*

harmony [ˈharməni] *n, pl* **-nies** : harmonie *f* — **harmonious** [harˈmoːniəs] *adj* : harmonieux — **harmonize** [ˈharməˌnaɪz] *v* **-nized; -nizing** *vt* : harmoniser — *vi* : s'harmoniser

harness [ˈharnəs] *n* : harnais *m* — **~** *vt* **1** : harnacher **2** UTILIZE : exploiter

harp [ˈharp] *n* : harpe *f* — **~** *vi* **~ on** : rabâcher

harpoon [harˈpuːn] *n* : harpon *m*

harpsichord [ˈharpsɪˌkord] *n* : clavecin *m*

harsh [ˈharʃ] *adj* **1** ROUGH : rude **2** SEVERE : dur, sévère **3** : cru (se dit des couleurs), rude (se dit des sons) — **harshness** [ˈharʃnəs] *n* : sévérité *f*

harvest [ˈharvəst] *n* : moisson *f*, récolte *f* — **~** *vt* : moissonner, récolter

has → **have**

hash ['hæʃ] vt **1** CHOP : hacher **2** ~ **over** DISCUSS : parler de, discuter — ~ n **1** : hachis m **2** JUMBLE : gâchis m

hasn't ['hæzənt] (contraction of **has not**) → **have**

hassle ['hæsəl] n : embêtements mpl, ennuis mpl — ~ vt : tracasser

haste ['heɪst] n : hâte f, précipitation f — **hasten** ['heɪsən] vt : hâter, précipiter — vi : se hâter, se dépêcher — **hastily** ['heɪstəli] adv : à la hâte — **hasty** ['heɪsti] adj **hastier; -est** : précipité

hat ['hæt] n : chapeau m

hatch ['hætʃ] n : écoutille f (d'un navire) — ~ vt **1** : couver, faire éclore **2** CONCOCT : tramer (un complot) — vi : éclore

hatchet ['hætʃət] n : hachette f

hate ['heɪt] n : haine f — ~ vt **hated; hating** : haïr — **hateful** ['heɪtfəl] adj : odieux — **hatred** ['heɪtrəd] n : haine f

haughty ['hɔti] adj **haughtier; -est** : hautain

haul ['hɔl] vt : tirer, traîner — ~ n **1** CATCH : prise f **2** LOOT : butin m **3** it's a long ~ : la route est longue

haunch ['hɔntʃ] n : hanche f (d'une personne), derrière m (d'un animal)

haunt ['hɔnt] vt : hanter

have ['hæv, in sense 2 as an auxiliary verb usu 'hæf] v had ['hæd]; having; has ['hæz] vt **1** : avoir **2** WANT : vouloir, prendre **3** RECEIVE : recevoir **4** ALLOW : permettre, tolérer **5** HOLD : tenir **6** ~ a sandwich : manger un sandwich — v aux **1** : avoir, être **2** ~ to : devoir **3** you've finished, haven't you? : tu as fini, n'est-ce pas?

haven ['heɪvən] n : refuge m, havre m

havoc ['hævək] n : ravages mpl, dégâts mpl

hawk[1] ['hɔk] n : faucon m (oiseau)

hawk[2] vt : colporter

hay ['heɪ] n : foin m — **hay fever** n : rhume m des foins — **haystack** ['heɪ,stæk] n : meule f de foin — **haywire** ['heɪ,waɪr] adj **go** ~ : se détraquer

hazard ['hæzərd] n **1** PERIL : risque m **2** CHANCE : hasard m — ~ vt : hasarder, risquer — **hazardous** ['hæzərdəs] adj : dangereux

haze ['heɪz] n : brume f

hazel ['heɪzəl] n : noisette f (couleur) — **hazelnut** ['heɪzəl,nʌt] n : noisette f

hazy ['heɪzi] adj **hazier; -est 1** : brumeux **2** VAGUE : vague, flou

he ['hi] pron **1** : il **2** (used for emphasis or contrast) : lui

head ['hɛd] n **1** : tête f **2** END, TOP : bout m (d'une table), chevet m (d'un lit) **3** LEADER : chef m **4** ~s or tails : pile ou face **5** per ~ : par personne — ~ adj MAIN : principal — ~ vt **1** LEAD : être en tête de **2** DIRECT

: diriger — vi : se diriger, aller — **headache** ['hɛd,eɪk] n : mal m de tête — **headband** ['hɛd,bænd] n : bandeau m — **headdress** ['hɛd,drɛs] n : coiffe f — **headfirst** ['hɛd-'fərst] adv : la tête la première — **heading** ['hɛdɪŋ] n : titre m, rubrique f — **headland** ['hɛdlənd, -,lænd] n : promontoire m, cap m — **headlight** ['hɛd,laɪt] n : phare m — **headline** ['hɛd,laɪn] n : (gros) titre m — **headlong** ['hɛd'lɔŋ] adv : à toute allure — **headmaster** ['hɛd,mæstər] n : directeur m (d'école) — **headmistress** ['hɛd-,mɪstrəs, -'mɪs-] n : directrice f (d'école) — **head-on** ['hɛd'ɑn, -'ɑn] adv & adj : de plein fouet — **headphones** ['hɛd,fo:nz] npl : casque m — **headquarters** ['hɛd-,kwɔrtərz] ns & pl : siège m (d'une compagnie), quartier m général (militaire) — **headstrong** ['hɛd,strɔŋ] adj : têtu, obstiné — **headwaiter** ['hɛd'weɪtər] n : maître m d'hôtel — **headway** ['hɛd,weɪ] n **1** : progrès m **2** make ~ : avancer, progresser — **heady** ['hɛdi] adj **headier; -est 1** : capiteux (se dit du vin) **2** EXCITING : grisant

heal ['hi:l] v : guérir

health ['hɛlθ] n : santé f — **healthy** ['hɛlθi] adj **healthier; -est** : sain, en bonne santé

heap ['hi:p] n : tas m — ~ vt : entasser

hear ['hɪr] v **heard** ['hərd]; **hearing** vt **1** : entendre **2** or ~ **about** : apprendre — vi **1** : entendre **2** ~ **from** : avoir des nouvelles de — **hearing** ['hɪrɪŋ] n **1** : ouïe f, audition f **2** : audience f (d'un tribunal) — **hearing aid** n : appareil m auditif — **hearsay** ['hɪr,seɪ] n : ouï-dire m

hearse ['hərs] n : corbillard m

heart ['hɑrt] n **1** : cœur m **2** at ~ : au fond **3** by ~ : par cœur **4** lose ~ : perdre courage — **heartache** ['hɑrt,eɪk] n : chagrin m, peine f — **heart attack** n : crise f cardiaque — **heartbeat** ['hɑrt,bi:t] n : battement m de cœur — **heartbroken** ['hɑrt-,bro:kən] adj be ~ : avoir le cœur brisé — **heartburn** ['hɑrt,bərn] n : brûlures fpl d'estomac

hearth ['hɑrθ] n : foyer m

heartily ['hɑrtəli] adv **1** eat ~ : manger avec appétit **2** laugh ~ : rire de bon cœur

heartless ['hɑrtləs] adj : sans cœur, cruel

hearty ['hɑrti] adj **heartier; -est 1** : cordial, chaleureux **2** : copieux (se dit d'un repas)

heat ['hi:t] v : chauffer — ~ n **1** : chaleur f **2** HEATING : chauffage m **3** PASSION : feu m, ardeur f — **heated** ['hi:təd] adj : animé, passionné — **heater** ['hi:tər] n : radiateur m, appareil m de chauffage

heath ['hi:θ] n : lande f

heathen [hi:ðən] adj : païen — ~ n, pl **-thens** or **-then** : païen m, païenne f

heather ['hɛðər] n : bruyère f

heave [ˈhiːv] v **heaved** or **hove** [ˈhoːv]; **heaving** vt **1** LIFT : lever, soulever (avec effort) **2** HURL : lancer **3** ~ **a sigh** : pousser un soupir — vi : se soulever — ~ n : effort m

heaven [ˈhɛvən] n : ciel m — **heavenly** [ˈhɛvənli] adj : céleste, divin

heavy [ˈhɛvi] adj **heavier; -est 1** : lourd, pesant **2** : gros (se dit du corps, du cœur, etc.) **3** ~ **sleep** : sommeil m profond **4** ~ **smoker** : grand fumeur m **5** ~ **traffic** : circulation f dense — **heavily** [ˈhɛvəli] adv : lourdement, pesamment — **heaviness** [ˈhɛvinəs] n : lourdeur f, pesanteur f — **heavyweight** [ˈhɛvi,weɪt] n : poids m lourd

Hebrew [ˈhiː,bruː] adj : hébreu — ~ n : hébreu m (langue)

heckle [ˈhɛkəl] vt **-led; -ling** : interrompre bruyamment

hectic [ˈhɛktɪk] adj : mouvementé, agité

he'd [ˈhiːd] (contraction of **he had** or **he would**) → **have, would**

hedge [ˈhɛdʒ] n : haie f — ~ v **hedged; hedging** vt ~ **one's bets** : se couvrir — vi : éviter de s'engager — **hedgehog** [ˈhɛdʒ,hɔɡ, -,hɑɡ] n : hérisson m

heed [ˈhiːd] vt : faire attention à, écouter — ~ n **take** ~ **of** : tenir compte de — **heedless** [ˈhiːdləs] adj : insouciant

heel [ˈhiːl] n : talon m

hefty [ˈhɛfti] adj **heftier; -est** : gros, lourd

heifer [ˈhɛfər] n : génisse f

height [ˈhaɪt] n **1** TALLNESS : taille f (d'une personne), hauteur f (d'un objet) **2** ALTITUDE : élévation f **3 the** ~ **of folly** : le comble de la folie **4 what is your** ~? : combien mesures-tu? — **heighten** [ˈhaɪtən] vt : augmenter, intensifier

heir [ˈær] n : héritier m, -tière f — **heiress** [ˈærəs] n : héritière f — **heirloom** [ˈær,luːm] n : objet m de famille

held → **hold**

helicopter [ˈhɛlə,kɑptər] n : hélicoptère m

hell [ˈhɛl] n : enfer m — **hellish** [ˈhɛlɪʃ] adj : infernal

he'll [ˈhiːl] (contraction of **he shall** or **he will**) → **shall, will**

hello [həˈloː, hɛ-] or Brit **hullo** [hʌˈleʊ] interj : bonjour!, allô! (au téléphone)

helm [ˈhɛlm] n : barre f

helmet [ˈhɛlmət] n : casque m

help [ˈhɛlp] vt **1** : aider, venir à l'aide de **2** PREVENT : empêcher **3** ~ **yourself** : servez-vous — ~ n **1** : aide f, secours m **2** STAFF : employés mpl, -ployées fpl **3** ~! : au secours! — **helper** [ˈhɛlpər] n : aide mf; assistant m, -tante f — **helpful** [ˈhɛlpfəl] adj : utile, serviable — **helping** [ˈhɛlpɪŋ] n SERVING : portion f — **helpless** [ˈhɛlpləs] adj : impuissant

hem [ˈhɛm] n : ourlet m — ~ vt **hemmed; hemming** : ourler

hemisphere [ˈhɛmə,sfɪr] n : hémisphère m

hemorrhage [ˈhɛmərɪdʒ] n : hémorragie f

hemorrhoids [ˈhɛmə,rɔɪdz, ˈhɛm,rɔɪdz] npl : hémorroïdes fpl

hemp [ˈhɛmp] n : chanvre m

hen [ˈhɛn] n : poule f

hence [ˈhɛnts] adv **1** : d'où, donc **2 ten years** ~ : d'ici dix ans — **henceforth** [ˈhɛnts,fɔrθ, ˌhɛnts'-] adv : dorénavant, désormais

henpeck [ˈhɛn,pɛk] vt : mener par le bout du nez

hepatitis [ˌhɛpəˈtaɪtəs] n, pl **-titides** [-ˈtɪtə,diːz] : hépatite f

her [ˈhər] adj : son, sa, ses — ~ [ˈhər, ər] pron **1** (used as a direct object) : la, l' **2** (used as an indirect object) : lui **3** (used as object of a preposition) : elle

herald [ˈhɛrəld] vt : annoncer

herb [ˈərb, ˈhərb] n : herbe f

herd [ˈhərd] n : troupeau m — ~ vt : mener, conduire — vi or ~ **together** : s'assembler

here [ˈhɪr] adv **1** : ici, là **2** NOW : alors **3** ~ **is**, ~ **are** : voici, voilà — **hereabouts** [ˈhɪrə,baʊts] or **hereabout** [-,baʊt] adv : par ici — **hereafter** [hɪrˈæftər] adv : ci-après — **hereby** [hɪrˈbaɪ] adv : par la présente

hereditary [həˈrɛdə,tɛri] adj : héréditaire — **heredity** [həˈrɛdəti] n : hérédité f

heresy [ˈhɛrəsi] n, pl **-sies** : hérésie f

herewith [hɪrˈwɪθ] adv : ci-joint

heritage [ˈhɛrətɪdʒ] n : héritage m, patrimoine m

hermit [ˈhərmət] n : ermite m

hernia [ˈhərniə] n, pl **-nias** or **-niae** [-niˌiː, -niˌaɪ] : hernie f

hero [ˈhiːˌroː, ˈhɪrˌoː] n, pl **-roes** : héros m — **heroic** [hɪˈroːɪk] adj : héroïque — **heroine** [ˈhɛroən] n : héroïne f — **heroism** [ˈhɛroˌɪzəm] n : héroïsme m

heron [ˈhɛrən] n : héron m

herring [ˈhɛrɪŋ] n, pl **-ring** or **-rings** : hareng m

hers [ˈhərz] pron **1** : le sien, la sienne, les siens, les siennes **2 some friends of** ~ : des amis à elle — **herself** [hərˈsɛlf] pron **1** (used reflexively) : se, s' **2** (used for emphasis) : elle-même **3** (used after a preposition) : elle, elle-même

he's [ˈhiːz] (contraction of **he is** or **he has**) → **be, have**

hesitant [ˈhɛzətənt] adj : hésitant, indécis — **hesitate** [ˈhɛzəˌteɪt] vi **-tated; -tating** : hésiter — **hesitation** [ˌhɛzəˈteɪʃən] n : hésitation f

heterogeneous [ˌhɛtərəˈdʒiːniəs, -njəs] adj : hétérogène

heterosexual [ˌhɛtəroʊˈsɛkʃʊəl] *adj* : hétérosexuel — **~** *n* : hétérosexuel *m*, -sexuelle *f*
hexagon [ˈhɛksəˌgɑn] *n* : hexagone *m*
hey [ˈheɪ] *interj* : hé!, ohé!
heyday [ˈheɪˌdeɪ] *n* : beaux jours *mpl*,
apogée *j*
hi [ˈhaɪ] *interj* : salut!
hibernate [ˈhaɪbərˌneɪt] *vi* **-nated; -nating**
: hiberner
hiccup [ˈhɪkəp] *vi* **-cuped; -cuping** : hoqueter — **~** *n* **have the ~s** : avoir le hoquet
hide[1] [ˈhaɪd] *n* : peau *f* (d'animal)
hide[2] *v* **hid** [ˈhɪd]; **hidden** [ˈhɪdən] *or* **hid**;
hiding *vt* : cacher — *vi* : se cacher —
hide–and–seek [ˈhaɪdəndˌsi:k] *n* : cache-
cache *m*
hideous [ˈhɪdiəs] *adj* : hideux, affreux
hideout [ˈhadˌaʊt] *n* : cachette *f*
hierarchy [ˈhaɪəˌrɑrki] *n, pl* **-chies** : hiérarchie *f* — **hierarchical** [ˌhaɪəˈrɑrkɪkəl] *adj*
: hiérarchique
high [ˈhaɪ] *adj* **1** : haut **2** : élevé (se dit des
prix, etc.) **3** INTOXICATED : parti *fam*,
drogué **4 ~ speed** : grande vitesse *f* **5 a
~ voice** : une voix aiguë — *adv* : haut
— **~** *n* : record *m*, niveau *m* élevé —
higher [ˈhaɪər] *adj* **1** : plus haut **2 ~ education** : études *fpl* supérieures — **highlight**
[ˈhaɪˌlaɪt] *n* : point *m* culminant — **~** *vt*
EMPHASIZE : souligner — **highly** [ˈhaɪli] *adv*
1 VERY : très, extrêmement **2 think ~ of**
: penser du bien de — **highness** [ˈhaɪnəs] *n*
His/Her Highness : son Altesse — **high
school** : lycée *m France*, école *f* secondaire *Can* — **high–strung** [ˈhaɪˈstrʌŋ]
adj : nerveux, très tendu — **highway** [ˈhaɪ-
ˌweɪ] *n* **1** : autoroute *f* **2** → **interstate**
hijack [ˈhaɪˌdʒæk] *vt* : détourner (un avion)
— **hijacker** [ˈhaɪˌdʒækər] *n* : pirate *m* de
l'air — **hijacking** [ˈhaɪˌdʒækɪŋ] *n* : détournement *m*
hike [ˈhaɪk] *v* **hiked; hiking** *vi* : faire une
randonnée — *vt or* **~ up** RAISE : augmenter — **~** *n* : randonnée *f* — **hiker**
[ˈhaɪkər] *n* : randonneur *m*, -neuse *f*
hilarious [hɪˈlæriəs, haɪ-] *adj* : désopilant,
hilarant — **hilarity** [hɪˈlærəti, haɪ-] *n* : hilarité *f*
hill [ˈhɪl] *n* : colline *f* — **hillside** [ˈhɪlˌsaɪd] *n*
: coteau *m* — **hilly** [ˈhɪli] *adj* **hillier; -est**
: vallonné, côteux *Can*
hilt [ˈhɪlt] *n* : poignée *f* (d'une épée)
him [ˈhɪm, əm] *pron* **1** (*used as a direct object*) : le, l' **2** (*used as an indirect object or
as object of a preposition*) : lui — **himself**
[hɪmˈsɛlf] *pron* **1** (*used reflexively*) : se, s'
2 (*used for emphasis*) : lui-même **3** (*used
after a preposition*) : lui, lui-même
hind [ˈhaɪnd] *adj* : de derrière

hinder [ˈhɪndər] *vt* : empêcher, entraver —
hindrance [ˈhɪndrənts] *n* : entrave *f*
hindsight [ˈhaɪndˌsaɪt] *n* **in ~** : avec du
recul
Hindu [ˌhɪnˌdu:] *adj* : hindou
hinge [ˈhɪndʒ] *n* : charnière *f*, gond *m* —
vi **hinged; hinging ~ on** : dépendre de
hint [ˈhɪnt] *n* **1** INSINUATION : allusion *f* **2**
TRACE : soupçon *m* **3** TIP : conseil *m* — **~**
vt : insinuer — *vi* **~ at** : faire une allusion à
hip [ˈhɪp] *n* : hanche *f*
hippie *or* **hippy** [ˈhɪpi] *n, pl* **hippies** : hippie
mf, hippy *mf*
hippopotamus [ˌhɪpəˈpɑtəməs] *n, pl*
-muses *or* **-mi** [-ˌmaɪ] : hippopotame *m*
hire [ˈhaɪr] *vt* **hired; hiring 1** : engager, embaucher **2** RENT : louer — **~** *n* **1** WAGES
: gages *mpl* **2 for ~** : à louer
his [ˈhɪz, ɪz] *adj* **1** : son, sa, ses **2 it's ~**
: c'est à lui — **~** *pron* **1** : le sien, la sienne,
les siens, les siennes **2 a friend of ~** : un
ami à lui
Hispanic [hɪˈspænɪk] *adj* : hispanique
hiss [ˈhɪs] *vi* : siffler — **~** *n* : sifflement *m*
history [ˈhɪstəri] *n, pl* **-ries 1** : histoire *f* **2**
: antécédents *mpl* (médicaux, etc.) — **histo-
rian** [hɪˈstɔriən] *n* : historien *m*, -rienne *f* —
historic [hɪˈstɔrɪk] *or* **historical** [-ɪkəl] *adj*
: historique
hit [ˈhɪt] *v* **hit; hitting** *vt* **1** : frapper (une
balle, etc.) **2** STRIKE : heurter **3** AFFECT
: toucher **4** REACH : atteindre — *vi* **1** : frapper **2** OCCUR : arriver — **~** *n* **1** : coup *m*
(aux sports, etc.) **2** SUCCESS : succès *m*
hitch [ˈhɪtʃ] *vt* **1** : accrocher **2** *or* **~ up**
RAISE : remonter **3 ~ a ride** : faire de
l'auto-stop — **~** *n* PROBLEM : problème *m*
— **hitchhike** [ˈhɪtʃˌhaɪk] *vi* **-hiked; -hiking**
: faire de l'auto-stop — **hitchhiker** [ˈhɪtʃ-
ˌhaɪkər] *n* : auto-stoppeur *m*, -peuse *f*
hitherto [ˈhɪðərˌtu:, ˌhɪðərˈ-] *adv* : jusqu'à
présent
HIV [ˌeɪtʃˌaɪˈvi:] *n* (*human immunodeficiency
virus*) : VIH *m*
hive [ˈhaɪv] *n* : ruche *f*
hives [ˈhaɪvz] *ns & pl* : urticaire *f*
hoard [ˈhɔrd] *n* : réserve *f*, provisions *fpl* —
~ *vt* : accumuler, amasser
hoarse [ˈhɔrs] *adj* **hoarser; -est** : rauque,
enroué
hoax [ˈhoːks] *n* : canular *m*
hobble [ˈhɑbəl] *vi* **-bled; -bling** : boitiller
hobby [ˈhɑbi] *n, pl* **-bies** : passe-temps *m*
hobo [ˈhoːˌboː] *n, pl* **-boes** : vagabond *m*,
-bonde *f*
hockey [ˈhɑki] *n* : hockey *m*
hoe [ˈhoː] *n* : houe *f*, binette *f* — **~** *vi* **hoed;
hoeing** : biner
hog [ˈhɔg, ˈhɑg] *n* : porc *m*, cochon *m* — **~**
vt **hogged; hogging** : monopoliser

hoist ['hɔɪst] vt : hisser — ~ n : palan m
hold[1] ['ho:ld] v **held** ['hɛld]; **holding** vt **1** : tenir **2** POSSESS : posséder **3** CONTAIN : contenir **4** or ~ **UP** SUPPORT : soutenir **5** : détenir (un prisonnier, etc.) **6** ~ **the line** : ne quittez pas **7** ~ **s.o's attention** : retenir l'attention de qqn — vi **1** LAST : durer, continuer **2** APPLY : tenir — ~ n **1** GRIP : prise f, étreinte f **2 get** ~ **of** : trouver — **holder** ['ho:ldər] n : détenteur m, -trice f; titulaire mf — **holdup** ['ho:ld,ʌp] n **1** : vol m à main armée **2** DELAY : retard m — **hold up** vt DELAY : retarder
hold[2] n : cale f (d'un navire ou d'un avion)
hole ['ho:l] n : trou m
holiday ['hɑlə,deɪ] n **1** : jour m férié **2** Brit VACATION : vacances fpl
holiness ['ho:linəs] n : sainteté f
holler ['hɑlər] vi : gueuler fam, hurler — ~ n : hurlement m
hollow ['hɑ,lo:] n : creux m — ~ adj **hollower; -est 1** : creux **2** FALSE : faux — ~ vt or ~ **out** : creuser
holly ['hɑli] n, pl **-lies** : houx m
holocaust ['hɑlə,kɔst, 'ho:-, 'hɔ-] n : holocauste m
holster ['ho:lstər] n : étui m de revolver
holy ['ho:li] adj **holier; -est 1** : saint **2** ~ **water** : eau f bénite
homage ['amɪdʒ, 'hɑ-] n : hommage m
home ['ho:m] n **1** RESIDENCE : maison f **2** FAMILY : foyer m, chez-soi m **3** → **funeral home, nursing home** — ~ adv **go** ~ : rentrer à la maison, rentrer chez soi — **homeland** ['ho:m,lænd] n : patrie f — **homeless** ['ho:mləs] n **the** ~ : les sans-abri — **homely** ['ho:mli] adj **homelier; -est 1** SIMPLE : simple, ordinaire **2** UGLY : laid — **homemade** ['ho:m'meɪd] adj : fait à la maison — **homemaker** ['ho:m,meɪkər] n : femme f au foyer — **home page** n : page f d'accueil — **home run** n : coup m de circuit Can — **homesick** ['ho:m,sɪk] adj **be** ~ : avoir le mal du pays — **homeward** ['ho:mwərd] or **homewards** [-wərdz] adv : vers la maison — **homeward** adj : de retour — **homework** ['ho:m,wərk] n : devoirs mpl — **homey** ['ho:mi] adj **homier; -est** COZY, INVITING : accueillant
homicide ['hɑmə,saɪd, 'ho:-] n : homicide m
homogeneous [,ho:mə'dʒi:niəs, -njəs] adj : homogène
homosexual [,ho:mə'sɛkʃuəl] adj : homosexuel — ~ n : homosexuel m, -sexuelle f — **homosexuality** [,ho:mə,sɛkʃu'æləti] n : homosexualité f
honest ['anəst] adj : honnête — **honestly** ['anəstli] adv : honnêtement — **honesty** ['anəsti] n : honnêteté f
honey ['hʌni] n, pl **-eys** : miel m — **honey-**

comb ['hʌni,ko:m] n : rayon m de miel — **honeymoon** ['hʌni,mu:n] n : lune f de miel
honk ['haŋk, 'hɔŋk] vi : klaxonner — ~ n : coup m de klaxon
honor or Brit **honour** ['anər] n : honneur m — ~ vt : honorer — **honorable** or Brit **honourable** ['anərəbəl] adj : honorable — **honorary** ['anə,reri] adj : honoraire, honorifique
hood ['hʊd] n **1** : capuchon m (d'un vêtement) **2** : capot m (d'une voiture)
hoodlum ['hʊdləm, 'hu:d-] n : voyou m
hoodwink ['hʊd,wɪŋk] vt : tromper
hoof ['hʊf, 'hu:f] n, pl **hooves** ['hʊvz, 'hu:vz] or **hoofs** : sabot m (d'un animal)
hook ['hʊk] n **1** : crochet m **2** FASTENER : agrafe f **3** → **fishhook** — ~ vt : accrocher — vi : s'accrocher
hoop ['hu:p] n : cerceau m
hoorah [hʊ'ra], **hooray** [hʊ'reɪ] → **hurrah**
hoot ['hu:t] vi **1** : hululer (se dit d'un hibou) **2** ~ **with laughter** : pouffer de rire — ~ n **1** : hululement m **2 I don't give a** ~ : je m'en fiche
hop ['hɑp] v **hopped; hopping** vi : sauter, sautiller — vt or ~ **over** : sauter — ~ n : saut m
hope ['ho:p] v **hoped; hoping** : espérer — ~ n : espoir m — **hopeful** ['ho:pfəl] adj **1** OPTIMISTIC : plein d'espoir **2** PROMISING : encourageant — **hopefully** ['ho:pfəli] adv **1** : avec espoir **2** ~ **it will work** : on espère que cela marche — **hopeless** ['ho:pləs] adj : désespéré — **hopelessly** ['ho:pləsli] adv **1** : complètement **2** ~ **in love** : éperdument amoureux
hops ['hɑps] nmpl : houblon m
horde ['hord] n : horde f, foule f
horizon [hə'raɪzən] n : horizon m — **horizontal** [,hɔrə'zantəl] adj : horizontal
hormone ['hɔr,mo:n] n : hormone f
horn ['hɔrn] n **1** : corne f (d'un animal) **2** : cor m (instrument de musique) **3** : klaxon m (d'un véhicule)
hornet ['hɔrnət] n : frelon m
horoscope ['hɔrə,sko:p] n : horoscope m
horrendous [hə'rɛndəs] adj : épouvantable — **horrible** ['hɔrəbəl] adj : horrible, affreux — **horrid** ['hɔrɪd] adj : horrible, hideux — **horrify** ['hɔrə,faɪ] vt **-fied; -fying** : horrifier — **horror** ['hɔrər] n : horreur f
hors d'oeuvre [ɔr'dərv] n, pl **hors d'oeuvres** [-'dərvz] : hors-d'œuvre m
horse ['hɔrs] n : cheval m — **horseback** ['hɔrs,bæk] n **on** ~ : à cheval — **horsefly** ['hɔrs,flaɪ] n, pl **-flies** : taon m — **horseman** ['hɔrsmən] n, pl **-men** [-mən, -,mɛn] : cavalier m — **horsepower** ['hɔrs,paʊər] n : cheval-vapeur m — **horseradish** ['hɔrs,rædɪʃ] n : raifort m — **horseshoe** ['hɔrs-**

‚ʃuː] *n* : fer *m* à cheval — **horsewoman** [ˈhɔrsˌwʊmən] *n, pl* **-women** [-ˌwɪmən] : cavalière *f*

horticulture [ˈhɔrtəˌkʌltʃər] *n* : horticulture *f*

hose [ˈhoʊz] *n 1 pl* **hoses** (tuyau *m* (d'arrosage, etc.) **2** *pl* **hose** STOCKINGS : bas *mpl* — ～ *vt* **hosed; hosing** : arroser —

hosiery [ˈhoʊʒəri, ˈhoʊzə-] *n* : bonneterie *f*

hospice [ˈhɑspəs] *n* : hospice *m*

hospital [ˈhɑsˌpɪtəl] *n* : hôpital *m* — **hospitable** [hɑsˈpɪtəbəl, ˈhɑˌspɪ-] *adj* : hospitalier — **hospitality** [ˌhɑspəˈtæləti] *n, pl* **-ties** : hospitalité *f* — **hospitalize** [ˈhɑsˌpɪtəˌlaɪz] *vt* **-ized; -izing** : hospitaliser

host¹ [ˈhoʊst] *n* a ～ **of** : une foule de

host² *n* **1** : hôte *mf* **2** : animateur *m*, -trice *f* (de radio, etc.) — ～ *vt* : animer (une émission de télévision, etc.)

host³ *n* EUCHARIST : hostie *f*

hostage [ˈhɑstɪʤ] *n* : otage *m*

hostel [ˈhɑstəl] *n* : auberge *f*

hostess [ˈhoʊstəs] *n* : hôtesse *f*

hostile [ˈhɑstəl, -ˌtaɪl] *adj* : hostile — **hostility** [hɑsˈtɪləti] *n, pl* **-ties** : hostilité *f*

hot [ˈhɑt] *adj* **hotter; hottest 1** : chaud **2** SPICY : épicé **3** ～ **news** : les dernières nouvelles **4 have a ～ temper** : s'emporter facilement **5 it's ～ today** : il fait chaud aujourd'hui

hot dog *n* : hot-dog *m*

hotel [hoʊˈtɛl] *n* : hôtel *m*

hotheaded [ˈhɑtˈhɛdəd] *adj* : impétueux

hound [ˈhaʊnd] *n* : chien *m* courant — ～ *vt* : traquer, poursuivre

hour [ˈaʊər] *n* : heure *f* — **hourglass** [ˈaʊərˌglæs] *n* : sablier *m* — **hourly** [ˈaʊərli] *adv & adj* : toutes les heures

house [ˈhaʊs] *n, pl* **houses** [ˈhaʊzəz, -səz] **1** HOME : maison *f* **2** : chambre *f* (en politique) **3 publishing ～** : maison *f* d'édition — ～ [ˈhaʊz] *vt* **housed; housing** : loger, héberger — **houseboat** [ˈhaʊsˌboʊt] *n* : péniche *f* aménagée — **housefly** [ˈhaʊsˌflaɪ] *n, pl* **-flies** : mouche *f* — **household** [ˈhaʊsˌhoʊld] *adj* **1** : ménager **2 ～ name** : nom *m* connu de tous — ～ *n* : ménage *m*, maison *f* — **housekeeper** [ˈhaʊsˌkiːpər] *n* : gouvernante *f* — **housekeeping** [ˈhaʊsˌkiːpɪŋ] *n* HOUSEWORK : ménage *m* — **housewarming** [ˈhaʊsˌwɔrmɪŋ] *n* : pendaison *f* de crémaillère — **housewife** [ˈhaʊsˌwaɪf] *n, pl* **-wives** : femme *f* au foyer, ménagère *f* — **housework** [ˈhaʊsˌwərk] *n* : travaux *mpl* ménagers, ménage *m* — **housing** [ˈhaʊzɪŋ] *n* : logement *m*

hovel [ˈhʌvəl, ˈhɑ-] *n* : taudis *m*

hover [ˈhʌvər] *vi* **1** : planer **2** *or* ～ **about** : rôder — **hovercraft** [ˈhʌvərˌkræft] *n* : aéroglisseur *m*

how [ˈhaʊ] *adv* **1** : comment **2** (*used in exclamations*) : comme, que **3** ～ **about . . . ?** : que dirais-tu de . . . ? **4** ～ **come** WHY : comment, pourquoi **5** ～ **much** : combien **6** ～ **do you do?** : comment allez-vous? **7** ～ **old are you?** : quel âge as-tu? — ～ *conj* : comment

however [haʊˈɛvər] *conj* **1** : de quelque manière que **2** ～ **you like** : comme vous voulez — ～ *adv* **1** NEVERTHELESS : cependant, toutefois **2** ～ **important it is** : si important que ce soit **3** ～ **you want** : comme tu veux

howl [ˈhaʊl] *vi* : hurler — ～ *n* : hurlement *m*

hub [ˈhʌb] *n* **1** CENTER : centre *m* **2** : moyeu *m* (d'une roue)

hubbub [ˈhʌˌbʌb] *n* : vacarme *m*, brouhaha *m*

hubcap [ˈhʌbˌkæp] *n* : enjoliveur *m*

huddle [ˈhʌdəl] *vi* **-dled; -dling** *or* ～ **together** : se blottir

hue [ˈhjuː] *n* : couleur *f*, teinte *f*

huff [ˈhʌf] *n* **be in a ～** : être fâché, être vexé

hug [ˈhʌg] *vt* **hugged; hugging 1** : serrer dans ses bras, étreindre **2** : serrer, longer (un mur, etc.) — ～ *n* : étreinte *f*

huge [ˈhjuːʤ] *adj* **huger; hugest** : énorme, immense

hull [ˈhʌl] *n* : coque *f* (d'un navire)

hullo *Brit* → **hello**

hum [ˈhʌm] *v* **hummed; humming** *vi* : bourdonner — *vt* : fredonner, chantonner — ～ *n* : bourdonnement *m*

human [ˈhjuːmən, ˈjuː-] *adj* **1** : humain **2** ～ **rights** : droits *mpl* de l'homme, droits *mpl* de la personne *Can* — ～ *n* : humain *m*, être *m* humain — **humane** [hjuːˈmeɪn, juː-] *adj* : humain — **humanitarian** [hjuːˌmænəˈteriən, juː-] *adj* : humanitaire — **humanity** [hjuːˈmænəti, juː-] *n, pl* **-ties** : humanité *f*

humble [ˈhʌmbəl] *adj* **humbler; -blest** : humble, modeste — ～ *vt* **-bled; -bling 1** : humilier **2** ～ **oneself** : s'humilier

humdrum [ˈhʌmˌdrʌm] *adj* : monotone, banal

humid [ˈhjuːməd, ˈjuː-] *adj* : humide — **humidity** [hjuːˈmɪdəˌti, juː-] *n, pl* **-ties** : humidité *f*

humiliate [hjuːˈmɪliˌeɪt, juː-] *vt* **-ated; -ating** : humilier — **humiliating** [hjuːˈmɪliˌeɪtɪŋ, juː-] *adj* : humiliant — **humiliation** [hjuːˌmɪliˈeɪʃən, juː-] *n* : humiliation *f* — **humility** [hjuːˈmɪləti, juː-] *n* : humilité *f*

humor *or Brit* **humour** [ˈhjuːmər, ˈjuː-] *n* **1** WIT : humour *m* **2** MOOD : humeur *f* — ～ *vt* : faire plaisir à, ménager — **humorist** [ˈhjuːmərɪst, ˈjuː-] *n* : humoriste *mf* — **humorous** [ˈhjuːmərəs, ˈjuː-] *adj* : plein d'humour, drôle

hump [ˈhʌmp] *n* : bosse *f*

hunch [ˈhʌntʃ] *vi* *or* ～ **over** : se pencher — ～ *n* : intuition *f*, petite idée *f*

hundred ['hʌndrəd] *n, pl* **-dreds** *or* **-dred** : cent *m* — ~ *adj* : cent — **hundredth** ['hʌndrədθ] *n* **1** : centième *mf* (dans une série) **2** : centième *m* (en mathématiques) — ~ *adj* : centième

hung → **hang**

hunger ['hʌŋgər] *n* : faim *f* — ~ *vi* ~ **for** : avoir envie de — **hungry** ['hʌŋgri] *adj* **hungrier; -est be** ~ : avoir faim

hunk ['hʌŋk] *n* : gros morceau *m*

hunt ['hʌnt] *vt* **1** : chasser **2** *or* ~ **for** : chercher — ~ *n* **1** : chasse *f* (sport) **2** SEARCH : recherche *f* — **hunter** ['hʌntər] *n* : chasseur *m*, -seuse *f* — **hunting** ['hʌntɪŋ] *n* : chasse *f*

hurdle ['hərdəl] *n* **1** : haie *f* (aux sports) **2** OBSTACLE : obstacle *m*

hurl ['hərl] *vt* : lancer, jeter

hurrah [hʊ'ra, -'rɔ] *interj* : hourra!

hurricane ['hərə,keɪn] *n* : ouragan *m*

hurry ['həri] *n* : hâte *f*, empressement *m* — ~ *v* **-ried; -rying** *vt* : presser, bousculer — *vi* **1** : se presser, se hâter **2** ~ **up!** : dépêche-toi! — **hurried** ['hərəd] *adj* : précipité — **hurriedly** ['hərədli] *adv* : à la hâte

hurt ['hərt] *v* **hurt; hurting** *vt* **1** INJURE : faire mal à, blesser **2** OFFEND : blesser — *vi* **1** : faire mal **2 my throat** ~**s** : j'ai mal à la gorge — ~ *adj* : blessé — ~ *n* **1** INJURY : blessure *f* **2** PAIN : douleur *f* — **hurtful** ['hərtfəl] *adj* : blessant

hurtle ['hərtəl] *vi* **-tled; -tling** : aller à toute vitesse

husband ['hʌzbənd] *n* : mari *m*

hush ['hʌʃ] *vt* *or* ~ **up** : faire taire — *vi* **1** : se taire **2** ~**!** : chut! — ~ *n* : silence *m*

husk ['hʌsk] *n* : enveloppe *f*

husky[1] ['hʌski] *adj* **huskier; -est** HOARSE : rauque

husky[2] *n, pl* **-kies** : chien *m* esquimau

husky[3] *n* BURLY : costaud

hustle ['həsəl] *v* **-tled; -tling** *vt* : presser, pousser — *vi* : se dépêcher — ~ *n* ~ **and bustle** : agitation *f*, grande activité *f*

hut ['hʌt] *n* : hutte *f*, cabane *f*

hutch ['hʌtʃ] *n* : clapier *m*

hyacinth ['haɪə,sɪnθ] *n* : jacinthe *f*

hybrid ['haɪbrɪd] *n* : hybride *m* — ~ *adj* : hybride

hydrant ['haɪdrənt] *n* *or* **fire** ~ : bouche *f* d'incendie

hydraulic [haɪ'drɔlɪk] *adj* : hydraulique

hydroelectric [ˌhaɪdroɪ'lɛktrɪk] *adj* : hydroélectrique

hydrogen ['haɪdrədʒən] *n* : hydrogène *m*

hyena [haɪ'iːnə] *n* : hyène *f*

hygiene ['haɪ,dʒiːn] *n* : hygiène *f* — **hygienic** [haɪ'dʒɛnɪk, -'dʒiː-; ˌhaɪdʒi:'ɛnɪk] *adj* : hygiénique

hymn ['hɪm] *n* : hymne *m*

hyperactive [ˌhaɪpər'æktɪv] *adj* : hyperactif

hyphen ['haɪfən] *n* : trait *m* d'union

hypnosis [hɪp'no:sɪs] *n, pl* **-noses** [-ˌsi:z] : hypnose *f* — **hypnotic** [hɪp'nɑtɪk] *adj* : hypnotique — **hypnotism** ['hɪpnə,tɪzəm] *n* : hypnotisme *m* — **hypnotize** ['hɪpnə,taɪz] *vt* **-tized; -tizing** : hypnotiser

hypochondriac [ˌhaɪpə'kɑndri,æk] *n* : hypocondriaque *mf*

hypocrisy [hɪ'pɑkrəsi] *n, pl* **-sies** : hypocrisie *f* — **hypocrite** ['hɪpə,krɪt] *n* : hypocrite *mf* — **hypocritical** [ˌhɪpə'krɪtɪkəl] *adj* : hypocrite

hypothesis [haɪ'pɑθəsɪs] *n, pl* **-eses** [-ˌsi:z] : hypothèse *f* — **hypothetical** [ˌhaɪpə-'θɛtɪkəl] *adj* : hypothétique

hysteria [hɪs'tɛriə, -'tɪr-] *n* : hystérie *f* — **hysterical** [hɪs'tɛrɪkəl] *adj* : hystérique

I

i ['aɪ] *n, pl* **i's** *or* **is** ['aɪz] : i *m*, neuvième lettre de l'alphabet

I ['aɪ] *pron* : je

ice ['aɪs] *n* **1** : glace *f* **2** ~ **cube** : glaçon *m* — ~ *v* **iced; icing** *vt* : glacer — *vi* *or* ~ **up** : se givrer — **iceberg** ['aɪs,bərg] *n* : iceberg *m* — **icebox** ['aɪs,bɑks] → **refrigerator** — **ice-cold** ['aɪs'ko:ld] *adj* : glacé — **ice cream** *n* : glace *f* *France*, crème *f* glacée *Can* — **ice-skate** *vi* **-skated; -skating** : patiner — **ice skate** ['aɪs,skeɪt] *n* : patin *m* (à glace) — **icicle** ['aɪ,sɪkəl] *n* : glaçon *m* — **icing** ['aɪsɪŋ] *n* : glaçage *m*

icon ['aɪ,kɑn, -kən] *n* : icône *f* (en informatique)

icy ['aɪsi] *adj* **icier; -est 1** : verglacé (se dit d'une route) **2** FREEZING : glacial, glacé

I'd ['aɪd] (*contraction of* **I should** *or* **I would**) → **should, would**

idea [aɪ'di:ə] *n* : idée *f*

ideal [aɪ'di:əl] *adj* : idéal — ~ *n* : idéal *m* — **idealist** [aɪ'di:ə,lɪst] *n* : idéaliste *mf* — **idealistic** [aɪˌdi:ə'lɪstɪk] *adj* : idéaliste —

idealize [aɪ'di:ə,laɪz] *vt* **-ized; -izing** : idéaliser

identity [aɪ'dɛntəti] *n, pl* **-ties** : identité *f* —
identical [aɪ'dɛntɪkəl] *adj* : identique —
identify [aɪ'dɛntə,faɪ] *v* **-fied; -fying** *vt* : identifier — *vi* ~ **with** : s'identifier à —
identification [aɪ,dɛntəfə'keɪʃən] *n* **1** : identification *f* **2** *or* ~ **card** : carte *f* d'identité

ideology [,aɪdi'ɑlədʒi, ,ɪ-] *n, pl* **-gies** : idéologie *f* — **ideological** [,aɪdiə'lɑdʒɪkəl, ,ɪ-] *adj* : idéologique

idiocy ['ɪdiəsi] *n, pl* **-cies** : idiotie *f*

idiom ['ɪdiəm] *n* **1** : expression *f* idiomatique **2** LANGUAGE : idiome *m* — **idiomatic** [,ɪdiə'mætɪk] *adj* : idiomatique

idiosyncrasy [,ɪdio'sɪŋkrəsi] *n, pl* **-sies** : particularité *f*

idiot ['ɪdiət] *n* : idiot *m*, -diote *f* — **idiotic** [,ɪdi'ɑtɪk] *adj* : idiot

idle ['aɪdəl] *adj* **idler; idlest 1** UNOCCUPIED : désœuvré, oisif **2** LAZY : paresseux **3** VAIN : vain **4 out of** ~ **curiosity** : par pure curiosité **5 stand** ~ : être à l'arrêt — ~ *v* **idled; idling** *vi* : tourner au ralenti (se dit d'un moteur) — *vt or* ~ **away** : gaspiller (son temps) — **idleness** ['aɪdəlnəs] *n* : oisiveté *f*

idol ['aɪdəl] *n* : idole *f* — **idolize** ['aɪdəl,aɪz] *vt* **-ized; izing** : idolâtrer

idyllic [aɪ'dɪlɪk] *adj* : idyllique

if ['ɪf] *conj* **1** : si **2** THOUGH : bien que **3** ~ **so** : dans ce cas-là **4** ~ **not** : sinon

igloo ['ɪ,glu:] *n, pl* **-loos** : igloo *m*

ignite [ɪg'naɪt] *v* **-nited; -niting** *vt* : enflammer — *vi* : prendre feu, s'enflammer — **ignition** [ɪg'nɪʃən] *n* **1** : allumage *m* **2** *or* ~ **switch** : contact *m*

ignorance ['ɪgnərənts] *n* : ignorance *f* — **ignorant** ['ɪgnərənt] *adj* : ignorant — **ignore** [ɪg'nor] *vt* **-nored; -noring** : ignorer

ilk ['ɪlk] *n* : espèce *f*

ill ['ɪl] *adj* **worse; worst 1** SICK : malade **2** BAD : mauvais — ~ *adv* **worse** ['wərs]; **worst** ['wərst] : mal — ~ *n* : mal *m* — **ill-advised** [,ɪləd'vaɪzd, -əd-] *adj* : peu judicieux — **ill at ease** *adj* : mal à l'aise

I'll ['aɪl] (*contraction of* **I shall** *or* **I will**) → **shall, will**

illegal [ɪl'li:gəl] *adj* : illégal

illegible [ɪl'lɛdʒəbəl] *adj* : illisible

illegitimate [,ɪlɪ'dʒɪtəmət] *adj* : illégitime — **illegitimacy** [,ɪlɪ'dʒɪtəməsi] *n* : illégitimité *f*

illicit [ɪl'lɪsət] *adj* : illicite

illiterate [ɪl'lɪtərət] *adj* : analphabète, illettré — **illiteracy** [ɪl'lɪtərəsi] *n, pl* **-cies** : analphabétisme *m*

ill-mannered [,ɪl'mænərd] *adj* : impoli

ill-natured [,ɪl'neɪtʃərd] *adj* : désagréable

illness ['ɪlnəs] *n* : maladie *f*

illogical [ɪl'lɑdʒɪkəl] *adj* : illogique

ill-treat [,ɪl'tri:t] *vt* : maltraiter

illuminate [ɪ'lu:mə,neɪt] *vt* **-nated; -nating** : éclairer — **illumination** [ɪ,lu:mə'neɪʃən] *n* : éclairage *m*

illusion [ɪ'lu:ʒən] *n* : illusion *f* — **illusory** [ɪ-'lu:səri, -zəri] *adj* : illusoire

illustrate ['ɪləs,treɪt] *v* **-trated; -trating** : illustrer — **illustration** [,ɪləs'treɪʃən] *n* : illustration *f* — **illustrative** [ɪ'lʌstrətɪv, 'ɪlə,streɪtɪv] *adj* : explicatif

illustrious [ɪ'lʌstriəs] *adj* : illustre

ill will *n* : malveillance *f*

I'm ['aɪm] (*contraction of* **I am**) → **be**

image ['ɪmɪdʒ] *n* : image *f* — **imagination** [ɪ'mædʒə'neɪʃən] *n* : imagination *f* — **imaginary** [ɪ'mædʒə,nɛri] *adj* : imaginaire — **imaginative** [ɪ'mædʒɪnətɪv] *adj* : imaginatif — **imagine** [ɪ'mædʒən] *vt* **-ined; -ining** : imaginer, s'imaginer

imbalance [ɪm'bælənts] *n* : déséquilibre *m*

imbecile ['ɪmbəsəl, -,sɪl] *n* : imbécile *mf*

imbue [ɪm'bju:] *vt* **-bued; -buing** : imprégner

imitation [,ɪmə'teɪʃən] *n* : imitation *f* — ~ *adj* : artificiel, faux — **imitate** ['ɪmə,teɪt] *vt* **-tated; -tating** : imiter — **imitator** ['ɪmə,teɪtər] *n* : imitateur *m*, -trice *f*

immaculate [ɪ'mækjələt] *adj* : impeccable

immaterial [,ɪmə'tɪriəl] *adj* : sans importance

immature [,ɪmə'tʃur, -'tjur, -'tur] *adj* : immature — **immaturity** [,ɪmə'tʃurəti, -'tjur-, -'tur-] *n, pl* **-ties** : immaturité *f*

immediate [ɪ'mi:diət] *adj* : immédiat — **immediately** [ɪ'mi:diətli] *adv* **1** : immédiatement **2** ~ **before** : juste avant

immense [ɪ'mɛnts] *adj* : immense — **immensity** [ɪ'mɛntsəti] *n, pl* **-ties** : immensité *f*

immerse [ɪ'mərs] *vt* **-mersed; -mersing** : plonger, immerger — **immersion** [ɪ-'mərʒən] *n* : immersion *f*

immigrate ['ɪmə,greɪt] *vi* **-grated; -grating** : immigrer — **immigrant** ['ɪmɪgrənt] *n* : immigrant *m*, -grante *f*; immigré *m*, -grée *f* — **immigration** [,ɪmə'greɪʃən] *n* : immigration *f*

imminent ['ɪmənənt] *adj* : imminent — **imminence** ['ɪmənənts] *n* : imminence *f*

immobile [ɪ'mo:bəl] *adj* **1** FIXED : fixe **2** MOTIONLESS : immobile — **immobilize** [ɪ-'mo:bə,laɪz] *vt* **-ized; -izing** : immobiliser

immoral [ɪ'mɔrəl] *adj* : immoral — **immorality** [,ɪmo'ræləti, ,ɪmə-] *n* : immoralité *f*

immortal [ɪ'mɔrtəl] *adj* : immortel — **immortality** [,ɪ,mɔr'tæləti] *n* : immortalité *f*

immune [ɪ'mju:n] *adj* : immunisé — **immunity** [ɪ'mju:nəti] *n, pl* **-ties** : immunité *f* —

improbable

immunization [ˌɪmjʊnəˈzeɪʃən] *n* : immunisation *f* — **immunize** [ˈɪmjʊˌnaɪz] *vt* -nized; -nizing : immuniser

imp [ˈɪmp] *n* 1 : lutin *m* 2 RASCAL : polisson *m*, -sonne *f*

impact [ˈɪmˌpækt] *n* : impact *m*

impair [ɪmˈpær] *vt* 1 WEAKEN : affaiblir 2 DAMAGE : détériorer

impart [ɪmˈpɑrt] *vt* : communiquer

impartial [ɪmˈpɑrʃəl] *adj* : impartial — **impartiality** [ɪmˌpɑrʃiˈæləti] *n* : impartialité *f*

impassable [ɪmˈpæsəbəl] *adj* : impraticable

impasse [ˈɪmˌpæs] *n* : impasse *f*

impassive [ɪmˈpæsɪv] *adj* : impassible

impatience [ɪmˈpeɪʃənts] *n* : impatience *f* — **impatient** [ɪmˈpeɪʃənt] *adj* : impatient — **impatiently** [ɪmˈpeɪʃəntli] *adv* : impatiemment

impeccable [ɪmˈpɛkəbəl] *adj* : impeccable

impede [ɪmˈpiːd] *vt* -peded; -peding : entraver, gêner — **impediment** [ɪmˈpɛdəmənt] *n* : entrave *f*, obstacle *m*

impel [ɪmˈpɛl] *vt* -pelled; -pelling 1 : inciter 2 PROPEL : pousser

impending [ɪmˈpɛndɪŋ] *adj* : imminent

impenetrable [ɪmˈpɛnətrəbəl] *adj* : impénétrable

imperative [ɪmˈpɛrətɪv] *adj* 1 COMMANDING : impérieux 2 NECESSARY : impératif — ~ *n* : impératif *m* (en grammaire)

imperceptible [ˌɪmpərˈsɛptəbəl] *adj* : imperceptible

imperfection [ɪmˌpərˈfɛkʃən] *n* : imperfection *f* — **imperfect** [ɪmˈpərfɪkt] *adj* : imparfait — ~ *n or* ~ **tense** : imparfait *m*

imperial [ɪmˈpɪriəl] *adj* : impérial — **imperialism** [ɪmˈpɪriəˌlɪzəm] *n* : impérialisme *m* — **imperious** [ɪmˈpɪriəs] *adj* : impérieux

impersonal [ɪmˈpərsənəl] *adj* : impersonnel

impersonate [ɪmˈpərsənˌeɪt] *vt* -ated; -ating : se faire passer pour — **impersonation** [ɪmˌpərsənˈeɪʃən] *n* : imitation *f* — **impersonator** [ɪmˈpərsənˌeɪtər] *n* : imitateur *m*, -trice *f*

impertinent [ɪmˈpərtənənt] *adj* : impertinent — **impertinence** [ɪmˈpərtənənts] *n* : impertinence *f*

impervious [ɪmˈpərviəs] *adj* ~ **to** : imperméable à

impetuous [ɪmˈpɛtʃuəs] *adj* : impétueux

impetus [ˈɪmpətəs] *n* : impulsion *f*

impinge [ɪmˈpɪndʒ] *vi* -pinged; -pinging 1 ~ **on** : affecter 2 ~ **on s.o.'s rights** : empiéter sur les droits de qqn

impish [ˈɪmpɪʃ] *adj* : espiègle

implant [ɪmˈplænt] *vt* : implanter — ~ [ˈɪmˌplænt] *n* : implant *m*

implausible [ɪmˈplɔzəbəl] *adj* : invraisemblable

implement [ˈɪmpləmənt] *n* : outil *m*, instru-

ment *m* — ~ [ˈɪmpləˌmɛnt] *vt* : mettre en œuvre, appliquer

implicate [ˈɪmpləˌkeɪt] *vt* -cated; -cating : impliquer — **implication** [ˌɪmpləˈkeɪʃən] *n* : implication *f*

implicit [ɪmˈplɪsət] *adj* 1 : implicite 2 UNQUESTIONING : absolu, total

implode [ɪmˈploːd] *vi* -ploded; -ploding : imploser

implore [ɪmˈplor] *vt* -plored; -ploring : implorer

imply [ɪmˈplaɪ] *vt* -plied; -plying : impliquer

impolite [ˌɪmpəˈlaɪt] *adj* : impoli

import [ɪmˈport] *vt* : importer (des marchandises) — ~ [ˈɪmˌport] *n* 1 IMPORTANCE : signification *f* 2 IMPORTATION : importation *f* — **importance** [ɪmˈpɔrtənts] *n* : importance *f* — **important** [ɪmˈpɔrtənt] *adj* : important — **importation** [ˌɪmˌpɔrˈteɪʃən] *n* : importation *f* — **importer** [ɪmˈpɔrtər] *n* : importateur *m*, -trice *f*

impose [ɪmˈpoːz] *v* -posed; -posing *vt* : imposer — *vi* 1 : s'imposer 2 ~ **on** : déranger — **imposing** [ɪmˈpoːzɪŋ] *adj* : imposant — **imposition** [ˌɪmpəˈzɪʃən] *n* : imposition *f*

impossible [ɪmˈpɑsəbəl] *adj* : impossible — **impossibility** [ɪmˌpɑsəˈbɪləti] *n, pl* -ties : impossibilité *f*

impostor *or* **imposter** [ɪmˈpɑstər] *n* : imposteur *m*

impotent [ˈɪmpətənt] *adj* : impuissant — **impotence** [ˈɪmpətənts] *n* : impuissance *f*

impound [ɪmˈpaʊnd] *vt* : saisir, confisquer

impoverished [ɪmˈpɑvərɪʃt] *adj* : appauvri

impracticable [ɪmˈpræktɪkəbəl] *adj* : impraticable

impractical [ɪmˈpræktɪkəl] *adj* : peu pratique

imprecise [ˌɪmprɪˈsaɪs] *adj* : imprécis

impregnable [ɪmˈprɛgnəbəl] *adj* : imprenable

impregnate [ɪmˈprɛgˌneɪt] *vt* -nated; -nating 1 FERTILIZE : féconder 2 SATURATE : imprégner

impress [ɪmˈprɛs] *vt* 1 IMPRINT : imprimer 2 AFFECT : impressionner 3 ~ **upon s.o.** : faire bien comprendre à qqn — **impression** [ɪmˈprɛʃən] *n* : impression *f* — **impressionable** [ɪmˈprɛʃənəbəl] *adj* : impressionnable — **impressive** [ɪmˈprɛsɪv] *adj* : impressionnant

imprint [ɪmˈprɪnt, ˈɪmˌ-] *vt* : imprimer — ~ [ˈɪmˌprɪnt] *n* MARK : empreinte *f*, marque *f*

imprison [ɪmˈprɪzən] *vt* : emprisonner — **imprisonment** [ɪmˈprɪzənmənt] *n* : emprisonnement *m*

improbable [ɪmˈprɑbəbəl] *adj* : improbable — **improbability** [ɪmˌprɑbəˈbɪləti] *n, pl* -ties : improbabilité *f*

impromptu

impromptu

impromptu [ɪmˈprɑmpˌtuː, -ˌtjuː] *adj* : impromptu

improper [ɪmˈprɑpər] *adj* **1** UNSEEMLY : peu convenable **2** INCORRECT : incorrect **3** INDECENT : indécent — **impropriety** [ˌɪmprəˈpraɪəti] *n, pl* **-ties** : inconvenance *f*

improve [ɪmˈpruːv] *v* **-proved; -proving** *vt* : améliorer — *vi* : s'améliorer, faire des progrès — **improvement** [ɪmˈpruːvmənt] *n* : amélioration *f*

improvise [ˈɪmprəˌvaɪz] *v* **-vised; -vising** : improviser — **improvisation** [ɪmˌprɑvəˈzeɪʃən, ˌɪmprəvə-] *n* : improvisation *f*

impudent [ˈɪmpjədənt] *adj* : impudent — **impudence** [ˈɪmpjədənts] *n* : impudence *f*

impulse [ˈɪmˌpʌls] *n* : impulsion *f* — **impulsive** [ɪmˈpʌlsɪv] *adj* : impulsif — **impulsiveness** [ɪmˈpʌlsɪvnəs] *n* : impulsivité *f*

impunity [ɪmˈpjuːnəti] *n* : impunité *f*

impure [ɪmˈpjʊr] *adj* : impur — **impurity** [ɪmˈpjʊrəti] *n, pl* **-ties** : impureté *f*

impute [ɪmˈpjuːt] *vt* **-puted; -puting** : imputer

in [ˈɪn] *prep* **1** : dans, en, à **2** ~ **1938** : en 1938 **3** ~ **an hour** : dans une heure **4** ~ **Canada** : au Canada **5** ~ **leather** : en cuir **6** ~ **my house** : chez moi **7** ~ **the hospital** : à l'hôpital **8** ~ **the sun** : au soleil **9** ~ **this way** : de cette manière **10 be** ~ **a hurry** : être pressé **11 be** ~ **luck** : avoir de la chance — ~ *adv* **1** INSIDE : dedans, à l'intérieur **2 be** ~ : être là, être chez soi **3 come** ~ : entrer **4 she's** ~ **for a surprise** : elle va être surprise **5** ~ **power** : au pouvoir — ~ *adj* : à la mode

inability [ˌɪnəˈbɪləti] *n, pl* **-ties** : incapacité *f*

inaccessible [ˌɪnɪkˈsɛsəbəl] *adj* : inaccessible

inaccurate [ɪnˈækjərət] *adj* : inexact

inactive [ɪnˈæktɪv] *adj* : inactif — **inactivity** [ˌɪnˌækˈtɪvəti] *n, pl* **-ties** : inactivité *f*

inadequate [ɪˈnædɪkwət] *adj* : insuffisant

inadvertently [ˌɪnədˈvərtəntli] *adv* : par inadvertance

inadvisable [ˌɪnædˈvaɪzəbəl] *adj* : déconseillé

inane [ɪˈneɪn] *adj* **inaner; -est** : inepte, stupide

inanimate [ɪˈnænəmət] *adj* : inanimé

inapplicable [ɪˈnæplɪkəbəl, ˌɪnəˈplɪkəbəl] *adj* : inapplicable

inappropriate [ˌɪnəˈproːpriət] *adj* : inopportun, peu approprié

inarticulate [ˌɪnɑrˈtɪkjələt] *adj* **1** : indistinct (se dit des mots, des sons, etc.) **2 be** ~ : ne pas savoir s'exprimer

inasmuch as [ˌɪnæzˈmʌtʃæz] *conj* : vu que

inaudible [ɪnˈɔdəbəl] *adj* : inaudible

inauguration [ɪˌnɔgjəˈreɪʃən, -gə-] *n* : inauguration *f* — **inaugural** [ɪˈnɔgjərəl, -gərəl]

adj : inaugural — **inaugurate** [ɪˈnɔgjəˌreɪt, -gə-] *vt* **-rated; -rating** : inaugurer

inborn [ˈɪnˌbɔrn] *adj* : inné

inbred [ˈɪnˌbrɛd] *adj* INNATE : inné

incalculable [ɪnˈkælkjələbəl] *adj* : incalculable

incapable [ɪnˈkeɪpəbəl] *adj* : incapable — **incapacitate** [ˌɪnkəˈpæsəˌteɪt] *vt* **-tated; -tating** : rendre incapable — **incapacity** [ˌɪnkəˈpæsəti] *n, pl* **-ties** : incapacité *f*

incarcerate [ɪnˈkɑrsəˌreɪt] *vt* **-ated; -ating** : incarcérer

incarnation [ˌɪnkɑrˈneɪʃən] *n* : incarnation *f*

incense[1] [ˈɪnsɛnts] *n* : encens *m*

incense[2] [ɪnˈsɛnts] *vt* **-censed; -censing** : mettre en fureur

incentive [ɪnˈsɛntɪv] *n* : motivation *f*

inception [ɪnˈsɛpʃən] *n* : commencement *m*

incessant [ɪnˈsɛsənt] *adj* : incessant — **incessantly** [ɪnˈsɛsəntli] *adv* : sans cesse

incest [ˈɪnˌsɛst] *n* : inceste *m* — **incestuous** [ɪnˈsɛstʃuəs] *adj* : incestueux

inch [ˈɪntʃ] *n* : pouce *m* — ~ *v* : avancer petit à petit

incident [ˈɪntsədənt] *n* : incident *m* — **incidental** [ˌɪntsəˈdɛntəl] *adj* : accessoire — **incidentally** [ˌɪntsəˈdɛntəli, -ˈdɛntli] *adv* : à propos

incinerate [ɪnˈsɪnəˌreɪt] *vt* **-ated; -ating** : incinérer — **incinerator** [ɪnˈsɪnəˌreɪtər] *n* : incinérateur *m*

incision [ɪnˈsɪʒən] *n* : incision *f*

incite [ɪnˈsaɪt] *vt* **-cited; -citing** : inciter

incline [ɪnˈklaɪn] *v* **-clined; -clining** *vt* **1** BEND : incliner **2 be** ~ **d to** : avoir tendance à — *vi* **1** LEAN : s'incliner **2** ~ **towards** : tendre vers — ~ [ˈɪnˌklaɪn] *n* : inclinaison *f* — **inclination** [ˌɪnkləˈneɪʃən] *n* : penchant *m*, inclination *f*

include [ɪnˈkluːd] *vt* **-cluded; -cluding** : inclure, comprendre — **inclusion** [ɪnˈkluːʒən] *n* : inclusion *f* — **inclusive** [ɪnˈkluːsɪv] *adj* : inclus, compris

incognito [ˌɪnˌkɑgˈniːˌto, ɪnˈkɑgnəˌtoː] *adv & adj* : incognito

incoherence [ˌɪnkoˈhɪrənts, -ˈhɛr-] *n* : incohérence *f* — **incoherent** [ˌɪnkoˈhɪrənt, -ˈhɛr-] *adj* : incohérent

income [ˈɪnˌkʌm] *n* : revenu *m* — **income tax** *n* : impôt *m* sur le revenu

incomparable [ɪnˈkɑmpərəbəl] *adj* : incomparable

incompatible [ˌɪnkəmˈpætəbəl] *adj* : incompatible — **incompatibility** [ˌɪnkəmˌpætəˈbɪləti] *n* : incompatibilité *f*

incompetent [ɪnˈkɑmpətənt] *adj* : incompétent — **incompetence** [ɪnˈkɑmpətənts] *n* : incompétence *f*

incomplete [ˌɪnkəmˈpliːt] *adj* : incomplet, inachevé

incomprehensible [ˌɪnˌkɑmpriˈhɛntsəbəl] *adj* : incompréhensible

inconceivable [ˌɪnkənˈsiːvəbəl] *adj* : inconcevable

inconclusive [ˌɪnkənˈkluːsɪv] *adj* : peu concluant

incongruous [ɪnˈkɑŋgruəs] *adj* : incongru

inconsiderate [ˌɪnkənˈsɪdərət] *adj* **1** THOUGHTLESS : inconsidéré **2** be ～ **to-ward** : manquer d'égards envers

inconsistent [ˌɪnkənˈsɪstənt] *adj* **1** ERRATIC : changeant **2** CONTRADICTORY : contradictoire — **inconsistency** [ˌɪnkənˈsɪstəntsi] *n, pl* **-cies** : incohérence *f*, contradiction *f*

inconspicuous [ˌɪnkənˈspɪkjuəs] *adj* : qui passe inaperçu

inconvenience [ˌɪnkənˈviːnjənts] *n* **1** BOTHER : dérangement *m* **2** DISADVANTAGE : inconvénient *m* — ～ *vt* **-nienced; -niencing** : déranger — **inconvenient** [ˌɪnkənˈviːnjənt] *adj* : incommode

incorporate [ɪnˈkɔrpəˌreɪt] *vt* **-rated; -rating** : incorporer

incorrect [ˌɪnkəˈrɛkt] *adj* : incorrect

increase [ˈɪnˌkriːs, ɪnˈkriːs] *n* : augmentation *f* — ～ [ɪnˈkriːs, ˈɪnˌkriːs] *v* **-creased; -creasing** : augmenter — **increasingly** [ɪnˈkriːsɪŋli] *adv* : de plus en plus

incredible [ɪnˈkrɛdəbəl] *adj* : incroyable

incredulous [ɪnˈkrɛdʒələs] *adj* : incrédule

incriminate [ɪnˈkrɪməˌneɪt] *vt* **-nated; -nating** : incriminer

incubator [ˈɪŋkjuˌbeɪtər, -ˌɪn-] *n* : incubateur *m*, couveuse *f*

incumbent [ɪnˈkʌmbənt] *n* : titulaire *mf*

incur [ɪnˈkər] *vt* **-curred; -curring** : encourir (une pénalité, etc.), contracter (une dette)

incurable [ɪnˈkjurəbəl] *adj* : incurable

indebted [ɪnˈdɛtəd] *adj* ～ **to** : redevable à

indecent [ɪnˈdiːsənt] *adj* : indécent — **indecency** [ɪnˈdiːsəntsi] *n, pl* **-cies** : indécence *f*

indecisive [ˌɪndɪˈsaɪsɪv] *adj* : indécis

indeed [ɪnˈdiːd] *adv* : vraiment, en effet

indefinite [ɪnˈdɛfənət] *adj* **1** : indéfini **2** VAGUE : imprécis — **indefinitely** [ɪnˈdɛfənətli] *adv* : indéfiniment

indelible [ɪnˈdɛləbəl] *adj* : indélébile

indent [ɪnˈdɛnt] *vt* : mettre en alinéa — **indentation** [ˌɪnˌdɛnˈteɪʃən] *n* DENT, NOTCH : creux *m*, bosse *f*

independent [ˌɪndəˈpɛndənt] *adj* : indépendant — **independence** [ˌɪndəˈpɛndənts] *n* : indépendance *f* — **independently** [ˌɪndəˈpɛndəntli] *adv* : de façon indépendante

indescribable [ˌɪndɪˈskraɪbəbəl] *adj* : indescriptible

indestructible [ˌɪndɪˈstrʌktəbəl] *adj* : indestructible

index [ˈɪnˌdɛks] *n, pl* **-dexes** *or* **-dices** [ˈɪndəˌsiːz] **1** : index *m* (d'un livre, etc.) **2**

INDICATOR : indice *m* **3** *or* ～ **finger** : index *m* — ～ *vt* : classer

Indian [ˈɪndiən] *adj* : indien

indication [ˌɪndəˈkeɪʃən] *n* : indication *f* — **indicate** [ˈɪndəˌkeɪt] *vt* **-cated; -cating** : indiquer — **indicative** [ɪnˈdɪkətɪv] *adj* : indicatif *m* — **indicator** [ˈɪndəˌkeɪtər] *n* : indicateur *m*

indict [ɪnˈdaɪt] *vt* : inculper — **indictment** [ɪnˈdaɪtmənt] *n* : inculpation *f*

indifferent [ɪnˈdɪfrənt, -ˈdɪfə-] *adj* **1** UNCONCERNED : indifférent **2** MEDIOCRE : médiocre — **indifference** [ɪnˈdɪfrənts, -ˈdɪfə-] *n* : indifférence *f*

indigenous [ɪnˈdɪdʒənəs] *adj* : indigène

indigestion [ˌɪndaɪˈdʒɛstʃən, -dɪ-] *n* : indigestion *f* — **indigestible** [ˌɪndaɪˈdʒɛstəbəl, -dɪ-] *adj* : indigeste

indignation [ˌɪndɪgˈneɪʃən] *n* : indignation *f* — **indignant** [ɪnˈdɪgnənt] *adj* : indigné — **indignity** [ɪnˈdɪgnəti] *n, pl* **-ties** : indignité *f*

indigo [ˈɪndɪˌgoː] *n, pl* **-gos** *or* **-goes** : indigo *m*

indirect [ˌɪndəˈrɛkt, -daɪ-] *adj* : indirect

indiscreet [ˌɪndɪˈskriːt] *adj* : indiscret — **indiscretion** [ˌɪndɪˈskrɛʃən] *n* : indiscrétion *f*

indiscriminate [ˌɪndɪˈskrɪmənət] *adj* **1** : sans discernement **2** RANDOM : fait au hasard

indispensable [ˌɪndɪˈspɛntsəbəl] *adj* : indispensable

indisputable [ˌɪndɪˈspjuːtəbəl] *adj* : incontestable

indistinct [ˌɪndɪˈstɪŋkt] *adj* : indistinct

individual [ˌɪndəˈvɪdʒuəl] *adj* **1** : individuel **2** SPECIFIC : particulier — *n* : individu *m* — **individuality** [ˌɪndəˌvɪdʒuˈæləti] *n, pl* **-ties** : individualité *f* — **individually** [ˌɪndəˈvɪdʒuəli, -dʒəli] *adv* : individuellement

indoctrinate [ɪnˈdɑktrəˌneɪt] *vt* **-nated; -nating** : endoctriner — **indoctrination** [ɪnˌdɑktrəˈneɪʃən] *n* : endoctrinement *m*

Indonesian [ˌɪndoˈniːʒən, -ʃən] *adj* : indonésien — ～ *n* : indonésien *m* (langue)

indoor [ˈɪnˌdor] *adj* **1** : d'intérieur **2** ～ **pool** : piscine *f* couverte **3** ～ **sports** : sports *mpl* pratiqués en salle — **indoors** [ˈɪnˈdorz] *adv* : à l'intérieur

induce [ɪnˈduːs, -ˈdjuːs] *vt* **-duced; -ducing** **1** PERSUADE : induire **2** CAUSE : provoquer — **inducement** [ɪnˈduːsmənt, -ˈdjuːs-] *n* : encouragement *m*

indulge [ɪnˈdʌldʒ] *v* **-dulged; -dulging** *vt* **1** GRATIFY : céder à **2** PAMPER : gâter — *vi* ～ **in** : se permettre — **indulgence** [ɪnˈdʌldʒənts] *n* : indulgence *f* — **indulgent** [ɪnˈdʌldʒənt] *adj* : indulgent

industrial [ɪnˈdʌstriəl] *adj* : industriel — **industrialize** [ɪnˈdʌstriəˌlaɪz] *vt* **-ized; -izing** : industrialiser — **industrious** [ɪnˈdʌstriəs] *adj* : industrieux, travailleur — **industry** ['ɪndəstri] *n, pl* **-tries** : industrie *f*

inebriated [ɪ'ni:bri,eɪtəd] *adj* : ivre

inedible [ɪ'nɛdəbəl] *adj* : immangeable

ineffective [,ɪnɪ'fɛktɪv] *adj* : inefficace — **ineffectual** [,ɪnɪ'fɛktʃuəl] *adj* : inefficace

inefficient [,ɪnɪ'fɪʃənt] *adj* **1** : inefficace **2** INCOMPETENT : incompétent — **inefficiency** [,ɪnɪ'fɪʃənsi] *n, pl* **-cies** : inefficacité *f*

ineligible [ɪn'ɛlədʒəbəl] *adj* : inéligible

inept [ɪ'nɛpt] *adj* : inepte

inequality [,ɪnɪ'kwɑləti] *n, pl* **-ties** : inégalité *f*

inert [ɪ'nərt] *adj* : inerte — **inertia** [ɪ'nərʃə] *n* : inertie *f*

inescapable [,ɪnɪ'skeɪpəbəl] *adj* : inéluctable

inevitable [ɪn'ɛvətəbəl] *adj* : inévitable — **inevitably** [-bli] *adv* : inévitablement

inexcusable [,ɪnɪk'skju:zəbəl] *adj* : inexcusable

inexpensive [,ɪnɪk'spɛntsɪv] *adj* : pas cher, bon marché

inexperienced [,ɪnɪk'spɪriəntst] *adj* : inexpérimenté

inexplicable [,ɪnɪk'splɪkəbəl] *adj* : inexplicable

infallible [ɪn'fæləbəl] *adj* : infaillible

infamous ['ɪnfəməs] *adj* : infâme, notoire

infancy ['ɪnfənsi] *n, pl* **-cies** : petite enfance *f* — **infant** ['ɪnfənt] *n* : petit enfant *m*, petite enfant *f*; nourrisson *m* — **infantile** ['ɪnfən,taɪl, -təl, -,ti:l] *adj* : infantile

infantry ['ɪnfəntri] *n, pl* **-tries** : infanterie *f*

infatuated [ɪn'fætʃu,eɪtəd] *adj* **be ~ with** : être épris de — **infatuation** [ɪn,fætʃu'eɪʃən] *n* : engouement *m*

infect [ɪn'fɛkt] *vt* : infecter — **infection** [ɪn'fɛkʃən] *n* : infection *f* — **infectious** [ɪn'fɛkʃəs] *adj* : infectieux, contagieux

infer [ɪn'fər] *vt* **-ferred; -ferring** : déduire — **inference** ['ɪnfərənts] *n* : déduction *f*

inferior [ɪn'fɪriər] *adj* : inférieur — ~ *n* : inférieur *m*, -rieure *f* — **inferiority** [ɪn,fɪri'ɔrəti] *n, pl* **-ties** : infériorité *f*

infernal [ɪn'fərnəl] *adj* : infernal — **inferno** [ɪn'fər,no:] *n, pl* **-nos** : brasier *m*

infertile [ɪn'fərtəl, -,taɪl] *adj* **1** : infertile **2** STERILE : stérile — **infertility** [,ɪnfər'tɪləti] *n* : infertilité *f*

infest [ɪn'fɛst] *vt* : infester

infidelity [,ɪnfə'dɛləti, -faɪ-] *n, pl* **-ties** : infidélité *f*

infiltrate [ɪn'fɪl,treɪt, 'ɪnfɪl-] *v* **-trated; -trating** *vt* : infiltrer — *vi* : s'infiltrer

infinite ['ɪnfənət] *adj* : infini — **infinitive** [ɪn'fɪnətɪv] *n* : infinitif *m* — **infinity** [ɪn'fɪnəti] *n, pl* **-ties** : infinité *f*

infirm [ɪn'fərm] *adj* : infirme — **infirmary** [ɪn'fərməri] *n, pl* **-ries** : infirmerie *f* — **infirmity** [ɪn'fərməti] *n, pl* **-ties** : infirmité *f*

inflame [ɪn'fleɪm] *v* **-flamed; -flaming** *vt* : enflammer — *vi* : s'enflammer — **inflammable** [ɪn'flæməbəl] *adj* : (in)flammable — **inflammation** [,ɪnflə'meɪʃən] *n* : inflammation *f* — **inflammatory** [ɪn'flæmə,tori] *adj* : incendiaire

inflate [ɪn'fleɪt] *v* **-flated; -flating** *vt* : gonfler — *vi* : se gonfler — **inflatable** [ɪn'fleɪtəbəl] *adj* : gonflable — **inflation** [ɪn'fleɪʃən] *n* : inflation *f* — **inflationary** [ɪn'fleɪʃə,nɛri] *adj* : inflationniste

inflexible [ɪn'flɛksɪbəl] *adj* : inflexible

inflict [ɪn'flɪkt] *vt* : infliger

influence ['ɪn,flu:ənts, ɪn'flu:ənts] *n* **1** : influence *f* **2 under the ~ of** : sous l'effet de — ~ *vt* **-enced; -encing** : influencer, influer sur — **influential** [,ɪnflu'ɛntʃəl] *adj* : influent

influenza [,ɪnflu'ɛnzə] *n* : grippe *f*

influx ['ɪn,flʌks] *n* : afflux *m*

inform [ɪn'fɔrm] *vt* : informer, renseigner — *vi* ~ **on** : dénoncer

informal [ɪn'fɔrməl] *adj* **1** : simple **2** CASUAL : familier, décontracté **3** UNOFFICIAL : officieux — **informally** [ɪn'fɔrməli] *adv* : sans cérémonie, simplement

information [,ɪnfər'meɪʃən] *n* : renseignements *mpl*, information *f* — **informative** [ɪn'fɔrmətɪv] *adj* : informatif — **informer** [ɪn'fɔrmər] *n* : indicateur *m*, -trice *f*

infrared [,ɪnfrə'rɛd] *adj* : infrarouge

infrastructure ['ɪnfrə,strʌktʃər] *n* : infrastructure *f*

infrequent [ɪn'fri:kwənt] *adj* : rare, peu fréquent — **infrequently** [ɪn'fri:kwəntli] *adv* : rarement

infringe [ɪn'frɪndʒ] *v* **-fringed; -fringing** *vt* : enfreindre — *vi* ~ **on** : empiéter sur — **infringement** [ɪn'frɪndʒmənt] *n* : infraction *f* (à la loi)

infuriate [ɪn'fjuri,eɪt] *vt* **-ated; -ating** : rendre furieux — **infuriating** [ɪn'fjuri,eɪtɪŋ] *adj* : exaspérant

infuse [ɪn'fju:z] *vt* **-fused; -fusing** : infuser — **infusion** [ɪn'fju:ʒən] *n* : infusion *f*

ingenious [ɪn'dʒi:njəs] *adj* : ingénieux — **ingenuity** [,ɪndʒə'nu:əti, -'nju:-] *n, pl* **-ties** : ingéniosité *f*

ingenuous [ɪn'dʒɛnjuəs] *adj* : ingénu, naïf

ingot ['ɪŋgət] *n* : lingot *m*

ingrained [ɪn'greɪnd] *adj* : enraciné

ingratiate [ɪn'greɪʃi,eɪt] *vt* **-ated; -ating** ~ **oneself with** : gagner les bonnes grâces de

ingratitude [ɪn'grætə,tu:d, -'tju:d] *n* : ingratitude *f*

ingredient [ɪn'gri:diənt] *n* : ingrédient *m*

inhabit [ɪn'hæbət] *vt* : habiter — **inhabitant** [ɪn'hæbətənt] *n* : habitant *m*, -tante *f*

inhale [ɪn'heɪl] v -haled; -haling vt : inhaler, respirer — vi : inspirer

inherent [ɪn'hɪrənt, -'hɛr-] adj : inhérent — **inherently** [ɪn'hɪrəntli, -'hɛr-] adv : fondamentalement

inherit [ɪn'hɛrət] vt : hériter de — **inheritance** [ɪn'hɛrəṭənts] n : héritage m

inhibit [ɪn'hɪbət] vt IMPEDE : entraver, gêner — **inhibition** [ˌɪnhə'bɪʃən, ˌɪnə-] n : inhibition f

inhuman [ɪn'hju:mən, -'ju:-] adj : inhumain — **inhumane** [ˌɪnhju'meɪn, -ju-] adj : cruel — **inhumanity** [ˌɪnhju'mænəṭi, -ju-] n, pl -ties : inhumanité f

initial [ɪ'nɪʃəl] adj : initial, premier — ~ n : initiale f — ~ vt -tialed or -tialled; -tialing or -tialling : parapher — **initially** [ɪ'nɪʃəli] adv : au départ

initiate [ɪ'nɪʃiˌeɪt] vt -ated; -ating 1 BEGIN : amorcer, entreprendre 2 ~ into : initier à — **initiation** [ɪˌnɪʃi'eɪʃən] n : initiation f — **initiative** [ɪ'nɪʃəṭɪv] n : initiative f

inject [ɪn'ʤɛkt] vt : injecter — **injection** [ɪn-'ʤɛkʃən] n : injection f

injure ['ɪnʤər] vt -jured; -juring 1 WOUND : blesser 2 HARM : nuire à 3 ~ oneself : se blesser — **injury** ['ɪnʤəri] n, pl -ries 1 WOUND : blessure f 2 WRONG : tort m

injustice [ɪn'ʤʌstəs] n : injustice f

ink ['ɪŋk] n : encre f — **inkwell** ['ɪŋk,wɛl] n : encrier m

inland ['ɪn,lænd, -lənd] adj : intérieur — ~ adv : à l'intérieur, vers l'intérieur

in–laws ['ɪn,lɔz] npl : beaux-parents mpl

inlet ['ɪn,lɛt, -lət] n : bras m de mer

inmate ['ɪn,meɪt] n 1 PRISONER : détenu m, -nue f 2 PATIENT : interné m, -née f

inn ['ɪn] n : auberge f

innards ['ɪnərdz] npl : entrailles fpl

innate [ɪ'neɪt] adj : inné

inner ['ɪnər] adj : intérieur, interne — **innermost** ['ɪnər,mo:st] adj : le plus profond

inning ['ɪnɪŋ] n : tour m de batte, manche f Can (au baseball)

innocence ['ɪnəsənts] n : innocence f — **innocent** ['ɪnəsənt] adj : innocent — ~ n : innocent m, -cente f

innocuous [ɪ'nɑkjəwəs] adj : inoffensif

innovate ['ɪnə,veɪt] v -vated; -vating : innover — **innovation** [ˌɪnə'veɪʃən] n : innovation f — **innovative** ['ɪnə,veɪṭɪv] adj : innovateur — **innovator** ['ɪnə,veɪṭər] n : innovateur m, -trice f

innumerable [ɪ'nu:mərəbəl, -'nju:-] adj : innombrable

inoculate [ɪ'nɑkjə,leɪt] vt -lated; -lating : inoculer — **inoculation** [ɪ,nɑkjə'leɪʃən] n : inoculation f

inoffensive [ˌɪnə'fɛntsɪv] adj : inoffensif

inpatient ['ɪn,peɪʃənt] n : malade m hospitalisé, malade f hospitalisée

input ['ɪn,pʊt] n 1 : contribution f 2 : entrée f (de données) — ~ vt -putted or -put; -putting : entrer (des données)

inquire [ɪn'kwaɪr] v -quired; -quiring vt : demander — vi 1 ~ about : se renseigner sur 2 ~ into : enquêter sur — **inquiry** [ɪn-'kwaɪri, 'ɪn,kwaɪri; 'ɪnkwəri, 'ɪŋ-] n, pl -ries 1 QUESTION : demande f 2 INVESTIGATION : enquête f — **inquisition** [ˌɪnkwə-'zɪʃən, ˌɪŋ-] n : inquisition f — **inquisitive** [ɪn'kwɪzəṭɪv] adj : curieux

insane [ɪn'seɪn] adj : fou — **insanity** [ɪn-'sænəṭi] n, pl -ties : folie f

insatiable [ɪn'seɪʃəbəl] adj : insatiable

inscribe [ɪn'skraɪb] vt -scribed; -scribing 1 : inscrire 2 DEDICATE : dédicacer — **inscription** [ɪn'skrɪpʃən] n : inscription f

inscrutable [ɪn'skru:ṭəbəl] adj : impénétrable

insect ['ɪn,sɛkt] n : insecte m — **insecticide** [ɪn'sɛktə,saɪd] n : insecticide m

insecure [ˌɪnsɪ'kjʊr] adj 1 UNSAFE : peu sûr 2 FEARFUL : anxieux — **insecurity** [ˌɪnsɪ-'kjʊrəṭi] n, pl -ties : insécurité f

insensitive [ɪn'sɛntsəṭɪv] adj : insensible — **insensitivity** [ɪn,sɛntsə'tɪvəṭi] n : insensibilité f

inseparable [ɪn'sɛpərəbəl] adj : inséparable

insert [ɪn'sərt] vt : insérer, introduire

inside [ɪn'saɪd, 'ɪn,saɪd] n 1 : intérieur m 2 ~s npl GUTS : entrailles fpl — ~ adv 1 : à l'intérieur 2 ~ out : à l'envers — ~ adj : intérieur — ~ prep : à l'intérieur de

insidious [ɪn'sɪdiəs] adj : insidieux

insight ['ɪn,saɪt] n : perspicacité f — **insightful** [ɪn'saɪtfəl] adj : perspicace

insignia [ɪn'sɪgniə] or **insigne** [-,ni:] n, pl -nia or -nias : insigne(s) m(pl)

insignificant [ˌɪnsɪg'nɪfɪkənt] adj : insignifiant

insincere [ˌɪnsɪn'sɪr] adj : pas sincère

insinuate [ɪn'sɪnjuˌeɪt] vt -ated; -ating : insinuer — **insinuation** [ɪn,sɪnju'eɪʃən] n : insinuation f

insipid [ɪn'sɪpəd] adj : insipide

insist [ɪn'sɪst] v : insister — **insistent** [ɪn-'sɪstənt] adj : insistant

insofar as [ˌɪnso'fɑræz] conj : dans la mesure où

insole ['ɪn,so:l] n : semelle f (intérieure)

insolence ['ɪntsələnts] n : insolence f — **insolent** ['ɪntsələnt] adj : insolent

insolvent [ɪn'sɑlvənt] adj : insolvable

insomnia [ɪn'sɑmniə] n : insomnie f

inspect [ɪn'spɛkt] vt : examiner, inspecter — **inspection** [ɪn'spɛkʃən] n : inspection f — **inspector** [ɪn'spɛktər] n : inspecteur m, -trice f

inspire [ɪn'spaɪr] *vt* **-spired; -spiring** : inspirer — **inspiration** [ˌɪnspə'reɪʃən] *n* : inspiration *f* — **inspirational** [ˌɪnspə'reɪʃənəl] *adj* : inspirant

instability [ˌɪnstə'bɪlətɪ] *n* : instabilité *f*

install [ɪn'stɔl] *vt* **-stalled; -stalling** : installer — **installation** [ˌɪnstɔ'leɪʃən] *n* : installation *f* — **installment** [ɪn'stɔlmənt] *n* **1** PAYMENT : versement *m*, acompte *m* **2** : épisode *m* (d'un feuilleton)

instance ['ɪnstənts] *n* **1** : cas *m*, exemple *m* **2 for ~** : par exemple

instant ['ɪnstənt] *n* : instant *m*, moment *m* — **~** *adj* **1** IMMEDIATE : immédiat, instantané **2 ~ coffee** : café *m* instantané — **instantaneous** [ˌɪnstən'teɪniəs] *adj* : instantané — **instantly** ['ɪnstəntli] *adv* : immédiatement, sur-le-champ

instead [ɪn'stɛd] *adv* **1** : plutôt **2 I went ~** : j'y suis allé à sa place — **instead of** *prep* : au lieu de, à la place de

instep ['ɪnˌstɛp] *n* : cou-de-pied *m*

instigate ['ɪnstəˌgeɪt] *vt* **-gated; -gating** : engager, provoquer — **instigation** [ˌɪnstə'geɪʃən] *n* : instigation *f* — **instigator** ['ɪnstəˌgeɪtər] *n* : instigateur *m*, -trice *f*

instill *or Brit* **instil** [ɪn'stɪl] *vt* **-stilled; -stilling** : inculquer

instinct ['ɪnˌstɪŋkt] *n* : instinct *m* — **instinctive** [ɪn'stɪŋktɪv] *or* **instinctual** [ɪn'stɪŋktʃʊəl] *adj* : instinctif

institute ['ɪnstəˌtuːt, -ˌtjuːt] *vt* **-tuted; -tuting** : instituer — **~** *n* : institut *m* — **institution** [ˌɪnstə'tuːʃən, -'tjuː-] *n* : institution *f*

instruct [ɪn'strʌkt] *vt* **1** TEACH : instruire **2** DIRECT : charger — **instruction** [ɪn'strʌkʃən] *n* : instruction *f* — **instructor** [ɪn'strʌktər] *n* : moniteur *m*, -trice *f*

instrument ['ɪnstrəmənt] *n* : instrument *m* — **instrumental** [ˌɪnstrə'mɛntəl] *adj* **1** : instrumental **2 be ~ in** : contribuer à

insufferable [ɪn'sʌfərəbəl] *adj* : insupportable

insufficient [ˌɪnsə'fɪʃənt] *adj* : insuffisant

insular ['ɪnsʊlər, -sjʊ-] *adj* **1** : insulaire **2** NARROW-MINDED : borné

insulate ['ɪnsəˌleɪt] *vt* **-lated; -lating** : isoler — **insulation** [ˌɪnsə'leɪʃən] *n* : isolation *f*

insulin ['ɪnsələn] *n* : insuline *f*

insult [ɪn'sʌlt] *vt* : insulter — **~** ['ɪnˌsʌlt] *n* : insulte *f*, injure *f*

insure [ɪn'ʃʊr] *vt* **-sured; -suring** : assurer — **insurance** [ɪn'ʃʊrənts] *n* : assurance *f*

insurmountable [ˌɪnsər'maʊntəbəl] *adj* : insurmontable

intact [ɪn'tækt] *adj* : intact

intake ['ɪnˌteɪk] *n* **1** : consommation *f* (de nourriture) **2** ADMISSION : admission *f*

intangible [ɪn'tændʒəbəl] *adj* : intangible

integral ['ɪntɪgrəl] *adj* **1** : intégral **2 be an ~ part of** : faire partie intégrante de

integrate ['ɪntəˌgreɪt] *v* **-grated; -grating** *vt* : intégrer — *vi* : s'intégrer

integrity [ɪn'tɛgrətɪ] *n* : intégrité *f*

intellect ['ɪntəˌlɛkt] *n* : intelligence *f* — **intellectual** [ˌɪntə'lɛktʃʊəl] *adj* : intellectuel — **~** *n* : intellectuel *m*, -tuelle *f* — **intelligence** [ɪn'tɛlədʒənts] *n* : intelligence *f* — **intelligent** [ɪn'tɛlədʒənt] *adj* : intelligent — **intelligible** [ɪn'tɛlədʒəbəl] *adj* : intelligible

intend [ɪn'tɛnd] *vt* **1 be ~ed for** : être destiné à **2 ~ to** : avoir l'intention de — **intended** [ɪn'tɛndəd] *adj* **1** PLANNED : voulu **2** INTENTIONAL : intentionnel

intense [ɪn'tɛnts] *adj* : intense — **intensely** [ɪn'tɛntsli] *adv* **1** : intensément **2** EXTREMELY : extrêmement — **intensify** [ɪn'tɛntsəˌfaɪ] *v* **-fied; -fying** *vt* : intensifier — *vi* : s'intensifier — **intensity** [ɪn'tɛntsətɪ] *n*, *pl* **-ties** : intensité *f* — **intensive** [ɪn'tɛntsɪv] *adj* : intensif

intent [ɪn'tɛnt] *n* : intention *f* — **~** *adj* **1** : absorbé, attentif **2 ~ on doing** : résolu à faire — **intention** [ɪn'tɛntʃən] *n* : intention *f* — **intentional** [ɪn'tɛntʃənəl] *adj* : intentionnel — **intently** [ɪn'tɛntli] *adv* : attentivement

interact [ˌɪntər'ækt] *vi* **1** : agir l'un sur l'autre **2 ~ with** : communiquer avec — **interaction** [ˌɪntər'ækʃən] *n* : interaction *f*

intercede [ˌɪntər'siːd] *vi* **-ceded; -ceding** : intercéder

intercept [ˌɪntər'sɛpt] *vt* : intercepter

interchange [ˌɪntər'tʃeɪndʒ] *vt* **-changed; -changing** EXCHANGE : échanger — **~** *n* ['ɪntərˌtʃeɪndʒ] **1** EXCHANGE : échange *m* **2** JUNCTION : échangeur *m* — **interchangeable** [ˌɪntər'tʃeɪndʒəbəl] *adj* : interchangeable

intercourse ['ɪntərˌkors] *n* : rapports *mpl* (sexuels)

interest ['ɪntrəst, -təˌrɛst] *n* : intérêt *m* — **~** *vt* : intéresser — **interesting** ['ɪntrəstɪŋ, -təˌrɛstɪŋ] *adj* : intéressant

interface ['ɪntərˌfeɪs] *n* : interface *f*

interfere [ˌɪntər'fɪr] *vi* **-fered; -fering 1** INTERVENE : intervenir **2 ~ in** : s'immiscer dans — **interference** [ˌɪntər'fɪrənts] *n* **1** : ingérence *f* **2** : interférence *f*, parasites *mpl* (à la radio, etc.)

interim ['ɪntərəm] *n* **1** : intérim *m* **2 in the ~** : entre-temps — **~** *adj* : provisoire

interior [ɪn'tɪriər] *adj* : intérieur — **~** *n* : intérieur *m*

interjection [ˌɪntər'dʒɛkʃən] *n* : interjection *f*

interlock [ˌɪntər'lɑk] *vi* : s'enclencher

intermediate [ˌɪntər'miːdiət] *adj* : intermédiaire — **intermediary** [ˌɪntər'miːdiˌɛri] *n*, *pl* **-aries** : intermédiaire *mf*

interminable [ɪn'tərmᵊnəbəl] *adj* : interminable

intermission [ˌɪntər'mɪʃən] *n* **1** : pause *f* **2** : entracte *m* (au théâtre)

intermittent [ˌɪntər'mɪtᵊnt] *adj* : intermittent

intern[1] ['ɪn,tərn, ɪn'tərn] *vt* CONFINE : interner

intern[2] ['ɪn,tərn] *n* : stagiaire *mf*

internal [ɪn'tərnᵊl] *adj* : interne — **internally** [ɪn'tərnᵊli] *adv* : intérieurement

international [ˌɪntər'næʃənᵊl] *adj* : international

Internet ['ɪntər,nɛt] *n* : Internet *m*

interpret [ɪn'tərprət] *vt* : interpréter — **interpretation** [ɪn,tərprə'teɪʃən] *n* : interprétation *f* — **interpreter** [ɪn'tərprətər] *n* : interprète *mf*

interrogate [ɪn'tɛrə,geɪt] *vt* **-gated; -gating** : interroger — **interrogation** [ɪn,tɛrə'geɪʃən] *n* QUESTIONING : interrogatoire *m* — **interrogative** [ˌɪntə'rɑgətɪv] *adj* : interrogatif

interrupt [ˌɪntə'rʌpt] *v* : interrompre — **interruption** [ˌɪntə'rʌpʃən] *n* : interruption *f*

intersect [ˌɪntər'sɛkt] *vt* : croiser, couper — *vi* : se croiser, se couper — **intersection** [ˌɪntər'sɛkʃən] *n* JUNCTION : croisement *m*, carrefour *m*

intersperse [ˌɪntər'spərs] *vt* **-spersed; -spersing** ~ **with** : parsemer de

interstate ['ɪntər,steɪt] *n or* ~ **highway** : autoroute *f*

intertwine [ˌɪntər'twaɪn] *vi* **-twined; -twining** : s'entrelacer

interval ['ɪntərvəl] *n* : intervalle *m*

intervene [ˌɪntər'viːn] *vi* **-vened; -vening** **1** : intervenir **2** HAPPEN : survenir — **intervention** [ˌɪntər'vɛntʃən] *n* : intervention *f*

interview ['ɪntər,vjuː] *n* **1** : entretien *m*, entrevue *f* **2** : interview *f* (à la télévision, etc.) — ~ *vt* **1** : faire passer une entrevue (pour un emploi) **2** : interviewer (à la télévision, etc.)

intestine [ɪn'tɛstən] *n* : intestin *m* — **intestinal** [ɪn'tɛstənᵊl] *adj* : intestinal

intimate[1] ['ɪntə,meɪt] *vt* **-mated; -mating** : laisser entendre

intimate[2] ['ɪntəmət] *adj* : intime — **intimacy** ['ɪntəməsi] *n, pl* **-cies** : intimité *f*

intimidate [ɪn'tɪmə,deɪt] *vt* **-dated; -dating** : intimider — **intimidation** [ɪn,tɪmə'deɪʃən] *n* : intimidation *f*

into ['ɪn,tuː] *prep* **1** : en, dans **2 bump** ~ : se cogner contre **3** (*used in mathematics*) **4** ~ **12 is 3** : 12 divisé par 4 fait 3

intolerable [ɪn'tɑlərəbəl] *adj* : intolérable — **intolerance** [ɪn'tɑlərənts] *n* : intolérance *f* — **intolerant** [ɪn'tɑlərənt] *adj* : intolérant

intoxicate [ɪn'tɑksə,keɪt] *vt* **-cated; -cating**

: enivrer — **intoxicated** [ɪn'tɑksə,keɪtəd] *adj* : ivre

intransitive [ɪn'træntsətɪv, -'trænzə-] *adj* : intransitif

intravenous [ˌɪntrə'viːnəs] *adj* : intraveineux

intrepid [ɪn'trepəd] *adj* : intrépide

intricate ['ɪntrɪkət] *adj* : compliqué — **intricacy** ['ɪntrɪkəsi] *n, pl* **-cies** : complexité *f*

intrigue ['ɪn,triːg, ɪn'triːg] *n* : intrigue *f* — ~ [ɪn'triːg] *v* **-trigued; -triguing** : intriguer — **intriguing** [ɪn'triːgɪŋ] *adj* : fascinant

intrinsic [ɪn'trɪnzɪk, -'trɪntsɪk] *adj* : intrinsèque

introduce [ˌɪntrə'duːs, -'djuːs] *vt* **-duced; -ducing** **1** : introduire **2** PRESENT : présenter — **introduction** [ˌɪntrə'dʌkʃən] *n* **1** : introduction *f* **2** PRESENTATION : présentation *f* — **introductory** [ˌɪntrə'dʌktəri] *adj* : d'introduction, préliminaire

introvert ['ɪntrə,vərt] *n* : introverti *m*, -tie *f* — **introverted** ['ɪntrə,vərtəd] *adj* : introverti

intrude [ɪn'truːd] *vi* **-truded; -truding** : déranger, s'imposer — **intruder** [ɪn'truːdər] *n* : intrus *m*, -truse *f* — **intrusion** [ɪn'truːʒən] *n* : intrusion *f* — **intrusive** [ɪn'truːsɪv] *adj* : importun, gênant

intuition [ˌɪntu'ɪʃən, -tju-] *n* : intuition *f* — **intuitive** [ɪn'tuːətɪv, -'tjuː-] *adj* : intuitif

inundate ['ɪnən,deɪt] *vt* **-dated; -dating** : inonder

invade [ɪn'veɪd] *vt* **-vaded; -vading** : envahir

invalid[1] [ɪn'væləd] *adj* : non valide, non valable

invalid[2] ['ɪnvələd] *n* : infirme *mf*, invalide *mf*

invaluable [ɪn'væljəbəl, -'væljuə-] *adj* : inestimable, précieux

invariable [ɪn'væriəbəl] *adj* : invariable

invasion [ɪn'veɪʒən] *n* : invasion *f*

invent [ɪn'vɛnt] *vt* : inventer — **invention** [ɪn'vɛntʃən] *n* : invention *f* — **inventive** [ɪn'vɛntɪv] *adj* : inventif — **inventor** [ɪn'vɛntər] *n* : inventeur *m*, -trice *f*

inventory ['ɪnvən,tɔri] *n, pl* **-ries** : inventaire *m*

invert [ɪn'vərt] *vt* : inverser, renverser

invertebrate [ɪn'vərtəbrət, -,breɪt] *adj* : invertébré — ~ *n* : invertébré *m*

invest [ɪn'vɛst] *v* : investir

investigate [ɪn'vɛstə,geɪt] *vt* **-gated; -gating** : enquêter sur, faire une enquête sur — **investigation** [ɪn,vɛstə'geɪʃən] *n* : investigation *f*, enquête *f*

investment [ɪn'vɛstmənt] *n* : investissement *m* — **investor** [ɪn'vɛstər] *n* : investisseur *m*, -seuse *f*

inveterate [ɪn'vɛtərət] *adj* : invétéré

invigorating [ɪn'vɪgə,reɪtɪŋ] *adj* : vivifiant, revigorant

invincible [ɪn'vɪntsəbəl] *adj* : invincible

invisible [ɪn'vɪzəbəl] *adj* : invisible
invitation [ˌɪnvə'teɪʃən] *n* : invitation *f* — **invite** [ɪn'vaɪt] *vt* **-vited; -viting** : inviter — **inviting** [ɪn'vaɪtɪŋ] *adj* : attrayant, engageant
invoice ['ɪnˌvɔɪs] *n* : facture *f*
invoke [ɪn'voːk] *vt* **-voked; -voking** : invoquer
involuntary [ɪn'vɑlənˌteri] *adj* : involontaire
involve [ɪn'vɑlv] *vt* **-volved; -volving** 1 ENTAIL : entraîner 2 CONCERN : concerner, toucher — **involved** [ɪn'vɑlvd] *adj* INTRICATE : complexe — **involvement** [ɪn'vɑlvmənt] *n* : participation *f*
invulnerable [ɪn'vʌlnərəbəl] *adj* : invulnérable
inward ['ɪnwərd] *adj* : intérieur — **~** *or* **inwards** ['ɪnwərdz] *adv* : vers l'intérieur
iodine ['aɪəˌdaɪn] *n* : iode *m*, teinture *f* d'iode
ion ['aɪən, 'aɪˌɑn] *n* : ion *m*
iota [aɪ'oːtə] *n* : brin *m*
IOU [ˌaɪˌoː'juː] *n* : reconnaissance *f* de dette
Iranian [ɪ'reɪniən, -'ræ-, -'rɑ-; aɪ'-] *adj* : iranien
Iraqi [ɪ'rɑki, -'ræ-] *adj* : irakien
irate [aɪ'reɪt] *adj* : furieux
iris ['aɪrəs] *n*, *pl* **irises** *or* **irides** ['aɪrəˌdiːz, 'ɪr-] : iris *m*
Irish ['aɪrɪʃ] *adj* : irlandais
irksome ['ərksəm] *adj* : irritant, agaçant
iron ['aɪərn] *n* 1 : fer *m* (métal) 2 : fer *m* à repasser — **~** *vt* PRESS : repasser — **ironing** ['aɪərnɪŋ] *n* : repassage *m*
irony ['aɪrəni] *n*, *pl* **-nies** : ironie *f* — **ironic** [aɪ'rɑnɪk] *or* **ironical** [-nɪkəl] *adj* : ironique
irrational [ɪ'ræʃənəl] *adj* : irrationnel
irreconcilable [ɪˌrekən'saɪləbəl] *adj* : irréconciliable, inconciliable
irrefutable [ˌɪrɪ'fjuːtəbəl, ɪr'rɛfjə-] *adj* : irréfutable
irregular [ɪ'regjələr] *adj* : irrégulier — **irregularity** [ɪˌregjə'lærəti] *n*, *pl* **-ties** : irrégularité *f*
irrelevant [ɪ'reləvənt] *adj* : sans rapport, non pertinent
irreparable [ɪ'repərəbəl] *adj* : irréparable
irreplaceable [ˌɪrɪ'pleɪsəbəl] *adj* : irremplaçable
irreproachable [ˌɪrɪ'proːtʃəbəl] *adj* : irréprochable
irresistible [ˌɪrɪ'zɪstəbəl] *adj* : irrésistible
irresolute [ɪ'rezəˌluːt] *adj* : irrésolu, indécis
irrespective of [ˌɪrɪ'spektɪvəv] *prep* : sans tenir compte de
irresponsible [ˌɪrɪ'spɑntsəbəl] *adj* : irresponsable — **irresponsibility** [ˌɪrɪˌspɑntsə'bɪləti] *n* : irresponsabilité *f*
irreverent [ɪ'revərənt] *adj* : irrévérencieux

irrigate ['ɪrəˌgeɪt] *vt* **-gated; -gating** : irriguer — **irrigation** [ˌɪrə'geɪʃən] *n* : irrigation *f*
irritate ['ɪrəˌteɪt] *vt* **-tated; -tating** : irriter **irritable** ['ɪrətəbəl] *adj* : irritable — **irritating** ['ɪrəˌteɪtɪŋ] *adj* : irritant, agaçant — **irritation** [ˌɪrə'teɪʃən] *n* : irritation *f*
is → **be**
Islam [ɪs'lɑm, ɪz-, -'læm; 'ɪsˌlɑm, 'ɪz-] *n* : islam *m* — **Islamic** [-mɪk] *adj* : islamique
island ['aɪlənd] *n* : île *f* — **isle** ['aɪl] *n* : île *f*, îlot *m*
isolate ['aɪsəˌleɪt] *vt* **-lated; -lating** : isoler — **isolation** [ˌaɪsə'leɪʃən] *n* : isolement *m*
Israeli [ɪz'reɪli] *adj* : israélien
issue ['ɪˌʃuː] *n* 1 MATTER : question *f*, problème *m* 2 : publication *f* (d'un livre), émission *f* (de timbres, etc.) 3 : numéro *m* (d'une revue, etc.) 4 **make an ~ of** : faire des histoires de — **~** *v* **-sued; -suing** *vt* 1 : émettre (un chèque, etc.), distribuer (des provisions, etc.), donner (un ordre) 2 PUBLISH : publier, sortir — *vi* **~ from** : provenir de
isthmus ['ɪsməs] *n* : isthme *m*
it ['ɪt] *pron* 1 (*as subject*) : il, elle 2 (*as direct object*) : le, la, l' 3 (*as indirect object*) : lui 4 (*as a nonspecific subject*) : ce, cela, ça 5 **it's snowing** : il neige 6 **that's ~** : c'est ça 7 **who is ~ ?** : qui c'est?
Italian [ɪ'tæliən, aɪ-] *adj* : italien — **~** *n* : italien *m* (langue)
italics [ɪ'tælɪks] *npl* : italique *m*
itch ['ɪtʃ] *n* : démangeaison *f* — **~** *vi* : avoir des démangeaisons — **itchy** ['ɪtʃi] *adj* **itchier; -est** : qui démange
it'd ['ɪtəd] (*contraction of* **it had** *or* **it would**) → **have, would**
item ['aɪtəm] *n* 1 : article *m*, chose *f* 2 : point *m* (d'un ordre du jour) 3 **news ~** : nouvelle *f* — **itemize** ['aɪtəˌmaɪz] *vt* **-ized; -izing** : détailler
itinerant [aɪ'tɪnərənt] *adj* : itinérant, ambulant
itinerary [aɪ'tɪnəˌreri] *n*, *pl* **-aries** : itinéraire *m*
it'll ['ɪtəl] (*contraction of* **it shall** *or* **it will**) → **shall, will**
its ['ɪts] *adj* : son, sa, ses
it's ['ɪts] *contraction of* **it is** *or* **it has** → **be, have**
itself [ɪtˌsɛlf] *pron* 1 (*used reflexively*) : se 2 (*for emphasis*) : lui-même, elle-même, soi-même
I've ['aɪv] (*contraction of* **I have**) → **have**
Ivorian ['aɪvəriən] *adj* : ivoirien
ivory ['aɪvəri] *n*, *pl* **-ries** : ivoire *m*
ivy ['aɪvi] *n*, *pl* **ivies** : lierre *m*

J

j ['dʒeɪ] *n*, *pl* **j's** *or* **js** ['dʒeɪz] : j *m*, dixième lettre de l'alphabet

jab ['dʒæb] *vt* **jabbed; jabbing 1** PIERCE : piquer **2** POKE : enfoncer — **~** *n* POKE : (petit) coup *m*

jabber ['dʒæbər] *vi* : jacasser, bavarder

jack ['dʒæk] *n* **1** : cric *m* (mécanisme) **2** : valet *m* (aux cartes) — **~** *vt or* **~ up** : soulever avec un cric

jackass ['dʒæk,æs] *n* : âne *m*

jacket ['dʒækət] *n* **1** : veste *f* **2** : jaquette *f* (d'un livre)

jackhammer ['dʒæk,hæmər] *n* : marteau-piqueur *m*

jackknife ['dʒæk,naɪf] *n*, *pl* **-knives** : couteau *m* de poche

jackpot ['dʒæk,pɑt] *n* : gros lot *m*

jaded ['dʒeɪdəd] *adj* : blasé

jagged ['dʒægəd] *adj* : dentelé

jail ['dʒeɪl] *n* : prison *f* — **~** *vt* : emprisonner, mettre en prison — **jailer** *or* **jailor** ['dʒeɪlər] *n* : geôlier *m*, -lière *f*

jam¹ ['dʒæm] *v* **jammed; jamming** *vt* **1** CRAM : entasser **2** OBSTRUCT : bloquer — *vi* : se bloquer, se coincer — **~** *n* **1** *or* **traffic ~** : embouteillage *m* **2** FIX : pétrin *m* *fam*

jam² *n* PRESERVES : confiture *f*

janitor ['dʒænətər] *n* : concierge *mf*

January ['dʒænju,ɛri] *n* : janvier *m*

Japanese [,dʒæpə'ni:z, -'ni:s] *adj* : japonais — **~** *n* : japonais *m* (langue)

jar¹ ['dʒɑr] *v* **jarred; jarring** *vi* **1** : rendre un son discordant **2** **~ on** : agacer (qqn) — *vt* JOLT : secouer — **~** *n* : secousse *f*

jar² *n* : bocal *m*, pot *m*

jargon ['dʒɑrgən] *n* : jargon *m*

jaundice ['dʒɔndɪs] *n* : jaunisse *f*

jaunt ['dʒɔnt] *n* : balade *f*

jaunty ['dʒɔnti] *adj* **-tier; -est** : allègre, insouciant

jaw ['dʒɔ] *n* : mâchoire *f* — **jawbone** ['dʒɔ-,bo:n] *n* : maxillaire *m*

jay ['dʒeɪ] *n* : geai *m*

jazz ['dʒæz] *n* : jazz *m* — **~** *vt or* **~ up** : animer — **jazzy** ['dʒæzi] *adj* **jazzier; jazziest** FLASHY : voyant, tapageur

jealous ['dʒɛləs] *adj* : jaloux — **jealousy** ['dʒɛləsi] *n*, *pl* **-sies** : jalousie *f*

jeans ['dʒi:nz] *npl* : jean *m*, blue-jean *m*

jeer ['dʒir] *vt* BOO : huer — *vi* **~ at** : se moquer de — **~** *n* : raillerie *f*

jelly ['dʒɛli] *n*, *pl* **-lies** : gelée *f* — **jellyfish** ['dʒɛli,fɪʃ] *n* : méduse *f*

jeopardy ['dʒɛpərdi] *n* : danger *m*, péril *m* —

jeopardize ['dʒɛpər,daɪz] *vt* **-dized; -dizing** : mettre en danger, compromettre

jerk ['dʒərk] *n* **1** JOLT : saccade *f*, secousse *f* **2** FOOL : idiot *m*, -diote *f* — **~** *vt* **1** YANK : tirer brusquement **2** JOLT : secouer

jersey ['dʒərzi] *n*, *pl* **-seys** : jersey *m* (tissu)

jest ['dʒɛst] *n* : plaisanterie *f* — **~** *vi* : plaisanter — **jester** ['dʒɛstər] *n* : bouffon *m*

Jesus ['dʒi:zəs, -zəz] *n* : Jésus *m*

jet ['dʒɛt] *n* **1** STREAM : jet *m* **2** *or* **~ airplane** : jet *m*, avion *m* à réaction — **jet–propelled** *adj* : à réaction

jettison ['dʒɛtəsən] *vt* **1** : jeter par-dessus bord **2** DISCARD : se débarrasser de

jetty ['dʒɛti] *n*, *pl* **-ties** : jetée *f*

jewel ['dʒu:əl] *n* : bijou *m* — **jeweler** *or* **jeweller** ['dʒu:ələr] *n* : bijoutier *m*, -tière *f*; joaillier *m*, -lière *f* — **jewelry** *or* Brit **jewellery** ['dʒu:əlri] *n* : bijoux *mpl*

Jewish ['dʒu:ɪʃ] *adj* : juif

jibe ['dʒaɪb] *vi* **jibed; jibing** AGREE : concorder

jiffy ['dʒɪfi] *n*, *pl* **-fies** : instant *m*

jig ['dʒɪg] *n* : gigue *f* (danse)

jiggle ['dʒɪgəl] *vt* **-gled; -gling** : secouer, agiter — **~** *n* : secousse *f*

jigsaw ['dʒɪg,sɔ] *n or* **~ puzzle** : puzzle *m*

jilt ['dʒɪlt] *vt* : laisser tomber

jingle ['dʒɪŋgəl] *v* **-gled; -gling** *vi* : tinter — **~** *vt* : faire tinter — **~** *n* : tintement *m*

jinx ['dʒɪŋks] *n* : mauvais sort *m*

jitters ['dʒɪtərz] *npl* **have the ~** : être nerveux — **jittery** ['dʒɪtəri] *adj* : nerveux

job ['dʒɑb] *n* **1** EMPLOYMENT : emploi *m* **2** TASK : travail *m*, tâche *f*

jockey ['dʒɑki] *n*, *pl* **-eys** : jockey *m*

jog ['dʒɑg] *vi* **jogged; jogging** : faire du jogging — **jogging** ['dʒɑgɪn] *n* : jogging *m*

join ['dʒɔɪn] *vt* **1** UNITE : joindre, unir **2** MEET : rejoindre **3** : devenir membre de (un club, etc.) — *vi or* **~ together** : s'unir, se joindre

joint [dʒɔɪnt] *n* **1** : articulation *f* (en anatomie) **2** : joint *m* (en menuiserie) — **~** *adj* : commun

joke ['dʒo:k] *n* : plaisanterie *f*, blague *f* — **~** *vi* **joked; joking** : plaisanter — **joker** ['dʒo:kər] *n* **1** : blagueur *m*, -gueuse *f* **2** : joker *m* (aux cartes)

jolly ['dʒɑli] *adj* **-lier; -est** : jovial, gai

jolt ['dʒo:lt] *vt* : secouer — **~** *n* **1** : secousse *f*, coup *m* **2** SHOCK : choc *m*

jostle ['dʒɑsəl] *v* **-tled; -tling** *vt* : bousculer — *vi* : se bousculer

jot ['dʒɑt] *vt* **jotted; jotting** *or* ~ **down** : prendre note de

journal ['dʒərnəl] *n* **1** DIARY : journal *m* (intime) **2** PERIODICAL : revue *f* — **journalism** ['dʒərnəl,ɪzəm] *n* ; journalisme *m* — **journalist** ['dʒərnəlɪst] *n* : journaliste *mf*

journey ['dʒərni] *n, pl* **-neys** : voyage *m*

jovial ['dʒo:viəl] *adj* : jovial

joy ['dʒɔɪ] *n* : joie *f* — **joyful** ['dʒɔɪfəl] *adj* : joyeux — **joyous** ['dʒɔɪəs] *adj* : joyeux

jubilant ['dʒu:bələnt] *adj* : débordant de joie — **jubilee** ['dʒu:bə,li:] *n* : jubilé *m*

Judaism ['dʒu:də,ɪzəm, 'dʒu:di-, 'dʒu:,deɪ-] *n* : judaïsme *m*

judge ['dʒʌdʒ] *vt* **judged; judging** : juger — ~ *n* : juge *m* — **judgment** *or* **judgement** ['dʒʌdʒmənt] *n* : jugement *m*

judicial [dʒʊ'dɪʃəl] *adj* : judiciaire — **judicious** [dʒʊ'dɪʃəs] *adj* : judicieux

jug ['dʒʌg] *n* : cruche *f*, pichet *m*

juggle ['dʒʌgəl] *vi* **-gled; -gling** : jongler — **juggler** ['dʒʌgələr] *n* : jongleur *m*, -gleuse *f*

juice ['dʒu:s] *n* : jus *m* — **juicy** ['dʒu:si] *adj* **juicier; juiciest** : juteux

July [dʒʊ'laɪ] *n* : juillet *m*

jumble ['dʒʌmbəl] *vt* **-bled; -bling** : mélanger — ~ *n* : fouillis *m*, désordre *m*

jumbo ['dʒʌm,bo:] *adj* : géant

jump ['dʒʌmp] *vi* **1** LEAP : sauter **2** START : sursauter **3** RISE : faire un bond **4** ~ **at** : saisir (une occasion, etc.) — *vt or* ~ **over** : sauter — ~ *n* **1** LEAP : saut *m* **2** INCREASE : hausse *f* — **jumper** ['dʒʌmpər] *n* **1** : sauteur *m*, -teuse *f* (aux sports) **2** : robe-

chasuble *f* (vêtement) — **jumpy** ['dʒʌmpi] *adj* **jumpier; jumpiest** : nerveux

junction ['dʒʌŋkʃən] *n* **1** : jonction *f* **2** : carrefour *m*, embranchement *m* (de deux routes) — **juncture** ['dʒʌŋktʃər] *n* : conjoncture *f*

June ['dʒu:n] *n* : juin *m*

jungle ['dʒʌŋgəl] *n* : jungle *f*

junior ['dʒu:njər] *adj* **1** YOUNGER : cadet, plus jeune **2** SUBORDINATE : subalterne — ~ *n* **1** : cadet *m*, -dette *f* **2** : étudiant *m*, -diante *f* de troisième année

junk ['dʒʌŋk] *n* : camelote *f fam*

Jupiter ['dʒu:pətər] *n* : Jupiter *f*

jurisdiction [,dʒʊrəs'dɪkʃən] *n* : juridiction *f*

jury ['dʒʊri] *n, pl* **-ries** : jury *m* — **juror** ['dʒʊrər] *n* : juré *m*, -rée *f*

just ['dʒʌst] *adj* : juste — ~ *adv* **1** BARELY : à peine **2** EXACTLY : exactement **3** ONLY : seulement **4 he has ~ arrived** : il vient d'arriver **5 it's ~ perfect** : c'est parfait

justice ['dʒʌstɪs] *n* **1** : justice *f* **2** JUDGE : juge *m*

justify ['dʒʌstə,faɪ] *vt* **-fied; -fying** : justifier — **justification** [,dʒʌstəfə'keɪʃən] *n* : justification *f*

jut ['dʒʌt] *vi* **jutted; jutting** *or* ~ **out** : dépasser, faire saillie

juvenile ['dʒu:və,naɪl, -vənəl] *adj* **1** YOUNG : jeune **2** CHILDISH : puéril — ~ *n* : jeune *mf*

juxtapose ['dʒʌkstə,po:z] *vt* **-posed; -posing** : juxtaposer

K

k ['keɪ] *n, pl* **k's** *or* **ks** ['keɪz] : k *m*, onzième lettre de l'alphabet

kangaroo [,kæŋgə'ru:] *n, pl* **-roos** : kangourou *m*

karat ['kærət] *n* : carat *m*

karate [kə'rɑti] *n* : karaté *m*

keel ['ki:l] *n* : quille *f* — ~ *vi or* ~ **over** : chavirer (se dit d'un bateau), s'écrouler (se dit d'une personne)

keen ['ki:n] *adj* **1** PENETRATING : vif, pénétrant **2** ENTHUSIASTIC : enthousiaste

keep ['ki:p] *v* **kept** ['kɛpt]; **keeping** *vt* **1** : garder **2** : tenir (une promesse, etc.) **3** DETAIN : retenir **4** PREVENT : empêcher **5** ~ **up** : maintenir — *vi* **1** STAY : se tenir, rester **2** LAST : se conserver, se garder **3** *or* ~ **on** CONTINUE : continuer — ~ **for**

~ **s** : pour de bon — **keeper** ['ki:pər] *n* : gardien *m*, -dienne *f* — **keeping** ['ki:pɪŋ] *n* **1** CARE : garde *f* **2 in ~ with** : en accord avec — **keepsake** ['ki:p,seɪk] *n* : souvenir *m*

keg ['kɛg] *n* : baril *m*, tonnelet *m*

kennel ['kɛnəl] *n* : niche *f*

kept → **keep**

kerchief ['kərtʃəf, -,tʃi:f] *n* : fichu *m*

kernel ['kərnəl] *n* **1** : amande *f* **2** CORE : noyau *m*, cœur *m*

kerosene *or* **kerosine** ['kɛrə,si:n, ,kɛrə'-] *n* : kérosène *m*, pétrole *m* lampant

ketchup ['kɛtʃəp, 'kæ-] *n* : ketchup *m*

kettle ['kɛtəl] *n* : bouilloire *f*

key ['ki:] *n* **1** : clé *f* **2** : touche *f* (d'un clavier) — ~ *adj* : clé — **keyboard** ['ki:-

kosher

‚bord] *n* : clavier *m* — **keyhole** ['ki:‚ho:l] *n* : trou *m* de serrure

khaki ['kæki, 'kɑ-] *adj* : kaki

kick ['kɪk] *vt* : donner un coup de pied à — *vi* : donner un coup de pied — ~ *n* 1 : coup *m* de pied 2 PLEASURE, THRILL : plaisir *m*

kid ['kɪd] *n* 1 GOAT : chevreau *m* 2 CHILD : gosse *mf France fam;* flot *m Can* — ~ *v* **kidded; kidding** *vi or* ~ **around** : blaguer, plaisanter — *vt* TEASE : taquiner — **kidnap** ['kɪd‚næp] *vt* **-napped** *or* **-naped** [-‚næpt]; **-napping** *or* **-naping** [-‚næpɪŋ] : kidnapper, enlever

kidney ['kɪd‚ni] *n, pl* **-neys** : rein *m*

kill ['kɪl] *v* : tuer — ~ *n* 1 KILLING : mise *f* à mort 2 PREY : proie *f* — **killer** ['kɪlər] *n* : meurtrier *m*, -trière *f*; tueur *m*, tueuse *f* — **killing** ['kɪlɪŋ] *n* : meurtre *m*

kiln ['kɪl, 'kɪln] *n* : four *m*

kilo ['ki:‚lo:] *n, pl* **-los** : kilo *m* — **kilogram** ['kɪlə‚græm, 'ki:-] *n* : kilogramme *m* — **kilometer** [kɪ'lɑmətər, 'kɪlə‚mi:-] *n* : kilomètre *m* — **kilowatt** ['kɪlə‚wɑt] *n* : kilowatt *m*

kin ['kɪn] *n* : parents *mpl*, famille *f*

kind ['kaɪnd] *n* : espèce *f*, genre *m*, sorte *f* — ~ *adj* : gentil, bienveillant

kindergarten ['kɪndər‚gɑrtən, -dən] *n* : jardin *m* d'enfants *France*, école *f* maternelle *Can*

kindhearted ['kaɪnd'hɑrtəd] *adj* : bon, qui a bon cœur

kindle ['kɪndəl] *v* **-dled; -dling** *vt* : allumer — *vi* : s'enflammer

kindly ['kaɪndli] *adj* **-lier; -est** : bienveillant — ~ *adv* 1 : avec gentillesse 2 OBLIGINGLY : gentiment — **kindness** ['kaɪndnəs] *n* : gentillesse *f*, bonté *f* — **kind of** *adv* SOMEWHAT : quelque peu

kindred ['kɪndrəd] *adj* 1 : apparenté 2 ~ **spirit** : âme *f* sœur

king ['kɪŋ] *n* : roi *m* — **kingdom** ['kɪŋdəm] *n* : royaume *m*

kink ['kɪŋk] *n* 1 TWIST : nœud *m* 2 FLAW : défaut *m*, problème *m*

kinship ['kɪn‚ʃɪp] *n* : parenté *f*

kiss ['kɪs] *vt* : embrasser, donner un baiser à — *vi* : s'embrasser — ~ *n* : baiser *m*

kit ['kɪt] *n* : trousse *f*

kitchen ['kɪtʃən] *n* : cuisine *f*

kite ['kaɪt] *n* : cerf-volant *m*

kitten ['kɪtən] *n* : chaton *m* — **kitty** ['kɪti] *n, pl* **-ties** FUND : cagnotte *f*

knack ['næk] *n* TALENT : don *m*

knapsack ['næp‚sæk] *n* : sac *m* à dos

knead ['ni:d] *vt* : pétrir

knee ['ni:] *n* : genou *m* — **kneecap** ['ni:-‚kæp] *n* : rotule *f*

kneel ['ni:l] *vi* **knelt** ['nɛlt] *or* **kneeled** ['ni:ld]; **kneeling** : s'agenouiller

knew → know

knife [naɪf] *n, pl* **knives** ['naɪvz] : couteau *m* — ~ *vt* **knifed** [naɪft]; **knifing** : donner un coup de couteau à

knight ['naɪt] *n* 1 : chevalier *m* 2 : cavalier *m* (aux échecs) — **knighthood** ['naɪt‚hu:d] *n* : titre *m* de chevalier

knit ['nɪt] *v* **knit** *or* **knitted** ['nɪtəd]; **knitting** : tricoter — **knitting** ['nɪtɪŋ] *n* : tricot *m*

knob ['nɑb] *n* : poignée *f*, bouton *m*

knock ['nɑk] *vt* 1 HIT : cogner, frapper 2 CRITICIZE : critiquer 3 ~ **down** *or* ~ **over** : renverser 4 ~ **out** : assommer — *vi* 1 : frapper (à la porte) 2 : cogner (se dit d'un moteur) 3 ~ **into** : heurter

knot ['nɑt] *n* : nœud *m* — ~ *vt* **knotted; knotting** : nouer, faire un nœud à — **knotty** ['nɑti] *adj* **-tier; -est** : épineux (se dit d'un problème)

know ['no:] *v* **knew** ['nu:, 'nju:]; **known** ['no:n]; **knowing** *vt* 1 : savoir 2 : connaître (une personne, un lieu) 3 UNDERSTAND : comprendre — *vi* 1 : savoir 2 ~ **about** : être au courant de, s'y connaître en (un sujet) — **knowing** ['no:ɪŋ] *adj* : entendu — **knowingly** ['no:ɪŋli] *adv* INTENTIONALLY : sciemment — **knowledge** ['nɑlɪdʒ] *n* 1 : connaissance *f* 2 LEARNING : connaissances *fpl*, savoir *m* — **knowledgeable** ['nɑlɪdʒəbəl] *adj* : bien informé

knuckle ['nʌkəl] *n* : jointure *f* du doigt, articulation *f* du doigt

Koran [kə'rɑn, -'ræn] *n* **the ~** : le Coran

Korean [kə'ri:ən] *adj* : coréen — ~ *n* : coréen *m* (langue)

kosher ['ko:ʃər] *adj* : kascher, casher

L

l [ˈɛl] n, pl l's or ls [ˈɛlz] : l m, douzième lettre de l'alphabet

lab [ˈlæb] → laboratory

label [ˈleɪbəl] n 1 TAG : étiquette f 2 BRAND : marque f — ~ vt -beled or -belled; -beling or -belling : étiqueter

labor or Brit labour [ˈleɪbər] n 1 : travail m 2 WORKERS : main-d'œuvre f 3 in ~ : en train d'accoucher — ~ vi 1 : travailler 2 STRUGGLE : avancer péniblement — vt : insister sur (un point)

laboratory [ˈlæbrəˌtori, ləˈbɔrə-] n, pl -ries : laboratoire m

laborer or Brit labourer [ˈleɪbərər] n : ouvrier m, -vrière f

laborious [ləˈboriəs] adj : laborieux

lace [ˈleɪs] n 1 : dentelle f 2 SHOELACE : lacet m — ~ vt laced; lacing 1 TIE : lacer 2 be laced with : être mêlé de (se dit d'une boisson)

lacerate [ˈlæsəˌreɪt] vt -ated; -ating : lacérer

lack [ˈlæk] vt : manquer de, ne pas avoir — vi or be lacking : manquer — ~ n : manque m, carence f

lackadaisical [ˌlækəˈdeɪzɪkəl] adj : apathique, indolent

lackluster [ˈlækˌlʌstər] adj : terne, fade

lacquer [ˈlækər] n : laque m

lacrosse [ləˈkrɔs] n : crosse f

lacy [ˈleɪsi] adj lacier; -est : de dentelle

lad [ˈlæd] n : gars m, garçon m

ladder [ˈlædər] n : échelle f

laden [ˈleɪdən] adj : chargé

ladle [ˈleɪdəl] n : louche f — ~ vt -dled; -dling : servir à la louche

lady [ˈleɪdi] n, pl -dies : dame f, madame f — ladybug [ˈleɪdiˌbʌg] n : coccinelle f — ladylike [ˈleɪdiˌlaɪk] adj : élégant, de dame

lag [ˈlæg] n 1 DELAY : retard m 2 INTERVAL : décalage m — ~ vi lagged; lagging : traîner, être en retard

lager [ˈlɑgər] n : bière f blonde

lagoon [ləˈguːn] n : lagune f

laid pp → lay[1]

lain pp → lie[1]

lair [ˈlær] n : tanière f

lake [ˈleɪk] n : lac m

lamb [ˈlæm] n : agneau m

lame [ˈleɪm] adj lamer; lamest 1 : boiteux 2 a ~ excuse : une excuse peu convaincante

lament [ləˈmɛnt] vt 1 MOURN : pleurer 2 DEPLORE : déplorer — ~ n : lamentation f — lamentable [ˈlæməntəbəl, ləˈmɛntə-] adj : lamentable

laminate [ˈlæməˌneɪt] vt -nated; -nating : laminer

lamp [ˈlæmp] n : lampe f — lamppost [ˈlæmpˌpost] n : réverbère m — lampshade [ˈlæmpˌʃeɪd] n : abat-jour m

lance [ˈlænts] n : lance f — ~ vt lanced; lancing : percer (en médecine)

land [ˈlænd] n 1 : terre f 2 COUNTRY : pays m 3 or plot of ~ : terrain m — ~ vt 1 : faire un atterrissage, débarquer (des passagers) 2 CATCH : attraper (un poisson) 3 SECURE : décrocher (un emploi, etc.) — vi 1 : atterrir (se dit d'un avion) 2 FALL : tomber — landing [ˈlændɪŋ] n 1 : atterrissage m (d'un avion) 2 : débarquement m (d'un navire) 3 : palier m (d'un escalier) — landlady [ˈlændˌleɪdi] n, pl -dies : propriétaire f — landlord [ˈlændˌlɔrd] n : propriétaire m — landmark [ˈlændˌmɑrk] n 1 : point m de repère 2 MONUMENT : monument m historique — landowner [ˈlændˌoːnər] n : propriétaire m foncier, propriétaire f foncière — landscape [ˈlændˌskeɪp] n : paysage m — ~ vt -scaped; -scaping : aménager — landslide [ˈlændˌslaɪd] n 1 : glissement m de terrain 2 or ~ victory : victoire f écrasante

lane [ˈleɪn] n 1 : voie f (d'une autoroute) 2 PATH, ROAD : chemin m

language [ˈlæŋgwɪʤ] n 1 : langue f 2 SPEECH : langage m

languid [ˈlæŋgwɪd] adj : languissant — languish [ˈlæŋgwɪʃ] vi : languir

lanky [ˈlæŋki] adj lankier; -est : grand et maigre, dégingandé

lantern [ˈlæntərn] n : lanterne f

lap [ˈlæp] n 1 : genoux mpl 2 : tour m de piste (aux sports) — ~ v lapped; lapping vt or ~ up : boire à petites gorgées — vi ~ against : clapoter

lapel [ləˈpɛl] n : revers m

lapse [ˈlæps] n 1 : trou m (de mémoire, etc.) 2 INTERVAL : laps m, intervalle m — ~ vi lapsed; lapsing 1 EXPIRE : expirer 2 ELAPSE : passer 3 ~ into : tomber dans

laptop [ˈlæpˌtɑp] adj : portable

larceny [ˈlɑrsəni] n, pl -nies : vol m

lard [ˈlɑrd] n : saindoux m

large [ˈlɑrʤ] adj larger; largest 1 : grand 2 at ~ : en liberté 3 by and ~ : en général — largely [ˈlɑrʤli] adv : en grande partie

lark [ˈlɑrk] n 1 : alouette f (oiseau) 2 for a ~ : comme divertissement

larva [ˈlɑrvə] n, pl -vae [-ˌviː, -ˌvaɪ] : larve f

larynx [ˈlærɪŋks] n, pl -rynges [ləˈrɪnˌʤiːz]

or **-ynxes** ['lærɪŋksəz] : larynx *m* — **laryn-gitis** [ˌlærənˈdʒaɪtəs] *n* : laryngite *f*

lasagna [ləˈzɑnjə] *n* : lasagnes *fpl*

laser ['leɪzər] *n* : laser *m*

lash ['læʃ] *vt* 1 WHIP : fouetter 2 BIND : at-tacher — *vi* ~ **out at** : invectiver contre — ~ *n* 1 BLOW : coup *m* de fouet 2 EYELASH : cil *m*

lass ['læs] *or* **lassie** ['læsi] *n* : fille *f*

lasso ['læˌsoː, læˈsuː] *n, pl* **-sos** *or* **-soes** : lasso *m*

last ['læst] *vi* : durer — ~ *n* 1 : dernier *m*, -nière *f* 2 **at** ~ : enfin, finalement — ~ *adv* 1 : pour la dernière fois, en dernière place 2 **arrive** ~ : arriver dernier — ~ *adj* 1 : dernier 2 ~ **year** : l'an passé — **lastly** ['læstli] *adv* : enfin, finalement

latch ['lætʃ] *n* : loquet *m*, serrure *f*

late ['leɪt] *adj* **later; latest** 1 : en retard 2 : avancé (se dit de l'heure) 3 DECEASED : défunt 4 RECENT : récent — ~ *adv* **later; latest** : en retard — **lately** ['leɪtli] *adv* : récemment, dernièrement — **lateness** ['leɪtnəs] *n* 1 : retard *m* 2 : heure *f* avancée

latent ['leɪtənt] *adj* : latent

lateral ['lætʒərəl] *adj* : latéral

latest ['leɪtəst] *n* **at the** ~ : au plus tard

lathe ['leɪð] *n* : tour *m*

lather ['læðər] *n* : mousse *f* — ~ *vt* : savon-ner — *vi* : faire mousser

Latin ['lætən] *adj* : latin — ~ *n* : latin *m* (langue)

latitude ['lætəˌtuːd, -ˌtjuːd] *n* : latitude *f*

latter ['lætər] *adj* 1 : dernier 2 SECOND : second — ~ *pron* **the** ~ : ce dernier, cette dernière, ces derniers

lattice ['lætəs] *n* : treillis *m*, treillage *m*

laugh ['læf] *vi* : rire — ~ *n* : rire *m* — **laughable** ['læfəbəl] *adj* : risible, ridicule — **laughter** ['læftər] *n* : rire *m*, rires *mpl*

launch ['lɔntʃ] *vt* : lancer — ~ *n* : lance-ment *m*

launder ['lɔndər] *vt* 1 : laver et repasser (du linge) 2 : blanchir (de l'argent) — **laundry** ['lɔndri] *n, pl* **-dries** 1 : linge *m* sale 2 : blanchisserie *f* (service) 3 **do the** ~ : faire la lessive

lava ['lɑvə, 'læ-] *n* : lave *f*

lavatory ['lævəˌtori] *n, pl* **-ries** BATHROOM : toilettes *fpl*

lavender ['lævəndər] *n* : lavande *f*

lavish ['lævɪʃ] *adj* 1 EXTRAVAGANT : prodigue 2 ABUNDANT : abondant 3 LUX-URIOUS : luxueux — ~ *vt* : prodiguer

law ['lɔ] *n* 1 : loi *f* 2 : droit *m* (profession, etc.) 3 **practice** ~ : exercer le droit — **lawful** ['lɔfəl] *adj* : légal, légitime

lawn ['lɔn] *n* : pelouse *f* — **lawn mower** *n* : tondeuse *f*

lawsuit ['lɔˌsuːt] *n* : procès *m*

lawyer ['lɔɪər, 'lɔjər] *n* : avocat *m*, -cate *f*

lax ['læks] *adj* : peu strict, relâché

laxative ['læksətɪv] *n* : laxatif *m*

lay¹ ['leɪ] *vt* **laid** ['leɪd]; **laying** 1 PLACE, PUT : mettre, placer 2 ~ **eggs** : pondre des œufs 3 ~ **off** : licencier (un employé) 4 ~ **out** PRESENT : présenter, exposer 5 ~ **out** DESIGN : concevoir (un plan)

lay² → **lie¹**

lay³ *adj* 1 SECULAR : laïc 2 NONPROFES-SIONAL : profane

layer ['leɪər] *n* : couche *f*

layman ['leɪmən] *n, pl* **-men** [-mən, -ˌmɛn] : profane *mf*, laïque *mf* (en religion)

layoff ['leɪˌɔf] *n* : licenciement *m*, renvoi *m*

layout ['leɪˌaʊt] *n* ARRANGEMENT : disposi-tion *f*

lazy ['leɪzi] *adj* **-zier; -est** : paresseux — **laziness** ['leɪzinəs] *n* : paresse *f*

lead¹ ['liːd] *v* **led** ['lɛd]; **leading** *vt* 1 GUIDE : conduire 2 DIRECT : diriger 3 HEAD : être à la tête de, aller au devant de — *vi* : mener, conduire (à) — ~ *n* 1 : devant *m* 2 **follow s.o.'s** ~ : suivre l'exemple de qqn

lead² ['lɛd] *n* 1 : plomb *m* (métal) 2 : mine *f* (d'un crayon) — **leaden** ['lɛdən] *adj* 1 : de plomb 2 HEAVY : lourd

leader ['liːdər] *n* : chef *m*; dirigeant *m*, -geante *f* — **leadership** ['liːdərˌʃɪp] *n* : di-rection *f*, dirigeants *mpl*

leaf ['liːf] *n, pl* **leaves** ['liːvz] 1 : feuille *f* 2 **turn over a new** ~ : tourner la page — ~ *vi* ~ **through** : feuilleter (se dit d'un livre, etc.) — **leaflet** ['liːflət] *n* : dépliant *m*, prospectus *m*

league ['liːg] *n* 1 : lieue *f* 2 **be in** ~ **with** : être de mèche avec

leak ['liːk] *vt* 1 : faire couler (un liquide ou un gaz) 2 : divulguer (un secret) — *vi* 1 : fuir, s'échapper (se dit d'un liquide ou d'un gaz) 2 : être divulgué (se dit de l'in-formation) — ~ *n* : fuite *f* — **leaky** ['liːki] *adj* **leakier; -est** : qui prend l'eau

lean¹ ['liːn] *v* **leaned** *or Brit* **leant** ['lɛnt]; **leaning** ['liːnɪŋ] *vi* 1 BEND : se pencher 2 ~ **against** : s'appuyer contre — *vt* : ap-puyer

lean² *adj* : mince (se dit d'une personne), maigre (se dit de la viande)

leaning ['liːnɪŋ] *n* : tendance *f*

leanness ['liːnnəs] *n* : minceur *f* (d'une per-sonne), maigreur *f* (de la viande)

leap ['liːp] *vi* **leaped** *or* **leapt** ['liːpt, 'lɛpt]; **leaping** : sauter, bondir — ~ *n* : saut *m*, bond *m* — **leap year** *n* : année *f* bissextile

learn ['lərn] *v* **learned** ['lərnd, 'lərnt] *or Brit* **learnt** ['lərnt]; **learning** : apprendre — **learned** ['lərnəd] *adj* : savant, érudit — **learner** ['lərnər] *n* : débutant *m*, -tante *f*;

étudiant *m*, -diante *f* — **learning** ['lərnıŋ] *n* : savoir *m*, érudition *f*

lease ['li:s] *n* : bail *m* — ~ *vt* **leased; leasing** : louer à bail

leash ['li:ʃ] *n* : laisse *f*

least ['li:st] *adj* **1** : moins **2** SLIGHTEST : moindre — ~ *n* **1 at** ~ : au moins **2 the** ~ : le moins — ~ *adv* : moins

leather ['lɛðər] *n* : cuir *m*

leave ['li:v] *v* **left** ['lɛft]; **leaving** *vt* **1** : quitter **2** : sortir de (un endroit) **3** ~ **out** : omettre — *vi* DEPART : partir — ~ *n or* ~ **of absence** : congé *m*

leaves → **leaf**

lecture ['lɛktʃər] *n* **1** TALK : conférence *f* **2** REPRIMAND : sermon *m*, réprimande *f* — ~ *v* **-tured; -turing** *vt* : sermonner — *vi* : donner un cours, donner une conférence

led → **lead**[1]

ledge ['lɛʤ] *n* : rebord *m* (d'une fenêtre, etc.), saillie *f* (d'une montagne)

leech ['li:tʃ] *n* : sangsue *f*

leek ['li:k] *n* : poireau *m*

leer ['lɪr] *vi* : jeter un regard lascif — ~ *n* : regard *m* lascif

leery ['lɪri] *adj* : méfiant

leeway ['li:ˌweɪ] *n* : liberté *f* d'action, marge *f* de manœuvre

left[1] → **leave**

left[2] ['lɛft] *adj* : gauche — ~ *adv* : à gauche — ~ *n* : gauche *f* — **left–handed** ['lɛft-ˈhandəd] *adj* : gaucher

leftovers ['lɛftˌoːvərz] *npl* : restes *mpl*

leg ['lɛg] *n* **1** : patte *f* (d'un animal), jambe *f* (d'une personne ou d'un pantalon), pied *m* (d'une table, etc.) **2** : étape *f* (d'un voyage)

legacy ['lɛgəsi] *n, pl* **-cies** : legs *m*

legal ['li:gəl] *adj* **1** LAWFUL : légitime, légal **2** JUDICIAL : juridique — **legality** [li'gæləti] *n, pl* **-ties** : légalité *f* — **legalize** ['li:gəˌlaɪz] *vt* **-ized; -izing** : légaliser

legend ['lɛʤənd] *n* : légende *f* — **legendary** ['lɛʤənˌdɛri] *adj* : légendaire

legible ['lɛʤəbəl] *adj* : lisible

legion ['li:ʤən] *n* : légion *f*

legislate ['lɛʤəsˌleɪt] *vi* **-lated; -lating** : légiférer — **legislation** [ˌlɛʤəsˈleɪʃən] *n* : législation *f* — **legislative** ['lɛʤəsˌleɪtɪv] *adj* : législatif — **legislature** ['lɛʤəsˌleɪtʃər] *n* : corps *m* législatif

legitimate [lɪˈʤɪtəmət] *adj* : légitime — **legitimacy** [lɪˈʤɪtəməsi] *n* : légitimité *f*

leisure ['li:ʒər, 'lɛ-] *n* **1** : loisir *m*, temps *m* libre **2 at your** ~ : à votre convenance — **leisurely** ['li:ʒərli, 'lɛ-] *adv* : lentement, sans se presser — ~ *adj* : lent

lemon ['lɛmən] *n* : citron *m* — **lemonade** [ˌlɛməˈneɪd] *n* : limonade *f*

lend ['lɛnd] *vt* **lent** ['lɛnt]; **lending** : prêter

length ['lɛŋkθ] *n* **1** : longueur *f* **2** DURATION : durée *f* **3 at** ~ FINALLY : finalement **4 at** ~ EXTENSIVELY : longuement **5 go to any** ~**s** : faire tout son possible — **lengthen** ['lɛŋkθən] *vt* **1** : rallonger **2** PROLONG : prolonger — *vi* : s'allonger — **lengthways** ['lɛŋkθˌweɪz] *or* **lengthwise** ['lɛŋkθ-ˌwaɪz] *adv* : dans le sens de la longueur — **lengthy** ['lɛŋkθi] *adj* **lengthier; -est** : long

lenient ['li:niənt] *adj* : indulgent — **leniency** ['li:niəntsi] *n* : indulgence *f*

lens ['lɛnz] *n* **1** : lentille *f* (d'un instrument) **2** → **contact lens**

Lent ['lɛnt] *n* : carême *m*

lentil ['lɛntəl] *n* : lentille *f*

leopard ['lɛpərd] *n* : léopard *m*

leotard ['li:əˌtard] *n* : justaucorps *m*

lesbian ['lɛzbiən] *n* : lesbienne *f*

less ['lɛs] *adv & adj* (*comparative of* **little**) : moins — ~ *pron* : moins — ~ *prep* MINUS : moins — **lessen** ['lɛsən] *v* : diminuer — **lesser** ['lɛsər] *adj* : moindre

lesson ['lɛsən] *n* **1** CLASS : classe *f*, cours *m* **2 learn one's** ~ : servir de leçon

lest ['lɛst] *conj* ~ **we forget** : de peur que nous n'oublions

let ['lɛt] *vt* **let; letting 1** ALLOW : laisser, permettre **2** RENT : louer **3** ~**'s go!** : allons-y! **4** ~ **down** DISAPPOINT : décevoir **5** ~ **in** : laisser entrer **6** ~ **off** FORGIVE : pardonner **7** ~ **up** ABATE : diminuer, arrêter

letdown ['lɛtˌdaʊn] *n* : déception *f*

lethal ['li:θəl] *adj* : mortel

lethargic [lɪˈθɑrʤɪk] *adj* : léthargique

let's ['lɛts] (*contraction of* **let us**) → **let**

letter ['lɛtər] *n* : lettre *f*

lettuce ['lɛtəs] *n* : laitue *f*

letup ['lɛtˌəp] *n* : pause *f*, répit *m*

leukemia [luˈki:miə] *n* : leucémie *f*

level ['lɛvəl] *n* **1** : niveau *m* **2 be on the** ~ : être franc — ~ *vt* **-eled** *or* **-elled; -eling** *or* **-elling 1** : niveler **2** AIM : diriger **3** RAZE : raser — ~ *adj* **1** FLAT : plat, plan **2** ~ **with** : au même niveau que — **levelheaded** ['lɛvəlˈhɛdəd] *adj* : sensé, équilibré

lever ['lɛvər, 'li:-] *n* : levier *m* — **leverage** ['lɛvərɪʤ, 'li:-] *n* **1** : force *f* de levier (en physique) **2** INFLUENCE : influence *f*

levity ['lɛvəti] *n* : légèreté *f*

levy ['lɛvi] *n, pl* **levies** : impôt *m* — ~ *vt* **levied; levying** : imposer, prélever (une taxe)

lewd ['lu:d] *adj* : lascif

lexicon ['lɛksɪˌkan] *n, pl* **-ica** [-kə] *or* **-icons** : lexique *m*

liable ['laɪəbəl] *adj* **1** : responsable **2** LIKELY : probable **3** SUSCEPTIBLE : sujet — **liability** [ˌlaɪəˈbɪləti] *n, pl* **-ties 1** RESPONSIBILITY : responsabilité *f* **2** DRAWBACK : désavantage *m* **3 liabilities** *npl* DEBTS : dettes *fpl*, passif *m*

liaison ['liːəˌzɑn, liˈeɪ-] *n* : liaison *f*

liar ['laɪər] *n* : menteur *m*, -teuse *f*

libel ['laɪbəl] *n* : diffamation *f* — ~ *vt* **-beled** *or* **-belled; -beling** *or* **-belling** : diffamer

liberal ['lɪbrəl, 'lɪbərəl] *adj* : libéral — ~ *n* : libéral *m*, -rale *f*

liberate ['lɪbəˌreɪt] *vt* **-ated; -ating** : libérer — **liberation** [ˌlɪbəˈreɪʃən] *n* : libération *f*

liberty ['lɪbərṭi] *n, pl* **-ties** : liberté *f*

library ['laɪˌbrɛri] *n, pl* **-braries** : bibliothèque *f* — **librarian** [laɪˈbrɛriən] *n* : bibliothécaire *mf*

lice → **louse**

license *or* **licence** *n* **1** PERMIT : permis *m* **2** FREEDOM : licence *f* **3** AUTHORIZATION : permission *f* — ~ ['laɪsənts] *vt* **-censed; -censing** : autoriser

lick ['lɪk] *vt* **1** : lécher **2** DEFEAT : battre (à plate couture) — ~ *n* : coup *m* de langue

licorice *or Brit* **liquorice** ['lɪkərɪʃ, -rəs] *n* : réglisse *f*

lid ['lɪd] *n* **1** : couvercle *m* **2** EYELID : paupière *f*

lie[1] ['laɪ] *vi* **lay** ['leɪ]; **lain** ['leɪn]; **lying** ['laɪɪŋ] **1** *or* ~ **down** : se coucher, s'allonger **2** BE : être, se trouver

lie[2] *vi* **lied; lying** ['laɪɪŋ] : mentir — ~ *n* : mensonge *m*

lieutenant [luˈtɛnənt] *n* : lieutenant *m*

life ['laɪf] *n, pl* **lives** ['laɪvz] : vie *f* — **lifeboat** ['laɪfˌboːt] *n* : canot *m* de sauvetage — **lifeguard** ['laɪfˌgɑrd] *n* : sauveteur *m* — **lifeless** ['laɪfləs] *adj* : sans vie — **lifelike** ['laɪfˌlaɪk] *adj* : naturel, réaliste — **lifelong** ['laɪfˌlɔŋ] *adj* : de toute une vie — **life preserver** *n* : gilet *m* de sauvetage — **lifestyle** ['laɪfˌstaɪl] *n* : mode *m* de vie — **lifetime** ['laɪfˌtaɪm] *n* : vie *f*

lift ['lɪft] *vt* **1** RAISE : lever **2** STEAL : voler — *vi* **1** CLEAR UP : se dissiper **2** *or* ~ **off** : décoller (se dit d'un avion, etc.) — ~ *n* **1** LIFTING : soulèvement *m* **2 give s.o. a ~** : emmener qqn en voiture — **liftoff** ['lɪftˌɔf] *n* : lancement *m*

light[1] ['laɪt] *n* **1** : lumière *f* **2** LAMP : lampe *f* **3** HEADLIGHT : phare *m* **4 do you have a ~?** : avez-vous du feu? — ~ *adj* **1** BRIGHT : bien illuminé **2** : clair (se dit des couleurs), blond (se dit des cheveux) — ~ *v* **lit** ['lɪt] *or* **lighted; lighting** *vt* **1** : allumer (un feu) **2** ILLUMINATE : éclairer — *vi or* ~ **up** : s'illuminer — **lightbulb** ['laɪtˌbʌlb] *n* : ampoule *f* — **lighten** ['laɪtən] *vt* BRIGHTEN : éclairer — **lighter** ['laɪtər] *n* : briquet *m* — **lighthouse** ['laɪtˌhaʊs] *n* : phare *m* — **lighting** ['laɪtɪŋ] *n* : éclairage *m* — **lightning** ['laɪtnɪŋ] *n* : éclairs *mpl*, foudre *f* — **light–year** ['laɪtˌjɪr] *n* : année-lumière *f*

light[2] *adj* : léger — **lighten** ['laɪtən] *vt* : al-

léger — **lightly** ['laɪtli] *adv* **1** : légèrement **2 let off ~** : traiter avec indulgence — **lightness** ['laɪtnəs] *n* : légèreté *f* — **lightweight** ['laɪtˌweɪt] *adj* : léger

like[1] ['laɪk] *v* **liked; liking** *vt* : aimer (qqn) **2** WANT : vouloir — *vi* **if you ~** : si vous voulez — **likes** *npl* : préférences *fpl*, goûts *mpl* — **likable** *or* **likeable** ['laɪkəbəl] *adj* : sympathique

like[2] *adj* SIMILAR : pareil — ~ *prep* : comme — ~ *conj* **1** AS : comme **2** AS IF : comme si — **likelihood** ['laɪkliˌhʊd] *n* : probabilité *f* — **likely** ['laɪkli] *adj* **-lier; -est** : probable — **liken** ['laɪkən] *vt* : comparer — **likeness** ['laɪknəs] *n* : ressemblance *f* — **likewise** ['laɪkˌwaɪz] *adv* **1** : de même **2** ALSO : aussi

liking ['laɪkɪŋ] *n* : goût *m* (pour une chose), affection *f* (pour une personne)

lilac ['laɪlək, -ˌlæk, -ˌlɑk] *n* : lilas *m*

lily ['lɪli] *n, pl* **lilies** : lis *m* — **lily of the valley** *n* : muguet *m*

lima bean ['laɪmə] *n* : haricot *m* de Lima

limb ['lɪm] *n* **1** : membre *m* (en anatomie) **2** : branche *f* (d'un arbre)

limber ['lɪmbər] *vi* ~ **up** : s'échauffer, faire des exercices d'assouplissement

limbo ['lɪmˌboː] *n, pl* **-bos** : limbes *mpl*

lime ['laɪm] *n* : lime *f*, citron *m* vert

limelight ['laɪmˌlaɪt] *n* **be in the ~** : être en vedette

limerick ['lɪmərɪk] *n* : poème *m* humoristique en cinq vers

limestone ['laɪmˌstoːn] *n* : pierre *f* à chaux, calcaire *m*

limit ['lɪmət] *n* : limite *f* — ~ *vt* : limiter, restreindre — **limitation** [ˌlɪməˈteɪʃən] *n* : limitation *f*, restriction *f* — **limited** ['lɪmətəd] *adj* : limité

limousine ['lɪməˌziːn, ˌlɪməˈ-] *n* : limousine *f*

limp[1] ['lɪmp] *vi* : boiter — ~ *n* **have a ~** : boiter

limp[2] *adj* : mou, flasque

line ['laɪn] *n* **1** : ligne *f* **2** ROPE : corde *f* **3** ROW : rangée *f* **4** QUEUE : file *f* **5** WRINKLE : ride *f* **6 drop s.o. a ~** : écrire un mot à qqn — ~ *v* **lined; lining** *vt* **1** : doubler (un vêtement, etc.), tapisser (un mur, etc.) **2** MARK : rayer, ligner **3** BORDER : border — *vi* ~ **up** : se mettre en ligne, faire la queue

lineage ['lɪniɪdʒ] *n* : lignée *f*

linear ['lɪniər] *adj* : linéaire

linen ['lɪnən] *n* : lin *m*

liner ['laɪnər] *n* **1** LINING : doublure *f* **2** SHIP : paquebot *m*

lineup ['laɪnˌʌp] *n* **1** *or* **police ~** : rangée *f* de suspects **2** : équipe *f* (aux sports)

linger ['lɪŋgər] *vi* **1** : s'attarder, flâner **2** PERSIST : persister

lingerie [ˌlɑndʒəˈreɪ] *n* : vêtement *m* intime féminin, lingerie *f*

lingo [ˈlɪŋgo] *n, pl* **-goes** JARGON : jargon *m*
linguistics [lɪŋˈgwɪstɪks] *n* : linguistique *f* —
linguist [ˈlɪŋgwɪst] *n* : linguiste *mf* — **linguistic** [lɪŋˈgwɪstɪk] *adj* : linguistique
lining [ˈlaɪnɪŋ] *n* : doublure *f*
link [ˈlɪŋk] *n* **1** : maillon *m* (d'une chaîne) **2** BOND : lien *m* **3** CONNECTION : liaison *f* — ~ *vt* : relier, lier — *vi or* ~ **up** : se rejoindre, se relier
linoleum [ləˈnoːliəm] *n* : linoléum *m*, prélart *m Can*
lint [ˈlɪnt] *n* : peluches *fpl*
lion [ˈlaɪən] *n* : lion *m* — **lioness** [ˈlaɪənɪs] *n* : lionne *f*
lip [ˈlɪp] *n* **1** : lèvre *f* **2** EDGE : rebord *m* — **lipstick** [ˈlɪpˌstɪk] *n* : rouge *m* à lèvres
liqueur [lɪˈkər, -ˈkʊr, -ˈkjʊr] *n* : liqueur *f*
liquid [ˈlɪkwəd] *adj* : liquide — ~ *n* : liquide *m* — **liquidate** [ˈlɪkwəˌdeɪt] *vt* **-dated; -dating** : liquider — **liquidation** [ˌlɪkwəˈdeɪʃən] *n* : liquidation *f*
liquor [ˈlɪkər] *n* : boissons *fpl* alcoolisées
lisp [ˈlɪsp] *vi* : zézayer — ~ *n* : zézaiement *m*
list[1] [ˈlɪst] *n* : liste *f* — ~ *vt* **1** ENUMERATE : faire une liste de, énumérer **2** INCLUDE : mettre (sur une liste)
list[2] *vi* : gîter (se dit d'un bateau)
listen [ˈlɪsən] *vi* **1** : écouter **2** ~ **to reason** : entendre raison — **listener** [ˈlɪsənər] *n* : auditeur *m*, -trice *f*
listless [ˈlɪstləs] *adj* : apathique
lit [ˈlɪt] *pp* → **light**[1]
litany [ˈlɪtəni] *n, pl* **-nies** : litanie *f*
liter [ˈliːtər] *n* : litre *m*
literacy [ˈlɪtərəsi] *n* : alphabétisation *f*
literal [ˈlɪtərəl] *adj* : littéral — **literally** [ˈlɪtərəli] *adv* : littéralement, au pied de la lettre
literate [ˈlɪtərət] *adj* : qui sait lire et écrire
literature [ˈlɪtərəˌtʃʊr, -tʃər] *n* : littérature *f* — **literary** [ˈlɪtəˌreri] *adj* : littéraire
lithe [ˈlaɪð, ˈlaɪθ] *adj* : agile et gracieux
litigation [ˌlɪtəˈgeɪʃən] *n* : litige *m*
litre → **liter**
litter [ˈlɪtər] *n* **1** RUBBISH : ordures *fpl* **2** : portée *f* (se dit d'un animal) **3** *or* **kitty** ~ : litière *f* (de chat) — ~ *vt* : mettre du désordre dans — *vi* : jeter des déchets
little [ˈlɪtəl] *adj* **littler** *or* **less** [ˈlɛs] *or* **lesser** [ˈlɛsər]; **littlest** *or* **least** [ˈliːst] **1** SMALL : petit **2** a ~ SOME : un peu de **3** he speaks ~ English : il ne parle presque pas l'anglais — ~ *adv* **less** [ˈlɛs]; **least** [ˈliːst] : peu — ~ *pron* **1** : peu *m* **2** ~ **by** ~ : peu à peu
liturgy [ˈlɪtərdʒi] *n, pl* **-gies** : liturgie *f* — **liturgical** [ləˈtərdʒɪkəl] *adj* : liturgique
live [ˈlɪv] *v* **lived; living** *vi* **1** : vivre **2** RESIDE : habiter **3** ~ **on** : vivre de — *vt*

: vivre, mener — ~ [ˈlaɪv] *adj* **1** : vivant **2** : sous tension (se dit d'un câble électrique) **3** : en direct (se dit d'un programme de télévision, etc.) — **livelihood** [ˈlaɪvliˌhʊd] *n* : subsistance *f*, gagne-pain *m* — **lively** [ˈlaɪvli] *adj* **-lier; -est** : animé, vivant — **liven** [ˈlaɪvən] *vt or* ~ **up** : animer, égayer — *vi* : s'animer
liver [ˈlɪvər] *n* : foie *m*
livestock [ˈlaɪvˌstak] *n* : bétail *m*
livid [ˈlɪvəd] *adj* **1** : livide **2** ENRAGED : furieux
living [ˈlɪvɪŋ] *adj* : vivant — ~ *n* **make a** ~ : gagner sa vie — **living room** *n* : salle *f* de séjour, salon *m*
lizard [ˈlɪzərd] *n* : lézard *m*
llama [ˈlamə, ˈja-] *n* : lama *m*
load [ˈloːd] *n* **1** CARGO : chargement *m* **2** BURDEN : charge *f*, poids *m* **3** ~s of : beaucoup de — ~ *vt* : charger
loaf[1] [ˈloːf] *n, pl* **loaves** [ˈloːvz] : pain *m*
loaf[2] *vi* : fainéanter, paresser — **loafer** [ˈloːfər] *n* **1** : fainéant *m*, fainéante *f* **2** : mocassin *m* (soulier)
loan [ˈloːn] *n* : emprunt *m*, prêt *m* — ~ *vt* : prêter
loathe [ˈloːð] *vt* **loathed; loathing** : détester — **loathsome** [ˈloːθsəm, ˈloːð-] *adj* : odieux
lobby [ˈlabi] *n, pl* **-bies 1** : vestibule *m* **2** *or* **political** ~ : groupe *m* de pression, lobby *m* — ~ *vt* **-bied; -bying** : faire pression sur
lobe [ˈloːb] *n* : lobe *m*
lobster [ˈlabstər] *n* : homard *m*
local [ˈloːkəl] *adj* : local — ~ *n* **the** ~**s** *npl* : les gens du coin — **locale** [loˈkæl] *n* : lieu *m* — **locality** [loˈkæləti] *n, pl* **-ties** : localité *f*
locate [ˈloːˌkeɪt] *vt* **-cated; -cating 1** SITUATE : situer, établir **2** FIND : trouver — **location** [loˈkeɪʃən] *n* : emplacement *m*, endroit *m*
lock[1] [ˈlak] *n* : mèche *f* (de cheveux)
lock[2] *n* **1** : serrure *f* (d'une porte, etc.) **2** : écluse *f* (d'un canal) — ~ *vt* **1** : fermer (à clé) **2** *or* ~ **up** CONFINE : enfermer — *vi* **1** : se fermer à clé **2** : se bloquer (se dit d'une roue, etc.) — **locker** [ˈlakər] *n* : vestiaire *m* — **locket** [ˈlakət] *n* : médaillon *m* — **locksmith** [ˈlakˌsmɪθ] *n* : serrurier *m*
locomotive [ˌloːkəˈmoːtɪv] *n* : locomotive *f*
locust [ˈloːkəst] *n* : criquet *m*, sauterelle *f*
lodge [ˈladʒ] *v* **lodged; lodging** *vt* **1** HOUSE : loger, héberger **2** FILE : déposer — *vi* : se loger — ~ *n* : pavillon *m* — **lodger** [ˈladʒər] *n* : locataire *mf*, pensionnaire *mf* — **lodging** [ˈladʒɪŋ] *n* **1** : hébergement *m* **2** ~**s** *npl* : logement *m*
loft [ˈlɔft] *n* : grenier *m* (d'une maison, à foin, etc.) — **lofty** [ˈlɔfti] *adj* **loftier; -est 1** : noble, élevé **2** HAUGHTY : hautain

log ['lɔg, 'lag] *n* **1** : bûche *f*, rondin *m* **2** RECORD : registre *m* de bord — ~ *vi* **logged; logging 1** : tronçonner (des arbres) **2** RECORD : enregistrer, noter **3** ~ **on** : entrer (dans le système) **4** ~ **off** : sortir (du système) — **logger** ['lɔgər, 'lɑ-] *n* : bûcheron *m*, -ronne *f*

logic ['lɑʤɪk] *n* : logique *f* — **logical** ['lɑʤɪkəl] *adj* : logique — **logistics** [lə-'ʤɪstɪks, lo-] *ns & pl* : logistique *f*

logo ['lo:ˌgo:] *n, pl* **logos** [-ˌgo:z] : logo *m*

loin ['lɔɪn] *n* : filet *m*

loiter ['lɔɪtər] *vi* : traîner, flâner

lollipop *or* **lollypop** ['lɑliˌpɑp] *n* : sucette *f* France, suçon *m* Can

lone ['lo:n] *adj* : solitaire — **loneliness** ['lo:nlinəs] *n* : solitude *f* — **lonely** ['lo:nli] *adj* **-lier; -est** : solitaire, seul — **loner** ['lo:nər] *n* : solitaire *mf* — **lonesome** ['lo:nsəm] *adj* : seul, solitaire

long[1] ['lɔŋ] *adj* **longer** ['lɔŋgər]; **longest** ['lɔŋgəst] : long — ~ *adv* **1** : longtemps **2 all day** ~ : toute la journée **3 as** ~ **as** : tant que **4 no** ~ **er** : ne...plus **5 so** ~! : à bientôt! — ~ *n* **1 before** ~ : dans peu de temps **2 the** ~ **and short of it** : l'essentiel *m*

long[2] *vi* ~ **for** : avoir envie de, désirer

longevity [lɑn'ʤɛvəti] *n* : longévité *f*

longing ['lɔŋɪŋ] *n* : envie *f*

longitude ['lɑnʤəˌtu:d, -ˌtju:d] *n* : longitude *f*

look ['lʊk] *vi* **1** : regarder **2** SEEM : sembler **3** ~ **after** : prendre soin (de) **4** ~ **for** EXPECT : attendre **5** ~ **for** SEEK : chercher **6** ~ **into** : enquêter **7** ~ **out** : faire attention **8** ~ **over** EXAMINE : examiner **9** ~ **up to** : respecter — *vt* : regarder — ~ *n* **1** : coup *m* d'œil, regard *m* **2** APPEARANCE : aspect *m*, air *m* — **lookout** ['lʊkˌaʊt] *n* **1** : poste *m* d'observation **2** WATCHMAN : guetteur *m* **3 be on the** ~ : faire le guet

loom[1] ['lu:m] *n* : métier *m* à tisser

loom[2] *vi* **1** APPEAR : surgir **2** APPROACH : être imminent

loop ['lu:p] *n* : boucle *f* — ~ *vt* : faire une boucle avec — **loophole** ['lu:pˌho:l] *n* : échappatoire *m*

loose ['lu:s] *adj* **looser; -est 1** MOVABLE : desserré **2** SLACK : lâche **3** ROOMY : ample **4** APPROXIMATE : approximatif **5** FREE : libre **6** IMMORAL : dissolu — **loosely** ['lu:sli] *adv* **1** : sans serrer **2** ROUGHLY : approximativement — **loosen** ['lu:sən] *vt* : desserrer

loot ['lu:t] *n* : butin *m* — ~ *vt* : piller, saccager — **looter** ['lu:tər] *n* : pillard *m*, -larde *f* — **looting** ['lu:tɪŋ] *n* : pillage *m*

lop ['lɑp] *vt* **lopped; lopping** : couper, élaguer

lopsided ['lɑpˌsaɪdəd] *adj* : de travers, croche Can

lord ['lɔrd] *n* **1** : seigneur *m*, noble *m* **2 the Lord** : le Seigneur

lore ['lor] *n* : savoir *m* populaire, tradition *f*

lose ['lu:z] *v* **lost** ['lɔst]; **losing** ['lu:zɪŋ] *vt* **1** : perdre **2** ~ **one's way** : se perdre **3** ~ **time** : retarder (se dit d'une horloge) — *vi* : perdre — **loser** ['lu:zər] *n* : perdant *m*, -dante *f* — **loss** ['lɔs] *n* **1** : perte *f* **2** DEFEAT : défaite *f* **3 be at a** ~ **for words** : ne pas savoir quoi dire — **lost** ['lɔst] *adj* **1** : perdu **2 get** ~ : se perdre

lot ['lɑt] *n* **1** FATE : sort *m* **2** PLOT : parcelle *f* **3 a** ~ **of** *or* ~**s of** : beaucoup, une montagne de

lotion ['lo:ʃən] *n* : lotion *f*

lottery ['lɑtəri] *n, pl* **-teries** : loterie *f*

loud ['laʊd] *adj* **1** : grand, fort **2** NOISY : bruyant **3** FLASHY : criard — ~ *adv* **1** : fort **2 out** ~ : à voix haute — **loudly** ['laʊdli] *adv* : à voix haute — **loudspeaker** ['laʊdˌspi:kər] *n* : haut-parleur *m*

lounge ['laʊnʤ] *vi* **lounged; lounging 1** : se vautrer **2** ~ **about** : flâner — ~ *n* : salon *m*

louse ['laʊs] *n, pl* **lice** ['laɪs] : pou *m* — **lousy** ['laʊzi] *adj* **lousier; -est 1** : pouilleux **2** BAD : piètre, très mauvais

love ['lʌv] *n* **1** : amour *m* **2 fall in** ~ : tomber amoureux — ~ *v* **loved; loving** : aimer — **lovable** ['lʌvəbəl] *adj* : adorable — **lovely** ['lʌvli] *adj* **-lier; -est** : beau, joli — **lover** ['lʌvər] *n* : amant *m*, -mante *f* — **loving** ['lʌvɪŋ] *adj* : affectueux

low ['lo:] *adj* **lower** ['lo:ər]; **lowest 1** : bas **2** SCARCE : limité **3** DEPRESSED : déprimé — ~ *adv* **1** : bas **2 turn the lights** ~ : baisser les lumières — ~ *n* **1** : point *m* bas **2** *or* ~ **gear** : première *f* — **lower** ['lo:ər] *adj* : inférieur, plus bas — ~ *vt* : baisser — **lowly** ['lo:li] *adj* **-lier; -est** : humble

loyal ['lɔɪəl] *adj* : loyal, fidèle — **loyalty** ['lɔɪəlti] *n, pl* **-ties** : loyauté *f*

lozenge ['lɑzənʤ] *n* : pastille *f*

lubricate ['lu:brəˌkeɪt] *vt* **-cated; -cating** : lubrifier — **lubricant** ['lu:brɪkənt] *n* : lubrifiant *m* — **lubrication** [ˌlu:brə'keɪʃən] *n* : lubrification *f*

lucid ['lu:səd] *adj* : lucide — **lucidity** [lu:-'sɪdəti] *n* : lucidité *f*

luck ['lʌk] *n* **1** : chance *f* **2 good** ~! : bonne chance! — **luckily** ['lʌkəli] *adv* : heureusement — **lucky** ['lʌki] *adj* **luckier; -est 1** : chanceux **2** ~ **charm** : porte-bonheur *m*

lucrative ['lu:krətɪv] *adj* : lucratif

ludicrous ['lu:dəkrəs] *adj* : ridicule, absurde

lug ['lʌg] *vt* **lugged; lugging** : traîner

luggage ['lʌgɪʤ] *n* : bagages *mpl*

lukewarm ['luːk'wɔrm] *adj* : tiède

lull ['lʌl] *vt* **1** CALM : calmer **2 ~ to sleep** : endormir — **~** *n* : période *f* de calme, pause *f*

lullaby ['lʌlə,baɪ] *n, pl* **-bies** : berceuse *f*

lumber ['lʌmbər] *n* : bois *m* — **lumberjack** ['lʌmbər,ʤæk] *n* : bûcheron *m*, -ronne *f*

luminous ['luːmənəs] *adj* : lumineux

lump ['lʌmp] *n* **1** CHUNK, PIECE : morceau *m*, motte *f* **2** SWELLING : bosse *f* **3** : grumeau *m* (dans une sauce) — **~** *vt or* **~ together** : réunir, regrouper — **lumpy** ['lʌmpi] *adj* **lumpier; -est** : grumeleux (se dit d'une sauce), bosselé (se dit d'un matelas)

lunacy ['luːnəsi] *n, pl* **-cies** : folie *f*

lunar ['luːnər] *adj* : lunaire

lunatic ['luːnə,tɪk] *n* : fou *m*

lunch ['lʌntʃ] *n* : déjeuner *m*, dîner *m* *Can*, lunch *m Can* — **~** *vi* : déjeuner, dîner *Can* — **luncheon** ['lʌntʃən] *n* : déjeuner *m*

lung ['lʌŋ] *n* : poumon *m*

lunge ['lʌnʤ] *vi* **lunged; lunging 1** : se précipiter **2 ~ at** : foncer sur

lurch[1] ['lərtʃ] *vi* **1** STAGGER : tituber **2** : faire une embardée (se dit d'une voiture)

lurch[2] *n* **leave in a ~** : laisser en plan

lure ['lʊr] *n* **1** BAIT : leurre *m* **2** ATTRACTION : attrait *m* — **~** *vt* **lured; luring** : attirer

lurid ['lʊrəd] *adj* **1** GRUESOME : épouvantable **2** SENSATIONAL : à sensation **3** GAUDY : criard

lurk ['lərk] *vi* : être tapi

luscious ['lʌʃəs] *adj* : délicieux, exquis

lush ['lʌʃ] *adj* : luxuriant, somptueux

lust ['lʌst] *n* **1** : luxure *f* **2** CRAVING : envie *f*, désir *m* — **~** *vi* **~ after** : désirer (une personne), convoiter (des richesses, etc.)

luster *or* **lustre** ['lʌstər] *n* : lustre *m*

lusty ['lʌsti] *adj* **lustier; -est** : robuste, vigoureux

luxurious [ˌlʌg'ʒʊriəs, ˌlʌk'ʃʊr-] *adj* : luxueux — **luxury** ['lʌkʃəri, 'lʌgʒə-] *n, pl* **-ries** : luxe *m*

lye ['laɪ] *n* : lessive *f*

lying → lie

lynch ['lɪntʃ] *vt* : lyncher

lynx ['lɪŋks] *n* : lynx *m*

lyric ['lɪrɪk] *or* **lyrical** ['lɪrɪkəl] *adj* : lyrique — **lyrics** *npl* : paroles *fpl* (d'une chanson)

M

m ['ɛm] *n, pl* **m's** *or* **ms** ['ɛmz] : m *m*, treizième lettre de l'alphabet

ma'am ['mæm] → **madam**

macabre [mə'kab, -'kabər, -'kabrə] *adj* : macabre

macaroni [ˌmækə'roːni] *n* : macaronis *mpl*

mace ['meɪs] *n* **1** : masse *f* (arme ou symbole) **2** : macis *m* (épice)

machete [mə'ʃɛti] *n* : machette *f*

machine [mə'ʃiːn] *n* : machine *f* — **machine gun** *n* : mitrailleuse *f* — **machinery** [mə'ʃiːnəri] *n, pl* **-eries 1** : machinerie *f* **2** WORKS : mécanisme *m*

mad ['mæd] *adj* **madder; maddest 1** INSANE : fou **2** FOOLISH : insensé **3** ANGRY : furieux

madam ['mædəm] *n, pl* **mesdames** [meɪ'dam] : madame *f*

madden ['mædən] *vt* : exaspérer

made → make

madly ['mædli] *adv* : comme un fou, follement — **madman** ['mæd,mæn, -mən] *n, pl* **-men** [-mən, -,mɛn] : fou *m* — **madness** ['mædnəs] *n* : folie *f*

Mafia ['mɑfiə] *n* : mafia *f*

magazine ['mægə,ziːn] *n* **1** PERIODICAL : revue *f* **2** : magasin *m* (d'une arme à feu)

maggot ['mægət] *n* : asticot *m*

magic ['mæʤɪk] *n* : magie *f* — **~** *or* **magical** ['mæʤɪkəl] *adj* : magique — **magician** [mə'ʤɪʃən] *n* : magicien *m*, -cienne *f*

magistrate ['mæʤə,streɪt] *n* : magistrat *m*

magnanimous [mæg'nænəməs] *adj* : magnanime

magnate ['mæg,neɪt, -nət] *n* : magnat *m*

magnet ['mægnət] *n* : aimant *m* — **magnetic** [mæg'nɛtɪk] *adj* : magnétique — **magnetism** ['mægnə,tɪzəm] *n* : magnétisme *m* — **magnetize** ['mægnə,taɪz] *vt* **-tized; -tizing** : magnétiser

magnificent [mæg'nɪfəsənt] *adj* : magnifique — **magnificence** [mæg'nɪfəsənts] *n* : splendeur *f*

magnify ['mægnə,faɪ] *vt* **-fied; -fying 1** ENLARGE : amplifier **2** EXAGGERATE : exagérer — **magnifying glass** *n* : loupe *f*

magnitude ['mægnə,tuːd, -,tjuːd] *n* : ampleur *f*

magnolia [mæg'noːljə] *n* : magnolia *m*

mahogany [mə'hɑgəni] *n, pl* **-nies** : acajou *m*

maid ['meɪd] *n* : servante *f,* bonne *f,* domestique *f* — **maiden name** *n* : nom *m* de jeune fille

mail ['meɪl] *n* **1** : poste *f* **2** LETTERS : correspondence *f* — ~ *vt* : envoyer par la poste — **mailbox** ['meɪl,bɑks] *n* : boîte *f* aux lettres — **mailman** ['meɪl,mæn, -mən] *n, pl* **-men** [-mən, -,mɛn] : facteur *m*

maim ['meɪm] *vt* : mutiler

main ['meɪn] *n* : canalisation *f* principale (d'eau ou de gaz) — ~ *adj* : principal — **mainframe** ['meɪn,freɪm] *n* : ordinateur *m* central — **mainland** ['meɪn,lænd, -lənd] *n* : continent *m* — **mainly** ['meɪnli] *adv* : principalement — **mainstay** ['meɪn,steɪ] *n* : soutien *m* prinicpal — **mainstream** ['meɪn,stri:m] *n* : courant *m* dominant — ~ *adj* : dominant, conventionnel

maintain [meɪn'teɪn] *vt* : entretenir, maintenir — **maintenance** ['meɪntənənts] *n* : entretien *m,* maintien *m*

maize ['meɪz] *n* : maïs *m*

majestic [mə'dʒɛstɪk] *adj* : majestueux — **majesty** ['mædʒəsti] *n, pl* **-ties** : majesté *f*

major ['meɪdʒər] *adj* **1** : très important, principal **2** : majeur (en musique) — ~ *n* **1** : commandant *m* (des forces armées) **2** : spécialité *f* (à l'université) — ~ *vi* **-jored; -joring** : se spécialiser — **majority** [mə'dʒɔrəti] *n, pl* **-ties** : majorité *f*

make ['meɪk] *v* **made** ['meɪd]; **making** *vt* **1** : faire **2** MANUFACTURE : fabriquer **3** CONSTITUTE : constituer **4** PREPARE : préparer **5** RENDER : rendre **6** COMPEL : obliger **7** ~ **a decision** : prendre une décision **8** ~ **a living** : gagner sa vie — *vi* **1** ~ **do** : se débrouiller **2** ~ **for** : se diriger vers **3** ~ **good** SUCCEED : réussir — ~ *n* BRAND : marque *f* — **make-believe** [,meɪkbə'li:v] *n* : fantaisie *f* — ~ *adj* : imaginaire — **make out** *vt* **1** : faire (un chèque, etc.) **2** DISCERN : distinguer **3** UNDERSTAND : comprendre — *vi* **how did you** ~? : comment ça s'est passé? — **maker** ['meɪkər] *n* MANUFACTURER : fabricant *m,* -cante *f* — **makeshift** ['meɪk,ʃɪft] *adj* : improvisé — **makeup** ['meɪk,ʌp] *n* **1** COMPOSITION : composition *f* **2** COSMETICS : maquillage *m* — **make up** *vt* **1** PREPARE : préparer **2** INVENT : inventer **3** CONSTITUTE : former — *vi* RECONCILE : faire la paix

maladjusted [,mælə'dʒʌstəd] *adj* : inadapté

malaria [mə'leriə] *n* : paludisme *m*

male ['meɪl] *n* : mâle *m,* homme *m* — ~ *adj* **1** : mâle **2** MASCULINE : masculin

malevolent [mə'lɛvələnt] *adj* : malveillant

malfunction [mæl'fʌŋkʃən] *vi* : mal fonctionner — ~ *n* : mauvais fonctionnement *m*

malice ['mælɪs] *n* : mauvaise intention *f,* rancœur *f* — **malicious** [mə'lɪʃəs] *adj* : malveillant

malign [mə'laɪn] *adj* : pernicieux — ~ *vt* : calomnier

malignant [mə'lɪgnənt] *adj* : malveillant

mall ['mɔl] *n or* **shopping** ~ : centre *m* commercial

malleable ['mæliəbəl] *adj* : malléable

mallet ['mælət] *n* : maillet *m*

malnutrition [,mælnʊ'trɪʃən, -njʊ-] *n* : malnutrition *f*

malpractice [,mæl'præktəs] *n* : négligence *f*

malt ['mɔlt] *n* : malt *m*

mama *or* **mamma** ['mɑmə] *n* : maman *f*

mammal ['mæməl] *n* : mammifère *m*

mammogram ['mæmə,græm] *n* : mammographie *f*

mammoth ['mæməθ] *adj* : gigantesque

man ['mæn] *n, pl* **men** ['mɛn] : homme *m* — ~ *vt* **manned; manning** : équiper en personnel

manage ['mænɪdʒ] *v* **-aged; -aging** *vt* **1** HANDLE : manier **2** DIRECT : gérer, diriger — *vi* COPE : se débrouiller — **manageable** ['mænɪdʒəbəl] *adj* : maniable — **management** ['mænɪdʒmənt] *n* : gestion *f,* direction *f* — **manager** ['mænɪdʒər] *n* : directeur *m,* -trice *f;* gérant *m,* -rante *f;* manager *m* (aux sports) — **managerial** [,mænə'dʒɪriəl] *adj* : de gestion

mandarin ['mændərən] *n or* ~ **orange** : mandarine *f*

mandate ['mæn,deɪt] *n* : mandat *m*

mandatory ['mændə,tɔri] *adj* : obligatoire

mane ['meɪn] *n* : crinière *f*

maneuver *or Brit* **manoeuvre** [mə'nu:vər, -'nju:-] *n* : manœuvre *f* — ~ *v* **-vered** *or Brit* **-vred; -vering** *or Brit* **-vring** : manœuvrer

mangle ['mæŋgəl] *vt* **-gled; -gling** : mutiler

mango ['mæŋ,go:] *n, pl* **-goes** : mangue *f*

mangy ['meɪndʒi] *adj* **mangier; -est** : galeux

manhandle ['mæn,hændəl] *vt* **-dled; -dling** : malmener

manhole ['mæn,ho:l] *n* : bouche *f* d'égout

manhood ['mæn,hʊd] *n* **1** : âge *m* d'homme **2** : virilité *f*

mania ['meɪniə, -njə] *n* : manie *f* — **maniac** ['meɪni,æk] *n* : maniaque *mf*

manicure ['mænə,kjʊr] *n* : manucure *f* — ~ *vt* **-cured; -curing** : faire les ongles de

manifest ['mænə,fɛst] *adj* : manifeste, patent — ~ *vt* : manifester — **manifesto** [,mænə'fɛs,to:] *n, pl* **-tos** *or* **-toes** : manifeste *m*

manipulate [mə'nɪpjə,leɪt] *vt* **-lated; -lating** : manipuler — **manipulation** [mə,nɪpjə'leɪʃən] *n* : manipulation *f*

mankind ['mæn'kaınd, -ˌkaınd] n : le genre humain, humanité f

manly ['mænli] adj -lier; -est : viril — **manliness** ['mænlinəs] n : virilité f

mannequin ['mænɪkən] n : mannequin m

manner ['mænər] n 1 : manière f 2 KIND : sorte f 3 ~s npl ETIQUETTE : manières fpl, éducation f — **mannerism** ['mænəˌrɪzəm] n : particularité f

manoeuvre Brit → **maneuver**

manor ['mænər] n : manoir m

manpower ['mænˌpaʊər] n : main-d'œuvre f

mansion ['mænʧən] n : château m

manslaughter ['mænˌslɔtər] n : homicide m involontaire

mantel ['mæntəl] or **mantelpiece** ['mæntəlˌpi:s] n : cheminée f

manual ['mænjʊəl] adj : manuel — ~ n : manuel m

manufacture [ˌmænjəˈfækʧər] n : fabrication f — ~ vt -tured; -turing : fabriquer — **manufacturer** [ˌmænjəˈfækʧərər] n : fabricant m, -cante f

manure [məˈnʊr, -ˈnjʊr] n : fumier m

manuscript ['mænjəˌskrɪpt] n : manuscrit m

many ['mɛni] adj **more** ['mor]; **most** ['mo:st] 1 : beaucoup de 2 as ~ : autant de 3 how ~ : combien 4 too ~ : trop de — ~ pron : beaucoup

map ['mæp] n : carte f, plan m — ~ vt **mapped; mapping** 1 : faire la carte de 2 or ~ **out** : élaborer

maple ['meɪpəl] n 1 : érable m 2 ~ **syrup** : sirop m d'érable

mar ['mar] vt **marred; marring** : estropier

marathon ['mærəˌθɑn] n : marathon m

marble ['marbəl] n 1 : marbre m 2 : billes fpl (à jouer)

march ['marʧ] n : marche f — ~ vi : marcher, défiler

March ['marʧ] n : mars m

mare ['mær] n : jument f

margarine ['marʤərən] n : margarine f

margin ['marʤən] n : marge f — **marginal** ['marʤənəl] adj : marginal

marigold ['mærəˌgo:ld] n : souci m

marijuana [ˌmærəˈhwɑnə] n : marijuana f

marinate ['mærəˌneɪt] v -nated; -nating : mariner

marine [məˈri:n] adj : marin — ~ n : fusilier m marin

marital ['mærətəl] adj 1 : conjugal 2 ~ **status** : état m civil

maritime ['mærəˌtaɪm] adj : maritime

mark ['mark] n 1 : marque f 2 STAIN : tache f 3 IMPRINT : trace f 4 TARGET : cible f 5 GRADE : note f — ~ vt 1 : marquer 2 STAIN : tacher 3 POINT OUT : signaler 4 : corriger (un examen, etc.) 5 COMMEMORATE : com-

mémorer 6 CHARACTERIZE : caractériser 7 ~ **off** : délimiter — **marked** ['markt] adj : marqué, notable — **markedly** ['markədli] adv : sensiblement — **marker** ['markər] n 1 : repère m 2 PEN : marqueur m

market ['markət] n : marché m — ~ vt : vendre, commercialiser — **marketable** ['markətəbəl] adj : vendable — **marketplace** ['markətˌpleɪs] n : marché m

marksman ['marksmən] n, pl -**men** [-mən, -ˌmɛn] : tireur m, -reuse f d'élite — **marksmanship** ['marksmənˌʃɪp] n : adresse f au tir

marmalade ['marməˌleɪd] n : marmelade f

maroon[1] [məˈru:n] vt : abandonner

maroon[2] n : rouge m foncé

marquee [marˈki:] n CANOPY : marquise f

marriage ['mærɪʤ] n 1 : mariage m 2 WEDDING : noces fpl — **married** ['mærid] adj 1 : marié 2 **get** ~ : se marier

marrow ['mæro:] n : moelle f

marry ['mæri] v -ried; -rying vt 1 : marier 2 WED : se marier avec, épouser — vi : se marier

Mars ['marz] n : Mars f

marsh ['marʃ] n 1 : marécage m 2 or **salt** ~ : marais m salant

marshal ['marʃəl] n : maréchal m (militaire), commissaire m (de police) — ~ vt -shaled or -shalled; -shaling or -shalling : rassembler

marshmallow ['marʃˌmɛlo:, -ˌmælo:] n : guimauve f

marshy ['marʃi] adj **marshier; -est** : marécageux

mart ['mart] n : marché m

martial ['marʃəl] adj : martial

martyr ['martər] n : martyr m, -tyre f — ~ vt : martyriser

marvel ['marvəl] n : merveille f — ~ vi -veled or -velled; -veling or -velling : s'émerveiller — **marvelous** ['marvələs] or **marvellous** adj : merveilleux

mascara [mæsˈkærə] n : mascara m

mascot ['mæsˌkɑt, -kət] n : mascotte f

masculine ['mæskjələn] adj : masculin — **masculinity** [ˌmæskjəˈlɪnəti] n : masculinité f

mash ['mæʃ] vt 1 CRUSH : écraser, aplatir 2 PUREE : faire une purée de, piler Can — **mashed potatoes** npl : purée f de pommes de terre, patates fpl Can

mask ['mæsk] n : masque m — ~ vt : masquer

masochism ['mæsəˌkɪzəm, 'mæzə-] n : masochisme m — **masochist** ['mæsəˌkɪst, 'mæzə-] n : masochiste mf — **masochistic** [ˌmæsəˈkɪstɪk] adj : masochiste

mason ['meɪsən] n : maçon m — **masonry** ['meɪsənri] n, pl -**ries** : maçonnerie f

masquerade [ˌmæskəˈreɪd] *n* : mascarade *f*
— ~ *vi* **-aded; -ading** ~ **as** : se déguiser
en, se faire passer pour

mass [ˈmæs] *n* **1** : masse *f* **2** MULTITUDE
: quantité *f* **3 the** ~**es** : les masses

Mass *n* : messe *f*

massacre [ˈmæsɪkər] *n* : massacre *m* — ~
vt **-cred; -cring** : massacrer

massage [məˈsɑʒ, -ˈsɑdʒ] *n* : massage *m* —
~ *vt* **-saged; -saging** : donner un massage
à, masser — **masseur** [mæˈsər] *n* : masseur
m — **masseuse** [mæˈsøz, -ˈsuːz] *n*
: masseuse *f*

massive [ˈmæsɪv] *adj* **1** BULKY : massif **2**
HUGE : énorme

mast [ˈmæst] *n* : mât *m*

master [ˈmæstər] *n* **1** : maître *m* **2** ~**'s degree** : maîtrise *f* — ~ *vt* : maîtriser — **mas-
terful** [ˈmæstərfəl] *adj* : magistral — **masterpiece** [ˈmæstərˌpiːs] *n* : chef *m* d'œuvre
— **mastery** [ˈmæstəri] *n* : maîtrise *f*

masturbate [ˈmæstərˌbeɪt] *vi* **-bated; -bat-
ing** : se masturber — **masturbation** [ˌmæs-
tərˈbeɪʃən] *n* : masturbation *f*

mat [ˈmæt] *n* **1** DOORMAT : paillasson *m* **2**
RUG : tapis *m*

match [ˈmætʃ] *n* **1** : allumette *f* **2** EQUAL
: égal *m*, égale *f* **3** GAME : match *m*, combat
m (de boxe) **4 be a good** ~ : être un bon
parti — ~ *vt* **1** *or* ~ **up** : appareiller **2**
EQUAL : égaler **3** : s'accorder avec, aller ensemble (vêtements, couleurs, etc.) — *vi*
: correspondre

mate [ˈmeɪt] *n* **1** COMPANION : compagnon
m, -pagne *f* **2** : mâle *m*, femelle *f* (d'un animal) — ~ *vi* **mated; mating** : s'accoupler

material [məˈtɪriəl] *adj* **1** : matériel **2** IM-
PORTANT : important — ~ *n* **1** : matière *f*
2 FABRIC : tissu *m*, étoffe *f* — **materialistic**
[məˌtɪriəˈlɪstɪk] *adj* : matérialiste — **materialize** [məˈtɪriəˌlaɪz] *vi* **-ized; -izing** : se
matérialiser

maternal [məˈtərnəl] *adj* : maternel — **maternity** [məˈtərnəti] *n*, *pl* **-ties** : maternité *f*
— ~ *adj* : de maternité

math [ˈmæθ] → **mathematics**

mathematics [ˌmæθəˈmætɪks] *ns & pl*
: mathématiques *fpl* — **mathematical**
[ˌmæθəˈmætɪkəl] *adj* : mathématique —
mathematician [ˌmæθəməˈtɪʃən] *n* : mathématicien *m*, -cienne *f*

matinee *or* **matinée** [ˌmætənˈeɪ] *n* : matinée
f (au cinéma)

matrimony [ˈmætrəˌmoːni] *n* : mariage *m* —
matrimonial [ˌmætrəˈmoːniəl] *adj* : matrimonial

matrix [ˈmeɪtrɪks] *n*, *pl* **-trices** [ˈmeɪtrəˌsiːz,
ˈmæ-] *or* **-trixes** [ˈmeɪtrɪksəz] : matrice *f*

matte [ˈmæt] *adj* : mat

matter [ˈmætər] *n* **1** SUBSTANCE : matière *f*

2 QUESTION : affaire *f*, question *f* **3 as a** ~
of fact : en fait, en réalité **4 for that** ~
: d'ailleurs **5 to make** ~**s worse** : pour ne
rien arranger **6 what's the** ~? : qu'est-ce
qu'il y a? — ~ *vi* : importer

mattress [ˈmætrəs] *n* : matelas *m*

mature [məˈtʊr, -ˈtjʊr, -ˈtʃʊr] *adj* **-turer; -est**
: mûr — ~ *vi* **-tured; -turing** : mûrir —
maturity [məˈtʊrəti, -ˈtjʊr-, -ˈtʃʊr-] *n* : maturité *f*

maul [ˈmɔl] *vt* : mutiler

mauve [ˈmoːv, ˈmɔv] *n* : mauve *m*

maxim [ˈmæksəm] *n* : maxime *f*

maximum [ˈmæksəməm] *n*, *pl* **-ma**
[ˈmæksəmə] *or* **-mums** : maximum *m* —
~ *adj* : maximum — **maximize** [ˈmæksə-
ˌmaɪz] *vt* **-mized; -mizing** : porter au maximum

may [ˈmeɪ] *v aux*, *past* **might** [ˈmaɪt]; *present
s & pl* **may 1** : pouvoir **2 come what** ~
: quoiqu'il arrive **3 it** ~ **rain** : il se peut
qu'il pleuve, il va peut-être pleuvoir **4** ~
the best man win : que le meilleur gagne

May [ˈmeɪ] *n* : mai *m*

maybe [ˈmeɪbi] *adv* : peut-être

mayhem [ˈmeɪˌhɛm, ˈmeɪəm] *n* : pagaille *f*

mayonnaise [ˈmeɪəˌneɪz] *n* : mayonnaise *f*

mayor [ˈmeɪər, ˈmɛr] *n* : maire *m*, mairesse *f*

maze [ˈmeɪz] *n* : labyrinthe *m*

me [ˈmiː] *pron* **1** : moi **2** : me, m' **3 give it
to** ~ : donne-le moi **4 will she come with**
~? : m'accompagnera-t-elle?

meadow [ˈmɛdoː] *n* : pré *m*, prairie *f*

meager *or* **meagre** [ˈmiːɡər] *adj* : maigre

meal [ˈmiːl] *n* **1** : repas *m* **2** : farine *f* (de
maïs, etc.) — **mealtime** [ˈmiːlˌtaɪm] *n*
: l'heure *f* du repas

mean[1] [ˈmiːn] *vt* **meant** [ˈmɛnt]; **meaning 1**
SIGNIFY : vouloir dire **2** INTEND : avoir l'intention de **3 be meant for** : être destiné à **4**
he didn't ~ **it** : il ne l'a pas fait exprès

mean[2] *adj* **1** UNKIND : méchant **2** STINGY
: mesquin

mean[3] *adj* AVERAGE : moyen — ~ *n*
: moyenne *f*

meander [miˈændər] *vi* **1** WIND : serpenter
2 WANDER : errer

meaning [ˈmiːnɪŋ] *n* : sens *m*, signification *f*
— **meaningful** [ˈmiːnɪŋfəl] *adj* : significatif
— **meaningless** [ˈmiːnɪŋləs] *adj* : sans signification

meanness [ˈmiːnnəs] *n* : méchanceté *f*

means [ˈmiːnz] *n* **1** : moyens *mpl* **2 by all**
~ : certainement **3 by** ~ **of** : au moyen de
4 by no ~ : d'aucune façon

meantime [ˈmiːnˌtaɪm] *n* **1** : intervalle *m* **2**
in the ~ : en attendant — ~ *adv* → **meanwhile**

meanwhile [ˈmiːnˌʍaɪl] *adv* : entre-temps
— ~ *n* → **meantime**

measles ['mi:zəlz] *npl* : rougeole *f*

measly ['mi:zli] *adj* **-slier; -est** : misérable, minable *fam*

measure ['mɛʒər, 'mei-] *n* : mesure *f* — ~ *v* **-sured; -suring** : mesurer — **measurable** ['mɛʒərəbəl, 'mei-] *adj* : mesurable — **measurement** ['mɛʒərmənt, 'mei-] *n* : mesure *f* — **measure up** *vi* ~ **to** : être à la hauteur de

meat ['mi:t] *n* : viande *f* — **meatball** ['mi:t-,bɔl] *n* : boulette *f* de viande — **meaty** ['mi:ti] *adj* **meatier; -est 1** : de viande **2** SUBSTANTIAL : substantiel

mechanic [mɪ'kænɪk] *n* : mécanicien *m*, -cienne *f* — **mechanical** [mɪ'kænɪkəl] *adj* : mécanique — **mechanics** [mɪ'kænɪks] *ns & pl* **1** : mécanique *f* **2** WORKINGS : mécanisme *m* — **mechanism** ['mɛkə,nɪzəm] *n* : mécanisme *m* — **mechanize** ['mɛkə,naɪz] *vt* **-nized; -nizing** : mécaniser

medal ['mɛdəl] *n* : médaille *f* — **medallion** [mə'dæljən] *n* : médaillon *m*

meddle ['mɛdəl] *vi* **-dled; -dling** : se mêler

media ['mi:diə] *or* **mass** ~ *npl* : les médias

median ['mi:diən] *adj* : médian

mediate ['mi:di,eɪt] *vi* **-ated; -ating** : servir de médiateur — **mediation** [,mi:di'eɪʃən] *n* : médiation *f* — **mediator** ['mi:di,eɪtər] *n* : médiateur *m*, -trice *f*

medical ['mɛdɪkəl] *adj* : médical — **medicated** ['mɛdə,keɪtəd] *adj* : médical, traitant — **medication** [,mɛdə'keɪʃən] *n* : médicaments *mpl* — **medicinal** [mə-'dɪsənəl] *adj* : médicinal — **medicine** ['mɛdəsən] *n* **1** : médecine *f* **2** MEDICATION : médicament *m*

medieval *or* **mediaeval** [mɪ'di:vəl, ,mi:-, ,mɛ-, -di'i:vəl] *adj* : médiéval

mediocre [,mi:di'o:kər] *adj* : médiocre — **mediocrity** [,mi:di'ɑkrəti] *n*, *pl* **-ties** : médiocrité *f*

meditate ['mɛdə,teɪt] *vi* **-tated; -tating** : méditer — **meditation** [,mɛdə'teɪʃən] *n* : méditation *f*

Mediterranean [,mɛdətə'reɪniən] *adj* : méditerranéen

medium ['mi:diəm] *n*, *pl* **-diums** *or* **-dia** ['mi:diə] **1** MEANS : moyen *m* **2** MEAN : milieu *m* **3** → **media** — ~ *adj* : moyen

medley ['mɛdli] *n*, *pl* **-leys 1** : mélange *m* **2** : pot-pourri *m* (de chansons)

meek ['mi:k] *adj* : docile

meet ['mi:t] *v* **met** ['mɛt]; **meeting** *vt* **1** ENCOUNTER : rencontrer **2** SATISFY : satisfaire **3 pleased to** ~ **you** : enchanté de faire votre connaissance — *vi* **1** : se rencontrer **2** ASSEMBLE : se réunir **3** : faire connaissance — ~ *n* : rencontre *f* (aux sports) — **meeting** ['mi:tɪŋ] *n* : réunion *f*

megabyte ['mɛgə,baɪt] *n* : mégaoctet *m*

megaphone ['mɛgə,fo:n] *n* : porte-voix *m*, mégaphone *m*

melancholy ['mɛlən,kɑli] *n*, *pl* **-cholies** : mélancolie *f* — ~ *adj* : mélancolique, triste

mellow ['mɛlo:] *adj* **1** : doux, moelleux **2** CALM : paisible — ~ *vt* : adoucir — *vi* : s'adoucir

melody ['mɛlədi] *n*, *pl* **-dies** : mélodie *f*

melon ['mɛlən] *n* : melon *m*

melt ['mɛlt] *vi* : fondre — *vt* : faire fondre

member ['mɛmbər] *n* : membre *m* — **membership** ['mɛmbər,ʃɪp] *n* **1** : adhésion *f* **2** MEMBERS : membres *mpl*

membrane ['mɛm,breɪn] *n* : membrane *f*

memory ['mɛmri, 'mɛmə-] *n*, *pl* **-ries 1** : mémoire *f* **2** RECOLLECTION : souvenir *m* — **memento** [mɪ'mɛn,to:] *n*, *pl* **-tos** *or* **-toes** : souvenir *m* — **memo** ['mɛmo:] *n*, *pl* **memos** *or* **memorandum** [,mɛmə-'rændəm] *n*, *pl* **-dums** *or* **-da** [-də] : mémorandum *m* — **memoirs** ['mɛm-,wɑrz] *npl* : mémoires *mpl* — **memorable** ['mɛmərəbəl] *adj* : mémorable — **memorial** [mə'moriəl] *adj* : commémoratif — ~ *n* : monument *m* (commémoratif) — **memorize** ['mɛmə,raɪz] *vt* **-rized; -rizing** : apprendre par cœur

men → **man**

menace ['mɛnəs] *n* : menace *f* — ~ *vt* **-aced; -acing** : menacer — **menacing** ['mɛnəsɪŋ] *adj* : menaçant

mend ['mɛnd] *vt* **1** : réparer, arranger **2** DARN : raccommoder — *vi* HEAL : guérir

menial ['mi:niəl] *adj* : servile, bas

meningitis [,mɛnən'ʤaɪtəs] *n*, *pl* **-gitides** [-'ʤɪtə,di:z] : méningite *f*

menopause ['mɛnə,pɔz] *n* : ménopause *f*

menstruate ['mɛnstru,eɪt] *vi* **-ated; -ating** : avoir ses règles — **menstruation** [,mɛnstru'eɪʃən] *n* : menstruation *f*, règles *fpl*

mental ['mɛntəl] *adj* : mental — **mentality** [mɛn'tæləti] *n*, *pl* **-ties** : mentalité *f*

mention ['mɛntʃən] *n* : mention *f* — ~ *vt* **1** : mentionner **2 don't** ~ **it** : il n'y a pas de quoi

menu ['mɛn,ju:] *n* : menu *m*

meow [mi:'au] *n* : miaulement *m*, miaou *m* — ~ *vi* : miauler

mercenary ['mərsən,ɛri] *n*, *pl* **-naries** : mercenaire *mf*

merchant ['mərtʃənt] *n* : marchand *m*, -chande *f*; commerçant *m*, -çante *f* — **merchandise** ['mərtʃən,daɪz, -,daɪs] *n* : marchandises *fpl*

merciful ['mərsɪfəl] *adj* : miséricordieux, compatissant — **merciless** ['mərsɪləs] *adj* : impitoyable

mercury ['mərkjəri] *n* : mercure *m*

Mercury ['mərkjəri] *n* : Mercure *f*

mercy ['mɛrsi] *n, pl* **-cies 1** : miséricorde *f*, compassion *f* **2 at the ~ of** : à la merci de

mere ['mɪr] *adj, superlative* **merest** : simple — **merely** ['mɪrli] *adv* : simplement

merge ['mərdʒ] *v* **merged; merging** *vi* : fusionner (se dit d'une compagnie), confluer (se dit d'une rivière, etc.) — *vt* : unir, fusionner — **merger** ['mərdʒər] *n* : union *f*, fusion *f*

merit ['mɛrət] *n* : mérite *m* — **~** *vt* : mériter

mermaid ['mər,meɪd] *n* : sirène *f*

merry ['mɛri] *adj* **-rier; -est** : allègre — **merry–go–round** ['mɛrigo,raʊnd] *n* : manège *m*

mesh ['mɛʃ] *n* : maille *f*

mesmerize ['mɛzmə,raɪz] *vt* **-ized; -izing** : hypnotiser

mess ['mɛs] *n* **1** : désordre *m* **2** MUDDLE : gâchis *m* **3** : cantine *f* (ambulante) — **~** *vt* **1 ~ up** : mettre en désordre **2** *or* **~ up** SOIL : salir **3 ~ up** BUNGLE : gâcher — *vi* **1 ~ around** PUTTER : bricoler **2 ~ with** PROVOKE : embêter

message ['mɛsɪdʒ] *n* : message *m* — **messenger** ['mɛsəndʒər] *n* : messager *m*, -gère *f*

messy ['mɛsi] *adj* **messier; -est** : désordonné

met → meet

metabolism [mə'tæbə,lɪzəm] *n* : métabolisme *m*

metal ['mɛt̬əl] *n* : métal *m* — **metallic** [mə'tælɪk] *adj* : métallique

metamorphosis [,mɛt̬ə'mɔrfəsɪs] *n, pl* **-phoses** [-'si:z] : métamorphose *f*

metaphor ['mɛt̬ə,fɔr, -fər] *n* : métaphore *f*

meteor ['mi:t̬iər, -ti̯ɔr] *n* : météore *m* — **meteorological** [,mi:t̬i̯ərə'ladʒɪkəl] *adj* : météorologique — **meteorologist** [,mi:t̬i̯ə'ralədʒɪst] *n* : météorologue *mf* — **meteorology** [,mi:t̬i̯ə'ralədʒi] *n* : météorologie *f*

meter *or Brit* **metre** ['mi:t̬ər] *n* **1** : mètre *m* **2** : compteur *m* (d'électricité, etc.)

method ['mɛθəd] *n* : méthode *f* — **methodical** [mə'θadɪkəl] *adj* : méthodique

meticulous [mə'tɪkjələs] *adj* : méticuleux

metric ['mɛtrɪk] *or* **metrical** [-trɪkəl] *adj* : métrique

metropolis [mə'trapələs] *n* : métropole *f* — **metropolitan** [,mɛtrə'palətən] *adj* : métropolitain

Mexican ['mɛksɪkən] *adj* : mexicain

mice → mouse

microbe ['maɪ,kro:b] *n* : microbe *m*

microfilm ['maɪkro,fɪlm] *n* : microfilm *m*

microphone ['maɪkrə,fo:n] *n* : microphone *m*

microscope ['maɪkrə,sko:p] *n* : microscope

m — **microscopic** [,maɪkrə'skapɪk] *adj* : microscopique

microwave ['maɪkrə,weɪv] *n or* **~ oven** : (four *m* à) micro-ondes *m*

mid ['mɪd] *adj* **1 ~-morning** . au milieu de la matinée **2 in ~-June** : à la mi-juin **3 she is in her ~ thirties** : elle est dans la trentaine — **midair** ['mɪd'ær] *n* **in ~** : en plein ciel — **midday** ['mɪd'deɪ] *n* : midi *m*

middle ['mɪdəl] *adj* : du milieu, au milieu — **~** *n* **1** : milieu *m*, centre *m* **2 in the ~ of** : au milieu de (un espace), en train de (faire une activité) — **middle–aged** *adj* : d'un certain age — **Middle Ages** *npl* : Moyen Âge *m* — **middle class** *n* : classe *f* moyenne — **Middle Eastern** *adj* : moyen-oriental — **middleman** ['mɪdəl,mæn] *n, pl* **-men** [-mən, -,mɛn] : intermédiaire *mf*

midget ['mɪdʒət] *n* : nain *m*, naine *f*

midnight ['mɪd,naɪt] *n* : minuit *m*

midriff ['mɪd,rɪf] *n* : diaphragme *m*

midst ['mɪdst] *n* **1 in the ~ of** : au milieu de **2 in our ~** : parmi nous

midsummer ['mɪd'sʌmər, -,sʌ-] *n* : milieu *m* de l'été

midway ['mɪd,weɪ] *adv* : à mi-chemin

midwife ['mɪd,waɪf] *n, pl* **-wives** [-,waɪvz] : sage-femme *f*

midwinter ['mɪd'wɪntər, -,win-] *n* : milieu *m* de l'hiver

miff ['mɪf] *vt* : vexer

might¹ ['maɪt] *(used to express permission or possibility or as a polite alternative to* **may***)* → **may**

might² *n* : force *f*, pouvoir *m* — **mighty** ['maɪt̬i] *adj* **mightier; -est 1** : fort, puissant **2** GREAT : énorme — **~** *adv* : très, rudement *fam*

migraine ['maɪ,greɪn] *n* : migraine *f*

migrate ['maɪ,greɪt] *vi* **-grated; -grating** : émigrer — **migrant** ['maɪgrənt] *n* : travailleur *m* saisonnier

mild ['maɪld] *adj* **1** GENTLE : doux **2** LIGHT : léger

mildew ['mɪl,du:, -,dju:] *n* : moisissure *f*

mildly ['maɪldli] *adv* : doucement, légèrement — **mildness** ['maɪldnəs] *n* : douceur *f*

mile ['maɪl] *n* : mille *m* — **mileage** ['maɪlɪdʒ] *n* : distance *f* parcourue (en milles), kilométrage *m* — **milestone** ['maɪl,sto:n] *n* : jalon *m*

military ['mɪlə,tɛri] *adj* : militaire — **~** *n* **the ~** : les forces armées — **militant** ['mɪlətənt] *adj* : militant — **~** *n* : militant *m*, -tante *f* — **militia** [mə'lɪʃə] *n* : milice *f*

milk ['mɪlk] *n* : lait *m* — **~** *vt* : traire (une vache, etc.) — **milky** ['mɪlki] *adj* **milkier; -est** : laiteux — **Milky Way** *n* **the ~** : la Voie lactée

mill ['mɪl] *n* **1** : moulin *m* **2** FACTORY : usine *f* — ～ *vt* : moudre — *vi or* ～ **about** : grouiller

millennium [məˈlɛniəm] *n, pl* **-nia** [-niə] *or* **-niums** : millénaire *m*

millon [ˈmɪljən] n : meunier *m*, ～icle *f*

milligram [ˈmɪləˌgræm] *n* : milligramme *m* — **millimeter** *or Brit* **millimetre** [ˈmɪləˌmiːtər] *n* : millimètre *m*

million [ˈmɪljən] *n, pl* **millions** *or* **million** : million *m* — ～ *adj* **a** ～ : un million de — **millionaire** [ˌmɪljəˈnær, ˈmɪljəˌnær] *n* : millionnaire *mf* — **millionth** [ˈmɪljənθ] *adj* : millionième

mime [ˈmaɪm] *n* **1** : mime *mf* **2** PANTOMIME : pantomime *f* — ～ *v* **mimed; miming** *vt* : imiter — *vi* : faire des mimiques — **mimic** *vt* **-icked; -icking** : imiter, singer

mince [ˈmɪnts] *vt* **minced; mincing 1** : hacher **2 not to** ～ **one's words** : ne pas mâcher ses mots

mind [ˈmaɪnd] *n* **1** : esprit *m* **2** INTELLECT : capacité *f* intellectuelle **3** OPINION : opinion *f* **4** REASON : raison *f* **5 have a** ～ **to** : avoir l'intention de — ～ *vt* **1** TEND : s'occuper de **2** OBEY : obéir à **3** WATCH : faire attention à **4 I don't** ～ **the heat** : la chaleur ne m'incommode pas — *vi* **1** OBEY : obéir **2 I don't** ～ : ça m'est égal — **mindful** [ˈmaɪndfəl] *adj* : attentif — **mindless** [ˈmaɪndləs] *adj* **1** SENSELESS : stupide **2** DULL : ennuyeux

mine[1] [ˈmaɪn] *pron* **1** : le mien, la mienne, les miens, les miennes **2 a friend of** ～ : un ami à moi

mine[2] *n* : mine *f* — ～ *vt* **mined; mining 1** : extraire (de l'or, etc.) **2** : miner (avec des explosifs) — **minefield** [ˈmaɪnˌfiːld] *n* : champ *m* de mines — **miner** [ˈmaɪnər] *n* : mineur *m*

mineral [ˈmɪnərəl] *n* : minéral *m*

mingle [ˈmɪŋɡəl] *v* **-gled; -gling** *vt* : mêler, mélanger — *vi* : se mêler (à, avec)

miniature [ˈmɪniəˌtʃʊr, ˈmɪniˌtʃʊr, -tʃər] *n* : miniature *f* — ～ *adj* : en miniature

minimal [ˈmɪnəməl] *adj* : minimal — **minimize** [ˈmɪnəˌmaɪz] *vt* **-mized; -mizing** : minimiser — **minimum** [ˈmɪnəməm] *adj* : minimum — ～ *n, pl* **-ma** [ˈmɪnəmə] *or* **-mums** : minimum *m*

minister [ˈmɪnəstər] *n* **1** : pasteur *m* (d'une église) **2** : ministre *m* (en politique) — ～ *vi* **to** : pourvoir à, donner des soins à — **ministerial** [ˌmɪnəˈstɪriəl] *adj* : ministériel — **ministry** [ˈmɪnəstri] *n, pl* **-tries** : ministère *m* (gouvernemental), sacerdoce *m* (religieux)

mink [ˈmɪŋk] *n, pl* **mink** *or* **minks** : vison *m*

minor [ˈmaɪnər] *adj* **1** : mineur **2** INSIGNIFICANT : sans importance — ～ *n* **1** : mineur *m*, -neure *f* **2** : matière *f* secondaire (à l'université) — **minority** [məˈnɔːrəti, maɪ-] *n, pl* **-ties** : minorité *f*

mint[1] [ˈmɪnt] *n* **1** : menthe *f* (plante) **2** : bonbon *m* à la menthe

mint[2] *n* **1 the Mint** : l'Hôtel *m* de la Monnaie **2 worth a** ～ : valoir une fortune — ～ *vt* : frapper (la monnaie) — ～ *adj* **in** ～ **condition** : comme neuf

minus [ˈmaɪnəs] *prep* **1** : moins **2** WITHOUT : sans — ～ *n or* ～ **sign** : moins *m*

minuscule *or* **miniscule** [ˈmɪnəsˌkjuːl] *adj* : minuscule

minute[1] [ˈmɪnət] *n* **1** : minute *f* **2** MOMENT : moment *m* **3** ～s *npl* : procès-verbal *m*

minute[2] [maɪˈnuːt, mɪ-, -ˈnjuːt] *adj* **-nuter; -est 1** TINY : minuscule **2** DETAILED : minutieux

miracle [ˈmɪrɪkəl] *n* : miracle *m* — **miraculous** [məˈrækjələs] *adj* : miraculeux

mirage [mɪˈrɑːʒ, *chiefly Brit* ˈmɪrˌɑːʒ] *n* : mirage *m*

mire [ˈmaɪr] *n* : boue *f*, fange *f*

mirror [ˈmɪrər] *n* : miroir *m*, glace *f* — ～ *vt* : refléter, réfléchir

mirth [ˈmərθ] *n* : allégresse *f*, gaieté *f*

misapprehension [ˌmɪsˌæprəˈhɛntʃən] *n* : malentendu *m*

misbehave [ˌmɪsbɪˈheɪv] *vi* **-haved; -having** : se conduire mal — **misbehavior** [ˌmɪsbɪˈheɪvjər] *n* : mauvaise conduite *f*

miscalculate [mɪsˈkælkjəˌleɪt] *v* **-lated; -lating** : mal calculer

miscarriage [ˌmɪsˈkæriʤ, ˈmɪsˌkæriʤ] *n* **1** : fausse couche *f* **2** ～ **of justice** : erreur *f* judiciaire

miscellaneous [ˌmɪsəˈleɪniəs] *adj* : divers, varié

mischief [ˈmɪstʃəf] *n* : espièglerie *f* — **mischievous** [ˈmɪstʃəvəs] *adj* : espiègle

misconception [ˌmɪskənˈsɛpʃən] *n* : concept *m* erroné

misconduct [mɪsˈkɑndəkt] *n* : mauvaise conduite *f*

misdeed [mɪsˈdiːd] *n* : méfait *m*

misdemeanor [ˌmɪsdɪˈmiːnər] *n* : délit *m* judiciaire

miser [ˈmaɪzər] *n* : avare *m*

miserable [ˈmɪzərəbəl] *adj* **1** UNHAPPY : malheureux **2** WRETCHED : misérable **3** ～ **weather** : temps *m* maussade

miserly [ˈmaɪzərli] *adj* : avare

misery [ˈmɪzəri] *n, pl* **-eries 1** : souffrance *f* **2** WRETCHEDNESS : misère *f*

misfire [mɪsˈfaɪr] *vi* **-fired; -firing** : échouer

misfit [ˈmɪsˌfɪt] *n* : inadapté *m*, -tée *f*

misfortune [mɪsˈfɔrtʃən] *n* : malheur *f*, infortune *f*

misgiving [mɪsˈɡɪvɪŋ] *n* : doute *m*

misguided [mɪsˈɡaɪdəd] *adj* : malencontreux, peu judicieux

mishap ['mɪs,hæp] *n* : contretemps *m*

misinform [,mɪsɪn'fɔrm] *vt* : mal renseigner

misinterpret [,ɪɪɪsɪn'tɔrprət] *vt* : mal interpréter

misjudge [mɪs'dʒʌdʒ] *vt* **-judged; -judging** : mal juger

mislay [mɪs'leɪ] *vt* **-laid** [-'leɪd]; **-laying** : égarer

mislead [mɪs'li:d] *vt* **-led** [-'lɛd]; **-leading** : tromper — **misleading** [mɪs'li:dɪŋ] *adj* : trompeur

misnomer [mɪs'no:mər] *n* : terme *m* impropre

misplace [mɪs'pleɪs] *vt* **-placed; -placing** : égarer, perdre

misprint ['mɪs,prɪnt, mɪs'-] *n* : faute *f* typographique, coquille *f*

miss ['mɪs] *vt* **1** : rater, manquer (une occasion, un vol, etc.) **2** OVERLOOK : laisser passer **3** AVOID : éviter **4** OMIT : sauter **5** I ~ **you** : tu me manques — ~ *n* **1** : coup *m* manqué **2** FAILURE : échec *m*

Miss ['mɪs] *n* : mademoiselle *f*

missile ['mɪsəl] *n* **1** : missile *m* **2** PROJECTILE : projectile *m*

missing ['mɪsɪŋ] *adj* : perdu, disparu

mission ['mɪʃən] *n* : mission *f* — **missionary** ['mɪʃə,nɛri] *n, pl* **-aries** : missionnaire *mf*

misspell [mɪs'spɛl] *vt* : mal orthographier, mal écrire

mist ['mɪst] *n* : brume *f*

mistake [mɪ'steɪk] *vt* **-took** [-'stʊk]; **-taken** [-'steɪkən]; **-taking 1** MISINTERPRET : mal comprendre **2** CONFUSE : confondre — ~ *n* **1** : faute *f*, erreur *f* **2 make a** ~ : se tromper — **mistaken** [mɪ'steɪkən] *adj* : erroné

mister ['mɪstər] *n* : monsieur *m*

mistletoe ['mɪsəl,to:] *n* : gui *m*

mistreat [mɪs'tri:t] *vt* : maltraiter

mistress ['mɪstrəs] *n* **1** : maîtresse *f* (de classe) **2** LOVER : amante *f*

mistrust [mɪs'trʌst] *n* : méfiance *f* — ~ *vt* : se méfier de

misty ['mɪsti] *adj* **mistier; -est** : brumeux

misunderstand [,mɪs,ʌndər'stænd] *vt* **-stood** [-'stʊd]; **-standing** : mal comprendre — **misunderstanding** [,mɪs,ʌndər'stændɪŋ] *n* : malentendu *m*

misuse [mɪs'ju:z] *vt* **-used; -using 1** : mal employer **2** MISTREAT : maltraiter — ~ [mɪs'ju:s] *n* : mauvais emploi *m*, abus *m*

mitigate ['mɪtə,geɪt] *vt* **-gated; -gating** : atténuer

mitt ['mɪt] *n* : gant *m* (de baseball) — **mitten** ['mɪtən] *n* : moufle *f*, mitaine *f* Can

mix ['mɪks] *vt* **1** : mélanger **2** ~ **up** : confondre — *vi* : se mélanger — ~ *n* : mélange *m* — **mixture** ['mɪkstʃər] *n* : mélange *m* — **mix-up** ['mɪks,ʌp] *n* : confusion *f*

moan ['mo:n] *n* : gémissement *m* — ~ *vi* : gémir

mob ['mɑb] *n* : foule *f* — ~ *vt* **mobbed; mobbing** : assaillir

mobile ['mo:bəl, -,bi:l, -,baɪl] *adj* : mobile — ~ ['mo:,bi:l] *n* : mobile *m* — **mobile home** *n* : auto-caravane *f* — **mobility** [mo:'bɪləti] *n* : mobilité *f* — **mobilize** ['mo:bə,laɪz] *vt* **-lized; -lizing** : mobiliser

moccasin ['mɑkəsən] *n* : mocassin *m*

mock ['mɑk, 'mɔk] *vt* : se moquer de — ~ *adj* : faux — **mockery** ['mɑkəri, 'mɔ-] *n, pl* **-eries** : moquerie *f*

mode ['mo:d] *n* : mode *m*

model ['mɑdəl] *n* **1** : modèle *m* **2** MOCK-UP : maquette *f* **3** : mannequin *m* (personne) — ~ *v* **-eled** *or* **-elled; -eling** *or* **-elling** *vt* **1** SHAPE : modeler **2** WEAR : porter — *vi* : travailler comme mannequin — ~ *adj* : modèle

modem ['mo:dəm, -,dɛm] *n* : modem *m*

moderate ['mɑdərət] *adj* : modéré — ~ *n* : modéré *m*, -rée *f* — ~ ['mɑdə,reɪt] *v* **-ated; -ating** *vt* : modérer — *vi* : se modérer — **moderation** [,mɑ'də'reɪʃən] *n* : modération *f* — **moderator** ['mɑdə,reɪtər] *n* : animateur *m*, -trice *f*

modern ['mɑdərn] *adj* : moderne — **modernize** ['mɑdər,naɪz] *vt* **-nized; -nizing** : moderniser

modest ['mɑdəst] *adj* : modeste — **modesty** ['mɑdəsti] *n* : modestie *f*

modify ['mɑdə,faɪ] *vt* **-fied; -fying** : modifier

moist ['mɔɪst] *adj* : humide — **moisten** ['mɔɪsən] *vt* : humecter — **moisture** ['mɔɪstʃər] *n* : humidité *f* — **moisturizer** ['mɔɪstʃə,raɪzər] *n* : crème *f* hydratante

molar ['mo:lər] *n* : molaire *f*

molasses [mə'læsəz] *n* : mélasse *f*

mold[1] ['mo:ld] *n* FORM : moule *m* — ~ *vt* : mouler, former

mold[2] *n* : moisissure *f* — **moldy** ['mo:ldi] *adj* **moldier, -est** : moisi

mole[1] ['mo:l] *n* : grain *m* de beauté (sur la peau)

mole[2] *n* : taupe *f* (animal)

molecule ['mɑlɪ,kju:l] *n* : molécule *f*

molest [mə'lɛst] *vt* **1** HARASS : importuner **2** : abuser (sexuellement)

molt ['mo:lt] *vi* : muer

molten ['mo:ltən] *adj* : en fusion

mom ['mɑm] *n* : maman *f*

moment ['mo:mənt] *n* : instant *m*, moment *m* — **momentarily** [,mo:mən'tɛrəli] *adv* **1** : momentanément **2** SOON : dans un instant, immédiatement — **momentary** ['mo:mən,tɛri] *adj* : momentané

momentous [mo:'mɛntəs] *adj* : très important

momentum [mo'mɛntəm] *n*, *pl* **-ta** [-tə] *or* **-tums** **1** : moment *m* (en physique) **2** IMPETUS : élan *m*

monarch ['mɑ,nɑrk, -nərk] *n* : monarque *m* — **monarchy** ['mɑ,nɑrki, -nər-] *n*, *pl* **-chies** : monarchie *f*

monastery ['mɑnə,stɛri] *n*, *pl* **-teries** : monastère *m*

Monday ['mʌn,deɪ, -di] *n* : lundi *m*

money ['mʌni] *n*, *pl* **-eys** *or* **-ies** [-iz] : argent *m* — **monetary** ['mɑnə,tɛri, 'mʌnə-] *adj* : monétaire — **money order** *n* : mandat-poste *m*

mongrel ['mɑŋgrəl, 'mʌŋ-] *n* : chien *m* métisse

monitor ['mɑnətər] *n* : moniteur *m* (d'un ordinateur, etc.) — ~ *vt* : surveiller

monk ['mʌŋk] *n* : moine *m*

monkey ['mʌŋki] *n*, *pl* **-keys** : singe *m* — **monkey wrench** *n* : clé *f* à molette

monogram ['mɑnə,græm] *n* : monogramme *m*

monologue ['mɑnə,lɔg] *n* : monologue *m*

monopoly [mə'nɑpəli] *n*, *pl* **-lies** : monopole *m* — **monopolize** [mə'nɑpə,laɪz] *vt* **-lized; -lizing** : monopoliser

monotonous [mə'nɑtənəs] *adj* : monotone — **monotony** [mə'nɑtəni] *n* : monotonie *f*

monster ['mɑnstər] *n* : monstre *m* — **monstrosity** [mɑn'strɑsəti] *n*, *pl* **-ties** : monstruosité *f* — **monstrous** ['mɑnstrəs] *adj* **1** : monstrueux **2** HUGE : gigantesque

month ['mʌnθ] *n* : mois *m* — **monthly** ['mʌnθli] *adv* : mensuellement — ~ *adj* : mensuel

monument ['mɑnjəmənt] *n* : monument *m* — **monumental** [,mɑnjə'mɛntəl] *adj* : monumental

moo ['mu:] *vi* : meugler — ~ *n* : meuglement *m*

mood ['mu:d] *n* : humeur *f* — **moody** ['mu:di] *adj* **moodier; -est** **1** GLOOMY : mélancolique, déprimé **2** IRRITABLE : de mauvaise humeur **3** TEMPERAMENTAL : d'humeur changeante

moon ['mu:n] *n* : lune *f* — **moonlight** ['mu:n,laɪt] *n* : clair *m* de lune

moor[1] ['mʊr] *n* : lande *f*

moor[2] *vt* : amarrer — **mooring** ['mʊrɪŋ] *n* : mouillage *m*

moose ['mu:s] *ns & pl* : orignal *m*

moot ['mu:t] *adj* : discutable

mop ['mɑp] *n* **1** : balai *m* à franges **2** *or* ~ **of hair** : tignasse *f* — ~ *vt* **mopped; mopping** : laver (le plancher, etc.)

mope ['mo:p] *vi* **moped; moping** : être déprimé

moped ['mo:,pɛd] *n* : cyclomoteur *m*, vélomoteur *m*

moral ['mɔrəl] *adj* : moral — ~ *n* **1** : morale *f* (d'une histoire, etc.) **2** ~**s** *npl* : mœurs *fpl* — **morale** [mə'ræl] *n* : moral *m* — **morality** [mə'ræləti] *n*, *pl* **-ties** : moralité *f*

morbid ['mɔrbɪd] *adj* : morbide

more ['mor] *adj* : plus de — ~ *adv* **1** : plus, davantage **2** ~ **and** ~ : de plus en plus **3** ~ **or less** : plus ou moins **4 once** ~ : encore une fois — ~ *n* **the** ~ : le plus — ~ *pron* : plus — **moreover** [mor'o:vər] *adv* : de plus

morgue ['mɔrg] *n* : morgue *f*

morning ['mɔrnɪŋ] *n* **1** : matin *m*, avant-midi *f* Can **2 good** ~ : bonjour **3 in the** ~ : pendant la matinée

Moroccan [mə'rɑkən] *adj* : marocain

moron ['mor,ɑn] *n* : imbécile *mf*

morose [mə'ro:s] *adj* : morose

morphine ['mor,fi:n] *n* : morphine *f*

morsel ['mɔrsəl] *n* **1** BITE : bouchée *f* **2** FRAGMENT : morceau *m*

mortal ['mɔrtəl] *adj* : mortel — ~ *n* : mortel *m*, -telle *f* — **mortality** [mor'tæləti] *n* : mortalité *f*

mortar ['mɔrtər] *n* : mortier *m*

mortgage ['mɔrgɪʤ] *n* : hypothèque *f* — ~ *vt* **-gaged; -gaging** : hypothéquer

mortify ['mɔrtə,faɪ] *vt* **-fied; -fying** : mortifier

mosaic [mo'zeɪɪk] *n* : mosaïque *f*

Moslem ['mɑzləm] → **Muslim**

mosque ['mɑsk] *n* : mosquée *f*

mosquito [mə'ski:to] *n*, *pl* **-toes** : moustique *m*, maringouin *m* Can

moss ['mɔs] *n* : mousse *f*

most ['mo:st] *adj* **1** : la plupart de **2 (the)** ~ : le plus — ~ *adv* : plus — ~ *n* : plus *m* — ~ *pron* : la plupart — **mostly** ['mo:stli] *adv* **1** MAINLY : principalement, surtout **2** USUALLY : normalement

motel [mo'tɛl] *n* : motel *m*

moth ['mɔθ] *n* : papillon *m* de nuit, mite *f*

mother ['mʌðər] *n* : mère *f* — ~ *vt* **1** : s'occuper de **2** SPOIL : dorloter — **motherhood** ['mʌðər,hʊd] *n* : maternité *f* — **mother-in-law** ['mʌðərɪn,lɔ] *n*, *pl* **mothers-in-law** : belle-mère *f* — **motherly** ['mʌðərli] *adj* : maternel — **mother-of-pearl** [,mʌðərəv-'pərl] *n* : nacre *f*

motif [mo'ti:f] *n* : motif *m*

motion ['mo:ʃən] *n* **1** : mouvement *m* **2** PROPOSAL : motion *f* **3 set in** ~ : mettre en marche — ~ *vi* ~ **to** : faire signe à — **motionless** ['mo:ʃənləs] *adj* : immobile — **motion picture** *n* : film *m*

motive ['mo:tɪv] *n* : motif *m* — **motivate** ['mo:tə,veɪt] *vt* **-vated; -vating** : motiver — **motivation** [,mo:tə'veɪʃən] *n* : motivation *f*

motor ['mo:tər] *n* : moteur *m* — **motorbike** ['mo:tər,baɪk] *n* : moto *f* — **motorboat**

['mo:ʈər,bo:t] *n* : canot *m* à moteur — **mo-torcycle** ['mo:ʈər,saɪkəl] *n* : motocyclette *f*, moto *f* — **motorcyclist** ['mo:ʈər,saɪkəlɪst] *n* : motocycliste *mf* — **motorist** ['mo:ʈərɪst] *n* : automobiliste *mf*

motto ['mɑʈo:] *n*, *pl* **-toes** : devise *f*

mould ['mo:ld] → **mold**

mound ['maʊnd] *n* **1** PILE : tas *m* **2** HILL : monticule *m*

mount[1] ['maʊnt] *n* **1** HORSE : monture *f* **2** SUPPORT : support *m* — ~ *vt* : monter sur (un cheval, etc.)

mount[2] *n* HILL : mont *m* — **mountain** ['maʊntən] *n* : montagne *f* — **mountainous** ['maʊnt'nəs] *adj* : montagneux

mourn ['morn] *vt* — **for s.o.** : pleurer qqn — *vi* : porter le deuil — **mournful** ['mornfəl] *adj* : triste — **mourning** ['mornɪŋ] *n* : deuil *m*

mouse ['maʊs] *n*, *pl* **mice** ['maɪs] : souris *f* — **mousetrap** ['maʊs,træp] *n* : souricière *f*

moustache ['mʌ,stæʃ, mə'stæʃ] → **mustache**

mouth ['maʊθ] *n* : bouche *f* (d'une personne, etc.), gueule *f* (d'un animal) — **mouthful** ['maʊθ,fʊl] *n* : bouchée *f* — **mouthpiece** ['maʊθ,pi:s] *n* : bec *m*, embouchure *f* (d'un instrument de musique)

move ['mu:v] *v* **moved; moving** *vi* **1** GO : aller **2** RELOCATE : déménager **3** STIR : bouger **4** ACT : agir — *vt* **1** : déplacer **2** AFFECT : émouvoir **3** TRANSPORT : transporter **4** PROPOSE : proposer — ~ *n* **1** MOVEMENT : mouvement *m* **2** RELOCATION : déménagement *m* **3** STEP : pas *m*, étape *m* — **movable** *or* **moveable** ['mu:vəbəl] *adj* : mobile — **movement** ['mu:vmənt] *n* : mouvement *m*

movie ['mu:vi] *n* **1** : film *m* **2** ~**s** *npl* : cinéma *m*

mow ['mo:] *vt* **mowed; mowed** *or* **mown** ['mo:n]; **mowing** : tondre — **mower** ['mo:ər] → **lawn mower**

Mr. ['mɪstər] *n*, *pl* **Messrs.** ['mɛsərz] : Monsieur *m*

Mrs. ['mɪsəz, -səs, *esp South* 'mɪzəz, -zəs] *n*, *pl* **Mesdames** [meɪ'dɑm, -'dæm] : Madame *f*

Ms. ['mɪz] *n* : Madame *f*, Mademoiselle *f*

much ['mʌtʃ] *adj* **more; most** : beaucoup de — ~ *adv* **more** ['mor]; **most** ['mo:st] **1** : beaucoup **2** as ~ : autant **3** how ~? : combien? **4** too ~ : trop — ~ *pron* : beaucoup

muck ['mʌk] *n* : saleté *f*

mucus ['mju:kəs] *n* : mucus *m*

mud ['mʌd] *n* : boue *f*, bouette *f* Can fam

muddle ['mʌdəl] *v* **-dled; -dling** *vt* **1** CONFUSE : confondre **2** JUMBLE : embrouiller

— *vi* ~ **through** : se tirer d'affaire — ~ *n* : désordre *m*, fouillis *m*

muddy ['mʌdi] *adj* **-dier; -est** : boueux

muffin ['mʌfən] *n* : muffin *m* Can

muffle ['mʌfəl] *vt* **muffled; muffling** : étouffer (des sons) — **muffler** ['mʌflər] *n* : silencieux *m* (d'un véhicule)

mug ['mʌg] *n* CUP : tasse *f* — ~ *vt* **mugged; mugging** : agresser, attaquer — **mugger** ['mʌgər] *n* : agresseur *m*

muggy ['mʌgi] *adj* **-gier; -est** : lourd et humide

mule ['mju:l] *n* : mule *f*, mulet *m*

mull ['mʌl] *vt or* ~ **over** : réfléchir sur

multicolored ['mʌlti,kʌlərd, 'mʌl,taɪ-] *adj* : multicolore

multimedia [,mʌlti'mi:diə, ,mʌl,taɪ-] *adj* : multimédia

multinational [,mʌlti'næʃənəl, ,mʌl,taɪ-] *adj* : multinational

multiple ['mʌltəpəl] *adj* : multiple — ~ *n* : multiple *m* — **multiplication** [,mʌltəplə'keɪʃən] *n* : multiplication *f* — **multiply** ['mʌltə,plaɪ] *v* **-plied; -plying** *vt* : multiplier — *vi* : se multiplier

multitude ['mʌltə,tu:d, -,tju:d] *n* : multitude *f*

mum ['mʌm] *adj* keep ~ : garder le silence

mumble ['mʌmbəl] *vi* **-bled; -bling** : marmonner

mummy ['mʌmi] *n*, *pl* **-mies** : momie *f*

mumps ['mʌmps] *ns & pl* : oreillons *mpl*

munch ['mʌntʃ] *v* : mâcher, mastiquer

mundane [,mʌn'deɪn, 'mʌn,-] *adj* : routinier, ordinaire

municipal [mju'nɪsəpəl] *adj* : municipal — **municipality** [mju,nɪsə'pælət̬i] *n*, *pl* **-ties** : municipalité *f*

munitions [mju'nɪʃənz] *npl* : munitions *fpl*

mural ['mjʊrəl] *n* : peinture *f* murale

murder ['mərdər] *n* : meurtre *m* — ~ *vt* : assassiner — **murderer** ['mərdərər] *n* : meurtrier *m*, -trière *f*; assassin *m* — **murderous** ['mərdərəs] *adj* : meurtrier

murky ['mərki] *adj* **murkier; -est** : obscur, sombre

murmur ['mərmər] *n* : murmure *m* — ~ *v* : murmurer

muscle ['mʌsəl] *n* : muscle *m* — ~ *vi* **-cled; -cling** *or* ~ **in** : s'ingérer avec force dans — **muscular** ['mʌskjələr] *adj* **1** : musculaire **2** STRONG : musclé

muse[1] ['mju:z] *n* : muse *f*

muse[2] *vi* **mused; musing** : méditer

museum [mju'zi:əm] *n* : musée *m*

mushroom ['mʌʃ,ru:m, -,rʊm] *n* : champignon *m* — ~ *vi* : proliférer, se multiplier

mushy ['mʌʃi] *adj* **mushier; -est** **1** SOFT : mou **2** SENTIMENTAL : mièvre

music ['mju:zɪk] n : musique f — **musical**
['mju:zɪkəl] adj : musical — n : comédie
f musicale — **musician** [mju'zɪʃən] n : musicien m, -cienne f
musket ['mʌskət] n : mousquet m
Muslim ['mʌzləm, 'mʊs-, 'mʊz-] adj
: musulman — ~ n : musulman m, -mane f
muslin ['mʌzlən] n : mousseline f
mussel ['mʌsəl] n : moule f
must ['mʌst] v aux 1 : devoir 2 she ~ try
: elle doit essayer 3 you ~ decide : il faut
que tu te décides — ~ n : nécessité f
mustache ['mʌˌstæʃ, mʌ'stæʃ] n : moustache f
mustard ['mʌstərd] n : moutarde f
muster ['mʌstər] vt : rassembler, réunir
musty ['mʌsti] adj **mustier; -est** : qui sent le
renfermé
mute ['mju:t] adj **muter; mutest** : muet —
~ n : muet m, muette f
mutilate ['mju:təˌleɪt] vt **-lated; -lating** : mutiler
mutiny ['mju:təni] n, pl **-nies** : mutinerie f —
~ vi **-nied; -nying** : se mutiner

mutter ['mʌtər] vi : marmonner
mutton ['mʌtən] n : viande f de mouton
mutual ['mju:tʃəl] adj 1 : mutuel 2 COM-
MON : commun — **mutually** ['mju:tʃʊəli,
-tʃəli] adv : mutuellement
muzzle ['mʌzəl] n 1 SNOUT : museau m 2
: muselière f (pour un chien, etc.) 3 : gueule
f (d'une arme à feu) — ~ vt **-zled; -zling**
: museler
my ['maɪ] adj : mon, ma, mes
myopia [maɪ'o:piə] n : myopie f — **myopic**
[maɪ'o:pɪk, -'ɑ-] adj : myope
myself [maɪ'self] pron 1 (reflexive) : me 2
(emphatic) : moi aussi 3 by ~ : tout seul
mystery ['mɪstəri] n, pl **-teries** : mystère
m — **mysterious** [mɪ'stɪriəs] adj : mystérieux
mystic ['mɪstɪk] adj or **mystical** ['mɪstɪkəl]
: mystique
mystify ['mɪstəˌfaɪ] vt **-fied; -fying** : rendre
perplexe
myth ['mɪθ] n : mythe m — **mythical**
['mɪθɪkəl] adj : mythique

N

n ['ɛn] n, pl **n's** or **ns** ['ɛnz] : n m, quatorzième lettre de l'alphabet
nab ['næb] vt **nabbed; nabbing** : pincer
fam
nag ['næg] v **nagged; nagging** vi COMPLAIN
: se plaindre — vt : harceler — **nagging**
['nægɪŋ] adj : persistant
nail ['neɪl] n 1 : clou m 2 FINGERNAIL
: ongle m — ~ vt or ~ **down** : clouer —
nail file n : lime f à ongles — **nail polish** n
: vernis m à ongles
naive or **naïve** [nɑ'i:v] adj **-iver; -est** : naïf
naked ['neɪkəd] adj : nu — **nakedness**
['neɪkədnəs] n : nudité f
name ['neɪm] n 1 : nom m 2 REPUTATION
: réputation f 3 what is your ~ ? : comment vous appelez-vous? — ~ vt **named;
naming** 1 : nommer 2 : fixer (une date, un
prix, etc.) — **nameless** ['neɪmləs] adj : sans
nom, anonyme — **namely** ['neɪmli] adv
: c'est-à-dire, savoir — **namesake** ['neɪm-
ˌseɪk] n : homonyme m
nap ['næp] vi **napped; napping** : faire un
somme — ~ n : somme m, sieste f
nape ['neɪp, 'næp] n : nuque f
napkin ['næpkən] n 1 : serviette f 2 → **sanitary napkin**

narcotic [nɑr'kɑtɪk] n 1 : narcotique m (en
pharmacie) 2 DRUG : stupéfiant m
narrate ['nærˌeɪt] vt **narrated; narrating**
: raconter, narrer — **narration** [næ'reɪʃən] n
: narration f — **narrative** ['nærətɪv] n : récit
m — **narrator** ['nærˌeɪtər] n : narrateur m,
-trice f
narrow ['nærˌo:] adj 1 : étroit 2 by a ~
margin : de justesse — ~ vt : limiter, réduire — vi : se rétrécir — **narrowly**
['næroli] adv : de justesse, de peu — **narrow–minded** [ˌnæro'maɪndəd] adj : étroit
d'esprit
nasal ['neɪzəl] adj : nasal
nasty ['næsti] adj **-tier; -est** 1 MEAN : mauvais, méchant 2 UNPLEASANT : désagréable,
sale 3 SERIOUS : grave — **nastiness**
['næstinəs] n : méchanceté f
nation ['neɪʃən] n : pays m, nation f — **national** ['næʃənəl] adj : national — **nationalism** ['næʃənəˌlɪzəm] n : nationalisme m
— **nationality** [ˌnæʃə'næləti] n, pl **-ties**
: nationalité f — **nationalize** ['næʃənəˌlaɪz]
vt **-ized; -izing** : nationaliser — **nationwide**
['neɪʃənˌwaɪd] adj : dans tout le pays
native ['neɪtɪv] adj 1 : natal (se dit d'un
pays, etc.) 2 INNATE : inné 3 ~ **language**

: langue *f* maternelle — ~ *n* **1** : natif *m*, -tive *f* **2 be a ~ of** : être originaire de — **Native American** *adj* : amérindien *m* — **nativity** [nə'tɪvəti, neɪ-] *n*, *pl* **-ties** : nativité *f*

natural ['nætʃərəl] *adj* **1** : naturel **2** INBORN : né, inné — **naturalize** ['nætʃərə‚laɪz] *vt* -**ized**; -**izing** : naturaliser — **naturally** ['nætʃərəli] *adv* **1** : naturellement **2** OF COURSE : bien sûr — **nature** ['neɪtʃər] *n* : nature *f*

naught ['nɔt] *n* **1** NOTHING : rien *m* **2** ZERO : zéro *m*

naughty ['nɔti] *adj* -**tier**; -**est** : méchant, vilain

nausea ['nɔziə, 'nɔʃə] *n* : nausée *f* — **nauseating** ['nɔzi‚eɪtɪŋ] *adj* : écœurant, nauséabond — **nauseous** ['nɔʃəs, -ziəs] *adj* : écœuré

nautical ['nɔtɪkəl] *adj* : nautique

naval ['neɪvəl] *adj* : naval

nave ['neɪv] *n* : nef *f* (d'une église)

navel ['neɪvəl] *n* : nombril *m*

navigate ['nævə‚geɪt] *v* -**gated**; -**gating** *vi* : naviguer — *vt* : naviguer sur (la mer, etc.), piloter (un avion), gouverner (un bateau) — **navigable** ['nævɪgəbəl] *adj* : navigable — **navigation** [‚nævə'geɪʃən] *n* : navigation *f* — **navigator** ['nævə‚geɪtər] *n* : navigateur *m*, -trice *f*

navy ['neɪvi] *n*, *pl* -**vies** : marine *f* — **navy blue** *adj* : bleu marine

near ['nɪr] *adv* **1** : près **2 nowhere ~ enough** : loin d'être suffisant — ~ *prep* : près de — ~ *adj* : proche — ~ *vt* : approcher de — **nearby** [nɪr'baɪ, 'nɪr‚baɪ] *adv* : tout près — ~ *adj* : voisin, proche — **nearly** ['nɪrli] *adv* : presque — **nearsighted** ['nɪr‚saɪtəd] *adj* : myope

neat ['ni:t] *adj* **1** TIDY : soigné, net **2** ORDERLY : bien rangé (se dit d'une chambre, etc.) **3** SKILLFUL : habile — **neatly** ['ni:tli] *adv* **1** : soigneusement **2** SKILLFULLY : habilement — **neatness** ['ni:tnəs] *n* : ordre *m*, propreté *f*

nebulous ['nɛbjʊləs] *adj* : nébuleux

necessary ['nɛsə‚sɛri] *adj* : nécessaire — **necessarily** [‚nɛsə'sɛrəli] *adv* : nécessairement, forcément — **necessitate** [nɪ'sɛsə‚teɪt] *vt* -**tated**; -**tating** : nécessiter, exiger — **necessity** [nɪ'sɛsəti] *n*, *pl* -**ties 1** : nécessité *f* **2 necessities** *npl* : choses *fpl* essentielles

neck ['nɛk] *n* **1** : cou *m* **2** COLLAR : col *m*, encolure *f* **3** : col *m*, goulot *m* (d'une bouteille) — **necklace** ['nɛkləs] *n* : collier *m* — **necktie** ['nɛk‚taɪ] *n* : cravate *f*

nectar ['nɛktər] *n* : nectar *m*

nectarine [‚nɛktə'ri:n] *n* : nectarine *f*

need ['ni:d] *n* **1** : besoin *m* **2 if ~ be** : si nécessaire, s'il le faut — ~ *vt* **1** : avoir besoin de **2 ~ to** : devoir — *v aux* **not ~ to** : ne pas être obligé de

needle ['ni:dəl] *n* : aiguille *f* — ~ *vt* -**dled**; -**dling** : agacer

needless ['ni:dləs] *adj* **1** : inutile **2 ~ to say** : il va sans dire

needlework ['ni:dəl‚wərk] *n* : travaux *mpl* d'aiguille

needy ['ni:di] *adj* **needier**; -**est** : dans le besoin

negative ['nɛgətɪv] *adj* : négatif — ~ *n* **1** : négatif *m* (en photographie) **2** : négation *f* (en grammaire)

neglect [nɪ'glɛkt] *vt* : négliger — ~ *n* : négligence *f*

negligee [‚nɛglə'ʒeɪ] *n* : négligé *m*

negligence ['nɛglɪʤənts] *n* : négligence *f*

negligent ['nɛglɪʤənt] *adj* : négligent

negligible ['nɛglɪʤəbəl] *adj* : négligeable

negotiate [nɪ'go:ʃi‚eɪt] *v* -**ated**; -**ating** : négocier — **negotiable** [nɪ'go:ʃəbəl, -ʃiə-] *adj* : négociable — **negotiation** [nɪ‚go:ʃi'eɪʃən, -si'eɪ-] *n* : négociation *f* — **negotiator** [nɪ'go:ʃi‚eɪtər, -si‚eɪ-] *n* : négociateur *m*, -trice *f*

Negro ['ni:‚gro:] *n*, *pl* -**groes** *sometimes considered offensive* : nègre *m*, négresse *f*

neigh ['neɪ] *vi* : hennir — ~ *n* : hennissement *m*

neighbor *or Brit* **neighbour** ['neɪbər] *n* : voisin *m*, -sine *f* — ~ *vt* : avoisiner — *vi* ~ **on** : être voisin de — **neighborhood** *or Brit* **neighbourhood** ['neɪbər‚hʊd] *n* **1** : quartier *m*, voisinage *m* **2 in the ~ of** : environ — **neighborly** *or Brit* **neighbourly** ['neɪbərli] *adj* : amical

neither ['ni:ðər, 'naɪ-] *conj* **1** ~ **... nor** : ni ... ni **2 ~ do I** : moi non plus — ~ *pron* : aucun — ~ *adj* : aucun (des deux)

neon ['ni:‚ɑn] *n* : néon *m*

nephew ['nɛ‚fju:, *chiefly Brit* 'nɛ‚vju:] *n* : neveu *m*

Neptune ['nɛp‚tu:n, -‚tju:n] *n* : Neptune *f*

nerve ['nərv] *n* **1** : nerf *m* **2** COURAGE : courage *m* **3** GALL : culot *m fam*, toupet *m fam* **4** ~**s** *npl* JITTERS : nerfs *mpl* — **nervous** ['nərvəs] *adj* : nerveux — **nervousness** ['nərvəsnəs] *n* : nervosité *f* — **nervy** ['nərvi] *adj* **nervier**; -**est** : effronté

nest ['nɛst] *n* : nid *m* — ~ *vi* : nicher

nestle ['nɛsəl] *vi* -**tled**; -**tling** : se blottir

net[1] ['nɛt] *n* : filet *m* — ~ *vt* **netted**; **netting** : prendre au filet (des poissons)

net[2] *adj* : net — ~ *vt* **netted**; **netting** YIELD : rapporter

nettle ['nɛtəl] *n* : ortie *f*

network ['nɛt‚wərk] *n* : réseau *m*

neurology [nʊ'rɑləʤi, njʊ-] *n* : neurologie *f*

neurosis [nʊ'ro:sɪs, njʊ-] *n*, *pl* -**roses** [-‚si:z]

: névrose *f* — **neurotic** [nʊˈrɑtɪk, njʊ-] *adj*
: névrosé

neuter [ˈnuːt̬ər, ˈnjuː-] *adj* : neutre — ~ *vt*
: châtrer

neutral [ˈnuːtrəl, ˈnjuː-] *adj* : neutre — ~ *n*
. point *m* mort, neutre *m Can* — **neutralize**
[ˈnuːtrəˌlaɪz, ˈnjuː-] *vt* **-ized; -izing** : neutraliser — **neutrality** [nuːˈtrælət̬i, njuː-] *n*
: neutralité *f*

neutron [ˈnuːˌtrɑn, ˈnjuː-] *n* : neutron *m*

never [ˈnɛvər] *adv* **1** : jamais **2 I ~ said a
word** : je n'ai rien dit — **nevermore**
[ˌnɛvərˈmor] *adv* : plus jamais, jamais plus
— **nevertheless** [ˌnɛvərðəˈlɛs] *adv* : néanmoins

new [ˈnuː, ˈnjuː] *adj* : neuf, nouveau — **newborn** [ˈnuːˌbɔrn, ˈnjuː-] *adj* : nouveau-né —
newcomer [ˈnuːˌkʌmər, ˈnjuː-] *n* : nouveau
venu *m*, nouvelle venue *f* — **newly** [ˈnuːli,
ˈnjuː-] *adv* : récemment — **newlywed**
[ˈnuːliˌwɛd, ˈnjuː-] *n* : nouveau marié *m*,
nouvelle mariée *f* — **news** [ˈnuːz, ˈnjuːz] *n*
: nouvelles *fpl* — **newscast** [ˈnuːzˌkæst,
ˈnjuːz-] *n* : journal *m* télévisé — **newscaster** [ˈnuːzˌkæstər, ˈnjuːz-] *n* : présentateur *m*, -trice *f* — **newsgroup** [ˈnuːzˌgruːp,
ˈnjuːz-] *n* : forum *m* (en informatique) —
newsletter [ˈnuːzˌlɛt̬ər, ˈnjuːz-] *n* : bulletin
m — **newspaper** [ˈnuːzˌpeɪpər, ˈnjuːz-] *n*
: journal *m* — **newsstand** [ˈnuːzˌstænd,
ˈnjuːz-] *n* : kiosque *m* à journaux

newt [ˈnuːt, ˈnjuːt] *n* : triton *m*

New Year's Day *n* : jour *m* de l'An

next [ˈnɛkst] *adj* **1** : prochain **2** FOLLOWING
: suivant — ~ *adv* **1** : la prochaine fois **2**
AFTERWARD : ensuite **3** NOW : maintenant
— **next door** [ˈnɛkstˈdor] *adv* : à côté —
next-door *adj* : voisin, d'à côté — **next to**
prep **1** BESIDE : à côté de **2** ~ **nothing**
: presque rien

nib [ˈnɪb] *n* : bec *m* (d'un stylo)

nibble [ˈnɪbəl] *vt* **-bled; -bling** : grignoter

nice [ˈnaɪs] *adj* **nicer; nicest 1** PLEASANT
: bon, agréable **2** KIND : gentil, aimable —
nicely [ˈnaɪsli] *adv* **1** WELL : bien **2** KINDLY
: gentiment — **niceness** [ˈnaɪsnəs] *n* : gentillesse *f* — **niceties** [ˈnaɪsət̬iz] *npl* : subtil-
ités *fpl*

niche [ˈnɪtʃ] *n* **1** : niche *f* **2 find one's ~**
: trouver sa voie

nick [ˈnɪk] *n* **1** NOTCH : entaille *f*, encoche *f*
2 in the ~ of time : juste à temps — ~ *vt*
: faire une entaille dans

nickel [ˈnɪkəl] *n* **1** : nickel *m* (métal) **2**
: pièce *f* de cinq cents

nickname [ˈnɪkˌneɪm] *n* : surnom *m* — ~ *vt*
: surnommer

nicotine [ˈnɪkəˌtiːn] *n* : nicotine *f*

niece [ˈniːs] *n* : nièce *f*

niggling [ˈnɪɡəliŋ] *adj* **1** PETTY : insignifiant
2 NAGGING : persistant

night [ˈnaɪt] *n* **1** : nuit *f*, soir *m* **2 at ~** : le
soir **3 tomorrow ~** : demain soir — ~
adj : de nuit — **nightclub** [ˈnaɪtˌklʌb] *n*
: boîte *f* de nuit — **nightfall** [ˈnaɪtˌfɔl] *n*
: tombée *f* de la nuit — **nightgown** [ˈnaɪt-
ˌɡaʊn] *n* : chemise *f* de nuit, robe *f* de nuit
Can — **nightingale** [ˈnaɪtənˌɡeɪl, ˈnaɪtɪŋ-]
n : rossignol *m* — **nightly** [ˈnaɪtli] *adv & adj*
: (de) tous les soirs — **nightmare** [ˈnaɪt-
ˌmær] *n* : cauchemar *m* — **nighttime** [ˈnaɪt-
ˌtaɪm] *n* : nuit *f*

nil [ˈnɪl] *n* NOTHING : zéro *m* — ~ *adj* : nul

nimble [ˈnɪmbəl] *adj* **-bler; -blest** : agile

nine [ˈnaɪn] *n* : neuf *m* — ~ *adj* : neuf —
nine hundred *adj* : neuf cents — **nineteen**
[naɪnˈtiːn] *n* : dix-neuf *m* — ~ *adj* : dix-
neuf — **nineteenth** [naɪnˈtiːnθ] *n* **1** : dix-
neuvième *mf* **2 January ~** : le dix-neuf
janvier — ~ *adj* : dix-neuvième — **nineti-
eth** [ˈnaɪntiəθ] *n* : quatre-vingt-dixième *mf*
— ~ *adj* : quatre-vingt-dixième — **ninety**
[ˈnaɪnti] *n, pl* **-ties** : quatre-vingt-dix *m* —
ninth [ˈnaɪnθ] *n* **1** : neuvième *mf* **2 March**
~ : le neuf mars — ~ *adj* : neuvième

nip [ˈnɪp] *vt* **nipped; nipping 1** BITE : mordre **2** PINCH : pincer — ~ *n* **1** BITE : morsure *f* **2** PINCH : pincement *m* **3 there's a
~ in the air** : il fait frisquet — **nippy**
[ˈnɪpi] *adj* **-pier; -est** : frisquet

nipple [ˈnɪpəl] *n* **1** : mamelon *m* (d'une
femme) **2** : tétine *f* (d'un biberon)

nitrogen [ˈnaɪtrədʒən] *n* : azote *m*

nitwit [ˈnɪtˌwɪt] *n* : imbécile *mf*

no [ˈnoː] *adv* **1** : non **2 ~ better** : pas
mieux **3 ~ bigger** : pas plus grand **4 ~
longer** : ne … plus — ~ *adj* **1** : pas de,
aucun **2 ~ parking** : stationnement interdit **3 ~ smoking** : défense de fumer — ~
n, pl **noes** *or* **nos** [ˈnoːz] : non *m*

noble [ˈnoːbəl] *adj* **-bler; -blest** : noble — ~
n : noble *mf* — **nobility** [noˈbɪlət̬i] *n* : noblesse *f*

nobody [ˈnoːbədi, -ˌbɑdi] *pron* : personne

nocturnal [nɑkˈtərnəl] *adj* : nocturne

nod [ˈnɑd] *v* **nodded; nodding** *vi* **1** : faire
un signe de la tête **2** *or* ~ **off** : s'endormir
— ~ *vt* ~ **one's head** : faire un signe de la
tête — ~ *n* : signe *m* de la tête

noise [ˈnɔɪz] *n* : bruit *m* — **noisily** [ˈnɔɪzəli]
adv : bruyamment — **noisy** [ˈnɔɪzi] *adj*
noisier; -est : bruyant

nomad [ˈnoːˌmæd] *n* : nomade *mf* — **nomadic** [noˈmædɪk] *adj* : nomade

nominal [ˈnɑmənəl] *adj* : nominal

nominate [ˈnɑməˌneɪt] *vt* **-nated; -nating 1**
PROPOSE : proposer **2** APPOINT : nommer
— **nomination** [ˌnɑməˈneɪʃən] *n* : nomination *f*

nonalcoholic [ˌnɑn͵ælkə'hɔlɪk] *adj* : non alcoolisé

nonchalant [ˌnɑnʃə'lɑnt] *adj* : nonchalant — **nonchalance** [ˌnɑnʃə'lɑnts] *n* : nonchalance *f*

noncommissioned officer [ˌnɑnkə'mɪʃənd] *n* : sous-officier *m*

noncommittal [ˌnɑnkə'mɪtəl] *adj* : évasif

nondescript [ˌnɑndɪ'skrɪpt] *adj* : quelconque

none ['nʌn] *pron* : aucun, aucune — ~ *adv* **1** ~ **too** : pas tellement **2** ~ **the worse** : pas plus mal

nonentity [ˌnɑn'ɛntəţi] *n, pl* **-ties** : être *m* insignifiant

nonetheless [ˌnʌnðə'lɛs] *adv* : néanmoins

nonexistent [ˌnɑnɪg'zɪstənt] *adj* : inexistant

nonfat [ˌnɑn'fæt] *adj* : sans matière grasse

nonfiction [ˌnɑn'fɪkʃən] *n* : œuvres *fpl* non romanesques

nonprofit [ˌnɑn'prɑfət] *adj* : à but non lucratif

nonsense ['nɑn͵sɛnts, -sənts] *n* : absurdités *fpl*, sottises *fpl* — **nonsensical** [nɑn'sɛntsɪkəl] *adj* : absurde

nonstop [ˌnɑn'stɑp] *adj* **1** : sans arrêt **2** ~ **flight** : vol *m* direct

noodle ['nu:dəl] *n* : nouille *f*

nook ['nʊk] *n* : coin *m*, recoin *m*

noon ['nu:n] *n* : midi *m* — ~ *adj* : de midi

no one *pron* : personne *f*

noose ['nu:s] *n* : nœud *m* coulant

nor ['nɔr] *conj* **1** : ni **2** ~ **can I** : moi non plus

norm ['nɔrm] *n* : norme *f* — **normal** ['nɔrməl] *adj* : normal — **normality** [nɔr'mæləţi] *n* : normalité *f* — **normally** ['nɔrməli] *adv* : normalement

north ['nɔrθ] *adv* : au nord, vers le nord — ~ *adj* : nord, du nord — ~ *n* **1** : nord *m* **2 the North** : le Nord — **North American** *adj* : nord-américain — ~ *n* : Nord-Américain *m*, -caine *f* — **northeast** [nɔrθ'i:st] *adv* : au nord-est, vers le nord-est — ~ *adj* : nord-est, du nord-est — ~ *n* : nord-est *m* — **northeastern** [nɔrθ'i:stərn] *adj* : nord-est, du nord-est — **northerly** ['nɔrðərli] *adj* : du nord — **northern** ['nɔrðərn] *adj* : nord, du nord — **northwest** [nɔrθ'wɛst] *adv* : au nord-ouest, vers le nord-ouest — ~ *adj* : nord-ouest, du nord-ouest — ~ *n* : nord-ouest *m* — **northwestern** [nɔrθ'wɛstərn] *adj* : nord-ouest, du nord-ouest

Norwegian [nɔr'wi:ʤən] *adj* : norvégien

nose ['no:z] *n* **1** : nez *m* **2 blow one's** ~ : se moucher — ~ *vi* **nosed; nosing** *or* ~ **around** : fouiner *fam* — **nosebleed** ['no:z͵bli:d] *n* : saignement *m* de nez — **nosedive** ['no:z͵daɪv] *n* : piqué *m*

nostalgia [nɑ'stælʤə, nə-] *n* : nostalgie *f* — **nostalgic** [-ʤɪk] *adj* : nostalgique

nostril ['nɑstrəl] *n* : narine *f* (d'une personne), naseau *m* (d'un animal)

nosey *or* **nosy** ['no:zi] *adj* **nosier; -est** : curieux, fureteur

not ['nɑt] *adv* **1** (*used to form a negative*) : ne...pas **2** (*used to replace a negative clause*) : non, pas **3** ~ **at all** : pas du tout **4 I hope** ~ : j'espère que non

notable ['no:ţəbəl] *adj* : notable — ~ *n* : notable *m* — **notably** ['no:ţəbli] *adv* : notamment

notary public ['no:ţəri] *n, pl* **notaries public** *or* **notary publics** : notaire *m*

notation [no'teɪʃən] *n* : notation *f*

notch ['nɑtʃ] *n* : entaille *f*, encoche *f*

note ['no:t] *vt* **noted; noting 1** NOTICE : remarquer **2** *or* ~ **down** : noter — ~ *n* **1** : note *f* **2** LETTER : mot *m* **3 an artist of** ~ : un artiste de renom — **notebook** ['no:t͵bʊk] *n* : carnet *m* — **noted** ['no:ţəd] *adj* : éminent, célèbre — **noteworthy** ['no:t͵wərði] *adj* : notable, remarquable

nothing ['nʌθɪŋ] *pron* : rien — ~ *adv* ~ **like** : pas du tout comme — ~ *n* **1** TRIFLE : rien *m* **2** ZERO : zéro *m*

notice ['no:ţɪs] *n* **1** : avis *m*, annonce *f* **2 be given one's** ~ : recevoir son congé **3 take** ~ **of** : faire attention à — ~ *vt* **-ticed; -ticing** : s'apercevoir de, remarquer — **noticeable** ['no:ţɪsəbəl] *adj* : visible

notify ['no:ţə͵faɪ] *vt* **-fied; -fying** : aviser, notifier — **notification** [ˌno:ţəfə'keɪʃən] *n* : avis *m*

notion ['no:ʃən] *n* **1** : notion *f*, idée *f* **2** ~**s** *npl* : mercerie *f*

notorious [no'to:riəs] *adj* : notoire — **notoriety** [ˌno:ţə'raɪəţi] *n, pl* **-ties** : notoriété *f*

notwithstanding [ˌnɑtwɪθ'stændɪŋ, -wɪð-] *adv* : néanmoins — ~ *prep* : malgré

nougat ['nu:gət] *n* : nougat *m*

nought ['nɔt, 'nɑt] → **naught**

noun ['naʊn] *n* : nom *m*, substantif *m*

nourish ['nərɪʃ] *vt* : nourrir — **nourishing** ['nərɪʃɪŋ] *adj* : nourrissant — **nourishment** ['nərɪʃmənt] *n* : nourriture *f*, alimentation *f*

novel ['nɑvəl] *adj* : nouveau, original — ~ *n* : roman *m* — **novelist** ['nɑvəlɪst] *n* : romancier *m*, -cière *f* — **novelty** ['nɑvəlţi] *n, pl* **-ties** : nouveauté *f*

November [no'vɛmbər] *n* : novembre *m*

novice ['nɑvɪs] *n* : novice *mf*; débutant *m*, -tante *f*

now ['naʊ] *adv* **1** : maintenant **2** ~ **and then** : de temps à autre — ~ *conj* ~ **that** : maintenant que — ~ *n* **1 by** ~ : déjà **2 for** ~ : pour le moment **3 up until** ~ : jusqu'à maintenant — **nowadays** ['naʊə͵deɪz] *adv* : de nos jours

nowhere ['no:ˌʰwɛr] *adv* **1** : nulle part **2** ~ **near** : loin de

noxious ['nɑkʃəs] *adj* : nocif

nozzle ['nɑzəl] *n* : ajutage *m*

nuance ['nu:ˌɑnts, 'nju:-] *n* ; nuance *f*

nucleus ['nu:kliəs, 'nju:-] *n, pl* **-clei** [-kliˌaɪ] : noyau *m* — **nuclear** ['nu:kliər, 'nju:-] *adj* : nucléaire

nude ['nu:d, 'nju:d] *adj* **nuder; nudest** : nu — ~ *n* : nu *m*

nudge ['nʌdʒ] *vt* **nudged; nudging** : donner un coup de coude à — ~ *n* : coup *m* de coude

nudity ['nu:dəti, 'nju:-] *n* : nudité *f*

nugget ['nʌgət] *n* : pépite *f*

nuisance ['nu:sənts, 'nju:-] *n* **1** ANNOYANCE : ennui *m* **2** PEST : peste *f*

null ['nʌl] *adj* ~ **and void** : nul et non avenu

numb ['nʌm] *adj* **1** : engourdi **2** ~ **with fear** : paralysé par la peur — ~ *vt* : engourdir

number ['nʌmbər] *n* **1** : nombre *m*, numéro *m* **2** NUMERAL : chiffre *m* **3 a** ~ **of** : un certain nombre de — ~ *vt* **1** : numéroter **2** INCLUDE : compter — **numeral** ['nu:mərəl, 'nju:-] *n* : chiffre *m* — **numerical** [nu-'merikəl, nyu-] *adj* : numérique — **numerous** ['nu:mərəs, 'nju:-] *adj* : nombreux

nun ['nʌn] *n* : religieuse *f*

nuptial ['nʌpʃəl] *adj* : nuptial

nurse ['nərs] *n* : infirmier *m*, -mière *f* — ~ *v* **nursed; nursing** *vt* **1** : soigner (un malade) **2** BREAST-FEED : allaiter — *vi* SUCKLE : téter — **nursery** ['nərsəri] *n, pl* **-eries 1** : crèche *f* France, garderie *f* Can **2** : pépinière *f* (pour les plantes) — **nursing home** *n* : maison *f* de retraite, centre *m* d'accueil *Can*

nurture ['nərtʃər] *vt* **-tured; -turing 1** : élever **2** : nourrir (des espoirs, etc.)

nut ['nʌt] *n* **1** : noix *f* **2** LUNATIC : fou *m*, folle *f* **3** ENTHUSIAST : mordu *m*, -due *f fam* **4** ~**s and bolts** : des écrous et des boulons — **nutcracker** ['nʌtˌkrækər] *n* : casse-noix *m* — **nutmeg** ['nʌtˌmɛg] *n* : muscade *f*

nutrient ['nu:triənt, 'nju:-] *n* : substance *f* nutritive — **nutrition** [nu'trɪʃən, nju-] *n* : nutrition *f*, alimentation *f* — **nutritional** [nu'trɪʃənəl, nju-] *adj* : nutritif — **nutritious** [nu'trɪʃəs, nju-] *adj* : nourrissant, nutritif

nuts ['nʌts] *adj* : fou, cinglé *fam*

nutshell ['nʌtˌʃɛl] *n* **1** : coquille *f* de noix **2 in a** ~ : en un mot

nuzzle ['nʌzəl] *v* **-zled; -zling** *vt* : frotter son nez contre — *vi* : se blottir

nylon ['naɪˌlɑn] *n* **1** : nylon *m* **2** ~**s** *npl* : bas *mpl* de nylon

nymph ['nɪmpf] *n* : nymphe *f*

O

o ['o:] *n, pl* **o's** *or* **os** ['o:z] **1** : o *m*, quinzième lettre de l'alphabet **2** ZERO : zéro *m*

O ['o:] → **oh**

oak ['o:k] *n, pl* **oaks** *or* **oak** : chêne *m*

oar ['or] *n* : rame *f*, aviron *m*

oasis [o'eɪsɪs] *n, pl* **oases** [-ˌsi:z] : oasis *f*

oath ['o:θ] *n, pl* **oaths** ['o:ðz, 'o:θs] **1** : serment *m* **2** SWEARWORD : juron *m*

oats ['o:ts] *npl* : avoine *f* — **oatmeal** ['o:tˌmi:l] *n* : farine *f* d'avoine

obedient [o'bi:diənt] *adj* : obéissant — **obedience** [o'bi:diənts] *n* : obéissance *f* — **obediently** [o'bi:diəntli] *adv* : docilement

obese [o'bi:s] *adj* : obèse — **obesity** [o'bi:səti] *n* : obésité *f*

obey [o'beɪ] *v* **obeyed; obeying** *vt* : obéir à — *vi* : obéir

obituary [ə'bɪtʃuˌɛri] *n, pl* **-aries** : nécrologie *f*

object ['ɑbdʒɪkt] *n* **1** : objet *m* **2** AIM : objectif *m*, but *m* **3** : complément *m* d'objet (en grammaire) — ~ [əb'dʒɛkt] *vi* : protester, s'opposer — *vt* : objecter — **objection** [əb'dʒɛkʃən] *n* : objection *f* — **objectionable** [əb'dʒɛkʃənəbəl] *adj* : désagréable — **objective** [əb'dʒɛktɪv] *adj* : objectif — ~ *n* : objectif *m*

oblige [ə'blaɪdʒ] *vt* **obliged; obliging 1** : obliger **2 be much** ~**d** : être très reconnaissant **3** ~ **s.o.** : rendre service à qqn — **obligation** [ˌɑblə'geɪʃən] *n* : obligation *f* — **obligatory** [ə'blɪgəˌtori] *adj* : obligatoire — **obliging** [ə'blaɪdʒɪŋ] *adj* : obligeant, aimable

oblique [o'bli:k] *adj* : oblique

obliterate [ə'blɪtəˌreɪt] *vt* **-ated; -ating** : effacer, détruire

oblivion [ə'blɪviən] *n* : oubli *m* — **oblivious** [ə'blɪviəs] *adj* : inconscient

oblong ['ɑˌblɔŋ] *adj* : oblong

obnoxious [ɑb'nɑkʃəs, əb-] *adj* : odieux

oboe ['o:ˌbo:] *n* : hautbois *m*

obscene [ab'si:n, əb-] *adj* : obscène — **obscenity** [ab'sɛnəṭi, əb-] *n, pl* **-ties** : obscénité *f*

obscure [ab'skjʊr, əb-] *vt* **-scured; -scuring 1** DARKEN : obscurcir **2** HIDE : cacher — ~ *adj* : obscur — **obscurity** [ab-'skjʊrəṭi, əb-] *n, pl* **-ties** : obscurité *f*

observe [əb'zərv] *vt* **-served; -serving** : observer — **observant** [əb'zərvənt] *adj* : observateur — **observation** [ˌabsər'veɪʃən, -zər-] *n* : observation *f* — **observatory** [əb-'zərvəˌtori] *n, pl* **-ries** : observatoire *m* — **observer** [əb'zərvər] *n* : observateur *m*, -trice *f*

obsess [əb'sɛs] *vt* : obséder — **obsession** [ab'sɛʃən, əb-] *n* : obsession *f* — **obsessive** [ab'sɛsɪv, əb-] *adj* : obsessionnel, obsédant

obsolete [ˌabsə'li:t, 'absəˌ-] *adj* : obsolète, démodé

obstacle ['abstɪkəl] *n* : obstacle *m*

obstetrics [əb'stɛtrɪks] *ns & pl* : obstétrique *f*

obstinate ['abstənət] *adj* : obstiné

obstruct [əb'strʌkt] *vt* **1** BLOCK : obstruer **2** HINDER : entraver — **obstruction** [əb-'strʌkʃən] *n* : obstruction *f*

obtain [əb'teɪn] *vt* : obtenir

obtrusive [əb'tru:sɪv] *adj* : trop voyant (se dit des choses), importun (se dit des personnes)

obtuse [ab'tu:s, əb-, -'tju:s] *adj* : obtus

obvious ['abviəs] *adj* : évident — **obviously** ['abviəsli] *adv* **1** CLEARLY : manifestement **2** OF COURSE : évidemment, bien sûr

occasion [ə'keɪʒən] *n* **1** : occasion *f* **2** EVENT : événement *m* — ~ *vt* : occasionner, provoquer — **occasional** [ə'keɪʒənəl] *adj* : occasionnel — **occasionally** [ə-'keɪʒənəli] *adv* : de temps en temps

occult [ə'kʌlt, 'aˌkʌlt] *adj* : occulte

occupy ['akjəˌpaɪ] *vt* **-pied; -pying 1** : occuper **2** ~ **oneself with** : s'occuper de — **occupancy** ['akjəpəntsi] *n, pl* **-cies** : occupation *f* — **occupant** ['akjəpənt] *n* : occupant *m*, -pante *f* — **occupation** [ˌakjə'peɪʃən] *n* **1** : occupation *f* **2** JOB : profession *f*, métier *m* — **occupational** [ˌakjə'peɪʃənəl] *adj* **1** : professionnel **2** ~ **hazard** : risque *m* du métier

occur [ə'kər] *vi* **occurred; occurring 1** HAPPEN : avoir lieu, se produire, arriver **2** APPEAR : se trouver **3** ~ **to s.o.** : venir à l'esprit de qqn — **occurrence** [ə'kərənts] *n* **1** EVENT : événement *m* **2** INSTANCE : cas *m*, apparition *f*

ocean ['oːʃən] *n* : océan *m* — **oceanic** [ˌoːʃi-'ænɪk] *adj* : océanique

ocher *or* **ochre** ['oːkər] *n* : ocre *mf*

o'clock [ə'klak] *adv* **1 at six** ~ : à six heures **2 it's ten** ~ : il est dix heures

octagon ['aktəˌgan] *n* : octogone *m*

octave ['aktɪv] *n* : octave *f*

October [ak'toːbər] *n* : octobre *m*

octopus ['aktəˌpʊs, -pəs] *n, pl* **-puses** *or* **-pi** [-ˌpaɪ] : pieuvre *f*

ocular ['akjələr] *adj* : oculaire — **oculist** ['akjəlɪst] *n* : oculiste *mf*

odd ['ad] *adj* **1** STRANGE : étrange, bizarre **2** : dépareillé (se dit d'une chaussette, etc.) **3** ~ **jobs** : travaux *mpl* divers **4** ~ **number** : nombre *m* impair **5 a hundred** ~ **dollars** : cent dollars et quelques — **oddity** ['adəṭi] *n, pl* **-ties** : étrangeté *f* — **oddly** ['adli] *adv* : étrangement — **odds** ['adz] *npl* **1** RATIO : cote *f* **2** CHANCES : chances *fpl* **3 at** ~**s** : en conflit — **odds and ends** *npl* : objets *mpl* divers

ode ['oːd] *n* : ode *f*

odious ['oːdiəs] *adj* : odieux

odor *or Brit* **odour** ['oːdər] *n* : odeur *f* — **odorless** *or Brit* **odourless** ['oːdərləs] *adj* : inodore

of [ˈʌv, ˈəv] *prep* **1** : de **2 five minutes** ~ **ten** : dix heures moins cinq **3 made** ~ **wood** : en bois **4 the eighth** ~ **April** : le huit avril

off ['ɔf] *adv* **1 be** ~ LEAVE : s'en aller **2 come** ~ : se détacher **3 cut** ~ : couper **4 day** ~ : jour *m* de congé **5 far** ~ : éloigné **6** ~ **and on** : par périodes **7 take** ~ REMOVE : enlever **8 ten miles** ~ : à dix milles d'ici **9 three weeks** ~ : en trois semaines — ~ *prep* **1** : de **2 be** ~ **duty** : être libre **3 be** ~ **the point** : ne pas être la question **4** ~ **center** : mal centré — ~ *adj* **1** OUT : éteint, fermé **2** CANCELED : annulé **3 on the** ~ **chance** : au cas où

offend [ə'fɛnd] *vt* : offenser — **offender** [ə-'fɛndər] *n* : délinquant *m*, -quante *f*; coupable *mf* — **offense** *or* **offence** [ə'fɛns, 'ɔˌfɛnts] *n* **1** INSULT : offense *f* **2** CRIME : délit *m* **3** : attaque *f* (aux sports) **4 take** ~ : s'offenser — **offensive** [ə'fɛntsɪv, 'ɔˌfɛnts-] *adj* : offensif — ~ *n* : offensive *f*

offer [ə'fɔr] *vt* : offrir, présenter — ~ *n* : proposition *f*, offre *f* — **offering** ['ɔfərɪŋ] *n* : offre *f*, offrande *f* (en réligion)

offhand ['ɔf'hænd] *adv* : spontanément, au pied levé — ~ *adj* : désinvolte

office ['ɔfəs] *n* **1** : bureau *m* **2** POSITION : fonction *f*, poste *m* — **officer** ['ɔfəsər] *n* **1** *or* **police** ~ : policier *m*, agent *m* (de police) **2** OFFICIAL : fonctionnaire *mf* **3** : officier *m* (dans l'armée) — **official** [ə'fɪʃəl] *adj* : officiel — ~ *n* : officiel *m*, -cielle *f*

offing ['ɔfɪŋ] *n* **in the** ~ : en perspective, imminent

offset ['ɔfˌsɛt] *vt* **-set; -setting** : compenser

offshore [ˈɔfˈʃor] *adv* : en mer — ~ *adj* : côtier, marin

offspring [ˈɔfˌsprɪŋ] *ns & pl* : progéniture *f*

often [ˈɔfən, ˈɔftən] *adv* **1** : souvent, fréquemment **2 every so ~** : de temps en temps

ogle [ˈoːgəl] *vt* **ogled; ogling** : lorgner

ogre [ˈoːgər] *n* : ogre *m*, ogresse *f*

oh [ˈoː] *interj* **1** : oh **2 ~ really?** : vraiment?

oil [ˈɔɪl] *n* **1** : huile *f* (d'olive, etc.) **2** PETROLEUM : pétrole *m* **3** or **heating ~** : mazout *m* — ~ *vt* : huiler, lubrifier — **oilskin** [ˈɔɪlˌskɪn] *n* : ciré *m* — **oily** [ˈɔɪli] *adj* **oilier; -est** : huileux

ointment [ˈɔɪntmənt] *n* : pommade *f*

OK *or* **okay** [ˌoːˈkeɪ] *adv* **1** WELL : bien **2** YES : oui — ~ *adj* **1** ALL RIGHT : bien **2 are you ~?** : ça va? — ~ *vt* **OK'd** *or* **okayed; OK'ing** *or* **okaying** : approuver — ~ *n* **1** APPROVAL : accord *m* **2 give the ~** : donner le feu vert

okra [ˈoːkrə, *south also* -kri] *n* : gombo *m*

old [ˈoːld] *adj* **1** : vieux **2** FORMER : ancien **3 any ~** : n'importe quel **4 be ten years ~** : avoir dix ans **5 ~ age** : vieillesse *f* **6 ~ man** : vieux *m* **7 ~ woman** : vieille *f* — ~ *n* **the ~** : les vieux, les personnes âgées — **old-fashioned** [ˈoːldˈfæʃənd] *adj* : démodé

olive [ˈɑlɪv, -ləv] *n* **1** : olive *f* (fruit) **2** or **~ green** : vert *m* olive

Olympic [oˈlɪmpɪk] *adj* : olympique — **Olympic Games** [oˈlɪmpɪk] *or* **Olympics** [-pɪks] *npl* : jeux *mpl* Olympiques

omelet *or* **omelette** [ˈɑmlət, ˈɑmə-] *n* : omelette *f*

omen [ˈoːmən] *n* : augure *m*, présage *m*

omit [oˈmɪt] *vt* **omitted; omitting** : omettre — **omission** [oˈmɪʃən] *n* : omission *f*

omnipotent [ɑmˈnɪpətənt] *adj* : omnipotent

on [ˈɑn, ˈɔn] *prep* **1** : sur **2 ~ fire** : en feu **3 ~ foot** : à pied **4 ~ Friday** : vendredi **5 ~ the plane** : dans l'avion **6 ~ the right** : à droite — ~ *adv* **1 from that moment ~** : à partir de ce moment-là **2 later ~** : plus tard **3 put ~** : mettre — ~ *adj* **1** : allumé (se dit d'une lumière), en marche (se dit d'un moteur), ouvert (se dit d'un robinet) **2 be ~** : avoir lieu (se dit d'un événement)

once [ˈwʌnts] *adv* **1** : une fois **2** FORMERLY : autrefois — ~ *n* **1** : une seule fois **2 at ~** SIMULTANEOUSLY : en même temps **3 at ~** IMMEDIATELY : tout de suite — ~ *conj* : dès que, une fois que

oncoming [ˈɑnˌkʌmɪŋ, ˈɔn-] *adj* : qui approche

one [ˈwʌn] *n* **1** : un *m* (numéro) **2 ~ o'clock** : une heure — ~ *adj* **1** : un, une **2**

ONLY : seul, unique **3** SAME : même — ~ *pron* **1** : un, une **2 ~ another** : l'un l'autre **3 ~ never knows** : on ne sait jamais **4 this ~** : celui-ci, celle-ci **5 that ~** : celui-là, celle-là **6 which ~?** : lequel? laquelle? — **oneself** [ˌwənˈsɛlf] *pron* **1** (*used reflexively*) : se **2** (*used for emphasis*) : soi-même **3** (*used after prepositions*) : soi **4 by ~** : seul — **one-sided** [ˈwʌnˈsaɪdəd] *adj* **1** UNEQUAL : inégal **2** BIASED : partial — **one-way** [ˈwʌnˈweɪ] *adj* **1** : à sens unique (se dit d'une route) **2 ~ ticket** : aller *m* simple

ongoing [ˈɑnˌgoːɪŋ] *adj* : continu, en cours

onion [ˈʌnjən] *n* : oignon *m*

online [ˈɑnˌlaɪn, ˈɔn-] *adj or adv* : en ligne

only [ˈoːnli] *adj* : seul, unique — ~ *adv* **1** : seulement, ne...que **2 if ~** : si, si seulement **3 ~ too well** : trop bien — ~ *conj* BUT : mais

onset [ˈɑnˌsɛt] *n* : début *m*

onslaught [ˈɑnˌslɔt, ˈɔn-] *n* : attaque *f*

onto [ˈɑnˌtuː, ˈɔn-] *prep* : sur

onus [ˈoːnəs] *n* : responsabilité *f*, charge *f*

onward [ˈɑnwərd, ˈɔn-] *adv & adj* **1** : en avant **2 from today ~** : à partir d'aujourd'hui

onyx [ˈɑnɪks] *n* : onyx *m*

ooze [ˈuːz] *vi* **oozed; oozing** : suinter

opal [ˈoːpəl] *n* : opale *f*

opaque [oˈpeɪk] *adj* : opaque

open [ˈoːpən] *adj* **1** : ouvert **2** FRANK : franc, sincère **3** CLEAR : dégagé **4** PUBLIC : public **5** UNCOVERED : découvert — ~ *vt* **1** : ouvrir **2** START : commencer — *vi* **1** : s'ouvrir **2** BEGIN : commencer **3 ~ onto** : donner sur — ~ *n* **1 in the ~** OUTDOORS : au grand air, dehors **2 in the ~** KNOWN : connu — **open-air** [ˈoːpənˈær] *adj* : en plein air — **opener** [ˈoːpənər] *n or* **can ~** : ouvre-boîtes — **opening** [ˈoːpənɪŋ] *n* **1** : ouverture *f* **2** START : début *m* **3** OPPORTUNITY : occasion *f* — ~ *adj* : premier, préliminaire — **openly** [ˈoːpənli] *adv* : ouvertement, franchement

opera [ˈɑprə, ˈɑpərə] *n* : opéra *m*

operate [ˈɑpəˌreɪt] *v* **-ated; -ating** *vi* **1** FUNCTION : fonctionner, marcher **2 ~ on s.o.** : opérer qqn — *vt* **1** : faire fonctionner (une machine) **2** MANAGE : diriger, gérer — **operation** [ˌɑpəˈreɪʃən] *n* **1** : opération *f* **2 in ~** : en marche, en service — **operational** [ˌɑpəˈreɪʃənəl] *adj* : opérationnel — **operative** [ˈɑpərətɪv, -ˌreɪ-] *adj* : en vigueur — **operator** [ˈɑpəˌreɪtər] *n* **1** : opérateur *m*, -trice *f* **2 telephone ~** : standardiste *mf*

opinion [əˈpɪnjən] *n* : opinion *f*, avis *m* — **opinionated** [əˈpɪnjəˌneɪtəd] *adj* : opiniâtre

opium [ˈoːpiəm] *n* : opium *m*

opossum [əˈpɑsəm] *n* : opossum *m*

opponent [ə'po:nənt] *n* : adversaire *mf*

opportunity [,apər'tu:nəti, -'tju:-] *n, pl* **-ties** : occasion *f* — **opportune** [,apər'tu:n, -'tju:n] *adj* : opportun — **opportunism** [,apər'tu:,nizəm, -'tju:-] *n* : opportunisme *m* — **opportunist** [,apər'tu:nist, -'tju:-] *n* : opportuniste *mf* — **opportunistic** [,apərtu:'nistik, -tju:-] *adj* : opportuniste

oppose [ə'po:z] *vt* **-posed; -posing** : s'opposer à — **opposed** [ə'po:zd] *adj* ~ **to** : opposé à

opposite ['apəzət] *adj* **1** FACING : d'en face **2** CONTRARY : opposé, inverse — ~ *n* : contraire *m* — ~ *adv* : en face — ~ *prep* : en face de — **opposition** [,apə'zɪʃən] *n* : opposition *f*

oppress [ə'prɛs] *vt* **1** PERSECUTE : opprimer **2** BURDEN : oppresser — **oppression** [ə-'prɛʃən] *n* : oppression *f* — **oppressive** [ə'prɛsɪv] *adj* : oppressif — **oppressor** [ə-'prɛsər] *n* : oppresseur *m*

opt ['apt] *vi* : opter

optic ['aptɪk] *or* **optical** ['aptɪkəl] *adj* : optique — **optician** [ap'tɪʃən] *n* : opticien *m*, -cienne *f*

optimism ['aptə,mɪzəm] *n* : optimisme *m* — **optimist** ['aptəmɪst] *n* : optimiste *mf* — **optimistic** [,aptə'mɪstɪk] *adj* : optimiste

optimum ['aptəməm] *adj* : optimum — ~ *n, pl* **-ma** ['aptəmə] : optimum *m*

option ['apʃən] *n* : option *f* — **optional** ['apʃənəl] *adj* : facultatif, optionnel

opulence ['apjələnts] *n* : opulence *f* — **opulent** [-lənt] *adj* : opulent

or ['ɔr] *conj* **1** (*indicating an alternative*) : ou **2** (*following a negative*) : ni **3** ~ **else** OTHERWISE : sinon

oracle ['ɔrəkəl] *n* : oracle *m*

oral ['ɔrəl] *adj* : oral

orange ['ɔrɪndʒ] *n* **1** : orange *f* (fruit) **2** : orange *m* (couleur)

orator ['ɔrətər] *n* : orateur *m*, -trice *f*

orbit ['ɔrbət] *n* : orbite *f* — ~ *vt* : graviter autour de

orchard ['ɔrtʃərd] *n* : verger *m*

orchestra ['ɔrkəstrə] *n* : orchestre *m*

orchid ['ɔrkɪd] *n* : orchidée *f*

ordain [ɔr'deɪn] *vt* **1** DECREE : décréter **2** : ordonner (en religion)

ordeal [ɔr'di:l, 'ɔr,di:l] *n* : épreuve *f*

order ['ɔrdər] *vt* **1** COMMAND : ordonner **2** REQUEST : commander (un repas, etc.) **3** ORGANIZE : organiser — ~ *n* **1** : ordre *m* **2** COMMAND, REQUEST : commande *f* **3 in good** ~ : en bon état **4 in** ~ **to** : afin de **5 out of** ~ : en panne — **orderly** ['ɔrdərli] *adj* **1** TIDY : en ordre, ordonné **2** DISCI-PLINED : discipliné

ordinary ['ɔrdən,ɛri] *adj* **1** USUAL : normal, habituel **2** AVERAGE : ordinaire, moyen —

ordinarily [,ɔrdən'ɛrəli] *adv* : d'ordinaire, d'habitude

ore ['ɔr] *n* : minerai *m*

oregano [ə'rɛgə,no:] *n* : origan *m*

organ ['ɔrgən] *n* **1** : orgue *m* (instrument de musique) **2** : organe *m* (du corps) — **organic** [ɔr'gænɪk] *adj* **1** : organique **2** NA-TUREL : biologique — **organism** ['ɔrgə-,nɪzəm] *n* : organisme *m* — **organist** ['ɔrgənɪst] *n* : organiste *mf* — **organize** ['ɔrgə,naɪz] *vt* **-nized; -nizing 1** : organiser **2 get organized** : s'organiser — **organiza-tion** [,ɔrgənə'zeɪʃən] *n* : organisation *f* — **organizer** ['ɔrgə,naɪzər] *n* : organisateur *m*, -trice *f*

orgasm ['ɔr,gæzəm] *n* : orgasme *m*

orgy ['ɔrdʒi] *n, pl* **-gies** : orgie *f*

Orient ['ori,ɛnt] *n* **the** ~ : l'Orient *m* — **ori-ent** *vt* : orienter — **oriental** [,ori'ɛntəl] *adj* : oriental, d'Orient — **orientation** [,ori-ɛn-'teɪʃən] *n* : orientation *f*

orifice ['ɔrəfəs] *n* : orifice *m*

origin ['ɔrədʒən] *n* : origine *f* — **original** [ə-'rɪdʒənəl] *adj* **1** : original **2** FIRST : premier — ~ *n* : original *m* — **originality** [ə,rɪdʒə-'næləti] *n* : originalité *f* — **originally** [ə'rɪdʒənəli] *adv* : à l'origine — **originate** [ə-'rɪdʒə,neɪt] *v* **-nated; -nating** *vt* : donner naissance à — *vi* : provenir, prendre nais-sance

ornament ['ɔrnəmənt] *n* : ornement *m* — **or-namental** [,ɔrnə'mɛntəl] *adj* : ornemental — **ornate** [ɔr'neɪt] *adj* : orné

ornithology [,ɔrnə'θalədʒi] *n, pl* **-gies** : or-nithologie *f*

orphan ['ɔrfən] *n* : orphelin *m*, -line *f*

orthodox ['ɔrθə,daks] *adj* : orthodoxe — **or-thodoxy** ['ɔrθə,daksi] *n, pl* **-doxies** : ortho-doxie *f*

orthopedic [,ɔrθə'pi:dɪk] *adj* : orthopédique — **orthopedics** [,ɔrθə'pi:dɪks] *ns & pl* : or-thopédie *f*

oscillate ['asə,leɪt] *vi* **-lated; -lating** : os-ciller — **oscillation** [,asə'leɪʃən] *n* : oscilla-tion *f*

ostensible [a'stɛntsəbəl] *adj* : apparent — **ostentation** [,astən'teɪʃən] *n* : ostentation *f*

osteopath ['astiə,pæθ] *n* : ostéopathe *mf*

ostracism ['astrə,sɪzəm] *n* : ostracisme *m* — **ostracize** ['astrə,saɪz] *vt* **-cized; -cizing** : mettre au ban de la société

ostrich ['astrɪtʃ, 'ɔs-] *n* : autruche *f*

other ['ʌðər] *adj* **1** : autre **2 every** ~ **day** : tous les deux jours **3 on the** ~ **hand** : d'autre part — ~ *pron* **1** : autre **2 the** ~**s** : les autres **3 someone or** ~ : quelqu'un — **other than** *prep* : autrement que, à part — **otherwise** ['ʌðər,waɪz] *adv* **1** : autrement **2** OR ELSE : sinon — ~ *adj* : autre

otter ['ɑtər] *n* : loutre *f*

ought ['ɔt] *v aux* **1** : devoir **2 you ~ to have done it** : tu aurais dû le faire

ounce ['aʊn̩s] *n* : once *f*

our ['ɑr, 'aʊr] *adj* : notre, nos — **ours** ['aʊrz, 'aʊrz] *pron* **1** : le nôtre, la nôtre **2 a friend of ~** : un de nos amis **3 that's ~** : c'est à nous — **ourselves** [ɑr'sɛlvz, aʊr-] *pron* **1** (*used reflexively*) : nous **2** (*used for emphasis*) : nous-mêmes

oust ['aʊst] *vt* : évincer

out ['aʊt] *adv* **1** OUTSIDE : dehors **2 cry ~** : crier **3 eat ~** : aller au restaurant **4 go ~** : sortir **5 turn ~** : éteindre — *prep* → **out of** — *adj* **1** ABSENT : absent, sorti **2** RELEASED : sorti **3** UNFASHIONABLE : démodé **4** EXTINGUISHED : éteint **5 the sun is ~** : il fait soleil

outboard motor ['aʊt,bord] *n* : hors-bord *m*

outbreak ['aʊt,breɪk] *n* : éruption *f* (d'une maladie, etc.), déclenchement *m* (des hostilités, etc.)

outburst ['aʊt,bərst] *n* : explosion *f*, accès *m*

outcast ['aʊt,kæst] *n* : paria *m*

outcome ['aʊt,kʌm] *n* : résultat *m*

outcry ['aʊt,kraɪ] *n, pl* **-cries** : tollé *m*

outdated ['aʊt'deɪtəd] *adj* : démodé

outdo [,aʊt'du:] *vt* **-did** [-'dɪd]; **-done** [-'dʌn]; **-doing** [-'du:ɪŋ]; **-does** [-'dʌz] : surpasser

outdoor ['aʊt'dor] *adj* : en plein air, de plein air — **outdoors** ['aʊt'dorz] *adv* : dehors

outer ['aʊtər] *adj* : extérieur — **outer space** *n* : espace *m* cosmique

outfit ['aʊt,fɪt] *n* **1** EQUIPMENT : équipement *m* **2** COSTUME : tenue *f* **3** GROUP : équipe *f* — *vt* **-fitted; -fitting** : équiper

outgoing ['aʊt,goɪŋ] *adj* **1** LEAVING : en partance (se dit d'un train, etc.), sortant (se dit d'une personne) **2** EXTROVERTED : ouvert **3 ~ mail** : courrier *m* à expédier

outgrow [,aʊt'gro:] *vt* **-grew** [-'gru:]; **-grown** [-'gro:n]; **-growing** : devenir trop grand pour

outing ['aʊtɪŋ] *n* : excursion *f*, sortie *f*

outlandish [aʊt'lændɪʃ] *adj* : bizarre

outlast [,aʊt'læst] *vt* : durer plus longtemps que

outlaw ['aʊt,lɔ] *n* : hors-la-loi *m* — *~ vt* : proscrire

outlay ['aʊt,leɪ] *n* : dépenses *fpl*

outlet ['aʊt,let, -lət] *n* **1** EXIT : sortie *f*, issue *f* **2** MARKET : débouché *m* **3** RELEASE : exutoire *m* **4** *or* **electrical ~** : prise *f* de courant **5** *or* **retail ~** : point *m* de vente

outline ['aʊt,laɪn] *n* **1** CONTOUR : contour *m* **2** SKETCH : esquisse *f* — *vt* **-lined; -lining 1** : souligner le contour de **2** SUMMARIZE : exposer dans ses grandes lignes

outlive [,aʊt'lɪv] *vt* **-lived; -living** : survivre à

outlook ['aʊt,lʊk] *n* : perspective *f*

outlying ['aʊt,laɪɪŋ] *adj* : écarté, périphérique

outmoded [,aʊt'mo:dəd] *adj* : démodé

outnumber [,aʊt'nʌmbər] *vt* : surpasser en nombre

out of *prep* **1** OUTSIDE : en dehors de **2** FROM : de **3 four ~ five** : quatre sur cinq **4 made ~ plastic** : fait en plastique **5 ~ control** : hors de contrôle **6 ~ money** : sans argent **7 ~ spite** : par dépit — **out-of-date** [,aʊtəv'deɪt] *adj* **1** OLD-FASHIONED : démodé **2** EXPIRED : périmé — **out-of-doors** [aʊtəv'dorz] → **outdoors**

outpost ['aʊt,po:st] *n* : avant-poste *m*

output ['aʊt,pʊt] *n* : rendement *m*, production *f*

outrage ['aʊt,reɪdʒ] *n* **1** AFFRONT : outrage *m*, affront *m* **2** ANGER : indignation *f* — *~ vt* **-raged; -raging** : outrager — **outrageous** [,aʊt'reɪdʒəs] *adj* **1** DISGRACEFUL : scandaleux **2** EXCESSIVE : outrancier

outright ['aʊt,raɪt] *adv* **1** COMPLETELY : complètement **2** INSTANTLY : sur le coup **3** FRANKLY : carrément — *~ adj* : total, absolu

outset ['aʊt,sɛt] *n* : début *m*, commencement *m*

outside [,aʊt'saɪd, 'aʊt,-] *n* : extérieur *m* — *~ adj* : extérieur — *~ adv* : à l'extérieur, dehors — *~ prep or ~ of* : en dehors de, à part — **outsider** [,aʊt'saɪdər] *n* : étranger *m*, -gère *f*

outskirts ['aʊt,skərts] *npl* : banlieue *f*, périphérie *f*

outspoken [,aʊt'spo:kən] *adj* : franc, direct

outstanding [,aʊt'stændɪŋ] *adj* **1** UNPAID : impayé **2** UNRESOLVED : en suspens **3** NOTABLE : exceptionnel

outstretched [,aʊt'strɛtʃt] *adj* : tendu

outstrip [,aʊt'strɪp] *vt* **-stripped; -stripping** : devancer

outward ['aʊtwərd] *or* **outwards** [-wərdz] *adv* **1** : vers l'extérieur **2 ~ bound** : en partance — *~ adj* : extérieur — **outwardly** ['aʊtwərdli] *adv* : en apparence

outweigh [,aʊt'weɪ] *vt* : l'emporter sur

outwit [,aʊt'wɪt] *vt* **-witted; -witting** : se montrer plus malin que

oval ['o:vəl] *adj* : ovale — *~ n* : ovale *m*

ovary ['o:vəri] *n, pl* **-ries** : ovaire *m*

ovation [o'veɪʃən] *n* : ovation *f*

oven ['ʌvən] *n* : four *m*

over ['o:vər] *adv* **1** ABOVE : au-dessus **2** MORE : de trop **3** AGAIN : encore **4 all ~** : partout **5 ask ~** : inviter **6 four times ~** : quatre fois de suite **7 ~ here** : ici **8 ~ there** : là-bas **9 start ~** : recommencer

— ～ *prep* **1** ABOVE : au-dessus de, par-dessus **2** MORE THAN : plus de **3** ACROSS : de l'autre côté de **4** DURING : pendant, au cours de **5** CONCERNING : au sujet de — ～ *adj* : fini, terminé

overall [ˌoːvərˈɔl] *adv* GENERALLY : en général — ～ *adj* : d'ensemble, total — **overalls** [ˈoːvərˌɔlz] *npl* : salopette *f*

overbearing [ˌoːvərˈbærɪŋ] *adj* : impérieux, autoritaire

overboard [ˈoːvərˌbord] *adv* : par-dessus bord

overburden [ˌoːvərˈbərdən] *vt* : surcharger

overcast [ˈoːvərˌkæst] *adj* : couvert

overcharge [ˌoːvərˈtʃɑrʤ] *vt* **-charged; -charging** : faire payer trop cher à

overcoat [ˈoːvərˌkoːt] *n* : pardessus *m*

overcome [ˌoːvərˈkʌm] *vt* **-came** [-ˈkeɪm]; **-come; -coming 1** CONQUER : vaincre, surmonter **2** OVERWHELM : accabler

overcook [ˌoːvərˈkʊk] *vt* : faire trop cuire

overcrowded [ˌoːvərˈkraʊdəd] *adj* : bondé

overdo [ˌoːvərˈduː] *vt* **-did** [-ˈdɪd]; **-done** [-ˈdʌn]; **-doing; -does** [-ˈdʌz] **1** : exagérer **2** → **overcook**

overdose [ˈoːvərˌdoːs] *n* : overdose *f*

overdraw [ˌoːvərˈdrɔ] *vt* **-drew** [-ˈdruː]; **-drawn** [-ˈdrɔn]; **-drawing** : mettre à découvert — **overdraft** [ˈoːvərˌdræft] *n* : découvert *m*

overdue [ˌoːvərˈduː] *adj* **1** UNPAID : arriéré **2** LATE : en retard

overestimate [ˌoːvərˈɛstəˌmeɪt] *vt* **-mated; -mating** : surestimer

overflow [ˌoːvərˈfloː] *v* : déborder — ～ [ˈoːvərˌfloː] *n* : trop-plein *m*, débordement *m*

overgrown [ˌoːvərˈgroːn] *adj* : envahi par la végétation

overhand [ˈoːvərˌhænd] *adv* : par-dessus la tête

overhang [ˌoːvərˈhæŋ] *vt* **-hung** [-ˈhʌŋ]; **-hanging** : surplomber

overhaul [ˌoːvərˈhɔl] *vt* : réviser (un moteur, etc.), remanier (un système, etc.)

overhead [ˌoːvərˈhɛd] *adv* : au-dessus — ～ *adj* : aérien — ～ *n* : frais *mpl* généraux

overhear [ˌoːvərˈhɪr] *vt* **-heard** [-ˈhərd]; **-hearing** : entendre par hasard

overheat [ˌoːvərˈhiːt] *vt* : surchauffer

overjoyed [ˌoːvərˈʤɔɪd] *adj* : ravi

overland [ˈoːvərˌlænd, -lənd] *adv & adj* : par voie de terre

overlap [ˌoːvərˈlæp] *v* **-lapped; -lapping** *vt* : chevaucher — *vi* : se chevaucher

overload [ˌoːvərˈloːd] *vt* : surcharger

overlook [ˌoːvərˈlʊk] *vt* **1** : donner sur (un jardin, la mer, etc.) **2** IGNORE : négliger, laisser passer

overly [ˈoːvərli] *adv* : trop

overnight [ˌoːvərˈnaɪt] *adv* **1** : (pendant) la nuit **2** SUDDENLY : du jour au lendemain — ～ [ˈoːvərˌnaɪt] *adj* **1** : de nuit, d'une nuit **2** SUDDEN : soudain

overpass [ˈoːvərˌpæs] *n* : voie *f* surélevée *Can*, pont *m* autoroutier

overpopulated [ˌoːvərˈpɑpjəˌleɪtəd] *adj* : surpeuplé

overpower [ˌoːvərˈpaʊər] *vt* **1** CONQUER : vaincre **2** OVERWHELM : accabler

overrate [ˌoːvərˈreɪt] *vt* **-rated; -rating** : surestimer

override [ˌoːvərˈraɪd] *vt* **-rode** [-ˈroːd]; **-ridden** [-ˈrɪdən]; **-riding 1** : passer outre à **2** ANNUL : annuler — **overriding** [oːvərˈraɪdɪŋ] *adj* : primordial

overrule [ˌoːvərˈruːl] *vt* **-ruled; -ruling** : rejeter

overrun [ˌoːvərˈrʌn] *vt* **-ran** [-ˈræn]; **-running 1** INVADE : envahir **2** EXCEED : dépasser

overseas [ˌoːvərˈsiːz] *adv* : à l'étranger, outre-mer — ～ [ˈoːvərˌsiːz] *adj* : à l'étranger, extérieur

oversee [ˌoːvərˈsiː] *vt* **-saw** [-ˈsɔ]; **-seen** [-ˈsiːn]; **-seeing** : surveiller

overshadow [ˌoːvərˈʃæˌdoː] *vt* : éclipser

oversight [ˈoːvərˌsaɪt] *n* : oubli *m*, omission *f*

oversleep [ˌoːvərˈsliːp] *vi* **-slept** [-ˈslɛpt]; **-sleeping** : se réveiller trop tard

overstep [ˌoːvərˈstɛp] *vt* **-stepped; -stepping** : outrepasser

overt [oːˈvərt, ˈoːˌvərt] *adj* : manifeste

overtake [ˌoːvərˈteɪk] *vt* **-took** [-ˈtʊk]; **-taken** [-ˈteɪkən]; **-taking** : dépasser

overthrow [ˌoːvərˈθroː] *vt* **-threw** [-ˈθruː]; **-thrown** [-ˈθroːn]; **-throwing** : renverser

overtime [ˈoːvərˌtaɪm] *n* **1** : heures *fpl* supplémentaires **2** : prolongations *fpl* (aux sports)

overtone [ˈoːvərˌtoːn] *n* : nuance *f*, sous-entendu *m*

overture [ˈoːvərˌtʃʊr, -tʃər] *n* : ouverture *f* (en musique)

overturn [ˌoːvərˈtərn] *vt* : renverser — *vi* : se renverser

overweight [ˌoːvərˈweɪt] *adj* : trop gros, obèse

overwhelm [ˌoːvərˈʰwɛlm] *vt* **1** : submerger, accabler **2** DEFEAT : écraser — **overwhelming** [ˌoːvərˈʰwɛlmɪŋ] *adj* : accablant, écrasant

overwork [ˌoːvərˈwərk] *vt* : surmener — ～ *n* : surmenage *m*

overwrought [ˌoːvərˈrɔt] *adj* : à bout de nerfs

owe [ˈoː] *vt* **owed; owing** : devoir — **owing to** *prep* : à cause de

owl [ˈaʊl] *n* : hibou *m*

own [ˈoːn] *adj* : propre — ～ *vt* : posséder,

avoir — *vi* ~ up : avouer — ~ *pron* **1 my (your, his/her, our, their)** ~ : le mien, la mienne; le tien, la tienne; le vôtre, la vôtre; le sien, la sienne; le nôtre, la nôtre; le leur, la leur **2 on one's** ~ : tout seul **3 to each his** ~ : chacun son goût — **owner** ['o:nər]

n : propriétaire *mf* — **ownership** ['o:nər-ˌʃɪp] *n* : possession *f*
ox ['aks] *n, pl* **oxen** ['aksən] : bœuf *m*
oxygen ['aksɪdʒən] *n* : oxygène *m*
oyster ['ɔɪstər] *n* : huître *f*
ozone ['o:ˌzo:n] *n* : ozone *m*

P

p ['pi:] *n, pl* **p's** *or* **ps** ['pi:z] : p *m*, seizième lettre de l'alphabet
pace ['peɪs] *n* **1** STEP : pas *m* **2** SPEED : allure *f* **3 keep** ~ **with** : suivre — ~ *v* **paced; pacing** *vt* : arpenter — *vi* ~ **to and fro** : faire les cent pas
pacify ['pæsəˌfaɪ] *vt* **-fied; -fying** : pacifier, apaiser — **pacifier** ['pæsəˌfaɪər] *n* : tétine *f*, sucette *f* — **pacifist** ['pæsəfɪst] *n* : pacifiste *mf*
pack ['pæk] *n* **1** PACKAGE : paquet *m* **2** BAG : sac *m* **3** GROUP : bande *f*, meute *f* (de chiens) **4** : jeu *m* (de cartes) — ~ *vt* **1** PACKAGE : emballer **2** FILL : remplir **3** : faire (ses bagages) — **package** ['pækɪdʒ] *vt* **-aged; -aging** : empaqueter — ~ *n* : paquet *m*, colis *m* — **packet** ['pækət] *n* : paquet *m*
pact ['pækt] *n* : pacte *m*
pad ['pæd] *n* **1** CUSHION : coussin *m* **2** TABLET : bloc *m* (de papier) **3 ink** ~ : tampon *m* encreur **4 launching** ~ : rampe *f* de lancement **5** : protection *f* (aux sports) — ~ *vt* **padded; padding** : rembourrer — **padding** ['pædɪŋ] *n* STUFFING : rembourrage *m*
paddle ['pædəl] *n* **1** : pagaie *f*, aviron *m Can* **2** : raquette *f* (aux sports) — ~ *vt* **-dled; -dling** : pagayer
padlock ['pædˌlak] *n* : cadenas *m* — ~ *vt* : cadenasser
pagan ['peɪgən] *n* : païen *m*, païenne *f* — ~ *adj* : païen
page[1] ['peɪdʒ] **paged; paging** *vt* : appeler
page[2] *n* : page *f* (d'un livre)
pageant ['pædʒənt] *n* : spectacle *m* — **pageantry** ['pædʒəntri] *n* : apparat *m*
paid → **pay**
pail ['peɪl] *n* : seau *m*
pain ['peɪn] *n* **1** : douleur *f* **2 take** ~**s** *npl* : se donner de la peine — ~ *vt* : peiner, faire souffrir — **painful** ['peɪnfəl] *adj* : douloureux — **painkiller** ['peɪnˌkɪlər] *n* : analgésique *m* — **painless** ['peɪnləs] *adj*

: indolore, sans douleur — **painstaking** ['peɪnˌsteɪkɪŋ] *adj* : soigneux, méticuleux
paint ['peɪnt] *v* : peindre, peinturer *Can* — ~ *n* : peinture *f* — **paintbrush** ['peɪnt-ˌbrʌʃ] *n* : pinceau *m* (d'un artiste), brosse *f* — **painter** ['peɪntər] *n* : peintre *m* — **painting** ['peɪntɪŋ] *n* : peinture *f*
pair ['pær] *n* **1** : paire *f* **2** COUPLE : couple *m* — ~ *vi* : accoupler
pajamas *or Brit* **pyjamas** [pə'dʒɑməz, -'dʒæ-] *npl* : pyjama *m*
pal ['pæl] *n* : copain *m*, -pine *f*
palace ['pæləs] *n* : palais *m*
palate ['pælət] *n* : palais *m* — **palatable** ['pælətəbəl] *adj* : savoureux
pale ['peɪl] *adj* **paler; palest** : pâle — ~ *vi* **paled; paling** : pâlir — **paleness** ['peɪlnəs] *n* : pâleur *f*
palette ['pælət] *n* : palette *f*
pallid ['pæləd] *adj* : pâle
palm[1] ['pɑm, 'pɑlm] *n* : paume *f* (de la main)
palm[2] *or* ~ **tree** : palmier *m* — **Palm Sunday** *n* : dimanche *m* des Rameaux
palpitate ['pælpəˌteɪt] *vi* **-tated; -tating** : palpiter — **palpitation** [ˌpælpə'teɪʃən] *n* : palpitation *f*
paltry ['pɔltri] *adj* **-trier; -est** : dérisoire
pamper ['pæmpər] *vt* : dorloter
pamphlet ['pæmpflət] *n* : dépliant *m*, brochure *f*
pan ['pæn] *n* **1** SAUCEPAN : casserole *f* **2** FRYING PAN : poêle *f*
pancake ['pænˌkeɪk] *n* : crêpe *f*
pancreas ['pæŋkriəs, 'pæn-] *n* : pancréas *m*
panda ['pændə] *n* : panda *m*
pandemonium [ˌpændə'mo:niəm] *n* : tumulte *m*
pander ['pændər] *vi* : flatter (bassement)
pane ['peɪn] *n* : vitre *f*, carreau *m*
panel ['pænəl] *n* **1** : panneau *m* **2** COMMITTEE : comité *m* **3** *or* **control** ~ : tableau *m* (de bord) — **paneling** ['pænəlɪŋ] *n* : lambris *m*
pang ['pæŋ] *n* : tiraillement *m*

panic ['pænɪk] *n* : panique *f* — ~ *v* **-icked; -icking** : paniquer

panorama [ˌpænəˈræmə, -ˈrɑ-] *n* : panorama *m* — **panoramic** [ˌpænəˈræmɪk, -ˈrɑ-] *adj* : panoramique

pansy ['pænzi] *n, pl* **-sies** : pensée *f*

pant ['pænt] *vi* : haleter

panther ['pænθər] *n* : panthère *f*

panties ['pæntiz] *npl* : (petite) culotte *f*, slip *m France*

pantomime ['pæntəˌmaɪm] *n* : pantomime *f*

pantry ['pæntri] *n, pl* **-tries** : garde-manger *m*

pants ['pænts] *npl* : pantalon *m*

panty hose ['pæntiˌhoːz] *npl* : collant *m*

papaya [pəˈpaɪə] *n* : papaye *f*

paper ['peɪpər] *n* **1** : papier *m* **2** DOCUMENT : document *m* **3** NEWSPAPER : journal *m* **4** : devoir *m* (scolaire) — ~ *vt* WALLPAPER : tapisser — ~ *adj* : de papier, en papier — **paperback** ['peɪpərˌbæk] *n* : livre *m* de poche — **paper clip** *n* : trombone *m* — **paperwork** ['peɪpərˌwərk] *n* : paperasserie *f*

par ['pɑr] *n* **1** EQUALITY : égalité *f* **2 on a** ~ **with** : de pair avec

parable ['pærəbəl] *n* : parabole *f*

parachute ['pærəˌʃuːt] *n* : parachute *m*

parade [pəˈreɪd] *n* **1** : défilé *m*, parade *f* (militaire) **2** DISPLAY : étalage *m* — ~ *v* **-raded; -rading** *vi* MARCH : défiler — *vt* DISPLAY : faire étalage de

paradise ['pærəˌdaɪs, -ˌdaɪz] *n* : paradis *m*

paradox ['pærəˌdɑks] *n* : paradoxe *m* — **paradoxical** [ˌpærəˈdɑksɪkəl] *adj* : paradoxal

paragraph ['pærəˌgræf] *n* : paragraphe *m*

parakeet ['pærəˌkiːt] *n* : perruche *f*

parallel ['pærəˌlɛl, -ləl] *adj* : parallèle — ~ *n* **1** : parallèle *f* (en géométrie) **2** SIMILARITY : parallèle *m* — ~ *vt* MATCH : égaler

paralysis [pəˈræləsɪs] *n, pl* **-yses** [-ˌsiːz] : paralysie *f* — **paralyze** *or Brit* **paralyse** ['pærəˌlaɪz] *vt* **-lyzed** *or Brit* **-lysed; -lyzing** *or Brit* **-lysing** : paralyser

parameter [pəˈræmətər] *n* : paramètre *m*

paramount ['pærəˌmaunt] *adj* : suprême

paranoia [ˌpærəˈnɔɪə] *n* : paranoïa *f* — **paranoid** ['pærəˌnɔɪd] *adj* : paranoïaque

parapet ['pærəpət, -ˌpɛt] *n* : parapet *m*

paraphernalia [ˌpærəfəˈneɪljə, -fər-] *ns & pl* : attirail *m*

paraphrase ['pærəˌfreɪz] *n* : paraphrase *f* — ~ *vt* **-phrased; -phrasing** : paraphraser

paraplegic ['pærəˈpliːdʒɪk] *n* : paraplégique *mf*

parasite ['pærəˌsaɪt] *n* : parasite *m*

parasol ['pærəˌsɔl] *n* : parasol *m*

paratrooper ['pærəˌtruːpər] *n* : parachutiste *m* (militaire)

parcel ['pɑrsəl] *n* : paquet *m*

parch ['pɑrtʃ] *vt* : dessécher

parchment ['pɑrtʃmənt] *n* : parchemin *m*

pardon ['pɑrdən] *n* **1** FORGIVENESS : pardon *m* **2** : grâce *f* (en droit) — ~ *vt* **1** FORGIVE : pardonner **2** ABSOLVE : gracier

parent ['pærənt] *n* **1** : mère *f*, père *m* **2** ~**s** *npl* : parents *mpl* — **parental** [pəˈrɛntəl] *adj* : parental

parenthesis [pəˈrɛnθəsəs] *n, pl* **-ses** [-ˌsiːz] : parenthèse *f*

parish ['pærɪʃ] *n* : paroisse *f* — **parishioner** [pəˈrɪʃənər] *n* : paroissien *m*, -sienne *f*

Parisian [pəˈrɪʒən, -ˈri-] *adj* : parisien

parity ['pærəti] *n, pl* **-ties** : parité *f*

park ['pɑrk] *n* : parc *m* — ~ *vt* : garer — *vi* : se garer, stationner

parka ['pɑrkə] *n* : parka *m*

parliament ['pɑrləmənt] *n* : parlement *m* — **parliamentary** [ˌpɑrləˈmɛntəri] *adj* : parlementaire

parlor *or Brit* **parlour** ['pɑrlər] *n* : salon *m*

parochial [pəˈroːkiəl] *adj* **1** : paroissial **2** PROVINCIAL : de clocher, provincial

parody ['pærədi] *n, pl* **-dies** : parodie *f* — ~ *vt* **-died; -dying** : parodier

parole [pəˈroːl] *n* : liberté *f* conditionnelle

parquet ['pɑrˌkeɪ, pɑrˈkeɪ] *n* : parquet *m*

parrot ['pærət] *n* : perroquet *m*

parry ['pæri] *vt* **-ried; -rying 1** : parer (un coup) **2** EVADE : éluder (une question)

parsley ['pɑrsli] *n* : persil *m*

parsnip ['pɑrsnɪp] *n* : panais *m*

part ['pɑrt] *n* **1** : partie *f* **2** PIECE : pièce *f* **3** ROLE : rôle *m* **4** SHARE : part *f* **5** SIDE : parti *m* **6** : raie *f* (entre les cheveux) — ~ *vi* **1** *or* ~ **company** : se séparer **2** ~ **with** : se défaire de — *vt* SEPARATE : séparer

partake [pɑrˈteɪk, pər-] *vi* **-took** [-ˈtʊk] **-taken** [-ˈteɪkən]; **-taking** ~ **in** : participer à

partial ['pɑrʃəl] *adj* **1** INCOMPLETE : partiel **2** BIASED : partial

participate [pərˈtɪsəˌpeɪt, pɑr-] *vi* **-pated; -pating** : participer — **participant** [pərˈtɪsəpənt, pɑr-] *n* : participant *m*, -pante *f*

participle ['pɑrtəˌsɪpəl] *n* : participe *m*

particle ['pɑrtɪkəl] *n* : particule *f*

particular [pərˈtɪkjələr] *adj* **1** : particulier **2** FUSSY : exigeant — ~ *n* **1 in** ~ : en particulier **2** ~**s** *npl* DETAILS : détails *mpl* — **particularly** [pərˈtɪkjələrli] *adv* : particulièrement

partisan ['pɑrtəzən, -sən] *n* : partisan *m*, -sane *f*

partition [pərˈtɪʃən, pɑr-] *n* **1** DISTRIBUTION : division *f* **2** DIVIDER : cloison *f* — ~ *vt* **1** : diviser **2** : cloisonner (une pièce)

partly ['pɑrtli] *adv* : en partie

partner ['pɑrtnər] *n* **1** ASSOCIATE : associé *m*, -ciée *f* **2** : partenaire *mf* (aux sports, en danse) — **partnership** ['pɑrtnər,ʃɪp] n : association f

party ['pɑrti] n, pl **-ties** 1 : parti m (politique) 2 PARTICIPANT : partie f 3 GATHERING : fête f 4 GROUP : groupe m

pass ['pæs] vi 1 MOVE : passer 2 **come to ~** : se passer, advenir 3 or **~ away** DIE : mourir 4 **~ out** FAINT : s'évanouir — vt 1 : passer 2 OVERTAKE : dépasser 3 : réussir (un examen) 4 **~ up** : laisser passer — ~ n 1 PERMIT : permis m, laissez-passer m 2 : passe f (aux sports) 3 or **mountain ~** : col m de montagne — **passable** ['pæsəbəl] adj ACCEPTABLE : passable — **passage** ['pæsɪdʒ] n 1 : passage m 2 CORRIDOR : couloir m — **passageway** ['pæsɪdʒ,weɪ] n : passage m, couloir m

passenger ['pæsəndʒər] n : passager m, -gère f

passerby [,pæsər'baɪ, 'pæsər,-] n, pl **passersby** : passant m, -sante f

passing ['pæsɪŋ] adj : passager

passion ['pæʃən] n : passion f — **passionate** ['pæʃənət] adj : passionné

passive ['pæsɪv] adj : passif

Passover ['pæs,o:vər] n : Pâque f (juive)

passport ['pæs,pɔrt] n : passeport m

password ['pæs,wərd] n : mot m de passe

past ['pæst] adj 1 : dernier, passé 2 FORMER : ancien — **~** prep 1 BEYOND : au-delà de 2 IN FRONT OF : devant 3 **half ~ one** : une heure et demie — **~** n : passé m — **~** adv : devant

pasta ['pɑstə, 'pæs-] n : pâtes fpl

paste ['peɪst] n 1 GLUE : colle f 2 DOUGH : pâte f — **~** vt **pasted; pasting** : coller

pastel [pæ'stɛl] n : pastel m — **~** adj : pastel

pasteurize ['pæstʃə,raɪz, 'pæstjə-] vt **-ized; -izing** : pasteuriser

pastime ['pæs,taɪm] n : passe-temps m

pastor ['pæstər] n : pasteur m

pastry ['peɪstri] n, pl **-tries** : pâtisserie f

pasture ['pæstʃər] n : pâturage m

pasty ['peɪsti] adj **-tier; -est** 1 DOUGHY : pâteux 2 PALLID : terreux

pat ['pæt] n 1 TAP : (petite) tape f 2 : noix f (de beurre, etc.) — **~** vt **patted; patting** : tapoter — **~** adv **have down ~** : connaître par cœur

patch ['pætʃ] n 1 : pièce f (d'étoffe) 2 : plaque f (de glace) — **~** vt 1 REPAIR : rapiécer 2 **~ up** : réparer — **patchy** ['pætʃi] adj **patchier; patchiest** : inégal, irrégulier

patent ['pætənt] adj 1 or **patented** [-təd] : breveté 2 ['pætənt, 'peɪt-] OBVIOUS : patent, évident — **~** ['pætənt] n : brevet m — **~** ['pætənt] vt : breveter

paternal [pə'tərnəl] adj : paternel — **paternity** [pə'tərnəti] n : paternité f

path ['pæθ, 'pɑθ] n 1 : allée f (dans un parc) 2 TRAIL : chemin m, sentier m 3 COURSE : trajectoire f

pathetic [pə'θɛtɪk] adj : pitoyable

pathology [pə'θɑlədʒi] n, pl **-gies** : pathologie f

pathway ['pæθ,weɪ] n : chemin m, sentier m

patience ['peɪʃənts] n : patience f — **patient** ['peɪʃənt] adj : patient — **~** n : patient m, -tiente f; malade mf — **patiently** ['peɪʃəntli] adv : patiemment

patio ['pæti,o:, 'pɑt-] n, pl **-tios** : patio m

patriot ['peɪtriət, -,ɑt] n : patriote mf — **patriotic** ['peɪtri'ɑtɪk] adj : patriote

patrol [pə'tro:l] n : patrouille f — **~** vi **-trolled; -trolling** : patrouiller

patron ['peɪtrən] n 1 SPONSOR : mécène m 2 CUSTOMER : client m, cliente f — **patronage** ['peɪtrənɪdʒ, 'pæ-] n 1 SPONSORSHIP : patronage m 2 CLIENTELE : clientèle f — **patronize** ['peɪtrə,naɪz, 'pæ-] vt **-ized; -izing** 1 SUPPORT : patronner, parrainer 2 : traiter avec condescendance

patter ['pætər] n : crépitement m

pattern ['pætərn] n 1 MODEL : modèle m 2 DESIGN : dessin m, motif m 3 NORM : mode m, norme f — **~** vt : modeler

paunch ['pɔntʃ] n : bedaine f

pause ['pɔz] n : pause f — **~** vi **paused; pausing** : faire une pause

pave ['peɪv] vt **paved; paving** : paver — **pavement** ['peɪvmənt] n : chaussée f

pavilion [pə'vɪljən] n : pavillon m

paw ['pɔ] n : patte f — **~** vt : tripoter

pawn¹ ['pɔn] n : gage m

pawn² vt : mettre en gage — **pawnbroker** ['pɔn,bro:kər] n : prêteur m, -teuse f sur gages — **pawnshop** ['pɔn,ʃɑp] n : mont-de-piété m France

pay ['peɪ] v **paid** ['peɪd]; **paying** vt 1 : payer 2 **~ attention to** : prêter attention à 3 **~ back** : rembourser 4 **~ one's respects** : présenter ses respects 5 **~ s.o. a visit** : rendre visite à qqn — vi : payer — **~** n : paie f, salaire m — **payable** ['peɪebəl] adj : payable — **paycheck** ['peɪ,tʃɛk] n : chèque m de paie — **payment** ['peɪmənt] n : paiement m

PC [,pi:'si:] n, pl **PCs** or **PC's** COMPUTER : PC m, micro-ordinateur m

pea ['pi:] n : pois m

peace ['pi:s] n : paix f — **peaceful** ['pi:sfəl] adj : paisible

peach ['pi:tʃ] n : pêche f

peacock ['pi:,kɑk] n : paon m

peak ['pi:k] n 1 SUMMIT : sommet m, pic m 2 APEX : apogée f — **~** adj : maximal — **~** vi : atteindre un sommet

peanut ['pi:,nʌt] *n* : cacahouète *f*
pear ['pær] *n* : poire *f*
pearl ['pərl] *n* : perle *f*
peasant ['pɛzənt] *n* : paysan *m*, -sanne *f*
peat ['pi:t] *n* : tourbe *f*
pebble ['pɛbəl] *n* : caillou *m*
pecan [pɪ'kɑn, -'kæn, 'pi:,kæn] *n* : noix *f* de pécan *France*, noix *f* de pacane *Can*
peck ['pɛk] *vt* : picorer — ~ *n* 1 : coup *m* de bec 2 KISS : bécot *m*
peculiar [pɪ'kju:ljər] *adj* 1 DISTINCTIVE : particulier 2 STRANGE : bizarre — **peculiarity** [pɪ,kju:l'jærəṭi, -,kju:li'ær-] *n*, *pl* **-ties** 1 DISTINCTIVENESS : particularité *f* 2 STRANGENESS : bizarrerie *f*
pedal ['pɛdəl] *n* : pédale *f* — ~ *vt* **-aled** *or* **-alled; -aling** *or* **-alling** : pédaler
pedantic [pɪ'dæntɪk] *adj* : pédant
peddle ['pɛdəl] *vt* **-dled; -dling** : colporter — **peddler** ['pɛdlər] *n* : colporteur *m*, -teuse *f*
pedestal ['pɛdəstəl] *n* : piédestal *m*
pedestrian [pə'dɛstriən] *n* : piéton *m* — ~ *adj* ~ **crossing** : passage *m* pour piétons
pediatrics [,pi:di'ætrɪks] *ns & pl* : pédiatrie *f* — **pediatrician** [,pi:diə'trɪʃən] *n* : pédiatre *mf*
pedigree ['pɛdə,gri:] *n* : pedigree *m* (d'un animal)
peek ['pi:k] *vi* GLANCE : jeter un coup d'œil — ~ *n* : coup *m* d'œil furtif
peel ['pi:l] *vt* : peler (un fruit), éplucher (un oignon, etc.) — *vi* 1 : peler (se dit de la peau) 2 : s'écailler (se dit de la peinture) — ~ *n* : pelure *f* (de pomme), écorce *f* (d'orange), épluchure *f* (de pomme de terre)
peep[1] ['pi:p] *vi* : pépier (se dit d'un oiseau) — ~ *n* : pépiement *m* (d'un oiseau)
peep[2] *vi* PEEK : jeter un coup d'œil — ~ *n* GLANCE : coup *m* d'œil
peer[1] ['pɪr] *n* : pair *m*
peer[2] *vi* : regarder attentivement
peeve ['pi:v] *vt* **peeved; peeving** : irriter — **peevish** ['pi:vɪʃ] *adj* : grincheux
peg ['pɛg] *n* 1 HOOK : patère *f* 2 STAKE : piquet *m*
pelican ['pɛlɪkən] *n* : pélican *m*
pellet ['pɛlət] *n* 1 BALL : boulette *f* 2 SHOT : plomb *m*
pelt[1] ['pɛlt] *n* : peau *f* (d'un animal)
pelt[2] *vt* THROW : bombarder
pelvis ['pɛlvɪs] *n*, *pl* **-vises** [-vɪsəz] *or* **-ves** [-,vi:z] : bassin *m*
pen[1] ['pɛn] *vt* **penned; penning** ENCLOSE : enfermer — ~ *n* : parc *m*, enclos *m*
pen[2] *n* : stylo *m*
penal ['pi:nəl] *adj* : pénal — **penalize** ['pi:nə,aız, 'pɛn-] *vt* **-ized; -izing** : pénaliser — **penalty** ['pɛnəlti] *n*, *pl* **-ties** 1 : peine *f* (en droit) 2 : pénalité *f* (aux sports)
penance ['pɛnənts] *n* : pénitence *f*

pencil ['pɛntsəl] *n* : crayon *m*
pending ['pɛndɪŋ] *adj* 1 UNDECIDED : en instance 2 IMMINENT : imminent — ~ *prep* 1 DURING : pendant 2 AWAITING : en attendant
penetrate ['pɛnə,treɪt] *v* **-trated; -trating** : pénétrer — **penetration** [,pɛnə'treɪʃən] *n* : pénétration *f*
penguin ['pɛŋgwɪn, 'pɛn-] *n* : manchot *m*
penicillin [,pɛnə'sɪlən] *n* : pénicilline *f*
peninsula [pə'nɪntsələ, -'nɪntʃʊlə] *n* : péninsule *f*
penis ['pi:nəs] *n*, *pl* **-nes** [-,ni:z] *or* **-nises** : pénis *m*
penitentiary [,pɛnə'tɛntʃəri] *n*, *pl* **-ries** : pénitencier *m*, prison *f*
pen name *n* : nom *m* de plume
penny ['pɛni] *n*, *pl* **-nies** : centime *m*, cent *m*, sou *m* — **penniless** ['pɛnɪləs] *adj* : sans le sou
pension ['pɛntʃən] *n* : pension *f*, retraite *f*
pensive ['pɛntsɪv] *adj* : pensif
pentagon ['pɛntə,gan] *n* : pentagone *m*
people ['pi:pəl] *ns & pl* 1 **people** *npl* : personnes *fpl*, gens *mfpl* 2 *pl* ~**s** : peuple *m* — ~ *vt* **-pled; -pling** : peupler
pep ['pɛp] *n* : entrain *m*
pepper ['pɛpər] *n* 1 : poivre *m* (condiment) 2 : poivron *m* (légume) — **peppermint** ['pɛpər,mɪnt] *n* : menthe *f* poivrée
per ['pər] *prep* 1 : par 2 ACCORDING TO : selon 3 **ten miles** ~ **hour** : dix miles à l'heure
perceive [pər'si:v] *vt* **-ceived; -ceiving** : percevoir
percent [pər'sɛnt] *adv* : pour cent — **percentage** [pər'sɛntɪdʒ] *n* : pourcentage *m*
perceptible [pər'sɛptəbəl] *adj* : perceptible
perception [pər'sɛpʃən] *n* : perception *f* — **perceptive** [pər'sɛptɪv] *adj* : perspicace
perch[1] ['pərtʃ] *n* : perchoir *m* — ~ *vi* : se percher
perch[2] *n* : perche *f* (poisson)
percolate ['pərkə,leɪt] *v* **-lated; -lating** *vi* SEEP : filtrer — *vt* : passer (du café) — **percolator** ['pərkə,leɪtər] *n* : cafetière *f* à pression
percussion [pər'kʌʃən] *n* : percussion *f*
perennial [pə'rɛniəl] *adj* 1 RECURRING : perpétuel 2 ~ **flowers** : fleurs *fpl* vivaces
perfect ['pərfɪkt] *adj* : parfait — ~ [pər'fɛkt] *vt* : perfectionner — **perfection** [pər'fɛkʃən] *n* : perfection *f* — **perfectionist** [pər'fɛkʃənɪst] *n* : perfectionniste *mf*
perforate ['pərfə,reɪt] *vt* **-rated; -rating** : perforer
perform [pər'fɔrm] *vt* 1 CARRY OUT : exécuter, faire 2 PRESENT : jouer — *vi* 1 ACT : jouer 2 FUNCTION : fonctionner — **performance** [pər'fɔr,mənts] *n* 1 EXECUTION

: exécution *f* **2** : interprétation *f* (d'un acteur), performance *f* (d'un athlète) **3** PRESENTATION : représentation *f* — **performer** [pər'fɔrmər] *n* : interprète *mf*
perfume ['pər,fju:m, pər'-] *n* : parfum *m*
perhaps [pər'hæps] *adv* : peut-être
peril ['perəl] *n* : péril *m* — **perilous** ['perələs] *adj* : périlleux
perimeter [pə'rɪmətər] *n* : périmètre *m*
period ['pɪriəd] *n* **1** : point *m* (signe de ponctuation) **2** TIME : période *f* **3** ERA : époque *f* **4** *or* **menstrual ~** : règles *fpl* — **periodic** [,pɪri'adɪk] *adj* : périodique — **periodical** [,pɪri'adɪkəl] *n* : périodique *m*
peripheral [pə'rɪfərəl] *adj* : périphérique
perish ['perɪʃ] *vi* : périr — **perishable** ['perɪʃəbəl] *adj* : périssable — **perishables** ['perɪʃəbəlz] *npl* : denrées *fpl* périssables
perjury ['pərdʒəri] *n* : faux témoignage *m*
perk ['pərk] *vi* **~ up** : se ragaillardir — **~** *n* : avantage *m* — **perky** ['pərki] *adj* **perkier; perkiest** : guilleret
permanence ['pərmənənts] *n* : permanence *f* — **permanent** ['pərmənənt] *adj* : permanent — **~** *n* : permanente *f*
permeate ['pərmi,eɪt] *vt* **-ated; -ating** : pénétrer
permission [pər'mɪʃən] *n* : permission *f* — **permissible** [pər'mɪsəbəl] *adj* : permis, admissible — **permissive** [pər'mɪsɪv] *adj* : permissif — **permit** [pər'mɪt] *v* **-mitted; -mitting** : permettre — **~** ['pər,mɪt, pər'-] *n* : permis *m*
peroxide [pə'rak,saɪd] *n* : peroxyde *m*
perpendicular [,pərpən'dɪkjələr] *adj* : perpendiculaire
perpetrate ['pərpə,treɪt] *vt* **-trated; -trating** : perpétrer — **perpetrator** ['pərpə,treɪtər] *n* : auteur *m* (d'un délit)
perpetual [pər'pɛtʃuəl] *adj* : perpétuel
perplex [pər'plɛks] *vt* : laisser perplexe — **perplexity** [pər'plɛksəti] *n*, *pl* **-ties** : perplexité *f*
persecute ['pərsɪ,kju:t] *vt* **-cuted; -cuting** : persécuter — **persecution** [,pərsɪ'kju:ʃən] *n* : persécution *f*
persevere [,pərsə'vɪr] *vi* **-vered; -vering** : persévérer — **perseverance** [,pərsə'vɪrənts] *n* : persévérance *f*
persist [pər'sɪst] *vi* : persister — **persistence** [pər'sɪstənts] *n* : persistance *f* — **persistent** [pər'sɪstənt] *adj* : persistant
person ['pərsən] *n* : personne *f* — **personal** ['pərsənəl] *adj* : personnel — **personality** [,pərsən'æləti] *n*, *pl* **-ties** : personnalité *f* — **personally** ['pərsənəli] *adv* : personnellement — **personnel** [,pərsə'nɛl] *n* : personnel *m*
perspective [pər'spɛktɪv] *n* : perspective *f*
perspiration [,pərspə'reɪʃən] *n* : trans-

piration *f* — **perspire** [pər'spaɪr] *vi* **-spired; -spiring** : transpirer
persuade [pər'sweɪd] *vt* **-suaded; -suading** : persuader — **persuasion** [pər'sweɪʒən] *n* **1** : persuasion *f* **2** BELIEF : conviction *f*
pertain [pər'teɪn] *vi* **~ to** : avoir rapport à — **pertinent** ['pərtənənt] *adj* : pertinent
perturb [pər'tərb] *vt* : troubler
pervade [pər'veɪd] *vt* **-vaded; -vading** : se répandre dans — **pervasive** [pər'veɪsɪv, -zɪv] *adj* : envahissant
perverse [pər'vərs] *adj* **1** CORRUPT : pervers **2** STUBBORN : obstiné — **pervert** ['pər,vərt] *n* : pervers *m*, -verse *f*
pessimism ['pɛsə,mɪzəm] *n* : pessimisme *m* — **pessimist** ['pɛsəmɪst] *n* : pessimiste *mf* — **pessimistic** [,pɛsə'mɪstɪk] *adj* : pessimiste
pest ['pɛst] *n* **1** : plante *f* ou animal *m* nuisible **2** NUISANCE : peste *f*
pester ['pɛstər] *vt* **-tered; -tering** : importuner, harceler
pesticide ['pɛstə,saɪd] *n* : pesticide *m*
pet ['pɛt] *n* **1** : animal *m* domestique **2** FAVORITE : chouchou *m fam* — **~** *vt* **petted; petting** : caresser
petal ['pɛtəl] *n* : pétale *m*
petition [pə'tɪʃən] *n* : pétition *f* — **~** *vt* : adresser une pétition à
petrify ['pɛtrə,faɪ] *vt* **-fied; -fying** : pétrifier
petroleum [pə'tro:liəm] *n* : pétrole *m*
petty ['pɛti] *adj* **-tier; -est 1** INSIGNIFICANT : insignifiant **2** MEAN : mesquin
petulant ['pɛtʃələnt] *adj* : irritable
pew ['pju:] *n* : banc *m* d'église
pewter ['pju:tər] *n* : étain *m*
pharmacy ['farməsi] *n*, *pl* **-cies** : pharmacie *f* — **pharmacist** [,farməsɪst] *n* : pharmacien *m*, -cienne *f*
phase ['feɪz] *n* : phase *f* — **~** *vt* **phased; phasing 1 ~ in** : introduire graduellement **2 ~ out** : discontinuer progressivement
phenomenon [fɪ'namə,nan, -nən] *n*, *pl* **-na** [-nə] *or* **-nons** : phénomène *m* — **phenomenal** [fɪ'namənəl] *adj* : phénoménal
philanthropy [fə'lænθrəpi] *n*, *pl* **-pies** : philanthropie *f* — **philanthropist** [fə'lænθrəpɪst] *n* : philanthrope *mf*
philosophy [fə'lasəfi] *n*, *pl* **-phies** : philosophie *f* — **philosopher** [fə'lasəfər] *n* : philosophe *mf*
phlegm ['flɛm] *n* : mucosité *f*
phobia ['fo:biə] *n* : phobie *f*
phone ['fo:n] → **telephone**
phonetic [fə'nɛtɪk] *adj* : phonétique
phony *or* **phoney** ['fo:ni] *adj* **-nier; -est** : faux — **~** *n*, *pl* **-nies** : charlatan *m*
phosphorus ['fasfərəs] *n* : phosphore *m*
photo ['fo:to:] *n*, *pl* **-tos** : photo *f* — **photocopier** ['fo:to,kapiər] *n* : photocopieur *m*,

photocopieuse f — **photocopy** ['fo:ţo,kapi] n, pl **-pies** : photocopie f — ~ vt **-copied; -copying** : photocopier — **photograph** ['fo:ţa,græf] n : photographie f, photo f — ~ vt : photographier — **photographer** [fə'tagrəfər] n : photographe mf — **photographic** [,fo:tə'græfɪk] adj : photographique — **photography** [fə'tagrəfi] n : photographie f

phrase ['freɪz] n : expression f — ~ vt **phrased; phrasing** : formuler, exprimer

physical ['fɪzɪkəl] adj : physique — ~ n : examen m médical

physician [fə'zɪʃən] n : médecin mf

physics ['fɪzɪks] ns & pl : physique f — **physicist** ['fɪzəsɪst] n : physicien m, -cienne f

physiology [,fɪzi'alədʒi] n : physiologie f

physique [fə'zi:k] n : physique m

piano [pi'æno:] n, pl **-anos** : piano m — **pianist** [pi'ænɪst, 'pi:ənɪst] n : pianiste mf

pick ['pɪk] vt 1 CHOOSE : choisir 2 GATHER : cueillir 3 REMOVE : enlever 4 ~ **a fight** : chercher la bagarre — vi 1 CHOOSE : choisir 2 ~ **on** : harceler — ~ n 1 CHOICE : choix m 2 BEST : meilleur m 3 or **pickax** ['pɪk,æks] : pic m

picket ['pɪkət] n 1 STAKE : piquet m 2 or ~ **line** : piquet m de grève — ~ vi : faire un piquet de grève

pickle ['pɪkəl] n 1 : cornichon m 2 JAM : pétrin m fam — ~ vt **-led; -ling** : conserver dans la saumure

pickpocket ['pɪk,pakət] n : voleur m, -leuse f à la tire

pickup ['pɪk,əp] n or ~ **truck** : camionnette f — **pick up** vt 1 LIFT : ramasser 2 LEARN : apprendre 3 RESUME : reprendre 4 TIDY : mettre en ordre 5 COLLECT : prendre — vi IMPROVE : s'améliorer

picnic ['pɪk,nɪk] n : pique-nique m — ~ vi **-nicked; -nicking** : pique-niquer

picture ['pɪktʃər] n 1 PAINTING : tableau m 2 DRAWING : dessin m 3 PHOTO : photo f, photographie f 4 IMAGE : image f 5 MOVIE : film m — ~ vt **-tured; -turing** 1 DEPICT : dépeindre 2 IMAGINE : s'imaginer — **picturesque** [,pɪktʃə'resk] adj : pittoresque

pie ['paɪ] n 1 : tarte f (dessert) 2 : pâté m, tourte f

piece ['pi:s] n 1 : pièce f 2 FRAGMENT : morceau m — ~ vt **pieced; piecing** or ~ **together** : rassembler — **piecemeal** ['pi:s,mi:l] adv : graduellement — ~ adj : fragmentaire

pier ['pɪr] n : jetée f

pierce ['pɪrs] vt **pierced; piercing** : percer — **piercing** ['pɪrsɪŋ] adj : perçant

piety ['paɪəţi] n, pl **-eties** : piété f

pig ['pɪg] n : porc m, cochon m

pigeon ['pɪdʒən] n : pigeon m — **pigeonhole** ['pɪdʒən,ho:l] n : casier m

piggyback ['pɪgi,bæk] adv & adj : sur le dos

pigment ['pɪgmənt] n : pigment m

pigpen ['pɪg,pen] n : porcherie f

pigtail ['pɪg,teɪl] n : natte f

pile[1] ['paɪəl] n HEAP : pile f, tas m — ~ v **piled; piling** vt 1 STACK : empiler 2 LOAD : remplir — vi 1 or ~ **up** : s'accumuler 2 CROWD : s'empiler

pile[2] n NAP : poil m (d'un tapis, etc.)

pilfer ['pɪlfər] vt : chaparder fam

pilgrim ['pɪlgrəm] n : pèlerin m, -rine f — **pilgrimage** ['pɪlgrəmɪdʒ] n : pèlerinage m

pill ['pɪl] n : pilule f, cachet m

pillage ['pɪlɪdʒ] n : pillage m — ~ vt **-laged; -laging** : piller

pillar ['pɪlər] n : pilier m

pillow ['pɪ,lo:] n : oreiller m — **pillowcase** ['pɪlo,keɪs] n : taie f d'oreiller

pilot ['paɪlət] n : pilote m — ~ vt : piloter — **pilot light** n : veilleuse f

pimple ['pɪmpəl] n : bouton m

pin ['pɪn] n 1 : épingle f 2 BROOCH : broche f 3 or **bowling** ~ : quille f — ~ vt **pinned; pinning** 1 FASTEN : épingler 2 or ~ **down** : fixer

pincers ['pɪntsərz] npl : tenailles fpl

pinch ['pɪntʃ] vt 1 : pincer 2 STEAL : piquer — vi : serrer — ~ n 1 SQUEEZE : pincement m 2 LITTLE : pincée f 3 in a ~ : à la rigueur

pine[1] ['paɪn] n : pin m

pine[2] vi **pined; pining** 1 LANGUISH : languir 2 ~ **for** : désirer ardemment

pineapple ['paɪn,æpəl] n : ananas m

pink ['pɪŋk] adj : rose — ~ n : rose m

pinnacle ['pɪnɪkəl] n : pinacle m

pinpoint ['pɪn,pɔɪnt] vt : préciser

pint ['paɪnt] n : pinte f

pioneer [,paɪə'nɪr] n : pionnier m, -nière f

pious ['paɪəs] adj : pieux

pipe ['paɪp] n 1 : tuyau m 2 : pipe f (pour fumer du tabac) — **pipeline** ['paɪp,laɪn] n : pipeline m

piquant ['pi:kənt, 'pɪkwənt] adj : piquant

pirate ['paɪrət] n : pirate m

pistachio [pə'stæʃi,o:, -'sta-] n, pl **-chios** : pistache f

pistol ['pɪstəl] n : pistolet m

piston ['pɪstən] n : piston m

pit ['pɪt] n 1 HOLE : trou m, fosse f 2 MINE : mine f 3 : creux m (de l'estomac) 4 : noyau m (d'un fruit) — ~ vt **pitted; pitting** 1 MARK : marquer 2 : dénoyauter (un fruit) 3 ~ **against** : opposer à

pitch ['pɪtʃ] vt 1 : dresser (une tente, etc.) 2 THROW : lancer — vi LURCH : tanguer (se dit d'un navire, etc.) — ~ n 1 DEGREE, LEVEL : degré m, niveau m 2 TONE : ton m 3

THROW : lancement *m* **4** *or* **sales ~** : boniment *m* de vente — **pitcher** ['pɪtʃər] *n* **1** JUG : cruche *f* **2** : artilleur *m* Can (au baseball) — **pitchfork** ['pɪtʃ,fɔrk] *n* : fourche *f*

pitfall ['pɪt,fɔl] *n* : piège *m*

pith ['pɪθ] *n* : moelle *f* — **pithy** ['pɪθi] *adj* **pithier; pithiest** : concis

pity ['pɪti] *n, pl* **pities 1** : pitié *f* **2 what a ~!** : quel dommage! — **~** *vt* **pitied; pitying** : avoir pitié de — **pitiful** ['pɪtɪfəl] *adj* : pitoyable — **pitiless** ['pɪtɪləs] *adj* : impitoyable

pivot ['pɪvət] *n* : pivot *m* — **~** *vi* : pivoter

pizza ['pi:tsə] *n* : pizza *f*

placard ['plækərd, -,kɑrd] *n* POSTER : affiche *f*

placate ['pleɪ,keɪt, 'plæ-] *vt* **-cated; -cating** : calmer

place ['pleɪs] *n* **1** : place *f* **2** LOCATION : endroit *m*, lieu *m* **3 in the first ~** : tout d'abord **4 take ~** : avoir lieu — **~** *vt* **placed; placing 1** PUT, SET : placer, mettre **2** RECOGNIZE : remettre **3 ~ an order** : passer une commande — **placement** ['pleɪsmənt] *n* : placement *m*

placid ['plæsəd] *adj* : placide

plagiarism ['pleɪʤə,rɪzəm] *n* : plagiat *m* — **plagiarize** ['pleɪʤə,raɪz] *vt* **-rized; -rizing** : plagier

plague ['pleɪg] *n* **1** : peste *f* **2** CALAMITY : fléau *m*

plaid ['plæd] *n* : tissu *m* écossais — **~** *adj* : écossais

plain ['pleɪn] *adj* **1** SIMPLE : simple **2** CLEAR : clair, évident **3** FRANK : franc **4** HOMELY : ordinaire — **~** *n* : plaine *f* — **plainly** ['pleɪnli] *adv* **1** SIMPLY : simplement **2** CLEARLY : clairement **3** FRANKLY : franchement

plaintiff ['pleɪntɪf] *n* : demandeur *m*, -deresse *f*; plaignant *m*, -gnante *f*

plan ['plæn] *n* **1** DIAGRAM : plan *m* **2** IDEA : projet *m* — **~** *v* **planned; planning** *vt* **1** INTEND : projeter **2** PREPARE : organiser — *vi* : faire des projets

plane¹ ['pleɪn] *n* **1** SURFACE : plan *m* **2** AIRPLANE : avion *m*

plane² *n* *or* **carpenter's ~** : rabot *m*

planet ['plænət] *n* : planète *f*

plank ['plæŋk] *n* : planche *f*

planning ['plænɪŋ] *n* : organisation *f*, planification *f*

plant ['plænt] *vt* : planter — **~** *n* **1** : plante *f* **2** FACTORY : usine *f*

plaque ['plæk] *n* : plaque *f*

plaster ['plæstər] *n* : plâtre *m* — **~** *vt* **1** : plâtrer **2** COVER : couvrir

plastic ['plæstɪk] *adj* **1** : de plastique, en plastique **2 ~ surgery** : chirurgie *f* esthétique — **~** *n* : plastique *m*

plate ['pleɪt] *n* **1** SHEET : plaque *f* **2** DISH : assiette *f* **3** ILLUSTRATION : planche *f* — **~** *vt* **plated; plating** : plaquer (avec un métal)

plateau [plæ'to:] *n, pl* **-teaus** *or* **-teaux** [-'to:z] : plateau *m*

platform ['plæt,fɔrm] *n* **1** STAGE : tribune *f*, estrade *f* **2** : quai *m* (d'une gare) **3** *or* **political ~** : plate-forme *f* (électorale)

platinum ['plætənəm] *n* : platine *m*

platoon [plə'tu:n] *n* : section *f* (dans l'armée)

platter ['plætər] *n* : plat *m*

plausible ['plɔzəbəl] *adj* : plausible

play ['pleɪ] *n* **1** : jeu *m* **2** DRAMA : pièce *f* de théâtre — **~** *vi* : jouer — *vt* **1** : jouer à (un jeu, un sport) **2** : jouer de (un instrument de musique) **3** PERFORM : jouer **4 ~ down** : minimiser **5 ~ up** EMPHASIZE : souligner — **player** ['pleɪər] *n* : joueur *m*, joueuse *f* — **playful** ['pleɪfəl] *adj* : enjoué — **playground** ['pleɪ,graʊnd] *n* : cour *f* de récréation — **playing card** *n* : carte *f* à jouer — **playmate** ['pleɪ,meɪt] *n* : camarade *mf* de jeu — **play–off** ['pleɪ,ɔf] *n* : match *m* crucial — **playpen** ['pleɪ,pɛn] *n* : parc *m* (pour bébés) — **plaything** ['pleɪ,θɪŋ] *n* : jouet *m* — **playwright** ['pleɪ,raɪt] *n* : dramaturge *mf*, auteur *m* dramatique

plea ['pli:] *n* **1** : défense *f* (en droit) **2** REQUEST : appel *m*, requête *f* — **plead** ['pli:d] *v* **pleaded** *or* **pled** ['plɛd]; **pleading** : plaider

pleasant ['plɛzənt] *adj* : agréable — **please** ['pli:z] *v* **pleased; pleasing** *vt* **1** GRATIFY : plaire à, faire plaisir à **2** SATISFY : contenter — *vi* : plaire, faire plaisir — **~** *adv* : s'il vous plaît — **pleasing** ['pli:zɪŋ] *adj* : agréable — **pleasure** ['plɛʒər] *n* : plaisir *m*

pleat ['pli:t] *n* : pli *m*

pledge ['plɛʤ] *n* **1** SECURITY : gage *m* **2** PROMISE : promesse *f* — **~** *vt* **pledged; pledging 1** PAWN : mettre en gage **2** PROMISE : promettre

plenty ['plɛnti] *n* **1** ABUNDANCE : abondance *f* **2 ~ of** : beaucoup de — **plentiful** ['plɛntɪfəl] *adj* : abondant

pliable ['plaɪəbəl] *adj* : flexible, malléable

pliers ['plaɪərz] *npl* : pinces *fpl*

plight ['plaɪt] *n* : situation *f* difficile

plod ['plɑd] *vi* **plodded; plodding 1** : marcher lourdement **2** LABOR : peiner

plot ['plɑt] *n* **1** LOT : lopin *m*, parcelle *f* (de terre) **2** STORY : intrigue *f* **3** CONSPIRACY : complot *m* — **~** *v* **plotted; plotting** *vt* : faire un plan de — *vi* CONSPIRE : comploter

plow *or* **plough** ['plaʊ] *n* **1** : charrue *f* **2** → **snowplow** — **~** *vt* **1** : labourer (la terre) **2** : déneiger

ploy ['plɔɪ] *n* : stratagème *m*

pluck ['plʌk] *vt* **1** : cueillir (une fleur) **2** : plumer (un oiseau) **3** : pincer (une corde) **4** ~ **one's eyebrows** : s'épiler les sourcils

plug ['plʌg] *n* **1** STOPPER : bouchon *m*, tampon *m* **2** : prise *f* (électrique) — ~ *vt* **plugged; plugging 1** BLOCK : boucher **2** ADVERTISE : faire de la publicité pour **3** ~ **in** : brancher

plum ['plʌm] *n* : prune *f*, pruneau *m Can*

plumb ['plʌm] *adj* : vertical, droit — **plumber** ['plʌmər] *n* : plombier *m* — **plumbing** ['plʌmɪŋ] *n* **1** : plomberie *f* **2** PIPES : tuyauterie *f*

plummet ['plʌmət] *vi* : tomber

plump ['plʌmp] *adj* : grassouillet, dodu

plunder ['plʌndər] *vt* : piller — ~ *n* : pillage *m*

plunge ['plʌndʒ] *v* **plunged; plunging** *vt* : plonger — *vi* **1** DIVE : plonger **2** DROP : chuter — ~ *n* **1** DIVE : plongeon *m* **2** DROP : chute *f* — **plunger** ['plʌndʒər] *n* : ventouse *f*

plural ['plʊrəl] *adj* : pluriel — ~ *n* : pluriel *m*

plus ['plʌs] *adj* : positif — ~ *n* **1** *or* ~ **sign** : plus *m* **2** ADVANTAGE : plus *m*, avantage *m* — ~ *prep* : plus — ~ *conj* AND : plus

plush ['plʌʃ] *n* : peluche *f* — ~ *adj* : somptueux

Pluto ['pluːˌtoː] *n* : Pluton *f*

plutonium [pluːˈtoːniəm] *n* : plutonium *m*

ply ['plaɪ] *vt* **plied; plying 1** USE : manier (un outil) **2** PRACTICE : exercer

plywood ['plaɪˌwʊd] *n* : contre-plaqué *m*

pneumatic [nʊˈmætɪk, njʊ-] *adj* : pneumatique

pneumonia [nʊˈmoːnjə, njʊ-] *n* : pneumonie *f*

poach[1] ['poːtʃ] *vt* : pocher (des œufs)

poach[2] *vt or* ~ **game** : braconner le gibier — **poacher** ['poːtʃər] *n* : braconnier *m*, -nière *f*

pocket ['pakət] *n* : poche *f* — ~ *vt* : empocher — **pocketbook** ['pakətˌbʊk] *n* PURSE : sac *m* à main, sacoche *f Can* — **pocketknife** ['pakətˌnaɪf] *n, pl* **-knives** : canif *m*

pod ['pad] *n* : cosse *f*

poem ['poːəm] *n* : poème *m* — **poet** ['poːət] *n* : poète *mf* — **poetic** [poˈɛtɪk] *or* **poetical** [-tɪkəl] *adj* : poétique — **poetry** ['poːətri] *n* : poésie *f*

poignant ['pɔɪnjənt] *adj* : poignant

point ['pɔɪnt] *n* **1** : point *m* **2** PURPOSE : utilité *f*, but *m* **3** TIP : pointe *f* **4** FEATURE : qualité *f* **5 at one** ~ : à un moment donné — ~ *vt* **1** AIM : braquer **2** *or* ~ **out** INDICATE : indiquer — **point-blank** ['pɔɪntˈblæŋk] *adv* : à bout portant — **pointer**

['pɔɪntər] *n* **1** ROD : baguette *f* **2** TIP : conseil *m* — **pointless** ['pɔɪntləs] *adj* : inutile — **point of view** *n* : point *m* de vue

poise ['pɔɪz] *n* **1** EQUILIBRIUM : équilibre *m* **2** COMPOSURE : assurance *f*

poison ['pɔɪzən] *n* : poison *m* — ~ *vt* : empoisonner — **poisonous** ['pɔɪzənəs] *adj* : vénéneux (se dit d'une plante), vénimeux (se dit d'un animal), toxique (se dit d'une substance)

poke ['poːk] *v* **poked; poking** *vt* **1** JAB : pousser **2** THRUST : fourrer *fam* — ~ *n* JAB : coup *m*

poker[1] ['poːkər] *n* : tisonnier *m* (pour le feu)

poker[2] *n* : poker *m* (jeu de cartes)

polar ['poːlər] *adj* : polaire — **polar bear** *n* : ours *m* polaire, ours *m* blanc — **polarize** ['poːləˌraɪz] *vt* **-ized; -izing** : polariser

pole[1] ['poːl] *n* ROD : perche *f*

pole[2] *n* : pôle *m* (en géographie)

police [pəˈliːs] *vt* **-liced; -licing** : surveiller — ~ *ns & pl* **the** ~ : la police — **policeman** [pəˈliːsmən] *n, pl* **-men** [-mən, -ˌmɛn] : policier *m* — **police officer** *n* : agent *m* de police — **policewoman** [pəˈliːsˌwʊmən] *n, pl* **-women** [-ˌwɪmən] : femme *f* policier

policy ['paləsi] *n, pl* **-cies 1** : politique *f* **2** *or* **insurance** ~ : police *f* d'assurance

polio ['poːliˌoː] *or* **poliomyelitis** [ˌpoːliˌoːˌmaɪəˈlaɪtəs] *n* : polio *f*, poliomyélite *f*

polish ['palɪʃ] *vt* : polir (se dit des chaussures, etc) — ~ *n* **1** LUSTER : poli *m*, éclat *m* **2** WAX : cire *f* (pour les meubles, etc.), cirage *m* (pour les chaussures) **3** **nail** ~ : vernis *m* à ongles

polite [pəˈlaɪt] *adj* **-liter; -est** : poli — **politeness** [pəˈlaɪtnəs] *n* : politesse *f*

political [pəˈlɪtɪkəl] *adj* : politique — **politician** [ˌpaləˈtɪʃən] *n* : politicien *m*, -cienne *f* — **politics** ['paləˌtɪks] *ns & pl* : politique *f*

polka ['poːlkə, 'poːkə] *n* : polka *f* — **polka dot** *n* : pois *m*, picot *m Can*

poll ['poːl] *n* **1** SURVEY : sondage *m* **2** ~**s** *npl* : urnes *fpl* — ~ *vt* **1** : obtenir (des voix) **2** CANVASS : sonder

pollen ['palən] *n* : pollen *m*

pollute [pəˈluːt] *vt* **-luted; -luting** : polluer — **pollution** [pəˈluːʃən] *n* : pollution *f*

polyester ['paliˌɛstər, ˌpali'-] *n* : polyester *m*

polymer ['paləmər] *n* : polymère *m*

pomegranate ['paməˌgrænət, 'pamˌgræ-] *n* : grenade *f* (fruit)

pomp ['pamp] *n* : pompe *f* — **pompous** ['pampəs] *adj* : pompeux

pond ['pand] *n* : étang *m*, mare *f*

ponder ['pandər] *vt* : considérer — *vi* ~ **over** : réfléchir à, méditer sur

pontoon [pan'tuːn] *n* : ponton *m*

pony ['poːni] *n, pl* **-nies** : poney *m* — **ponytail** ['poːniˌteɪl] *n* : queue *f* de cheval

poodle ['puːdəl] *n* : caniche *m*

pool ['puːl] *n* **1** PUDDLE : flaque *f* (d'eau), mare *f* (de sang) **2** RESERVE : fonds *m* commun **3** BILLIARDS : billard *m* américain **4** *or* **swimming ~** : piscine *f* — *vt* : mettre en commun

poor ['pʊr, 'pɔr] *adj* **1** : pauvre **2** INFERIOR : mauvais — **poorly** ['pʊrli, 'pɔr-] *adv* BADLY : mal

pop[1] ['pap] *v* **popped; popping** *vt* **1** BURST : faire éclater **2** PUT : mettre — *vi* **1** BURST : éclater, exploser **2 ~ in** : faire une petite visite **3** *or* **~ out** : sortir **4 ~ up** APPEAR : surgir — *n* **1** : bruit *m* sec **2** SODA : boisson *f* gazeuse — *adj* : pop

pop[2] *n or* **~ music** : musique *f* pop

popcorn ['pap,kɔrn] *n* : pop-corn *m*

pope ['poːp] *n* : pape *m*

poplar ['paplər] *n* : peuplier *m*

poppy ['papi] *n, pl* **-pies** : coquelicot *m*

popular ['papjələr] *adj* : populaire — **popularity** [,papjə'lærəti] *n* : popularité *f* — **popularize** ['papjələ,raɪz] *vt* **-ized; -izing** : populariser

populate ['papjə,leɪt] *vt* **-lated; -lating** : peupler — **population** [,papjə'leɪʃən] *n* : population *f*

porcelain ['pɔrsələn] *n* : porcelaine *f*

porch ['pɔrtʃ] *n* : porche *m*

porcupine ['pɔrkjə,paɪn] *n* : porc-épic *m*

pore[1] ['pɔr] *vi* **pored; poring ~ over** : étudier de près

pore[2] *n* : pore *m*

pork ['pɔrk] *n* : porc *m*

pornography [pɔr'nagrəfi] *n* : pornographie *f* — **pornographic** [,pɔrnə'græfɪk] *adj* : pornographique

porous ['pɔrəs] *adj* : poreux

porpoise ['pɔrpəs] *n* : marsouin *m*

porridge ['pɔrɪdʒ] *n* : porridge *m France*, gruau *m Can*

port[1] ['pɔrt] *n* HARBOR : port *m*

port[2] *n or* **~ side** : bâbord *m*

port[3] *n or* **~ wine** : porto *m*

portable ['pɔrtəbəl] *adj* : portatif

porter ['pɔrtər] *n* : porteur *m*, -teuse *f*

portfolio [pɔrt'foːli,o] *n, pl* **-lios** : portefeuille *m*

porthole ['pɔrt,hoːl] *n* : hublot *m*

portion ['pɔrʃən] *n* : portion *f*

portrait ['pɔrtrət, -,treɪt] *n* : portrait *m*

portray [pɔr'treɪ] *vt* DEPICT : représenter

Portuguese [,pɔrtʃə'giːz, -'giːs] *adj* : portugais — *n* : portugais *m* (langue)

pose ['poːz] *v* **posed; posing** *vt* : poser — *vi* **1** : poser **2 ~ as** : se faire passer pour — *n* : pose *f*

posh ['paʃ] *adj* : chic

position [pə'zɪʃən] *n* **1** : position *f* **2** JOB : poste *m* — **~** *vt* **1** PLACE : placer **2** ORIENT : positionner

positive ['pazətɪv] *adj* **1** : positif **2** SURE : sûr, certain

possess [pə'zɛs] *vt* : posséder — **possession** [pə'zɛʃən] *n* **1** : possession *f* **2 ~s** *npl* BELONGINGS : biens *mpl* — **possessive** [pə'zɛsɪv] *adj* : possessif

possible ['pasəbəl] *adj* : possible — **possibility** [,pasə'bɪləti] *n, pl* **-ties** : possibilité *f* — **possibly** ['pasəbli] *adv* : peut-être, possiblement *Can*

post[1] ['poːst] *n* POLE : poteau *m*

post[2] *n* POSITION : poste *m*

post[3] *n* MAIL : poste *f*, courrier *m* — *vt* **1** MAIL : poster **2 keep ~ed** : tenir au courant — **postage** ['poːstɪdʒ] *n* : affranchissement *m* — **postal** ['poːstəl] *adj* : postal — **postcard** ['poːst,kard] *n* : carte *f* postale

poster ['poːstər] *n* : poster *m*, affiche *f*

posterity [pa'stɛrəti] *n* : postérité *f*

posthumous ['pastʃəməs] *adj* : posthume

postman ['poːstmən, -,mæn] *n, pl* **-men** [-mən, -,mɛn] → **mailman** — **post office** *n* : bureau *m* de poste

postpone [,poːst'poːn] *vt* **-poned; -poning** : remettre, reporter — **postponement** [,poːst'poːnmənt] *n* : renvoi *m*, remise *f*

postscript ['poːst,skrɪpt] *n* : post-scriptum *m*

posture ['pastʃər] *n* : posture *f*

postwar [,poːst'wɔr] *adj* : d'après-guerre

pot ['pat] *n* **1** SAUCEPAN : marmite *f*, casserole *f* **2** CONTAINER : pot *m*

potassium [pə'tæsiəm] *n* : potassium *m*

potato [pə'teɪto] *n, pl* **-toes** : pomme *f* de terre, patate *f fam*

potent ['poːtənt] *adj* **1** POWERFUL : puissant **2** EFFECTIVE : efficace

potential [pə'tɛntʃəl] *adj* : potentiel — **~** *n* : potentiel *m*

pothole ['pat,hoːl] *n* : nid-de-poule *m*

potion ['poːʃən] *n* : potion *f*

pottery ['patəri] *n, pl* **-teries** : poterie *f*

pouch ['pautʃ] *n* **1** BAG : petit sac *m* **2** : poche *f* (des marsupiaux)

poultry ['poːltri] *n* : volaille *f*

pounce ['paunts] *vi* **pounced; pouncing** : bondir

pound[1] ['paund] *n* **1** : livre *f* (unité de mesure) **2** : livre *f* sterling

pound[2] *n* SHELTER : fourrière *f*

pound[3] *vt* **1** CRUSH : piler **2** HAMMER : marteler **3** BEAT : battre — *vi* BEAT : battre

pour ['pɔr] *vt* : verser — *vi* **1** FLOW : couler **2** RAIN : pleuvoir à verse

pout ['paut] *vi* : faire la moue — *n* : moue *f*

poverty ['pavərti] *n* : pauvreté *f*

powder ['paʊdər] vt **1** : poudrer **2** CRUSH : pulvériser — **~** n : poudre f — **powdery** ['paʊdəri] adj : poudreux

power ['paʊər] n **1** AUTHORITY : pouvoir m **2** ABILITY : capacité f **3** STRENGTH : puissance f **4** CURRENT : courant m — **~** vt : faire fonctionner, faire marcher — **powerful** ['paʊərfəl] adj : puissant — **powerless** ['paʊərləs] adj : impuissant

practical ['præktɪkəl] adj : pratique — **practically** ['præktɪkli] adv : pratiquement

practice or **practise** ['præktəs] v **-ticed** or **-tised**; **-ticing** or **-tising** vt **1** : pratiquer **2** : exercer (une profession) — vi **1** : s'exercer **2** TRAIN : s'entraîner — **~** n **1** : pratique f **2** : exercice m (d'une profession) **3** TRAINING : entraînement m — **practitioner** [præk'tɪʃənər] n : praticien m, -cienne f

pragmatic [præg'mætɪk] adj : pragmatique

prairie ['preɪri] n : prairie f

praise ['preɪz] vt **praised; praising** : louer — **~** n : louange f — **praiseworthy** ['preɪz,wərði] adj : louable, digne d'éloges

prance ['prænts] vt **pranced; prancing** : caracoler (se dit d'un cheval), cabrioler (se dit d'une personne)

prank ['præŋk] n : farce f

prawn ['prɔn] n : crevette f (rose)

pray ['preɪ] vi : prier — **prayer** ['prɛr] n : prière f

preach ['pri:tʃ] v : prêcher — **preacher** ['pri:tʃər] n : pasteur m

precarious [prɪ'kæriəs] adj : précaire

precaution [prɪ'kɔʃən] n : précaution f

precede [prɪ'si:d] vt **-ceded; -ceding** : précéder — **precedence** ['prɛsədənts, prɪ'si:dənts] n **1** : préséance f **2** PRIORITY : priorité f — **precedent** ['prɛsədənt] n : précédent m

precinct ['pri:,sɪŋkt] n **1** DISTRICT : arrondissement m (en France), circonscription f (au Canada) **2** **~s** npl : environs mpl

precious ['prɛʃəs] adj : précieux

precipice ['prɛsəpəs] n : précipice m

precipitate [prɪ'sɪpə,teɪt] v **-tated; -tating** : précipiter — **precipitation** [prɪ,sɪpə'teɪʃən] n **1** HASTE : précipitation f, hâte f **2** : précipitations fpl (en météorologie)

precise [prɪ'saɪs] adj : précis — **precisely** [prɪ'saɪsli] adv : précisément — **precision** [prɪ'sɪʒən] n : précision f

preclude [prɪ'klu:d] vt **-cluded; -cluding** : empêcher

precocious [prɪ'koʃəs] adj : précoce

preconceived [,pri:kən'si:vd] adj : préconçu

predator ['prɛdətər] n : prédateur m

predecessor ['prɛdə,sɛsər, 'pri:-] n : prédécesseur m

predicament [prɪ'dɪkəmənt] n : situation f difficile

predict [prɪ'dɪkt] vt : prédire — **predictable** [prɪ'dɪktəbəl] adj : prévisible — **prediction** [prɪ'dɪkʃən] n : prédiction f

predispose [,pri:dɪ'spo:z] vt : prédisposer

predominant [prɪ'damənənt] adj : prédominant

preen ['pri:n] vt : lisser (ses plumes)

prefabricated [,pri:'fæbrə,keɪtəd] adj : préfabriqué

preface ['prɛfəs] n : préface f

prefer [prɪ'fər] vt **-ferred; -ferring** : préférer — **preferable** ['prɛfərəbəl] adj : préférable — **preference** ['prɛfrənts, 'prɛfər-] n : préférence f — **preferential** [,prɛfə'rɛntʃəl] adj : pré-férentiel

prefix ['pri:,fɪks] n : préfixe m

pregnancy ['prɛgnənsi] n, pl **-cies** : grossesse f — **pregnant** ['prɛgnənt] adj : enceinte

prehistoric [,pri:hɪs'tɔrɪk] or **prehistorical** [-ɪkəl] adj : préhistorique

prejudice ['prɛdʒədəs] n **1** HARM : préjudice m **2** BIAS : préjugés mpl — **~** vt **-diced; -dicing 1** : porter préjudice à (en droit) **2** be **~d** : avoir des préjugés

preliminary [prɪ'lɪmə,nɛri] adj : préliminaire

prelude ['prɛ,lu:d, 'prɛl,ju:d, 'preɪ,lu:d, 'pri:-] n : prélude m

premature [,pri:mə'tʊr, -'tjʊr, -'tʃʊr] adj : prématuré

premeditated [prɪ'mɛdə,teɪtəd] adj : prémédité

premier [prɪ'mɪr, -'mjɪr; 'pri:miər] n : premier — **~** n → **prime minister**

premiere [prɪ'mjɛr, -'mɪr] n : première f (d'un spectacle)

premise ['prɛmɪs] n **1** : prémisse f (d'un raisonnement) **2 ~s** npl : lieux mpl

premium ['pri:miəm] n : prime f

preoccupied [pri'akjə,paɪd] adj : préoccupé

prepare [prɪ'pær] v **-pared; -paring** vt : préparer — vi : se préparer — **preparation** [,prɛpə'reɪʃən] n **1** PREPARING : préparation f **2 ~s** npl ARRANGEMENTS : préparatifs mpl — **preparatory** [prɪ'pærə,tori] adj : préparatoire

prepay [,pri:'peɪ] vt **-paid; -paying** : payer d'avance

preposition [,prɛpə'zɪʃən] n : préposition f

preposterous [prɪ'pastərəs] adj : absurde, insensé

prerequisite [pri'rɛkwəzət] n : préalable m

prerogative [prɪ'ragətɪv] n : prérogative f

prescribe [prɪ'skraɪb] vt **-scribed; -scribing** : prescrire — **prescription** [prɪ'skrɪpʃən] n : prescription f

presence ['prɛzənts] n : présence f

present[1] ['prɛzənt] adj **1** CURRENT : actuel

2 ATTENDING : présent — ~ *n or* ~ **time** : présent *m*

present² ['prɛzənt] *n* GIFT : cadeau *m* — ~ [prɪ'zɛnt] *vt* : présenter — **presentation** [ˌpriˌzɛn'teɪʃən, ˌprɛzən-] *n* : présentation *f*

presently ['prɛzəntli] *adv* **1** SOON : bientôt **2** NOW : actuellement, en ce moment

preserve [prɪ'zərv] *vt* **-served; -serving 1** PROTECT : préserver **2** MAINTAIN : conserver — ~ *n* **1** *or* **game** ~ : réserve *f* **2** ~**s** *npl* : confitures *fpl* — **preservation** [ˌprɛzər'veɪʃən] *n* : préservation *f*, maintien *m* — **preservative** [prɪ'zərvətɪv] *n* : agent *m* de conservation

president ['prɛzədənt] *n* : président *m* — **presidency** ['prɛzədəntsi] *n, pl* **-cies** : présidence *f* — **presidential** [ˌprɛzə-'dɛntʃəl] *adj* : présidentiel

press ['prɛs] *n* : presse *f* — ~ *vt* **1** PUSH : presser, appuyer sur **2** IRON : repasser — *vi* **1** PUSH : appuyer **2** CROWD : se presser — **pressing** ['prɛsɪŋ] *adj* : urgent — **pressure** ['prɛʃər] *n* : pression *f* — ~ *vt* **-sured; -suring** : pousser, faire pression sur

prestige [prɛ'stiʒ, -'stiːdʒ] *n* : prestige *m* — **prestigious** [prɛ'stɪdʒəs, -'sti-, prə-] *adj* : prestigieux

presume [prɪ'zuːm] *vt* **-sumed; -suming** : présumer — **presumably** [prɪ'zuːməbli] *adv* : vraisemblablement — **presumption** [prɪ'zʌmpʃən] *n* : présomption *f* — **presumptuous** [prɪ'zʌmptʃuəs] *adj* : présomptueux

pretend [prɪ'tɛnd] *vt* **1** PROFESS : prétendre **2** FEIGN : faire semblant de — *vi* : faire semblant — **pretense** *or* **pretence** ['priːˌtɛns, prɪ'tɛnts] *n* **1** CLAIM : prétention *f* **2** PRETEXT : prétexte *m* — **pretentious** [prɪ-'tɛntʃəs] *adj* : prétentieux

pretext ['priːˌtɛkst] *n* : prétexte *m*

pretty ['prɪti] *adj* **-tier; -est** : joli, beau — ~ *adv* FAIRLY : assez

pretzel ['prɛtsəl] *n* : bretzel *m*

prevail [prɪ'veɪl] *vi* : prévaloir — **prevalent** ['prɛvələnt] *adj* : répandu

prevent [prɪ'vɛnt] *vt* : empêcher — **prevention** [prɪ'vɛntʃən] *n* : prévention *f* — **preventive** [prɪ'vɛntɪv] *adj* : préventif

preview ['priːˌvjuː] *n* : avant-première *f*

previous ['priːviəs] *adj* : antérieur, précédent — **previously** ['priːviəsli] *adv* : antérieurement, auparavant

prey ['preɪ] *ns & pl* : proie *f* — **prey on** *vt* : faire sa proie de

price ['praɪs] *n* : prix *m* — ~ *vt* **priced; pricing** : fixer un prix sur — **priceless** ['praɪsləs] *adj* : inestimable

prick ['prɪk] *n* : piqûre *f* — ~ *vt* **1** : piquer **2** ~ **up one's ears** : dresser l'oreille — **prickly** ['prɪkəli] *adj* **-lier; -est** : épineux

pride ['praɪd] *n* : fierté *f*, orgueil *m* — ~ *vt* **prided; priding** ~ **oneself on** : être fier de

priest ['priːst] *n* : prêtre *m* — **priesthood** ['priːstˌhʊd] *n* : prêtrise *f*

prim ['prɪm] *adj* **primmer; primmest** : guindé

primary ['praɪˌmɛri, 'praɪməri] *adj* **1** FIRST : primaire **2** PRINCIPAL : principal — **primarily** [praɪ'mɛrəli] *adv* : principalement

prime¹ ['praɪm] *vt* **primed; priming 1** LOAD : charger **2** PREPARE : apprêter **3** COACH : préparer

prime² *n* **the** ~ **of life** : la force de l'âge — ~ *adj* **1** MAIN : principal **2** EXCELLENT : excellent — **prime minister** *n* : Premier ministre *m*

primer¹ ['praɪmər] *n* : apprêt *m*

primer² ['prɪmər] *n* : premier livre *m* de lecture

primitive ['prɪmətɪv] *adj* : primitif

primrose ['prɪmˌroːz] *n* : primevère *f*

prince ['prɪnts] *n* : prince *m* — **princess** ['prɪntsəs, 'prɪnˌsɛs] *n* : princesse *f*

principal ['prɪntsəpəl] *adj* : principal — ~ *n* **1** DIRECTOR : directeur *m*, -trice *f* **2** : principal *m* (d'une dette), capital *m* (d'une somme)

principle ['prɪntsəpəl] *n* : principe *m*

print ['prɪnt] *n* **1** MARK : empreinte *f* **2** LETTER : caractère *m* **3** ENGRAVING : gravure *f* **4** : imprimé *m* (d'un tissu) **5** : épreuve *f* (en photographie) **6 in** ~ : disponible — ~ *vt* : imprimer (un texte, etc.) — *vi* : écrire en lettres moulées — **printer** ['prɪntər] *n* **1** : imprimeur *m* (personne) **2** : imprimante *f* (machine) — **printing** ['prɪntɪŋ] *n* **1** : imprimerie *f* (technique) **2** IMPRESSION : impression *f* **3** LETTERING : écriture *f* en lettres moulées

prior ['praɪər] *adj* **1** : antérieur, précédent **2** ~ **to** : avant — **priority** [praɪ'ɔrəti] *n, pl* **-ties** : priorité *f*

prison ['prɪzən] *n* : prison *f* — **prisoner** ['prɪzənər] *n* : prisonnier *m*, -nière *f*

privacy ['praɪvəsi] *n, pl* **-cies** : intimité *f* — **private** ['praɪvət] *adj* **1** : privé **2** PERSONAL : personnel — ~ *n* : (simple) soldat *m* — **privately** ['praɪvətli] *adv* : en privé

privilege ['prɪvlɪdʒ, 'prɪvə-] *n* : privilège *m* — **privileged** ['prɪvlɪdʒd, 'prɪvə-] *adj* : privilégié

prize ['praɪz] *n* : prix *m* — ~ *adj* : primé — ~ *vt* **prized; prizing** : priser — **prizewinning** ['praɪzˌwɪnɪŋ] *adj* : primé, gagnant

pro ['proː] *n* **1** → **professional 2 the** ~**s and cons** : le pour et le contre

probability [ˌprɑbə'bɪləti] *n, pl* **-ties** : probabilité *f* — **probable** ['prɑbəbəl] *adj* : probable — **probably** [-bli] *adv* : probablement

probation [proˈbeɪʃən] *n* : période *f* d'essai (d'un employé)

probe [ˈproːb] *n* **1** : sonde *f* (en médecine) **2** INVESTIGATION : enquête *f* — ~ *vt* **probed; probing** : sonder

problem [ˈprɑbləm] *n* : problème *m*

procedure [prəˈsiːdʒər] *n* : procédure *f*

proceed [proˈsiːd] *vi* **1** ACT : procéder **2** CONTINUE : continuer **3** ADVANCE : avancer, aller — **proceedings** [proˈsiːdɪŋz] *npl* **1** EVENTS : événements *mpl* **2** *or* legal ~ : poursuites *fpl* — **proceeds** [ˈproːˌsiːdz] *npl* : recette *f*

process [ˈprɑˌsɛs, ˈproː-] *n, pl* **-cesses** [ˈprɑˌsɛsəz, ˈproː-, -səsəz, -səˌsiːz] **1** : processus *m* **2** METHOD : procédé *m* **3** in the ~ of : en train de — ~ *vt* : traiter — **procession** [prəˈsɛʃən] *n* : procession *f*

proclaim [proˈkleɪm] *vt* : proclamer — **proclamation** [ˌprɑkləˈmeɪʃən] *n* : proclamation *f*

procrastinate [prəˈkræstəˌneɪt] *vi* **-nated; -nating** : remettre à plus tard

procure [prəˈkjʊr] *vt* **-cured; -curing** : obtenir

prod [ˈprɑd] *vt* **prodded; prodding** : pousser

prodigal [ˈprɑdɪɡəl] *adj* : prodigue

prodigious [prəˈdɪdʒəs] *adj* : prodigieux

prodigy [ˈprɑdədʒi] *n, pl* **-gies** : prodige *m*

produce [prəˈduːs, -ˈdjuːs] *vt* **-duced; -ducing 1** : produire **2** SHOW : présenter **3** CAUSE : causer — ~ [ˈprɑˌduːs, ˈproː-, -ˌdjuːs] *n* : produits *mpl* agricoles — **producer** [prəˈduːsər, -ˈdjuː-] *n* : producteur *m*, -trice *f* — **product** [ˈprɑˌdʌkt] *n* : produit *m* — **productive** [prəˈdʌktɪv] *adj* : productif

profane [proˈfeɪn] *adj* **1** SECULAR : profane **2** IRREVERENT : sacrilège — **profanity** [proˈfænəti] *n, pl* **-ties** : juron *m*

profess [prəˈfɛs] *vt* : professer — **profession** [prəˈfɛʃən] *n* : profession *f* — **professional** [prəˈfɛʃənəl] *adj* : professionnel — ~ *n* : professionnel *m*, -nelle *f* — **professor** [prəˈfɛsər] *n* : professeur *m*

proficiency [prəˈfɪʃəntsi] *n, pl* **-cies** : compétence *f* — **proficient** [prəˈfɪʃənt] *adj* : compétent

profile [ˈproːˌfaɪl] *n* : profil *m*

profit [ˈprɑfət] *n* : profit *m*, bénéfice *m* — ~ *vi* **from** : tirer profit de — *vt* BENEFIT : profiter à — **profitable** [ˈprɑfətəbəl] *adj* : profitable

profound [prəˈfaʊnd] *adj* : profond

profuse [prəˈfjuːs] *adj* **1** ABUNDANT : abondant **2** LAVISH : prodigue — **profusion** [prəˈfjuːʒən] *n* : profusion *f*

prognosis [prɑɡˈnoːsɪs] *n, pl* **-ses** [-ˌsiːz] : pronostic *m*

program *or Brit* **programme** [ˈproːˌɡræm, -ɡrəm] *n* **1** : programme *m* **2** television ~ : émission *f* de télévision — ~ *vt* **-grammed** *or* **-gramed; -gramming** *or* **-graming** : programmer

progress [ˈprɑɡrəs, -ˌɡrɛs] *n* **1** : progrès *m* **2** in ~ : en cours — ~ [prəˈɡrɛs] *vi* : progresser — **progressive** [prəˈɡrɛsɪv] *adj* **1** : progressiste (en politique, etc.) **2** : progressif

prohibit [proˈhɪbət] *vt* : interdire — **prohibition** [ˌproːəˈbɪʃən, ˌproːhə-] *n* : prohibition *f*

project [ˈprɑˌdʒɛkt, -dʒɪkt] *n* : projet *m* — ~ [prəˈdʒɛkt] *vt* : projeter — *vi* PROTRUDE : faire saillie — **projectile** [prəˈdʒɛktəl, -ˌtaɪl] *n* : projectile *m* — **projection** [prəˈdʒɛkʃən] *n* **1** : projection *f* **2** BULGE : saillie *f* — **projector** [prəˈdʒɛktər] *n* : projecteur *m*

proliferate [prəˈlɪfəˌreɪt] *vi* **-ated; -ating** : proliférer — **proliferation** [prəˌlɪfəˈreɪʃən] *n* : prolifération *f* — **prolific** [prəˈlɪfɪk] *adj* : prolifique

prologue [ˈproːˌlɔɡ, -ˌlɑɡ] *n* : prologue *m*

prolong [prəˈlɔŋ] *vt* : prolonger

prom [ˈprɑm] *n* : bal *m* d'étudiants

prominent [ˈprɑmənənt] *adj* **1** : proéminent **2** IMPORTANT : important — **prominence** [ˈprɑmənənts] *n* **1** : proéminence *f* **2** IMPORTANCE : importance *f*

promiscuous [prəˈmɪskjuəs] *adj* : de mœurs légères

promise [ˈprɑməs] *n* : promesse *f* — ~ *v* **-mised; -mising** : promettre — **promising** [ˈprɑməsɪŋ] *adj* : prometteur

promote [prəˈmoːt] *vt* **-moted; -moting** : promouvoir — **promoter** [prəˈmoːtər] *n* : promoteur *m*, -trice *f* — **promotion** [prəˈmoːʃən] *n* : promotion *f*

prompt [ˈprɑmpt] *vt* **1** INCITE : inciter **2** CAUSE : provoquer — ~ *adj* **1** QUICK : prompt **2** PUNCTUAL : ponctuel

prone [ˈproːn] *adj* **1** APT : sujet, enclin **2** FLAT : à plat ventre

prong [ˈprɔŋ] *n* : dent *f*

pronoun [ˈproːˌnaʊn] *n* : pronom *m*

pronounce [prəˈnaʊnts] *vt* **-nounced; -nouncing** : prononcer — **pronouncement** [prəˈnaʊntsmənt] *n* : déclaration *f* — **pronunciation** [prəˌnʌntsiˈeɪʃən] *n* : prononciation *f*

proof [ˈpruːf] *n* **1** EVIDENCE : preuve *f* **2** PRINT : épreuve *f* — **proofread** [ˈpruːfˌriːd] *vt* **-read** [-ˌrɛd]; **-reading** : corriger les épreuves de

prop [ˈprɑp] *n* **1** SUPPORT : étai *m* **2** ~s *npl* : accessoires *mpl* — ~ *vt* **propped; propping 1** LEAN : appuyer **2** ~ up SUPPORT : étayer

propaganda [ˌprɑpəˈɡændə, ˌproː-] *n* : propagande *f*

propagate ['prɑpə,ɡeɪt] v **-gated; -gating** vt
: propager — vi : se propager
propel [prə'pɛl] vt **-pelled; -pelling**
: propulser — **propeller** [prə'pɛlər] n
: hélice f
propensity [prə'pɛntsəti] n, pl **-ties** : pro-
pension f
proper ['prɑpər] adj **1** SUITABLE : convenable **2** REAL : vrai **3** CORRECT : correct **4**
~ **name** : nom propre — **properly**
['prɑpərli] adv : correctement
property ['prɑpərti] n, pl **-ties 1** POSSES-
SIONS : biens mpl, propriété f **2** REAL ES-
TATE : biens mpl immobiliers **3** QUALITY
: propriété f
prophet ['prɑfət] n : prophète m —
prophecy ['prɑfəsi] n, pl **-cies** : prophétie f
— **prophesy** ['prɑfə,saɪ] vt **-sied; -sying**
: prophétiser — **prophetic** [prə'fɛtɪk] adj
: prophétique
proponent [prə'po:nənt] n : partisan m,
-sane f
proportion [prə'porʃən] n **1** : proportion f
2 SHARE : part f — **proportional** [prə-
'porʃənəl] adj : proportionnel — **propor-
tionate** [prə'porʃənət] adj : proportionnel
proposal [prə'po:zəl] n : proposition f
propose [prə'po:z] v **-posed; -posing** vt
: proposer — vi : faire une demande en
mariage — **proposition** [,prɑpə'zɪʃən] n
: proposition f
proprietor [prə'praɪətər] n : propriétaire mf
propriety [prə'praɪəti] n, pl **-ties** : convenance f
propulsion [prə'pʌlʃən] n : propulsion f
prose ['pro:z] n : prose f
prosecute ['prɑsɪ,kju:t] vt **-cuted; -cuting**
: poursuivre — **prosecution** [,prɑsɪ-
'kju:ʃən] n : poursuites fpl judiciaires —
prosecutor ['prɑsɪ,kju:tər] n : procureur m
prospect ['prɑ,spɛkt] n **1** VIEW : vue f **2**
POSSIBILITY : perspective f **3** ~**s** : es-
pérances fpl — **prospective** [prə'spɛktɪv,
'prɑ,spɛk-] adj : éventuel
prosper ['prɑspər] vt : prospérer — **prosperity** [prɑ'spɛrəti] n : prospérité f — **pros-
perous** ['prɑspərəs] adj : prospère
prostitute ['prɑstə,tu:t, -,tju:t] n : prostituée
f — **prostitution** [,prɑstə'tu:ʃən, -'tju:-] n
: prostitution f
prostrate ['prɑ,streɪt] adj **1** : allongé à plat
ventre **2** STRICKEN : prostré
protagonist [pro'tæɡənɪst] n : protagoniste
mf
protect [prə'tɛkt] vt : protéger — **protection**
[prə'tɛkʃən] n : protection f — **protective**
[prə'tɛktɪv] adj : protecteur — **protector**
[prə'tɛktər] n : protecteur m, -trice f
protein ['pro:,ti:n] n : protéine f
protest ['pro:,tɛst] n **1** DEMONSTRATION

: manifestation f **2** OBJECTION : protestation
f — ~ [pro'tɛst] v : protester — **Protestant**
['prɑtəstənt] n : protestant m, -tante f —
protester or **protestor** ['pro:,tɛstər, prɑ'-]
n : manifestant m, -tante f
protocol ['pro:tə,kɔl] n : protocole m
protrude [pro'tru:d] vi **-truded; -truding**
: dépasser
proud ['praʊd] adj **1** : fier **2** ARROGANT
: orgueilleux
prove ['pru:v] v **proved; proved** or **proven**
['pru:vən]; **proving** vt : prouver — vi
: s'avérer, se montrer
proverb ['prɑ,vərb] n : proverbe m
provide [prə'vaɪd] v **-vided; -viding** vt
: fournir — vi ~ **for** SUPPORT : subvenir
aux besoins de — **provided** [prə'vaɪdəd] or
~ **that** conj : à condition que — **providence** ['prɑvədənts] n : providence f
province ['prɑvɪnts] n **1** : province f **2**
SPHERE : domaine m — **provincial** [prə-
'vɪntʃəl] adj : provincial
provision [prə'vɪʒən] n **1** SUPPLYING : approvisionnement m **2** STIPULATION : stipulation f **3** ~**s** npl : provisions fpl — **provisional** [prə'vɪʒənəl] adj : provisoire
provoke [prə'vo:k] vt **-voked; -voking**
: provoquer — **provocative** [prə'vɑkətɪv]
adj : provocant, provocateur
prow ['praʊ] n : proue f
prowess ['praʊəs] n : prouesse f
prowl ['praʊl] vi : rôder — ~ n **be on the**
~ : rôder — **prowler** ['praʊlər] n : rôdeur
m, -deuse f
proximity [prɑk'sɪməti] n : proximité f —
proxy ['prɑksi] n, pl **proxies** : procuration f
prude ['pru:d] n : prude f
prudence ['pru:dənts] n : prudence f — **prudent** ['pru:dənt] adj : prudent
prune¹ ['pru:n] n : pruneau m
prune² vt **pruned; pruning** : élaguer, tailler
pry ['praɪ] v **pried; prying** vi ~ **into** : mettre son nez dans — vt or ~ **open** : forcer
avec un levier
psalm ['sɑm, 'sɑlm] n : psaume m
pseudonym ['su:də,nɪm] n : pseudonyme m
psychiatry [sə'kaɪətri, saɪ-] n : psychiatrie f
— **psychiatric** [,saɪki'ætrɪk] adj : psychiatrique — **psychiatrist** [sə'kaɪətrɪst, saɪ-] n
: psychiatre mf
psychic ['saɪkɪk] adj : psychique
psychoanalysis [,saɪkoə'næləsɪs] n : psychanalyse — **psychoanalyst** [,saɪko-
'ænəlɪst] n : psychanalyste mf — **psychoanalyze** [,saɪko'ænəl,aɪz] vt **-lyzed; -lyzing**
: psychanalyser
psychology [saɪ'kɑlədʒi] n, pl **-gies** : psychologie f — **psychological** [,saɪkə-
'lɑdʒɪkəl] adj : psychologique — **psychologist** [saɪ'kɑlədʒɪst] n : psychologue mf

psychotherapy [ˌsaɪkoʹθɛrəpi] *n* : psychothérapie *f*

puberty [ʹpju:bərti] *n* : puberté *f*

public [ʹpʌblɪk] *adj* : public — **~** *n* : public *m* — **publication** [ˌpʌbləʹkeɪʃən] *n* : publication *f* — **publicity** [pəʹblɪsəti] *n* : publicité *f* — **publicize** [ʹpʌbləˌsaɪz] *vt* **-cized; -cizing** : rendre public, faire connaître

publish [ʹpʌblɪʃ] *vt* : publier — **publisher** [ʹpʌblɪʃər] *n* 1 : éditeur *m*, -trice *f* 2 : maison *f* d'édition (entreprise)

puck [ʹpʌk] *n* : palet *m*, rondelle *f* Can (au hockey)

pucker [ʹpʌkər] *vt* : plisser — *vi* : se plisser

pudding [ʹpʊdɪŋ] *n* : pudding *m*, pouding *m*

puddle [ʹpʌdəl] *n* : flaque *f* (d'eau)

puff [ʹpʌf] *vi* 1 BLOW : souffler 2 PANT : haleter 3 **~** up SWELL : enfler — *vt or* **~ out** : gonfler — **~** *n* 1 : bouffée *f* 2 cream **~** : chou *m* à la crème 3 *or* **powder ~** : houppette *f* — **puffy** [ʹpʌfi] *adj* **puffier; puffiest** : enflé, bouffi

pull [ʹpʊl, ʹpʌl] *vt* 1 : tirer 2 STRAIN : se froisser 3 EXTRACT : arracher 4 DRAW : sortir 5 **~** off : enlever 6 **~** oneself together : se ressaisir 7 **~** up RAISE : remonter — *vi* 1 **~** away : se retirer 2 **~** out of : quitter 3 **~** through RECOVER : s'en tirer 4 **~** together COOPERATE : agir en concert 5 **~** up STOP : s'arrêter — **~** *n* 1 TUG : coup *m* 2 INFLUENCE : influence *f* — **pulley** [ʹpʊli] *n*, *pl* **-leys** : poulie *f* — **pullover** [ʹpʊlˌoːvər] *n* : chandail *m*, pullover *m* France

pulmonary [ʹpʊlməˌnɛri, ʹpʌl-] *adj* : pulmonaire

pulp [ʹpʌlp] *n* : pulpe *f*

pulpit [ʹpʊlˌpɪt] *n* : chaire *f*

pulsate [ʹpʌlˌseɪt] *vi* **-sated; -sating** 1 BEAT : palpiter 2 VIBRATE : vibrer — **pulse** [ʹpʌls] *n* : pouls *m*

pummel [ʹpʌməl] *vt* **-meled; -meling** : bourer de coups

pump[1] [ʹpʌmp] *n* : pompe *f* — **~** *vt* 1 : pomper (de l'eau) 2 **~** up : gonfler

pump[2] *n* SHOE : escarpin *m*

pumpernickel [ʹpʌmpərˌnɪkəl] *n* : pain *m* noir

pumpkin [ʹpʌmpkɪn, ʹpʌŋkən] *n* : citrouille *f*, potiron *m* France

pun [ʹpʌn] *n* : jeu *m* de mots

punch[1] [ʹpʌntʃ] *vt* 1 : donner un coup de poing à 2 PERFORATE : poinçonner — **~** *n* BLOW : coup *m* de poing

punch[2] *n* : punch *m* (boisson)

punctual [ʹpʌŋktʃuəl] *adj* : ponctuel — **punctuality** [ˌpʌŋktʃuʹæləti] *n* : ponctualité *f*

punctuate [ʹpʌŋktʃuˌeɪt] *vt* **-ated; -ating** : ponctuer — **punctuation** [ˌpʌŋktʃuʹeɪʃən] *n* : ponctuation *f*

puncture [ʹpʌŋktʃər] *n* 1 HOLE : perforation *f* 2 PRICK : piqûre *f* — **~** *vt* **-tured; -turing** 1 PIERCE : perforer 2 : crever (un ballon, un pneu, etc.)

pungent [ʹpʌndʒənt] *adj* : âcre

punish [ʹpʌnɪʃ] *vt* : punir — **punishment** [ʹpʌnɪʃmənt] *n* : punition *f* — **punitive** [ʹpju:nətɪv] *adj* : punitif

puny [ʹpju:ni] *adj* **-nier; -est** : chétif

pup [ʹpʌp] *n* : chiot *m*, jeune animal *m*

pupil[1] [ʹpju:pəl] *n* STUDENT : élève *mf*

pupil[2] *n* : pupille *f* (de l'œil)

puppet [ʹpʌpət] *n* : marionnette *f*

puppy [ʹpʌpi] *n*, *pl* **-pies** : chiot *m*

purchase [ʹpərtʃəs] *vt* **-chased; -chasing** : acheter — **~** *n* : achat *m*

pure [ʹpjʊr] *adj* **purer; purest** : pur

puree [pjuʹreɪ, -ʹri:] *n* : purée *f*

purely [ʹpjʊrli] *adv* : purement

purgatory [ʹpərgəˌtori] *n*, *pl* **-ries** : purgatoire *m* — **purge** [ʹpərdʒ] *vt* **purged; purging** : purger — **~** *n* : purge *f*

purify [ʹpjʊrəˌfaɪ] *vt* **-fied; -fying** : purifier — **purifier** [ʹpjʊrəˌfaɪər] *n* : purificateur *m*

puritan [ʹpju:rətən] *n* : puritain *m*, -taine *f* — **puritanical** [ˌpju:rəʹtænɪkəl] *adj* : puritain

purity [ʹpjʊrəti] *n* : pureté *f*

purple [ʹpərpəl] *adj* : violet, pourpre — **~** *n* : violet *m*, pourpre *m*

purpose [ʹpərpəs] *n* 1 AIM : intention *f*, but *m* 2 DETERMINATION : résolution *f* 3 on **~** : exprès — **purposeful** [ʹpərpəsfəl] *adj* 1 MEANINGFUL : significatif 2 INTENTIONAL : réfléchi 3 DETERMINED : résolu — **purposely** [ʹpərpəsli] *adv* : exprès

purr [ʹpər] *n* : ronronnement *m* — **~** *vi* : ronronner

purse [ʹpərs] *n* 1 *or* **change ~** : porte-monnaie *m* 2 HANDBAG : sac *m* à main, sacoche *f* Can

pursue [pərʹsu:] *vt* **-sued; -suing** : poursuivre — **pursuer** [pərʹsu:ər] *n* : poursuivant *m*, -vante *f* — **pursuit** [pərʹsu:t] *n* 1 : poursuite *f* 2 OCCUPATION : activité *f*

pus [ʹpʌs] *n* : pus *m*

push [ʹpʊʃ] *vt* 1 : pousser 2 PRESS : appuyer sur 3 THRUST : enfoncer 4 **~** away : repousser — *vi* 1 : pousser 2 **~** on : continuer 3 **~** (oneself) : s'exercer — **~** *n* 1 SHOVE : poussée *f* 2 EFFORT : effort *m* — **pushy** [ʹpʊʃi] *adj* **pushier; pushiest** : arriviste

pussycat [ʹpʊsiˌkæt] *n* : minet *m*, minou *m* *fam*

put [ʹpʊt] *v* **put; putting** *vt* 1 : mettre 2 PLACE : placer, poser 3 EXPRESS : dire 4 **~** forward PROPOSE : avancer, proposer —

putrefy 308

vi **~ up with** TOLERATE : supporter — **put away** *vt* **1** STORE : ranger **2** *or* **~ aside** : mettre de côté — **put down** *vt* **1** : poser, déposer **2** WRITE : mettre (par écrit) — **put off** *vt* POSTPONE : remettre à plus tard, retarder — **put on** *vt* **1** ASSUME : prendre **2** PRESENT : monter (un spectacle, etc.) **3** WEAR : mettre — **put out** *vt* **1** EXTINGUISH, TURN OFF : éteindre **2** INCONVENIENCE : déranger — **put up** *vt* **1** BUILD : ériger **2** LODGE : loger **3** HANG : accrocher

putrefy [ˈpjuːtrəˌfaɪ] *v* **-fied; -fying** *vt* : putréfier — *vi* : se putréfier
putty [ˈpʌti] *n, pl* **-ties** : mastic *m*
puzzle [ˈpʌzəl] *vt* **-zled; -zling** CONFUSE : intriguer, laisser perplexe — **~** *n* **1** : casse-tête *m* **2** *or* **jigsaw ~** : puzzle *m* **3** MYSTERY : énigme *f*, mystère *m*
pyjamas *Brit* → **pajamas**
pylon [ˈpaɪˌlɑn, -lən] *n* : pylône *m*
pyramid [ˈpɪrəˌmɪd] *n* : pyramide *f*
python [ˈpaɪˌθɑn, -θən] *n* : python *m*

Q

q [ˈkjuː] *n, pl* **q's** *or* **qs** [ˈkjuːz] : q *m*, dix-septième lettre de l'alphabet
quack[1] [ˈkwæk] *vi* : faire des coin-coin
quack[2] *n* CHARLATAN : charlatan *m*
quadruped [ˈkwɑdrəˌpɛd] *n* : quadrupède *m*
quadruple [kwɑˈdruːpəl, -ˈdrʌ-; ˈkwɑ-drə-] *v* **-pled; -pling** : quadrupler — **~** *adj* : quadruple
quagmire [ˈkwæɡˌmaɪr, ˈkwɑɡ-] *n* : bourbier *m*
quail [ˈkweɪl] *n, pl* **quail** *or* **quails** : caille *f*
quaint [ˈkweɪnt] *adj* **1** ODD : bizarre **2** PICTURESQUE : pittoresque
quake [ˈkweɪk] *vi* **quaked; quaking** : trembler
qualify [ˈkwɑləˌfaɪ] *v* **-fied; -fying** *vt* **1** LIMIT : poser des conditions sur **2** AUTHORIZE : qualifier, autoriser **3** MODERATE : mitiger — *vi* : se qualifier — **qualification** [ˌkwɑləfəˈkeɪʃən] *n* **1** : qualification *f* **2** LIMITATION : réserve *f* **3** ABILITY : compétence *f* — **qualified** [ˈkwɑləˌfaɪd] *adj* : qualifié, compétent
quality [ˈkwɑləti] *n, pl* **-ties** : qualité *f*
qualm [ˈkwɑm, ˈkwɑlm, ˈkwɔm] *n* : scrupule *m*
quandary [ˈkwɑndri] *n, pl* **-ries** : dilemme *m*
quantity [ˈkwɑntəti] *n, pl* **-ties** : quantité *f*
quarantine [ˈkwɔrənˌtiːn] *n* : quarantaine *f* — **~** *vt* **-tined; -tining** : mettre en quarantaine
quarrel [ˈkwɔrəl] *n* : dispute *f*, querelle *f* — **~** *vi* **-reled** *or* **-relled; -reling** *or* **-relling** : se quereller, se disputer — **quarrelsome** [ˈkwɔrəlsəm] *adj* : querelleur
quarry [ˈkwɔri] *n, pl* **-ries** EXCAVATION : carrière *f*
quart [ˈkwɔrt] *n* : quart *m* de gallon
quarter [ˈkwɔrtər] *n* **1** : quart *m* **2** : (pièce de) vingt-cinq cents *m* **3** DISTRICT : quartier

m **4** : trimestre *m* (de l'année fiscale) **5 ~ after three** : trois heures et quart **6 ~s** *npl* LODGINGS : logement *m* — **~** *vt* : diviser en quatre — **quarterly** [ˈkwɔrtərli] *adv* : tous les trois mois, trimestriellement — **~** *adj* : trimestriel — **~** *n, pl* **-lies** : publication *f* trimestrielle
quartet [kwɔrˈtɛt] *n* : quatuor *m*
quartz [ˈkwɔrts] *n* : quartz *m*
quash [ˈkwɑʃ, ˈkwɔʃ] *vt* : étouffer, réprimer
quaver [ˈkweɪvər] *vi* : trembloter
quay [ˈkiː, ˈkeɪ, ˈkweɪ] *n* WHARF : quai *m*
queasy [ˈkwiːzi] *adj* **-sier; -est** : nauséeux
Quebecer [kwɪˈbɛkər] *adj* : québécois
Quebecois *or* **Québécois** [kebeˈkwɑ] *adj* : québécois
queen [ˈkwiːn] *n* : reine *f*
queer [ˈkwɪr] *adj* ODD : étrange, bizarre
quell [ˈkwɛl] *vt* SUPPRESS : réprimer
quench [ˈkwɛntʃ] *vt* **1** EXTINGUISH : éteindre **2 ~ one's thirst** : étancher la soif
query [ˈkwɪri, ˈkwɛr-] *n, pl* **-ries** : question *f* — **~** *vt* **-ried; -rying** ASK : poser une question à
quest [ˈkwɛst] *n* : quête *f*
question [ˈkwɛstʃən] *n* : question *f* — **~** *vt* **1** ASK : poser une question à **2** INTERROGATE : questionner **3** DOUBT : mettre en doute — **questionable** [ˈkwɛstʃənəbəl] *adj* : discutable — **question mark** *n* : point *m* d'interrogation — **questionnaire** [ˌkwɛstʃəˈnær] *n* : questionnaire *m*
queue [ˈkjuː] *n* LINE : queue *f*, file *f* — **~** *vi* **queued; queuing** *or* **queueing** : faire la queue
quibble [ˈkwɪbəl] *vi* **-bled; -bling** : chicaner — **~** *n* : chicane *f*
quick [ˈkwɪk] *adj* : rapide — **~** *adv* : rapidement, vite — **quicken** [ˈkwɪkən] *vt* : accélérer — **~** *vi* : s'accélérer — **quickly**

['kwɪkli] *adv* : rapidement, vite — **quickness** ['kwɪknəs] *n* : rapidité *f*, vitesse *f* — **quicksand** ['kwɪk,sænd] *n* : sables *mpl* mouvants

quiet ['kwaɪət] *n* **1** : silence *m* **2** CALM : calme *m* — ~ *adj* **1** SILENT : silencieux **2** CALM : tranquille — ~ *vt* **1** SILENCE : faire taire **2** CALM : calmer — *vi or* ~ **down** : se calmer — **quietly** ['kwaɪətli] *adv* **1** SILENTLY : sans bruit, doucement **2** CALMLY : tranquillement

quilt ['kwɪlt] *n* : édredon *m*

quintet [kwɪn'tɛt] *n* : quintette *m* — **quintuple** [kwɪn'tu:pəl, -'tju:-, -'tʌ-; 'kwɪntə-] *adj* : quintuple

quip ['kwɪp] *n* : raillerie *f*

quirk ['kwərk] *n* : bizarrerie *f* — **quirky** ['kwərki] *adj* **quirkier; quirkiest** : excentrique

quit ['kwɪt] *v* **quit; quitting** *vt* **1** LEAVE : quitter **2** STOP : arrêter — *vi* **1** GIVE UP : abandonner **2** RESIGN : démissionner

quite ['kwaɪt] *adv* **1** COMPLETELY : tout à fait **2** RATHER : assez **3** POSITIVELY : vraiment

quits ['kwɪts] *adj* **1** : quitte **2** **we called it** ~ : nous y avons renoncé

quiver ['kwɪvər] *vi* : trembler

quiz ['kwɪz] *n*, *pl* **quizzes** TEST : interrogation *f* — ~ *vt* **quizzed; quizzing** : questionner, interroger

quota ['kwo:tə] *n* : quota *m*

quotation [kwo'teɪʃən] *n* **1** CITATION : citation *f* **2** ESTIMATE : devis *m* — **quotation marks** *npl* : guillemets *mpl* — **quote** ['kwo:t] *vt* **quoted; quoting 1** CITE : citer **2** STATE : indiquer (un prix) **3** : coter (un prix à la Bourse) — ~ *n* **1** → **quotation 2** ~**s** *npl* → **quotation marks**

quotient ['kwo:ʃənt] *n* : quotient *m*

R

r ['ɑr] *n*, *pl* **r's** *or* **rs** ['ɑrz] : r *m*, dix-huitième lettre de l'alphabet

rabbi ['ræ,baɪ] *n* : rabbin *m*

rabbit ['ræbət] *n*, *pl* **-bit** *or* **-bits** : lapin *m*, -pine *f*

rabies ['reɪbi:z] *ns & pl* : rage *f* — **rabid** ['ræbɪd] *adj* **1** : enragé (se dit d'un chien) **2** FURIOUS : furieux

raccoon [ræ'ku:n] *n*, *pl* **-coon** *or* **-coons** : raton *m* laveur

race[1] ['reɪs] *n* **1** : race *f* **2 human** ~ : genre *m* humain

race[2] *n* : course *f* (à pied, etc.) — ~ *vi* **raced; racing** : courir — **racehorse** ['reɪs,hɔrs] *n* : cheval *m* de course — **racetrack** ['reɪs,træk] *n* : hippodrome *m*

racial ['reɪʃəl] *adj* : racial — **racism** ['reɪ,sɪzəm] *n* : racisme *m* — **racist** ['reɪsɪst] *n* : raciste *mf*

rack ['ræk] *n* **1** SHELF : étagère *f* **2 luggage** ~ : porte-bagages *m* — ~ *vt* **1** ~**ed with** : tourmenté par **2** ~ **one's brains** : se creuser les méninges

racket[1] ['rækət] *n* : raquette *f* (de tennis, etc.)

racket[2] *n* **1** DIN : vacarme *m* **2** SWINDLE : escroquerie *f*

racy ['reɪsi] *adj* **racier; -est** : osé, risqué

radar ['reɪ,dɑr] *n* : radar *m*

radiant ['reɪdiənt] *adj* : radieux — **radiance** ['reɪdiənts] *n* : éclat *m* — **radiate** ['reɪdi,eɪt]

v **-ated; -ating** *vt* : irradier — *vi* : rayonner — **radiation** [,reɪdi'eɪʃən] *n* : rayonnement *m* — **radiator** ['reɪdi,eɪtər] *n* : radiateur *m*

radical ['rædɪkəl] *adj* : radical — ~ *n* : radical *m*, -cale *f*

radii → **radius**

radio ['reɪdi,o:] *n*, *pl* **-dios** : radio *f* — ~ *vt* : transmettre par radio — **radioactive** ['reɪdio'æktɪv] *adj* : radioactif

radish ['rædɪʃ] *n* : radis *m*

radius ['reɪdiəs] *n*, *pl* **radii** [-di,aɪ] : rayon *m*

raffle ['ræfəl] *vt* **-fled; -fling** : mettre en tombola — ~ *n* : tombola *f*

raft ['ræft] *n* : radeau *m*

rafter ['ræftər] *n* : chevron *m*

rag ['ræg] *n* **1** : chiffon *m*, guenille *f Can* **2 in** ~**s** : en haillons

rage ['reɪdʒ] *n* **1** : colère *f*, rage *f* **2 be all the** ~ : faire fureur — ~ *vi* **raged; raging 1** : être furieux **2** : hurler (se dit du vent, etc.)

ragged ['rægəd] *adj* **1** UNEVEN : inégal **2** TATTERED : en loques

raid ['reɪd] *n* **1** : invasion *f*, raid *m* **2** *or* **police** ~ : descente *f*, rafle *f* — ~ *vt* INVADE : envahir

rail[1] ['reɪl] *vi* ~ **at** : invectiver contre

rail[2] *n* **1** BAR : barre *f* **2** HANDRAIL : balustrade *f* **3** TRACK : rail *m* **4 by** ~ : par train — **railing** ['reɪlɪŋ] *n* **1** : rampe *f* (d'un escalier), balustrade *f* (d'un balcon) **2** RAILS : grille *f* — **railroad** ['reɪl,ro:d] *n*

: chemin *m* de fer — **railway** ['reɪl₁weɪ] →
railroad
rain ['reɪn] *n* : pluie *f* — ~ *vi* : pleuvoir —
rainbow ['reɪn₁bo:] *n* : arc-en-ciel *m* —
raincoat ['reɪn₁ko:t] *n* : imperméable *m*
— **rainfall** ['reɪn₁fɔl] *n* : précipitations *fpl*
— **rainy** ['reɪni] *adj* **rainier; -est** : pluvieux
raise ['reɪz] *vt* **raised; raising 1** : lever **2**
REAR : élever **3** GROW : cultiver **4** IN-
CREASE : augmenter **5** : soulever (des ob-
jections) **6** ~ **money** : collecter des fonds
— ~ *n* : augmentation *f*
raisin ['reɪzən] *n* : raisin *m* sec
rake ['reɪk] *n* : râteau *m* — ~ *vt* **raked; rak-
ing** : ratisser
rally ['ræli] *v* **-lied; -lying** *vi* : se rallier, se
rassembler — *vt* : rallier, rassembler — ~
n, pl **-lies** : ralliement *m*, rassemblement *m*
ram ['ræm] *n* : bélier *m* (mouton) — ~ *vt*
rammed; ramming 1 CRAM : fourrer **2** *or*
~ **into** : percuter
RAM ['ræm] *n* (*random-access memory*)
: RAM *f*
ramble ['ræmbəl] *vi* **-bled; -ling 1** WANDER
: se balader **2** *or* ~ **on** : divaguer — ~ *n*
: randonnée *f*, excursion *f*
ramp ['ræmp] *n* **1** : rampe *f* **2** : passerelle *f*
(pour accéder à un avion)
rampage ['ræm₁peɪʤ] *vi* **-paged; -paging**
: se déchaîner
rampant ['ræmpənt] *adj* : déchaîné
ramshackle ['ræm₁ʃækəl] *adj* : délabré
ran → **run**
ranch ['rænʧ] *n* : ranch *m*
rancid ['rænʦɪd] *adj* : rance
rancor *or Brit* **rancour** ['ræŋkər] *n* : rancœur *f*, rancune *f*
random ['rændəm] *adj* **1** : aléatoire **2 at** ~
: au hasard
rang → **ring**
range ['reɪnʤ] *n* **1** : chaîne *f* (de montagnes)
2 STOVE : cuisinière *f* **3** VARIETY : gamme *f*
4 SCOPE : portée *f* — ~ *vi* **ranged; ranging**
1 EXTEND : s'étendre **2** ~ **from ... to ...**
: varier entre ... et ... — **ranger** ['reɪnʤər] *n*
or **forest** ~ : garde *m* forestier
rank[1] ['ræŋk] *adj* : fétide
rank[2] *n* **1** ROW : rang *m* **2** : grade *m* (militaire) **3** ~**s** : simples soldats *mpl* **4 the** ~
and file : la base — ~ *vt* RATE : classer,
ranger — *vi* : se classer, compter
rankle ['ræŋkəl] *vi* **-kled; -kling** : rester sur
le cœur
ransack ['ræn₁sæk] *vt* **1** SEARCH : fouiller
2 LOOT : saccager
ransom ['rænʦəm] *n* : rançon *f* — ~ *vt*
: payer une rançon pour
rant ['rænt] *vi or* ~ **and rave** : fulminer
rap[1] ['ræp] *n* KNOCK : coup *m* sec — ~ *v*
rapped; rapping : cogner

rap[2] *n or* ~ **music** : rap *m*
rapacious [rə'peɪʃəs] *adj* : rapace
rape ['reɪp] *vt* **raped; raping** : violer — ~ *n*
: viol *m*
rapid ['ræpɪd] *adj* : rapide — **rapids**
['ræpɪdz] *npl* : rapides *mpl*
rapture ['ræpʧər] *n* : extase *f*
rare ['rær] *adj* **rarer; rarest 1** FINE : exceptionnel **2** UNCOMMON : rare **3** : saignant (se
dit de la viande) — **rarely** ['rærli] *adv*
: rarement — **rarity** ['rærəṭi] *n, pl* **-ties**
: rareté *f*
rascal ['ræskəl] *n* : polisson *m*, -sonne *f*
rash[1] ['ræʃ] *adj* : irréfléchi
rash[2] *n* : rougeurs *fpl*
raspberry ['ræz₁bɛri] *n, pl* **-ries** : framboise
f
rat ['ræt] *n* : rat *m*
rate ['reɪt] *n* **1** PACE : vitesse *f*, rythme *m* **2**
: taux *m* (d'intérêt, etc.) **3** PRICE : tarif *m* **4
at any** ~ : de toute manière — ~ *vt* **rated;
rating 1** REGARD : considérer **2** RANK
: classer
rather ['ræðər, 'rʌ-, 'rɑ-] *adv* **1** FAIRLY
: assez, plutôt **2 I'd** ~ **decide** : je préférerais décider
ratify ['ræṭə₁faɪ] *vt* **-fied; -fying** : ratifier
— **ratification** [₁ræṭəfə'keɪʃən] *n* : ratification *f*
rating ['reɪṭɪŋ] *n* **1** : classement *m*, cote *f* **2**
~**s** *npl* : indice *m* d'écoute
ratio ['reɪʃio] *n, pl* **-tios** : rapport *m*, proportion *f*
ration ['ræʃən, 'reɪʃən] *n* **1** : ration *f* **2** ~**s**
npl : vivres *mpl* — ~ *vt* **rationed; ra-
tioning** : rationner
rational ['ræʃənəl] *adj* : rationnel — **rationale** [₁ræʃə'næl] *n* : logique *f*, raisons *fpl* —
rationalize ['ræʃənə₁laɪz] *vt* **-ized; -izing**
: rationaliser
rattle ['ræṭəl] *v* **-tled; -tling** *vi* : faire du bruit
— *vt* **1** SHAKE : agiter **2** UPSET : déconcerter **3** ~ **off** : débiter à toute vitesse —
~ *n* **1** : succession *f* de bruits secs **2** *or*
baby's ~ : hochet *m* — **rattlesnake**
['ræṭəl₁sneɪk] *n* : serpent *m* à sonnettes
ravage ['rævɪʤ] *vt* **-aged; -aging** : ravager
— **ravages** ['rævɪʤəz] *npl* : ravages *mpl*
rave ['reɪv] *vi* **raved; raving 1** : délirer **2** ~
about : parler avec enthousiasme de
raven ['reɪvən] *n* : grand corbeau *m*
ravenous ['rævənəs] *adj* **1** HUNGRY : affamé **2** VORACIOUS : vorace
ravine [rə'vi:n] *n* : ravin *m*
ravishing ['rævɪʃɪŋ] *adj* : ravissant
raw ['rɔ] *adj* **rawer; rawest 1** UNCOOKED
: cru **2** INEXPERIENCED : novice **3** CHAFED
: à vif (se dit d'une plaie) **4** : cru et humide
(se dit de la température) **5** ~ **materials**
: matières *fpl* premières

ray ['reɪ] *n* : rayon *m* (de lumière), lueur *f* (d'espoir, etc.)

rayon ['reɪˌɑn] *n* : rayonne *f*

raze ['reɪz] *vt* **razed; razing** : raser, détruire

razor ['reɪzər] *n* : rasoir *m* — **razor blade** *n* : lame *f* de rasoir

reach ['riːtʃ] *vt* **1** : atteindre **2** *or* ~ **out** : tendre **3** : parvenir à (une entente, etc.) **4** CONTACT : rejoindre — *vi* EXTEND : s'étendre — ~ *n* **1** : portée *f*, proximité *f* **2 within** ~ : à portée de la main

react [ri'ækt] *vi* : réagir — **reaction** [ri-'ækʃən] *n* : réaction *f* — **reactionary** [ri-'ækʃəˌnɛri] *adj* : réactionnaire — ~ *n, pl* **-ries** : réactionnaire *mf* — **reactor** [ri-'æktər] *n* : réacteur *m*

read ['riːd] *v* **read** ['rɛd]; **reading** *vt* **1** : lire **2** INTERPRET : interpréter **3** SAY : dire **4** IN-DICATE : indiquer — *vi* : se lire — **readable** ['riːdəbəl] *adj* : lisible — **reader** ['riːdər] *n* : lecteur *m*, -trice *f*

readily ['rɛdəli] *adv* **1** WILLINGLY : volontiers **2** EASILY : facilement

reading ['riːdɪŋ] *n* : lecture *f*

readjust [ˌriːə'dʒʌst] *vt* : réajuster — *vi* : se réadapter

ready ['rɛdi] *adj* **readier; -est 1** : prêt, disposé **2** AVAILABLE : disponible **3 get** ~ : se préparer — ~ *vt* **readied; readying** : préparer

real ['riːl] *adj* **1** : véritable, réel **2** GENUINE : authentique — ~ *adv* VERY : très — **real estate** *n* : biens *mpl* immobiliers — **realistic** [ˌriːə'lɪstɪk] *adj* : réaliste — **reality** [ri-'æləti] *n, pl* **-ties** : réalité *f*

realize ['riːəˌlaɪz] *vt* **-ized; -izing 1** : se rendre compte de **2** ACHIEVE : réaliser

really ['rɪli, 'riː-] *adv* : vraiment

realm ['rɛlm] *n* **1** KINGDOM : royaume *m* **2** SPHERE : domaine *m*

reap ['riːp] *vt* : moissonner, récolter

reappear [ˌriːə'pɪr] *vi* : réapparaître

rear[1] ['rɪr] *vt* : élever (des enfants, etc.)

rear[2] *n* : arrière *m*, derrière *m* — ~ *adj* : postérieur

rearrange [ˌriːə'reɪndʒ] *vt* **-ranged; -ranging** : réarranger

reason ['riːzən] *n* : raison *f* — ~ *vi* : raisonner — **reasonable** ['riːzənəbəl] *adj* : raisonnable — **reasoning** ['riːzənɪŋ] *n* : raisonnement *m*

reassure [ˌriːə'ʃʊr] *vt* **-sured; -suring** : rassurer — **reassurance** [ˌriːə'ʃʊrənts] *n* : réconfort *m*

rebate ['riːˌbeɪt] *n* : ristourne *f*

rebel ['rɛbəl] *n* : rebelle *mf* — ~ [rɪ'bɛl] *vi* **-belled; -belling** : se rebeller — **rebellion** [rɪ'bɛljən] *n* : rébellion *f* — **rebellious** [rɪ-'bɛljəs] *adj* : rebelle

rebirth [ˌriː'bərθ] *n* : renaissance *f*

reboot [ˌriː'buːt] *vt* : réamorcer, redémarrer (en informatique)

rebound ['riːˌbaʊnd, riː'baʊnd] *vi* : rebondir — ~ ['riːˌbaʊnd] *n* : rebond *m*

rebuff [rɪ'bʌf] *vt* : rabrouer — ~ *n* : rebuffade *f*

rebuild [ˌriː'bɪld] *vt* **-built** [-'bɪlt]; **-building** : reconstruire

rebuke [rɪ'bjuːk] *vt* **-buked; -buking** : reprocher — ~ *n* : réprimande *f*

rebut [rɪ'bʌt] *vt* **-butted; -butting** : réfuter — **rebuttal** [rɪ'bʌtəl] *n* : réfutation *f*

recall [rɪ'kɔl] *vt* **1** : rappeler (au devoir, etc.) **2** REMEMBER : se rappeler **3** REVOKE : annuler — ~ [rɪ'kɔl, 'riːˌkɔl] *n* : rappel *m*

recapitulate [ˌriːkə'pɪtʃəˌleɪt] *v* **-lated; -lating** : récapituler

recapture [ˌriː'kæptʃər] *vt* **-tured; -turing 1** : reprendre **2** RELIVE : revivre

recede [rɪ'siːd] *vi* **-ceded; -ceding** : se retirer

receipt [rɪ'siːt] *n* **1** : reçu *m* **2** ~**s** *npl* : recettes *fpl*

receive [rɪ'siːv] *vt* **-ceived; -ceiving** : recevoir — **receiver** [rɪ'siːvər] *n* : récepteur *m*, combiné *m*

recent ['riːsənt] *adj* : récent — **recently** [-li] *adv* : récemment

receptacle [rɪ'sɛptɪkəl] *n* : récipient *m*

reception [rɪ'sɛpʃən] *n* : réception *f* — **receptionist** [rɪ'sɛpʃənɪst] *n* : réceptionniste *mf* — **receptive** [rɪ'sɛptɪv] *adj* : réceptif

recess ['riːˌsɛs, rɪ'sɛs] *n* **1** ALCOVE : recoin *m* **2** BREAK : récréation *f* (scolaire) — **recession** [rɪ'sɛʃən] *n* : récession *f*

recharge [ˌriː'tʃɑrdʒ] *vt* **-charged; -charging** : recharger — **rechargeable** [ˌriː-'tʃɑrdʒəbəl] *adj* : rechargeable

recipe ['rɛsəˌpi] *n* : recette *f*

recipient [rɪ'sɪpiənt] *n* : récipiendaire *mf*

reciprocal [rɪ'sɪprəkəl] *adj* : réciproque

recite [rɪ'saɪt] *vt* **-cited; -citing 1** : réciter (un poème, etc.) **2** LIST : énumérer — **recital** [rɪ'saɪtəl] *n* : récital *m*

reckless ['rɛkləs] *adj* : imprudent — **recklessness** ['rɛkləsnəs] *n* : imprudence *f*

reckon ['rɛkən] *vt* : estimer, penser — **reckoning** ['rɛkənɪŋ] *n* : calculs *mpl*

reclaim [rɪ'kleɪm] *vt* : récupérer

recline [rɪ'klaɪn] *vi* **-clined; -clining** : s'allonger — **reclining** [rɪ'klaɪnɪŋ] *adj* : réglable (se dit d'un siège)

recluse ['rɛˌkluːs, rɪ'kluːs] *n* : reclus *m*, -cluse *f*

recognition [ˌrɛkɪg'nɪʃən] *n* : reconnaissance *f* — **recognizable** [ˌrɛkəg,naɪzəbəl] *adj* : reconnaissable — **recognize** ['rɛkɪg-ˌnaɪz] *vt* **-nized; -nizing** : reconnaître

recoil [rɪ'kɔɪl] *vi* : reculer — ~ ['riːˌkɔɪl, rɪ'-] *n* : recul *m* (d'une arme à feu)

recollect [ˌrɛkə'lɛkt] v : se souvenir — **recollection** [ˌrɛkə'lɛkʃən] n : souvenir m

recommend [ˌrɛkə'mɛnd] vt : recommander — **recommendation** [ˌrɛkəmən'deɪʃən] n : recommandation f

reconcile ['rɛkən͵saɪl] v -ciled; -ciling vt 1 : réconcilier (des personnes), concilier (des dates, etc.) 2 ~ **oneself to** : se résigner à — vi MAKE UP : se réconcilier — **reconciliation** [ˌrɛkən͵sɪli'eɪʃən] n : réconciliation f

reconsider [ˌriːkən'sɪdər] vt : reconsidérer

reconstruct [ˌriːkən'strʌkt] vt : reconstruire

record [rɪ'kɔrd] vt 1 : enregistrer 2 WRITE DOWN : noter — ~ ['rɛkərd] n 1 DOCUMENT : dossier m 2 REGISTER : registre m 3 HISTORY : passé m 4 : disque m (de musique) 5 or police ~ : casier m judiciaire 6 world ~ : record m mondial — **recorder** [rɪ'kɔrdər] n 1 : flûte f à bec 2 or tape ~ : magnétophone m — **recording** [rɪ'kɔrdɪŋ] n : enregistrement m

recount[1] [rɪ'kaʊnt] vt NARRATE : raconter

recount[2] ['riː͵kaʊnt, ͵rɪ'-] vt : recompter (des votes, etc.) — ~ n : décompte m

recourse ['riː͵kors, rɪ'-] n 1 : recours m 2 have ~ to : recourir à

recover [rɪ'kʌvər] vt : récupérer — vi RECUPERATE : se remettre, se rétablir — **recovery** [rɪ'kʌvəri] n, pl -ries : rétablissement m

recreation [ˌrɛkri'eɪʃən] n : loisirs mpl, récréation f — **recreational** [ˌrɛkri'eɪʃənəl] adj : récréatif

recruit [rɪ'kruːt] vt : recruter — ~ n : recrue f — **recruitment** [rɪ'kruːtmənt] n : recrutement m

rectangle ['rɛk͵tæŋgəl] n : rectangle m — **rectangular** [rɛk'tæŋgjələr] adj : rectangulaire

rectify ['rɛktə͵faɪ] vt -fied; -fying : rectifier

rector ['rɛktər] n : pasteur m — **rectory** ['rɛktəri] n, pl -ries : presbytère m

rectum ['rɛktəm] n, pl -tums or -ta [-tə] : rectum m

recuperate [rɪ'kuːpə͵reɪt, -'kjuː-] v -ated; -ating vt : récupérer — vi : se rétablir

recur [rɪ'kər] vi -curred; -curring : réapparaître — **recurrence** [rɪ'kərənts] n : répétition f — **recurrent** [rɪ'kərənt] adj : qui se répète

recycle [rɪ'saɪkəl] vt -cled; -cling : recycler

red ['rɛd] adj : rouge — ~ n : rouge m — **redden** ['rɛdən] v : rougir — **reddish** ['rɛdɪʃ] adj : rougeâtre

redecorate [ˌriː'dɛkə͵reɪt] vt -rated; -rating : repeindre

redeem [rɪ'diːm] vt : racheter, sauver — **redemption** [rɪ'dɛmpʃən] n : rédemption f

red–handed ['rɛd'hændəd] adv & adj : la main dans le sac

redhead ['rɛd͵hɛd] n : roux m, rousse f

red–hot ['rɛd'hɑt] adj : brûlant

redness ['rɛdnəs] n : rougeur f

redo [ˌriː'duː] vt -did [-dɪd]; -done [-'dʌn]; -doing : refaire

red tape n : paperasserie f

reduce [rɪ'duːs, -'djuːs] vt -duced; -ducing : réduire — **reduction** [rɪ'dʌkʃən] n : réduction f

redundant [rɪ'dʌndənt] adj : superflu

reed ['riːd] n : roseau m

reef ['riːf] n : récif m

reek ['riːk] vi : empester

reel ['riːl] n : bobine f (de fil, etc.) — ~ vt ~ **in** : enrouler (une ligne de pêche), ramener (un poisson) — vi 1 STAGGER : tituber 2 SPIN : tournoyer

reestablish [ˌriːɪ'stæblɪʃ] vt : rétablir

refer [rɪ'fər] v -ferred; -ferring vt DIRECT : renvoyer — vi ~ **to** 1 : faire allusion à 2 CONSULT : consulter

referee [ˌrɛfə'riː] n : arbitre m — ~ v -eed; -eeing : arbitrer

reference ['rɛfrənts, 'rɛfə-] n 1 : référence f 2 in ~ **to** : en ce qui concerne

refill [ˌriː'fɪl] vt : remplir à nouveau — ~ ['riː͵fɪl] n : recharge f, cartouche f (d'encre)

refine [rɪ'faɪn] vt -fined; -fining : raffiner — **refined** [rɪ'faɪnd] adj : raffiné — **refinement** [rɪ'faɪnmənt] n : raffinement m — **refinery** [rɪ'faɪnəri] n, pl -eries : raffinerie f

reflect [rɪ'flɛkt] vt : réfléchir (la lumière), refléter (une image, etc.) — vi 1 PONDER : réfléchir 2 ~ **badly on** : faire du tort à — **reflection** [rɪ'flɛkʃən] n 1 : réflexion f 2 IMAGE : reflet m

reflex ['riː͵flɛks] n : réflexe m

reflexive [rɪ'flɛksɪv] adj : réfléchi

reform [rɪ'fɔrm] vt : réformer — ~ n : réforme f — **reformer** [rɪ'fɔrmər] n : réformateur m, -trice f

refrain[1] [rɪ'freɪn] vi ~ **from** : se retenir de

refrain[2] n : refrain m (en musique)

refresh [rɪ'frɛʃ] vt : rafraîchir — **refreshments** [rɪ'frɛʃmənts] npl : rafraîchissements mpl

refrigerate [rɪ'frɪʤə͵reɪt] vt -ated; -ating : réfrigérer — **refrigeration** [rɪ͵frɪʤə'reɪʃən] n : réfrigération f — **refrigerator** [rɪ'frɪʤə͵reɪtər] n : réfrigérateur m

refuel [ˌriː'fjuːəl] v -eled or -elled; -eling or -elling vt : ravitailler en carburant — vi : se ravitailler

refuge ['rɛ͵fjuːʤ] n : refuge m, abri m — **refugee** [ˌrɛfjʊ'ʤiː] n : réfugié m, -giée f

refund [rɪ'fʌnd, 'riː͵fʌnd] vt : rembourser — ~ n : remboursement m

refurbish [rɪ'fərbɪʃ] vt : remettre à neuf

refuse[1] [rɪ'fjuːz] vt -fused; -fusing 1 : refuser 2 ~ **to do sth** : se refuser à faire qqch — **refusal** [rɪ'fjuːzəl] n : refus m

refuse² ['rɛ,fju:s, -,fju:z] *n* : ordures *fpl*, déchets *mpl*

refute [rɪ'fju:t] *vt* **-futed; -futing** : réfuter

regain [ri:'geɪn] *vt* : retrouver

regal ['ri:gəl] *adj* : royal, majestueux — **regalia** [rɪ'geɪljə] *n* : insignes *mpl*, vêtements *mpl* de cérémonie

regard [rɪ'gɑrd] *n* **1** : égard *m*, considération *f* **2** ESTEEM : estime *f* **3** ~s *npl* : amitiés *fpl* **4 with** ~ **to** : en ce qui concerne — ~ *vt* **1** HEED : tenir compte de **2** ESTEEM : estimer **3 as** ~s : en ce qui concerne **4** ~ **as** : considérer — **regarding** [rɪ'gɑrdɪŋ] *prep* : concernant — **regardless** [rɪ'gɑrdləs] *adv* : malgré tout — **regardless of** *prep* **1** : sans tenir compte de **2** IN SPITE OF : malgré

regime [reɪ'ʒi:m, rɪ-] *n* : régime *m* — **regimen** ['rɛdʒəmən] *n* : régimen *m*

regiment ['rɛdʒəmənt] *n* : régiment *m*

region ['ri:dʒən] *n* : région *f* — **regional** ['ri:dʒənəl] *adj* : régional

register ['rɛdʒəstər] *n* : registre *m* — ~ *vt* **1** : inscrire, enregistrer **2** SHOW : exprimer **3** RECORD : indiquer (la température, etc.) **4** : immatriculer (un véhicule) — *vi* ENROLL : s'inscrire — **registration** [,rɛdʒə'streɪʃən] *n* **1** : inscription *f*, enregistrement *m* **2** ~ **number** : numéro *m* d'immatriculation — **registry** ['rɛdʒəstri] *n, pl* **-tries** : registre *m*

regret [rɪ'grɛt] *vt* **-gretted; -gretting** : regretter — ~ *n* **1** REMORSE : remords *m* **2** SORROW : regret *m* — **regrettable** [rɪ'grɛtəbəl] *adj* : lamentable

regular ['rɛgjələr] *adj* **1** : régulier **2** CUSTOMARY : habituel — ~ *n* : habitué *m*, -tuée *f* — **regularity** [,rɛgjə'lærəti] *n, pl* **-ties** : régularité *f* — **regularly** ['rɛgjələrli] *adv* : régulièrement — **regulate** ['rɛgjə,leɪt] *vt* **-lated; -lating** : régler — **regulation** [,rɛgjə'leɪʃən] *n* **1** RULE : règlement *m*, règle *f* **2** CONTROL : réglementation *f*

rehabilitate [,ri:hə'bɪlə,teɪt, ,ri:ə-] *vt* **-tated; -tating** : réhabiliter — **rehabilitation** [,ri:hə,bɪlə'teɪʃən, ,ri:ə-] *n* : réhabilitation *f*

rehearse [rɪ'hərs] *vt* **-hearsed; -hearsing** : répéter — **rehearsal** [rɪ'hərsəl] *n* : répétition *f*

reign ['reɪn] *n* : règne *m* — ~ *vi* : régner

reimburse [,ri:əm'bərs] *vt* **-bursed; -bursing** : rembourser — **reimbursement** [,ri:əm'bərsmənt] *n* : remboursement *m*

rein ['reɪn] *n* : rêne *f*

reindeer ['reɪn,dɪr] *n* : renne *m*

reinforce [,ri:ən'fors] *vt* **-forced; -forcing** : renforcer — **reinforcement** [,ri:ən'forsmənt] *n* : renfort *m*

reinstate [,ri:ən'steɪt] *vt* **-stated; -stating** : rétablir (dans ses fonctions)

reiterate [ri'ɪtə,reɪt] *vt* **-ated; -ating** : réitérer

reject [rɪ'dʒɛkt] *vt* : rejeter — **rejection** [rɪ'dʒɛkʃən] *n* : rejet *m*

rejoice [rɪ'dʒɔɪs] *vi* **-joiced; -joicing** : se réjouir

rejuvenate [rɪ'dʒu:və,neɪt] *vt* **-nated; -nating** : rajeunir

rekindle [,ri:'kɪndəl] *vt* **-dled; -dling** : raviver, ranimer

relapse ['ri:,læps, rɪ'læps] *n* : rechute *f* — ~ [rɪ'læps] *vi* **-lapsed; -lapsing** : rechuter

relate [rɪ'leɪt] *v* **-lated; -lating** *vt* **1** TELL : raconter **2** ASSOCIATE : relier — *vi* **1** ~ **to** : se rapporter à **2** ~ **to** : s'entendre (avec) **3** ~ **to** : apprécier, comprendre — **related** [rɪ'leɪtəd] *adj* ~ **to** : apparenté à — **relation** [rɪ'leɪʃən] *n* **1** : rapport *m*, lien *m* **2** RELATIVE : parent *m*, -rente *f* **3 in** ~ **to** : par rapport à **4** ~s *npl* : rapports *mpl*, relations *fpl* — **relationship** [rɪ'leɪʃən,ʃɪp] *n* **1** : rapport *m*, relations *fpl* **2** KINSHIP : liens *mpl* de parenté — **relative** ['rɛlətɪv] *n* : parent *m*, -rente *f* — ~ *adj* : relatif — **relatively** ['rɛlətɪvli] *adv* : relativement

relax [rɪ'læks] *vt* : détendre — *vi* : se détendre — **relaxation** [,ri:,læk'seɪʃən] *n* : détente *f*, relaxation *f*

relay ['ri:,leɪ] *n* **1** : relève *m* **2** *or* ~ **race** : course *f* de relais — ~ ['ri:,leɪ, rɪ'leɪ] *vt* **-layed; -laying** : relayer, transmettre

release [rɪ'li:s] *vt* **-leased; -leasing 1** FREE : libérer, mettre en liberté **2** : relâcher (une bride, etc.) **3** EMIT : émettre **4** : publier (un livre), sortir (un nouveau film) — ~ *n* **1** : libération *f* **2** : sortie *f* (d'un film), parution *f* (d'un livre)

relegate ['rɛlə,geɪt] *vt* **-gated; -gating** : reléguer

relent [rɪ'lɛnt] *vi* **1** GIVE IN : céder **2** ABATE : se calmer — **relentless** [rɪ'lɛntləs] *adj* : implacable

relevant ['rɛləvənt] *adj* : pertinent — **relevance** ['rɛləvənts] *n* : pertinence *f*

reliable [rɪ'laɪəbəl] *adj* : fiable, sûr — **reliability** [rɪ,laɪə'bɪləti] *n, pl* **-ties** : fiabilité *f* — **reliance** [rɪ'laɪənts] *n* **1** : dépendance *f* **2** TRUST : confiance *f*

relic ['rɛlɪk] *n* : relique *f*

relief [rɪ'li:f] *n* **1** : soulagement *m* **2** AID : aide *f*, secours *m* **3** : relief *m* (d'une carte géographique) **4** REPLACEMENT : relève *f* — **relieve** [rɪ'li:v] *vt* **-lieved; -lieving 1** : soulager **2** REPLACE : relayer (qqn) **3** ~ **s.o. of** : libérer qqn de

religion [rɪ'lɪdʒən] *n* : religion *f* — **religious** [rɪ'lɪdʒəs] *adj* : religieux

relinquish [rɪ'lɪŋkwɪʃ, -'lɪn-] *vt* : renoncer à

relish ['rɛlɪʃ] *n* **1** : condiment *m* à base de cornichons **2 with** ~ : avec un plaisir évident — ~ *vt* : savourer

relocate [,ri:'lo:,keɪt, ,ri:lo'keɪt] *v* **-cated;**

-cating *vt* : transférer — *vi* : déménager, s'établir ailleurs — **relocation** [ˌriːloʊˈkeɪʃən] *n* : déménagement *m*

reluctance [rɪˈlʌktənts] *n* : réticence *f* — **reluctant** [rɪˈlʌktənt] *adj* : réticent — **reluctantly** [rɪˈlʌktəntli] *adv* : à contrecœur

rely [rɪˈlaɪ] *vi* **-lied; -lying** ~ **on** 1 : dépendre de 2 TRUST : se fier à

remain [rɪˈmeɪn] *vi* : rester — **remainder** [rɪˈmeɪndər] *n* : reste *m*, restant *m* — **remains** [rɪˈmeɪnz] *npl* : restes *mpl*

remark [rɪˈmɑrk] *n* : remarque *f*, observation *f* — ~ *vt* 1 : remarquer 2 SAY : mentionner — *vi* ~ **on** : observer que — **remarkable** [rɪˈmɑrkəbəl] *adj* : remarquable

remedy [ˈrɛmədi] *n, pl* **-dies** : remède *m* — ~ *vt* **-died; -dying** : remédier à — **remedial** [rɪˈmiːdiəl] *adj* : de rattrapage

remember [rɪˈmɛmbər] *vt* 1 : se rappeler, se souvenir de 2 ~ **to** : ne pas oublier de — *vi* : se rappeler, se souvenir — **remembrance** [rɪˈmɛmbrənts] *n* : souvenir *m*

remind [rɪˈmaɪnd] *vt* ~ **s.o. of sth** : rappeler qqch à qqn — **reminder** [rɪˈmaɪndər] *n* : rappel *m*

reminisce [ˌrɛməˈnɪs] *vi* **-nisced; -niscing** : se rappeler le bon vieux temps — **reminiscent** [ˌrɛməˈnɪsənt] *adj* ~ **of** : qui rappelle, qui fait penser à

remission [rɪˈmɪʃən] *n* : rémission *f*

remit [rɪˈmɪt] *vt* **-mitted; -mitting** : envoyer (de l'argent)

remnant [ˈrɛmnənt] *n* 1 : reste *m*, restant *m* 2 TRACE : vestige *m*

remorse [rɪˈmɔrs] *n* : remords *m* — **remorseful** [rɪˈmɔrsfəl] *adj* : plein de remords

remote [rɪˈmoːt] *adj* **-moter; -est** 1 : lointain, éloigné 2 ALOOF : distant — **remote control** *n* : télécommande *f*

remove [rɪˈmuːv] *vt* **-moved; -moving** 1 : enlever, ôter 2 DISMISS : renvoyer 3 ELIMINATE : supprimer, dissiper — **removable** [rɪˈmuːvəbəl] *adj* : amovible — **removal** [rɪˈmuːvəl] *n* : élimination *f*

remunerate [rɪˈmjuːnəˌreɪt] *vt* **-ated; -ating** : rémunérer

render [ˈrɛndər] *vt* : rendre

rendition [rɛnˈdɪʃən] *n* : interprétation *f*

renegade [ˈrɛnɪˌgeɪd] *n* : renégat *m*, -gate *f*

renew [rɪˈnuː, -ˈnjuː] *vt* 1 : renouveler 2 RESUME : reprendre — **renewal** [rɪˈnuːəl, -ˈnjuː-] *n* : renouvellement *m*

renounce [rɪˈnaʊnts] *vt* **-nounced; -nouncing** : renoncer à

renovate [ˈrɛnəˌveɪt] *vt* **-vated; -vating** : rénover — **renovation** [ˌrɛnəˈveɪʃən] *n* : rénovation *f*

renown [rɪˈnaʊn] *n* : renommée *f*, renom *m* — **renowned** [rɪˈnaʊnd] *adj* : renommé, célèbre

rent [ˈrɛnt] *n* 1 : loyer *m* (somme d'argent) 2 **for** ~ : à louer — ~ *vt* : louer — **rental** [ˈrɛntəl] *n* : location *f* — ~ *adj* : de location — **renter** [ˈrɛntər] *n* : locataire *mf*

renunciation [rɪˌnʌntsiˈeɪʃən] *n* : renonciation *f*

reorganize [ˌriːˈɔrgəˌnaɪz] *vt* **-nized; -nizing** : réorganiser — **reorganization** [ˌriːˌɔrgənəˈzeɪʃən] *n* : réorganisation *f*

repair [rɪˈpær] *vt* : réparer — ~ *n* 1 : réparation *f* 2 **in bad** ~ : en mauvais état

repay [rɪˈpeɪ] *vt* **-paid; -paying** : rembourser (un emprunt), rendre (une faveur, etc.)

repeal [rɪˈpiːl] *vt* : abroger, révoquer — ~ *n* : abrogation *f*, révocation *f*

repeat [rɪˈpiːt] *vt* : répéter — ~ *n* 1 : répétition *f* 2 : rediffusion *f* (se dit d'une émission) — **repeatedly** [rɪˈpiːtədli] *adv* : à plusieurs reprises

repel [rɪˈpɛl] *vt* **-pelled; -pelling** : repousser — **repellent** [rɪˈpɛlənt] *adj* : repoussant

repent [rɪˈpɛnt] *vi* : se repentir — **repentance** [rɪˈpɛntənts] *n* : repentir *m*

repercussion [ˌriːpərˈkʌʃən, ˌrɛpər-] *n* : répercussion *f*

repertoire [ˈrɛpərˌtwɑr] *n* : répertoire *m*

repetition [ˌrɛpəˈtɪʃən] *n* : répétition *f* — **repetitious** [ˌrɛpəˈtɪʃəs] *adj* : répétitif — **repetitive** [rɪˈpɛtətɪv] *adj* : répétitif

replace [rɪˈpleɪs] *vt* **-placed; -placing** 1 : remettre (à sa place) 2 SUBSTITUTE : remplacer 3 EXCHANGE : échanger — **replacement** [rɪˈpleɪsmənt] *n* 1 : remplacement *m* 2 SUBSTITUTE : remplaçant *m*, -çante *f* 3 ~ **part** : pièce *f* de rechange

replenish [rɪˈplɛnɪʃ] *vt* 1 : réapprovisionner 2 : remplir (de nouveau)

replica [ˈrɛplɪkə] *n* : réplique *f*

reply [rɪˈplaɪ] *vi* **-plied; -plying** : répondre, répliquer — ~ *n, pl* **-plies** : réponse *f*, réplique *f*

report [rɪˈport] *n* 1 : rapport *m*, compte rendu *m* 2 *or* **news** ~ : reportage *m* 3 **weather** ~ : bulletin *m* (météorologique) — ~ *vt* 1 RELATE : raconter 2 ~ **an accident** : signaler un accident — *vi* ~ **to s.o.** : se présenter à qqn — **report card** *n* : bulletin *m* scolaire — **reporter** [rɪˈportər] *n* : journaliste *mf*, reporter *m*

reprehensible [ˌrɛprɪˈhɛntsəbəl] *adj* : répréhensible

represent [ˌrɛprɪˈzɛnt] *vt* : représenter — **representation** [ˌrɛprɪˌzɛnˈteɪʃən, -zən-] *n* : représentation *f* — **representative** [ˌrɛprɪˈzɛntətɪv] *adj* : représentatif — ~ *n* : représentant *m*, -tante *f*

repress [rɪˈprɛs] *vt* : réprimer — **repression** [rɪˈprɛʃən] *n* : répression *f*

reprieve [rɪˈpriːv] *n* : sursis *m*

reprimand ['rɛprə‚mænd] *n* : réprimande *f*
— ~ *vt* : réprimander

reprint [ri'prɪnt] *vt* : réimprimer — ~ ['ri:‚prɪnt, ri'prɪnt] *n* : réimpression *f*

reprisal [rɪ'praɪzəl] *n* : représailles *fpl*

reproach [rɪ'pro:tʃ] *n* **1** : reproche *m* **2 beyond** ~ : irréprochable — ~ *vt* : reprocher à — **reproachful** [rɪ'pro:tʃfəl] *adj* : de reproche

reproduce [‚ri:prə'du:s, -'dju:s] *v* **-duced; -ducing** *vt* : reproduire — *vi* : se reproduire — **reproduction** [‚ri:prə'dʌkʃən] *n* : reproduction *f*

reptile ['rɛp‚taɪl] *n* : reptile *m*

republic [rɪ'pʌblɪk] *n* : république *f* — **republican** [rɪ'pʌblɪkən] *n* : républicain *m*, -caine *f* — ~ *adj* : républicain

repudiate [rɪ'pju:di‚eɪt] *vt* **-ated; -ating** : répudier

repugnant [rɪ'pʌgnənt] *adj* : répugnant — **repugnance** [rɪ'pʌgnənts] *n* : répugnance *f*

repulse [rɪ'pʌls] *vt* **-pulsed; -pulsing** : repousser — **repulsive** [rɪ'pʌlsɪv] *adj* : repoussant

reputation [‚rɛpjə'teɪʃən] *n* : réputation *f* — **reputable** ['rɛpjətəbəl] *adj* : de bonne réputation — **reputed** [rɪ'pju:təd] *adj* : réputé

request [rɪ'kwɛst] *n* : demande *f* — ~ *vt* : demander

require [rɪ'kwaɪr] *vt* **-quired; -quiring 1** CALL FOR : requérir **2** NEED : avoir besoin de — **requirement** [rɪ'kwaɪrmənt] *n* **1** NEED : besoin *m* **2** DEMAND : exigence *f* — **requisite** ['rɛkwəzɪt] *adj* : nécessaire

resale ['ri:‚seɪl, ‚ri:'seɪl] *n* : revente *f*

rescind [rɪ'sɪnd] *vt* : annuler, abroger

rescue ['rɛs‚kju:] *vt* **-cued; -cuing** : sauver, secourir — ~ *n* : sauvetage *m* — **rescuer** ['rɛs‚kju:ər] *n* : sauveteur *m*, secouriste *mf*

research [rɪ'sərtʃ, 'ri:‚sərtʃ] *n* : recherches *fpl* — ~ *vt* : faire des recherches sur — **researcher** [rɪ'sərtʃər, 'ri:‚-] *n* : chercheur *m*, -cheuse *f*

resemble [rɪ'zɛmbəl] *vt* **-bled; -bling** : ressembler à — **resemblance** [rɪ'zɛmblənts] *n* : ressemblance *f*

resent [rɪ'zɛnt] *vt* : en vouloir à, s'offenser de — **resentful** [rɪ'zɛntfəl] *adj* : éprouver du ressentiment — **resentment** [rɪ'zɛntmənt] *n* : ressentiment *m*

reserve [rɪ'zərv] *vt* **-served; -serving** : réserver — ~ *n* : réserve *f* — **reservation** [‚rɛzər'veɪʃən] *n* **1** : réserve *f* (indienne) **2** RESERVING : réservation *f* — **reserved** [rɪ'zərvd] *adj* : réservé, discret — **reservoir** ['rɛzər‚vwar, -‚vwɔr, -‚vɔr] *n* : réservoir *m*

reset [‚ri:'sɛt] *vt* **-set; -setting** : remettre à l'heure (une montre), remettre à zéro (un compteur)

residence ['rɛzədənts] *n* : résidence *f* — **reside** [rɪ'zaɪd] *vi* **-sided; -siding** : résider — **resident** ['rɛzədənt] *adj* : résidant — ~ *n* : résident *m*, -dente *f* — **residential** [‚rɛzə'dɛntʃəl] *adj* : résidentiel

residue ['rɛzə‚du:, -‚dju:] *n* : résidu *m*

resign [rɪ'zaɪn] *vt* **1** QUIT : démissionner **2** ~ **oneself to** : se résigner à — **resignation** [‚rɛzɪg'neɪʃən] *n* **1** : démission *f* **2** ACCEPTANCE : résignation *f*

resilient [rɪ'zɪljənt] *adj* **1** : résistant **2** ELASTIC : élastique — **resilience** [rɪ'zɪljənts] *n* **1** : résistance *f* **2** ELASTICITY : élasticité *f*

resin ['rɛzən] *n* : résine *f*

resist [rɪ'zɪst] *vt* : résister à — **resistance** [rɪ'zɪstənts] *n* : résistance *f* — **resistant** [rɪ'zɪstənt] *adj* : résistant

resolve [rɪ'zalv] *vt* **-solved; -solving 1** : résoudre **2** ~ **to do** : décider de faire — ~ *n* : résolution *f*, détermination *f* — **resolution** [‚rɛzə'lu:ʃən] *n* : résolution *f* — **resolute** ['rɛzə‚lu:t] *adj* : résolu

resonance ['rɛzənənts] *n* : résonance *f* — **resonant** ['rɛzənənt] *adj* : résonant

resort [rɪ'zɔrt] *n* **1** : recours *m* **2** : centre *m* touristique, station *f* (de ski, etc.) — ~ *vi* ~ **to** : recourir à, avoir recours à

resound [rɪ'zaʊnd] *vi* : résonner, retentir — **resounding** [rɪ'zaʊndɪŋ] *adj* : retentissant

resource ['ri:‚sɔrs, ri'sɔrs] *n* : ressource *f* — **resourceful** [rɪ'sɔrsfəl, -'zɔrs-] *adj* : ingénieux, débrouillard

respect [rɪ'spɛkt] *n* **1** : respect *m* **2** ~**s** *npl* : respects *mpl*, hommages *mpl* **3 in** ~ **to** : en ce qui concerne **4 in some** ~**s** : à certains égards — ~ *vt* : respecter — **respectable** [rɪ'spɛktəbəl] *adj* : respectable — **respectful** [rɪ'spɛktfəl] *adj* : respectueux — **respective** [rɪ'spɛktɪv] *adj* : respectif — **respectively** [rɪ'spɛktɪvli] *adv* : respectivement

respiratory ['rɛspərə‚tori, rɪ'spaɪrə-] *adj* : respiratoire

respite ['rɛspɪt, rɪ'spaɪt] *n* : répit *m*, sursis *m*

response [rɪ'spants] *n* : réponse *f* — **respond** [rɪ'spand] *vi* : répondre — **responsibility** [rɪ‚spantsə'bɪləti] *n*, *pl* **-ties** : responsabilité *f* — **responsible** [rɪ'spantsəbəl] *adj* : responsable — **responsive** [rɪ'spantsɪv] *adj* : réceptif

rest¹ ['rɛst] *n* **1** : repos *m* **2** SUPPORT : appui *m* **3** : silence *m* (en musique) **4** ~ **area** : aire *f* de repos, halte *f* routière *Can* — ~ *vi* **1** : se reposer **2** LEAN : s'appuyer **3** ~ **on** DEPEND : dépendre de — *vt* **1** : reposer **2** LEAN : appuyer

rest² *n* REMAINDER : reste *m*

restaurant ['rɛstə‚rant, -rənt] *n* : restaurant *m*

restful ['rɛstfəl] *adj* : reposant, paisible

restless ['rɛstləs] *adj* : inquiet, agité
restore [rɪ'stor] *vt* **-stored; -storing 1** RETURN : retourner **2** REESTABLISH : rétablir **3** REPAIR : restaurer — **restoration** [ˌrɛstə'reɪʃən] *n* **1** : rétablissement *m* **2** REPAIR : restauration *f*
restrain [rɪ'streɪn] *vt* **1** : retenir **2** ~ **oneself** : se retenir — **restrained** [rɪ'streɪnd] *adj* : contenu, maîtrisé — **restraint** [rɪ'streɪnt] *n* **1** : restriction *f*, contrainte *f* **2** SELF-CONTROL : retenue *f*, maîtrise *f* de soi
restrict [rɪ'strɪkt] *vt* : restreindre — **restriction** [rɪ'strɪkʃən] *n* : restriction *f* — **restrictive** [rɪ'strɪktɪv] *adj* : restrictif
result [rɪ'zʌlt] *vi* **1** ~ **from** : résulter de **2** ~ **in** : avoir pour résultat — ~ *n* **1** : résultat *m* **2 as a** ~ **of** : à la suite de
resume [rɪ'zu:m] *v* **-sumed; -suming** : reprendre
résumé *or* **resume** *or* **resumé** ['rɛzəˌmeɪ, ˌrɛzə'-] *n* : curriculum vitæ
resumption [rɪ'zʌmpʃən] *n* : reprise *f*
resurgence [rɪ'sərdʒənts] *n* : réapparition *f*
resurrection [ˌrɛzə'rɛkʃən] *n* : résurrection *f* — **resurrect** [ˌrɛzə'rɛkt] *vt* : ressusciter
resuscitate [rɪ'sʌsəˌteɪt] *vt* **-tated; -tating** : réanimer
retail ['ri:ˌteɪl] *vt* : vendre au détail — ~ *n* : vente *f* au détail — ~ *adj* : de détail — ~ *adv* : au détail — **retailer** ['ri:ˌteɪlər] *n* : détaillant *m*, -lante *f*
retain [rɪ'teɪn] *vt* : retenir
retaliate [rɪ'tæliˌeɪt] *vi* **-ated; -ating** : riposter — **retaliation** [rɪˌtæli'eɪʃən] *n* : riposte *f*, représailles *fpl*
retarded [rɪ'tɑrdəd] *adj* : arriéré
retention [rɪ'tɛntʃən] *n* : rétention *f*
reticence ['rɛtəsənts] *n* : réticence *f* — **reticent** ['rɛtəsənt] *adj* : réticent, hésitant
retina ['rɛtənə] *n, pl* **-nas** *or* **-nae** [-ənˌi:, -ənˌaɪ] : rétine *f*
retire [rɪ'taɪr] *vi* **-tired; -tiring 1** WITHDRAW : se retirer **2** : prendre sa retraite **3** : aller se coucher — **retirement** [rɪ'taɪrmənt] *n* : retraite *f*
retort [rɪ'tɔrt] *vt* : rétorquer, riposter — ~ *n* : riposte *f*
retrace [ˌri:'treɪs] *vt* **-traced; -tracing** ~ **one's steps** : revenir sur ses pas
retract [rɪ'trækt] *vt* **1** WITHDRAW : retirer **2** : rentrer (ses griffes, etc.) — **retractable** [rɪ'træktəbəl] *adj* : escamotable
retrain [ˌri:'treɪn] *vt* : recycler
retreat [rɪ'tri:t] *n* **1** : retraite *f* **2** REFUGE : refuge *m* — ~ *vi* : se retirer, reculer
retribution [ˌrɛtrə'bju:ʃən] *n* : châtiment *m*
retrieve [rɪ'tri:v] *vt* **-trieved; -trieving** : retrouver, récupérer — **retrieval** [rɪ'tri:vəl] *n* : récupération *f*
retroactive [ˌrɛtro'æktɪv] *adj* : rétroactif

retrospect ['rɛtrəˌspɛkt] *n* **in** ~ : avec le recul — **retrospective** [ˌrɛtrə'spɛktɪv] *adj* : rétrospectif
return [rɪ'tərn] *vi* **1** : retourner, revenir **2** REAPPEAR : réapparaître — *vt* **1** : rapporter, rendre **2** YIELD : produire — ~ *n* **1** : retour *m* **2** YIELD : rapport *m*, rendement *m* **3 in** ~ **for** : en échange de **4** *or* **tax** ~ : déclaration *f* d'impôts — ~ *adj* : de retour
reunite [ˌri:ju'naɪt] *vt* **-nited; -niting** : réunir — **reunion** [ri'ju:njən] *n* : réunion *f*
revamp [ˌri:'væmp] *vt* : retaper (une maison), réviser (un texte)
reveal [rɪ'vi:l] *vt* **1** : révéler **2** SHOW : laisser voir
revel ['rɛvəl] *vi* **-eled** *or* **-elled; -eling** *or* **-elling** ~ **in** : se délecter de
revelation [ˌrɛvə'leɪʃən] *n* : révélation *f*
revelry ['rɛvəlri] *n, pl* **-ries** : festivités *fpl*, réjouissances *fpl*
revenge [rɪ'vɛndʒ] *vt* **-venged; -venging** : venger — ~ *n* **1** : vengeance *f* **2 take** ~ **on** : se venger sur
revenue ['rɛvəˌnu:, -ˌnju:] *n* : revenu *m*
reverberate [rɪ'vərbəˌreɪt] *vi* **-ated; -ating** : retentir, résonner
reverence ['rɛvərənts] *n* : révérence *f*, vénération *f* — **revere** [rɪ'vɪr] *vt* **-vered; -vering** : révérer, vénérer — **reverend** ['rɛvərənd] *adj* : révérend — **reverent** ['rɛvərənt] *adj* : respectueux
reverse [rɪ'vərs] *adj* : inverse, contraire — ~ *v* **-versed; -versing** *vt* **1** : inverser **2** CHANGE : renverser, annuler — *vi* : faire marche arrière (se dit d'une voiture) — ~ *n* **1** BACK : dos *m*, envers *m* **2** *or* ~ **gear** : marche *f* arrière **3 the** ~ : le contraire — **reversal** [rɪ'vərsəl] *n* **1** : renversement *m* **2** CHANGE : revirement *m* **3** SETBACK : revers *m* — **reversible** [rɪ'vərsəbəl] *adj* : réversible — **revert** [rɪ'vərt] *vi* ~ **to** : revenir à
review [rɪ'vju:] *n* **1** : révision *f* **2** OVERVIEW : résumé *m* **3** : critique *f* **4** : revue *f* (militaire) — ~ *vt* **1** EXAMINE : examiner **2** : repasser (une leçon) **3** : faire la critique de (un roman, etc.) — **reviewer** [rɪ'vju:ər] *n* : critique *mf*
revile [rɪ'vaɪl] *vt* **-viled; -viling** : injurier
revise [rɪ'vaɪz] *vt* **-vised; -vising 1** : réviser, corriger **2** : modifier (une politique) — **revision** [rɪ'vɪʒən] *n* : révision *f*
revive [rɪ'vaɪv] *v* **-vived; -viving** *vt* **1** : ranimer, raviver **2** : réanimer (une personne) **3** RESTORE : rétablir — *vi* COME TO : reprendre connaissance — **revival** [rɪ'vaɪvəl] *n* : renouveau *m*, renaissance *f*
revoke [rɪ'vo:k] *vt* **-voked; -voking** : révoquer
revolt [ri'vo:lt] *vt* : révolter, dégoûter — *vi* ~ **against** : se révolter contre — ~ *n* : ré-

volte *f*, insurrection *f* — **revolting** [rɪ-ˈvoːltɪŋ] *adj* : révoltant, dégoûtant

revolution [ˌrɛvəˈluːʃən] *n* : révolution *f* — **revolutionary** [ˌrɛvəˈluːʃənˌɛri] *adj* : révolutionnaire — **~** *n, pl* **-aries** : révolutionnaire *mf* — **revolutionize** [ˌrɛvəˈluːʃənˌaɪz] *vt* **-ized; -izing** : révolutionner

revolve [rɪˈvɑlv] *v* **-volved; -volving** *vt* : faire tourner — *vi* : tourner

revolver [rɪˈvɑlvər] *n* : revolver *m*

revulsion [rɪˈvʌlʃən] *n* : répugnance *f*

reward [rɪˈwɔrd] *vt* : récompenser — **~** *n* : récompense *f*

rewrite [ˌriːˈraɪt] *vt* **-wrote** [-ˈroːt]; **-written** [-ˈrɪtən]; **-writing** : récrire

rhetoric [ˈrɛt̬ərɪk] *n* : rhétorique *f* — **rhetorical** [rɪˈtɔrɪkəl] *adj* : rhétorique

rheumatism [ˈruːməˌtɪzəm, ˈrʊ-] *n* : rhumatisme *m*

rhino [ˈraɪˌnoː] *n, pl* **-no** *or* **-nos** → **rhinoceros** — **rhinoceros** [raɪˈnɑsərəs] *n, pl* **-noceros** *or* **-noceros** *or* **-noceri** [-ˌraɪ] : rhinocéros *m*

rhubarb [ˈruːˌbɑrb] *n* : rhubarbe *f*

rhyme [ˈraɪm] *n* **1** : rime *f* **2** VERSE : vers *m* — **~** *vi* **rhymed; rhyming** : rimer

rhythm [ˈrɪðəm] *n* : rythme *m* — **rhythmic** [ˈrɪðmɪk] *or* **rhythmical** [-mɪkəl] *adj* : rythmique

rib [ˈrɪb] *n* : côte *f* (en anatomie) — **~** *vt* **ribbed; ribbing** : taquiner

ribbon [ˈrɪbən] *n* : ruban *m*

rice [ˈraɪs] *n* : riz *m*

rich [ˈrɪtʃ] *adj* **1** : riche **2 ~ meal** : repas *m* lourd — **riches** [ˈrɪtʃəz] *npl* : richesses *fpl* — **richness** [ˈrɪtʃnəs] *n* : richesse *f*

rickety [ˈrɪkət̬i] *adj* : branlant

ricochet [ˈrɪkəˌʃeɪ] *n* : ricochet *m* — **~** *vi* **-cheted** [-ˌʃeɪd] *or* **-chetted** [-ˌʃɛt̬əd]; **-cheting** [-ˌʃeɪɪŋ] *or* **-chetting** [-ˌʃɛt̬ɪŋ] : ricocher

rid [ˈrɪd] *vt* **rid; ridding 1** : débarrasser **2 ~ oneself of** : se débarrasser de — **riddance** [ˈrɪdən̩ts] *n* **good ~!** : bon débarras!

riddle[1] [ˈrɪdəl] *n* : énigme *f*, devinette *f*

riddle[2] *vt* **-dled; -dling 1** : cribler **2 ~ with** : plein de

ride [ˈraɪd] *v* **rode** [ˈroːd]; **ridden** [ˈrɪdən]; **riding** *vt* **1** : monter (à cheval, à bicyclette), prendre (le bus, etc.) **2** TRAVEL : parcourir — *vi* **1** *or* **~ horseback** : monter à cheval **2** : aller (en auto, etc.) — **~** *n* **1** : tour *m*, promenade *f* **2** : manège *m* (à la foire) **3 give s.o. a ~** : conduire qqn en voiture — **rider** [ˈraɪdər] *n* **1** : cavalier *m*, -lière *f* **2** CYCLIST : cycliste *mf*, motocycliste *mf*

ridge [ˈrɪdʒ] *n* : chaîne *f* (de montagnes)

ridiculous [rəˈdɪkjələs] *adj* : ridicule — **ridicule** [ˈrɪdəˌkjuːl] *n* : ridicule *m*, dérision *f* — **~** *vt* **-culed; -culing** : ridiculiser

rife [ˈraɪf] *adj* **be ~ with** : être abondant en

rifle[1] [ˈraɪfəl] *vi* **-fled; -fling ~ through** : fouiller dans

rifle[2] *n* : carabine *f*, fusil *m*

rift [ˈrɪft] *n* **1** : fente *f*, fissure *f* **2** BREACH : désaccord *m*

rig[1] [ˈrɪg] *vt* : truquer (une élection)

rig[2] *vt* **rigged; rigging 1** : gréer (un navire) **2** EQUIP : équiper **3** *or* **~ out** DRESS : habiller **4** *or* **~ up** : bricoler — **~** *n* **1** : gréement *m* **2** *or* **oil ~** : plateforme *f* pétrolière — **rigging** [ˈrɪgɪŋ, -gən] *n* : gréement *m*

right [ˈraɪt] *adj* **1** JUST : bien, juste **2** CORRECT : exact **3** APPROPRIATE : convenable **4** STRAIGHT : droit **5 be ~** : avoir raison **6** → **right-hand** — **~** *n* **1** GOOD : bien *m* **2** ENTITLEMENT : droit *m* **3 on the ~** : à droite **4** *or* **~ side** : droite *f* — **~** *adv* **1** WELL : bien, comme il faut **2** EXACTLY : précisément **3** DIRECTLY : droit **4** IMMEDIATELY : tout de suite **5** COMPLETELY : tout à fait **6** *or* **to the ~** : à la droite — **~** *vt* **1** RESTORE : redresser **2 ~ a wrong** : réparer un tort — **right angle** *n* : angle *m* droit — **righteous** [ˈraɪtʃəs] *adj* : juste, droit — **rightful** [ˈraɪtʃəl] *adj* : légitime — **right-hand** [ˈraɪt-ˈhænd] *adj* **1** : du côté droit **2 ~ man** : bras *m* droit — **right-handed** [ˈraɪtˈhændəd] *adj* : droitier — **rightly** [ˈraɪtli] **1** : à juste titre **2** CORRECTLY : correctement — **right-of-way** [ˌraɪt̬əˈweɪ, -əv-] *n, pl* **rights-of-way** : priorité *f* (sur la route) — **right-wing** [ˈraɪtˈwɪŋ] *adj* : de droite (en politique)

rigid [ˈrɪdʒɪd] *adj* : rigide

rigor *or Brit* **rigour** [ˈrɪgər] *n* : rigueur *f* — **rigorous** [ˈrɪgərəs] *adj* : rigoureux

rim [ˈrɪm] *n* **1** EDGE : bord *m* **2** : jante *f* (d'une roue)

rind [ˈraɪnd] *n* : écorce *f* (de citron, etc.)

ring[1] [ˈrɪŋ] *v* **rang** [ˈræŋ]; **rung** [ˈrʌŋ]; **ringing** *vi* **1** : sonner **2** RESOUND : résonner — *vt* : sonner (une cloche, etc.) — **~** *n* **1** : son *m*, tintement *m* **2** CALL : coup *m* de téléphone

ring[2] *n* **1** : bague *f*, anneau *m* **2** CIRCLE : cercle *m* **3** *or* **boxing ~** : ring *m* (de boxe) **4** NETWORK : réseau *m* (clandestin) — **~** *vt* **ringed; ringing** : encercler — **ringleader** [ˈrɪŋˌliːdər] *n* : meneur *m*, -neuse *f*

rink [ˈrɪŋk] *n* : piste *f*, patinoire *f*

rinse [ˈrɪnts] *vt* **rinsed; rinsing** : rincer — **~** *n* : rinçage *m*

riot [ˈraɪət] *n* : émeute *f* — **~** *vi* : faire une émeute — **rioter** [ˈraɪət̬ər] *n* : émeutier *m*, -tière *f*

rip [ˈrɪp] *v* **ripped; ripping** *vt* **1** : déchirer **2 ~ off** : arracher — *vi* : se déchirer — **~** *n* : déchirure *f*

ripe [ˈraɪp] *adj* **riper; ripest** : mûr, prêt — **ripen** [ˈraɪpən] *v* : mûrir

ripple ['rɪpəl] v **-pled; -pling** vi : onduler (se dit de l'eau) — vt : rider — ~ n : ondulation f, ride f

rise ['raɪz] vi **rose** ['ro:z]; **risen** ['rɪzən]; **rising 1** : se lever (se dit d'une personne du soleil, etc.) **2** INCREASE : augmenter, monter **3** ~ **up** REBEL : se soulever (contre) — ~ n **1** ASCENT : montée f **2** INCREASE : augmentation f **3** INCLINE : pente f — **riser** ['raɪzər] n **1 early** ~ : lève-tôt mf **2 late** ~ : lève-tard mf

risk ['rɪsk] n : risque m — ~ vt : risquer — **risky** ['rɪski] adj **riskier; -est** : risqué, hasardeux

rite ['raɪt] n : rite m — **ritual** ['rɪtʃuəl] adj : rituel — ~ n : rituel m

rival ['raɪvəl] n : rival m, -vale f — ~ adj : rival — ~ vt **-valed** or **-valled; -valing** or **-valling** : rivaliser avec — **rivalry** ['raɪvəlri] n, pl **-ries** : rivalité f

river ['rɪvər] n : rivière f, fleuve m — ~ adj : fluvial

rivet ['rɪvət] n : rivet m — ~ vt **1** : river, fixer **2 be** ~**ed by** : être fasciné par

road ['ro:d] n **1** : route f **2** STREET : rue f **3** PATH : chemin m — **roadblock** ['ro:d,blak] n : barrage m routier — **roadside** ['ro:d-,saɪd] n : bord m de la route — **roadway** ['ro:d,weɪ] n : chaussée f

roam ['ro:m] vi : errer

roar ['ror] vi **1** : rugir **2** ~ **with laughter** : éclater de rire — vt : hurler — ~ n **1** : rugissement m **2** : grondement m (d'un avion, etc.)

roast ['ro:st] vt : rôtir (de la viande, etc.), griller (des noix, etc.) — ~ n : rôti m — **roast beef** n : rosbif m

rob ['rab] vt **robbed; robbing 1** : dévaliser (une banque), cambrioler (une maison) **2** STEAL : voler — **robber** ['rabər] n : voleur m, -leuse f — **robbery** ['rabəri] n, pl **-beries** : vol m

robe ['ro:b] n **1** : toge f (d'un juge) **2** → **bathrobe**

robin ['rabən] n : rouge-gorge m

robot ['ro:,bat, -bət] n : robot m

robust [ro'bʌst, 'ro:,bʌst] adj : robuste

rock[1] ['rak] vt **1** : bercer (un enfant), balancer (un berceau) **2** SHAKE : secouer — vi : se balancer — ~ n or ~ **music** : musique f rock

rock[2] n **1** : roche f, roc m **2** BOULDER : rocher m **3** STONE : pierre f

rocket ['rakət] n : fusée f

rocking chair n : fauteuil m à bascule

rocky ['raki] adj **rockier; -est 1** : rocheux **2** SHAKY : précaire

rod ['rad] n **1** : baguette f (de bois), tige f (de métal) **2** or **fishing** ~ : canne f à pêche

rode → **ride**

rodent ['ro:dənt] n : rongeur m

rodeo ['ro:di,o:, ro'deɪ,o:] n, pl **-deos** : rodéo m

roe ['ro:] n : œufs mpl de poisson

roe deer n : chevreuil m

role ['ro:l] n : rôle m

roll ['ro:l] n **1** : rouleau m **2** LIST : liste f **3** BUN : petit pain m **4** : roulement m (de tambour) — ~ vt **1** : rouler **2** ~ **down** : baisser **3** ~ **out** : dérouler **4** ~ **up** : retrousser (ses manches) — vi **1** : (se) rouler **2** ~ **over** : se retourner — **roller** ['ro:lər] n : rouleau m — **roller coaster** ['ro:lər,ko:stər] n : montagnes fpl russes — **roller-skate** ['ro:lər,skeɪt] vi **-skated; -skating** : faire du patin à roulettes — **roller skates** npl : patins mpl à roulettes

Roman ['ro:mən] adj : romain — **Roman Catholic** adj : catholique

romance [ro'mænts, 'ro:,mænts] n **1** : roman m d'amour **2** AFFAIR : liaison f amoureuse

romantic [ro'mæntɪk] adj : romantique

roof ['ru:f, 'ruf] n, pl **roofs** ['ru:fs, 'rufs, 'ru:vz, 'ruvz] **1** : toit m **2** ~ **of the mouth** : palais m — **roofing** ['ru:fɪŋ, 'rufɪŋ] n : toiture f — **rooftop** ['ru:f,tap, 'ruf-] n → **roof**

rook ['ruk] n : tour f (aux échecs)

rookie ['ruki] n : novice mf

room ['ru:m, 'rum] n **1** : chambre f (à coucher), salle f (de conférence) **2** SPACE : espace m **3** OPPORTUNITY : possibilité f — **roommate** ['ru:m,meɪt, 'rum-] n : camarade mf de chambre — **roomy** ['ru:mi, 'rumi] adj **roomier; -est** : spacieux

roost ['ru:st] n : perchoir m — ~ vi : se percher — **rooster** ['ru:stər, 'rus-] n : coq m

root[1] ['ru:t, 'rut] n **1** : racine f **2** SOURCE : origine f **3** CORE : fond m, cœur m — vt ~ **out** : extirper

root[2] vi ~ **for** SUPPORT : encourager

rope ['ro:p] n : corde f — ~ vt **roped; roping 1** : attacher (avec une corde) **2** ~ **off** : interdire l'accès à

rosary ['ro:zəri] n, pl **-ries** : chapelet m

rose[1] → **rise**

rose[2] ['ro:z] n : rose f (fleur), rose m (couleur) — **rosebush** ['ro:z,buʃ] n : rosier m

rosemary ['ro:z,mɛri] n, pl **-maries** : romarin m

Rosh Hashanah [,raʃha'ʃanə, ,ro:ʃ-] n : le Nouvel An juif

rostrum ['rastrəm] n, pl **-tra** [-trə] or **-trums** : tribune f

rosy ['ro:zi] adj **rosier; -est 1** : rose, rosé **2** PROMISING : prometteur

rot ['rat] v **rotted; rotting** : pourrir — ~ n : pourriture f

rotary ['ro:təri] adj : rotatif — ~ n : rond-point m

rotate ['ro:ˌteɪt] v **-tated; -tating** vi : tourner
— vt **1** : tourner **2** ALTERNATE : faire à tour
de rôle — **rotation** [ro'teɪʃən] n : rotation f
rote ['ro:t] n **by ~** : par cœur
rotten ['ratən] adj **1** : pourri **2** BAD : mauvais
rouge ['ru:ʒ] n : rouge m à joues
rough ['rʌf] adj **1** COARSE : rugueux **2**
RUGGED : accidenté **3** CHOPPY : agité **4**
DIFFICULT : difficile **5** FORCEFUL : brusque
6 APPROXIMATE : approximatif **7 ~ draft**
: brouillon m — **~** vt **1** → **roughen 2 ~**
up BEAT : tabasser fam — **roughage**
['rʌfɪʤ] n : fibres mpl alimentaires —
roughen ['rʌfən] vt : rendre rugueux —
roughly ['rʌfli] adv **1** : rudement **2** ABOUT
: environ — **roughness** ['rʌfnəs] n : ru-
gosité f
roulette [ˌru:'lɛt] n : roulette f
round ['raʊnd] adj : rond — **~** adv →
around — **~** n **1** : série f (de négociations, etc.) **2** : manche f (d'un match) **3 ~**
of applause : salve f d'applaudissements
4 ~s npl : visites fpl (d'un médecin, etc.),
rondes fpl (d'un policier, etc.) — **~** vt **1**
TURN : tourner **2 ~ off** : arrondir **3 ~ off**
or **~ out** COMPLETE : compléter **4 ~ up**
GATHER : rassembler — **~** prep → **around**
— **roundabout** ['raʊndəˌbaʊt] adj : indirect — **round–trip** ['raʊndˌtrɪp] n : voyage
m aller et retour — **roundup** ['raʊndˌʌp] n
: rassemblement m
rouse ['raʊz] vt **roused; rousing 1** AWAKEN
: réveiller **2** EXCITE : susciter
rout ['raʊt] n : déroute f — **~** vt : mettre en
déroute
route ['ru:t, 'raʊt] n **1** : route f **2** or **deliv-**
ery ~ : tournée f de livraison
routine [ru:'ti:n] n : routine f — **~** adj : routinier
row[1] ['ro:] vi : ramer
row[2] ['ro:] n **1** : file f (de gens), rangée f (de
maisons, etc.) **2 in a ~** SUCCESSIVELY : de
suite
row[3] ['raʊ] n **1** RACKET : vacarme m **2**
QUARREL : dispute f
rowboat ['ro:ˌbo:t] n : bateau m à rames
rowdy ['raʊdi] adj **-dier; -est** : tapageur
royal ['rɔɪəl] adj : royal — **royalty** ['rɔɪəlti] n,
pl **-ties 1** : royauté f **2 royalties** npl : droits
mpl d'auteur
rub ['rʌb] v **rubbed; rubbing** vt **1** : frotter **2**
~ in : faire pénétrer — vi **1 ~ against**
: frotter contre **2 ~ off** : enlever (en frot-
tant) — **~** n : friction f, massage m
rubber ['rʌbər] n : caoutchouc m — **rubber**
band n : élastique m — **rubber stamp** n
: tampon m (de caoutchouc) — **rubbery**
['rʌbəri] adj : caoutchouteux

rubbish ['rʌbɪʃ] n **1** : ordures fpl, déchets
mpl **2** NONSENSE : bêtises fpl
rubble ['rʌbəl] n : décombres mpl
ruby ['ru:bi] n, pl **-bies** : rubis m
rudder ['rʌdər] n : gouvernail m
ruddy ['rʌdi] adj **-dier; -est** : rougeaud
rude ['ru:d] adj **ruder; rudest 1** IMPOLITE
: grossier **2** ABRUPT : brusque — **rudely**
['ru:dli] adv : grossièrement — **rudeness**
['ru:dnəs] n : manque m d'éducation
rudiment ['ru:dəmənt] n : rudiment m —
rudimentary [ˌru:də'mɛntəri] adj : rudimentaire
ruffle ['rʌfəl] vt **-fled; -fling 1** : ébouriffer
(ses cheveux), hérisser (ses plumes) **2** VEX
: contrarier — **~** n : volant m (d'une jupe,
etc.)
rug ['rʌg] n : tapis m, carpette f
rugged ['rʌgəd] adj **1** : accidenté (se dit
d'un terrain), escarpé (se dit d'une montagne) **2** STURDY : robuste
ruin ['ru:ən] n : ruine f — **~** vt : ruiner
rule ['ru:l] n **1** : règle f, règlement m **2** CON-
TROL : autorité f **3 as a ~** : en général —
~ v **ruled; ruling** vt **1** GOVERN : gouverner **2** : juger, décider (d'un juge) **3 ~**
out : écarter — vi : gouverner, régner —
ruler ['ru:lər] n **1** : dirigeant m, -geante f;
souverain m, -raine f **2** : règle f (pour
mesurer) — **ruling** ['ru:lɪŋ] n VERDICT : décision f
rum ['rʌm] n : rhum m
rumble ['rʌmbəl] vi **-bled; -bling 1** : gronder **2** : gargouiller (se dit de l'estomac) —
~ n : grondement m
rummage ['rʌmɪʤ] vi **-maged; -maging ~**
in : fouiller dans
rumor or Brit **rumour** ['ru:mər] n : rumeur f
— **~** vt **be ~ed that** : il paraît que
rump ['rʌmp] n **1** : croupe f (d'un animal)
2 or **~ steak** : romsteck m
run ['rʌn] v **ran** ['ræn]; **run; running** vi **1**
: courir **2** FUNCTION : marcher **3** LAST
: durer **4** : déteindre (se dit des couleurs) **5**
EXTEND : passer (se dit d'un câble) **6** : se
présenter (comme candidat) **7 ~ away**
: s'enfuir **8 ~ into** ENCOUNTER : rencontrer **9 ~ into** HIT : heurter **10 ~ late**
: être en retard **11 ~ out of** : manquer de
12 ~ over : écraser — vt **1** : courir **2** OP-
ERATE : faire marcher **3** : faire couler (de
l'eau) **4** MANAGE : diriger **5 ~ a fever**
: faire de la température — **~** n **1** : course
f **2** TRIP : tour m, excursion f **3** SERIES
: série f **4 in the long ~** : à la longue —
runaway ['rʌnəˌweɪ] n : fugitif m, -tive f —
~ adj : fugueur — **rundown** ['rʌnˌdaʊn] n
: résumé m — **run–down** ['rʌn'daʊn] adj **1**
: délabré **2** EXHAUSTED : fatigué
rung[1] → **ring**[1]

rung[2] [ˈrʌŋ] *n* : barreau *m* (d'une échelle, etc.)

runner [ˈrʌnər] *n* : coureur *m*, -reuse *f* — **runner–up** [ˌrʌnərˈʌp] *n*, *pl* **runners–up** : second *m*, -conde *f* — **running** [ˈrʌnɪŋ] *adj* 1 FLOWING : courant 2 CONTINUOUS : continuel 3 CONSECUTIVE : de suite

runway [ˈrʌnˌweɪ] *n* : piste *f* (d'envol ou d'atterrissage)

rupture [ˈrʌptʃər] *n* : rupture *f* — ~ *v* **-tured; -turing** *vt* : rompre — *vi* : se rompre

rural [ˈrʊrəl] *adj* : rural

ruse [ˈruːs, ˈruːz] *n* : ruse *f*, stratagème *m*

rush[1] [ˈrʌʃ] *n* 1 : jonc *m* (plante) 2 **in a ~** : pressé

rush[2] *vi* : se précipiter — *vt* 1 : presser, bousculer 2 ATTACK : prendre d'assaut 3 : transporter d'urgence (à l'hôpital, etc.) — ~ *n* 1 : hâte *f*, empressement *m* 2 : bouffée *f* (d'air), torrent *m* (d'eau) — **rush hour** *n* : heure *f* de pointe

russet [ˈrʌsət] *adj* : roux

Russian [ˈrʌʃən] *adj* : russe — ~ *n* : russe (langue)

rust [ˈrʌst] *n* : rouille *f* — ~ *vi* : se rouiller — *vt* : rouiller

rustic [ˈrʌstɪk] *adj* : rustique, champêtre

rustle [ˈrʌsəl] *vi* **-tled; -tling** bruire — ~ *n* : bruissement *m*

rusty [ˈrʌsti] *adj* **rustier; -est** : rouillé

rut [ˈrʌt] *n* 1 : ornière *f* 2 **be in a ~** : s'enliser dans une routine

ruthless [ˈruːθləs] *adj* : impitoyable, cruel

rye [ˈraɪ] *n* : seigle *m*

S

s [ˈɛs] *n*, *pl* **s's** *or* **ss** [ˈɛsəz] : s *m*, dix-neuvième lettre de l'alphabet

Sabbath [ˈsæbəθ] *n* 1 : sabbat *m* (judaïsme) 2 : dimanche *m* (christianisme)

sabotage [ˈsæbəˌtɑːʒ] *n* : sabotage *m* — ~ *vt* **-taged; -taging** : saboter

sack [ˈsæk] *n* : sac *m* — ~ *vt* 1 FIRE : virer *fam* 2 PLUNDER : saccager

sacred [ˈseɪkrəd] *adj* : sacré

sacrifice [ˈsækrəˌfaɪs] *n* : sacrifice *m* — ~ *vt* **-ficed; -ficing** : sacrifier

sad [ˈsæd] *adj* **sadder; saddest** : triste — **sadden** [ˈsædən] *vt* : attrister

saddle [ˈsædəl] *n* : selle *f* — ~ *vt* **-dled; -dling** : seller

sadistic [səˈdɪstɪk] *adj* : sadique

sadness [ˈsædnəs] *n* : tristesse *f*

safari [səˈfɑri, -ˈfær-] *n* : safari *m*

safe [ˈseɪf] *adj* **safer; safest** 1 : sûr 2 UNHARMED : en sécurité 3 CAREFUL : prudent 4 **~ and sound** : sain et sauf — ~ *n* : coffre-fort *m* — **safeguard** [ˈseɪfˌgɑrd] *n* : sauvegarde *f* — ~ *vt* : sauvegarder — **safely** [ˈseɪfli] *adv* 1 : sûrement 2 **arrive ~** : bien arriver — **safety** [ˈseɪfti] *n*, *pl* **-ties** : sécurité *f* — **safety belt** *n* : ceinture *f* de sécurité — **safety pin** *n* : épingle *f* de sûreté

sag [ˈsæg] *vi* **sagged; sagging** : s'affaisser

sage[1] [ˈseɪdʒ] *n* : sauge *f* (plante)

sage[2] *n* : sage *m*

said → **say**

sail [ˈseɪl] *n* 1 : voile *f* (d'un bateau) 2 **go for a ~** : faire un tour en bateau 3 **set ~** : prendre la mer — ~ *vi* : naviguer — *vt* 1 : manœuvrer (un bateau) 2 **~ the seas** : parcourir les mers — **sailboat** [ˈseɪlˌboːt] *n* : voilier *m* — **sailor** [ˈseɪlər] *n* : marin *m*, matelot *m*

saint [ˈseɪnt, *before a name* ˌseɪnt *or* sənt] *n* : saint *m*, sainte *f*

sake [ˈseɪk] *n* 1 **for goodness' ~!** : pour l'amour de Dieu! 2 **for the ~ of** : pour le bien de

salad [ˈsæləd] *n* : salade *f*

salary [ˈsæləri] *n*, *pl* **-ries** : salaire *m*

sale [ˈseɪl] *n* 1 : vente *f* 2 **for ~** : à vendre 3 **on ~** : en solde — **salesman** [ˈseɪlzmən] *n*, *pl* **-men** [-mən, -ˌmɛn] : vendeur *m*, représentant *m* — **saleswoman** [ˈseɪlzˌwʊmən] *n*, *pl* **-women** [-ˌwɪmən] : vendeuse *f*, représentante *f*

salient [ˈseɪljənt] *adj* : saillant

saliva [səˈlaɪvə] *n* : salive *f*

salmon [ˈsæmən] *ns & pl* : saumon *m*

salon [səˈlɑn, ˈsæˌlɑn] *n* : salon *m*

saloon [səˈluːn] *n* : bar *m*

salt [ˈsɔlt] *n* : sel *m* — ~ *vt* : saler — **saltwater** [ˈsɔltˌwɔtər, -ˌwɑ-] *adj* : de mer — **salty** [ˈsɔlti] *adj* **saltier; -est** : salé

salute [səˈluːt] *vt* **-luted; -luting** : saluer — ~ *n* : salut *m*

salvage [ˈsælvɪdʒ] *vt* **-vaged; -vaging** : sauver, récupérer

salvation [sælˈveɪʃən] *n* : salut *m*

salve [ˈsæv, ˈsav] *n* : onguent *m*, pommade *f*

same [ˈseɪm] *adj* 1 : même 2 **be the ~ (as)** : être comme 3 **the ~ thing (as)** : la même chose (que) — ~ *pron* 1 **all the ~** : pareil

2 the ~ : le même — ~ *adv* the ~ : pareil

sample ['sæmpəl] *n* : échantillon *m* — ~ *vt* **-pled; -pling** : essayer

sanctify ['sæŋktə,faɪ] *vt* **-fied; -fying** : sanctifier

sanction ['sæŋkʃən] *n* : sanction *f* — ~ *vt* : sanctionner

sanctuary ['sæŋktʃu,ɛri] *n, pl* **-aries** : sanctuaire *m*

sand ['sænd] *n* : sable *m* — ~ *vt* **1** : sabler (une route) **2** : poncer (du bois)

sandal ['sændəl] *n* : sandale *f*

sandpaper ['sænd,peɪpər] *n* : papier *m* de verre — ~ *vt* : poncer

sandwich ['sænd,wɪtʃ] *n* : sandwich *m* — ~ *vt* ~ **between** : mettre entre

sandy ['sændi] *adj* **sandier; -est** : sablonneux

sane ['seɪn] *adj* **saner; -est 1** : sain d'esprit **2** SENSIBLE : raisonnable

sang → **sing**

sanitary ['sænəteri] *adj* **1** : sanitaire **2** HYGIENIC : hygiénique — **sanitary napkin** *n* : serviette *f* hygiénique — **sanitation** [,sænə'teɪʃən] *n* : système *m* sanitaire

sanity ['sænəti] *n* : équilibre *m* mental

sank → **sink**

Santa Claus ['sæntə,klɔz] *n* : père *m* Noël

sap[1] ['sæp] *n* : sève *f* (d'un arbre)

sap[2] *vt* **sapped; sapping** : saper, miner

sapphire ['sæ,faɪr] *n* : saphir *m*

sarcasm ['sɑr,kæzəm] *n* : sarcasme *m* — **sarcastic** [sɑr'kæstɪk] *adj* : sarcastique

sardine [sɑr'di:n] *n* : sardine *f*

sash ['sæʃ] *n* : large ceinture *f* (d'une robe), écharpe *f* (d'un uniforme)

sat → **sit**

satellite ['sætə,laɪt] *n* : satellite *m*

satin ['sætən] *n* : satin *m*

satire ['sæ,taɪr] *n* : satire *f* — **satiric** [sə-'tɪrɪk] *or* **satirical** [-ɪkəl] *adj* : satirique

satisfaction [,sætəs'fækʃən] *n* : satisfaction *f* — **satisfactory** [,sætəs'fæktəri] *adj* : satisfaisant — **satisfy** ['sætəs,faɪ] *vt* **-fied; -fying** : satisfaire — **satisfying** ['sætəs-,faɪɪŋ] *adj* : satisfaisant

saturate ['sætʃə,reɪt] *vt* **-rated; -rating 1** : saturer **2** DRENCH : tremper

Saturday ['sætər,deɪ, -di] *n* : samedi *m*

Saturn ['sætərn] *n* : Saturne *f*

sauce ['sɔs] *n* : sauce *f* — **saucepan** ['sɔs,pæn] *n* : casserole *f* — **saucer** ['sɔsər] *n* : soucoupe *f*

Saudi ['saʊdi] *or* **Saudi Arabian** ['saʊdə-'reɪbiən] *adj* : saoudien

sauna ['sɔnə, 'saʊnə] *n* : sauna *m*

saunter ['sɔntər, 'sɑn-] *vi* : se promener

sausage ['sɔsɪdʒ] *n* : saucisse *f* (crue), saucisson *m* (cuit)

sauté [sɔ'teɪ, so:-] *vt* **-téed** *or* **-téd; -téing** : faire revenir

savage ['sævɪdʒ] *adj* : sauvage, féroce — ~ *n* : sauvage *mf* — **savagery** ['sævɪdʒri, -dʒəri] *n, pl* **-ries** : férocité *f*

save ['seɪv] *vt* **saved; saving 1** RESCUE : sauver **2** RESERVE : garder **3** : gagner (du temps), économiser (de l'argent) **4** : sauvegarder (en informatique) — ~ *prep* EXCEPT : sauf

savior ['seɪvjər] *n* : sauveur *m*

savor ['seɪvər] *vt* : savourer — **savory** ['seɪvəri] *adj* : savoureux

saw[1] → **see**

saw[2] ['sɔ] *n* : scie *f* — ~ *vt* **sawed; sawed** *or* **sawn** ['sɔn]; **sawing** : scier — **sawdust** ['sɔ,dʌst] *n* : sciure *f* — **sawmill** ['sɔ,mɪl] *n* : scierie *f*

saxophone ['sæksə,fo:n] *n* : saxophone *m*

say ['seɪ] *v* **said** ['sɛd]; **saying; says** ['sɛz] *vt* **1** : dire **2** INDICATE : indiquer (se dit d'une montre, etc.) — *vi* **1** : dire **2 that is to** ~ : c'est-à-dire — ~ *n, pl* **says** ['seɪz] **1 have no** ~ : ne pas avoir son mot à dire **2 have one's** ~ : dire son mot — **saying** ['seɪɪŋ] *n* : dicton *m*

scab ['skæb] *n* **1** : croûte *f*, gale *f* *Can* **2** STRIKEBREAKER : jaune *mf*

scaffold ['skæfəld, -,fo:ld] *n* : échafaudage *m* (en construction)

scald ['skɔld] *vt* : ébouillanter

scale[1] ['skeɪl] *n* : pèse-personne *m*, balance *f*

scale[2] *n* : écaille *f* (d'un poisson, etc.) — ~ *vt* **scaled; scaling** : écailler

scale[3] *n* : gamme *f* (en musique), échelle *f* (salariale)

scallion ['skæljən] *n* : ciboule *f*, échalote *f*

scallop ['skɑləp, 'skæ-] *n* : coquille *f* Saint-Jacques

scalp ['skælp] *n* : cuir *m* chevelu

scam ['skæm] *n* : escroquerie *f*

scan ['skæn] *vt* **scanned; scanning 1** EXAMINE : scruter **2** SKIM : lire attentivement **3** : balayer (en informatique)

scandal ['skændəl] *n* : scandale *m* — **scandalous** ['skændələs] *adj* : scandaleux

Scandinavian [,skændə'neɪviən] *adj* : scandinave

scant ['skænt] *adj* : insuffisant

scapegoat ['skeɪp,go:t] *n* : bouc *m* émissaire

scar ['skɑr] *n* : cicatrice *f* — ~ *v* **scarred; scarring** *vt* : laisser une cicatrice sur — *vi* : se cicatriser

scarce ['skɛrs] *adj* **scarcer; scarcest** : rare — **scarcely** ['skɛrsli] *adv* : à peine — **scarcity** ['skɛrsəti] *n, pl* **-ties** : pénurie *f*

scare ['skɛr] *vt* **scared; scaring 1** : faire peur à **2 be** ~**d of** : avoir peur de — ~ *n* **1** FRIGHT : peur *f* **2** PANIC : panique *f* — **scarecrow** ['skɛr,kro:] *n* : épouvantail *m* scarf [ˈskɑrf] n, pl scarves [ˈskɑrvz] or scarfs : écharpe f, foulard m

scarlet [ˈskɑrlət] adj : écarlate — scarlet fever n : scarlatine f

scary [ˈskɛri] adj scarier, -est : qui fait peur

scathing [ˈskeɪðɪŋ] adj : cinglant

scatter [ˈskæt̬ər] vt 1 STREW : éparpiller 2 DISPERSE : disperser — vi : se disperser

scavenger [ˈskævəndʒər] n : charognard m, -gnarde f

scenario [səˈnæriˌoː, -ˈnɑr-] n, pl -ios : scénario m

scene [ˈsiːn] n 1 : scène f 2 behind the ~s : dans les coulisses — scenery [ˈsiːnəri] n, pl -eries 1 : décor m 2 LANDSCAPE : paysages mpl — scenic [ˈsiːnɪk] adj : pittoresque

scent [ˈsɛnt] n 1 : arôme m 2 PERFUME : parfum m 3 TRAIL : piste f — scented [ˈsɛnt̬əd] adj : parfumé

sceptic [ˈskɛptɪk] → skeptic

schedule [ˈskɛˌdʒuːl, -dʒəl, esp Brit ˈʃedˌjuːl] n 1 : programme m 2 TIMETABLE : horaire m 3 behind ~ : en retard 4 on ~ : à l'heure — vt -uled; -uling : prévoir

scheme [ˈskiːm] n 1 PLAN : plan m 2 PLOT : intrigue f — vi schemed; scheming : conspirer

schizophrenia [ˌskɪtsəˈfriːniə, ˌskɪzə-, -ˈfriː-] n : schizophrénie f

scholar [ˈskɑlər] n : savant m, -vante f; érudit m, -dite f — scholarship [ˈskɑlərˌʃɪp] n : bourse f

school¹ [ˈskuːl] n : banc m (de poissons)

school² n 1 : école f, lycée m 2 COLLEGE : université f 3 DEPARTMENT : faculté f — ~ vt : instruire — schoolboy [ˈskuːlˌbɔɪ] n : écolier m — schoolgirl [ˈskuːlˌgərl] n : écolière f

science [ˈsaɪənts] n : science f — scientific [ˌsaɪənˈtɪfɪk] adj : scientifique — scientist [ˈsaɪənt̬ɪst] n : scientifique mf

scissors [ˈsɪzərz] npl : ciseaux mpl

scoff [ˈskɑf] vi ~ at : se moquer de

scold [ˈskoːld] vt : gronder, réprimander

scoop [ˈskuːp] n 1 : pelle f 2 : exclusivité f (en journalisme) — ~ vt 1 : enlever (avec une pelle) 2 ~ out : évider 3 ~ up : ramasser

scooter [ˈskuːt̬ər] n 1 : trottinette f 2 or motor ~ : scooter m

scope [ˈskoːp] n 1 RANGE : étendue f, portée f 2 OPPORTUNITY : possibilités fpl

scorch [ˈskɔrtʃ] vt : roussir

score [ˈskor] n, pl scores 1 : score m, pointage m Can (aux sports) 2 RATING : note f, résultat m 3 : partition f (en musique) 4 keep ~ : marquer les points — ~ vt scored; scoring 1 : marquer (un point) 2 : obtenir (une note)

scorn [ˈskɔrn] n : mépris m, dédain m — ~ vt : mépriser, dédaigner — scornful [ˈskɔrnfəl] adj : méprisant

scorpion [ˈskɔrpiən] n : scorpion m

scotch [ˈskɑtʃ] n or ~ whiskey : scotch m — Scottish [ˈskɑt̬əʃ] adj : écossais

scoundrel [ˈskaʊndrəl] n : chenapan m

scour [ˈskaʊər] vt 1 SCRUB : récurer 2 SEARCH : parcourir

scourge [ˈskərdʒ] n : fléau m

scout [ˈskaʊt] n : éclaireur m, -reuse f; scout m, scoute f

scowl [ˈskaʊl] vi : faire la grimace — ~ n : air m renfrogné

scram [ˈskræm] vi scrammed; scramming : filer fam

scramble [ˈskræmbəl] vt -bled; -bling : brouiller, mêler — ~ n : bousculade f, ruée f — scrambled eggs npl : œufs mpl brouillés

scrap [ˈskræp] n 1 PIECE : bout m 2 or ~ metal : ferraille f 3 ~s npl LEFTOVERS : restes mpl — ~ vt scrapped; scrapping : mettre au rebut

scrapbook [ˈskræpˌbʊk] n : album m de coupures de journaux

scrape [ˈskreɪp] v scraped; scraping vt 1 : racler 2 : s'écorcher (le genou, etc.) 3 or ~ off : enlever en grattant — vi 1 ~ against : érafler 2 ~ by : se débrouiller — ~ n 1 : éraflure f 2 PREDICAMENT : pétrin m fam — scraper [ˈskreɪpər] n : grattoir m

scratch [ˈskrætʃ] vt 1 : égratigner 2 MARK : rayer 3 : se gratter (la tête, etc.) 4 ~ out : biffer — ~ n 1 : éraflure f, égratignure f 2 from ~ : à partir de zéro

scrawny [ˈskrɔni] adj -nier; -niest : maigre

scream [ˈskriːm] vi : hurler, crier — ~ n : hurlement m, cri m

screech [ˈskriːtʃ] n 1 : cri m perçant 2 : crissement m (de pneus, etc.) — ~ vi 1 : pousser un cri 2 : crisser (se dit des pneus, etc.)

screen [ˈskriːn] n 1 : écran m (de télévision, etc.) 2 PARTITION : paravent m 3 or window ~ : moustiquaire f — ~ vt 1 SHIELD : protéger 2 HIDE : cacher 3 EXAMINE : passer au crible

screw [ˈskruː] n : vis f — ~ vt 1 : visser 2 ~ up RUIN : bousiller — screwdriver [ˈskruːˌdraɪvər] n : tournevis m

scribble [ˈskrɪbəl] v -bled; -bling : gribouiller, griffonner — ~ n : gribouillage m

script [ˈskrɪpt] n : scénario m (d'un film, etc.)

scroll [ˈskroːl] n : rouleau m (de parchemin) — ~ vi : défiler (en informatique)

scrub [ˈskrʌb] vt scrubbed; scrubbing SCOUR : récurer — ~ n : nettoyage m

scruple [ˈskruːpəl] n : scrupule m — scrupulous [ˈskruːpjələs] adj : scrupuleux

scrutiny ['skru:təni] *n, pl* **-nies** : analyse *f* attentive

scuffle ['skʌfəl] *n* : bagarre *f*

sculpture ['skʌlptʃər] *n* : sculpture *f* — **sculptor** ['skʌlptər] *n* : sculpteur *m*

scum ['skʌm] *n* : écume *f*

scurry ['skəri] *vi* **-ried; -rying** : se précipiter

scuttle ['skʌtəl] *vt* **-tled; -tling** : saborder (un navire)

scythe ['saɪð] *n* : faux *f*

sea ['si:] *n* **1** : mer *f* **2 at** ~ : en mer — ~ *adj* : de mer — **seafood** ['si:,fu:d] *n* : fruits *mpl* de mer — **seagull** ['si:,gʌl] *n* : mouette *f*

seal[1] ['si:l] *n* : phoque *m*

seal[2] *n* **1** STAMP : sceau *m* **2** CLOSURE : fermeture *f* (hermétique) — ~ *vt* : sceller, cacheter

seam ['si:m] *n* : couture *f*

search ['sərtʃ] *vt* : fouiller — *vi* ~ **for** : chercher — ~ *n* **1** : recherche *f* **2** EXAMINATION : fouille *f*

seashell ['si:,ʃɛl] *n* : coquillage *m* — **seashore** ['si:,ʃor] *n* : bord *m* de la mer — **seasick** ['si:,sɪk] *adj* **be** ~ : avoir le mal de mer — **seasickness** ['si:,sɪknəs] *n* : mal *m* de mer

season ['si:zən] *n* : saison *f* — ~ *vt* : assaisonner, épicer — **seasonal** ['si:zənəl] *adj* : saisonnier — **seasoned** ['si:zənd] *adj* : expérimenté — **seasoning** ['si:zənɪŋ] *n* : assaisonnement *m*

seat ['si:t] *n* **1** : siège *m* **2** : fond *m* (de pantalon) **3 take a** ~ : asseyez-vous — ~ *vt* **1 be** ~**ed** : s'asseoir **2 the bus** ~**s 30** : l'autobus peut accueillir 30 personnes — **seat belt** *n* : ceinture *f* de sécurité

seaweed ['si:,wi:d] *n* : algue *f* marine

secede [sɪ'si:d] *vi* **-ceded; -ceding** : faire sécession

secluded [sɪ'klu:dəd] *adj* : isolé — **seclusion** [sɪ'klu:ʒən] *n* : isolement *m*

second ['sɛkənd] *adj* : second, deuxième — ~ *or* **secondly** ['sɛkəndli] *adv* : deuxièmement — ~ *n* **1** : deuxième *mf*; second *m*, -conde *f* **2** MOMENT : seconde *f* **3 have** ~**s** : prendre une deuxième portion (de nourriture) — ~ *vt* : affirmer, appuyer — **secondary** ['sɛkən,dɛri] *adj* : secondaire — **secondhand** ['sɛkənd'hænd] *adj* : d'occasion — **second-rate** ['sɛkənd'reɪt] *adj* : médiocre

secret ['si:krət] *adj* : secret — ~ *n* : secret *m* — **secrecy** ['si:krəsi] *n, pl* **-cies** : secret *m*

secretary ['sɛkrə,tɛri] *n, pl* **-taries 1** : secrétaire *mf* **2** : ministre *m* (du gouvernement)

secrete [sɪ'kri:t] *vt* **-creted; -creting** : sécréter

secretive ['si:krətɪv, sɪ'kri:tɪv] *adj* : cachottier — **secretly** ['si:krətli] *adv* : en secret

sect ['sɛkt] *n* : secte *f*

section ['sɛkʃən] *n* : section *f*, partie *f*

sector ['sɛktər] *n* : secteur *m*

secular ['sɛkjələr] *adj* : séculier, laïque

secure [sɪ'kjur] *adj* **-curer; -est** : sûr, en sécurité — ~ *vt* **-cured; -curing 1** FASTEN : attacher **2** GET : obtenir — **security** [sɪ'kjurəti] *n, pl* **-ties 1** : sécurité *f* **2** GUARANTEE : garantie *f* **3 securities** *npl* : valeurs *fpl*

sedan [sɪ'dæn] *n* : berline *f*

sedative ['sɛdətɪv] *n* : calmant *m*, sédatif *m*

sedentary ['sɛdən,tɛri] *adj* : sédentaire

seduce [sɪ'du:s, -'dju:s] *vt* **-duced; -ducing** : séduire — **seduction** [sɪ'dʌkʃən] *n* : séduction *f* — **seductive** [sɪ'dʌktɪv] *adj* : séduisant

see ['si:] *v* **saw** ['sɔ]; **seen** ['si:n]; **seeing** *vt* **1** : voir **2** UNDERSTAND : comprendre **3** ESCORT : accompagner **4** ~ **through** : mener à terme **5** ~ **you later** : au revoir — *vi* **1** : voir **2** UNDERSTAND : comprendre **3 let's** ~ : voyons **4** ~ **to** : s'occuper de

seed ['si:d] *n, pl* **seed** *or* **seeds 1** : graine *f* **2** SOURCE : germe *m* — **seedling** ['si:dlɪŋ] *n* : semis *m*, jeune plant *m* — **seedy** ['si:di] *adj* **seedier; seediest** SQUALID : miteux

seek ['si:k] *v* **sought** ['sɔt]; **seeking** *vt* **1** *or* ~ **out** : chercher **2** REQUEST : demander — *vi* : rechercher

seem ['si:m] *vi* : paraître, sembler, avoir l'air

seep ['si:p] *vi* : suinter

seesaw ['si:,sɔ] *n* : balançoire *f*, bascule *f*

seethe ['si:ð] *vi* **seethed; seething** : bouillonner (de rage)

segment ['sɛgmənt] *n* : segment *m*

segregate ['sɛgrɪ,geɪt] *vt* **-gated; -gating** : séparer — **segregation** [,sɛgrɪ'geɪʃən] *n* : ségrégation *f*

seize ['si:z] *vt* **seized; seizing 1** GRASP : saisir **2** CAPTURE : prendre — **seizure** ['si:,ʒər] *n* : attaque *f*, crise *f* (en médecine)

seldom ['sɛldəm] *adv* : rarement

select [sə'lɛkt] *adj* : privilégié — ~ *vt* : choisir, sélectionner — **selection** [sə'lɛkʃən] *n* : sélection *f*

self ['sɛlf] *n, pl* **selves** ['sɛlvz] **1** : moi *m* **2 her better** ~ : son meilleur côté — **self-addressed** [,sɛlfə'drɛst] *adj* ~ **envelope** : enveloppe *f* affranchie —**self-assured** [,sɛlfə'ʃurd] *adj* : sûr de soi — **self-centered** [,sɛlf'sɛntərd] *adj* : égocentrique — **self-confidence** [,sɛlf'kanfədenʦ] *n* : confiance *f* en soi — **self-confident** [,sɛlf-'kanfədənt] *adj* : sûr de soi — **self-conscious** [,sɛlf'kanʧəs] *adj* : gêné, timide — **self-control** [,sɛlfkən'tro:l] *n* : maîtrise *f* de soi — **self-defense** [,sɛlfdɪ'fɛnʦ] *n* : autodéfense *f* — **self-employed** [,sɛlfɪm-'plɔɪd] *adj* : qui travaille à son compte —

self–esteem [ˌsɛlfɪˈstiːm] *n* : amour-propre *m* — **self–evident** [ˌsɛlfˈɛvədənt] *adj* : qui va de soi — **self–explanatory** [ˌsɛlfɪkˈsplænəˌtori] *adj* : explicite — **self–help** [ˌsɛlfˈhɛlp] *n* : initiative *f* personnelle — **self important** [ˌsɛlfɪmˈpɔrtənt] *adj* : vaniteux — **self–interest** [ˌsɛlfˈɪntrəst, -təˌrɛst] *n* : intérêt *m* personnel — **selfish** [ˈsɛlfɪʃ] *adj* : égoïste — **selfishness** [ˈsɛlfɪʃnəs] *n* : égoïsme *m* — **self–pity** [ˌsɛlfˈpɪti] *n*, *pl* **-ties** : apitoiement *m* sur soi-même — **self–portrait** [ˌsɛlfˈpɔrtrət] *n* : autoportrait *m* — **self–respect** [ˌsɛlfrɪˈspɛkt] *n* : amour *m* propre — **self–righteous** [ˌsɛlfˈraɪtʃəs] *adj* : suffisant — **self–service** [ˌsɛlfˈsərvɪs] *n* : libre-service *m* — **self–sufficient** [ˌsɛlfsəˈfɪʃənt] *adj* : autosuffisant — **self–taught** [ˌsɛlfˈtɔt] *adj* : autodidacte

sell [ˈsɛl] *v* **sold** [ˈsoːld]; **selling** *vt* : vendre — *vi* : se vendre — **seller** [ˈsɛlər] *n* : vendeur *m*, -deuse *f*

selves → **self**

semantics [sɪˈmæntɪks] *ns & pl* : sémantique *f*

semblance [ˈsɛmblənts] *n* : semblant *m*, apparence *f*

semester [səˈmɛstər] *n* : semestre *m*

semicolon [ˈsɛmiˌkoːlən, ˈsɛˌmaɪ-] *n* : point-virgule *m*

semifinal [ˈsɛmiˌfaɪnəl, ˈsɛˌmaɪ-] *n* : demi-finale *f*

seminary [ˈsɛməˌnɛri] *n*, *pl* **-naries** : séminaire *m* — **seminar** [ˈsɛməˌnar] *n* : séminaire *m*

senate [ˈsɛnət] *n* : sénat *m* — **senator** [ˈsɛnətər] *n* : sénateur *m*

send [ˈsɛnd] *vt* **sent** [ˈsɛnt]; **sending** 1 : envoyer, expédier 2 ~ **away for** : commander 3 ~ **back** : renvoyer (de la marchandise, etc.) 4 ~ **for** : appeler, faire venir — **sender** [ˈsɛndər] *n* : expéditeur *m*, -trice *f*

Senegalese [ˌsɛnəgəˈliːz, -ˈliːs] *adj* : sénégalais

senile [ˈsiːˌnaɪl] *adj* : sénile — **senility** [sɪˈnɪləti] *n* : sénilité *f*

senior [ˈsiːnjər] *n* 1 SUPERIOR : supérieur *m* 2 : étudiant *m*, -diante *f* de dernière année (en éducation) 3 *or* ~ **citizen** : personne *f* du troisième âge 4 **be s.o.'s** ~ : être plus âgé que qqn — ~ *adj* 1 : haut placé 2 ELDER : aîné, plus âgé — **seniority** [ˌsiːˈnjɔrəti] *n* : ancienneté *f*

sensation [sɛnˈseɪʃən] *n* : sensation *f* — **sensational** [sɛnˈseɪʃənəl] *adj* : sensationnel

sense [ˈsɛnts] *n* 1 : sens *m* 2 FEELING : sensation *f* 3 COMMON SENSE : bon sens *m* 4 **make** ~ : être logique — ~ *vt* **sensed**; **sensing** : sentir — **senseless** [ˈsɛntsləs]

adj : insensé — **sensible** [ˈsɛntsəbəl] *adj* : raisonnable, pratique — **sensibility** [ˌsɛntsəˈbɪləti] *n*, *pl* **-ties** : sensibilité *f* — **sensitive** [ˈsɛntsətɪv] *adj* 1 : sensible 2 TOUCHY : susceptible — **sensitivity** [ˌsɛntsəˈtɪvəti] *n*, *pl* **-ties** : sensibilité *f*

sensor [ˈsɛnˌsɔr, ˈsɛntsər] *n* : détecteur *m* — **sensual** [ˈsɛntʃuəl] *adj* : sensuel — **sensuous** [ˈsɛntʃuəs] *adj* : sensuel

sent → **send**

sentence [ˈsɛntənts, -ənz] *n* 1 : phrase *f* 2 JUDGMENT : sentence *f*, condamnation *f* — ~ *vt* **-tenced**; **-tencing** : condamner

sentiment [ˈsɛntəmənt] *n* 1 : sentiment *m* 2 BELIEF : opinion *f*, avis *m* — **sentimental** [ˌsɛntəˈmɛntəl] *adj* : sentimental — **sentimentality** [ˌsɛntəˌmɛnˈtæləti] *n*, *pl* **-ties** : sentimentalité *f*

sentry [ˈsɛntri] *n*, *pl* **-tries** : sentinelle *f*

separation [ˌsɛpəˈreɪʃən] *n* : séparation *f* — **separate** [ˈsɛpəˌreɪt] *v* **-rated**; **-rating** *vt* 1 : séparer 2 DISTINGUISH : distinguer — *vi* : se séparer — ~ [ˈsɛprət, ˈsɛpə-] *adj* 1 : séparé 2 DETACHED : à part 3 DISTINCT : distinct — **separately** [ˈsɛprətli, ˈsɛpə-] *adv* : séparément

September [sɛpˈtɛmbər] *n* : septembre *m*

sequel [ˈsiːkwəl] *n* : continuation *f*, suite *f*

sequence [ˈsiːkwənts] *n* 1 ORDER : ordre *m*, suite *f* 2 : série *f*, succession *f* (de nombres)

serene [səˈriːn] *adj* : serein, calme — **serenity** [səˈrɛnəti] *n* : sérénité *f*

sergeant [ˈsardʒənt] *n* : sergent *m*

serial [ˈsɪriəl] *adj* : en série — ~ *n* : feuilleton *m* — **series** [ˈsɪrˌiːz] *n*, *pl* : série *f*

serious [ˈsɪriəs] *adj* : sérieux — **seriously** [ˈsɪriəsli] *adv* 1 : sérieusement 2 GRAVELY : gravement 3 **take** ~ : prendre au sérieux

sermon [ˈsərmən] *n* : sermon *m*

serpent [ˈsərpənt] *n* : serpent *m*

servant [ˈsərvənt] *n* : domestique *mf*

serve [ˈsərv] *v* **served**; **serving** *vi* 1 : servir 2 ~ **as** : servir de — *vt* 1 : servir (une personne, etc.), desservir (une région, etc.) 2 ~ **time** : purger une peine — **server** [ˈsərvər] *n* 1 WAITER : serveur *m*, -veuse *f* : serveur *m* (en informatique)

service [ˈsərvəs] *n* 1 : service *m* 2 CEREMONY : office *m* (en religion) 3 MAINTENANCE : entretien *m* 4 **armed** ~**s** : forces *fpl* armées — ~ *vt* **-viced**; **-vicing** : réviser (un véhicule, etc.) — **serviceman** [ˈsərvəsˌmæn, -mən] *n*, *pl* **-men** [-mən, -ˌmɛn] : militaire *m* — **service station** *n* : station-service *f*, poste *m* d'essence — **serving** [ˈsərvɪŋ] *n* : portion *f*, ration *f*

session [ˈsɛʃən] *n* : séance *f*, session *f*

set [ˈsɛt] *n* 1 : ensemble *m*, série *f*, jeu *m* 2 : set *m* (au tennis) 3 *or* **stage** ~ : scène *f*, plateau *m* **4** *or* **television** ~ : poste *m* de télévision — ~ *v* **set; setting** *vt* **1** *or* ~ **down** : mettre, placer **2** : régler (une montre) **3** FIX : fixer (un rendez-vous, etc.) **4** ~ **fire to** : mettre le feu à **5** ~ **free** : mettre en liberté **6** ~ **off** : déclencher (une alarme), faire détoner (une bombe) **7** ~ **out to do sth** : se proposer de faire qqch **8** ~ **up** ASSEMBLE : installer **9** ~ **up** ESTABLISH : établir — *vi* **1** : prendre (se dit de la gélatine, etc.) **2** : se coucher (se dit du soleil) **3** ~ **in** BEGIN : commencer **4** ~ **off** *or* ~ **out** : partir (en voyage) — ~ *adj* **1** FIXED : fixe **2** READY : prêt — **setback** ['sɛt,bæk] *n* : revers *m* — **setting** ['sɛtɪŋ] *n* **1** : réglage *m* (d'une machine) **2** MOUNTING : monture *f* (d'un bijou) **3** SCENE : décor *m*

settle ['sɛtəl] *v* **settled; settling** *vi* **1** : se poser (se dit d'un oiseau), se déposer (se dit de la poussière) **2** ~ **down** RELAX : se calmer **3** ~ **for** : se contenter de **4** ~ **in** : s'installer — *vt* **1** DECIDE : fixer, décider **2** RESOLVE : résoudre **3** PAY : régler (un compte) **4** CALM : calmer **5** COLONIZE : coloniser — **settlement** ['sɛtəlmənt] *n* **1** PAYMENT : règlement *m* **2** COLONY : colonie *f*, village *m* **3** AGREEMENT : accord *m* — **settler** ['sɛtələr] *n* : colonisateur *m*, -trice *f*; colon *m*

seven ['sɛvən] *n* : sept *m* — ~ *adj* : sept — **seven hundred** *adj* : sept cents — **seventeen** [,sɛvən'ti:n] *n* : dix-sept *m* — ~ *adj* : dix-sept — **seventeenth** [,sɛvən'ti:nθ] *n* **1** : dix-septième *m* **2** April ~ : le dix-sept avril — ~ *adj* : dix-septième — **seventh** [,sɛvənθ] *n* **1** : septième *mf* **2** July ~ : le sept juillet — ~ *adj* : septième — **seventieth** ['sɛvəntiəθ] *n* : soixante-dixième *mf* — ~ *adj* : soixante-dixième — **seventy** ['sɛvənti] *n*, *pl* **-ties** : soixante-dix *m* — ~ *adj* : soixante-dix

sever ['sɛvər] *vt* **-ered; -ering** **1** : couper **2** BREAK : rompre

several ['sɛvrəl, 'sɛvə-] *adj & pron* : plusieurs

severance ['sɛvrənts, 'sɛvə-] *n* **1** : rupture *f* **2** ~ **pay** : indemnité *f* de départ

severe [sə'vɪr] *adj* **-verer; -verest** **1** : sévère **2** SERIOUS : grave — **severely** [sə'vɪrli] *adv* **1** : sévèrement **2** SERIOUSLY : gravement

sew ['so:] *v* **sewed; sewn** ['so:n] *or* **sewed; sewing** : coudre

sewer ['su:ər] *n* : égout *m* — **sewage** ['su:ɪdʒ] *n* : eaux *fpl* d'égout

sewing ['so:ɪŋ] *n* : couture *f*

sex ['sɛks] *n* **1** : sexe *m* **2** INTERCOURSE : relations *fpl* sexuelles — **sexism** ['sɛk,sɪzəm] *n* : sexisme *m* — **sexist** ['sɛksɪst] *adj* : sexiste — **sexual** ['sɛkʃuəl] *adj* : sexuel —

sexuality [,sɛkʃu'æləti] *n* : sexualité *f* — **sexy** ['sɛksi] *adj* **sexier; sexiest** : sexy

shabby ['ʃæbi] *adj* **-bier; -biest** **1** WORN : miteux **2** UNFAIR : mal, injuste

shack ['ʃæk] *n* : cabane *f*

shackles ['ʃækəlz] *npl* : fers *mpl*, chaînes *fpl*

shade ['ʃeɪd] *n* **1** : ombre *f* **2** : ton *m* (d'une couleur) **3** NUANCE : nuance *f* **4** *or* **lampshade** : abat-jour *m* **5** WINDOW ~ : store *m* — ~ *vt* **shaded; shading** : protéger de la lumière — **shadow** ['ʃædo:] *n* : ombre *f* — **shadowy** ['ʃædowi] *adj* INDISTINCT : vague — **shady** ['ʃeɪdi] *adj* **shadier; shadiest** **1** : ombragé **2** DISREPUTABLE : suspect

shaft ['ʃæft] *n* **1** : tige *f* (d'une flèche, etc.) **2** HANDLE : manche *m* **3** AXLE : arbre *m* **4** *or* **mine** ~ : puits *m*

shaggy ['ʃægi] *adj* **-gier; -est** : poilu

shake ['ʃeɪk] *v* **shook** ['ʃʊk]; **shaken** ['ʃeɪkən]; **shaking** *vt* **1** : secouer **2** MIX : agiter **3** ~ **hands with s.o.** : serrer la main à qqn **4** ~ **one's head** : secouer la tête **5** ~ **up** UPSET : ébranler — *vi* : trembler — ~ *n* **1** : secousse *f* **2** → **handshake** — **shaker** ['ʃeɪkər] *n* **1** salt ~ : salière *f* **2** pepper ~ : poivrière *f* — **shaky** ['ʃeɪki] *adj* **shakier; shakiest** **1** : tremblant **2** UNSTABLE : peu ferme

shall ['ʃæl] *v aux*, *past* **should** ['ʃʊd]; *pres sing & pl* **shall** **1** (*expressing volition or futurity*) → **will 2** (*expressing possibility or obligation*) → **should 3** ~ **we go?** : nous y allons?

shallow ['ʃælo:] *adj* **1** : peu profond **2** SUPERFICIAL : superficiel

sham ['ʃæm] *n* : faux-semblant *m*

shambles ['ʃæmbəlz] *ns & pl* : désordre *m*

shame ['ʃeɪm] *n* **1** : honte *f* **2 what a** ~! : quel dommage! — ~ *vt* **shamed; shaming** : faire honte à — **shameful** ['ʃeɪmfəl] *adj* : honteux

shampoo [ʃæm'pu:] *vt* : se laver (les cheveux) — ~ *n*, *pl* **-poos** : shampooing *m*

shan't ['ʃænt] (*contraction of shall not*) → **shall**

shape ['ʃeɪp] *v* **shaped; shaping** *vt* **1** : façonner **2** DETERMINE : déterminer **3 be** ~**d like** : avoir la forme de — *vi or* ~ **up** : prendre forme — ~ *n* **1** : forme *f* **2 get in** ~ : se mettre en forme — **shapeless** ['ʃeɪpləs] *adj* : informe

share ['ʃɛr] *n* **1** : portion *f*, part *f* **2** : action *f* (d'une compagnie) — ~ *v* **shared; sharing** *vt* **1** : partager **2** DIVIDE : diviser — *vi* : partager — **shareholder** ['ʃɛr,ho:ldər] *n* : actionnaire *mf*

shark ['ʃɑrk] *n* : requin *m*

sharp ['ʃɑrp] *adj* **1** : affilé **2** POINTY : pointu **3** ACUTE : aigu **4** HARSH : dur, sévère **5** CLEAR : net **6** : dièse (en musique)

— ~ *adv* **at two o'clock** ~ : à deux heures pile — ~ *n* : dièse *m* (en musique) — **sharpen** ['ʃɑrpən] *vt* : aiguiser (un couteau, etc.), tailler (un crayon) — **sharpener** ['ʃɑrpənər] *n* : aiguisoir *m*, ⸺ *or* pencil ⸺ : taille-crayon *m*

sharply ['ʃɑrpli] *adv* : brusquement

shatter ['ʃæt̬ər] *vt* **1** : briser, fracasser **2** DEVASTATE : détruire — *vi* : se briser, se fracasser

shave ['ʃeɪv] *v* **shaved**; **shaved** *or* **shaven** ['ʃeɪvən]; **shaving** *vt* **1** : raser **2** SLICE : couper — *vi* : se raser — ~ *n* : rasage — **shaver** ['ʃeɪvər] *n* : rasoir *m*

shawl ['ʃɔl] *n* : châle *m*

she ['ʃiː] *pron* : elle

sheaf ['ʃiːf] *n, pl* **sheaves** ['ʃiːvz] : gerbe *f* (de céréales), liasse *f* (de papiers)

shear ['ʃɪr] *vt* **sheared**; **sheared** *or* **shorn** ['ʃɔrn]; **shearing** : tondre — **shears** ['ʃɪrz] *npl* : cisailles *fpl*

sheath ['ʃiːθ] *n, pl* **sheaths** ['ʃiːðz, 'ʃiːθs] : fourreau *m* (d'épée), gaine *f* (de poignard)

shed[1] ['ʃɛd] *v* **shed**; **shedding** *vt* **1** : verser (des larmes) **2** : perdre (ses poils, etc.) **3** ~ **light on** : éclairer — *vi* : perdre ses poils, muer

shed[2] *n* : abri *m*, remise *f*

she'd ['ʃiːd] (*contraction of* **she had** *or* **she would**) → **have, would**

sheen ['ʃiːn] *n* : lustre *m*, éclat *m*

sheep ['ʃiːp] *n, pl* **sheep** : mouton *m* — **sheepish** ['ʃiːpɪʃ] *adj* : penaud

sheer ['ʃɪr] *adj* **1** PURE : pur **2** STEEP : escarpé

sheet ['ʃiːt] *n* **1** : drap *m* (de lit) **2** : feuille *f* (de papier) **3** : plaque *f* (de glace, etc.)

shelf ['ʃɛlf] *n, pl* **shelves** ['ʃɛlvz] : étagère *f*, rayon *m*

shell ['ʃɛl] *n* **1** : coquillage *m* **2** : carapace *f* (d'un crustacé, etc.) **3** : coquille *f* (d'œuf, etc.) **4** POD : cosse *f* **5** MISSILE : obus *m* — ~ *vt* **1** : décortiquer (des noix), écosser (des pois) **2** BOMBARD : bombarder

she'll ['ʃiːl, 'ʃɪl] (*contraction of* **she shall** *or* **she will**) → **shall, will**

shellfish ['ʃɛlˌfɪʃ] *n* : crustacé *m*

shelter ['ʃɛltər] *n* **1** : abri *m*, refuge *m* **2** **take** ~ : se réfugier — ~ *vt* **1** PROTECT : protéger **2** HARBOR : abriter

shepherd ['ʃɛpərd] *n* : berger *m*

sherbet ['ʃərbət] *n* : sorbet *m*

sheriff ['ʃɛrɪf] *n* : shérif *m*

sherry ['ʃɛri] *n, pl* **-ries** : xérès *m*

she's ['ʃiːz] (*contraction of* **she is** *or* **she has**) → **be, have**

shield ['ʃiːld] *n* : bouclier *m* — ~ *vt* : protéger

shier, shiest → **shy**

shift ['ʃɪft] *vt* : bouger, changer — *vi* **1** : se

déplacer, bouger **2** CHANGE : changer **3** *or* ~ **gears** : changer de vitesse — ~ *n* **1** : changement *m* **2** : équipe *f* (au travail)

shimmer ['ʃɪmər] *vi* : briller, reluire

shin ['ʃɪn] *n* : tibia *m*

shine ['ʃaɪn] *v* **shone** ['ʃoɪn] *or* **shined**; **shining** *vi* : briller — *vt* POLISH : cirer (des chaussures) — ~ *n* : éclat *m*

shingle ['ʃɪŋɡəl] *n* : bardeau *m* — **shingles** ['ʃɪŋɡəlz] *npl* : zona *m*

shiny ['ʃaɪni] *adj* **shinier; shiniest** : brillant

ship ['ʃɪp] *n* : bateau *m*, navire *m* — ~ *vt* **shipped; shipping** : expédier (par bateau), transporter (par avion) — **shipbuilding** ['ʃɪpˌbɪldɪŋ] *n* : construction *f* navale — **shipment** ['ʃɪpmənt] *n* : cargaison *f*, chargement *m* — **shipping** ['ʃɪpɪŋ] *n* : transport *m* (maritime) — **shipwreck** ['ʃɪpˌrɛk] *n* : naufrage *m* — ~ *vt* **be ~ed** : faire naufrage — **shipyard** ['ʃɪpˌjɑrd] *n* : chantier *m* naval

shirt ['ʃərt] *n* : chemise *f*

shiver ['ʃɪvər] *vi* : frissonner — ~ *n* : frisson *m*

shoal ['ʃoːl] *n* : banc *m* (de poissons, etc.)

shock ['ʃɑk] *n* **1** : choc *m* **2** *or* **electric** ~ : décharge *f* (électrique) — ~ *vt* : choquer, scandaliser — **shock absorber** *n* : amortisseur *m* — **shocking** ['ʃɑkɪŋ] *adj* : choquant

shoddy ['ʃɑdi] *adj* **-dier; -est** : de mauvaise qualité

shoe ['ʃuː] *n* : chaussure *f*, soulier *m* — **shoelace** ['ʃuːˌleɪs] *n* : lacet *m* — **shoemaker** ['ʃuːˌmeɪkər] *n* : cordonnier *m*, -nière *f*

shone → **shine**

shook → **shake**

shoot ['ʃuːt] *v* **shot** ['ʃɑt]; **shooting** *vt* **1** : tirer (une balle, etc.) **2** : lancer (un regard) **3** PHOTOGRAPH : photographier **4** FILM : tourner — *vi* **1** : tirer **2** ~ **by** : passer en trombe — ~ *n* : rejeton *m*, pousse *f* (d'une plante) — **shooting star** *n* : étoile *f* filante

shop ['ʃɑp] *n* **1** : magasin *m*, boutique *f* **2** WORKSHOP : atelier *m* — ~ *vi* **shopped; shopping 1** : faire des courses **2 go shopping** : faire les magasins — **shopkeeper** ['ʃɑpˌkiːpər] *n* : commerçant *m*, -çante *f*; marchand *m*, -chande *f* — **shoplift** ['ʃɑpˌlɪft] *vt* : voler à l'étalage — **shoplifter** ['ʃɑpˌlɪftər] *n* : voleur *m*, -leuse *f* à l'étalage — **shopper** ['ʃɑpər] *n* : personne *f* qui fait ses courses

shore ['ʃɔr] *n* : rivage *m*, bord *m*

shorn → **shear**

short ['ʃɔrt] *adj* **1** : court **2** : petit, de petite taille **3** CURT : brusque **4 a ~ time ago** : il y a peu de temps **5 be ~ of** : être à court de — ~ *adv* **1 fall** ~ : ne pas atteindre **2**

stop ~ : s'arrêter net — **shortage** ['ʃɔrtɪʤ] n : manque m, carence f — **shortcake** ['ʃɔrt,keɪk] n : tarte f sablée — **shortcoming** ['ʃɔrt,kʌmɪŋ] n : défaut m — **shortcut** ['ʃɔrt,kʌt] n : raccourci m — **shorten** ['ʃɔrtən] vt : raccourcir — **shorthand** ['ʃɔrt,hænd] n : sténographie f — **short-lived** ['ʃɔrt'lɪvd, -'laɪvd] adj : éphémère — **shortly** ['ʃɔrtli] adv : bientôt — **shortness** ['ʃɔrtnəs] n 1 : petite taille f 2 ~ **of breath** : manque m de souffle — **shorts** npl : short m, pantalons mpl courts — **shortsighted** ['ʃɔrt,saɪtəd] → **nearsighted**

shot ['ʃɑt] n 1 : coup m (de feu) 2 : coup m, tir m (aux sports) 3 ATTEMPT : essai m, tentative f 4 PHOTOGRAPH : photo f 5 INJECTION : piqûre f 6 : verre m (de liqueur) — **shotgun** ['ʃɑt,gʌn] n : fusil m

should ['ʃʊd] past of **shall 1 if she** ~ **call** : si elle appelle **2 I** ~ **have gone** : j'aurais dû y aller **3 they** ~ **arrive soon** : ils devraient arriver bientôt **4 what** ~ **we do?** : qu'allons nous faire?

shoulder ['ʃoːldər] n 1 : épaule f 2 : accotement m (d'une chaussée) — **shoulder blade** n : omoplate f

shouldn't ['ʃʊdənt] (contraction of should not) → **should**

shout ['ʃaʊt] v : crier — ~ n : cri m

shove ['ʃʌv] vt **shoved; shoving** : pousser, bousculer — ~ n **give s.o. a** ~ : pousser qqn

shovel ['ʃʌvəl] n : pelle f — ~ vt **-veled** or **-velled; -veling** or **-velling** : pelleter

show ['ʃoː] v **showed; shown** ['ʃoːn] or **showed; showing** vt 1 : montrer 2 TEACH : enseigner 3 PROVE : démontrer 4 ESCORT : accompagner 5 : passer (une émission, un film, etc.) 6 ~ **off** : faire étalage de — vi 1 : se voir 2 ~ **off** : faire le fier 3 ~ **up** ARRIVE : arriver — ~ n 1 : démonstration f 2 EXHIBITION : exposition f 3 : spectacle m (de théâtre), émission f (de télévision, etc.) — **showdown** ['ʃoː,daʊn] n : confrontation f

shower ['ʃaʊər] n 1 : douche f 2 : averse f (de pluie, etc.) 3 PARTY : fête f — ~ vt 1 SPRAY : arroser 2 ~ **s.o. with** : couvrir qqn de — vi : prendre une douche

showy ['ʃoːi] adj **showier; showiest** : tape-à-l'œil

shrank → **shrink**

shrapnel ['ʃræpnəl] ns & pl : éclats mpl d'obus

shred ['ʃrɛd] n 1 : brin m, parcelle f 2 **in** ~**s** : en lambeaux — ~ vt **shredded; shredding 1** : déchirer **2** GRATE : râper

shrewd ['ʃruːd] adj : astucieux

shriek ['ʃriːk] vi : pousser un cri perçant — ~ n : cri m perçant

shrill ['ʃrɪl] adj : perçant, strident

shrimp ['ʃrɪmp] n : crevette f

shrine ['ʃraɪn] n : lieu m saint

shrink ['ʃrɪŋk] v **shrank** ['ʃræŋk]; **shrunk** ['ʃrʌŋk] or **shrunken** ['ʃrʌŋkən]; **shrinking** : rétrécir

shrivel ['ʃrɪvəl] vi **-eled** or **-elled; -eling** or **-elling** or ~ **up** : se dessécher, se rider

shroud ['ʃraʊd] n 1 : linceul m 2 VEIL : voile m — ~ vt : envelopper

shrub ['ʃrʌb] n : arbuste m, arbrisseau m

shrug ['ʃrʌg] vi **shrugged; shrugging** : hausser les épaules

shrunk → **shrink**

shudder ['ʃʌdər] vi : frissonner, frémir — ~ n : frisson m

shuffle ['ʃʌfəl] v **-fled; -fling** vt : mélanger (des papiers), battre (des cartes) — vi : marcher en traînant les pieds

shun ['ʃʌn] vt **shunned; shunning** : éviter, esquiver

shut ['ʃʌt] v **shut; shutting** vt 1 CLOSE : fermer 2 → **turn off 3** ~ **up** CONFINE : enfermer — vi 1 or ~ **down** : fermer 2 ~ **up** : se taire — **shutter** ['ʃʌtər] n or **window** ~ : volet m (d'une fenêtre)

shuttle ['ʃʌtəl] n 1 : navette f (à l'aéroport, etc.) 2 → **space shuttle** — ~ v **-tled; -tling** : transporter — **shuttlecock** ['ʃʌtəl,kɑk] n : volant m

shy ['ʃaɪ] adj **shier** or **shyer** ['ʃaɪər]; **shiest** or **shyest** ['ʃaɪəst] : timide, gêné — ~ vi **shied; shying** or ~ **away** : éviter — **shyness** ['ʃaɪnəs] n : timidité f

sibling ['sɪblɪŋ] n : frère m, sœur f

sick ['sɪk] adj 1 : malade 2 **be** ~ VOMIT : vomir 3 **be** ~ **of** : en avoir assez de 4 **feel** ~ : avoir des nausées — **sicken** ['sɪkən] vt DISGUST : écœurer — **sickening** ['sɪkənɪŋ] adj : écœurant — **sick leave** n : congé m de maladie

sickle ['sɪkəl] n : faucille f

sickly ['sɪkli] adj **-lier; -est** : maladif — **sickness** ['sɪknəs] n : maladie f

side ['saɪd] n 1 : bord m 2 : côté m (d'une personne), flanc m (d'un animal) 3 : côté m, camp m (de l'opposition, etc.) 4 ~ **by** ~ : côte à côte 5 **take** ~**s** : prendre parti — ~ adj : latéral — vi ~ **with** : prendre le parti de — **sideboard** ['saɪd,bord] n : buffet m — **sideburns** ['saɪd,bərnz] npl : favoris mpl — **side effect** n : effet m secondaire — **sideline** ['saɪd,laɪn] n : travail m d'appoint — **sidewalk** ['saɪd,wɔk] n : trottoir m — **sideways** ['saɪd,weɪz] adv & adj : de côté — **siding** ['saɪdɪŋ] n : revêtement m extérieur

siege ['siːʤ, 'siːʒ] n : siège m

sieve ['sɪv] n : tamis m, crible m

sift ['sɪft] vt 1 : tamiser 2 or ~ **through** : examiner

sigh ['saɪ] *vi* : soupirer — ~ *n* : soupir *m*

sight ['saɪt] *n* **1** : vue *f* **2** SPECTACLE : spectacle *m* **3** : centre *m* d'intérêt (touristique) **4 catch ~ of** : apercevoir — **sightseer** ['saɪt,siːər] *n* : touriste *mf*

sign ['saɪn] *n* **1** : signe *m* **2** NOTICE : panneau *m*, enseigne *f* — ~ *vt* : signer (un chèque, etc.) — *vi* **1** : signer **2 ~ up** ENROLL : s'inscrire

signal ['sɪgnəl] *n* : signal *m* — ~ *v* **-naled** *or* **-nalled; -naling** *or* **-nalling** *vt* **1** : faire signe à **2** INDICATE : signaler — *vi* **1** : faire des signes **2** : mettre son clignotant (dans un véhicule)

signature ['sɪgnə,tʃʊr] *n* : signature *f*

significance [sɪg'nɪfɪkənts] *n* **1** : signification *f*, sens *m* **2** IMPORTANCE : importance *f* — **significant** [sɪg'nɪfɪkənt] *adj* **1** : significatif **2** IMPORTANT : considérable — **significantly** [sɪg'nɪfɪkəntli] *adv* : sensiblement — **signify** ['sɪgnə,faɪ] *vt* **-fied; -fying** : signifier — **sign language** *n* : langage *m* des signes — **signpost** ['saɪn,poːst] *n* : poteau *m* indicateur

silence ['saɪlənts] *n* : silence *m* — ~ *vt* **-lenced; -lencing** : faire taire — **silent** ['saɪlənt] *adj* **1** : silencieux **2** : muet (se dit d'un film, etc.)

silhouette [,sɪlə'wɛt] *n* : silhouette *f*

silicon ['sɪlɪkən, -,kɑn] *n* : silicium *m*

silk ['sɪlk] *n* : soie *f* — **silky** ['sɪlki] *adj* **silkier; -est** : soyeux

sill ['sɪl] *n* : rebord *m* (d'une fenêtre), seuil *m* (d'une porte)

silly ['sɪli] *adj* **-lier; -est** : stupide, bête

silt ['sɪlt] *n* : limon *m*

silver ['sɪlvər] *n* **1** : argent *m* **2** → **silverware** — ~ *adj* : d'argent, en argent — **silverware** ['sɪlvər,wær] *n* : argenterie *f*, coutellerie *f* *Can* — **silvery** ['sɪlvəri] *adj* : argenté

similar ['sɪmələr] *adj* : semblable, pareil — **similarity** [,sɪmə'lærəṭi] *n*, *pl* **-ties** : ressemblance *f*, similarité *f*

simmer ['sɪmər] *vi* : mijoter

simple ['sɪmpəl] *adj* **-pler; -plest 1** : simple **2** EASY : facile — **simplicity** [sɪm'plɪsəṭi] *n* : simplicité *f* — **simplify** ['sɪmplə,faɪ] *vt* **-fied; -fying** : simplifier — **simply** ['sɪmpli] *adv* **1** : simplement **2** ABSOLUTELY : absolument

simulate ['sɪmjə,leɪt] *vt* **-lated; -lating** : simuler

simultaneous [,saɪməl'teɪniəs] *adj* : simultané

sin ['sɪn] *n* : péché *m* — ~ *vi* **sinned; sinning** : pécher

since ['sɪnts] *adv* **1** *or* ~ **then** : depuis **2 long ~** : il y a longtemps — ~ *conj* **1** : depuis que **2** BECAUSE : puisque, comme **3 it's been years ~ ...** : il y a des années que ... — ~ *prep* : depuis

sincere [sɪn'sɪr] *adj* **-cerer; -cerest** : sincère — **sincerely** [sɪn'sɪrli] *adv* : sincèrement — **sincerity** [sɪn'sɛrəṭi] *n* : sincérité *f*

sinful ['sɪnfəl] *adj* : immoral

sing ['sɪŋ] *v* **sang** ['sæŋ] *or* **sung** ['sʌŋ]; **sung; singing** : chanter — **singer** ['sɪŋər] *n* : chanteur *m*, -teuse *f*

single ['sɪŋgəl] *adj* **1** : seul, unique **2** UNMARRIED : célibataire **3 every ~ day** : tous les jours **4 every ~ time** : chaque fois — ~ *vt* **-gled; -gling ~ out 1** SELECT : choisir **2** DISTINGUISH : distinguer

singular ['sɪŋgjələr] *adj* : singulier — ~ *n* : singulier *m*

sinister ['sɪnəstər] *adj* : sinistre

sink ['sɪŋk] *v* **sank** ['sæŋk] *or* **sunk** ['sʌŋk]; **sunk; sinking** *vi* **1** : couler **2** DROP : baisser, tomber — *vt* **1** : couler **2 ~ sth into** : enfoncer qqch dans — ~ *n* **1** *or* **bathroom ~** : lavabo *m* **2** *or* **kitchen ~** : évier *m*

sinner ['sɪnər] *n* : pécheur *m*, -cheresse *f*

sip ['sɪp] *vt* **sipped; sipping** : boire à petites gorgées, siroter *fam* — ~ *n* : petite gorgée *f*

siphon ['saɪfən] *n* : siphon *m* — ~ *vt* : siphonner

sir ['sər] *n* **1** (*as a form of address*) : monsieur *m* **2** (*in titles*) : sir *m*

siren ['saɪrən] *n* : sirène *f*

sirloin ['sər,lɔɪn] *n* : aloyau *m*

sissy ['sɪsi] *n*, *pl* **-sies** : poule *f* mouillée *fam*

sister ['sɪstər] *n* : sœur *f* — **sister-in-law** ['sɪstərɪn,lɔ] *n*, *pl* **sisters-in-law** : belle-sœur *f*

sit ['sɪt] *v* **sat** ['sæt]; **sitting** *vi* **1** *or* ~ **down** : s'asseoir **2** LIE : être, se trouver **3** MEET : siéger **4** *or* ~ **up** : se redresser — *vt* : asseoir

site ['saɪt] *n* **1** : site *m*, emplacement *m* **2** LOT : terrain *m*

sitting room → **living room**

situated ['sɪtʃʊ,eɪṭəd] *adj* : situé — **situation** [,sɪtʃʊ'eɪʃən] *n* : situation *f*

six ['sɪks] *n* : six *m* — ~ *adj* : six — **six hundred** *adj* : six cents — **sixteen** [sɪks'tiːn] *n* : seize *m* — ~ *adj* : seize — **sixteenth** [sɪks'tiːnθ] *n* **1** : seizième *mf* **2 October ~** : le seize octobre — ~ *adj* : seizième — **sixth** ['sɪksθ, 'sɪkst] *n* **1** : sixième *mf* **2 March ~** : le six mars — ~ *adj* : sixième — **sixtieth** ['sɪkstiəθ] *n* : soixantième *mf* — ~ *adj* : soixantième — **sixty** ['sɪksti] *n*, *pl* **-ties** : soixante *m* — ~ *adj* : soixante

size ['saɪz] *n* **1** : taille *f* (d'un vêtement), pointure *f* (de chaussures, etc.) **2** EXTENT : ampleur *f* — ~ *vt* **sized; sizing** *or* ~ **up** : jauger, évaluer

sizzle ['sɪzəl] *vi* **-zled; -zling** : grésiller

skate ['skeɪt] *n* : patin *m* — ~ *vi* **skated; skating** : patiner, faire du patin — **skateboard** ['skeɪt,bord] *n* : planche *f* à roulettes — **skater** ['skeɪtər] *n* : patineur *m*, neuse *f*

skeleton ['skɛlətən] *n* : squelette *m*

skeptical ['skɛptɪkəl] *adj* : sceptique

sketch ['skɛtʃ] *n* : esquisse *f*, croquis *m* — ~ *vt* : esquisser

skewer ['skju:ər] *n* : brochette *f*, broche *f*

ski ['ski:] *n*, *pl* **skis** : ski *m* — ~ *vi* **skied; skiing** : faire du ski

skid ['skɪd] *n* : dérapage *m* — ~ *vi* **skidded; skidding** : déraper, patiner

skier ['ski:ər] *n* : skieur *m*, skieuse *f*

skill ['skɪl] *n* **1** : habileté *f*, dextérité *f* **2** TECHNIQUE : technique *f* **3** ~**s** *npl* : compétences *fpl* — **skilled** ['skɪld] *adj* : habile

skillet ['skɪlət] *n* : poêle *f* (à frire)

skillful *or Brit* **skilful** ['skɪlfəl] *adj* : habile, adroit

skim ['skɪm] *vt* **skimmed; skimming 1** : écumer (de la soupe), écrémer (du lait) **2** : effleurer (une surface) **3** *or* ~ **through** : parcourir (un livre, etc.) — ~ *adj* : écrémé

skimpy ['skɪmpi] *adj* **skimpier; skimpiest 1** : maigre (se dit d'une portion) **2** : étriqué (se dit d'un vêtement)

skin ['skɪn] *n* **1** : peau *f* **2** : pelure *f* (de pomme, etc.) — ~ *vt* **skinned; skinning 1** : dépouiller (un animal) **2** : s'écorcher (le genou, etc.) — **skin diving** *n* : plongée *f* sous-marine — **skinny** ['skɪni] *adj* **-nier; -est** : maigre

skip ['skɪp] *v* **skipped; skipping** *vi* : sautiller — *vt* OMIT : sauter — ~ *n* : petit saut *m*, petit bond *m*

skirmish ['skərmɪʃ] *n* : escarmouche *f*

skirt ['skərt] *n* : jupe *f*

skull ['skʌl] *n* : crâne *m*

skunk ['skʌŋk] *n* : mouffette *f*

sky ['skaɪ] *n*, *pl* **skies** : ciel *m* — **skylight** ['skaɪ,laɪt] *n* : lucarne *f* — **skyline** ['skaɪ,laɪn] *n* : horizon *m* — **skyscraper** ['skaɪ,skreɪpər] *n* : gratte-ciel *m*

slab ['slæb] *n* : dalle *f*, bloc *m*

slack ['slæk] *adj* **1** LOOSE : mou, lâche **2** CARELESS : négligent — **slacks** ['slæks] *npl* : pantalon *m* — **slacken** ['slækən] *vt* : relâcher

slain → **slay**

slam ['slæm] *n* : claquement *m* (de porte) — ~ *v* **slammed; slamming** *vt* **1** : claquer (une porte, etc.) **2** *or* ~ **down** : flanquer **3** *or* ~ **shut** : fermer brusquement — *vi* ~ **into** : heurter

slander ['slændər] *vt* : calomnier, diffamer — ~ *n* : calomnie *f*, diffamation *f*

slang ['slæŋ] *n* : argot *m*

slant ['slænt] *n* : pente *f*, inclinaison *f* — ~ *vi* : pencher, s'incliner

slap ['slæp] *vt* **slapped; slapping** : gifler, donner une claque à — ~ *n* : gifle *f*, claque *f*

slash ['slæʃ] *vt* : entailler

slat ['slæt] *n* : lame *f*, lamelle *f*

slate ['sleɪt] *n* : ardoise *f*

slaughter ['slɔtər] *n* : massacre *m* — ~ *vt* **1** : abattre (des animaux) **2** MASSACRE : massacrer — **slaughterhouse** ['slɔtər,haʊs] *n* : abattoir *m*

slave ['sleɪv] *n* : esclave *mf* — **slavery** ['sleɪvəri] *n* : esclavage *m*

sled ['slɛd] *n* : traîneau *m*, luge *f*

sledgehammer ['slɛdʒ,hæmər] *n* : masse *f*

sleek ['sli:k] *adj* : lisse, luisant

sleep ['sli:p] *n* **1** : sommeil *m* **2 go to** ~ : s'endormir — ~ *vi* **slept** ['slɛpt]; **sleeping** : dormir — **sleeper** ['sli:pər] *n* **be a light** ~ : avoir le sommeil léger — **sleepless** ['sli:pləs] *adj* **have a** ~ **night** : passer une nuit blanche — **sleepwalker** ['sli:p-,wɔkər] *n* : somnambule *mf* — **sleepy** ['sli:pi] *adj* **sleepier; -est 1** : somnolent **2 be** ~ : avoir sommeil

sleet ['sli:t] *n* : grésil *m* — ~ *vi* : grésiller

sleeve ['sli:v] *n* : manche *f* — **sleeveless** ['sli:vləs] *adj* : sans manches

sleigh ['sleɪ] *n* : traîneau *m*, carriole *f* *Can*

slender ['slɛndər] *adj* : svelte, mince

slept → **sleep**

slice ['slaɪs] *vt* **sliced; slicing** : trancher — ~ *n* : tranche *f*, rondelle *f*

slick ['slɪk] *adj* SLIPPERY : glissant

slide ['slaɪd] *v* **slid** ['slɪd]; **sliding** ['slaɪdɪŋ] *vi* : glisser — *vt* : faire glisser — ~ *n* **1** : glissoire *f* **2** : toboggan *m* (dans un terrain de jeu) **3** : diapositive *f* (en photographie) **4** DECLINE : baisse *f*

slier, sliest → **sly**

slight ['slaɪt] *adj* **1** SLENDER : mince **2** MINOR : léger — ~ *vt* : offenser — **slightly** ['slaɪtli] *adv* : légèrement, un peu

slim ['slɪm] *adj* **slimmer; slimmest 1** : svelte **2 a** ~ **chance** : une faible chance — ~ *v* **slimmed; slimming** : maigrir

slime ['slaɪm] *n* MUD : vase *f*, boue *f*

sling ['slɪŋ] *vt* **slung** ['slʌŋ]; **slinging** THROW : lancer — ~ *n* **1** : fronde *f* **2** : écharpe *f* (en médecine) — **slingshot** ['slɪŋ,ʃɑt] *n* : lance-pierres *m*

slip[1] ['slɪp] *v* **slipped; slipping** *vi* **1** SLIDE : glisser **2** ~ **away** : partir furtivement **3** ~ **up** : faire une gaffe — *vt* **1** : glisser **2** ~ **into** : enfiler (un vêtement, etc.) — ~ *n* **1** MISTAKE : erreur *f* **2** : jupon *m* **3 a** ~ **of the tongue** : un lapsus

slip[2] *n* ~ **of paper** : bout *m* (de papier)

slipper ['slɪpər] *n* : pantoufle *f*

slippery ['slɪpəri] *adj* **-perier; -est** : glissant

slit ['slɪt] *n* **1** OPENING : fente *f* **2** CUT : incision *f* — *vt* **slit; slitting** : couper

slither ['slɪðər] *vi* : ramper

sliver ['slɪvər] *n* : éclat *m* (de bois)

slogan ['slo:gən] *n* : slogan *m*

slope ['slo:p] *vi* **sloped; sloping** : pencher — *n* : pente *f*

sloppy ['slɑpi] *adj* **-pier; -piest 1** CARELESS : peu soigné **2** UNKEMPT : débraillé

slot ['slɑt] *n* **1** : fente *f* **2** GROOVE : rainure *f*

sloth ['slɔθ, 'slo:θ] *n* : paresse *f*

slouch ['slaʊtʃ] *vi* : marcher avec les épaules rentrées

slow ['slo:] *adj* **1** : lent **2** be ~ : retarder (se dit d'une horloge) — ~ *adv* → **slowly** — ~ *vt* : retarder — *vi or* ~ **down** : ralentir — **slowly** ['slo:li] *adv* : lentement — **slowness** ['slo:nəs] *n* : lenteur *f*

slug ['slʌg] *n* : limace *f* (mollusque)

sluggish ['slʌgɪʃ] *adj* : lent

slum ['slʌm] *n* : taudis *m*

slumber ['slʌmbər] *vi* : sommeiller — ~ *n* : sommeil *m*

slump ['slʌmp] *vi* **1** DROP : baisser, chuter **2** COLLAPSE : s'effondrer — ~ *n* : crise *f* (économique)

slung → **sling**

slur¹ ['slər] *n* : calomnie *f*, diffamation *f*

slur² *vt* **slurred; slurring** : mal articuler (ses mots)

slurp ['slərp] *v* : boire bruyamment

slush ['slʌʃ] *n* : neige *f* fondue, gadoue *f* Can

sly ['slaɪ] *adj* **slier** ['slaɪər]; **sliest** ['slaɪəst] **1** : rusé, sournois **2** on the ~ : en cachette

smack¹ ['smæk] *vi* ~ **of** : sentir

smack² *vt* **1** : donner une claque à **2** KISS : donner un baiser à — ~ *n* **1** SLAP : claque *f*, gifle *f* **2** KISS : gros baiser *m* — ~ *adv* : juste, exactement

small ['smɔl] *adj* : petit — **smallpox** ['smɔl-ˌpɑks] *n* : variole *f*

smart ['smɑrt] *adj* **1** : intelligent **2** STYLISH : élégant

smash ['smæʃ] *n* **1** COLLISION : choc *m* **2** BANG, CRASH : fracas *m* — ~ *vt* BREAK : fracasser — *vi* **1** SHATTER : se briser **2** ~ **into** : s'écraser contre

smattering ['smætərɪŋ] *n* : notions *fpl* vagues

smear ['smɪr] *n* : tache *f* — ~ *vt* **1** : barbouiller, faire des taches sur **2** ~ **sth on** : enduire qqch de

smell ['smɛl] *v* **smelled** ['smɛld] *or* **smelt** ['smɛlt]; **smelling** : sentir — ~ *n* **1** : odorat *m* **2** ODOR : odeur *f* — **smelly** ['smɛli] *adj* **smellier; -est** : qui sent mauvais

smile ['smaɪl] *vi* **smiled; smiling** : sourire — ~ *n* : sourire *m*

smirk ['smərk] *n* : petit sourire *m* satisfait

smitten ['smɪtən] *adj* be ~ **with** : être épris de

smock ['smɑk] *n* : blouse *f*, sarrau *m*

smog ['smɑg, 'smɔg] *n* : smog *m*

smoke ['smo:k] *n* : fumée *f* — ~ *v* **smoked; smoking** : fumer — **smoke detector** *n* : détecteur *m* de fumée — **smoker** ['smo:kər] *n* : fumeur *m*, -meuse *f* — **smokestack** ['smo:kˌstæk] *n* : cheminée *f* — **smoky** ['smo:ki] *adj* **smokier; -est** : enfumé

smolder ['smo:ldər] *vi* : couver

smooth ['smu:ð] *adj* : lisse (se dit d'une surface, etc.), calme (se dit de la mer), doux (se dit de la peau, etc.) — ~ *or* ~ **out** *vt* : défroisser — **smoothly** ['smu:ðli] *adv* : sans heurts

smother ['smʌðər] *vt* **1** : recouvrir (un feu) **2** : étouffer (qqn)

smudge ['smʌdʒ] *vt* **smudged; smudging** : salir, faire des taches sur — ~ *n* : tache *f*, bavure *f*

smug ['smʌg] *adj* **smugger; smuggest** : suffisant

smuggle ['smʌgəl] *vt* **-gled; -gling** : faire passer en contrebande — **smuggler** ['smʌgələr] *n* : contrebandier *m*, -dière *f*

snack ['snæk] *n* : casse-croûte *m*, collation *f*

snag ['snæg] *n* : accroc *m* — ~ *vt* **snagged; snagging** : faire un accroc à (un bas)

snail ['sneɪl] *n* : escargot *m*

snake ['sneɪk] *n* : serpent *m*

snap ['snæp] *v* **snapped; snapping** *vi* **1** BREAK : se casser, se briser **2** ~ **at** : répondre brusquement à — *vt* **1** BREAK : casser, briser **2** ~ **one's fingers** : claquer des doigts **3** ~ **open/shut** : s'ouvrir, se fermer d'un coup sec — ~ *n* **1** : claquement *m* **2** FASTENER : bouton-pression *m* **3** be a ~ : être facile — **snappy** ['snæpi] *adj* **-pier; -piest 1** FAST : vite **2** STYLISH : élégant — **snapshot** ['snæpˌʃɑt] *n* : instantané *m*

snare ['snær] *n* : piège *m*

snarl¹ ['snɑrl] *vi* TANGLE : enchevêtrer

snarl² *vi* GROWL : grogner — ~ *n* : grognement *m*

snatch ['snætʃ] *vt* : saisir

sneak ['sni:k] *vi* : se glisser, se faufiler — *vt* : faire furtivement — **sneakers** ['sni:kərz] *npl* : tennis *mpl* France, espadrilles *fpl* Can — **sneaky** ['sni:ki] *adj* **sneakier; -est** : sournois

sneer ['snɪr] *vi* : ricaner — ~ *n* : ricanement *m*

sneeze ['sni:z] *vi* **sneezed; sneezing** : éternuer — ~ *n* : éternuement *m*

snide ['snaɪd] *adj* : sarcastique

sniff ['snɪf] *vi* : renifler — ~ *n* : inhalation *f*

— **sniffle** ['snɪfəl] *vi* **-fled; -fling** : renifler
— **sniffles** ['snɪfəlz] *npl* **have the** ~ : être
enrhumé

snip ['snɪp] *n* : coup *m* de ciseaux — ~ *vt*
snipped; snipping : couper

snivel ['snɪvəl] *vi* **-eled** *or* **-elled; -eling** *or*
-elling : pleurnicher *fam*

snob ['snab] *n* : snob *mf* — **snobbish**
['snabɪʃ] *adj* : snob

snoop ['snu:p] *vi or* ~ **around** : fouiner

snooze ['snu:z] *vi* **snoozed; snoozing**
: sommeiller — ~ *n* : petit somme *m*,
sieste *f*

snore ['snor] *vi* **snored; snoring** : ronfler
— ~ *n* : ronflement *m*

snort ['snɔrt] *vi* : grogner (se dit d'un cochon, d'une personne) — ~ *n* : grognement *m*

snout ['snaʊt] *n* : museau *m*, groin *m*

snow ['sno:] *n* : neige *f* — ~ *vi* : neiger —
snowbank ['sno:ˌbæŋk] *n* : banc *m* de
neige *Can* — **snowfall** ['sno:ˌfɔl] *n* : chute *f*
de neige — **snowflake** ['sno:ˌfleɪk] *n* : flocon *m* de neige — **snowman** ['sno:ˌmæn] *n*
: bonhomme *m* de neige — **snowplow**
['sno:ˌplaʊ] *n* : chasse-neige *m* — **snowshoe** ['sno:ˌʃu:] *n* : raquette *f* — **snowstorm** ['sno:ˌstorm] *n* : tempête *f* de neige
— **snowy** ['sno:i] *adj* **snowier; -est** 1
: neigeux 2 : enneigé (se dit d'une montagne, etc.)

snub ['snʌb] *vt* **snubbed; snubbing**
: rabrouer — ~ *n* : rebuffade *f*

snuff ['snʌf] *vt or* ~ **out** : moucher (une
chandelle)

snug ['snʌg] *adj* **snugger; snuggest** 1
: confortable, douillet 2 TIGHT : ajusté —
snuggle ['snʌgəl] *vi* **-gled; -gling** : se blottir

so ['so:] *adv* 1 LIKEWISE : aussi 2 THUS
: ainsi 3 THEREFORE : alors 4 *or* ~ **much**
: tant 5 *or* ~ **very** : si 6 **and** ~ **on** : et
cetera 7 **I think** ~ : je pense que oui 8 **I
told you** ~ : je te l'avais bien dit — ~
conj 1 THEREFORE : donc 2 *or* ~ **that**
: pour que 3 ~ **what?** : et alors? — ~ *adj*
TRUE : vrai — ~ *pron or* ~ : plus ou
moins

soak ['so:k] *vt* 1 : tremper 2 ~ **up** : absorber — ~ *n* : trempage *m*

soap ['so:p] *n* : savon *m* — ~ *vt* ~ **up**
: savonner — **soapy** ['so:pi] *adj* **soapier;
-est** : savonneux

soar ['sor] *vi* 1 : planer 2 INCREASE : monter (en flèche)

sob ['sab] *vi* **sobbed; sobbing** : sangloter
— ~ *n* : sanglot *m*

sober ['so:bər] *adj* 1 : sobre 2 SERIOUS
: sérieux — **sobriety** [sə'braɪəti, so-] *n* 1
: sobriété *f* 2 SERIOUSNESS : sérieux *m*

so-called ['so:'kɔld] *adj* : présumé

soccer ['sakər] *n* : football *m France*, soccer
m Can

social ['so:ʃəl] *adj* : social — ~ *n* : réunion
f — **sociable** ['so:ʃəbəl] *adj* : sociable —
socialism ['so:ʃəˌlɪzəm] *n* : socialisme *m* —
socialist ['so:ʃəlɪst] *n* : socialiste *mf* — ~
adj : socialiste — **socialize** ['so:ʃəˌlaɪz] *v*
-ized; -izing *vt* : socialiser — *vi* ~ **with**
: fréquenter des gens — **society** [sə'saɪəti]
n, *pl* **-eties** : société *f* — **sociology** [ˌso:si-
'alədʒi] *n* : sociologie *f*

sock[1] ['sak] *n*, *pl* **socks** *or* **sox** : chaussette *f*

sock[2] *vt* : donner un coup de poing à

socket ['sakət] *n* 1 *or* **electric** ~ : prise *f*
de courant 2 *or* **eye** ~ : orbite *f*

soda ['so:də] *n* 1 *or* ~ **pop** : boisson *f*
gazeuse, soda *m France*, liqueur *f Can* 2 *or*
~ **water** : soda *m*

sodium ['so:diəm] *n* : sodium *m*

sofa ['so:fə] *n* : canapé *m*

soft ['sɔft] *adj* 1 : mou 2 SMOOTH : doux —
softball ['sɔftˌbɔl] *n* : balle-molle *f Can* —
soft drink *n* : boisson *f* non alcoolisée, boisson *f* gazeuse — **soften** ['sɔfən] *vt* 1 : amollir, ramollir 2 EASE : adoucir, atténuer — *vi*
1 : se ramollir 2 EASE : s'adoucir — **softly**
['sɔftli] *adv* : doucement — **softness**
['sɔftnəs] *n* : douceur *f* — **software** ['sɔft-
ˌwær] *n* : logiciel *m*

soggy ['sagi] *adj* **-gier; -est** : détrempé

soil ['sɔɪl] *vt* : salir, souiller — ~ *n* DIRT
: terre *f*

solace ['saləs] *n* : consolation *f*

solar ['so:lər] *adj* : solaire

sold → **sell**

solder ['sadər, 'sɔ-] *n* : soudure *f* — ~ *vt*
: souder

soldier ['so:ldʒər] *n* : soldat *m*

sole[1] ['so:l] *n* : sole *f* (poisson)

sole[2] *n* : plante *f* (du pied), semelle *f* (d'un
soulier)

sole[3] *adj* : seul — **solely** ['so:li] *adv*
: uniquement

solemn ['saləm] *adj* : solennel — **solemnity**
[sə'lɛmnəti] *n*, *pl* **-ties** : solennité *f*

solicit [sə'lɪsɪt] *vt* : solliciter

solid ['saləd] *adj* 1 : solide 2 UNBROKEN
: continu 3 ~ **gold** : *or* massif 4 **two** ~
hours : deux heures de suite — ~ *n*
: solide *m* — **solidarity** [ˌsalə'dærəti] *n*
: solidarité *f* — **solidify** [sə'lɪdəˌfaɪ] *v* **-fied;
-fying** *vt* : solidifier — *vi* : se solidifier —
solidity [sə'lɪdəti] *n*, *pl* **-ties** : solidité *f*

solitary ['saləˌteri] *adj* : solitaire — **solitude**
['saləˌtu:d, -ˌtju:d] *n* : solitude *f*

solo ['so:ˌlo:] *n*, *pl* **-los** : solo *m* — **soloist**
['so:loɪst] *n* : soliste *mf*

solution [sə'lu:ʃən] *n* : solution *f* — **soluble**
['saljəbəl] *adj* : soluble — **solve** ['salv] *vt*

solved; solving : résoudre — **solvent** [ˈsɑlvənt] *n* : solvent *m*

somber [ˈsɑmbər] *adj* : sombre

some [ˈsʌm] *adj* **1** (*of unspecified identity*) : un **2** (*of an unspecified amount*) : de, un peu de **3** (*of an unspecified number*) : certains **4** SEVERAL : quelques **5** *that was* ∼ *game!* : ça c'était un match! — ∼ *pron* **1** SEVERAL : certains, quelques-uns **2** *do you want* ∼? : en voulez vous? — ∼ *adv* ∼ *twenty people* : une vingtaine de personnes — **somebody** [ˈsʌmbədi, -ˌbɑdi] *pron* : quelqu'un — **someday** [ˈsʌmˌdeɪ] *adv* : un jour — **somehow** [ˈsʌmˌhaʊ] *adv* **1** : pour quelque raison **2** ∼ *or other* : d'une manière ou d'une autre — **someone** [ˈsʌmˌwʌn] *pron* : quelqu'un

somersault [ˈsʌmərˌsɔlt] *n* : culbute *f*

something [ˈsʌmθɪŋ] *pron* **1** : quelque chose **2** ∼ *else* : autre chose — **sometime** [ˈsʌmˌtaɪm] *adv* **1** : un jour, un de ces jours **2** ∼ *next month* : dans le courant du mois à venir — **sometimes** [ˈsʌmˌtaɪmz] *adv* : quelquefois, parfois — **somewhat** [ˈsʌmˌhwɑt, -ˌhwʌt] *adv* : un peu — **somewhere** [ˈsʌmˌhwɛr] *adv* **1** : quelque part **2** ∼ *around* : autour de **3** ∼ *else* → **elsewhere**

son [ˈsʌn] *n* : fils *m*

song [ˈsɔŋ] *n* : chanson *f*

son–in–law [ˈsʌnɪnˌlɔ] *n, pl* **sons–in–law** : gendre *m*, beau-fils *m*

soon [ˈsuːn] *adv* **1** : bientôt **2** SHORTLY : sous peu **3** *as* ∼ *as* : aussitôt que **4** ∼ *after* : peu après **5** ∼ *er or later* : tôt ou tard **6** *the* ∼ *er the better* : le plus tôt sera le mieux

soot [ˈsʊt, ˈsuːt, ˈsʌt] *n* : suie *f*

soothe [ˈsuːð] *vt* **soothed; soothing 1** : calmer, apaiser **2** RELIEVE : soulager

sophisticated [səˈfɪstəˌkeɪtəd] *adj* **1** : perfectionné **2** WORLDLY : sophistiqué

sophomore [ˈsɑfˌmor, ˈsɑfəˌmor] *n* : étudiant *m*, -diante *f* de deuxième année

soprano [səˈpræˌnoː] *n, pl* **-nos** : soprano *mf*

sorcerer [ˈsorsərər] *n* : sorcier *m* — **sorcery** [ˈsorsəri] *n* : sorcellerie *f*

sordid [ˈsordɪd] *adj* : sordide

sore [ˈsor] *adj* **sorer; sorest 1** : douloureux **2** ∼ *loser* : mauvais perdant **3** ∼ *throat* : mal *m* de gorge — ∼ *n* : plaie *f* — **sorely** [ˈsorli] *adv* : grandement — **soreness** [ˈsornəs] *n* : douleur *f*

sorrow [ˈsɑrˌoː] *n* : chagrin *m*, peine *f*

sorry [ˈsɑri] *adj* **-rier; -est 1** PITIFUL : lamentable **2** *feel* ∼ *for* : plaindre **3** *I'm* ∼ : je suis désolé, je regrette

sort [ˈsort] *n* **1** : genre *m*, sorte *f* **2** *a* ∼ *of* : une espèce de — ∼ *vt* : trier, classer — **sort of** *adv* **1** SOMEWHAT : plutôt **2** MORE OR LESS : plus ou moins

SOS [ˌɛsˌoːˈɛs] *n* : S.O.S. *m*

so–so [ˈsoːˈsoː] *adv* : comme ci comme ça — ∼ *adj* : moyen

soufflé [suːˈfleɪ] *n* : soufflé *m*

sought → **seek**

soul [ˈsoːl] *n* **1** : âme *f* **2** *not a* ∼ : pas un chat

sound[1] [ˈsaʊnd] *adj* **1** HEALTHY : sain **2** FIRM : solide **3** SENSIBLE : logique **4** *a* ∼ *sleep* : un sommeil profond **5** *safe and* ∼ : sain et sauf

sound[2] *n* **1** : son *m* **2** NOISE : bruit *m* — ∼ *vt* : sonner, retentir — *vi* **1** : sonner **2** SEEM : sembler, paraître

sound[3] *n* CHANNEL : détroit *m* — ∼ *vt* : sonder

soundproof [ˈsaʊndˌpruːf] *adj* : insonorisé

soup [ˈsuːp] *n* : soupe *f*

sour [ˈsaʊər] *adj* : aigre — ∼ *vt* : aigrir

source [ˈsors] *n* : source *f*, origine *f*

south [ˈsaʊθ] *adv* : au sud, vers le sud — ∼ *adj* : (du) sud — ∼ *n* : sud *m* — **southeast** [saʊˈθiːst] *adv* : au sud-est, vers le sud-est — ∼ *adj* : (du) sud-est — ∼ *n* : sud-est *m* — **southeastern** [saʊˈθiːstərn] *adj* → **southeast** — **southerly** [ˈsʌðərli] *adv & adj* : (du) sud — **southern** [ˈsʌðərn] *adj* : du sud, méridional — **southwest** [saʊθˈwest] *adv* : au sud-ouest, vers le sud-ouest — ∼ *adj* : (du) sud-ouest — ∼ *n* : sud-ouest *m* — **southwestern** [saʊθˈwestərn] *adj* → **southwest**

souvenir [ˌsuːvəˈnɪr, ˈsuːvəˌ-] *n* : souvenir *m*

sovereign [ˈsɑvərən] *n* : souverain *m*, -raine *f* — ∼ *adj* : souverain — **sovereignty** [ˈsɑvərənti] *n, pl* **-ties** : souveraineté *f*

sow[1] [ˈsaʊ] *n* : truie *f*

sow[2] [ˈsoː] *vt* **sowed; sown** [ˈsoːn] *or* **sowed; sowing** : semer

sox → **sock**

soybean [ˈsɔɪˌbiːn] *n* : graine *f* de soja

spa [ˈspɑ] *n* : station *f* thermale

space [ˈspeɪs] *n* **1** : espace *m* **2** ROOM, SPOT : place *f* — ∼ *vt* **spaced; spacing** *or* ∼ *out* : espacer — **spaceship** [ˈspeɪsˌʃɪp] *n* : vaisseau *m* spatial — **space shuttle** *n* : navette *f* spatiale — **spacious** [ˈspeɪʃəs] *adj* : spacieux, ample

spade[1] [ˈspeɪd] *n* SHOVEL : bêche *f*, pelle *f*

spade[2] *n* : pique *f* (aux cartes)

spaghetti [spəˈgɛti] *n* : spaghetti *mpl*

span [ˈspæn] *n* **1** PERIOD : espace *m* **2** : travée *f* (d'un pont) — ∼ *vt* **spanned; spanning 1** : couvrir (une période) **2** CROSS : s'étendre sur

spaniel [ˈspænjəl] *n* : épagneul *m*

Spanish [ˈspænɪʃ] *adj* : espagnol — ∼ *n* : espagnol *m* (langue)

spank [ˈspæŋk] *vt* : donner une fessée à

spare [ˈspær] *vt* **spared; sparing 1** PARDON

: pardonner **2** SAVE : épargner **3 can you ~ a dollar?** : avez-vous un dollar à me prêter? **4 I can't ~ the time** : je n'ai pas le temps **5 ~ no expense** : ne pas ménager ses efforts — **~** *adj* **1** : de rechange **2** EXCESS : de trop — **~** *n or* **~ part** : pièce *f* de rechange — **spare time** *n* : temps *m* libre — **sparing** ['spærɪŋ] *adj* : économe

spark ['spɑrk] *n* : étincelle *f* — **~** *vt* : éveiller, susciter — **sparkle** ['spɑrkəl] *vi* -**kled; -kling** : étinceler, scintiller — **~** *n* : scintillement *m* — **spark plug** *n* : bougie *f*

sparrow ['spæro:] *n* : moineau *m*

sparse ['spɑrs] *adj* **sparser; sparsest** : clairsemé, épars — **sparsely** ['spɑrsli] *adv* : peu

spasm ['spæzəm] *n* : spasme *m*

spat¹ ['spæt] → **spit**

spat² *n* QUARREL : prise *f* de bec

spatter ['spætər] *vt* : éclabousser

spawn ['spɒn] *vi* : frayer — *vt* : engendrer, produire — **~** *n* : frai *m*

speak ['spi:k] *v* **spoke** ['spo:k]; **spoken** ['spo:kən]; **speaking** *vi* **1** : parler **2 ~ out against** : dénoncer **3 ~ up** : parler plus fort **4 ~ up for** : défendre — *vt* **1** : dire **2** : parler (une langue) — **speaker** ['spi:kər] *n* **1** : personne *f* qui parle (une langue) **2** ORATOR : orateur *m*, -trice *f* **3** LOUDSPEAKER : haut-parleur *m*

spear ['spɪr] *n* : lance *f* — **spearhead** ['spɪr-ˌhɛd] *n* : fer *m* de lance — **~** *vt* : mener, être à la tête de — **spearmint** ['spɪrˌmɪnt] *n* : menthe *f* verte

special ['spɛʃəl] *adj* : spécial, particulier — **specialist** ['spɛʃəlɪst] *n* : spécialiste *mf* — **specialize** ['spɛʃəˌlaɪz] *vi* -**ized; -izing** : se spécialiser — **specially** ['spɛʃəli] *adv* : spécialement — **specialty** ['spɛʃəlti] *n, pl* -**ties** : spécialité *f*

species ['spi:ˌʃi:z, -ˌsi:z] *ns & pl* : espèce *f*

specify ['spɛsəˌfaɪ] *vt* -**fied; -fying** : spécifier — **specific** [spɪ'sɪfɪk] *adj* : précis, explicite — **specifically** [spɪ'sɪfɪkli] *adv* **1** : spécialement **2** EXPLICITLY : expressément

specimen ['spɛsəmən] *n* : spécimen *m*, échantillon *m*

speck ['spɛk] *n* **1** SPOT : tache *f* **2** BIT : brin *m* — **speckled** ['spɛkəld] *adj* : tacheté, moucheté

spectacle ['spɛktɪkəl] *n* **1** : spectacle *m* **2 ~s** *npl* GLASSES : lunettes *fpl* — **spectacular** [spɛk'tækjələr] *adj* : spectaculaire — **spectator** ['spɛkˌteɪtər] *n* : spectateur *m*, -trice *f*

specter *or* **spectre** ['spɛktər] *n* : spectre *m*

spectrum ['spɛktrəm] *n, pl* -**tra** [-trə] *or* -**trums 1** : spectre *m* **2** RANGE : gamme *f*

speculation [ˌspɛkjə'leɪʃən] *n* : conjectures *fpl*, spéculations *fpl*

speech ['spi:tʃ] *n* **1** : parole *f* **2** ADDRESS : discours *m* — **speechless** ['spi:tʃləs] *adj* : muet

speed ['spi:d] *n* **1** : vitesse *f* **2** VELOCITY : rapidité *f* — **~** *v* **sped** ['spɛd] *or* **speeded; speeding** *vi* **1** : faire un excès de vitesse **2 ~ off** : aller à toute vitesse — *vt or* **~ up** : accélérer — **speed limit** *n* : limitation *f* de vitesse — **speedometer** [spɪ'dɑmətər] *n* : compteur *m* (de vitesse) — **speedy** ['spi:di] *adj* **speedier; -est** : rapide

spell¹ ['spɛl] *vt* **1** : écrire, orthographier **2** *or* **~ out** : épeler **3** MEAN : signifier

spell² *n* ENCHANTMENT : sortilège *m*

spell³ *n* : période *f* (de temps)

spellbound ['spɛlˌbaʊnd] *adj* : captivé

spelling ['spɛlɪŋ] *n* : orthographe *f*

spend ['spɛnd] *vt* **spent** ['spɛnt]; **spending 1** : dépenser (de l'argent) **2** : passer (ses vacances, etc.)

sperm ['spərm] *n, pl* **sperm** *or* **sperms** : sperme *m*

sphere ['sfɪr] *n* : sphère *f* — **spherical** ['sfɪrɪkəl, 'sfɛr-] *adj* : sphérique

spice ['spaɪs] *n* : épice *f* — **~** *vt* **spiced; spicing** : assaisonner — **spicy** ['spaɪsi] *adj* **spicier; -est** : épicé, piquant

spider ['spaɪdər] *n* : araignée *f*

spigot ['spɪɡət, -kət] *n* : robinet *m*

spike ['spaɪk] *n* **1** : gros clou *m* **2** POINT : pointe *f* — **spiky** ['spaɪki] *adj* -**kier; -est** : pointu

spill ['spɪl] *vt* : renverser, répandre — *vi* : se répandre

spin ['spɪn] *v* **spun** ['spʌn]; **spinning** *vi* : tourner, tournoyer — *vt* **1** : faire tourner **2** : filer (de la laine) — **~** *n* **1** : tour *m* **2 go for a ~** : faire une balade (en auto)

spinach ['spɪnɪtʃ] *n* : épinards *mpl*

spinal cord ['spaɪnəl] *n* : moelle *f* épinière

spindle ['spɪndəl] *n* : fuseau *m* (en textile)

spine ['spaɪn] *n* **1** : colonne *f* vertébrale **2** : piquant *m* (d'un animal) **3** : dos *m* (d'un livre)

spinster ['spɪntstər] *n* : vieille fille *f*

spiral ['spaɪrəl] *adj* : en spirale — **~** *n* : spirale *f* — **~** *vi* -**raled** *or* -**ralled; -raling** *or* -**ralling** : aller en spirale

spire ['spaɪr] *n* : flèche *f*

spirit ['spɪrət] *n* **1** : esprit *m* **2 in good ~s** : de bonne humeur **3 ~s** *npl* : spiritueux *mpl* — **spirited** ['spɪrətəd] *adj* : animé — **spiritual** ['spɪrɪtʃuəl, -tʃəl] *adj* : spirituel — **spirituality** [ˌspɪrɪtʃu'æləti] *n* : spiritualité *f*

spit¹ ['spɪt] *n* : broche *f*

spit² *v* **spit** *or* **spat** ['spæt]; **spitting** : cracher — **~** *n* SALIVA : salive *f*

spite ['spaɪt] *n* **1** : rancune *f* **2 in ~ of** : malgré — **~** *vt* **spited; spiting** : contrarier — **spiteful** ['spaɪtfəl] *adj* : rancunier

splash ['splæʃ] *vt* : éclabousser — *vi or* ~
about : patauger — ~ *n* 1 : éclaboussement *m* 2 : plouf *m* (bruit)
splatter ['splætər] → **spatter**
splice ['splaɪs] *n* : raccord *f* (épissure)
splendid ['splɛndəd] *adj* : splendide — ~
splendor *or Brit* **splendour** ['splɛndər] *n*
: splendeur *f*
splint ['splɪnt] *n* : attelle *f*
splinter ['splɪntər] *n* : éclat *m* — ~ *vi* : se
briser en éclats
split ['splɪt] *v* **split**; **splitting** *vt* 1 : fendre
(du bois), déchirer (un pantalon) 2 *or* ~ **up**
: diviser — *vi* ~ **up** : se séparer — ~ *n* 1
CRACK : fente *f* 2 *or* ~ **seam** : déchirure *f*
splurge ['splərdʒ] *vi* **splurged**; **splurging**
: faire des folles dépenses
spoil ['spɔɪl] *vt* **spoiled** *or* **spoilt** ['spɔɪlt];
spoiling 1 RUIN : gâcher 2 PAMPER : gâter
— **spoils** ['spɔɪlz] *npl* : butin *m*
spoke[1] ['spoːk] → **speak**
spoke[2] *n* : rayon *m* (d'une roue)
spoken → **speak**
spokesman ['spoːksmən] *n, pl* **-men** [-mən,
-ˌmɛn] : porte-parole *m* — **spokeswoman**
['spoːksˌwʊmən] *n, pl* **-women** [-ˌwɪmən]
: porte-parole *f*
sponge ['spʌndʒ] *n* : éponge *f* — ~ *vt*
sponged; **sponging** : éponger — **spongy**
['spʌndʒi] *adj* **spongier**; **-est** : spongieux
sponsor ['spantsər] *n* : parrain *m* (d'une
cause, etc.) — ~ *vt* : patronner — **sponsorship** ['spantsərˌʃɪp] *n* : parrainage *m*,
patronage *m*
spontaneity ['spantəˈniːəti, -ˈneɪ-] *n* : spontanéité *f* — **spontaneous** [spanˈteɪniəs] *adj*
: spontané
spooky ['spuːki] *adj* **spookier**; **-est** : qui
donne la chair de poule
spool ['spuːl] *n* : bobine *f*
spoon ['spuːn] *n* : cuillère *f* — **spoonful**
['spuːnˌfʊl] *n* : cuillerée *f*
sporadic [spəˈrædɪk] *adj* : sporadique
sport ['sport] *n* 1 : sport *m* 2 **be a good** ~
: avoir l'esprit d'équipe — **sportsman**
['sportsmən] *n, pl* **-men** [-mən, -ˌmɛn]
: sportif *m* — **sportswoman** ['sportsˌwʊmən] *n, pl* **-women** [-ˌwɪmən] : sportive
f — **sporty** ['sporti] *adj* **sportier**; **-est**
: sportif
spot ['spat] *n* 1 : tache *f* 2 DOT : pois *m* 3
PLACE : endroit *m*, lieu *m* 4 **in a tight** ~
: dans l'embarras 5 **on the** ~ INSTANTLY
: immédiatement — ~ *vt* **spotted**; **spotting** 1 STAIN : tacher 2 DETECT, NOTICE
: apercevoir, repérer — **spotless** ['spatləs]
adj : impeccable — **spotlight** ['spatˌlaɪt] *n*
1 : projecteur *m*, spot *m* 2 **be in the** ~
: être le centre de l'attention — **spotty**
['spati] *adj* **-tier**; **-est** : irrégulier

spouse ['spaʊs] *n* : époux *m*, épouse *f*
spout ['spaʊt] *vi* : jaillir — ~ *n* : bec *m*
(d'une cruche)
sprain ['spreɪn] *n* : entorse *f*, foulure *f* — ~
vt : **se faire une entorse à, se fouler** (la
cheville, etc.)
sprawl ['sprɔl] *vi* 1 : être affalé (dans un fauteuil, etc.) 2 EXTEND : s'étendre — ~ *n*
: étendue *f*
spray[1] ['spreɪ] *n* BOUQUET : gerbe *f*, bouquet
m
spray[2] *n* 1 MIST : gouttelettes *fpl* fines 2 *or*
aerosol ~ : vaporisateur *m*, bombe *f* 3 *or*
~ **bottle** : atomiseur *m* — ~ *vt* : vaporiser, pulvériser
spread ['sprɛd] *v* **spread**; **spreading** *vt* 1
: propager (une nouvelle), répandre (de l'information) 2 *or* ~ **out** : écarter 3 : étaler,
tartiner (avec de la confiture, etc.) — *vi* 1
: se propager (se dit d'une maladie) 2 *or* ~
out : s'étendre (se dit d'un feu) — ~ *n* 1
: propagation *f*, diffusion *f* 2 PASTE : pâte *f* à
tartiner — **spreadsheet** ['sprɛdˌʃiːt] *n*
: tableur *m*
spree ['spriː] *n* **go on a spending** ~ : faire
de folles dépenses
sprightly ['spraɪtli] *adj* **-lier**; **-est** : vif,
alerte
spring ['sprɪŋ] *v* **sprang** ['spræŋ] *or* **sprung**
['sprʌŋ]; **sprung**; **springing** *vi* 1 : sauter,
bondir 2 ~ **from** : surgir de — *vt* 1 ACTIVATE : actionner 2 ~ **sth on s.o.** : surprendre qqn avec qqch — ~ *n* 1 : puits *m*
2 : printemps *m* (saison) 3 LEAP : bond *m*,
saut *m* 4 RESILIENCE : élasticité *f* 5 : ressort
m (mécanisme) 6 *or* **bedspring** : sommier
m — **springboard** ['sprɪŋˌbord] *n* : tremplin *m* — **springtime** ['sprɪŋˌtaɪm] *n*
: printemps *m* — **springy** ['sprɪŋi] *adj*
springier; **-est** : élastique
sprinkle ['sprɪŋkəl] *v* **-kled**; **-kling** *vt* 1 : arroser 2 DUST : saupoudrer — ~ *n* : petite
averse *f* — **sprinkler** ['sprɪŋkˈlər] *n* : arroseur *m*
sprint ['sprɪnt] *vi* : courir — ~ *n* : sprint *m*
(aux sports)
sprout ['spraʊt] *vi* : germer, pousser — ~ *n*
: pousse *f*
spruce[1] ['spruːs] *vt* **spruced**; **sprucing** ~
up : embellir
spruce[2] *n* : épicéa *m*
spun → **spin**
spur ['spər] *n* 1 : éperon *m* 2 STIMULUS : incitation *f* 3 **on the** ~ **of the moment** : sur
le coup — ~ *vt* **spurred**; **spurring** 1 *or* ~
on : éperonner (un cheval) 2 ~ **on** MOTIVATE : motiver
spurn ['spərn] *vt* : repousser, rejeter
spurt[1] ['spərt] *vi* : jaillir — ~ *n* : jaillissement *m*, jet *m*

spurt[2] *n* **1** : sursaut *m* (d'énérgie, etc.) **2 work in ~s** : travailler par à-coups

spy ['spaɪ] *vi* **spied; spying ~ on** : espionner — **~** *n* : espion *m*

squabble ['skwɑbəl] *n* : dispute *f*, querelle *f* — **~** *vi* **-bled; -bling** : se disputer, se chamailler

squad ['skwɑd] *n* : peloton *m* (militaire), brigade *f* (de police)

squadron ['skwɑdrən] *n* : escadron *m* (de soldats), escadre *f* (de navires ou d'avions)

squalid ['skwɑlɪd] *adj* : sordide

squalor ['skwɑlər] *n* : conditions *fpl* sordides

squander ['skwɑndər] *vt* : gaspiller

square ['skwær] *n* **1** : carré *m* **2** : place *f* (d'une ville) — **~** *adj* **squarer; squarest 1** : carré **2** EVEN : quitte — **~** *vt* **squared; squaring** : carrer (un nombre) — **square root** *n* : racine *f* carrée

squash[1] ['skwɑʃ, 'skwɔʃ] *vt* : écraser, aplatir

squash[2] *n*, *pl* **squashes** *or* **squash** : courge *f*

squat ['skwɑt] *vi* **squatted; squatting** : s'accroupir — **~** *adj* **squatter; squattest** : trapu

squawk ['skwɔk] *n* : cri *m* rauque — **~** *vi* : pousser des cris rauques

squeak ['skwi:k] *vi* : grincer — **~** *n* : grincement *m*

squeal ['skwi:l] *vi* **1** : pousser des cris aigus **2** : crisser (se dit des pneus), grincer (se dit des freins) **3 ~ on** : dénoncer — **~** *n* : petit cri *m* aigu

squeamish ['skwi:mɪʃ] *adj* : impressionnable, délicat

squeeze ['skwi:z] *vt* **squeezed; squeezing 1** : presser, serrer **2** : extraire (du jus) — **~** *n* : pression *f*, resserrement *m*

squid ['skwɪd] *n*, *pl* **squid** *or* **squids** : calmar *m*

squint ['skwɪnt] *vi* : loucher

squirm ['skwərm] *vi* : se tortiller

squirrel ['skwərəl] *n* : écureuil *m*

squirt ['skwərt] *vt* : lancer un jet de — *vi* : jaillir — **~** *n* : jet *m*

stab ['stæb] *n* **1** : coup *m* de couteau **2 ~ of pain** : élancement *m* **3 take a ~ at sth** : tenter de faire qqch — **~** *vt* **stabbed; stabbing 1** KNIFE : poignarder **2** THRUST : planter

stable ['steɪbəl] *n* **1** : étable *f* (pour le bétail) **2** *or* **horse ~** : écurie *f* — **~** *adj* **-bler; -est** : stable — **stability** [stə'bɪləti] *n*, *pl* **-ties** : stabilité *f* — **stabilize** ['steɪbə,laɪz] *vt* **-lized; -lizing** : stabiliser

stack ['stæk] *n* : tas *m*, pile *f* — **~** *vt* : entasser, empiler

stadium ['steɪdiəm] *n*, *pl* **-dia** [-diə] *or* **-diums** : stade *m*

staff ['stæf] *n*, *pl* **staffs** ['stæfs, 'stævz] *or* **staves** ['stævz, 'steɪvz] **1** : bâton *m* **2** *pl* **staffs** PERSONNEL : personnel *m*

stag ['stæg] *n*, *pl* **stags** *or* **stag** : cerf *m*

stage ['steɪʤ] *n* **1** : scène *f* (au théâtre) **2** PHASE : étape *f* **3 the ~** : le théâtre — **~** *vt* **staged; staging 1** : mettre en scène **2** ORGANIZE : organiser

stagger ['stægər] *vi* : tituber, chanceler — *vt* **1** : échelonner **2 be ~ed by** : être stupéfié par — **staggering** ['stægərɪŋ] *adj* : stupéfiant

stagnant ['stægnənt] *adj* : stagnant — **stagnate** ['stæg,neɪt] *vi* **-nated; -nating** : stagner

stain ['steɪn] *vt* **1** : tacher **2** : teindre (du bois) — **~** *n* **1** : tache *f* **2** DYE : teinture *f* — **stainless steel** ['steɪnləs] *n* : acier *m* inoxydable

stair ['stær] *n* **1** STEP : marche *f* **2 ~s** *npl* : escalier *m* — **staircase** ['stær,keɪs] *n* : escalier *m* — **stairway** ['stær,weɪ] *n* : escalier *m*

stake ['steɪk] *n* **1** POST : poteau *m*, pieu *m*, piquet *m* **2** INTEREST : intérêts *mpl* **3 be at ~** : être en jeu — **~** *vt* **staked; staking 1** BET : miser, parier **2 ~ a claim to** : revendiquer

stale ['steɪl] *adj* **staler; stalest 1** : rassis **2** OLD : vieux **3** STUFFY : vicié

stalk[1] ['stɔk] *n* : tige *f* (d'une plante)

stalk[2] *vt* : traquer, suivre

stall[1] ['stɔl] *n* **1** : stalle *f* (d'un cheval, etc.) **2** STAND : stand *m*, kiosque *m* — **~** *vi* : caler (se dit d'un moteur)

stall[2] *vt* : retarder

stallion ['stæljən] *n* : étalon *m*

stalwart ['stɔlwərt] *adj* **1** STRONG : robuste **2 ~ supporter** : partisan *m* inconditionnel

stamina ['stæmənə] *n* : résistance *f*

stammer ['stæmər] *vi* : bégayer — **~** *n* : bégaiement *m*

stamp ['stæmp] *n* **1** SEAL : cachet *m* **2** MARK : tampon *m* **3** *or* **postage ~** : timbre *m* — **~** *vt* **1** : affranchir (une lettre, etc.) **2** IMPRINT : estamper **3** MINT : frapper (la monnaie) **4 ~ one's feet** : taper des pieds

stampede [stæm'pi:d] *n* : débandade *f*, ruée *f*

stance ['stænts] *n* : position *f*

stand ['stænd] *v* **stood** ['stʊd]; **standing** *vi* **1** : être debout **2** BE : être, se trouver **3** CONTINUE : rester valable **4** LIE, REST : reposer **5 ~ back** : reculer **6 ~ out** : ressortir **7** *or* **~ up** : se mettre debout — *vt* **1** PLACE : mettre **2** ENDURE : supporter **3 ~ a chance** : avoir de bonnes chances — **stand by** *vt* **1** : s'en tenir à (une promesse, etc.) **2** SUPPORT : appuyer — **stand for** *vt* **1** MEAN : signifier **2** PERMIT : tolérer —

stand up vi 1 ~ **for** : défendre 2 ~ **up to** : tenir tête à — **stand** n 1 RESISTANCE : résistance f 2 STALL : stand m 3 BASE : pied m 4 POSITION : position f 5 ~s npl : tribune f

standard ['stændʊrd] n 1 . norme f 2 BANNER : étendard m 3 CRITERION : critère m 4 ~ **of living** : niveau m de vie — ~ adj : standard

standing ['stændɪŋ] n 1 RANK : position f, standing m 2 DURATION : durée f

standpoint ['stænd,pɔɪnt] n : point m de vue

standstill ['stænd,stɪl] n 1 **be at a** ~ : être paralysé 2 **come to a** ~ : s'arrêter

stank → **stink**

stanza ['stænzə] n : strophe f

staple[1] ['steɪpəl] n : produit m de base — ~ adj : principal, de base

staple[2] n : agrafe f — ~ vt **-pled; -pling** : agrafer — **stapler** ['steɪplər] n : agrafeuse f

star ['star] n : étoile f — ~ v **starred; starring** vt FEATURE : avoir pour vedette — vi ~ **in** : être la vedette de

starboard ['starbərd] n : tribord m

starch ['startʃ] vt : amidonner — ~ n 1 : amidon m 2 : fécule f (aliment)

stardom ['stardəm] n : célébrité f

stare ['stær] vi **stared; staring** : regarder fixement — ~ n : regard m fixe

starfish ['star,fɪʃ] n : étoile f de mer

stark ['stark] adj 1 PLAIN : austère 2 HARSH : sévère, dur

starling ['starlɪŋ] n : étourneau m

starry ['stari] adj **-rier; -est** : étoilé

start ['start] vi 1 : débuter, commencer 2 SET OUT : partir 3 JUMP : sursauter 4 or ~ **up** : démarrer — vt 1 : commencer 2 CAUSE : provoquer 3 or ~ **up** ESTABLISH : établir 4 or ~ **up** : mettre en marche (un moteur, etc.) — ~ n 1 : commencement m, début m 2 **get an early** ~ : commencer tôt 3 **give s.o. a** ~ : faire sursauter qqn — **starter** ['startər] n : démarreur m (d'un véhicule)

startle ['startəl] vt **-tled; -tling** : surprendre

starve ['starv] v **starved; starving** vi : mourir de faim — vt : affamer — **starvation** [star'veɪʃən] n : faim f

state ['steɪt] n 1 : état m 2 **the States** : les États-Unis — ~ vt **stated; stating** 1 SAY : déclarer 2 REPORT : exposer — **statement** ['steɪtmənt] n 1 : déclaration f 2 or **bank** ~ : relevé m de compte — **statesman** ['steɪtsmən] n, pl **-men** [-mən, -,mɛn] : homme m d'État

static ['stætɪk] adj : statique — ~ n : parasites mpl (en radio, etc.)

station ['steɪʃən] n 1 : gare f (de train) 2 : chaîne f (de télévision), poste m (de radio)

3 → **fire station, police station** — ~ vt : poster, placer — **stationary** ['steɪʃə,nɛri] adj : stationnaire

stationery ['steɪʃə,nɛri] n : papeterie f, papier m à lettres

station wagon n : familiale f

statistic [stə'tɪstɪk] n : statistique f

statue ['stæ,tʃu:] n : statue f

stature ['stætʃər] n : stature f, taille f

status ['steɪtəs, 'stæ-] n 1 : statut m 2 or **marital** ~ : situation f (de famille) 3 or **social** ~ : rang m (social)

statute ['stæ,tʃu:t] n : loi f, règle f

staunch ['stɔntʃ] adj : dévoué

stay[1] ['steɪ] vi 1 REMAIN : rester, demeurer 2 LODGE : séjourner 3 ~ **awake** : rester éveillé 4 ~ **in** : rester à la maison — ~ n : séjour m

stay[2] n SUPPORT : soutien m

stead ['stɛd] n **in s.o.'s** ~ : à la place de qqn — **steadfast** ['stɛd,fæst] adj 1 FIRM : ferme 2 LOYAL : fidèle — **steady** ['stɛdi] adj **steadier; -est** 1 FIRM, SURE : ferme, stable 2 FIXED : fixe 3 CONSTANT : constant — ~ vt **steadied; steadying** : stabiliser

steak ['steɪk] n : bifteck m, steak m

steal ['sti:l] v **stole** ['sto:l]; **stolen** ['sto:lən]; **stealing** : voler

stealthy ['stɛlθi] adj **stealthier; -est** : furtif

steam ['sti:m] n 1 : vapeur f 2 **let off** ~ : se défouler — vt 1 : cuire à la vapeur 2 or ~ **up** : s'embuer

steel ['sti:l] n 1 : acier m 2 ~ **industry** : sidérurgie — ~ adj : en acier, d'acier

steep[1] ['sti:p] adj : raide, à pic

steep[2] vt : infuser (du thé, etc.)

steeple ['sti:pəl] n : clocher m, flèche f

steer[1] ['stɪr] n : bœuf m

steer[2] vt 1 : conduire (une voiture, etc.), gouverner (un navire) 2 GUIDE : diriger — **steering wheel** n : volant m

stem ['stɛm] n : tige f (d'une plante), pied m (d'un verre) — ~ vi ~ **from** : provenir de

stench ['stɛntʃ] n : puanteur f

step ['stɛp] n 1 : pas m 2 RUNG, STAIR : marche f 3 ~ **by** ~ : petit à petit 4 **take** ~s : prendre des mesures 5 **watch your** ~ : faites attention (à la marche) — ~ vi **stepped; stepping** 1 : faire un pas 2 ~ **back** : reculer 3 ~ **down** RESIGN : se retirer 4 ~ **in** : intervenir 5 ~ **out** : sortir (pour un moment) 6 ~ **this way** : par ici — **step up** vt INCREASE : augmenter

stepbrother ['stɛp,brʌðər] n : beau-frère m — **stepdaughter** ['stɛp,dɔtər] n : belle-fille f — **stepfather** ['stɛp,faðər, -,fa-] n : beau-père m

stepladder ['stɛp,lædər] n : escabeau m

stepmother ['stɛp,mʌðər] n : belle-mère f

— **stepsister** ['stɛp,sɪstər] *n* : belle-sœur *f*
—**stepson** ['stɛp,sʌn] *n* : beau-fils *m*
stereo ['stɛri,o:, 'stɪr-] *n, pl* **stereos** : stéréo *f* — ~ *adj* : stéréo
stereotype ['stɛriə,taɪp, 'stɪr-] *vt* -**typed**; -**typing** : stéréotyper — ~ *n* : stéréotype *m*
sterile ['stɛrəl] *adj* : stérile — **sterility** [stə'rɪləti] *n* : stérilité *f* — **sterilization** [,stɛrələ'zeɪʃən] *n* : stérilisation *f* — **sterilize** ['stɛrə,laɪz] *vt* -**ized**; -**izing** : stériliser
sterling silver ['stərlɪŋ] *n* : argent *m* fin
stern[1] ['stərn] *adj* : sévère
stern[2] *n* : poupe *f*
stethoscope ['stɛθə,sko:p] *n* : stéthoscope *m*
stew ['stu:, 'stju:] *n* : ragoût *m* — ~ *vi* 1 : cuire 2 FRET : être préoccupé
steward ['stu:ərd, 'stju:-] *n* 1 : administrateur *m*, -trice *f* 2 : steward *m* (d'un avion, etc.) — **stewardess** ['stu:ərdəs, 'stju:-] *n* : hôtesse *f*
stick[1] ['stɪk] *n* 1 : bâton *m* 2 WALKING STICK : canne *f*
stick[2] *v* **stuck** ['stʌk]; **sticking** *vt* 1 : coller 2 STAB : enfoncer 3 PUT : mettre 4 ~ **out** : sortir, tirer (la langue) — *vi* 1 : se coller 2 JAM : se bloquer 3 ~ **around** : rester 4 ~ **out** PROTRUDE : dépasser 5 ~ **up for** : défendre — **sticker** ['stɪkər] *n* : autocollant *m* — **sticky** ['stɪki] *adj* **stickier**; -**est** : collant
stiff ['stɪf] *adj* 1 RIGID : rigide, raide 2 STILTED : guindé 3 : courbaturé (se dit des muscles) — **stiffen** ['stɪfən] *vt* : renforcer, raidir — *vi* : se durcir, se raidir — **stiffness** ['stɪfnəs] *n* : raideur *f*, rigidité *f*
stifle ['staɪfəl] *vt* -**fled**; -**fling** : étouffer
stigmatize ['stɪgmə,taɪz] *vt* -**tized**; -**tizing** : stigmatiser
still ['stɪl] *adj* 1 : immobile 2 SILENT : tranquille — ~ *adv* 1 : encore, toujours 2 NEVERTHELESS : quand même, tout de même 3 **sit ~!** : reste tranquille! — ~ *n* : quiétude *f*, calme *m* — **stillness** ['stɪlnəs] *n* : calme *m*, silence *m*
stilt ['stɪlt] *n* : échasse *f* — **stilted** ['stɪltəd] *adj* : forcé
stimulate ['stɪmjə,leɪt] *vt* -**lated**; -**lating** : stimuler — **stimulant** ['stɪmjələnt] *n* : stimulant *m* — **stimulation** [,stɪmjə-'leɪʃən] *n* : stimulation *f* — **stimulus** ['stɪmjələs] *n, pl* -**li** [-,laɪ] : stimulant *m*
sting ['stɪŋ] *v* **stung** ['stʌŋ]; **stinging** : piquer — ~ *n* : piqûre *f* — **stinger** ['stɪŋər] *n* : dard *m*, aiguillon *m*
stingy ['stɪndʒi] *adj* **stingier**; -**est** : avare, pingre — **stinginess** ['stɪndʒinəs] *n* : avarice *f*
stink ['stɪŋk] *vi* **stank** ['stæŋk] *or* **stunk**

['stʌŋk]; **stunk**; **stinking** : puer — ~ *n* : puanteur *f*
stint ['stɪnt] *vi* ~ **on** : lésiner sur — ~ *n* : période *f* (de travail)
stipulate ['stɪpjə,leɪt] *vt* -**lated**; -**lating** : stipuler — **stipulation** [,stɪpjə'leɪʃən] *n* : stipulation *f*
stir ['stər] *v* **stirred**; **stirring** *vt* 1 : agiter, remuer 2 MOVE : émouvoir 3 INCITE : inciter 4 *or* ~ **up** PROVOKE : susciter — *vi* : remuer, bouger — ~ *n* COMMOTION : émoi *m*
stirrup ['stərəp, 'stɪr-] *n* : étrier *m*
stitch ['stɪtʃ] *n* : point *m* (en couture, en médecine) — ~ *v* : coudre
stock ['stɑk] *n* 1 INVENTORY : réserve *f*, stock *m* 2 SECURITIES : actions *fpl*, valeurs *fpl* 3 ANCESTRY : lignée *f*, souche *f* 4 BROTH : bouillon *m* 5 **out of** ~ : épuisé 6 **take** ~ **of** : évaluer — ~ *vt* : approvisionner — *vi* ~ **up on** : s'approvisionner en — **stockbroker** ['stɑk,bro:kər] *n* : agent *m* de change
stocking ['stɑkɪŋ] *n* : bas *m*
stock market *n* : Bourse *f*
stocky ['stɑki] *adj* **stockier**; -**est** : trapu
stodgy ['stɑdʒi] *adj* **stodgier**; -**est** 1 DULL : lourd 2 OLD-FASHIONED : vieux-jeu
stoic ['sto:ɪk] *n* : stoïque *mf* — ~ *or* **stoical** [-ɪkəl] *adj* : stoïque
stoke ['sto:k] *vt* **stoked**; **stoking** : alimenter (un feu, etc.)
stole[1] ['sto:l] → **steal**
stole[2] *n* : étole *f*
stolen → **steal**
stomach ['stʌmɪk] *n* : estomac *m* — ~ *vt* : supporter, tolérer — **stomachache** ['stʌmɪk,eɪk] *n* : mal *m* de ventre
stone ['sto:n] *n* 1 : pierre *f* 2 : noyau *m* (d'un fruit) — ~ *vt* **stoned**; **stoning** : lapider — **stony** ['sto:ni] *adj* **stonier**; -**est** : pierreux
stood → **stand**
stool ['stu:l] *n* : tabouret *m*
stoop ['stu:p] *vi* 1 : se baisser, se pencher 2 ~ **to** : s'abaisser à
stop ['stɑp] *v* **stopped**; **stopping** *vt* 1 PLUG : boucher 2 PREVENT : empêcher 3 HALT : arrêter, mettre fin à 4 CEASE : cesser de — *vi* 1 : s'arrêter, stopper 2 CEASE : cesser 3 ~ **by** : passer — ~ *n* 1 : arrêt *m*, halte *f* 2 **come to a** ~ : s'arrêter 3 **put a** ~ **to** : mettre fin à — **stoplight** ['stɑp,laɪt] *n* : feu *m* rouge — **stopper** ['stɑpər] *n* : bouchon *m*
store ['stor] *vt* **stored**; **storing** : emmagasiner, entreposer — ~ *n* 1 SUPPLY : réserve *f*, provision *f* 2 SHOP : magasin *m* — **storage** ['storɪdʒ] *n* : entreposage *m* — **storehouse** ['stor,haʊs] *n* : entrepôt *m* — **storekeeper** ['stor,ki:pər] *n* : commerçant

m, -çante *f* — **storeroom** [ˈstorˌruːm, -ˌrʊm] *n* : magasin *m*, réserve *f*

stork [ˈstɔrk] *n* : cigogne *f*

storm [ˈstɔrm] *n* : orage *m*, tempête *f* — ～ *vi* 1 RAGE : tempêter 2 ～ **out** : partir furieux — vt DIVOMIT : prendre d'assaut — **stormy** [ˈstɔrmi] *adj* **stormier; -est** : orageux

story[1] [ˈstori] *n*, *pl* **stories** 1 TALE : conte *m* 2 ACCOUNT : histoire *f*, récit *m* 3 RUMOR : rumeur *f*

story[2] *n* FLOOR : étage *m*

stout [ˈstaʊt] *adj* 1 RESOLUTE : tenace 2 STURDY : fort 3 FAT : corpulent

stove [ˈstoːv] *n* 1 : poêle *m* (pour chauffer) 2 RANGE : cuisinière *f*

stow [ˈstoː] *vt* 1 : ranger 2 LOAD : charger — *vi* ～ **away** : voyager clandestinement

straddle [ˈstrædəl] *vt* **-dled; -dling** : s'asseoir à califourchon sur

straggle [ˈstrægəl] *vi* **-gled; -gling** : traîner — **straggler** [ˈstrægələr] *n* : traînard *m*, -narde *f*

straight [ˈstreɪt] *adj* 1 : droit 2 : raide (se dit des cheveux) 3 HONEST : franc — ～ *adv* 1 DIRECTLY : (tout) droit, directement 2 FRANKLY : carrément — **straightaway** [ˌstreɪtəˈweɪ] *adv* : immédiatement — **straighten** [ˈstreɪtən] *vt* 1 : redresser, rendre droit 2 *or* ～ **up** : ranger — **straightforward** [streɪtˈfɔrwərd] *adj* 1 FRANK : franc, honnête 2 CLEAR : clair, simple

strain [ˈstreɪn] *vt* 1 : se forcer (la voix), se fatiguer (les yeux), se froisser (un muscle) 2 FILTER : égoutter 3 ～ **oneself** : faire un grand effort — *vi* : s'efforcer — ～ *n* 1 STRESS : stress *m*, tension *f* 2 SPRAIN : foulure *f* — **strainer** [ˈstreɪnər] *n* : passoire *f*

strait [ˈstreɪt] *n* 1 : détroit *m* 2 **in dire** ～**s** : aux abois

strand[1] [ˈstrænd] *vt* **be left** ～**ed** : être abandonné

strand[2] *n* : fil *m*, brin *m*

strange [ˈstreɪndʒ] *adj* **stranger; strangest** 1 : étrange, bizarre 2 UNFAMILIAR : inconnu — **strangely** [ˈstreɪndʒli] *adv* : étrangement — **strangeness** [ˈstreɪndʒnəs] *n* : étrangeté *f* — **stranger** [ˈstreɪndʒər] *n* : étranger *m*, -gère *f*

strangle [ˈstræŋgəl] *vt* **-gled; -gling** : étrangler

strap [ˈstræp] *n* 1 : courroie *f*, sangle *f* 2 *or* **shoulder** ～ : bretelle *f* — ～ *vt* **strapped; strapping** : attacher — **strapless** [ˈstræpləs] *n* : sans bretelles — **strapping** [ˈstræpɪŋ] *adj* : robuste, costaud *fam*

strategy [ˈstrætədʒi] *n*, *pl* **-gies** : stratégie *f* — **strategic** [strəˈtiːdʒɪk] *adj* : stratégique

straw [ˈstrɔ] *n* 1 : paille *f* 2 **the last** ～ : le comble

strawberry [ˈstrɔˌberi] *n*, *pl* **-ries** : fraise *f*

stray [ˈstreɪ] *n* : animal *m* errant — ～ *vi* 1 : errer, vagabonder 2 DEVIATE : s'écarter — ～ *adj* : errant, perdu

streak [ˈstriːk] *n* 1 : raie *f*, bande *f* 2 VEIN : veine *f*

stream [ˈstriːm] *n* 1 : ruisseau *m* 2 FLOW : flot *m*, courant *m* — ～ *vi* : couler — **streamer** [ˈstriːmər] *n* 1 : banderole *f* 2 : serpentin *m* (de papier) — **streamlined** [ˈstriːmˌlaɪnd] *adj* 1 : aérodynamique 2 EFFICIENT : efficace

street [ˈstriːt] *n* : rue *f* — **streetcar** [ˈstriːtˌkɑr] *n* : tramway *m* — **streetlight** [ˈstriːtˌlaɪt] *n* : réverbère *m*

strength [ˈstreŋkθ] *n* 1 : force *f* 2 TOUGHNESS : résistance *f* 3 INTENSITY : intensité *f* 4 ～**s and weaknesses** : qualités et faiblesses — **strengthen** [ˈstreŋkθən] *vt* 1 : fortifier 2 REINFORCE : renforcer 3 INTENSIFY : intensifier

strenuous [ˈstrenjuəs] *adj* 1 : énergique 2 ARDUOUS : ardu — **strenuously** [ˈstrenjuəsli] *adv* : vigoureusement

stress [ˈstres] *n* 1 : stress *m*, tension *f* 2 EMPHASIS : accent *m* — ～ *vt* 1 EMPHASIZE : mettre l'accent sur 2 *or* ～ **out** : stresser — **stressful** [ˈstresfəl] *adj* : stressant

stretch [ˈstretʃ] *vt* 1 : étirer (des muscles, un élastique, etc.) 2 EXTEND : tendre 3 ～ **the truth** : exagérer — *vi* 1 : s'étirer 2 ～ **out** EXTEND : s'étendre — ～ *n* 1 : étirement *m* 2 EXPANSE : étendue *f* 3 : période *f* (de temps) — **stretcher** [ˈstretʃər] *n* : civière *f*, brancard *m*

strew [ˈstruː] *vt* **strewed; strewed** *or* **strewn** [ˈstruːn]; **strewing** : éparpiller

stricken [ˈstrɪkən] *adj* ～ **with** : affligé de (une émotion), atteint de (une maladie)

strict [ˈstrɪkt] *adj* : strict — **strictly** *adv* ～ **speaking** : à proprement parler

stride [ˈstraɪd] *vi* **strode** [ˈstroːd]; **stridden** [ˈstrɪdən]; **striding** : marcher à grandes enjambées — ～ *n* 1 : grand pas *m*, enjambée *f* 2 **make great** ～**s** : faire de grands progrès

strident [ˈstraɪdənt] *adj* : strident

strife [ˈstraɪf] *n* : conflit *m*

strike [ˈstraɪk] *v* **struck** [ˈstrʌk]; **struck**; **striking** *vt* 1 HIT : frapper 2 *or* ～ **against** : heurter 3 *or* ～ **out** DELETE : rayer 4 : sonner (l'heure) 5 IMPRESS : impressionner 6 : découvrir (de l'or, du pétrole) 7 **it** ～**s me that ...** : il m'apparaît que ... 8 ～ **up** START : commencer — *vi* 1 : frapper 2 ATTACK : attaquer 3 : faire grève — ～ *n* 1 BLOW : coup *m* 2 : grève *f* (des transports, etc.) 3 ATTACK : attaque *f* 4 : prise *f* *Can* (au baseball) — **striker** [ˈstraɪkər] *n*

: gréviste *mf* — **striking** ['straɪkɪŋ] *adj*
: frappant, saisissant

string ['strɪŋ] *n* **1** : ficelle *f* **2** SERIES : suite
f **3** ~**s** *npl* : cordes *fpl* (d'un orchestre) —
~ *vi* **strung** ['strʌŋ]; **stringing** : enfiler —
string bean *n* : haricot *m* vert

stringent ['strɪndʒənt] *adj* : rigoureux, strict

strip[1] ['strɪp] *v* **stripped; stripping** *vt* RE-
MOVE : enlever — *vi* UNDRESS : se déshabiller

strip[2] *n* : bande *f*

stripe ['straɪp] *n* : rayure *f*, bande *f* —
striped ['straɪpt, 'straɪpəd] *adj* : rayé, à
rayures

strive ['straɪv] *vi* **strove** ['stro:v]; **striven**
['strɪvən] *or* **strived; striving 1** ~ **for** : lutter pour **2** ~ **to** : s'efforcer de

strode → **stride**

stroke ['stro:k] *vt* **stroked; stroking** : caresser — ~ *n* : attaque *f* (cérébrale)

stroll ['stro:l] *vi* : se promener — ~ *n*
: promenade *f* — **stroller** ['stro:lər] *n*
: poussette *f* (pour enfants)

strong ['strɔŋ] *adj* : fort, robuste — **stronghold** ['strɔŋ,ho:ld] *n* : bastion *m* —
strongly ['strɔŋli] *adv* **1** DEEPLY : profondément **2** TOTALLY : totalement **3** VIG-
OROUSLY : énergiquement

strove → **strive**

struck → **strike**

structure ['strʌktʃər] *n* : structure *f* — **structural** ['strʌktʃərəl] *adj* : structural

struggle ['strʌɡəl] *vi* **-gled; -gling 1** : lutter,
se débattre **2** STRIVE : s'efforcer — ~ *n*
: lutte *f*

strung → **string**

strut ['strʌt] *vi* **strutted; strutting** : se pavaner

stub ['stʌb] *n* : mégot *m* (de cigarette), bout
m (de crayon, etc.), talon *m* (de chèque) —
~ *vt* **stubbed; stubbing** ~ **one's toe** : se
cogner le doigt de pied

stubble ['stʌbəl] *n* : barbe *f* de plusieurs
jours

stubborn ['stʌbərn] *adj* **1** : têtu, obstiné **2**
PERSISTENT : tenace

stuck → **stick** — **stuck–up** ['stʌk'ʌp] *adj*
: prétentieux

stud[1] ['stʌd] *n* : étalon *m*

stud[2] *n* **1** NAIL : clou *m* **2** : montant *m* (en
construction)

student ['stu:dənt, 'stju:-] *n* : élève *m*, élève
f (au primaire); étudiant *m*, -diante *f* (universitaire) — **studio** ['stu:di,o:, 'stju:-] *n, pl*
-dios : studio *m*, atelier *m* — **study** ['stʌdi]
n, pl **studies** *f* : étude *f* **2** OFFICE : bureau
m — ~ *v* **studied; studying** : étudier —
studious ['stu:diəs, 'stju:-] *adj* : studieux

stuff ['stʌf] *n* **1** : affaires *fpl*, choses *fpl* **2**
MATTER, SUBSTANCE : chose *f* — ~ *vt* **1**

FILL : rembourrer **2** CRAM : fourrer —
stuffing ['stʌfɪŋ] *n* : rembourrage *m* —
stuffy ['stʌfi] *adj* **stuffier; -est 1** STODGY
: ennuyeux **2** : bouché (se dit du nez) **3** ~
room : pièces *fpl* mal aérées

stumble ['stʌmbəl] *vi* **-bled; -bling 1**
: trébucher **2** ~ **across** *or* ~ **upon**
: tomber sur

stump ['stʌmp] *n* **1** : moignon *m* (d'un
membre) **2** *or* **tree** ~ : souche *f* — ~ *vt*
: laisser perplexe

stun ['stʌn] *vt* **stunned; stunning 1** : assommer (avec un coup) **2** ASTONISH : étonner

stung → **sting**

stunk → **stink**

stunning ['stʌnɪŋ] *adj* **1** : incroyable, sensationnel **2** STRIKING : frappant

stunt[1] ['stʌnt] *vt* : rabougrir

stunt[2] *n* : prouesse *f* (acrobatique)

stupid ['stu:pəd, 'stju:-] *adj* **1** : stupide **2**
SILLY : bête — **stupidity** [stʊ'pɪdəti, stju-]
n, pl **-ties** : stupidité *f*

sturdy ['stərdi] *adj* **-dier; -est 1** : fort, résistant **2** ROBUST : robuste — **sturdiness**
['stərdinəs] *n* : solidité *f*

stutter ['stʌtər] *vi* : bégayer — ~ *n* : bégaiement *m*

sty ['staɪ] *n* **1** *pl* **sties** PIGPEN : porcherie *f* **2**
pl **sties** *or* **styes** : orgelet *m*

style ['staɪl] *n* **1** : style *m* **2** FASHION : mode
f — ~ *vt* **styled; styling** : coiffer (les
cheveux) — **stylish** ['staɪlɪʃ] *adj* : chic, élégant

suave ['swɑv] *adj* : raffiné et affable

subconscious [ˌsʌb'kɑntʃəs] *adj* : subconscient — ~ *n* : subconscient *m*

subdivision [ˌsʌbdə,vɪʒən] *n* : subdivision *f*

subdue [səb'du:, -'dju:] *vt* **-dued; -duing 1**
CONQUER : subjuguer **2** CONTROL
: dominer **3** SOFTEN : atténuer — **subdued**
[səb'du:,d, -'dju:d] *adj* : atténué

subject ['sʌbdʒɪkt] *n* **1** : sujet *m* **2** TOPIC
: matière *f* — ~ *adj* **1** : asservi **2** ~ **to**
: sujet à — ~ [səb'dʒɛkt] *vt* ~ **to** : soumettre à — **subjective** [səb'dʒɛktɪv] *adj*
: subjectif

subjunctive [səb'dʒʌnktɪv] *n* : subjonctif *m*

sublet ['sʌb,lɛt] *vt* **-let; -letting** : sous-louer

sublime [sə'blaɪm] *adj* : sublime

submarine ['sʌbmə,ri:n, ˌsʌbmə'-] *n* : sous-
marin *m*

submerge [səb'mərdʒ] *vt* **-merged; -merg-
ing** : submerger

submit [səb'mɪt] *v* **-mitted; -mitting** *vi* **1**
YIELD : se rendre **2** ~ **to** : se soumettre à
— *vt* : soumettre — **submission** [səb-
'mɪʃən] *n* : soumission *f* — **submissive**
[səb'mɪsɪv] *adj* : soumis

subordinate [sə'bɔrdənət] *adj* : subordonné

— ~ *n* : subordonné *m*, -née *f* — ~ [sə-'bɔrdən,eɪt] *vt* -**nated; -nating** : subordonner

subpoena [sə'pi:nə] *n* : assignation *f*

subscribe [səb'skraɪb] *vi* -**scribed; -scribing** ~ **to** : s'abonner à (un magazine, etc.) — **subscriber** [səb'skraɪbər] *n* : abonné *m*, -née *f* — **subscription** [səb'skrɪpʃən] *n* : abonnement *m*

subsequent ['sʌbsɪkwənt, -sə,kwɛnt] *adj* **1** : subséquent, suivant **2** ~ **to** : postérieur à — **subsequently** ['sʌbsɪ,kwɛntli, -,kwənt-] *adv* : par la suite

subservient [səb'sərviənt] *adj* : servile

subside [səb'saɪd] *vi* -**sided; -siding** : s'atténuer

subsidiary [səb'sɪdi,ɛri] *adj* : secondaire — ~ *n, pl* -**aries** : filiale *f*

subsidy ['sʌbsədi] *n, pl* -**dies** : subvention *f* — **subsidize** ['sʌbsə,daɪz] *vt* -**dized; -dizing** : subventionner

subsistence [səb'sɪstənts] *n* : subsistance *f* — **subsist** [səb'sɪst] *vi* : subsister

substance ['sʌbstənts] *n* : substance *f*

substandard [,sʌb'stændərd] *adj* : inférieur

substantial [səb'stænʧəl] *adj* : substantiel — **substantially** [səb'stænʧəli] *adv* : considérablement

substitute ['sʌbstə,tu:t, -,tju:t] *n* **1** : remplaçant *m*, -çante *f*; suppléant *m*, -pléante *f* **2** : succédané *m* (d'une chose) — ~ *vt* -**tuted; -tuting** : substituer, remplacer

subtitle ['sʌb,taɪtəl] *n* : sous-titre *m*

subtle ['sʌtəl] *adj* -**tler; -tlest** : subtil — **subtlety** ['sʌtəlti] *n, pl* -**ties** : subtilité *f*

subtraction [səb'trækʃən] *n* : soustraction *f* — **subtract** [səb'trækt] *vt* : soustraire

suburb ['sʌ,bərb] *n* **1** : quartier *m* résidentiel **2** **the** ~**s** : la banlieue — **suburban** [sə'bərbən] *adj* : de banlieue

subversive [səb'vərsɪv] *adj* : subversif

subway ['sʌb,weɪ] *n* : métro *m*

succeed [sək'si:d] *vt* : succéder à — *vi* : réussir — **success** [sək'sɛs] *n* : réussite *f*, succès *m* — **successful** [sək'sɛsfəl] *adj* : réussi — **successfully** [sək'sɛsfəli] *adv* : avec succès

succession [sək'sɛʃən] *n* **1** : succession *f* **2** **in** ~ : successivement, de suite — **successive** [sək'sɛsɪv] *adj* : successif — **successor** [sək'sɛsər] *n* : successeur *m*

succinct [sək'sɪŋkt, sə'sɪŋkt] *adj* : succinct

succumb [sə'kʌm] *vi* : succomber

such ['sʌʧ] *adj* **1** : tel, pareil **2** ~ **as** : comme **3** ~ **a pity!** : quel dommage! — ~ *pron* **1** : tel **2 as** ~ : comme tel — ~ *adv* **1** VERY : très **2** ~ **a nice man!** : un homme si gentil! **3** ~ **that** : de façon à ce que

suck ['sʌk] *vt* **1** *or* ~ **on** : sucer **2** *or* ~ **up**

: absorber (un liquide), aspirer (avec une machine) — **suckle** ['sʌkəl] *v* -**led; -ling** *vt* : allaiter — *vi* : téter — **suction** ['sʌkʃən] *n* : succion *f*

sudden ['sʌdən] *adj* **1** : soudain, subit **2 all of a** ~ : tout à coup — **suddenly** ['sʌdənli] *adv* ~ : soudainement, subitement

suds ['sʌdz] *npl* : mousse *f* (de savon)

sue ['su:] *vt* **sued; suing** : poursuivre en justice

suede ['sweɪd] *n* : daim *m*, suède *m*

suet ['su:ət] *n* : graisse *f* de rognon

suffer ['sʌfər] *vi* : souffrir — **suffering** ['sʌfərɪŋ] *n* : souffrance *f*

suffice [sə'faɪs] *vi* -**ficed; -ficing** : être suffisant, suffir — **sufficient** [sə'fɪʃənt] *adj* : suffisant — **sufficiently** [sə'fɪʃəntli] *adv* : suffisamment

suffix ['sʌ,fɪks] *n* : suffixe *m*

suffocate ['sʌfə,keɪt] *v* -**cated; -cating** *vt* : asphyxier, suffoquer — *vi* : s'asphyxier, suffoquer

suffrage ['sʌfrɪʤ] *n* : suffrage *m*

sugar ['ʃʊgər] *n* : sucre *m* — **sugarcane** ['ʃʊgər,keɪn] *n* : canne *f* à sucre — **sugarhouse** ['ʃʊgər,haʊs] *n* : cabane *f* (à sucre) *Can*

suggestion [səg'ʤɛsʧən, sə-] *n* : suggestion *f*, proposition *f* — **suggest** [səg'ʤɛst, sə-] *vt* **1** : proposer, suggérer **2** INDICATE : laisser supposer

suicide ['su:ə,saɪd] *n* **1** : suicide *m* **2 commit** ~ : se suicider — **suicidal** [,su:ə-'saɪdəl] *adj* : suicidaire

suit ['su:t] *n* **1** : complet *m* (d'homme), tailleur *m* (de femme) **2** : couleur *f* (aux cartes) — ~ *vt* : convenir à, aller à — **suitable** ['su:təbəl] *adj* : convenable, approprié — **suitcase** ['su:t,keɪs] *n* : valise *f*

suite ['swi:t] *n* : suite *f*

suitor ['su:tər] *n* : prétendant *m*

sulfur *or Brit* **sulphur** ['sʌlfər] *n* : soufre *m*

sulk ['sʌlk] *vi* : bouder — **sulky** ['sʌlki] *adj* **sulkier; -est** : boudeur

sullen ['sʌlən] *adj* : maussade, morose

sulphur *Brit* → **sulfur**

sultry ['sʌltri] *adj* -**trier; -est 1** : étouffant, lourd **2** SENSUAL : sensuel

sum ['sʌm] *n* : somme *f* — ~ *vt* **summed; summing** ~ **up** : résumer — **summarize** ['sʌmə,raɪz] *v* -**rized; -rizing** *vt* : résumer — *vi* : se résumer — **summary** ['sʌməri] *n, pl* -**ries** : sommaire *m*, résumé *m*

summer ['sʌmər] *n* : été *m*

summit ['sʌmət] *n* : sommet *m*, cime *f*

summon ['sʌmən] *vt* **1** : appeler (qqn), convoquer (une réunion) **2** : citer (en droit) — **summons** ['sʌmənz] *n, pl* **summonses** SUBPOENA : assignation *f*

sumptuous ['sʌmpʧuəs] *adj* : somptueux

sun [ˈsʌn] *n* : soleil *m* — **sunbathe** [ˈsʌnˌbeɪð] *vi* **-bathed; -bathing** : prendre un bain de soleil — **sunburn** [ˈsʌnˌbərn] *n* : coup *m* de soleil

Sunday [ˈsʌnˌdeɪ, -di] *n* : dimanche *m*

sunflower [ˈsʌnˌflaʊər] *n* : tournesol *m*

sung → **sing**

sunglasses [ˈsʌnˌglæsəz] *npl* : lunettes *fpl* de soleil

sunk → **sink**

sunlight [ˈsʌnˌlaɪt] *n* : (lumière *f* du) soleil *m* — **sunny** [ˈsʌni] *adj* **-nier; -est** : ensoleillé — **sunrise** [ˈsʌnˌraɪz] *n* : lever *m* du soleil — **sunset** [ˈsʌnˌset] *n* : coucher *m* du soleil — **sunshine** [ˈsʌnˌʃaɪn] *n* : (lumière *f* du) soleil *m* — **suntan** [ˈsʌnˌtæn] *n* : hâle *m*, bronzage *m*

super [ˈsuːpər] *adj* : super *fam*, génial

superb [sʊˈpərb] *adj* : superbe

superficial [ˌsuːpərˈfɪʃəl] *adj* : superficiel

superfluous [sʊˈpərfluəs] *adj* : superflu

superintendent [ˌsuːpərɪnˈtendənt] *n* **1** : commissaire *m* (de police) **2** *or* **building** ~ : concierge *mf* **3** *or* **school** ~ : inspecteur *m*, -trice *f*

superior [sʊˈpɪriər] *adj* : supérieur — ~ *n* : supérieur *m*, -rieure *f* — **superiority** [sʊˌpɪriˈɔrəti] *n*, *pl* **-ties** : supériorité *f*

superlative [sʊˈpərlətɪv] *n* : superlatif *m*

supermarket [ˈsuːpərˌmɑrkət] *n* : supermarché *m*

supernatural [ˌsuːpərˈnætʃərəl] *adj* : surnaturel

superpower [ˈsuːpərˌpaʊər] *n* : superpuissance *f*

supersede [ˌsuːpərˈsiːd] *vt* **-seded; -seding** : remplacer, supplanter

superstition [ˌsuːpərˈstɪʃən] *n* : superstition *f* — **superstitious** [ˌsuːpərˈstɪʃəs] *adj* : superstitieux

supervise [ˈsuːpərˌvaɪz] *vt* **-vised; -vising** : surveiller, superviser — **supervision** [ˌsuːpərˈvɪʒən] *n* : surveillance *f*, supervision *f* — **supervisor** [ˈsuːpərˌvaɪzər] *n* : surveillant *m*, -lante *f*

supper [ˈsʌpər] *n* : dîner *m*, souper *m* *Can*

supplant [səˈplænt] *vt* : supplanter

supple [ˈsʌpəl] *adj* **-pler; -plest** : souple

supplement [ˈsʌpləmənt] *n* : supplément *m* — ~ [ˈsʌpləˌment] *vt* : compléter, augmenter

supply [səˈplaɪ] *vt* **-plied; -plying 1** : fournir **2** ~ **with** : approvisionner en — ~ *n*, *pl* **-plies 1** : provision *f*, réserve *f* **2** ~ **and demand** : l'offre et la demande **3 supplies** *npl* : provisions *fpl*, vivres *mpl* **4 supplies** *npl* : fournitures *fpl* (de bureau, etc.) — **supplier** [səˈplaɪər] *n* : fournisseur *m*, -seuse *f*

support [səˈport] *vt* **1** BACK : soutenir, appuyer **2** : subvenir aux besoins de (une famille, etc.) **3** PROP UP : supporter — ~ *n* **1** : appui *m*, soutien *m* **2** PROP : support *m* — **supporter** [səˈportər] *n* **1** : partisan *m*, -sane *f* **2** FAN : supporter *m*

suppose [səˈpoːz] *vt* **-posed; -posing 1** : supposer **2 be** ~**d to do sth** : être censé faire qqch — **supposedly** [səˈpoːzədli] *adv* : soi-disant

suppress [səˈpres] *vt* **1** : réprimer **2** WITHHOLD : supprimer

supreme [sʊˈpriːm] *adj* : suprême — **supremacy** [sʊˈprɛməsi] *n*, *pl* **-cies** : suprématie *f*

sure [ˈʃʊr] *adj* **surer; surest 1** : sûr **2 make** ~ **that** : s'assurer que — ~ *adv* **1** OF COURSE : bien sûr **2 it** ~ **is hot!** : quelle chaleur! — **surely** [ˈʃʊrli] *adv* : sûrement

surfing [ˈsərfɪŋ] *n* : surf *m*

surface [ˈsərfəs] *n* **1** : surface *f* **2** AREA : superficie *f* — ~ *vi* **-faced; -facing** : faire surface, remonter à la surface — *vt* : revêtir (une chaussée)

surfboard [ˈsərfˌbord] *n* : planche *f* de surf

surfeit [ˈsərfət] *n* : excès *m*

surfing [ˈsərfɪŋ] *n* : surf *m*

surge [ˈsərdʒ] *vi* **surged; surging** : déferler — ~ *n* **1** : déferlement *m* (de la mer), ruée *f* (de personnes, etc.) **2** INCREASE : augmentation *f* (subite)

surgeon [ˈsərdʒən] *n* : chirurgien *m*, -gienne *f* — **surgery** [ˈsərdʒəri] *n*, *pl* **-geries** : chirurgie *f* — **surgical** [ˈsərdʒɪkəl] *adj* : chirurgical

surly [ˈsərli] *adj* **-lier; -est** : revêche, bourru

surname [ˈsərˌneɪm] *n* : nom *m* de famille

surpass [sərˈpæs] *vt* : surpasser

surplus [ˈsərˌplʌs] *n* : excédent *m*, surplus *m*

surprise [səˈpraɪz, sər-] *n* **1** : surprise *f* **2 take by** ~ : prendre au dépourvu — ~ *vt* **-prised; -prising** : surprendre — **surprising** [səˈpraɪzɪŋ, sər-] *adj* : surprenant

surrender [səˈrendər] *vt* : rendre, céder — *vi* : se rendre — ~ *n* : capitulation *f*, reddition *f*

surround [səˈraʊnd] *vt* : entourer — **surroundings** [səˈraʊndɪŋz] *npl* : environs *mpl*, alentours *mpl*

surveillance [sərˈveɪlənts, -ˈveɪljənts, -ˈveɪənts] *n* : surveillance *f*

survey [sərˈveɪ] *vt* **-veyed; -veying 1** : arpenter (un terrain) **2** INSPECT : inspecter **3** POLL : sonder — ~ [ˈsərˌveɪ] *n*, *pl* **-veys 1** INSPECTION : inspection *f* **2** POLL : sondage *m* — **surveyor** [sərˈveɪər] *n* : arpenteur *m*, -teuse *f*

survive [sərˈvaɪv] *v* **-vived; -viving** *vi* : survivre — *vt* : survivre à — **survival** [sərˈvaɪvəl] *n* : survie *f* — **survivor** [sərˈvaɪvər] *n* : survivant *m*, -vante *f*

susceptible [sə'sɛptəbəl] *adj* ~ **to** : prédisposé à

suspect ['sʌs,pɛkt, sə'spɛkt] *adj* : suspect — ~ ['sʌs,pɛkt] *n* : suspect *m*, -pecte *f* — ~ [sə'spɛkt] *vt* 1 : douter de, se méfier de 2 ~ of : soupçonner qqn de

suspend [sə'spɛnd] *vt* : suspendre — **suspenders** [sə'spɛndərz] *npl* : bretelles *fpl* — **suspense** [sə'spɛnts] *n* 1 : incertitude *f* 2 : suspense *m* (au cinéma, etc.)

suspicion [sə'spɪʃən] *n* : soupçon *m* — **suspicious** [sə'spɪʃəs] *adj* 1 QUESTIONABLE : suspect 2 DISTRUSTFUL : soupçonneux

sustain [sə'steɪn] *vt* 1 SUPPORT : soutenir 2 NOURISH : nourrir 3 SUFFER : subir

swagger ['swægər] *vi* : se pavaner

swallow[1] ['swɑːlo:] *vt* 1 : avaler 2 *or* ~ **up** : engloutir — ~ *n* : gorgée *f*

swallow[2] *n* : hirondelle *f*

swam → **swim**

swamp ['swɑmp] *n* : marais *m*, marécage *m* — ~ *vt* : inonder — **swampy** ['swɑmpi] *adj* **swampier; -est** : marécageux

swan ['swɑn] *n* : cygne *m*

swap ['swɑp] *vt* **swapped; swapping** : échanger — ~ *n* : échange *m*

swarm ['swɔrm] *n* : essaim *m* (d'abeilles, etc.) — ~ *vi* ~ **with** : grouiller de

swat ['swɑt] *vt* **swatted; swatting** : écraser (un insecte)

sway ['sweɪ] *n* 1 : balancement *m* 2 INFLUENCE : influence *f* — ~ *vi* : se balancer — *vt* : influencer

swear ['swær] *v* **swore** ['swor]; **sworn** ['sworn]; **swearing** *vi* CURSE : jurer — *vt* VOW : jurer — **swearword** ['swær,wərd] *n* : juron *m*

sweat ['swɛt] *vi* **sweat** *or* **sweated; sweating** : transpirer — ~ *n* : sueur *f*, transpiration *f*

sweater ['swɛtər] *n* : pull-over *m France*, chandail *m*

sweaty ['swɛti] *adj* **sweatier; -est** : en sueur

sweep ['swiːp] *v* **swept** ['swɛpt] **sweeping** *vt* 1 : balayer 2 *or* ~ **aside** : écarter — *vi* : balayer — ~ *n* 1 : coup *m* de balai 2 SCOPE : étendue *f* — **sweeping** ['swiːpɪŋ] *adj* 1 WIDE : large 2 EXTENSIVE : de grande portée

sweet ['swiːt] *adj* 1 : doux, sucré 2 PLEASANT : agréable, gentil — ~ *n* : bonbon *m*, dessert *m* — **sweeten** ['swiːtən] *vt* : sucrer — **sweetener** ['swiːtənər] *n* : édulcorant *m* — **sweetheart** ['swiːt,hɑrt] *n* 1 : petit ami *m*, petite amie *f* 2 (*used as a term of address*) : chéri *m*, -rie *f* — **sweetness** ['swiːtnəs] *n* : douceur *f* — **sweet potato** *n* : patate *f* douce

swell ['swɛl] *vi* **swelled; swelled** *or* **swollen** ['swoːlən, 'swʌl-]; **swelling** 1 *or* ~ **up** : enfler, gonfler 2 INCREASE : augmenter — ~ *n* : houle *f* (de la mer) — **swelling** ['swɛlɪŋ] *n* : enflure *f*, gonflement *m*

sweltering ['swɛltərɪŋ] *adj* : étouffant

swept → **sweep**

swerve ['swərv] *vi* **swerved; swerving** : faire une embardée — ~ *n* : embardée *f*

swift ['swɪft] *adj* : rapide — **swiftly** ['swɪftli] *adv* : rapidement

swim ['swɪm] *vi* **swam** ['swæm]; **swum** ['swʌm]; **swimming** 1 : nager 2 REEL : tourner — ~ *n* 1 : baignade *f* 2 **go for a** ~ : aller se baigner — **swimmer** ['swɪmər] *n* : nageur *m*, -geuse *f*

swindle ['swɪndəl] *vt* **-dled; -dling** : escroquer — ~ *n* : escroquerie *f* — **swindler** ['swɪndələr] *n* : escroc *m*

swine ['swaɪn] *ns & pl* : porc *m*

swing ['swɪŋ] *v* **swung** ['swʌŋ]; **swinging** *vt* : balancer, faire osciller — *vi* 1 : se balancer, osciller 2 SWIVEL : tourner — ~ *n* 1 : va-et-vient *m*, balancement *m* 2 : balançoire *f* (dans un terrain de jeu) 3 **be in full** ~ : battre son plein

swipe ['swaɪp] *vt* **swiped; swiping** 1 : passer dans un lecteur de cartes 2 STEAL : piquer *fam*

swirl ['swərl] *vi* : tourbillonner — ~ *n* : tourbillon *m*

swish ['swɪʃ] *vi* RUSTLE : faire un bruit léger

Swiss ['swɪs] *adj* : suisse

switch ['swɪtʃ] *n* 1 CHANGE : changement *m* 2 : interrupteur *m* (d'électricité), bouton *m* (d'une radio ou d'une télévision) — ~ *vt* 1 CHANGE : changer de 2 ~ **on** : ouvrir, allumer 3 ~ **off** : couper, fermer, éteindre — *vi* SWAP : échanger — **switchboard** ['swɪtʃ,bord] *n or* **telephone** ~ : standard *m*

swivel ['swɪvəl] *vi* **-eled** *or* **-elled; -eling** *or* **-elling** : pivoter

swollen → **swell**

swoop ['swuːp] *vi* ~ **down on** : s'abattre sur — ~ *n* : descente *f* en piqué

sword ['sord] *n* : épée *f*

swordfish ['sord,fɪʃ] *n* : espadon *m*

swore, sworn → **swear**

swum → **swim**

swung → **swing**

syllable ['sɪləbəl] *n* : syllabe *f*

syllabus ['sɪləbəs] *n, pl* **-bi** [-,baɪ] *or* **-buses** : programme *m* (d'études)

symbol ['sɪmbəl] *n* : symbole *m* — **symbolic** [sɪm'bɑlɪk] *adj* : symbolique — **symbolism** ['sɪmbə,lɪzəm] *n* : symbolisme *m* — **symbolize** ['sɪmbə,laɪz] *vt* **-ized; -izing** : symboliser

symmetry ['sɪmətri] *n, pl* **-tries** : symétrie *f* — **symmetrical** [sə'mɛtrɪkəl] *adj* : symétrique

sympathy ['sɪmpəθi] *n, pl* **-thies 1** COMPAS- SION : sympathie *f* **2** UNDERSTANDING : compréhension *f* **3** CONDOLENCES : con- doléances *fpl* — **sympathetic** [ˌsɪmpə- 'θεɪ̯k] *adj* **1** COMPASSIONATE : compa- tissant **2** UNDERSTANDING : compréhensif — **sympathize** ['sɪmpəˌθaɪz] *vi* **-thized; -thizing ～ with 1** PITY : plaindre **2** UN- DERSTAND : comprendre

symphony ['sɪmↄfəni] *n, pl* **-nies** : sym- phonie *f*

symposium [sɪm'poːziəm] *n, pl* **-sia** [-ziə] *or* **-siums** : symposium *m*

symptom ['sɪmptəm] *n* : symptôme *m*

synagogue ['sɪnəˌgɑg, -ˌgↄg] *n* : synagogue *f*

synchronize ['sɪŋkrəˌnaɪz, 'sɪn-] *vt* **-nized; -nizing** : synchroniser

syndrome ['sɪnˌdroːm] *n* : syndrome *m*

synonym ['sɪnəˌnɪm] *n* : synonyme *m* — **synonymous** [sə'nɑnəməs] *adj* : syn- onyme

syntax ['sɪnˌtæks] *n* : syntaxe *f*

synthesis ['sɪnθəsɪs] *n, pl* **-ses** [-ˌsiːz] : syn- thèse *f* — **synthetic** [sɪn'θεɪ̯k] *adj* : synthé- tique

syringe [sə'rɪndʒ, 'sɪrɪndʒ] *n* : seringue *f*

syrup ['sərəp, 'sɪrəp] *n* : sirop *m*

system ['sɪstəm] *n* **1** : système *m* **2** BODY : organisme *m* **3 digestive ～** : appareil *m* digestif — **systematic** [ˌsɪstə'mæɪ̯k] *adj* : systématique

T

t ['tiː] *n, pl* **t's** *or* **ts** ['tiːz] : t *m*, vingtième let- tre de l'alphabet

tab ['tæb] *n* **1** FLAP : languette *f* **2 keep ～s on** : surveiller

table ['teɪbəl] *n* : table *f* — **tablecloth** ['teɪbəlˌklↄθ] *n* : nappe *f* — **tablespoon** ['teɪbəlˌspuːn] *n* : cuillère *f* à soupe

tablet ['tæblət] *n* **1** : bloc-notes *m* **2** PILL : comprimé *m*

tabloid ['tæˌblↄɪd] *n* : quotidien *m* populaire, tabloïde *m*

taboo [tə'buː, tæ-] *adj* : tabou — **～** *n, pl* **-boos** : tabou *m*

tacit ['tæsɪt] *adj* : tacite

taciturn ['tæsɪˌtərn] *adj* : taciturne

tack ['tæk] *vt* **1** ATTACH : clouer **2 ～ on** ADD : ajouter

tackle ['takəl] *n* **1** GEAR : équipement *m*, matériel *m* **2** : plaquage *m* (au football) — **～** *vt* **-led; -ling 1** : plaquer (au football) **2** CONFRONT : s'attaquer à

tacky ['tæki] *adj* **tackier; tackiest 1** STICKY : collant **2** GAUDY : de mauvais goût

tact ['tækt] *n* : tact *m* — **tactful** ['tæktfəl] *adj* : plein de tact

tactical ['tæktɪkəl] *adj* : tactique — **tactic** ['tæktɪk] *n* : tactique *f* — **tactics** ['tæktɪks] *ns & pl* : tactique *f*

tactless ['tæktləs] *adj* : qui manque de tact

tadpole ['tædˌpoːl] *n* : têtard *m*

tag[1] ['tæg] *n* LABEL : étiquette *f* — **～** *v* **tagged; tagging** *vt* LABEL : étiqueter — *vi* **～ along** : suivre

tag[2] *vt* : toucher (au jeu de chat)

tail ['teɪl] *n* **1** : queue *f* **2 ～s** *npl* : pile *f*

(d'une pièce de monnaie) — **～** *vt* FOLLOW : suivre

tailor ['teɪlər] *n* : tailleur *m* — **～** *vt* **1** : faire sur mesure (un vêtement) **2** ADAPT : adapter

taint ['teɪnt] *vt* : entacher, souiller

Taiwanese [ˌtaɪwə'niːz, -'niːs] *adj* : tai- wanais

take ['teɪk] *v* **took** ['tʊk]; **taken** ['teɪkən]; **taking** *vt* **1** : prendre **2** BRING : emmener **3** CARRY : porter **4** REQUIRE : demander **5** ACCEPT : accepter **6** BEAR : supporter **7** : passer (un examen) **8 I ～ it that** : je sup- pose que **9 ～ a walk** : se promener **10 ～ apart** DISMANTLE : démonter **11 ～ back** : retirer **12 ～ in** ALTER : reprendre **13 ～ in** UNDERSTAND : saisir **14 ～ in** DECEIVE : tromper **15 ～ off** REMOVE : enlever **16 ～ on** : assumer (une responsabilité) **17 ～ over** : prendre le pouvoir **18 ～ place** : avoir lieu **19 ～ up** SHORTEN : raccourcir **20 ～ up** OCCUPY : prendre — *vi* **1** WORK : faire effet **2 ～ off** DEPART : s'en aller **3 ～ off** : décoller (se dit d'un avion) — *n* **1** PROCEEDS : recette *f* **2** : prise *f* (au cinéma) — **takeoff** ['teɪkˌↄf] *n* : décollage *m* (d'un avion) — **takeover** ['teɪkˌoːvər] *n* : prise *f* de contrôle (d'une compagnie)

talcum powder ['tælkəm] *n* : talc *m*

tale ['teɪl] *n* : conte *m*, histoire *f*

talent ['tælənt] *n* : talent *m* — **talented** ['tæləntəd] *adj* : talentueux, doué

talk ['tↄk] *vt* **1** : parler **2 ～ about** : parler de **3 ～ to/with** : parler avec — *vi* **1** SPEAK : parler **2 ～ over** : parler de, discuter —

~ *n* **1** CONVERSATION : entretien *m*, conversation *f* **2** SPEECH : discours *m*, exposé *m* — **talkative** ['tɔkətɪv] *adj* : bavard

tall ['tɔl] *adj* **1** : grand **2 how ~ are you?** : combien mesures-tu?

tally ['tæli] *n, pl* **-lies** : compte *m* — ~ *v* **-lied; -lying** *vt* RECKON : calculer — *vi* MATCH : correspondre

tambourine [ˌtæmbə'ri:n] *n* : tambourin *m*

tame ['teɪm] *adj* **tamer; tamest 1** : apprivoisé **2** : docile — ~ *vt* **tamed; taming** : apprivoiser, dompter

tamper ['tæmpər] *vi* ~ **with** : forcer (une serrure), falsifier (un document)

tampon ['tæmˌpɑn] *n* : tampon *m* (hygiénique)

tan ['tæn] *v* **tanned; tanning** *vt* : tanner (du cuir) — *vi* : bronzer — ~ *n* **1** SUNTAN : bronzage *m* **2** : brun *m* clair (couleur)

tang ['tæŋ] *n* : goût *m* piquant

tangent ['tændʒənt] *n* : tangente *f*

tangerine ['tændʒəˌri:n, ˌtændʒə'-] *n* : mandarine *f*

tangible ['tændʒəbəl] *adj* : tangible

tangle ['tæŋɡəl] *v* **-gled; -gling** *vt* : enchevêtrer — *vi* : s'emmêler — ~ *n* : enchevêtrement *m*

tango ['tæŋˌgo:] *n, pl* **-gos** : tango *m*

tank ['tæŋk] *n* **1** : réservoir *m*, cuve *f* **2** : char *m* (militaire) — **tanker** ['tæŋkər] *n* **1** *or* **oil ~** : pétrolier *m* **2** *or* ~ **truck** : camion-citern *m*

tantalizing ['tæntəˌlaɪzɪŋ] *adj* : alléchant

tantrum ['tæntrəm] *n* **throw a ~** : piquer une crise

tap[1] ['tæp] *n* FAUCET : robinet *m* — ~ *vt* **tapped; tapping** : mettre sur écoute

tap[2] *v* **tapped; tapping** *vt* TOUCH : tapoter, taper — *vi* : taper légèrement — ~ *n* : petit coup *m*

tape ['teɪp] *n or* **adhesive ~** : ruban *m* adhésif — ~ *vt* **taped; taping 1** : coller avec un ruban adhésif **2** RECORD : enregistrer — **tape measure** *n* : mètre *m* ruban

taper ['teɪpər] *vi* **1** : s'effiler **2** *or* ~ **off** : diminuer

tapestry ['tæpəstri] *n, pl* **-tries** : tapisserie *f*

tar ['tɑr] *n* : goudron *m* — ~ *vt* **tarred; tarring** : goudronner

tarantula [tə'ræntʃələ, -'ræntələ] *n* : tarentule *f*

target ['tɑrɡət] *n* **1** : cible *f* **2** GOAL : objectif *m*, but *m*

tariff ['tærɪf] *n* : tarif *m* douanier

tarnish ['tɑrnɪʃ] *vt* : ternir — *vi* : se ternir

tarpaulin [tɑr'pɔlən, 'tɑrpə-] *n* : bâche *f*

tart[1] ['tɑrt] *adj* SOUR : aigre

tart[2] *n* : tartelette *f*

tartan ['tɑrtən] *n* : tartan *m*, tissu *m* écossais

task ['tæsk] *n* : tâche *f*

tassel ['tæsəl] *n* : gland *m*

taste ['teɪst] *v* **tasted; tasting** *vt* : goûter (à) — *vi* ~ **like** : avoir le goût de — ~ *n* : goût *m* — **tasteful** ['teɪstfəl] *adj* : de bon goût — **tasteless** ['teɪstləs] *adj* **1** FLAVORLESS : sans goût **2** COARSE : de mauvais goût — **tasty** ['teɪsti] *adj* **tastier; tastiest** : savoureux

tattered ['tætərd] *adj* : en lambeaux

tattle ['tætəl] *vi* **-tled; -tling** ~ **on s.o.** : dénoncer qqn

tattoo [tæ'tu:] *vt* : tatouer — ~ *n* : tatouage *m*

taught → **teach**

taunt ['tɔnt] *n* : raillerie *f* — ~ *vt* : railler

taut ['tɔt] *adj* : tendu

tavern ['tævərn] *n* : taverne *f*

tax ['tæks] *vt* **1** : imposer (une personne), taxer (de l'argent, des marchandises) **2** STRAIN : mettre à l'épreuve — ~ *n* : taxe *f*, impôt *m* — **taxable** ['tæksəbəl] *adj* : imposable — **taxation** [tæk'seɪʃən] *n* : taxation *f*, imposition *f* — **tax-exempt** ['tæksɪɡ'zɛmpt, -ɛg-] *adj* : exempt d'impôts

taxi ['tæksi] *n, pl* **taxis** : taxi *m*

taxpayer ['tæksˌpeɪər] *n* : contribuable *mf*

tea ['ti:] *n* : thé *m*

teach ['ti:tʃ] *v* **taught** ['tɔt]; **teaching** *vt* **1** : enseigner (un sujet) **2** ~ **s.o. to** : apprendre qqn à — *vi* : enseigner — **teacher** ['ti:tʃər] *n* : instituteur *m*, -trice *f* (à l'école primaire); professeur *m* — **teaching** ['ti:tʃɪŋ] *n* : enseignement *m*

teacup ['ti:ˌkʌp] *n* : tasse *f* à thé

team ['ti:m] *n* : équipe *f* — ~ *vi* ~ **up with** : faire équipe avec — ~ *adj* : d'équipe — **teammate** ['ti:mˌmeɪt] *n* : coéquipier *m*, -pière *f* — **teamwork** ['ti:mˌwərk] *n* : travail *m* d'équipe

teapot ['ti:ˌpɑt] *n* : théière *f*

tear[1] ['tær] *v* **tore** ['tor]; **torn** ['torn]; **tearing** *vt* **1** RIP : déchirer **2** ~ **down** : démolir **3** ~ **off** *or* ~ **out** : arracher **4** ~ **up** : déchirer — *vi* **1** : se déchirer **2** RUSH : se précipiter — ~ *n* : déchirure *f*

tear[2] ['tɪr] *n* : larme *f* — **tearful** ['tɪrfəl] *adj* : larmoyant

tease ['ti:z] *vt* **teased; teasing** : taquiner — ~ *n* : taquin *m*, -quine *f*

teaspoon ['ti:ˌspu:n] *n* : petite cuillère *f*, cuillère *f* à café

technical ['tɛknɪkəl] *adj* : technique — **technicality** [ˌtɛknə'kæləti] *n, pl* **-ties** : détail *m* technique — **technician** [tɛk'nɪʃən] *n* : technicien *m*, -cienne *f*

technique [tɛk'ni:k] *n* : technique *f*

technological [ˌtɛknə'lɑdʒɪkəl] *adj* : technologique — **technology** [tɛk'nɑlədʒi] *n, pl* **-gies** : technologie *f*

tedious ['ti:diəs] *adj* : fastidieux — **tedium** ['ti:diəm] : ennui *m*

teem ['ti:m] *vi* ~ **with** : foisonner de, abonder en

teenage ['ti:n₁eɪʤ] *or* **teenaged** [-₁eɪʤd] *adj* : adolescent, d'adolescence — **teenager** ['ti:n₁eɪʤər] *n* : adolescent *m*, -cente *f* — **teens** ['ti:nz] *npl* : adolescence *f*

teepee → **tepee**

teeter ['ti:tər] *vi* : chanceler

teeth → **tooth** — **teethe** ['ti:ð] *vi* **teethed; teething** : faire ses dents

telecommunication [₁tɛləkə₁mju:nə'keɪʃən] *n* : télécommunication *f*

telegram ['tɛlə₁græm] *n* : télégramme *m*

telegraph ['tɛlə₁græf] *n* : télégraphe *m*

telephone ['tɛlə₁fo:n] *n* : téléphone *m* — *v* **-phoned; -phoning** *vt* : téléphoner à — *vi* : appeler, téléphoner

telescope ['tɛlə₁sko:p] *n* : télescope *m*

televise ['tɛlə₁vaɪz] *vt* **-vised; -vising** : téléviser — **television** ['tɛlə₁vɪʒən] *n* **1** : télévision *f* **2** *or* ~ **set** : téléviseur *m*

tell ['tɛl] *v* **told** ['to:ld]; **telling** *vt* **1** : dire **2** RELATE : raconter **3** DISTINGUISH : distinguer **4** ~ **s.o. off** : réprimander qqn — *vi* **1** : dire **2** KNOW : savoir **3** SHOW : se faire sentir **4** ~ **on s.o.** : dénoncer qqn — **teller** ['tɛlər] *n or* **bank** ~ : caissier *m*, -sière *f*

temp ['tɛmp] *n* : intérimaire *mf; occasionnel *m*, -nelle *f Can*

temper ['tɛmpər] *vt* MODERATE : tempérer — ~ *n* **1** MOOD : humeur *f* **2 lose one's** ~ : se mettre en colère — **temperament** ['tɛmpərmənt, -prə-, -pərə-] *n* : tempérament *m* — **temperamental** [₁tɛmpər'mɛntəl, -prə-, -pərə-] *adj* : capricieux — **temperate** ['tɛmpərət] *adj* **1** MILD : tempéré **2** MODERATE : modéré

temperature ['tɛmpər₁ʧur, -prə-, -ʧər] *n* **1** : température *f* **2 have a** ~ : avoir de la température

temple ['tɛmpəl] *n* **1** : temple *m* **2** : tempe *f* (en anatomie)

tempo ['tɛm₁po:] *n, pl* **-pi** [-₁pi:] *or* **-pos** **1** : tempo *m* **2** PACE : rythme *m*

temporarily [₁tɛmpə'rɛrəli] *adv* : temporairement — **temporary** ['tɛmpə₁rɛri] *adj* : temporaire

tempt ['tɛmpt] *vt* : tenter — **temptation** [tɛmp'teɪʃən] *n* : tentation *f*

ten ['tɛn] *n* : dix *m* — ~ *adj* : dix

tenacious [tə'neɪʃəs] *adj* : tenace — **tenacity** [tə'næsəti] *n* : ténacité *f*

tenant ['tɛnənt] *n* : locataire *mf*

tend¹ ['tɛnd] *vt* : s'occuper de

tend² *vi* ~ **to** : avoir tendance à — **tendency** ['tɛndənʦi] *n, pl* **-cies** : tendance *f*

tender¹ ['tɛndər] *adj* **1** : tendre **2** PAINFUL : douloureux

tender² *vt* : présenter — ~ *n* **1** : soumission *f* **2 legal** ~ : cours *m* légal

tenderloin ['tɛndər₁lɔɪn] *n* : filet *m* (de porc, etc.)

tenderness ['tɛndərnəs] *n* : tendresse *f*

tendon ['tɛndən] *n* : tendon *m*

tenet ['tɛnət] *n* : principe *m*

tennis ['tɛnəs] *n* : tennis *m*

tenor ['tɛnər] *n* : ténor *m*

tense¹ ['tɛnʦ] *n* : temps *m* (en grammaire)

tense² *v* **tensed; tensing** *vt* : tendre — *vi or* ~ **up** : se raidir — ~ *adj* **tenser; tensest** : tendu — **tension** ['tɛnʧən] *n* : tension *f*

tent ['tɛnt] *n* : tente *f*

tentacle ['tɛntɪkəl] *n* : tentacule *m*

tentative ['tɛntətɪv] *adj* **1** HESITANT : hésitant **2** PROVISIONAL : provisoire

tenth ['tɛnθ] *n* **1** : dixième *mf* **2 September** ~ : le dix septembre — ~ *adj* : dixième

tenuous ['tɛnjuəs] *adj* : ténu

tepee ['ti:₁pi:] *n* : tipi *m*

tepid ['tɛpɪd] *adj* : tiède

term ['tərm] *n* **1** WORD : terme *m* **2** : trimestre *m* (scolaire) **3 be on good** ~**s** : être en bons termes — ~ *vt* : appeler, nommer

terminal ['tərmənəl] *adj* : terminal — ~ *n* **1** : borne *f* (en électricité) **2** *or* **computer** ~ : terminal *m* **3** : terminus *m* (de train, de bus)

terminate ['tərmə₁neɪt] *v* **-nated; -nating** *vi* : se terminer — *vt* : terminer — **termination** [₁tərmə'neɪʃən] *n* : fin *f*

terminology [₁tərmə'nɑləʤi] *n, pl* **-gies** : terminologie *f*

termite ['tər₁maɪt] *n* : termite *m*

terrace ['tɛrəs] *n* : terrasse *f*

terrain [tə'reɪn] *n* : terrain *m*

terrestrial [tə'rɛstriəl] *adj* : terrestre

terrible ['tɛrəbəl] *adj* : terrible, épouvantable — **terribly** ['tɛrəbli] *adv* : terriblement

terrier ['tɛriər] *n* : terrier *m*

terrific [tə'rɪfɪk] *adj* **1** FRIGHTFUL : terrible **2** EXCELLENT : formidable

terrify ['tɛrə₁faɪ] *vt* **-fied; -fying** : terrifier — **terrifying** ['tɛrə₁faɪɪŋ] *adj* : terrifiant

territory ['tɛrə₁tori] *n, pl* **-ries** : territoire *m* — **territorial** [₁tɛrə'toriəl] *adj* : territorial

terror ['tɛrər] *n* : terreur *f* — **terrorism** ['tɛrər₁ɪzəm] *n* : terrorisme *m* — **terrorist** ['tɛrərɪst] *n* : terroriste *mf* — **terrorize** ['tɛrər₁aɪz] *vt* **-ized; -izing** : terroriser

terse ['tərs] *adj* **terser; tersest** : concis, succinct

test ['tɛst] *n* **1** TRIAL : épreuve *f* **2** EXAM : examen *m*, test *m* **3 blood** ~ : analyse *f* de sang — ~ *vt* **1** TRY : essayer **2** QUIZ : examiner, tester **3** : analyser (le sang, etc.), examiner (les yeux, etc.)

testament ['tɛstəmənt] n 1 WILL : testament m 2 the Old/New Testament : l'Ancien, le Nouveau Testament
testicle ['tɛstɪkəl] n : testicule m
testify ['tɛstə‚faɪ] v -fied; -fying 1 : témoigner m) 2
testimony ['tɛstə‚moːni] n, pl -nies : témoignage m
test tube n : éprouvette f
tetanus ['tɛtənəs] n : tétanos m
tether ['tɛðər] vt : attacher
text ['tɛkst] n : texte m — **textbook** ['tɛkst‚buk] n : manuel m scolaire
textile ['tɛk‚staɪl, 'tɛkstəl] n : textile m
texture ['tɛkstʃər] n : texture f
than ['ðæn] conj : que — ~ prep : que, de
thank ['θæŋk] vt 1 : remercier 2 ~ you : merci — **thankful** ['θæŋkfəl] adj : reconnaissant — **thankfully** ['θæŋkfəli] adv 1 : avec reconnaissance 2 FORTUNATELY : heureusement — **thankless** ['θæŋkləs] adj : ingrat — **thanks** ['θæŋks] npl 1 : remerciements mpl 2 ~ to : grâce à
Thanksgiving [θæŋks'gɪvɪn, 'θæŋks‚-] n : jour m d'Action de Grâces
that ['ðæt] pron, pl those ['ðoːz] 1 : cela, ce, ça 2 (more distant) : celui-là, celle-là, ceux-là, celles-là 3 WHO : qui 4 (used to introduce relative clauses) : que 5 is ~ you? : c'est toi? 6 ~ is : c'est-à-dire — ~ conj 1 : que 2 in order ~ : afin que — ~ adj, pl those 1 : ce, cet, cette, ces 2 ~ one : celui-là, celle-là — ~ adv VERY : tellement, très
thaw ['θɔ] vt : dégeler (des aliments) — vi 1 : se dégeler 2 MELT : fondre — ~ n : dégel m
the [ðə, before vowel sounds usu ðiː] art 1 : le, la, l', les 2 PER : le, la 3 ~ English : les Anglais — ~ adv 1 : le 2 ~ sooner ~ better : le plus tôt sera le mieux
theater or **theatre** ['θiːətər] n : théâtre m — **theatrical** [θiˈætrɪkəl] adj : théâtral
theft ['θɛft] n : vol m
their ['ðɛr] adj : leur — **theirs** ['ðɛrz] pron 1 : le leur, la leur, les leurs 2 some friends of ~ : des amis à eux
them ['ðɛm] pron 1 (used as direct object) : les 2 (used as indirect object) : leur 3 (used as object of a preposition) : eux, elles
theme ['θiːm] n : thème m
themselves [ðəmˈsɛlvz, ðɛm-] pron 1 (used reflexively) : se 2 (used emphatically) : eux-mêmes, elles-mêmes 3 (used after a preposition) : eux, elles, eux-mêmes, elles-mêmes 4 by ~ : tous seuls, toutes seules
then ['ðɛn] adv 1 : alors 2 NEXT : ensuite, puis 3 BESIDES : et puis — ~ adj : d'alors, de l'époque
theology [θiˈɑlədʒi] n, pl -gies : théologie f
theorem ['θiːərəm, 'θɪrəm] n : théorème m

— **theoretical** [‚θiːəˈrɛtɪkəl] adj : théorique — **theory** ['θiːəri, 'θɪri] n, pl -ries : théorie f
therapeutic [‚θɛrəˈpjuːtɪk] adj : thérapeutique — **therapist** ['θɛrəpɪst] n : thérapeute m) — **therapy** ['θɛrəpi] n, pl -pies : thérapie f
there ['ðær] adv 1 or over ~ : là-bas 2 down/up ~ : là-dessous, là-haut 3 in ~ : là-dedans 4 ~, it's done! : voilà, c'est fini! 5 who's ~? : qui est là? — ~ pron 1 ~ is/are : il y a 2 ~ are three of us : nous sommes trois — **thereabouts** or **thereabout** [ðærəˈbaʊts, -ˈbaʊt, 'ðærə‚-] adv : dans les environs, par là — **thereafter** [ðærˈæftər] adv : par la suite — **thereby** [ðærˈbaɪ, 'ðær‚baɪ] adv : ainsi — **therefore** ['ðær‚for] adv : donc, par conséquent
thermal ['θərməl] adj : thermal, thermique
thermometer [θərˈmɑmətər] n : thermomètre m
thermos ['θərməs] n : thermos mf
thermostat ['θərmə‚stæt] n : thermostat m
thesaurus [θɪˈsɔrəs] n, pl -sauri [-'sɔr‚aɪ] or -sauruses [-'sɔrəsəz] : dictionnaire m analogique, dictionnaire m des synonymes
these → **this**
thesis ['θiːsɪs] n, pl theses ['θiːsiːz] : thèse f
they ['ðeɪ] pron 1 : ils, elles 2 as ~ say : comme on dit 3 there ~ are : les voici — **they'd** ['ðeɪd] (contraction of they had or they would) → have, would — **they'll** ['ðeɪl, 'ðɛl] (contraction of they shall or they will) → shall, will — **they're** ['ðɛr] (contraction of they are) → be — **they've** ['ðeɪv] (contraction of they have) → have
thick ['θɪk] adj 1 : épais 2 DENSE : bête 3 a ~ accent : un accent prononcé 4 two inches ~ : deux pouces d'épaisseur — ~ n in the ~ of : au plus fort de — **thicken** ['θɪkən] vt : épaissir (une sauce, etc.) — vi : s'épaissir — **thicket** ['θɪkət] n : fourré m — **thickness** ['θɪknəs] n : épaisseur f, grosseur f
thief ['θiːf] n, pl thieves ['θiːvz] : voleur m, -leuse f
thigh ['θaɪ] n : cuisse f
thimble ['θɪmbəl] n : dé m à coudre
thin ['θɪn] adj thinner; thinnest 1 : mince 2 SPARSE : clairsemé 3 WATERY : clair (se dit d'une soupe, etc.) — ~ v thinned; thinning vt DILUTE : diluer — vi : s'éclaircir
thing ['θɪn] n 1 : chose f 2 ~s npl BELONGINGS : affaires fpl 3 for one ~ : en premier lieu 4 how are ~s? : comment ça va? 5 the important ~ is... : l'important c'est...
think ['θɪŋk] v thought ['θɔt]; thinking vt 1 : penser 2 BELIEVE : croire 3 ~ up : inventer — vi 1 : penser 2 ~ about or ~ of CONSIDER : penser à 3 ~ of REMEMBER : se rappeler

thinness [ˈθɪnnəs] n : minceur f

third [ˈθərd] adj : troisième — ∼ or **thirdly** [-li] adv : troisième, troisièmement — ∼ n **1** : troisième mf (dans une série) **2** : tiers m (en mathématiques) **3** December ∼ : le trois décembre — **Third World** n : le tiers-monde

thirst [ˈθərst] n : soif f — **thirsty** [ˈθərsti] adj **thirstier; thirstiest 1** : assoiffé **2 be** ∼ : avoir soif

thirteen [ˌθərˈtiːn] n : treize m — ∼ adj : treize — **thirteenth** [ˌθərˈtiːnθ] n **1** : treizième mf **2 January** ∼ : le treize janvier — ∼ adj : treizième

thirty [ˈθərti] n, pl **-ties** : trente m — ∼ adj : trente — **thirtieth** [ˈθərtiəθ] n **1** : trentième mf **2 May** ∼ : le trente mai — ∼ adj : trentième

this [ˈðɪs] pron, pl **these 1** : ce, ceci **2** (in comparisons) : celui-ci, celle-ci, ceux-ci, celles-ci **3** ∼ **is your room** : voici ta chambre — ∼ adj, pl **these** [ˈðiːz] **1** : ce, cet, cette, ces **2** ∼ **one** : celui-ci, celle-ci **3** ∼ **way** : par ici — ∼ adv : si, aussi

thistle [ˈθɪsəl] n : chardon m

thorn [ˈθɔrn] n : épine f — **thorny** [ˈθɔrni] adj **thornier; thorniest** : épineux

thorough [ˈθəˌroː] adj **1** : consciencieux **2** COMPLETE : complet — **thoroughly** [ˈθəroli] adv **1** : à fond **2** COMPLETELY : absolument — **Thoroughbred** [ˈθəroˌbred] n : pur-sang m — **thoroughfare** [ˈθəroˌfær] n : voie f publique

those → **that**

though [ˈðoː] conj : bien que, quoique — ∼ adv **1** : cependant, pourtant **2 as** ∼ : comme si

thought [ˈθɔt] → **think** — ∼ n **1** : pensée f **2** IDEA : idée f — **thoughtful** [ˈθɔtfəl] adj **1** : pensif **2** KIND : aimable — **thoughtless** [ˈθɔtləs] adj **1** : irréfléchi **2** RUDE : manquer d'égard (envers qqn)

thousand [ˈθaʊzənd] n, pl **-sands** or **-sand** : mille m — ∼ adj : mille — **thousandth** [ˈθaʊzəntθ] n : millième mf — ∼ adj : millième

thrash [ˈθræʃ] vi or ∼ **about** : se débattre

thread [ˈθrɛd] n : fil m — ∼ vt : enfiler (une aiguille, des perles, etc.) — **threadbare** [ˈθrɛdˌbær] adj : usé

threat [ˈθrɛt] n : menace f — **threaten** [ˈθrɛtən] v : menacer — **threatening** [ˈθrɛtənɪŋ] adj : menaçant

three [ˈθriː] n : trois m — ∼ adj : trois — **three hundred** adj : trois cent

threshold [ˈθrɛʃˌhoːld, -ˌoːld] n : seuil m

threw → **throw**

thrift [ˈθrɪft] n : économie f — **thrifty** [ˈθrɪfti] adj **thriftier; thriftiest** : économe

thrill [ˈθrɪl] vt : transporter (de joie) — ∼ n : frisson m — **thriller** [ˈθrɪlər] n : thriller m — **thrilling** [ˈθrɪlɪŋ] adj : excitant

thrive [ˈθraɪv] vi **throve** [ˈθroːv] or **thrived; thriven** [ˈθrɪvən] **1** FLOURISH : réussir **2** PROSPER : prospérer

throat [ˈθroːt] n : gorge f

throb [ˈθrɑb] vi **throbbed; throbbing 1** : battre, palpiter **2** VIBRATE : vibrer **3** ∼ **with pain** : lanciner

throes [ˈθroːz] npl **1** : agonie f **2 in the** ∼ **of** : en proie à

throne [ˈθroːn] n : trône m

throng [ˈθrɔŋ] n : foule f

through [ˈθruː] prep **1** : à travers **2** BECAUSE OF : à cause de **3** BY : par **4** DURING : pendant **5 Monday** ∼ **Friday** : du lundi au vendredi **6** → **throughout** — ∼ adv **1** : à travers **2** COMPLETELY : complètement **3 let** ∼ : laisser passer — ∼ adj **1 be** ∼ : avoir terminé **2** ∼ **traffic** : trafic en transit — **throughout** [θruːˈaʊt] prep **1** : partout dans **2** DURING : pendant

throw [ˈθroː] vt **threw** [ˈθruː]; **thrown** [ˈθroːn]; **throwing 1** : lancer (une balle, etc.) **2** CONFUSE : déconcerter **3** ∼ **a party** : organiser une fête **4** ∼ **away** or ∼ **out** : jeter — ∼ n TOSS : lancer m, jet m — **throw up** vt : vomir, renvoyer Can fam, restituer Can fam

thrush [ˈθrʌʃ] n : grive f (oiseau)

thrust [ˈθrʌst] vt **thrust; thrusting 1** : enfoncer, planter **2** ∼ **upon** : imposer à — ∼ n : poussée f

thud [ˈθʌd] n : bruit m sourd

thug [ˈθʌg] n : voyou m

thumb [ˈθʌm] n : pouce m — ∼ vt or ∼ **through** : feuilleter — **thumbnail** [ˈθʌmˌneɪl] n : ongle m du pouce — **thumbtack** [ˈθʌmˌtæk] n : punaise f

thump [ˈθʌmp] vt : cogner — vi : battre fort (se dit du cœur) — ∼ n : bruit m sourd

thunder [ˈθʌndər] n : tonnerre m — ∼ vi : tonner — ∼ vt SHOUT : vociférer — **thunderbolt** [ˈθʌndərˌboːlt] n : foudre f — **thunderous** [ˈθʌndərəs] adj : étourdissant — **thunderstorm** [ˈθʌndərˌstorm] n : orage m

Thursday [ˈθərzˌdeɪ, -di] n : jeudi m

thus [ˈðʌs] adv **1** : ainsi, donc **2** ∼ **far** : jusqu'à présent

thwart [ˈθwɔrt] vt : contrecarrer

thyme [ˈtaɪm, ˈθaɪm] n : thym m

thyroid [ˈθaɪˌrɔɪd] n : thyroïde f

tic [ˈtɪk] n : tic m (nerveux)

tick¹ [ˈtɪk] n : tique f (insecte)

tick² n **1** : tic-tac m (bruit) **2** CHECK : coche f — ∼ vi : faire tic-tac — vt **1** or ∼ **off** CHECK : cocher **2** ∼ **off** ANNOY : agacer

ticket [ˈtɪkət] n **1** : billet m (d'avion, de train, etc.), ticket m (d'autobus, de métro) **2** or **parking** ∼ : contravention f

tickle ['tɪkəl] v **-led; -ling** vt **1** : chatouiller
2 AMUSE : amuser — vi : chatouiller — ~ n
: chatouillement m — **ticklish** ['tɪkəlɪʃ] adj
: chatouilleux

tidal wave ['taɪdəl] n : raz-de-marée m

tidbit ['tɪd‚bɪt] n : détail m intéressant

tide ['taɪd] n : marée f — ~ vt **tided; tiding**
~ **over** : dépanner

tidy ['taɪdi] adj **-dier; -est** NEAT : propre —
~ vt **-died; -dying** or ~ **up** : ranger

tie ['taɪ] n **1** : attache f, cordon m **2** BOND
: lien m **3** : match m nul (aux sports) **4**
NECKTIE : cravate f — ~ v **tied; tying** or
tieing vt **1** : attacher **2** ~ **a knot** : faire un
nœud — vi : faire match nul, être ex æquo

tier ['tɪr] n : étage m, gradin m (d'un stade)

tiger ['taɪgər] n : tigre m

tight ['taɪt] adj **1** : serré, étroit **2** TAUT
: tendu **3** STINGY : avare **4 a** ~ **seal** : une
fermeture étanche — ~ adv **closed** ~
: bien fermé — **tighten** ['taɪtən] vt : serrer,
resserrer — **tightly** ['taɪtli] adv : fermement,
bien — **tightrope** ['taɪt‚ro:p] n : corde f
raide — **tights** ['taɪts] npl : collants mpl

tile ['taɪl] n : carreau m, tuile f — ~ vt **tiled;
tiling** : carreler, poser des tuiles sur

till[1] ['tɪl] prep & conj → **until**

till[2] vt : labourer

till[3] n : tiroir-caisse m

tilt ['tɪlt] n **1** : inclinaison f **2 at full** ~ : à
toute vitesse — ~ vt : pencher, incliner —
vi : se pencher, s'incliner

timber ['tɪmbər] n **1** : bois m de construction
2 BEAM : poutre f

time ['taɪm] n **1** : temps m **2** AGE : époque f
3 : rythme m (en musique) **4 at** ~**s** : parfois **5 at this** ~ : en ce moment **6 for the**
~ **being** : pour le moment **7 from** ~ **to**
~ : de temps à autre **8 have a good** ~
: amusez-vous bien **9 on** ~ : à l'heure **10**
several ~**s** : plusieurs fois **11** ~ **after** ~
: à maintes reprises **12 what** ~ **is it?**
: quelle heure est-il? — ~ vt **timed; timing**
1 SCHEDULE : prévoir, fixer **2**
: chronométrer (une course, etc.) — **time-
less** ['taɪmləs] adj : éternel — **timely**
['taɪmli] adj **-lier; -est** : opportun — **timer**
['taɪmər] n : minuteur m (en cuisine) —
times ['taɪmz] prep **3** ~ **4 is 12** : 3 fois 4
égale 12 — **timetable** ['taɪm‚teɪbəl] n : horaire m

timid ['tɪmɪd] adj : timide

tin ['tɪn] n **1** : étain m (métal) **2** or ~ **can**
: boîte f — **tinfoil** ['tɪn‚fɔɪl] n : papier m
d'aluminium

tinge ['tɪndʒ] vt **tinged; tingeing** or **tinging**
['tɪndʒɪŋ] : teinter — ~ n : teinte f

tingle ['tɪŋgəl] vi **-gled; -gling** : picoter —
~ n : picotement m

tinker ['tɪŋkər] vi ~ **with** : bricoler

tinkle ['tɪŋkəl] vi **-kled; -kling** : tinter — ~
n : tintement m

tint ['tɪnt] n : teinte f — ~ vt : teinter

tiny ['taɪni] adj **-nier; -niest** : minuscule

tip[1] ['tɪp] v **tipped; tipping** vt **1** TILT : incliner **2** or ~ **over** : renverser — vi
: pencher

tip[2] n END : pointe f, bout m (d'un crayon)

tip[3] n ADVICE : conseil m, tuyau m fam — ~
vt ~ **off** : prévenir

tip[4] vt : donner un pourboire à — ~ n GRA-
TUITY : pourboire m

tipsy ['tɪpsi] adj **-sier; -est** : gris fam,
éméché fam

tiptoe ['tɪp‚to:] n **on** ~ : sur la pointe des
pieds — ~ vi **-toed; -toeing** : marcher sur
la pointe des pieds

tire[1] ['taɪr] n : pneu m

tire[2] v **tired; tiring** vt : fatiguer — vi : se fatiguer — **tired** ['taɪrd] adj **1** : fatigué **2 be**
~ **of** : en avoir assez de — **tiresome**
['taɪrsəm] adj : ennuyeux

tissue ['tɪ‚ʃu:] n **1** : tissu m (en biologie) **2**
: mouchoir m en papier, papier m mouchoir
Can

title ['taɪtəl] n : titre m — ~ vt **-tled; -tling**
: intituler

to ['tu:] prep **1** : à **2** TOWARD : vers **3** IN
ORDER TO : afin de, pour **4** UP TO : jusqu'à
5 a quarter ~ **three** : trois heures moins le
quart **6 be nice** ~ **him** : sois gentil envers
lui **7 ten** ~ **the box** : dix par boîte **8 two**
~ **four years old** : entre deux et quatre ans
9 want ~ **do** : vouloir faire — ~ adv **1**
come ~ : reprendre connaissance **2 go** ~
and fro : aller et venir

toad ['to:d] n : crapaud m

toast ['to:st] vt **1** : griller (du pain), toaster
Can **2** : boire à la santé de (une personne)
— ~ n **1** : toast m, pain m grillé, rôtie f **2**
drink a ~ **to** : porter un toast à — **toaster**
['to:stər] n : grille-pain m

tobacco [tə'bæko:] n, pl **-cos** : tabac m

toboggan [tə'bagən] n : toboggan m, traîne
f Can

today [tə'deɪ] adv : aujourd'hui — ~ n : aujourd'hui m

toddler ['tadələr] n : bambin m, -bine f

toe ['to:] n : orteil m, doigt m de pied — **toe-
nail** ['to:‚neɪl] n : ongle m d'orteil

together [tə'gɛðər] adv **1** : ensemble **2** ~
with : ainsi que

toil ['tɔɪl] n : labeur m — ~ vi : peiner

toilet ['tɔɪlət] n BATHROOM : toilettes fpl, toilette f Can — **toilet paper** n : papier m hygiénique — **toiletries** ['tɔɪlətriz] npl : arti-
cles mpl de toilette

token ['to:kən] n **1** SIGN : signe m, marque f
2 : jeton m (pour le métro, etc.)

told → **tell**

tolerable ['tɑlərəbəl] *adj* : tolérable — **tolerance** ['tɑlərənts] *n* : tolérance *f* — **tolerant** ['tɑlərənt] *adj* : tolérant — **tolerate** ['tɑlə,reɪt] *vt* **-ated; -ating** : tolérer

toll[1] ['to:l] *n* **1** : pénge *m* **2 death** ~ : nombre *m* de morts **3 take a** ~ **on** : affecter

toll[2] *v* RING : sonner

tomato [tə'meɪto, -'mɑ-] *n, pl* **-toes** : tomate *f*

tomb ['tu:m] *n* : tombeau *m* — **tombstone** ['tu:m,sto:n] *n* : pierre *f* tombale

tomorrow [tə'mɑro] *adv* : demain — ~ *n* : demain *m*

ton ['tʌn] *n* : tonne *f*

tone ['to:n] *n* **1** : ton *m* **2** BEEP : tonalité *f* — ~ *vt* **toned; toning** *or* ~ **down** : atténuer

tongs ['tɑŋz, 'tɔŋz] *npl* : pinces *fpl*

tongue ['tʌŋ] *n* : langue *f*

tonic ['tɑnɪk] *n* : tonique *m*

tonight [tə'naɪt] *adv* : ce soir — ~ *n* : ce soir, cette nuit

tonsil ['tɑntsəl] *n* : amygdale *f*

too ['tu:] *adv* **1** ALSO : aussi **2** VERY : très

took → **take**

tool ['tu:l] *n* : outil *m* — **toolbox** ['tu:l,bɑks] *n* : boîte *f* à outils

toot ['tu:t] *vi* : klaxonner — ~ *n* : coup *m* de klaxon

tooth ['tu:θ] *n, pl* **teeth** ['ti:θ] : dent *f* — **toothache** ['tu:θ,eɪk] *n* : mal *m* de dents — **toothbrush** ['tu:θ,brʌʃ] *n* : brosse *f* à dents — **toothpaste** ['tu:θ,peɪst] *n* : dentifrice *m*

top[1] ['tɑp] *n* **1** : haut *m* **2** SUMMIT : cime *f* **3** COVER : couvercle *m* **4 on** ~ **of** : sur — ~ *vt* **topped; topping 1** COVER : couvrir **2** SURPASS : dépasser — ~ *adj* **1** : de haut, du haut **2** LEADING : premier, principal **3 the** ~ **floor** : le dernier étage

top[2] *n* : toupie *f* (jouet)

topic ['tɑpɪk] *n* : sujet *m* — **topical** ['tɑpɪkəl] *adj* : d'actualité

topple ['tɑpəl] *v* **-pled; -pling** *vi* : basculer — *vt* : renverser

torch ['tɔrtʃ] *n* : torche *f*

tore → **tear**[1]

torment ['tɔr,mɛnt] *n* : tourment *m* — ~ ['tɔr,mɛnt, tɔr'-] *vt* : tourmenter

torn → **tear**[1]

tornado [tɔr'neɪdo] *n, pl* **-does** *or* **-dos** : tornade *f*

torpedo [tɔr'pi:do] *n, pl* **-does** : torpille *f* — ~ *vt* : torpiller

torrent ['tɔrənt] *n* : torrent *m*

torrid ['tɔrɪd] *adj* : torride

torso ['tɔr,so:] *n, pl* **-sos** *or* **-si** [-,si:] : torse *m*

tortoise ['tɔrtəs] *n* : tortue *f* — **tortoiseshell** ['tɔrtəs,ʃɛl] *n* : écaille *f*

tortuous ['tɔrtʃuəs] *adj* : tortueux

torture ['tɔrtʃər] *n* : torture *f* — ~ *vt* **-tured; -turing** : torturer

toss ['tɔs, 'tɑs] *vt* : tirer, lancer — *vi* ~ **and turn** : se tourner et se retourner — ~ *n* : lancer *m*

tot ['tɑt] *n* : petit enfant *m*

total ['to:təl] *adj* : total — ~ *n* : total *m* — ~ *vt* **-taled** *or* **-talled; -taling** *or* **-talling** : totaliser, additionner

totalitarian [,to:,tælə'tɛriən] *adj* : totalitaire

touch ['tʌtʃ] *vt* **1** : toucher **2** AFFECT : émouvoir **3** ~ **up** : retoucher — *vi* : se toucher — ~ *n* **1** : toucher *m* (sens) **2** HINT : touche *f* **3 a** ~ **of** : un peu de **4 keep in** ~ : demeurer en contact — **touchdown** ['tʌtʃ,daʊn] *n* **1** : atterrissage *m* (d'un avion) **2** : but *m* (au football américain) — **touchy** ['tʌtʃi] *adj* **touchier; touchiest 1** : susceptible **2 a** ~ **subject** : un sujet épineux

tough ['tʌf] *adj* **1** : dur **2** STRONG : solide **3** STRICT : sévère **4** DIFFICULT : difficile — **toughen** ['tʌfən] *vt or* ~ **up** : endurcir — *vi* : s'endurcir — **toughness** ['tʌfnəs] *n* : dureté *f*

tour ['tʊr] *n* **1** : tour *m* (d'une ville, etc.), visite *f* (d'un musée, etc.) **2 go on** ~ : faire une tournée — ~ *vi* **1** TRAVEL : voyager **2** : être en tournée (se dit d'une équipe, etc.) — *vt* : visiter — **tourist** ['tʊrɪst, 'tər-] *n* : touriste *mf*

tournament ['tərnəmənt, 'tʊr-] *n* : tournoi *m*

tousle ['taʊzəl] *vt* **-sled; -sling** : ébouriffer (les cheveux)

tout ['taʊt] *vt* : vanter les mérites de

tow ['to:] *vt* : remorquer — ~ *n* : remorquage *m*

toward ['tord, tə'word] *or* **towards** ['tordz, tə'wordz] *prep* : vers

towel ['taʊəl] *n* : serviette *f*

tower ['taʊər] *n* : tour *f* — ~ *vi* ~ **over** : dominer — **towering** ['taʊərɪŋ] *adj* : imposant

town ['taʊn] *n* **1** VILLAGE : village *m* **2** CITY : ville *f* — **township** ['taʊn,ʃɪp] *n* **1** : municipalité *f* **2** : canton *m* Can (division territoriale)

tow truck ['to:,trʌk] *n* : dépanneuse *f*, remorqueuse *f* Can

toxic ['tɑksɪk] *adj* : toxique

toy ['tɔɪ] *n* : jouet *m* — ~ *vi* ~ **with** : jouer avec

trace ['treɪs] *n* : trace *f* — ~ *vt* **traced; tracing 1** : tracer, calquer (un dessin) **2** FOLLOW : suivre **3** LOCATE : retrouver

track ['træk] *n* **1** : piste *f* **2** FOOTPRINT : trace *f* **3** *or* **railroad** ~ : voie *f* ferrée **4 keep** ~ **of** : suivre — ~ *vt* : suivre la trace de, suivre la piste de

tract[1] ['trækt] *n* **1** EXPANSE : étendue *f* **2** : appareil *m* (en physiologie)

tract[2] *n* LEAFLET : brochure *f*

traction ['trækʃən] *n* : traction *f*

tractor ['træktər] *n* **1** : tracteur *m* **2** *or* **tractor–trailer** : semi-remorque *m*

trade ['treɪd] *n* **1** PROFESSION : métier *m* **2** COMMERCE : commerce *m* **3** INDUSTRY : industrie *f* **4** EXCHANGE : échange *m* — ~ *v* **traded; trading 1** : faire du commerce — *vt* ~ **sth for** : échanger qqch pour — **trademark** ['treɪd,mɑrk] *n* : marque *f* de fabrique

tradition [trə'dɪʃən] *n* : tradition *f* — **traditional** [trə'dɪʃənəl] *adj* : traditionnel

traffic ['træfɪk] *n* **1** : circulation *f* (routière) **2 drug** ~ : trafic *m* de drogue — ~ *vi* **-ficked; -ficking** : trafiquer — **traffic light** *n* : feu *m* (de signalisation)

tragedy ['trædʒədi] *n, pl* **-dies** : tragédie *f* — **tragic** ['trædʒɪk] *adj* : tragique

trail ['treɪl] *vi* **1** DRAG : traîner **2** LAG : être à la traîne **3** ~ **off** : s'estomper — *vt* **1** : traîner **2** PURSUE : suivre la piste de — ~ *n* **1** : trace *f*, piste *f* **2** PATH : sentier *m*, chemin *m* — **trailer** ['treɪlər] *n* **1** : remorque *f* **2** CAMPER : caravane *f*, roulotte *f* Can

train ['treɪn] *n* **1** : train *m* **2** : traîne *f* (d'une robe) **3** SERIES : suite *f*, série *f* **4** ~ **of thought** : fil *m* des pensées — ~ *vt* **1** : former, entraîner (un athlète, etc.) **2** AIM : braquer — *vi* : s'entraîner (aux sports) — **trainer** ['treɪnər] *n* **1** : entraîneur *m*, -neuse *f* (aux sports) **2** : dresseur *m*, -seuse *f* (d'animaux)

trait ['treɪt] *n* : trait *m*

traitor ['treɪtər] *n* : traître *m*, -tresse *f*

tramp ['træmp] *vi* : marcher (d'un pas lourd) — ~ *n* VAGRANT : clochard *m*, -charde *f*

trample ['træmpəl] *vt* **-pled; -pling** : piétiner

trampoline [,træmpə'li:n, 'træmpə,-] *n* : trampoline *m*

trance ['trænts] *n* : transe *f*

tranquillity *or* **tranquility** [træŋ'kwɪləti] *n* : tranquillité *f* — **tranquilizer** ['træŋkwə-,laɪzər] *n* : tranquillisant *m*

transaction [træn'zækʃən] *n* : transaction *f*

transcribe [træn'skraɪb] *vt* **-scribed; -scribing** : transcrire — **transcript** ['træn-,skrɪpt] *n* : transcription *f*

transfer [træn*t*s'fər, 'træn*t*s,fər] *v* **-ferred; -ferring** *vt* **1** : transférer **2** : muter (un employé) — *vi* **1** : être transféré **2** : changer (d'université) — ~ ['træn*t*s,fər] *n* **1** : transfert *m*, mutation *f* **2** : virement *m* (de fonds)

transform [træn*t*s'fɔrm] *vt* : transformer — **transformation** [,træn*t*sfər'meɪʃən] *n* : transformation *f*

transfusion [træn*t*s'fju:ʒən] *n* : transfusion *f*

transgression [træn*t*s'grɛʃən, trænz-] *n* : transgression *f* — **transgress** [træn*t*s-'grɛs, trænz-] *vt* : transgresser

transient ['trænʃənt, 'trænsiənt] *adj* : transitoire, passager

transit ['trænˌsɪt, 'trænzɪt] *n* **1** : transit *m* **2** TRANSPORTATION : transport *m* — **transition** [træn'sɪʃən, -'zɪʃ-] *n* : transition *f* — **transitive** ['træn*t*sətɪv, 'trænzə-] *adj* : transitif — **transitory** ['træn*t*sə,tori, 'trænzə-] *adj* : transitoire, passager

translate ['trænts,leɪt, trænz-; 'trænts,-, 'trænz,-] *vt* **-lated; -lating** : traduire — **translation** [trænts'leɪʃən, trænz-] *n* : traduction *f* — **translator** [trænts'leɪtər, trænz-; 'trænts,-, 'trænz,-] *n* : traducteur *m*, -trice *f*

translucent [trænts'lu:sənt, trænz-] *adj* : translucide

transmit [trænts'mɪt, trænz-] *vt* **-mitted; -mitting** : transmettre — **transmission** [trænts'mɪʃən, trænz-] *n* : transmission *f* — **transmitter** [trænts'mɪtər, trænz-; 'trænts,-, 'trænts,-] *n* : émetteur *m*

transparent [trænts'pærənt] *adj* : transparent — **transparency** [trænts'pærəntsi] *n, pl* **-cies** : transparence *f*

transplant [trænts'plænt] *vt* : transplanter — ~ ['trænts,plænt] *n* : transplantation *f*

transport [trænts'port, 'trænts,-] *vt* : transporter — ~ ['trænts,port] *n* : transport *m* — **transportation** [,trænts pər'teɪʃən] *n* : transport *m*

transpose [trænts'po:z] *vt* **-posed; -posing** : transposer

trap ['træp] *n* : piège *m* — ~ *vt* **trapped; trapping** : prendre au piège, attraper — **trapdoor** ['træp'dor] *n* : trappe *f*

trapeze [træ'pi:z] *n* : trapèze *m*

trappings ['træpɪŋz] *npl* SIGNS : attributs *mpl*

trash ['træʃ] *n* : déchets *mpl*, ordures *fpl*

trauma ['trɔmə, 'traʊ-] *n* : traumatisme *m* — **traumatic** [trə'mætɪk, trɔ-, traʊ-] *adj* : traumatisant

travel ['trævəl] *vi* **-eled** *or* **-elled; -eling** *or* **-elling 1** : voyager **2** SPREAD : circuler, se répandre **3** MOVE : aller, rouler — ~ *n* : voyages *mpl* — **traveler** *or* **traveller** ['trævələr] *n* : voyageur *m*, -geuse *f*

trawl ['trɔl] *vi* : pêcher au chalut — **trawler** ['trɔlər] *n* : chalutier *m*

tray ['treɪ] *n* : plateau *m*

treachery ['trɛtʃəri] *n, pl* **-eries** : traîtrise *f* — **treacherous** ['trɛtʃərəs] *adj* **1** : traître **2** DANGEROUS : dangereux

tread ['trɛd] *v* **trod** ['trɑd]; **trodden** ['trɑdən] *or* **trod; treading** *vt* ~ **water** : nager sur place — *vi or* ~ **on** : marcher sur — ~ *n* **1** STEP : pas *m* **2** : bande *f* de roulement (d'un pneu) — **treadmill** ['trɛd-,mɪl] *n* : exerciseur *m*

treason ['tri:zən] *n* : trahison *f*

treasure ['trɛʒər, 'treɪ-] *n* : trésor *m* — ~ *vt* **-sured; -suring** : tenir beaucoup à — **treas-**

urer ['trɛʒərər, 'trɛɪ-] *n* : trésorier *m*, -rière *f* — **treasury** ['trɛʒəri, 'trɛɪ-] *n, pl* **-suries** **1** : trésorerie *f* **2 Treasury** : ministère *m* des Finances

treat ['triːt] *vt* **1** : traiter **2 ~ s.o. to sth** : offrir qqch à qqn — **~** *n* : régal *m*, plaisir *m*

treatise ['triːtəs] *n* : traité *m*

treatment ['triːtmənt] *n* : traitement *m*

treaty ['triːti] *n, pl* **-ties** : traité *m*

treble ['trɛbəl] *adj* **1** TRIPLE : triple **2** : de soprano (en musique) — **treble clef** *n* : clé *f* de sol

tree ['triː] *n* : arbre *m*

trek ['trɛk] *n* : randonnée *f*

trellis ['trɛlɪs] *n* : treillis *m*, treillage *m*

tremble ['trɛmbəl] *vi* **-bled; -bling** : trembler

tremendous [trɪ'mɛndəs] *adj* **1** HUGE : énorme **2** EXCELLENT : formidable

tremor ['trɛmər] *n* : tremblement *m*

trench ['trɛntʃ] *n* : tranchée *f*

trend ['trɛnd] *n* **1** : tendance *f* **2** FASHION : mode *f* — **trendy** ['trɛndi] *adj* **trendier; trendiest** : à la mode

trepidation [ˌtrɛpə'deɪʃən] *n* : inquiétude *f*

trespass ['trɛspəs, -ˌpæs] *vi* : s'introduire illégalement

trial ['traɪəl] *n* **1** HEARING : procès *m* **2** TEST : essai *m* **3** ORDEAL : épreuve *f* — **~** *adj* : d'essai

triangle ['traɪˌæŋɡəl] *n* : triangle *m* — **triangular** [traɪ'æŋɡjələr] *adj* : triangulaire

tribe ['traɪb] *n* : tribu *f* — **tribal** ['traɪbəl] *adj* : tribal

tribulation [ˌtrɪbjə'leɪʃən] *n* : tourment *m*

tribunal [traɪ'bjuːnəl, trɪ-] *n* : tribunal *m*

tribute ['trɪbˌjuːt] *n* : hommage *m* — **tributary** ['trɪbjəˌtɛri] *n, pl* **-taries** : affluent *m*

trick ['trɪk] *n* **1** PRANK : farce *f*, tour *m* **2** KNACK : truc *m*, astuce *f* — **~** *vt* : duper — **trickery** ['trɪkəri] *n* : tromperie *f*

trickle ['trɪkəl] *vi* **-led; -ling** DRIP : dégouliner — **~** *n* : filet *m* (d'eau)

tricky ['trɪki] *adj* **trickier; trickiest 1** SLY : rusé **2** DIFFICULT : difficile

tricycle ['traɪsəkəl, -ˌsɪkəl] *n* : tricycle *m*

trifle ['traɪfəl] *n* : bagatelle *f*, rien *m* — **trifling** ['traɪflɪŋ] *adj* : insignifiant

trigger ['trɪɡər] *n* : détente *f*, gâchette *f* — **~** *vt* : déclencher

trillion ['trɪljən] *n* : billion *m*

trilogy ['trɪlədʒi] *n, pl* **-gies** : trilogie *f*

trim ['trɪm] *vt* **trimmed; trimming 1** CUT : tailler **2** ADORN : décorer — **~** *adj* **trimmer; trimmest 1** SLIM : mince **2** NEAT : soigné — **~** *n* **1** HAIRCUT : coupe *f* **2** DECORATION : garniture *f* — **trimmings** ['trɪmɪŋs] *npl* : garniture *f*

Trinity ['trɪnəti] *n* : Trinité *f*

trinket ['trɪŋkət] *n* : babiole *f*

trio ['triːˌoː] *n, pl* **trios** : trio *m*

trip ['trɪp] *v* **tripped; tripping** *vi* : trébucher, s'enfarger *Can* — *vt* **1** : faire trébucher (une personne) **2** ACTIVATE : déclencher — **~** *n* **1** : voyage *m* **2** STUMBLE : trébuchement *m*

tripe ['traɪp] *n* : tripes *fpl* (d'un animal)

triple ['trɪpəl] *v* **-pled; -pling** : tripler — **~** *n* : triple *m* — **~** *adj* : triple — **triplets** ['trɪpləts] *npl* : triplés *mpl* — **triplicate** ['trɪplɪkət] *n* **in ~** : en trois exemplaires

tripod ['traɪˌpɑd] *n* : trépied *m*

trite ['traɪt] *adj* **triter; tritest** : banal

triumph ['traɪəmpf] *n* : triomphe *m* — **~** *vi* : triompher — **triumphal** [traɪ'ʌmpfəl] *adj* : triomphal — **triumphant** [traɪ'ʌmpfənt] *adj* : triomphant

trivial ['trɪviəl] *adj* : insignifiant — **trivia** ['trɪviə] *ns & pl* : futilités *fpl* — **triviality** [ˌtrɪvi'æləti] *n, pl* **-ties** : insignifiance *f*

trod, trodden → **tread**

trolley ['trɑli] *n, pl* **-leys** : tramway *m*

trombone [trɑm'boːn] *n* : trombone *m*

troop ['truːp] *n* **1** GROUP : bande *f*, groupe *m* **2 ~s** *npl* : troupes *fpl* — **trooper** ['truːpər] *n* **1** : soldat *m* **2** or **state ~** : gendarme *m* *France*, policier *m*

trophy ['troːfi] *n, pl* **-phies** : trophée *m*

tropic ['trɑpɪk] *n* **1** : tropique *m* **2 the ~s** : les tropiques *mpl* — **~** *or* **tropical** ['trɑpɪkəl] *adj* : tropical

trot ['trɑt] *n* : trot *m* — **~** *vi* **trotted; trotting** : trotter

trouble ['trʌbəl] *vt* **-bled; -bling 1** WORRY : inquiéter **2** BOTHER : déranger — **~** *n* **1** PROBLEMS : ennuis *mpl* **2** EFFORT : mal *m*, peine *f* **3 be in ~** : avoir des ennuis **4 I had ~ doing it** : j'ai eu du mal à le faire — **troublemaker** ['trʌbəlˌmeɪkər] *n* : fauteur *m*, -trice *f* de troubles — **troublesome** ['trʌbəlsəm] *adj* : gênant, pénible

trough ['trɔf] *n, pl* **troughs** ['trɔfs, 'trɔvz] **1** : abreuvoir *m* (pour les animaux) **2** *or* **feeding ~** : auge *f*

trousers ['trauzərz] *npl* : pantalon *m*

trout ['traut] *ns & pl* : truite *f*

trowel ['trauəl] *n* : truelle *f* (pour le mortier), déplantoir *m* (pour le jardinage)

truant ['truːənt] *n* : élève *mf* absentéiste

truce ['truːs] *n* : trêve *f*

truck ['trʌk] *n* : camion *m* — **trucker** ['trʌkər] *n* : camionneur *m*, -neuse *f*; routier *m*

trudge ['trʌdʒ] *vi* **trudged; trudging** : marcher péniblement

true ['truː] *adj* **truer; truest 1** FACTUAL : vrai **2** LOYAL : fidèle **3** GENUINE : authentique

truffle ['trʌfəl] *n* : truffe *f*

truly ['truːli] *adv* : vraiment

trump [ˈtrʌmp] *n* : atout *m*

trumpet [ˈtrʌmpət] *n* : trompette *f*

trunk [ˈtrʌŋk] *n* **1** STEM, TORSO : tronc *m* **2** : trompe *f* (d'un éléphant) **3** : coffre *m* (d'une voiture) **4** SUITCASE : malle *f* **5** ~**s** *npl* : maillot *m* de bain

trust [ˈtrʌst] *n* **1** CONFIDENCE : confiance *f* **2** HOPE : espoir *m* **3** : trust *m* (en finances) **4** in ~ : par fidéicommis — ~ *vi* **1** HOPE : espérer **2** ~ in : faire confiance à — *vt* **1** ENTRUST : confier **2** I ~ **him** : j'ai confiance en lui — **trustee** [ˌtrʌsˈtiː] *n* : fidéicommissaire *mf* — **trustworthy** [ˈtrʌst-ˌwərði] *adj* : digne de confiance

truth [ˈtruːθ] *n*, *pl* **truths** [ˈtruːðz, ˈtruːθs] : vérité *f* — **truthful** [ˈtruːθfəl] *adj* : sincère, vrai

try [ˈtraɪ] *v* **tried; trying** *vt* **1** ATTEMPT : essayer **2** : juger (un accusé) **3** TEST : éprouver, mettre à l'épreuve **4** TASTE : goûter — *vi* : essayer — ~ *n*, *pl* **tries** : essai *m* — **trying** [ˈtraɪɪŋ] *adj* : pénible — **tryout** [ˈtraɪ-ˌaʊt] *n* : essai *m*

tsar [ˈzɑr, ˈtsɑr, ˈsɑr] → **czar**

T–shirt [ˈtiːˌʃərt] *n* : tee-shirt *m*, t-shirt *m*

tub [ˈtʌb] *n* **1** VAT : cuve *f* **2** CONTAINER : pot *m* **3** BATHTUB : baignoire *f*

tuba [ˈtuːbə, ˈtjuː-] *n* : tuba *m*

tube [ˈtuːb, ˈtjuːb] *n* **1** : tube *m* **2** *or* inner ~ : chambre *f* à air **3** the ~ : la télé

tuberculosis [tʊˌbərkjəˈloːsəs, tjʊ-] *n*, *pl* **-loses** [-ˌsiːz] : tuberculose *f*

tubing [ˈtuːbɪŋ, ˈtjuː-] *n* : tubes *mpl* — **tubular** [ˈtuːbjələr, ˈtjuː-] *adj* : tubulaire

tuck [ˈtʌk] *vt* **1** *or* ~ **away** : ranger **2** ~ **in** : rentrer (une chemise, etc.) — ~ *n* : pli *m*

Tuesday [ˈtuːzˌdeɪ, ˈtjuːz-, -di] *n* : mardi *m*

tuft [ˈtʌft] *n* : touffe *f* (de cheveux, d'herbe, etc.)

tug [ˈtʌg] *vt* **tugged; tugging** *or* ~ **at** : tirer sur — ~ *n* : petit coup *m* — **tugboat** [ˈtʌg-ˌboːt] *n* : remorqueur *m* — **tug-of-war** [ˌtʌgəˈwɔr] *n*, *pl* **tugs-of-war** : lutte *f* à la corde

tuition [tʊˈɪʃən, ˈtjuː-] *n* : frais *mpl* de scolarité

tulip [ˈtuːlɪp, ˈtjuː-] *n* : tulipe *f*

tumble [ˈtʌmbəl] *vi* **-bled; -bling** : tomber — ~ *n* : chute *f* — **tumbler** [ˈtʌmblər] *n* : verre *m* droit

tummy [ˈtʌmi] *n*, *pl* **-mies** : ventre *m*

tumor *or* *Brit* **tumour** [ˈtuːmər, ˈtjuː-] *n* : tumeur *f*

tumult [ˈtuːˌmʌlt ˈtjuː-] *n* : tumulte *m* — **tumultuous** [tʊˈmʌltʃʊəs, tjuː-] *adj* : tumultueux

tuna [ˈtuːnə ˈtjuː-] *n*, *pl* **-na** *or* **-nas** : thon *m*

tune [ˈtuːn, ˈtjuːn] *n* **1** MELODY : air *m* **2** in ~ : accordé, juste **3** out of ~ : désac-

cordé, faux — ~ *v* **tuned; tuning** *vt* **1** : accorder (un piano, etc.) **2** *or* ~ **up** : régler (un moteur) — *vi* ~ **in** : se mettre à l'écoute — **tuner** [ˈtuːnər, ˈtjuː-] *n* : accordeur *m* (de pianos, etc.)

tunic [ˈtuːnɪk, ˈtjuː-] *n* : tunique *f*

Tunisian [tuːˈniːʒən, tjuːˈnɪziən] *adj* : tunisien

tunnel [ˈtʌnəl] *n* : tunnel *m* — ~ *vi* **-neled** *or* **-nelled; -neling** *or* **-nelling** : creuser un tunnel

turban [ˈtərbən] *n* : turban *m*

turbine [ˈtərbən, -ˌbaɪn] *n* : turbine *f*

turbulent [ˈtərbjələnt] *adj* : turbulent — **turbulence** [ˈtərbjələnts] *n* : turbulence *f*

turf [ˈtərf] *n* : gazon *m*

turkey [ˈtərki] *n*, *pl* **-keys** : dinde *f*

Turkish [ˈtərkɪʃ] *adj* : turc — ~ *n* : turc *m* (langue)

turmoil [ˈtərˌmɔɪl] *n* : désarroi *m*, confusion *f*

turn [ˈtərn] *vt* **1** : tourner **2** SPRAIN : tordre **3** ~ **down** REFUSE : refuser **4** ~ **down** LOWER : baisser **5** : rendre **6** ~ **into** : convertir en **7** ~ **off** : éteindre (la lumière, etc.), couper (le contact, etc.) **8** ~ **out** EXPEL : expulser **9** ~ **out** PRODUCE : produire **10** ~ **out** → **turn off 11** *or* ~ **over** FLIP : retourner **12** ~ **over** TRANSFER : remettre **13** ~ **s.o.'s stomach** : soulever le cœur à qqn **14** ~ **up** RAISE : augmenter — *vi* **1** ROTATE : tourner **2** BECOME : devenir **3** SOUR : tourner **4** CHANGE : se transformer **5** HEAD : se diriger **6** *or* ~ **around** : se retourner **7** ~ **in** RETIRE : se coucher **8** ~ **in** DELIVER : livrer **9** ~ **into** : se changer en **10** ~ **out** COME : venir **11** ~ **out** RESULT : se terminer **12** ~ **out to be** : s'avérer, se révéler **13** ~ **up** APPEAR : se présenter — ~ *n* **1** ROTATION : tour *m* **2** CHANGE : changement *m* **3** CURVE : virage *m* **4** DEED : service *m* **5** **wait your** ~ : attendez votre tour

turnip [ˈtərnəp] *n* : navet *m*

turnout [ˈtərnˌaʊt] *n* : participation *f* — **turnover** [ˈtərnˌoːvər] *n* **1** REVERSAL : renversement *m* **2** : roulement *m* (du personnel) **3** **apple** ~ : chausson *m* aux pommes — **turnpike** [ˈtərnˌpaɪk] *n* : autoroute *f* à péage — **turntable** [ˈtərnˌteɪbəl] *n* : platine *f*

turpentine [ˈtərpənˌtaɪn] *n* : térébenthine *f*

turret [ˈtərət] *n* : tourelle *f*

turtle [ˈtərtəl] *n* : tortue *f* — **turtleneck** [ˈtərtəlˌnɛk] *n* : col *m* roulé, col *m* montant

tusk [ˈtʌsk] *n* : défense *f* (d'un animal)

tutor [ˈtuːtər, ˈtjuː-] *n* : précepteur *m*, -trice *f*; professeur *m* particulier — ~ *vt* : donner des cours particuliers à

tuxedo [ˌtəkˈsiːˌdoː] *n*, *pl* **-dos** *or* **-does** : smoking *m*

TV [ˌtiːˈviː, ˈtiːˌviː] → **television**

twang [ˈtwæŋ] *n* : ton *m* nasillard (de la voix)

tweed [ˈtwiːd] *n* : tweed *m*

tweet [ˈtwiːt] *n* : pépiement *m* — ~ *vi* : pépier

tweezers [ˈtwiːzərz] *ns & pl* : pince *f* à épiler

twelve [ˈtwɛlv] *n* : douze *m* — ~ *adj* : douze — **twelfth** [ˈtwɛlfθ] *n* **1** : douzième *mf* **2 February** ~ : le douze février — ~ *adj* : douzième

twenty [ˈtwʌnti, ˈtwɛn-] *n, pl* **-ties** : vingt *m* — ~ *adj* : vingt — **twentieth** [ˈtwʌntiəθ, ˈtwɛn-] *n* **1** : vingtième *mf* **2 March** ~ : le vingt mars — ~ *adj* : vingtième

twice [ˈtwaɪs] *adv* **1** : deux fois **2** ~ **as much** : deux fois plus

twig [ˈtwɪg] *n* : brindille *f*

twilight [ˈtwaɪˌlaɪt] *n* : crépuscule *m*

twin [ˈtwɪn] *n* : jumeau *m*, -melle *f* — ~ *adj* : jumeau

twine [ˈtwaɪn] *n* : ficelle *f*

twinge [ˈtwɪndʒ] *n* : élancement *m* (de douleur)

twinkle [ˈtwɪŋkəl] *vi* **-kled; -kling 1** : scintiller (se dit des étoiles, etc.) **2** : pétiller (se dit des yeux) — ~ *n* : scintillement *m* (des étoiles), pétillement *m* (des yeux)

twirl [ˈtwərl] *vt* : faire tournoyer — *vi* : tournoyer — ~ *n* : tournoiement *m*

twist [ˈtwɪst] *vt* **1** TURN : tourner **2** SPRAIN : tordre **3** DISTORT : déformer — *vi* **1** : serpenter (se dit d'une route) **2** COIL : s'enrouler **3** ~ **and turn** : se tortiller **4** ~ **off** : dévisser — ~ *n* **1** TURN : tour *m* **2** BEND : tournant *m* **3 a** ~ **of fate** : un coup du sort — **twister** [ˈtwɪstər] → **tornado**

twitch [ˈtwɪtʃ] *vi* : se contracter — ~ *n or* **nervous** ~ : tic *m* (nerveux)

two [ˈtuː] *n, pl* **twos** : deux *m* — ~ *adj* : deux — **twofold** [ˈtuːˌfoːld] *adj* : double — ~ *adv* : doublement — **two hundred** *adj* : deux cents

tycoon [taɪˈkuːn] *n* : magnat *m*

tying → **tie**

type [ˈtaɪp] *n* **1** KIND : type *m* **2** : caractère *m* (d'imprimerie) — ~ *v* **typed; typing** : taper (à la machine) — **typewriter** [ˈtaɪpˌraɪtər] *n* : machine *f* à écrire, dactylo *f Can*

typhoon [taɪˈfuːn] *n* : typhon *m*

typical [ˈtɪpɪkəl] *adj* : typique — **typify** [ˈtɪpəˌfaɪ] *vt* **-fied; -fying** : être typique de

typist [ˈtaɪpɪst] *n* : dactylo *mf*

typography [taɪˈpɑgrəfi] *n* : typographie *f*

tyranny [ˈtɪrəni] *n, pl* **-nies** : tyrannie *f* — **tyrant** [ˈtaɪrənt] *n* : tyran *m*

tzar [ˈzɑr, ˈtsɑr, ˈsɑr] → **czar**

U

u [ˈjuː] *n, pl* **u's** *or* **us** [ˈjuːz] : u *m*, vingt et unième lettre de l'alphabet

udder [ˈʌdər] *n* : pis *m*

UFO [ˌjuːˌɛfˈoː, ˈjuːˌfoː] *n* (*unidentified flying object*), *pl* **UFO's** *or* **UFOs** : ovni *m*

ugly [ˈʌgli] *adj* **-lier; -est** : laid — **ugliness** [ˈʌglinəs] *n* : laideur *f*

ulcer [ˈʌlsər] *n* : ulcère *f*

ulterior [ˌʌlˈtɪriər] *adj* ~ **motive** : arrière-pensée *f*

ultimate [ˈʌltəmət] *adj* **1** : ultime, final **2** SUPREME : suprême — **ultimately** [ˈʌltəmətli] *adv* **1** : finalement, en fin de compte **2** EVENTUALLY : par la suite

ultimatum [ˌʌltəˈmeɪtəm, -ˈmɑ-] *n, pl* **-tums** *or* **-ta** [-tə] : ultimatum *m*

ultraviolet [ˌʌltrəˈvaɪələt] *adj* : ultraviolet

umbilical cord [ˌʌmˈbɪlɪkəl] *n* : cordon *m* ombilical

umbrella [ˌʌmˈbrɛlə] *n* : parapluie *m*

umpire [ˈʌmˌpaɪr] *n* : arbitre *m* — ~ *vt* **-pired; -piring** : arbitrer

umpteenth [ˈʌmpˌtinθ, ˌʌmpˈ-] *adj* : énième

unable [ˌʌnˈeɪbəl] *adj* **1** : incapable **2 be** ~ **to** : ne pas pouvoir

unabridged [ˌʌnəˈbrɪdʒd] *adj* : intégral

unacceptable [ˌʌnɪkˈsɛptəbəl] *adj* : inacceptable

unaccountable [ˌʌnəˈkaʊntəbəl] *adj* : inexplicable

unaccustomed [ˌʌnəˈkʌstəmd] *adj* **be** ~ **to** : ne pas avoir l'habitude de

unadulterated [ˌʌnəˈdʌltəˌreɪtəd] *adj* : pur, naturel

unaffected [ˌʌnəˈfɛktəd] *adj* **1** : indifférent **2** NATURAL : sans affectation

unafraid [ˌʌnəˈfreɪd] *adj* : sans peur

unaided [ˌʌnˈeɪdəd] *adj* : sans aide

unanimous [juˈnænəməs] *adj* : unanime

unannounced [ˌʌnəˈnaʊnst] *adj* : inattendu, sans se faire annoncer

unarmed [ˌʌnˈɑrmd] *adj* : non armé, sans armes

unassuming [ˌʌnəˈsuːmɪŋ] *adj* : modeste

unattached [ˌʌnəˈtætʃt] *adj* **1** : détaché **2** UNMARRIED : libre

unattractive

354

unattractive [ˌʌnəˈtræktɪv] *adj* : peu attrayant

unauthorized [ˌʌnˈɔːθəˌraɪzd] *adj* : non autorisé

unavailable [ˌʌnəˈveɪləbəl] *adj* : indisponible

unavoidable [ˌʌnəˈvɔɪdəbəl] *adj* : inévitable

unaware [ˌʌnəˈwær] *adj* 1 : ignorant 2 **be ~ of** : ignorer, ne pas être conscient de

unbalanced [ˌʌnˈbæləntst] *adj* : déséquilibré

unbearable [ˌʌnˈbærəbəl] *adj* : insupportable

unbelievable [ˌʌnbəˈliːvəbəl] *adj* : incroyable

unbending [ˌʌnˈbendɪŋ] *adj* : inflexible

unbiased [ˌʌnˈbaɪəst] *adj* : impartial

unborn [ˌʌnˈbɔrn] *adj* : qui n'est pas encore né

unbreakable [ˌʌnˈbreɪkəbəl] *adj* : incassable

unbroken [ˌʌnˈbroːkən] *adj* 1 INTACT : intact 2 CONTINUOUS : continu

unbutton [ˌʌnˈbʌtən] *vt* : déboutonner

uncalled-for [ˌʌnˈkɔldˌfɔr] *adj* : déplacé, injustifié

uncanny [ənˈkæni] *adj* 1 STRANGE : mystérieux, troublant 2 REMARKABLE : remarquable

unceasing [ˌʌnˈsiːsɪŋ] *adj* : incessant

uncertain [ˌʌnˈsərtən] *adj* : incertain — **uncertainty** [ˌʌnˈsərtənti] *n, pl* **-ties** : incertitude *f*

unchanged [ˌʌnˈtʃeɪndʒd] *adj* : inchangé — **unchanging** [ˌʌnˈtʃeɪndʒɪŋ] *adj* : immuable

uncivilized [ˌʌnˈsɪvəˌlaɪzd] *adj* : barbare

uncle [ˈʌŋkəl] *n* : oncle *m*

unclear [ˌʌnˈklɪr] *adj* : peu clair

uncomfortable [ˌʌnˈkʌmpfərtəbəl] *adj* 1 : inconfortable 2 AWKWARD : mal à l'aise

uncommon [ˌʌnˈkɑmən] *adj* : rare, peu commun

uncompromising [ˌʌnˈkɑmprəˈmaɪzɪŋ] *adj* : intransigeant

unconcerned [ˌʌnkənˈsərnd] *adj* : indifférent

unconditional [ˌʌnkənˈdɪʃənəl] *adj* : inconditionnel

unconscious [ˌʌnˈkɑnʃəs] *adj* : inconscient

uncontrollable [ˌʌnkənˈtroːləbəl] *adj* : incontrôlable

unconventional [ˌʌnkənˈventʃənəl] *adj* : peu conventionnel

uncouth [ˌʌnˈkuːθ] *adj* : grossier

uncover [ˌʌnˈkʌvər] *vt* : découvrir

undecided [ˌʌndɪˈsaɪdəd] *adj* : indécis

undeniable [ˌʌndɪˈnaɪəbəl] *adj* : indéniable

under [ˈʌndər] *adv* 1 : en dessous 2 LESS : moins 3 *or* **~ anesthetic** : sous anesthésie — **~** *prep* 1 BELOW, BENEATH : sous, en dessous de 2 ACCORDING TO : d'après, selon

underage [ˌʌndərˈeɪdʒ] *adj* : mineur

underclothes [ˈʌndərˌkloːz, -ˌkloːðz] *npl* → **underwear**

undercover [ˌʌndərˈkʌvər] *adj* : secret

underdeveloped [ˌʌndərdɪˈvɛləpt] *adj* : sous-développé

underestimate [ˌʌndərˈɛstəˌmeɪt] *vt* **-mated; -mating** : sous-estimer

undergo [ˌʌndərˈgoː] *vt* **-went** [-ˈwɛnt]; **-gone** [-ˈgɔn]; **-going** : subir, éprouver

undergraduate [ˌʌndərˈgrædʒuət] *n* : étudiant *m*, -diante *f* de premier cycle; étudiant *m*, -diante *f* qui prépare une licence *France*

underground [ˌʌndərˈgraʊnd] *adv* : sous terre — **~** [ˈʌndərˌgraʊnd] *adj* 1 : souterrain 2 SECRET : clandestin — **~** [ˈʌndərˌgraʊnd] *n* SUBWAY : métro *m*

undergrowth [ˈʌndərˌgroːθ] *n* : sous-bois *m*, broussailles *fpl*

underhanded [ˌʌndərˈhændəd] *adj* SLY : sournois

underline [ˈʌndərˌlaɪn] *vt* **-lined; -lining** : souligner

underlying [ˌʌndərˈlaɪɪŋ] *adj* : sous-jacent

undermine [ˌʌndərˈmaɪn] *vt* **-mined; -mining** : saper, miner

underneath [ˌʌndərˈniːθ] *prep* : sous, au-dessous de — **~** *adv* : en dessous, dessous

underpants [ˈʌndərˌpænts] *npl* : caleçon *m*, slip *m France*

underpass [ˈʌndərˌpæs] *n* : voie *f* inférieure (de l'autoroute), passage *m* souterrain (pour piétons)

underprivileged [ˌʌndərˈprɪvlɪdʒd] *adj* : défavorisé

undershirt [ˈʌndərˌʃərt] *n* : maillot *m* de corps

understand [ˌʌndərˈstænd] *vt* **-stood** [-ˈstʊd]; **-standing** 1 : comprendre 2 BELIEVE : croire — **understandable** [ˌʌndərˈstændəbəl] *adj* : compréhensible — **understanding** [ˌʌndərˈstændɪŋ] *n* 1 : compréhension *f* 2 AGREEMENT : entente *f*, accord *m* — **~** *adj* : compréhensif

understudy [ˈʌndərˌstʌdi] *n, pl* **-dies** : doublure *f* (au théâtre)

undertake [ˌʌndərˈteɪk] *vt* **-took** [-ˈtʊk]; **-taken** [-ˈteɪkən]; **-taking** : entreprendre (une tâche), assumer (une responsabilité) — **undertaker** [ˈʌndərˌteɪkər] *n* : entrepreneur *m* de pompes funèbres — **undertaking** [ˈʌndərˌteɪkɪŋ, ˌʌndərˈ-] *n* : entreprise *f*

undertone [ˈʌndərˌtoːn] *n* : voix *f* basse

undertow [ˈʌndərˌtoː] *n* : courant *m* sous-marin

underwater [ˌʌndərˈwɔtər, -ˈwɑ-] *adj* : sous-marin — **~** *adv* : sous l'eau

under way [ˌʌndərˈweɪ] *adv* : en cours, en route

underwear ['ʌndər,wær] *n* : sous-vêtements *mpl*

underwent → **undergo**

underworld ['ʌndər,wərld] *n or* **criminal ~** : milieu *m*, pègre *f*

undesirable [,ʌndɪ'zaɪrəbəl] *adj* : indésirable

undisputed [,ʌndɪ'spju:təd] *adj* : incontesté

undo [,ʌn'du:] *vt* **-did; -done; -doing 1** UNFASTEN : défaire, détacher **2 ~ a wrong** : réparer un tort

undoubtedly [,ʌn'dautədli] *adv* : sans aucun doute

undress [,ʌn'drɛs] *vt* : déshabiller — *vi* : se déshabiller

undue [,ʌn'du:, -'dju:] *adj* : excessif, démesuré

undulate ['ʌndʒə,leɪt] *vi* **-lated; -lating** : onduler

unduly [,ʌn'du:li] *adv* : excessivement

unearth [,ʌn'ɛrθ] *vt* : déterrer

uneasy [,ʌn'i:zi] *adj* **1** : mal à l'aise, gêné **2** WORRIED : inquiet **3** UNSTABLE : précaire — **uneasily** [,ʌn'i:zəli] *adv* : avec inquiétude — **uneasiness** [,ʌn'i:zinəs] *n* : inquiétude *f*

uneducated [,ʌn'ɛdʒə,keɪtəd] *adj* : sans éducation

unemployed [,ʌnɪm'plɔɪd] *adj* : en chômage, sans travail — **unemployment** [,ʌnɪm'plɔɪmənt] *n* : chômage *m*

unequal [,ʌn'i:kwəl] *adj* : inégal

uneven [,ʌn'i:vən] *adj* **1** : inégal **2** ODD : impair

unexpected [,ʌnɪk'spɛktəd] *adj* : inattendu, imprévu

unfailing [,ʌn'feɪlɪŋ] *adj* **1** CONSTANT : infaillible **2** INEXHAUSTIBLE : inépuisable

unfair [,ʌn'fær] *adj* : injuste — **unfairly** [,ʌn'færli] *adj* : injustement — **unfairness** [,ʌn'færnəs] *n* : injustice *f*

unfaithful [,ʌn'feɪθfəl] *adj* : infidèle — **unfaithfulness** [,ʌn'feɪθfəlnəs] *n* : infidélité *f*

unfamiliar [,ʌnfə'mɪljər] *adj* **1** : inconnu, peu familier **2 be ~ with** : mal connaître

unfasten [,ʌn'fæsən] *vt* : déboucler (une ceinture)

unfavorable [,ʌn'feɪvərəbəl] *adj* : défavorable

unfeeling [,ʌn'fi:lɪŋ] *adj* : insensible

unfinished [,ʌn'fɪnɪʃd] *adj* : inachevé

unfit [,ʌn'fɪt] *adj* : inapte, impropre

unfold [,ʌn'fo:ld] *vt* **1** : déplier **2** REVEAL : dévoiler — *vi* : se dérouler

unforeseen [,ʌnfor'si:n] *adj* : imprévu

unforgettable [,ʌnfər'gɛtəbəl] *adj* : inoubliable

unforgivable [,ʌnfər'gɪvəbəl] *adj* : impardonnable

unfortunate [,ʌn'fɔrtʃənət] *adj* **1** UNLUCKY : malheureux **2** REGRETTABLE : regrettable, fâcheux — **unfortunately** [,ʌn'fɔrtʃənətli] *adv* : malheureusement

unfounded [,ʌn'faundəd] *adj* : sans fondement

unfurl [,ʌn'fərl] *vt* : déployer

unfurnished [,ʌn'fərnɪʃt] *adj* : non meublé

ungainly [,ʌn'geɪnli] *adj* : gauche

ungodly [,ʌn'gɑdli, -'gɑd-] *adj* UNSEEMLY : indu, impossible

ungrateful [,ʌn'greɪtfəl] *adj* : ingrat

unhappy [,ʌn'hæpi] *adj* **-pier; -est 1** SAD : malheureux, triste **2** DISSATISFIED : mécontent — **unhappiness** [,ʌn'hæpinəs] *n* : tristesse *f*

unharmed [,ʌn'hɑrmd] *adj* : indemne

unhealthy [,ʌn'hɛlθi] *adj* **-healthier; -healthiest 1** : insalubre, malsain **2** SICKLY : malade, maladif

unheard-of [,ʌn'hərdəv] *adj* : sans précédent, inconnu

unhook [,ʌn'huk] *vt* **1** REMOVE : décrocher **2** UNFASTEN : dégrafer

unhurt [,ʌn'hərt] *adj* : indemne

unicorn ['ju:nə,kɔrn] *n* : licorne *f*

unification [,ju:nəfə'keɪʃən] *n* : unification *f*

uniform ['ju:nə,fɔrm] *adj* : uniforme — *n* : uniforme *m* — **uniformity** [,ju:nə'fɔrməti] *n, pl* **-ties** : uniformité *f*

unify ['ju:nə,faɪ] *vt* **-fied; -fying** : unifier

unilateral [,ju:nə'lætərəl] *adj* : unilatéral

uninhabited [,ʌnɪn'hæbətəd] *adj* : inhabité

union ['ju:njən] *n* **1** : union *f* **2 or labor ~** : syndicat *m*

unique [ju'ni:k] *adj* : unique — **uniquely** [ju'ni:kli] *adv* : exceptionnellement

unison ['ju:nəsən, -zən] *n* **in ~** : à l'unisson

unit ['ju:nɪt] *n* **1** : unité *f* **2** GROUP : groupe *m*

unite [ju'naɪt] *v* **united; uniting** *vt* : unir — *vi* : s'unir — **unity** ['ju:nəti] *n, pl* **-ties** : unité *f*

universe ['ju:nə,vərs] *n* : univers *m* — **universal** [,ju:nə'vərsəl] *adj* : universel

university [,ju:nə'vərsəti] *n, pl* **-ties** : université *f*

unjust [,ʌn'dʒʌst] *adj* : injuste — **unjustified** [,ʌn'dʒʌstə,faɪd] *adj* : injustifié

unkempt [,ʌn'kɛmpt] *adj* : en désordre, négligé

unkind [,ʌn'kaɪnd] *adj* : peu aimable, pas gentil — **unkindness** [,ʌn'kaɪndnəs] *n* : méchanceté *f*

unknown [,ʌn'no:n] *adj* : inconnu

unlawful [,ʌn'lɔfəl] *adj* : illégal

unless [ən'lɛs] *conj* : à moins que, à moins de

unlike [,ʌn'laɪk] *adj* : différent — **~** *prep* **1** : différent de **2** : contrairement à — **unlikelihood** [,ʌn'laɪkli,hud] *n* : improbabilité *f* —

unlikely [ˌʌnˈlaɪkli] *adj* **-lier; -liest** : improbable

unlimited [ˌʌnˈlɪmətəd] *adj* : illimité

unload [ˌʌnˈloːd] *vt* : décharger

unlock [ˌʌnˈlɑk] *vt* : ouvrir, débarrer *Can* (une porte, etc.)

unlucky [ˌʌnˈlʌki] *adj* **-luckier; -luckiest** **1** : malchanceux **2** : qui porte malheur (se dit d'un numéro)

unmarried [ˌʌnˈmærid] *adj* : célibataire

unnecessary [ˌʌnˈnɛsəˌsɛri] *adj* : inutile

unnerving [ˌʌnˈnərvɪŋ] *adj* : déconcertant

unnoticed [ˌʌnˈnoːtəst] *adj* : inaperçu

unoccupied [ˌʌnˈɑkjəˌpaɪd] *adj* **1** IDLE : inoccupé **2** EMPTY : libre

unofficial [ˌʌnəˈfɪʃəl] *adj* : officieux, non officiel

unpack [ˌʌnˈpæk] *vi* : défaire ses bagages

unparalleled [ˌʌnˈpærəˌlɛld] *adj* : sans égal, sans pareil

unpleasant [ˌʌnˈplɛzənt] *adj* : désagréable

unplug [ˌʌnˈplʌg] *vt* **-plugged; -plugging** **1** UNCLOG : déboucher **2** DISCONNECT : débrancher

unpopular [ˌʌnˈpɑpjələr] *adj* : impopulaire

unprecedented [ˌʌnˈprɛsəˌdɛntəd] *adj* : sans précédent

unpredictable [ˌʌnprɪˈdɪktəbəl] *adj* : imprévisible

unprepared [ˌʌnprɪˈpærd] *adj* : mal préparé

unqualified [ˌʌnˈkwɑləˌfaɪd] *adj* : non qualifié

unquestionable [ˌʌnˈkwɛsʧənəbəl] *adj* : incontestable

unravel [ˌʌnˈrævəl] *vt* **-eled** *or* **-elled; -eling** *or* **elling** : démêler, dénouer

unreal [ˌʌnˈriːl] *adj* : irréel — **unrealistic** [ˌʌnˌriːəˈlɪstɪk] *adj* : irréaliste

unreasonable [ˌʌnˈriːzənəbel] *adj* : déraisonnable

unrecognizable [ˌʌnˈrɛkəgˌnaɪzəbˈl] *adj* : méconnaissable

unrelated [ˌʌnrɪˈleɪtəd] *adj* : sans rapport

unrelenting [ˌʌnrɪˈlɛntɪŋ] *adj* : implacable

unreliable [ˌʌnrɪˈlaɪəbəl] *adj* : peu fiable, peu sûr

unrepentant [ˌʌnrɪˈpɛntənt] *adj* : impénitent

unrest [ˌʌnˈrɛst] *n* : agitation *f*, troubles *mpl*

unripe [ˌʌnˈraɪp] *adj* : pas mûr, vert

unrivaled *or* **unrivalled** [ˌʌnˈraɪvəld] *adj* : sans égal, incomparable

unroll [ˌʌnˈroːl] *vt* : dérouler

unruly [ˌʌnˈruːli] *adj* : indiscipliné

unsafe [ˌʌnˈseɪf] *adj* : dangereux

unsatisfactory [ˌʌnˌsætəsˈfæktəri] *adj* : peu satisfaisant

unscrew [ˌʌnˈskruː] *vt* : dévisser

unseemly [ˌʌnˈsiːmli] *adj* **-lier; -est** : inconvenant

unseen [ˌʌnˈsiːn] *adj* : invisible

unsettle [ˌʌnˈsɛtəl] *vt* **-tled; -tling** DISTURB : perturber — **unsettled** [ˌʌnˈsɛtəld] *adj* **1** UNSTABLE : instable **2** DISTURBED : troublé

unsightly [ˌʌnˈsaɪtli] *adj* : laid

unskilled [ˌʌnˈskɪld] *adj* : non spécialisé — **unskillful** [ˌʌnˈskɪlfəl] *adj* : malhabile

unsound [ˌʌnˈsaʊnd] *adj* : peu judicieux

unspeakable [ˌʌnˈspiːkəbəl] *adj* **1** : indicible **2** TERRIBLE : atroce

unstable [ˌʌnˈsteɪbəl] *adj* : instable

unsteady [ˌʌnˈstɛdi] *adj* **1** : instable **2** SHAKY : tremblant

unsuccessful [ˌʌnsəkˈsɛsfəl] *adj* **1** : infructueux **2** be ~ : échouer

unsuitable [ˌʌnˈsuːtəbəl] *adj* : qui ne convient pas, inapproprié — **unsuited** [ˌʌnˈsuːtəd] *adj* : inapte

unsure [ˌʌnˈʃʊr] *adj* **1** : incertain **2** be ~ of oneself : manquer de confiance en soi

unsuspecting [ˌʌnsəˈspɛktɪŋ] *adj* : qui ne se doute de rien

unthinkable [ˌʌnˈθɪŋkəbəl] *adj* : impensable, inconcevable

untidy [ˌʌnˈtaɪdi] *adj* **-dier; -est** : en désordre

untie [ˌʌnˈtaɪ] *vt* **-tied; -tying** *or* **-tieing** : dénouer, défaire

until [ˌʌnˈtɪl] *prep* **1** UP TO : jusqu'à **2** BEFORE : avant — ~ *conj* : jusqu'à ce que, avant que, avant de

untimely [ˌʌnˈtaɪmli] *adj* **1** : prématuré **2** INOPPORTUNE : déplacé

untoward [ˌʌnˈtɔrd, -ˈtoːərd, -təˈwɔrd] *adj* : fâcheux

untroubled [ˌʌnˈtrʌbəld] *adj* **1** : tranquille **2** be ~ by : ne pas être affecté par

untrue [ˌʌnˈtruː] *adj* : faux

unused *adj* [ˌʌnˈjuːzd, *in sense 1 usually* -ˈjuːst] **1** UNACCUSTOMED : pas habitué **2** NEW : neuf, nouveau

unusual [ˌʌnˈjuːʒʊəl] *adj* : peu commun, rare — **unusually** [ˌʌnˈjuːʒʊəli] *adv* : exceptionnellement

unveil [ˌʌnˈveɪl] *vt* : dévoiler

unwanted [ˌʌnˈwɑntəd] *adj* : non désiré

unwarranted [ˌʌnˈwɔrəntəd] *adj* : injustifié

unwelcome [ˌʌnˈwɛlkəm] *adj* : inopportun

unwell [ˌʌnˈwɛl] *adj* : indisposé

unwieldy [ˌʌnˈwiːldi] *adj* : encombrant

unwilling [ˌʌnˈwɪlɪŋ] *adj* : peu disposé — **unwillingly** [ˌʌnˈwɪlɪŋli] *adv* : à contrecœur

unwind [ˌʌnˈwaɪnd] *v* **-wound; -winding** *vt* : dérouler — *vi* **1** : se dérouler **2** RELAX : se détendre

unwise [ˌʌnˈwaɪz] *adj* : imprudent

unworthy [ˌʌnˈwərði] *adj* ~ of : indigne de

unwrap [ˌʌnˈræp] *vt* **-wrapped; -wrapped** : déballer

up [ˈʌp] *adv* **1** ABOVE : en haut **2** UPWARDS : vers le haut **3 farther** ~ : plus loin **4 go** ~ : augmenter, monter **5 speak** ~ : par-

ler plus fort **6 stand** ~ : se lever **7** ~
until : jusqu'à — ~ *adj* **1** AWAKE : levé **2**
INCREASING : qui augmente **3** UP-TO-DATE
: au courant, à jour **4** FINISHED : fini **5 be**
~ **for** : être prêt pour **6 what's** ~?
: qu'est-ce qui se passe? — ~ *prep* **1** : en
haut de **2 go** ~ : monter **3 sail** ~ **the**
river : remonter la rivière en bateau **4** ~ **to**
: jusqu'à — ~ *v* **upped; upping** *vt* : augmenter — *vi* ~ **and leave** : partir sans mot
dire

upbringing [ˈʌpˌbrɪŋɪŋ] *n* : éducation *f*

upcoming [ˌʌpˈkʌmɪŋ] *adj* : prochain, à
venir

update [ˌʌpˈdeɪt] *vt* **-dated; -dating** : mettre
à jour — ~ [ˈʌpˌdeɪt] *n* : mise *f* à jour

upgrade [ˈʌpˌgreɪd, ˌʌpˈ-] *vt* **-graded;**
-grading 1 IMPROVE : améliorer **2** PRO-
MOTE : promouvoir

upheaval [ˌʌpˈhiːvəl] *n* : bouleversement *m*

uphill [ˌʌpˈhɪl] *adv* go ~ : monter — ~
[ˈʌpˌhɪl] *adj* **1** ASCENDING : qui monte **2**
DIFFICULT : pénible

uphold [ˌʌpˈhoːld] *vt* **-held; -holding**
: soutenir, maintenir

upholstery [ˌʌpˈhoːlstəri] *n, pl* **-steries**
: rembourrage *m*

upkeep [ˈʌpˌkiːp] *n* : entretien *m*

upon [əˈpɔn, əˈpɑn] *prep* **1** : sur **2** ~ **leav-**
ing : en partant

upper [ˈʌpər] *adj* : supérieur

upper class *n* : aristocratie *f*

upper hand *n* have the ~ : avoir le dessus

uppermost [ˈʌpərˌmoːst] *adj* : le plus haut,
le plus élevé

upright [ˈʌpˌraɪt] *adj* : droit — ~ *n* : montant *m* (en construction)

uprising [ˈʌpˌraɪzɪŋ] *n* : soulèvement *m*

uproar [ˈʌpˌroːr] *n* : tumulte *m*

uproot [ˌʌpˈruːt, -ˈrʊt] *vt* : déraciner

upset [ˌʌpˈsɛt] *vt* **-set; -setting 1** OVER-
TURN : renverser **2** DISRUPT : déranger **3**
ANNOY : ennuyer — ~ *adj* **1** DISTRESSED
: bouleversé **2** ANNOYED : ennuyé, vexé **3**
have an ~ **stomach** : avoir l'estomac
dérangé — ~ [ˈʌpˌsɛt] *n* : bouleversement
m

upshot [ˈʌpˌʃɑt] *n* : résultat *m*

upside down *adv* **1** : à l'envers **2 turn** ~
: mettre sens dessus dessous — **upside-**
down [ˌʌpˌsaɪdˈdaʊn] *adj* : à l'envers

upstairs [ˌʌpˈstærz, ˈʌpˌ-] *adv* : en haut — ~ [ˈʌp-
ˌstærz, ˌʌpˈ-] *adj* : d'en haut, à l'étage — ~
[ˈʌpˌstærz, ˌʌpˈ-] *ns & pl* : étage *m*

upstart [ˈʌpˌstɑrt] *n* : arriviste *mf*

upstream [ˈʌpˈstriːm] *adv* : en amont

up–to–date [ˌʌptəˈdeɪt] *adj* **1** : à jour **2**
MODERN : moderne

uptown [ˈʌpˈtaʊn] *adv* : dans les quartiers
résidentiels

upturn [ˈʌpˌtərn] *n* : amélioration *f,* reprise *f*
(économique)

upward [ˈʌpwərd] *or* **upwards** [-wərdz] *adv*
1 : vers le haut **2** ~ **of** : plus de — **upward**
adj : ascendant

uranium [juˈreɪniəm] *n* : uranium *m*

Uranus [juˈreɪnəs, ˈjʊrənəs] *n* : Uranus *f*

urban [ˈərbən] *adj* : urbain

urbane [ˌərˈbeɪn] *adj* : raffiné, courtois

urge [ˈərdʒ] *vt* **urged; urging** : pousser, inciter — ~ *n* **1** DESIRE : envie *f* **2** IMPULSE
: pulsion *f* — **urgency** [ˈərdʒəntsi] *n, pl*
-cies : urgence *f* — **urgent** [ˈərdʒənt] *adj* **1**
: urgent **2 be** ~ : presser

urinal [ˈjʊrənəl, *esp Brit* jʊrˈaɪnəl] *n* : urinoir
m

urine [ˈjʊrən] *n* : urine *f* — **urinate** [ˈjʊrə-
ˌneɪt] *vi* **-nated; -nating** : uriner

urn [ˈərn] *n* : urne *f*

us [ˈʌs] *pron* : nous

usable [ˈjuːzəbəl] *adj* : utilisable

usage [ˈjuːsɪdʒ, -zɪdʒ] *n* : usage *m*

use [ˈjuːz] *v* **used** [ˈjuːzd; *in phrase "used*
to" usually ˈjuːstu]; **using** *vt* **1** : employer,
utiliser, se servir de **2** CONSUME : consommer **3** ~ **up** : épuiser — *vi* **she** ~**d to**
dance : elle dansait avant — ~ [ˈjuːs] *n* **1**
: emploi *m,* usage *m* **2** USEFULNESS : utilité
f **3 in** ~ : occupé **4 what's the** ~? : à
quoi bon? — **used** [ˈjuːzd] *adj* **1** SECOND-
HAND : d'occasion **2 be** ~ **to** : avoir
l'habitude de, être habitué à — **useful** [ˈjuː-
ˌsfəl] *adj* : utile, pratique — **usefulness**
[ˈjuːsfəlnəs] *n* : utilité *f* — **useless** [ˈjuːsləs]
adj : inutile — **user** [ˈjuːzər] *n* : usager *m;*
utilisateur *m,* -trice *f*

usher [ˈʌʃər] *vt* **1** : conduire, accompagner
2 ~ **in** : inaugurer — ~ *n* : huissier *m* (à
un tribunal); placeur *m,* -ceuse *f* (au théâtre)

usual [ˈjuːʒəl] *adj* **1** : habituel **2 as** ~
: comme d'habitude — **usually** [ˈjuːʒəli]
adv : habituellement, d'habitude

usurp [juˈsərp, -ˈzərp] *vt* : usurper

utensil [juˈtɛntsəl] *n* : ustensile *m*

uterus [ˈjuːtərəs] *n, pl* **uteri** [-ˌraɪ] : utérus *m*

utility [juˈtɪləti] *n, pl* **-ties 1** : utilité *f* **2** *or*
public ~ : service *m* public

utilize [ˈjuːtəˌlaɪz] *vt* **-lized; -lizing** : utiliser

utmost [ˈʌtˌmoːst] *adj* **1** FARTHEST : extrême **2 of** ~ **importance** : de la plus
haute importance — ~ *n* **do one's** ~
: faire tout son possible

utopia [juˈtoːpiə] *n* : utopie *f* — **utopian** [juˈ-
ˈtoːpiən] *adj* : utopique

utter¹ [ˈʌtər] *adj* : absolu, total

utter² *vt* : émettre (un son), pousser (un cri)
— **utterance** [ˈʌtərənts] *n* : déclaration *f,*
paroles *fpl*

utterly [ˈʌtərli] *adv* : complètement

V

v [ˈviː] n, pl **v's** or **vs** [ˈviːz] : v m, vingt-deu-
xième lettre de l'alphabet

vacant [ˈveɪkənt] adj **1** AVAILABLE : libre **2**
UNOCCUPIED : vacant — **vacancy** [ˈveɪ-
kəntsi] n, pl **-cies 1** : chambre f disponible
2 : poste m vacant **3 no ~** : complet

vacate [ˈveɪˌkeɪt] vt **-cated; -cating** : quitter

vacation [veɪˈkeɪʃən, və-] n : vacances fpl

vaccination [ˌvæksəˈneɪʃən] n : vaccination
f — **vaccinate** [ˈvæksəˌneɪt] vt **-nated;
-nating** : vacciner — **vaccine** [vækˈsiːn,
ˈvækˌ-] n : vaccin m

vacuum [ˈvæˌkjuːm, -kjəm] n, pl **vacuums**
or **vacua** [ˈvækjuə] : vide m — **~** vt
: passer l'aspirateur sur — **vacuum cleaner**
n : aspirateur m, balayeuse f Can

vagina [vəˈdʒaɪnə] n, pl **-nae** [-ˌniː, -ˌnaɪ] or
-nas : vagin m

vagrant [ˈveɪgrənt] n : vagabond m, -bonde f

vague [ˈveɪg] adj **vaguer; vaguest** : vague

vain [ˈveɪn] adj **1** FUTILE : vain **2** CON-
CEITED : vaniteux

valentine [ˈvælənˌtaɪn] n : carte f de Saint–
Valentin

valiant [ˈvæljənt] adj : vaillant

valid [ˈvæləd] adj : valable, valide — **validate** [ˈvæləˌdeɪt] vt **-dated; -dating**
: valider

valley [ˈvæli] n, pl **-leys** : vallée f

valor or Brit **valour** [ˈvælər] n : bravoure f

value [ˈvælˌjuː] n : valeur f — **~** vt **valued;
valuing 1** : estimer, évaluer **2** APPRECIATE
: apprécier — **valuable** [ˈvæljuəbəl, -jəbəl]
adj **1** : de valeur **2** WORTHWHILE : précieux
— **valuables** [ˈvæljuəbəlz, -jəbəlz] npl : objets mpl de valeur

valve [ˈvælv] n : valve f (d'un pneu),
soupape f

vampire [ˈvæmˌpaɪr] n : vampire m

van [ˈvæn] n : camionnette f, fourgonnette
f

vandal [ˈvændəl] n : vandale mf — **vandalism** [ˈvændəlˌɪzəm] n : vandalisme m —
vandalize [ˈvændəlˌaɪz] vt **-ized; -izing**
: saccager

vane [ˈveɪn] n or **weather ~** : girouette f

vanguard [ˈvænˌgɑrd] n : avant-garde f

vanilla [vəˈnɪlə, -ˈnɛ-] n : vanille f

vanish [ˈvænɪʃ] vi : disparaître

vanity [ˈvænəti] n, pl **-ties** : vanité f

vantage point [ˈvæntɪdʒ] n : point m de vue

vapor [ˈveɪpər] n : vapeur f

variable [ˈvɛriəbəl] adj : variable — **~** n
: variable f — **variant** [ˈvɛriənt] n : variante
f — **variation** [ˌvɛriˈeɪʃən] n : variation f —

varied [ˈvɛrid] adj : varié, divers — **variety**
[vəˈraɪəti] n, pl **-eties 1** DIVERSITY : variété
f **2** SORT : espèce f, sorte f — **various**
[ˈvɛriəs] adj : divers, varié

varnish [ˈvɑrnɪʃ] n : vernis m — **~** vt
: vernir

vary [ˈvɛri] v **varied; varying** : varier

vase [ˈveɪs, ˈveɪz, ˈvɑz] n : vase m

vast [ˈvæst] adj : vaste — **vastness**
[ˈvæstnəs] n : immensité f

vat [ˈvæt] n : cuve f, bac m

vault [ˈvɔlt] n **1** ARCH : voûte f **2** or **bank
~** : chambre f forte

VCR [ˌviːˌsiːˈɑr] n (videocassette recorder)
: magnétoscope m

veal [ˈviːl] n : veau m

veer [ˈvɪr] vi : virer

vegetable [ˈvɛdʒtəbəl, ˈvɛdʒətə-] adj **1**
: végétal **2 ~ soup** : soupe f aux légumes
— **~** n : légume m — **vegetarian** [ˌvɛdʒə-
ˈtɛriən] n : végétarien m, -rienne f — **vegetation** [ˌvɛdʒəˈteɪʃən] n : végétation f

vehement [ˈviːəmənt] adj : véhément

vehicle [ˈviəkəl, ˈviːˌhɪkəl] n : véhicule m

veil [ˈveɪl] n : voile m — **~** vt : voiler

vein [ˈveɪn] n **1** : veine f **2** : filon m (d'un
minéral, etc.) **3** : nervure f (d'une feuille)

velocity [vəˈlɑsəti] n, pl **-ties** : vélocité f

velvet [ˈvɛlvət] n : velours m — **velvety**
[ˈvɛlvəti] adj : velouté

vending machine [ˈvɛndɪŋ-] n : distributeur
m automatique

vendor [ˈvɛndər] n : vendeur m, -deuse f

veneer [vəˈnɪr] n **1** : placage m (de bois) **2**
FACADE : vernis m

venerable [ˈvɛnərəbəl] adj : vénérable —
venerate [ˈvɛnəˌreɪt] vt **-ated; -ating**
: vénérer

venereal [vəˈnɪriəl] adj : vénérien

venetian blind [vəˈniːʃən] n : store m véni-
tien

vengeance [ˈvɛndʒənts] n **1** : vengeance f **2
take ~ on** : se venger sur — **vengeful**
[ˈvɛndʒfəl] adj : vengeur, vindicatif

venison [ˈvɛnəsən, -zən] n : venaison f

venom [ˈvɛnəm] n : venin m — **venomous**
[ˈvɛnəməs] adj : venimeux

vent [ˈvɛnt] vt : décharger — **~** n **1** : orifice
m, conduit m **2** or **air ~** : bouche f d'aéra-
tion — **ventilate** [ˈvɛntəlˌeɪt] vt **-lated; -lat-
ing** : ventiler — **ventilation** [ˌvɛntəlˈeɪʃən]
n : ventilation f

venture [ˈvɛntʃər] v **-tured; -turing** vt RISK
: risquer — vi or **~ out** : s'aventurer — **~**
n : entreprise f

Venus [ˈviːnəs] *n* : Vénus *f*

veranda *or* **verandah** [vəˈrændə] *n* : véranda *f*

verb [ˈvərb] *n* : verbe *m* — **verbal** [ˈvərbəl] *adj* : verbal — **verbatim** [vərˈbeiṭəm] *adv & adj* : mot pour mot

verdict [ˈvərdɪkt] *n* : verdict *m*

verge [ˈvərdʒ] *n* **1** EDGE : bordure *f* **2 on the ~ of** : sur le point de

verify [ˈvɛrəˌfaɪ] *vt* **-fied; -fying** : vérifier

vermin [ˈvərmən] *ns & pl* : vermine *f*

versatile [ˈvərsəṭəl] *adj* : polyvalent

verse [ˈvərs] *n* **1** STANZA : strophe *f* **2** POETRY : vers *mpl* **3** : verset *m* (de la Bible) — **versed** [ˈvərst] *adj* **be well ~ in** : être versé dans

version [ˈvərʒən] *n* : version *f*

versus [ˈvərsəs] *prep* : contre

vertebra [ˈvərṭəbrə] *n, pl* **-brae** [-ˌbreɪ, -ˌbriː] *or* **-bras** : vertèbre *f*

vertical [ˈvərṭɪkəl] *adj* : vertical — **~** *n* : verticale *f*

vertigo [ˈvərṭɪˌgoː] *n, pl* **-goes** *or* **-gos** : vertige *m*

very [ˈvɛri] *adv* **1** : très **2 ~ much** : beaucoup — **~** *adj* **1** EXACT : même **2 at the ~ least** : tout au moins **3 the ~ thought!** : quelle idée!

vessel [ˈvɛsəl] *n* **1** : vaisseau *m* **2** CONTAINER : récipient *m*

vest [ˈvɛst] *n* : gilet *m*

vestige [ˈvɛstɪdʒ] *n* : vestige *m*

veteran [ˈvɛṭərən, ˈvɛtrən] *n* : vétéran *m*, ancien combattant *m*

veterinarian [ˌvɛṭərəˈnɛriən, ˌvɛtrə-] *n* : vétérinaire *mf*

veto [ˈviːṭo] *n, pl* **-toes** : veto *m* — **~** *vt* : mettre son veto à

vex [ˈvɛks] *vt* **vexed; vexing** : vexer, contrarier

via [ˈvaɪə, ˈviːə] *prep* : via, par

viable [ˈvaɪəbəl] *adj* : viable

vial [ˈvaɪəl] *n* : ampoule *f*

vibrant [ˈvaɪbrənt] *adj* : vibrant — **vibrate** [ˈvaɪˌbreɪt] *vi* **-brated; -brating** : vibrer — **vibration** [vaɪˈbreɪʃən] *n* : vibration *f*

vicar [ˈvɪkər] *n* : vicaire *m*

vice [ˈvaɪs] *n* : vice *m*

vice president *n* : vice-président *m*, -dente *f*

vice versa [ˌvaɪsiˈvərsə, ˌvaɪsˈvər-] *adv* : vice versa

vicinity [vəˈsɪnəṭi] *n, pl* **-ties** : environs *mpl*

vicious [ˈvɪʃəs] *adj* **1** SAVAGE : brutal **2** MALICIOUS : méchant

victim [ˈvɪktəm] *n* : victime *f*

victor [ˈvɪktər] *n* : vainqueur *m* — **victorious** [vɪkˈtoːriəs] *adj* : victorieux — **victory** [ˈvɪktəri] *n, pl* **-ries** : victoire *f*

video [ˈvɪdiˌoː] *n* : vidéo *f* — **~** *adj* : vidéo — **videocassette** [ˌvɪdioːkəˈsɛt] *n* : vidéo-

cassette *f* — **videotape** [ˈvɪdio̯ˌteɪp] *n* : bande *f* vidéo — **~** *vt* **-taped; -taping** : enregistrer (sur magnétoscope)

vie [ˈvaɪ] *vi* **vied; vying** [ˈvaɪɪŋ] **~ for** : lutter pour

Vietnamese [viˌɛtnəˈmiːz, -ˈmiːs] *adj* : vietnamien

view [ˈvjuː] *n* **1** : vue *f* **2** OPINION : opinion *f*, avis *m* **3 come into ~** : apparaître **4 in ~ of** : vu, étant donné — **~** *vt* **1** : voir **2** CONSIDER : considérer — **viewer** [ˈvjuːər] *or* **television ~** : téléspectateur *m*, -trice *f* — **viewpoint** [ˈvjuːˌpɔɪnt] *n* : point *m* de vue

vigil [ˈvɪdʒəl] *n* : veille *f* — **vigilance** [ˈvɪdʒələnts] *n* : vigilance *f* — **vigilant** [ˈvɪdʒələnt] *adj* : vigilant, attentif

vigor *or Brit* **vigour** [ˈvɪgər] *n* : vigueur *f* — **vigorous** [ˈvɪgərəs] *adj* : vigoureux

vile [ˈvaɪl] *adj* **viler; vilest 1** BASE : vil **2** AWFUL : abominable, exécrable

villa [ˈvɪlə] *n* : villa *f*

village [ˈvɪlɪdʒ] *n* : village *m* — **villager** [ˈvɪlɪdʒər] *n* : villageois *m*, -geoise *f*

villain [ˈvɪlən] *n* : scélérat *m*, -rate *f*; méchant *m*, -chante *f*

vindicate [ˈvɪndəˌkeɪt] *vt* **-cated; -cating** : justifier

vindictive [vɪnˈdɪktɪv] *adj* : vindicatif

vine [ˈvaɪn] *n* : vigne *f*

vinegar [ˈvɪnɪgər] *n* : vinaigre *m*

vineyard [ˈvɪnjərd] *n* : vignoble *m*

vintage [ˈvɪntɪdʒ] *n* **1** *or* **~ wine** : vin *m* de grand cru **2** *or* **~ year** : millésime *m*

vinyl [ˈvaɪnəl] *n* : vinyle *m*

violate [ˈvaɪəˌleɪt] *vt* **-lated; -lating** : violer — **violation** [ˌvaɪəˈleɪʃən] *n* : violation *f*

violence [ˈvaɪələnts] *n* : violence *f* — **violent** [ˈvaɪələnt] *adj* : violent

violet [ˈvaɪələt] *adj* : violet — **~** *n* **1** : violette *f* (plante) **2** : violet *m* (couleur)

violin [ˌvaɪəˈlɪn] *n* : violon *m* — **violinist** [ˌvaɪəˈlɪnɪst] *n* : violoniste *mf*

VIP [ˌviːˌaɪˈpiː] *n, pl* **VIPs** [-ˈpiːz] (*very important person*) : personnage *m* de marque

viper [ˈvaɪpər] *n* : vipère *f*

virgin [ˈvərdʒən] *adj* : vierge — **~** *n* : vierge *f* — **virginity** [vərˈdʒɪnəṭi] *n, pl* **-ties** : virginité *f*

virile [ˈvɪrəl, -ˌaɪl] *adj* : viril

virtual [ˈvərtʃuəl] *adj* : virtuel (en informatique) — **virtually** [ˈvərtʃuəli] *adv* : pratiquement

virtue [ˈvərˌtʃuː] *n* **1** : vertu *f* **2 by ~ of** : en raison de

virtuoso [ˌvərtʃuˈoːˌsoː, -ˌzoː] *n, pl* **-sos** *or* **-si** [-ˌsiː, -ˌziː] : virtuose *mf*

virtuous [ˈvərtʃuəs] *adj* : vertueux

virulent [ˈvɪrələnt, -jələnt] *adj* : virulent

virus [ˈvaɪrəs] *n* : virus *m*

visa ['viːzə, -sə] *n* : visa *m*

viscous ['vɪskəs] *adj* : visqueux

vise *or Brit* **vice** ['vaɪs] *n* : étau *m*

visible ['vɪzəbəl] *adj* : visible — **visibility** [ˌvɪzə'bɪləṭi] *n, pl* **-ties** : visibilité *f*

vision ['vɪʒən] *n* : vision *f* — **visionary** ['vɪʒəˌnɛri] *adj* : visionnaire

visit ['vɪzət] *vt* : rendre visite à (qqn), visiter (un lieu) — **~** *n* : visite *f* — **visitor** ['vɪzəṭər] *n* : visiteur *m*, -teuse *f*

visor ['vaɪzər] *n* : visière *f*

vista ['vɪstə] *n* : vue *f*

visual ['vɪʒuəl] *adj* : visuel — **visualize** ['vɪʒuəˌlaɪz] *vt* **-ized; -izing** : visualiser

vital ['vaɪṭəl] *adj* **1** : vital **2** ESSENTIAL : essentiel — **vitality** [vaɪ'tæləṭi] *n, pl* **-ties** : vitalité *f*

vitamin ['vaɪṭəmən] *n* : vitamine *f*

vivacious [və'veɪʃəs, vaɪ-] *adj* : vif, animé

vivid ['vɪvəd] *adj* : vivant, vif

vocabulary [voː'kæbjəˌlɛri] *n, pl* **-laries** : vocabulaire *m*

vocal ['voːkəl] *adj* **1** : vocal **2** OUTSPOKEN : franc — **vocal cords** *npl* : cordes *fpl* vocales — **vocalist** ['voːkəlɪst] *n* : chanteur *m*, -teuse *f*

vocation [voː'keɪʃən] *n* **1** : vocation *f* (religieuse) **2** OCCUPATION : profession *f*, métier *m* — **vocational** [voː'keɪʃənəl] *adj* : professionnel

vodka ['vadkə] *n* : vodka *m*

vogue ['voːg] *n* **1** : vogue *f*, mode *f* **2 be in ~** : être à la mode

voice ['vɔɪs] *n* : voix *f* — **~** ['vɔɪs] *vt* **voiced; voicing** : exprimer, formuler

void ['vɔɪd] *adj* **1** NULL : nul **2 ~ of** : dépourvu de — **~** *n* : vide *m* — **~** *vt* ANNUL : annuler

volatile ['valəṭəl] *adj* : volatil, instable

volcano [val'keɪˌnoː, vɔl-] *n, pl* **-noes** *or* **-nos** : volcan *m* — **volcanic** [val'kænɪk, vɔl-] *adj* : volcanique

volley ['vali] *n, pl* **-leys** : volée *f* — **volleyball** ['valiˌbɔl] *n* : volley-ball *m*

volt ['voːlt] *n* : volt *m* — **voltage** ['voːltɪdʒ] *n* **1** : voltage *m* **2 high ~** : de haute tension

volume ['valjəm, -ˌjuːm] *n* : volume *m*

voluntary ['valənˌtɛri] *adj* **1** : volontaire **2** UNPAID : bénévole — **volunteer** [ˌvalən'tɪr] *n* : volontaire *mf* — **~** *vt* : offrir — *vi* : se porter volontaire

voluptuous [və'lʌptʃuəs] *adj* : volup-tueux

vomit ['vamət] *n* : vomi *m* — **~** *v* : vomir

voracious [vɔ'reɪʃəs, və-] *adj* : vorace

vote ['voːt] *n* **1** : vote *m* **2** SUFFRAGE : droit *m* de vote — **~** *v* **voted; voting** : voter — **voter** ['voːṭər] *n* : électeur *m*, -trice *f* — **voting** ['voːṭɪŋ] *n* : scrutin *m*, vote *m*

vouch ['vautʃ] *vi* **~ for** : répondre de — **voucher** ['vautʃər] *n* : bon *m*

vow ['vau] *n* : vœu *m*, serment *m* — **~** *vt* : jurer

vowel ['vauəl] *n* : voyelle *f*

voyage ['vɔɪɪdʒ] *n* : voyage *m*

vulgar ['vʌlgər] *adj* **1** COMMON : vulgaire **2** CRUDE : grossier — **vulgarity** [ˌvʌl'gærəṭi] *n, pl* **-ties** : vulgarité *f*

vulnerable ['vʌlnərəbəl] *adj* : vulnérable — **vulnerability** [ˌvʌlnərə'bɪləṭi] *n* : vulnérabilité *f*

vulture ['vʌltʃər] *n* : vautour *m*

vying → **vie**

W

w ['dʌbəlˌjuː] *n, pl* **w's** *or* **ws** [-ˌjuːz] : w *m*, vingt-troisième lettre de l'alphabet

wad ['wad] *n* : tampon *m* (d'ouate, etc.), liasse *f* (de billets)

waddle ['wadəl] *vi* **-dled; -dling** : se dandiner

wade ['weɪd] *v* **waded; wading** *vi* : patauger — *vt or* **~ across** : traverser

wafer ['weɪfər] *n* : gaufrette *f*

waffle ['wafəl] *n* : gaufre *f*

waft ['waft, 'wæft] *vi* : flotter

wag ['wæg] *vt* **wagged; wagging** : agiter, remuer

wage ['weɪdʒ] *n or* **wages** *npl* : salaire *m*, paie *f* — **~** *vt* **waged; waging ~ war** : faire la guerre

wager ['weɪdʒər] *n* : pari *m* — **~** *v* : parier

wagon ['wægən] *n* : chariot *m*

wail ['weɪl] *vi* : se lamenter — **~** *n* : lamentation *f*

waist ['weɪst] *n* : taille *f* — **waistline** ['weɪstˌlaɪn] *n* : taille *f*

wait ['weɪt] *vi* : attendre — *vt* **1** AWAIT : attendre **2 ~ tables** : servir à table — **~** *n* **1** : attente *f* **2 lie in ~ for** : guetter — **waiter** ['weɪṭər] *n* : serveur *m*, garçon *m* — **waiting room** *n* : salle *f* d'attente — **waitress** ['weɪtrəs] *n* : serveuse *f*

waive ['weɪv] *vt* **waived; waiving** : renoncer à

wake[1] ['weɪk] *v* **woke** ['woːk]; **woken**

['wo:kən] *or* **waked; waking** *vi or* ~ **up** : se réveiller — *vt* : réveiller — ~ *n* : veillée *f* funèbre

wake² *n* **1** : sillage *m* (laissé par un bateau) **2 in the** ~ **of** : à la suite de

waken ['weɪkən] *vt* : réveiller — *vi* : se réveiller

walk ['wɔk] *vi* **1** : marcher, aller à pied **2** STROLL : se promener — *vt* **1** : faire à pied **2** : raccompagner (qqn), promener (un chien) — ~ *n* **1** : marche *f*, promenade *f* **2** PATH : chemin *m* **3** GAIT : démarche *f* (d'une personne) — **walker** ['wɔkər] *n* : marcheur *m*, -cheuse *f*; promeneur *m*, -neuse *f* — **walking stick** *n* : canne *f* — **walkout** ['wɔk,aʊt] *n* STRIKE : grève *f* — **walk out** *vi* **1** STRIKE : faire la grève **2** LEAVE : partir, sortir **3** ~ **on** : quitter, abandonner

wall ['wɔl] *n* **1** : mur *m* (extérieur), paroi *f* (intérieur) **2** : remparts *mpl* (d'une ville)

wallet ['wɑlət] *n* : portefeuille *m*

Walloon [wɑ'lu:n] *adj* : wallon

wallop ['wɑləp] *vt* : donner une raclée à — ~ *n* : raclée *f*

wallow ['wɑ,lo:] *vi* **1** : se vautrer **2** ~ **in** : s'apitoyer sur

wallpaper ['wɔl,peɪpər] *n* : tapisserie *f* — ~ *vt* : tapisser

walnut ['wɔl,nʌt] *n* **1** : noyer *m* (arbre) **2** : noix *f* (fruit)

walrus ['wɔlrəs, 'wɑl-] *n, pl* **-rus** *or* **-ruses** : morse *m*

waltz ['wɔlts] *n* : valse *f* — ~ *vi* : valser

wan ['wɑn] *adj* **wanner; wannest** : blême, pâle

wand ['wɑnd] *n* : baguette *f* (magique)

wander ['wɑndər] *vi* **1** : se promener, se balader **2** STRAY : errer — *vt* : parcourir — **wanderer** ['wɑndərər] *n* : vagabond *m*, -bonde *f*

wane ['weɪn] *vi* **waned; waning** : diminuer — ~ *n* **be on the** ~ : être sur le déclin

want ['wɑnt, 'wɔnt] *vt* **1** DESIRE : vouloir **2** NEED : avoir besoin de **3** LACK : manquer de **4** ~**ed** : recherché par la police — ~ *n* **1** NEED : besoin *m* **2** LACK : manque *m* **3** DESIRE : désir *m* **4 for** ~ **of** : faute de — **wanting** ['wɑntɪŋ, 'wɔn-] *adj* **be** ~ : manquer

wanton ['wɑntən, 'wɔn-] *adj* **1** LEWD : lascif **2** ~ **cruelty** : cruauté *f* gratuite

war ['wɔr] *n* : guerre *f*

ward ['wɔrd] *n* **1** : salle *f* (d'un hôpital, etc.) **2** : circonscription *f* électorale **3** ~ **of the court** : pupille *f* — ~ *vt or* ~ **off** : parer, éviter — **warden** ['wɔrdən] *n* **1** : gardien *m*, -dienne *f* **2** *or* **prison** ~ : directeur *m*, -trice *f* de prison

wardrobe ['wɔrd,ro:b] *n* **1** CLOSET : armoire *f*, penderie *f* **2** CLOTHES : garde-robe *f*

warehouse ['wær,haʊs] *n* : entrepôt *m*, magasin *m* — **wares** ['wærz] *npl* : marchandises *fpl*

warfare ['wɔr,fær] *n* : guerre *f*

warhead ['wɔr,hɛd] *n* : ogive *f*

warily ['wærəli] *adv* : avec précaution

warlike ['wɔr,laɪk] *adj* : guerrier, belliqueux

warm ['wɔrm] *adj* **1** : chaud **2** LUKEWARM : tiède **3** CARING : chaleureux **4 I feel** ~ : j'ai chaud — ~ *vt or* ~ **up** : chauffer, réchauffer — *vi* **1** *or* ~ **up** : se réchauffer **2** ~ **to** : se prendre de sympathie pour (qqn), s'enthousiasmer pour (qqch) — **warm-blooded** ['wɔrm'blʌdəd] *adj* : à sang chaud — **warmhearted** ['wɔrm-'hɑrtəd] *adj* : chaleureux — **warmly** ['wɔrmli] *adv* **1** : chaleureusement **2 dress** ~ : s'habiller chaudement — **warmth** ['wɔrmpθ] *n* **1** : chaleur *f* **2** AFFECTION : affection *f*

warn ['wɔrn] *vt* **1** : avertir **2** INFORM : aviser — **warning** ['wɔrnɪŋ] *n* **1** : avertissement *m* **2** NOTICE : avis *m*

warp ['wɔrp] *vt* **1** : voiler (bois, etc.) **2** DISTORT : déformer

warrant ['wɔrənt] *n* **1** : autorisation *f* **2 arrest** ~ : mandat *m* d'arrêt — ~ *vt* : justifier — **warranty** ['wɔrənti, ,wɔrən'ti:] *n, pl* **-ties** : garantie *f*

warrior ['wɔriər] *n* : guerrier *m*, -rière *f*

warship ['wɔr,ʃɪp] *n* : navire *m* de guerre

wart ['wɔrt] *n* : verrue *f*

wartime ['wɔr,taɪm] *n* : temps *m* de guerre

wary ['wæri] *adj* **warier; -est 1** : prudent, circonspect **2 be** ~ **of** : se méfier de

was → **be**

wash ['wɔʃ, 'wɑʃ] *vt* **1** : laver, se laver **2** ~ **away** : emporter — *vi* : se laver — ~ *n* **1** : lavage *m* **2** LAUNDRY : linge *m* sale — **washable** ['wɔʃəbəl, 'wɑ-] *adj* : lavable — **washcloth** ['wɔʃ,klɔθ, 'wɑʃ-] *n* : gant *m* de toilette, débarbouillette *f* Can — **washed-out** ['wɔʃ'aʊt, 'wɑʃt-] *adj* **1** : décoloré **2** EXHAUSTED : épuisé — **washer** ['wɔʃər, 'wɑ-] *n* **1** → **washing machine 2** : rondelle *f*, joint *m* — **washing machine** *n* : machine *f* à laver — **washroom** ['wɔʃ-,ru:m, 'wɑʃ-, -,rʊm] *n* : toilettes *fpl*

wasn't ['wʌzənt] (*contraction of* **was not**) → **be**

wasp ['wɑsp] *n* : guêpe *f*

waste ['weɪst] *v* **wasted; wasting** *vt* : gaspiller, perdre — *vi or* ~ **away** : dépérir — ~ *adj* : de rebut — ~ *n* **1** : gaspillage *m* (d'argent), perte *f* (de temps) **2** RUBBISH : déchets *mpl*, ordures *fpl* — **wastebasket** ['weɪst,bæskət] *n* : corbeille *f* à papier — **wasteful** ['weɪstfəl] *adj* : gaspilleur — **wasteland** ['weɪst,lænd, -lənd] *n* : terre *f* inculte

watch ['wɑtʃ] *vi* **1** : regarder **2** *or* **keep ~** : faire le guet **3 ~ out** : faire attention — *vt* **1** : regarder **2** *or* **~ over** : veiller — **~** *n* **1** : montre *f* **2** SURVEILLANCE : surveillance *f* — **watchdog** ['wɑtʃ,dɔg] *n* : chien *m* de garde, chienne *f* de garde — **watchful** ['wɑtʃfəl] *adj* : vigilant — **watchman** ['wɑtʃmən] *n*, *pl* **-men** [-mən, -,mɛn] : gardien *m*

water ['wɔtər, 'wɑ-] *n* : eau *f* — **~** *vt* **1** : arroser (un jardin, etc.) **2** *or* **~ down** DILUTE : diluer, couper (du vin, etc.) — *vi* **1** : larmoyer (se dit des yeux) **2 my mouth is ~ing** : j'ai l'eau à la bouche — **watercolor** ['wɔtər,kʌlər, 'wɑ-] *n* : aquarelle *f* — **watercress** ['wɔtər,krɛs, 'wɑ-] *n* : cresson *m* — **waterfall** ['wɔtər,fɔl, 'wɑ-] *n* : chute *f* (d'eau), cascade *f* — **water lily** *n* : nénuphar *m* — **watermark** ['wɔtər,mɑrk, 'wɑ-] : filigrane *m* — **watermelon** ['wɔtər,mɛlən, 'wɑ-] *n* : pastèque *f*, melon *m* d'eau — **waterproof** ['wɔtər,pru:f, 'wɑ-] *adj* : imperméable — **watershed** ['wɔtər,ʃɛd, 'wɑ-] *n* **1** : ligne *m* de partage des eaux **2** : moment *m* critique — **waterskiing** ['wɔtər,ski:ɪŋ, 'wɑ-] *n* : ski *m* nautique — **watertight** ['wɔtər,tɑɪt, 'wɑ-] *adj* : étanche — **waterway** ['wɔtər,weɪ, 'wɑ-] *n* : cours *m* d'eau navigable — **waterworks** ['wɔtər'wərks, wɑ-] *npl* : système *m* hydraulique — **watery** ['wɔtəri, 'wɑ-] *adj* **1** : larmoyant (se dit des yeux) **2** DILUTED : trop liquide, dilué

watt ['wɑt] *n* : watt *m* — **wattage** ['wɑtɪdʒ] *n* : puissance *f* en watts

wave ['weɪv] *v* **waved; waving** *vi* **1** : faire un signe de la main **2** : flotter au vent (se dit d'un drapeau) — *vt* **1** SHAKE : agiter, brandir **2** CURL : onduler **3** SIGNAL : faire signe à — **~** *n* **1** : vague *f* (d'eau) **2** CURL : ondulation *f* **3** : onde (en physique) **4** : geste *m* de la main **4** SURGE : vague *f* — **wavelength** ['weɪv,lɛŋkθ] *n* : longueur *f* d'onde

waver ['weɪvər] *vi* : vaciller, chanceler

wavy ['weɪvi] *adj* **wavier; -est** : ondulé

wax[1] ['wæks] *vi* : croître (se dit de la lune)

wax[2] *n* : cire *f* — **~** *vt* : cirer (le plancher, etc.), farter (des skis) — **waxy** ['wæksi] *adj* **waxier; -est** : cireux

way ['weɪ] *n* **1** : chemin *m* **2** MEANS : façon *f*, manière *f* **3 by the ~** : à propos **4 by ~ of** : par, via **5 come a long ~** : faire de grands progrès **6 get in the ~** : gêner le passage **7 get one's own ~** : arriver à ses fins **8 out of the ~** REMOTE : éloigné, isolé **9 which ~ did he go?** : où est-il passé?

we ['wi:] *pron* : nous

weak ['wi:k] *adj* : faible — **weaken** ['wi:kən] *vt* : affaiblir — *vi* : s'affaiblir, faiblir — **weakling** ['wi:klɪŋ] *n* : mauviette *f* — **weakly** ['wi:kli] *adv* : faiblement — **weakness** ['wi:knəs] *n* **1** : faiblesse *f* **2** FLAW : défaut *m*

wealth ['wɛlθ] *n* **1** : richesse *f* **2 a ~ of** : une profusion de — **wealthy** ['wɛlθi] *adj* **wealthier; -est** : riche

wean ['wi:n] *vt* : sevrer (un bébé)

weapon ['wɛpən] *n* : arme *f*

wear ['wær] *v* **wore** ['wor]; **worn** ['worn]; **wearing** *vt* **1** : mettre, porter **2 ~ oneself out** : s'épuiser **3** *or* **~ out** : user — *vi* **1** LAST : durer **2 ~ off** : diminuer **3 ~ out** : s'user, se détériorer — **~** *n* **1** USE : usage *m* **2** CLOTHES : vêtements *mpl* — **wear and tear** : usure *f*

weary ['wɪri] *adj* **-rier; -est** : fatigué, las — **~** *vt* **-ried; -rying** : lasser, fatiguer — **weariness** ['wɪrinəs] *n* : lassitude *f* — **wearisome** ['wɪrisəm] *adj* : fastidieux

weasel ['wi:zəl] *n* : belette *f*

weather ['wɛðər] *n* **1** : temps *m* **2 be under the ~** : ne pas être dans son assiette — **~** *vt* OVERCOME : surmonter — **weatherbeaten** ['wɛðər,bi:tən] *adj* **1** : battu, usé (par les intempéries) **2** : hâlé (se dit d'un visage) — **weatherman** ['wɛðər,mæn] *n*, *pl* **-men** [-mən, -,mɛn] : météorologiste *mf* — **weather vane** *n* : girouette *f*

weave ['wi:v] *v* **wove** ['wo:v] *or* **weaved; woven** ['wo:vən] *or* **weaved; weaving** *vt* **1** : tisser **2 ~ one's way through** : se faufiler à travers — *vi* : tisser — **~** *n* : tissage *m*

web ['wɛb] *n* **1** : toile *f* (d'araignée) **2** : palmure *f* (d'un oiseau) **3** NETWORK : réseau *m* **4 Web → World Wide Web**

webbed ['wɛbd] *adj* : palmé

webmaster ['wɛb,mæstər] *n* : webmestre *m*

wed ['wɛd] *v* **wedded; wedding** *vt* : se marier à, épouser — *vi* : marier

we'd ['wi:d] (*contraction of* **we had, we should,** *or* **we would**) → **have, should, would**

wedding ['wɛdɪŋ] *n* : mariage *m*, noces *fpl*

wedge ['wɛdʒ] *n* **1** : cale *f* **2** PIECE : morceau *m* (de fromage), part *m* (de gâteau, etc.) — **~** *vt* **wedged; wedging 1** : caler, fixer **2** CRAM : enfoncer

Wednesday ['wɛnz,deɪ, -di] *n* : mercredi *m*

wee ['wi:] *adj* **1** : très petit **2 in the ~ hours** : aux petites heures (du matin)

weed ['wi:d] *n* : mauvaise herbe *f* — **~** *vt* **1** : désherber **2 ~ out** : se débarrasser de

week ['wi:k] *n* : semaine *f* — **weekday** ['wi:k,deɪ] *n* : jour *m* de semaine — **weekend** ['wi:k,ɛnd] *n* : fin *f* de semaine, weekend *m* — **weekly** ['wi:kli] *adv* : à la semaine, chaque semaine — **~** *adj* : hebdomadaire — **~** *n*, *pl* **-lies** : hebdomadaire *m*

weep ['wi:p] *vi* **wept** ['wɛpt]; **weeping**

: pleurer — **weeping willow** n : saule m pleureur — **weepy** ['wi:pi] adj **weepier; -est** : au bord des larmes

weigh ['weɪ] vt 1 : peser 2 CONSIDER : considérer 3 ~ **down** : accabler — vi 1 : peser 2 ~ **on s.o.'s mind** : préoccuper qqn

weight ['weɪt] n 1 : poids m 2 IMPORTANCE : influence f 3 gain : engraisser 4 lose ~ : maigrir — **weighty** ['weɪti] adj **weightier; -est** 1 HEAVY : pesant, lourd 2 IMPORTANT : de poids

weird ['wɪrd] adj 1 : mystérieux 2 STRANGE : étrange, bizarre

welcome ['wɛlkəm] vt **-comed; -coming** : accueillir, souhaiter la bienvenue à — ~ adj 1 : bienvenu 2 **you're** ~ : de rien, je vous en prie — ~ n : accueil m

weld ['wɛld] vt : souder — ~ n : soudure f

welfare ['wɛl,fær] n 1 WELL-BEING : bien-être m 2 AID : aide f sociale, assistance f publique

well[1] ['wɛl] n : puits m (d'eau, de pétrole, etc.) — ~ vi or ~ **up** : monter, jaillir

well[2] adv **better** ['bɛtər]; **best** ['bɛst] 1 : bien 2 **as** ~ : aussi — ~ adj : bien — ~ interj 1 (used to introduce a remark) : bon, bien, enfin 2 (used to express surprise) : ça alors!, eh bien!

we'll ['wi:l, wɪl] (contraction of **we shall** or **we will**) → **shall, will**

well–being ['wɛl'bi:ɪŋ] n : bien-être m — **well–bred** ['wɛl'brɛd] adj : bien élevé, poli — **well–done** ['wɛl'dʌn] adj 1 : bien fait 2 : bien cuit (se dit de la viande, etc.) — **well–known** ['wɛl'no:n] adj : bien connu — **well–meaning** ['wɛl'mi:nɪŋ] adj : bien intentionné — **well–off** ['wɛl'ɔf] adj : prospère — **well–rounded** [,wɛl'raʊndəd] adj : complet — **well–to–do** [,wɛltə'du:] adj : riche, aisé

Welsh ['wɛlʃ] adj : gallois — ~ n : gallois m (langue)

welt ['wɛlt] n : zébrure f, marque f (sur la peau)

went → **go**

wept → **weep**

were → **be**

we're ['wɪr, 'wər, 'wi:ər] (contraction of **we are**) → **be**

weren't ['wərənt, 'wərnt] (contraction of **were not**) → **be**

west ['wɛst] adv : à l'ouest, vers l'ouest — ~ adj : ouest, d'ouest — ~ n 1 : ouest m 2 **the West** : l'Ouest m, l'Occident m — **westerly** ['wɛstərli] adv : vers l'ouest — ~ adj : à l'ouest, d'ouest — **western** ['wɛstərn] adj 1 : ouest, de l'ouest, occidental 2 **Western** : de l'Ouest, occidental — **Westerner** ['wɛstərnər] n : habitant m,

-tante f de l'Ouest — **westward** ['wɛstwərd] adv & adj : vers l'ouest

wet ['wɛt] adj **wetter; wettest** 1 : mouillé 2 RAINY : pluvieux 3 ~ **paint** : peinture f fraîche — ~ vt **wet** or **wetted; wetting** : mouiller, humecter

we've ['wi:v] (contraction of **we have**) → **have**

whack ['hwæk] vt : donner une claque à — ~ n : coup m, claque f

whale ['hweɪl] n, pl **whales** or **whale** : baleine f

wharf ['hwɔrf] n, pl **wharves** ['hwɔrvz] : quai m

what ['hwɑt, 'hwʌt] adj 1 (used in questions and exclamations) : quel 2 WHATEVER : tout — ~ pron 1 (used in questions) : qu'est-ce que, qu'est-ce qui 2 (used in indirect statements) : ce que, ce qui 3 ~ **does it cost?** : combien est-ce que ça coûte? 4 ~ **for?** : pourquoi? 5 ~ **if** : et si — **whatever** [hwɑt'ɛvər, ,hwʌt-] adj 1 : n'importe quel 2 **there's no chance** ~ : il n'y a pas la moindre possibilité 3 **nothing** ~ : rien du tout — ~ pron 1 ANYTHING : (tout) ce que 2 (used in questions) : qu'est-ce que, qu'est-ce qui 3 ~ **it may be** : quoi que ce soit — **whatsoever** [,hwɑtso'ɛvər, ,hwʌt-] adj & pron → **whatever**

wheat ['hwi:t] n : blé m

wheedle ['hwi:dəl] vt **-dled; -dling** : enjôler

wheel ['hwi:l] n 1 : roue f 2 or **steering** ~ : volant m — ~ vt : pousser (quelque chose sur des roulettes) — **wheelbarrow** ['hwi:l,bær,o:] n : brouette f — **wheelchair** ['hwi:l,tʃær] n : fauteuil m roulant

wheeze ['hwi:z] vi **wheezed; wheezing** : respirer bruyamment

when ['hwɛn] adv : quand — ~ conj 1 : quand, lorsque 2 **the days** ~ **I go to the bank** : les jours où je vais à la banque — ~ pron : quand — **whenever** [hwɛn'ɛvər] adv : quand (donc) — ~ conj 1 : chaque fois que 2 ~ **you like** : quand vous voulez

where ['hwɛr] adv 1 : où 2 ~ **are you going?** : où vas-tu? — ~ conj & pron : où — **whereabouts** ['hwɛrə,baʊts] adv : où (donc) — ~ ns & pl **know s.o.'s** ~ : savoir où se trouve qqn

whereas [hwɛr'æz] conj : alors que, tandis que

wherever [hwɛr'ɛvər] conj 1 : n'importe où 2 WHERE : où, où donc

whet ['hwɛt] vt **whetted; whetting** 1 : affûter, aiguiser (un couteau) 2 ~ **one's appetite** : ouvrir l'appétit

whether ['hwɛðər] conj 1 : si 2 **we doubt** ~ **he'll show up** : nous doutons qu'il vienne 3 ~ **you like it or not** : que cela te plaise ou non

which ['*h*wɪtʃ] *adj* **1** : quel **2 in ~ case** : auquel cas — **~** *pron* **1** (*used in questions*) : lequel, quel **2** (*used in relative clauses*) : qui, que — **whichever** [*h*wɪtʃ-'ɛvər] *adj* : peu importe quel — **~** *pron* : quel que

whiff ['*h*wɪf] *n* **1** ɴᴜꜰꜰ ? ᴠᴀᴘᴏᴜʀ ? **2** ꜱᴍᴇʟʟ : odeur *f*

while ['*h*waɪl] *n* **1** : temps *m*, moment *m* **2 be worth one's ~** : valoir la peine **3 in a ~** : sous peu — **~** *conj* **1** : pendant que **2** ᴡʜᴇʀᴇᴀꜱ : tandis que, alors que **3** ᴀʟ-ᴛʜᴏᴜɢʜ : bien que — **~** *vt* **whiled; whiling ~ away** : (faire) passer

whim ['*h*wɪm] *n* : caprice *m*, lubie *f*

whimper ['*h*wɪmpər] *vi* : gémir, pleurnicher *fam* — **~** *n* : gémissement *m*

whimsical ['*h*wɪmzɪkəl] *adj* : capricieux, fantasque

whine ['*h*waɪn] *vi* **whined; whining 1** ᴡʜɪᴍᴘᴇʀ : gémir **2** ᴄᴏᴍᴘʟᴀɪɴ : se plaindre — **~** *n* : gémissement *m*

whip ['*h*wɪp] *v* **whipped; whipping** *vt* **1** : fouetter **2** ʙᴇᴀᴛ : battre (des œufs, etc.) — *vi* ꜰʟᴀᴘ : battre, claquer — **~** *n* : fouet *m*

whir ['*h*wər] *vi* **whirred; whirring** : ronronner, vrombir

whirl ['*h*wərl] *vi* : tourner, tourbillonner — **~** *n* : tourbillon *m* — **whirlpool** ['*h*wərl-ˌpuːl] *n* : tourbillon *m* (d'eau) — **whirlwind** ['*h*wərlˌwɪnd] *n* : tourbillon *m* (de vent)

whisk ['*h*wɪsk] *vt* **1** : fouetter (des œufs) **2** *or* **~ away** : enlever — **~** *n* : fouet *m* (en cuisine)

whisker ['*h*wɪskər] *n* **1** : poil *m* de barbe **2 ~s** *npl* : barbe *f* (d'un homme), moustaches *fpl* (d'un chat, etc.)

whiskey *or* **whisky** ['*h*wɪski] *n*, *pl* **-keys** *or* **-kies** : whisky *m*

whisper ['*h*wɪspər] *v* : chuchoter — **~** *n* : chuchotement *m*

whistle ['*h*wɪsəl] *v* **-tled; -tling** : siffler — **~** *n* **1** : sifflement *m* (son) **2** : sifflet *m* (objet)

white ['*h*waɪt] *adj* **whiter; -est** : blanc — **~** *n* **1** : blanc *m* (couleur) **2** *or* **~ person** : Blanc *m*, Blanche *f* — **white–collar** ['*h*waɪt'kɑlər] *adj* : de bureau — **whiten** ['*h*waɪtən] *v* : blanchir — **whiteness** ['*h*waɪtnəs] *n* : blancheur *f* — **whitewash** ['*h*waɪtˌwɔʃ] *n* : lait *m* de chaux

whittle ['*h*wɪtəl] *vt* **-tled; -tling ~ down** : réduire

whiz *or* **whizz** ['*h*wɪz] *vi* **whizzed; whizzing 1** ʙᴜᴢᴢ : bourdonner **2 ~ by** : passer à toute vitesse — **~** *or* **whizz** *n*, *pl* **whizzes** : expert *m*, as *m* — **whiz kid** *n* : jeune prodige *m*

who ['*h*uː] *pron* **1** (*used in direct and indirect questions*) : qui, qui est-ce qui **2** (*used in relative clauses*) : qui — **whoever** [*h*uː-

'ɛvər] *pron* **1** : qui que ce soit, quiconque **2** (*used in questions*) : qui

whole ['*h*oːl] *adj* **1** : entier **2** ɪɴᴛᴀᴄᴛ : intact **3 a ~ lot** : beaucoup — **~** *n* **1** : tout *m*, ensemble *m* **2 as a ~** : dans son ensemble **3 on the ~** : en général — **wholehearted** ['*h*oːl'hɑrtəd] *adj* : sincère — **wholesale** ['*h*oːlˌseɪl] *n* : vente *f* en gros — **~** *adj* : de gros — **~** *adv* : en gros — **wholesaler** ['*h*oːlˌseɪlər] *n* : grossiste *mf* — **wholesome** ['*h*oːlsəm] *adj* : sain — **whole wheat** *adj* : de blé entier — **wholly** ['*h*oːli] *adv* : entièrement

whom ['*h*uːm] *pron* **1** (*used in direct and indirect questions*) : qui, à qui **2** (*used in relative clauses*) : que

whooping cough ['*h*uːpɪŋ] *n* : coqueluche *f*

whore ['*h*or] *n* : prostituée *f*

whose ['*h*uːz] *adj* **1** (*used in questions*) : de qui, à qui **2** (*used in relative clauses*) : dont — **~** *pron* : à qui

why ['*h*waɪ] *adv* : pourquoi — **~** *n*, *pl* **whys** : pourquoi *m* — **~** *conj* : pourquoi — **~** *interj* (*used to express surprise*) : mais!, tiens!

wick ['wɪk] *n* : mèche *f*

wicked ['wɪkəd] *adj* **1** : méchant **2** ᴍɪꜱᴄʜɪᴇ-ᴠᴏᴜꜱ : espiègle **3** ᴛᴇʀʀɪʙʟᴇ : terrible — **wickedness** ['wɪkədnəs] *n* : méchanceté *f*

wicker ['wɪkər] *n* : osier *m*

wide ['waɪd] *adj* **wider; widest 1** : de large, de largeur **2** ᴠᴀꜱᴛ : étendu, vaste — **~** *adv* **1 ~ apart** : très écarté **2 far and ~** : partout **3 open ~** : ouvrir grand (la bouche) — **wide–awake** ['waɪdə'weɪk] *adj* : éveillé, alerte — **widely** ['waɪdli] *adv* : largement — **widen** ['waɪdən] *vt* : élargir — **widespread** ['waɪd'sprɛd] *adj* : généralisé

widow ['wɪˌdoː] *n* : veuve *f* — **~** *vt* : devenir veuf — **widower** ['wɪdowər] *n* : veuf *m*

width ['wɪdθ] *n* : largeur *f*

wield ['wiːld] *vt* **1** : manier **2** ᴇxᴇʀᴛ : exercer

wife ['waɪf] *n*, *pl* **wives** ['waɪvz] : femme *f*, épouse *f*

wig ['wɪg] *n* : perruque *f*

wiggle ['wɪgəl] *v* **-gled; -gling** *vi* : remuer — *vt* : faire bouger (ses orteils, etc.)

wigwam ['wɪgˌwɑm] *n* : wigwam *m*

wild ['waɪld] *adj* **1** : sauvage **2** ᴜɴʀᴜʟʏ : indiscipliné **3** ʀᴀɴᴅᴏᴍ : au hasard **4** ꜰʀᴀɴ-ᴛɪᴄ : frénétique **5** ᴏᴜᴛʀᴀɢᴇᴏᴜꜱ : extravagant — **~** *adv* **1** → **wildly 2 run ~** : se déchaîner — **wild boar** *n* : sanglier *m* — **wilderness** ['wɪldərnəs] *n* : région *f* sauvage — **wildfire** ['waɪldˌfaɪr] *n* **1** : feu *m* de forêt **2 spread like ~** : se répandre comme une traînée de poudre — **wildflower** ['waɪldˌflauər] *n* : fleur *f* des champs —

wildlife [ˈwaɪldˌlaɪf] *n* : faune *f* — **wildly** [ˈwaɪldli] *adv* **1** FRANTICALLY : frénétiquement **2** EXTREMELY : extrêmement

will[1] [ˈwɪl] *v, past* **would** [ˈwʊd]; *pres sing & pl* **will** *vt* WISH : vouloir — *v aux* **1** tomorrow we ~ go shopping : demain nous irons faire les magasins **2** he ~ get angry over nothing : il se fâche pour des riens **3** I ~ go despite them : j'irai malgré eux **4** I won't do it : je ne le ferai pas **5** that ~ be the mailman : ça doit être le facteur **6** the back seat ~ hold three people : le siège arrière peut accommoder trois personnes **7** accidents ~ happen : les accidents arrivent **8** you ~ do as I say : je t'ordonne de faire ce que je te dis

will[2] *n* **1** : volonté *f* **2** TESTAMENT : testament *m* **3** free ~ : de son propre gré — **willful** *or* **wilful** [ˈwɪlfəl] *adj* **1** OBSTINATE : volontaire **2** INTENTIONAL : délibéré — **willing** [ˈwɪlɪŋ] *adj* **1** : complaisant **2** be ~ to : être prêt à, être disposé à — **willingly** [ˈwɪlɪŋli] *adv* : volontiers, de bon cœur — **willingness** [ˈwɪlɪŋnəs] *n* : bonne volonté *f*

willow [ˈwɪˌloː] *n* : saule *m*

willpower [ˈwɪlˌpaʊər] *n* : volonté *f*

wilt [ˈwɪlt] *vi* : se faner

wily [ˈwaɪli] *adj* **wilier; -est** : rusé, malin

win [ˈwɪn] *v* **won** [ˈwʌn]; **winning** *vi* : gagner — *vt* **1** : gagner, remporter **2** ~ over : convaincre — ~ *n* : victoire *f*

wince [ˈwɪnts] *vi* **winced; wincing** : tressaillir — ~ *n* : tressaillement *m*

winch [ˈwɪntʃ] *n* : treuil *m*

wind[1] [ˈwɪnd] *n* **1** : vent *m* **2** BREATH : souffle *m* **3** : gaz *mpl* intestinaux **4** get ~ of : apprendre

wind[2] [ˈwaɪnd] *v* **wound** [ˈwaʊnd]; **winding** *vi* : serpenter — *vt* **1** COIL : enrouler **2** ~ a clock : remonter une horloge

wind down *vi* RELAX : se détendre

windfall [ˈwɪndˌfɔl] *n* : bénéfice *m* inattendu

winding [ˈwaɪndɪŋ] *adj* : sinueux

wind instrument *n* : instrument *m* à vent

windmill [ˈwɪndˌmɪl] *n* : moulin *m* à vent

window [ˈwɪnˌdoː] *n* : fenêtre *f* (d'une maison), vitre *f* (d'une voiture), guichet *m* (dans une banque, etc.), vitrine *f* (d'un magasin) — **windowpane** [ˈwɪnˌdoːˌpeɪn] *n* : vitre *f*, carreau *m* — **windowsill** [ˈwɪndoˌsɪl] *n* : rebord *m* de fenêtre

windpipe [ˈwɪndˌpaɪp] *n* : trachée *f*

windshield [ˈwɪndˌfiːld] *n* **1** : pare-brise *m* **2** ~ wiper : essuie-glace *m*

wind up [ˈwaɪndˌʌp] *vt* : terminer, conclure — *vi* : finir

windy [ˈwɪndi] *adj* **windier; -est 1** : venteux **2** it's ~ : il vente

wine [ˈwaɪn] *n* : vin *m* — **wine cellar** *n* : cave *f* à vin

wing [ˈwɪŋ] *n* : aile *f*

wink [ˈwɪŋk] *vi* : faire un clin d'œil — ~ *n* **1** : clin *m* d'œil **2** not sleep a ~ : ne pas fermer l'œil

winner [ˈwɪnər] *n* : gagnant *m*, -gnante *f* — **winning** [ˈwɪnɪŋ] *adj* : gagnant — **winnings** [ˈwɪnɪŋz] *npl* : gains *mpl*

winter [ˈwɪntər] *n* : hiver *m* — ~ *adj* : d'hiver — **wintergreen** [ˈwɪntərˌgriːn] *n* : gaulthérie *f* — **wintertime** [ˈwɪntərˌtaɪm] *n* : hiver *m* — **wintry** [ˈwɪntri] *adj* **-trier; -est** : hivernal

wipe [ˈwaɪp] *vt* **wiped; wiping 1** : essuyer **2** ~ away : effacer (un souvenir) **3** ~ out : détruire — ~ *n* : coup *m* d'éponge

wire [ˈwaɪr] *n* **1** : fil *m* métallique **2** : câble *m* (électrique ou téléphonique) — ~ *vt* **wired; wiring 1** : faire l'installation électrique de **2** BIND : relier, attacher — **wireless** [ˈwaɪrləs] *adj* : sans fil — **wiring** [ˈwaɪrɪŋ] *n* : installation *f* électrique — **wiry** [ˈwaɪri] *adj* **wirier; -est** : mince et musclé

wisdom [ˈwɪzdəm] *n* : sagesse *f* — **wisdom tooth** *n* : dent *f* de sagesse

wise [ˈwaɪz] *adj* **wiser; wisest 1** : sage **2** SENSIBLE : prudent — **wisecrack** [ˈwaɪzˌkræk] *n* : vanne *f* — **wisely** [ˈwaɪzli] *adv* : sagement

wish [ˈwɪʃ] *vt* **1** : souhaiter, désirer **2** ~ s.o. well : souhaiter le meilleur à qqn — *vi* **1** : souhaiter, vouloir **2** as you ~ : comme vous voulez — ~ *n* **1** : souhait *m*, désir *m*, vœu *m* **2** best ~es *npl* : meilleurs vœux *mpl* — **wishful** [ˈwɪʃfəl] *adj* **1** : désireux **2** ~ thinking : illusions *fpl*

wishy-washy [ˈwɪʃiˌwɔʃi, -ˌwɑʃi] *adj* : faible, insipide

wisp [ˈwɪsp] *n* **1** : mèche *f* (de cheveux) **2** HINT : trace *f*, soupçon *m*

wistful [ˈwɪstfəl] *adj* : mélancolique

wit [ˈwɪt] *n* **1** CLEVERNESS : ingénuosité *f* **2** HUMOR : esprit *m* **3** at one's ~'s end : désespéré **4** scared out of one's ~s : mort de peur

witch [ˈwɪtʃ] *n* : sorcière *f* — **witchcraft** [ˈwɪtʃˌkræft] *n* : sorcellerie *f*

with [ˈwɪð, ˈwɪθ] *prep* **1** : avec **2** I'm going ~ you : je vais avec toi **3** it varies ~ the season : ça varie selon la saison **4** the girl ~ red hair : la fille aux cheveux roux **5** ~ all his faults, he's still my friend : malgré tous ses défauts, il est quand même mon ami

withdraw [wɪðˈdrɔ, wɪθ-] *v* **-drew** [-ˈdruː]; **-drawn** [-ˈdrɔn]; **-drawing** *vt* : retirer, rétracter (une parole, etc.) — *vi* LEAVE : se retirer — **withdrawal** [wɪðˈdrɔəl, wɪθ-] *n* : retrait *m* — **withdrawn** [wɪðˈdrɔn, wɪθ-] *adj* : renfermé, replié sur soi-même

wither [ˈwɪðər] *vi* : se faner, se flétrir

withhold [wɪθˈhoːld, wɪθ-] *vt* **-held** [-ˈhɛld]; **-holding** : retenir (des fonds), refuser (la permission, etc.)

within [wɪˈðɪn, wɪθ-] *adv* : à l'intérieur — ~ *prep* **1** : dans, à l'intérieur de **2** (*in expressions of distances*) : à moins de **3** (*in expressions of time*) : en moins de **4** ~ **reach** : à (la) portée de la main

without [wɪˈðaʊt, wɪθ-] *adv* **do** ~ : se passer de — ~ *prep* : sans

withstand [wɪθˈstænd, wɪð-] *vt* **-stood** [-ˈstʊd]; **-standing 1** BEAR : supporter **2** RESIST : résister à

witness [ˈwɪtnəs] *n* **1** : témoin *m* **2** EVIDENCE : témoignage *m* **3** **bear** ~ : témoigner — ~ *vt* **1** SEE : être témoin de **2** : servir de témoin lors de (une signature)

witty [ˈwɪti] *adj* **-tier; -est** : ingénieux

wives → **wife**

wizard [ˈwɪzərd] *n* **1** : magicien *m*, sorcier *m* **2 a math** ~ : un génie en mathématiques

wobble [ˈwɑbəl] *vi* **-bled; -bling 1** : branler, osciller **2** : trembler (se dit de la voix, etc.) — **wobbly** [ˈwɑbəli] *adj* : bancal

woe [ˈwoː] *n* **1** : affliction *f* **2** ~**s** *npl* TROUBLES : peines *fpl* — **woeful** [ˈwoːfəl] *adj* : triste

woke, woken → **wake**

wolf [ˈwʊlf] *n, pl* **wolves** [ˈwʊlvz] : loup *m*, louve *f* — ~ *vt or* ~ **down** : engloutir, engouffrer

woman [ˈwʊmən] *n, pl* **women** [ˈwɪmən] : femme *f* — **womanly** [ˈwʊmənli] *adj* : féminin

womb [ˈwuːm] *n* : utérus *m*

won → **win**

wonder [ˈwʌndər] *n* **1** MARVEL : merveille *f* **2** AMAZEMENT : émerveillement *m* — ~ *vi* : penser, songer — *vt* : se demander — **wonderful** [ˈwʌndərfəl] *adj* : merveilleux, formidable

won't [ˈwoːnt] (*contraction of* **will not**) → **will**

woo [ˈwuː] *vt* **1** COURT : courtiser, faire la cour à **2** : rechercher les faveurs de (un client, etc.)

wood [ˈwʊd] *n* **1** : bois *m* (matière) **2** *or* ~**s** *npl* FOREST : bois *m* — ~ *adj* : de bois, en bois — **woodchuck** [ˈwʊdˌtʃʌk] *n* : marmotte *f* d'Amérique — **wooded** [ˈwʊdəd] *adj* : boisé — **wooden** [ˈwʊdən] *adj* : en bois, de bois — **woodpecker** [ˈwʊdˌpɛkər] *n* : pic *m* — **woodwind** [ˈwʊdˌwɪnd] *n* : bois *m* (en musique) — **woodwork** [ˈwʊdˌwərk] *n* : boiseries *fpl* (en menuiserie)

wool [ˈwʊl] *n* : laine *f* — **woolen** *or* **woollen** [ˈwʊlən] *adj* **1** : de laine, en laine **2** ~**s** *npl* : lainages *mpl* — **woolly** [ˈwʊli] *adj* **-lier; -est** : laineux

woozy [ˈwuːzi] *adj* **-zier; -est** : qui a la tête qui tourne

word [ˈwərd] *n* **1** : mot *m* **2** NEWS : nouvelles *fpl* **3** ~**s** *npl* : texte *m*, paroles *fpl* (d'une chanson, etc.) **4 have a** ~ **with s.o.** : parler avec qqn **5 keep one's** ~ : tenir sa parole — ~ *vt* : formuler, rédiger — **wording** [ˈwərdɪŋ] *n* : termes *mpl* (d'un document) — **word processing** *n* : traitement *m* de texte — **word processor** *n* : machine *f* à traitement de textes — **wordy** [ˈwərdi] *adj* **wordier; -est** : prolixe

wore → **wear**

work [ˈwərk] *n* **1** LABOR : travail *m* **2** EMPLOYMENT : travail *m*, emploi *m* **3** : œuvre *f* (d'art, etc.) **4** ~**s** *npl* FACTORY : usine *f* **5** ~**s** *npl* MECHANISM : rouages *mpl* (d'une horloge, etc.) — ~ *v* **worked** [ˈwərkt] *or* **wrought** [ˈrɔt]; **working** *vt* **1** : faire travailler (qqn) **2** OPERATE : faire marcher — *vi* **1** : travailler **2** FUNCTION : fonctionner **3** SUCCEED : réussir — **workbench** [ˈwərkˌbɛntʃ] *n* : établi *m* — **worked up** *adj* : nerveux — **worker** [ˈwərkər] *n* : travailleur *m*, -leuse *f*; employé *m*, -ployée *f* — **working** [ˈwərkɪŋ] *adj* **1** : qui travaille (se dit d'une personne), de travail (de sit d'un vêtement, etc.) **2 be in** ~ **order** : en état de marche — **working class** *n* : classe *f* ouvrière — **workman** [ˈwərkmən] *n, pl* **-men** [-mən, -ˌmɛn] : ouvrier *m* — **workmanship** [ˈwərkmənˌʃɪp] *n* : habileté *f*, dextérité *f* — **workout** [ˈwərkˌaʊt] *n* : exercices *mpl* physiques — **work out** *vt* **1** DEVELOP : élaborer **2** SOLVE : résoudre — *vi* **1** TURN OUT : marcher **2** SUCCEED : fonctionner, bien tourner **3** EXERCISE : s'entraîner, faire de l'exercice — **workshop** [ˈwərkˌʃɑp] *n* : atelier *m* — **work up** *vt* **1** EXCITE : stimuler **2** GENERATE : produire

world [ˈwərld] *n* **1** : monde *m* **2 think the** ~ **of s.o.** : tenir qqn en haute estime — ~ *adj* : du monde, mondial — **worldly** [ˈwərldli] *adj* : matériel, de ce monde — **worldwide** [ˈwərldˈwaɪd] *adv* : partout dans le monde — ~ *adj* : mondial, universel

World Wide Web *n* : Web *m*

worm [ˈwərm] *n* **1** : ver *m* **2** ~**s** *npl* : vers *mpl* (intestinaux)

worn → **wear** — **worn-out** [ˈwornˈaʊt] *adj* **1** USED : usé, fini **2** EXHAUSTED : épuisé, éreinté

worry [ˈwəri] *v* **-ried; -rying** *vt* : inquiéter, préoccuper — *vi* : s'inquiéter — ~ *n, pl* **-ries** : inquiétude *f*, souci *m* — **worried** [ˈwəri:d] *adj* : inquiet — **worrisome** [ˈwərisəm] *adj* : inquiétant

worse [ˈwərs] *adv* (*comparative of* **bad** *or of* **ill**) : moins bien, plus mal — ~ *adj* (*comparative of* **bad** *or of* **ill**) **1** : pire, plus mauvais **2 get** ∼ : s'empirer — ∼ *n* **1 the** ∼ : le pire **2 take a turn for the** ∼ : s'aggraver, empirer — **worsen** ['wərsən] *vi* : empirer, rempirer *Can fam* — *vt* : aggraver

worship ['wərʃəp] *v* **-shiped** *or* **-shipped; -shiping** *or* **-shipping** *vt* : adorer, vénérer — *vi* : pratiquer une religion — ∼ *n* : adoration *f*, culte *m* — **worshiper** *or* **worshipper** ['wərʃəpər] *n* : fidèle *mf* (en religion)

worst ['wərst] *adv* (*superlative of* **ill** *or of* **bad** *or* **badly**) : plus mal — ∼ *adj* (*superlative of* **bad** *or of* **ill**) : pire, plus mauvais — ∼ *n* **the** ∼ : le pire

worth ['wərθ] *n* **1** : valeur *f* (monétaire) **2** MERIT : mérite *m* **3 ten dollars'** ∼ **of gas** : dix dollars d'essence — ∼ *prep* **1 be** ∼ **doing** : valoir l'effort **2 it's** ∼ **$ 10** : cela vaut 10 $ — **worthless** ['wərθləs] *adj* **1** : sans valeur **2** USELESS : inutile — **worthwhile** [wərθ'*h*waɪl] *adj* : qui en vaut la peine — **worthy** ['wərði] *adj* **-thier; -est** : digne

would ['wʊd] *past of* **will 1 he** ∼ **often take his children to the park** : il amenait souvent ses enfants au parc **2 I** ∼ **go if I had the money** : j'irais si j'avais les moyens **3 I** ∼ **rather go alone** : je préférerais y aller seul **4 she** ∼ **have won if she hadn't tripped** : elle aurait gagné si elle n'avait pas trébuché **5** ∼ **you kindly help them?** : auriez-vous la gentillesse de les aider? — **wouldn't** ['wʊd^ənt] (*contraction of* **would not**) → **would**

wound[1] ['wu:nd] *n* : blessure *f* — ∼ *vt* : blesser

wound[2] ['waʊnd] → **wind**

wove, woven → **weave**

wrangle ['ræŋgəl] *vi* **-gled; -gling** : se disputer

wrap ['ræp] *vt* **wrapped; wrapping 1** : envelopper, emballer **2** *or* ∼ **up** FINISH : conclure — ∼ *n* → **wrapper** — **wrapper** ['ræpər] *n* : papier *m*, emballage *m* — **wrapping** ['ræpɪŋ] *n* : emballage *m*

wrath ['ræθ] *n* : furie *f*, colère *f*

wreath ['ri:θ] *n, pl* **wreaths** ['ri:ðz, 'ri:θs] : couronne *f* (de fleurs, etc.)

wreck ['rɛk] *n* **1** WRECKAGE : épave *f* (d'un navire) **2** ACCIDENT : accident *m* (de voiture), écrasement *m* (d'avion) **3 be a nervous** ∼ : être à bout — ∼ *vt* : détruire (une automobile), faire échouer (un navire) — **wreckage** ['rɛkɪdʒ] *n* **1** : épave *f* (d'un navire) **2** : décombres *mpl* (d'un édifice)

wren ['rɛn] *n* : roitelet *m*

wrench ['rɛntʃ] *vt* PULL : tirer brusquement — ∼ *n* **1** TUG : secousse *f* **2** *or* **monkey** ∼ : clef *f*

wrestle ['rɛsəl] *vi* **-tled; -tling** : lutter, pratiquer la lutte (aux sports) — **wrestler** ['rɛslər] *n* : lutteur *m*, -teuse *f* — **wrestling** ['rɛsəlɪŋ] *n* : lutte *f* (sport)

wretch ['rɛtʃ] *n* : pauvre diable *m* — **wretched** ['rɛtʃəd] *adj* **1** : misérable **2** ∼ **weather** : temps *m* affreux

wriggle ['rɪgəl] *vi* **-gled; -gling** : gigoter

wring ['rɪŋ] *vt* **wrung** ['rʌŋ]; **wringing 1** *or* ∼ **out** : essorer (du linge) **2** TWIST : tordre

wrinkle ['rɪŋkəl] *n* : ride *f* — ∼ *v* **-kled; -kling** *vt* : rider — *vi* : se rider

wrist ['rɪst] *n* : poignet *m* — **wristwatch** ['rɪst‚wɑtʃ] *n* : montre-bracelet *f*

writ ['rɪt] *n* : ordonnance *f* (en droit)

write ['raɪt] *v* **wrote** ['ro:t]; **written** ['rɪt^ən]; **writing** : écrire — **write down** *vt* : mettre par écrit, noter — **write off** *vt* CANCEL : annuler — **writer** ['raɪtər] *n* : écrivain *m*, écrivaine *f Can*

writhe ['raɪð] *vi* **writhed; writhing** : se tordre, se tortiller

writing ['raɪtɪŋ] *n* : écriture *f*

wrong ['rɔŋ] *n* **1** : mal *m* **2** INJUSTICE : tort *m* — ∼ *adj* **wronger; wrongest 1** : mal **2** UNSUITABLE : inapproprié **3** INCORRECT : mauvais, faux **4 be** ∼ : se tromper, avoir tort **5 what's** ∼? : qu'est-ce qui ne va pas? — ∼ *adv* **1** : à tort **2** INCORRECTLY : mal — ∼ *vt* **wronged; wronging** : faire du tort à — **wrongful** ['rɔŋfəl] *adj* **1** UNJUST : injustifié **2** UNLAWFUL : illégal — **wrongly** ['rɔŋli] *adv* : à tort

wrote → **write**

wrought iron ['rɔt] *n* : fer *m* forgé

wrung → **wring**

wry ['raɪ] *adj* **wrier** ['raɪər]; **wriest** ['raɪəst] : narquois

XYZ

x [ˈɛks] *n*, *pl* **x's** *or* **xs** [ˈɛksəz] : x *m*, vingt–quatrième lettre de l'alphabet

xenophobia [ˌzɛnəˈfoːbiə, ˌziː-] *n* : xénophobie *f*

Xmas [ˈkrɪsməs] → Christmas

X ray [ˈɛksˌreɪ] *n* **1** : rayon *m* X **2** *or* **photograph** : radiographie *f* — **x–ray** *vt* : radiographier

xylophone [ˈzaɪləˌfoːn] *n* : xylophone *m*

y [ˈwaɪ] *n*, *pl* **y's** *or* **ys** [ˈwaɪz] : y *m*, vingt–cinquième lettre de l'alphabet

yacht [ˈjɑt] *n* : yacht *m*

yam [ˈjæm] *n* SWEET POTATO : patate *f* douce

yank [ˈjæŋk] *vt* : tirer d'un coup sec — **~** *n* : coup *m* sec

yap [ˈjæp] *vi* **yapped; yapping 1** : japper **2** CHATTER : jacasser — **~** *n* : jappement *m*

yard [ˈjɑrd] *n* **1** : yard *m*, verge *f Can* (unité de mesure) **2** COURTYARD : cour *f* **3** : jardin *m* (d'une maison) — **yardstick** [ˈjɑrdˌstɪk] *n* **1** : mètre *m* **2** CRITERION : critère *m*

yarn [ˈjɑrn] *n* **1** : fil *m* (à tisser) **2** TALE : histoire *f*

yawn [ˈjɔn] *vi* : bâiller — **~** *n* : bâillement *m*

year [ˈjɪr] *n* **1** : an *m*, année *f* **2 he's ten ~s old** : il a dix ans **3 I haven't seen them in ~s** : je ne les ai pas vus depuis des années — **yearbook** [ˈjɪrˌbʊk] *n* : recueil *m* annuel, annuaire *m* — **yearly** [ˈjɪrli] *adv* **1** : annuellement **2 three times ~** : trois fois par an — **~** *adj* : annuel

yearn [ˈjərn] *vi* **~ for** : désirer ardemment — **yearning** [ˈjərnɪŋ] *n* : désir *m* ardent

yeast [ˈjiːst] *n* : levure *f*

yell [ˈjɛl] *vi* : crier — *vt* : crier, hurler — **~** *n* : cri *m*, hurlement *m*

yellow [ˈjɛlo] *adj* : jaune — **~** *n* : jaune *m* — **~** *v* : jaunir — **yellowish** [ˈjɛloɪʃ] *adj* : jaunâtre

yelp [ˈjɛlp] *n* : glapissement *m* — **~** *vi* : glapir

yes [ˈjɛs] *adv* **1** : oui **2 you're not ready, are you? ~, I am** : vous n'êtes pas prêt? mais si, je le suis — **~** *n* : oui *m*

yesterday [ˈjɛstərˌdeɪ, -di] *adv* : hier — **~** *n* **1** : hier *m* **2 the day before ~** : avant–hier *m*

yet [ˈjɛt] *adv* **1** : encore **2 has he come ~?** : est-il déjà arrivé? **3 not ~** : pas encore **4 ~ more problems** : encore des problèmes **5** NEVERTHELESS : néanmoins — **~** *conj* : mais

yield [ˈjiːld] *vt* **1** PRODUCE : produire, rapporter **2 ~ the right of way** : céder le pas-

sage — *vi* **1** GIVE : céder **2** SURRENDER : se rendre — **~** *n* : rendement *m*, rapport *m*

yoga [ˈjoːgə] *n* : yoga *m*

yogurt [ˈjoːgərt] *n* : yaourt *m*, yogourt *m*

yoke [ˈjoːk] *n* : joug *m*

yolk [ˈjoːk] *n* : jaune *m* (d'œuf)

you [ˈjuː] *pron* **1** (*used as subject — singular*) : tu (familier), vous (forme polie) **2** (*used as subject — plural*) : vous **3** (*used as the direct or indirect object of a verb*) : te (familier), vous (forme polie), vous (pluriel) **4** (*used as the object of a preposition*) : toi (familier), vous (forme polie), vous (pluriel) **5 ~ never know** : on ne sait jamais — **you'd** [ˈjuːd, ˈjʊd] (*contraction of you had or you would*) → have, would — **you'll** [ˈjuːl, ˈjʊl] (*contraction of you shall or you will*) → shall, will

young [ˈjʌŋ] *adj* **younger** [ˈjʌŋgər]; **youngest** [-gəst] **1** : jeune **2 my ~er brother** : mon frère cadet **3 she is the ~est** : elle est la plus jeune — **~** *npl* : jeunes *mfpl* (personnes), petits *mpl* (animaux) — **youngster** [ˈjʌŋkstər] *n* **1** : jeune *mf* **2** CHILD : enfant *mf*

your [ˈjʊr, ˈjoːr, jər] *adj* **1** (*familiar singular*) : ta, ton **2** (*formal singular*) : votre **3** (*familiar plural*) : tes **4** (*formal plural*) : vos **5 on ~ left** : à votre gauche

you're [ˈjʊr, ˈjoɪr, ˈjər, ˈjuɪər] (*contraction of you are*) → be

yours [ˈjʊrz, ˈjoːrz] *pron* **1** (*familiar singular*) : le tien, la tienne **2** (*formal singular*) : le vôtre, la vôtre **3** (*familiar plural*) : les tiens, les tiennes **4** (*formal plural*) : les vôtres

yourself [jərˈsɛlf] *pron*, *pl* **yourselves** [jərˈsɛlvz] **1** (*used reflexively*) : tu (familier), vous (forme polie), vous (pluriel) **2** (*used for emphasis*) : toi–même (familier), vous–même (forme polie), vous–mêmes (pluriel)

youth [ˈjuːθ] *n*, *pl* **youths** [ˈjuːðz, ˈjuːθs] **1** : jeunesse *f* **2** BOY : jeune *m* **3 today's ~** : les jeunes d'aujourd'hui — **youthful** [ˈjuːθfəl] *adj* **1** : juvénile, de jeunesse **2** YOUNG : jeune

you've [ˈjuːv] (*contraction of you have*) → have

yowl [ˈjæʊl] *vi* : hurler (se dit d'un chien ou d'une personne) — **~** *n* : hurlement *m*

yule [ˈjuːl] *n* : Noël *m* — **yuletide** [ˈjuːlˌtaɪd] *n* : temps *m* de Noël

z [ˈziː] *n*, *pl* **z's** *or* **zs** : z *m*, vingt-sixième lettre de l'alphabet

zany [ˈzeɪni] *adj* **-nier; -est** : farfelu *fam*

zeal [ˈziːl] *n* : zèle *m*, ferveur *f* — **zealous** [ˈzɛləs] *adj* : zélé

zebra [ˈziːbrə] *n* : zèbre *m*

zed [ˈzɛd] *Brit* → **z**

zenith [ˈziːnəθ] *n* : zénith *m*

zero [ˈzɪro, ˈzɪro] *n, pl* **-ros** : zéro *m* — *adj* : zéro, nul

zest [ˈzɛst] *n* **1** : enthousiasme *m*, entrain *m* **2** FLAVOR : piquant *m*

zigzag [ˈzɪɡˌzæɡ] *n* : zigzag *m* — ~ *vi* **-zagged; -zagging** : zigzaguer

zinc [ˈzɪŋk] *n* : zinc *m*

zip [ˈzɪp] *v* **zipped; zipping** *vt or* ~ **up** : fermer avec une fermeture à glissière — *vi* SPEED : filer à toute allure — **zip code** *n* : code *m* postal — **zipper** [ˈzɪpər] *n* : fermeture *f* à glissière

zodiac [ˈzoːdiˌæk] *n* : zodiaque *m*

zone [ˈzoːn] *n* : zone *f*

zoo [ˈzuː] *n, pl* **zoos** : zoo *m* — **zoology** [zoˈɑləʤi, zuː-] *n* : zoologie *f*

zoom [ˈzuːm] *vi* : passer comme une trombe — ~ *n or* ~ **lens** : zoom *m*

zucchini [zʊˈkiːni] *n, pl* **-ni** *or* **-nis** : courgette *f*

Common French Abbreviations

AB, Alb.	Alberta	**AB, Alta.**	Alberta
ALÉNA	Accord de libre-échange nord-américain	**NAFTA**	North American Free Trade Agreement
AP	assistance publique (France)	—	welfare services
ap. J.-C.	après Jésus-Christ	**AD**	anno Domini
a/s	aux soins de	**c/o**	care of
av.	avenue	**ave.**	avenue
av. J.-C.	avant Jésus-Christ	**BC**	before Christ
avr.	avril	**Apr.**	April
BC	Colombie-Britannique	**BC, B.C.**	British Columbia
bd	boulevard	**blvd.**	boulevard
BD	bande dessinée	—	comic strip
BN	Bibliothèque nationale	—	national library
BP	boîte postale	**P.O.B.**	post office box
B.S.	bien-être social (Canada)	—	welfare services
c	centime	**c, ct.**	cent
C	centigrade, Celsius	**C**	centigrade, Celsius
CA	comptable agréé (Canada)	**CPA**	certified public accountant
CA	courant alternatif	**AC**	alternating current
c.-à-d.	c'est-à-dire	**i.e.**	that is
C.-B.	Colombie-Britannique	**BC, B.C.**	British Columbia
CC	courant continu	**DC**	direct current
CE	Communauté européenne	**EC**	European Community
CEE	Communauté européenne économique	**EEC**	European Economic Community
cg	centigramme	**cg**	centigram
Cie	compagnie	**Co.**	company
cm	centimètre	**cm**	centimeter
C.P.	case postale (Canada)	**P.O.B**	post office box
CV	curriculum vitae	**CV**	curriculum vitae
déc.	décembre	**Dec.**	December
dép., dépt.	département	**dept.**	department
DG	directeur général	**CEO**	chief executive officer
dim.	dimanche	**Sun.**	Sunday
dir.	directeur	**dir.**	director
DOM	Département(s) d'outre-mer	—	French overseas department
dr.	droite	**rt.**	right
Dr	docteur	**Dr.**	doctor
E	Est, est	**E**	East, east
ECG	électrocardiogramme	**EKG**	electrocardiogram
éd.	édition	**ed.**	edition

FRENCH ABBREVIATION AND EXPANSION		ENGLISH EQUIVALENT	
EPS	éducation physique et sportive	**PE**	physical education
etc.	et caetera, et cetera	**etc.**	et cetera
É.-U.	États-Unis	**U.S.**	United States
F	Fahrenheit	**F**	Fahrenheit
F	franc	**fr.**	franc
FAB	franco à bord	**FOB**	free on board
févr.	février	**Feb.**	February
FMI	Fonds monétaire international	**IMF**	International Monetary Fund
g	gauche	**l., L**	left
g	gramme	**g**	gram
h	heure(s)	**hr.**	hour
HS	hors service	—	out of order
i.e.	c'est-à-dire	**i.e.**	that is
IPC	indice des prix à la consommation	**CPI**	consumer price index
Î.P.-É.	île-du-Prince-Édouard	**PE, P.E.I.**	Prince Edward Island
janv.	janvier	**Jan.**	January
jeu.	jeudi	**Thurs.**	Thursday
juill.	juillet	**Jul.**	July
kg	kilogramme	**kg**	kilogram
km	kilomètre	**km**	kilometer
l	litre	**l**	liter
lun.	lundi	**Mon.**	Monday
m	mètre	**m.**	meter
M.	monsieur	**Mr.**	mister
mar.	mardi	**Tues.**	Tuesday
MB, Man.	Manitoba	**MB, Man.**	Manitoba
mer.	mercredi	**Wed.**	Wednesday
MLF	mouvement de libération des femmes	—	—
Mlle	Mademoiselle	**Ms., Miss**	—
Mme	Madame	**Ms., Mrs.**	—
MST	maladie sexuellement transmissible	**STD**	sexually transmitted disease
N	Nord, nord	**N**	North, north
N°, n°	numéro	**no.**	number
NB, N.-B.	Nouveau-Brunswick	**NB, N.B.**	New Brunswick
n.d.	non disponible	**NA**	not available
NL, T.-N.-L.	Terre-Neuve et Labrador	**NL**	Newfoundland and Labrador
nov.	novembre	**Nov.**	November
NS, N.-É.	Nouvelle-Écosse	**NS, N.S.**	Nova Scotia
NT	Territoires du Nord-Ouest	**NT, N.T.**	Northwest Territories
NU	Nunavut	**Nu**	Nunavut
O	Ouest, ouest	**W**	West, west

FRENCH ABBREVIATION AND EXPANSION		ENGLISH EQUIVALENT	
oc	ondes courtes	**s-w**	short wave
oct.	octobre	**Oct.**	October
OIT	Organisation internationale du travail	**ILO**	International Labor Organization
OMS	Organisation mondiale de la santé	**WHO**	World Health Organization
ON, Ont.	Ontario	**ON, Ont.**	Ontario
ONG	organisation non gouvernementale	**NGO**	nongovernmental organization
ONU	Organisation des Nations Unies	**UN**	United Nations
OTAN	Organisation du traité de l'Atlantique Nord	**NATO**	North Atlantic Treaty Organization
OVNI, ovni	objet volant non identifié	**UFO**	unidentified flying object
p.	page	**p.**	page
PCV	paiement contre vérification	—	collect call
PDG	président-directeur général	**CEO**	chief executive officer
PE	Île-du-Prince-Édouard	**PE, P.E.I.**	Prince Edward Island
p. ex.	par exemple	**e.g.**	for example
PIB	produit intérieur brut	**GDP**	gross domestic product
PNB	produit national brut	**GNP**	gross national product
P.-S.	post-scriptum	**P.S.**	postscript
QC	Québec	**QC, Que.**	Quebec
QG	quartier général	**HQ**	headquarters
QI	quotient intellectuel	**IQ**	intelligence quotient
R-D	recherche-développement	**R and D**	research and development
réf.	référence	**ref.**	reference
RF	République Française	—	France
RN	route nationale	—	interstate highway
RV	rendez-vous	**rdv., R.V.**	rendezvous
s.	siècle	**c., cent.**	century
S	Sud, sud	**S, so.**	South, south
SA	société anonyme	**Inc.**	incorporated (company)
sam.	samedi	**Sat.**	Saturday
SARL	société à responsabilité limitée	**Ltd.**	limited (corporation)
Sask.	Saskatchewan	**SK, Sask.**	Saskatchewan
SDF	sans domicile fixe	—	homeless (person)
sept.	septembre	**Sept.**	September
SK	Saskatchewan	**SK, Sask.**	Saskatchewan
SM	Sa Majesté	**HM**	His Majesty, Her Majesty
SME	Système monétaire européen	—	European Monetary System
St	saint	**St.**	Saint
Ste	sainte	**St.**	Saint
SVP	s'il vous plaît	**pls.**	please

FRENCH ABBREVIATION AND EXPANSION		ENGLISH EQUIVALENT	
t	tonne	**t., tn.**	ton
tél.	téléphone	**tel.**	telephone
T.-N.	Terre-Neuve	**NF, Nfld**	Newfoundland
T.N.-O.	Territoires du Nord-Ouest	**NT, N.T.**	Northwest Territories
TVA	taxe à valeur ajoutée	**VAT**	value-added tax
UE	Union européenne	**EU**	European Union
univ.	université	**U., univ.**	university
V., v.	voir	**vid.**	see
ven.	vendredi	**Fri.**	Friday
vol.	volume	**vol.**	volume
VPC	vente par correspondance	—	mail-order selling
W-C	water closet	**w.c.**	water closet
YT, Yuk.	Yukon	**YT, Y.T.**	Yukon Territory